Solid Edge 2026

Basics and Beyond

Online Instructor

AF520420

Solid Edge 2026 Basics and Beyond

© Copyright 2026@Kishore

This book may not be duplicated in any way without the express written consent of the publisher, except in the form of brief excerpts or quotations for review. The information contained herein is for the reader's personal use and may not be incorporated in any commercial programs, other books, database, or any software without the publisher's written consent. Making copies of this book or any portion for a purpose other than your own is a violation of copyright laws.

Limit of Liability/Disclaimer of Warranty:
The author and publisher make no representations or warranties concerning the accuracy or completeness of this work's contents and specifically disclaim all warranties, including without limitation warranties of fitness for a particular purpose. The advice and strategies contained herein may not be suitable for every situation. Neither the publisher nor the author shall be liable for damages arising here from.

Trademarks:
All brand names and product names used in this book are trademarks, registered trademarks, or their respective holders' trade names. The author and publisher are not associated with any product or vendor mentioned in this book.

Solid Edge 2026 Basics and Beyond

Contact us for resource files

online.books999@gmail.com

Contents

Introduction

Welcome to the *Solid Edge 2026 Basics and Beyond* book. This book is written to assist students, designers, and engineering professionals. It covers the important features and functionalities of Solid Edge using relevant examples and exercises.

This book is written for new users, who can use it as a self-study resource to learn Solid Edge. Also, experienced users can use it as a reference. This book focuses on modeling, assembly modeling, drawings, sheet metal design, and surface design.

Topics covered in this Book

- Chapter 1, "Getting Started with Solid Edge 2026", gives an introduction to Solid Edge. The user interface and terminology are discussed in this chapter.
- Chapter 2, "Sketch Techniques," explores the sketching commands in Solid Edge. You will learn to create parametric sketches.
- Chapter 3, "Extrude and Revolve features," teaches you to create basic 3D geometry using the Extrude and Revolve commands.
- Chapter 4, "Placed Features," covers the features which can be created without using sketches.
- Chapter 5, "Patterned Geometry," explores the commands to create patterned and mirrored geometry.
- Chapter 6, "Sweep Features," covers the commands to create swept and helical features.
- Chapter 7, "Loft Features," covers the Loft command and its core features.
- Chapter 8, "Additional Features and Multibody Parts," covers additional commands to create complex geometry. Also, the multibody parts are covered.
- Chapter 9, "Modifying Parts," explores the commands and techniques to modify the part geometry.
- Chapter 10, "Assemblies," explains you to create assemblies using the bottom-up and top-down design approaches.
- Chapter 11, "Drawings," covers how to create 2D drawings from 3D parts and assemblies.
- Chapter 12, "Sheet Metal Design," covers how to create sheet metal parts and flat patterns.
- Chapter 13, "Surface Design," covers how to create complex shapes and designs using surface modeling tools.
- Chapter 14, "Subdivision Modeling," covers creating complex shapes and designs using subdivision modeling tools.

Chapter 1: Getting Started with Solid Edge 2026

Introduction to Solid Edge 2026

Solid Edge 2026 is a parametric and feature-based system that allows you to create 3D parts, assemblies, and 2D drawings. The design process in Solid Edge is shown below.

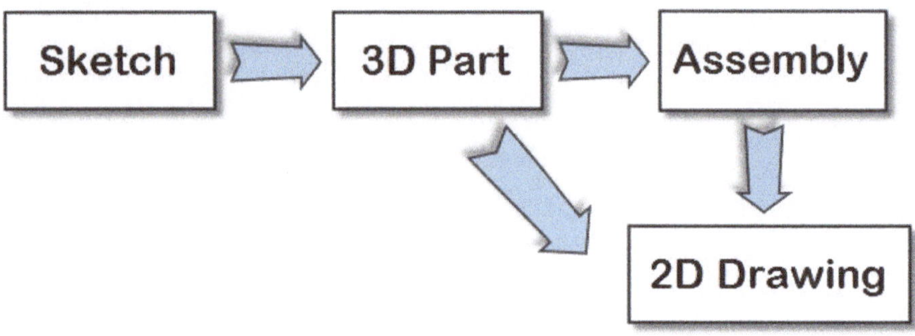

In Solid Edge, everything is controlled by parameters, dimensions, or relationships. For example, if you want to change the hole's position shown in the figure, you need to change the dimension or relation that controls its position.

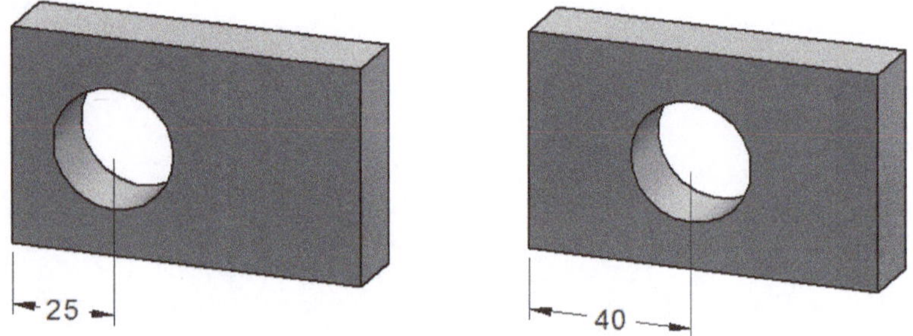

The parameters and relationships that you set up allow you to have control over the design intent. The design intent describes how your 3D model will behave when you apply dimensions and relationships to it. For example, if you want to position the hole at the center of the block, one way is to add dimensions between the hole and the adjacent edges. However, when you change the block's size, the hole will not be at the center.

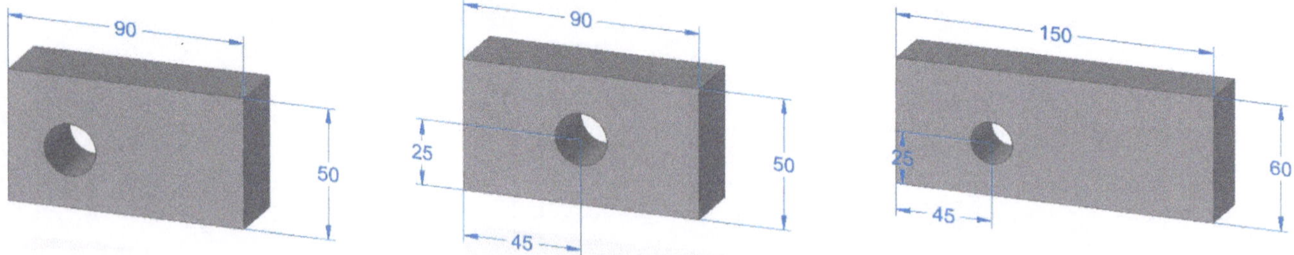

You can make the hole to be at the center, even if the size of the block changes. You need to apply the **Horizontal/Vertical** relationships between the hole and midpoints of the adjacent edges. Even if you change the block's size, the hole will always remain at the center.

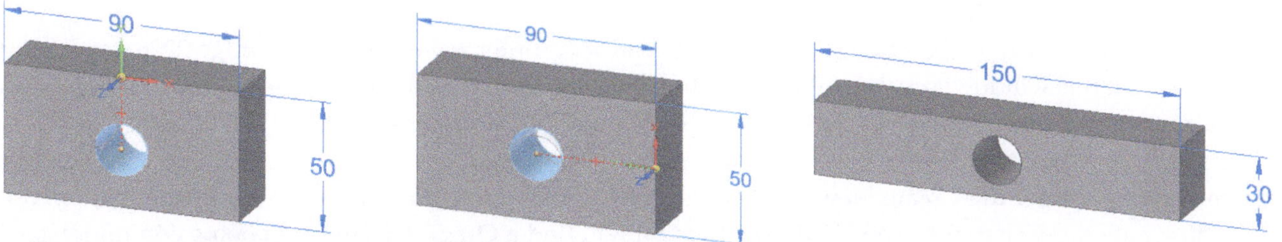

The other big advantage of Solid Edge is the associativity between parts, assemblies and drawings. When you make changes to a part's design, the changes will occur in any assembly that it is a part of. Also, the 2D drawing will update automatically.

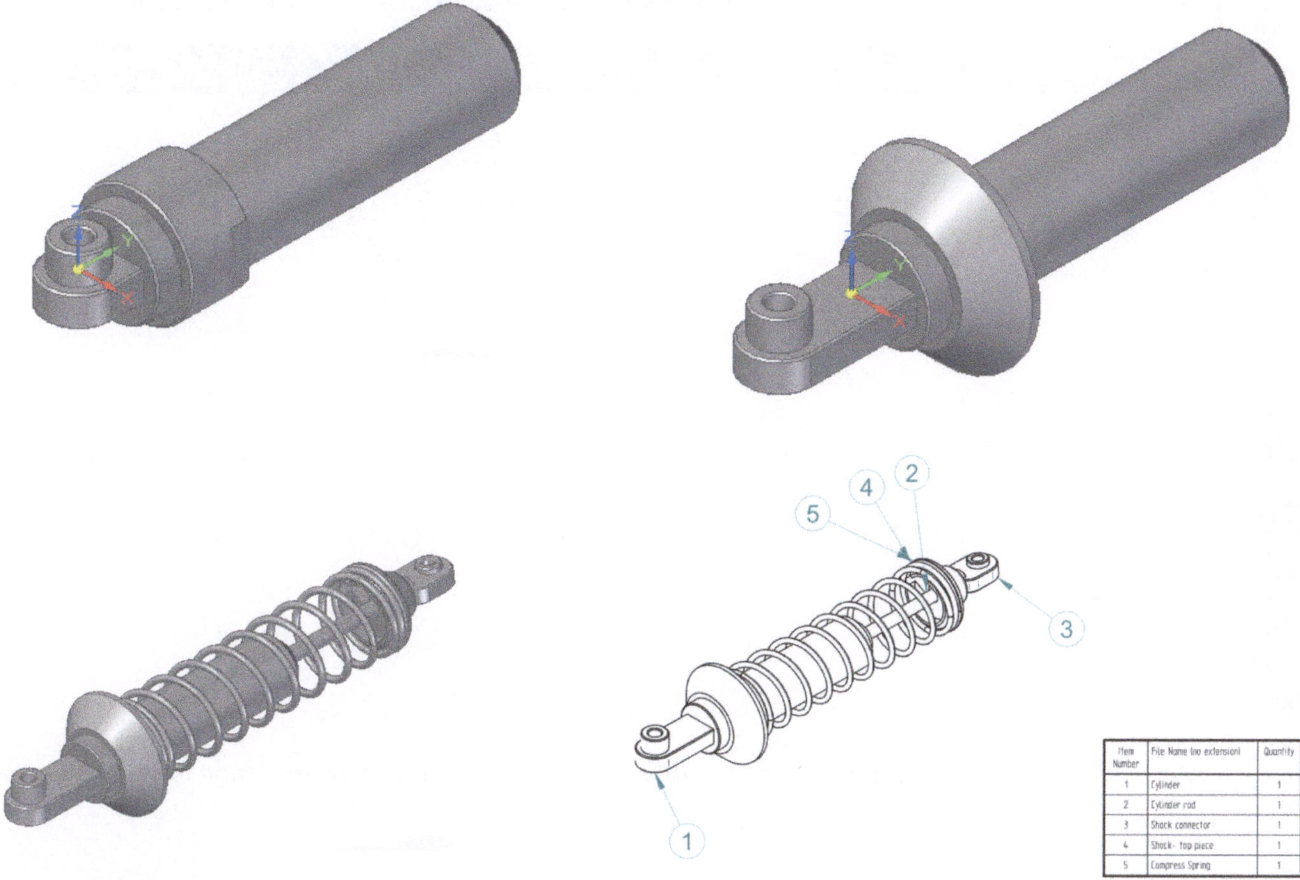

Item Number	File Name (no extension)	Quantity
1	Cylinder	1
2	Cylinder rod	1
3	Shock connector	1
4	Shock- top piece	1
5	Compress Spring	1

Installing Solid Edge 2026

To install **Solid Edge 2026**, click the **autostart** icon in the Solid Edge 2026 disc; the **Solid Edge** window appears. Click the **Solid Edge** link on the **Solid Edge** window; the **Solid Edge Installation Wizard** starts. On the **Solid Edge 2026** window, type-in the **User name** and **Organisation**, and then select the **Modeling standard**. You can select a modeling standard, which your company or client uses. This book uses the **ISO Metric** modeling standard to create all parts, assemblies, and drawings. Click **Install** after selecting the modeling standard. Close the **Solid Edge** window after the installation is complete.

Starting Solid Edge 2026

To start Solid Edge 2026, click the Solid Edge 2026 icon on your computer screen. The Solid Edge 2026 application window appears. On this window, several options and tutorials are displayed to quickly get started. You can view video tutorials to learn about creating parts, assemblies, drawings, and running simulation workflows.

On the main window, under the **Create New** section, select New Part, New Sheet Metal, New Assembly, or New Draft based on what you wish to work on. Additionally, you will find a **Quick UI Tour** that helps you understand the interface. Use the File menu on the left for options like New, Open, Print, Settings, and Tools to further navigate and customize your experience with Solid Edge 2026.

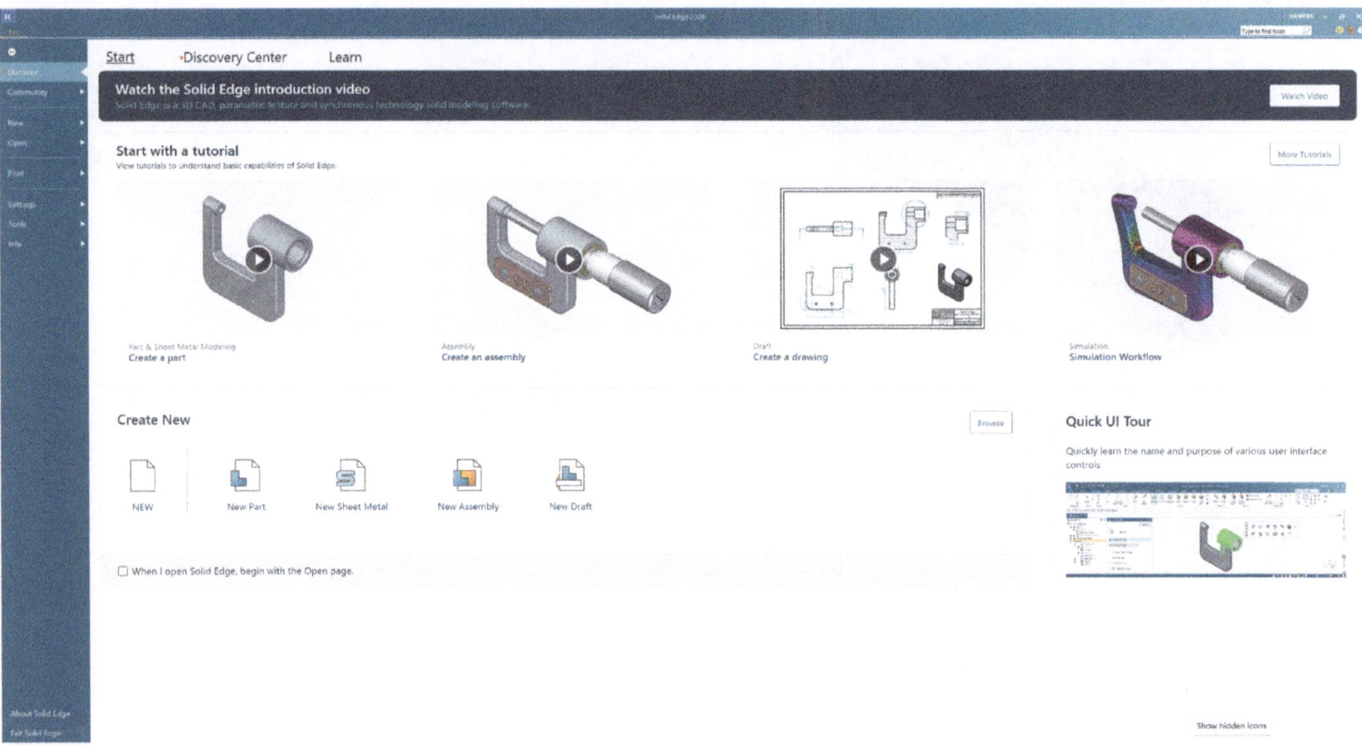

On the File Menu, click the **New** option, and then click **ISO Metric Part** under the **Create** section to start a new part document.

*You can change the templates displayed on the **New** page by clicking **Edit List**. On the **Template List Creation** dialog, select a modeling standard from the **Standard Templates** section. You can change the templates' order by selecting them from the **Templates** section and clicking the **Move Up** and **Move Down** arrows. Likewise, you can change the **Name** and **Description** of the template and click **Apply**. Click **OK** on the **Template List Creation** dialog to apply the changes.*

File Types

Various file types that can be created in Solid Edge are given below.

- **Part (.par)**
- **Assembly (.asm)**
- **Draft (.dft)**

- Sheet Metal (.psm)
- Weldment (.pwd)

User Interface

The following image shows the **Solid Edge 2026** application window.

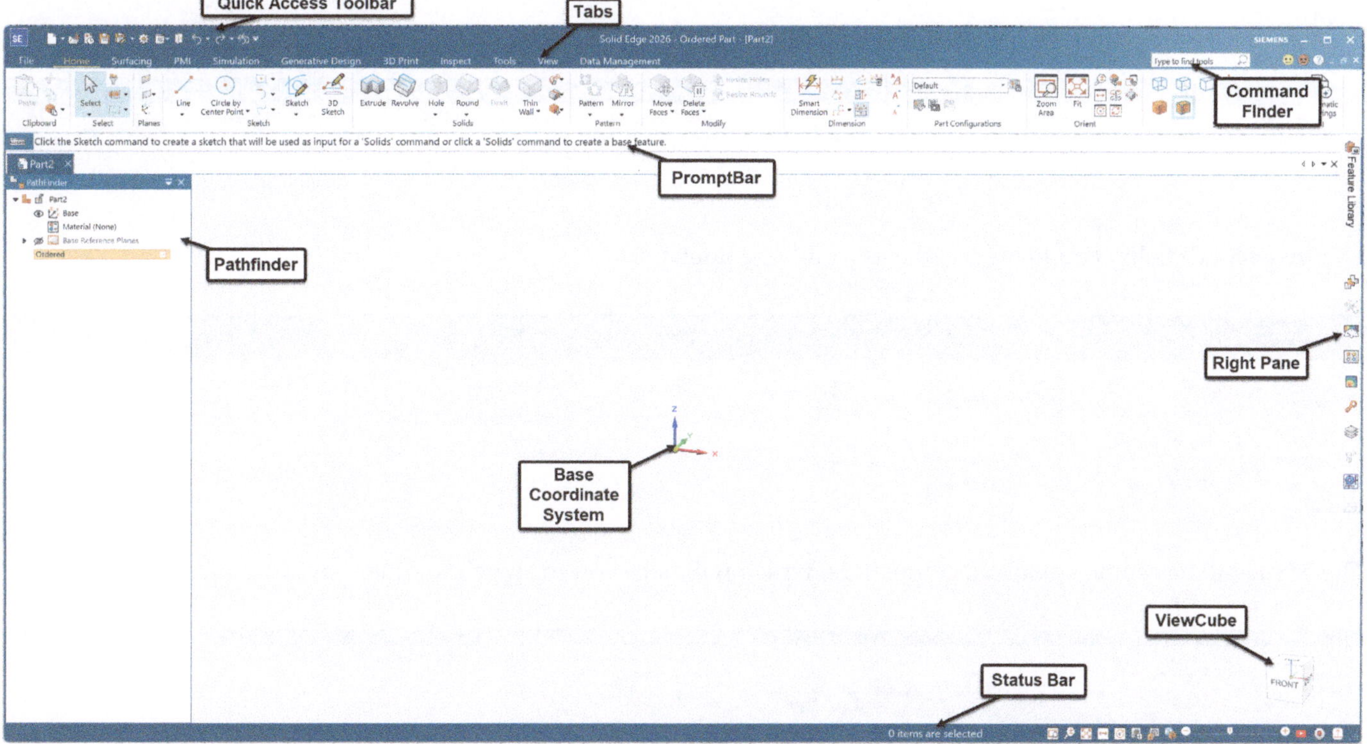

Environments in Solid Edge

There are five main environments available in Solid Edge: **Part (Synchronous** and **Ordered)**, **Assembly**, **Draft**, **Weldment**, and **Sheet Metal (Synchronous** and **Ordered)**. Also, there some additional environments to create exploded views, renderings, structures, piping, and wire harnesses.

Part environment (Synchronous and Ordered)

This environment has all the commands to create a 3D part model. It is available in two modes: **Synchronous** and **Ordered**. The **Synchronous** mode allows you to create and edit models directly. The **Ordered** mode allows you to create History-based models. In this mode, every feature or sketch that you create is stored in the Pathfinder. You can always go back and edit the feature or sketch. It has a ribbon located at the top of the screen. The ribbon is arranged in a hierarchy of tabs, panels, and commands. Panels such as **Draw**, **Relate**, and **Dimension** consists of commands, which are grouped based on their usage. Panels, in turn, are grouped into various tabs. For example, the panels such as **Draw**, **Relate**, and **Dimension** is located in the **Home** tab.

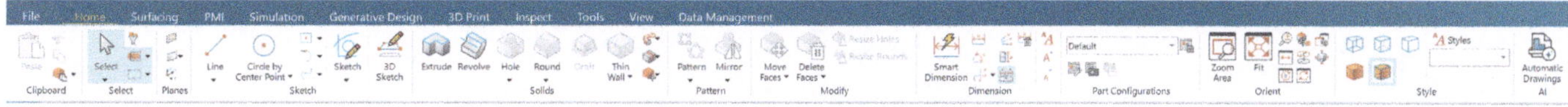

Assembly environment

This environment is used to create assemblies. The **Home** tab of the Ribbon has various commands, which will allow you to assemble and modify the components.

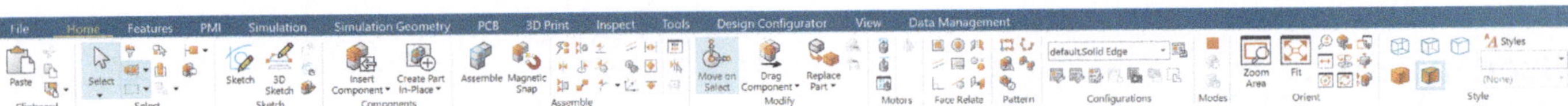

The **Features** tab has commands, which will help you to create cutouts, holes and other features at the assembly level.

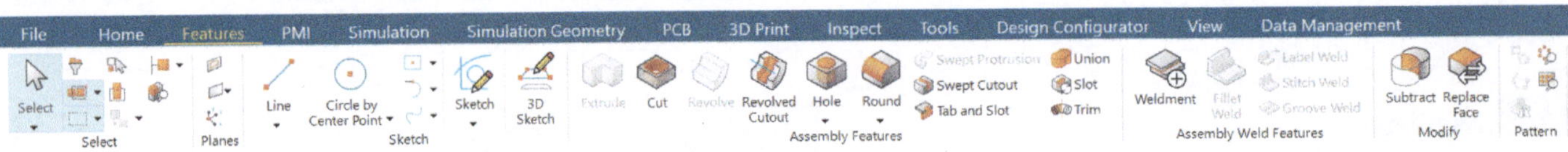

The **Inspect** tab helps you to inspect the assembly geometry.

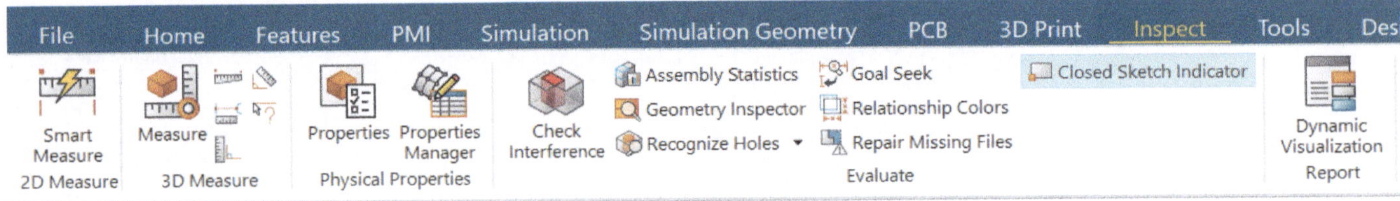

The **Tools** tab has some advanced commands, which will help you to switch to other environments.

Draft environment

This environment has all the commands to generate 2D drawings of parts and assemblies.

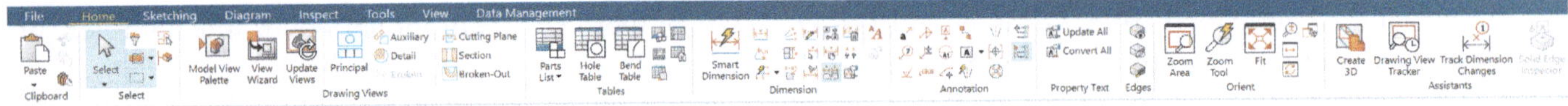

Sheet Metal environment

This environment has commands to create sheet metal parts.

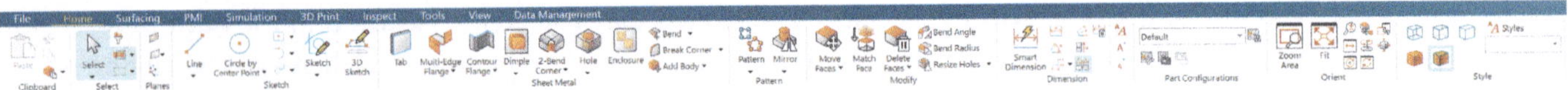

The **Command Finder** bar is used to search for any command available in Solid Edge 2026. You can type any keyword in the **Command Finder** bar and find a list of commands related to it.

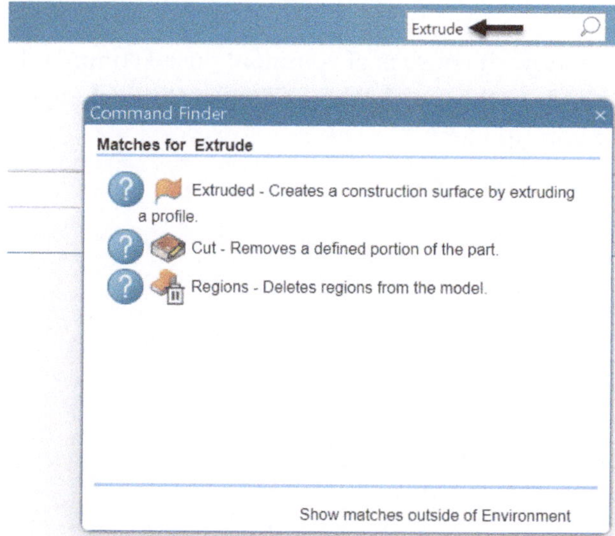

The other components of the user interface are discussed next.

File Menu

The **File Menu** appears when you click on the **File** tab of ribbon located at the top left corner of the window. The **File Menu** consists of a list of self-explanatory menus. Click on the **Open** menu to see a list of recently opened documents under the **Files** section.

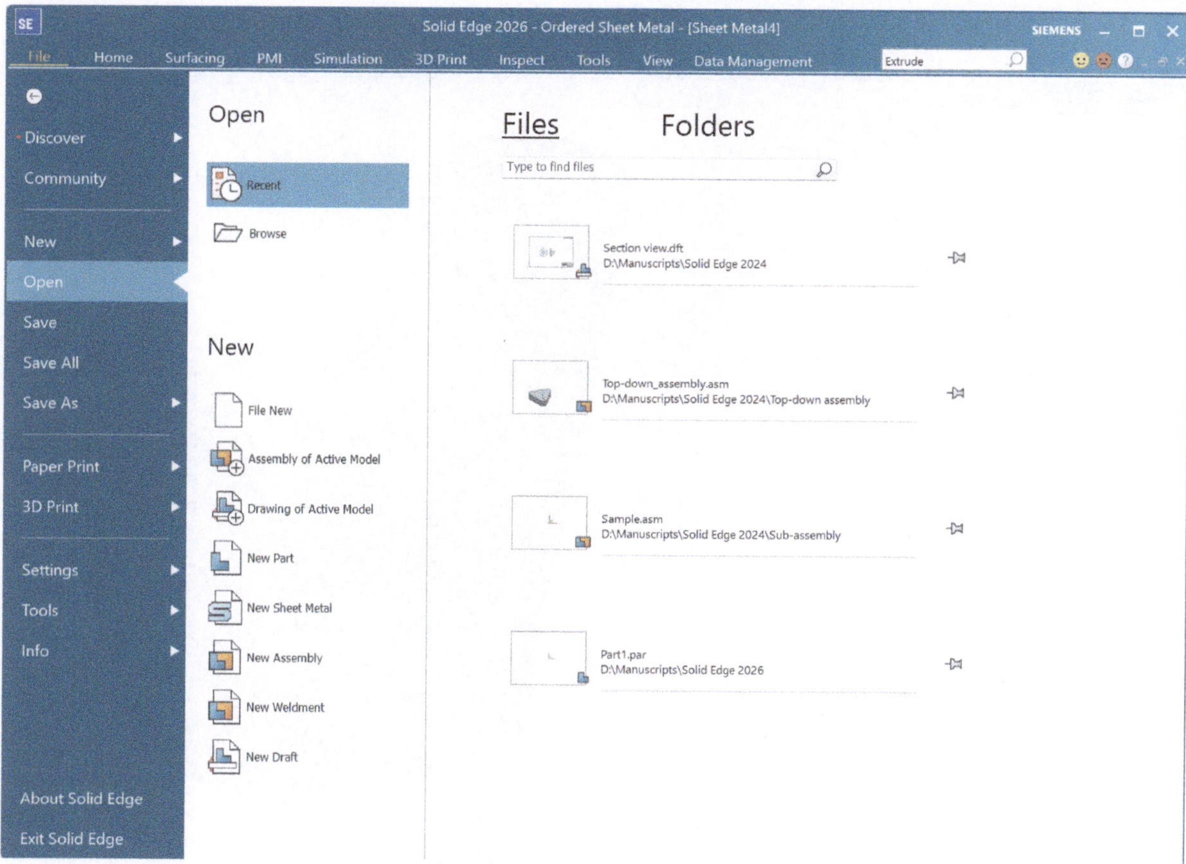

Quick Access Toolbar

The Quick Access Toolbar is located at the top left corner of the window. It consists of commonly used commands such as **New**, **Save**, **Open**, and **Save As**. You can add more commands to the **Quick Access Toolbar** by clicking on the down-arrow next to it and then selecting commands from the pop-up menu.

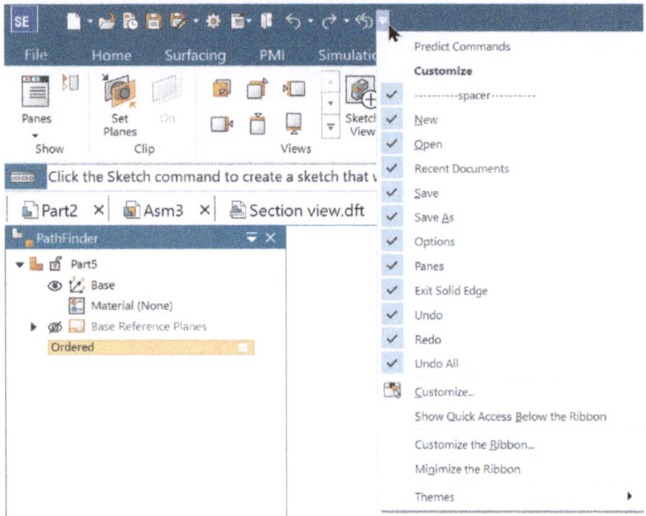

Graphics Window

Graphics window is the blank space located below the ribbon. You can draw sketches and create 3D geometry in the Graphics window. The left corner of the graphics window has a **Pathfinder**. Using the **Pathfinder**, you can access the features of the 3D model.

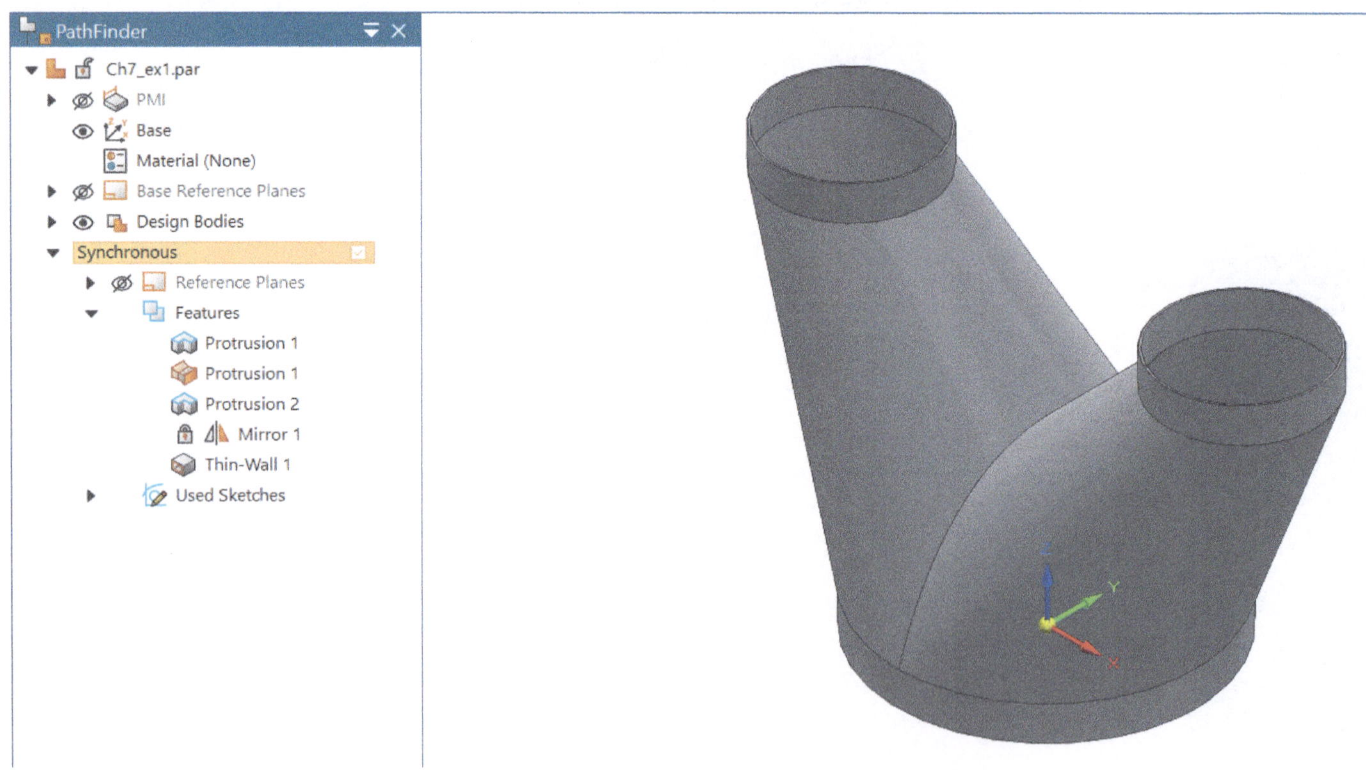

Prompt Bar

Prompt Bar is located below the Ribbon. It is useful when you activate a command. It displays various prompts while working with any command. These prompts are a series of steps needed to create a feature successfully.

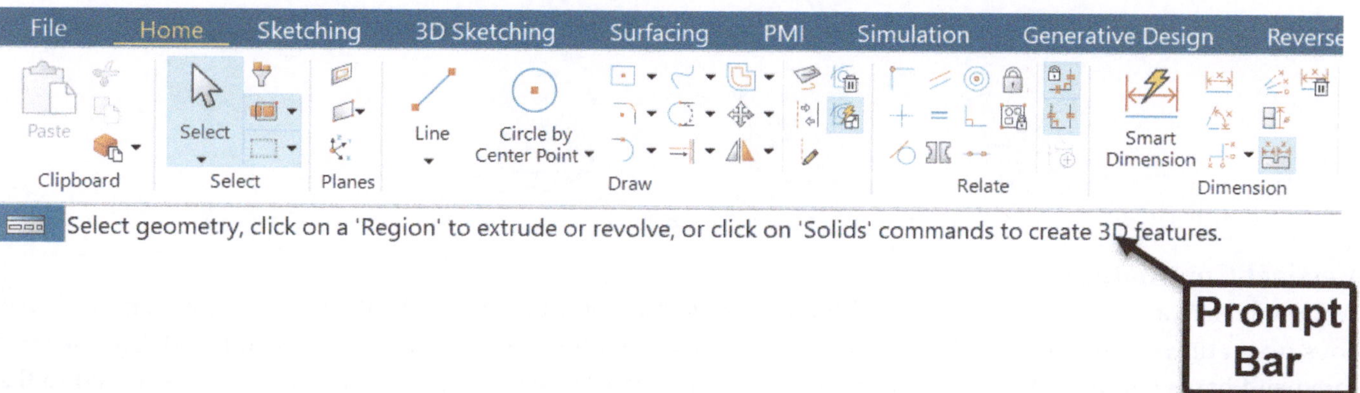

Status Bar

Status Bar is located at the bottom of the Solid Edge window. It contains many icons, which help you to visualize the 3D model. You can use the **Record** and **Upload to Youtube** icons to create and upload videos. To add more icons to the Status Bar, click the right mouse button on it and select the pop-up menu options.

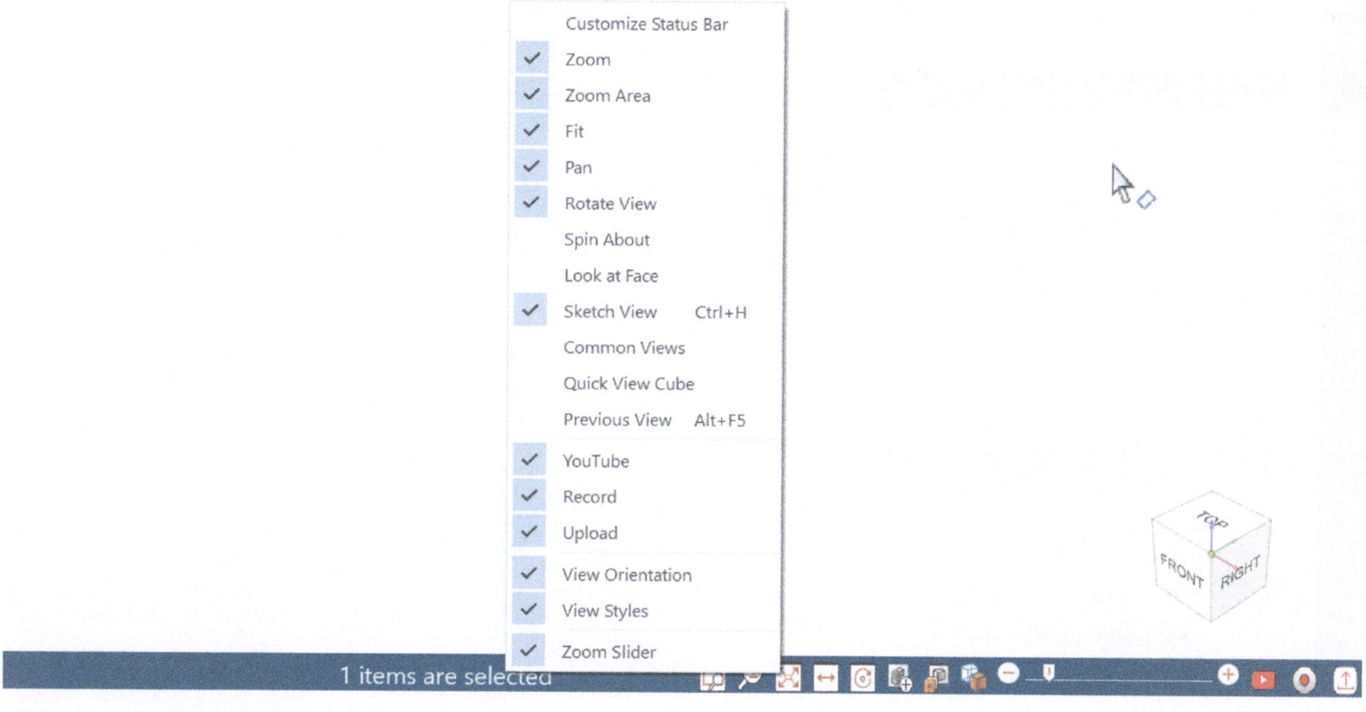

Quick View Cube

It is located at the bottom right corner of the graphics window. It is used to set the view orientation of the model.

Vertical Command bar

When you activate any command in Solid Edge, a contextual productivity tool called the vertical command bar pops up on the screen. It displays the options and steps to complete the execution of the command. This vertical command bar is strategically positioned to the right of the **PathFinder** panel and is magnetically anchored to the upper edge of the graphics window. The options on the Vertical Command bar are thoughtfully arranged vertically. This arrangement aids in locating the desired command, particularly if you are utilizing a widescreen monitor. If you want to put the command bar somewhere else on the screen, you can choose to attach it to either the top or bottom of the graphics window. To do this, just double-click on the command bar's title bar, and it will stick to the left side of the window. However, keep in mind that doing this will make the graphics window a bit smaller because some of the screen space will be used by the command bar.

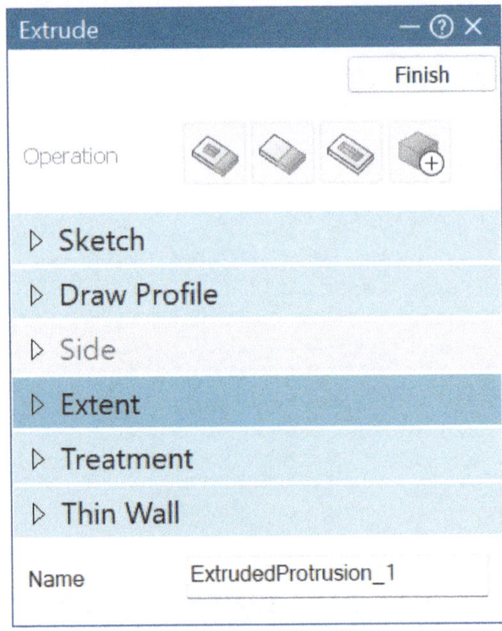

Changing the display of the Ribbon

You can add or remove more commands to the ribbon by clicking the right mouse button and selecting **Customize the Ribbon**. On the **Customize** dialog, click on the options in the right-side box, and then click **Add** or **Remove**. After making the required changes, close the dialog and click **Yes** to save the changes.

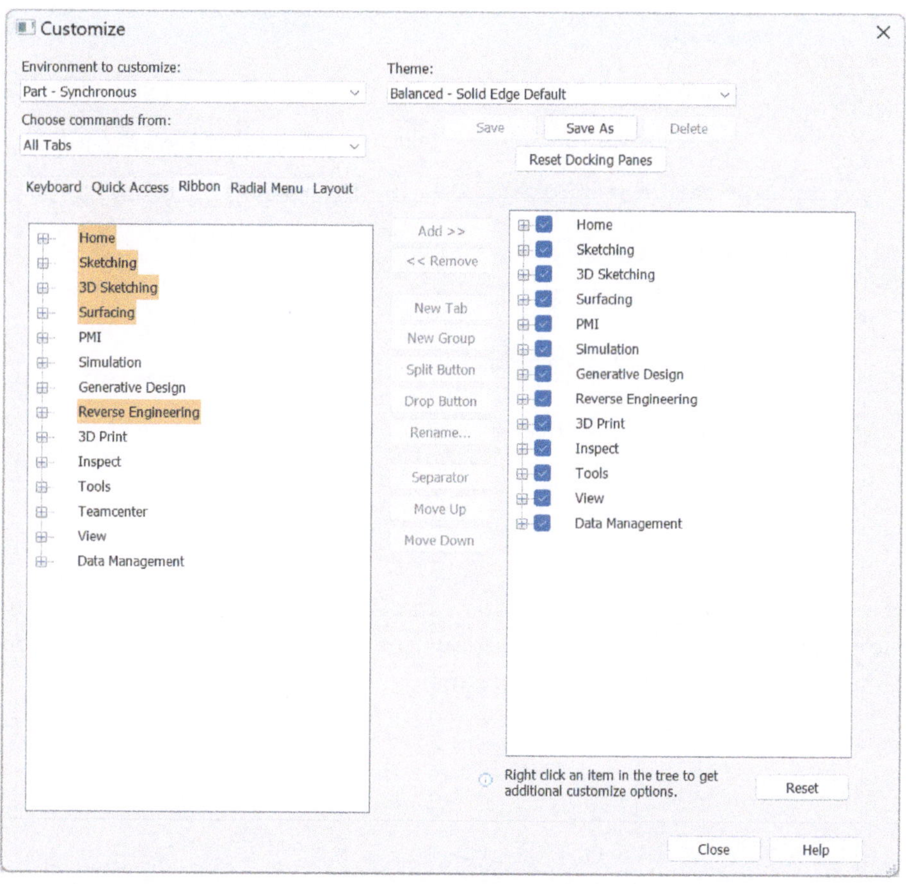

You can minimize the ribbon by clicking the right mouse button on the ribbon and selecting **Minimize the Ribbon**.

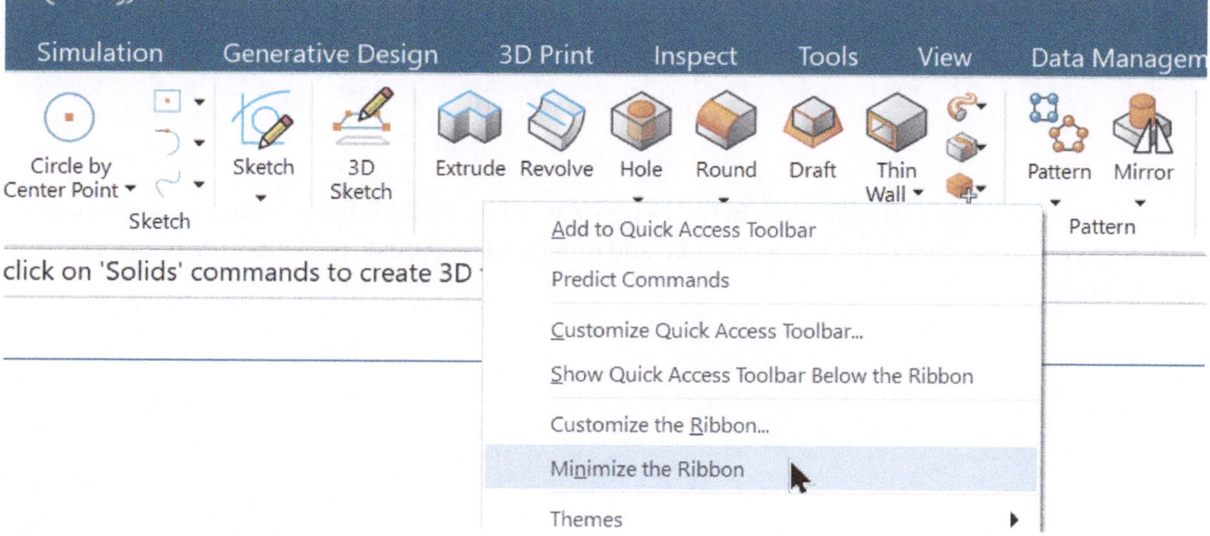

Dialogs

Dialogs are part of the Solid Edge user interface. Using a dialog, you can easily specify many settings and options. Examples of dialogs are shown below.

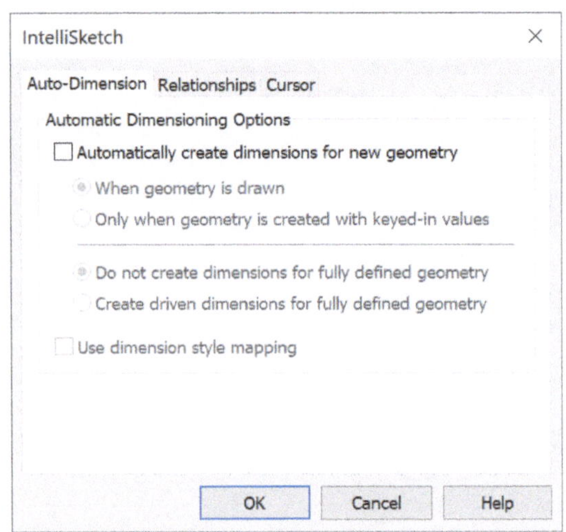

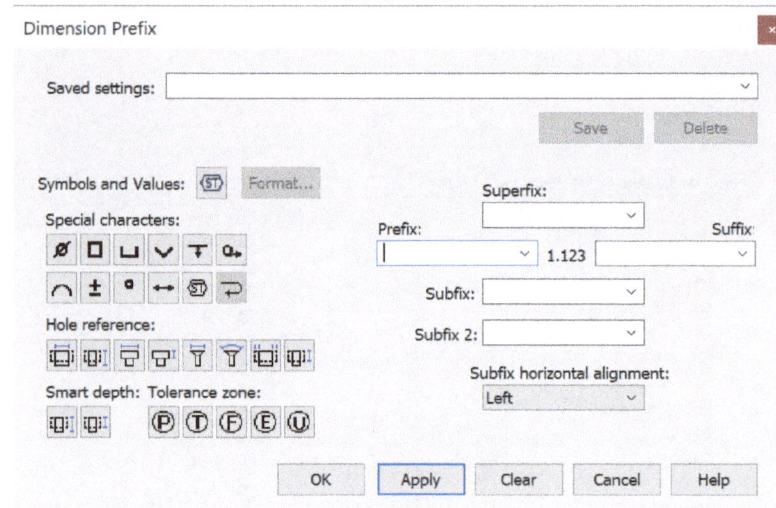

Radial Menus

Radial Menus provide you with another way of activating commands. You can display Radial Menus by clicking the right mouse button and dragging the pointer. A Radial Menu has various commands arranged radially. You can add or remove commands to the Radial Menu by using the **Customize** dialog.

Shortcut Menus

Shortcut Menus are displayed when you right-click in the graphics window. Solid Edge provides various shortcut menus in order to help you access some options very easily and quickly. The options in shortcut menus vary based on the environment.

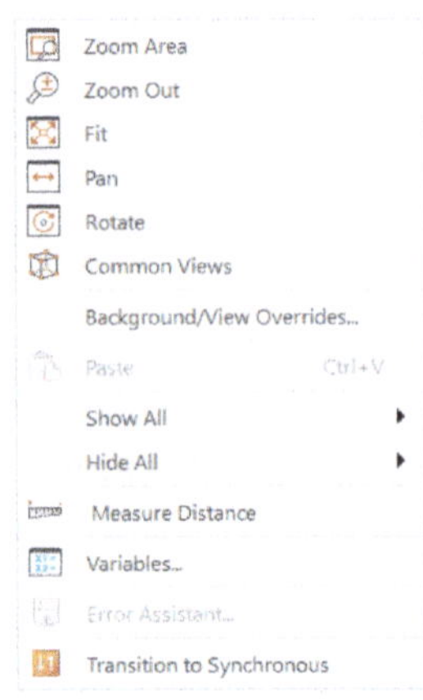

Starting a new document

You can start a new document directly from the File Menu or by using the **New** dialog. On the initial screen, the File tab located at the top left corner. On the File Menu, click the **New** option and click on the required template to start a part, assembly, drawing, weldment or sheet metal document.

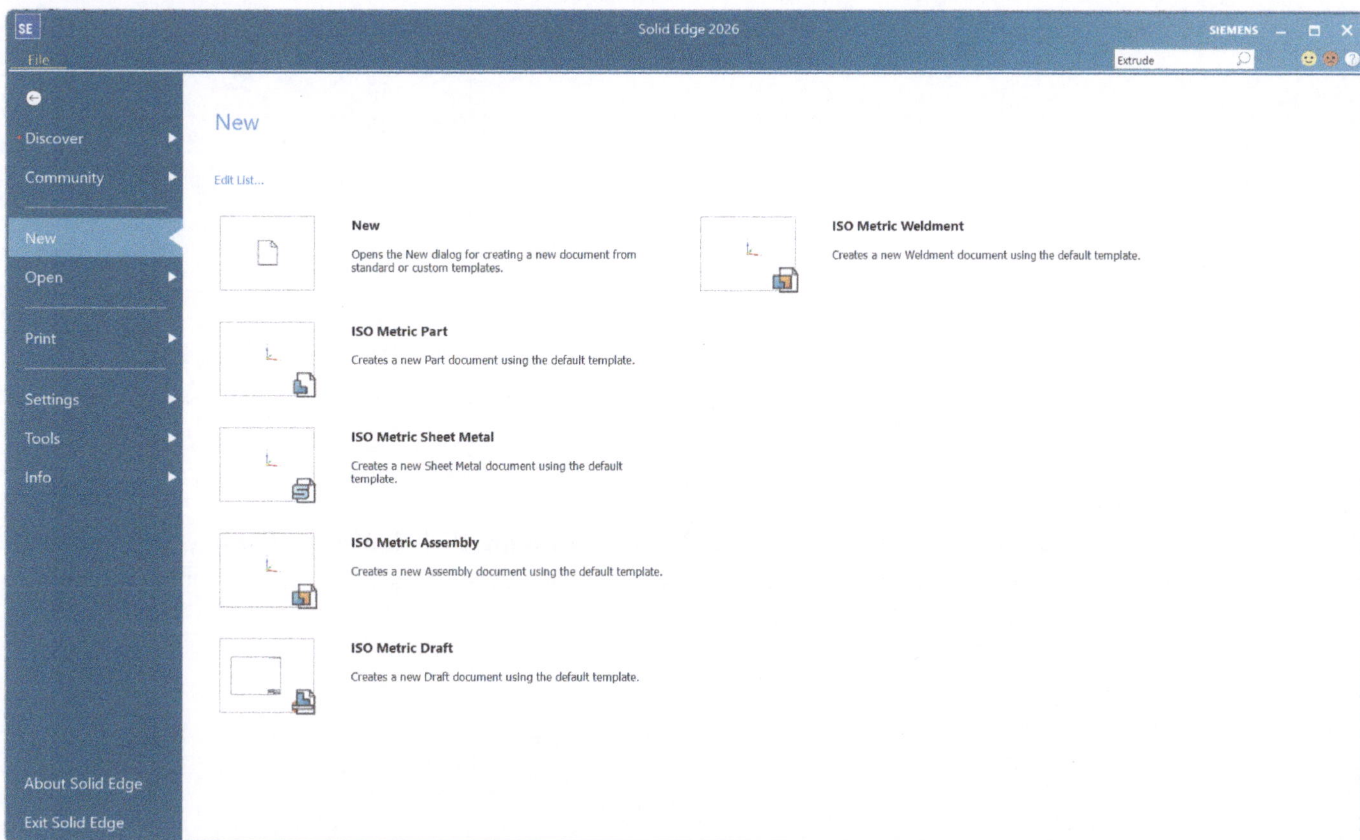

The New dialog

To start a new document using the **New** dialog, click the **New** button on anyone of the following:

- **Quick Access Toolbar**
- **File Menu**

The **New** dialog appears when you click the **New** button. In this dialog, select the standard from the **Standard Templates** section. The templates related to the selected standard will appear. Select the .asm, .dft, .par, or .psm to start an assembly, drafting, part, or sheet metal file, respectively.

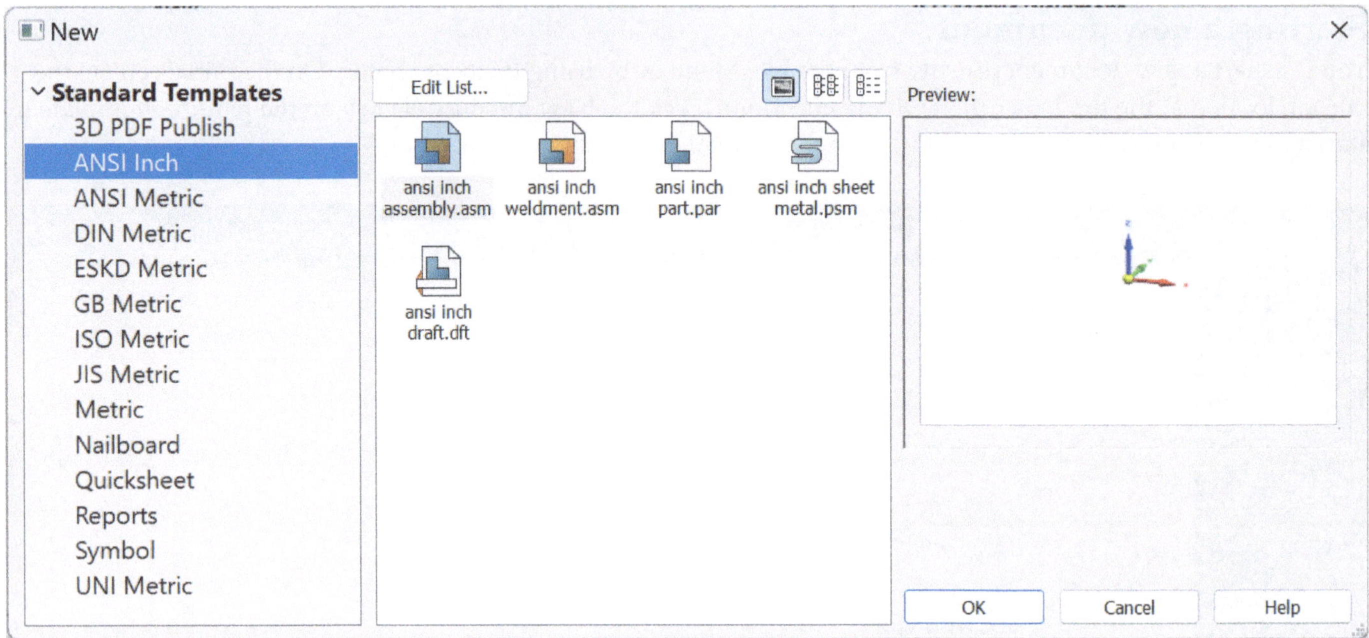

Solid Edge Options

You can customize Solid Edge as per your requirement. On the **File Menu**, click **Settings > Options** to open the **Solid Edge Options** dialog. On this dialog, you can set options on each of the pages. The options on this dialog vary depending upon the environment that you are in.

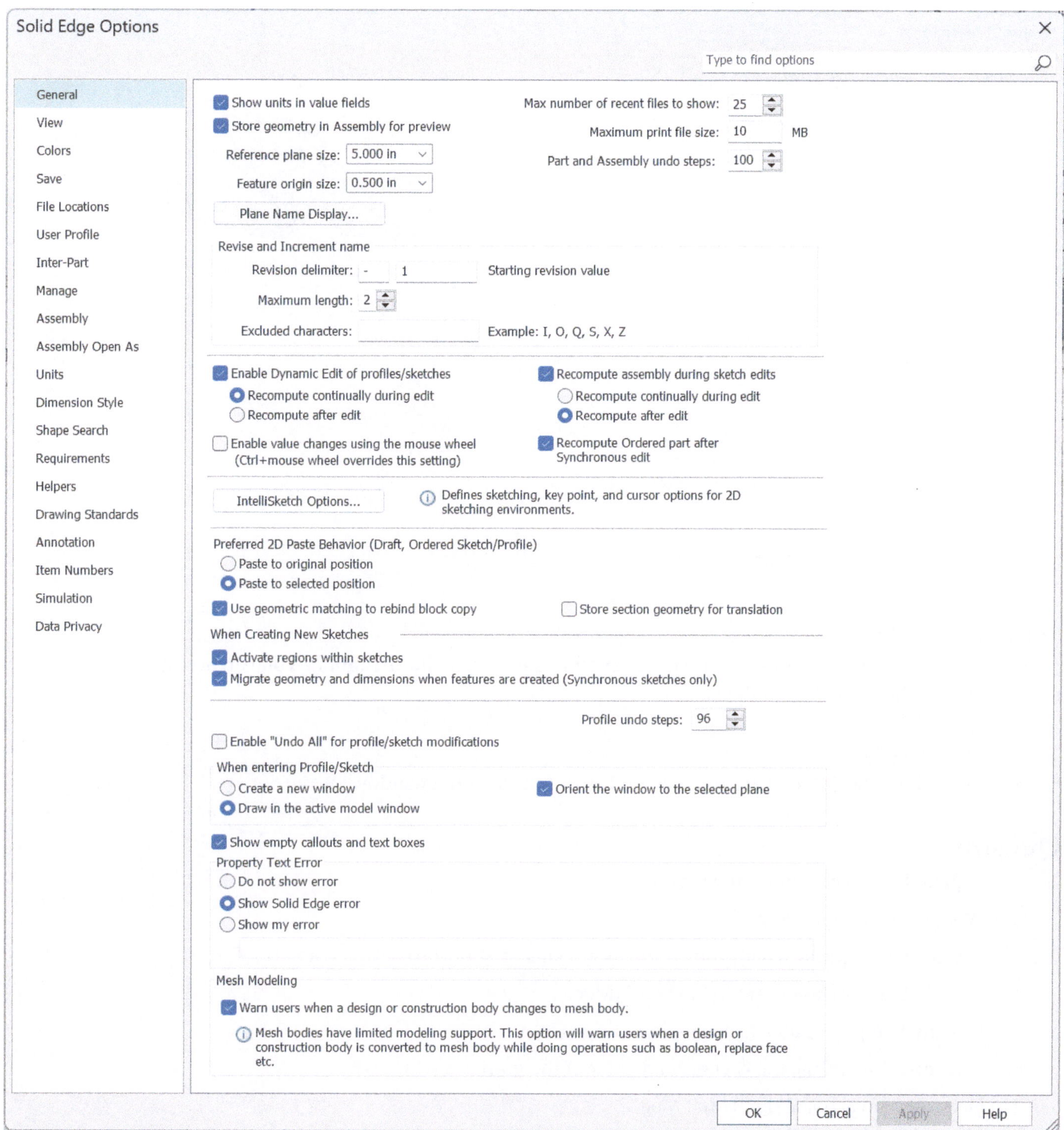

View Overrides dialog

The **View Overrides** dialog helps you to change the background color, rendering, and light settings. On the ribbon, click **View > Style > View Overrides** to open this dialog. On this dialog, click the **Background** tab and set the **Type** to **Solid**. Next, select **White** from the drop-down; the background color is changed to white.

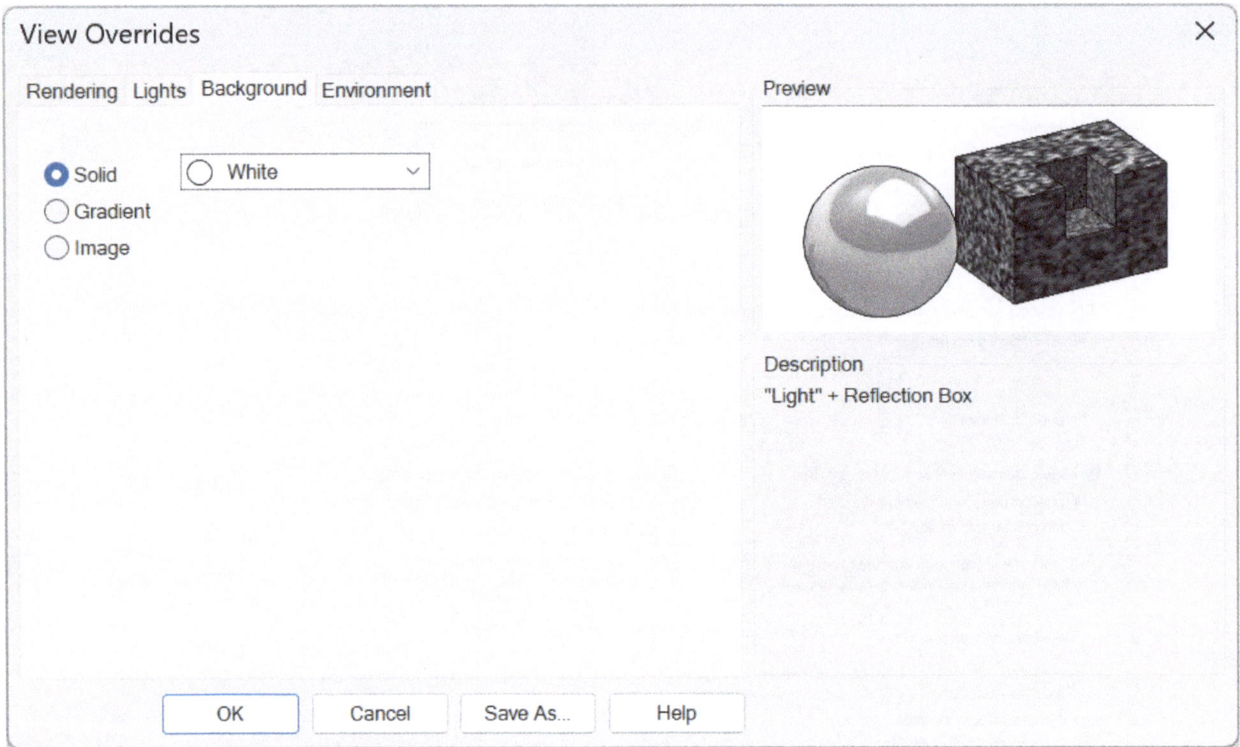

Solid Edge Help

Solid Edge offers you a help system that goes beyond basic command definition. You can access Solid Edge help by using any of the following methods:

- Press the F1 key.
- Click on the **Solid Edge Help** option on the right side of the window.

Questions

1. Explain how to customize the Ribbon.
2. What is the design intent?
3. Give one example of where you would establish a relationship between a part's features.
4. Explain the term 'associativity' in Solid Edge.
5. List any two procedures to access Solid Edge Help.
6. How can you change the background color of the graphics window?
7. How can you activate the Radial Menu?
8. How is Solid Edge a parametric modeling application?

Chapter 2: Sketch Techniques

This chapter covers the methods and commands to create sketches in the part environment. The commands and methods are discussed in the context of the part environment. In Solid Edge, the part environment is divided into two separate modes: Synchronous and Ordered.

In Solid Edge, you create a rough sketch and then apply dimensions and constraints that define its shape and size. The dimensions define the length, size, and angle of a sketch element, whereas constraints define the relations between sketch elements.

The topics covered in this chapter are:

- Create sketches in the Part environment (Synchronous and Ordered mode)
- Use relationships and dimensions to control the shape and size of a sketch
- Learn sketching commands
- Learn commands and options that help you to create sketches easily

Create Sketches in the Ordered mode

Ordered is the default mode activated in the Part environment. This mode offers a separate environment called the Sketching environment. To open this environment, select **Home > Sketch > Sketch** on the ribbon; the Sketch environment will open, showing the Sketch command bar with **Coincident Plane** as the default option. Click on a **Base Reference Plane** from the graphics window. You will notice that the **Line** command is activated by default. You can start sketching lines or select any other sketching command. After completing the sketch, select **Home > Close > Close Sketch** on the ribbon. Next, enter the sketch's name and then click the **Finish** button on the **Sketch** command bar.

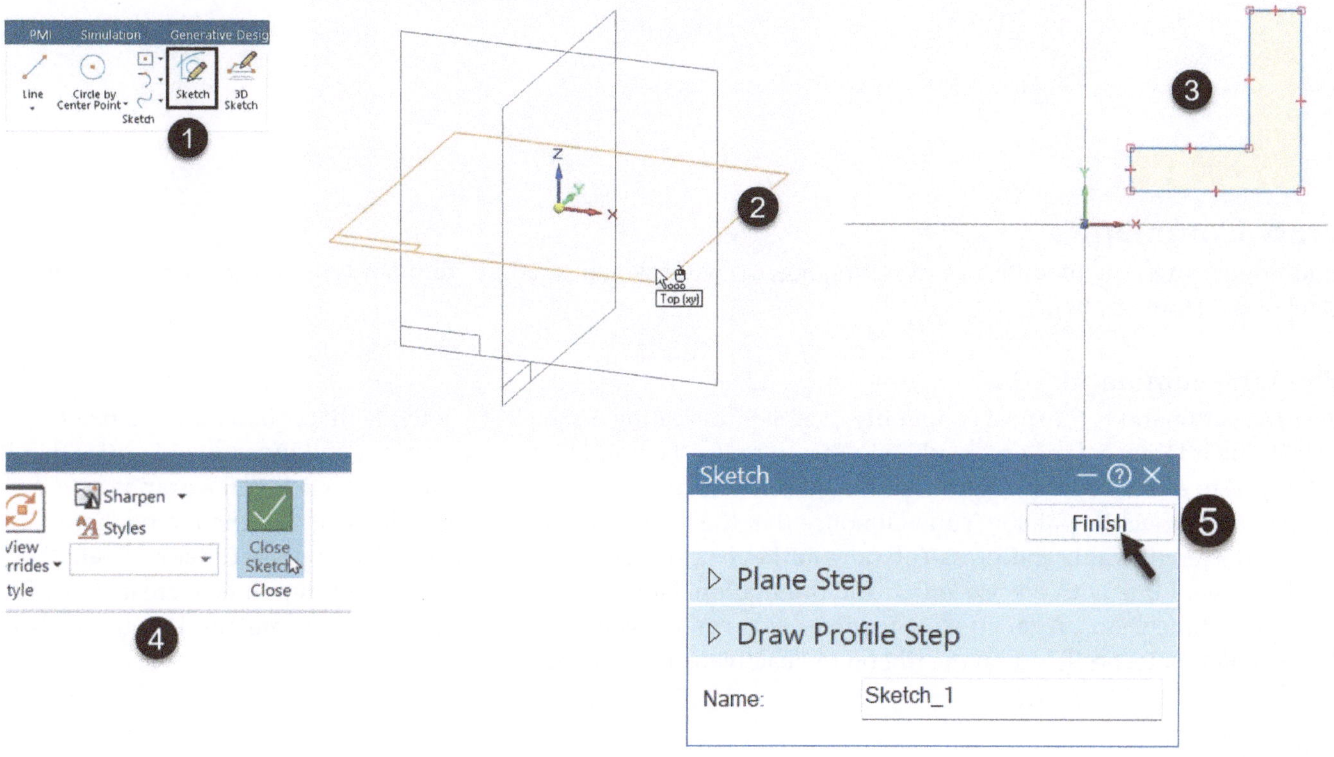

Create Sketches in the Synchronous mode

The Synchronous mode was the default mode in previous versions of Solid Edge. You can activate this mode by right-clicking and selecting **Transition to Synchronous** or selecting **Tools > Model > Synchronous** on the ribbon. The process of creating sketches in this mode is very simple. You need to select a sketch command and then define a plane on which you want to create the sketch. The sketch commands are available in the **Sketching** or **Home** tab of the ribbon. To create a sketch, check the **Base Reference Planes** option under the **PathFinder** to display the **Base Reference Planes**. Next, select any of the sketch command (For example, the **Line** command) from **Sketching > Draw** panel and place the pointer on any one of the Base Reference Planes. You will notice that a lock symbol appears on the plane. Click on the lock symbol (or) press F3 on your keyboard to lock the plane. You can now start drawing sketches on the locked plane. After creating the sketch, press the Esc key and click on the lock icon at the top right corner. The plane will be unlocked.

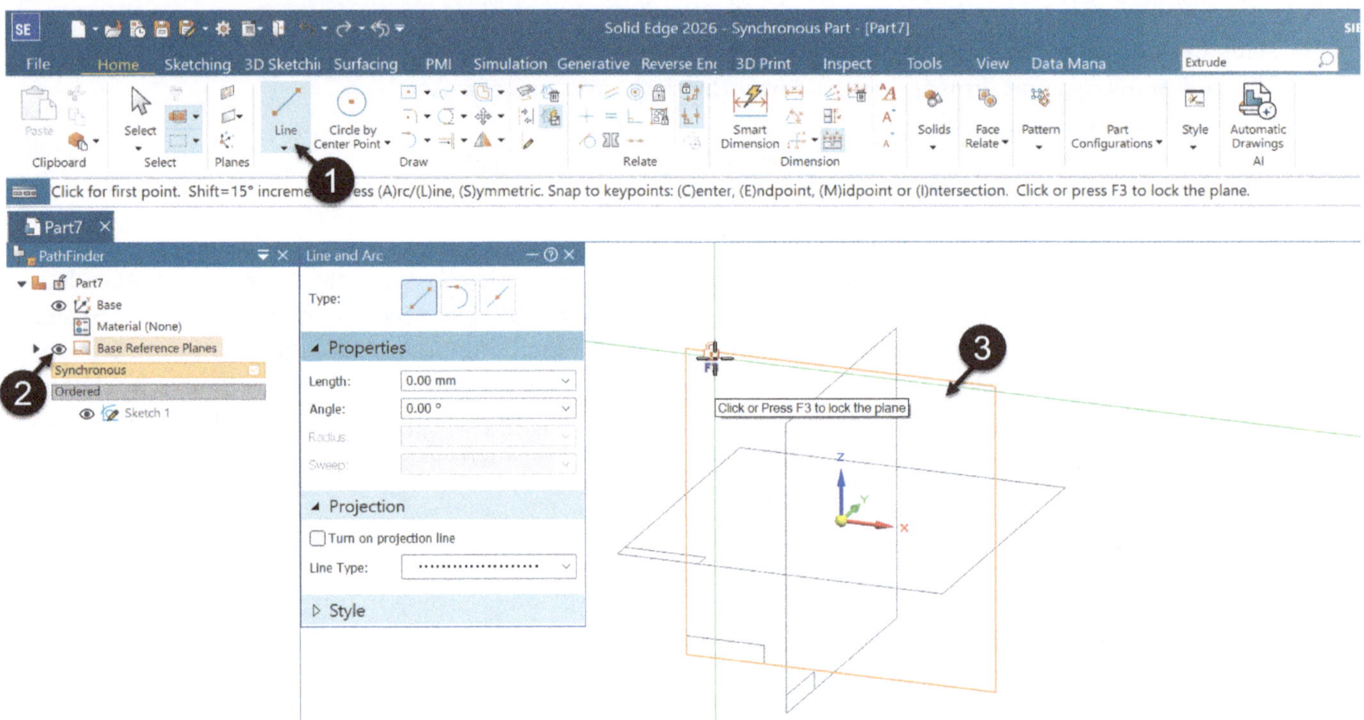

Draw Commands

Solid Edge provides you with a set of commands to create sketches. These commands are located on the **Draw** panel of the **Home** ribbon.

The Line command

The **Line** command is the most commonly used while creating a sketch. To activate this command, you need to click **Home > Draw > Line** on the ribbon. As you move the pointer in the graphics window, you will notice that it is changed to a crosshairs set. It indicates that the command is active. To create a line, click in the graphics window and move the pointer. You will notice that the length and angle dimensions are attached to the line. Type-in the length value and press **Tab** on your keyboard. Type-in the angle value and press **Enter** to create the line. It creates a line with precise length and orientation. However, you can simply select points to create lines and then apply dimensions. After creating the lines, you can press **Esc** to deactivate the **Line** command. You can also click **Home > Select > Select** on the ribbon to deactivate a command.

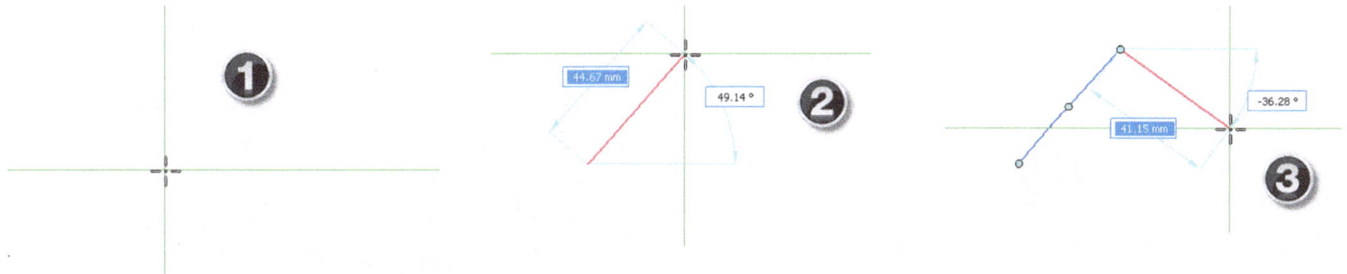

The **Line** command can also be used to draw arcs continuous with lines. Click the **Arc** icon from the command bar to draw this type of arc. The figure below shows the procedure to draw arcs connected to lines.

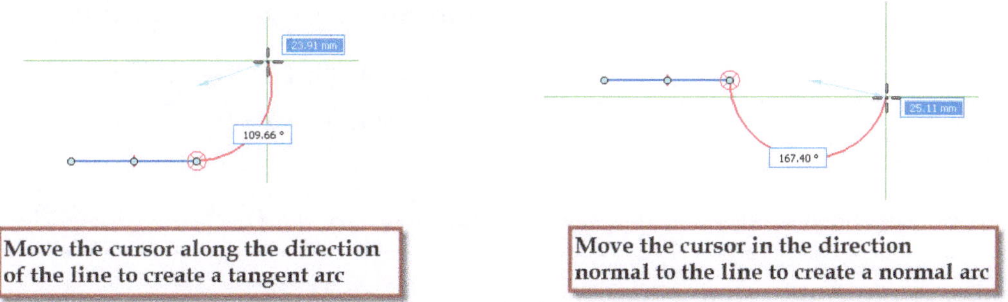

To delete a line, select it and press the **Delete** key. To select more than one line, press and hold the **Ctrl** key and then click on the line segments; the lines will be highlighted. You can also select multiple lines by dragging a box from left to right. Press and hold the left mouse button and drag a box from left to right; the lines inside or crossing the box boundary will be selected. Dragging a box from right to left will only select the lines that are inside the box.

Using Grid and Snap settings

If you are new to Solid Edge, the grid and snap settings will help you create sketches easily. A grid is similar to a graph paper on your computer screen, whereas the snap mode forces the pointer to select the grid points. You can locate sketch points easily and accurately using the grid and snap settings. To use these settings, you need to activate the **Show Grid** and **Snap to Grid** icons on the **Draw** panel of the ribbon. Next, activate a drawing command and start drawing the sketch. You will notice that you can select the grid points easily. It makes it easy to create sketches.

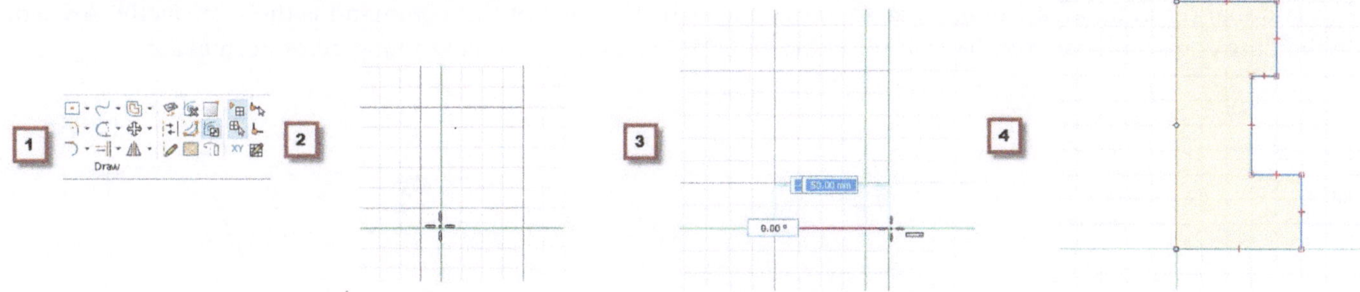

You can change the spacing between the grid points using the **Grid Options** dialog. Select **Sketching > Draw > Grid Options** on the ribbon to open this dialog. Next, modify the **Major line spacing value** to change the distance between the dark grid lines. Change the **Minor spaces per major** value to change the number of lighter grid lines between two major lines (dark lines). Examine the other options in this dialog. Most of them are self-explanatory.

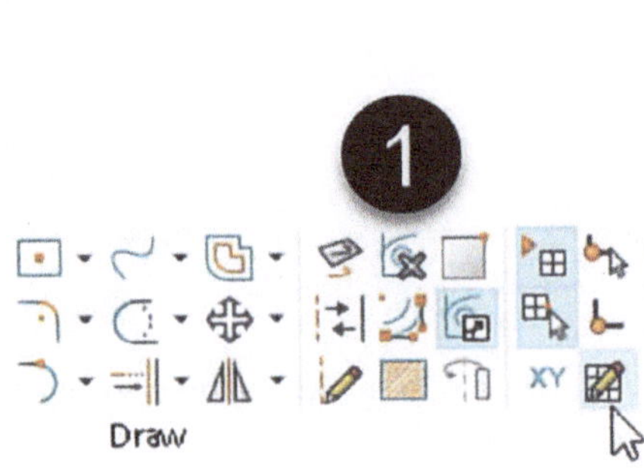

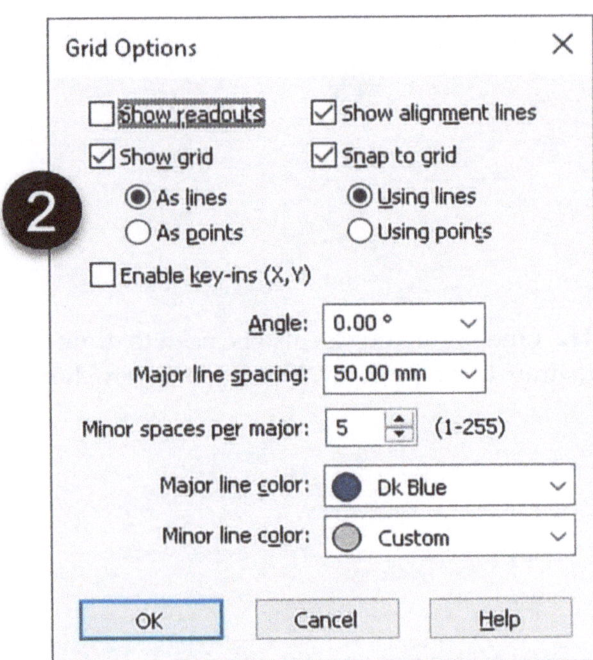

Drawing a Symmetric Line

You can create a symmetric line using the **Line** command. Activate this command, press **S**, and click to define the midpoint of the line. Move the pointer and click to define the endpoint; a symmetric line is created about the specified midpoint.

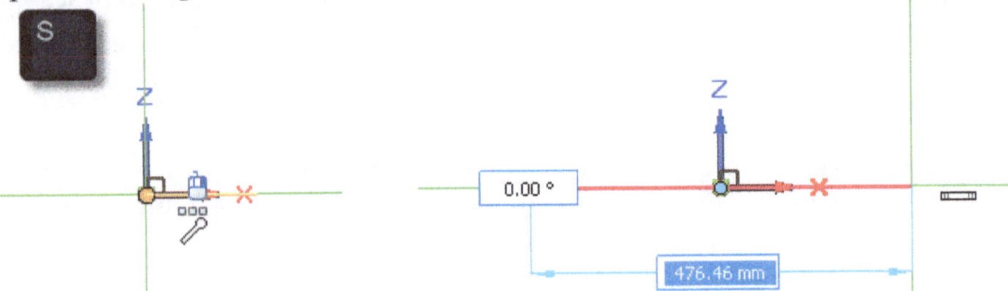

The Tangent Arc command

This command creates an arc tangent to another entity. The working of this command is the same as the **Arc** icon on the **Line** command bar. You have to select the endpoint of a line and create a tangent or normal arc.

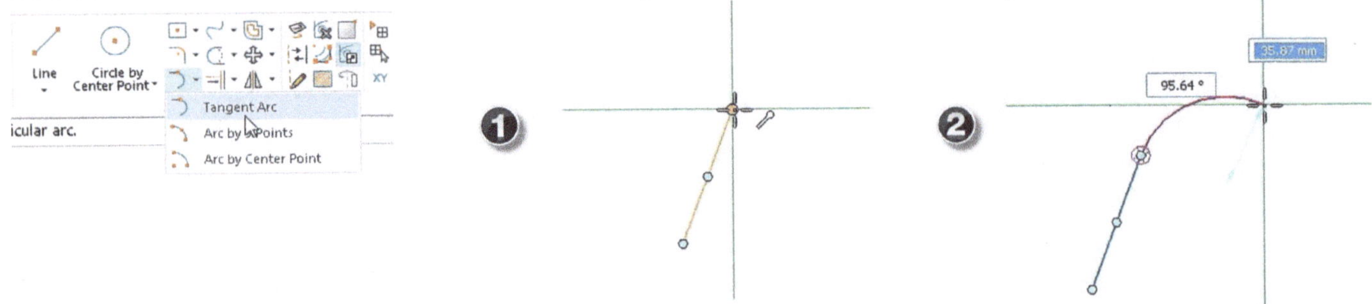

The Arc by 3 Points command

This command creates an arc by defining its start, end, and radius. Activate this command (click **Home > Draw > Tangent Arc > Arc by 3 Points** on the ribbon) and click to define the start point of the arc. Click again to define the endpoint. After defining the arc's start and end, you have to define the size and position of the arc. Move the pointer and click to define the radius and position of the arc (or) type-in the radius value in the dimension box attached to the pointer.

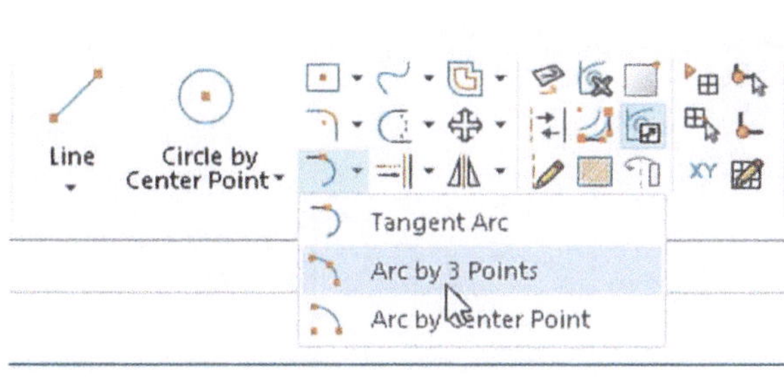

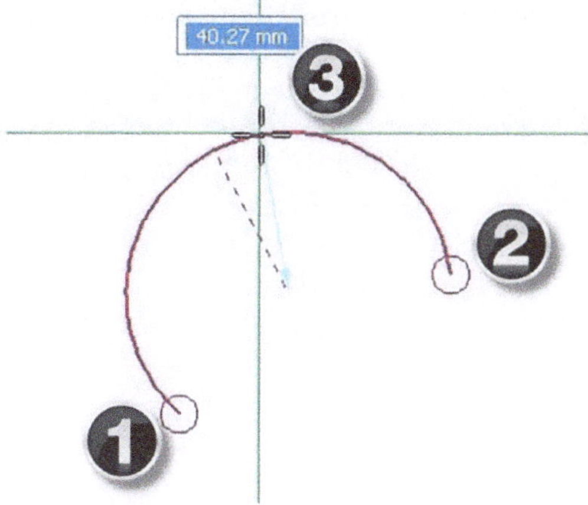

The Arc by Center Point command

This command creates an arc by defining its center, start and endpoints. Activate this command (click **Home > Draw > Tangent Arc > Arc by Center Point** on the ribbon) and click to define the center point. Next, move the pointer, and you will notice that a line appears between the center and the mouse pointer. This line is the radius of the arc. Now, click to define the start point of the arc and move the pointer. You will notice that an arc is drawn from the start point. Now, type-in the radius value and press Tab. Type-in the arc angle and press Enter (or) simply move the pointer and click.

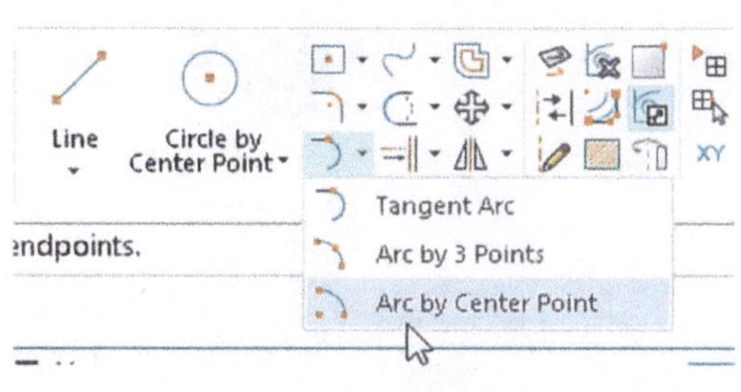

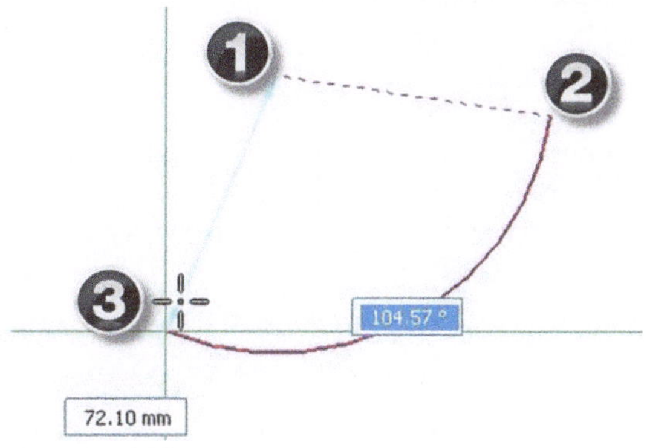

The Rectangle by Center command

This command creates a rectangle by defining its center and one corner point. Centered rectangles are particularly useful when you need to create symmetrical shapes. By defining the center point, you can ensure that the rectangle is perfectly balanced on both sides.

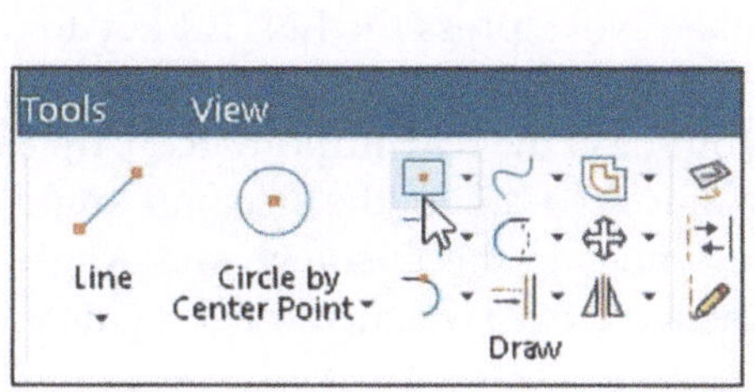

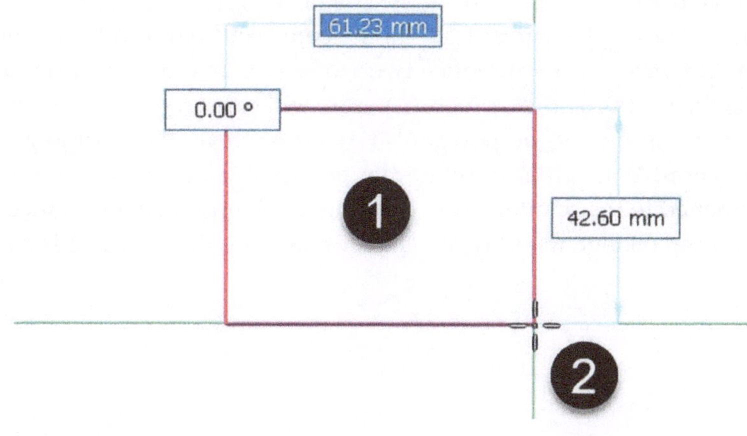

The Rectangle by 2 Points command

This command creates a rectangle by defining its diagonal corners. This command can be used for defining the boundaries of machine parts, circuit boards, and structural members.

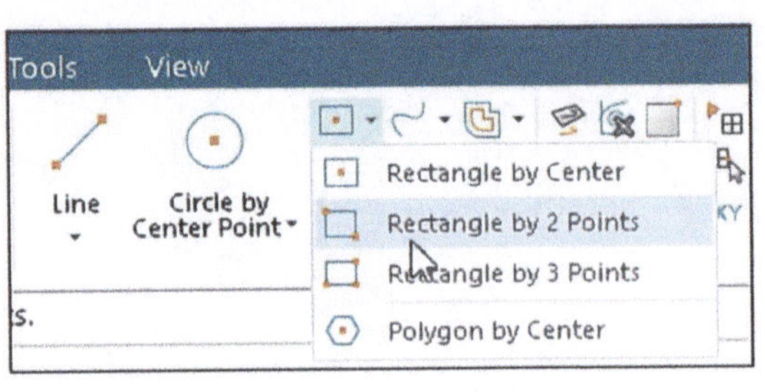

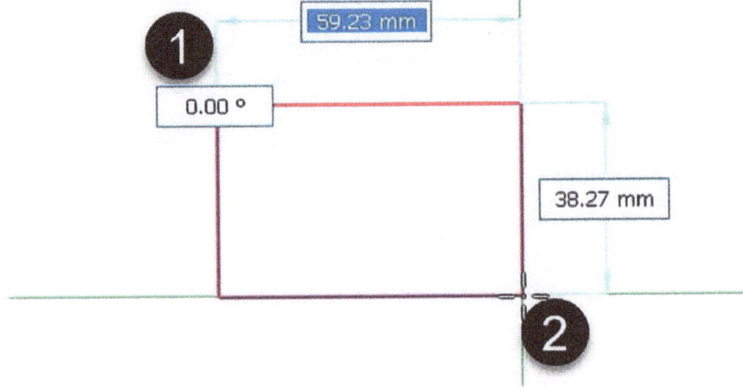

The Rectangle by 3 Points command

This command creates an inclined rectangle. The first two points define the length and inclination angle of the rectangle. The third point defines its width.

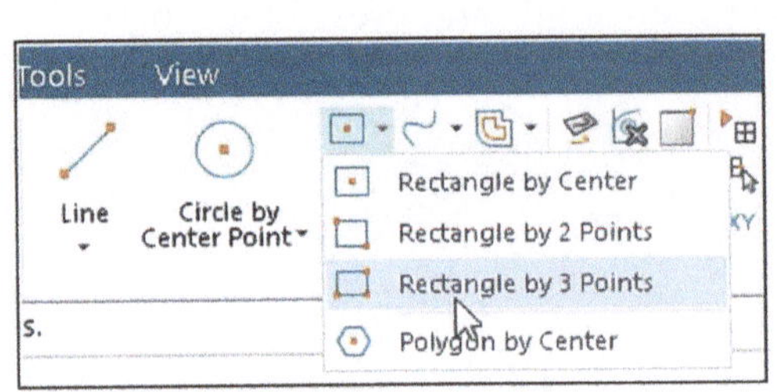

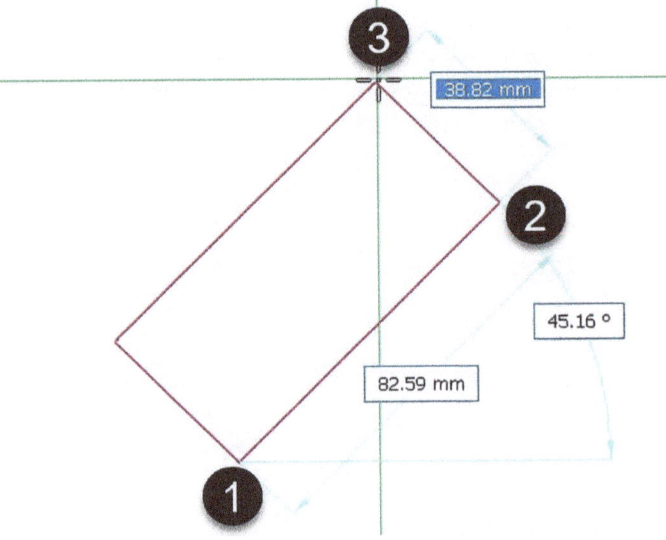

The Polygon by Center command

This command provides a simple way to create a polygon with any number of sides. As soon as you activate this command, a command bar pops up. Now, click in the graphics window to define the center of the polygon. As you move the pointer away from the center, you will see a preview of the polygon. To change the polygon's number of sides, click in the **Sides** field on the command bar and type a new number. Next, press the ENTER key to update the preview. You will notice two icons available on the command bar: **By Vertex** and **By Midpoint**. If you select the **By Vertex** icon, a polygon's vertex will be attached to the pointer. If you select the **By Midpoint** icon, the pointer will be on one of the polygon's flat sides. Next, click in the graphics window to define the size and angle of the polygon. You can also define the polygon's size and angle by entering values in the **Distance** and **Angle** fields attached to the pointer. After creating a polygon, you will notice that a dashed circle is created touching its vertices. You can change the polygon size by changing the size of this circle.

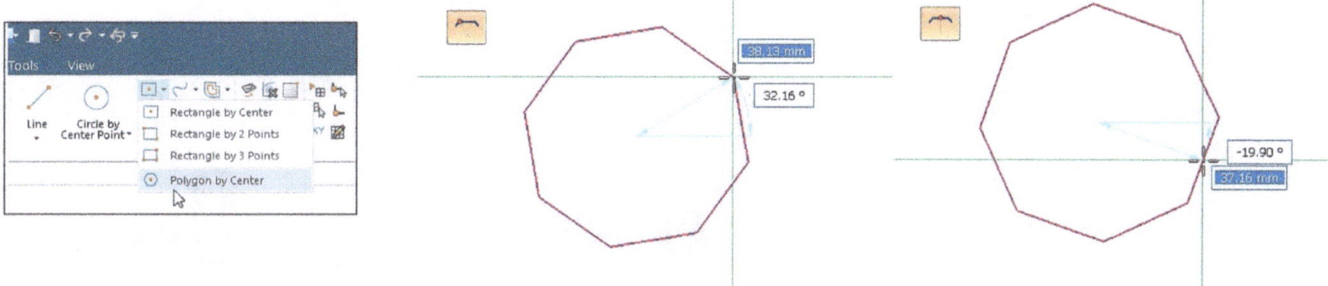

The Circle by Center Point command

This command is a common way to draw a circle. Activate this command (click **Home > Draw > Circle by Center Point** on the ribbon) and click to locate the circle's center. Next, move the pointer, and then click again to define the diameter of the circle. You can also enter the diameter or radius value of the circle on the command bar.

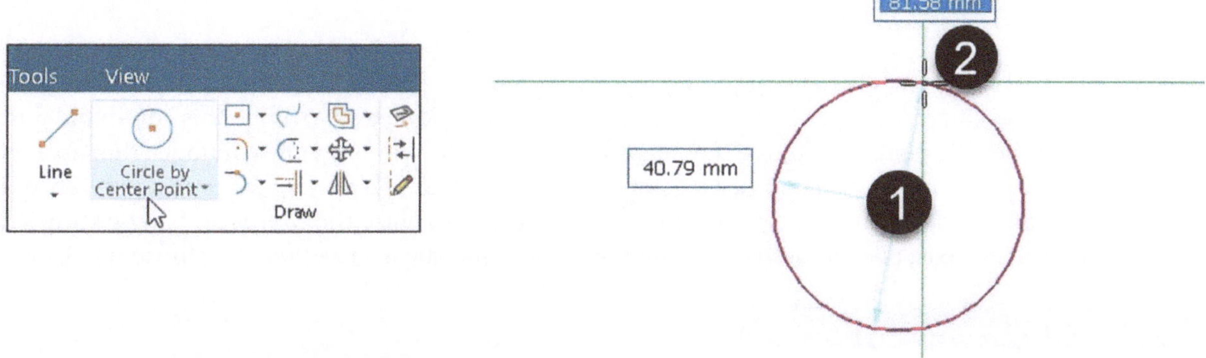

The Circle by 3 Points command

This command creates a circle by using three points. Activate this command and select three points from the graphics window. You can also select existing points from the sketch geometry. The first two points define the location of the circle, and the third point defines its diameter.

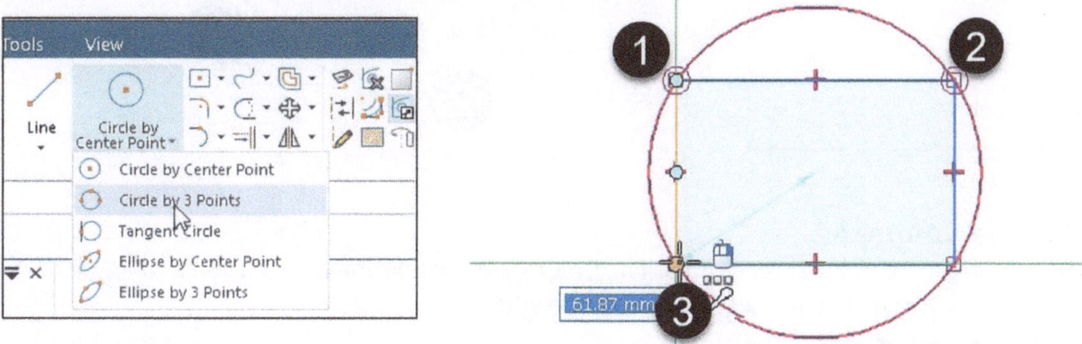

The Tangent Circle command

This command creates a circle by using two tangent points. Activate this command and select two lines, arcs, or circles; a circle will be drawn tangent to them.

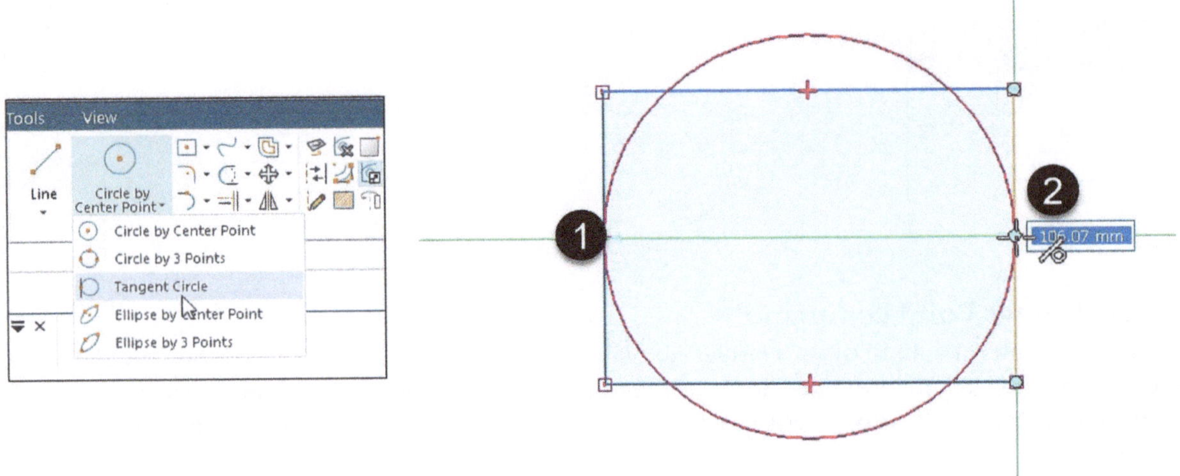

The Ellipse by Center Point command

This command creates an ellipse using a center point and major and minor axes. Activate this command and click to define the center of the ellipse. As you move the pointer away from the center, you will notice that an axis is displayed. It can be either the major or the minor axis of the ellipse. When you click to place it, a preview of the ellipse appears, and you can define the other axis. Note that you can also enter the radius and angle values of the axis. After defining the first axis, click to define the other axis (or) enter the axis radius; the ellipse will be drawn.

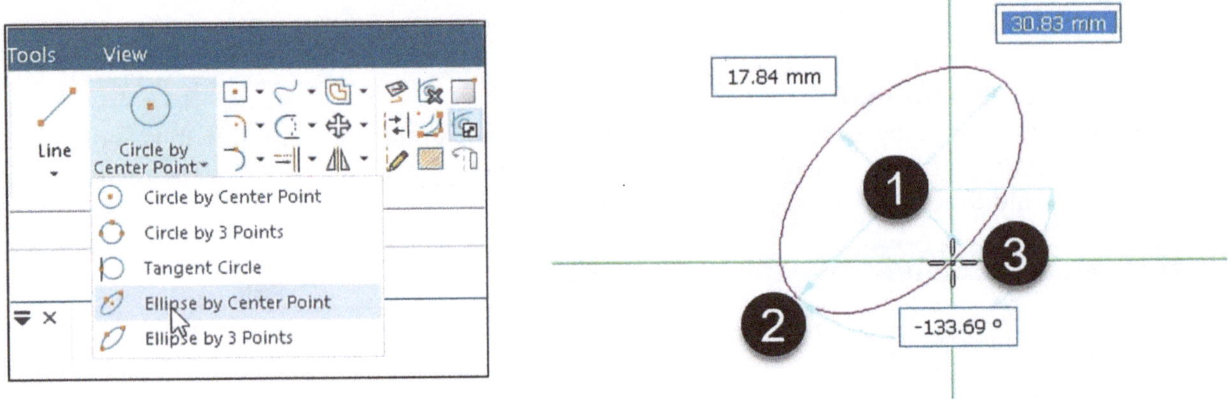

The Ellipse by 3 Points command

This command creates an ellipse by using three points. The first two points define the location and angle of the first axis of the ellipse. The third point defines the second axis of the ellipse.

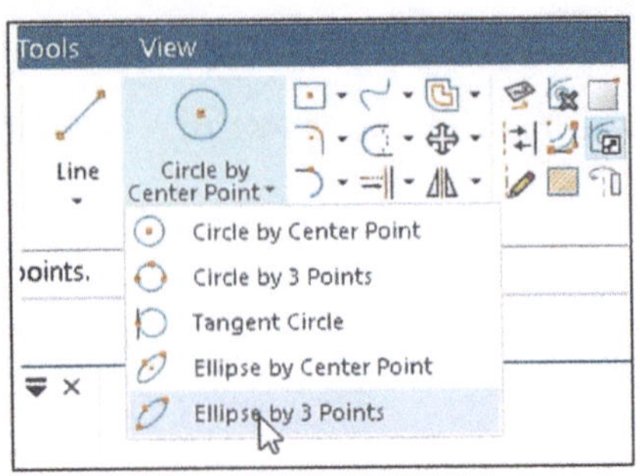

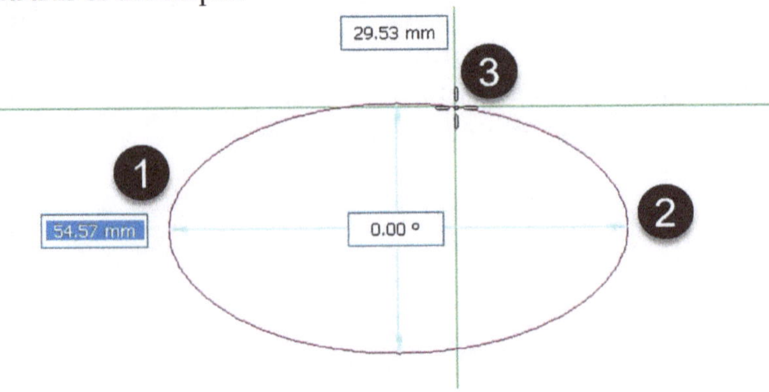

The Curve command

This command creates a smooth B-spline curve along with the selected points. B-Splines are non-uniform curves, which are used to create irregular shapes. You can select points or press the left mouse button and drag to create a curve.

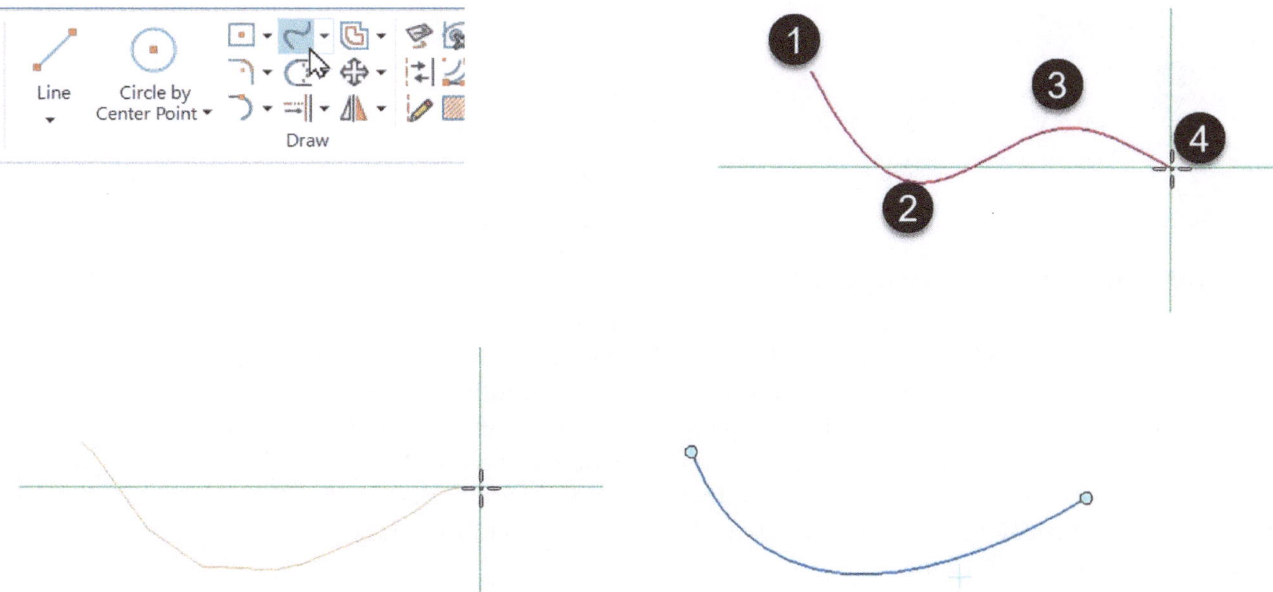

You also use the **Close Curve** option to create a closed curve.

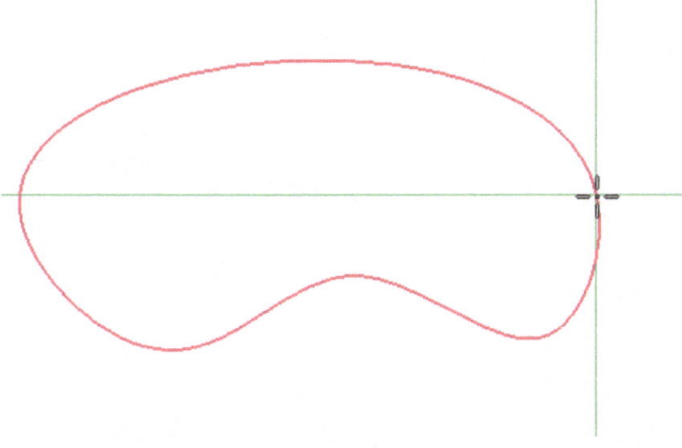

Press **Esc** to deactivate this command, and then select the curve; you will notice that control vertices are displayed on the curve. Click and drag the control vertices to edit the curve shape. You can use the **Add/Remove Points** option on the command bar to add more points or remove the curve points.

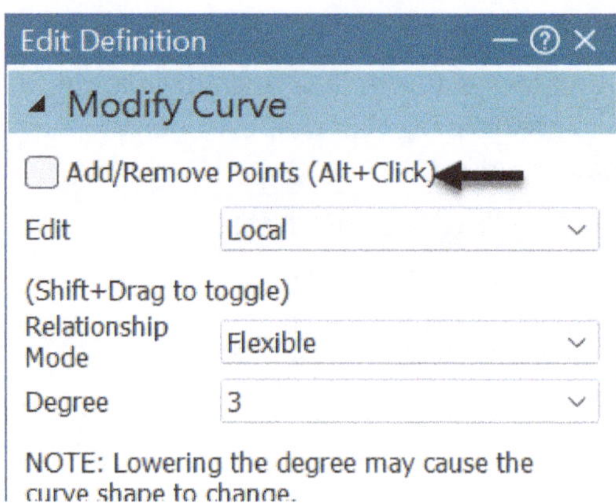

The Smart Dimension command

It is generally considered good practice to ensure that every sketch you create is fully constrained before moving on to create features. The term 'fully-constrained' means that the sketch has a definite shape and size. You can fully-constrain a sketch by using dimensions and relations. You can add dimensions to a sketch by using the **Smart Dimension** command. You can use this command to add all dimensions such as length, angle, and diameter. This command creates a dimension based on the geometry you select. For instance, to dimension a circle, activate the **Smart Dimension** command and then click on the circle. Next, move the pointer and click again to position the dimension; you will notice that a box pops up. You can type in a value in this box and then press Enter to update the dimension.

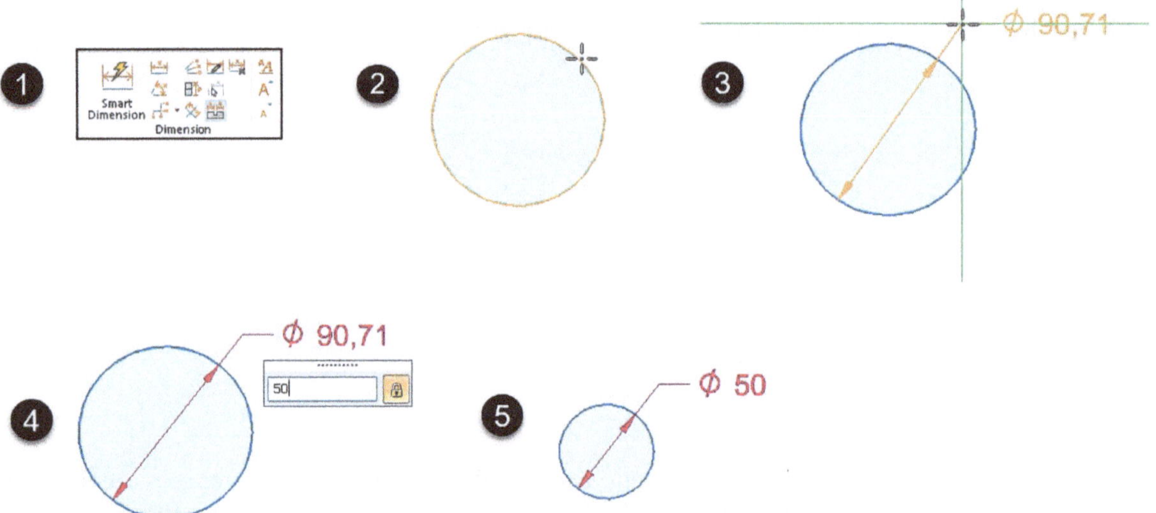

If you click a line, this command automatically creates a linear dimension. Click once more to position the dimension, and then type-in a value and press Enter; the dimension will be updated.

You can use the **Angle** option on the **Smart Dimension** command bar to add an angle dimension.

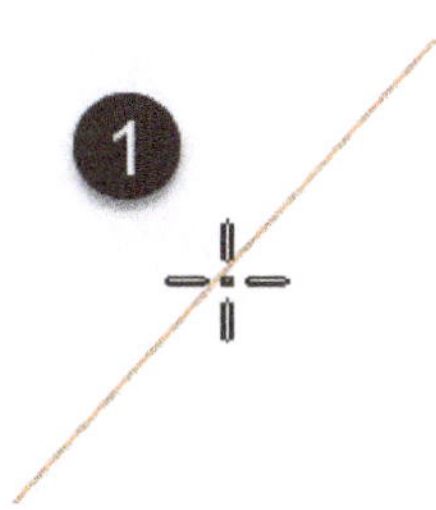

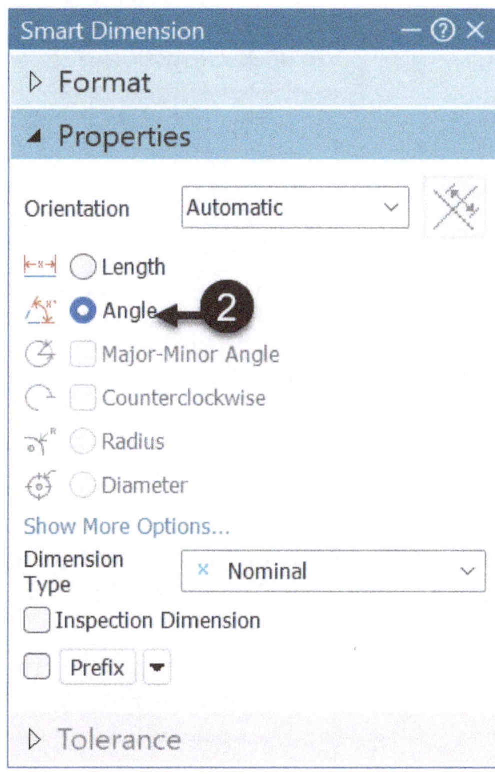

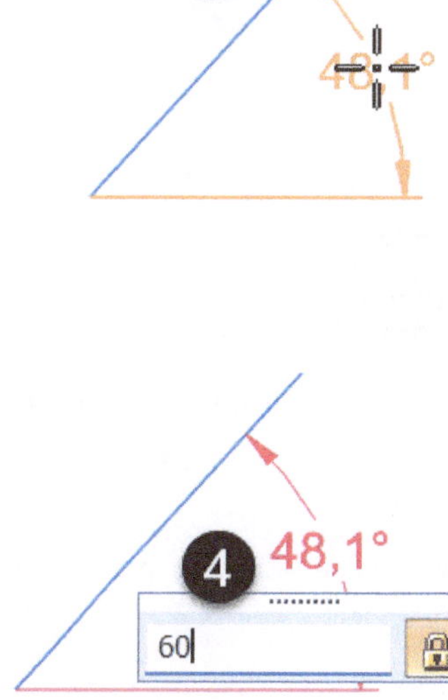

The Distance Between command

This command creates a linear dimension between two points. Activate this command and select the **Horizontal/Vertical** option on the command bar. Select the endpoints of a line and move the pointer to establish a vertical or horizontal dimension.

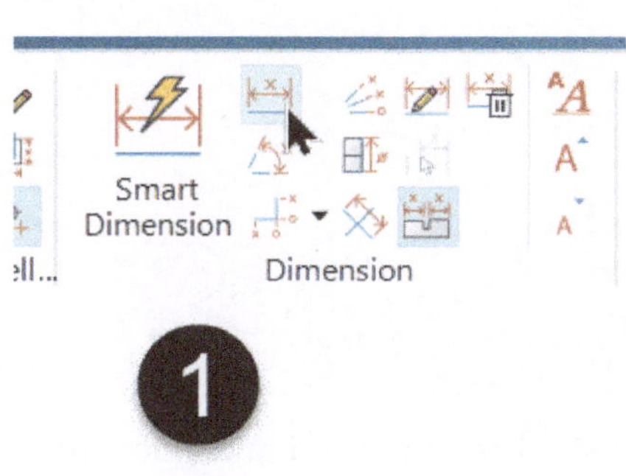

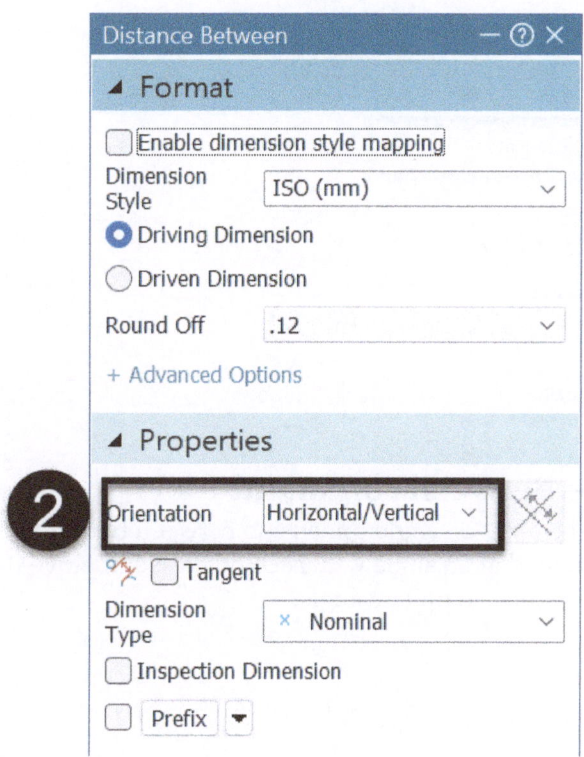

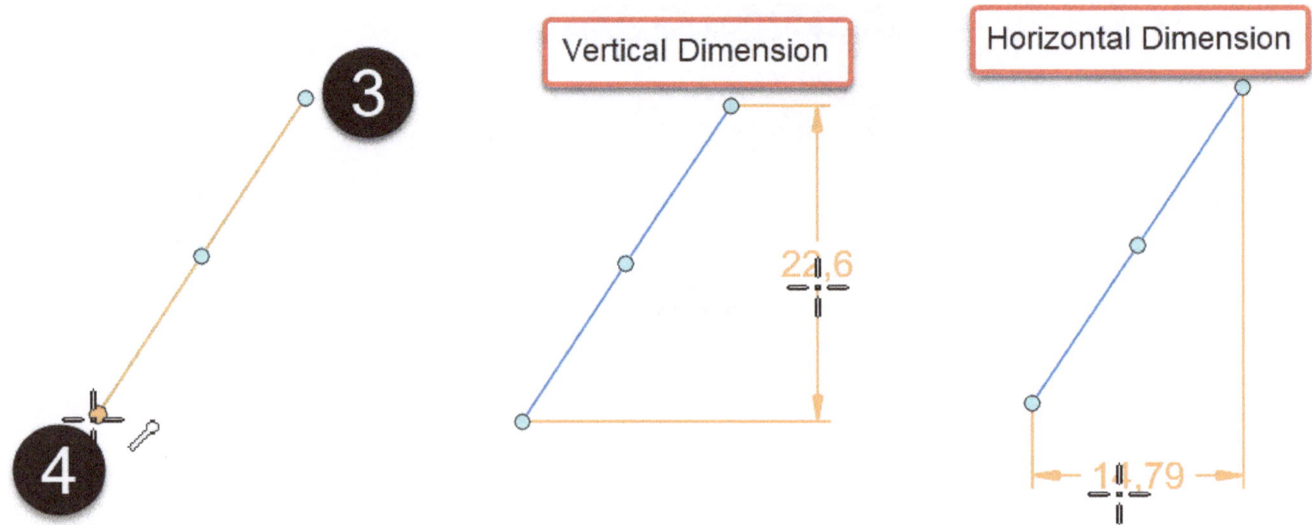

If you want the line's true length, select the **By 2 Points** option on the command bar. Next, select the endpoints of a line, and move the pointer and position the dimension. Type-in a value in the box and press Enter to update the dimension.

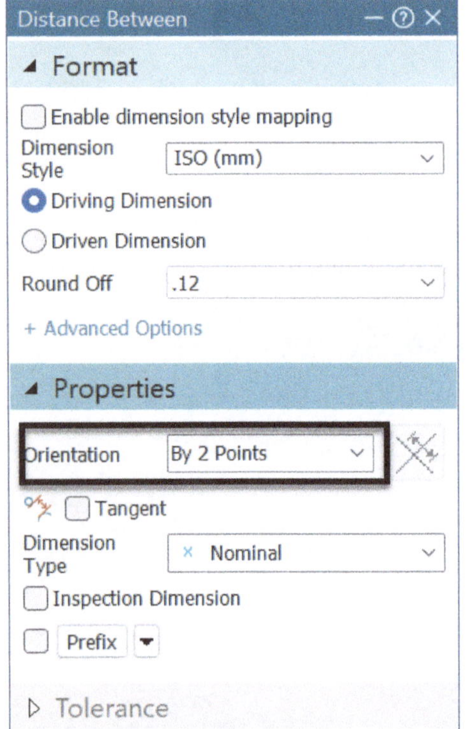

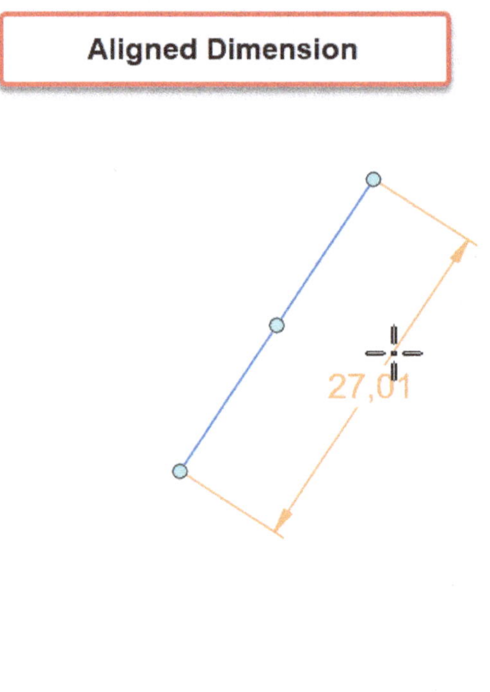

The Angle Between command

This command creates an angle dimension between two selected elements. Activate this command and select the elements positioned at an angle with each other. Next, move the pointer and position the dimension. Type-in a value and press Enter to update angle.

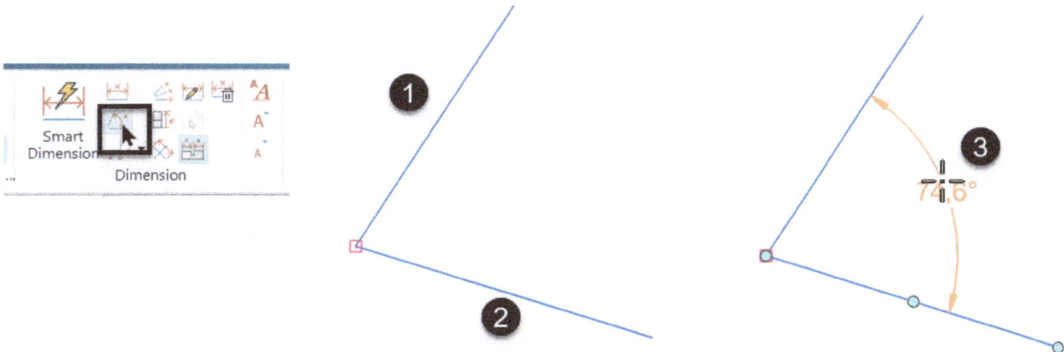

In the **Angle Between** dialog, the **Major-Minor Angle** option allows you to switch between the larger (major) or smaller (minor) angle formed by the intersecting elements. By default, Solid Edge displays the minor angle, but you can check this option to measure the major angle, depending on your design needs.

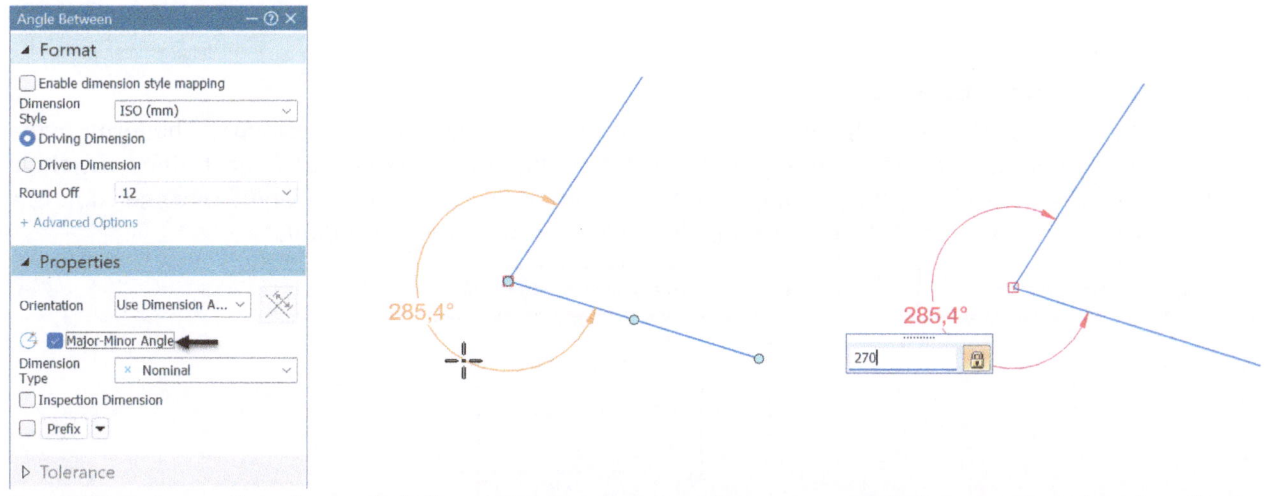

In addition to creating the angled dimension between two lines, you can define an arc angle using the **Angle Between** command. Activate this command and select the endpoints of the arc. Next, click on the center point of the arc, move the pointer, and position the angle dimension.

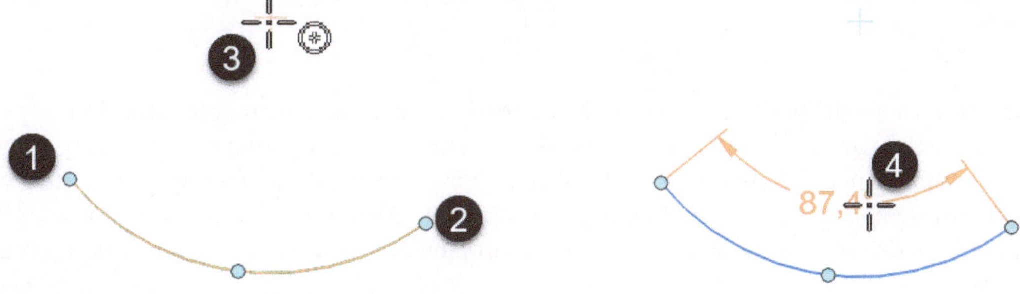

Auto-Scale Sketch

The **Auto-Scale Sketch** option (On the ribbon, click **Sketching** tab > **Draw** group > **Auto-Scale Sketch**) automatically scales the sketch when you edit its first dimension. This can be useful for keeping the sketch's proportions consistent while you make adjustments. This option is active by default, and it is deactivated when you add the second dimension to the sketch.

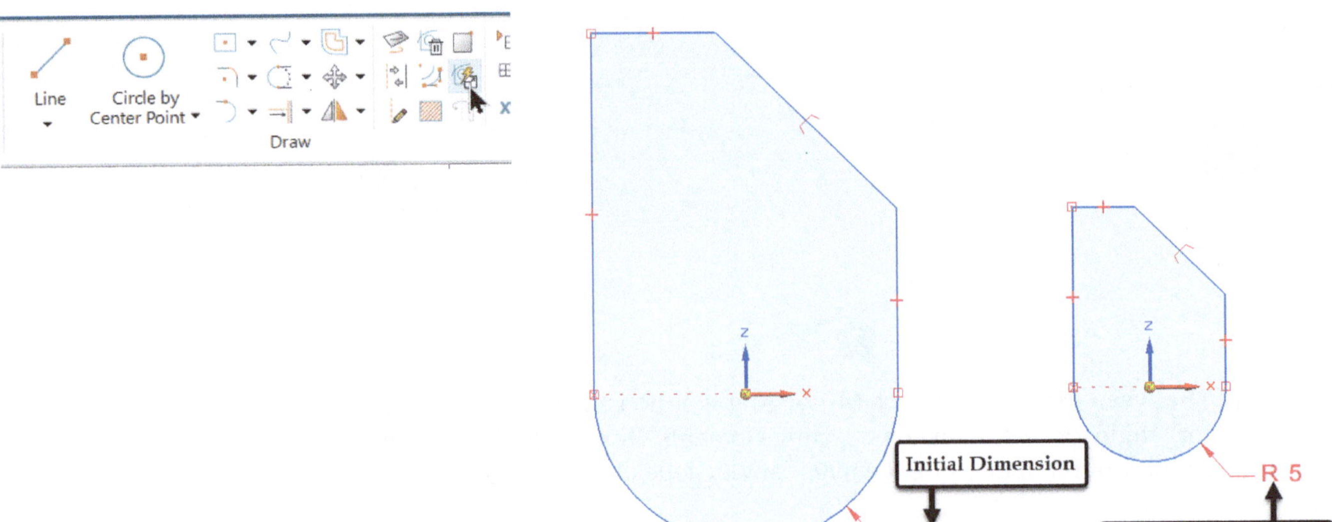

Driving Vs Driven dimensions

When creating sketches for a part, Solid Edge will not allow you to over-constrain the geometry. The term 'over-constrain' means adding more dimensions than required. The following figure shows a fully constrained sketch. If you add another dimension to this sketch (e.g., diagonal dimension), it appears blue. This type of dimension is a driven dimension. You cannot double-click and edit this dimension because it is redundant.

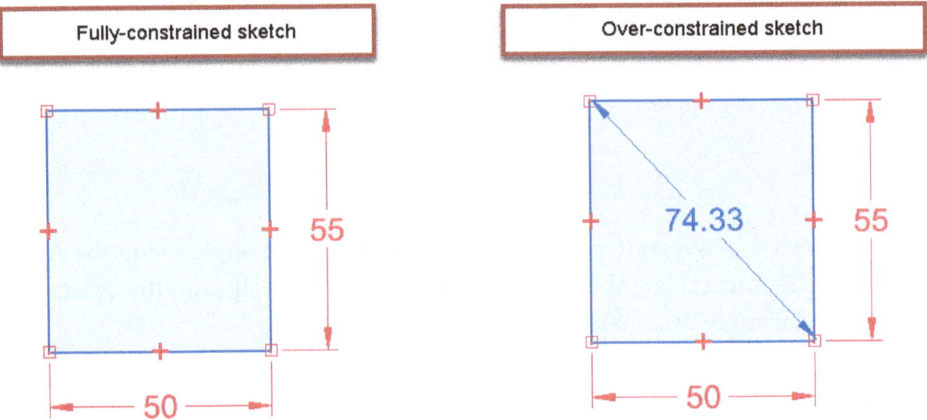

Existing driving dimensions (dimensions in red color) already define the sketch geometry. Driving dimensions are so named because they drive the geometry of the sketch. Double-clicking one of the driving dimensions and changing the value will change the geometry of the sketch. For example, if you change the width's value, the driven dimension automatically goes along the diagonal updates. Also, note that the dimensions, which are initially created, will be driving dimensions, whereas the dimensions created after fully defining the sketch are driven dimensions.

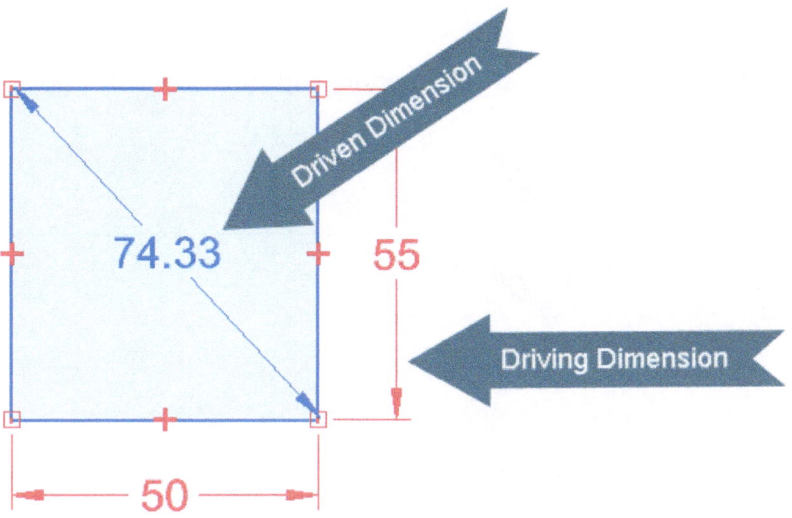

IntelliSketch Auto-Dimensions

Solid Edge provides you with an option to create dimensions automatically. You can do it using the **IntelliSketch** dialog. Click **Sketching > IntelliSketch > IntelliSketch Options** to activate this dialog. On this dialog, select the **Auto-Dimension** tab, and then select the **Automatically create dimensions for new geometry** option. This feature can save time and effort by automatically creating dimensions for new geometry.

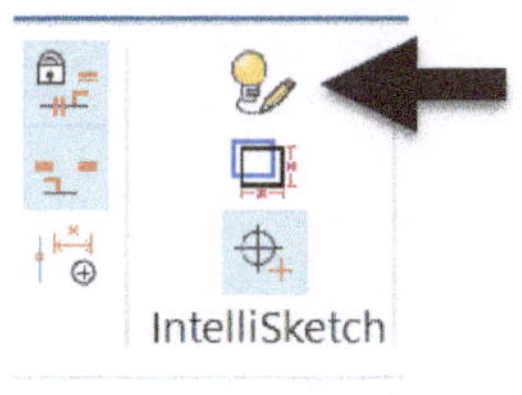

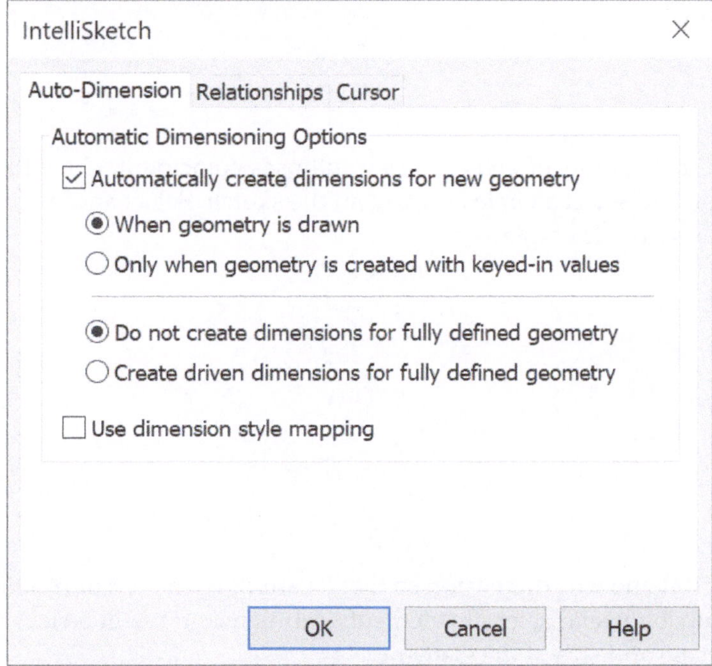

Also, there are other options on the **IntelliSketch** dialog to define the conditions to create automatic dimensions. These options are self-explanatory. Click **OK** after defining the settings in this dialog.

Geometric Relations

Geometric Relations are used to control the shape of a sketch by establishing relationships between the sketch elements. The geometric relations are available on the **Relate** panel of the **Home** tab and are explained next.

Connect

This relation connects a point to another point or element. Activate this button, and then select two points; the selected points will be connected.

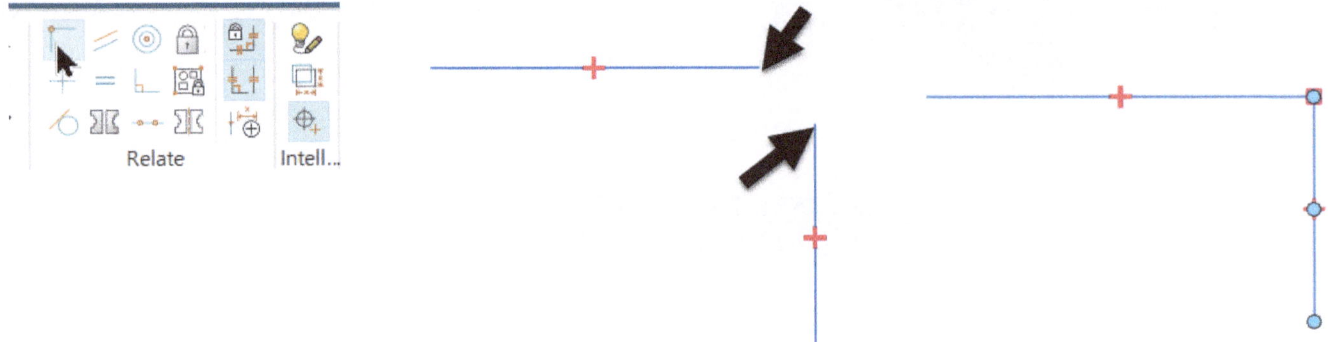

Parallel

This relation makes two lines parallel to each other. Click the **Parallel** button on the **Relate** group of the ribbon, and then select two lines from the sketch; the first line is parallel to the second line.

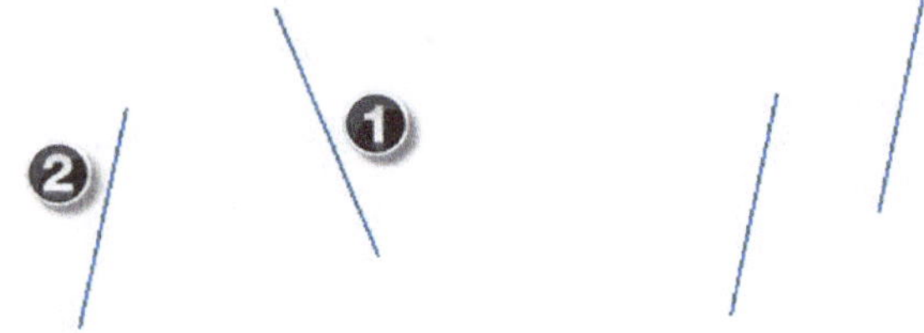

Concentric

This relation makes the center points of arcs, circles or ellipses coincident. Click the **Concentric** button on the **Relate** group of the ribbon and select a circle or arc from the sketch. Select another circle or arc. The first circle/arc will be concentric with the second circle/arc.

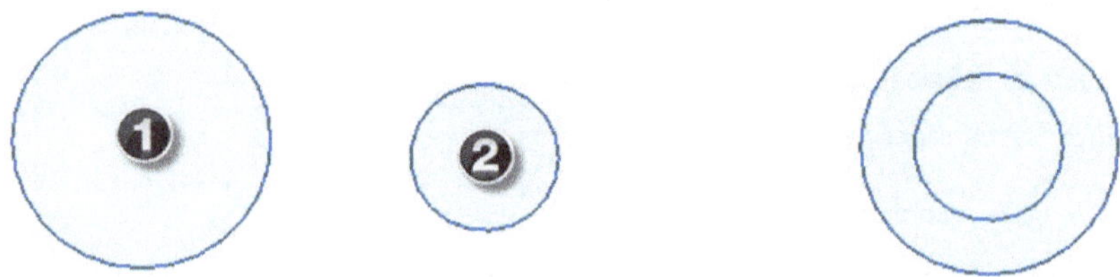

Lock

This relation locks a sketch element or dimension so that it cannot be moved or modified. Click the **Lock** button on the **Relate** group of the ribbon and select an element or dimension; it will be locked at its current position. Also, you cannot change the shape and size of the element.

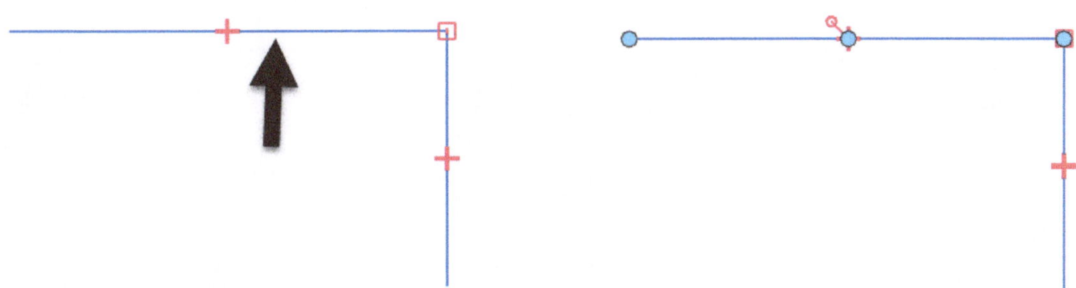

Horizontal/Vertical

The **Horizontal/Vertical** command makes a line or two points of a sketch horizontal or vertical. Click the **Horizontal/Vertical** button on the **Relate** group of the ribbon and select a line or lines; the lines positioned at an angle below 45-degrees will be made horizontal. The lines positioned at an angle above 45-degrees will be made vertical.

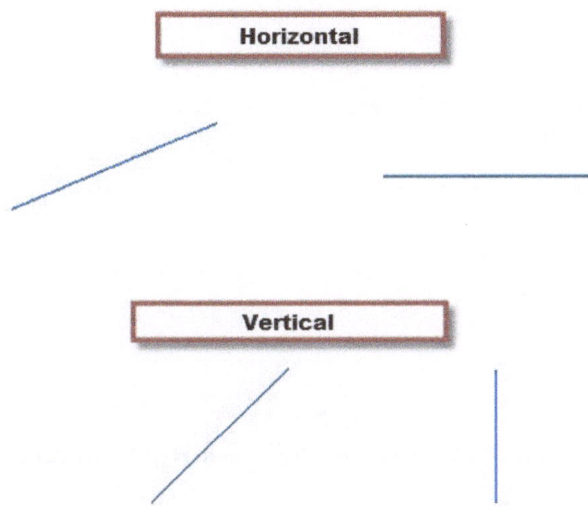

Equal

This relation makes the selected objects equal in magnitude. For example, click the **Equal** button on the **Relate** group of the ribbon and select two circles; the diameter of the selected circles will become equal. If you select two lines, the length of the two lines will be equal.

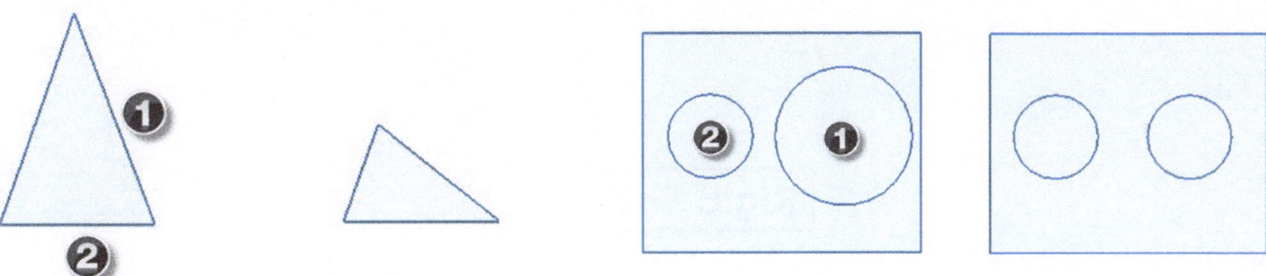

Perpendicular

This relation makes two lines perpendicular to each other. Click the **Perpendicular** button on the **Relate** group of the ribbon and select two lines from the sketch. The first line will be made perpendicular to the second line.

Rigid Set

This relation makes the selected objects act as a single unit. Click the **Rigid Set** button on the **Relate** group of the ribbon and select two or more objects from the sketch. Click the **Accept** button on the command bar. The selected objects will be made into a rigid set.

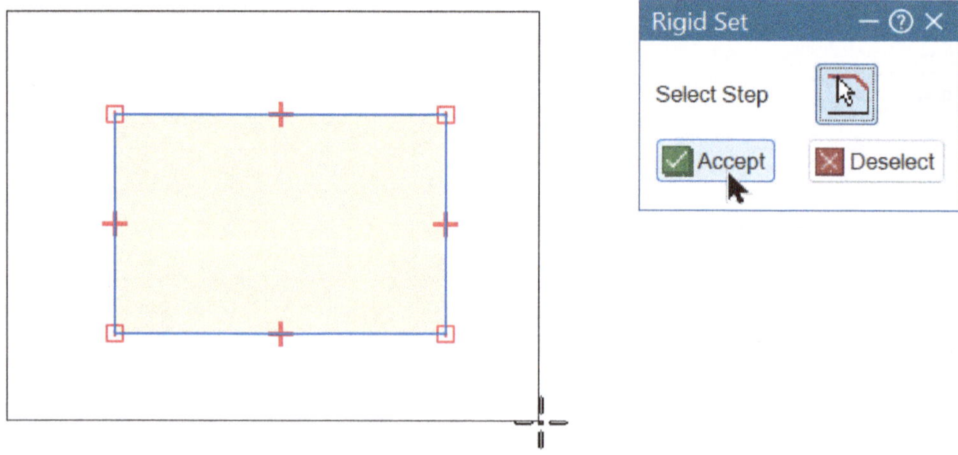

Now, click and drag any one of the objects from the rigid set. You will notice that the entire set will be dragged.

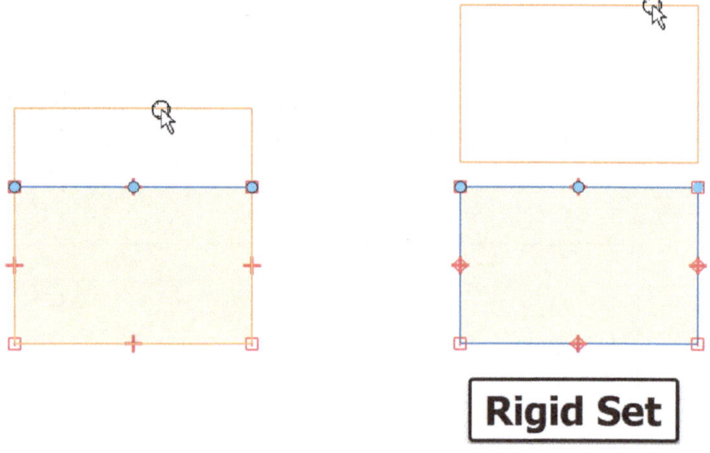

Tangent

This relation makes an arc, circle, or line tangent to another arc or circle. Click the **Tangent** button on the **Relate** group of the ribbon and select a circle, arc, or line. Select another circle, arc, or line. The first object will be tangent to the second object.

You can also make a curve continuous with another curve or arc using the **Tangent** relation.

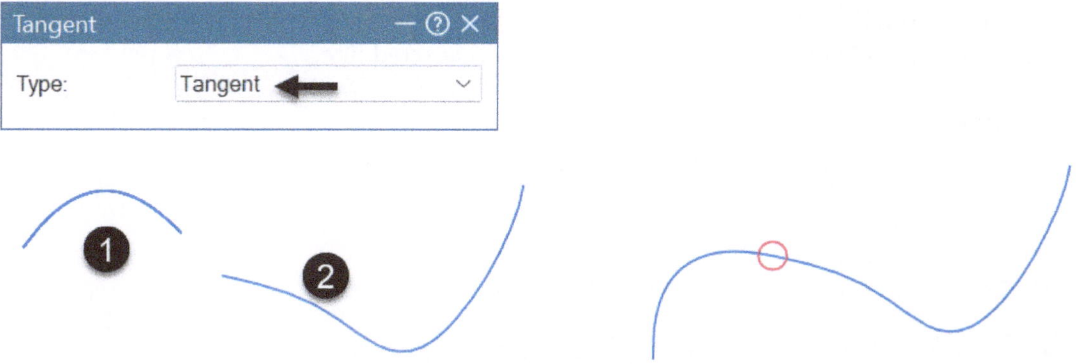

The **Tangent + Equal Curvature** option not only makes the curve or arc smoothly connect to another but also ensures that it matches the length of the other curve or arc. This means they are not only touching but are also of the same size.

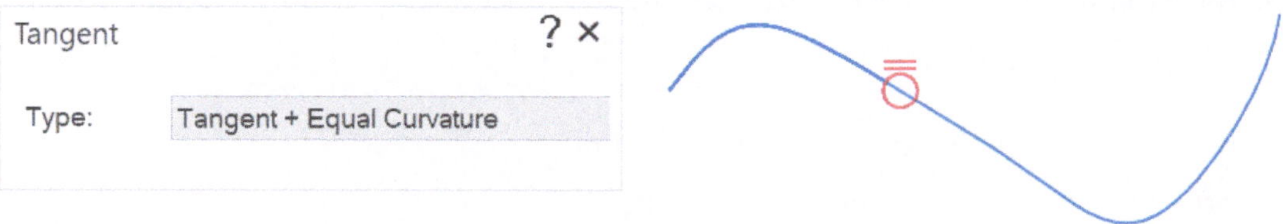

The **Parallel Tangent Vectors** option allows you to create a smooth curve or arc that smoothly connects to another curve or arc while also making their tangent vectors (Control polygon lines) parallel to each other. Select the splines and click the **Show Polygon** icon on the command bar to display the control polygon lines. You'll notice that these control polygon lines run in parallel to each other.

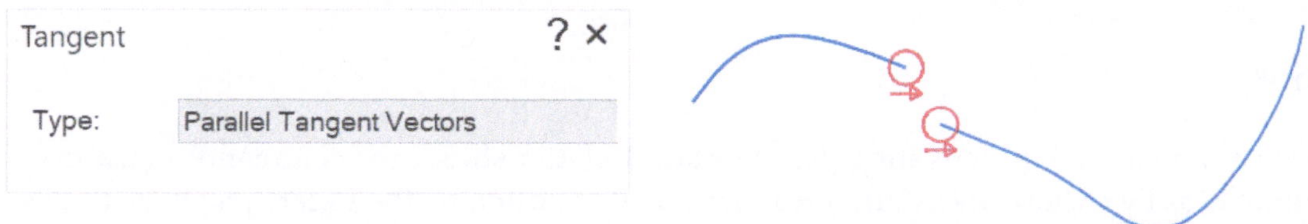

The **Parallel Tangent Vectors + Equal Curvature** option merges the functionalities of both the **Parallel Tangent Vectors** and **Equal Curvature** options. In other words, it combines the features of these two tools into one.

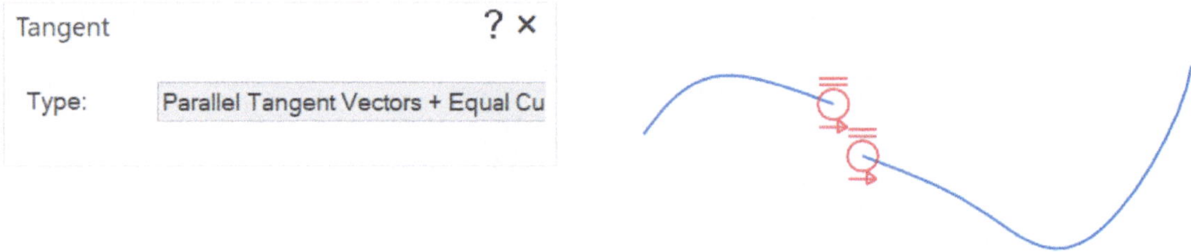

Symmetric

This relation makes two objects symmetric about a line. The objects will have the same size, position and orientation about a line. For example, if you select two circles about a line, they will become equal in size, aligned horizontally, and positioned at an equal distance from the line. Activate the **Symmetric** button and select the symmetry line. Select two objects from the sketch. They will be made symmetric about the selected line.

Collinear

The **Collinear** relation forces a line to be collinear to another line. The lines are not required to touch each other.

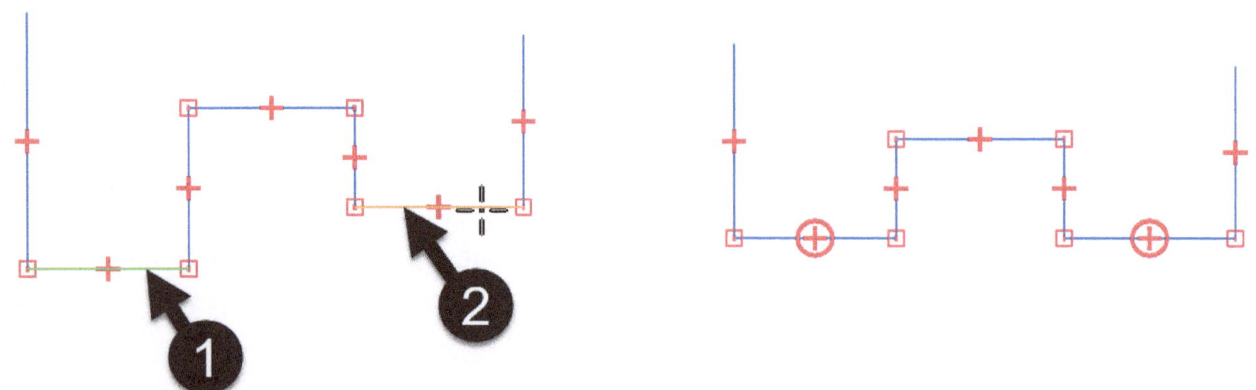

Maintain Relationships

Relations can also be applied automatically by activating the **Maintain Relationships** command. Activate or deactivate **Maintain Relationships** by clicking the **Maintain Relationships** button on the **Relate** panel. With this command, relations are applied automatically when the sketch elements are created. You can define which relations to apply automatically by using the **IntelliSketch Options** dialog. Click **Sketching > IntelliSketch >**

IntelliSketch Options, and then select the **Relationships** tab on the **IntelliSketch Options** dialog. In this tab, select the relations to be created while sketching elements, and then click **OK**.

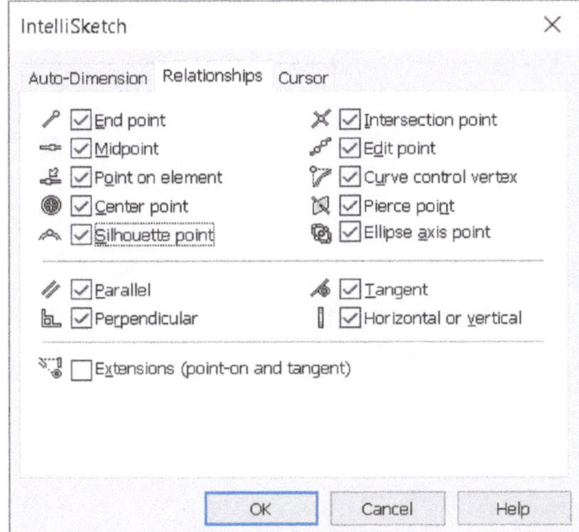

Relationship Handles

As relations are created, they can be viewed using the **Relationship Handles** button located on the **Relate** panel. When dealing with complicated sketches involving numerous relations, you can deactivate this button to turn off all relationship handles.

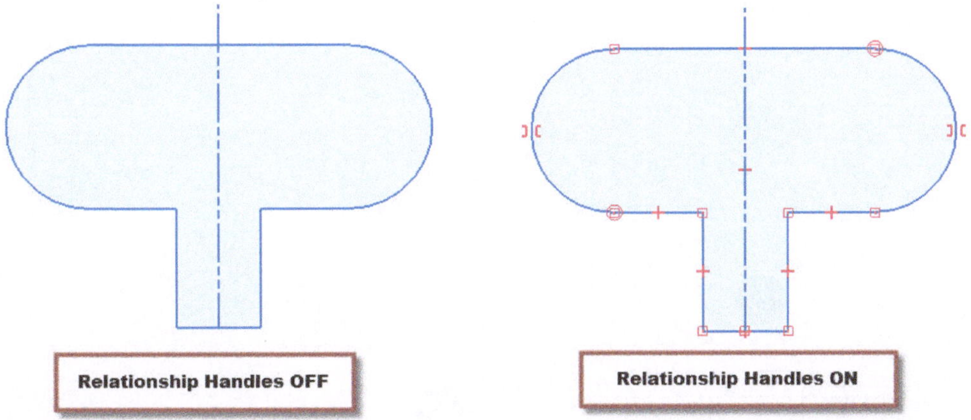

Relationship Assistant

In addition to the **Smart Dimension** command and other geometric relations, Solid Edge provides you with the **Relationship Assistant** command. This command automatically applies relations and dimensions to fully-constrain a sketch. To activate this command, click **Home > Relate > Relationship Assistant** on the ribbon. A command bar pops up. Select the **Options** icon on the command bar to open the **Relationship Assistant** dialog. On this dialog, click the **Geometry** tab, and then select the relations to be applied. Similarly, click the **Dimension** tab and select the dimensions to be applied. You can also select the **Dimension Scheme** such as **Stack**, **Chain**, and **Coordinate**. Click **OK** on the **Relationship Assistant** dialog and select the objects to apply relations and dimensions. Next, click the **Accept** button on the command bar and then select the origins of the horizontal and vertical dimensions. The relations and dimensions will be created automatically.

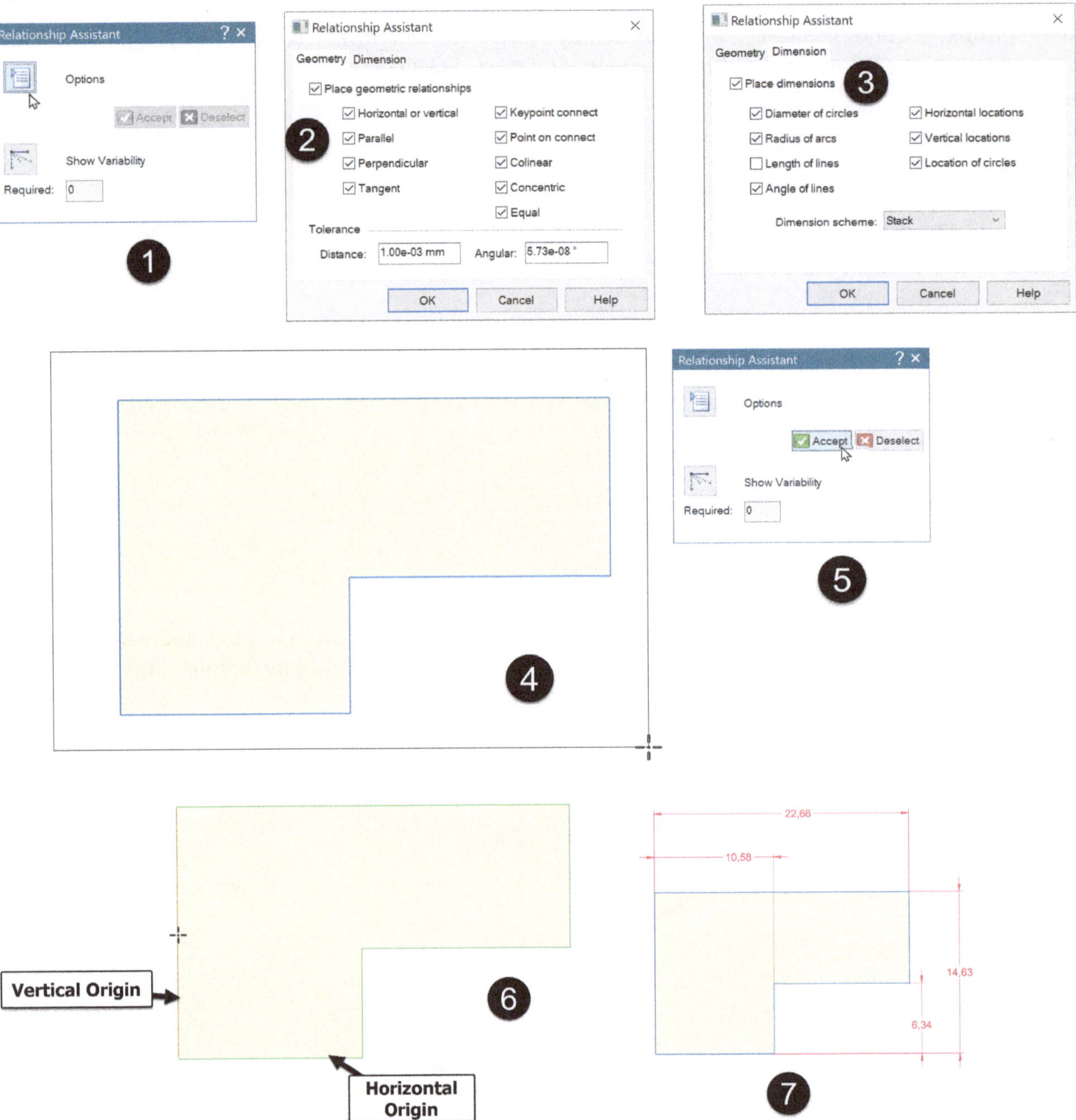

The Construction command

This command converts a sketch element into a construction element. Construction elements are reference elements that support you in creating a sketch of the desired shape and size. Activate the **Construction** command from the **Draw** panel and click on a sketch element. The selected element will be converted to a construction element. You can also convert the construction element to a sketch element by activating the **Construction** command and clicking on the element.

The Create as Construction command

The **Create as Construction** command serves a specific purpose in sketching. It allows you to generate construction geometry within your sketches. This construction geometry plays a crucial role in assisting you to establish the shape and dimensions of a part or assembly. However, it's important to note that this construction geometry is not incorporated into the final design. Activate the **Create as Construction** command from the **Draw** panel. Next, activate anyone of the draw commands and create the construction elements. After creating the construction elements, deactivate the **Create as Construction** command by again clicking on it.

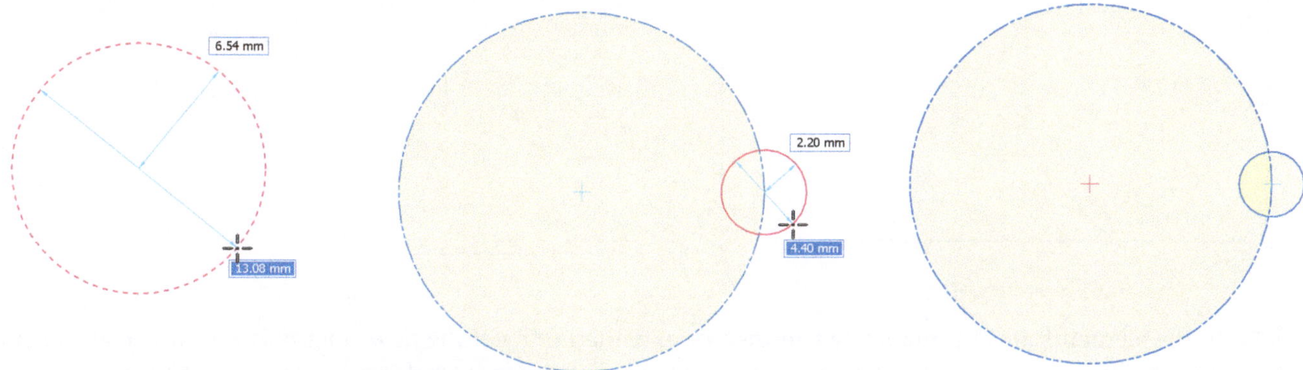

The Symmetric Diameter command

This command is very useful while creating a sketch for a revolved feature. It creates a dimension by measuring the distance between two lines or points and then multiplying it by two. Activate the **Symmetric Diameter** command from the **Dimension** panel, and then select the dimension origin. You need to ensure that the dimension origin is locked at its location. Now, select the line up to which the dimension is to be created. Click to position the dimension, and then change the value.

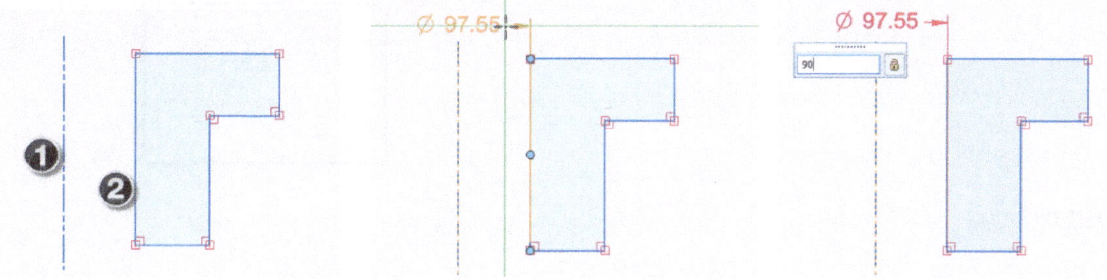

The Fillet command

This command rounds a sharp corner created by the intersection of two lines, arcs, circles, and rectangle or polygon vertices. Click the **Fillet** drop-down > **Fillet** on the **Draw** panel and select the elements' ends to be filleted. Type-in a radius value in the **Radius** box of the command bar and press Enter. The elements to be filleted are not required to form an intersection.

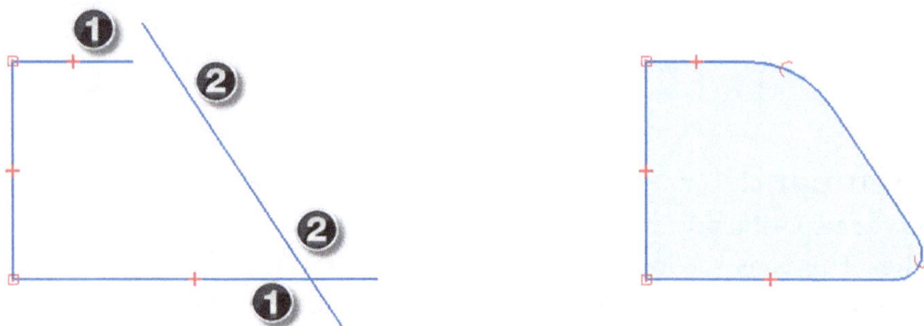

You can also drag the pointer across the elements to fillet the corner.

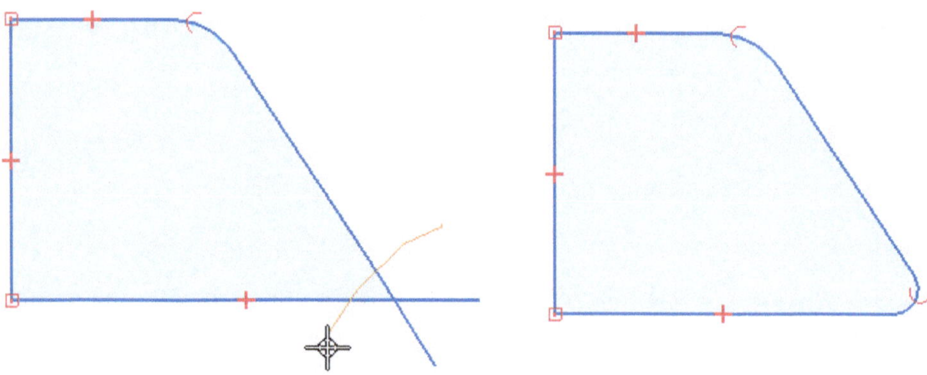

By default, the elements are automatically trimmed or extended to meet the new fillet radius's end. You can check the **No Trim** option on the command bar if you do not want to trim or extend the necessary elements.

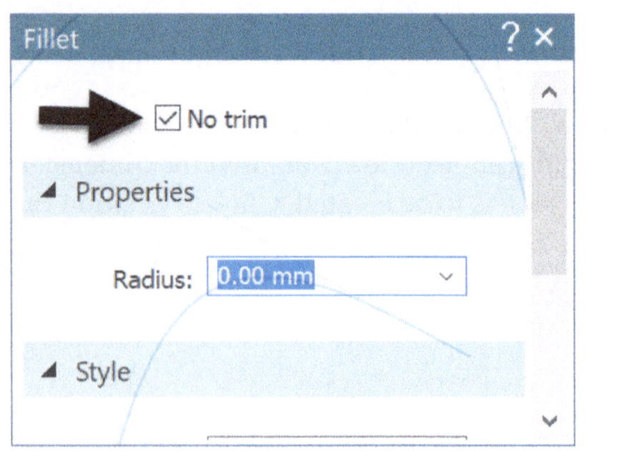

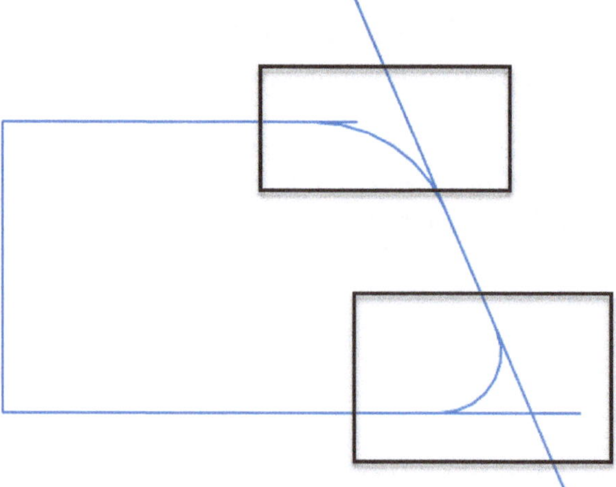

The Chamfer command

This command replaces a sharp corner with an angled line. Click the **Fillet** drop-down > **Chamfer** on the **Draw** panel and select the elements' ends to be chamfered. Type-in the chamfer angle in the **Angle** box on the command bar and press Enter. Next, move the pointer and click to create the chamfer. Instead, you can also use the **Setback A** and **Setback B** boxes on the command bar to define the chamfer size.

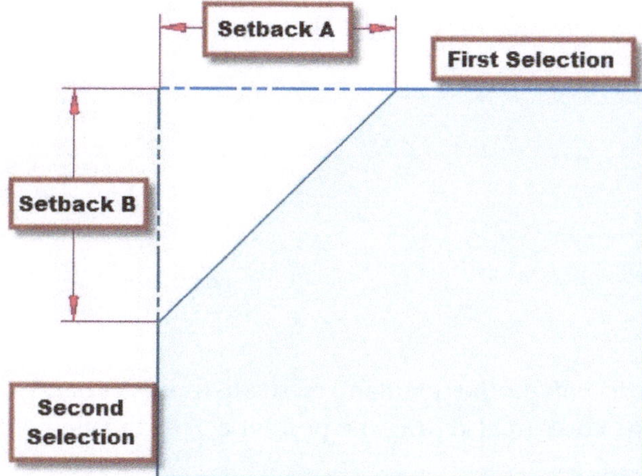

The Split command

This command splits an element into two elements. Click **Extend** drop-down > **Split** on the **Draw** panel and click the element to split. Next, select a split point on the element. In the case of a circle or ellipse, you must select two split points.

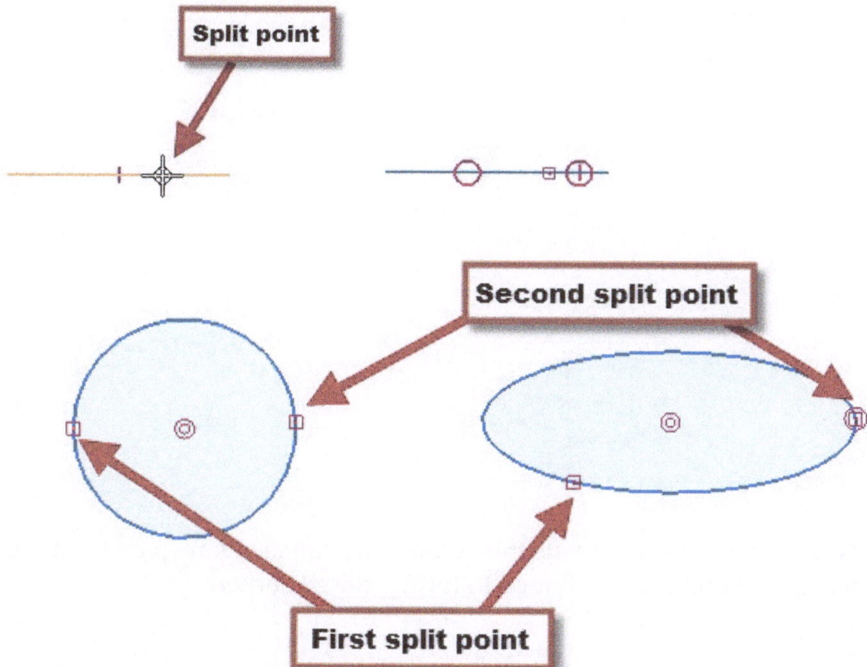

The **Split** command is also available in the 3D Sketching environment.

The Extend to Next command

This command extends elements such as lines, arcs, and curves until they intersect another boundary edge element.

Click the **Extend to Next** icon on the **Draw** panel and click on the element to extend. It will extend up to the next element.

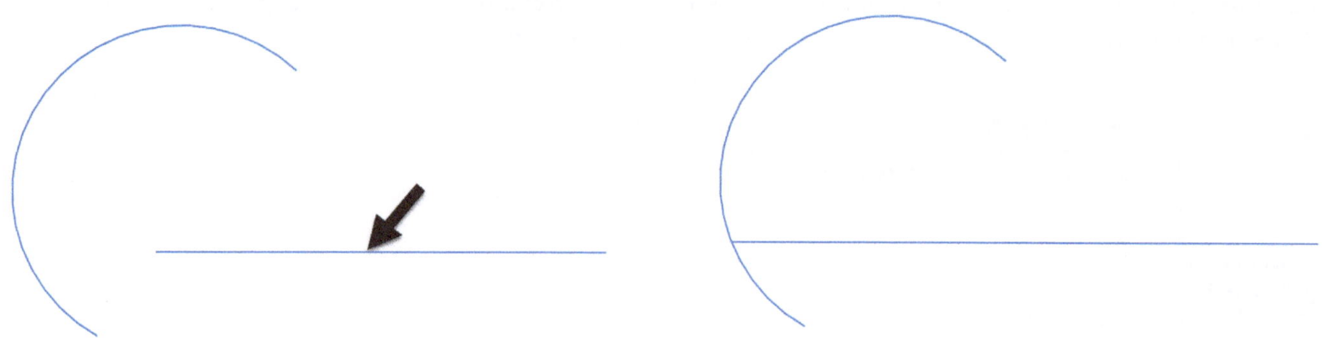

The Trim command

This command trims the end of an element back to the intersection of another element. Activate this command from the **Draw** panel and select the element or elements to trim. You can also drag the pointer across the elements to trim.

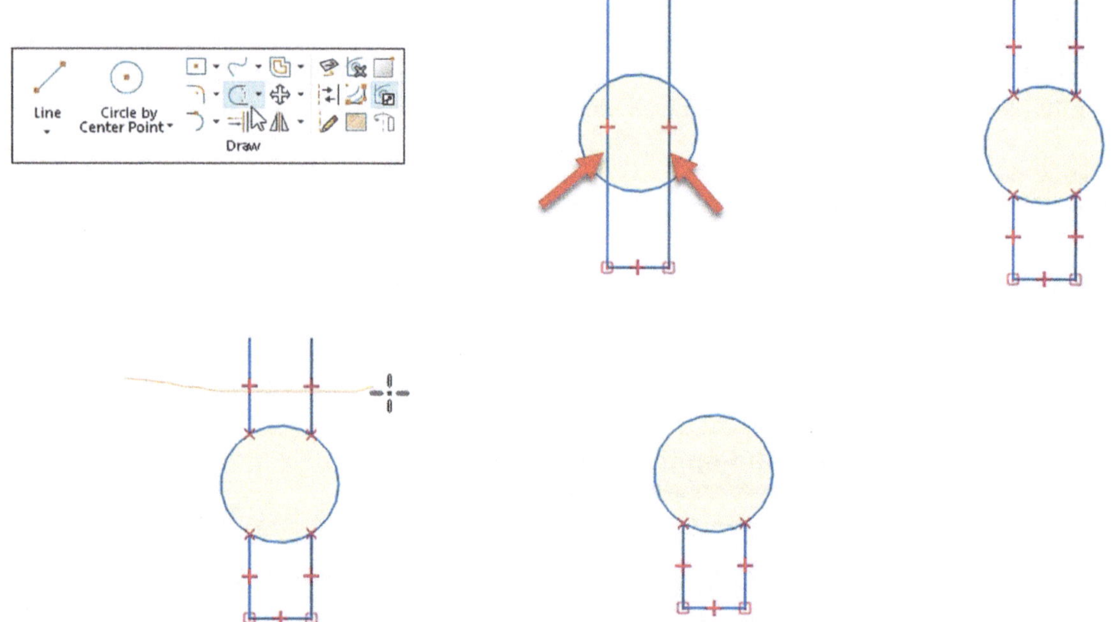

The Trim Corner command

This command trims and extends elements to form a corner. Activate this command from the **Draw** panel and select two intersecting elements. The elements will be trimmed and extended to form a closed corner.

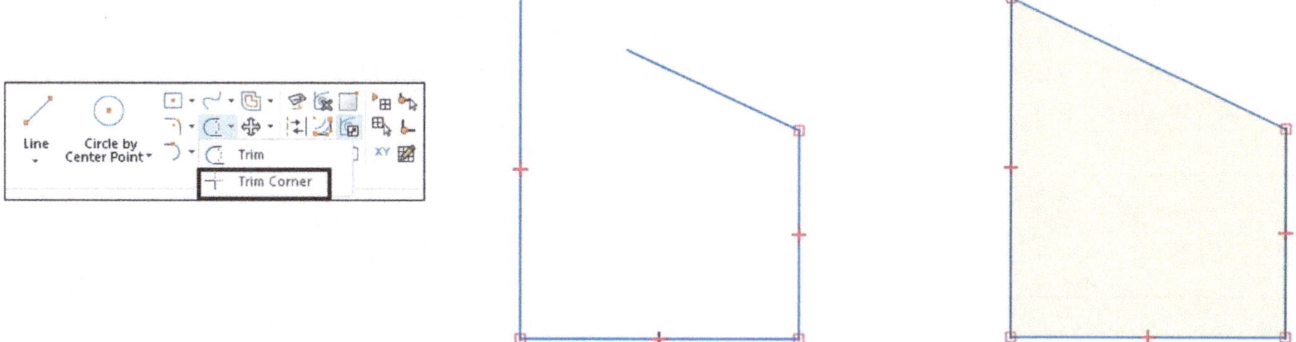

The Offset command

This command creates a parallel copy of a selected element or chain of elements. Activate this command from the **Draw** panel and select an element or chain of elements to offset. You can use the **Single** or **Chain** option from the **Select** drop-down on the command bar to select a single element or chain of elements. After selecting the element, type-in a value in the **Distance** field on the command bar and click the **Accept** button. Click to define the side of the offset. A parallel copy of the elements will be created, and you can click again to create another parallel copy. Click the right mouse button after creating parallel copies. Press **Esc** to deactivate this command.

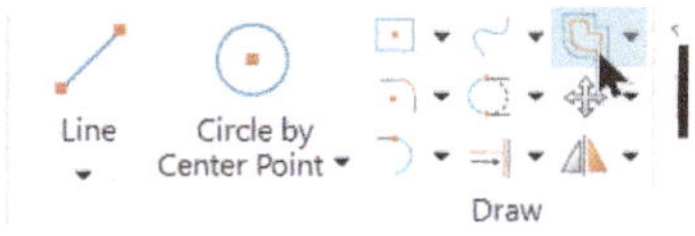

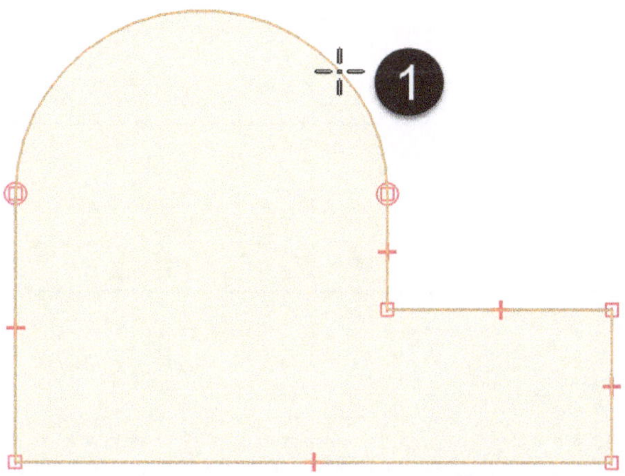

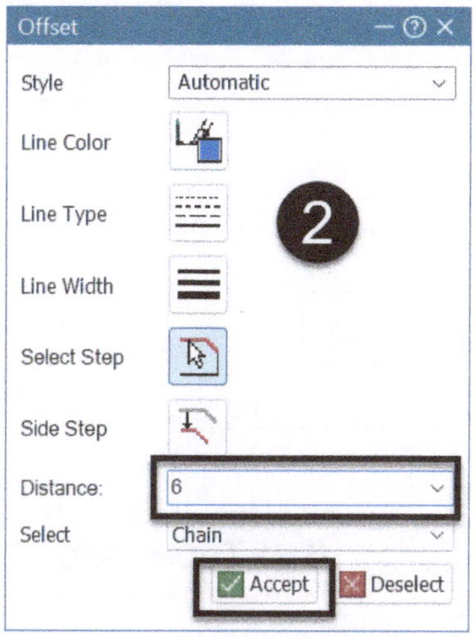

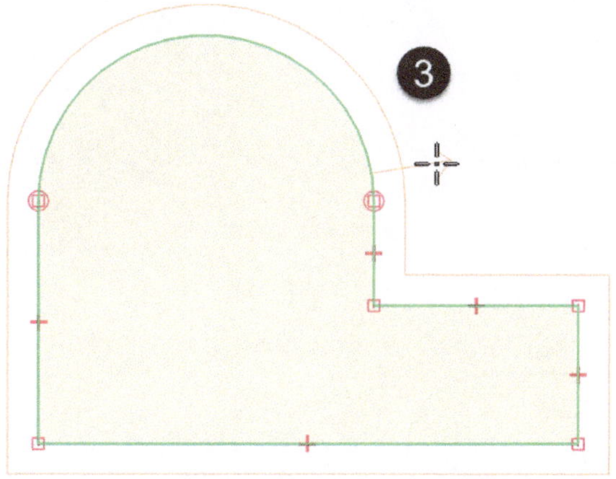

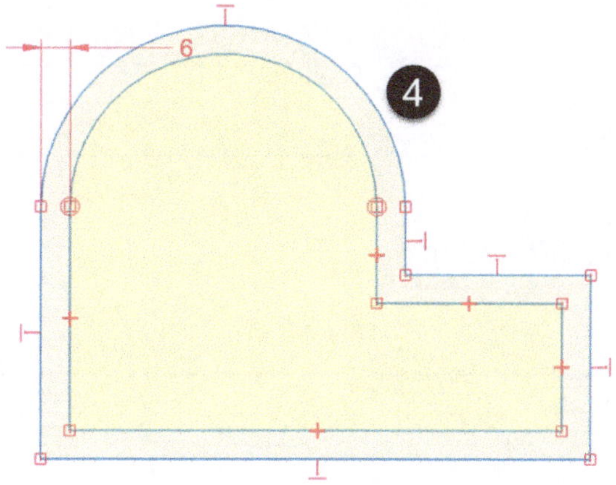

The Symmetric Offset command

This command creates a parallel copy on both sides of a selected element or chain of elements. It is helpful while creating a sketch slot. Activate this command from the **Offset** drop-down on the **Draw** panel. The **Symmetric Offset Options** dialog pops up on the screen.

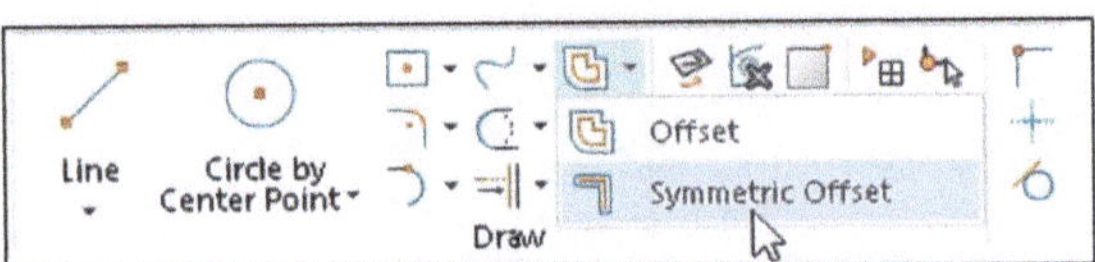

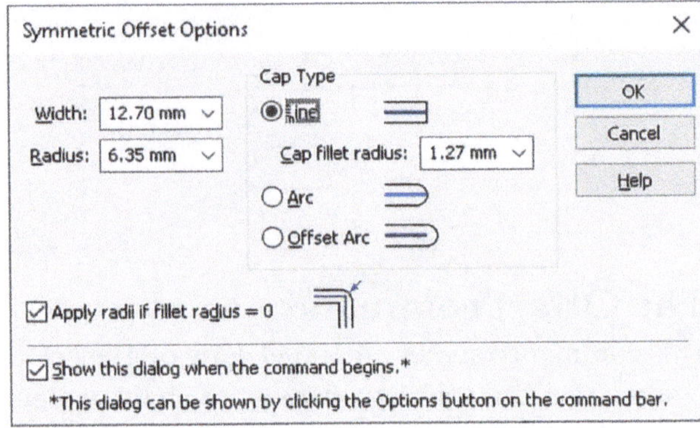

The options on this dialog are illustrated below. Set the required options on the dialog and click **OK**. Next, select an open sketch (line or arc) and click the **Accept** button to create the symmetric offset.

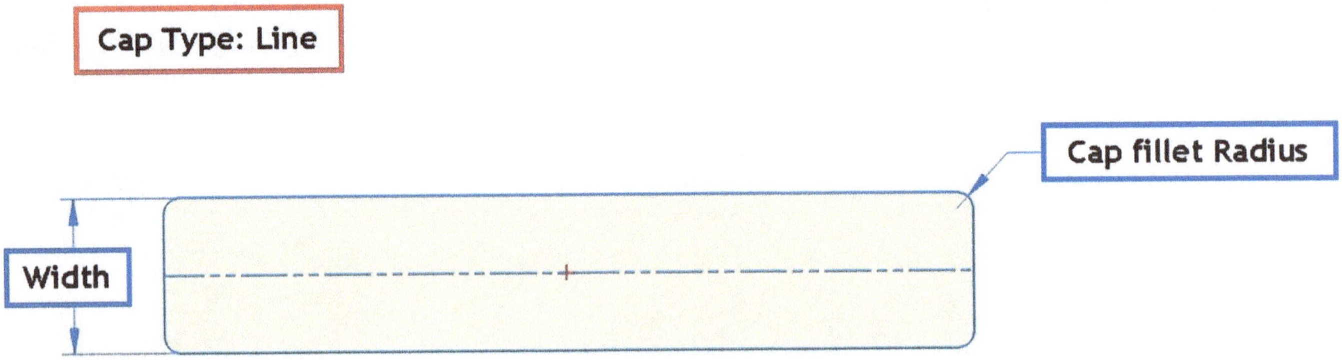

Cap Type: Line

Cap fillet Radius

Width

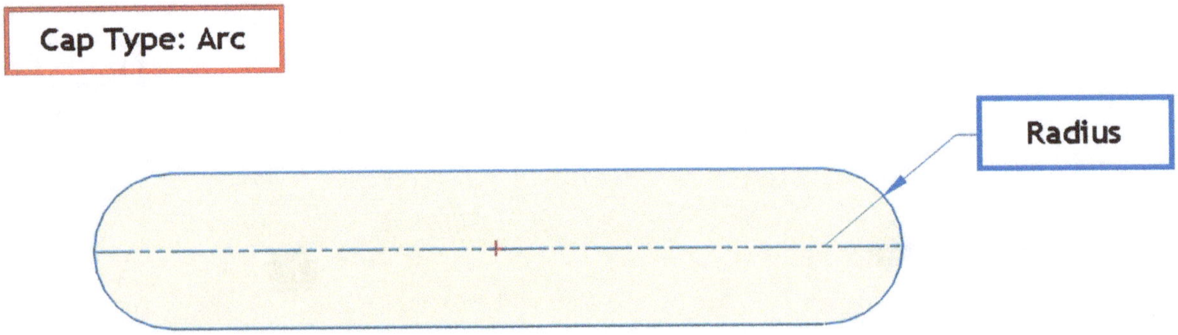

Cap Type: Arc

Radius

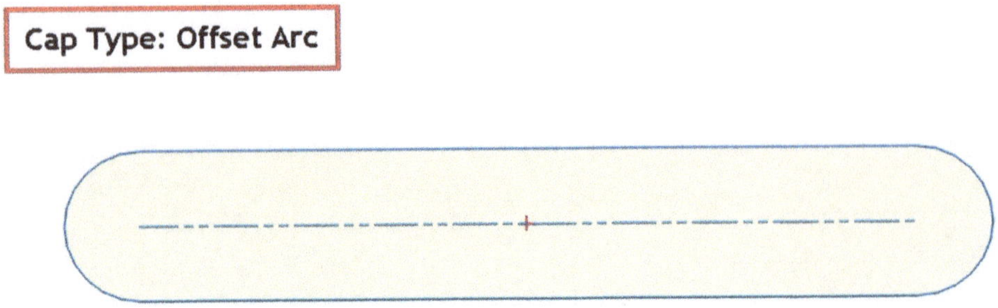

Cap Type: Offset Arc

The Move command

This command relocates one or more elements from one position in the sketch to any other position you specify. Activate this command from the **Draw** panel, and then click on the elements to move. Next, you must select a base point and click at a new location.

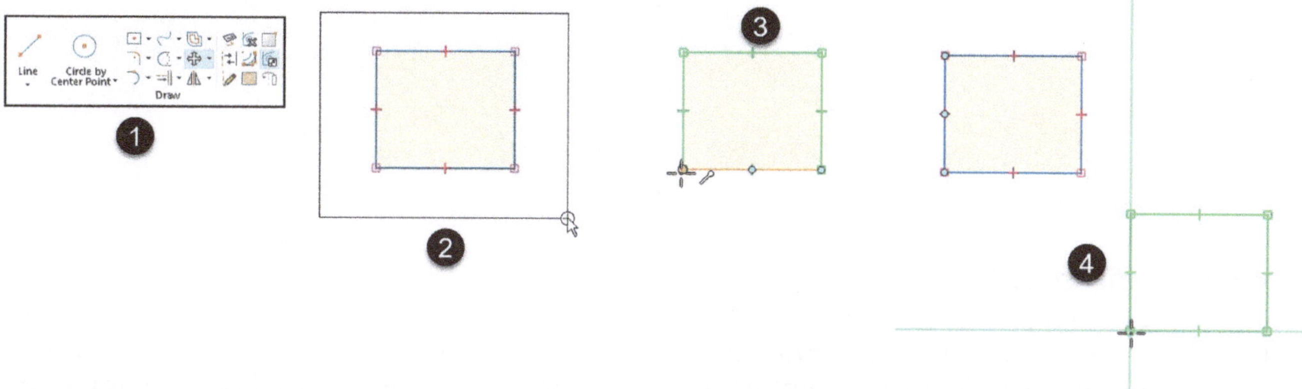

The **Copy** option on the **Move** command bar can be used to copy and move the selected elements.

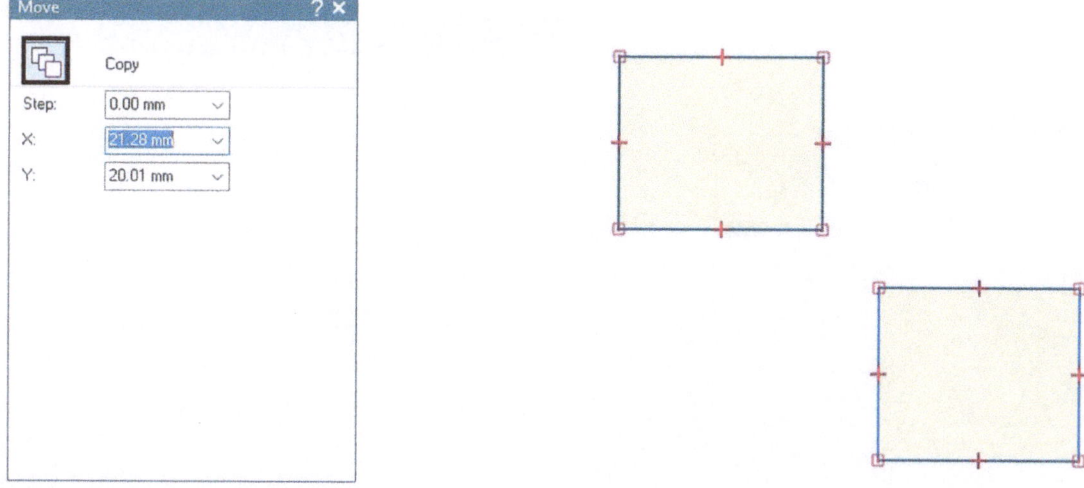

The Rotate command

This command rotates the selected elements to any position. Click **Move** drop-down > **Rotate** on the **Draw** panel, and then select the elements to rotate. Next, you must define a base point and a point from which the object will be rotated. Move the pointer and click to define the rotation angle. You can use the **Copy** option on the command bar to copy and rotate the selected elements.

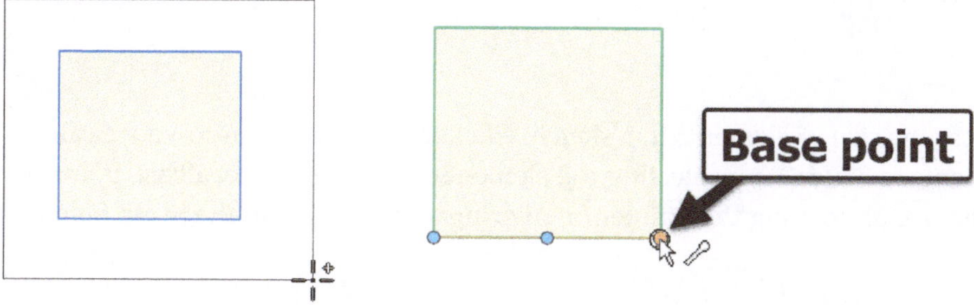

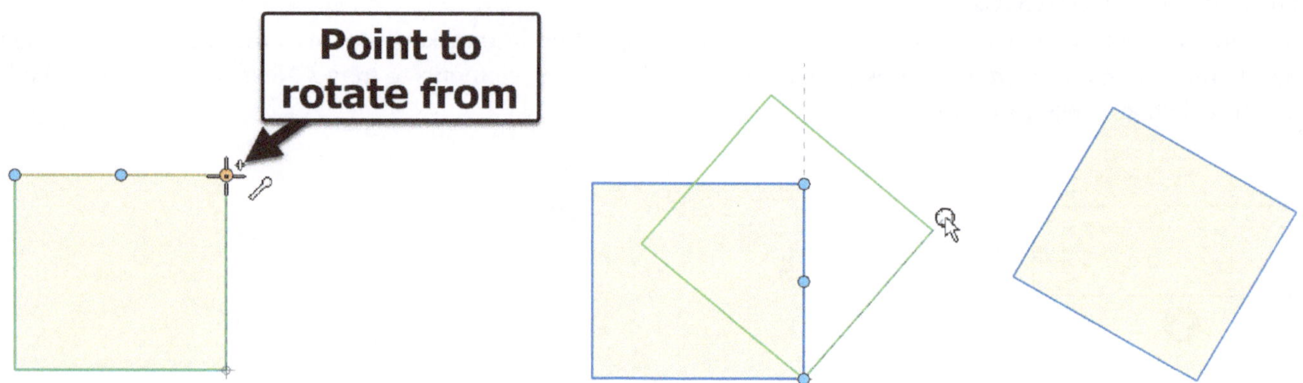

The Mirror command

This command creates a mirror image of the selected elements. You have the option to retain or delete the original elements. Activate this command from the **Draw** panel, and then select the elements to mirror. Next, you have to create two points defining the mirror-line. To retain the original elements, you must ensure that the **Copy** option is active on the command bar.

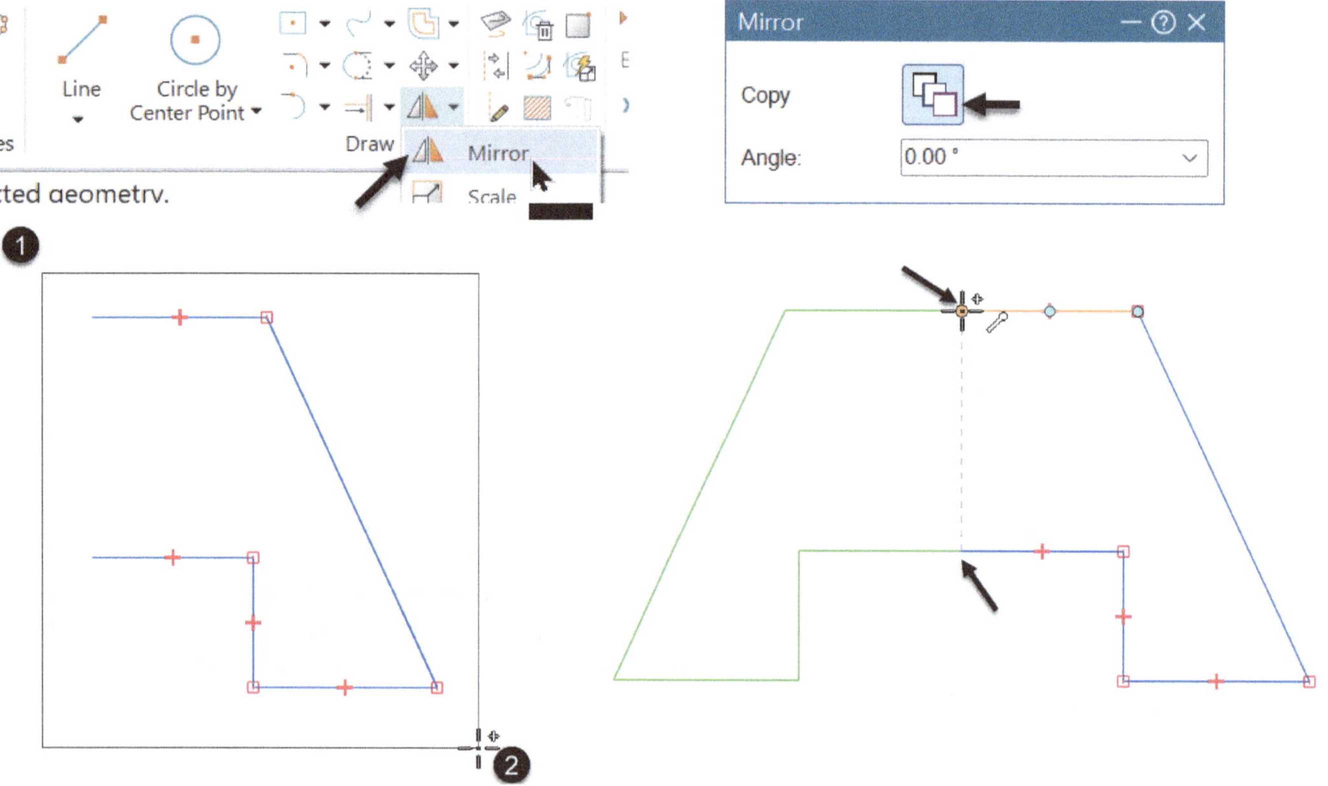

The Scale command

This command increases or decreases the size of elements in a sketch. Click the **Mirror** drop-down > **Scale** on the **Draw** panel and select the elements to scale. After selecting the elements, you must select a base point. You can then scale the selected elements' size by moving the pointer or entering a scale value in the **Scale** field on the command bar.

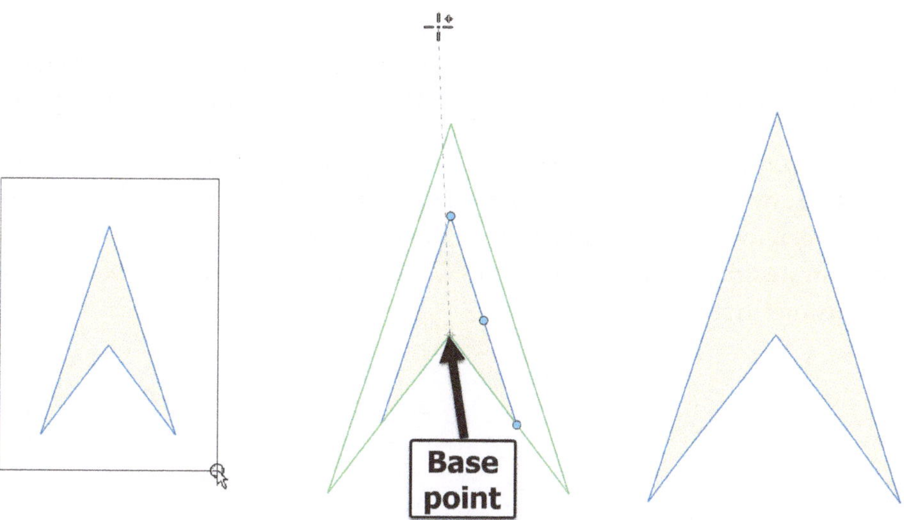

The Stretch command

This command moves a portion of the sketch while still preserving other parts of it. Click **Mirror** drop-down > **Stretch** on the **Draw** panel, and then drag a box to select the elements to be stretched. Select a base point and move the pointer to stretch the selected elements.

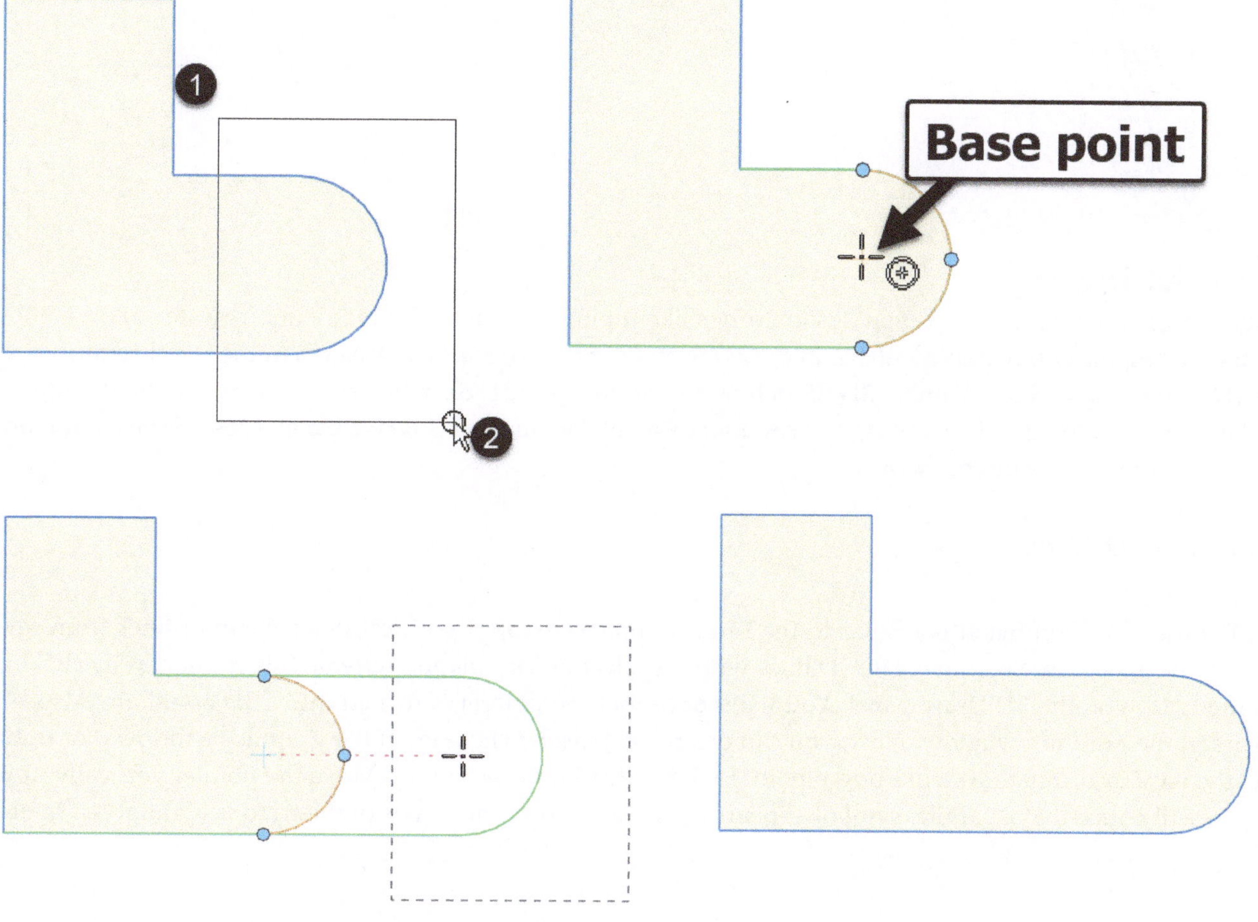

The Draw command

This command helps you to create sketches by using a pen, mouse, or finger. It converts a freehand sketch into an accurate sketch. Activate this command (On the ribbon, click **Home** tab > **Draw** panel > **Line** drop-down > **Free Sketch**). Next, draw a freehand sketch on your touch-enabled screen using a pen or finger. If you do not have a touch screen, you can use the mouse to draw a freehand sketch. If you use a mouse, then press and hold the left mouse button, and then drag it on the screen to create a sketch. Release the mouse after drawing the sketch; the freehand sketch is converted into an accurate drawing using lines, arcs, circles, ellipses, or splines. Next, you can fully define the sketch by adding dimensions to it.

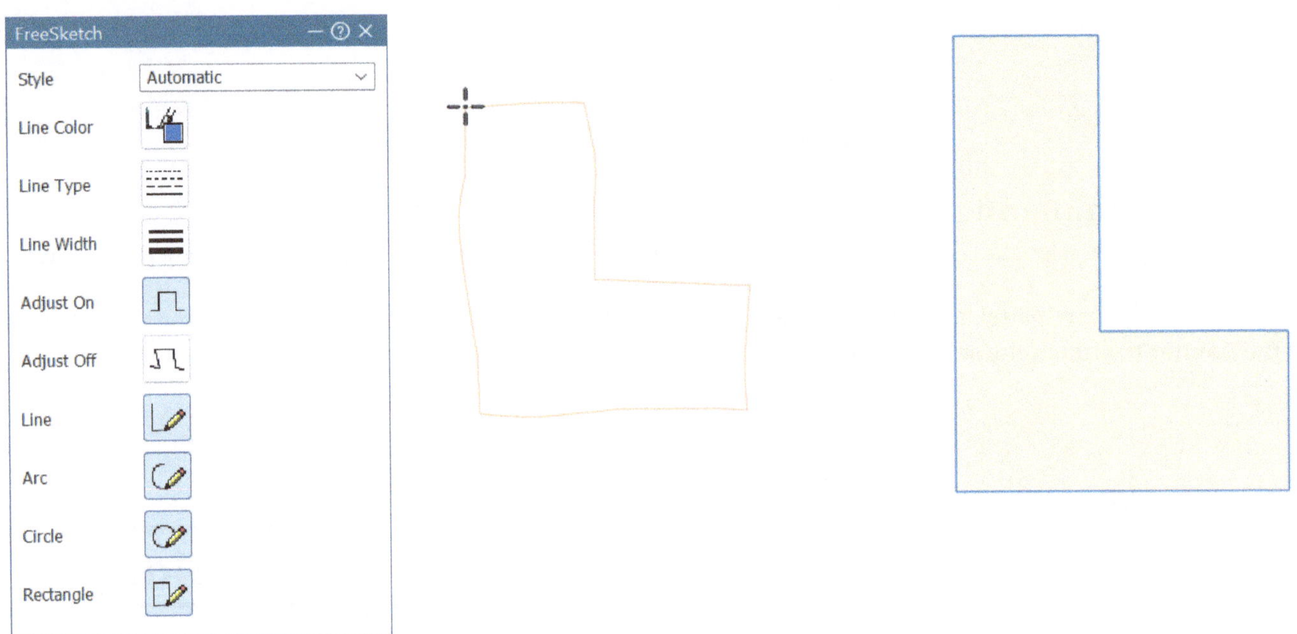

3D Sketching

3D Sketching in Solid Edge helps you design things like piping, tubing, and weldments. You can create a 3D sketch by using the commands available in the 3D Sketching tab. To start a 3D sketch in the Synchronous mode, click **3D Sketching > New Sketch > 3D Sketch** on the ribbon. The 3D Sketches entry is listed in the Pathfinder. Now, you can create a 3D sketch using the commands available on the **3D Draw** panel. Most of the commands are similar to the 2D **Draw** commands.

Creating a 3D Line

The **3D Line** command is similar to the **Line** command except that it creates a chain of lines from selected points in the 3D space. You can create 3D lines without selecting any plane. Activate this command by clicking the **3D Line** button on the **3D Draw** panel. You will notice that the pointer is turned into a 3D crosshair. Also, a triad appears in the graphics window. Now, you can create 3D lines by clicking on the graphics window. For example, select the Base Coordinate system's origin point to define the line's start point. Move the pointer vertically upward, and you will notice that a parallel symbol appears on the line. Also, the Z-axis of the triad is highlighted in orange.

It means that the line is drawn parallel to the Z-axis. Click to define the endpoint of the line.

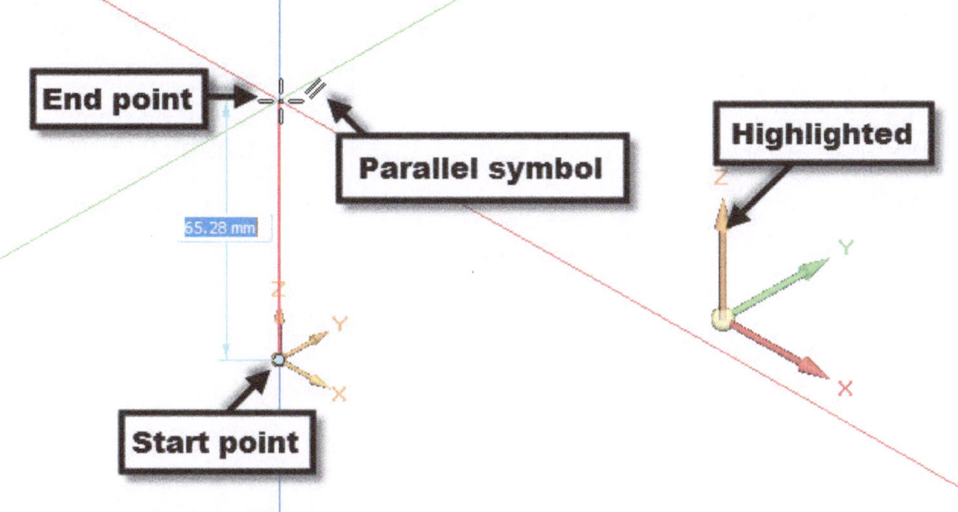

Now, move the pointer along the red line of the crosshairs. You will notice that the line is drawn parallel to the X-axis. Click to define the endpoint of the line.

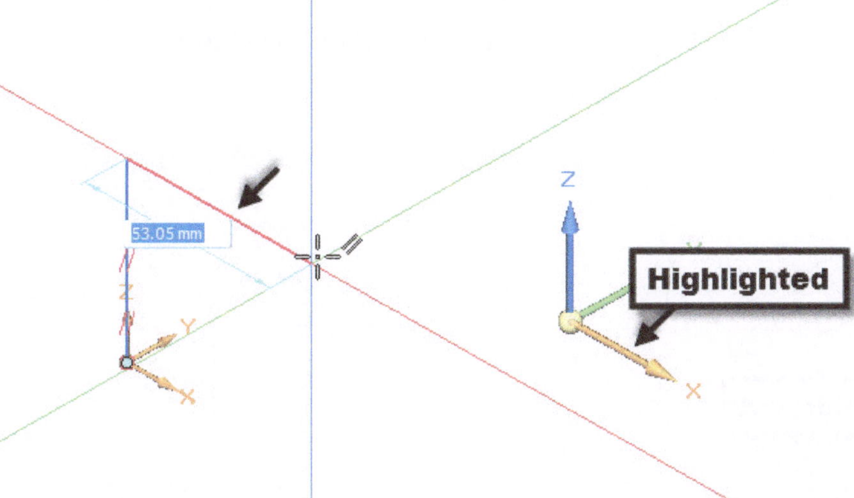

Move the pointer along the green line of the crosshairs. This draws a line parallel to the Y-axis. Click to define the endpoint of the line.

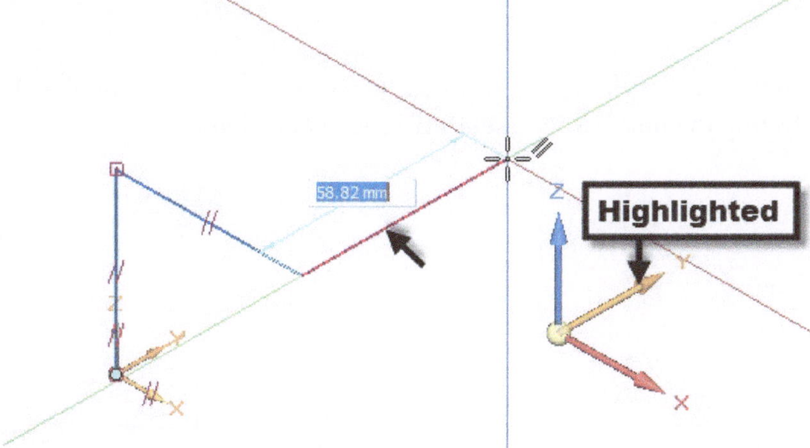

Likewise, create some more lines in the Z, X, and Y-axes. Press Esc to deactivate the **3D Line** command. When you rotate the view, you can see the 3D Line created.

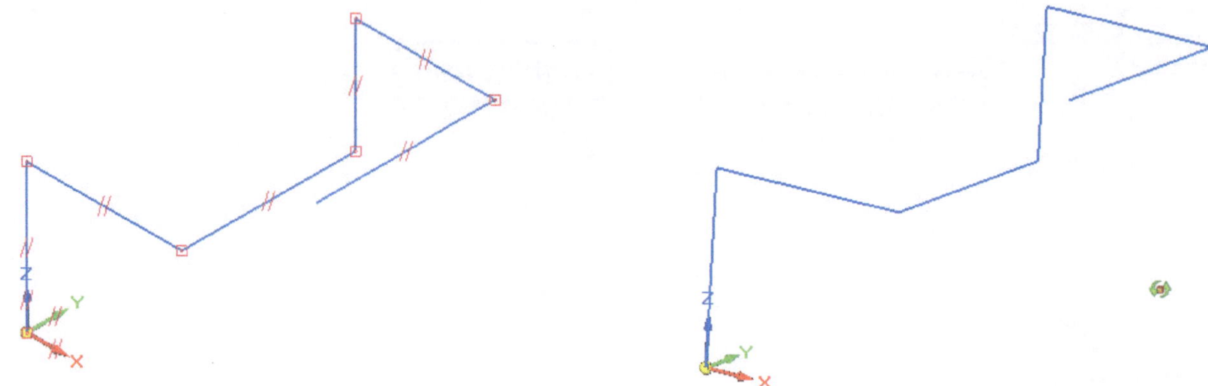

Adding Relationships and Dimensions

Adding Relationships in 3D Sketching is similar to that in 2D sketching except for two additional commands: **On Plane** and **Coaxial**. The **On Plane** command moves the selected sketch element onto a plane. Click the **On Plane** button on the **3D Relate** panel. Select the 3D sketch element and the plane. The selected sketch element will be moved to the selected plane.

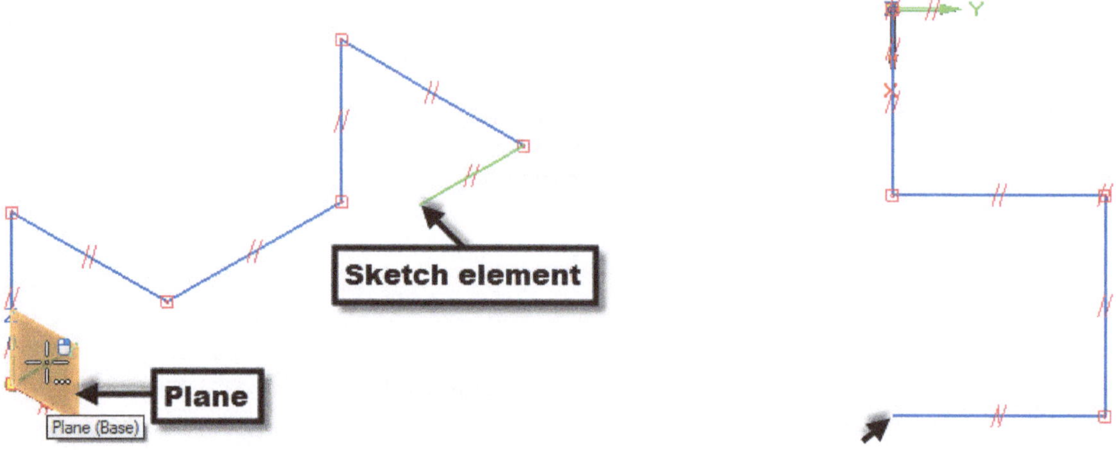

The **Coaxial** command makes the center of the circle coaxial with a line. Click the **Coaxial** button on the **3D Relate** panel and select an arc or circle. After selecting the first element, select the second element.

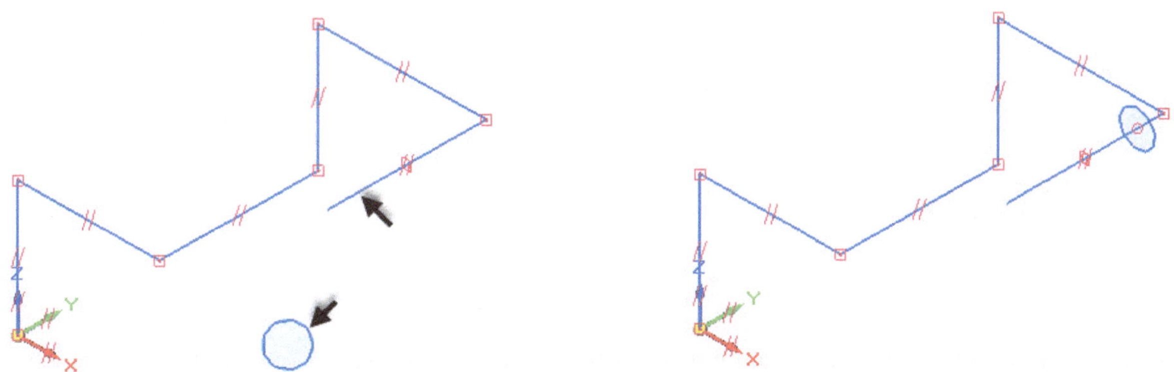

Use the **Smart Dimension** command to apply dimensions to the 3D sketch. Activate this command and select the sketch element. However, if you select the endpoints of two elements, the dimension will be displayed aligned to them. Press **N** on your keyboard to change the orientation of the dimension.

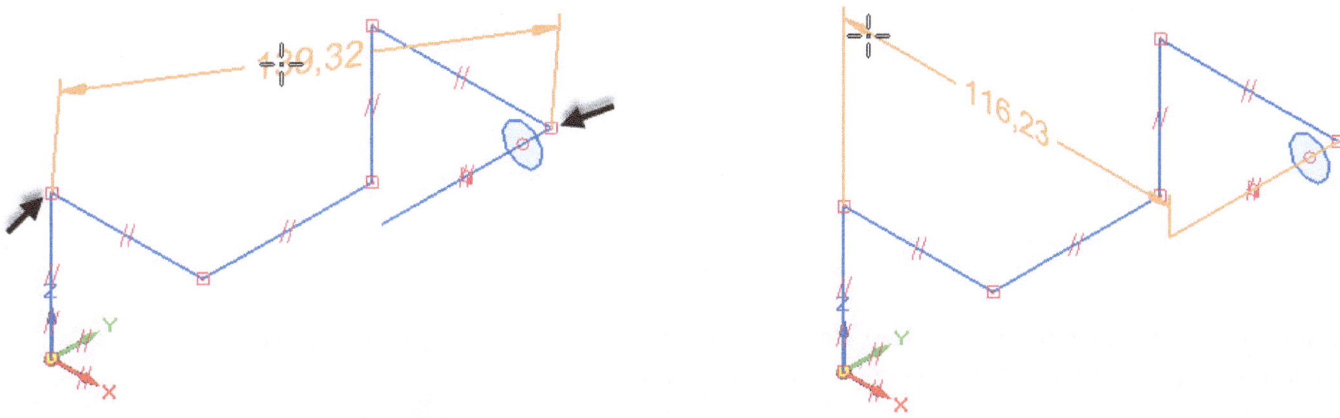

Drawing a 3D Sketch element by Locking a plane

To create a 3D sketch by locking a plane, you can use the default planes or create new planes. For this example, you will create a new plane and use it to draw a 3D sketch. On the ribbon, click **3D Sketching > Planes > Coincident Plane**, and then select the XZ plane from the Base coordinate system. You will notice the steering wheel on the new plane. Click on the torus of the steering wheel and move the pointer. Type-in 135 and press Enter. The plane will be rotated by 135 degrees.

Click the **3D Line** button on the **3D Draw** panel. On the command bar, click the **Lock Sketch Plane** icon and select the plane. Select the origin point of the Base coordinate system to define the start point. Move the pointer upward, and then type-in 50 and -90 in the Length and Angle boxes, respectively and press Enter. Move the pointer along the horizontal crosshair and enter 50 and 0 in the length box and angle boxes, respectively. Likewise, create another vertically inclined line of 50 mm length. Press F3 to unlock the plane.

Now, move the pointer along the crosshairs' green line, type 100 in the length box, and press Enter. Complete the sketch by creating other lines, as shown below. Press Esc to deactivate the command.

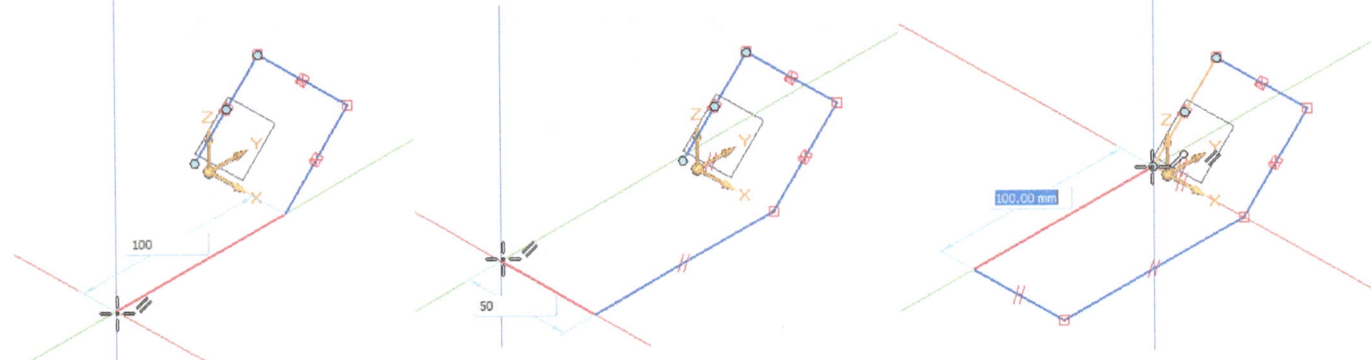

To add fillets to the sketch, click the **3D Fillet** button on the **3D Draw** panel. Type-in a value in the radius box and press Enter. Select the corners of the sketch to fillet them.

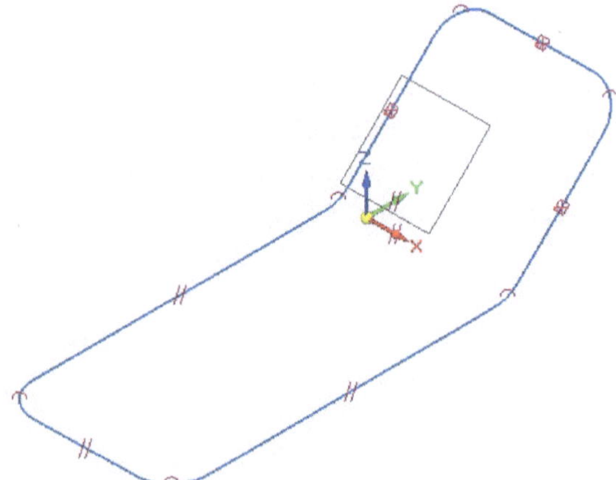

In the Ordered Environment, you have to open the 3D Sketching environment to create a 3D sketch. On the ribbon, click **Home > Sketch > 3D Sketch**. Use the drawing commands and create the 3D sketching. Click the **Close 3D Sketch** button after completing the sketch.

The Routing Path command

The **Routing Path** command creates a 3D sketch path between the two selected points. Activate this command (on the ribbon, click **3D Sketching** tab > **Draw** panel > **Routing Path**) and then select two points; Solid Edge displays a 3D sketch path between the selected points. On the command bar, click the **Next** icon to display the next path between the selected points. Click **Accept** if you are satisfied with the result.

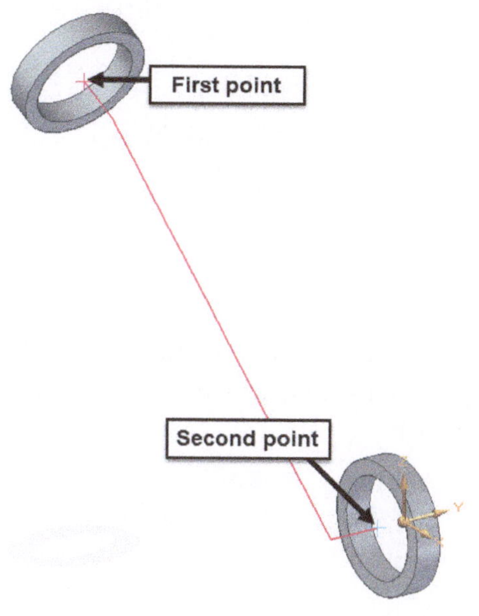

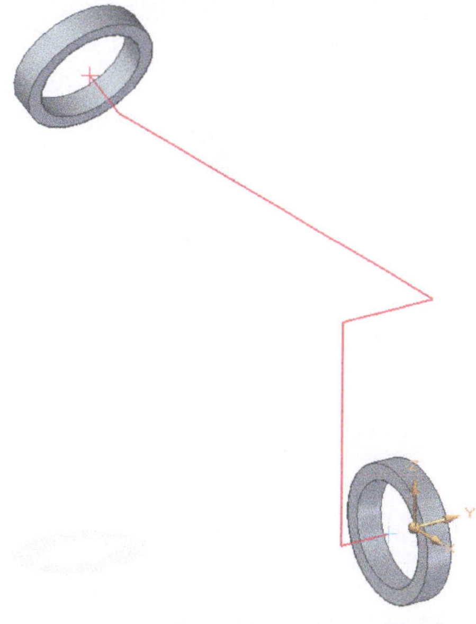

Examples

Example 1 (Millimetres)

In this example, you will draw the sketch shown below.

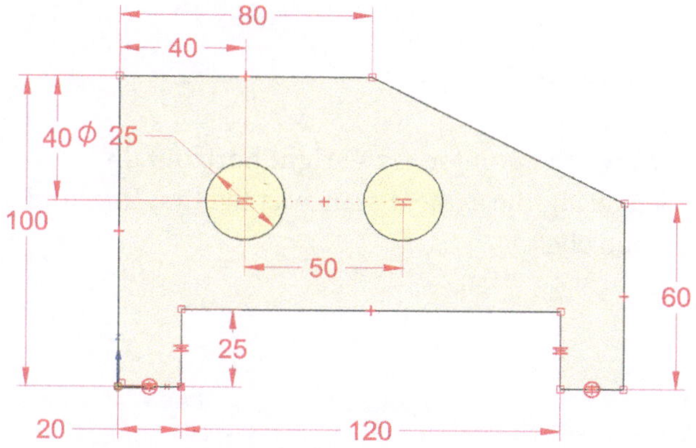

1. Start **Solid Edge 2026** by clicking the **Solid Edge 2026** icon on your desktop.
2. Click **File > New > New**; The **New** dialog appears.

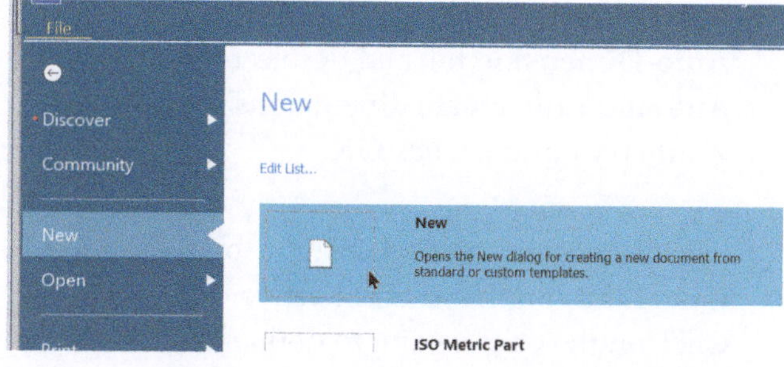

3. Select **ISO Metric > iso metric part.par**. Next, click **OK**; a new part file is opened.

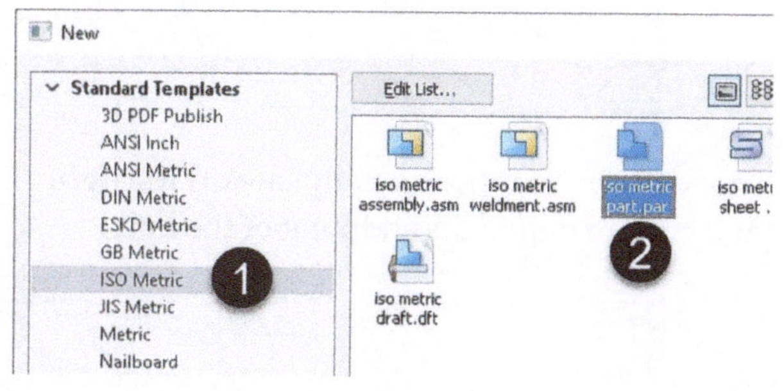

4. Click **Continue with Ordered** button on the **Ordered as default** dialog; the Ordered environment is set as the default environment.
5. To start a new sketch, click **Home > Sketch > Sketch** on the ribbon.
6. Select the Front (xz) plane from the base reference planes displayed in the graphics window; the sketch is started and the sketch plane is oriented normal to the screen.

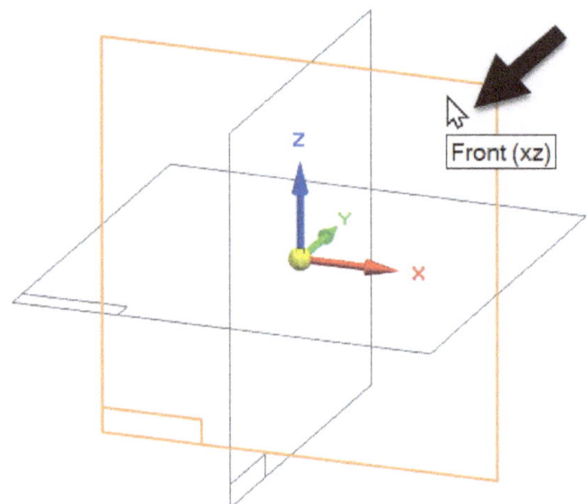

7. On the ribbon, click **Home > Intellisketch > Intellisketch Options** . Next, click the **Auto-Dimension** tab and deselect the **Automatically create dimensions for new geometry** option. Click **OK**.
8. Click **Home > Draw > Line** on the ribbon, if the **Line** command is not active.
9. Click on the origin point to define the first point of the line.

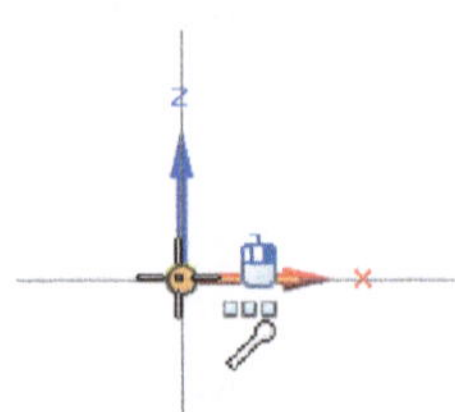

10. Move the pointer horizontally toward the right and click to define the endpoint of the line.

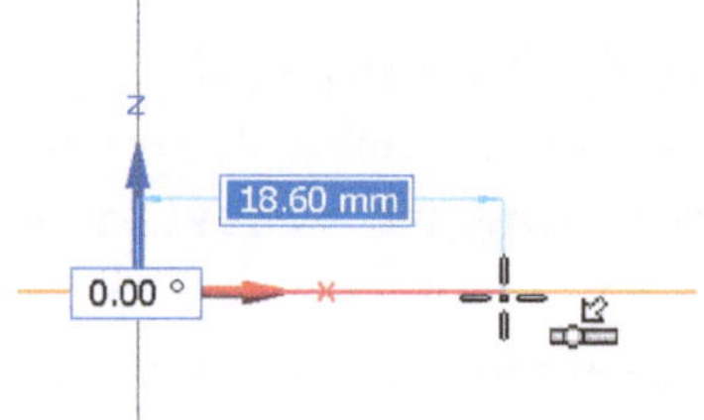

11. Move the pointer vertically upward. Click to define the second line.

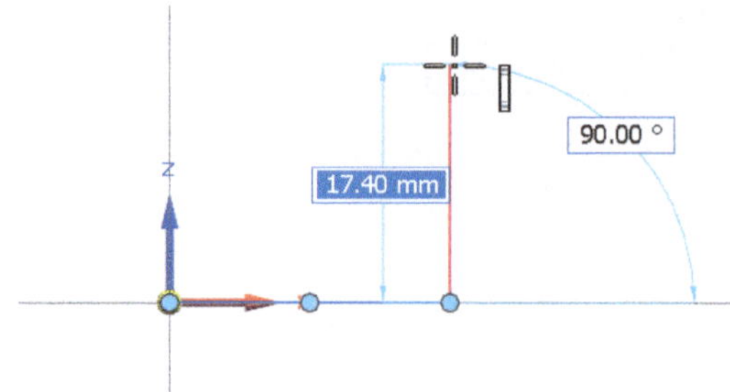

12. Move the pointer horizontally toward the right, covering twice the distance of the previous line, and then click.

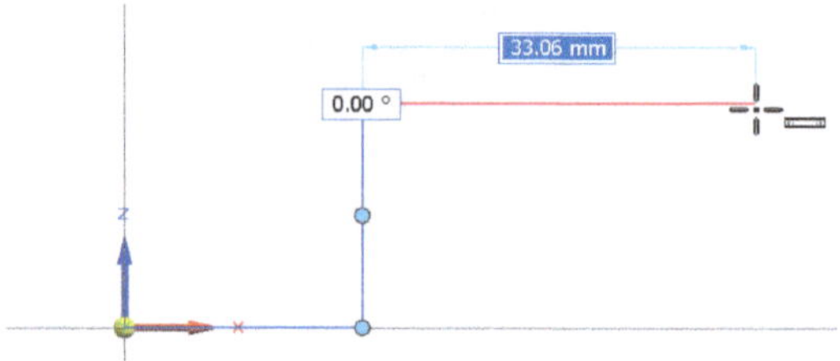

13. Move the pointer vertically downward and click when a dotted line appears from the origin point.

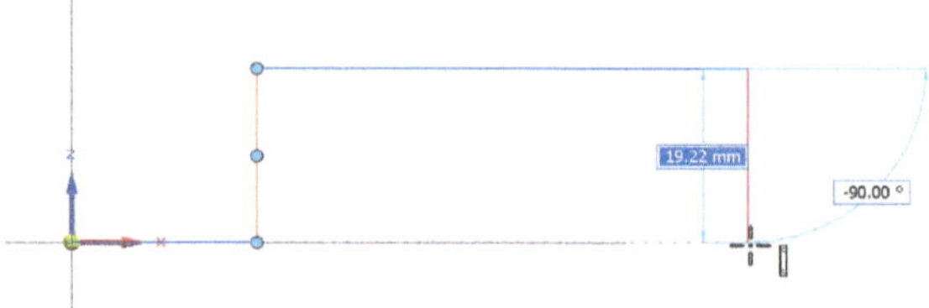

14. Move the pointer to the right horizontally, covering the same distance as the first line, and then click.

15. Move the pointer vertically upward and click to create vertical line.

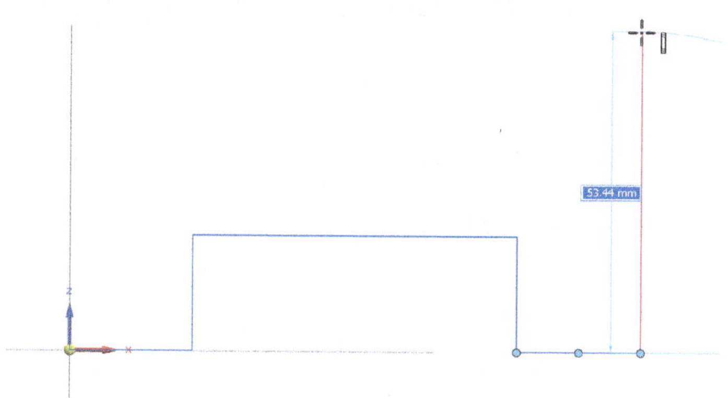

16. To create an inclined line, move the pointer in the top-left direction and click.

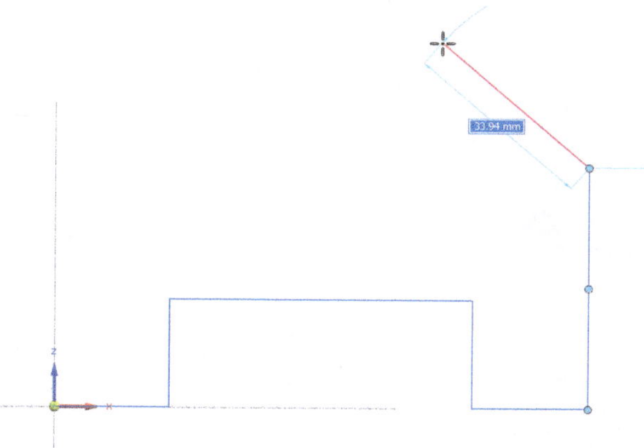

17. Move the pointer to left horizontally, and click when a dotted line appears from the origin point.

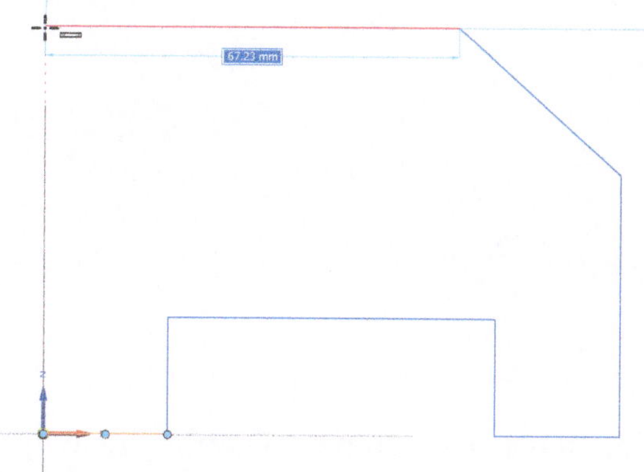

18. Move the pointer vertically down and select the origin point to create a closed sketch.

19. Click **Home > Relate > Collinear** on the ribbon and click on the two horizontal lines at the bottom; they become collinear.

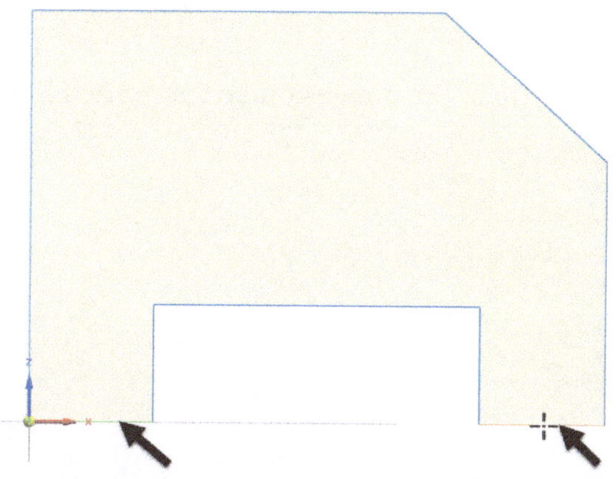

20. Click **Home > Relate > Equal** on the ribbon and click on the two horizontal lines at the bottom; they become equal in length.
21. Select the small vertical lines to make their lengths equal.

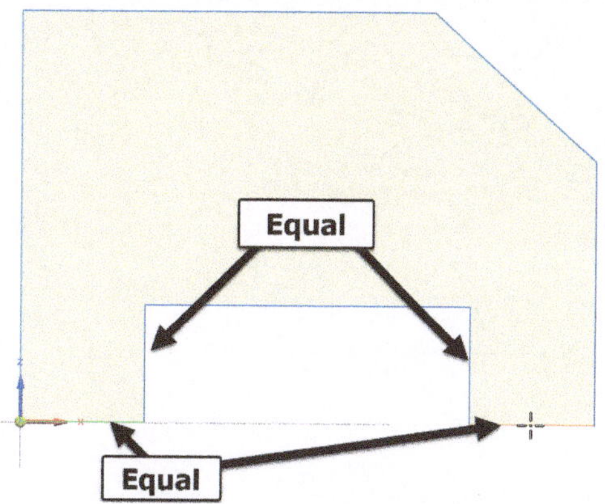

22. Click **Home > Dimension > Smart Dimension** on the ribbon and click on the lower left horizontal line. Move the mouse pointer downward and click to locate the dimension.

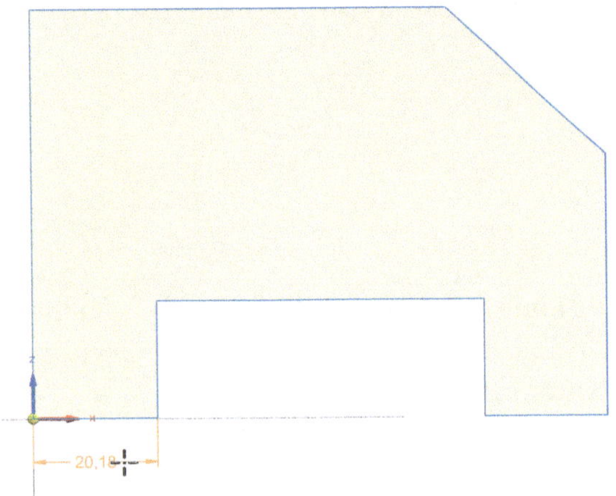

23. Type-in **20** in the dimension box and press Enter.

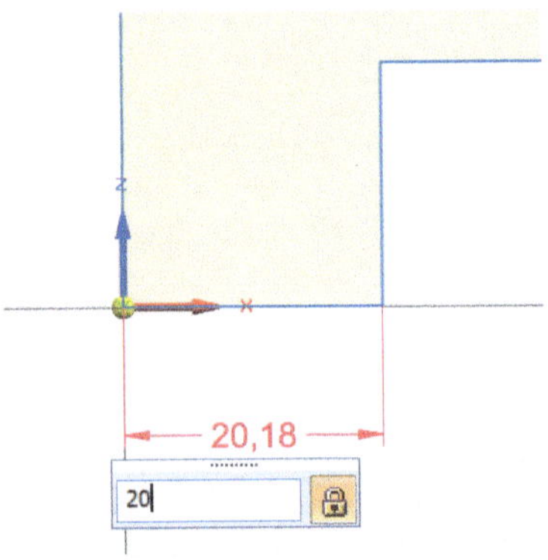

24. Click on the small vertical line located on the left side. Move the mouse pointer towards the right and click to position the dimension.

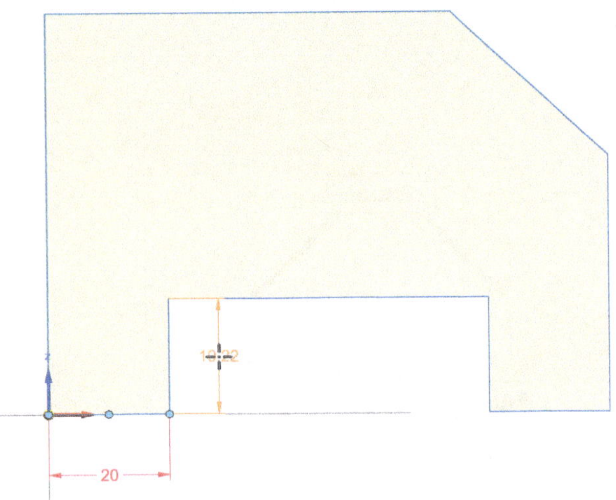

25. Type-in **25** in the dimension box and press Enter.

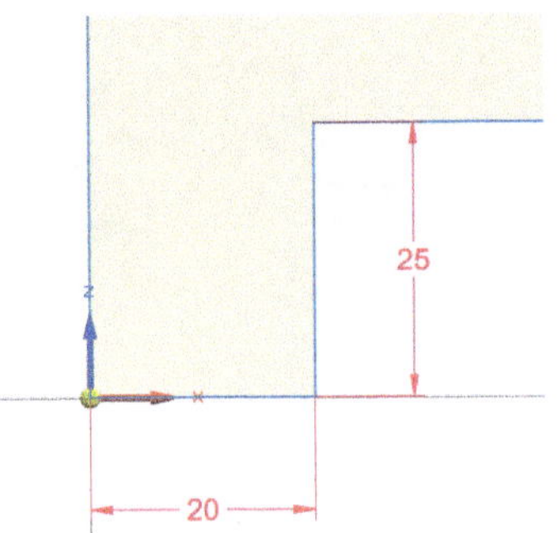

26. Create other dimensions in the sequence, shown below. Press Esc to deactivate the **Smart Dimension** command.

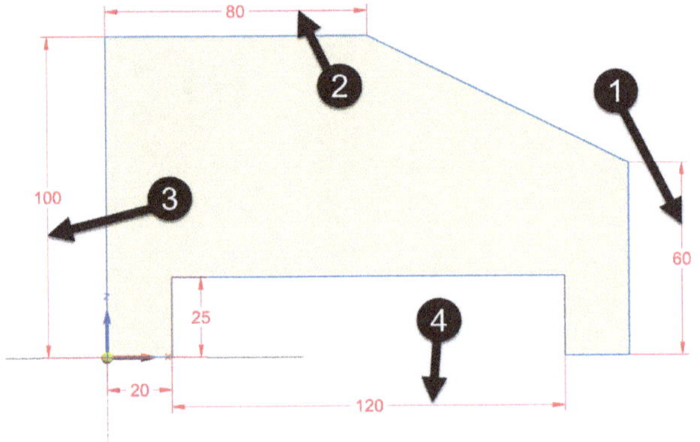

27. Arrange the dimensions, as shown.

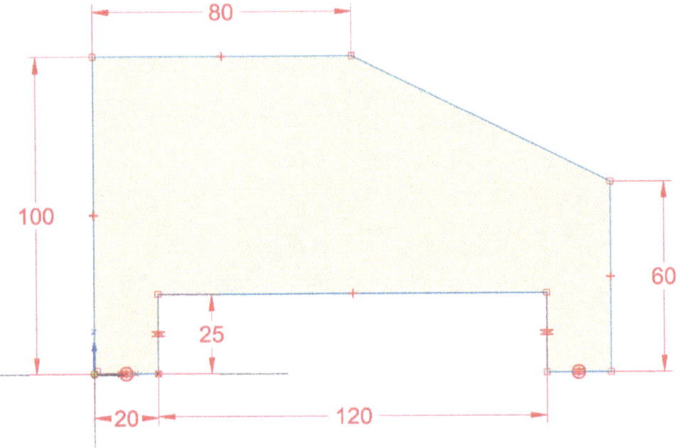

28. On the ribbon, click **Home > Draw > Circle by Center Point**. Click inside the sketch region to define the center point of the circle. Move the mouse pointer and click to define the diameter. Likewise, create another circle.

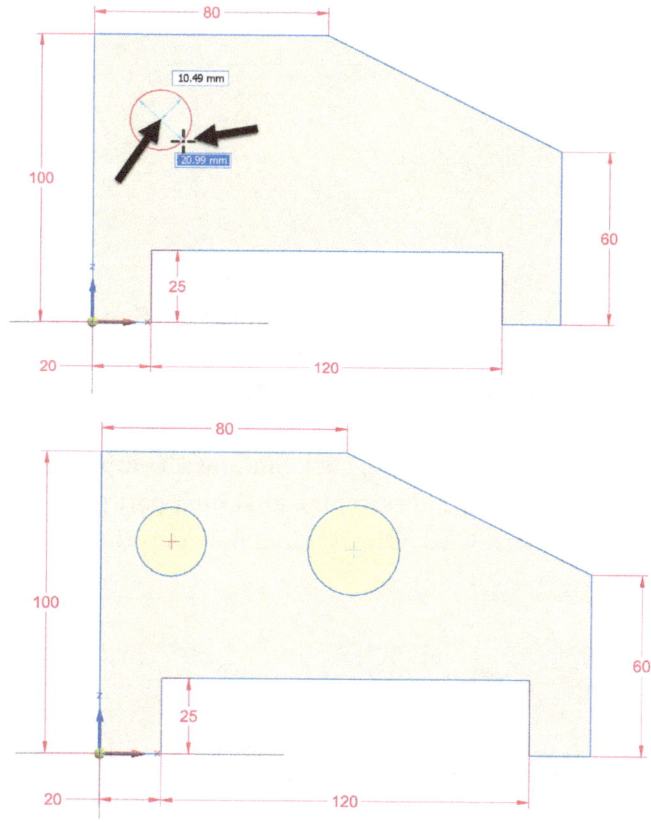

29. On the ribbon, click **Home > Relate > Horizontal/Vertical** . Click on the center points of the two circles to make them horizontally aligned.

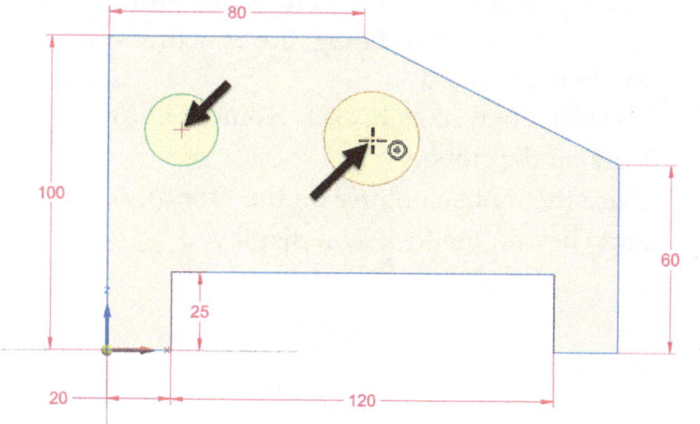

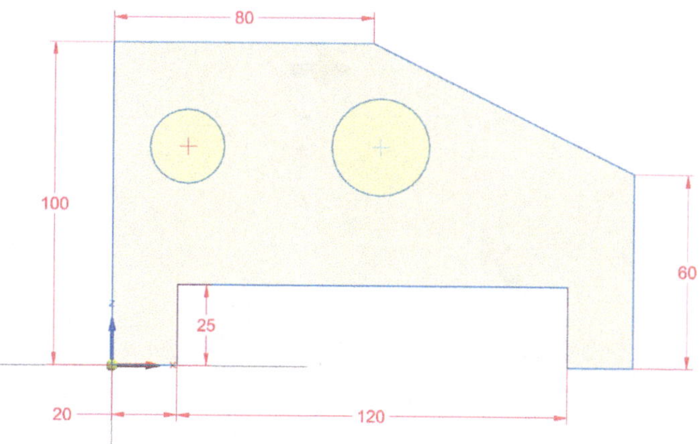

30. On the ribbon, click **Home > Relate > Equal** , and then click on the two circles. The diameters of the circles will become equal.

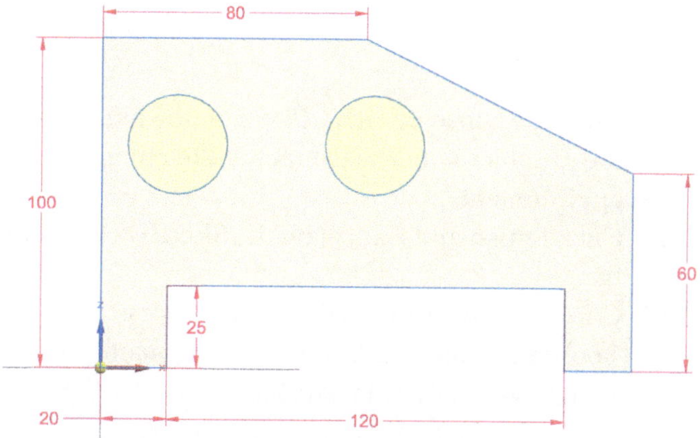

31. Activate the **Smart Dimension** command and click on any one of the circles. Move the mouse pointer and click to position the dimension. Type 25 in the dimension box and press Enter.

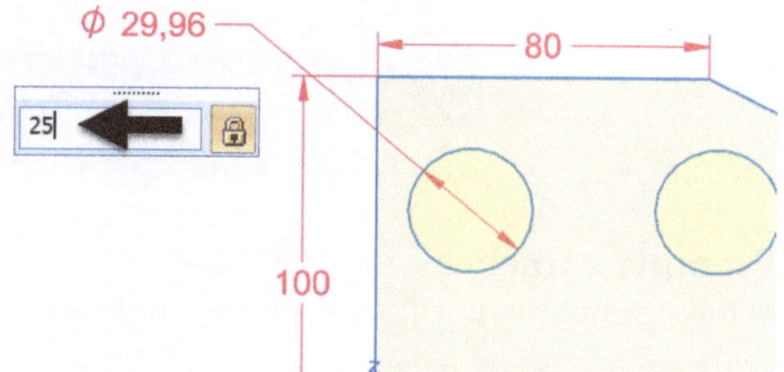

32. Activate the **Smart Dimension** command and select left circle. Next select the left vertical line and move the pointer upward, and then click. Type **40** in the dimension box and press ENTER.
33. Likewise create other dimensions between the circles and the adjacent line, as shown below.

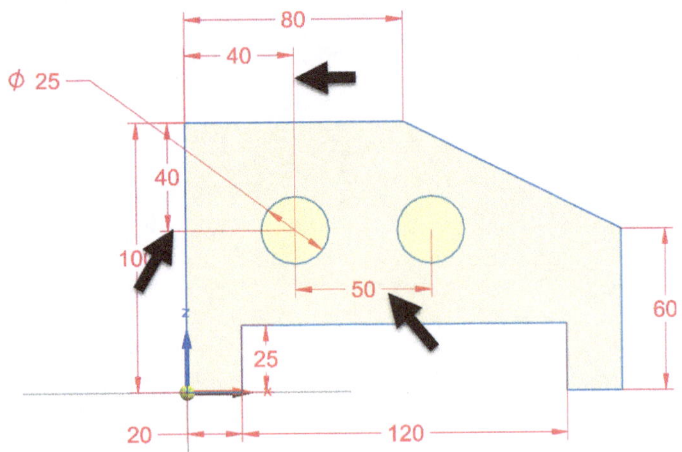

34. On the ribbon, click **Home > Intellisketch** group > **Relationship Colors** , if it not already active. The color of the sketch elements is turned into black indicating that the sketch is fully defined.
35. Click the **Close Sketch** icon on the left side of the graphics window to exit the sketching environment.
36. Click **Finish** and **Cancel** on the **Sketch** command bar.
37. Click the **Save** icon on the **Quick Access Toolbar**. Define the location and file name and click **Save** to save the part file.

38. Click **Close Window** on the top right corner to close the part file.

Example 2 (Inches)

In this example, you will draw the sketch shown below.

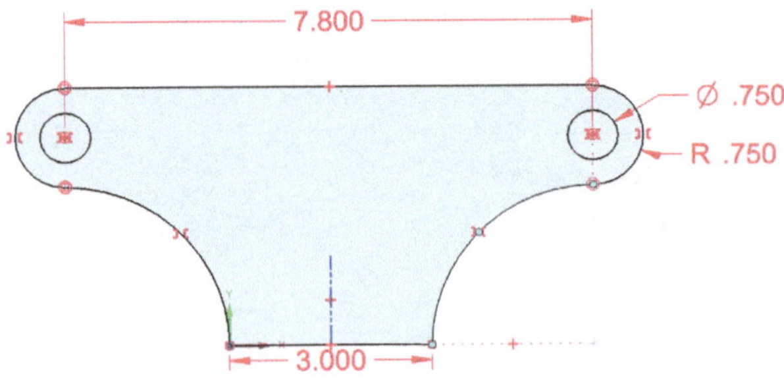

1. Start **Solid Edge 2026** by clicking the **Solid Edge 2026** icon on your desktop.
2. On the File Menu, click the **New** > **New** icon; the **New** dialog is opened.
3. On the **New** dialog, click **Standard Templates > ANSI Inch** and select the **ansi inch part.par** template. Click **OK** to start a new part file.

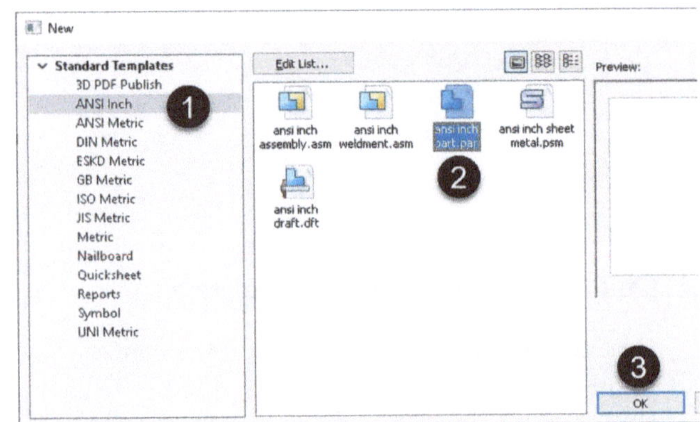

4. Click **Continue with Synchronous** button on the Ordered as default dialog; the Synchronous mode is activated.
5. To start a new sketch, click **Home > Draw > Line** on the ribbon.
6. Place the mouse pointer on the Front(xy) plane and click on the lock icon displayed.

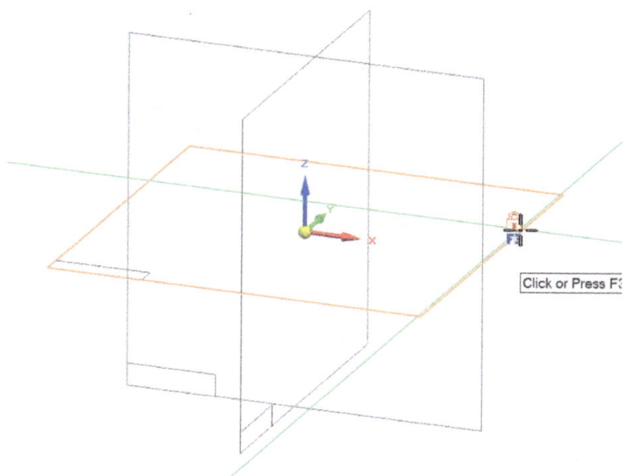

7. Click the **Sketch View** icon located at the bottom of the window. It orients the sketch plane normal to the screen.
8. Click on the origin point to define the first point of the line. Move the mouse pointer horizontally and click to draw a line.

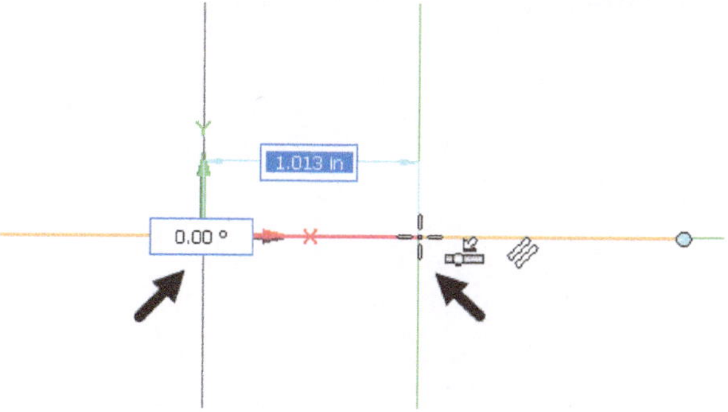

9. On the **Line and Arc** command bar, select **Type > Arc(a)**.
10. Take the mouse pointer to the endpoint of the line.
11. Move it upwards and right. Next, click to create the arc.

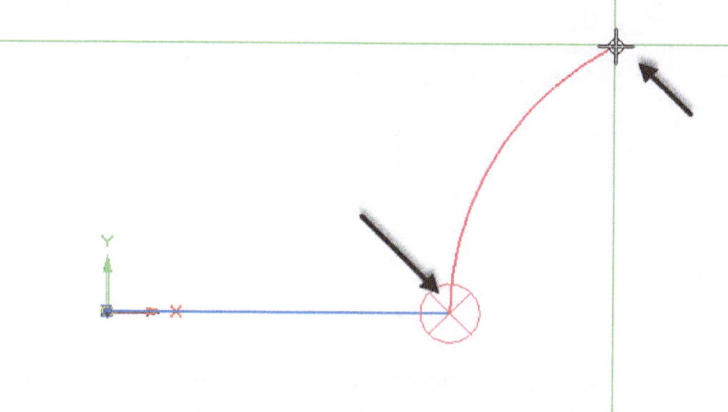

12. Again, select **Type > Arc(a)** on the **Line and Arc** command bar.
13. Move the pointer to the endpoint of the arc, and then move it upwards right.

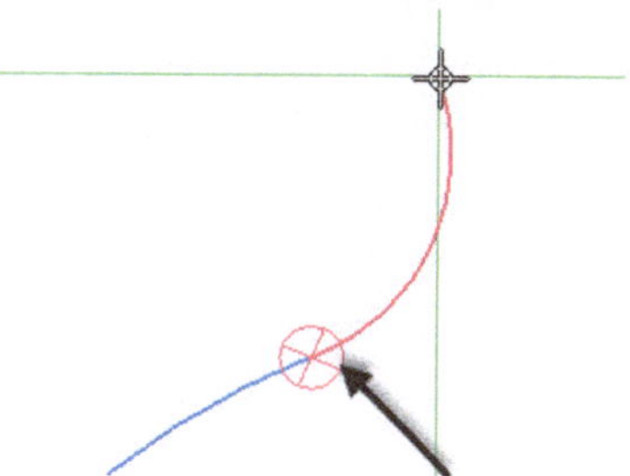

14. Move the pointer toward the left and click when a vertical dotted line appears, as shown below.

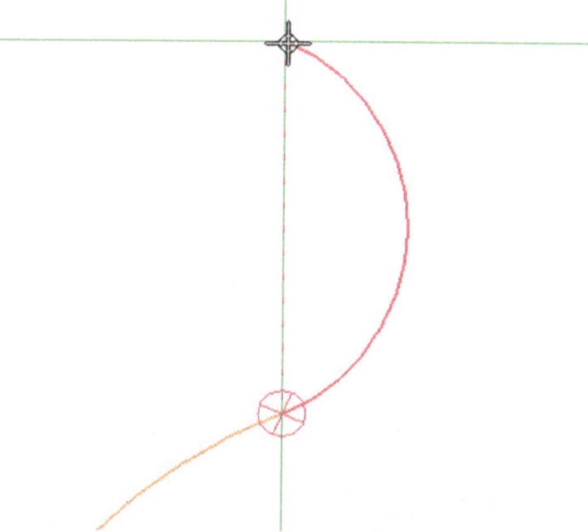

15. Move the mouse pointer horizontally toward the left and click to create a horizontal line. Note that the length of the new line should be greater than that of the lower horizontal line.
16. Select **Type >Arc(a)** on the **Line and Arc** command bar and move it downward left.
17. Move the pointer toward the right and click when a vertical dotted line appears, as shown below.

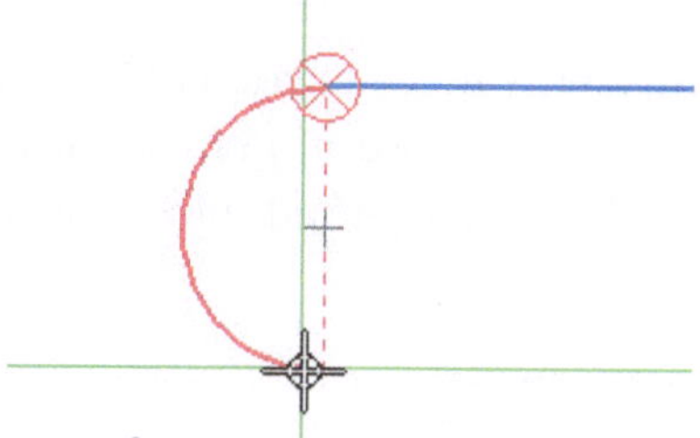

18. Select **Type >Arc(a)** on the **Line and Arc** command bar. Next, move the pointer to the endpoint of the previous arc.
19. Move the mouse pointer downwards right and click on the origin to close the sketch.

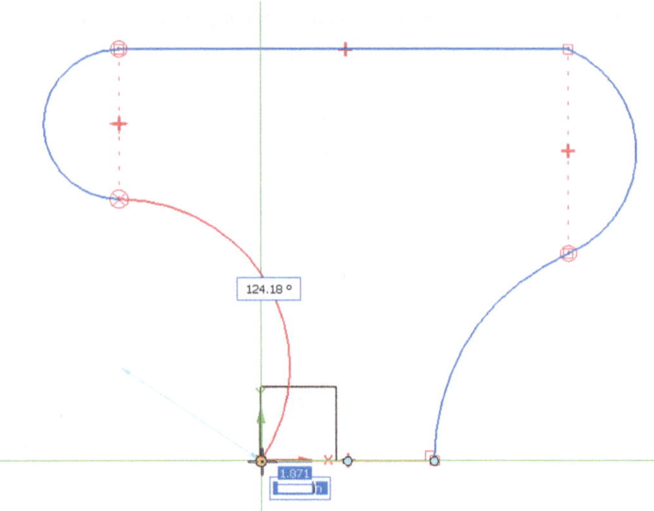

20. Click the right mouse button to end the chain.
21. Click on the midpoint of the lower horizontal line. Move the mouse pointer vertically up and click to create a vertical line.

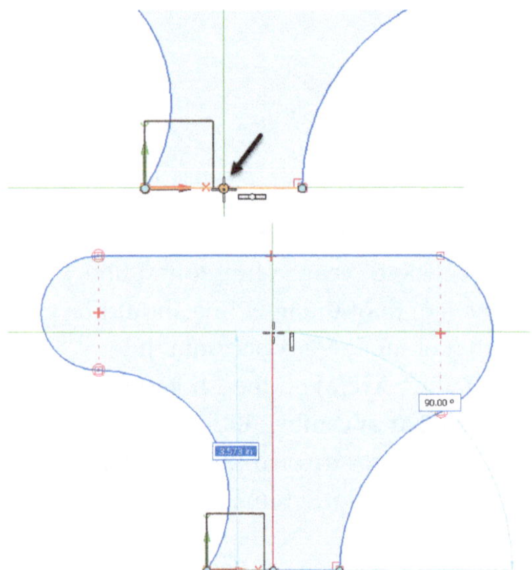

22. Click on the vertical line located at the center.
23. Select the Construction option from the Context toolbar. The line is converted into a construction element.

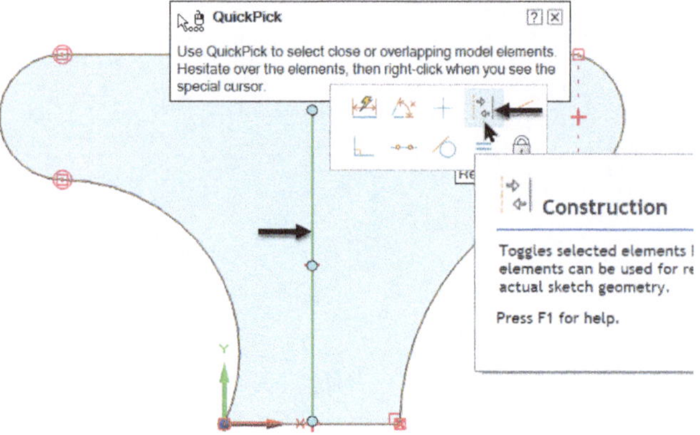

24. Activate the **Circle by Center Point** command and draw a circle on the construction line's right side.
25. On the ribbon, click **Home > Relate > Concentric**. Click on the circle and the small arc on the right side. The circle and arc are made concentric.

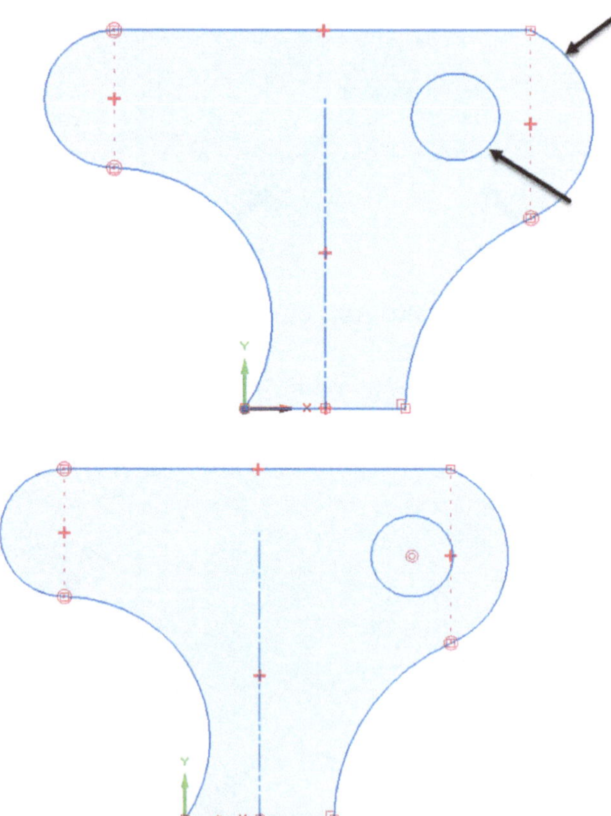

26. Likewise, create another circle concentric to the small arc located on the construction line's left side.

27. On the ribbon, click **Home > Relate > Tangent**  .
28. Select the small arc on the right side and the horizontal line.

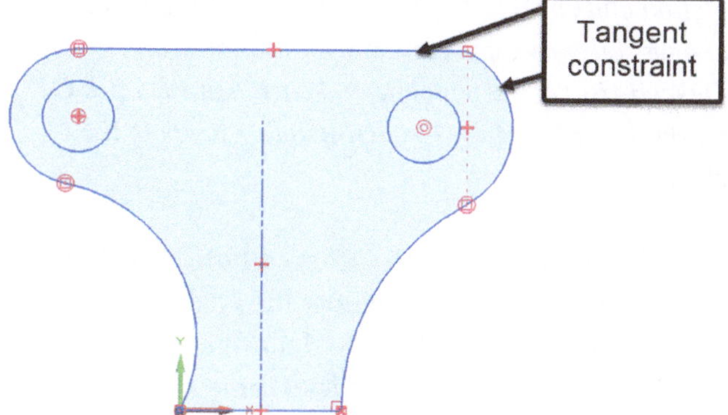

29. On the ribbon, click **Home > Relate > Symmetric** . Click on the construction line located at the center. The line will act as a symmetry line.

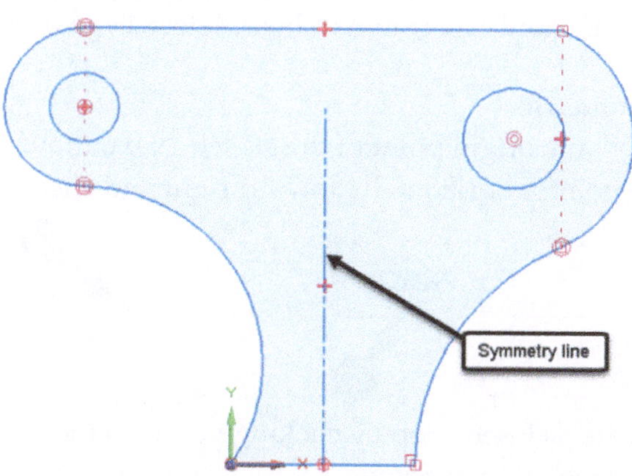

30. Click on the large arcs on both sides of the symmetry line. The arcs are made symmetric about the construction line.
31. Likewise, make the small arcs and circles symmetric about the construction line.

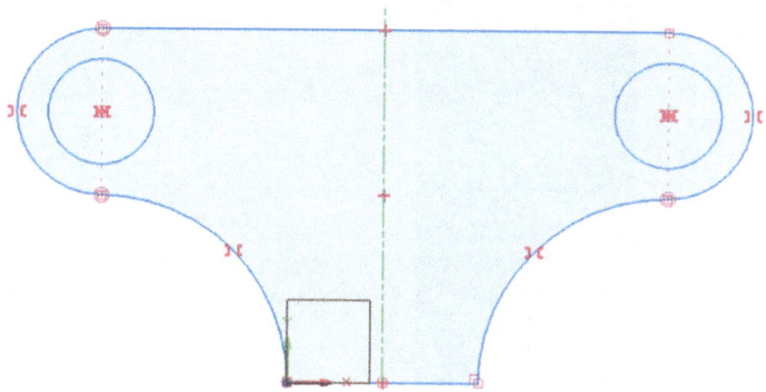

32. Activate the **Smart Dimension** command and apply dimensions to the sketch in the sequence, as shown below.

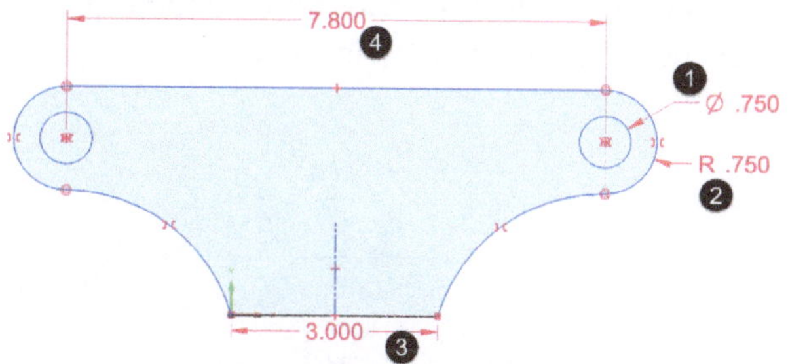

33. On the ribbon, click **Home > Relate > Horizontal/Vertical** .
34. Select the right end point of the lower horizontal line and centerpoint of the right large arc; the centerpoint of arc and the horizontal line are horizontally aligned.

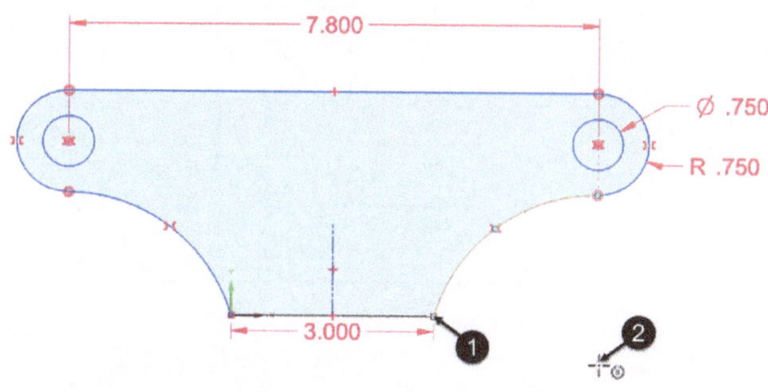

35. On the status bar, click the **Fit** icon to fit the drawing in the graphics window.
36. To save the file, click **File > Save**. Define the location and file name, and then click **Save**; the part file is saved.

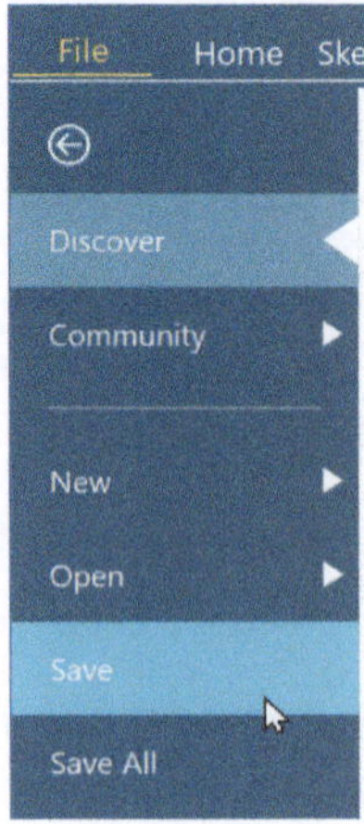

37. To close the file, click **Close** on the top right corner of the graphics window.

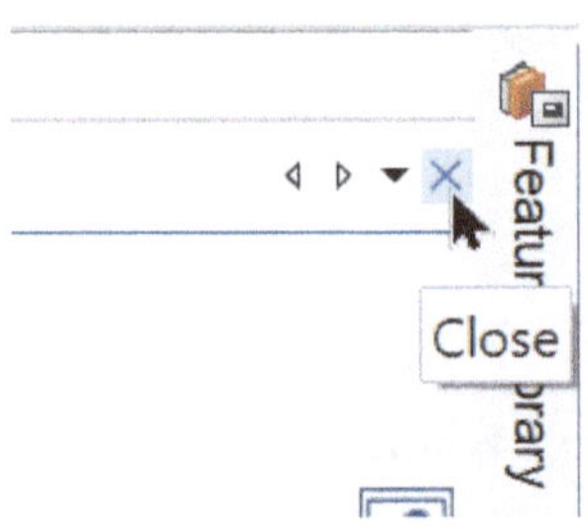

Example 3 (Millimetres)

In this example, you will draw the sketch shown below.

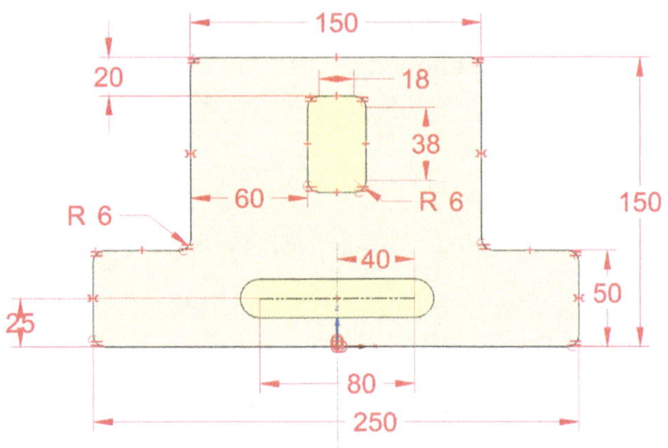

1. Start **Solid Edge 2026**, if not already opened.
2. To start a new part file, click **File Menu > New > ISO Metric Part.**

*Tip: You can change the templates displayed on the **New** page by clicking **Edit List**. On the **Template List Creation** dialog, select a modeling standard from the **Standard Templates** section. You can change the templates' order by selecting them from the **Templates** section and clicking the **Move Up** and **Move Down** arrows. Likewise, you can change the **Name** and **Description** of the template and click **Apply**. Click **OK** on the **Template List Creation** dialog to apply the changes.*

3. Click **Continue with Ordered** button on the **Ordered as default** dialog; the Ordered environment is set as the default environment.
4. To start a new sketch, click **Home > Sketch > Sketch** on the ribbon.
5. Select the Front (xz) plane from the base reference planes displayed in the graphics window; the sketch is started and the sketch plane is oriented normal to the screen.
6. Click **Home > Draw > Line** on the ribbon. On the **Line and Arc** command bar, select **Type > Symmetric** .
7. Select the origin point of the sketch. Next, move the pointer horizontally toward right and click.

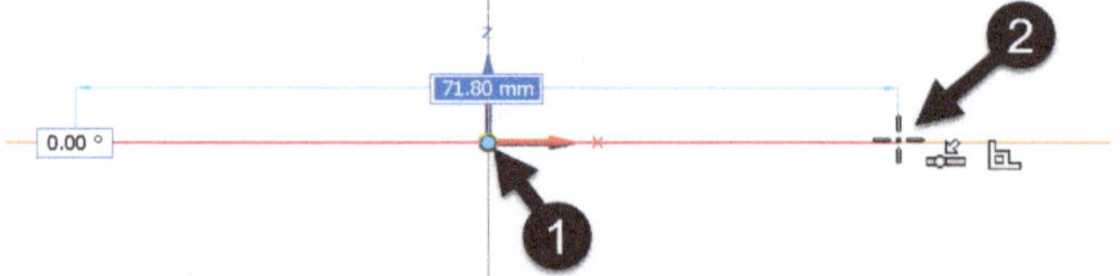

8. Create a closed-loop by clicking points in the sequence shown below.

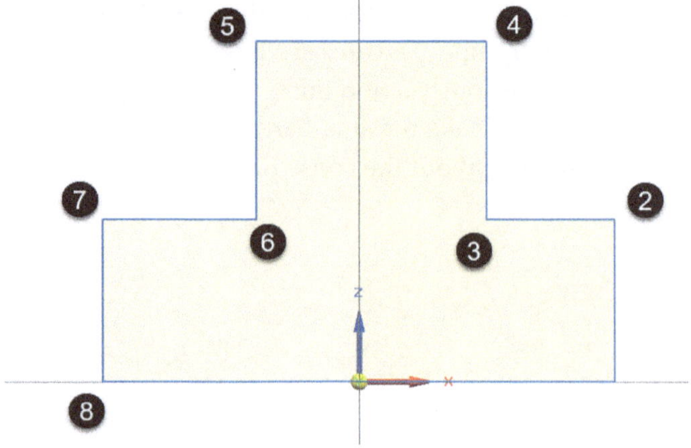

9. Click **Home > Draw > Fillet** on the ribbon. Type-in **6** in the **Radius** box on the command bar and press Enter.

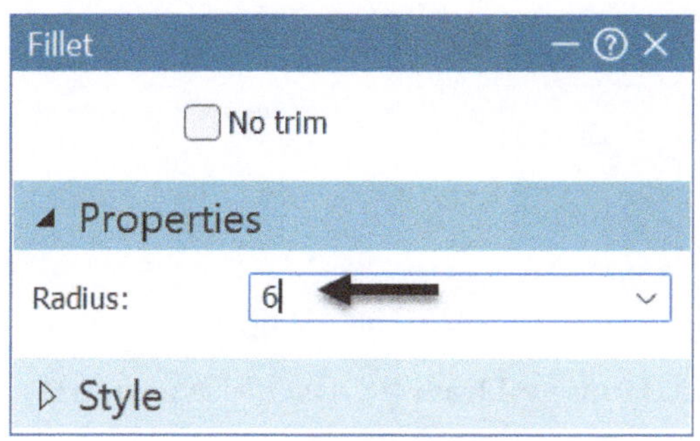

10. Create fillets by clicking on the corners of the sketch.

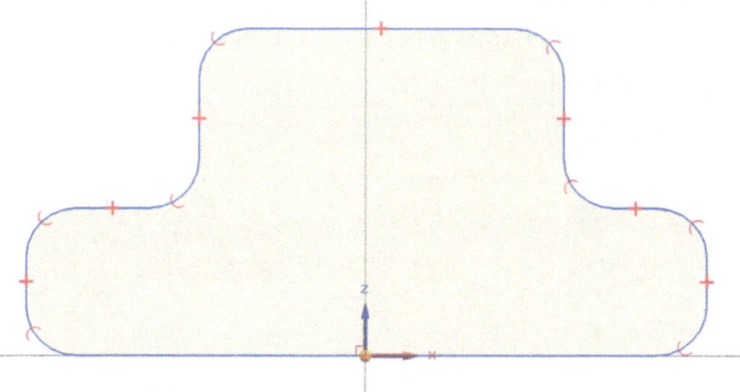

11. Click **Home > Relate > Symmetric** on the ribbon. Click on the Z-axis to define the symmetric axis.
12. Click on the small vertical lines to make them symmetric.
13. Click on the other vertical lines to make them symmetric.

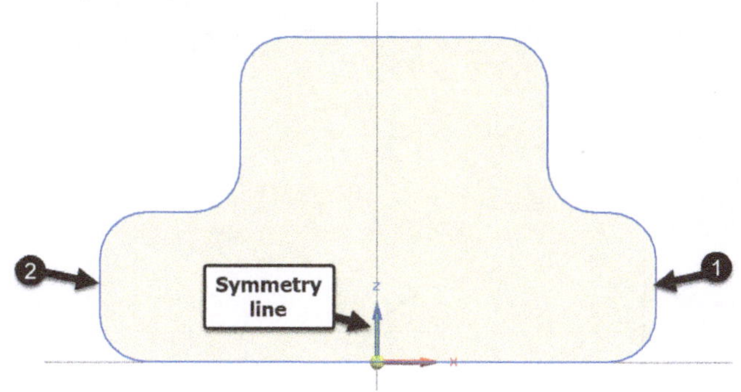

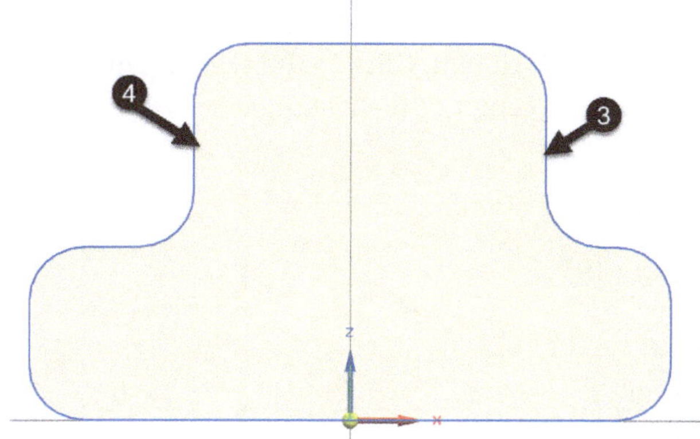

14. On the ribbon, click **Home > Relate > Collinear** . Click on the lower horizontal line and the X-axis to make them collinear.
15. On the ribbon, click **Home > Relate > Equal** . Select the lower left corner fillet and the fillet located next to it.
16. Likewise, select the other sets of the fillet, as shown.

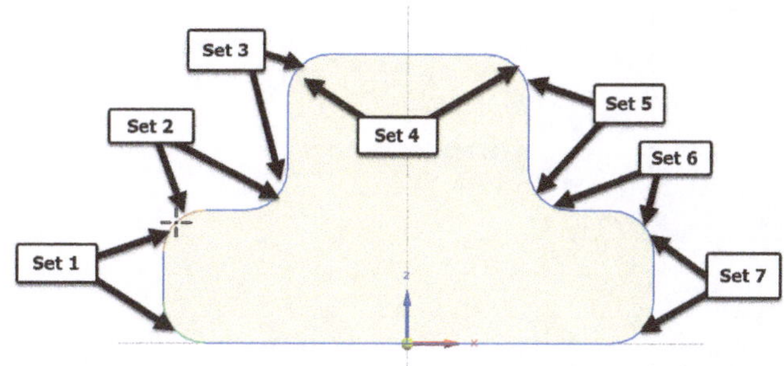

17. Activate the **Smart Dimension** command and apply dimensions in the sequence shown below.

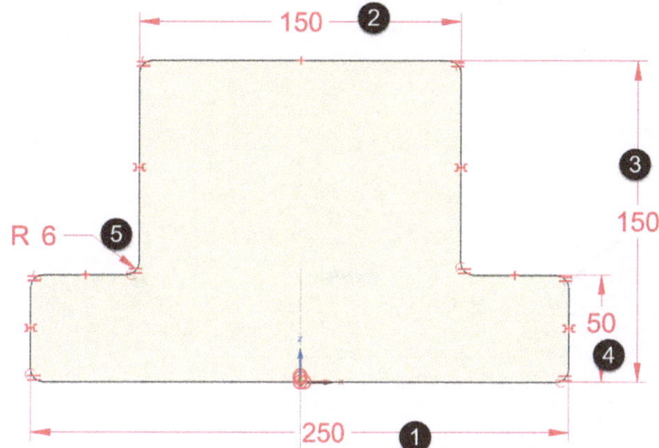

18. Click **Home > Draw > Rectangle by Center** on the ribbon. Click in the sketch region to define the center of the rectangle.

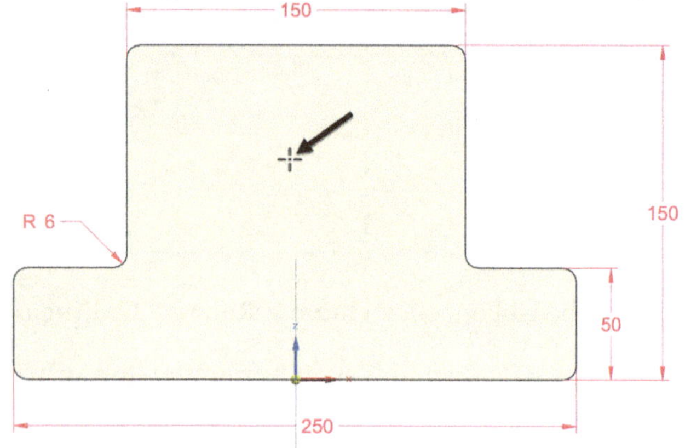

19. Move the mouse pointer toward the top right and click to define the corner of the rectangle.

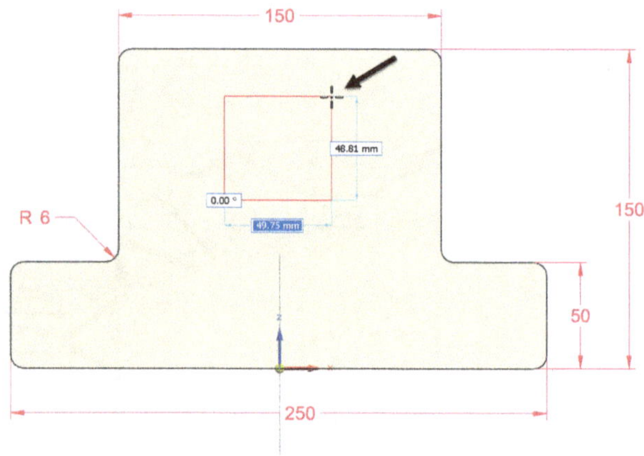

20. Activate the **Line** command and draw a horizontal line inside the loop.

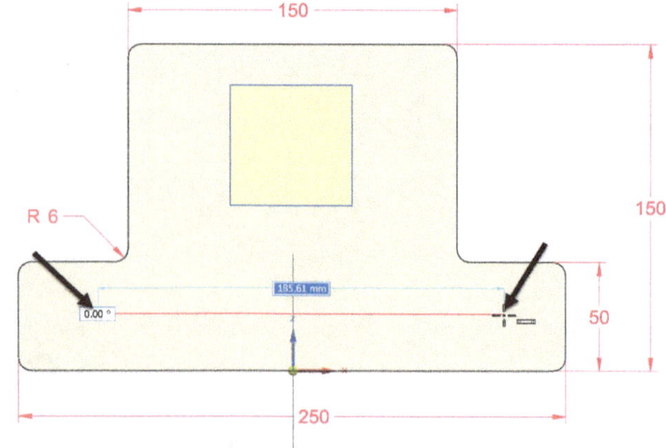

21. Activate the **Smart Dimension** command and apply dimensions in the sequence shown below.

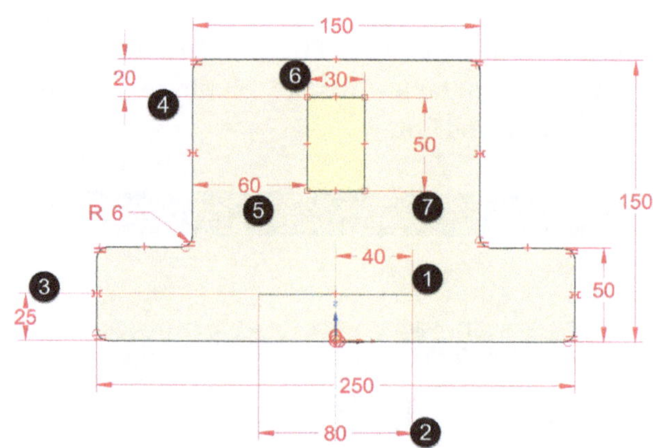

22. Click **Home > Draw > Offset > Symmetric Offset** on the ribbon; the **Symmetric Offset Options** dialog pops up.

23. On this dialog, type-in **20** in the **Width** box and select the **Offset Arc** option. Click **OK** to close the dialog.

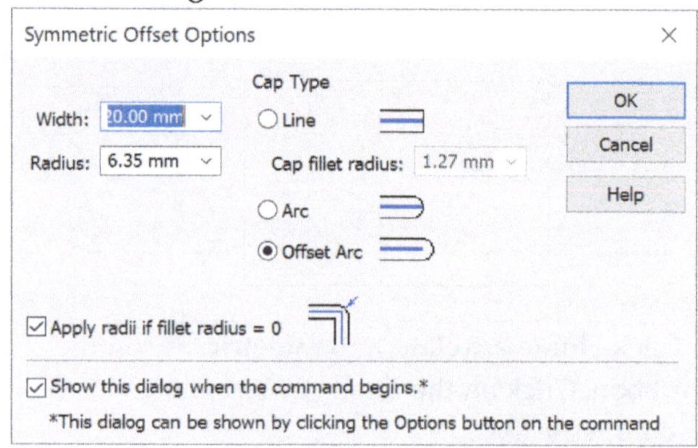

24. Select the horizontal line and click the **Accept** button on the command bar.

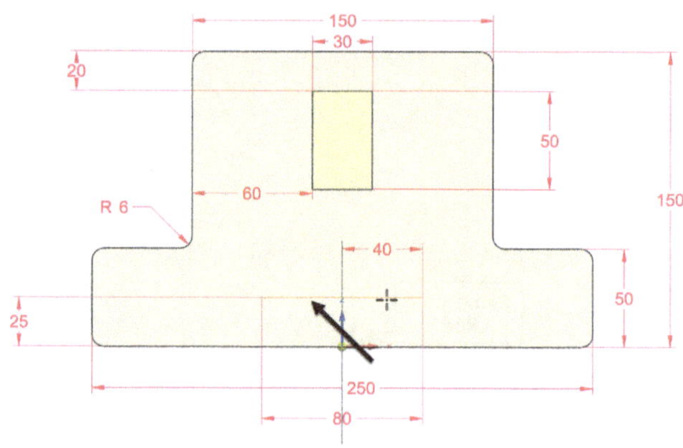

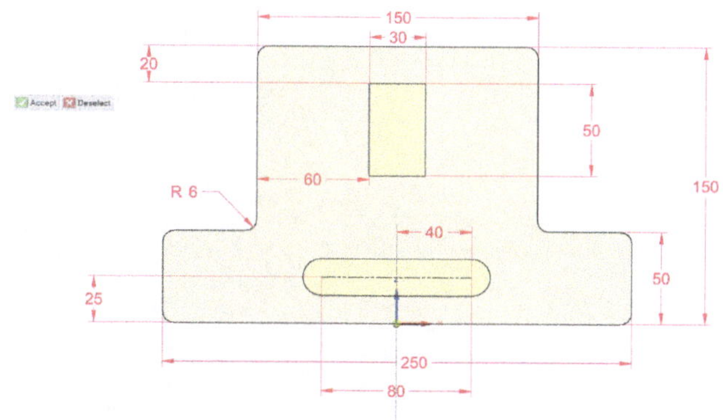

25. Click **Home > Draw > Fillet** on the ribbon. Type-in **6** in the **Radius** box on the command bar and press Enter.
26. Create fillets by clicking on the corners of the rectangle. Next, apply the **Equal** relation between the fillets of the rectangle.
27. Click **Home > Dimension > Smart Dimension** and select anyone of the fillets. Type **6** in the dimension box and press ENTER.

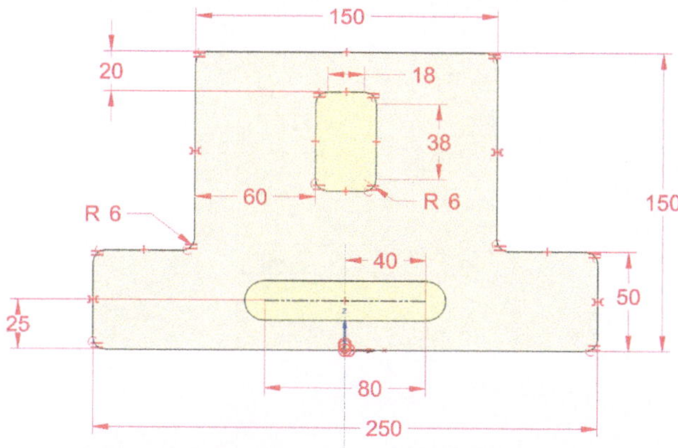

28. Click **Home > Close > Close Sketch** on the ribbon. Next, click **Finish** and **Cancel** on the **Sketch** command bar.
29. Save and close the file.

Questions

1. What is the procedure to create sketches in Synchronous mode?
2. List any two sketch *Relationships* in Solid Edge.
3. Which command orients the sketch normal to the screen?
4. What is the procedure to create sketches in Ordered mode?
5. Which command allows you to apply dimensions to a sketch automatically?
6. Describe the two methods to create ellipses.
7. How do you define the shape and size of a sketch?
8. How do you create a tangent arc using the **Line** command?
9. Which command is used to apply multiple types of dimensions to a sketch?
10. List any two commands to create circles?

Exercises

Exercise 1

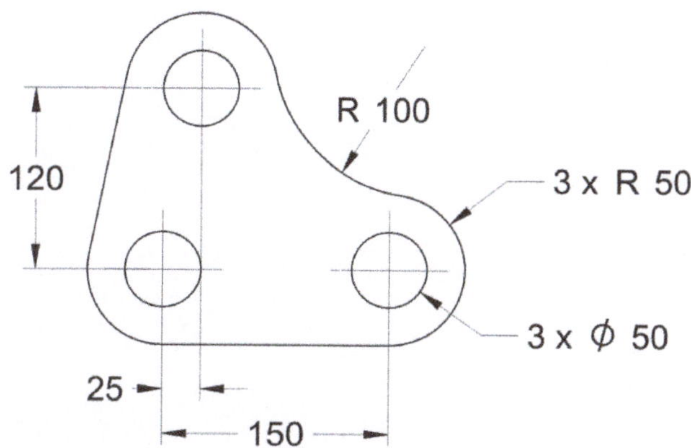

Exercise 2

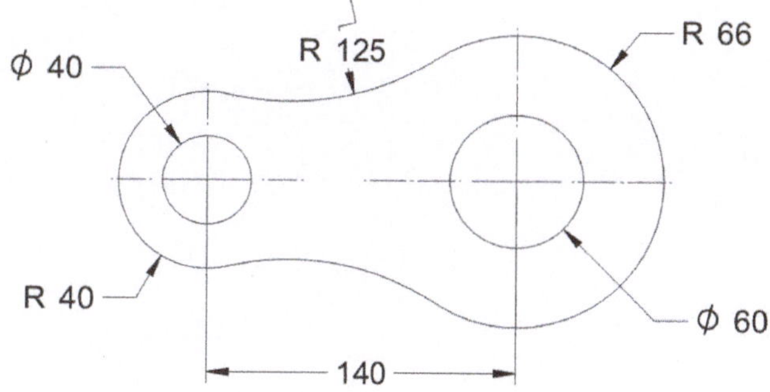

Exercise 3

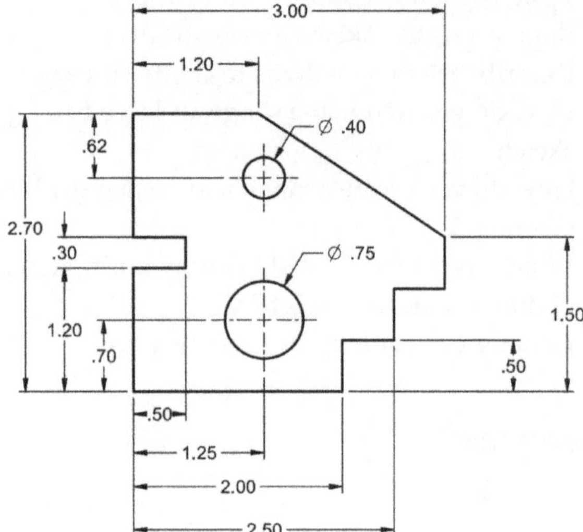
3.00
1.20
Ø .40
.62
2.70
.30
Ø .75
1.50
1.20
.70
.50
.50
1.25
2.00
2.50

Chapter 3: Extrude and Revolve Features

This chapter covers the methods and commands to create extruded and revolved features.

The topics covered in this chapter are:

- Constructing *Extrude* and *Revolve* features in the Part environment (Synchronous and Ordered mode)
- Creating Reference Planes
- Additional Options in the *Extrude* and *Revolve* commands

Extrude Features (Ordered)

Extrude is the process of taking a two-dimensional profile and converting it into 3D by giving it some thickness. A simple example of this would be taking a circle and converting it into a cylinder. Activate the **Extrude** command from the **Solids** panel on the **Home** tab of the ribbon. The **Extrude** command bar pops up on the screen. Select the **Select from Sketch** and **Chain** options on the **Extrude** command bar. Click on the sketch profile and click the green check on the **Sketch** section of the command bar; this completes the sketch selection step and activates the **Extent** step. In this step, you will define the side and extent of the **Extrude** feature. In the **Extent** section, the **Direction > One-sided Extent** option is activated by default. Now, move the pointer on either side of sketch plane to add thickness to the sketch profile. Next, type-in a value in the **Distance** box on the command bar and press Enter to define the extrusion distance.

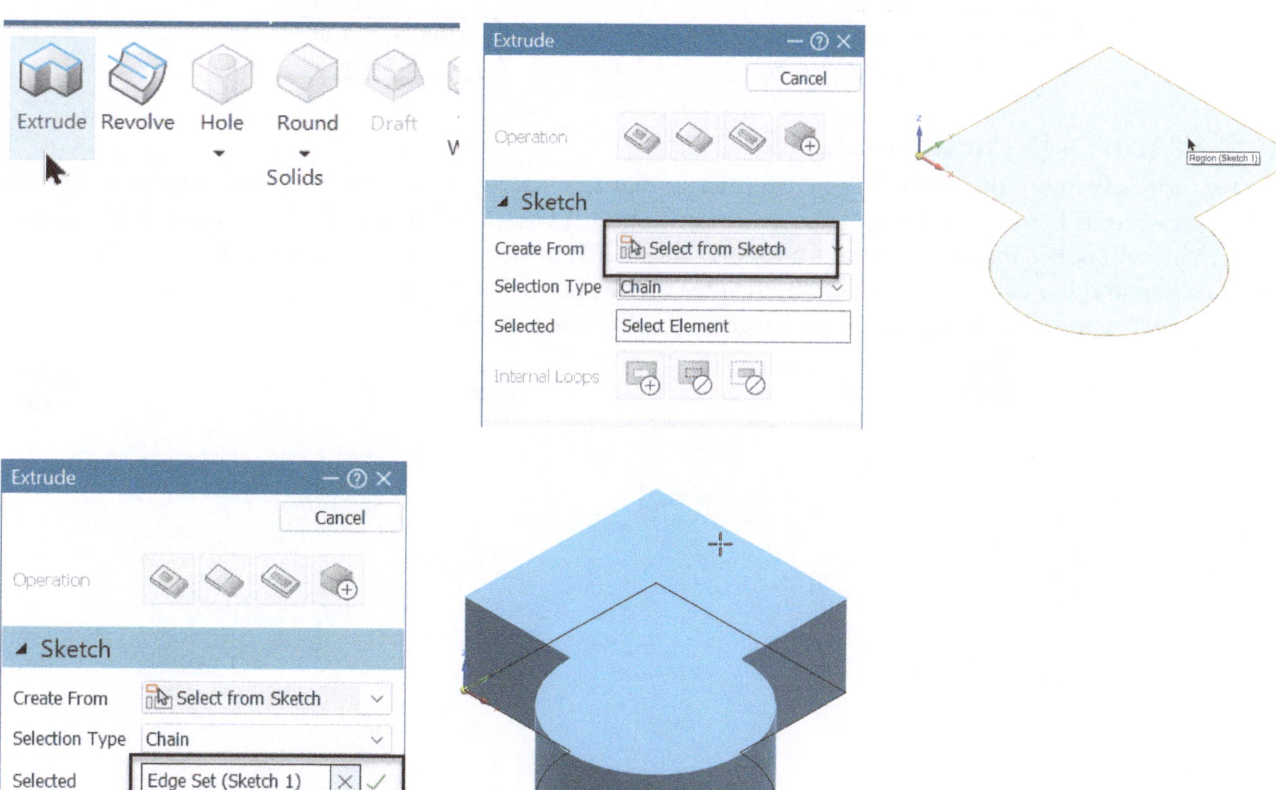

Use the **Direction > Symmetric Extent** option on the command bar to add equal thickness on both sides of the sketch. Use the **Direction > Non-Symmetric Extent** option to add separate thickness on either side of the sketch profile. To do this, click the **Non-Symmetric Extent** button under the **Extent** section and move the pointer on anyone of the side of the sketch plane and click or enter a value in the Distance box; the Direction 1 is defined. Next, move the pointer on the other side of the sketch and click or enter a value in the **Distance** box; the Direction 2 is defined. Next, click **Finish** and **Cancel** on the **Extrude** command bar.

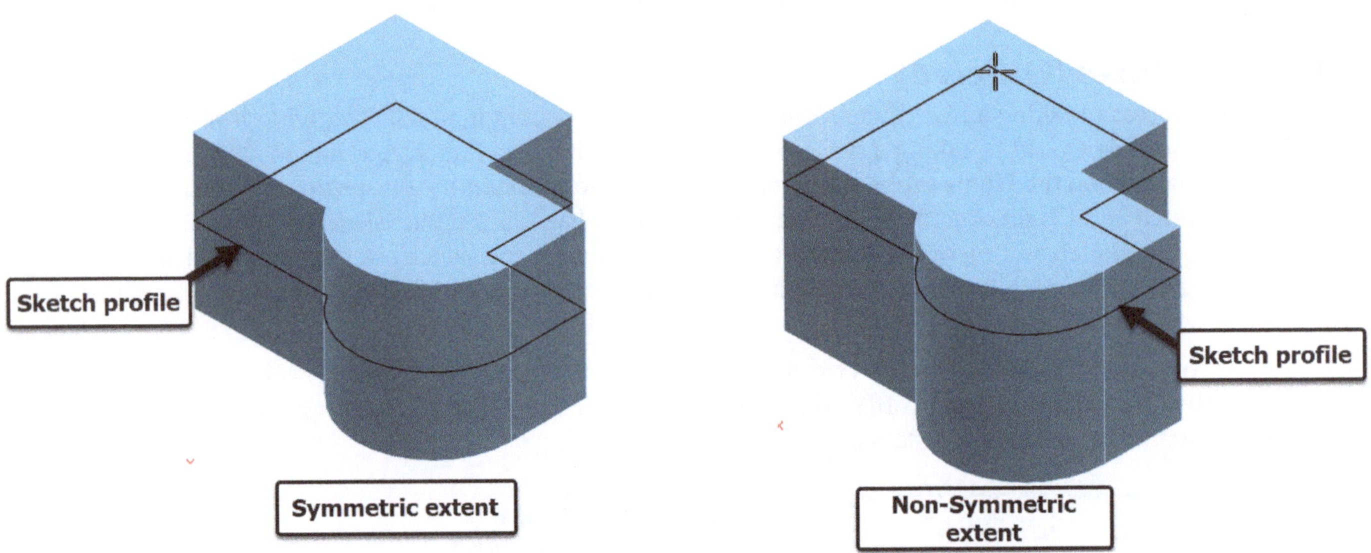

Extrude Features (Synchronous)

Creating Extrude features in the mode is **Synchronous** similar to **Ordered**. Once you have created a sketch profile or profiles you want to *Extrude*, click inside the sketch to display a two-sided arrow. Click the arrow and move the pointer. You will notice that a thickness is added to the sketch profile. Use the **Symmetric Extent** option on the **Extrude** command bar to add thickness to both sides of the sketch. Next, type-in a value in the box that appears on the extrusion, and then press Enter to create the *Extrude* feature.

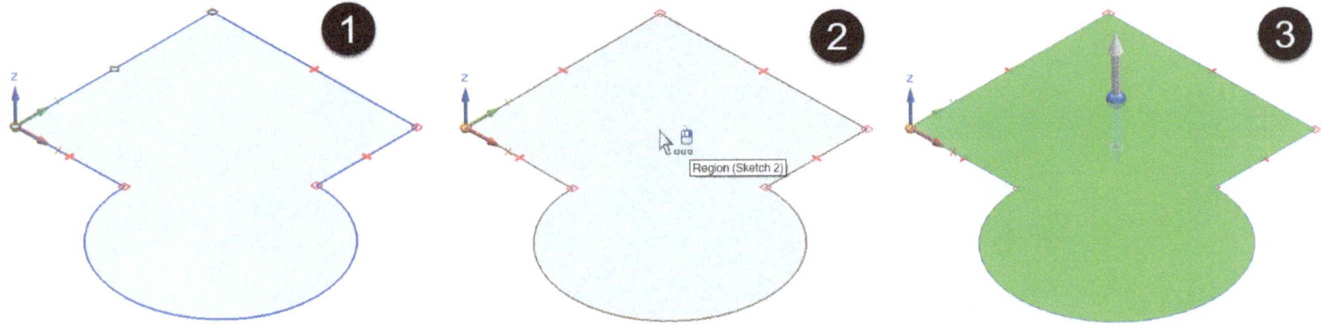

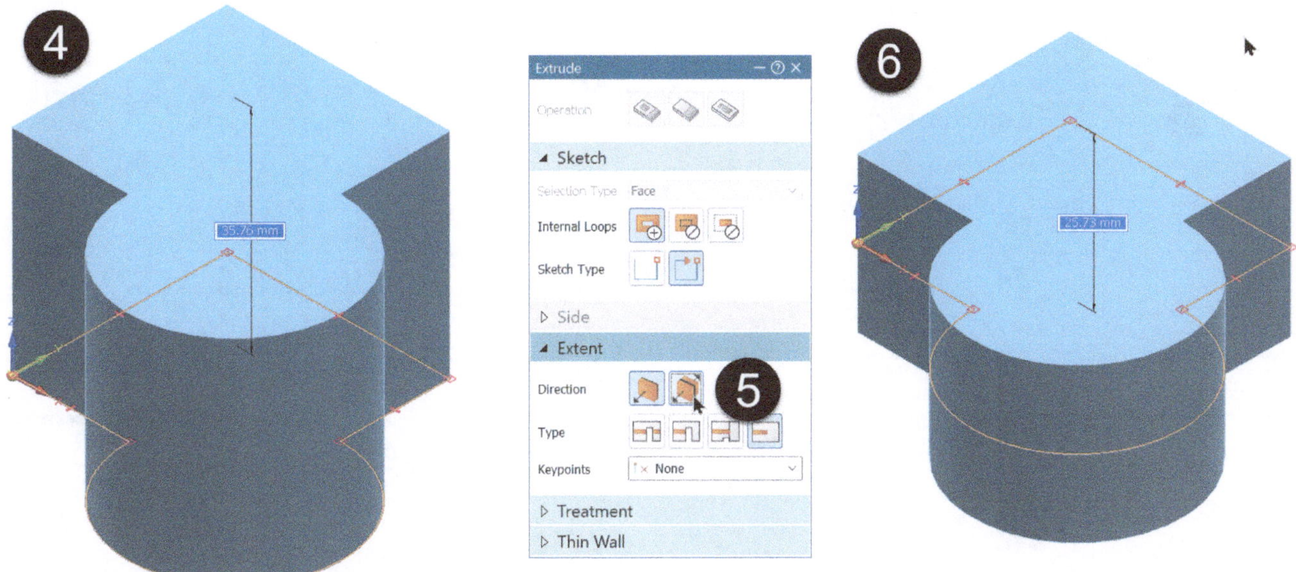

Revolve Features (Ordered)

Revolve is the process of taking a two-dimensional profile and revolving it about a centerline to create a 3D geometry (axially symmetric shapes). While creating a sketch for the *Revolve* feature, it is important to think about the cross-sectional shape defining the 3D geometry once it revolves around an axis. For instance, the following geometry has a hole in the center. It could be created with a separate *Cut* or *Hole* feature. To make that hole part of the *Revolve* feature, you need to sketch the axis of revolution to leave a space between the profile and the axis.

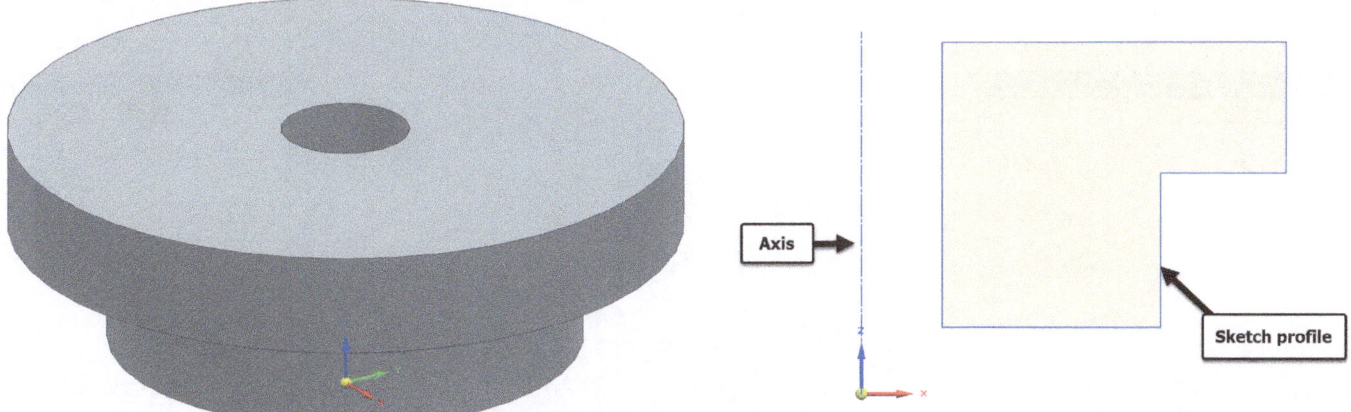

Activate the **Revolve** command (click **Home > Solids > Revolve** on the ribbon), and then select the sketching plane. Next, draw the cross-section and axis of revolution. Click **Home > Draw > Axis of Revolution** on the ribbon and select a line to define the revolution axis. Click the **Close sketch** button on the ribbon. Next, expand the Extent section and type-in a value in the **Angle** field on the **Revolve** command bar (or) click the **Revolve 360** icon in the **Extent** section to revolve up to 360 degrees. Next, click **Finish** to create the *Revolve* feature. Click **Cancel** to deactivate this command.

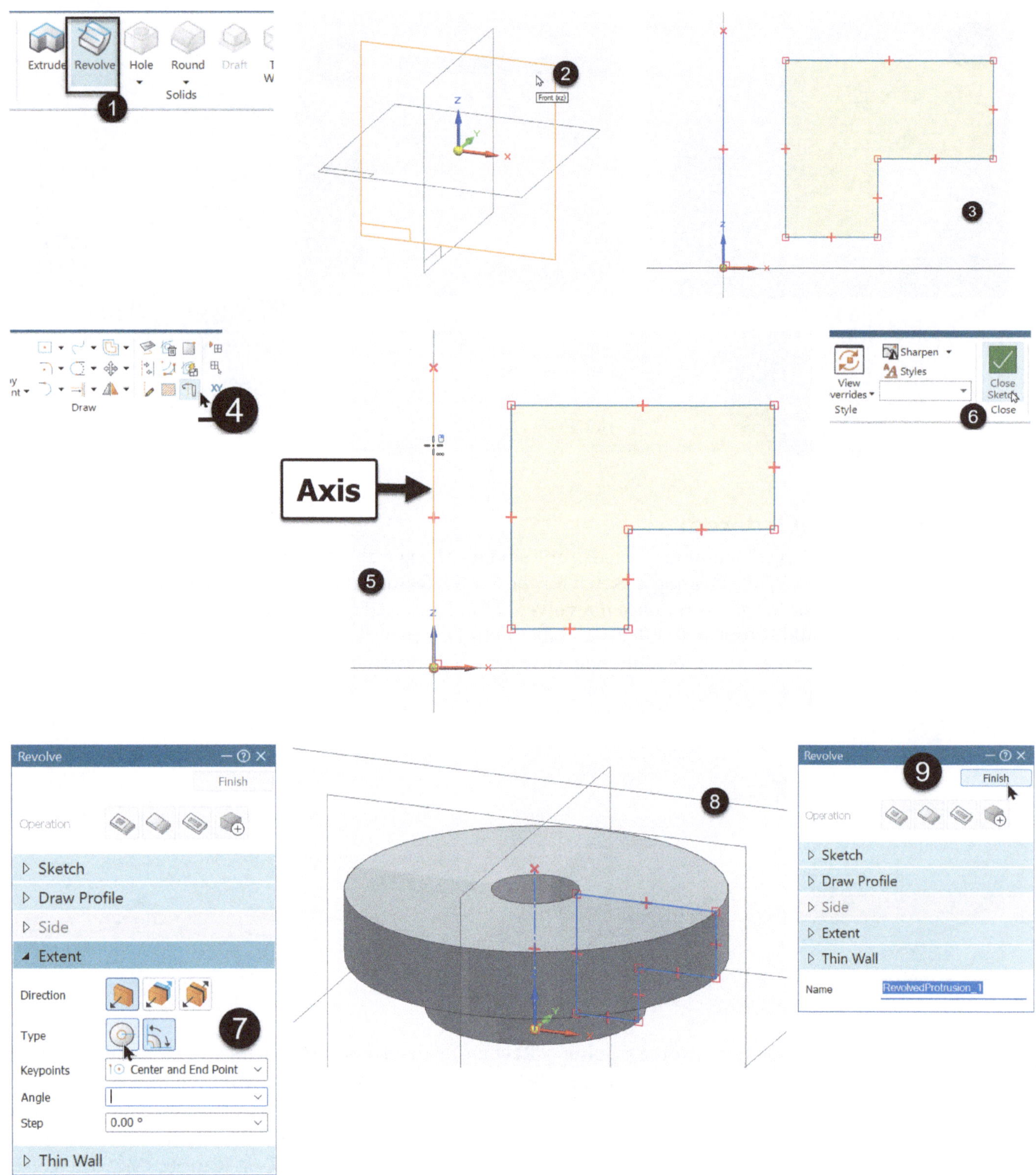

Revolve Features (Synchronous)

The process of creating the *Revolve* feature in the **Synchronous** mode is a little bit different from **Ordered**. After completing the sketch, click inside the sketch region. The *Extrude Handle* appears on the sketch region. Activate the **Revolve** command from the command bar (click the drop-down available at top of the Select command bar and select **Revolve**). You will notice that the *Extrude Handle* is changed to *Revolve Handle* (a two-sided arrow with a torus and spear in the middle). Click the spear on the *Revolve Handle* and drag and place it on the axis of revolution. Click the torus on the *Revolve Handle* and move the pointer to revolve the sketch. Type-in an angle value and press Enter to create the *Revolve* feature. Select **Type > 360** on the **Extent** section of the command bar to revolve the sketch up to 360 degrees.

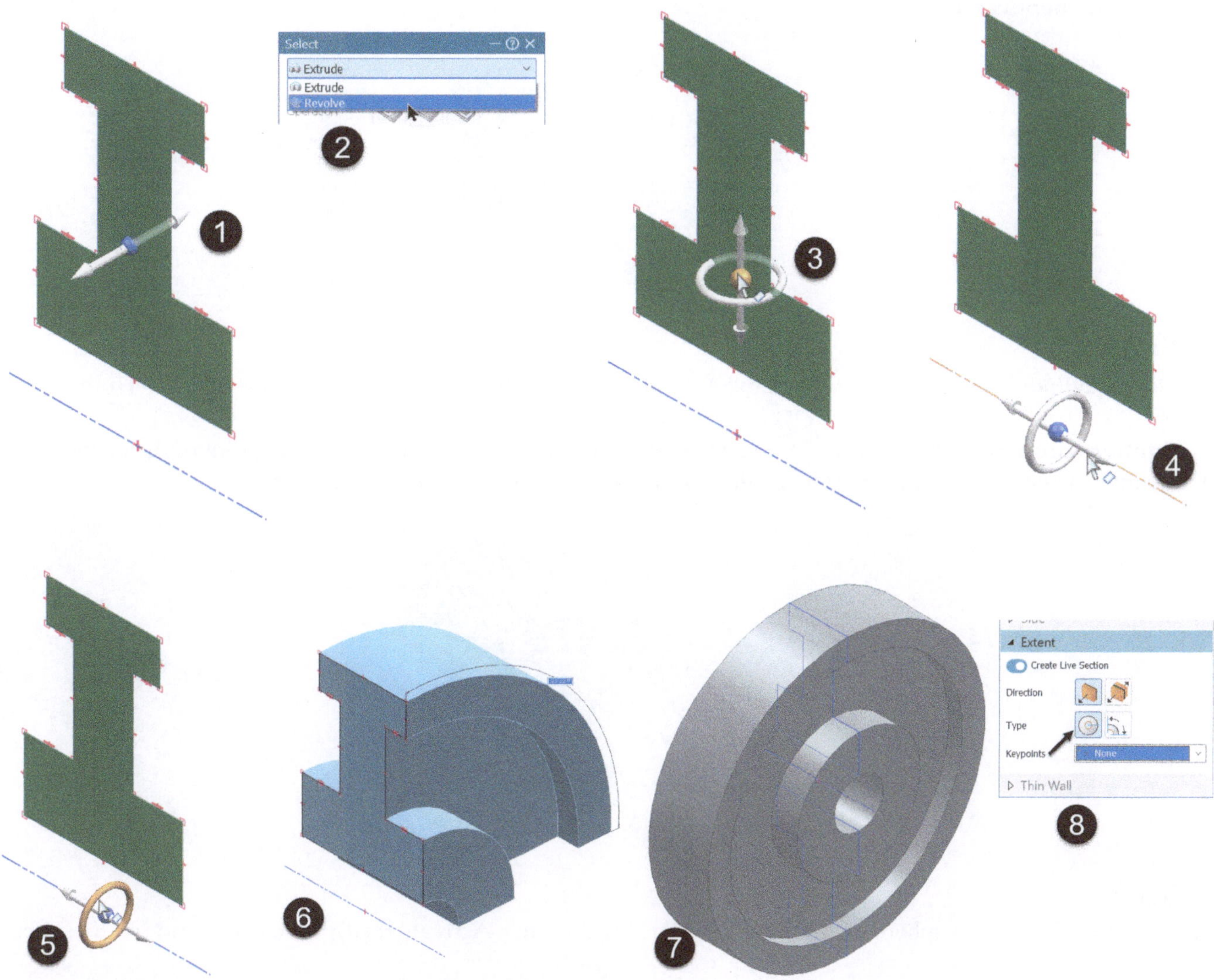

Primitive Shapes (Synchronous only)

Solid Edge provides you with commands to create primitive shapes such as boxes, cylinders, and spheres. These commands are available in the Synchronous mode only.

Box

This command creates a box by using a rectangular sketch. You can create rectangles using three options: **by Center**, **by 2 points**, and **by 3 points**. These options are discussed earlier in Chapter 2 in the **Rectangles** section.

Activate this command (on the ribbon, click **Home > Solids > Primitives** drop-down **> Box**) and set the **Selection Type** on the **Box** command bar. For example, set the **Selection type** to **by Center** and select a plane. Click to define the center point of the rectangle. Move the pointer and click to define the corner point (or) type-in values in the length, width, and angle dimension boxes by pressing the Tab key. Move the pointer and click (or) type-in the extrusion depth and press Enter.

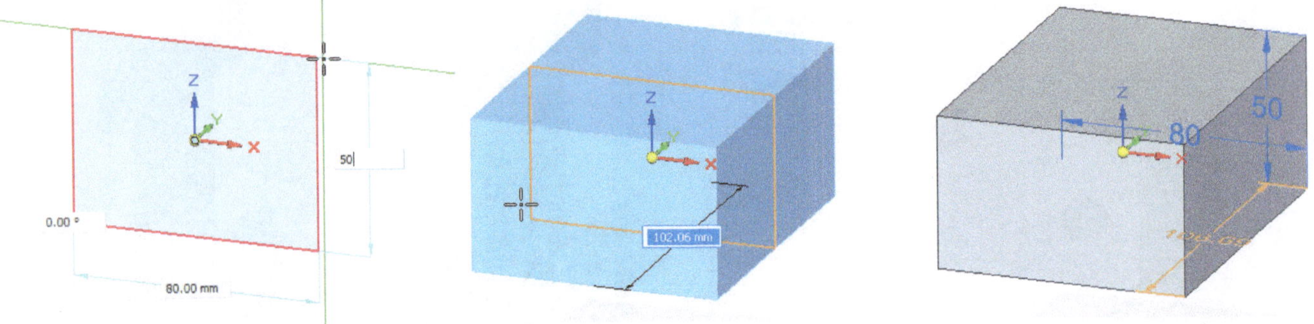

Cylinder

Creating a cylinder is similar to that of a box. Activate the **Cylinder** command (on the ribbon, click **Home > Solids > Primitives** drop-down **> Cylinder**) and select a plane. Click to define the center point of the cylinder. Next, define the extrusion depth by entering a value (or) by moving the pointer and clicking.

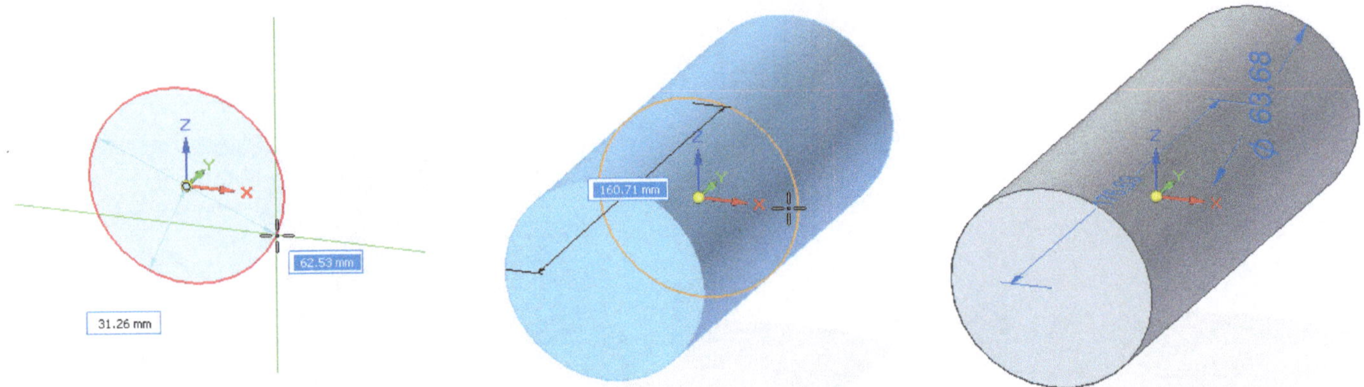

Sphere

This command creates a sphere by defining the center and radius. Activate the **Sphere** command (on the ribbon, click **Home > Solids > Primitives** drop-down **> Sphere**) and click to define the center point of the sphere. You can also select a plane and define a point on it. Next, define the radius by entering a value (or) moving the pointer and clicking.

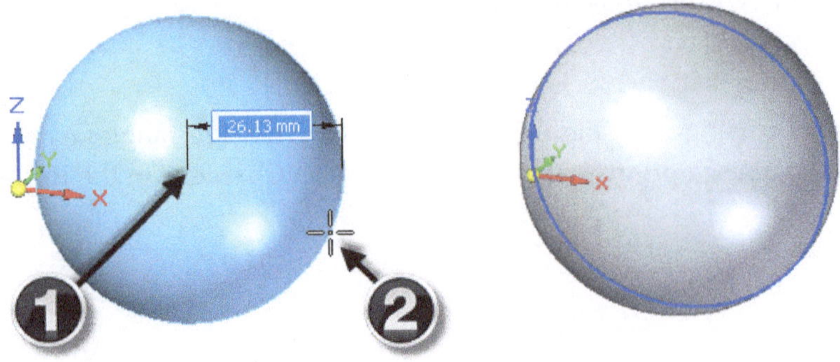

Creating Planes

Each time you start a new part file, Solid Edge automatically creates default reference planes (Base Reference Planes) along with the default coordinate system. Planes and coordinate system make up a specific type of feature in Solid Edge, known as Reference features. These features act as supports to your 3D geometry. In addition to the default reference features, you can create your additional planes and coordinate systems too. Until now, you have known to create sketches on any of the default reference planes. If you want to create sketches and geometry at locations other than default reference planes, you can manually create new reference planes. You can do so by using the commands available in the **Planes** panel of the **Home** tab.

Coincident Plane (Ordered)

This command creates a reference plane, which is coincident with a selected face or plane. To use it, go to **Home > Planes > Coincident Plane** on the ribbon, then hover your cursor over a flat face or an existing plane. A new plane will appear, with its origin at the bottom left corner. You can adjust where this plane's origin is displayed by using the n, b, t, or f keys on your keyboard (n = next, b = back, t = toggle, f = flip, p = base plane). Once you've set the plane's origin, click to select the face or plane, and a plane that matches it will be created.

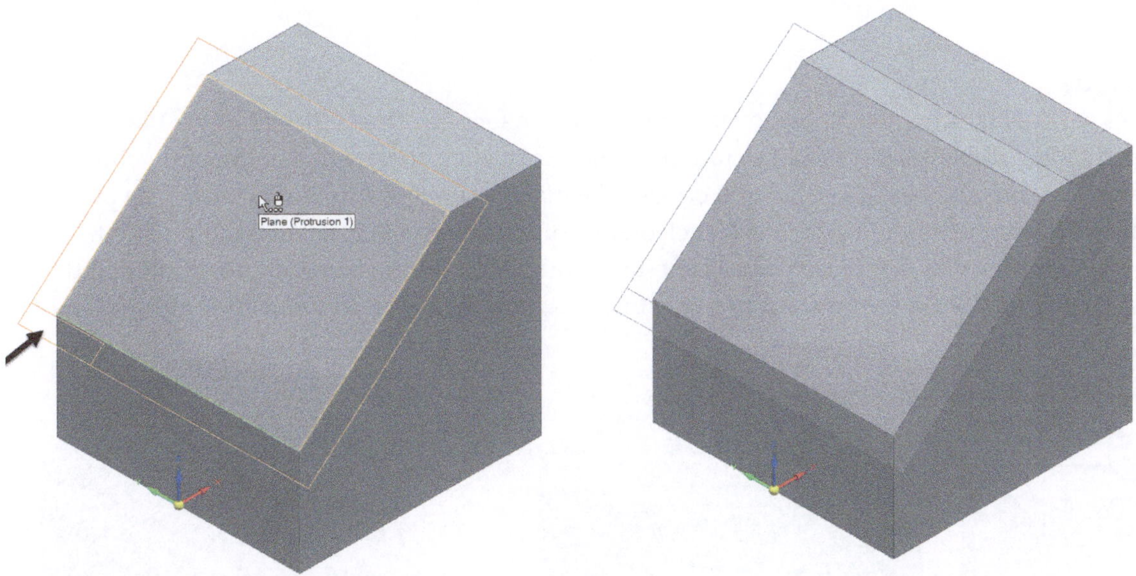

Parallel (Ordered)

This command creates a reference plane, which will be parallel to a face or another plane. Click **Home > Planes > More Planes > Parallel** on the ribbon and select a flat face. Drag the pointer (or) type-in a value in the **Distance** box available on the Parallel command bar and press Enter on the Keyboard. Next, move the pointer and click on either side of the selected face to create the parallel plane.

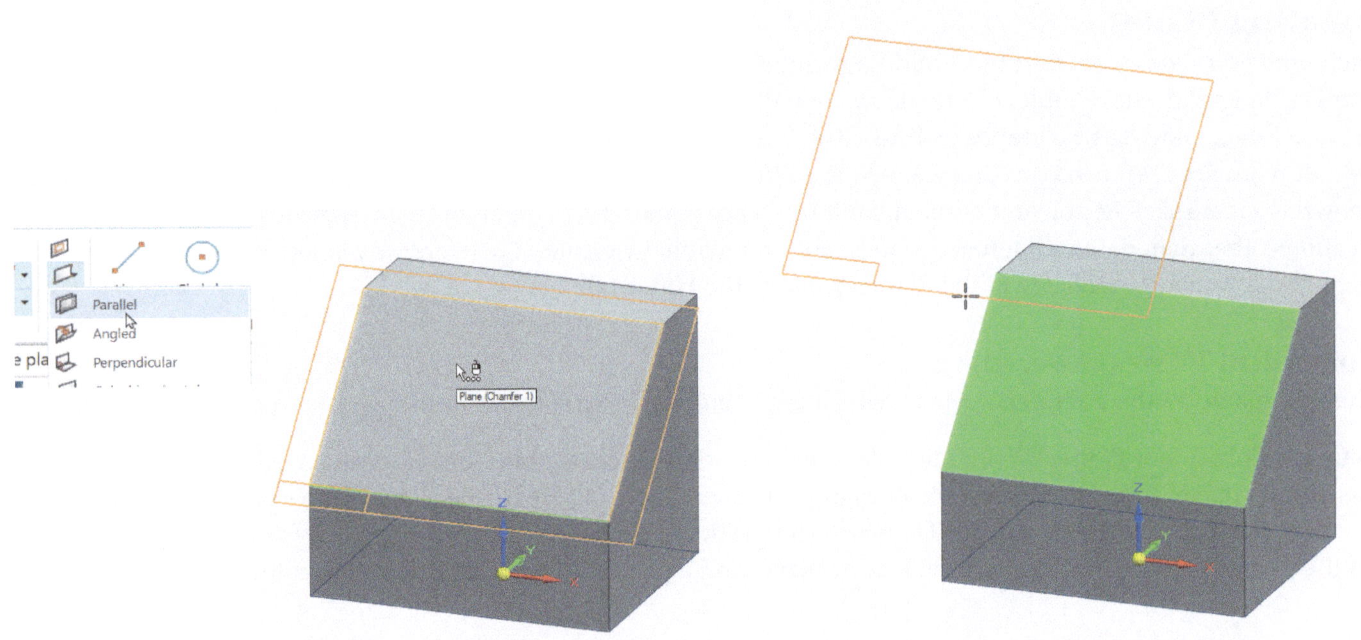

Angled (Ordered)

This command creates a plane, which will be positioned at an angle to a face or plane. Click **Home > Planes > More Planes > Angled** on the ribbon and select a flat face or plane. Next, click on the edge of the part geometry to define the rotation axis. You can also select a plane that crosses the plane you picked in the last step. The point where these two planes meet is the rotation axis. Next, click on one of the endpoints located along the rotation axis to establish the origin for the new reference plane. Type-in a value in the **Angle** box and press Enter on the Keyboard. Position the cursor on the side you want to rotate towards, and then click to create the angled plane.

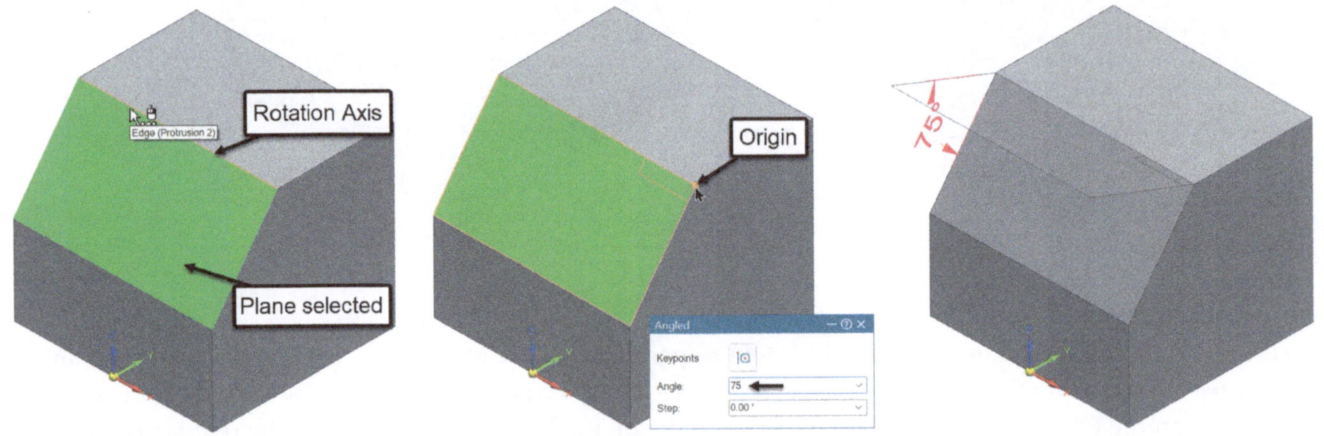

Perpendicular (Ordered)

This command creates a plane, which will be positioned at an angle to a face or plane. Click **Home > Planes > More Planes > Perpendicular** on the ribbon and select a flat face or plane. Next, click on the edge of the part geometry to define the rotation axis. You can also select a plane that crosses the plane you picked in the last step. The point where these two planes meet is the rotation axis. Next, click on one of the endpoints located along the rotation axis to establish the origin for the new reference plane. Position the cursor on the side you want to rotate towards, and then click to create the perpendicular plane.

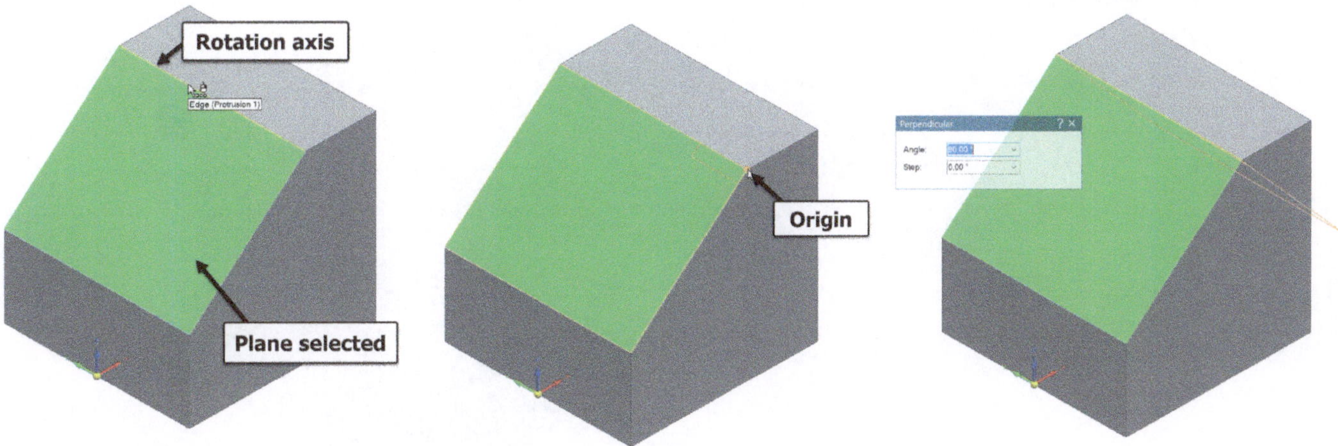

Normal to Curve

This command creates a reference plane, which will be normal (perpendicular) to a line, curve, or edge. Activate this command (click **Home > Planes > More Planes > Normal to Curve** on the ribbon), and then select an edge, line, curve, arc, or circle. Drag the pointer and click on a point to define the plane's location (or) type-in a value in the **Position** box (or) type-in a distance value in the **Distance** box and press Enter.

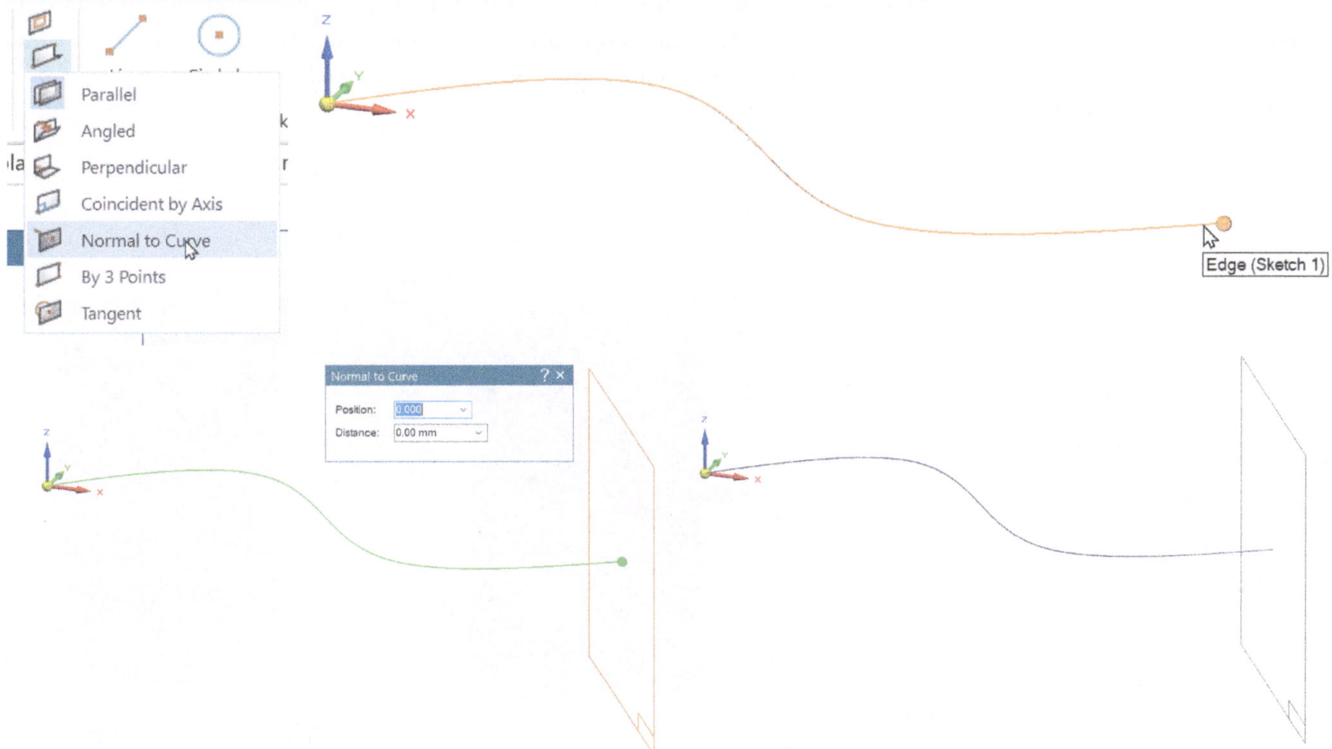

By 3 Points

This command creates a reference plane passing through three points. Activate this command (click **Home > Planes > More Planes > By 3 Points** on the ribbon), and then select three points from the model geometry. A plane will be placed passing through these points.

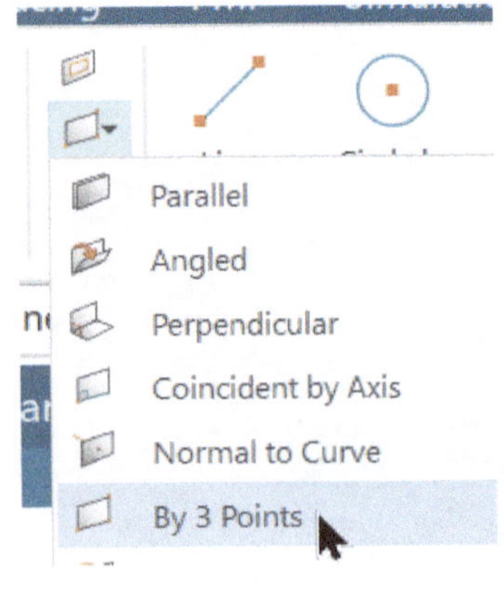

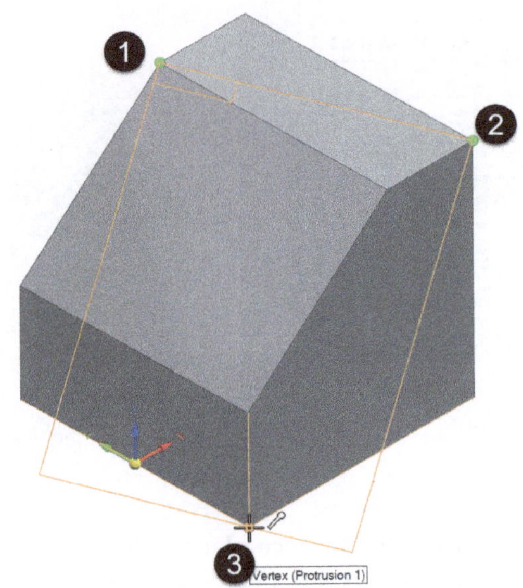

Tangent

This command creates a plane tangent to a curved face. Activate this command (click **Home > Planes > More Planes > Tangent** on the ribbon) and select a curved face. A plane tangent to the selected face appears. Drag the pointer and click to define the tangent plane's position (or) type-in an angle value and press Enter.

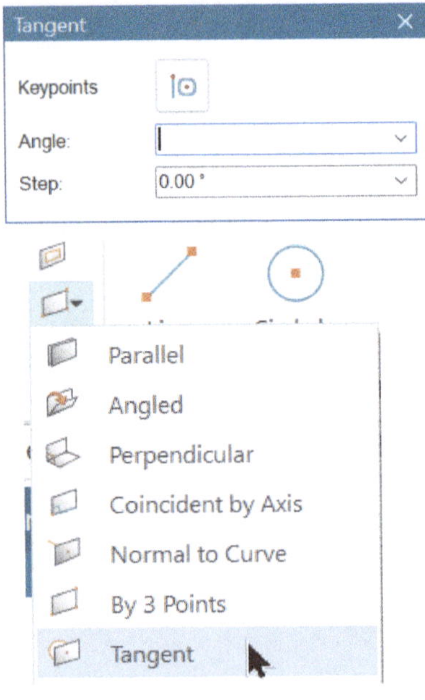

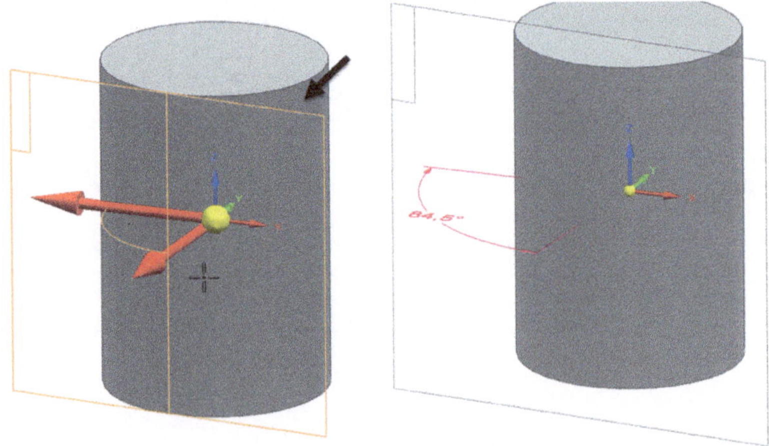

Coincident by Axis

This command creates a plane, which is coincident with a selected face or plane. Activate this command (click **Home > Planes > More Planes > Coincident by Axis** on the ribbon) and select a flat face or plane. Next, select a part edge to define the plane's x-axis and then select a point to define the x-axis origin.

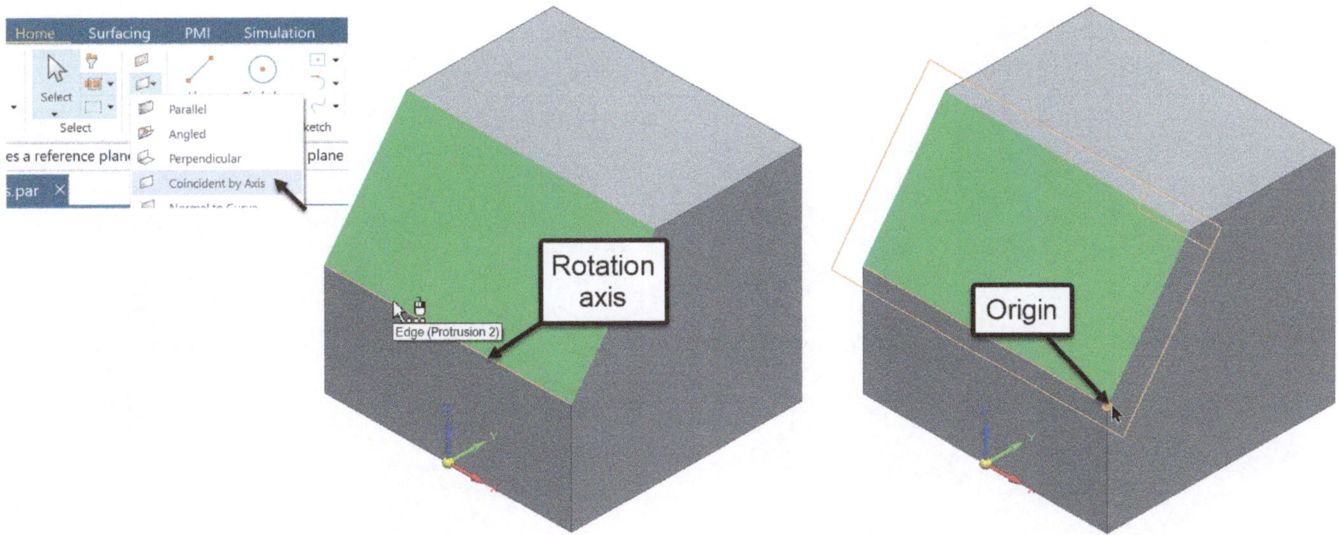

Mid

This command creates a new reference plane positioned exactly halfway between two selected planar faces or existing planes. Activate this command (click **Home > Planes > More Planes > Mid** on the ribbon) and click on the two faces or planes between which you want to create the new plane. Solid Edge automatically calculates the midpoint distance and generates a new plane equidistant from both selections.

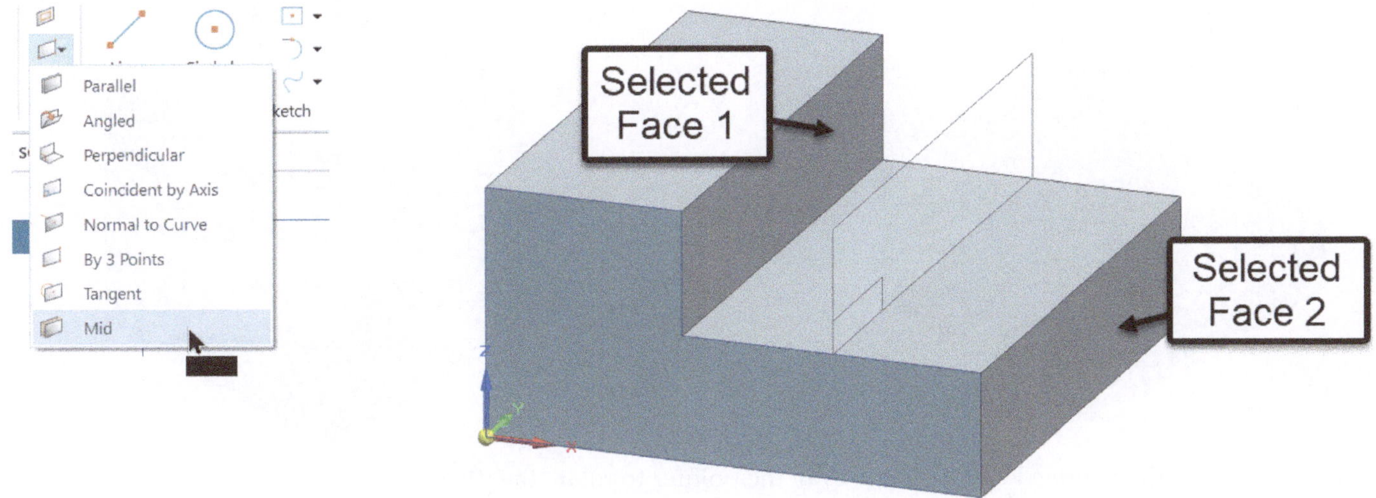

Coincident Plane (Synchronous)

Activate **Coincident Plane** command (click **Home > Planes > Coincident Plane** on the ribbon) and click on a face or plane. A plane coincident with the selected face will be placed. Also, the *Steering Wheel* tool appears on the plane.

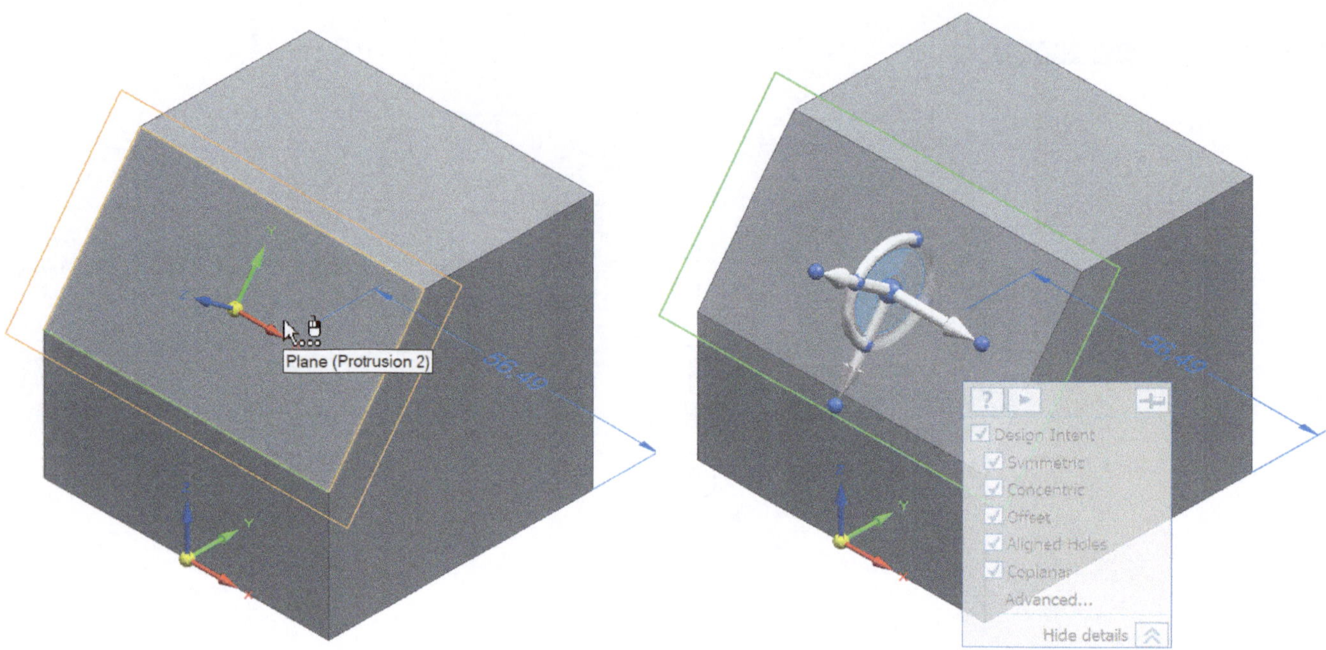

Click on any Steering Wheel tool's arrows and drag the pointer to change the plane's location.

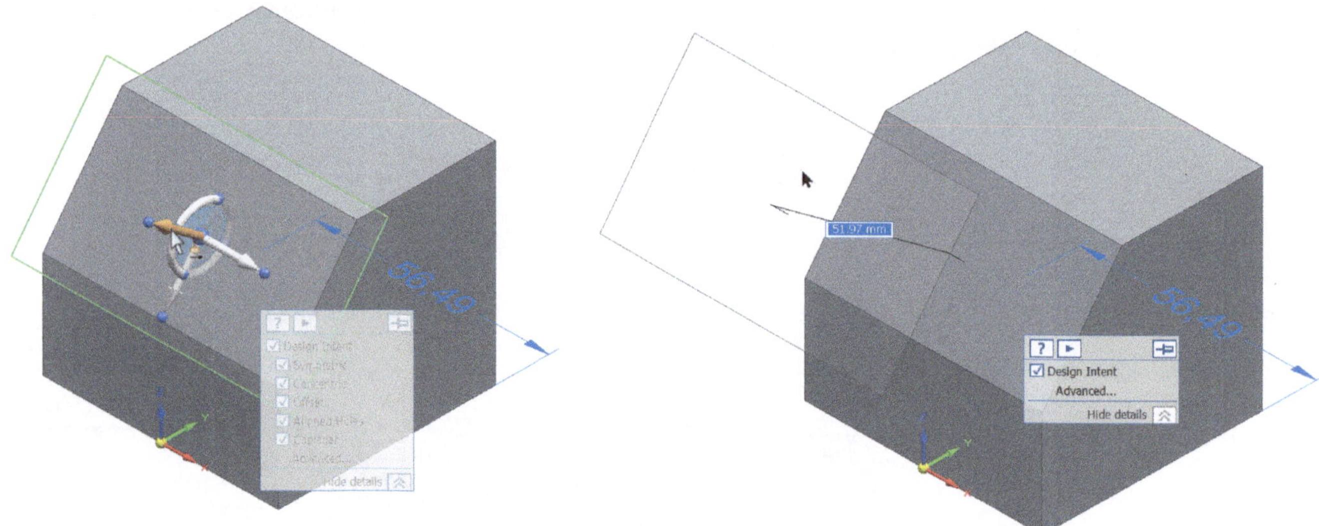

Click the torus of the *Steering Wheel* tool and drag the pointer to rotate the plane.

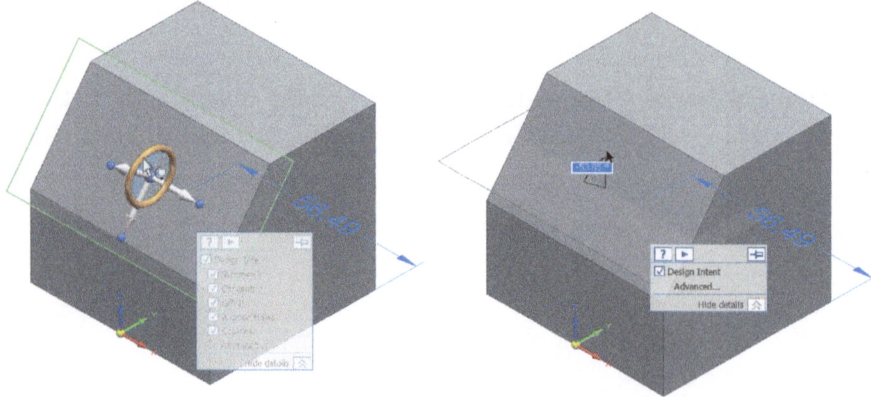

Coordinate System (Ordered)

This command creates a new coordinate system in addition to the default one. Click **Home > Planes > Coordinate System** on the ribbon; the **Coordinate System Options** dialog pops up on the screen. On this dialog, select the **Key-in (relative to another coordinate system)** option to set the direction of the new coordinate system in relation to an existing one. Select the **Geometry** option to set the orientation of a new coordinate system in relation to the geometry of the model. When you create a coordinate system tied to the model, it stays linked to the model's geometry. This means that if the model's geometry undergoes any orientation changes, the coordinate system will automatically adjust accordingly. Click **OK** on the **Coordinate System Options** dialog.

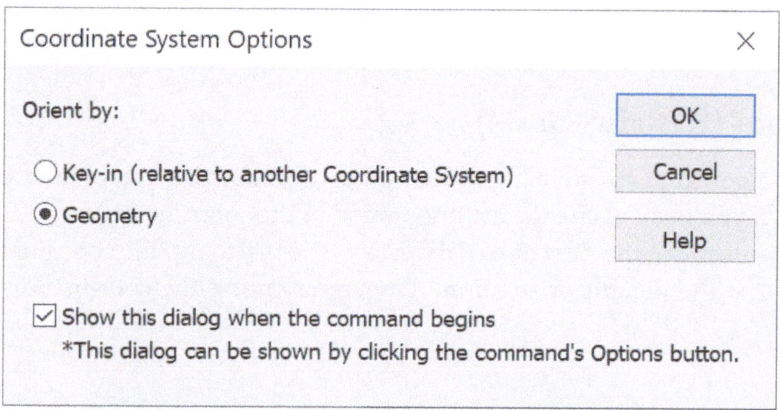

After selecting the required option from the **Coordinate System Options** dialog, you need to define the origin of the new coordinate system. You have two options for this based on the selection made from the **Coordinate System Options** dialog. If you have selected the **Geometry** option, you need to select a keypoint from the model geometry. If you have selected the **Key-in** option, you need input coordinates as offsets from the existing coordinate system using the X, Y, and Z boxes.

Next, select an edge or line to determine the vector for the first axis of the new coordinate system. Click the green check on the **First Axis Step** section. Next, move the pointer and click to define the direction of the first axis.

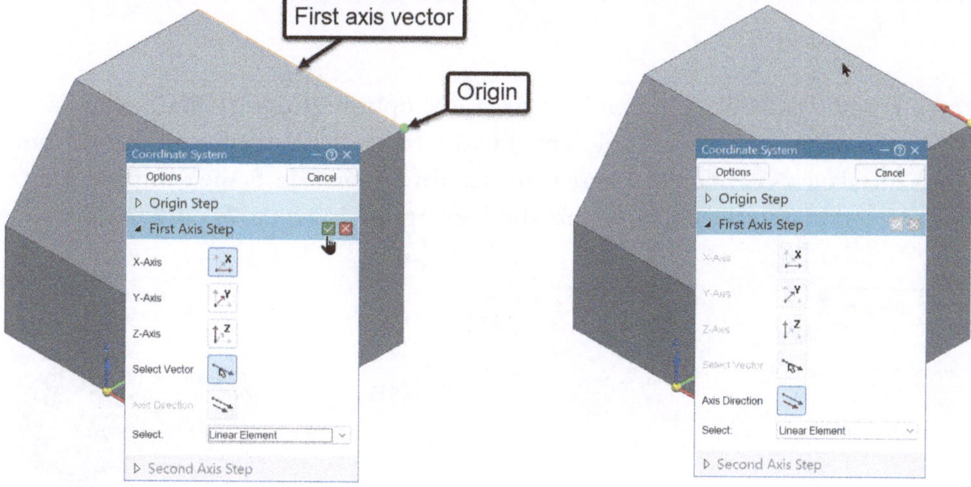

Likewise, specify the vector and axis direction for the second axis of the new coordinate system. Click **Finish** to complete the new coordinate system creation.

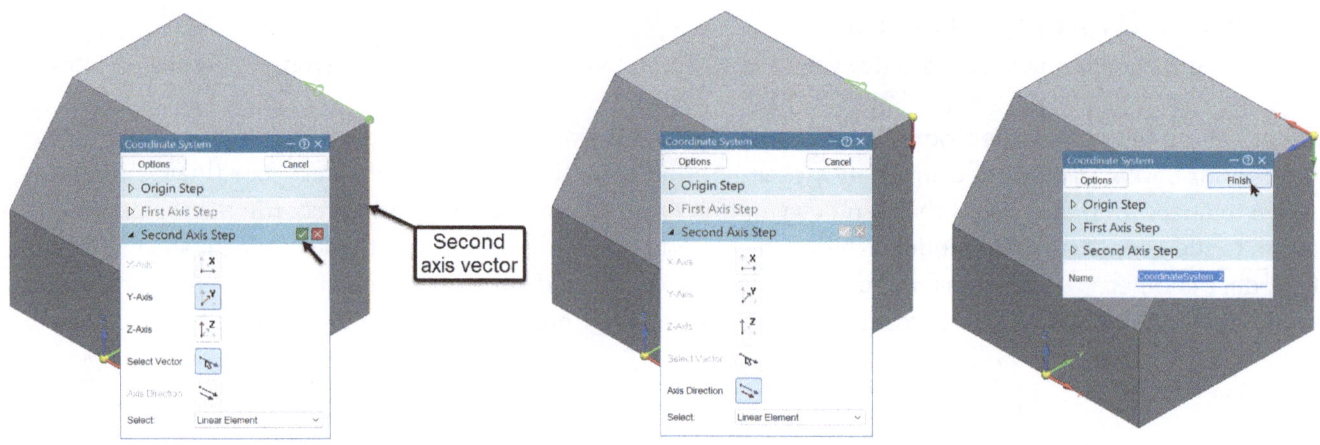

Coordinate System (Synchronous)

Click **Home > Planes > Coordinate System** on the ribbon and position the pointer on a point or face, or line. Use the orientation keys if you want to change the orientation of the coordinate system. For example, press F to flip the coordinate system by reversing the direction of the z-axis. Press T to flip the coordinate system by reversing the x-axis. Press G to return to the default orientation. After re-orienting the coordinate system, click to define its location.

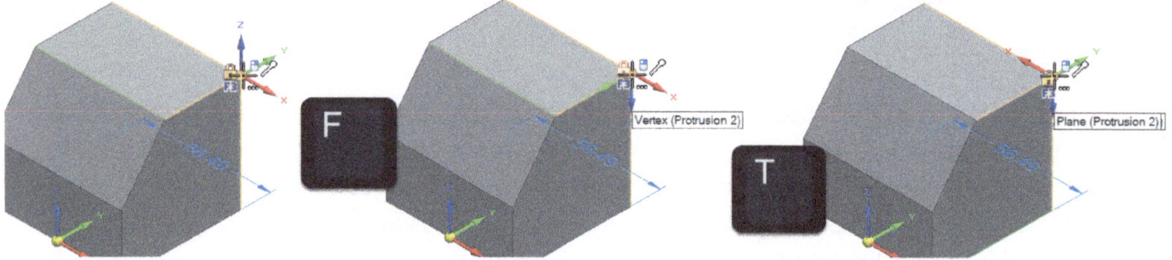

Additional options of the Extrude command

The **Extrude** command has some additional options to create 3D geometry and complex features. Some of these options are inactive by default and are activated after you have created the first feature of the part.

Selection Type options

The **Selection Type** drop-down menu on the **Extrude** command bar has three options: **Single**, **Chain**, and **Face**. Note that the **Selection Type** drop-down menu is available only when you activate the **Extrude** command from the ribbon. The **Single** option selects the sketch's elements, whereas the **Chain** option selects the complete loop. The **Face** option selects the region enclosed by the sketch. Note that the **Face** option is available only in the **Synchronous** Mode.

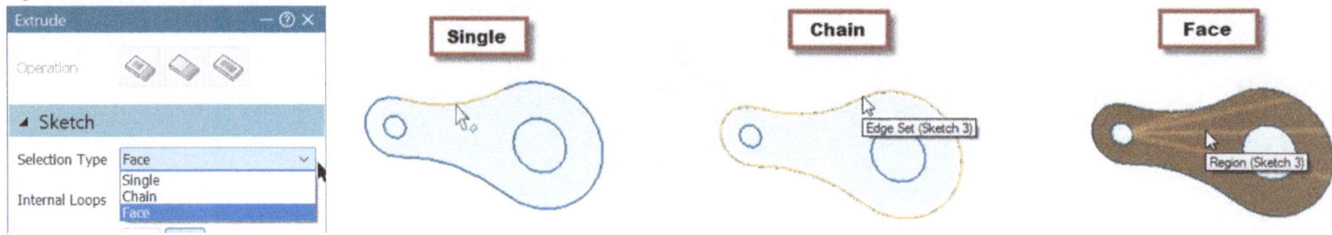

Include Internal Loops

This option is useful while working with a sketch having internal loops. If you select this option, the sketch's internal loops will be detected while creating the *Extrude* feature.

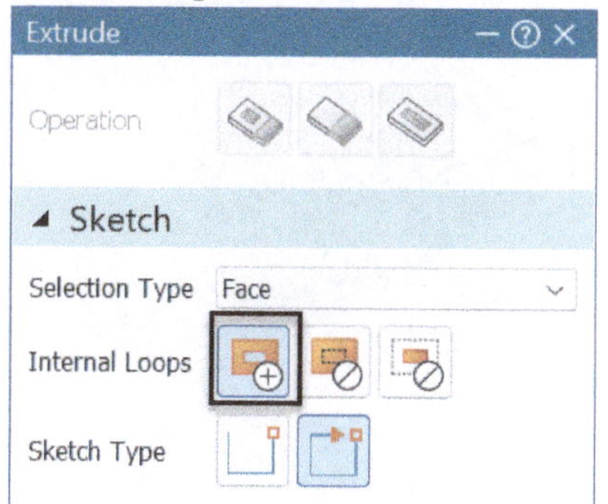

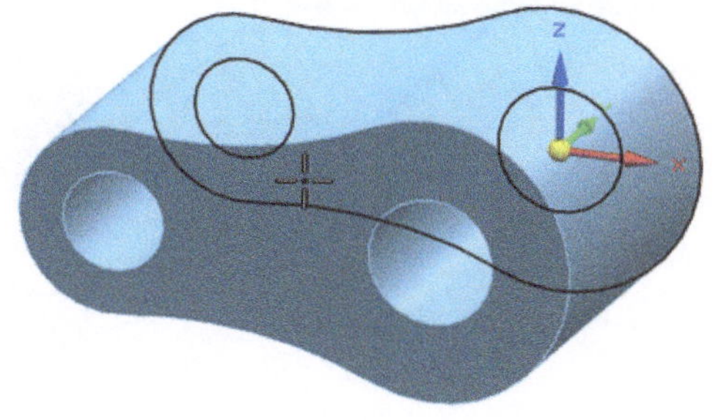

Exclude Internal Loops

This option ignores the internal loops of a sketch.

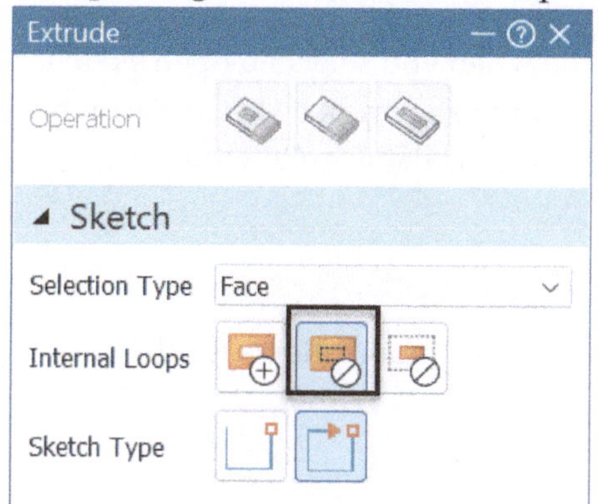

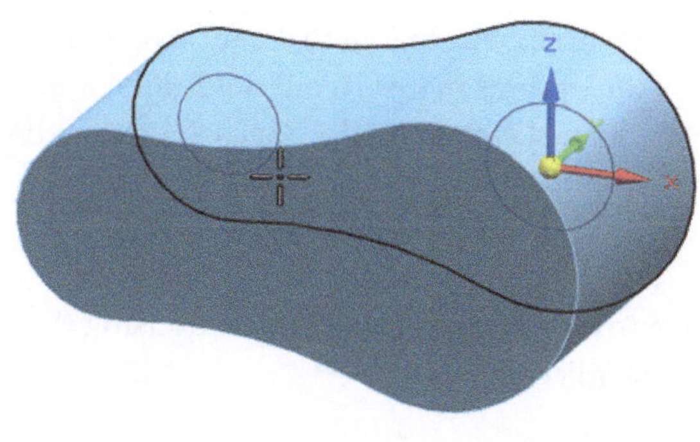

Use Only Internal Loops

This option considers only the internal loops of the sketch.

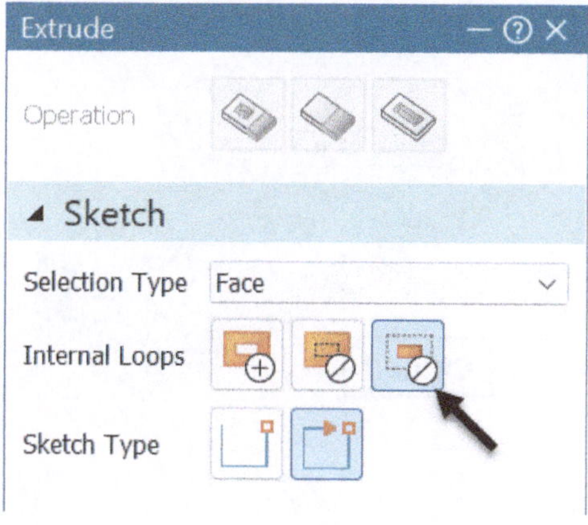

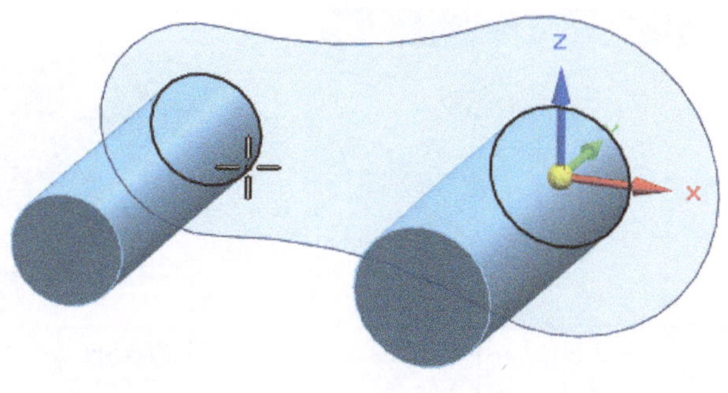

Add

The **Add** option adds material to the geometry.

Cut

This **Cut** option removes material from the part geometry.

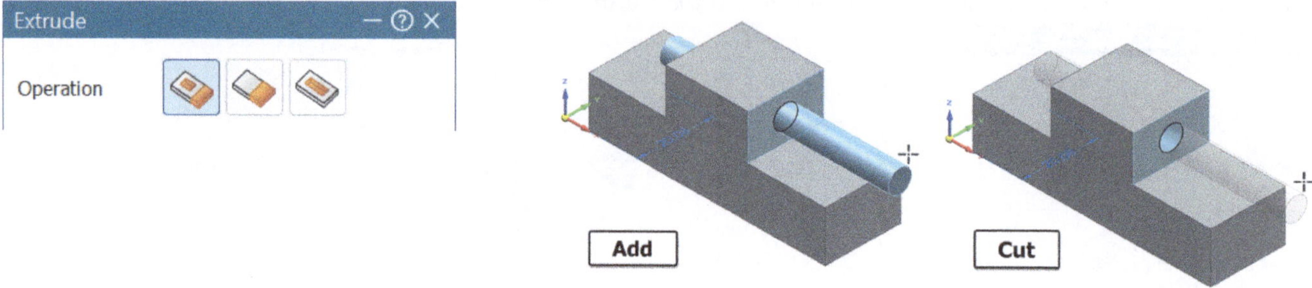

Automatic

This **Automatic** option adds or removes material based on the extrusion direction.

Sketch Type

The Sketch Type options help you to create an extrusion using an open sketch. When you select an open sketch for extrusion, the options in this flyout determine if nearby model edges are treated as part of a sketch area when connecting an open sketch to model edges. Note that the **Sketch Type** options are available only in the Synchronous environment.

Open

This option extrudes an open sketch without using the adjacent edges. Enabling this option allows for the modification of adjacent faces.

Closed

Converts an open sketch into a closed one by using the adjacent edges and then extrudes the sketch. When you enable this option, it only impacts faces that are entirely within the protrusion.

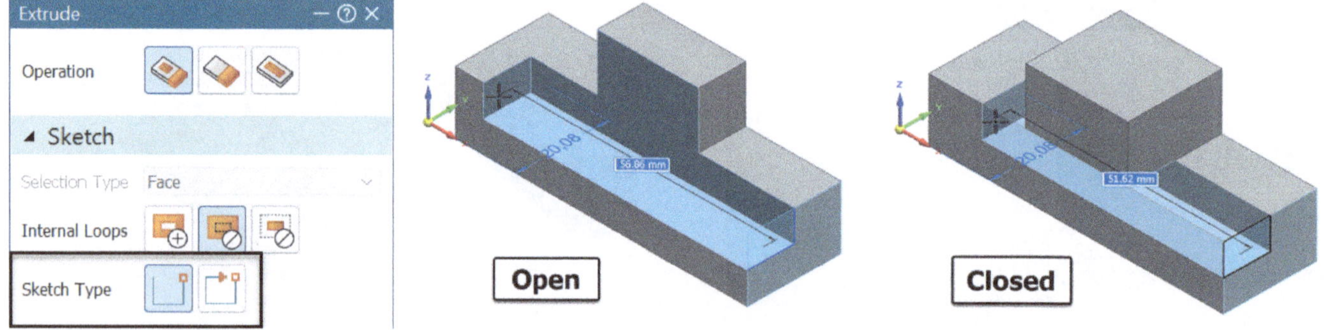

Side

This option defines the side of the sketch to extrude. On the command bar, set the **Selection Type** to **Chain** and select an open sketch. Right click to accept the sketch. Use the arrow that appears on the selected sketch to define the sketch's side to be extruded. Move the pointer to extrude the sketch. You can click the **Side** button to change the side to be extruded.

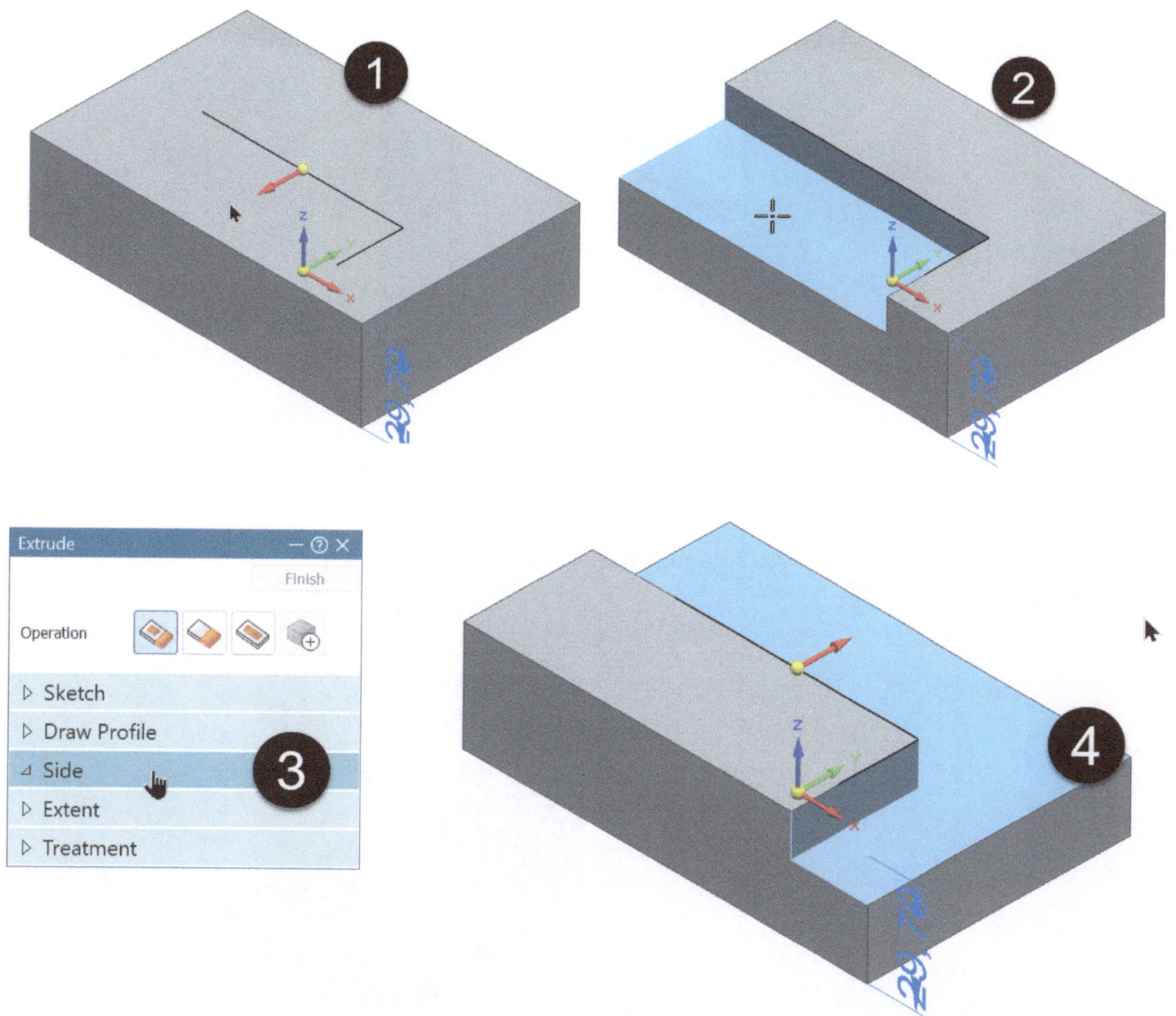

Extent Type options

The **Extent** section on the command bar has four options: **Finite**, **Through All**, **Through Next**, and **From-To**. The **Finite** option extrudes the sketch up to the distance that you specify. The **Through All** option extrudes the sketch throughout the 3D geometry.

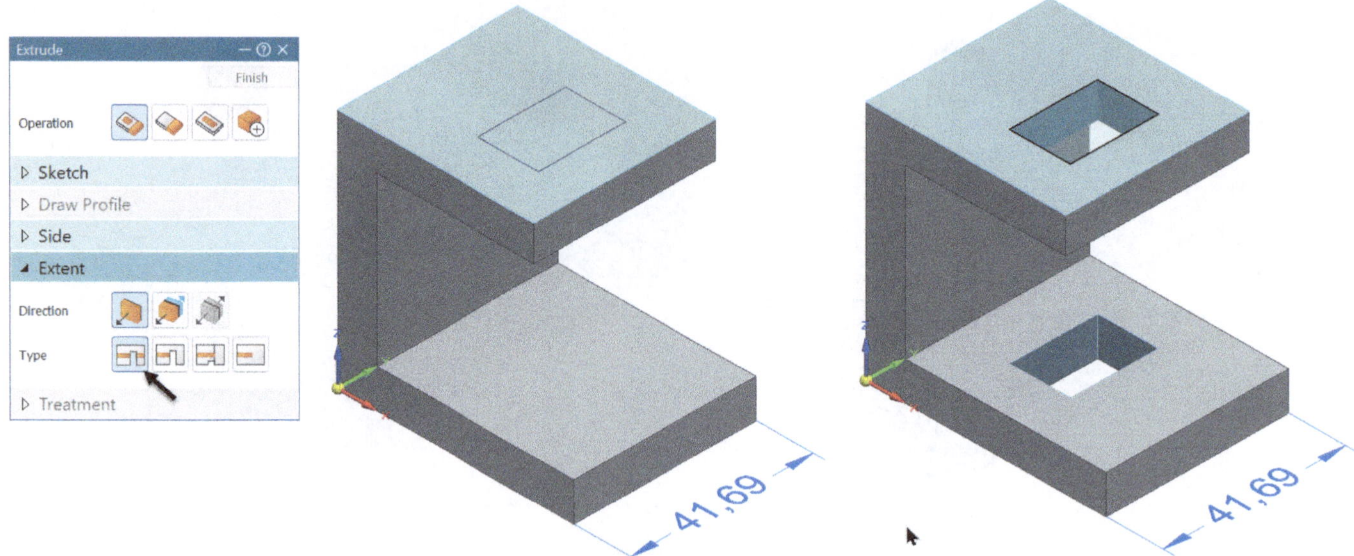

The **Through Next** option extrudes the sketch through the face next to the sketch plane.

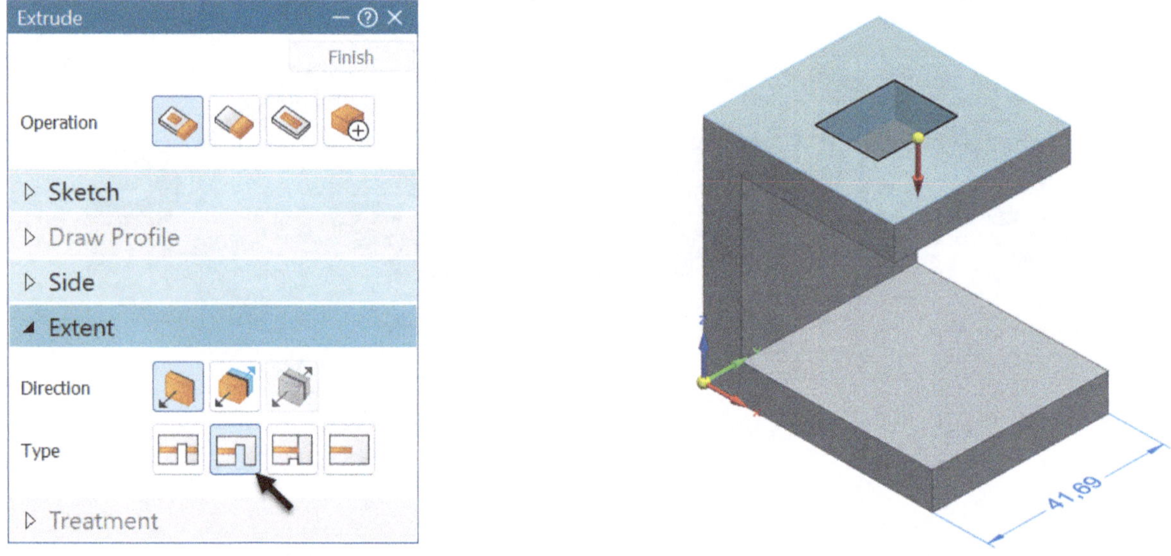

The **From-To Extent** option extrudes the sketch from the sketch plane up to a selected face. Click inside the sketch region, and then click on the arrow handle. On the **Extrude** command bar, select **From-To extent** from the **Extent Step** section. The 'From' surface is selected automatically, and you need to select the 'To' surface. Select the 'To' Surface from the model geometry; the sketch will be extruded up to the selected surface. Additionally, you can apply offsets to these boundaries. To do this enter a value in the **Offset (From)** box to start the extrusion at a specific distance from the selected start face, and enter a value in the **Offset (To)** box to stop the extrusion at a specific distance from the selected end face.

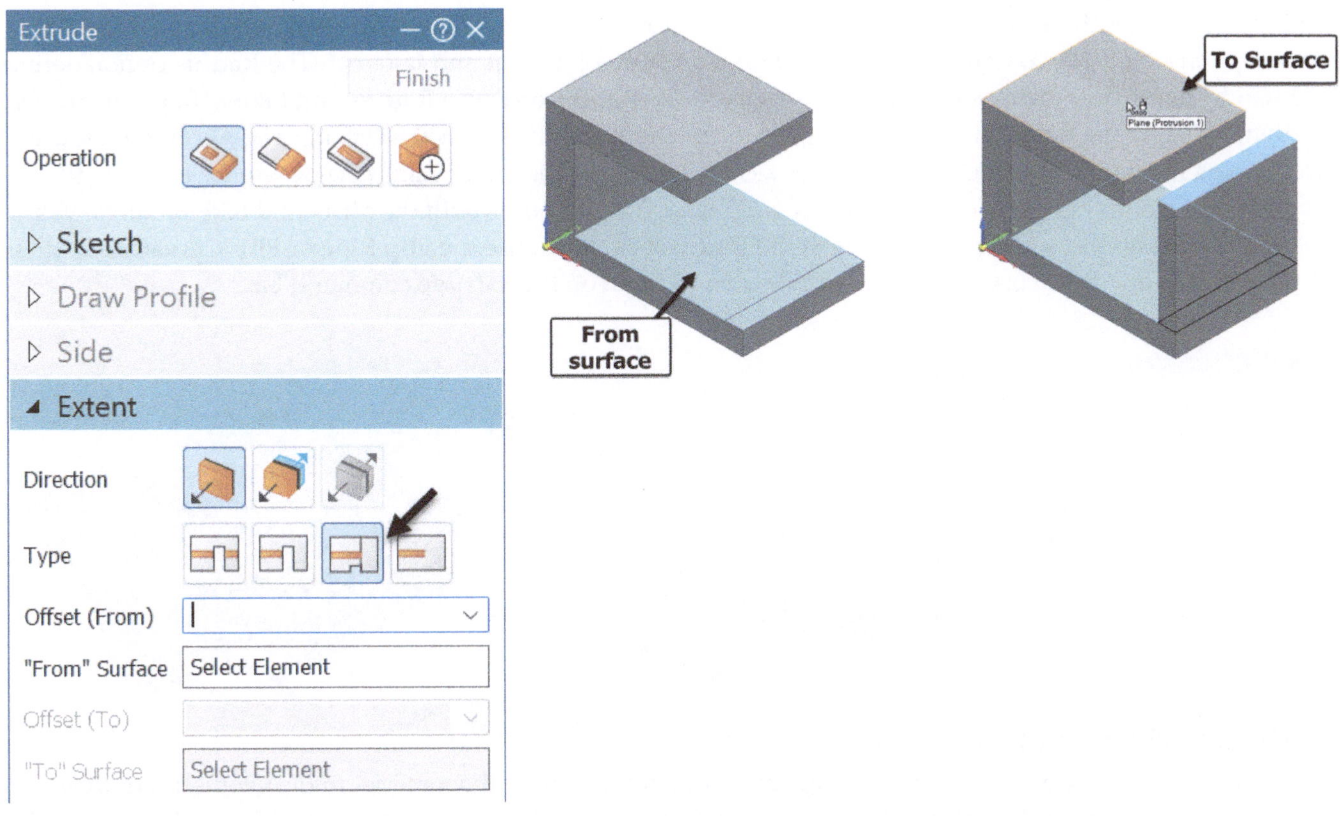

Treatments

The **Treatments** section on the command bar has three options: **No Treatment**, **Draft**, and **Crown**. The **No Treatment** option creates the *Extrude* feature without any treatment. The **Draft** option applies a draft to the *Extrude* feature. Activate this option and type-in a value in the **Angle 1** box. Click the **Flip Side** button below the **Angle** box to flip the draft angle. If you select the **Symmetric Extent** or **Non-Symmetric Extent** option from the **Extent** section, you can define the draft in the second direction.

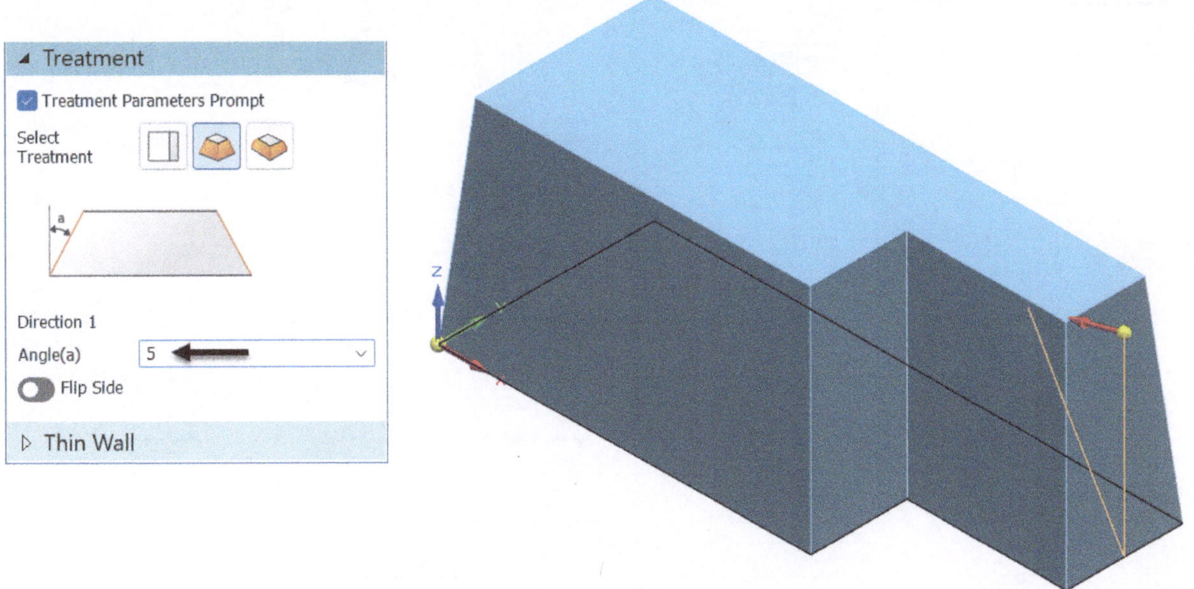

The **Crown** option in the **Treatment Step** section adds a crown to the *Extrude* feature. Next, the **Type** drop-down has five options: **No Crown, Radius, Radius and take-off, Offset, Offset and take-off**. The **Radius** option defines the crown by using the crown radius that you specify in the **Radius** box. The **Radius and take-off** option creates the crown by using the radius and take-off angle values. The take-off value is the starting angle crown measured from the sketch plane. The **Offset** option creates a crown by using the offset value (the difference between the start and end sections of the crown). The **Offset and take-off** option uses both the offset and take-off angle values. Select the **Radius** option and type-in a value in the **Radius** box. Next, use the **Flip Side** or **Flip Curvature** buttons to flip the crown or crown curvature. Click **Preview** and **Finish** on the **Extrude** command bar.

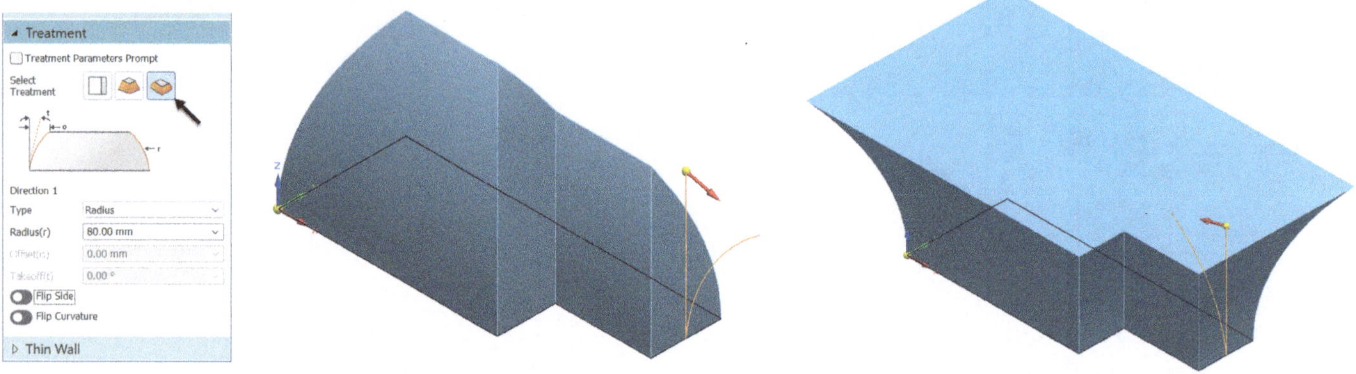

Applying Material to the Model

Solid Edge allows you to apply a material to the model easily. To apply the material to the geometry, double-click the **Material** option under the **PathFinder** tree. On the **Material Table** dialog, expand the **Material** tree and select a material. The material **Properties** of the selected material appear on the right-side. Click the **Apply to Model** button. The selected material will be applied to the model. If you want to remove the material, right-click on the **Material** option under **PathFinder** and select **Remove Material**.

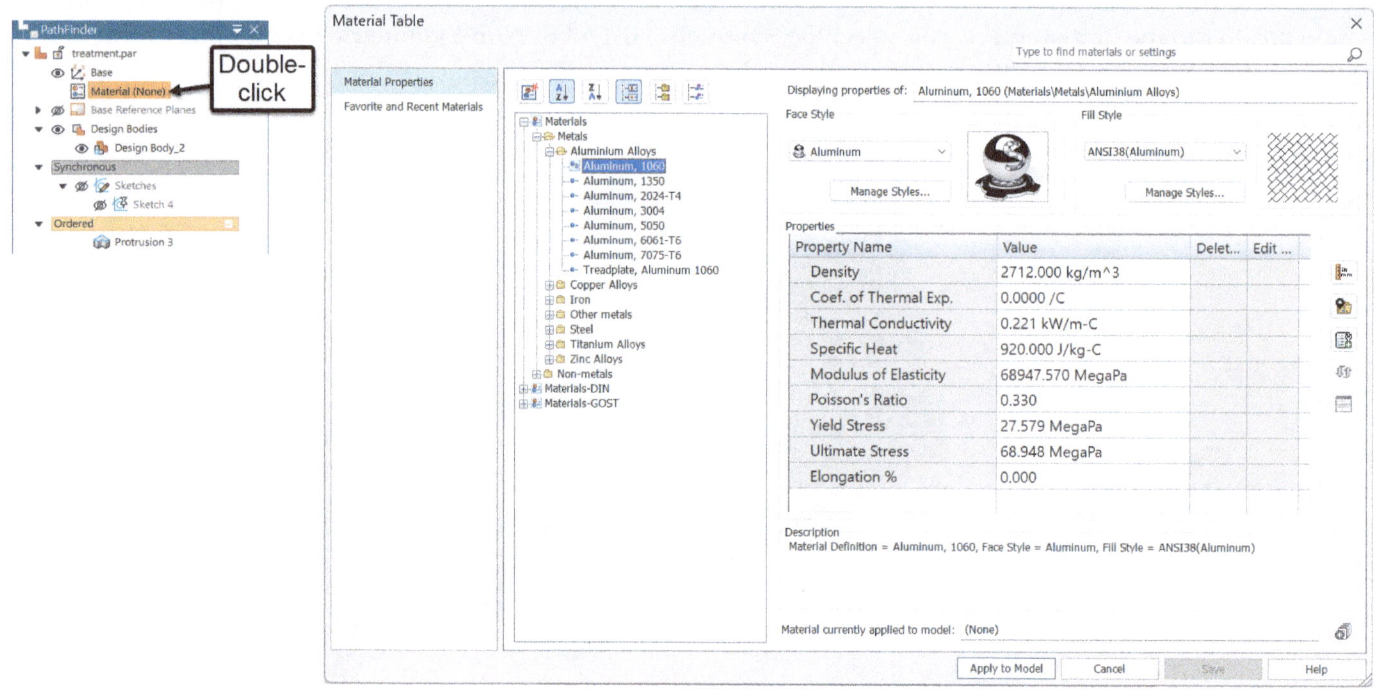

Examples

Example 1 (Millimetres)

In this example, you will create the part shown below.

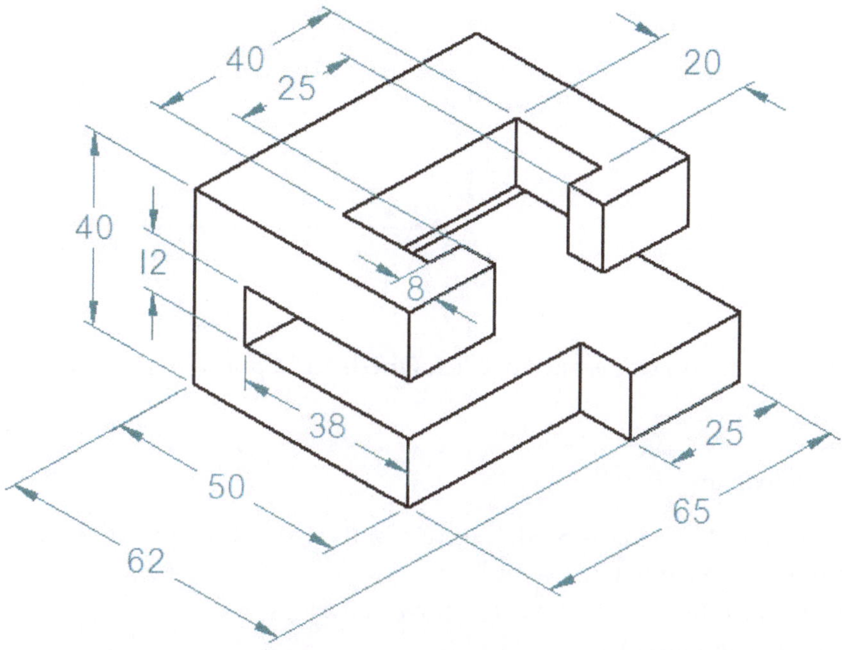

1. Start **Solid Edge 2026**.
2. On the **Start** page, under the **Create New** section, click **New** button.
3. On the **New** dialog, **iso metric.par** template and click **OK**; a new part file is opened.
4. Click **Continue with Ordered** button on the **Ordered as default** dialog; the Ordered environment is set as the default environment.
5. To start a new sketch, click **Home > Sketch > Sketch** on the ribbon.
6. Select the Front (xz) plane from the base reference planes displayed in the graphics window; the sketch is started and the sketch plane is oriented normal to the screen.
7. On the ribbon, click **Home > Draw > Rectangle by Center > Rectangle by 2 Points** .
8. Click the origin point to define the first corner of the rectangle.
9. Move the mouse pointer toward the top right corner and click to define the second corner.
10. Use the **Smart Dimension** command and apply dimensions to the rectangle.

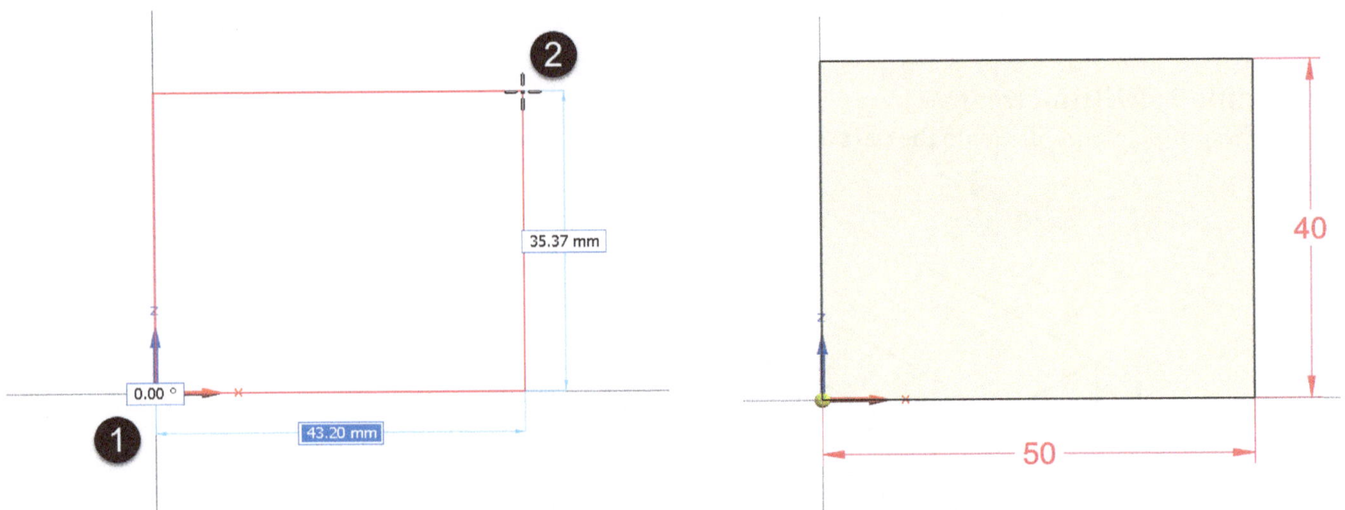

11. Click the **Close Sketch** button on the ribbon to exit the sketch. Click **Finish** and **Cancel** on the **Sketch** command bar.

12. On the ribbon, click **Home > Solids > Extrude** .

13. Select the rectangle and click the green check on the **Sketch** section of the **Extrude** command bar.
14. On the **Extent** section, click the **Direction** > **Symmetric Extent** icon.
15. Type-in **65** in the **Distance** box on the **Extrude** command bar and press Enter.
16. Click **Finish** and **Cancel** on the **Extrude** command bar.

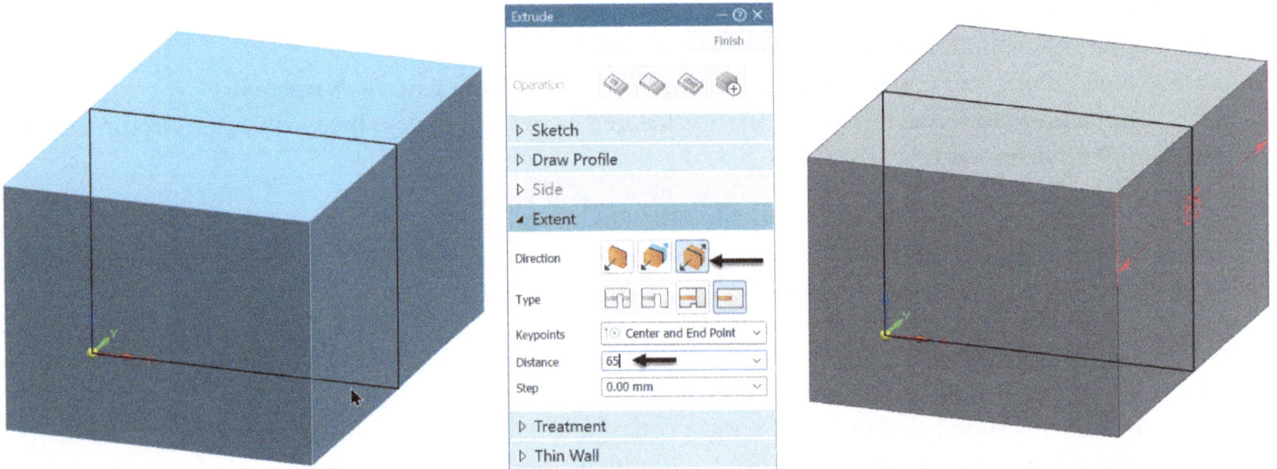

17. On the ribbon, click **Home > Solids > Extrude** . Next, select **Coincident Plane** option from the **Create From Options** drop-down available under the **Sketch Step** section of the **Extrude** command bar.
18. Click on the front face of the part geometry.

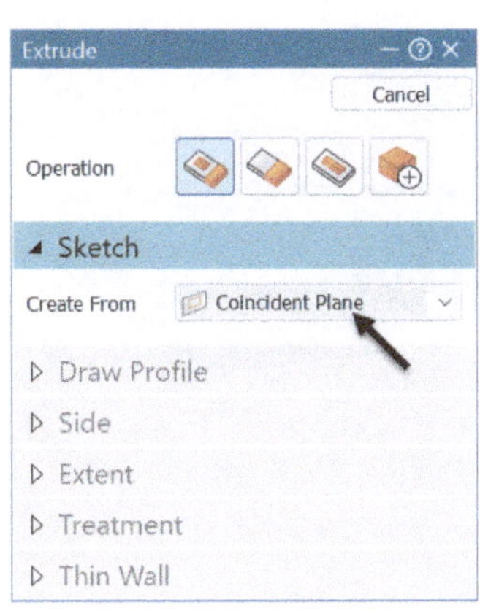

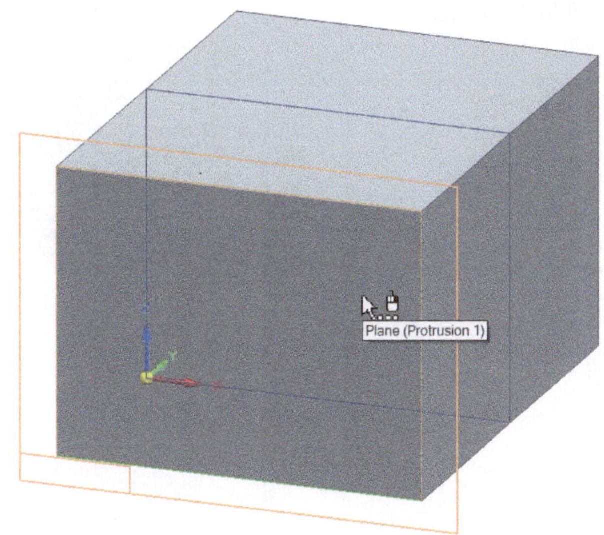

19. On the ribbon, click **Home > Draw > Rectangle by Center > Rectangle by 2 Points** .
20. Click on the right vertical edge of the model to define the first corner of the rectangle.
21. Move the pointer toward left and click to specify the second corner of the rectangle.
22. Activate the **Smart Dimension** command and select the right vertical edge of the rectangle.
23. Move the pointer toward right and click. Type 12 in the dimension box and press ENTER.
24. Select the horizontal edge of the rectangle, move the pointer downward, and click.
25. Type 38 and press ENTER.
26. Select the top horizontal edge of the rectangle and the top edge of the model. Move the pointer toward right and click to place the dimension. Type 14 and press ENTER.
27. Click the **Close Sketch** button on the ribbon.

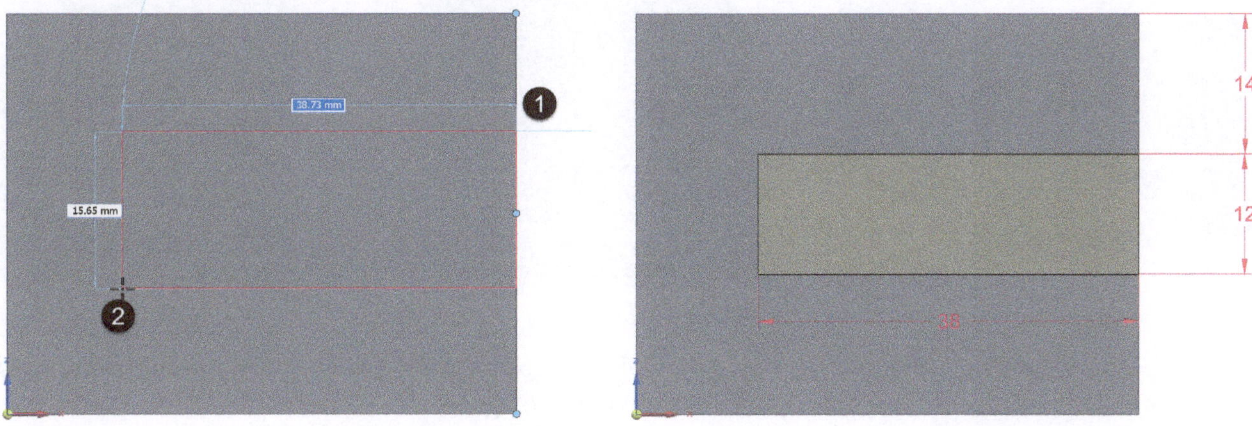

28. On the command bar, click the **Ones-sided Extent** button and the **Through All** button under the **Extent** section.
29. Move the mouse pointer toward the part geometry and click. Click **Finish** on the **Extrude** command bar to create the extruded cut.

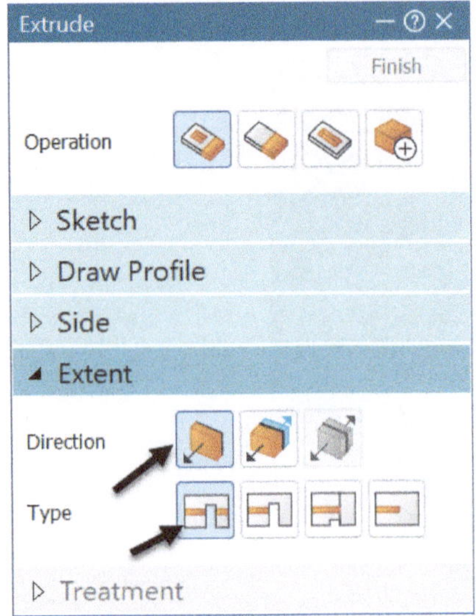

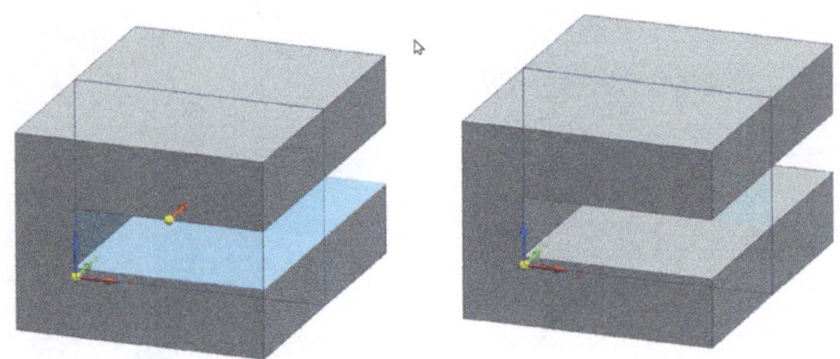

30. With the **Extrude** command still active, click on the top face of the part geometry.
31. Click **Home > Draw > Line** on the ribbon. On the **Extrude** command bar, select **Symmetric (s)** from the **Type** drop-down.
32. Place the pointer on the right vertical edge of the top face and select its midpoint.
33. Move the pointer vertically upward and click on the vertical edge to create a line.
34. Move the pointer horizontally toward left and click.
35. Likewise, create other entities of the sketch, as shown.

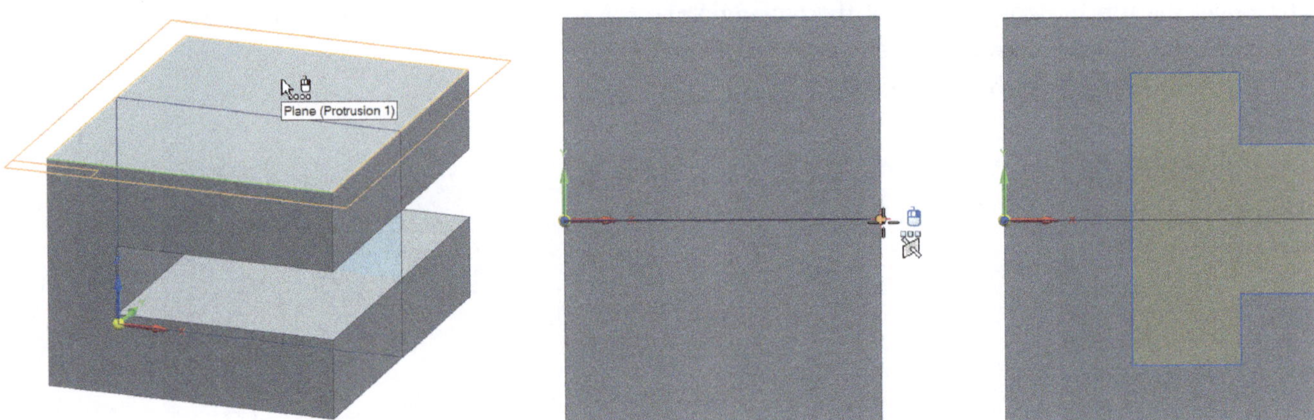

36. Click **Home > Relate > Symmetric** on the ribbon. Click on the X-axis to define the symmetric axis.
37. Click on the horizontal lines in the sequence shown in the figure.
38. Use the **Smart Dimension** command to apply the dimension to the sketch.

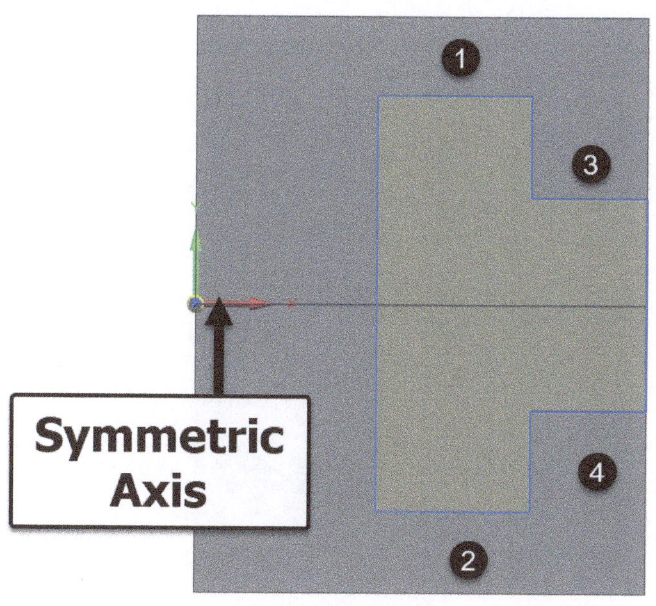

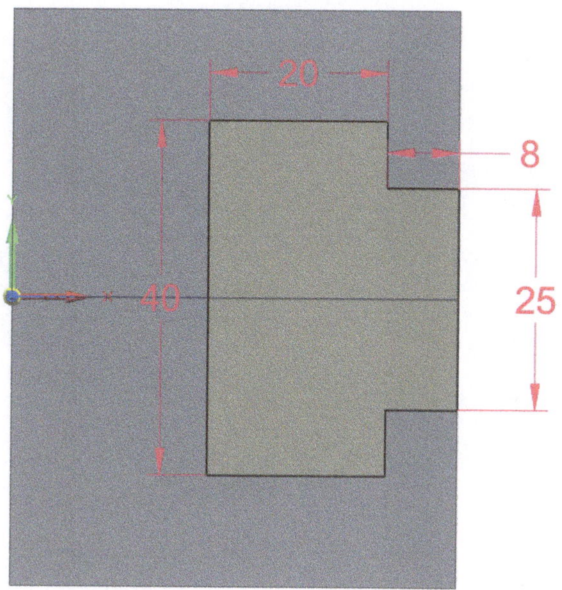

39. Click the **Close Sketch** button on the ribbon.
40. On the command bar, click the **Ones-sided Extent** button and the **Through Next** button under the **Extent** section.
41. Move the mouse pointer downward and click.
42. Click **Finish** to create the extruded cut.

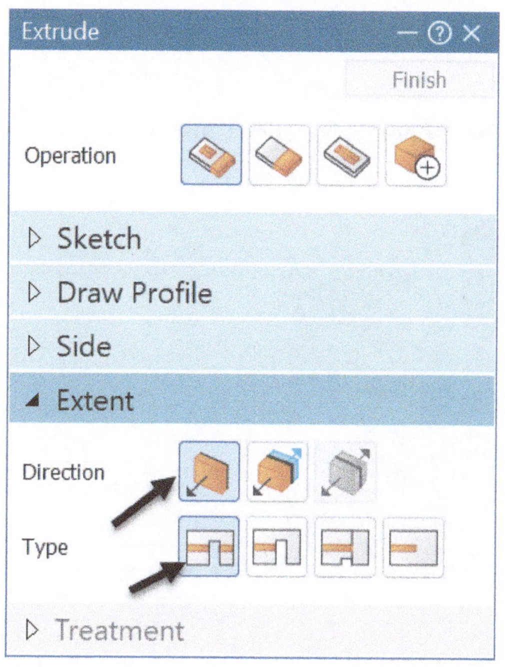

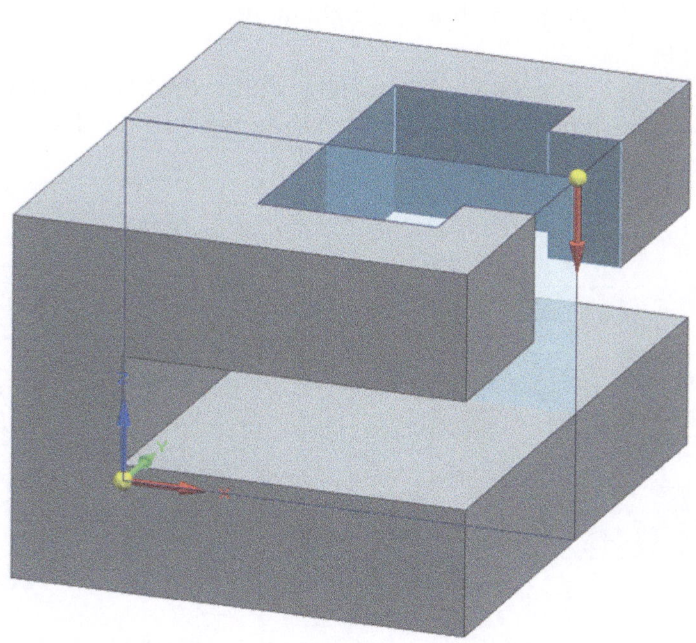

43. Click on the horizontal face, as shown in the figure.
44. Activate the **Rectangle by 2 Points** command and draw the sketch. Apply dimensions to the sketch. Next, click the **Close Sketch** button on the ribbon.

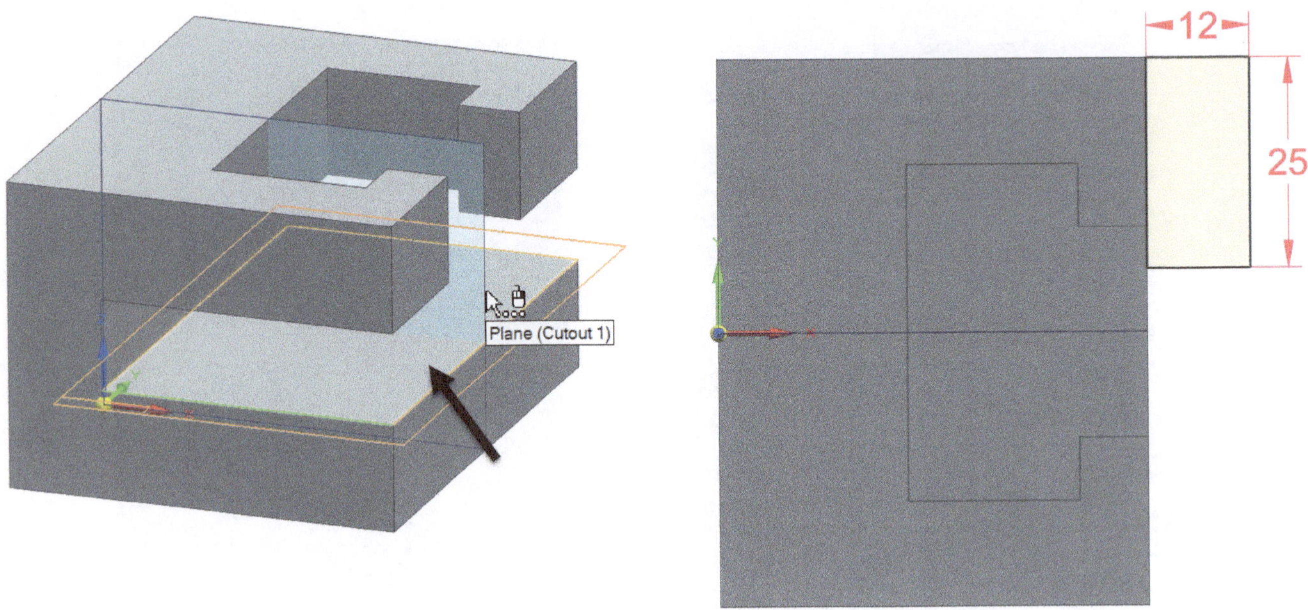

45. On the command bar, click **Operation** > **Add** .
46. On the command bar, click the **From/To Extent** button under the **Extent** section.
47. Select the flat horizontal face of the extruded cut feature to define the "**From**" surface.
48. Press and hold the middle and right mouse buttons, and then drag the pointer such that the bottom face is visible.
49. Select the bottom face of the model to define the "**To**" surface.
50. Click **Finish** on the command bar to add the extruded feature to the model. Next, click **Cancel** to close the Extrude command bar.

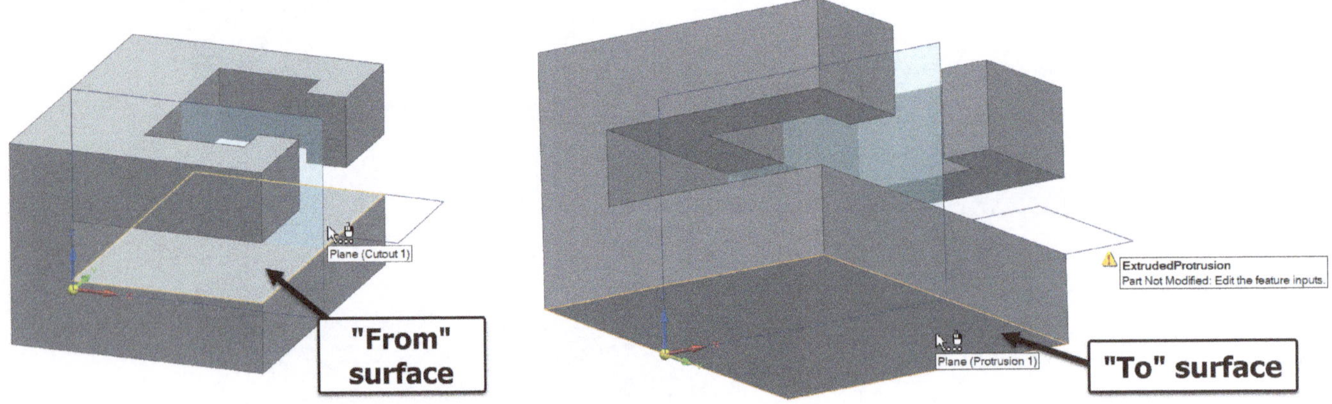

51. On the bottom-right corner of the window, click **View Orientation > Trimetric View**; the view orientation is changed to trimetric.

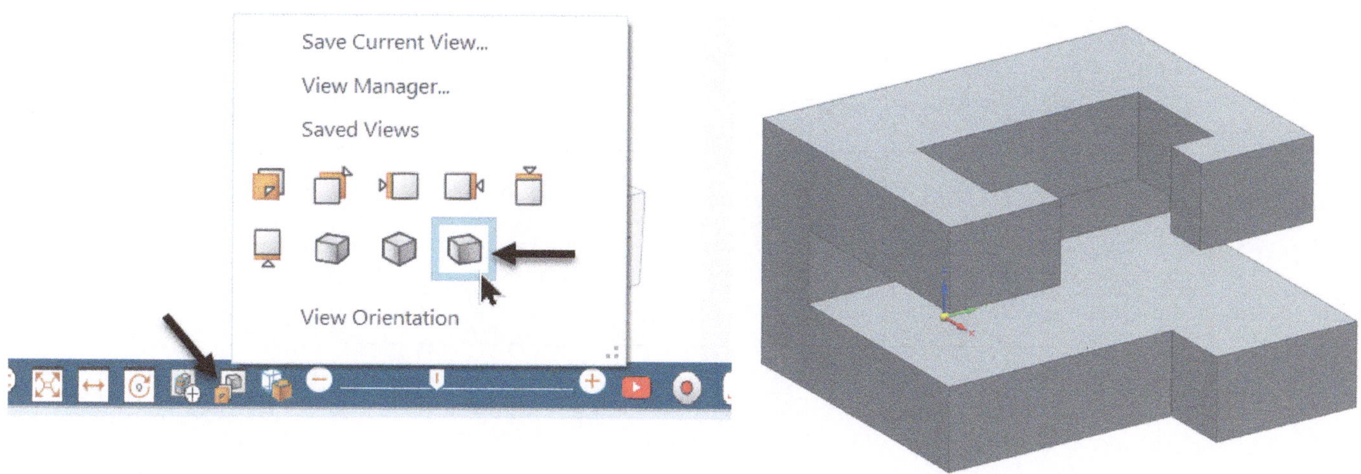

52. Save and close the file.

Example 2 (Inches)

In this example, you will create the part shown below.

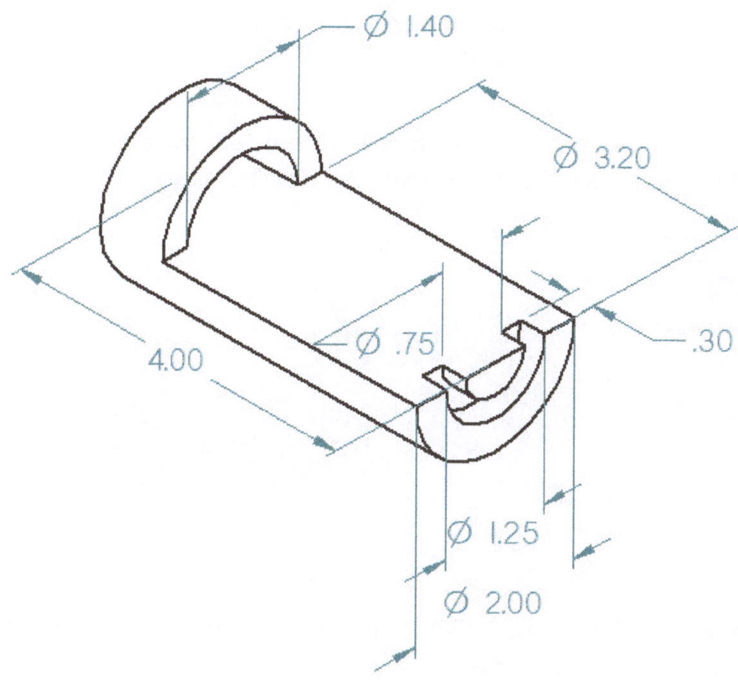

1. Start **Solid Edge 2026.**
2. On the **Quick Access Toolbar**, click **New**; the **New** dialog appears.
3. On the **New** dialog, click **Standard Templates > ANSI Inch** and select the **ansi inch part.par** template. Click **OK** to start a new part file.
4. Click **Continue with Ordered** button on the **Ordered as default** dialog; the Ordered environment is set as the default environment.
5. To start a new sketch, click **Home > Sketch > Sketch** on the ribbon.
6. Select the Front (xz) plane from the base reference planes displayed in the graphics window; the sketch is started and the sketch plane is oriented normal to the screen.

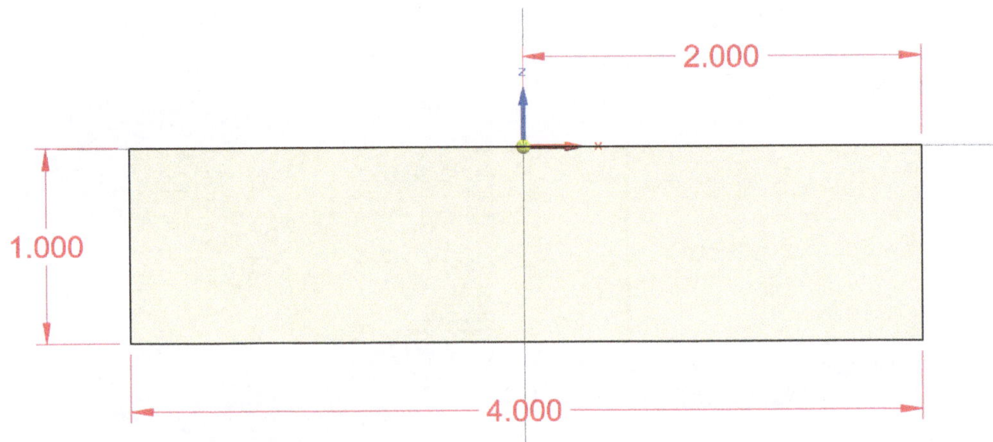

7. Click the **Close Sketch** button on the ribbon to exit the sketch. Click **Finish** and **Cancel** on the **Sketch** command bar.
8. On the ribbon, click **Home > Solids > Revolve**. Next, select **Select from Sketch** option from the **Create From Options** drop-down available under the **Sketch** section of the **Revolve** command bar.
9. Select the sketch and rectangular sketch and click the green check on the **Sketch** section.
10. Select the top horizontal edge of the rectangle to define the axis of revolution.
11. Click **Extent** section on the **Revolve** command bar and click the **Symmetric Extent** button.
12. Type-in **180** in the **Angle** box and Press **Enter**. Next, click **Finish** to create the *Revolve* feature.

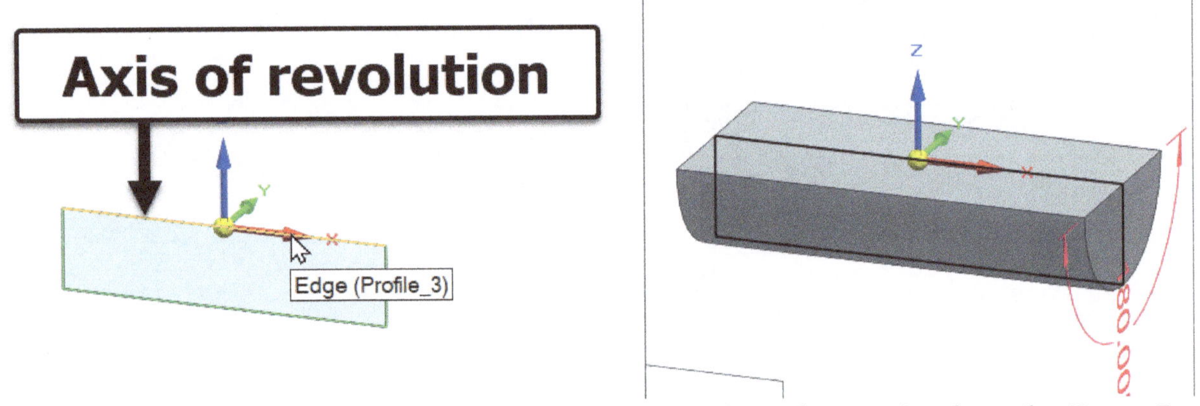

13. With the **Revolve** command still active, select the **Coincident Plane** option from the **Create-From Options** drop-down under the **Sketch** section of the **Revolve** command bar.
14. Click on top face of the part geometry to start the sketch.
15. On the ribbon, click **Home > Draw > Rectangle** drop-down > **Rectangle by 2 Points** .
16. Select the left right vertical edge. Next, move the pointer toward bottom-left corner and click, as shown.

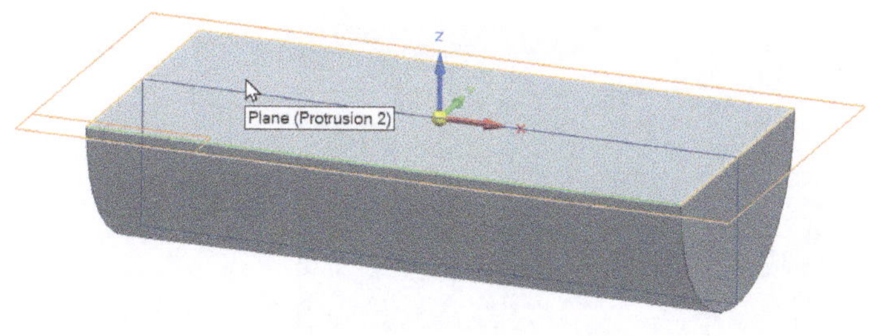

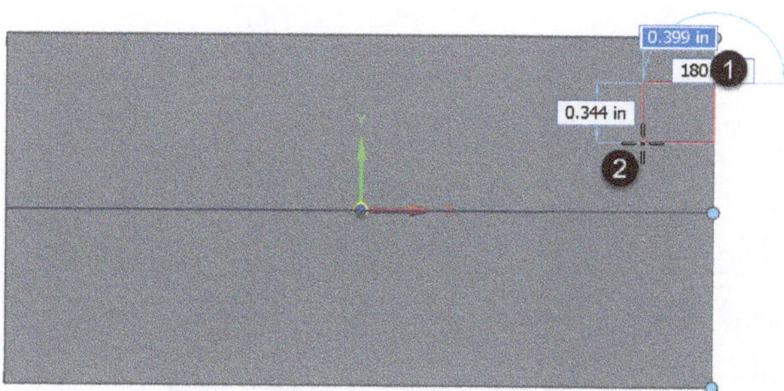

17. On the ribbon, click **Home > Dimension > Symmetric Diameter** . Next, the X-axis of the coordinate system and select the lower horizontal edge of the rectangle.
18. Type 0.75 in the Dimension edit box and press ENTER.
19. Select the top horizontal edge of the rectangle. Next, type 1.25 in the **Dimension** edit box and press ENTER.

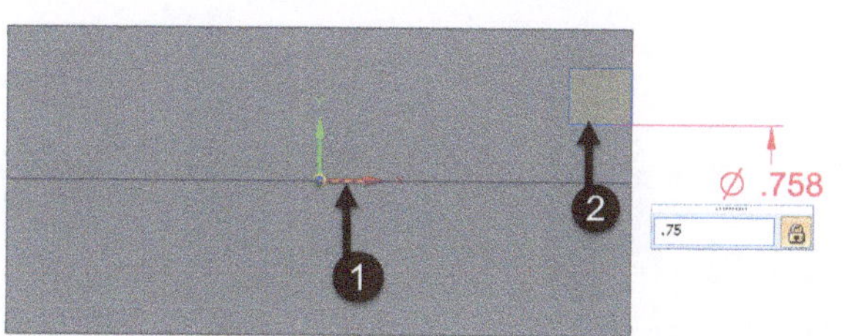

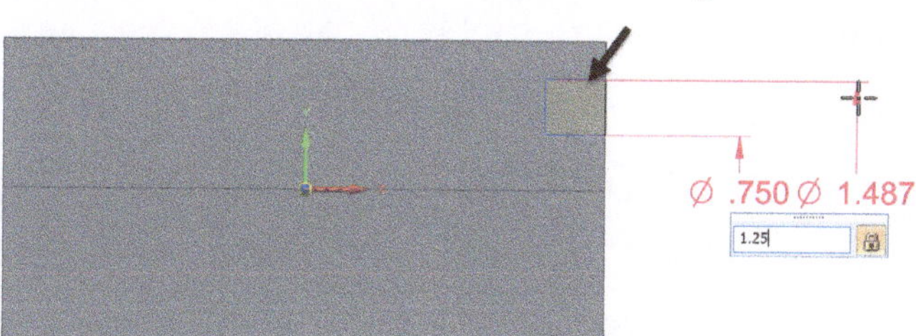

20. On the ribbon, click **Home > Dimension > Smart Dimension.** Next, select the top horizontal line of the rectangle.

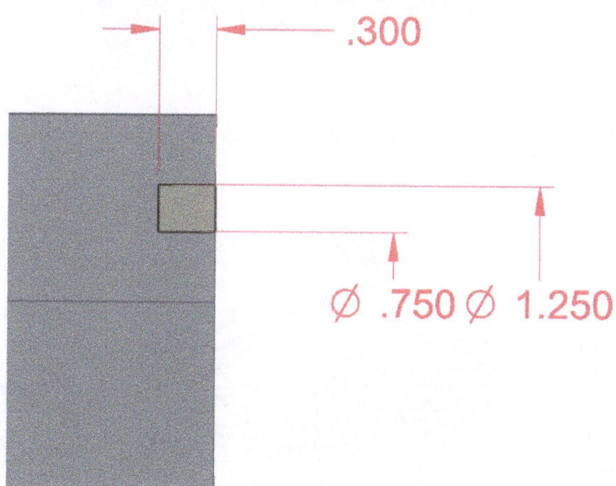

21. On the ribbon, click **Home > Draw > Line.** Next, select the sketch origin, move the pointer toward right and select the midpoint of the right vertical edge, as shown.
22. On the ribbon, click **Home > Draw > Axis of Revolution** . Next, select the newly created horizontal line.

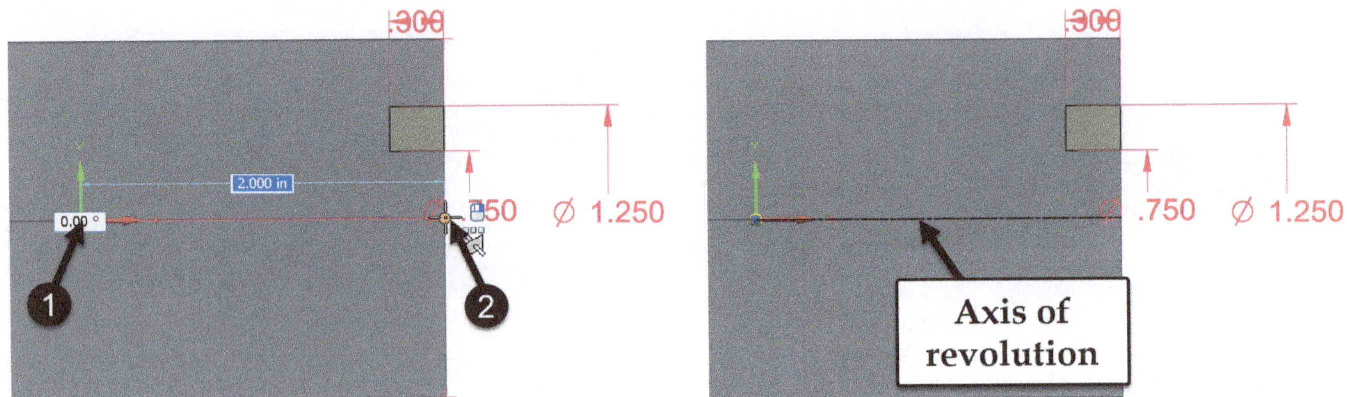

23. On the command bar, click the **Extent** section and activate the **One-sided Extent** icon.
24. Type-in **180** in the **Angle** box. Move the pointer downward and click to create the revolved cut. Next, click **Finish**.

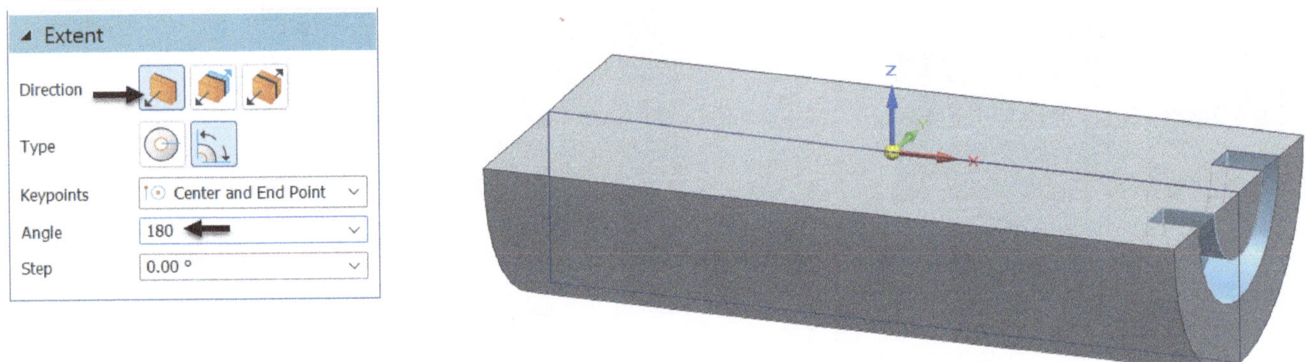

25. Draw a sketch on the top face of the part geometry.
26. Revolve the sketch to create the third feature. Next, click **Finish** and **Cancel** on the **Revolve** Command bar.

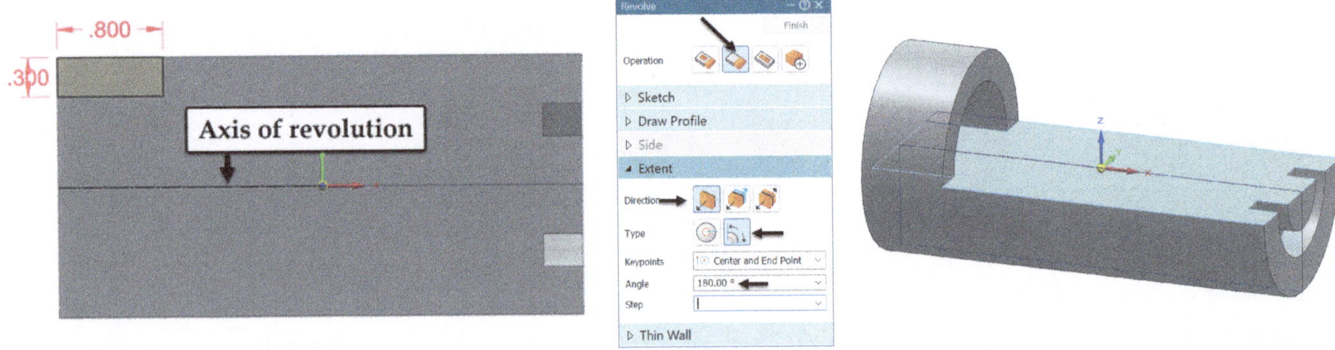

27. Save and close the file.

Questions

1. List the two methods to create *Extrude* features in Synchronous mode.
2. List the two methods to create *Revolve* features in Synchronous mode.
3. How do you create parallel planes in Synchronous mode?

4. List the three options to extrude sketches containing internal loops.
5. What are the treatment options available on the **Extrude** command bar?
6. List the four extent types available on the **Extrude** command bar.

Exercises

Exercise 1 (Millimetres)

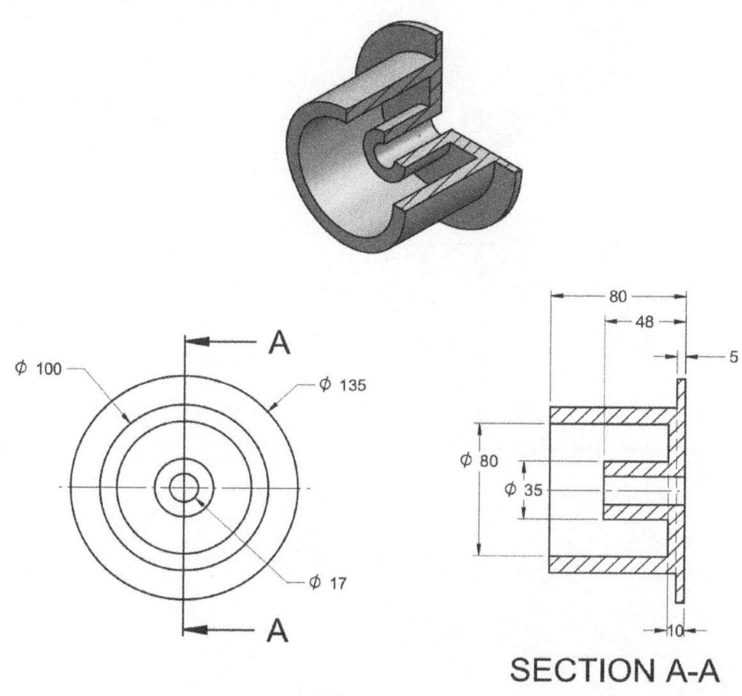

Exercise 2 (Inches)

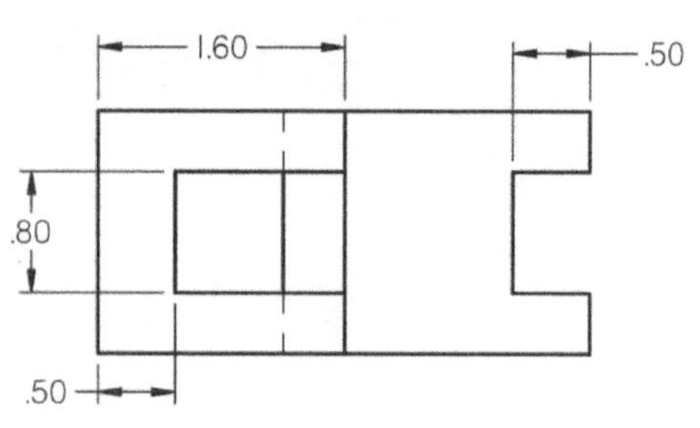

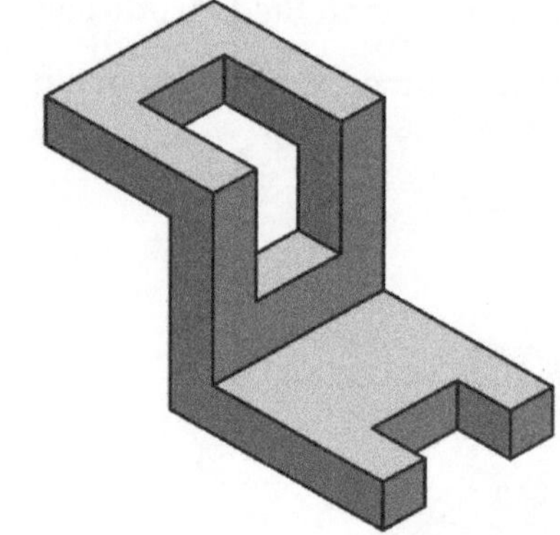

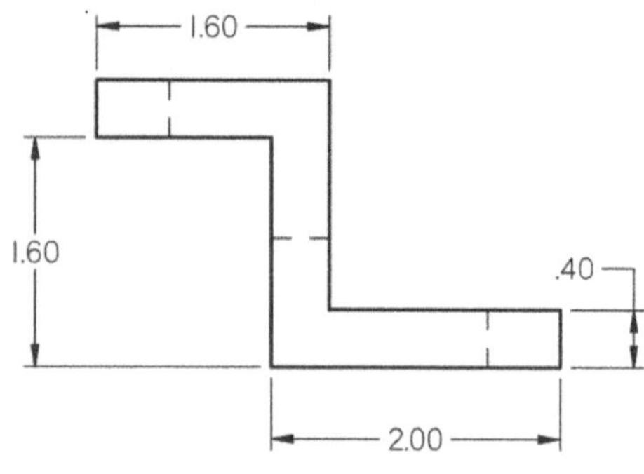

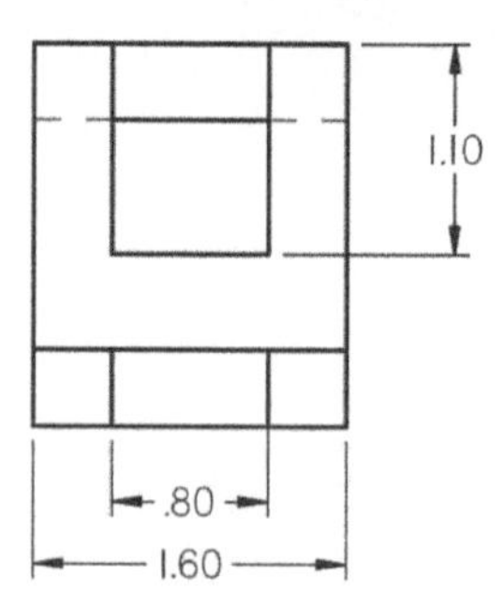

Exercise 3 (Millimetres)

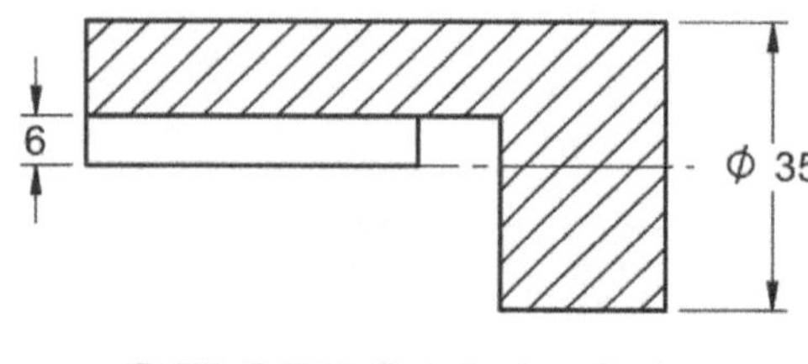

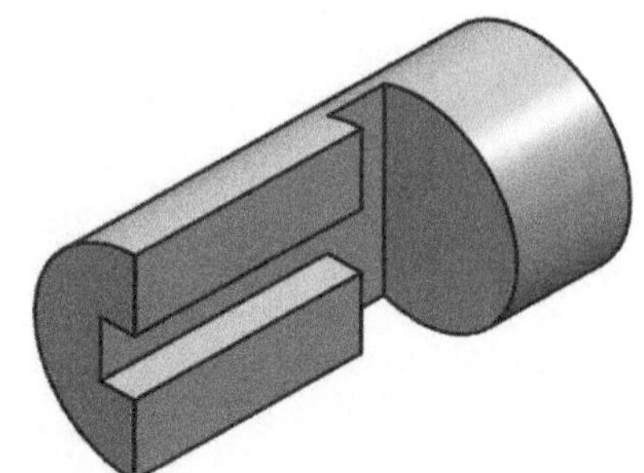

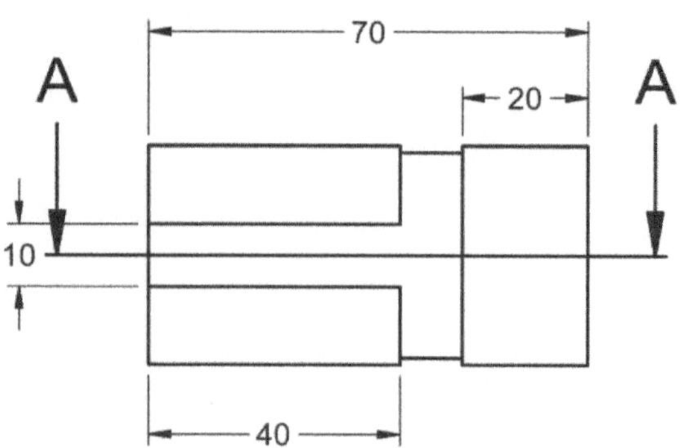

Chapter 4: Placed Features

So far, all of the features that were covered in previous chapters were based on two-dimensional sketches. However, there are certain features in Solid Edge that do not require a sketch at all. Features that do not require a sketch are called placed features. You can simply place them on your models. You must have some existing geometry to create placed features. Unlike a sketch-based feature, you cannot use a placed feature as the first feature of a model. For example, in order to create a *Fillet* feature, you must have an already existing edge. Now, you will learn how to add placed features to your design.

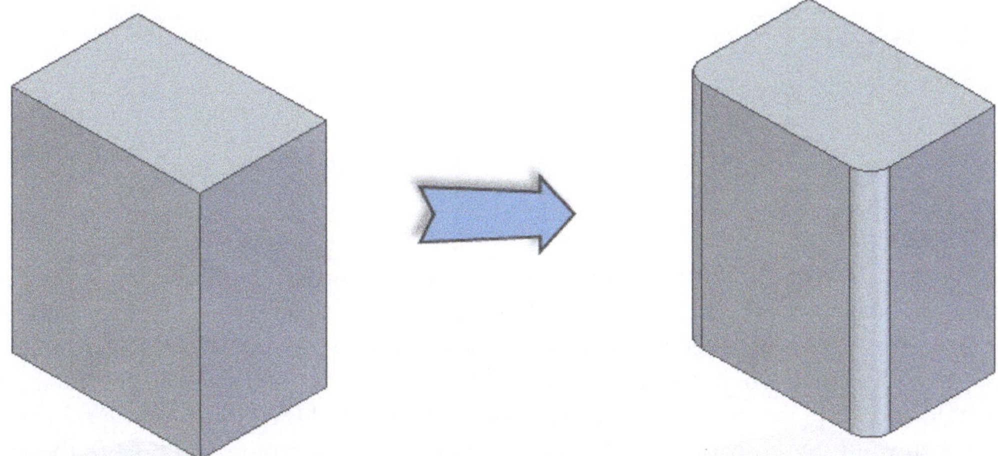

The topics covered in this chapter are:

- *Holes*
- *Threads*
- *Slots*
- *Rounds* and *Blends*
- *Chamfers*
- *Drafts*
- *Shells*

Hole

You know it is possible to use the *Extrude* command to create cuts and remove material. However, if you want to drill holes of standard sizes, the **Hole** command is a better way to do this. The reason for this is that it has many hole types already predefined for you. All you have to do is choose the correct hole type and size. The other benefit is when you create a 2D drawing, Solid Edge can automatically place the correct hole annotation.

Hole (Ordered)

Click **Home > Solids > Hole** on the ribbon, and you will notice that a command bar pops up. Click the **Hole Options** button on the command bar to open the **Hole Options** dialog. The options on this dialog help you to create different types of holes.

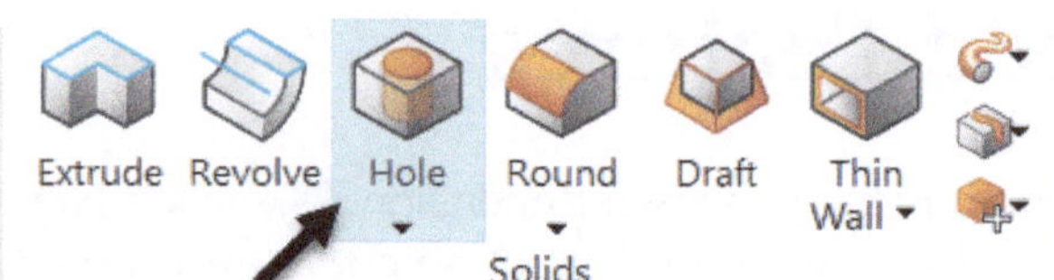

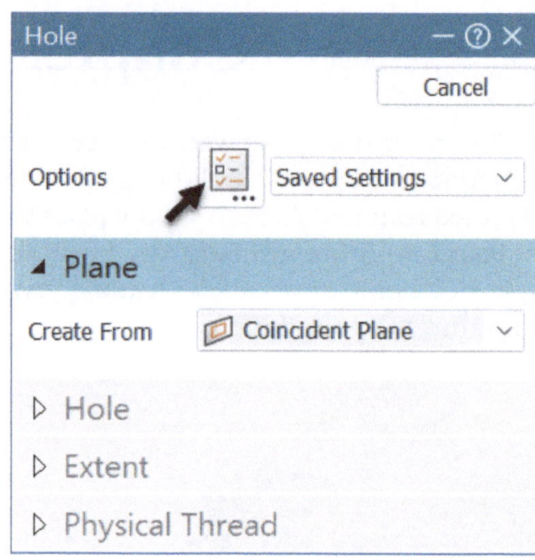

Create a Simple Hole feature

To create a simple hole feature, select the **Simple** button from the top left corner and set the **Standard** of the hole. Next, select the **Sub type** based on what the hole is meant to do. Choose **Drill Size** when you want the diameter driven by standard drill-bit sizes, choose **Dowel** when the hole is intended for a dowel pin used for accurate part location, or choose **General Screw Clearance** when the hole is intended to let a screw/bolt pass through without threading. Set the **Size** of the hole and **Hole Extents** type. Suppose you have selected **Finite Extent**, type-in a value in the **Hole depth** box. If you want a V-bottom hole, check the **V-bottom angle** option and type in the angle box value. Choose **Dimension to Flat** to specify that the hole depth is measured from the flat part where the V-shaped bottom angle begins. Choose **Dimension to V** to indicate that the hole depth extends to the V bottom. If you want to add a chamfer to the hole, check the **Start Chamfer** option. Type-in the chamfer offset and angle values. Click **OK** to close the dialog.

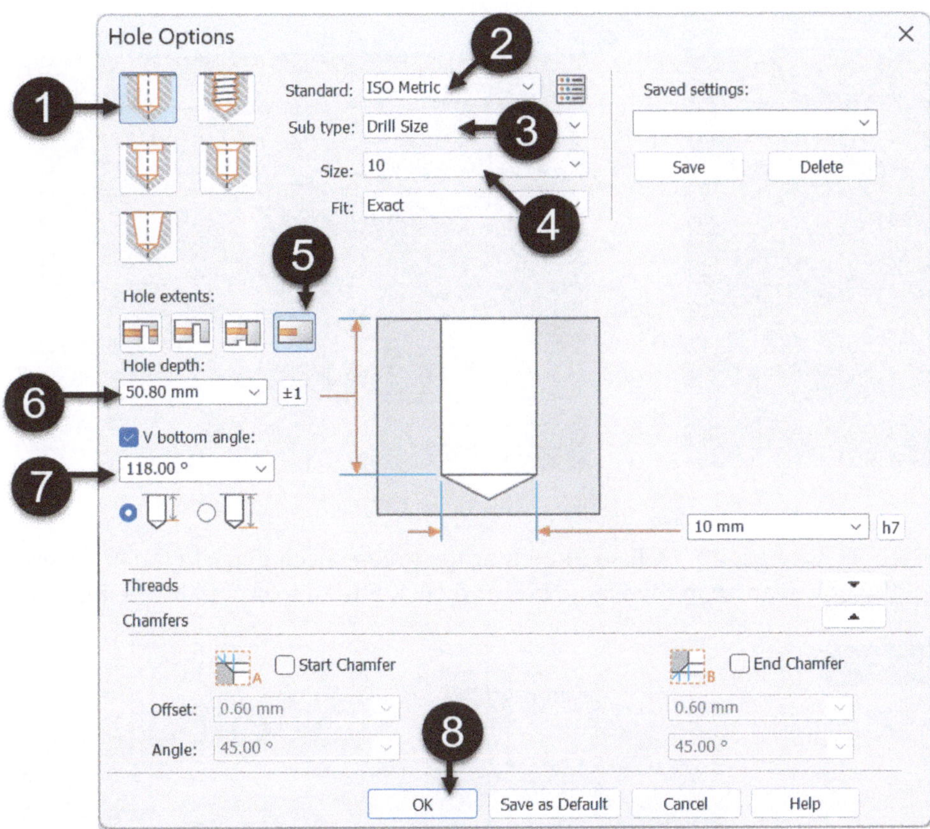

Next, set the reference plane for the profile sketch. To do this, select an option from the **Create From Options** drop-down on the **Hole** Command bar and define the reference plance of the profile sketch.

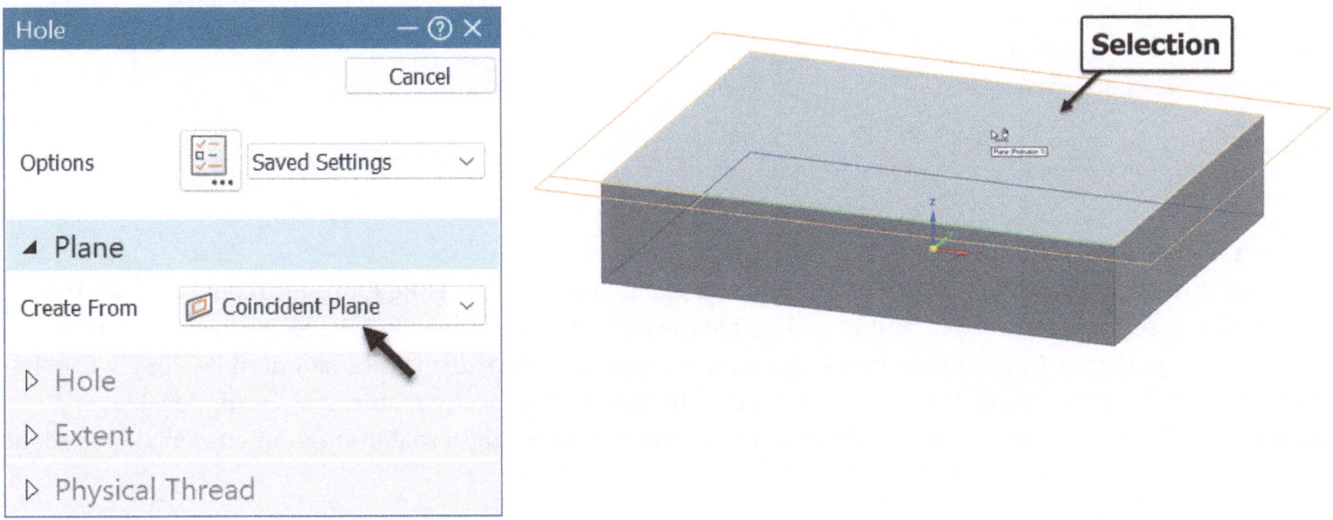

Next, use the **Hole Circle** command to position one or more hole circles. You can also align their center points horizontally or vertically, taking advantage of automatic alignment when placing circles close to each other. You can also opt for symmetrical alignment.

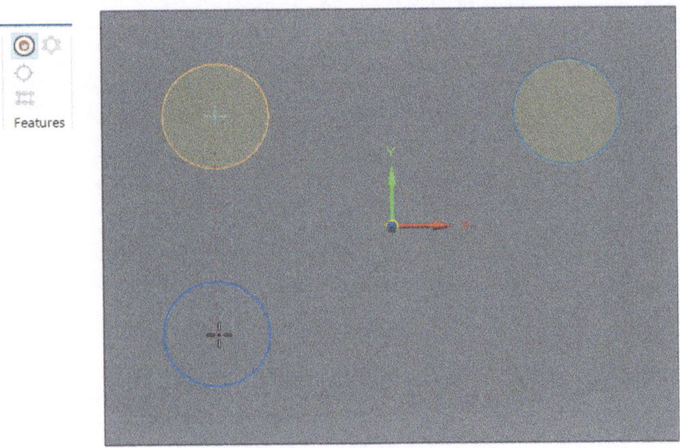

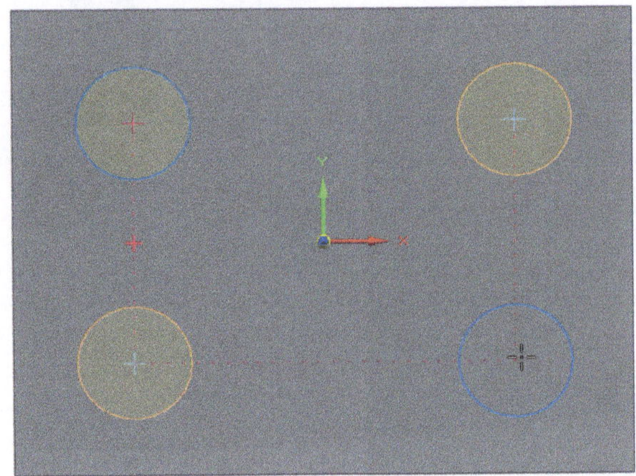

Finish the sketch by clicking **Home** tab > **Close** group > **Close Sketch** or the green check mark in the graphics window. Lastly, specify the name of the hole feature in the **Name** box and click **Finish** to complete the feature.

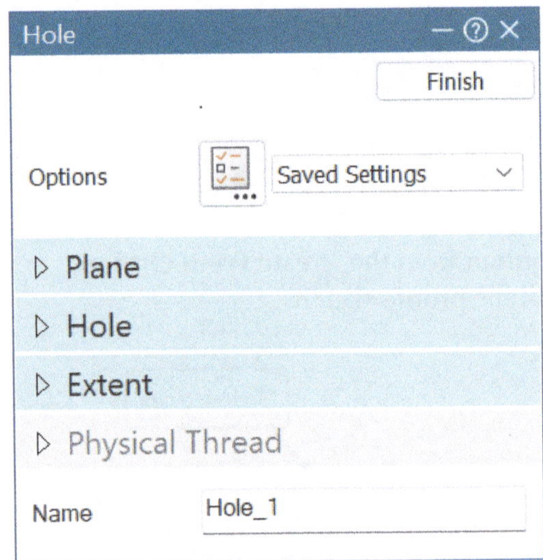

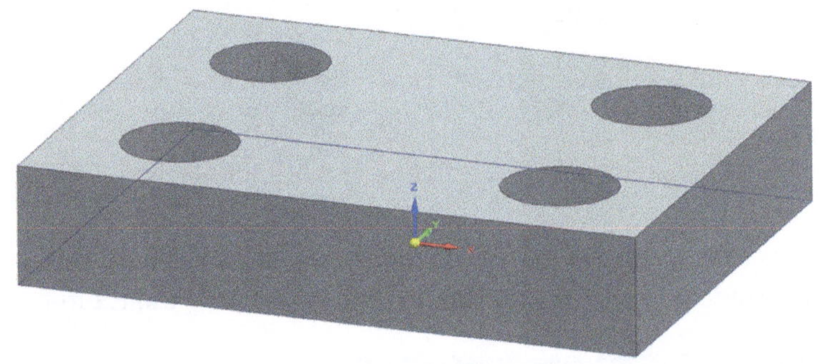

Create a Threaded Hole feature

To create a threaded hole feature, activate the **Hole** command and open the **Hole Options** dialog. On the **Hole Options** dialog, select the **Threaded** button and define the hole **Standard**. Next, set the **Sub type** to match the desired thread geometry. Choose **Standard Thread** for straight, parallel threads (like standard ISO or UNC bolts), choose **Straight Pipe Thread** for parallel pipe threads where sealing typically requires an O-ring/gasket, or choose **Tapered Pipe Thread** for threads that taper to create a pressure-tight seal through interference. Define the other parameters such as Size and Hole extents.

Under the **Threads** section, select the **Tap drill diameter**, **Internal minor diameter**, or **Nominal diameter** option. For instance, if you choose the **Nominal diameter** option, the hole size in the geometry will match the thread's nominal diameter. The nominal diameter is a standard label representing the approximate size of components like bolts or screws. While it may not exactly reflect the physical dimensions, this option ensures consistency with the designated nominal diameter, simplifying communication and standardization in engineering and manufacturing. Selecting the **Tap drill diameter** option places a hole in the model with dimensions that precisely match the tap drill diameter specifications. Selecting the **Internal Minor Diameter** option creates a hole in the model to match the specified internal minor diameter. This diameter is the smallest within the internal threads of a threaded hole or feature.

Next, define the **Thread direction**, and **Thread extent**. You can define **Thread extent** up to the hole extent or by entering a value. Specify the thread pitch value and click **OK** on the dialog.

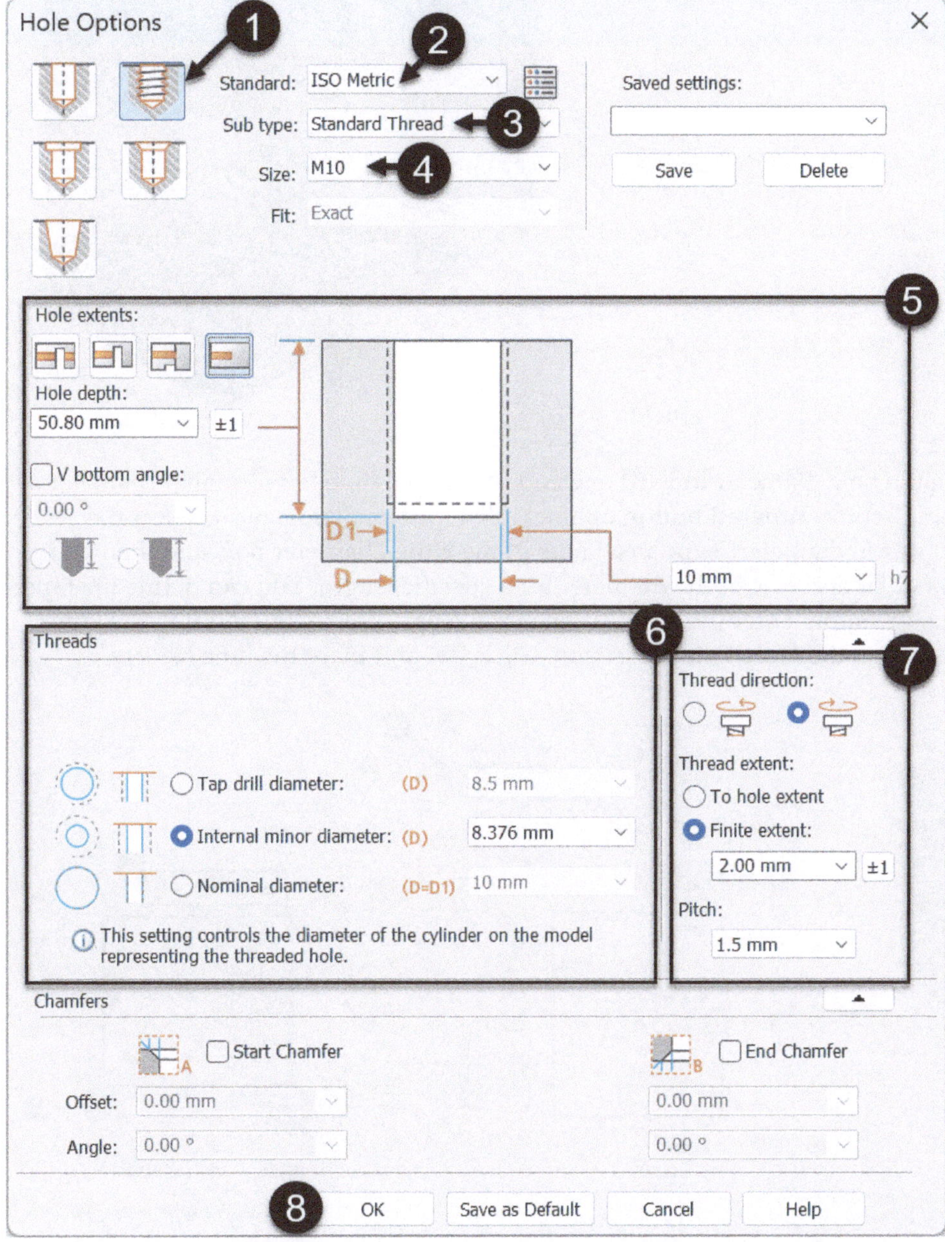

First, establish the reference plane for the profile sketch and define the hole position(s). Within the **Hole** command bar, extend the **Physical Thread Step** section and select the **Physical Thread** button. A message box titled **Physical Thread** will emerge, indicating potential performance effects. Confirm by clicking **Yes** on the message box.

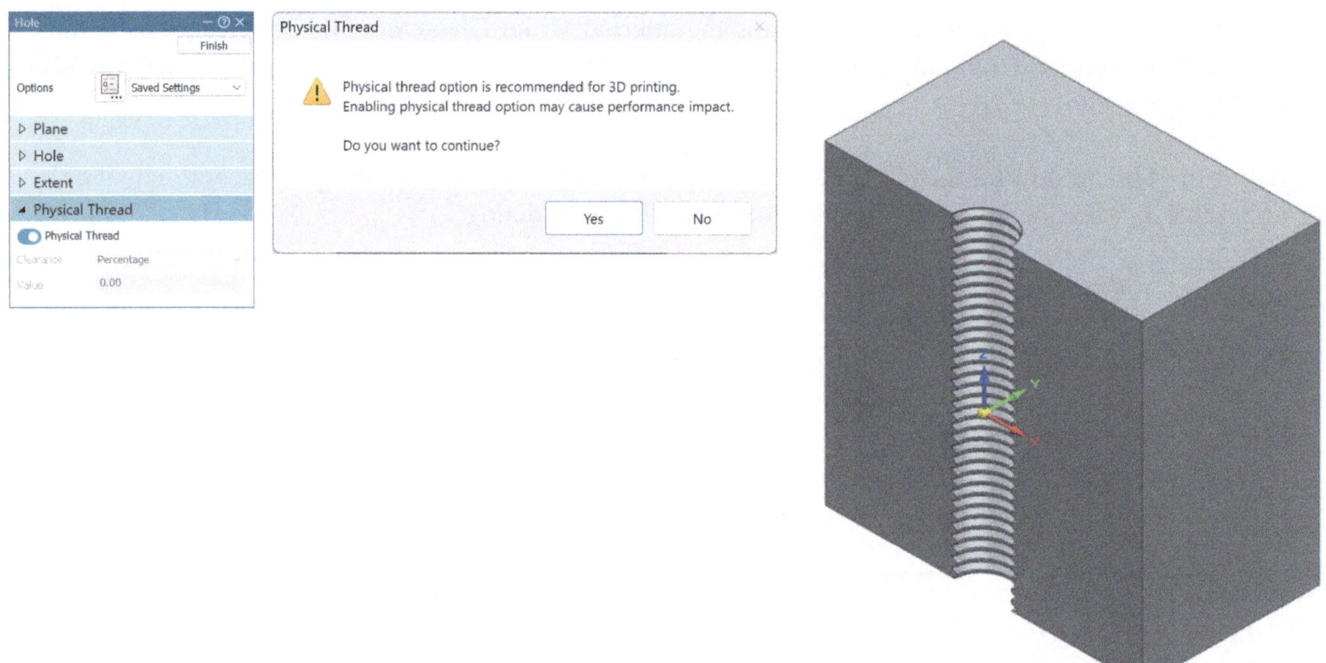

Create a Tapered Hole feature

Tapering is the process of decreasing the hole diameter toward one end. A tapered hole has a smaller diameter at the bottom. To create a tapered hole, select the **Tapered** button on the **Hole Options** dialog. Next, select the option to define the bottom diameter or top diameter. Type-in a value in the **Hole Diameter** box, and then define the taper ratio. The taper ratio is the rate of decrease in the diameter for a specific length. You can define the taper using the **Decimal (R/L)**, **Ratio (R: L),** or simply enter the taper angle in the **Angle** box. After defining the taper, specify the hole depth and end condition in the **Hole Extents** section. Click **OK** and place the hole feature.

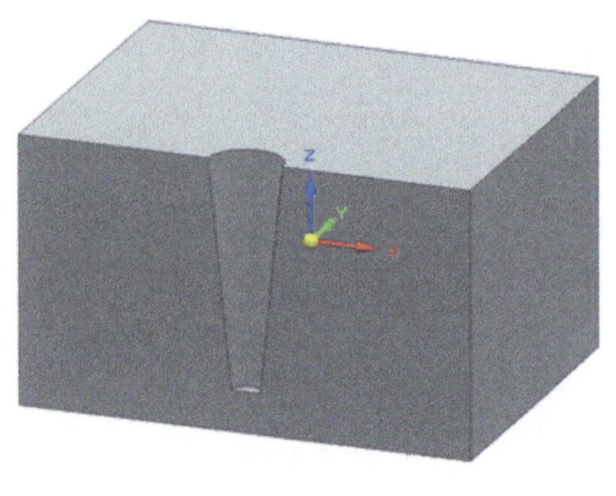

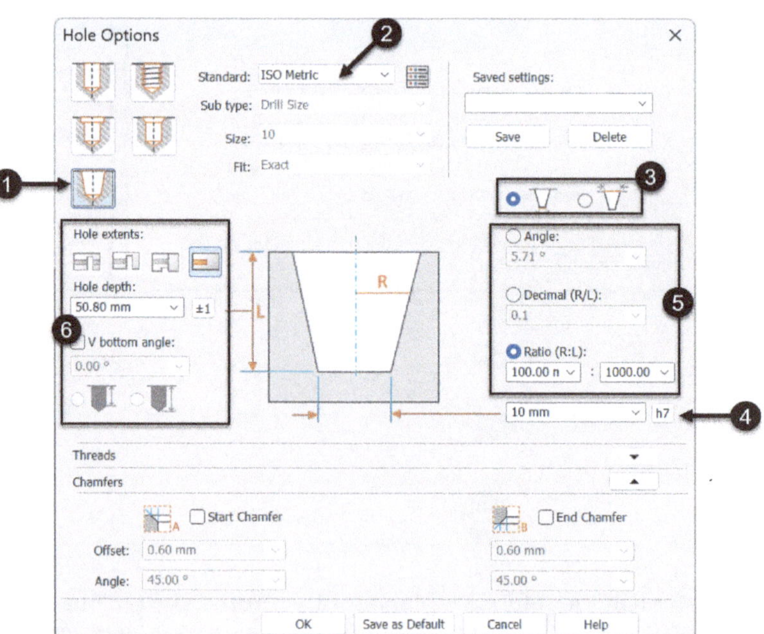

Create a Counterbore Hole feature

A counterbore hole is a large diameter hole added at the opening of another hole. This counterbore hole is used to accommodate a fastener below the level of the workpiece surface. The three types of counterbore holes that can be created in Solid Edge are shown in the figure.

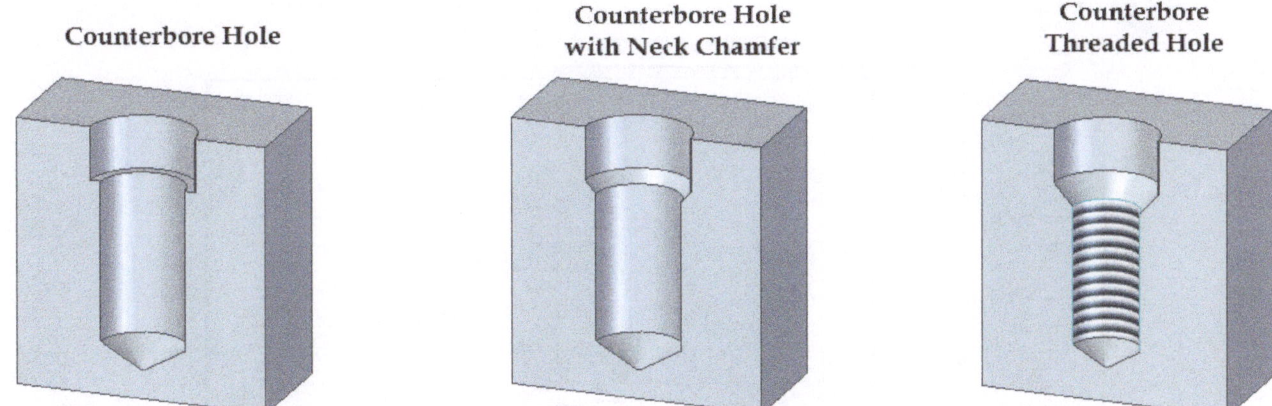

To create a counterbore hole, select the **Counterbore** button on the **Hole Options** dialog. Next, define the counterbore subtype, hole size, fit, counterbore diameter, and counterbore depth. Check the **Neck Chamfer** option under the **Chamfer** section if you want a V-bottomed counterbore hole. Check the **Thread** option under the **Thread** section and define the thread parameters to add a thread to the hole. Click **OK** and place the hole.

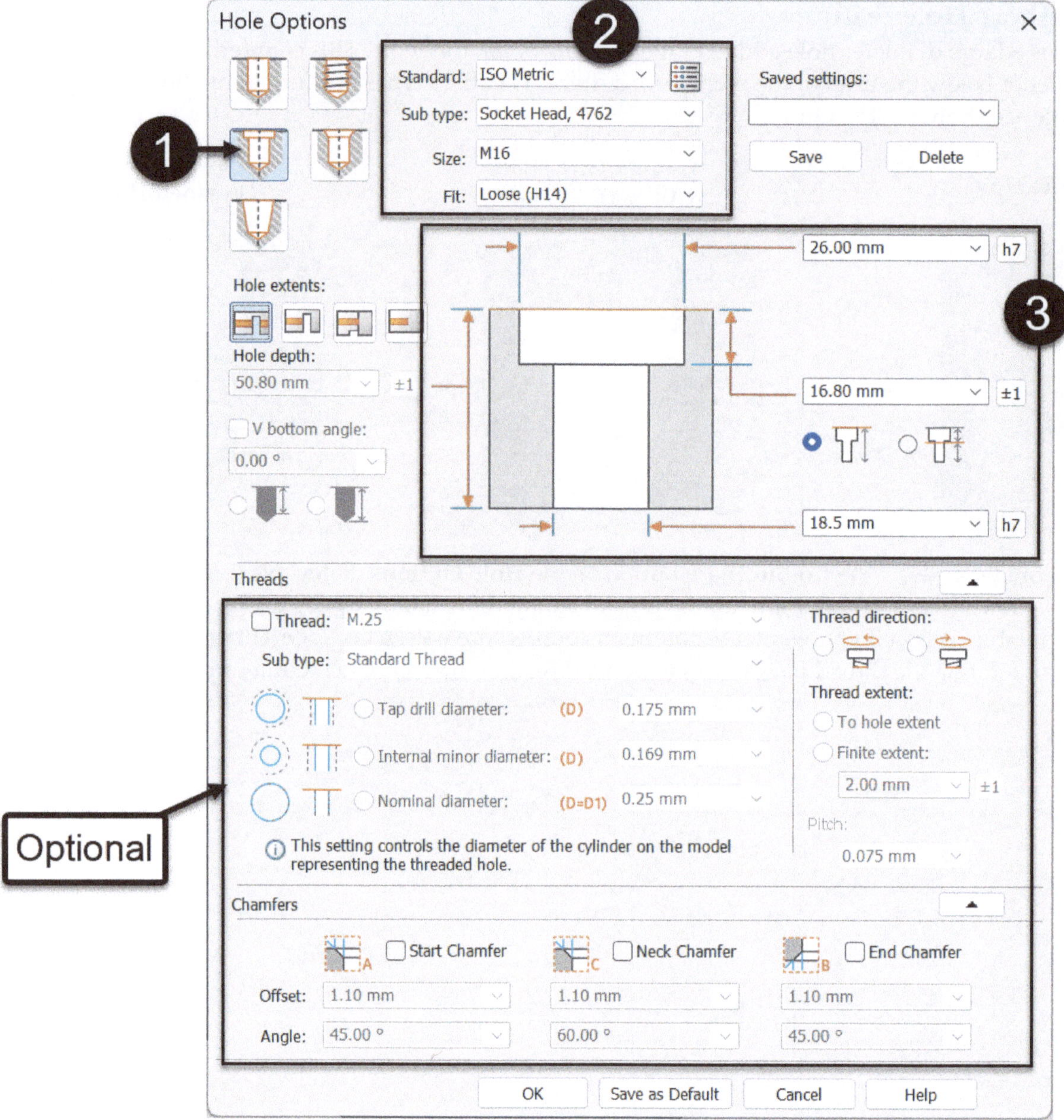

Create a Countersink Hole feature

A countersunk hole has an enlarged V-shaped opening to accommodate a fastener below the workpiece surface level. To create a countersink hole, select the **Countersink** button on the **Hole Options** dialog. Type-in values in the **Diameter**, **Countersink diameter** and **Countersink angle** boxes. You can also check the **Head clearance** option if you want to provide head clearance. Set the hole depth and end condition in the **Hole Extents** section. Click **OK** and place the hole.

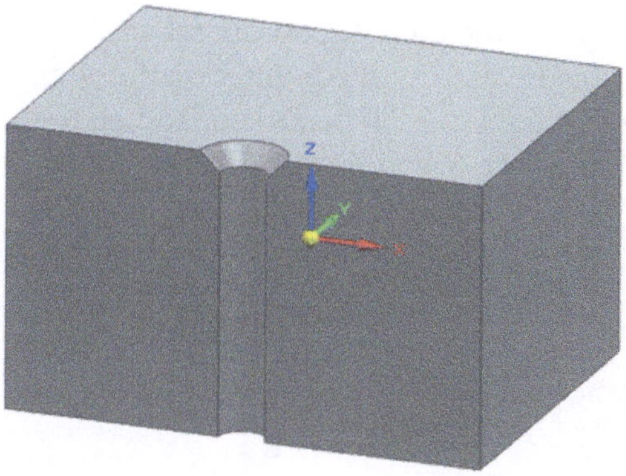

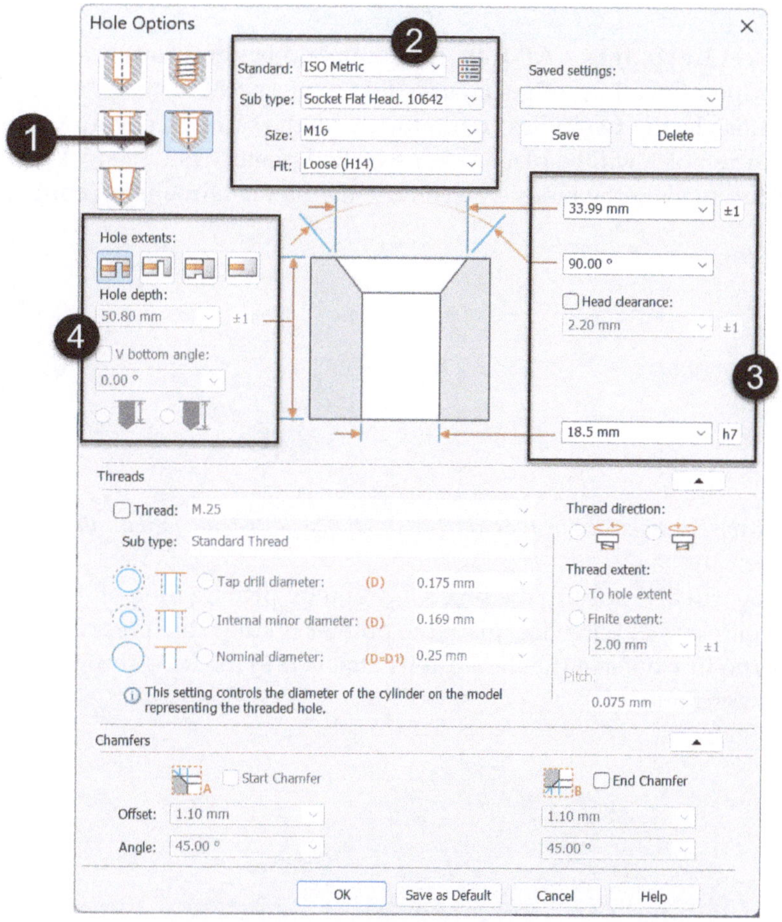

Hole (Synchronous)

Click **Home > Solids > Hole** on the ribbon, and you will notice that a command bar pops up. Click the **Hole Options** icon on the command bar to open the **Hole Options** dialog. The options on this dialog are discussed earlier. Specify the settings on the **Hole Options** dialog and click **OK**.

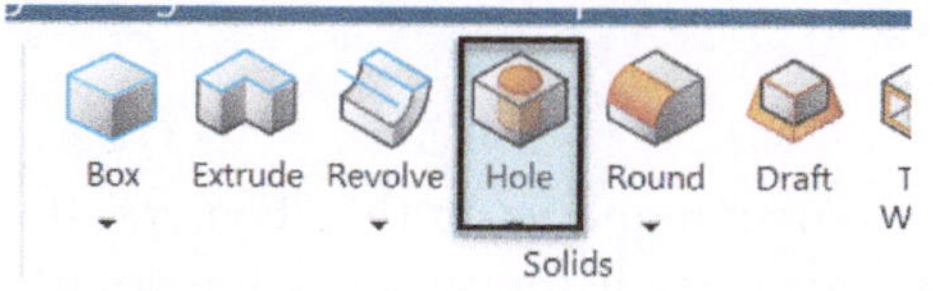

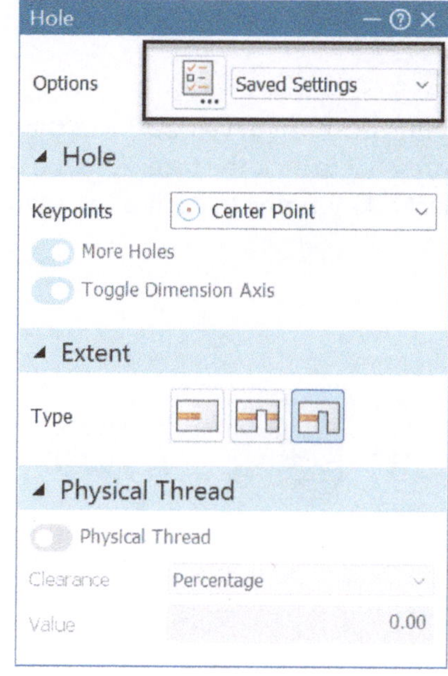

Select **Keypoints** > **All** from the command bar and start selecting points from the model. You can select an endpoint of a line, edge or curve (or) center point of an arc or circular edge by placing the pointer on the edge. After placing two holes continuously on the same face, you will notice that the face will be locked, and all the future holes will be placed on the locked plane. Click the lock icon on the screen if you want to unlock the face. After placing the holes, you can use the **Smart Dimension** command to position the hole.

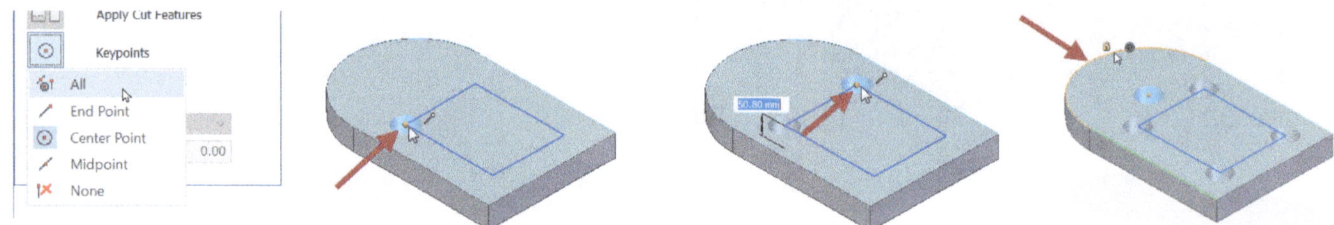

Note: *The hole size in the example should be adjusted based on the model size.*

You can also specify the hole's location by placing the pointer with the hole preview on the adjacent edge and then press E. Likewise, place the pointer on the edge perpendicular to previously selected, and then press Enter. Type-in values in the dimensions attached to the hole and press Enter. Press Tab to switch between the dimensions.

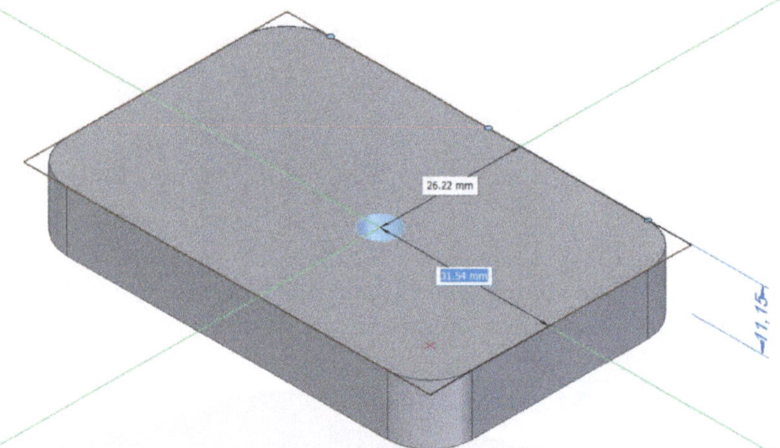

If you want to place a hole on a cylindrical or curved surface, there is an easy technique to do this. Position the pointer on the cylindrical face and press **F3** to lock the face. A plane tangent to the face will appear. Drag the pointer and type-in an angle value (or) select a key point to define the plane orientation. Now, place holes on the locked plane.

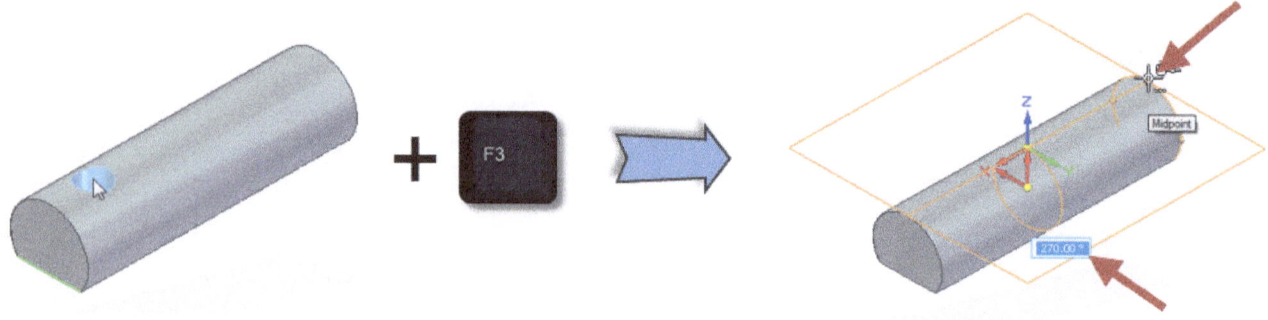

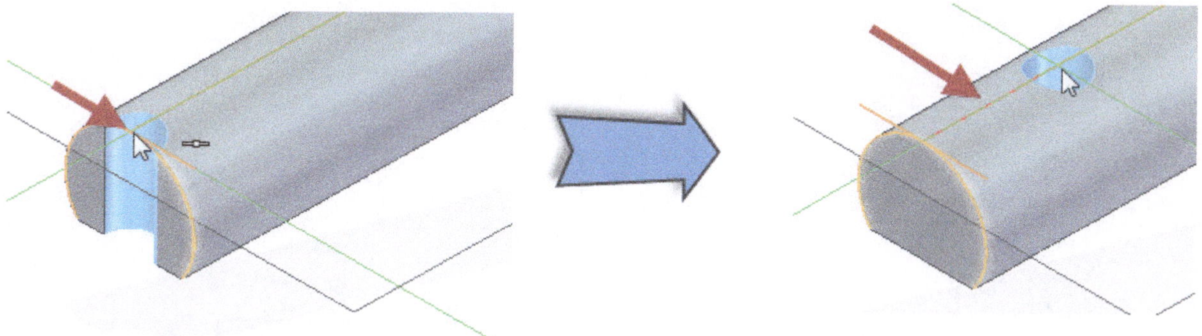

Modify Holes

After placing holes, you may be required to modify them or add more holes to the set. To modify a hole, you must select it and click on the hole diameter. A box appears with the hole parameters. Change the hole parameters by entering new values in the box. You can use the command bar options to change the hole type. Click and drag the arrows displayed on the holes to change the location of the hole.

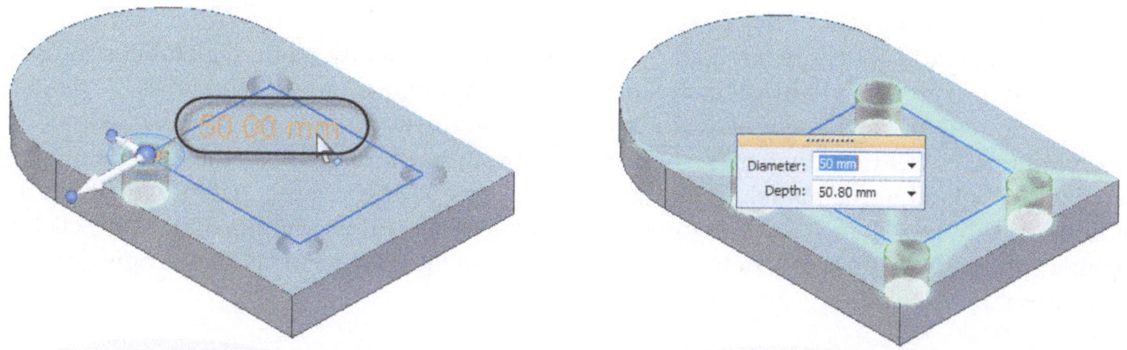

You will notice that all the holes placed at a time are grouped under one set in the Pathfinder. If you modify one hole in the set, all the other holes will also be modified. Use the **More holes** option on the command bar to add more holes to the hole set.

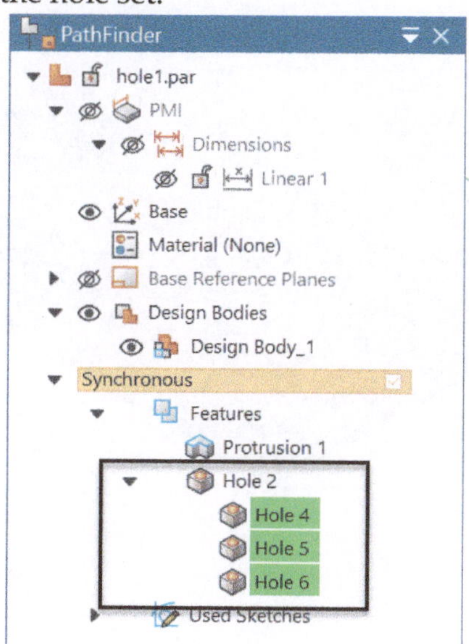

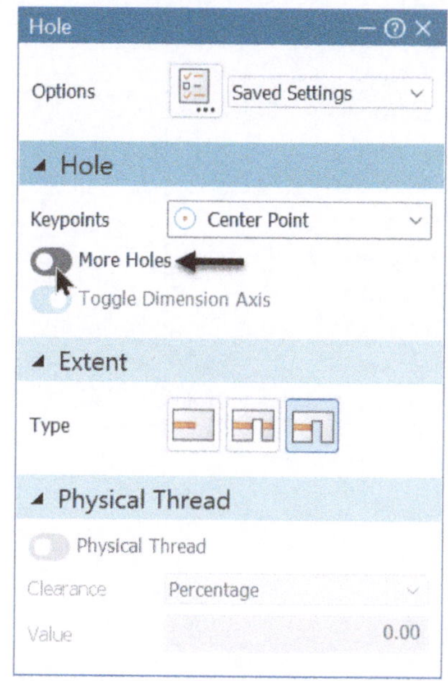

If you want to remove a hole from the set, click the right mouse button on it in the Pathfinder and select **Separate**. The hole will be separated.

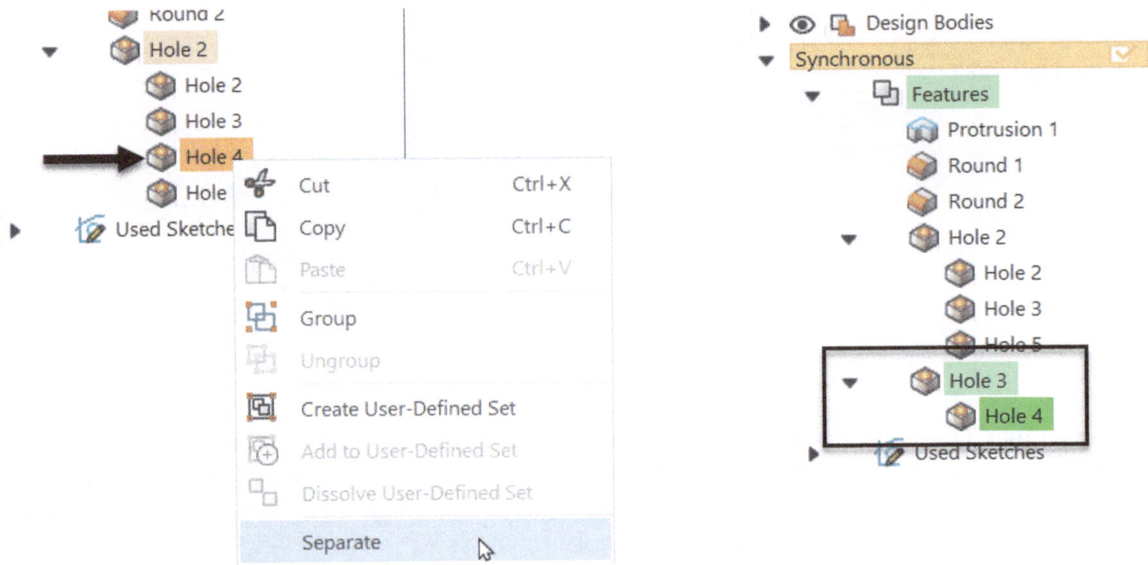

Recognize Holes (Synchronous)

This command converts the cylindrical features created by using the cutting operation into the **Hole** features. This command is also helpful to convert the cylindrical cut features in the imported geometry into holes. Activate this command (click **Home > Solids > Hole > Recognize Holes** on the ribbon). The **Hole Recognition** dialog pops up and displays all the cylindrical cut features that are recognized as holes. As you place the pointer over the holes in the dialog, they will be highlighted in the model. Click the **Hole Options** buttons on the dialog to open the **Hole Options** dialog of individual holes. Change the hole type and diameter (if required) in this dialog and click **OK**. Uncheck the **Recognize** options if you do not want to recognize the holes. Click **OK** on the **Hole Recognition** dialog to convert the cut features into holes.

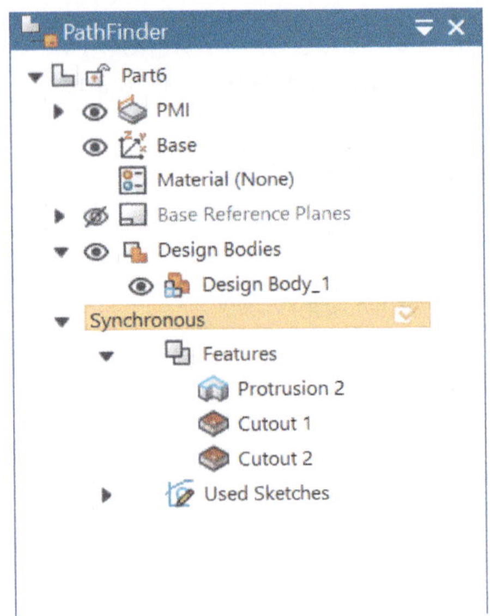

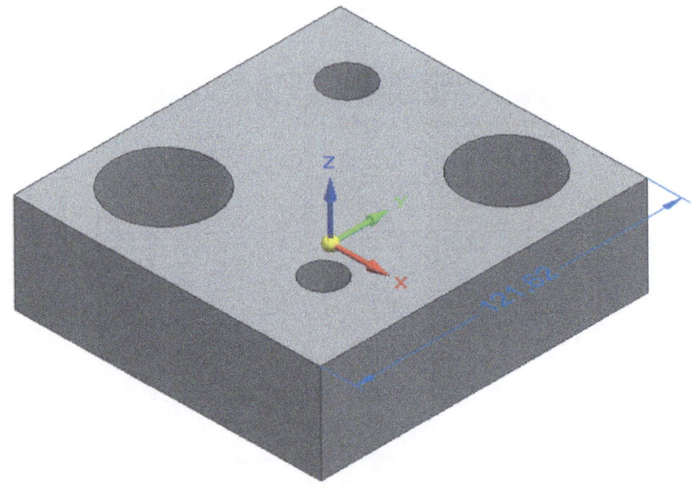

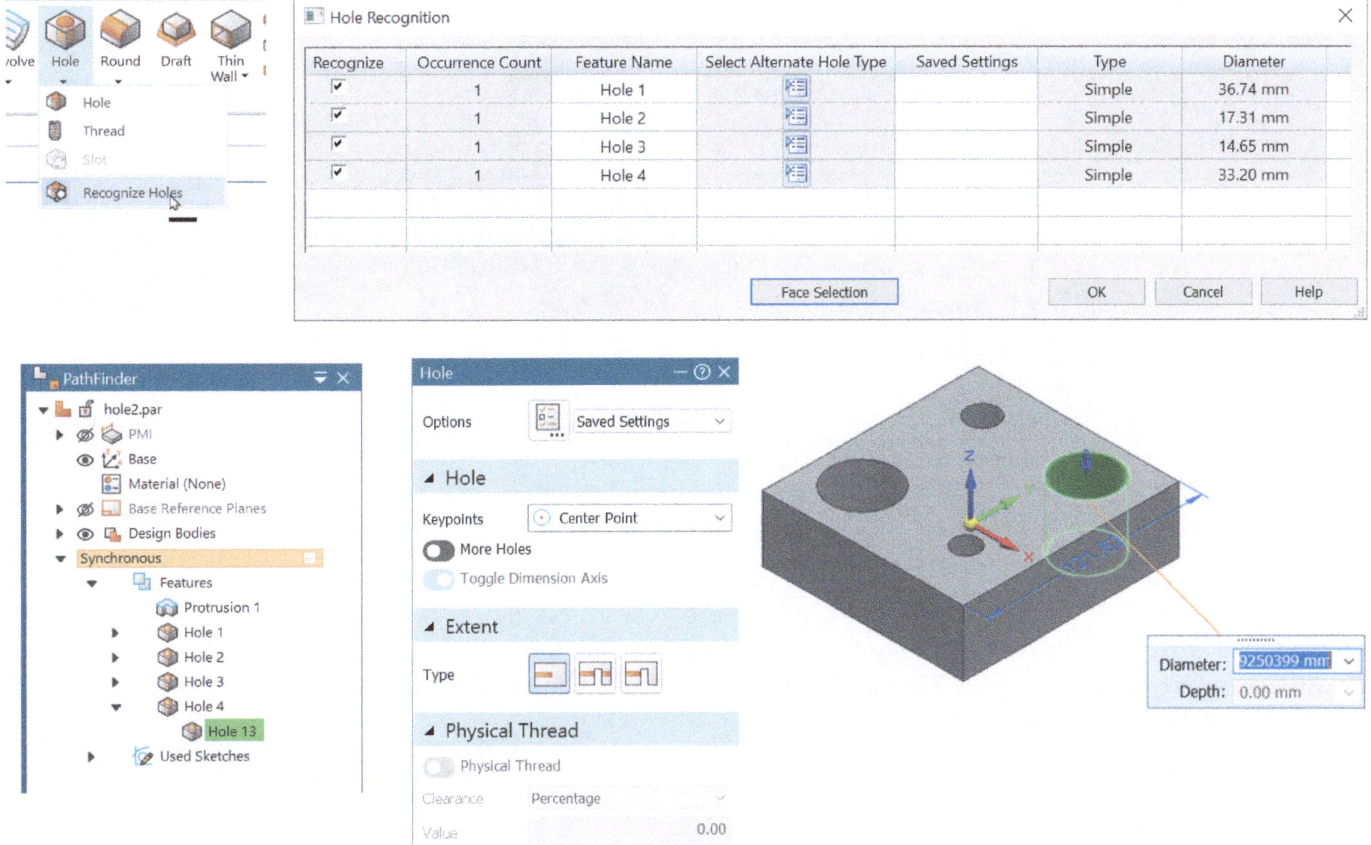

Thread (Ordered)

This command in Solid Edge facilitates the addition of a reference thread feature to a cylindrical face, enhancing the 3D geometry. When creating a 2D drawing later on, Solid Edge can automatically place the correct thread annotation, streamlining the annotation process.

To activate this command, navigate to the ribbon and click on **Home > Solids > Hole > Thread**. This action triggers the **Thread Options** dialog, where you can set thread parameters like type, standard, size, and thread diameter. After configuring these settings, click the **OK** button to proceed.

Select a cylindrical face to establish the reference for the thread. It's important to note that the diameter of the cylindrical face must correspond to a specific value listed in the Solid Edge hole database. This ensures alignment with specified thread sizes, promoting a smooth integration into your design.

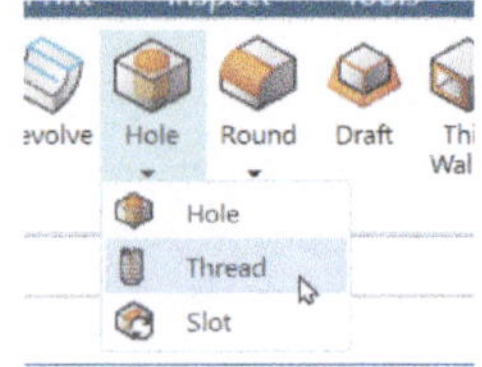

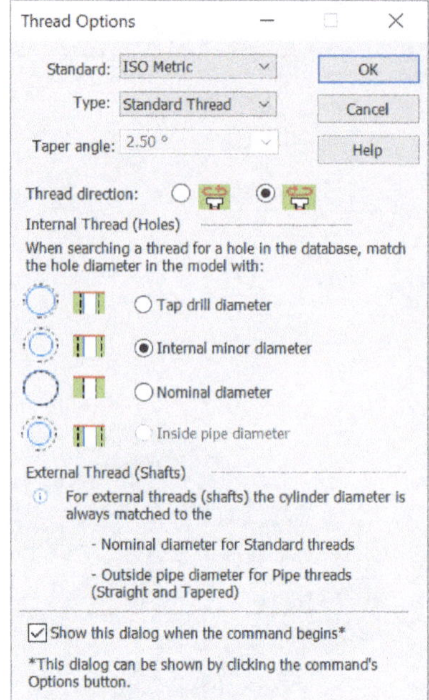

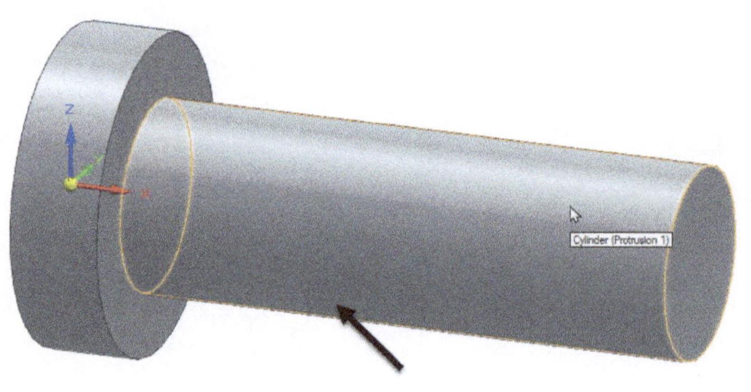

Moving forward, choose the circular edge of the cylindrical face to define the starting point of the thread. The **Parameters** section activates on the **Thread** command bar, where you can define parameters, such as **Offset**, **Depth**, **Value**, **Size**, and **Pitch**.

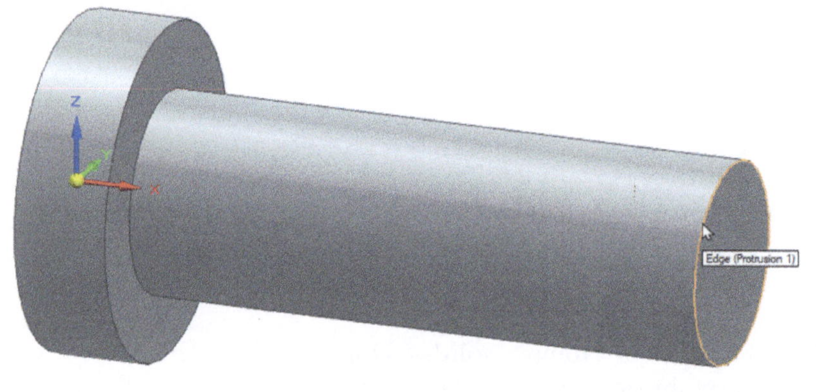

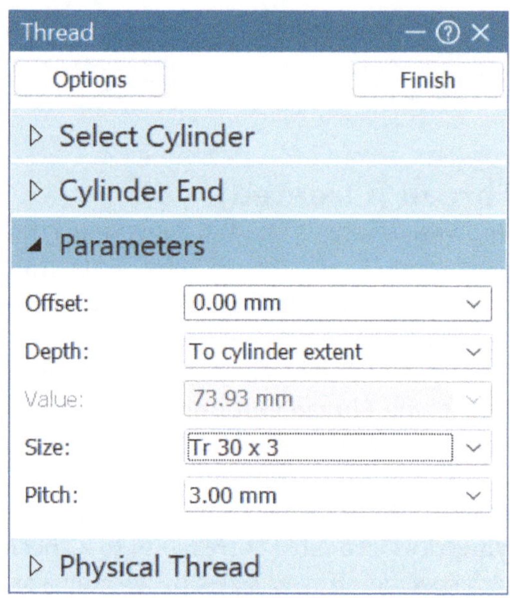

Expand the **Physical Thread** section and click on the **Physical Thread** button. Next, click **Yes** the **Physical Thread** message box. Specify the thread clearance by selecting **Percentage** or **Absolute** from the **Clearance** drop-down, then input the desired value in the **Value** box. This clearance value is crucial for ensuring interference-free engagement of threads, achieved by adjusting the thread's internal or external diameter.

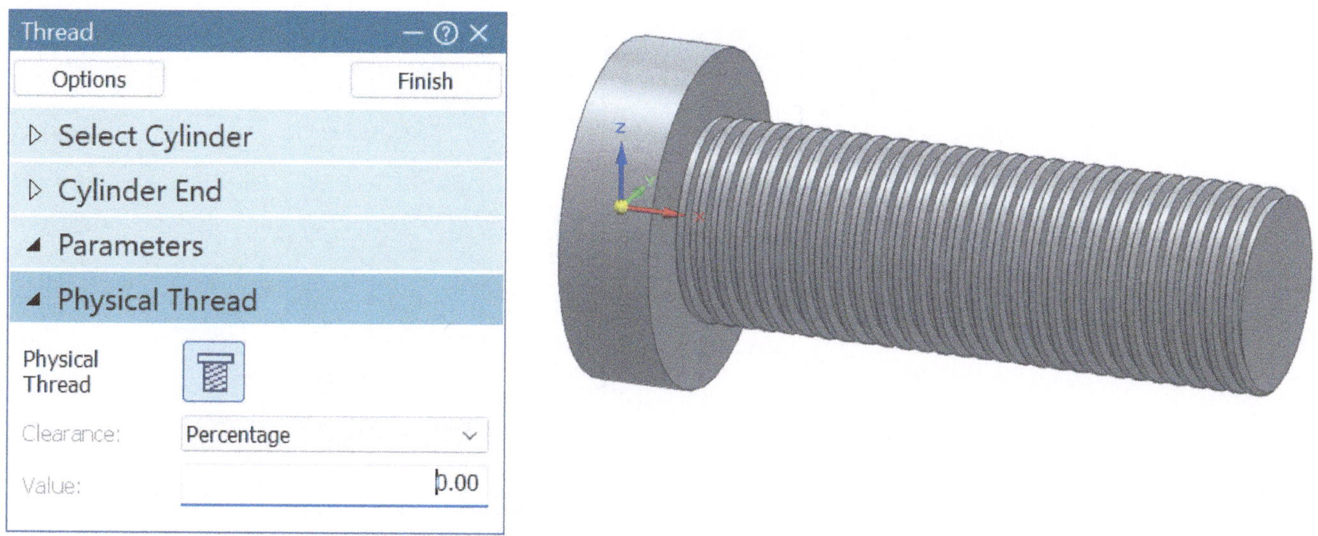

Upon completing these steps, click **Finish** to finalize the thread feature.

Thread (Synchronous)

This command adds a reference thread feature to a cylindrical face. The thread features are added to a 3D geometry so that when you create a 2D drawing, Solid Edge can automatically place the correct thread annotation. Activate this command (click **Home > Solids > Hole > Thread** on the ribbon) and click the **Options** icon on the **Thread** command bar. The **Thread Options** dialog pops up. Set the thread parameters such as type, standard, size, and thread diameter, and then click the **OK** button. Set the **Extent Type** on the command bar and select a cylindrical face. The **Change Diameter** message appears. Click **OK** to change the diameter of the cylindrical face to suit the selected thread size. Type-in the thread length and press Enter if you have set the **Extent Type** to **Finite Value**.

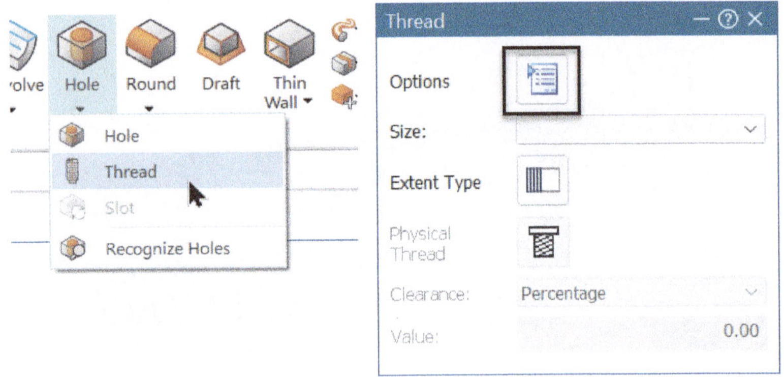
Hole
Round
Draft
Thin Wall
Hole
Thread
Slot
Recognize Holes
Thread
Options
Size:
Extent Type
Physical Thread
Clearance:
Percentage
Value:
0.00

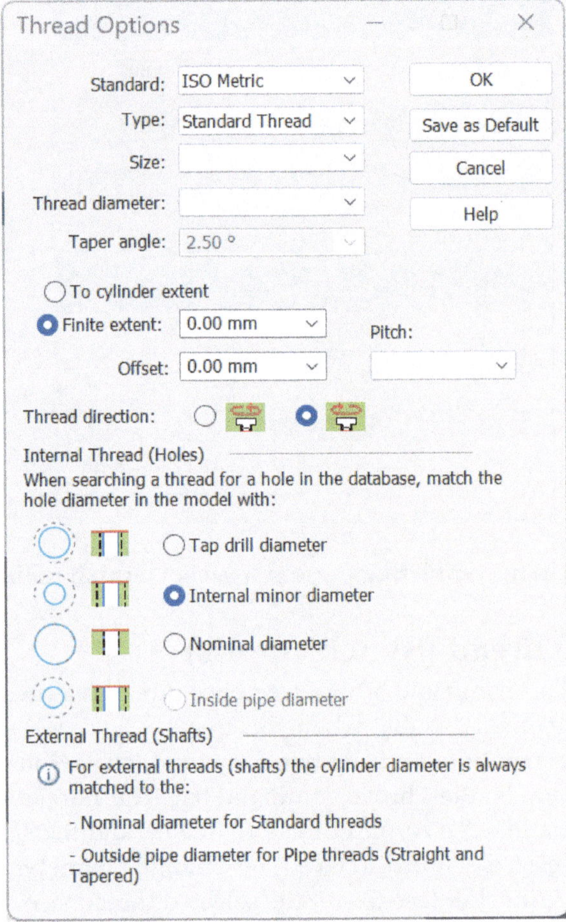
Thread Options
Standard: ISO Metric
Type: Standard Thread
Size:
Thread diameter:
Taper angle: 2.50 °
OK
Save as Default
Cancel
Help
To cylinder extent
Finite extent: 0.00 mm
Offset: 0.00 mm
Pitch:
Thread direction:
Internal Thread (Holes)
When searching a thread for a hole in the database, match the hole diameter in the model with:
Tap drill diameter
Internal minor diameter
Nominal diameter
Inside pipe diameter
External Thread (Shafts)
For external threads (shafts) the cylinder diameter is always matched to the:
- Nominal diameter for Standard threads
- Outside pipe diameter for Pipe threads (Straight and Tapered)

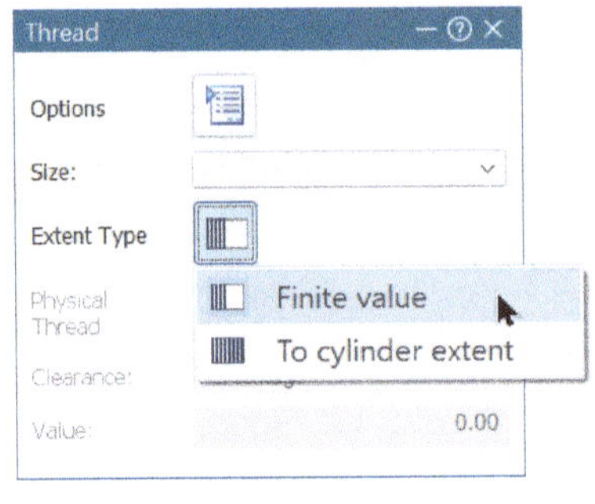
Thread
Options
Size:
Extent Type
Physical Thread
Clearance:
Value:
0.00
Finite value
To cylinder extent

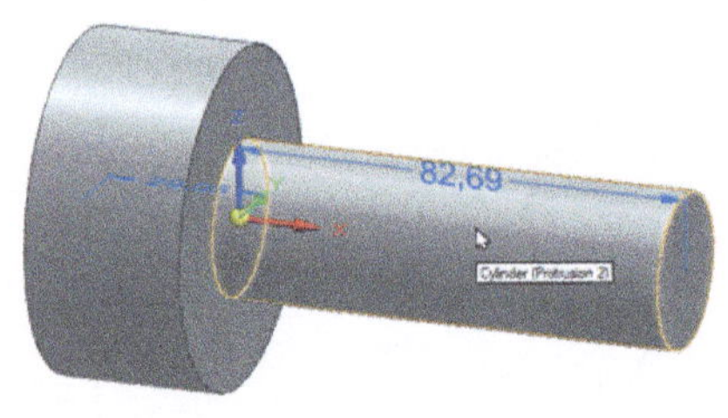
82,69

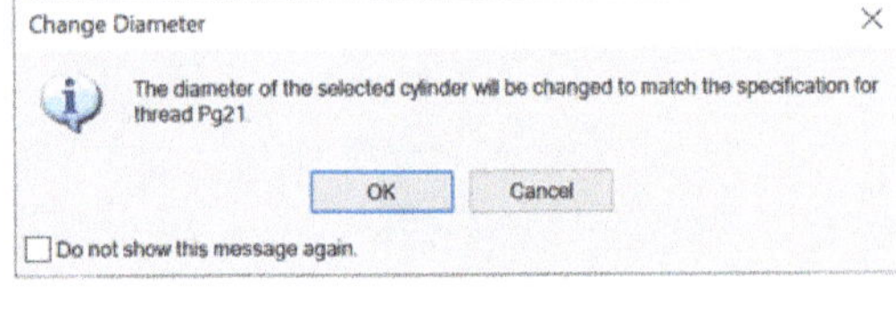
Change Diameter
The diameter of the selected cylinder will be changed to match the specification for thread Pg21
OK
Cancel
Do not show this message again.

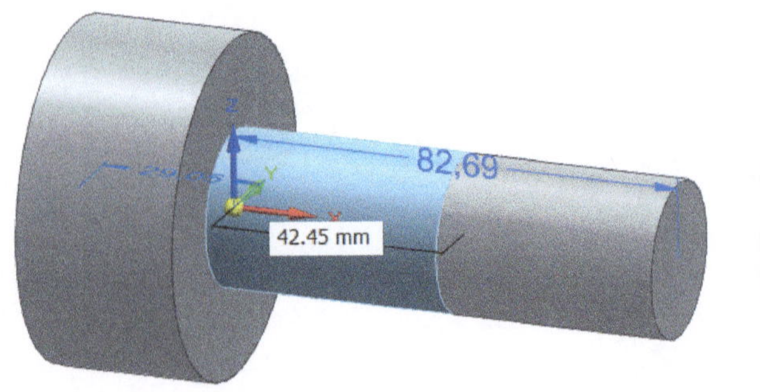
82,69
42.45 mm

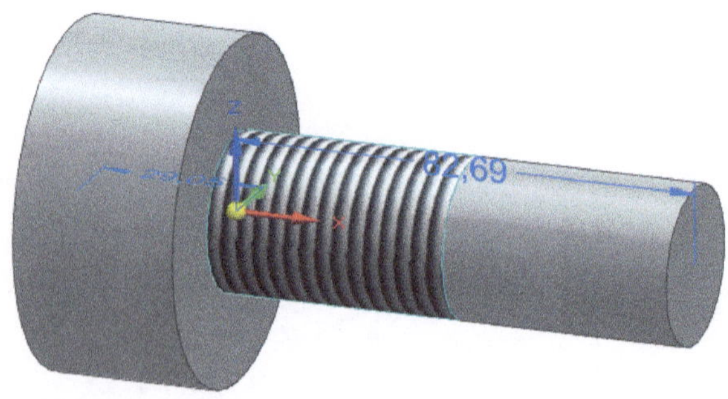
82,69

Round (Ordered)

To enhance the part's design, utilize the **Round** command, a powerful tool for smoothing the edges. With this command, you have the flexibility to apply a constant rounding radius, a variable radius, or a combination of both approaches.

When applying the **Round** feature, consider not only edges but also the option to create blends between faces or a combination of edges and faces.

Click **Home > Solids > Round** on the ribbon and click **Options > Constant Radius**. Next, click **Round Parameters** on the **Round** command bar; the **Round Parameters** section is expanded. The options in this section are discussed next.

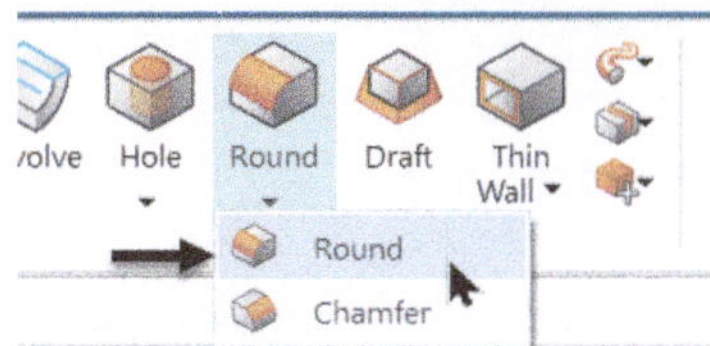

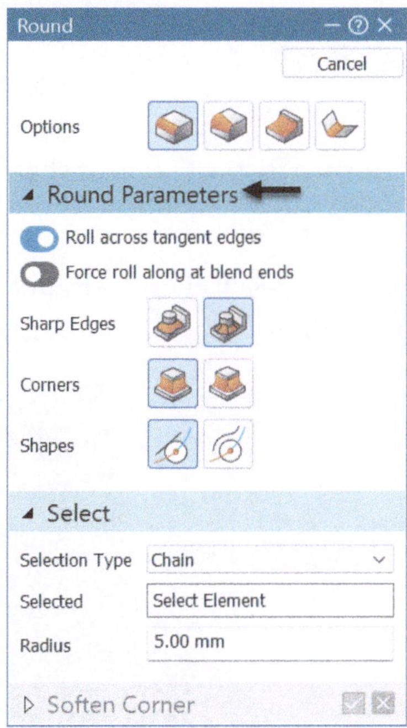

Roll Across Tangent Edges: When adjusting the round, this option ensures a seamless transition by allowing it to roll smoothly across tangent edges it interacts with.

Force Roll along At Blend Ends: This option customizes the blend to either conform closely to the original edge or create a cliff-like effect at its ends by exerting control over its rolling behavior.

Cap Sharp Edges: The **Cap Sharp Edges** option changes how the round is created where the selected edge meets the surrounding faces. When this option is turned on, Solid Edge extends the round across the sharp transition and blends it smoothly into the adjacent faces, creating a continuous **cap** surface.

Roll Along Sharp Edges: This option controls how the round follows sharp outer edges of the model. When this option is turned on, the round keeps the same radius and rolls smoothly over the sharp corner, continuing along the adjoining faces without adding extra material or creating a cap.

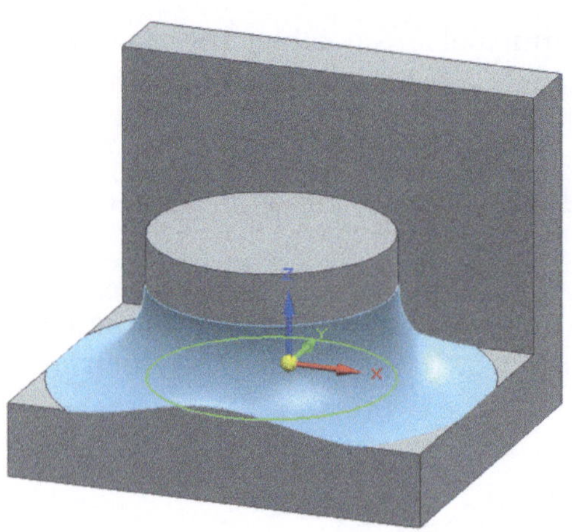

Cap Sharp Edges

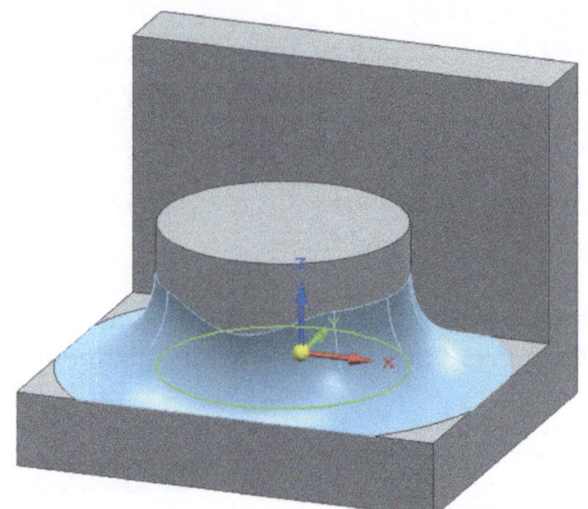

Roll Along Sharp Edges

Miter at Corner: This option adapts the blend to form a distinct seam at sharp corners it encounters, ensuring a precise and deliberate outcome in these areas.

Roll Around Corners: This option refines the blend to gracefully roll around any sharp corners it comes across, maintaining a smooth and continuous flow in the design.

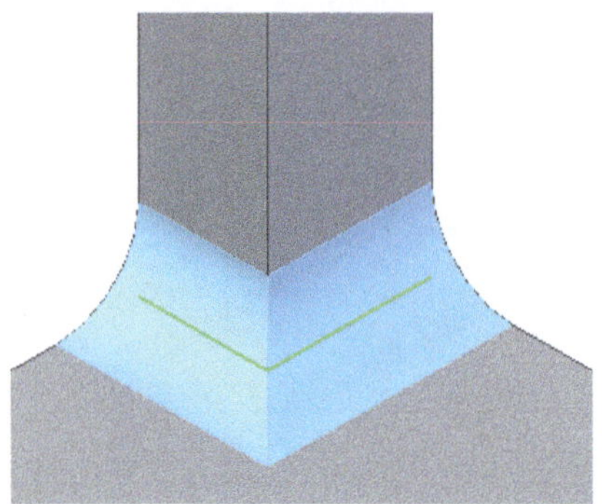

Miter at Corner

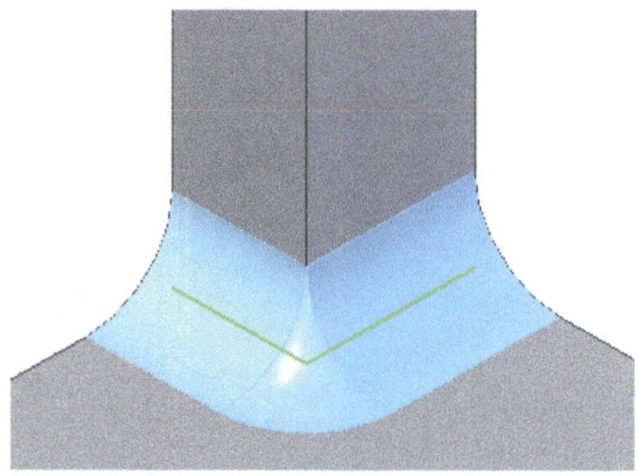

Roll Around Corners

Specify your preferences in the **Round Parameters** section and proceed to select the edges you wish to round. Next, confirm your choices by clicking the green checkmark in the **Select** section. Use the **Preview** button to assess the anticipated outcome before finalizing the process.

For a comprehensive understanding of the rounded feature, ensure that the selected edges align with your design specifications. Once you are satisfied with the preview, proceed to click the **Finish** button, thereby concluding the round feature implementation.

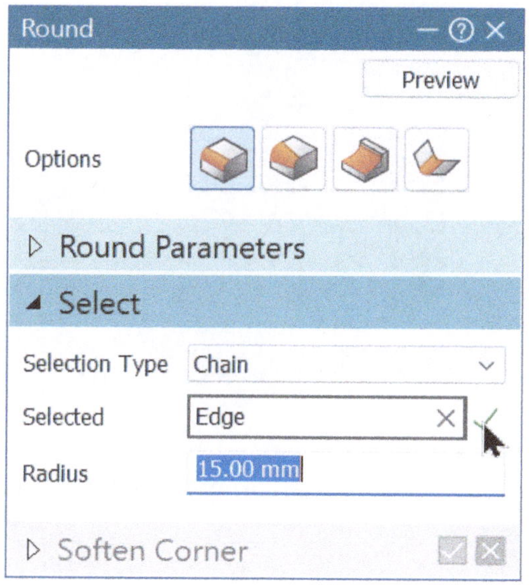

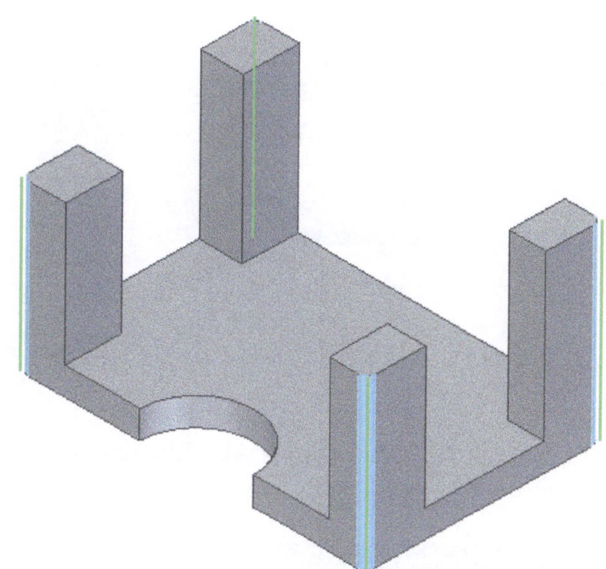

Round (Synchronous)

This command breaks the sharp edges of a model and rounds them. It does not need a sketch to create a round. All you need to have is model edges. Activate this command (click **Home > Solids > Round** on the ribbon) and select edges. As you start selecting edges, you will see a preview of the geometry. You can select the edges located at the back of the model without rotating it. By mistake, if you have selected a wrong edge, you can deselect it by holding the CTRL key and selecting the edge again. You can change the radius by typing a value in the box displayed on the selected edge. As you change the radius, all the selected edges will be updated because they are all part of one instance. If you want the edges to have different radii, you must create rounds in separate instances. Select the required number of edges and right-click to finish this feature. The *Round* feature will be listed in the Pathfinder.

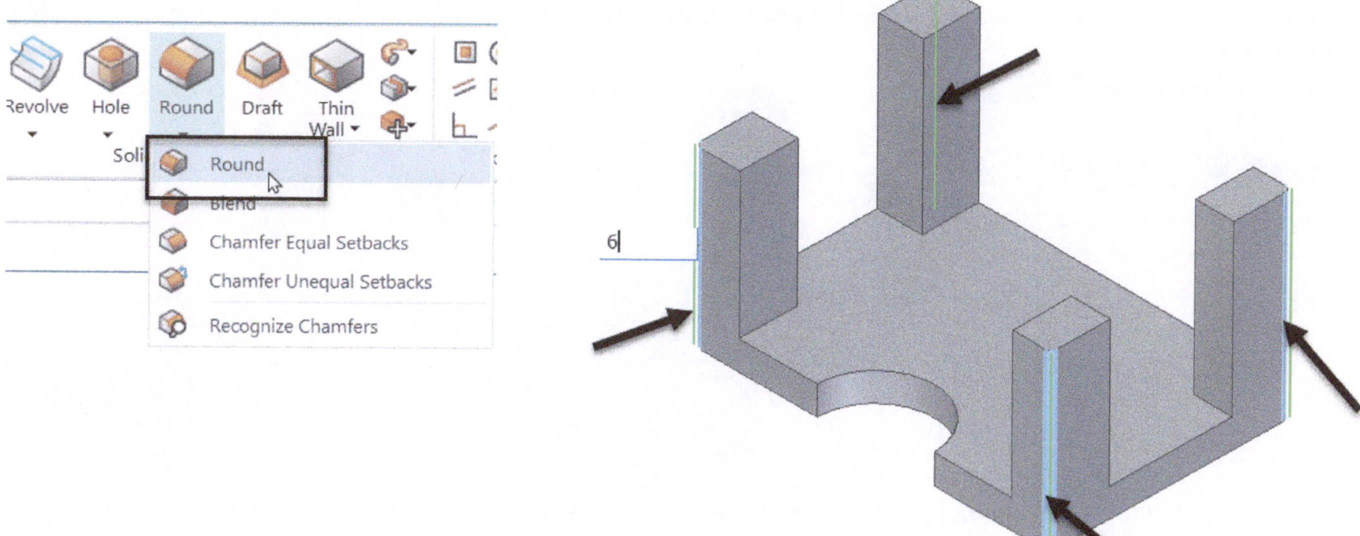

After creating the *Round* feature, the command will still be active to create more *Round* features. Now, if you select the **Loop** option from the **Selection Type** drop-down on the **Round** command bar, the pointer will select a loop of edges on a face. Select a loop and change the radius. As you press Enter, all of the edges will be rounded.

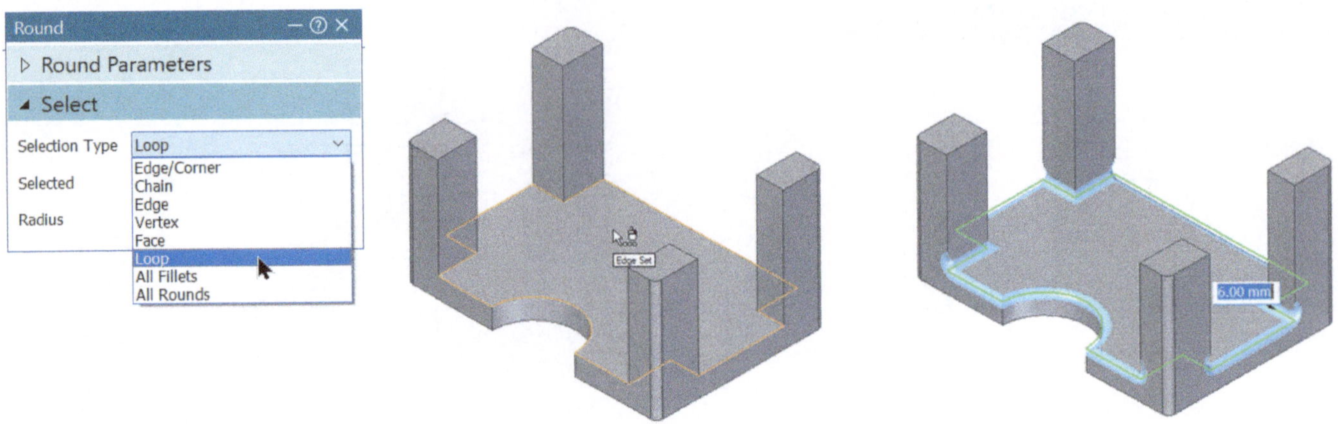

If you select the **Selection Type > All Fillets** option on the command bar, all fillets (concave corners) will be created on the model.

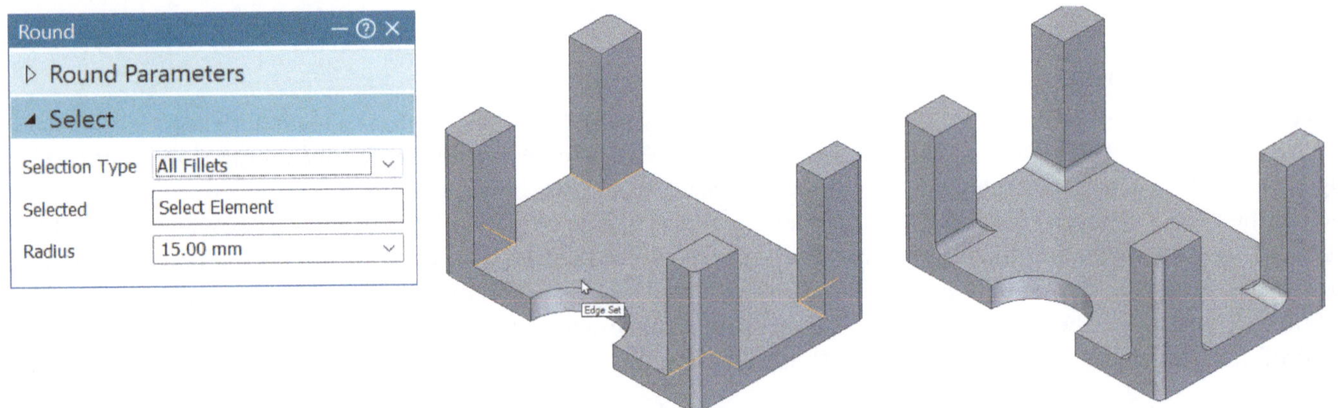

If you select the **Selection Type > All Rounds** option on the dialog bar, all rounds (convex corners) will be created on the model.

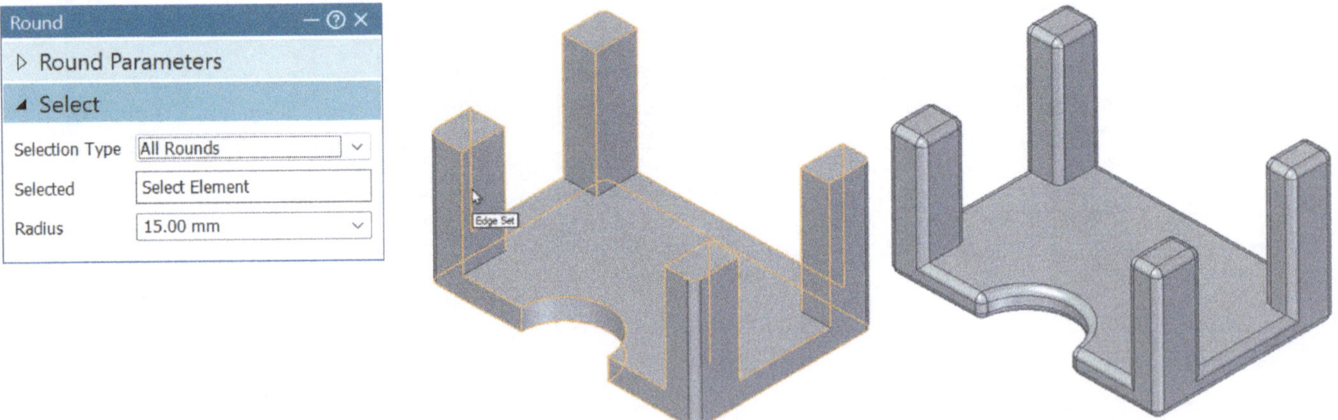

If you ever needed to change the radius of a *Round* feature, select it from the Pathfinder or the model, and then click the diameter value appearing on the feature. Next, type in a new value in the box that pops up on the *Round* feature and press Enter. To remove a *Round* feature, right-click on it, and then select **Delete**.

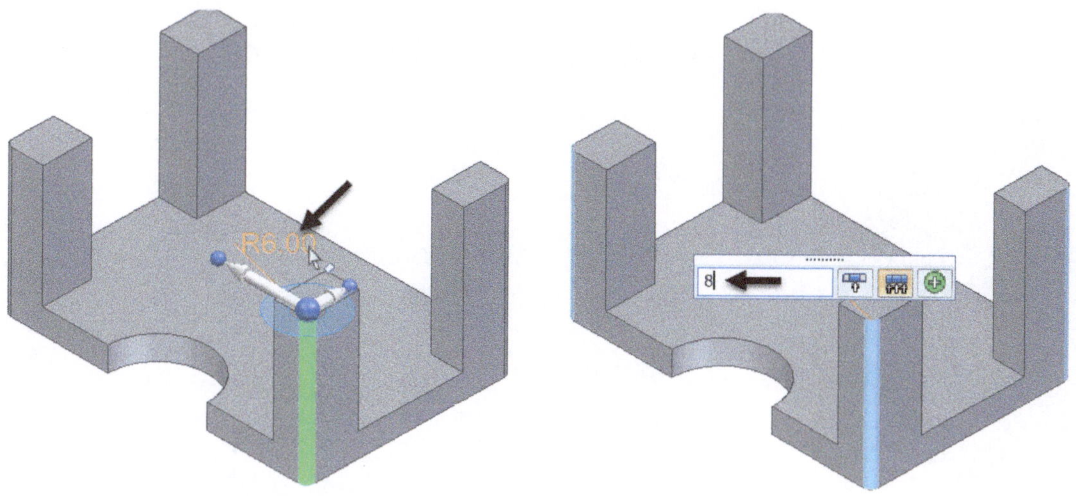

Blend (Synchronous)

This command creates a variable radius blend, blend between two faces, and surface blend. These three types of blends are explained next.

Variable Radius Blend

Navigate to the **Home** tab and find the **Solids** group. Within this group, click the **Round** drop-down and select the **Blend** command. On the **Blend** command bar, select **Options** > **Variable radius.** Choose the edges that you intend to round and click the **Accept** button on the **Select** section.

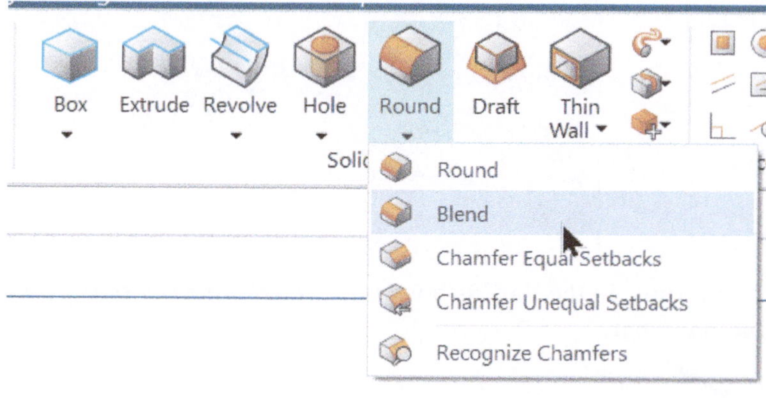

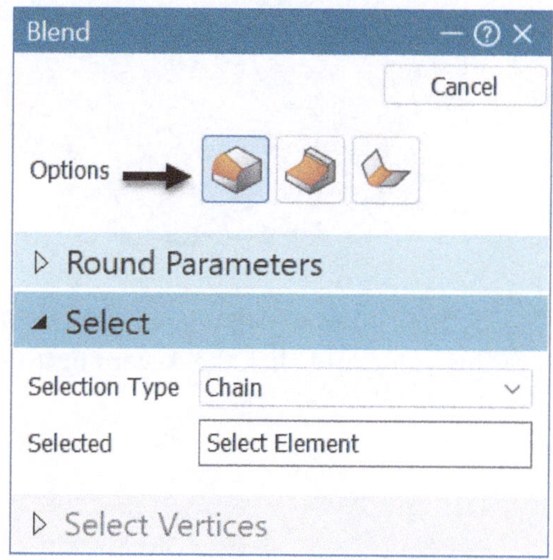

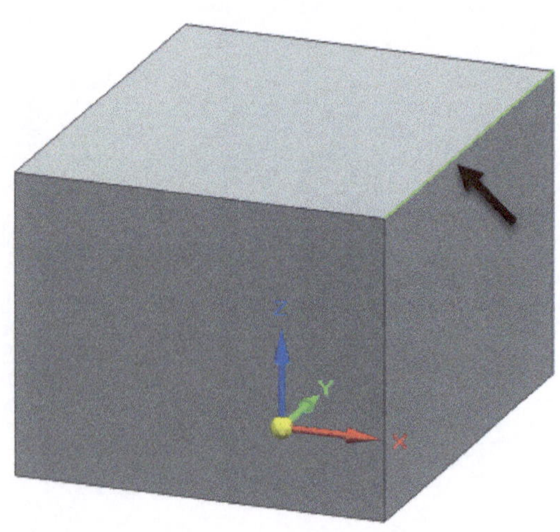

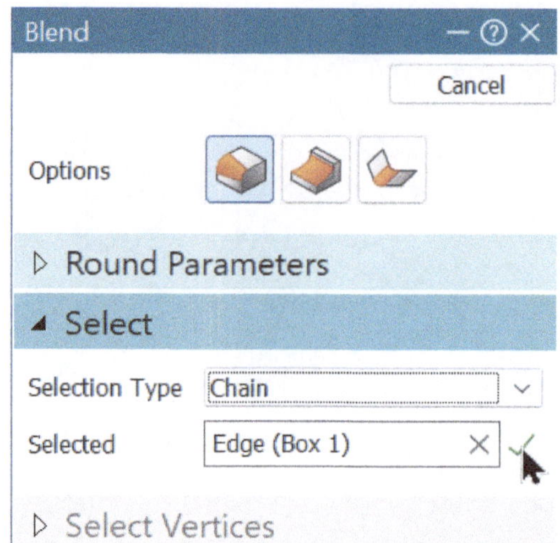

Define the end to which you want to apply the starting radius. In the **Radius** box of the **Select Vertices** step, input a radius value and press ENTER.

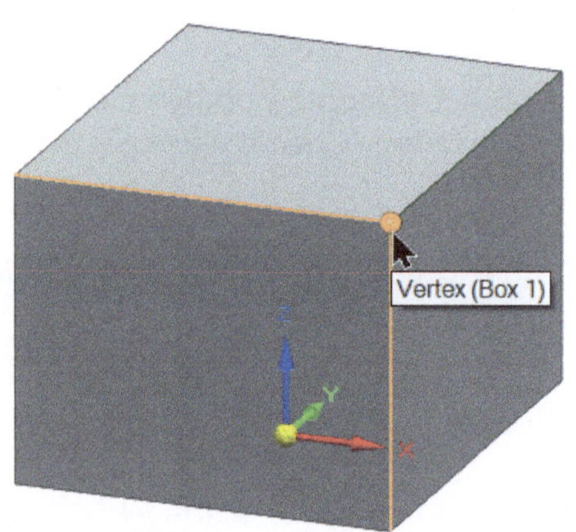

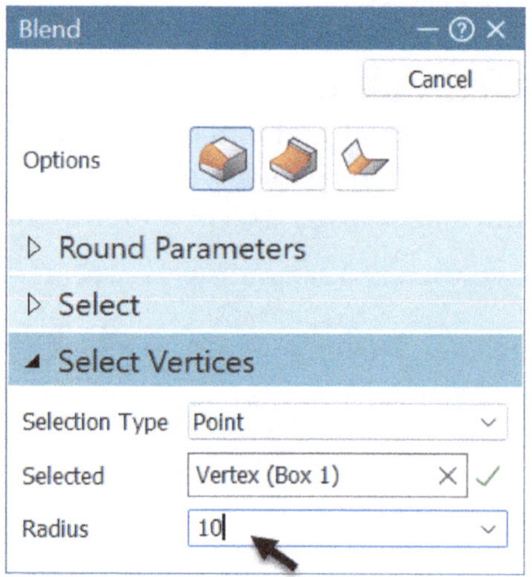

Specify the end to which you want to apply the ending radius. In the **Radius** box of the **Select Vertices** step, input a radius value and click the **Accept** button on the command bar.

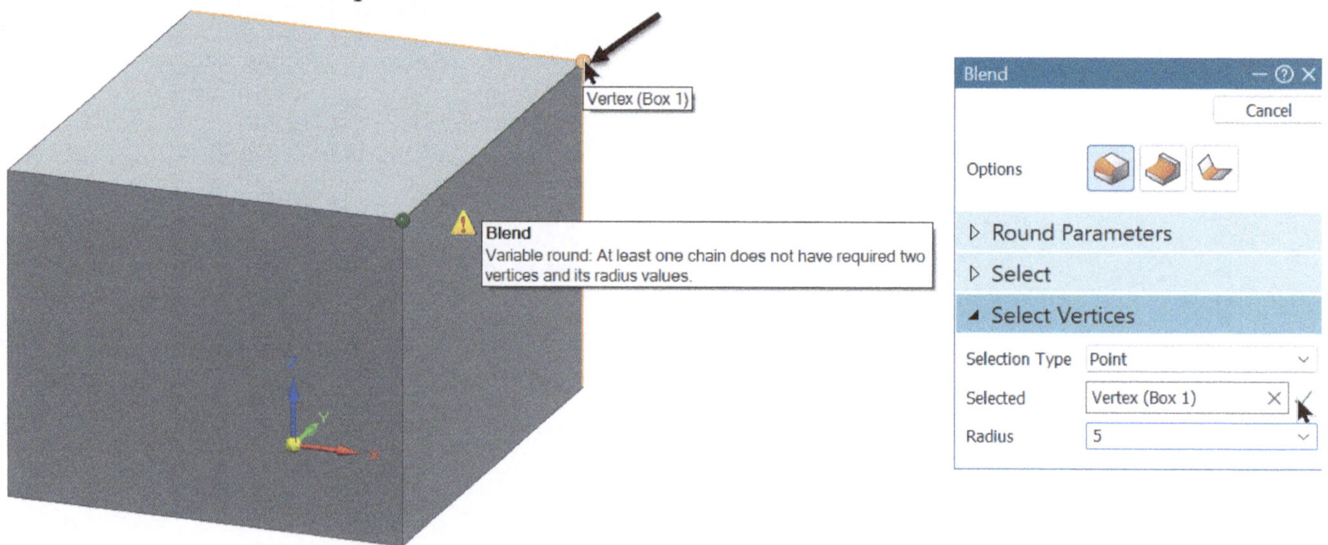

Return to the **Blend** command bar and click the **Finish** button.

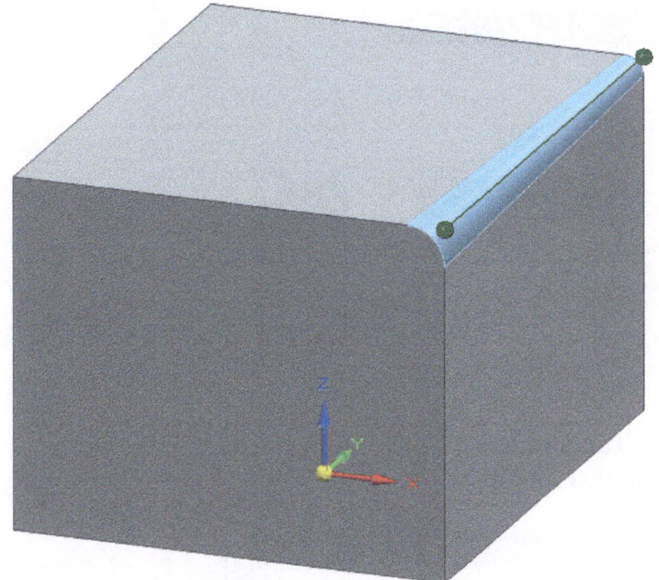

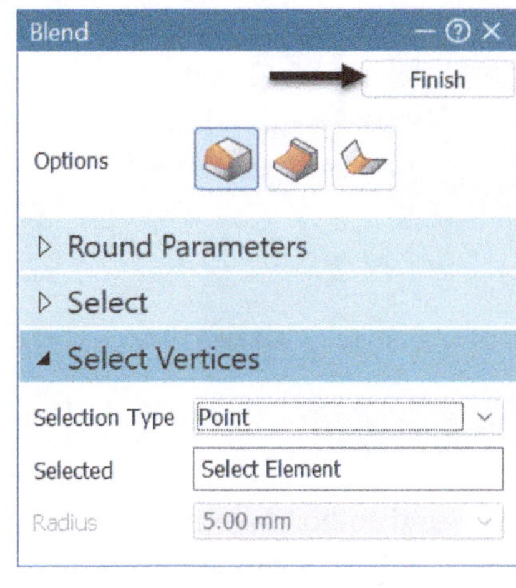

Blend between faces

Navigate to the **Home** tab and find the **Solids** group. Within this group, click the **Round** drop-down and select the **Blend** command. On the **Blend** command bar, opt for **Blend**. Next, select an option from the **Shape** drop-down in the **Select Step** section. Choose the faces that you intend to blend. In the **Radius** box of the **Select Vertices** step, input a radius value and click the **Accept** button on the command bar.

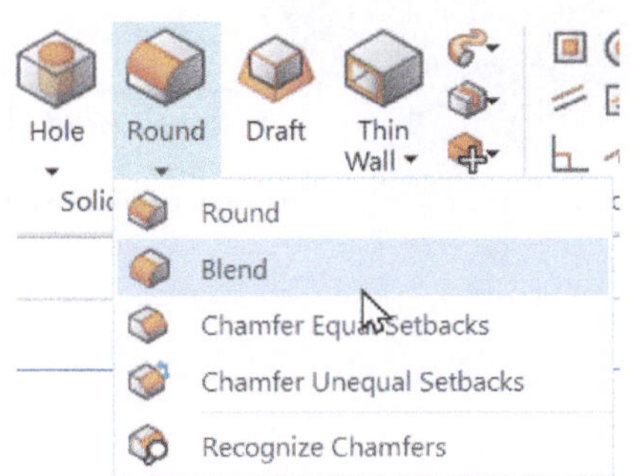

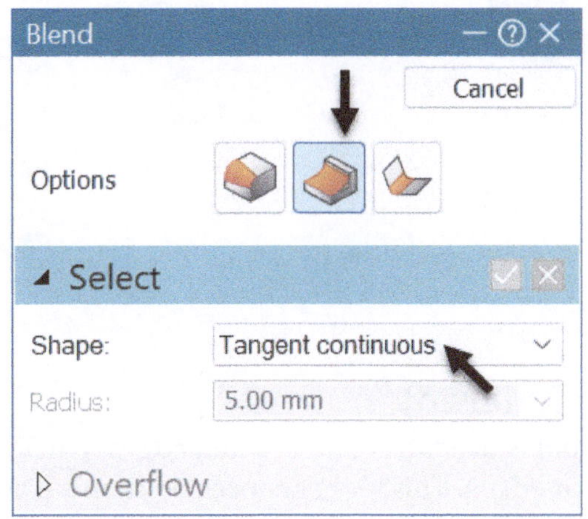

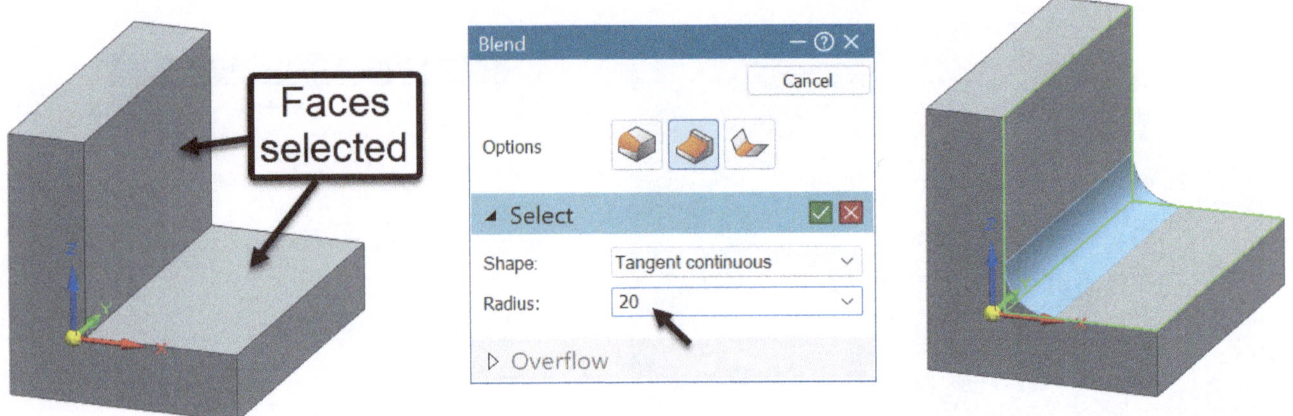

If you want the blend to be tangent to an edge, select the **Tangent Hold Line** option on the **Blend** command bar and select edges on eitherside every input face or just a single input face. The blend will be created tangent to the selected hold lines.

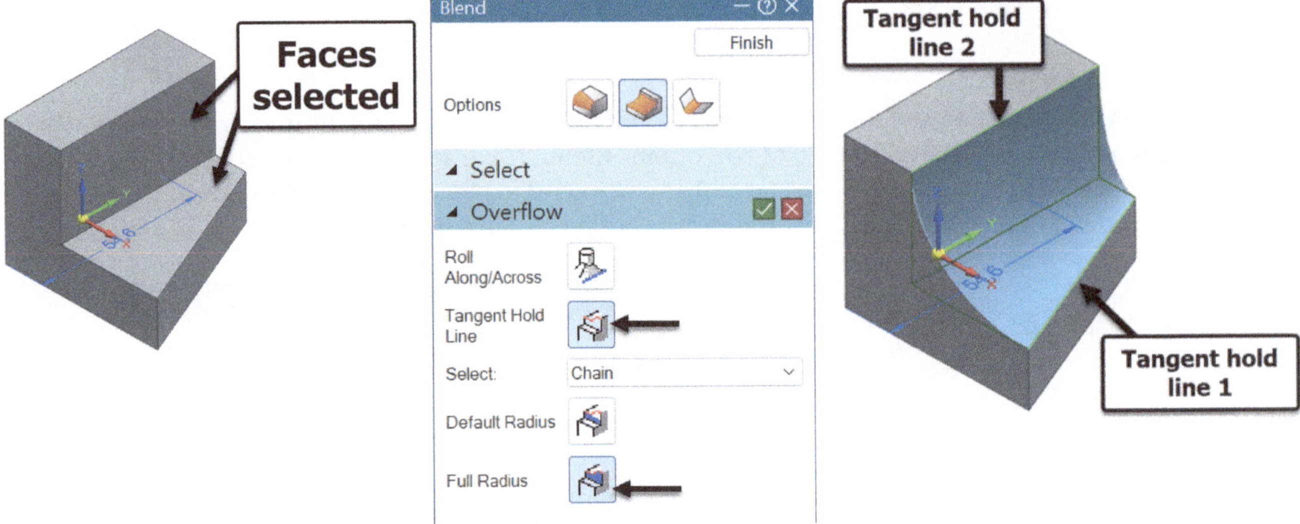

Chamfer (Ordered)

The **Chamfer** tool is used to create beveled edges in a 3D model, proving beneficial for introducing gradual slopes between faces or edges. This tool enhances both visual aesthetics and functional aspects by addressing the need for smoother transitions in geometric features. It is especially useful in scenarios where sharp edges may be impractical or uncomfortable. The **Chamfer** tool allows for precise control over dimensions, using three options: **Equal setbacks**, **Angle and setback**, and **2 Setbacks**.

Chamfer with Equal setbacks

To apply this type of chamfer, start by navigating to the **Home** tab and locating the **Solids** group. Within this group, access the **Round** drop-down and select the **Chamfer** command. On the **Chamfer** command bar, click **Options > Equal Setbacks**. This choice allows you to establish a consistent setback distance for the chamfer, promoting uniformity and symmetry along the edges. Subsequently, choose the specific edge you wish to chamfer. Input the desired distance value in the **Setback** box on the **Chamfer** command bar and execute the chamfer by clicking the green check. To finalize the process, click **Finish**.

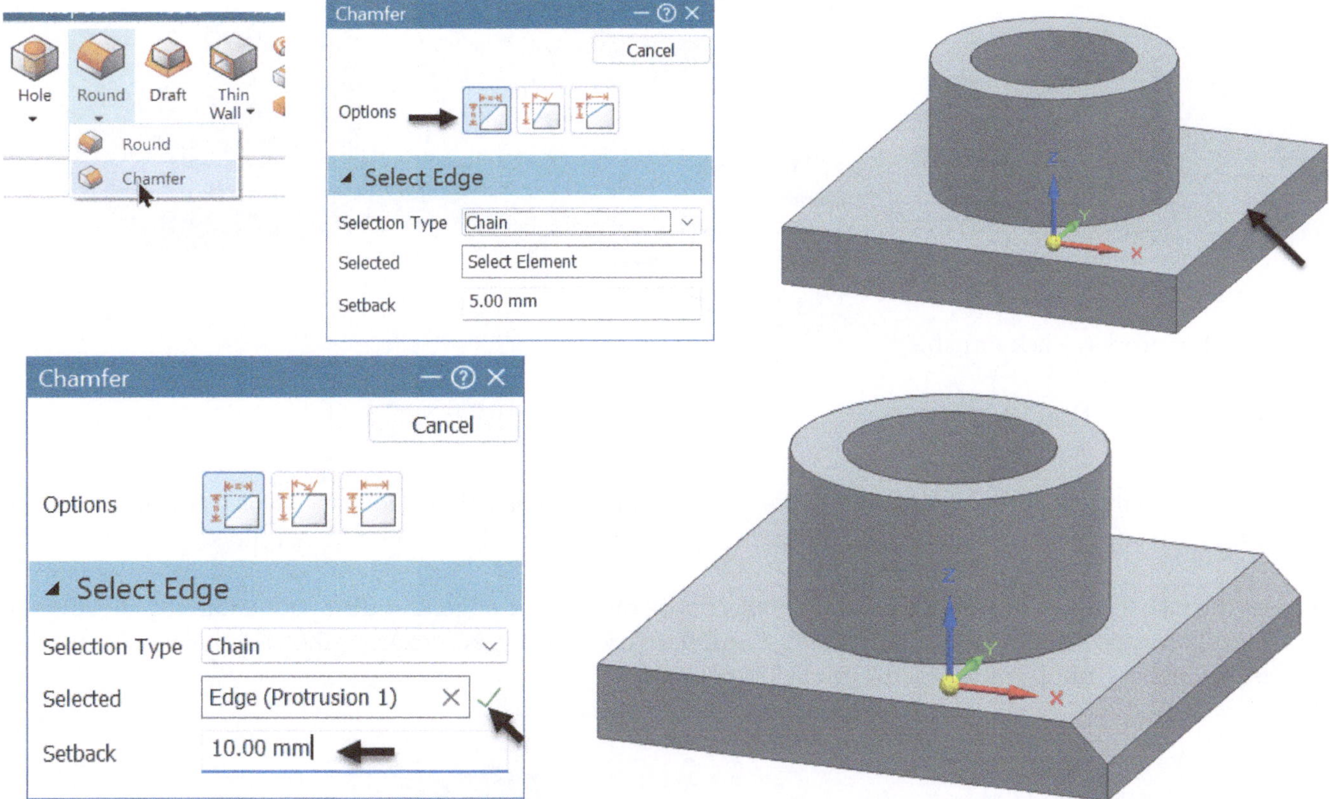

Chamfer with Angle and Setback

To apply this type chamfer, start by selecting the **Chamfer** command. On the **Chamfer** command bar, click **Options** > **Angle and Setback**. This option allows you to establish a setback distance for one face and specify the chamfer angle. The setback on the opposite adjacent face is automatically calculated. Next, select the face adjacent to which the chamfer is to be added. Next, pick the specific edge you want to chamfer and click the green check. Enter the desired distance and angle values in the **Setback** and **Angle** boxes, respectively. Execute the chamfer by clicking the green check.

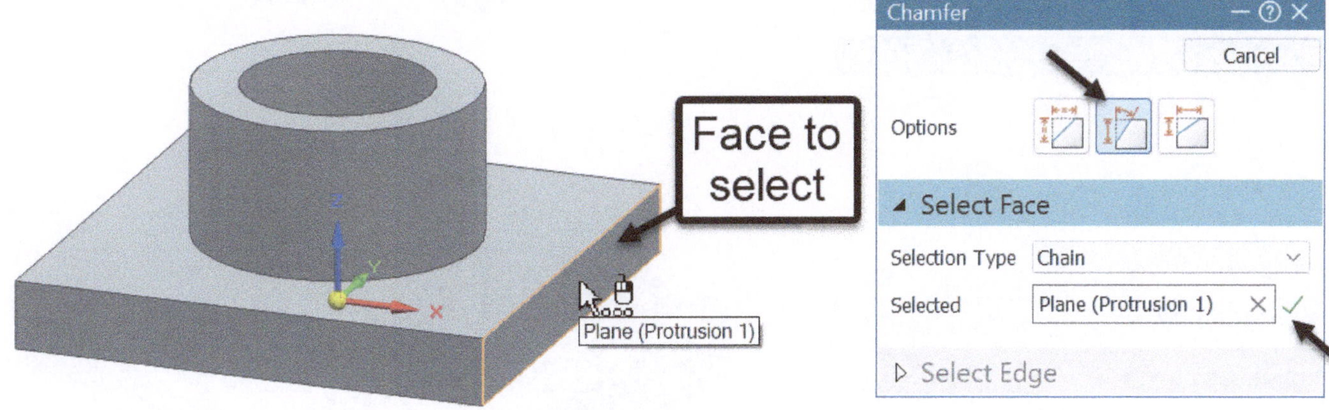

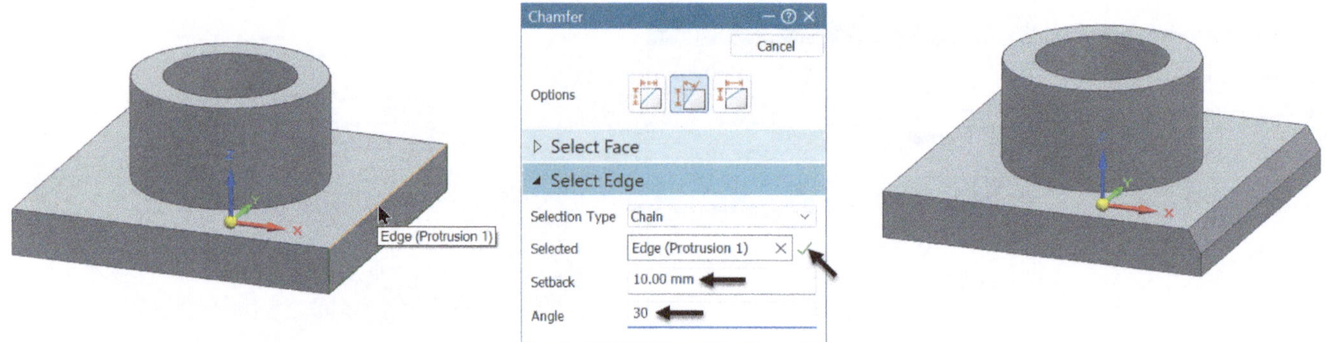

To complete the process, click **Finish**.

Chamfer with 2 Setbacks

Start by clicking on the **Chamfer** command and then click **Options > The 2 Setbacks** 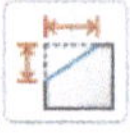 . This lets you set setback distances for each adjacent face separately, automatically calculating angles for tailored chamfers.

Now, pick the face where you want the chamfer, then choose the specific edge. Confirm your choice by clicking the green check. Enter the setback values in **Setback 1** and **Setback 2** boxes, and execute the chamfer by clicking the green check. Finally, complete the process by clicking **Finish**.

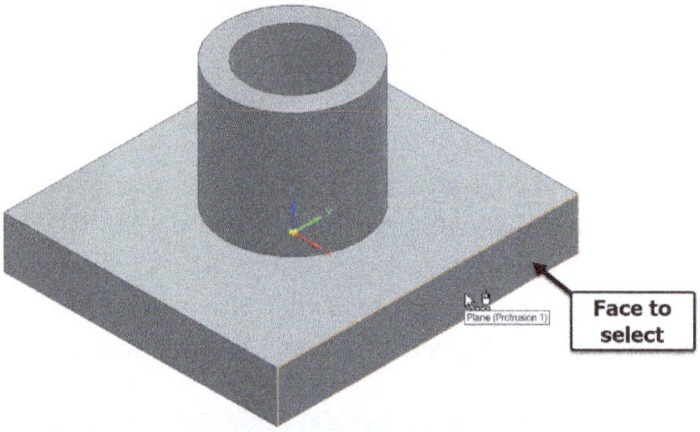

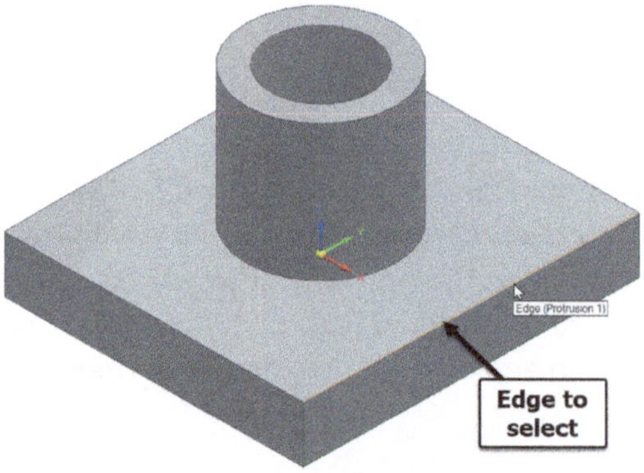

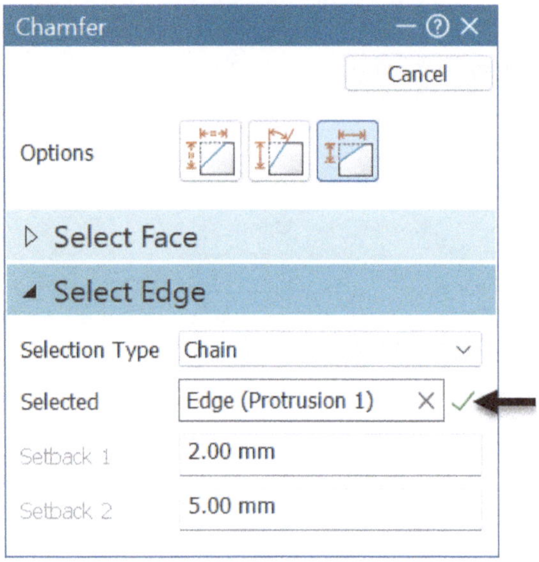

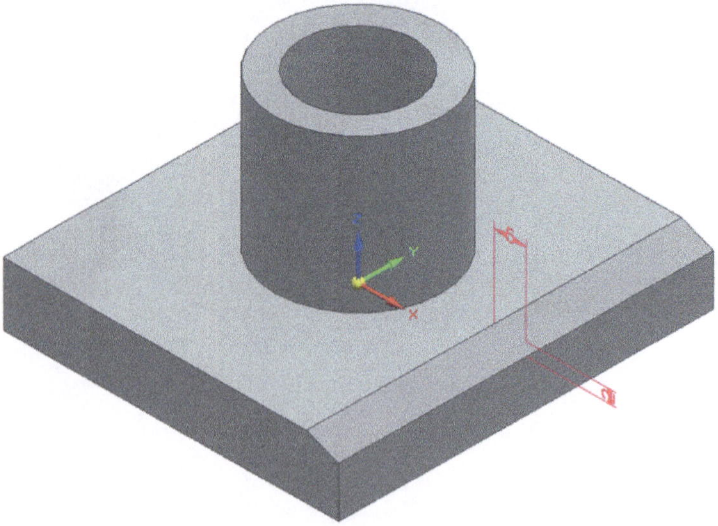

Chamfer Equal Setbacks (Synchronous)

The **Chamfer** and **Round** commands are commonly used to break sharp edges. The difference is that the **Chamfer Equal Setbacks** command adds a 45-degree bevel face to the model, whereas the **Round** command adds a curved face. A chamfer is also a placed feature. Activate this command (click **Home > Round > Chamfer Equal Setbacks** on the ribbon) and select an edge to chamfer. Type-in the distance value in the box attached to the chamfer and press Enter to create the chamfer.

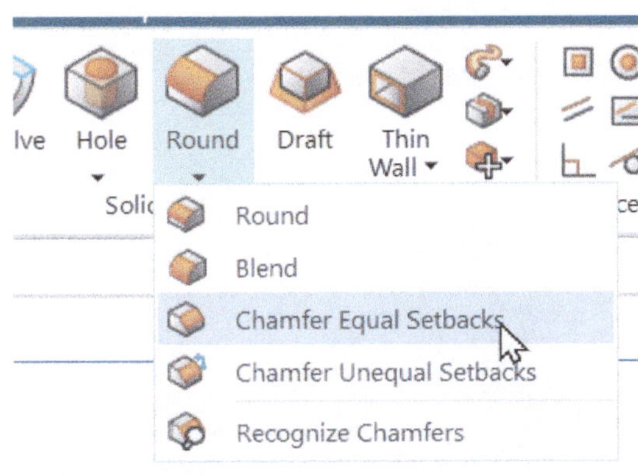

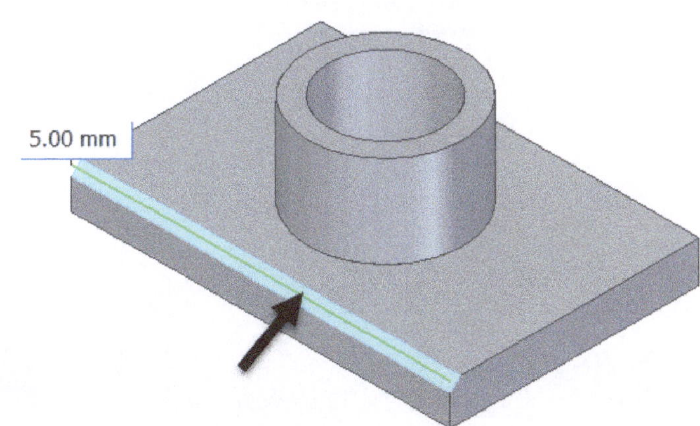

Tthe **Chamfer Equal Setbacks** command gives a good result for non-planar edges.

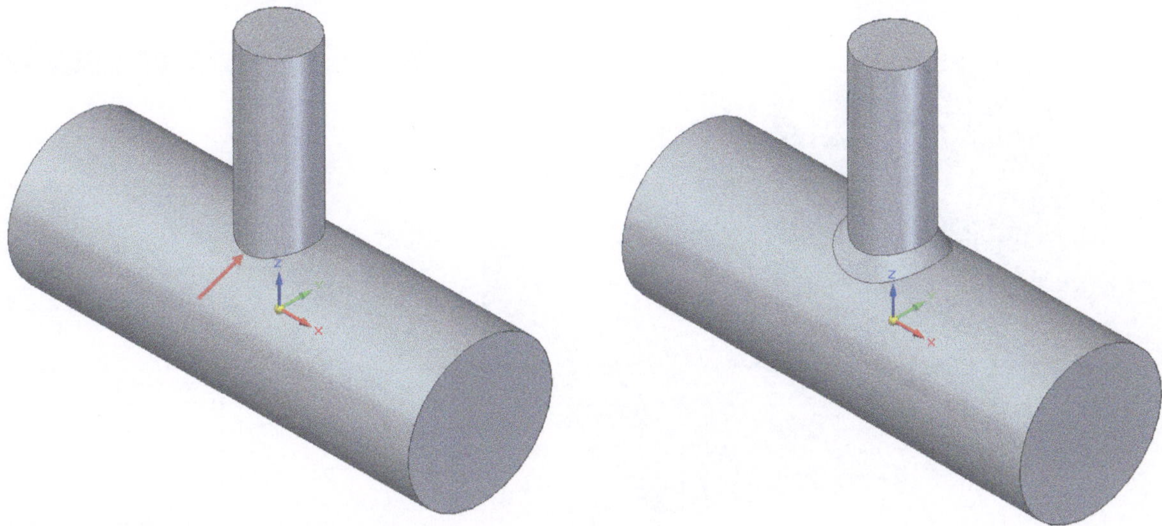

Chamfer Unequal Setbacks (Synchronous)

This command will be useful if you want a chamfer to have different setbacks on both sides of the edge. On the ribbon, click **Home > Solids > Chamfer Unequal Setbacks**. Next, select **Options > Angle and Setback**. Next, you need to select both a face and an edge. First, you need to select a face, which acts as a reference. Click the green check on the command bar, and then type-in the **Setback** and **Angle** value. Solid Edge measures the setback distance and angle concerning the selected face. Select the edge to be chamfered, click the green check, and then click **Finish**.

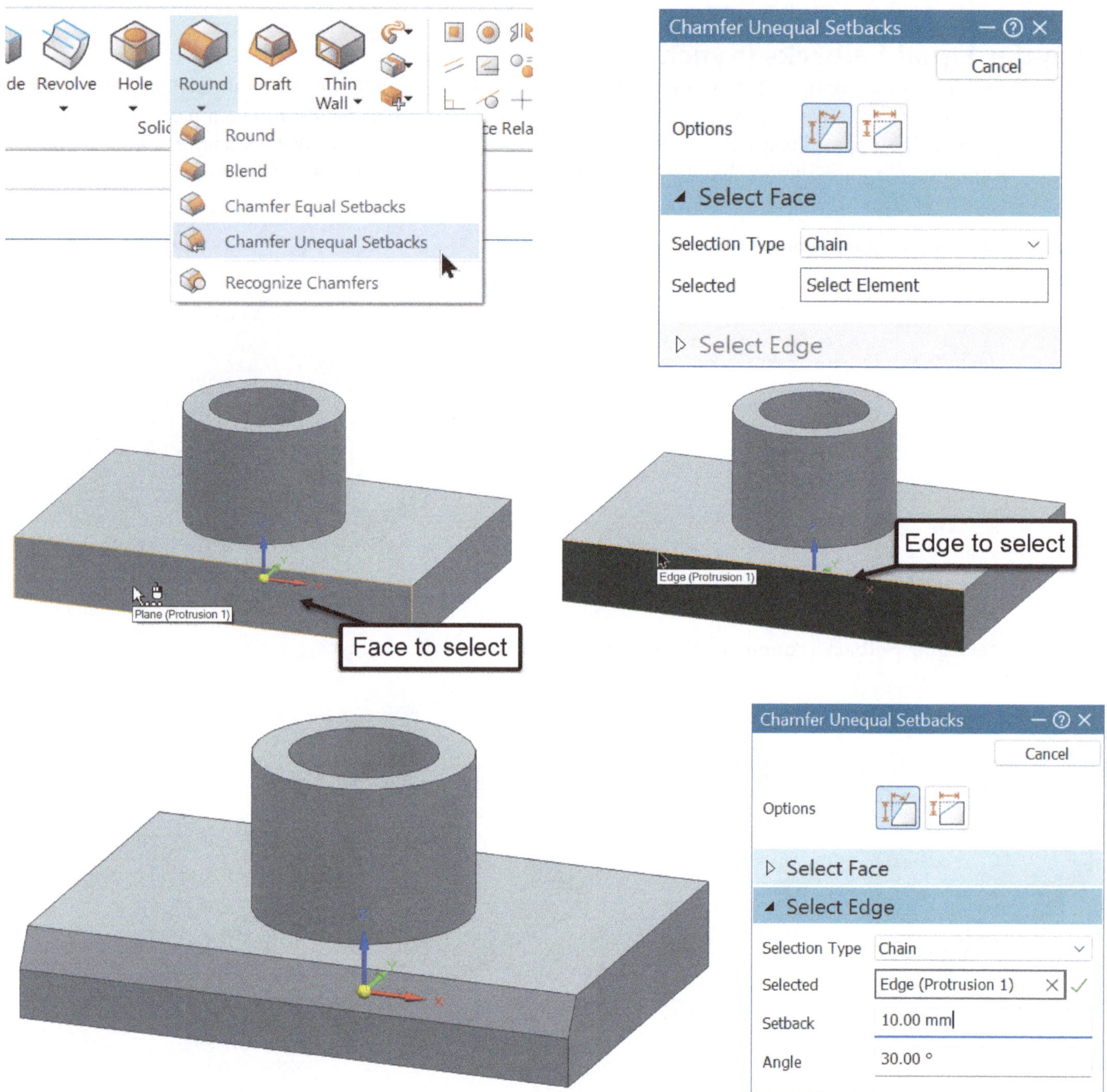

Tip: You can create rounds and chamfers by selecting the edges of multiple bodies of a part.

Draft (Ordered)

The **Draft** command is used in the context of creating drafts on part faces. Draft refers to the taper or angle applied to a part face, typically in the mold design or casting process. Adding draft to faces facilitates the ejection of parts from molds and helps prevent undercuts.

Access the **Draft** command on the **Home** tab in the **Solids** group. On the **Draft** command bar, click **Draft Options**, and use the **Draft Options** dialog box to specify the reference or starting point for the draft feature. The options on this dialog are discussed next.

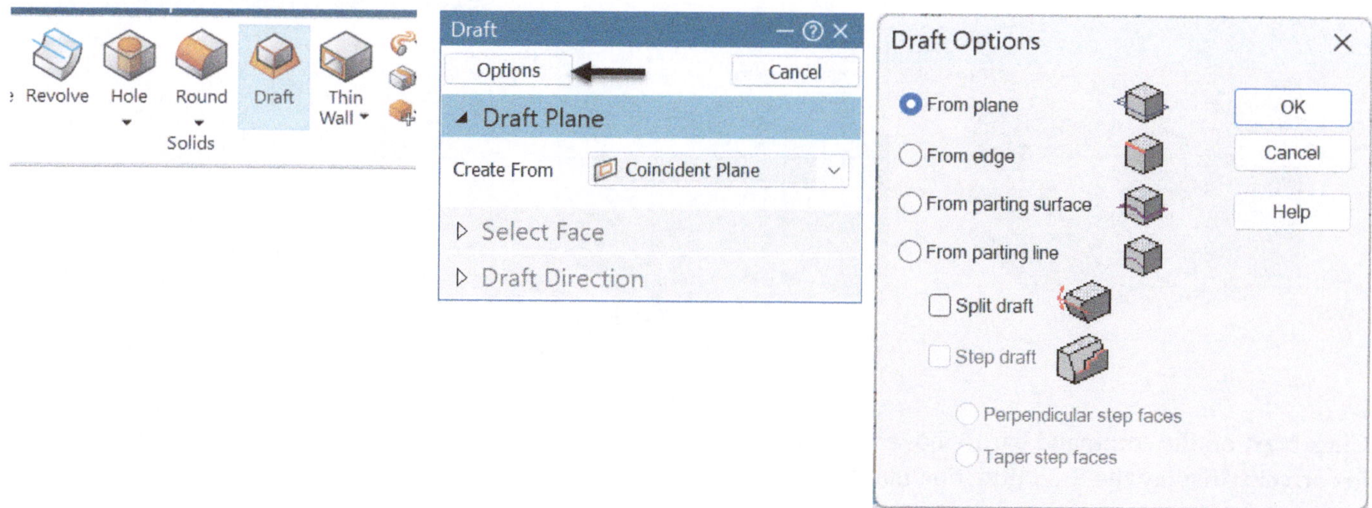

From plane
You can set the draft angle by choosing this option and specifying it based on a reference plane or a planar face.

From edge
To determine the draft angle from a specific part edge, choose this option.

From parting surface
You can set the draft angle by choosing this option and specifying it with respect to a designated construction surface.

From parting line
This option allows you to establish the draft angle by referencing a construction curve.

Split draft
If you check this option, it allows you to add draft angles to the part in two directions at the same time. This means you can make adjustments on both sides of the part simultaneously.

Step draft
This feature is only applicable when choosing **From Parting Line** or **From Edge**. The **Step draft** option is designed to ensure a consistent draft angle, particularly in cases involving a multi-segmented parting line. This option automatically fills gaps to maintain a uniform draft angle along the parting line. It is important to be aware that the parting line should not intersect with the draft plane.

Perpendicular step faces
Selecting this option ensures that step faces remain perpendicular to the draft face during a **Step Draft** operation

Taper step faces
This option makes step faces tapered with respect to the draft face during a Step Draft operation.

Click **OK** on the **Draft Options** dialog and define the draft plane if you have selected the **From Plane** option. If you have selected the **From Edge**, From **Parting Surface**, or **From Parting Line** option, select the relevant parting geometry. Choose the faces for drafting and set the draft angle. Next, click **Accept** on the command bar.

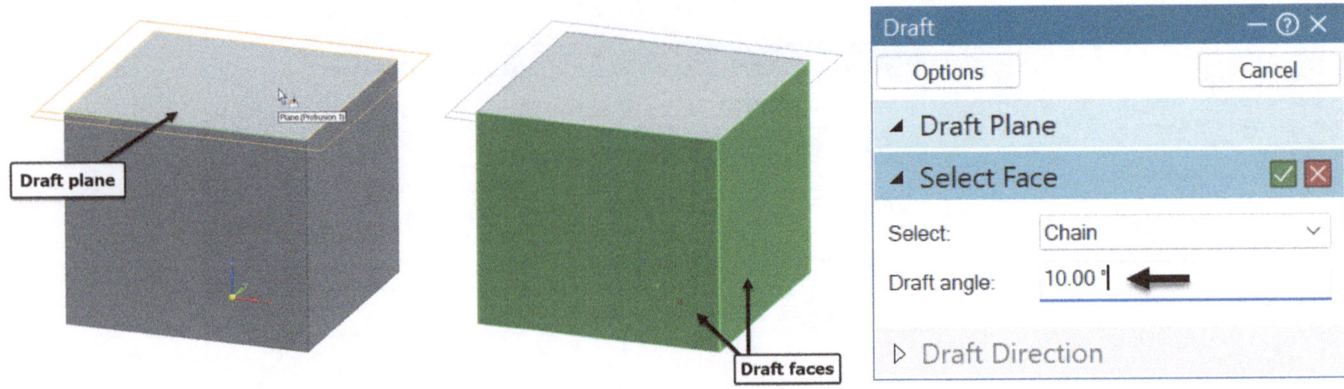

Click **Next** on the command bar to move to the **Draft Direction** Step. Position the cursor in the graphics window to correctly display the draft direction handle, and click to confirm.

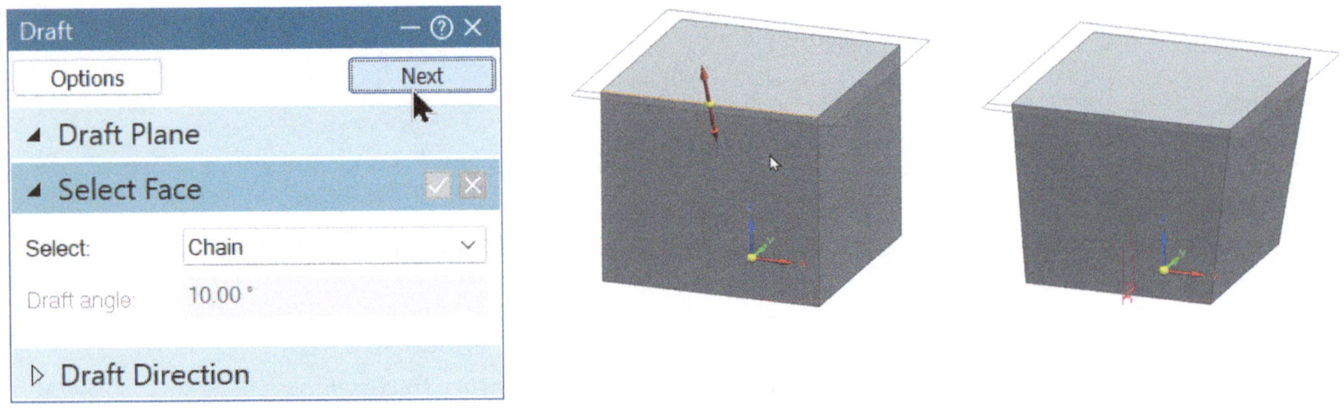

Finish the feature by clicking the **Finish** button.

Draft (Synchronous)

When creating cast or plastic parts, you are often required to add a draft on them so that they can be molded. A draft is an angle or taper applied to parts' faces to make it easier to remove them from a mold. When creating *Extrude* features, you can predefine the draft angle. However, most of the time, it is easier to apply the draft after creating the features. Activate the **Draft** command from the **Solids** panel. Select a face that will act as a reference plane for the draft. The draft angle will be measured with reference to this face. After selecting the reference plane, select the faces to draft. There are four options (**Chain**, **Face**, **Loop**, and **All Normal Faces**) on the command bar, which will help you select the faces to draft. As you select the faces to draft, a two-sided arrow will appear along with a box. Use this two-sided arrow to define the direction of pull, and then type-in a value (angle) in the box.

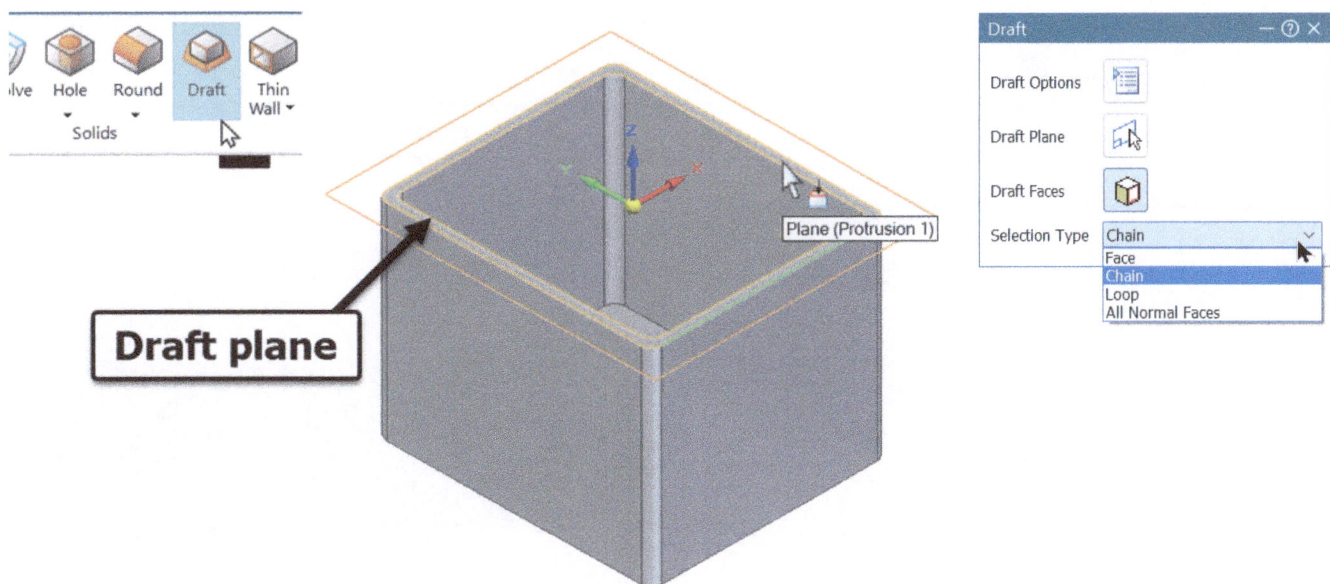

Press Enter to create the *Draft* feature.

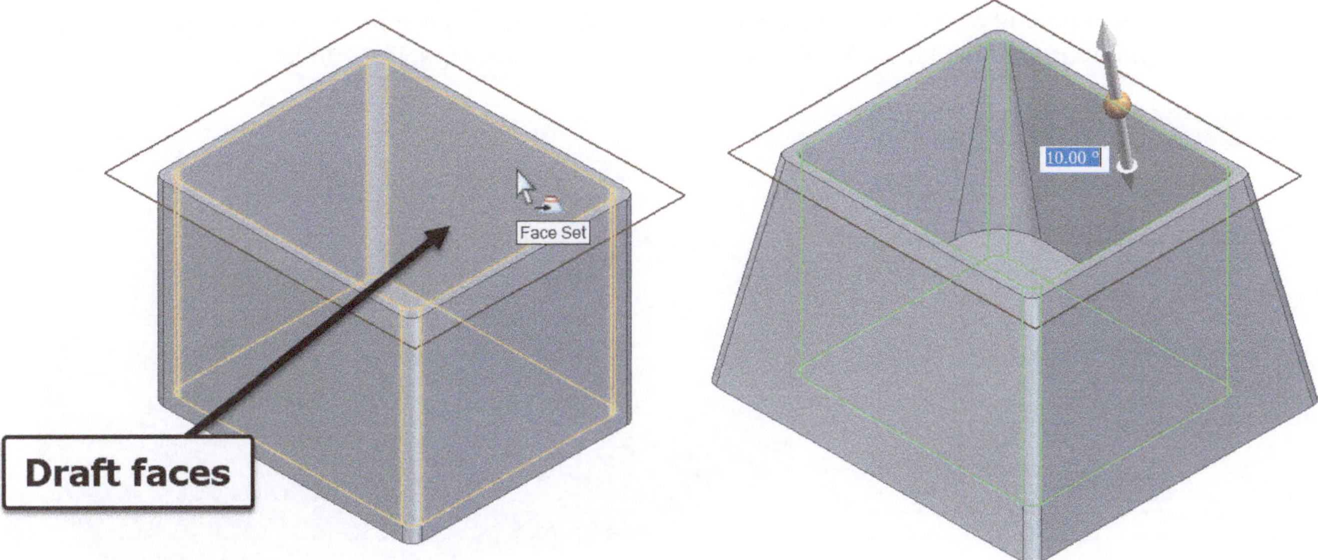

Thin Wall (Ordered)

In Solid Edge, you can create a thin-walled enclosure around a solid part using the "**Thin Wall**" command. This feature is particularly useful when designing components that require a hollow interior, which can serve various purposes such as minimizing material usage, reducing overall part weight, or accommodating elements like wires or fluid passages.

To initiate the Thin Wall feature, go to the **Home** tab on the ribbon and locate the **Thin Wall** command within the **Thin Wall** drop-down of the **Solids** group. On the command bar, modify the offset direction by selecting **Offset Inside, Offset Outside**, or **Symmetrical**. Click the preferred button and then specify the common wall thickness. Input the desired value in the **Common Thickness** box, which will be uniformly applied to most or all of the part walls.

If there are specific faces you want to keep open, navigate to the **Open Faces** section. Select the faces to remain open and then click the **Accept** button on the command bar.

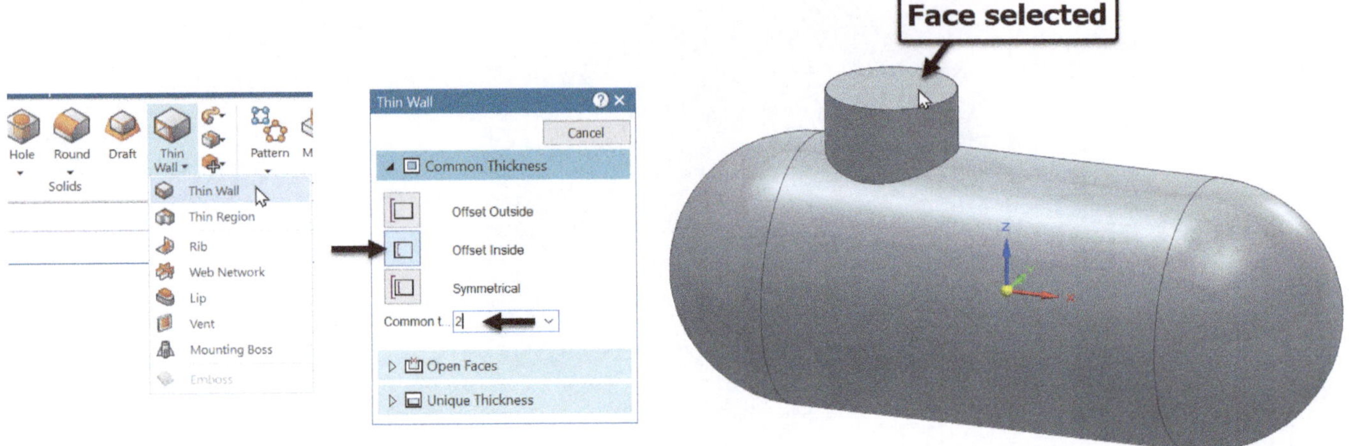

Preview the feature by clicking the **Preview** button. If the previewed feature doesn't meet your requirements, you can revisit any step for adjustments. You have the flexibility to preview and modify the feature multiple times before finalizing. It's important to note that open walls are optional, and you can preview the feature at any point after defining the common wall thickness. Now, make necessary offset changes, if required.

For varying wall thickness, choose the **Unique Thickness** button on the command bar. This action takes you to the **Unique Thickness** step, where you can select faces and input distinct thickness values in the **Unique Thickness** box. Next, click **Preview** to preview the feature. If everything seems fine, complete the feature by clicking the **Finish** button.

Thin Wall (Synchronous)

The **Thin Wall** is another useful command that can be applied directly to a solid model. It allows you to take a solid geometry and make it hollow. It can be a powerful and time-saving technique when designing parts that call for thin walls such as bottles, tanks, and containers. This command is easy to use. You should have a solid part and then activate this command from the **Solids** panel. Now, select the faces to remove, and then type-in the wall thickness in the box that appears on the model. Click the arrow on the model to specify whether the thickness is added inside or outside the model. Right-click to finish the feature.

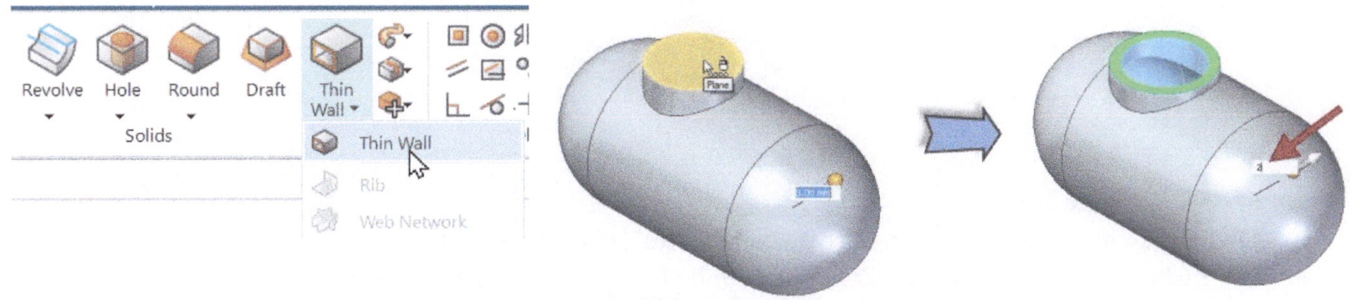

Examples

Example 1 (Millimetres)

In this example, you will create the part shown below.

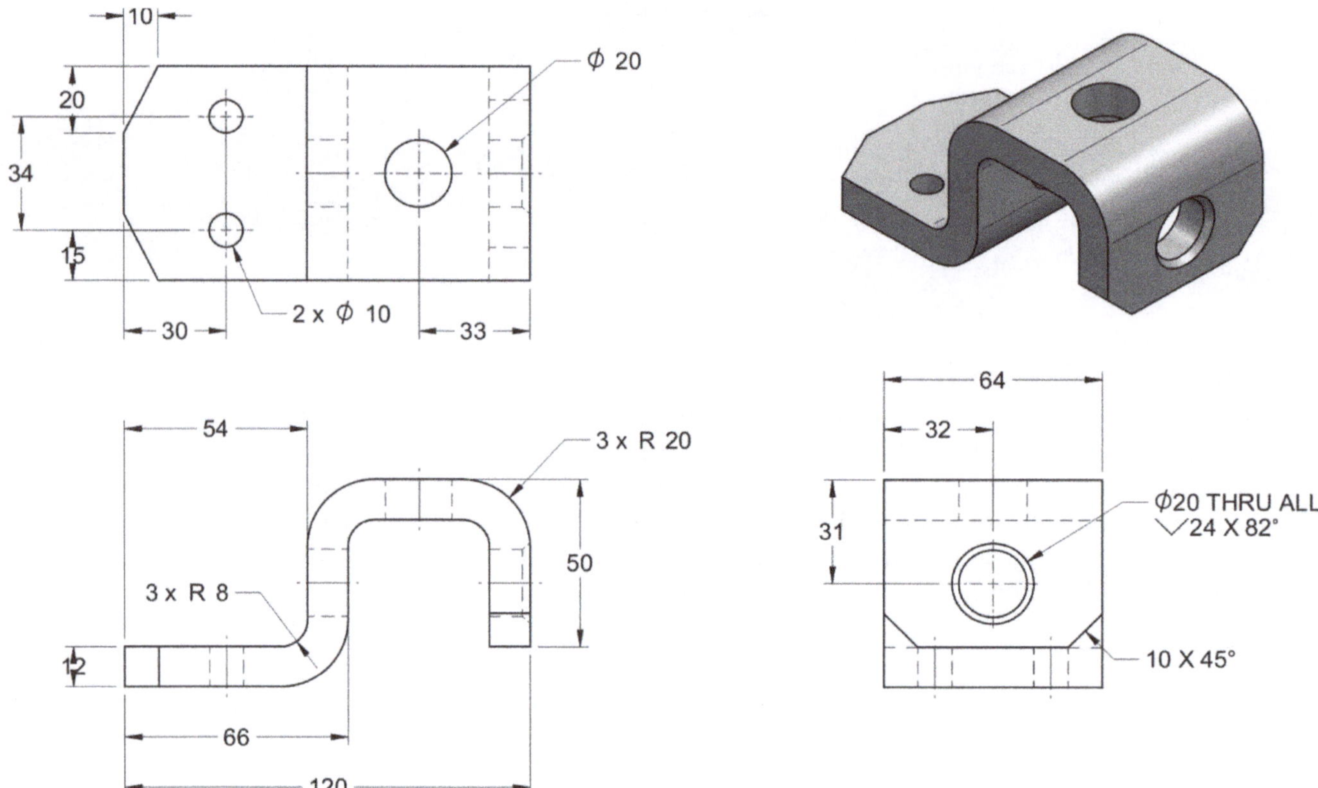

1. Start **Solid Edge 2026.**
2. On the **Discover** page, under the **Create New** section, click **New** button.
3. On the **New** dialog, **iso metric.par** template and click **OK**; a new part file is opened.
4. Click **Continue with Ordered** button on the **Ordered as default** dialog; the Ordered environment is set as the default environment.
5. To start a new sketch, click **Home > Sketch > Sketch** on the ribbon.
6. Select the Front (xz) plane from the base reference planes displayed in the graphics window; the sketch is started and the sketch plane is oriented normal to the screen.
7. On the ribbon, click **Home > Draw > Line** and draw the sketch, as shown below. Click **Close Sketch** on the **Close** group of the ribbon. Next, click **Finish** on **Sketch** command bar.
8. Create the *Extrude* feature of 64 mm thickness.

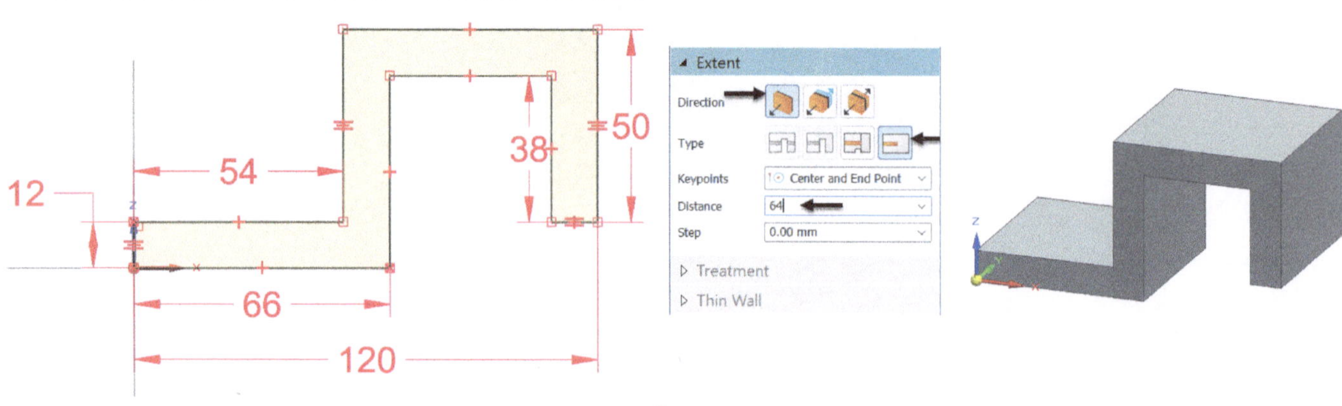

9. On the ribbon, click **Home > Solids > Hole**  .

10. On the command bar, click the **Options** button; the **Hole Options** dialog pops up.
11. On this dialog, select the **Countersink** button and set the **Standard** to **mm**.
12. Type-in 20, 24, and 82 in the **Hole Diameter**, **Countersink Diameter**, **Countersink Angle** boxes.
13. Set the **Hole Extents** type to **Through All**. Click **OK** to close the dialog.
14. Click on the right-side face of the model, as shown.

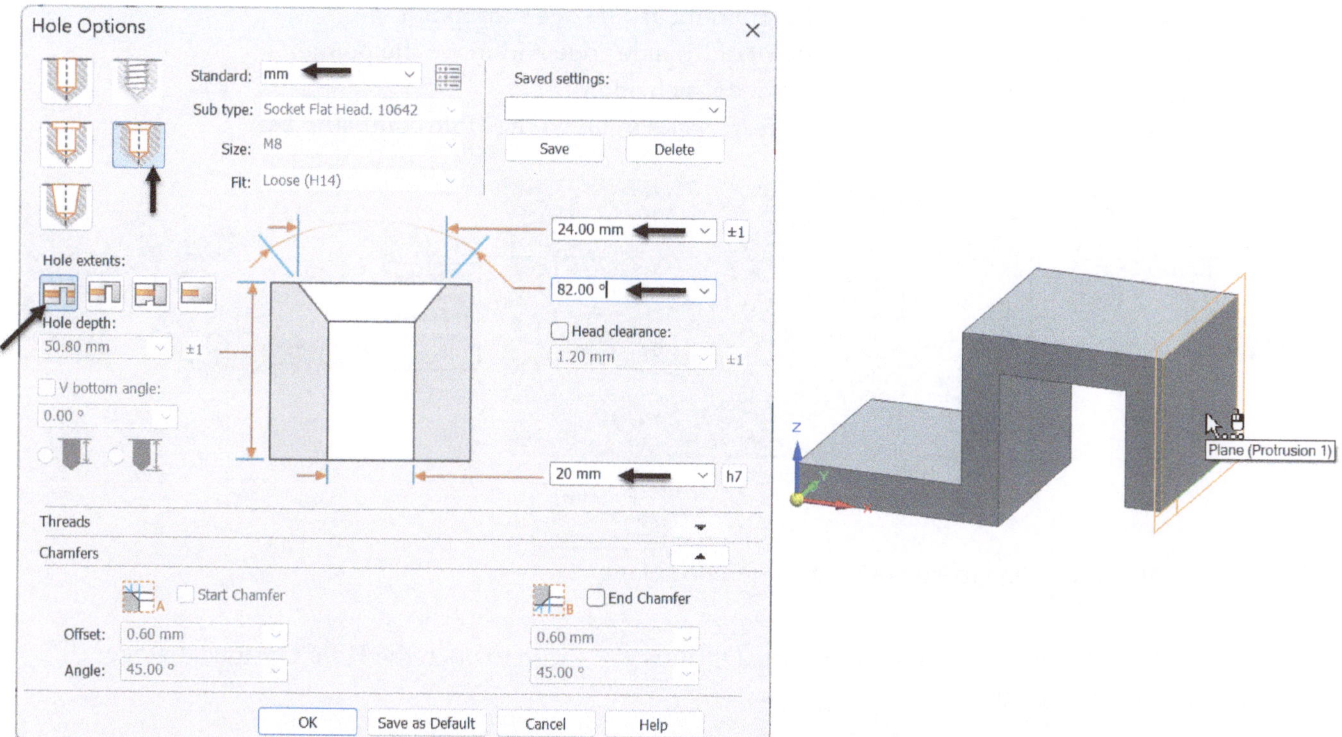

15. Place the hole circle and add dimensions between its center and the adjacent edges, as shown.
16. Click **Close Sketch** on the **Close** group of the ribbon.

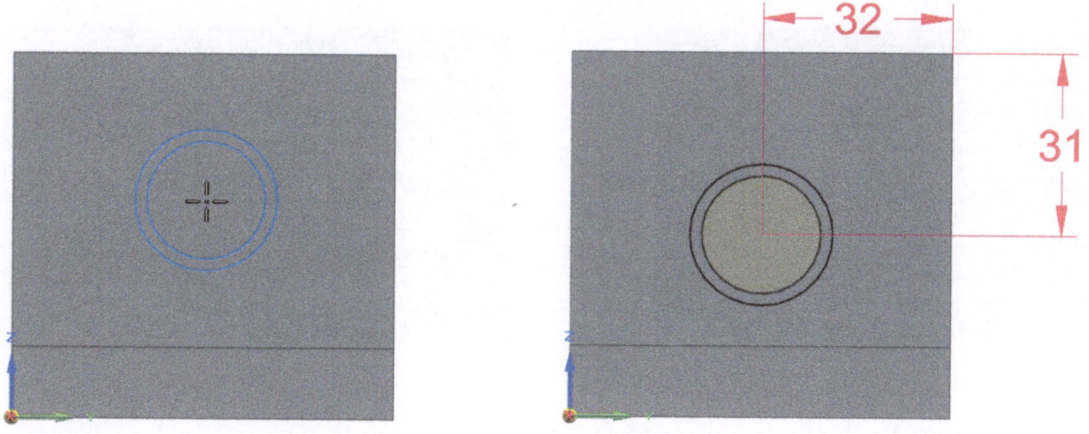

17. Click **Finish** on the **Hole** command bar.
18. With the **Hole** command still active, click on the top face of the part geometry.

19. Click the **Options** icon on the **Hole Circle** command bar; the **Hole Options** dialog pops up.
20. On this dialog, select the **Simple** button and set the **Standard** to **mm**.
21. Enter 20 in the **Hole Diameter** box.
22. Set the **Hole extents** type to **Through All**. Click **OK** to close the dialog.
23. Place the mouse pointer on the midpoint of the front edge.
24. Move the pointer and notice a dotted line from the front edge's midpoint.
25. Likewise, place the pointer on the midpoint of the side edge and move the pointer.
26. Click when both the dotted lines intersect with each other.
27. Click **Close Sketch** on the **Close** group. Next, click **Finish** on the **Hole** command bar.

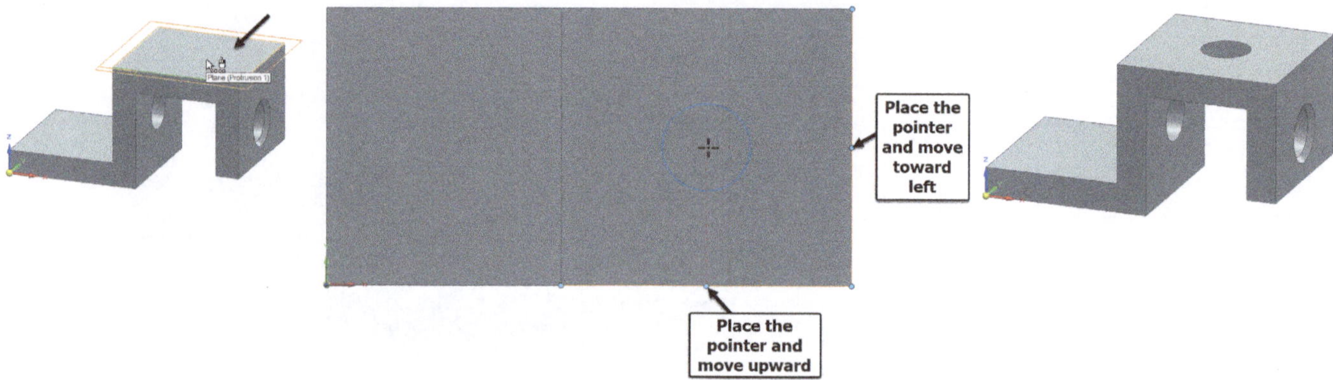

28. Click on the lower top face to define the reference plane.
29. On the **Hole Circle** command bar, click the **Options** icon to open the **Hole Options** dialog.
30. Set the **Standard** to **mm**
31. Select the **Simple** button and set the **Hole Diameter** to **10**. Click **OK** on the dialog.
32. Place two hole circles on the lower top face of the model, as shown.
33. Add dimensions between the centers of the hole circles and the adjacent edges, as shown.

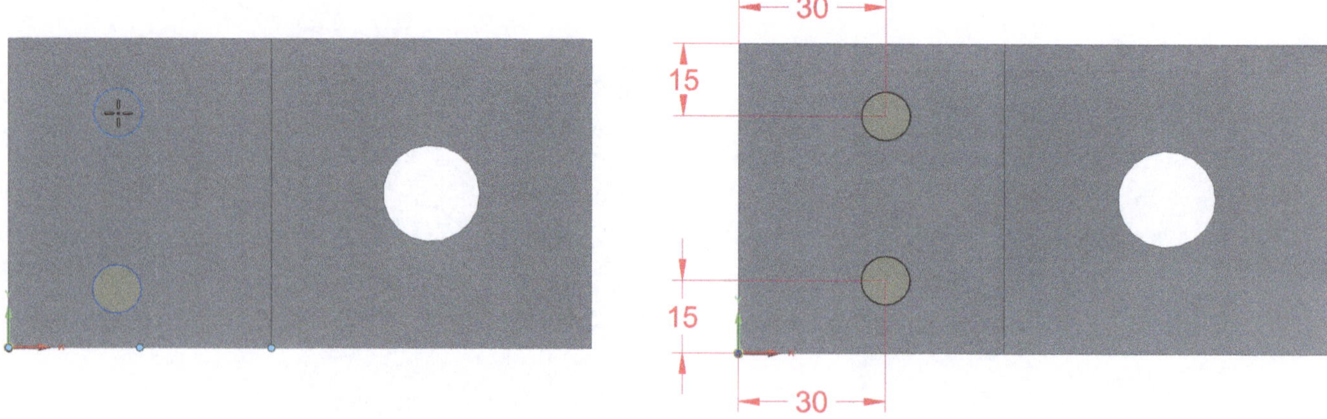

34. Click **Close Sketch** on the **Close** group of the ribbon.
35. Click **Finish** on the **Hole** command bar. Click **Cancel** on the command bar.

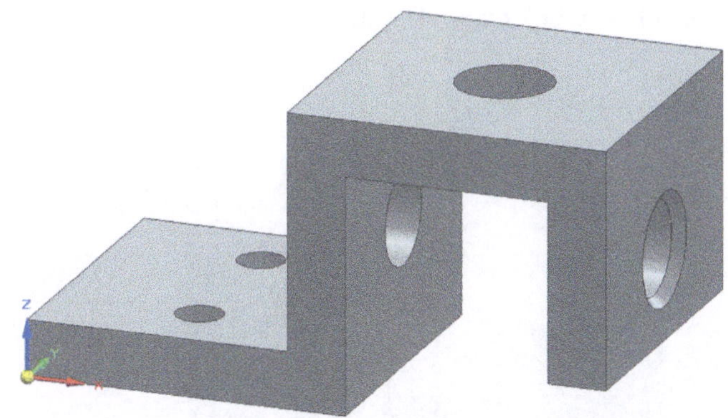

36. Click **Home > Solids > Round > Chamfer** on the ribbon.
37. On the command bar, click the **Options** > **2 Setbacks**.

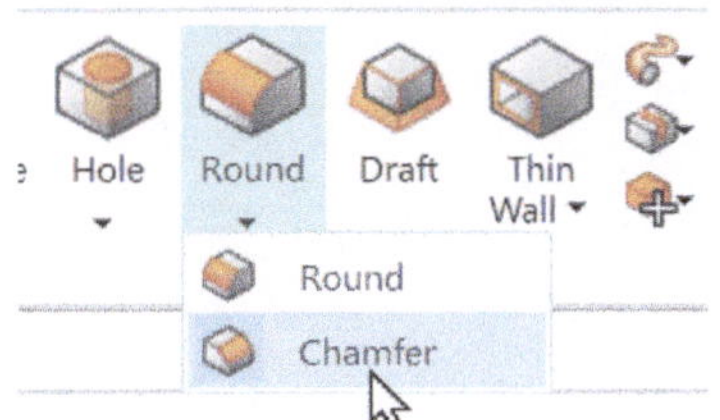

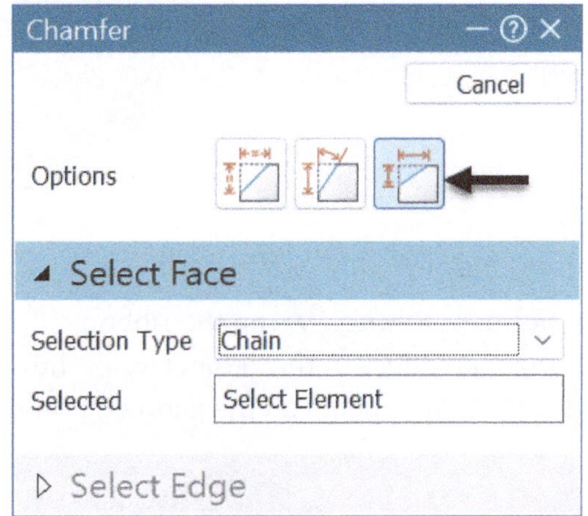

38. Click on the top-left corner of the Front face of the ViewCube.
39. Click on the front face of the model and click the green check on the command bar.
40. Click on the side edges of the selected face, as shown in the figure.

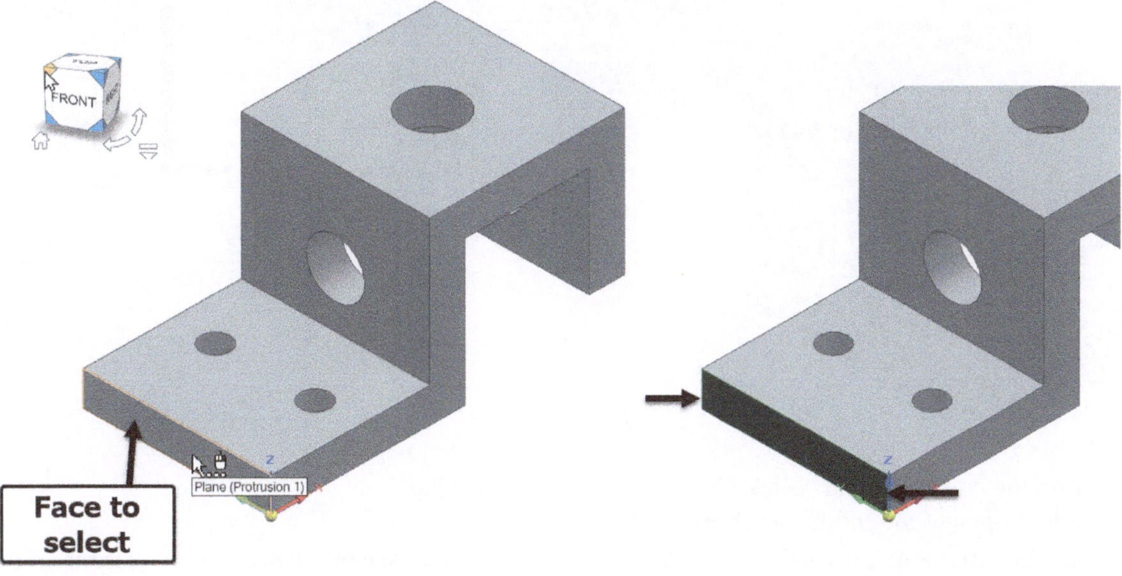

41. Set the **Setback 1** and **Setback 2** to **20** and **10**, respectively. Click the green check.

42. Click the green check, and then **Finish** on the command bar. Click **Cancel** on the command bar.

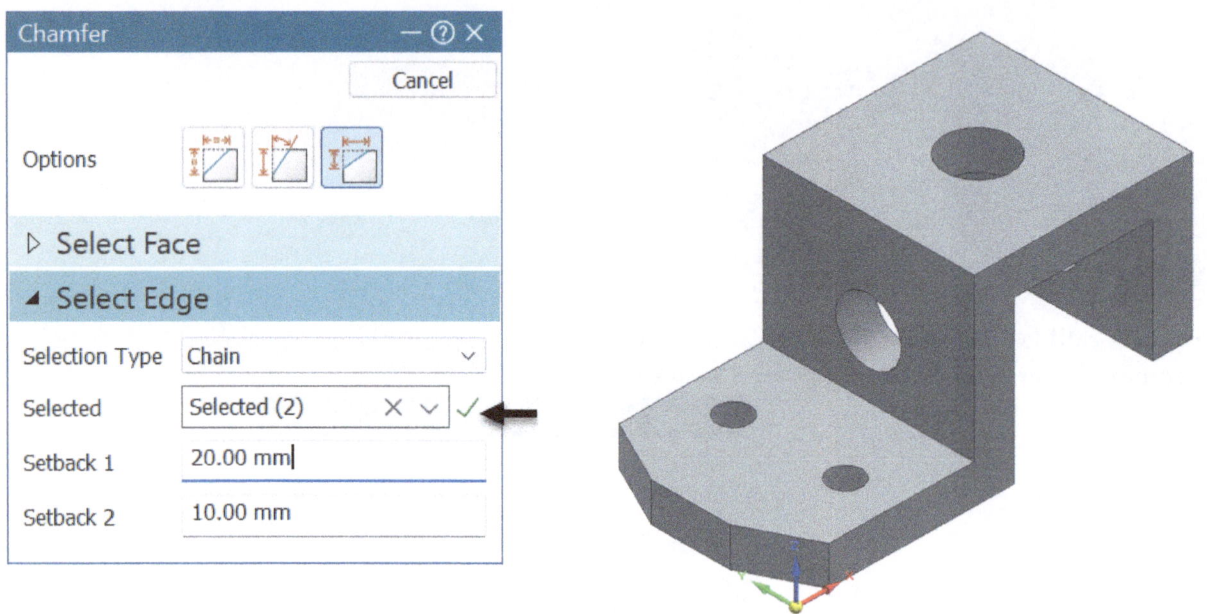

43. Click **Home > Solids > Round** on the ribbon.
44. Click on the horizontal edges of the geometry, as shown below.
45. Type-in **8** in the box that appears on the geometry, and then click the **Accept** button on the command bar.

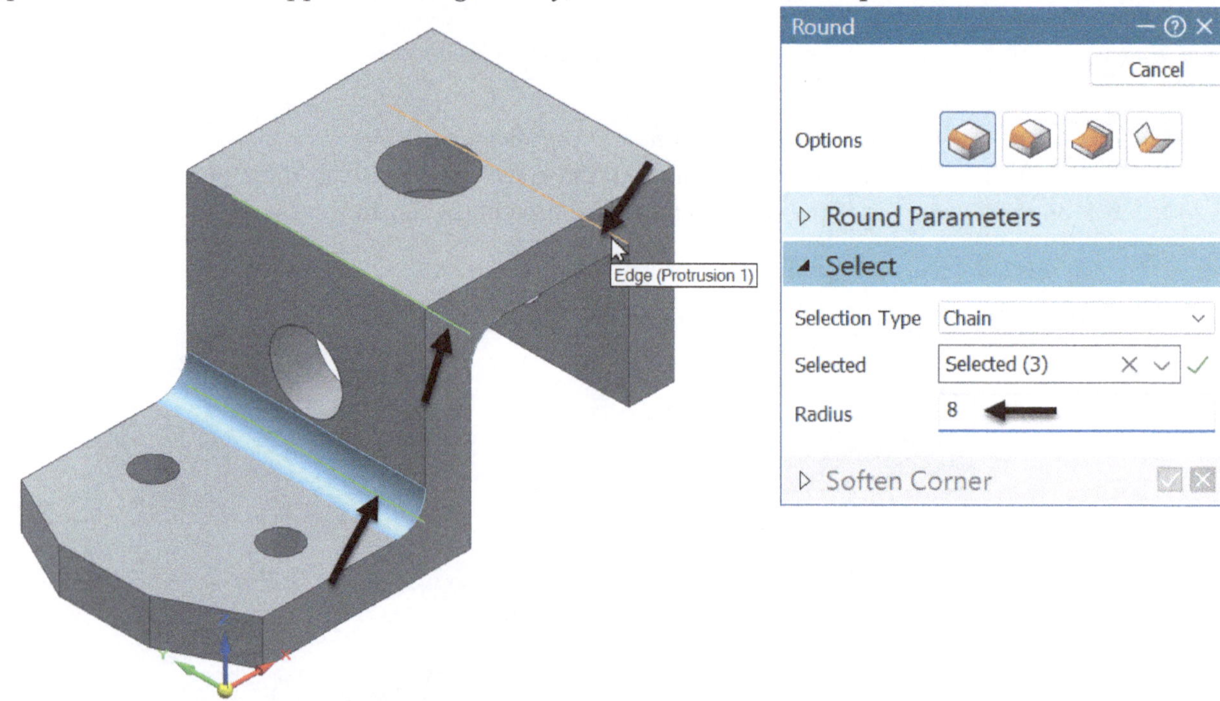

46. Click **Preview** on the command bar. Click **Finish** on the command bar.
47. Click on the outer edges of the model, as shown below.
48. Type-in **20** in the box that appears on the geometry, and then click the **Accept** button on the command bar.
49. Click **Preview** and **Finish** on the command bar. Next, click **Cancel** on the command bar.

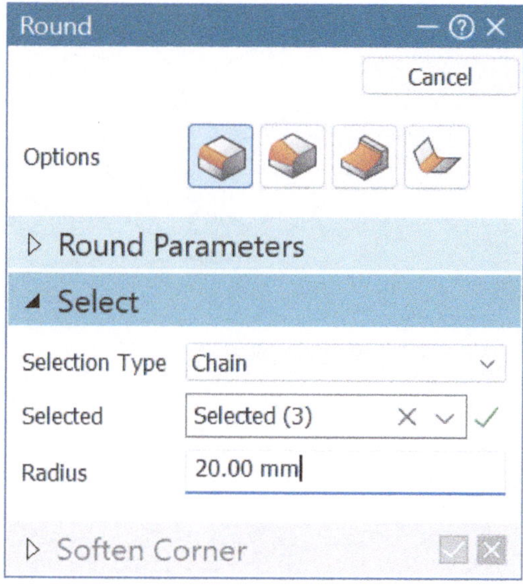

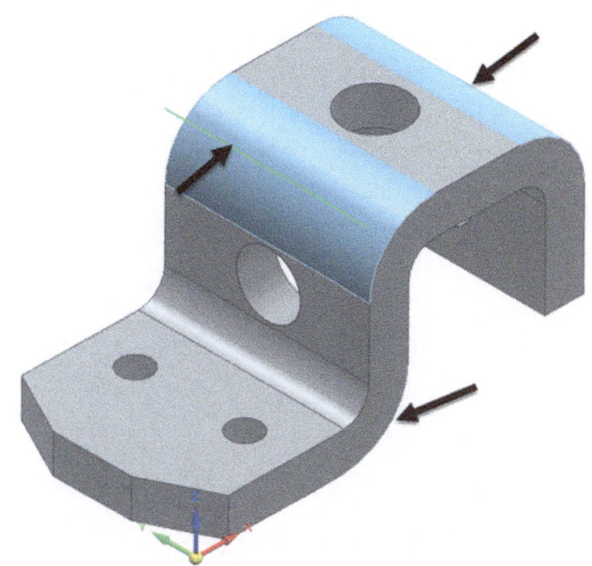

50. Change the orientation of the model view to **Isometric** by clicking the **Home** icon below the **Quick View Cube**.
51. Click **Home > Solids > Round > Chamfer** on the ribbon.
52. Click the **Options** > **Equal Setbacks** on the command bar.
53. Type 10 in the **Setback** box on the **Chamfer** command bar.
54. Click on the lower corners of the part geometry.

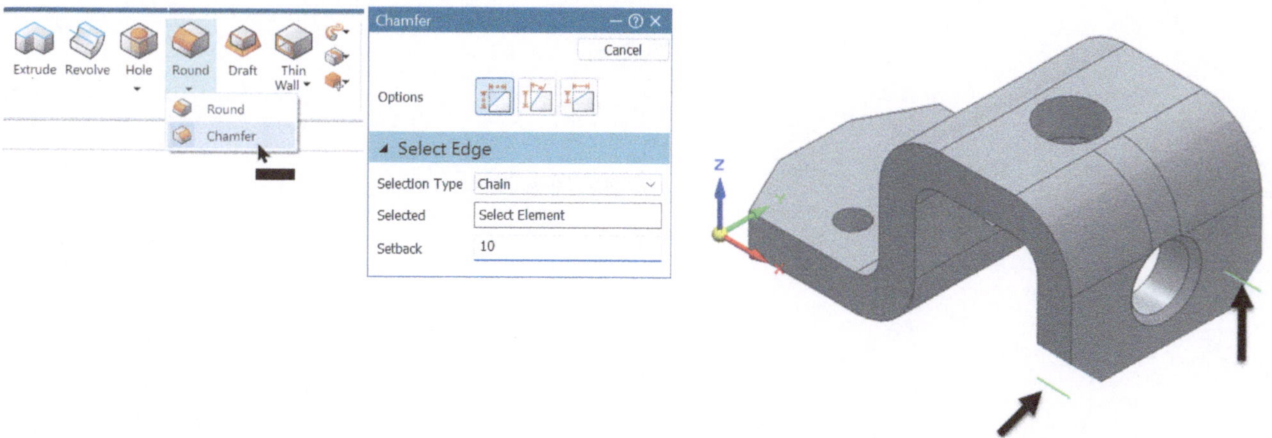

55. Click the green check on the command bar.
56. Click **Preview** and **Finish** on the command bar. Next, click **Cancel** on the command bar.
57. Save and close the file.

Example 2 (Millimeters)

In this example, you will create the part shown below.

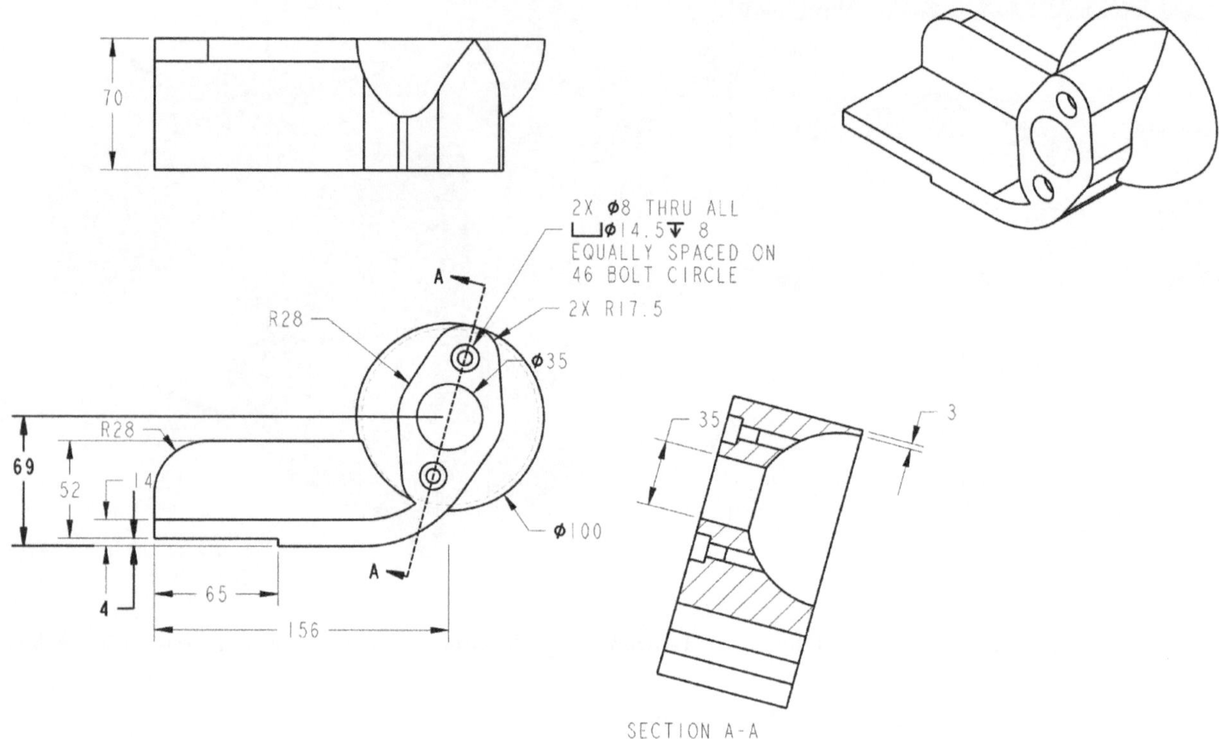
70
2X ⌀8 THRU ALL
⌴⌀14.5↧ 8
EQUALLY SPACED ON
46 BOLT CIRCLE
A
R28
2X R17.5
⌀35
R28
69
52
14
4
65
156
⌀100
35
3
SECTION A-A

Creating the First Feature

1. Start **Solid Edge 2026.**
2. On the Quick Access Toolbar, click the **New** button.
3. environment is set as the default environment.
4. Select **ISO Metric > iso metric part.par**. Next, click **OK**; a new part file is opened.
5. Click **Continue with Ordered** button on the **Ordered as default** dialog; the Ordered.
6. On the ribbon, click **Home > Solids > Revolve** and select the **Front(xz)** plane.

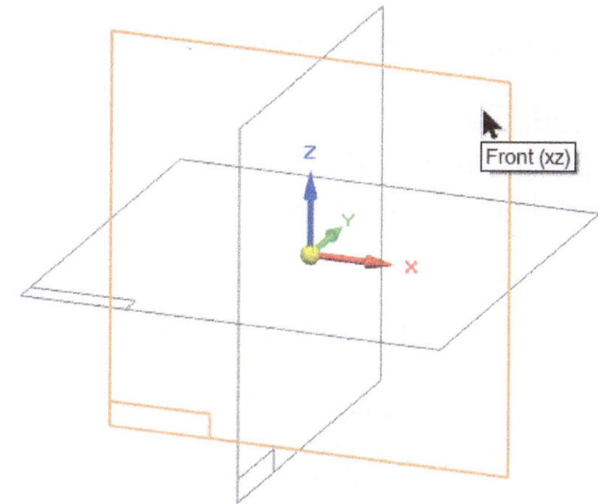

7. Click **Home > Draw > Circle** drop-down **> Circle by Center Point** on the ribbon.
8. Click on the origin point to define the centerpoint.
9. Move the pointer outward and click.
10. On the ribbon, click **Home** tab > **Draw** panel > **Line.**
11. Click on the intersection point between the circle and the vertical axis.

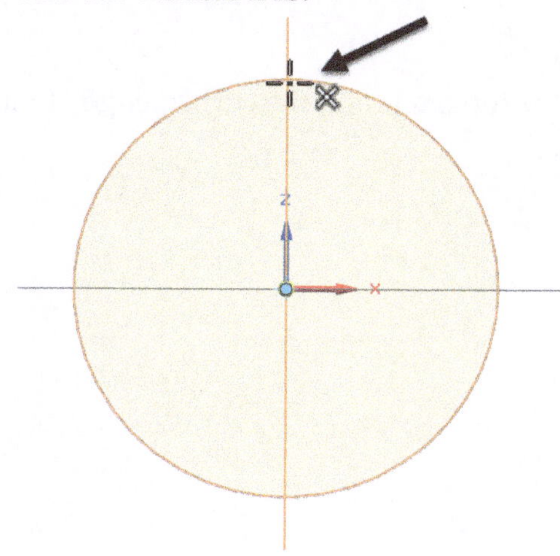

12. Move the pointer downward and click on the intersection point between the circle and the vertical axis.

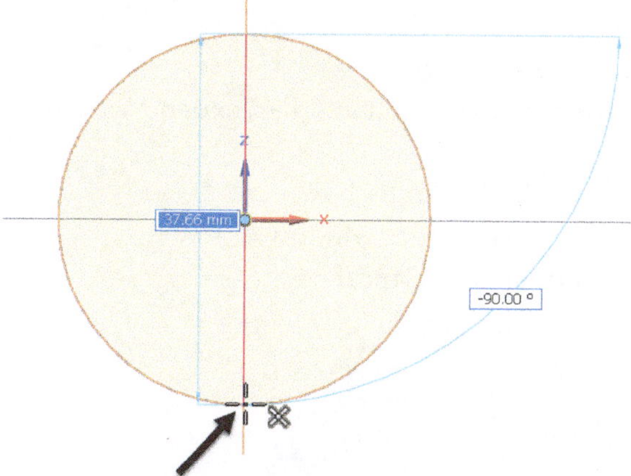

13. On the ribbon, click **Home** tab > **Draw** panel > **Trim** .
14. Click on the element to trim, as shown.

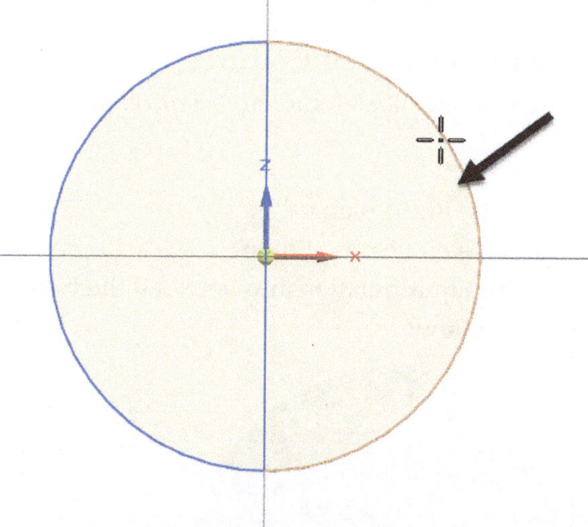

15. Add dimension to the vertical line, as shown.

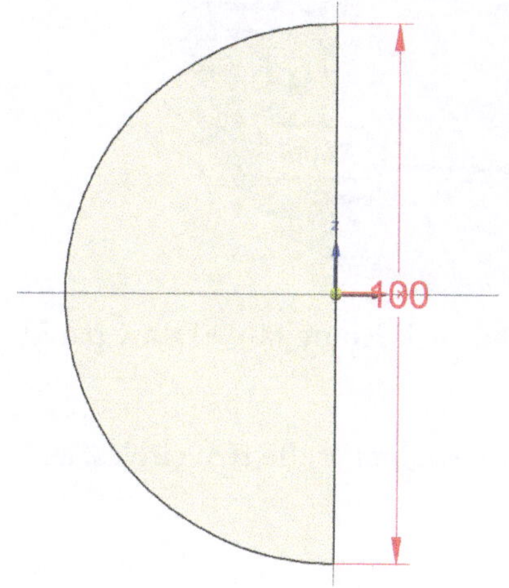

16. On the ribbon, click **Home** tab > **Draw** > **Axis of Revolution** .
17. Select the vertical line to define the axis of revolution.
18. Click **Close Sketch**.
19. On the **Revolve** command bar, expand **Extend** section.
20. Type 180 in the **Angle** box.
21. Click in the graphics window.
22. Click **Finish** and **Cancel**.

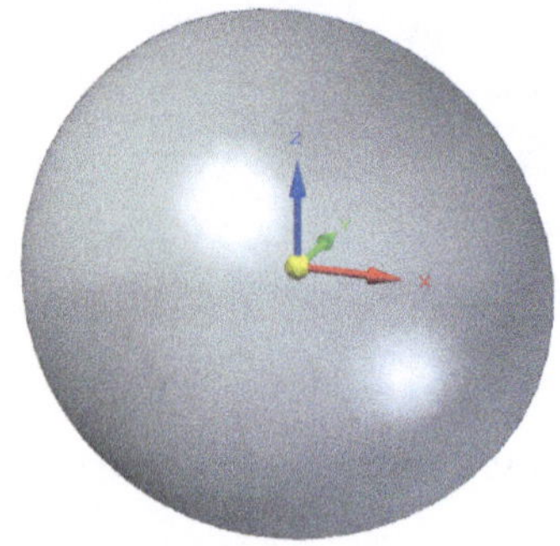

Creating the Extruded Features

1. On the ribbon, click **Home** tab > **Solids** panel > **Extrude** .
2. Click on the Front plane.
3. Create three circles, as shown.
4. Apply the **Equal** relationship between the two circles, as shown.

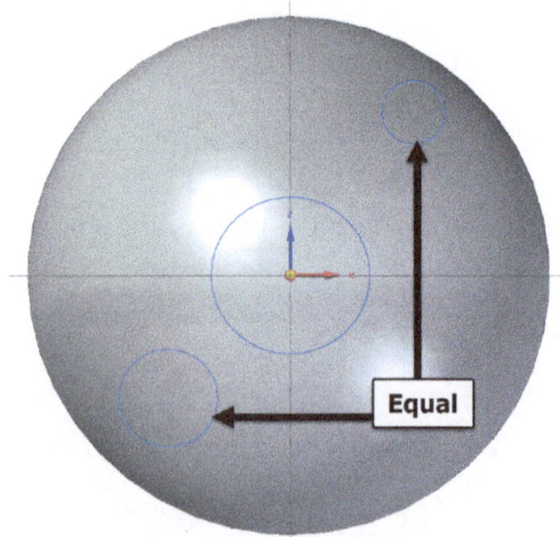

5. On the ribbon, click **Home** tab > **Draw** panel > **Line** .
6. Select the centerpoints of the two circles, as shown.

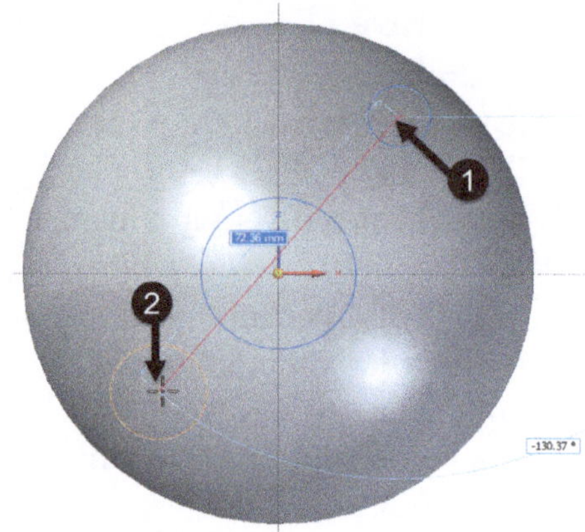

7. Press ESC.
8. On the ribbon, click **Home** tab > **Draw** panel > **Construction** .
9. Select the newly created line.
10. On the ribbon, click **Home** tab > **Relate** panel > **Connect** .
11. Select the centerpoint of the large circle.
12. Select the midpoint of the construction line.

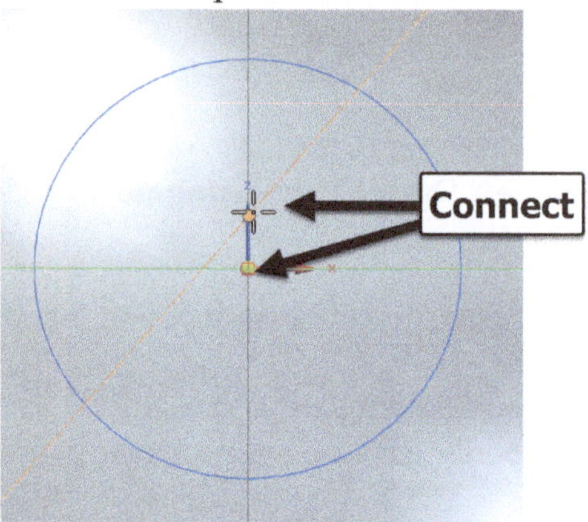

13. On the ribbon, click **Sketch** tab > **Relate** group > **Tangent** .
14. Select the top circle and the curved edge of the model.

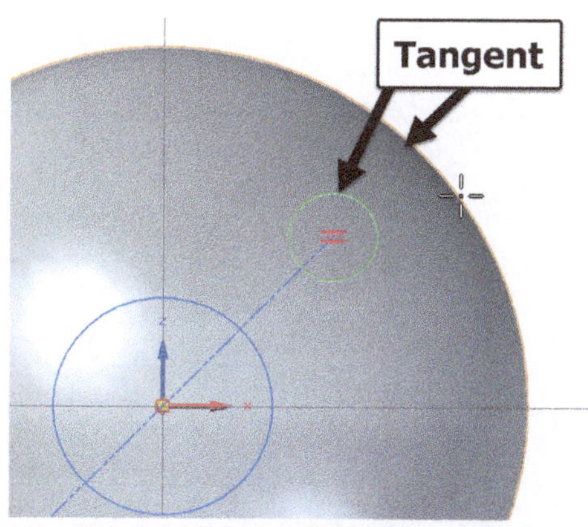

15. On the ribbon, click **Sketch** tab > **Dimension** group > **Smart Dimension**.
16. Create the dimensions, as shown.

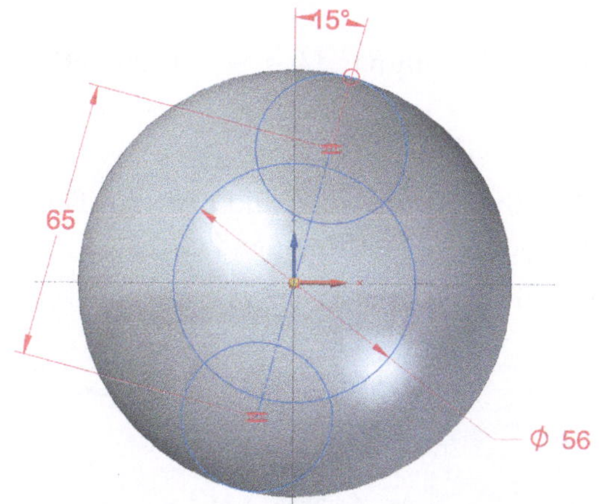

17. Click **Home > Draw > Line** on the ribbon.
18. Select the two circles, as shown.

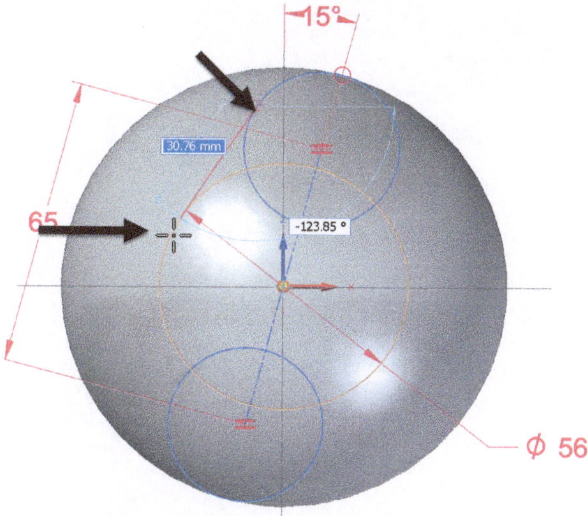

19. Press ESC.
20. On the ribbon, click **Home** tab > **Relate** group > **Tangent**.
21. Select the line and the circle connected to it; the tangent relationship is applied between the line and circle.

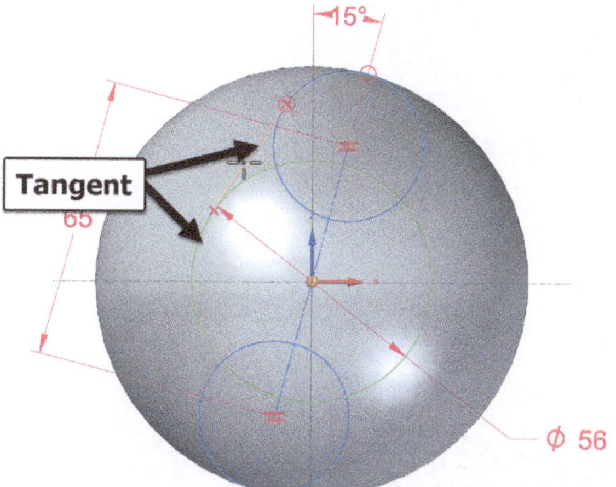

22. Likewise, apply the **Tangent** relationship between the line and other circle, if not already applied.

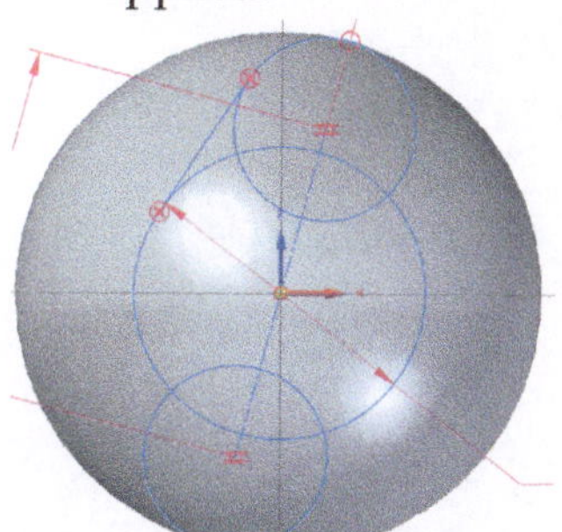

23. Likewise, create three more tangent lines, as shown.

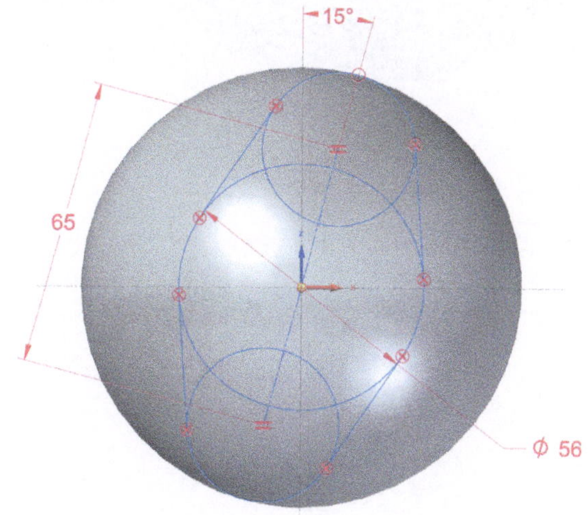

24. On the ribbon, click **Home** tab > **Draw** group > **Trim** drop-down **> Trim** .
25. Select the inner segments of the circles, as shown.

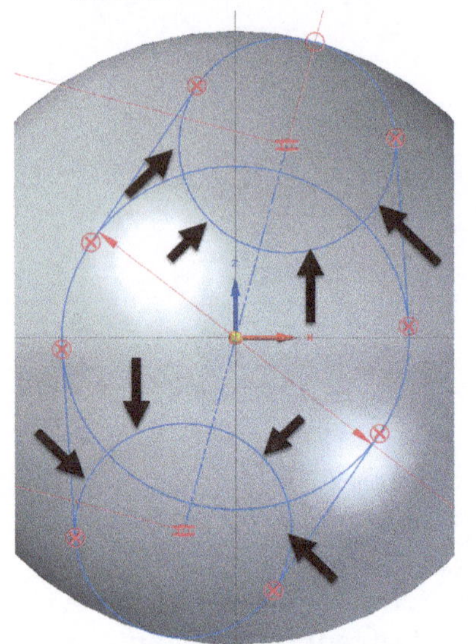

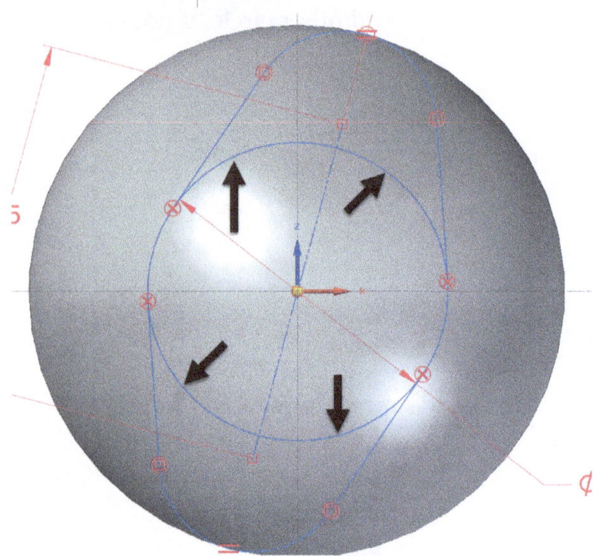

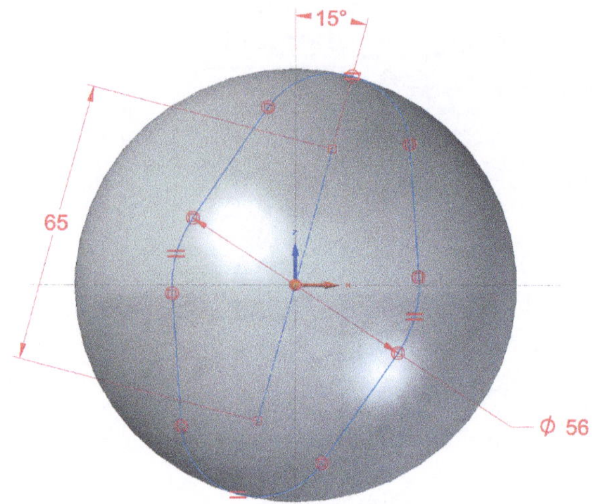

26. Click **Close Sketch** on the **Home** tab of the ribbon.
27. On the **Extrude** command bar, select **Operation > Add** .
28. Type **70** in the **Distance** box and press ENTER.
29. Move the pointer toward left and click.
30. Click **Finish**.

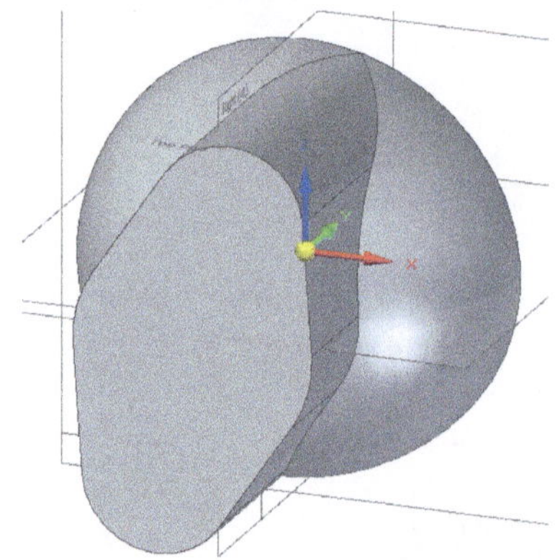

31. Click on the Front plane.

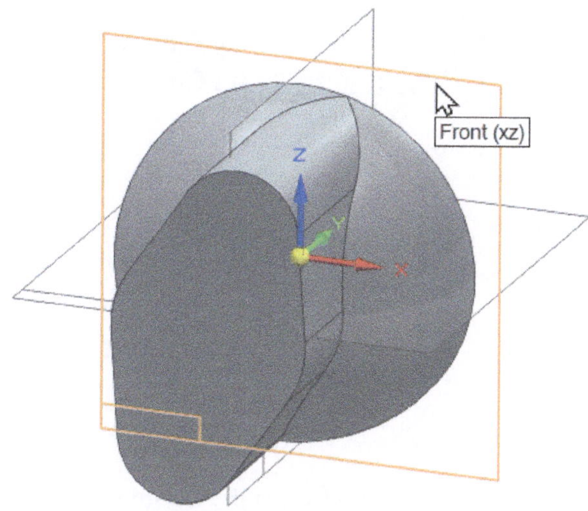

32. On the ribbon, click **Home** tab > **Draw** panel > **Line** .
33. Create four lines, as shown.

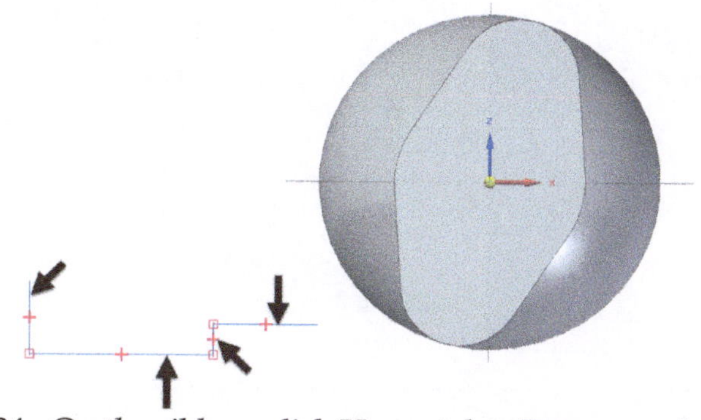

34. On the ribbon, click **Home** tab > **Draw** panel > **Arc** drop-down > **Arc by 3 Points** .
35. Select the end point of the right horizontal line.
36. Select the circular edge of the model, as shown.
37. Move the pointer downward and click.

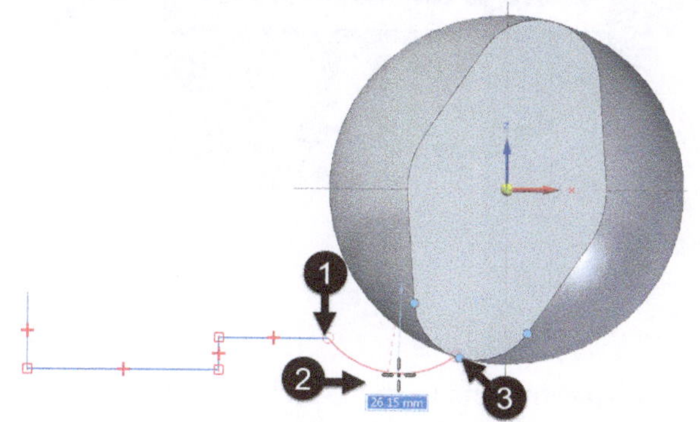

38. On the ribbon, click **Home** tab > **Relate** panel > **Tangent** .
39. Select the newly created arc and the circular edge.

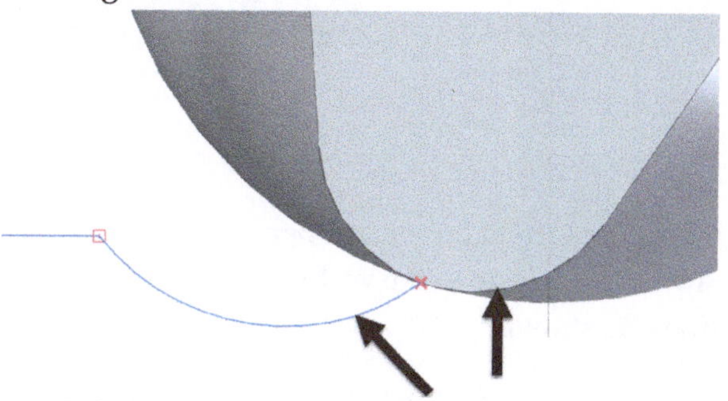

40. Select the newly created arc and the horizontal line.

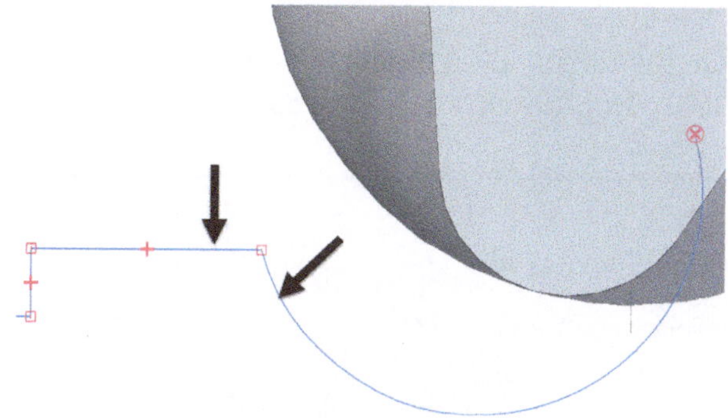

41. On the ribbon, click **Home** tab > **Draw** panel > **Offset** .
42. Select the **Single** option from the **Select** drop-down.

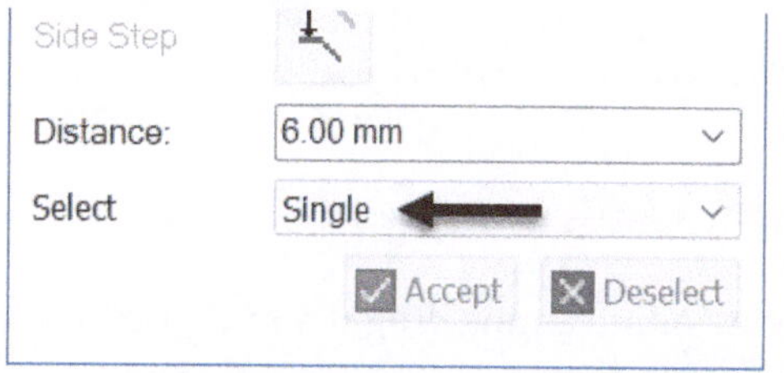

43. Select the arc and horizontal line, as shown.

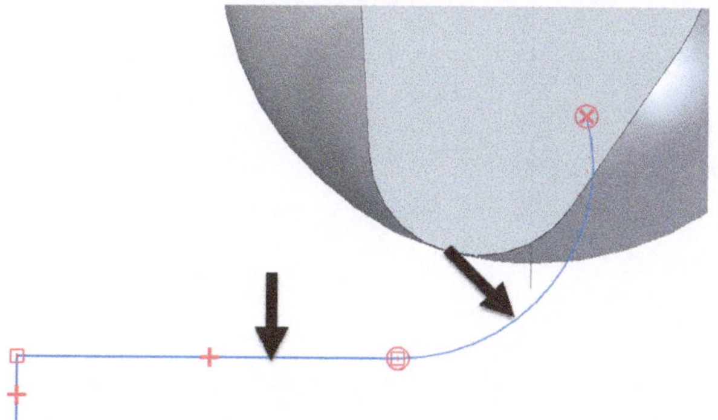

44. Type-in a value in the **Distance** box and press ENTER.

45. Move the pointer upward and click.

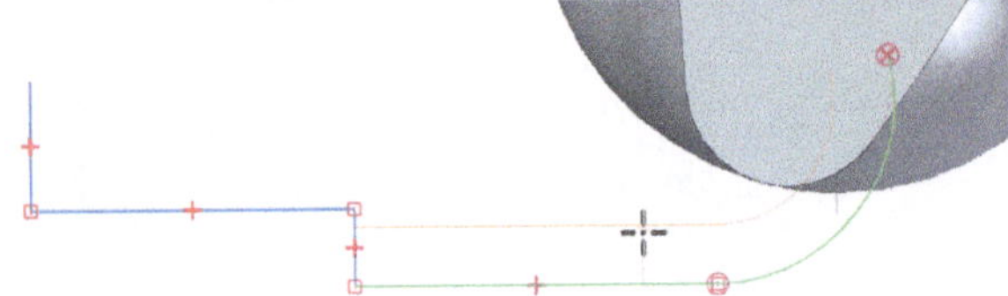

46. Close the **Offset** command bar.
47. Add dimensions to the vertical and horizontal lines, as shown.

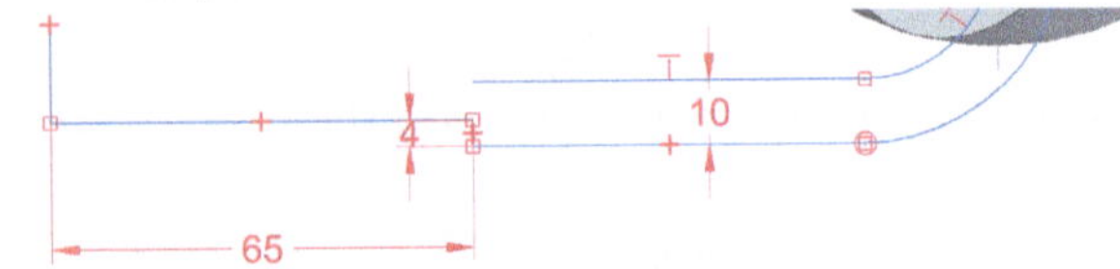

48. On the ribbon, click **Home** tab > **Draw** panel > **Trim** drop-down > **Trim Corner**.

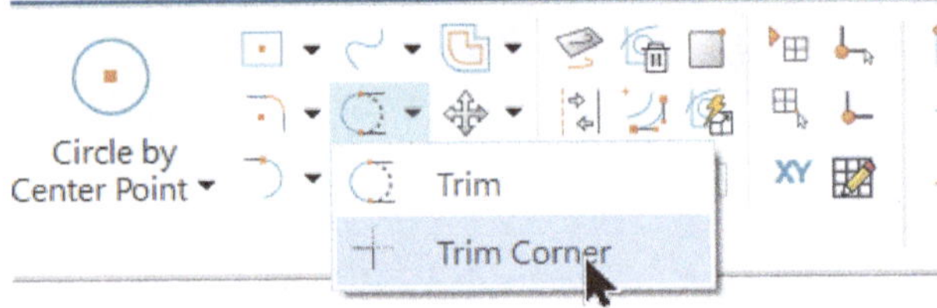

49. Select vertical and horizontal lines, as shown.

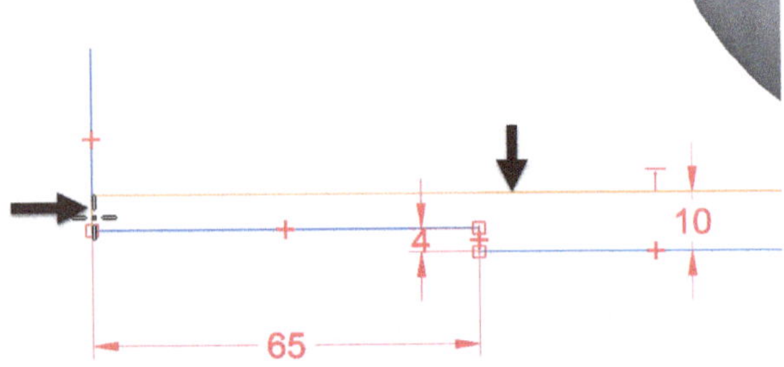

50. Create a line connecting the end points of the arcs, as shown.

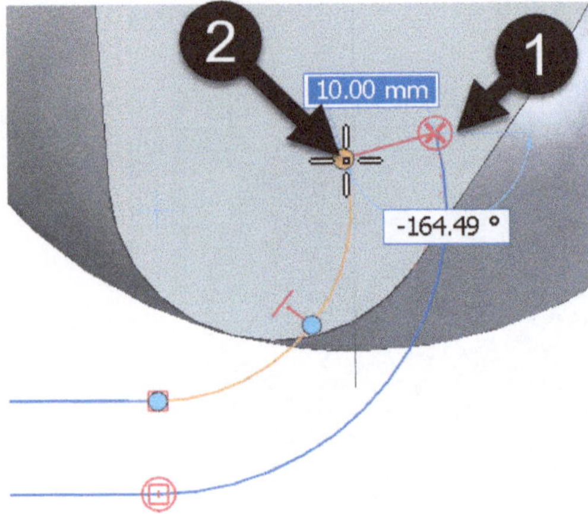

51. On the ribbon, click **Home** tab > **Relate** panel > **Connect** .
52. Select the endpoint of the arc and the quadrant point of the circular edge.

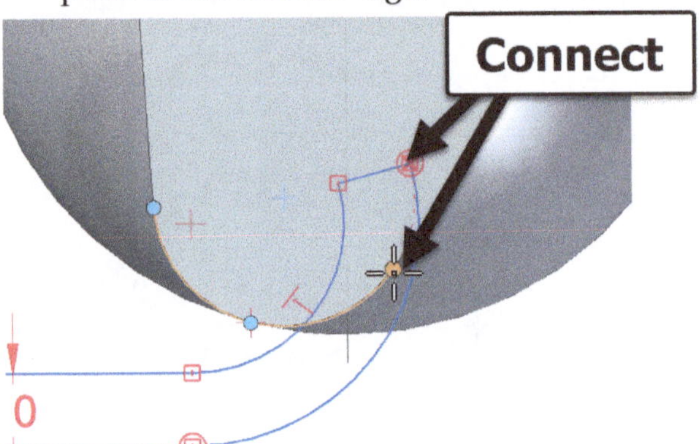

53. On the ribbon, click **Home** tab > **Relate** panel > **Perpendicular** .
54. Select the arc and the line, as shown.

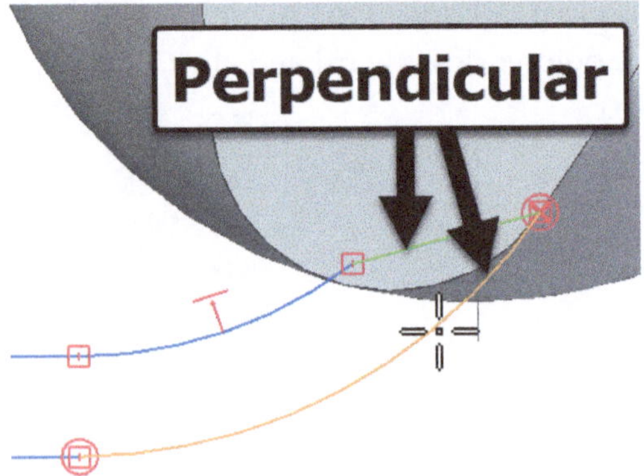

55. Add dimensions to the sketch, as shown.

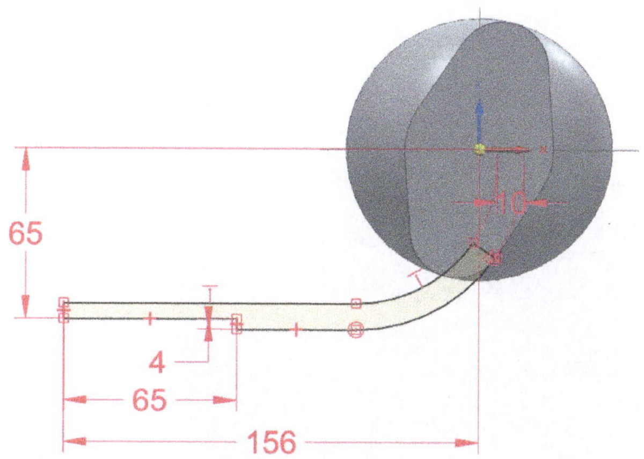

56. Click **Close Sketch** on the ribbon.
57. On the command bar, expand the Extent section and click **Type** > **From/To Extent** .
58. Select the Front plane to define the From plane of the extrusion.
59. Select the flat end face of the extruded feature, as shown.

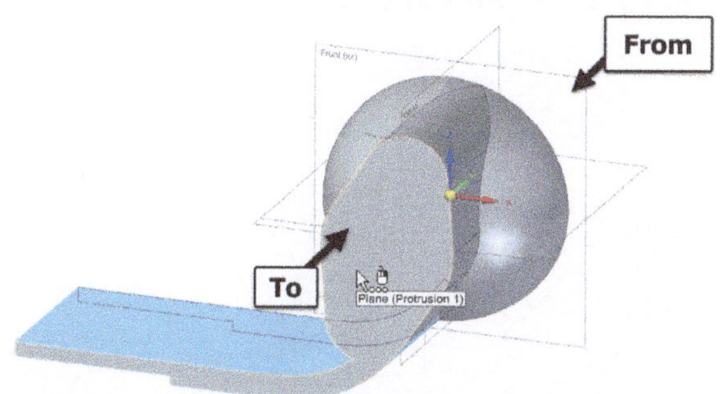

60. Click **Finish** on the command bar.
61. Click on the Front plane.

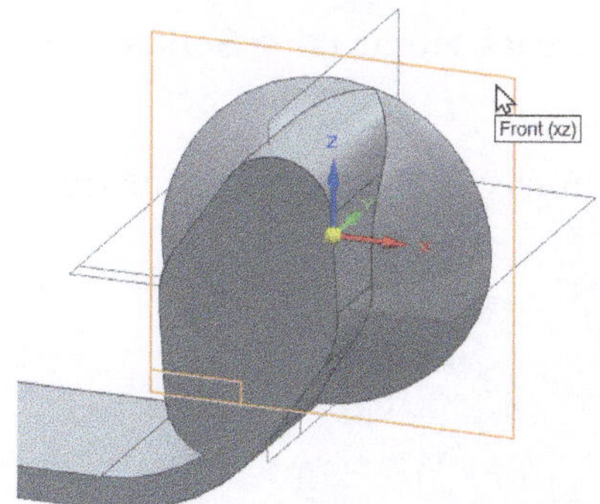

62. On the ribbon, click **Home** tab > **Draw** panel > **Line** .
63. Create two lines, as shown.

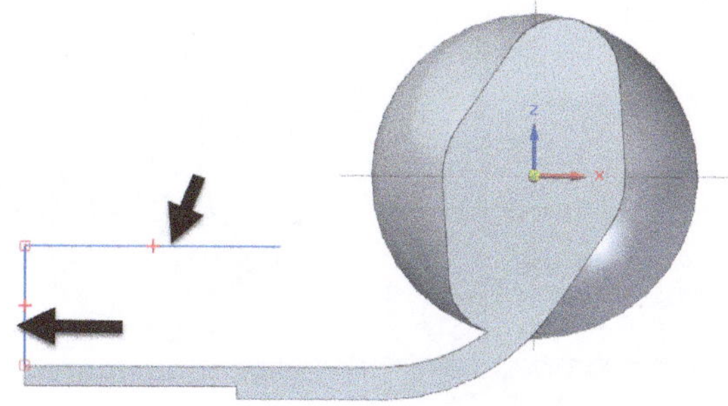

64. On the ribbon, click **Home** tab > **Draw** panel > **Project to Sketch** .
65. Select the horizontal and curved edges, as shown.

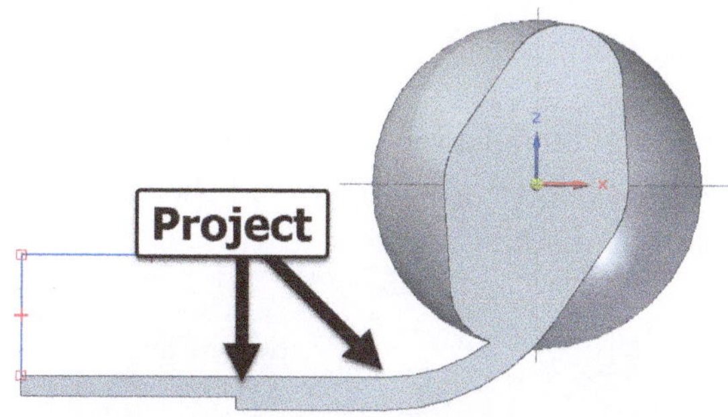

66. Press ESC.
67. Select the endpoint of the horizontal line, and then drag it toward right; the horizontal line is lengthened.

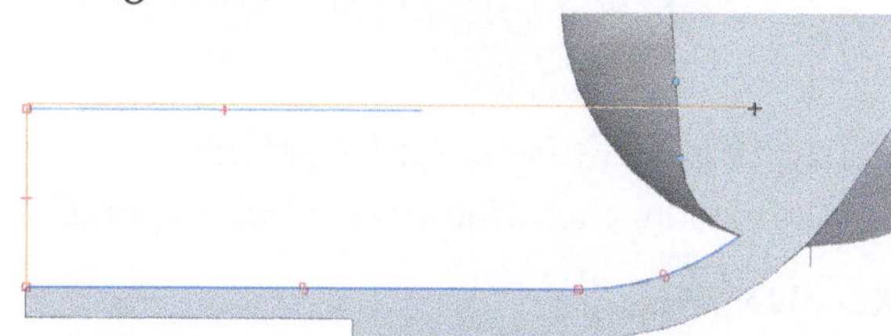

68. On the ribbon, click **Home** tab > **Draw** panel > **Trim** drop-down > **Trim Corner** .
69. Select the end portion of the horizontal and arc.

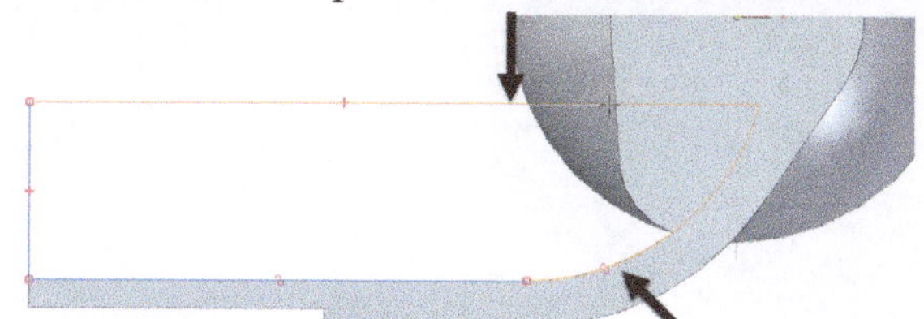

70. Add a fillet and dimensions to the sketch, as shown.

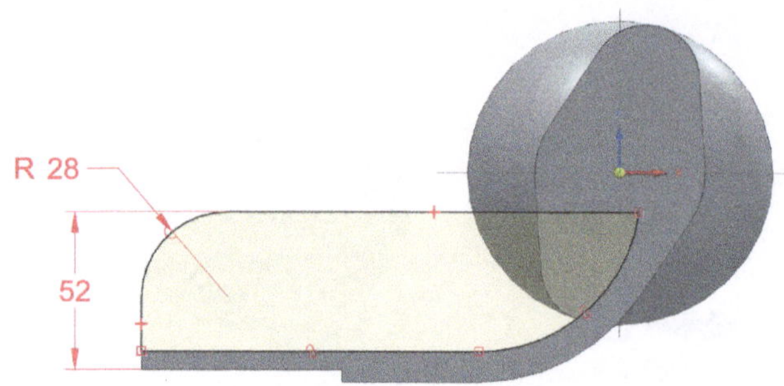

71. Click **Close sketch** on the ribbon.
72. On the **Extrude** command bar, select **Operation > Add** .
73. On the command bar, click the **Finite Extent** 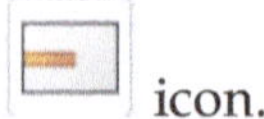 icon.
74. Type **12** in the **Distance** box and press ENTER.
75. Move the pointer toward left and click.
76. Click **Finish** and **Cancel**.

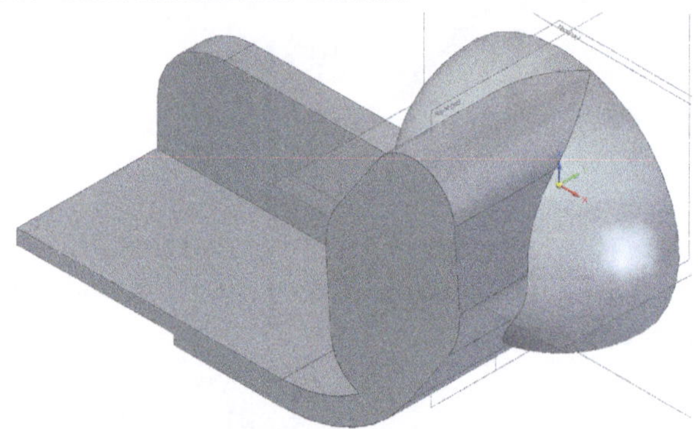

Creating the Revolved Cut Feature

1. On the ribbon, click **Home** tab > **Solids** panel > **Revolve**.
2. Select the Front plane.

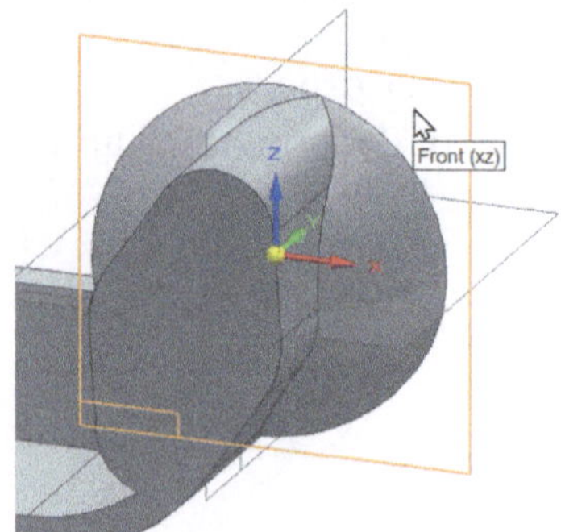

3. Create an arc and line, as shown.
4. On the ribbon, click **Home** tab > **Draw** > **Axis of Revolution**.
5. Specify the vertical line as the axis revolution.

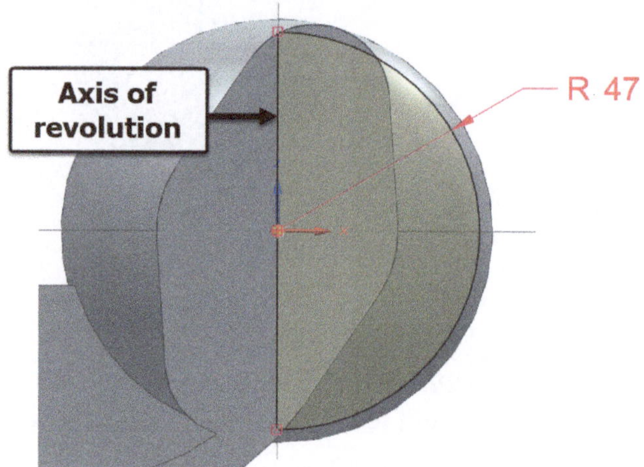

6. Click **Close Sketch** on the ribbon.
7. Expand the **Extent** section on the command bar.
8. Click the **Revolve 360** icon on the command bar.
9. Click **Finish** and **Cancel**.

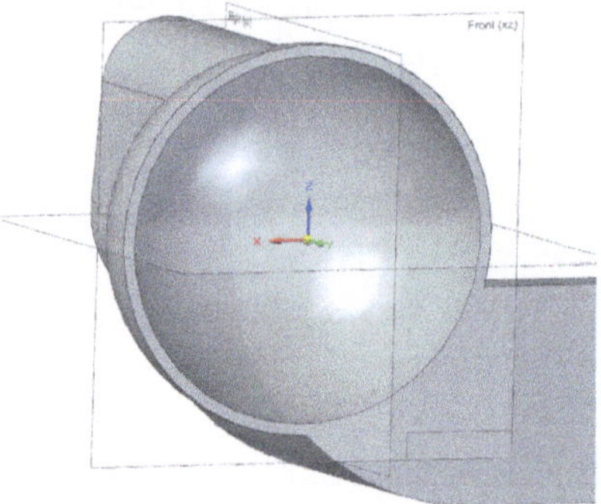

Creating the Hole Features

1. On the ribbon, click **Home** tab > **Solids** panel > **Hole**.
2. Select the front face of the model geometry.

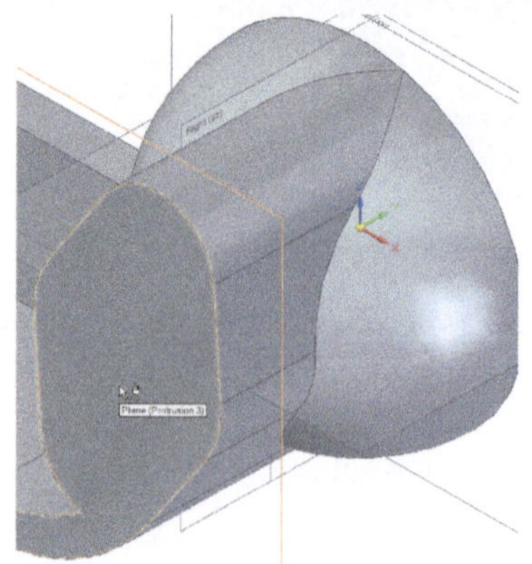

3. On the ribbon, click **Home** tab > **Features** panel > **Hole Circle** .
4. Select the sketch origin.

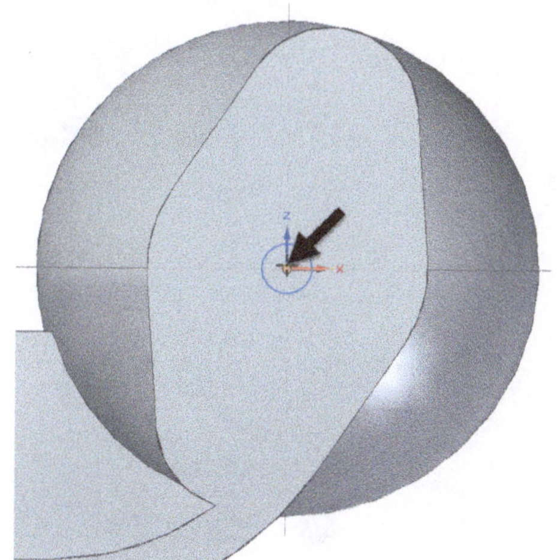

5. Click **Close Sketch**.
6. Click the **Hole Options** icon on the command bar.
7. Select **Standard > mm.**
10. Click the **Through All** icon under the **Hole extents** section.
11. Type **35** in the **Hole Diameter** box.
12. Click **OK**.
13. Click **Close Sketch** on the ribbon.
14. Click **Finish**.

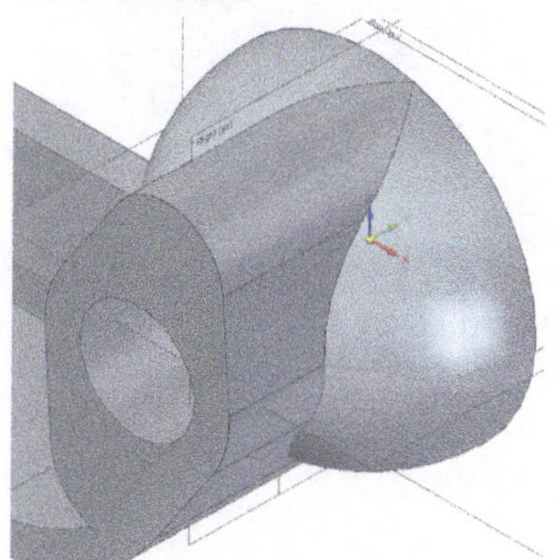

15. Select the front face of the model geometry.
16. Place the two hole circles.
17. Apply the **Concentric** relationship between the hole circles and the circular edges, as shown.

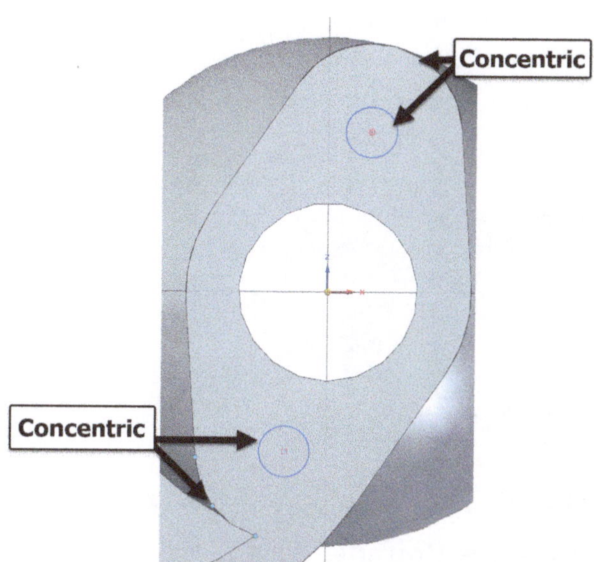

18. Click the **Close Sketch** button on the ribbon.
8. Click the **Hole Options** icon on the command bar.
9. Click the **Counterbore** button on the top-left corner of the dialog.
10. Select **Standard > ISO Metric.**
11. Select **M8** from the **Size** drop-down.
19. Click the **Through All** icon under the **Hole extents** section.

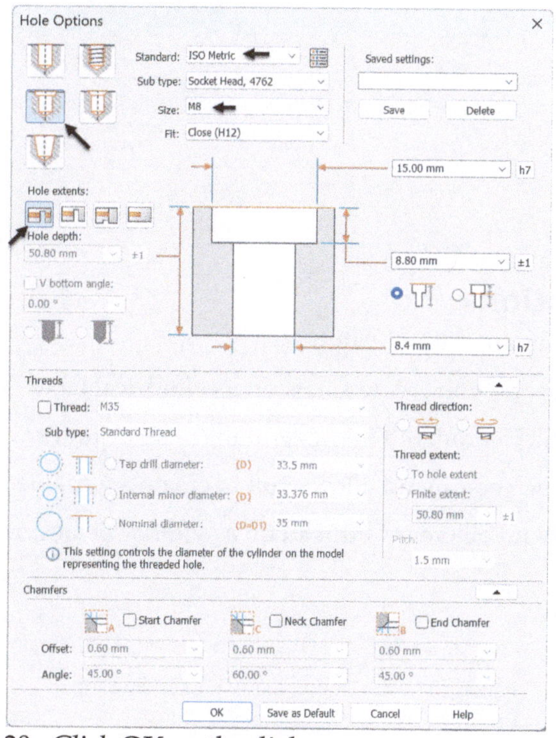

20. Click **OK** on the dialog.

21. Click **Close Sketch**.
22. Click the **Finish** and **Cancel**.

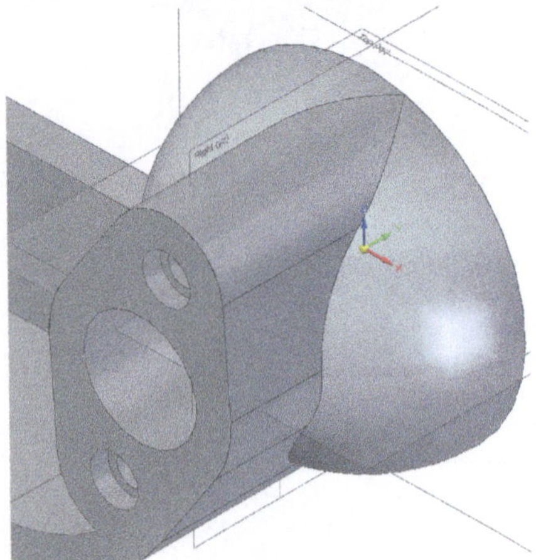

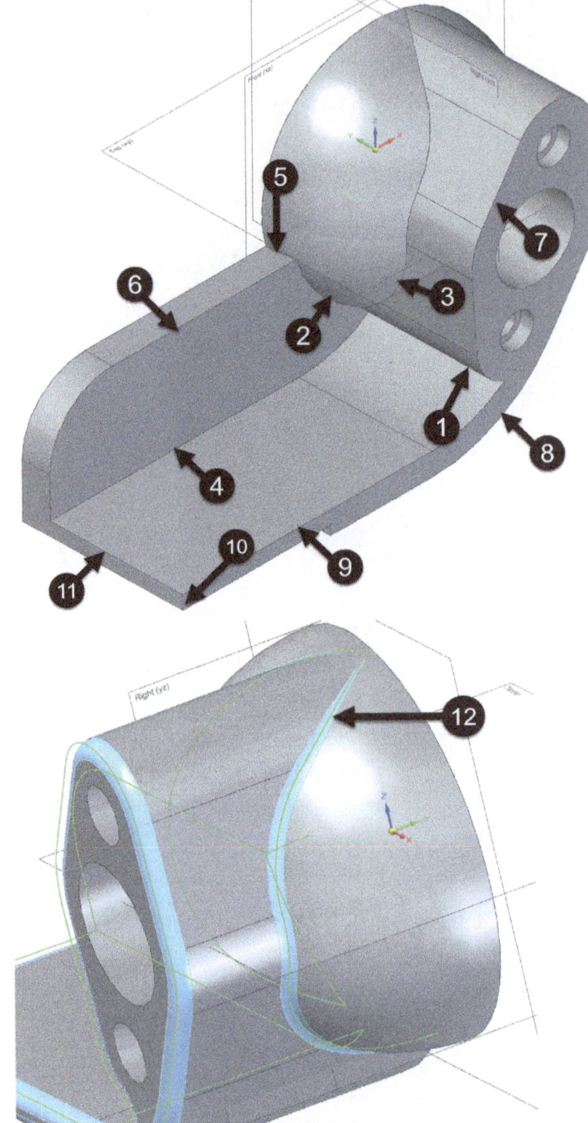

Creating the Rounds

1. On the ribbon, click **Home > Solids > Round**.
2. Type **4** in the **Radius** box.
3. Select the edges in the sequence, as shown.
4. Click **Accept**, **Preview**, **Finish**, and **Cancel**.
5. Save and close the file.

Questions

1. What are placed features?
2. How do you create a hole on a cylindrical face?
3. Which command allows you to create chamfer with unequal setbacks?
4. Which command allows you to create a variable radius blend?
5. When you create a thread on a cylindrical face, will the cylinder's diameter remains the same or not?

Exercises

Exercise 1 (Millimetres)

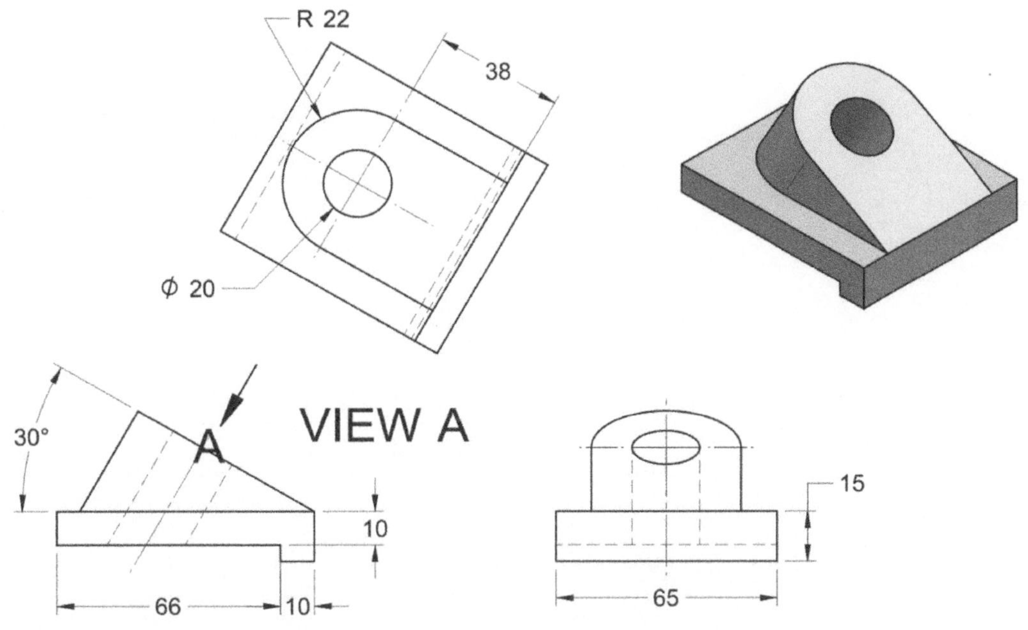

Exercise 2 (Inches)

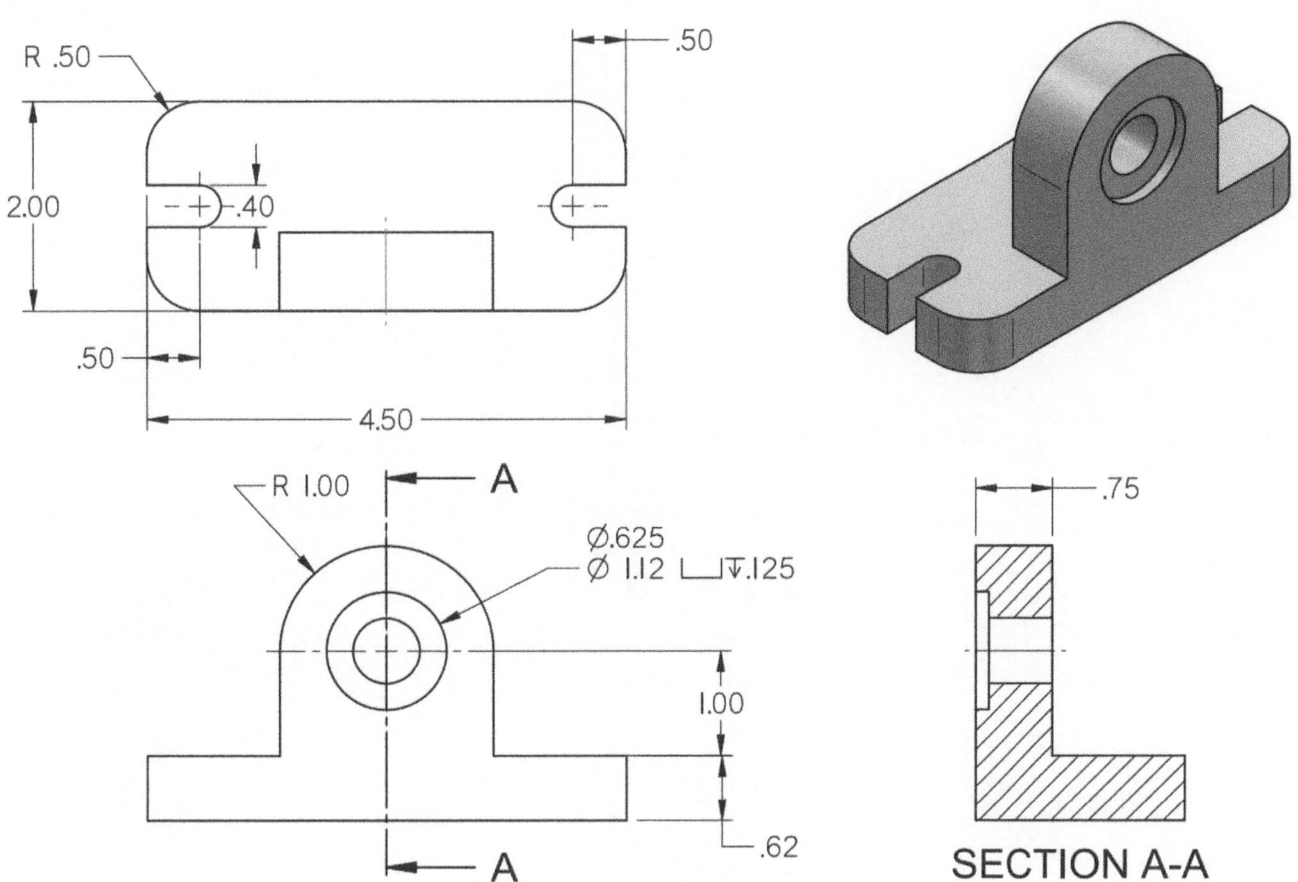

Chapter 5: Patterned Geometry

When designing a part geometry, frequently, there are symmetry elements in each part, or there are at least a few features that are repeated multiple times. In these situations, Solid Edge offers you some commands that save you time. For example, you can use mirror features to design symmetric parts, making the part quicker. You only have to design a portion of the part and use the mirror feature to create the remaining geometry.

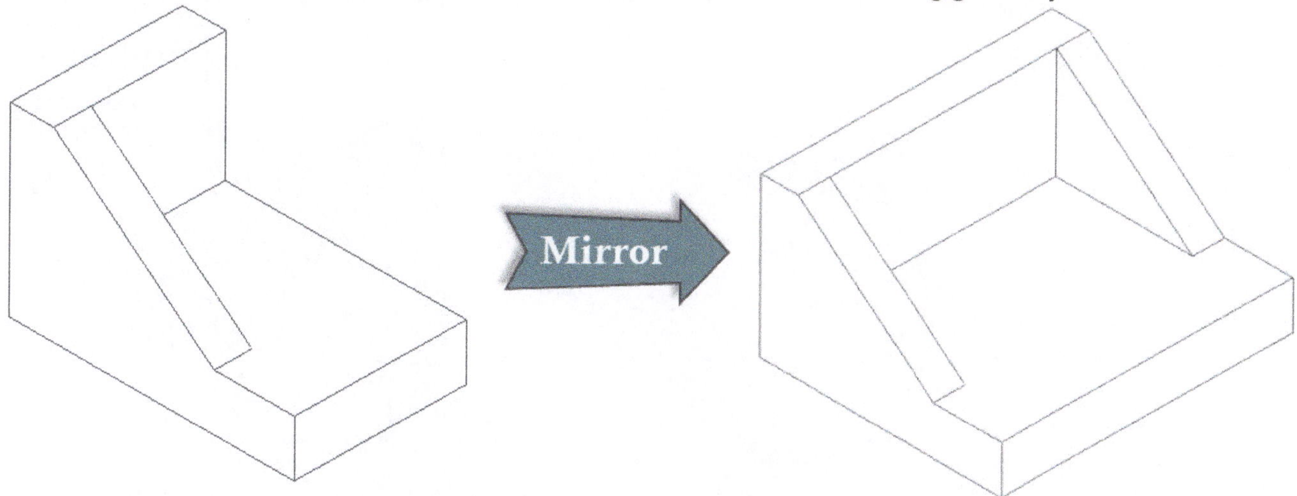

Also, there are some pattern commands to replicate a feature throughout a part quickly. They save you from creating additional features individually and help you modify the design easily. If the design changes, you only need to change the first feature, and the rest of the pattern features will update automatically. In this chapter, you will learn to create the mirrored and pattern geometries using the commands available in Solid Edge.

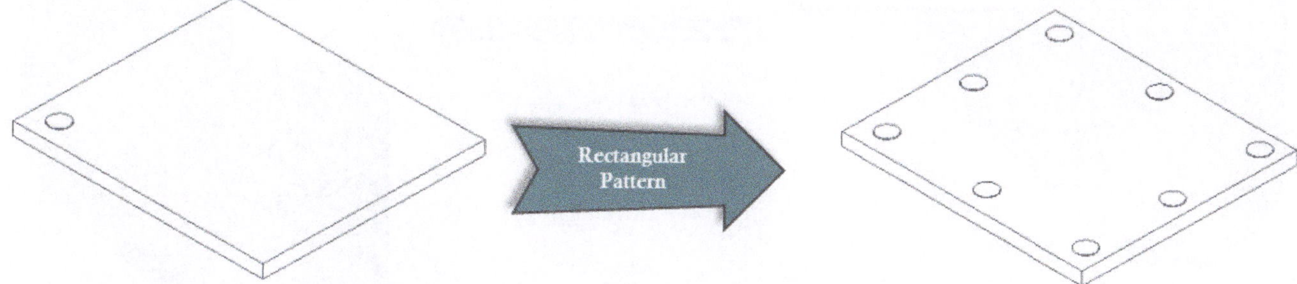

The topics covered in this chapter are:

- *Mirror* features
- *Rectangular Patterns*
- *Circular Patterns*
- *Along Curve Patterns*
- *Fill Patterns*
- *Recognize Hole Patterns*

Mirror Copy Feature (Ordered)

The **Mirror Copy Feature** command creates symmetrical components or features in parts by reflecting selected entities across a specified plane. This generates a mirrored version of the entities. The command is used in product design, where symmetry occurs frequently. It maintains consistency and reduces the time required to model both sides of a symmetrical object.

To mirror elements, access the **Home** tab and navigate to the **Pattern** group. Select **Mirror Copy Feature** from the **Mirror** drop-down menu. Select the elements in the part to mirror. For features such as rounds and drafts, select the parent feature first. Click **Accept** on the **Select Features** section in the command bar. The **Plane** section then activates.

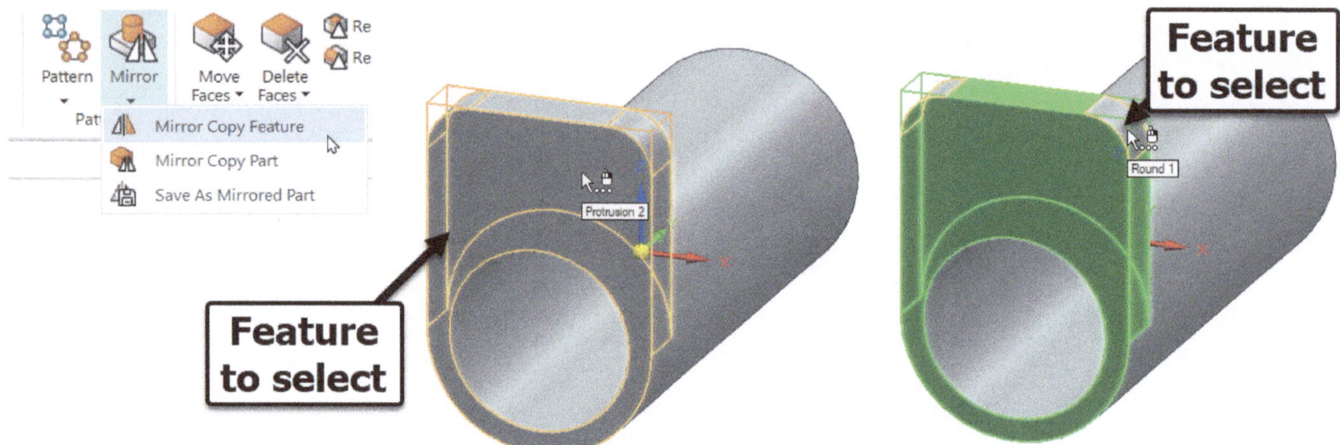

Select an option from the **Create From** drop-down, and then define the mirroring plane around which the selected elements will be mirrored for the desired effect. Conclude the mirroring operation by clicking the **Finish** button.

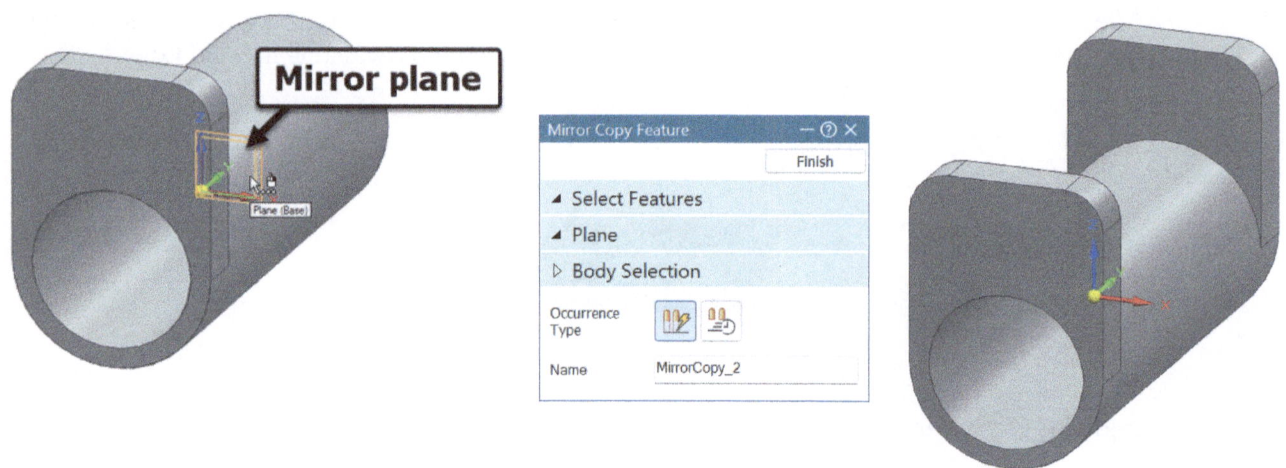

Mirror Copy Part (Ordered)

If your part is entirely symmetric, you can save time by creating only half of it and then mirroring the entire geometry instead of duplicating individual features. To do this efficiently, you can utilize the **Mirror Copy Part** command. Activate this command by navigating to the ribbon and clicking on **Home > Pattern > Mirror > Mirror Copy Part**. Once the command is active, click on the solid part you want to mirror.

Next, select the face that will serve as the axis for mirroring the geometry. If desired, you have the option to use the **Remove Original** button to eliminate the original part, leaving only the mirrored half. After configuring these settings, click **Finish** to execute the mirror copy part operation.

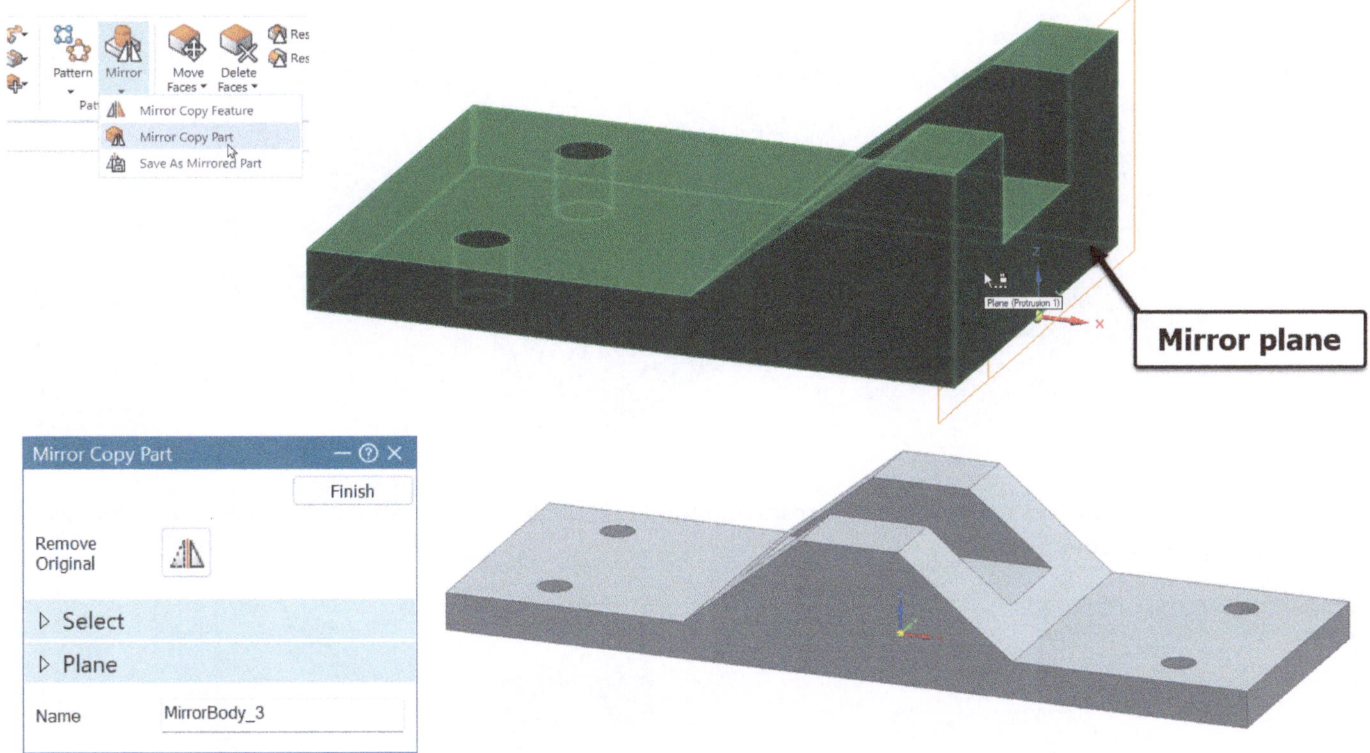

Mirror (Synchronous)

If you are designing a symmetric part, you can save time by using the **Mirror** command. Using this command, you can replicate the individual features of the entire body. To mirror features (3D geometry), you need to have a face or plane to use as a reference. You can use a model face, default plane, or create a new plane if it does not exist where it is needed.

Click on the features to be mirrored in the Pathfinder and activate the **Mirror** command (click **Home > Pattern > Mirror** on the ribbon). Now, select the reference plane about which the features are to be mirrored.

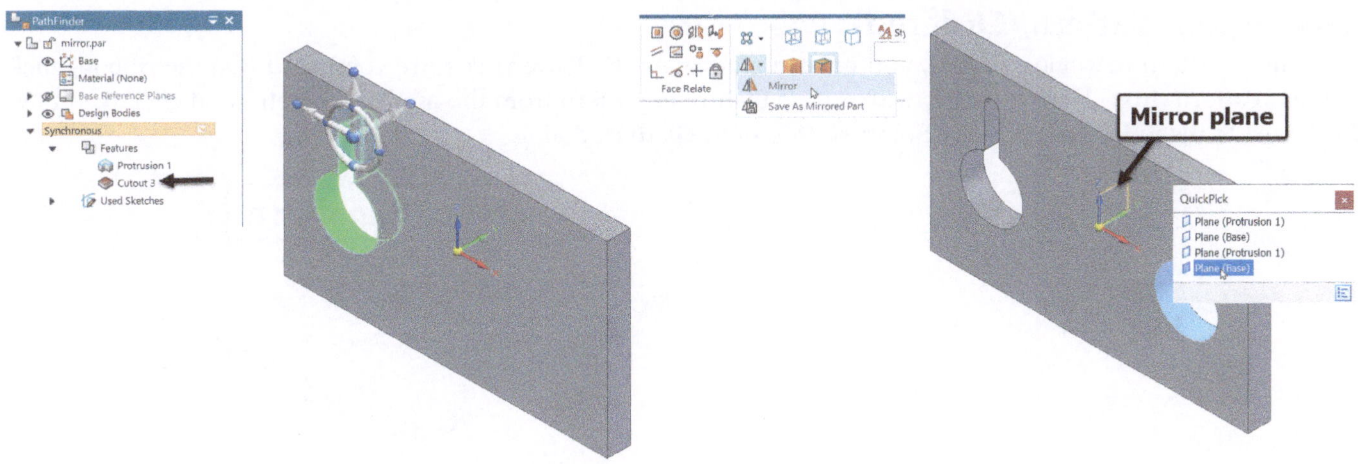

Now, if you make changes to the original feature, the mirror feature will be updated automatically.

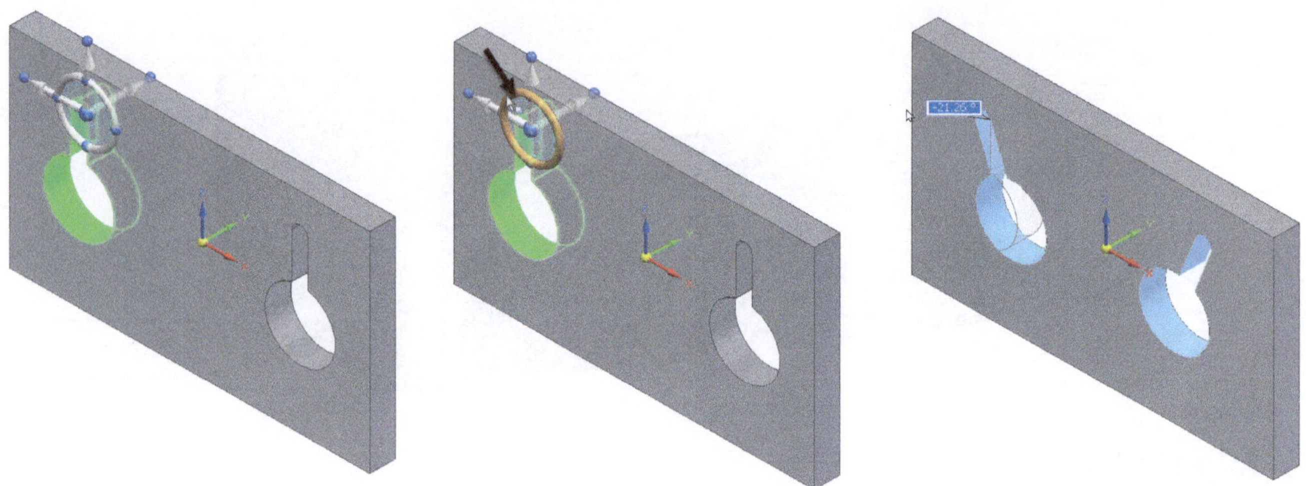

If you select the **Detach Faces** option on the **Mirror** command bar, the feature's faces will be mirrored but detached from the rest of the model.

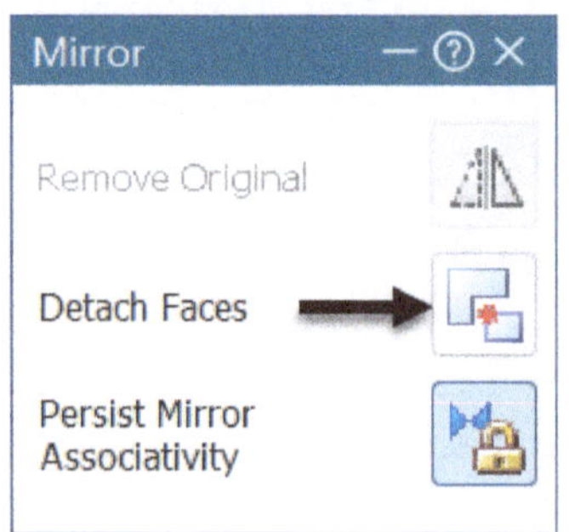

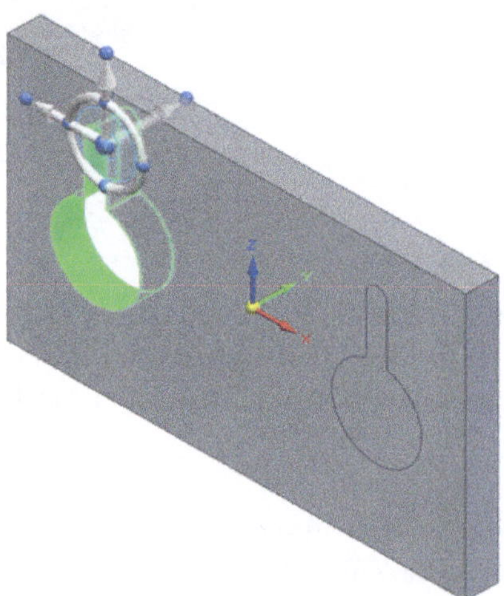

Rectangular Pattern (Ordered)

To create a pattern in a linear layout, you must first activate the **Pattern Feature** command (On the ribbon, click **Home > Pattern** drop-down **> Pattern**). Select the feature to pattern from the model geometry and click the green check next to the **Selected** box in the **Select** section of the **Pattern** dialog.

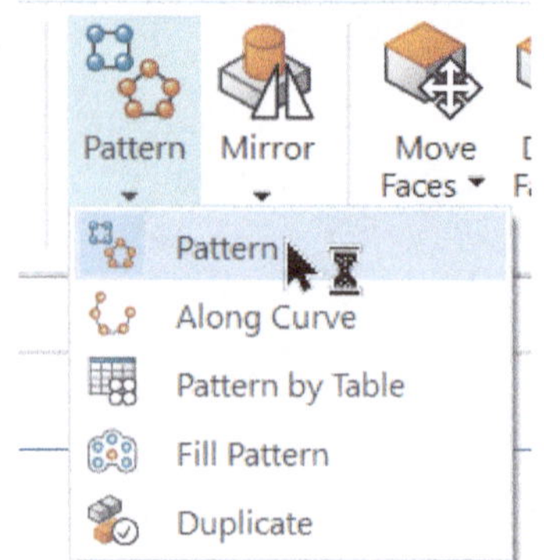

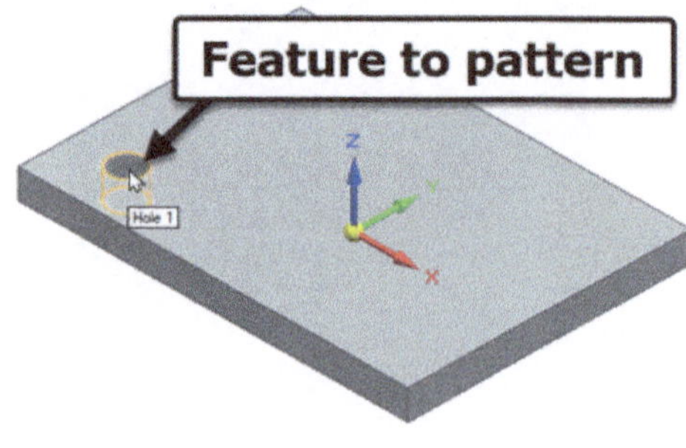

On the **Pattern** dialog, select **Pattern Type > Rectangular**. Next, you need to create the outline of the pattern profile according to your design. You can do this by first selecting the **Placement Type**: **Quick Pattern** or **By Sketch**. For example, select **Placement Type > By Sketch**. Next, specify the plane where you intend to arrange the pattern; the model is oriented parallel to the selected plane, allowing you to sketch the pattern profile.

Specify the first corner of the rectangular pattern. This point serves as the default reference point, indicated by a bold X symbol. This reference point determines the position of the entire feature pattern relative to it and the parent feature. Move the pointer diagonally and click to specify the second corner of the rectangular pattern.

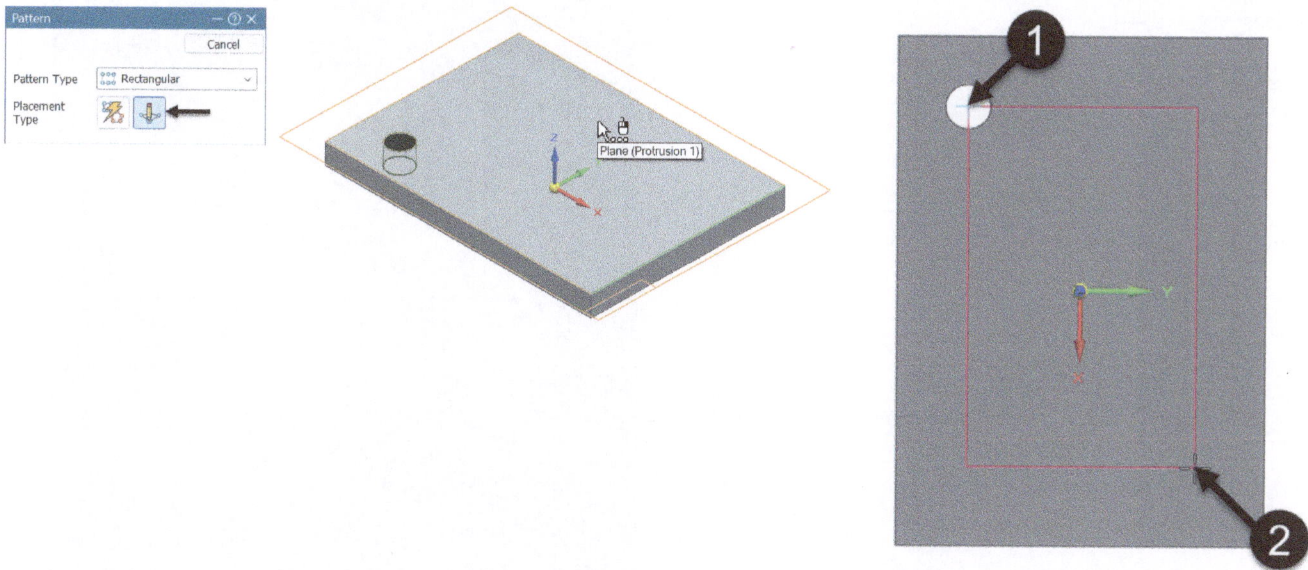

Next, select the pattern type from the **Rectangular Pattern** command bar. There are three options in this drop-down: **Fit**, **Fill**, and **Fixed**.

In the **Fit** option, specify the number of occurrences in the x and y directions, as well as the height and width of the pattern. This provides precise control over the pattern layout.

When using the **Fit** option, the command bar automatically calculates the X Spacing and Y Spacing values. These values define the spacing between occurrences in the horizontal (x) and vertical (y) directions.

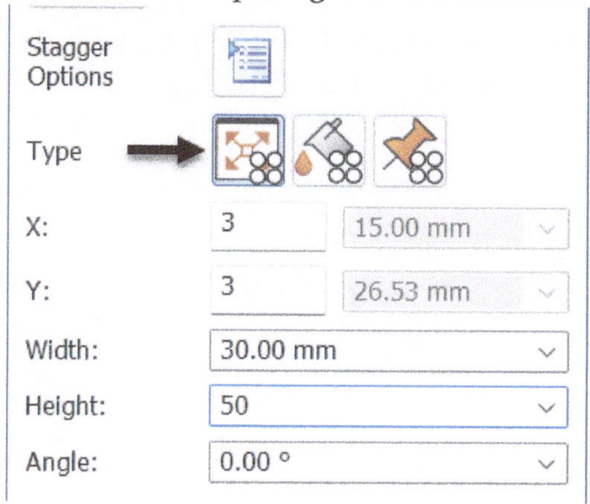

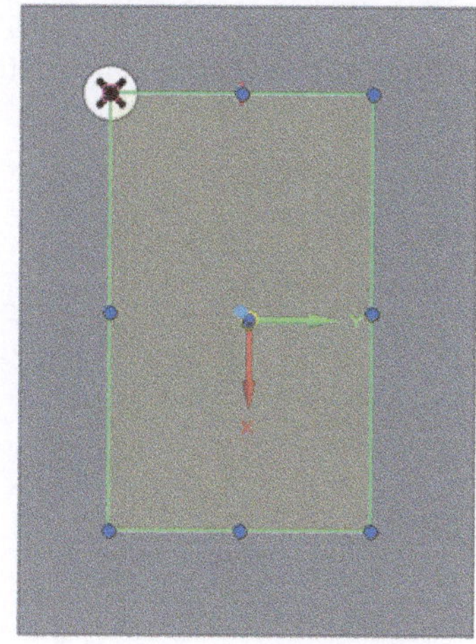

When you select the **Fill** option, you need to enter values in the x and y spacing boxes. Also, you need to type-in values in the **Height** and **Width** boxes. The **X** Count and **Y** Count values on the command bar are automatically calculated and remain fixed as whole numbers.

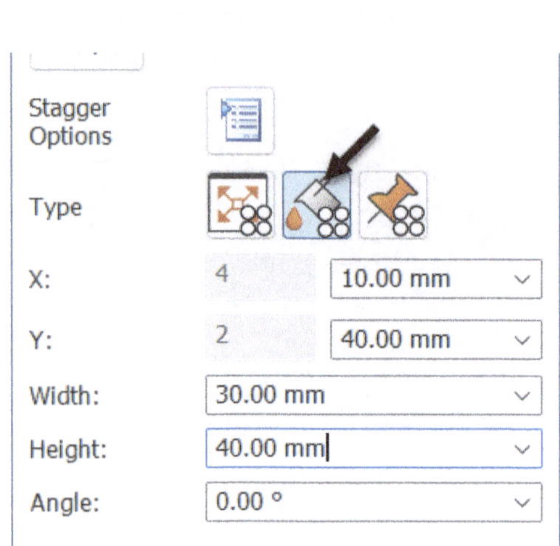

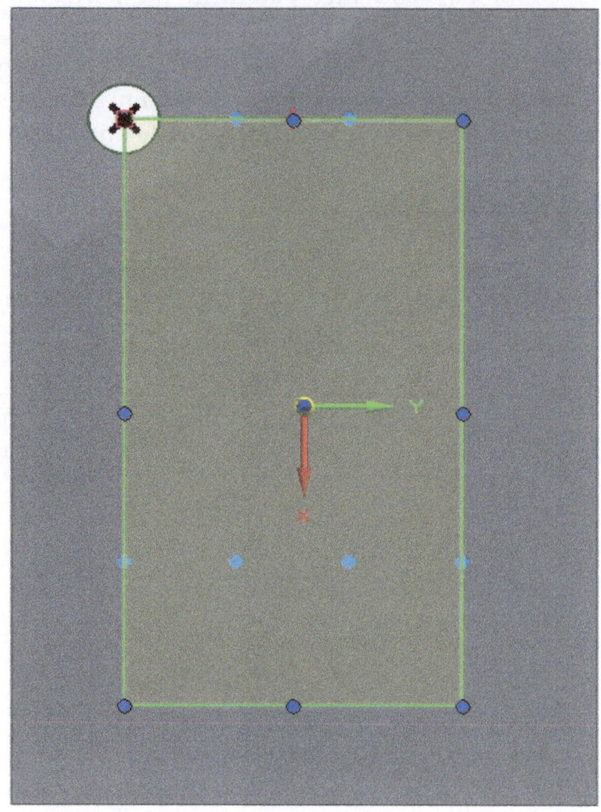

Next, adjust the width and height of the pattern profile by entering values in the **Width** and **Height** boxes available on the **Rectangular Pattern** command bar. Optionally, you can also change the angle of the rectangular pattern by entering a value in the **Angle** box.

When you choose the **Fixed** setting, you can determine the number of occurrences in both the **X** and **Y** boxes. Additionally, it's necessary to specify the **X** and **Y** spacing.

As you input these parameters, the **Width** and **Height** values displayed on the command bar are automatically calculated. This calculation is based on the parameters you've set, ensuring that the dimensions align precisely with your specifications.

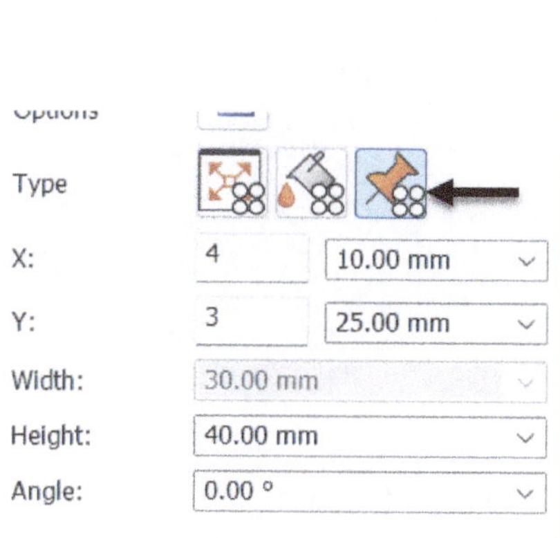

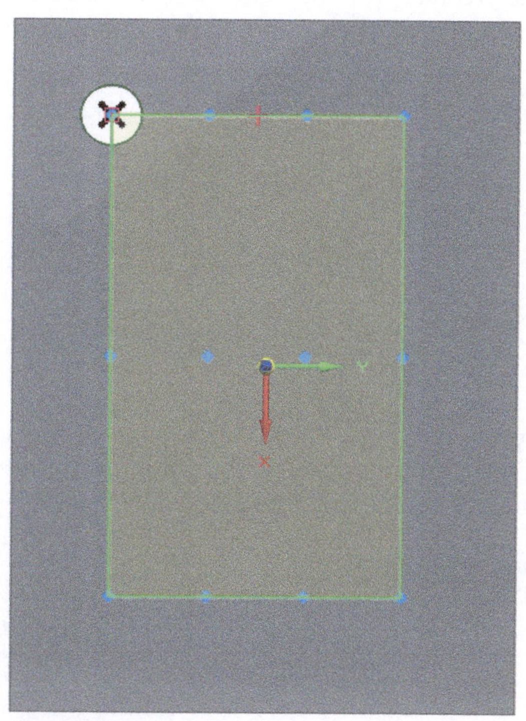

Use the **Suppress Occurrence** button if you need to suppress any individual occurrence in the rectangular pattern. Upon completing the sketch, click the **Close Sketch** button on the ribbon to proceed. Click on the **Finish** button situated on the command bar to finalize the pattern arrangement.

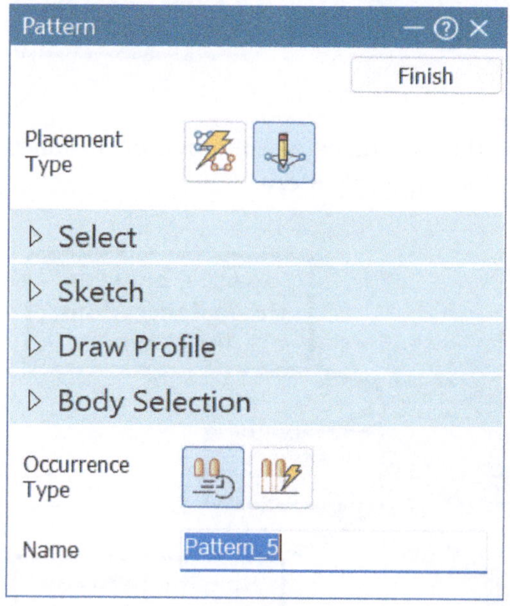

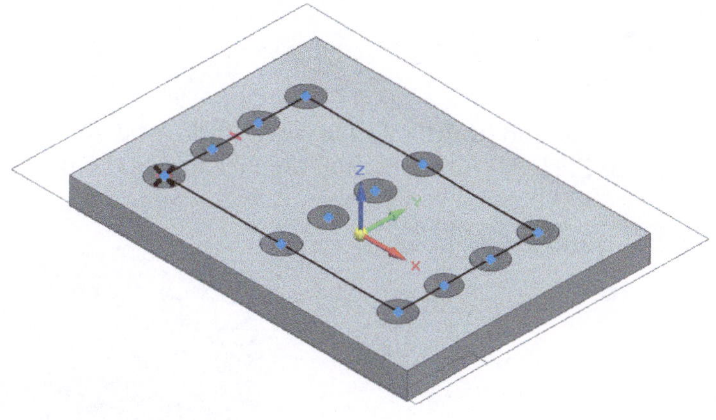

Rectangular Pattern (Synchronous)

This command creates a rectangular pattern of a feature. To create a rectangular pattern, you must first select the feature to pattern and activate the **Rectangular** command (click **Home > Pattern > Rectangular** on the command bar). Next, define the second corner of the rectangular pattern by moving the pointer diagonally and clicking on the model's face. You will notice that a pattern preview appears on the model.

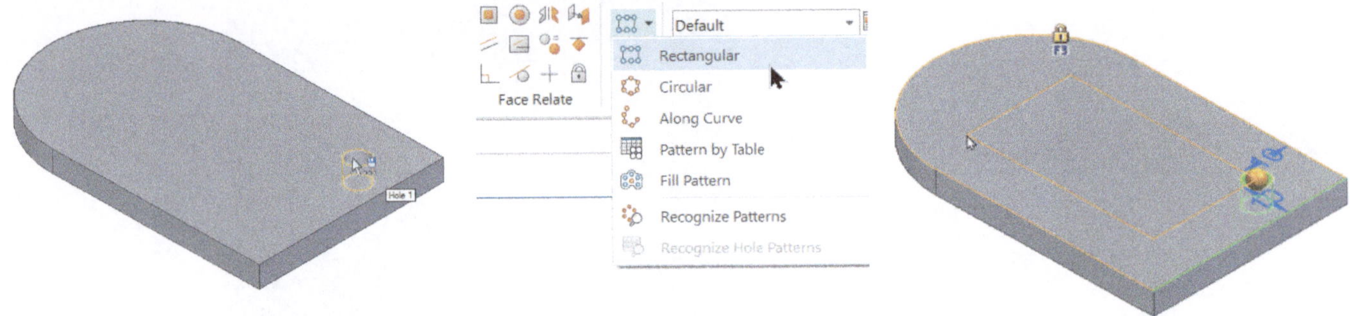

Now, select the **Fit** option from the **Fill Style** drop-down and set the pattern's parameters (Total Spacing along X-axis and Y-axis, X Count, and Y Count). If you want to suppress some instances, click the **Suppress Instance** option on the command bar and select the green dots from the pattern preview. Next, click the **Accept** button on the command bar.

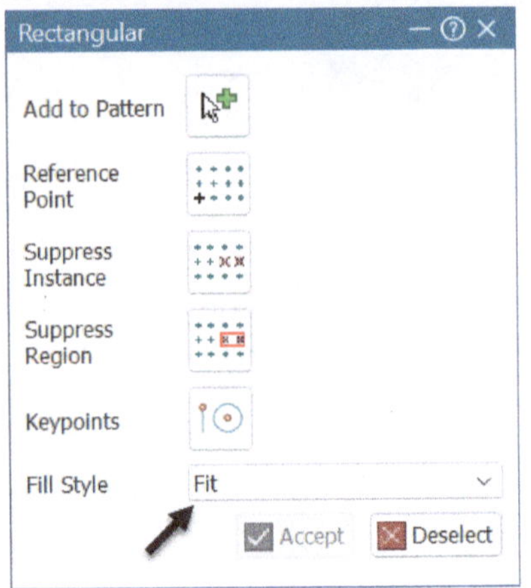

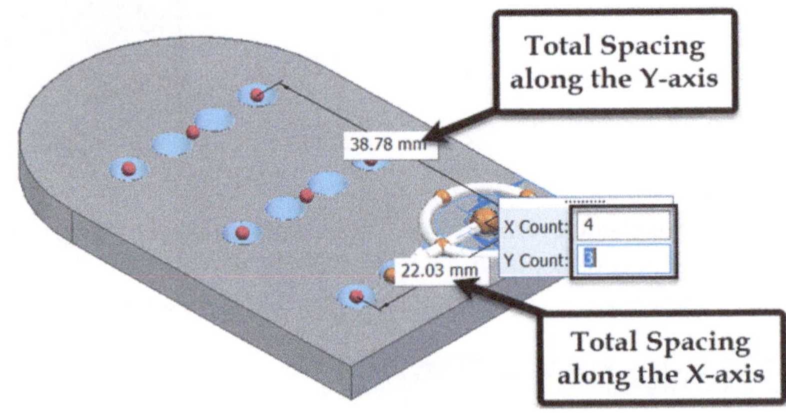

Select the **Fixed** option from the **Fill Style** drop-down if you want to enter the spacing between individual instances of the pattern. Click the **Accept** button on the command bar to finish the rectangular pattern.

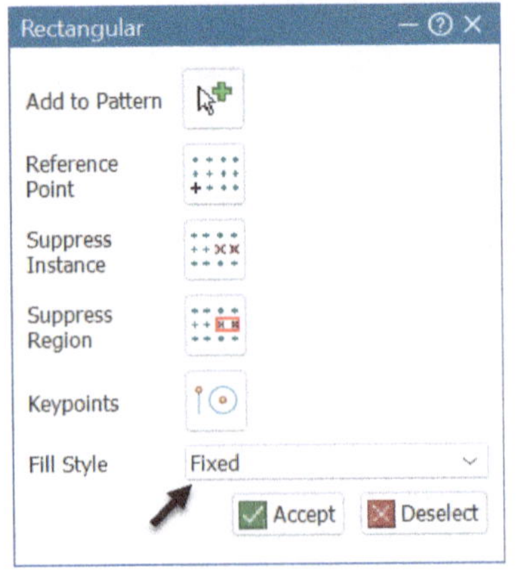

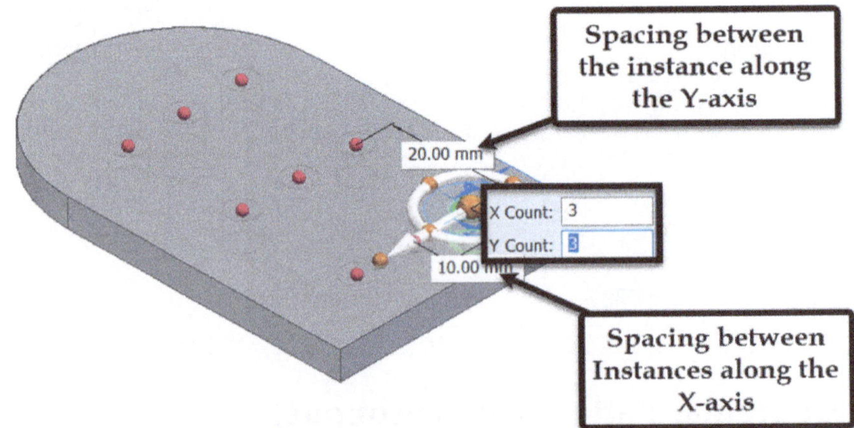

If you want to modify the rectangular pattern, just select it from the model or Pathfinder. A pattern annotation (for example, Pattern 3X2) appears on it. Select the annotation and then modify the pattern parameters. You can use the **Add to Pattern** option on the command bar to add more features to the pattern.

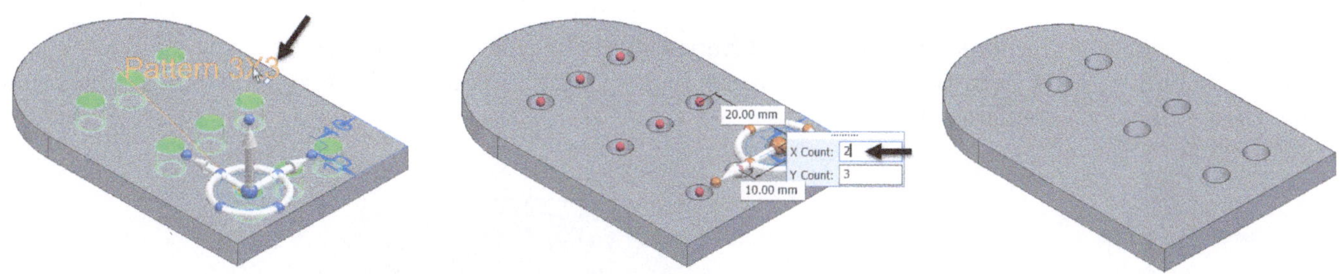

Circular Pattern (Ordered)

Creating a circular pattern is accomplished by replicating features or components along a circular trajectory. This process allows you to efficiently duplicate design elements in a symmetrical arrangement. Navigate to the **Home** tab and access the **Pattern** command in the **Pattern** drop-down of the **Pattern** group. Select the feature to pattern from the model geometry and click the green check next to the **Selected** box in the **Select** section of the **Pattern** dialog.

On the **Pattern** dialog, select **Pattern Type > Circular**. Next, select **Placement Type > By Sketch**. Next, specify the plane where you intend to arrange the pattern; the model is oriented parallel to the selected plane, allowing you to sketch the pattern profile.

Select the feature to pattern from the model geometry and click the **Accept** button. Next, specify the plane where you intend to arrange the pattern; the model is oriented parallel to the selected plane, allowing you to sketch the pattern profile.

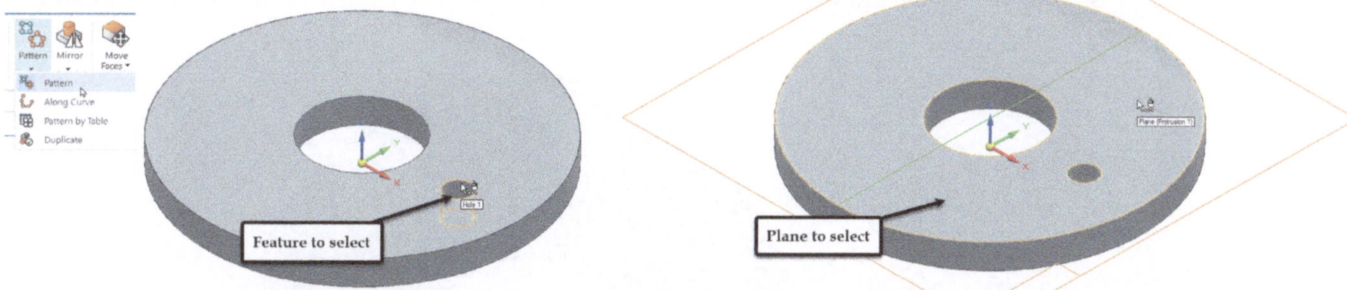

Click to identify the center point for the circular pattern. Specify the radius (start point) of the pattern circle by clicking. You can also enter a value in the **Radius** box available on the **Circular Pattern** command bar. Determine the direction for placing the pattern along the circle by clicking.

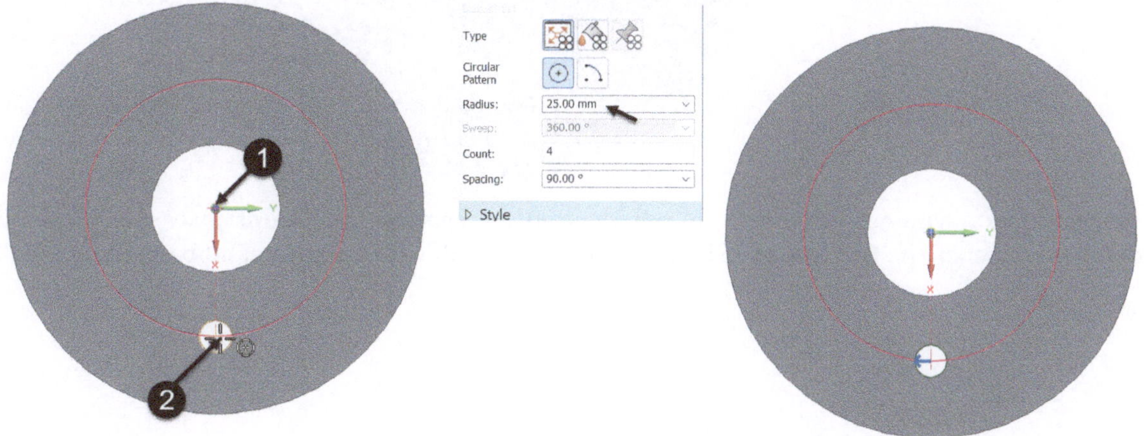

Next, select the pattern type from the **Type** section. There are three options: **Fit**, **Fill**, and **Fixed**.

When select the **Fit** option, you have to define the **Count** and the **Radius** of the pattern circle. If you click the **Partial Circle** button, you must also specify the **Sweep** angle of the arc. Notably, the angular **Spacing** value found on the command bar is automatically calculated.

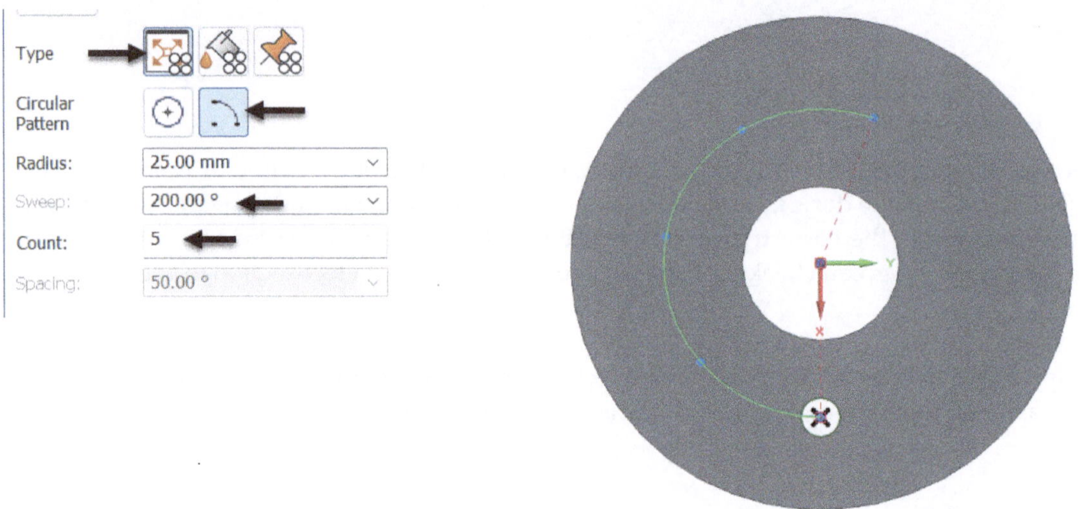

When you select the **Fill** option, you need to enter values in the **Radius** and **Spacing** boxes. If you click the **Partial Circle** button, you must also specify the arc's sweep angle in the **Sweep** box. The **Count** value on the command bar, automatically computed.

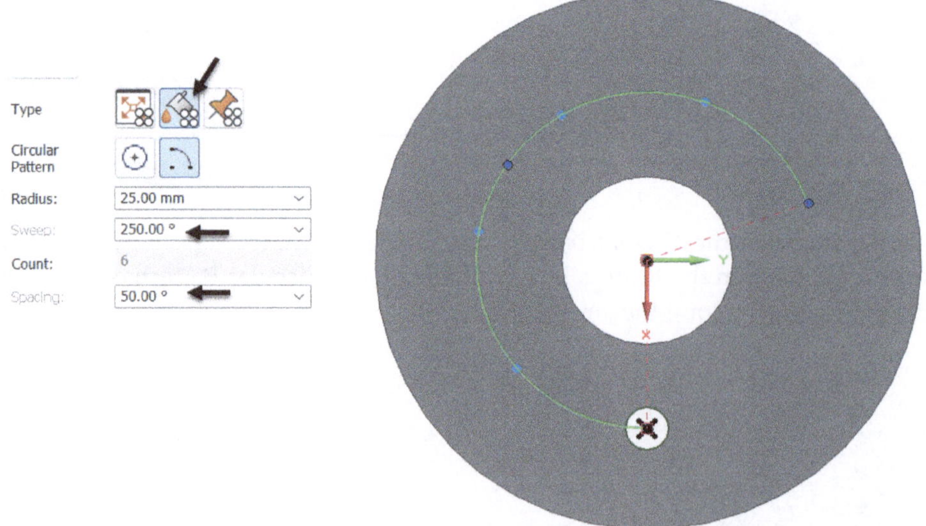

When you select the **Fill** option, you need to enter values in the **Radius**, **Spacing** and **Count** boxes. Note that this option is selected only if you click the **Partial Circle** button. The **Sweep** value on the command bar, automatically computed.

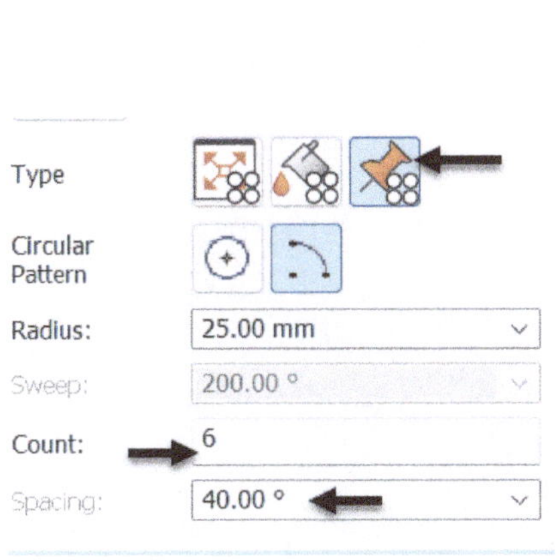

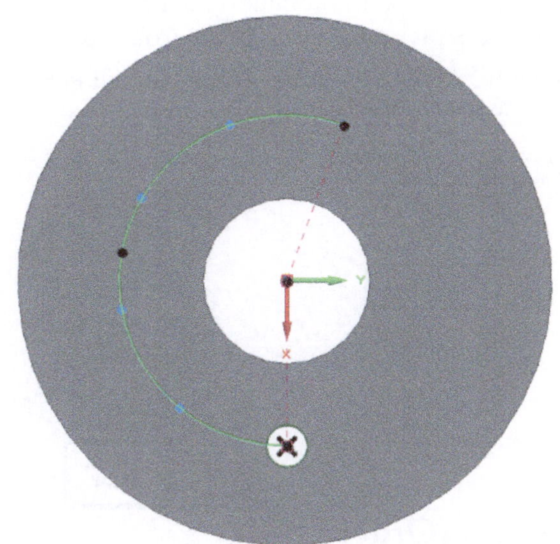

Conclude the sketch by clicking **Close Sketch**. Click **Finish** on the command bar.

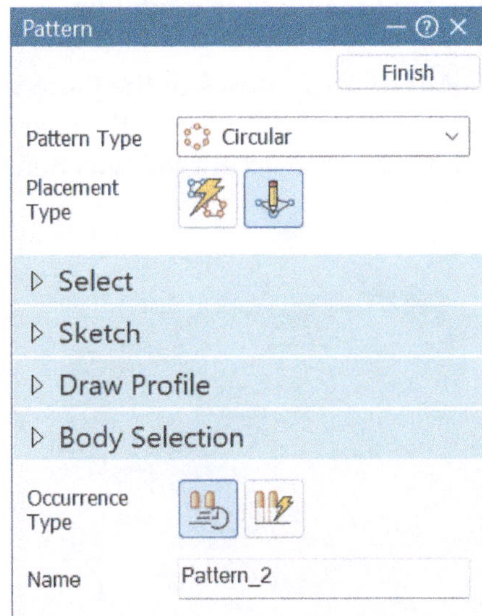

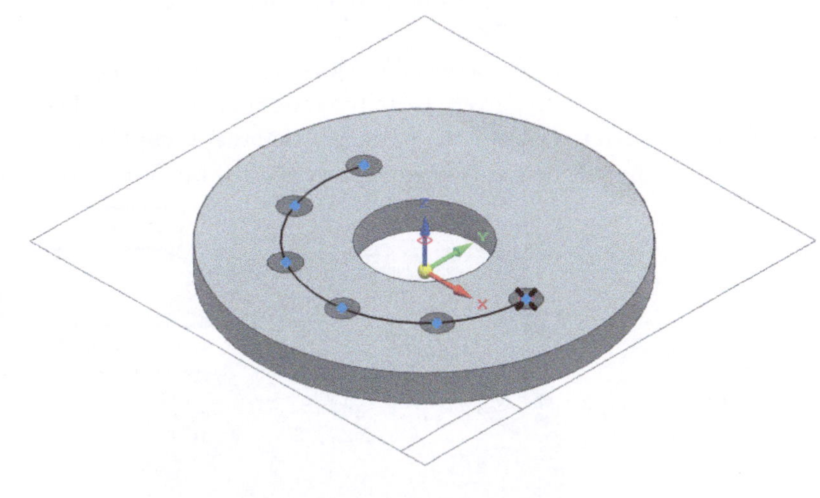

Circular Pattern (Synchronous)

This command creates a pattern of selected features circularly. Select the feature to pattern and activate the **Circular** command (click **Home > Pattern > Rectangular > Circular** on the ribbon). Next, define the axis of the circular pattern by selecting a key point.

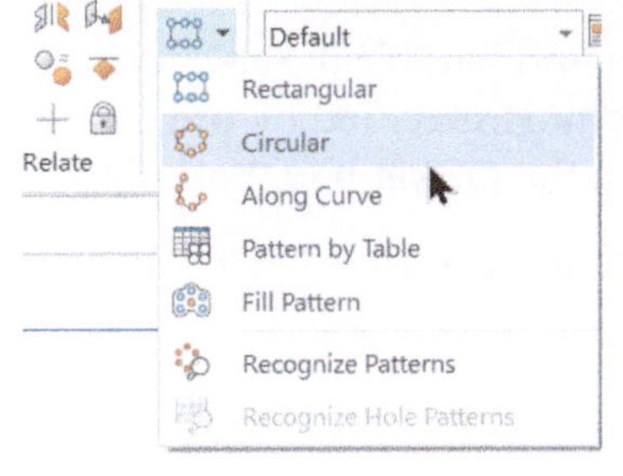

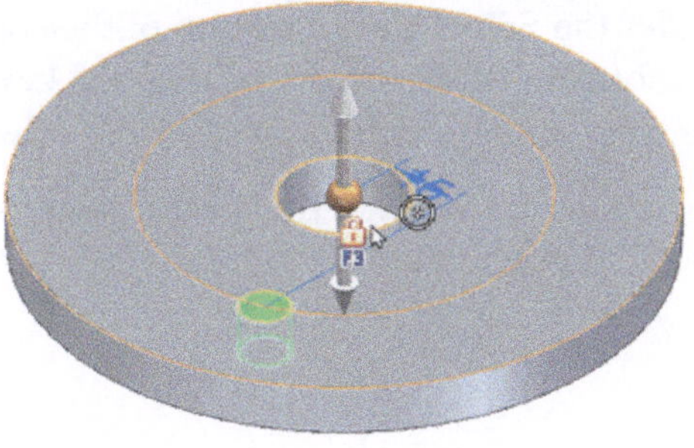

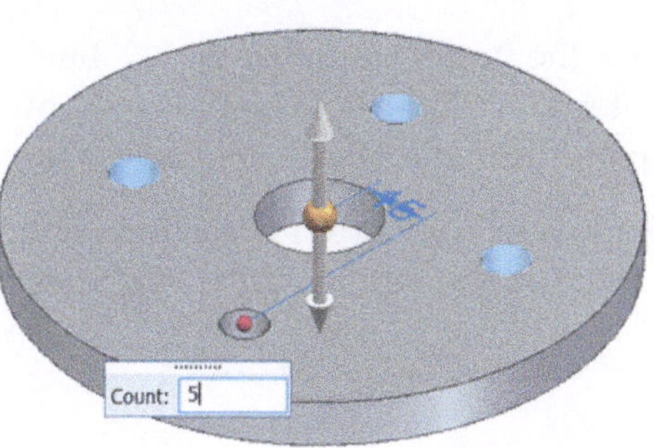

Use the **Circle/Arc Pattern** option on the command bar to create an arc pattern. Next, select the **Fit** option from the **Fill Style** drop-down. Next, type-in values in the **Count** and **Total Angle** boxes. If you select the **Fixed** option, you specify both the quantity of occurrences and the angular spacing between the individual occurrences. Click the **Accept** button to create the circular pattern.

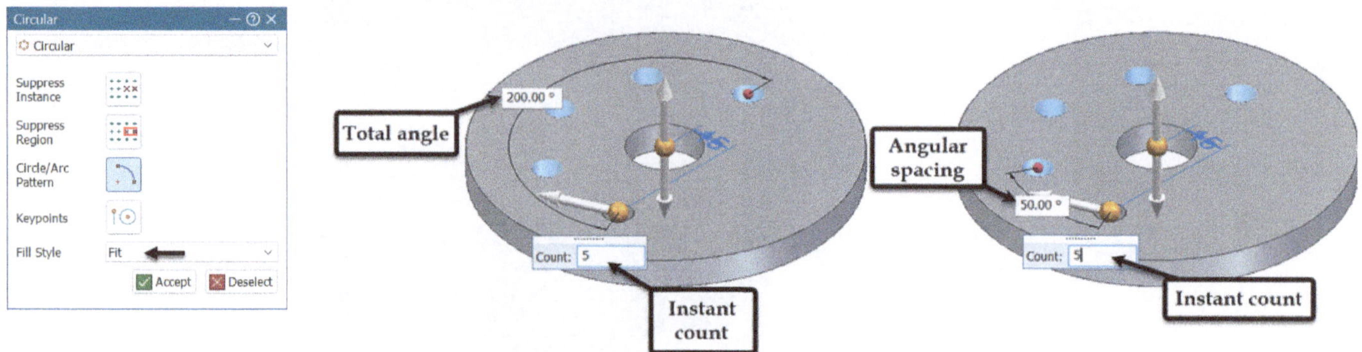

Along Curve Pattern (Ordered)

The **Along Curve Pattern** command replicates features along a selected curve in your design. It is useful for placing elements such as steps on spiral staircases, parts on curved railings, and details on curved surfaces. It also supports tasks like hose routing, piping layouts, wave-like patterns, and basic terrain or landscape modeling.

Navigate to the **Home** tab and access the **Along Curve Pattern** command in the **Pattern** drop-down of the **Pattern** group. Select the feature to pattern from the model geometry and click the **Accept** button. Next, specify the curve along which you plan to arrange the pattern. Click the **Accept** button on the command bar to accept the selection. Select a point on the selected curve/edge to define the anchor point of the pattern.

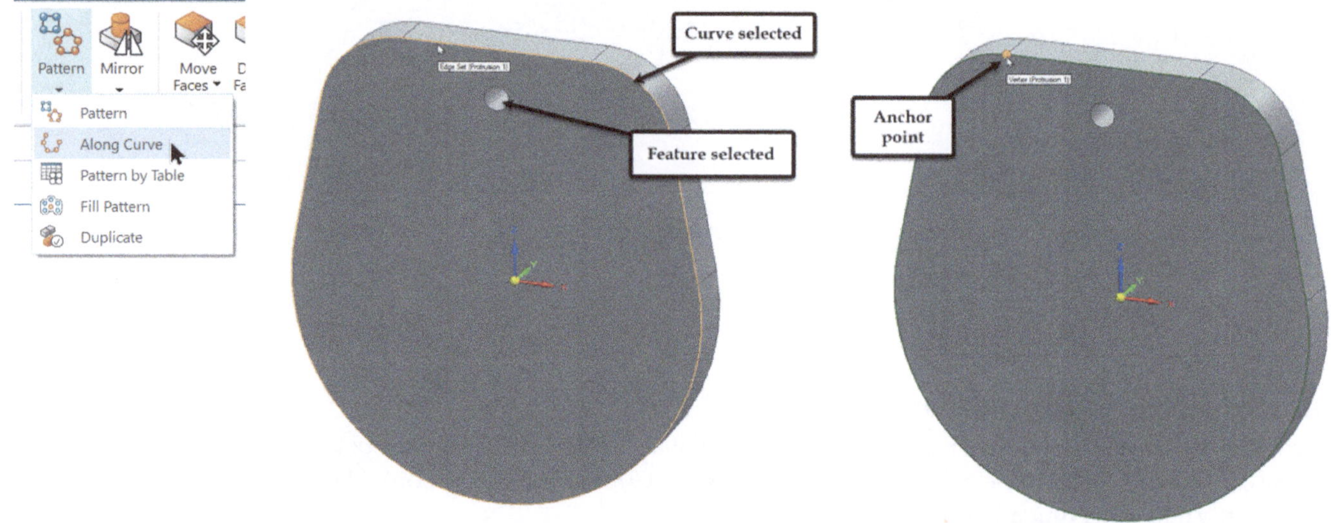

Click the **Project onto Curve** button under the **Select Curve** section of the command bar. Next, select the centerpoint of the hole feature, as shown; the offset distance from the selected keypoint is specified by projecting a point from the selected element. However, you can also enter a fixed offset value in the **Offset** box. You can toggle the **Flip Pattern Direction** button to change the direction of the pattern along the curve. Next, click **Accept** on the command bar; the **Spacing** section is activated.

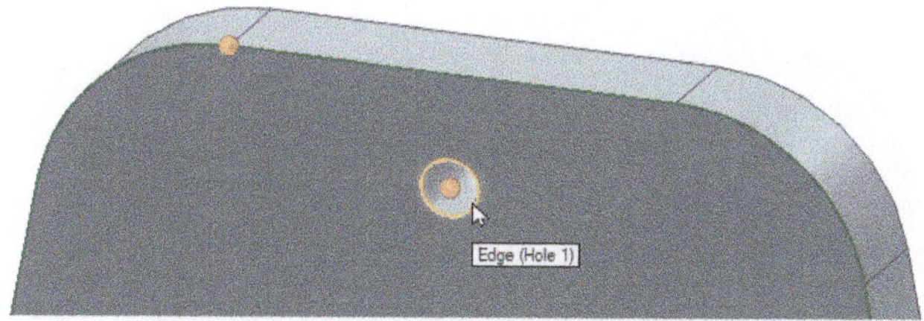

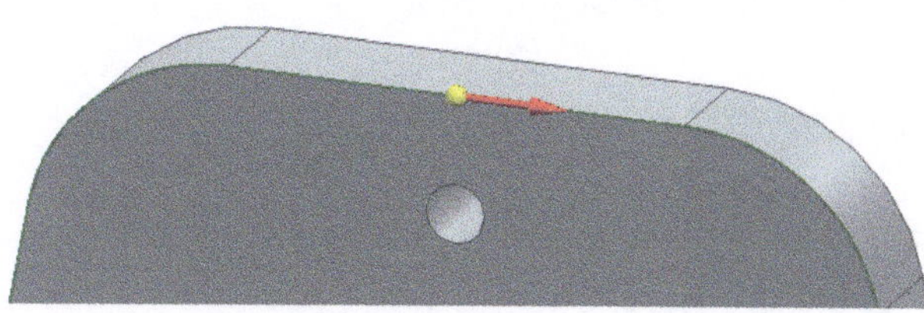

Next, select an option from the **Pattern type** drop-down available on the command bar. There are four options in this drop-down: **Fit**, **Fill**, **Fixed**, and **Chord Length**.

When you select the **Fit** option, you just need to enter the number of occurrences in the **Count** box. As a result, the count value indicates the total number of occurrences along the selected curve length, including the parent. The resulting spacing value is then determined automatically.

The **Fill** option allows you to enter only the **Spacing** value; the number of occurrences are determined automatically.

Moving on to the **Fixed** pattern type, it allows you to enter both **Count** and **Spacing** values.

The **Chord Length** pattern type allows you specify three values: **Count**, **Spacing**, and **Skip**. The **Count** value signifies the total occurrences along the curve length, including the parent. The **Spacing** value is defined as the chord length between two points. The **Skip** value allows you to omit the occurences in between the pattern along the curve. A 0 skip will not skip any occurrence in the pattern. Whereas, the 1 skip value omits alternating occurrences. A Skip value of 2 means that after the parent occurrence, two instances are skipped in the pattern, and the fourth occurrence is then displayed. This pattern continues in a similar manner throughout the series.

Click the **Next** button to activate the **Alignment** section. In this section, specify the orientation of the occurrences using the **Occurrence Orientation** drop-down. For this example, select the **Follow Curve** option; the orientation of the parent component to precisely matched with the curvature of the specified curve. Click **Preview** and **Finish** to complete the feature.

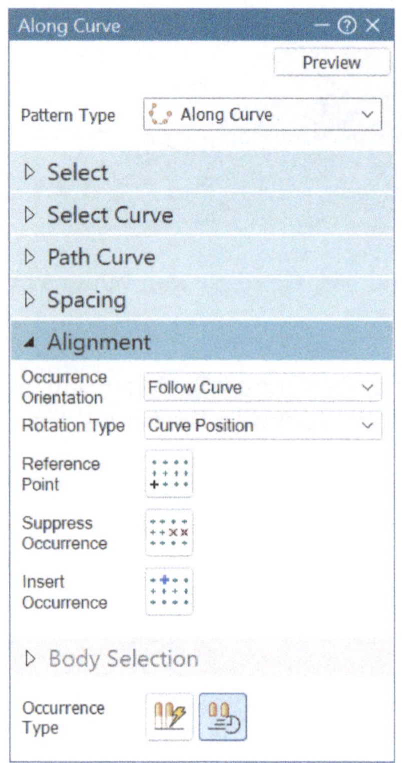

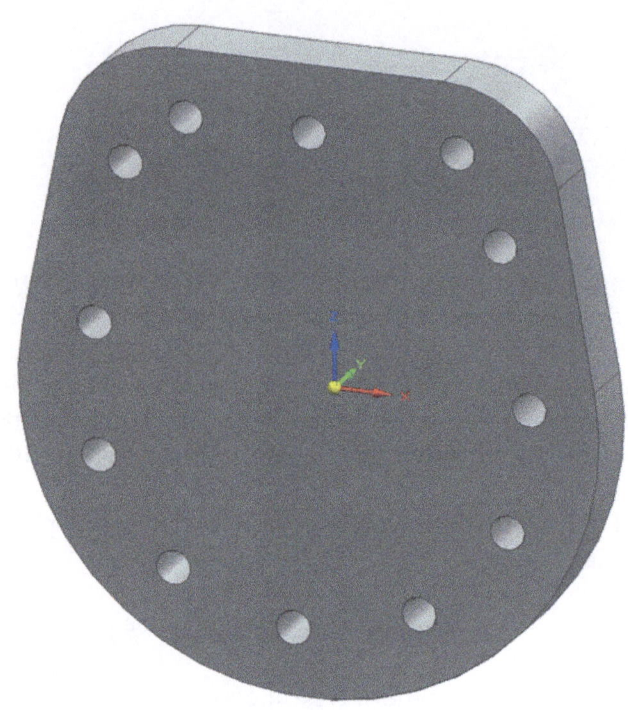

Along Curve Pattern (Synchronous)

This command creates a pattern along a selected curve or edge. Activate this command (click **Home > Pattern > Rectangular > Along Curve** on the ribbon).

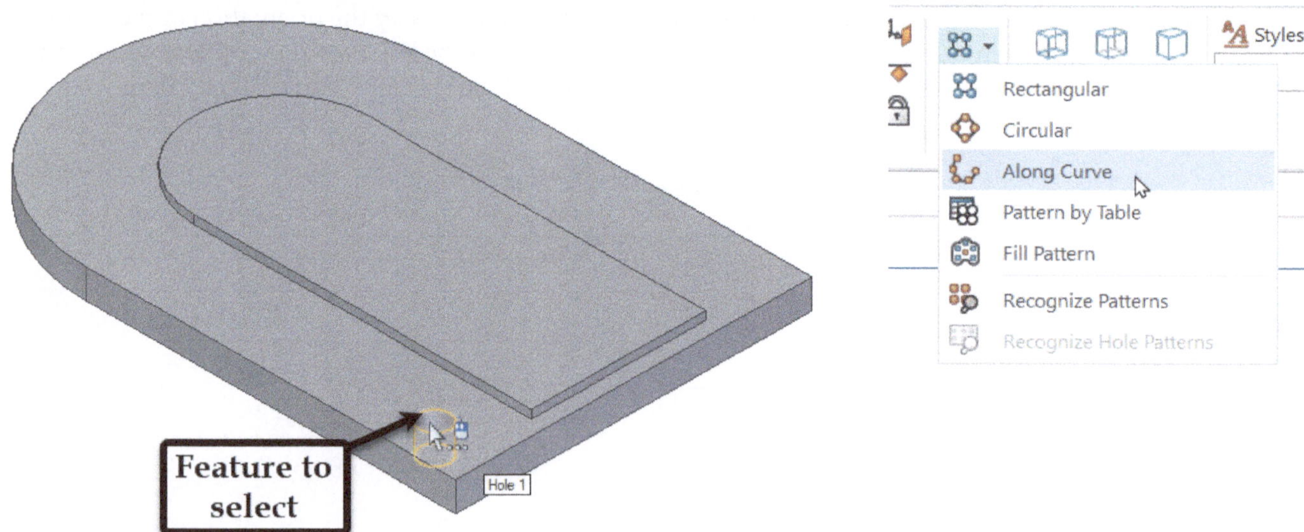

Next, set the **Selection Type** on the command bar and click on a curve or edge. Click the **Accept** button on the command bar to accept the selection. Select a point on the selected curve/edge to define the anchor point of the pattern.

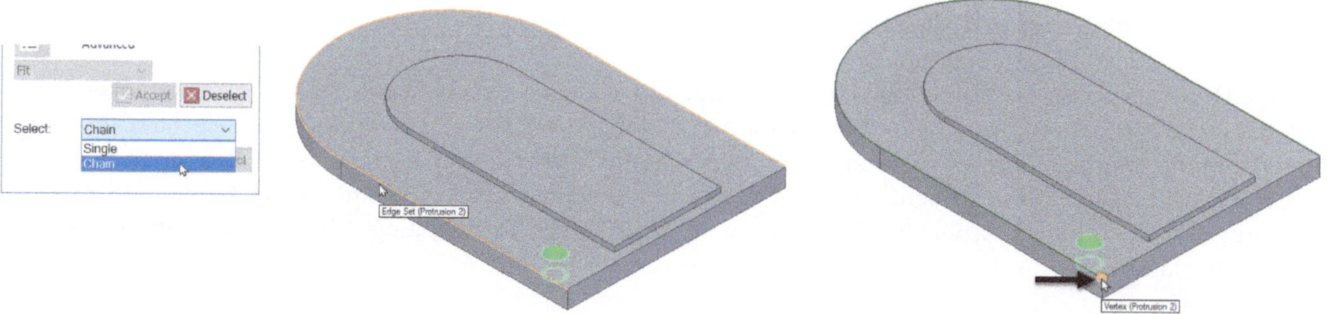

Click to define the side of the pattern. On the command bar, click the **Advanced** icon to display a box.

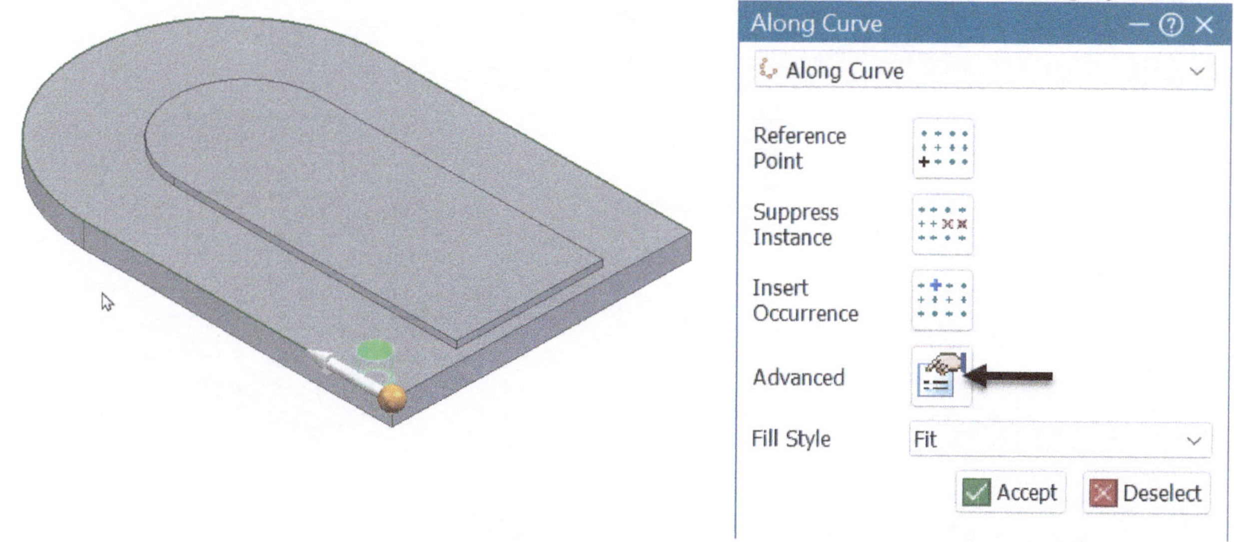

On this box, set the **Transformation Type** to **Follow Curve** and **Rotation Type** to **Curve Position**. Click the **Accept** button on the box and type-in a value in the **Count** box. On the command bar, set the **Fill Style** to **Fit** and click the **Accept** button to create the curve pattern.

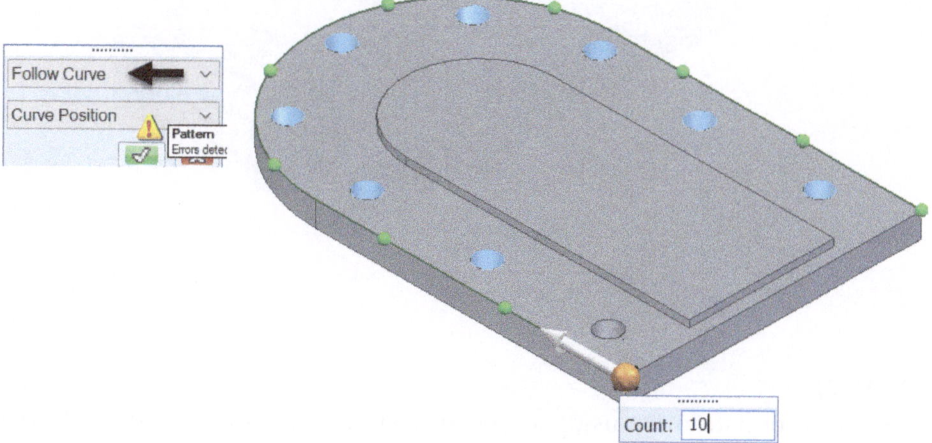

Pattern by Table (Ordered)

The **Pattern by Table** command empowers you to create a pattern with instances precisely determined based on the coordinate locations specified in an Excel spreadsheet. In this process, you use the first and second columns of the spreadsheet to specify the X and Y coordinates of the pattern instance. Then, the third column allows you to determine the orientation angle for each pattern instance.

Go to the **Home** tab, then navigate to the **Pattern** group, and select **Pattern by Table** from the **Pattern** drop-down. Select the feature to pattern from the graphics window, and then click the green check. Next, select a coordinate system from the graphics window to define the pattern's X and Y orientation. Next, click the **Browse** button and locate the Excel spreadsheet document you want to use. If you wish to embed the spreadsheet in the file, make sure to uncheck the **Link** box. Click the **Close** button on the **Instance Table** dialog. Click **Preview** and **Finish** to complete the pattern.

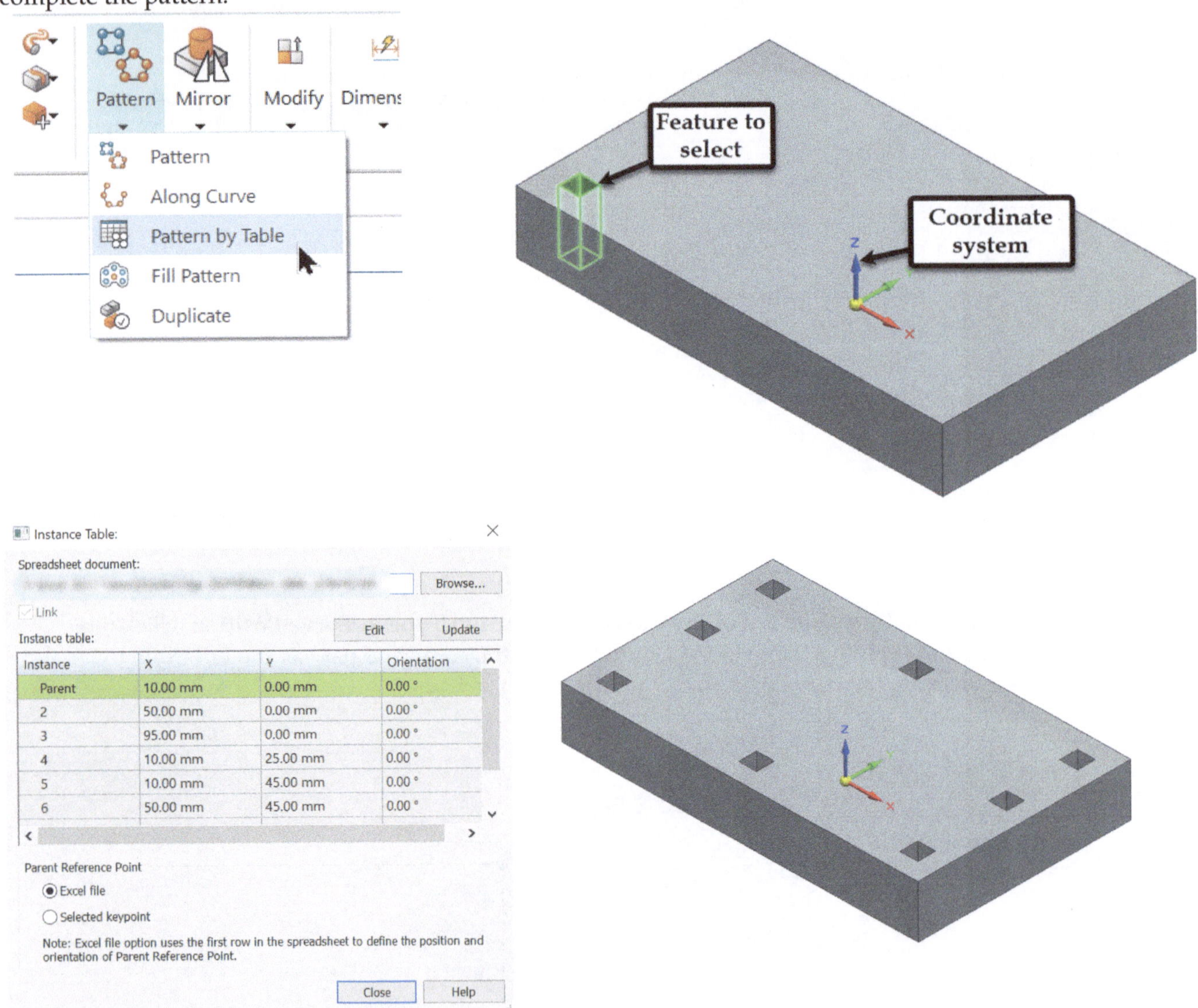

Pattern by Table (Synchronous)

The **Pattern by Table** command creates a feature pattern by using a spreadsheet to define the pattern instances' location. This command uses the first two columns of a spreadsheet to define the instance's X and Y coordinates. The value in the third column is used to define the orientation angle of the pattern instance. Select the feature to pattern from the model and activate the **Pattern by Table** command (On the ribbon, click **Home > Pattern > Pattern drop-down > Pattern by Table**). On the command bar, click the **Options** icon to open the **Pattern by Table**

Options dialog. In this dialog, specify the units using the **Use units from current document** or **Use custom units** options. If you select the **Use custom units** option, then you can define **Units** and **Round-off** values from the table available on the dialog. Click **OK** after defining the units.

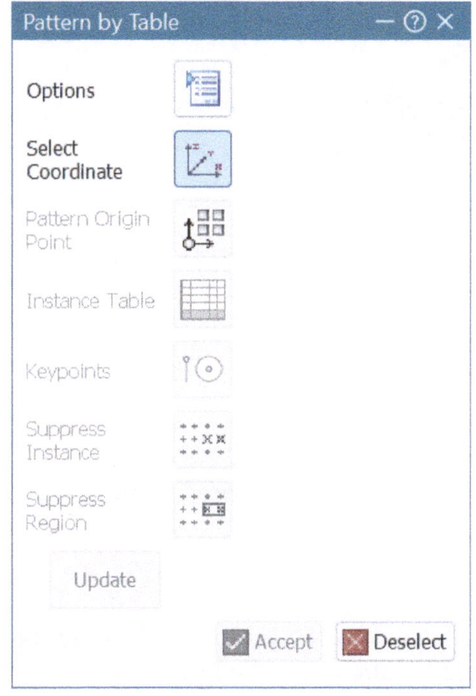

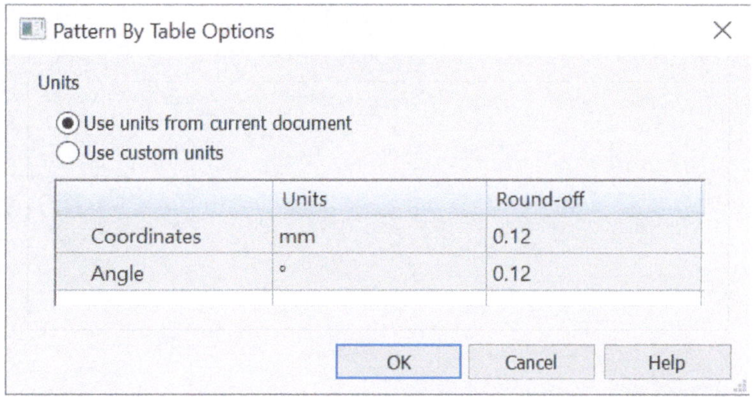

Select the coordinate system from the graphics window; the **Instance Table** dialog pops up on the screen. On this dialog, click the **Browse** button, select the spreadsheet, and click **Open**. You can use the **Edit** and **Update** buttons to make changes to the spreadsheet. On the **Instance Table** dialog, select the **Excel file** or **Selected keypoint** option from the **Parent Reference Point** section. Select a key point from the model to define the parent reference point if you have set the **Parent Reference Point** to **Selected keypoint**. Click **Close** on the dialog. Next, click the **Accept** button on the command bar to create the pattern.

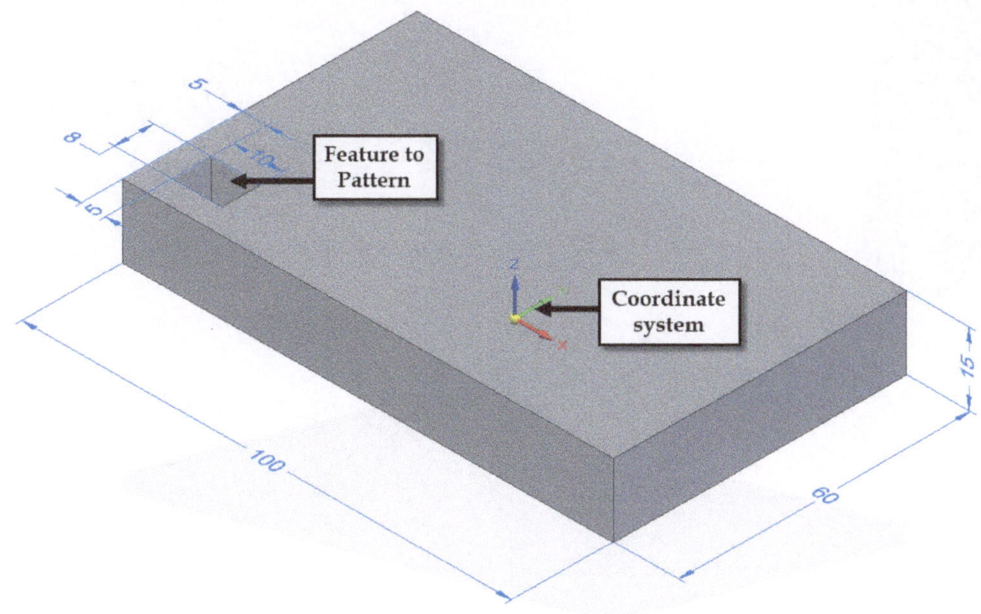

Spreadsheet

	A	B	C	D
1	10	0	0	
2	50	0	0	
3	90	0	0	
4	10	21	0	
5	10	42	0	
6	50	42	0	
7	90	21	0	
8	90	42	0	
9				

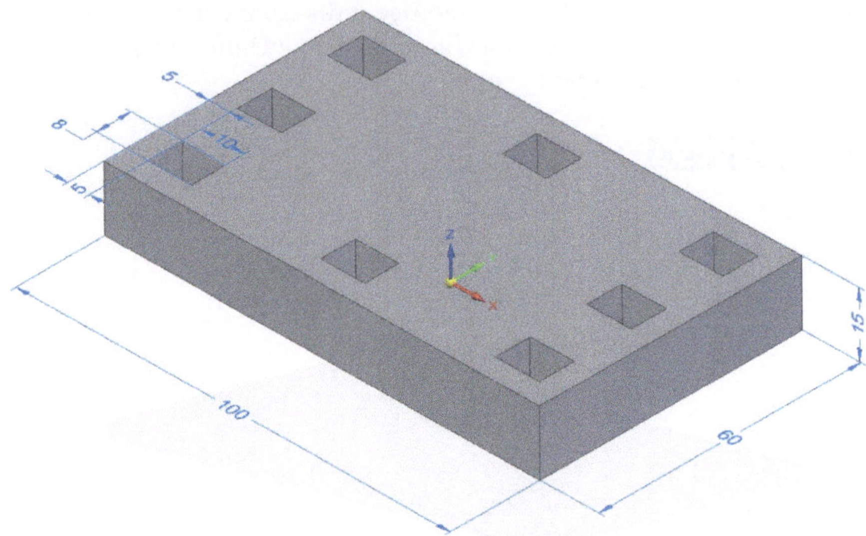

Fill Pattern (Synchronous)

This command creates a pattern of a feature by filling it in a defined region. You can create three different types of fill patterns: **Rectangular**, **Staggered**, and **Radial**.

Rectangular Fill Pattern

Select the feature from the geometry and activate the **Fill Pattern** command (click **Home > Pattern > Rectangular > Fill Pattern** on the ribbon). Select the face or region on which to create the fill pattern. Set the **Fill Style** to **Rectangular** and click the **Accept** button on the command bar. Type-in the spacing values between the pattern instances.

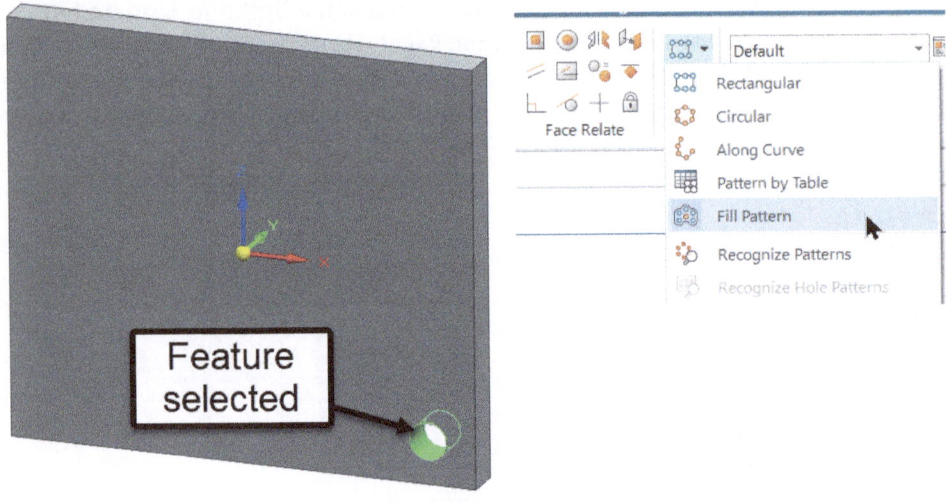

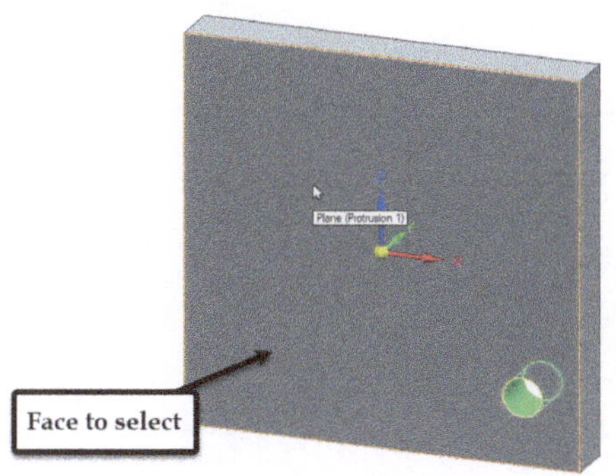

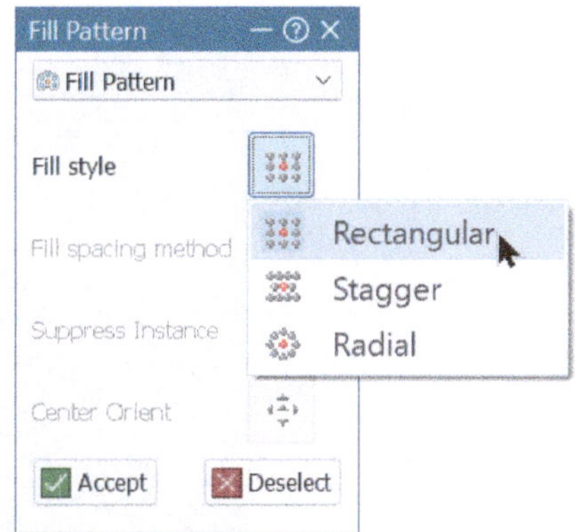

On the command bar, click the **Suppress Instance** icon to suppress the unwanted instances. You have the option to select individual occurrences by clicking on them. Alternatively, you can choose a group of occurrences by clicking and dragging over them.

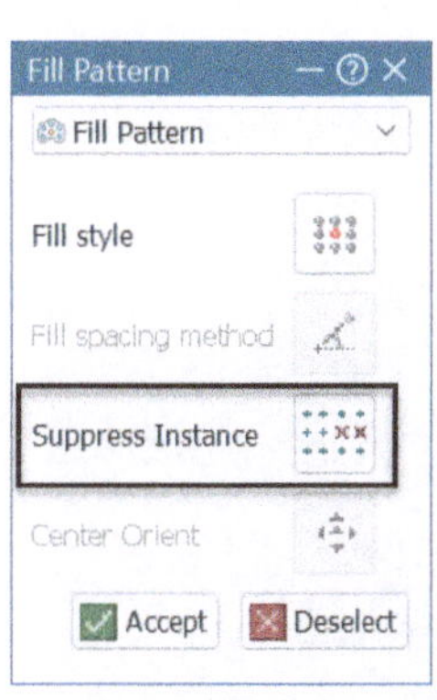

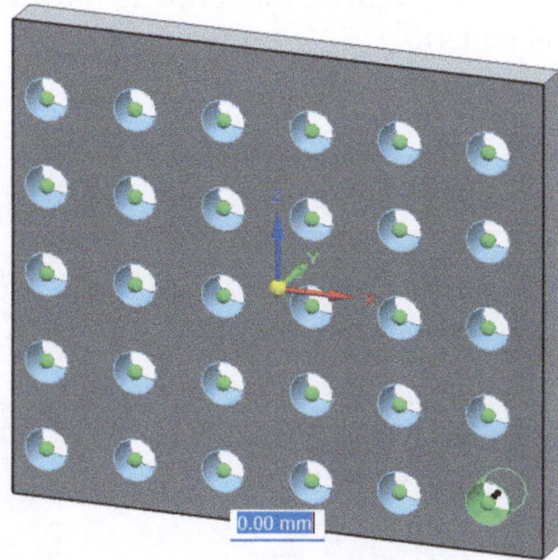

When you enable the **Use Occurrence Footprint** option (which is the default setting), Solid Edge analyzes the shape and dimensions of the patterned object to decide if it falls within the defined fill region. By turning off **Use Occurrence Footprint**, you enable the use of the occurrence marker method for determining the object's location within the fill region. This provides an alternative approach for pattern placement. In this method, occurrences are marked individually, and their collective arrangement defines the pattern.

Click the **Allow Boundary Touching** icon to include the instances that are outside the region and touching the boundary. Click the green dots on the instances to suppress them. On the command bar, click the **Accept** button after suppressing the instances.

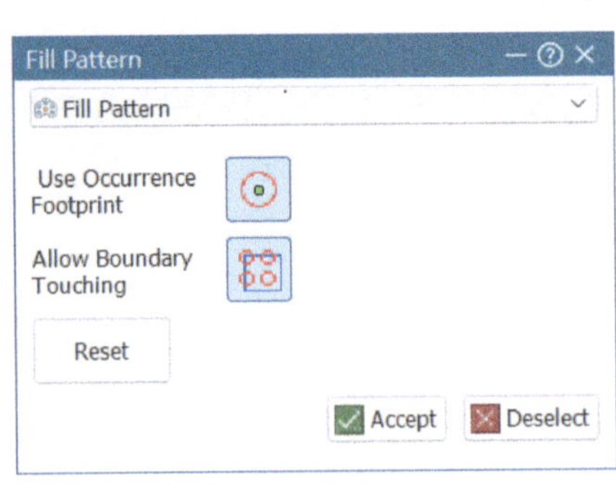

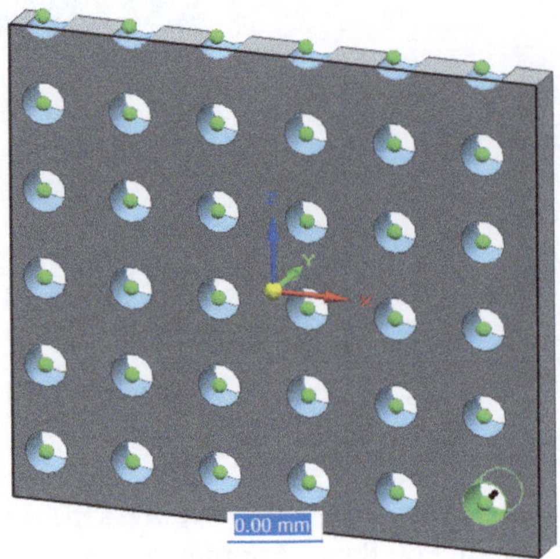

Click and drag the pattern boundaries to increase or decrease the fill pattern region. After defining the required settings, right-click to create the rectangular fill pattern.

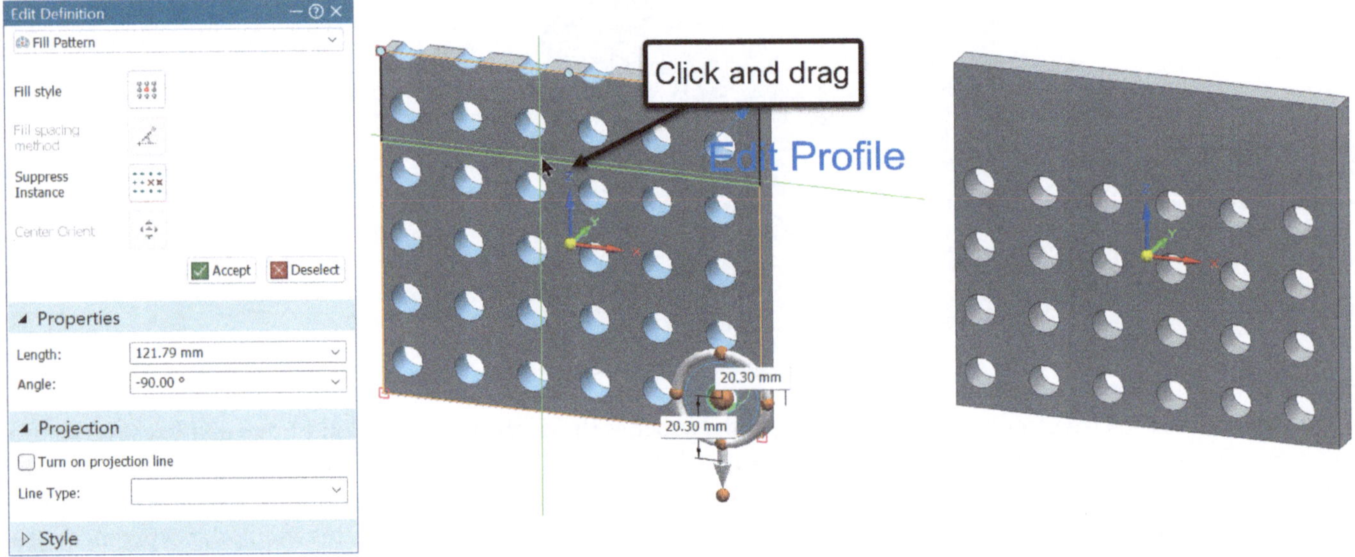

Staggered Fill Pattern

In this type of pattern, the features are arranged in a perforation fashion. To create a staggered fill pattern, set the **Fill Style** to **Stagger** on the command bar.

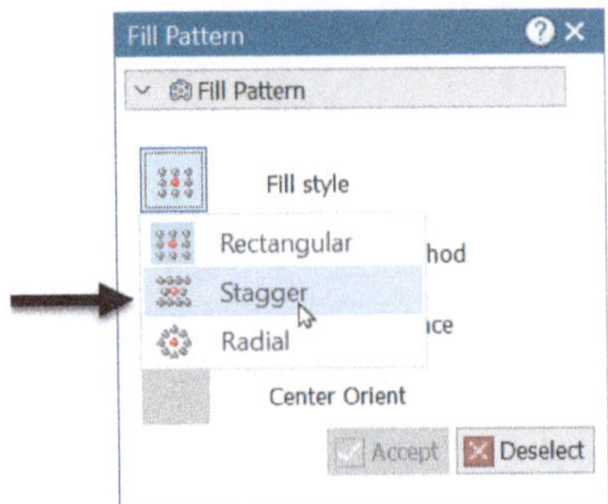

Click on the face fill and define the spacing between the instances. You can do this by using the **Fill spacing** methods. There are three methods to define the spacing between the instances: **Polar**, **Linear Offset**, and **Complex Linear Offset**. The **Polar** method creates a pattern using (a) rotation angle between two rows and (b) distance between the instances. The **Linear Offset** method creates a pattern using (c) spacing between two rows and (d) stagger offset. The **Complex Linear Offset** method creates a pattern by using (e) spacing between two instances in a row, (f) spacing between rows, and (g) stagger offset. Select a **Fill spacing method** and click the **Accept** button.

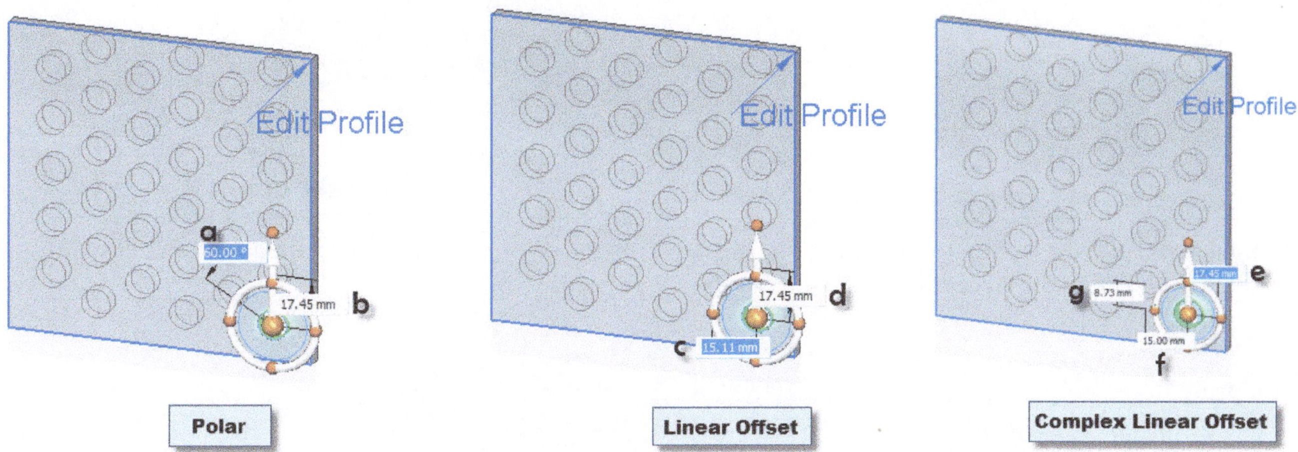

Specify the spacing parameters and click the **Accept** button to create the staggered pattern.

Radial Fill Pattern

In this type of pattern, the features are filled in a radial fashion inside the selected region. To create a radial fill pattern, set the **Fill Style** to **Radial** on the command bar.

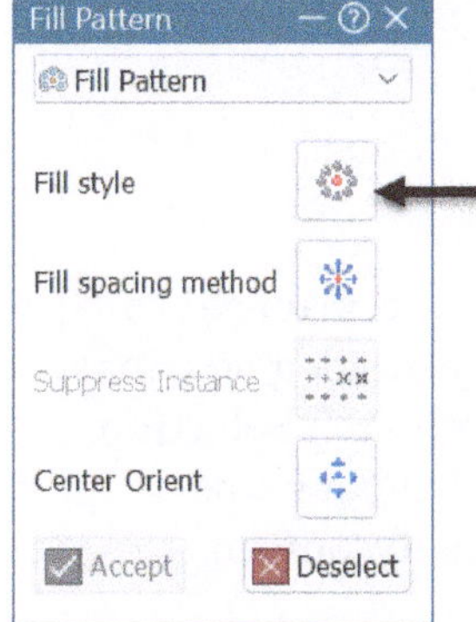

Next, define the spacing between the instances. This can be done by using the **Fill spacing methods**. There are two methods to define the spacing between the instances: **Target Spacing** and **Occurrence Count**. The **Target Spacing** method creates a pattern using (a) spacing between the rings and (b) spacing between the instances. The **Occurrence Count** method creates a pattern using (a) the number of instances per ring and (b) spacing between the rings.

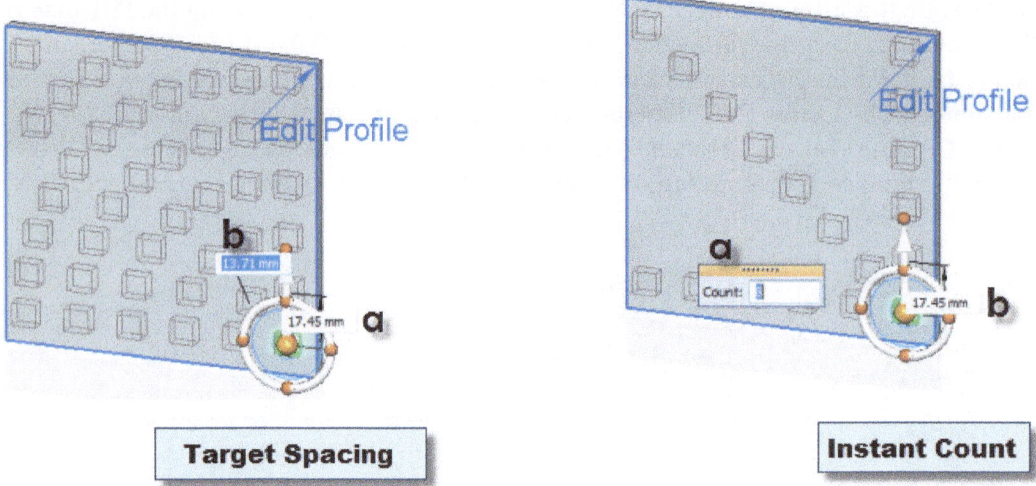

Target Spacing

Instant Count

Use the **Center Orient** option to orient the feature towards the center of the radial fill pattern. Specify the spacing parameters and click the **Accept** button to create the fill pattern.

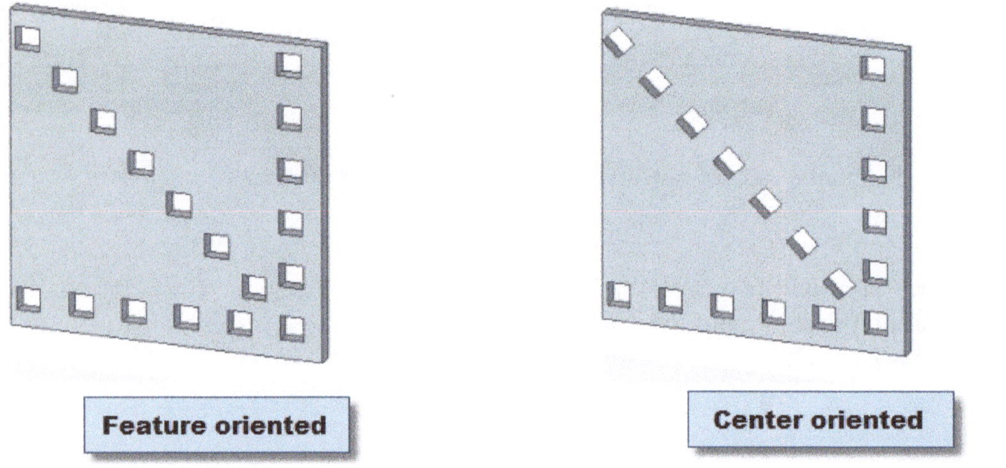

Feature oriented

Center oriented

Fill Pattern (Ordered)

Creates an array of patterned instances that populate a selected region, starting from a central occurrence. To create a fill pattern, click **Home > Pattern > Pattern drop-down > Fill Pattern** command. In the dialog box, make sure the **Pattern Type** is set to **Fill Pattern**. In the Select section, choose the required option from the **Selection Type** drop-down, for example **Feature** or another available type. Next, select the feature or element in the graphics window that you want to pattern. After the element is selected, click the green check to confirm.

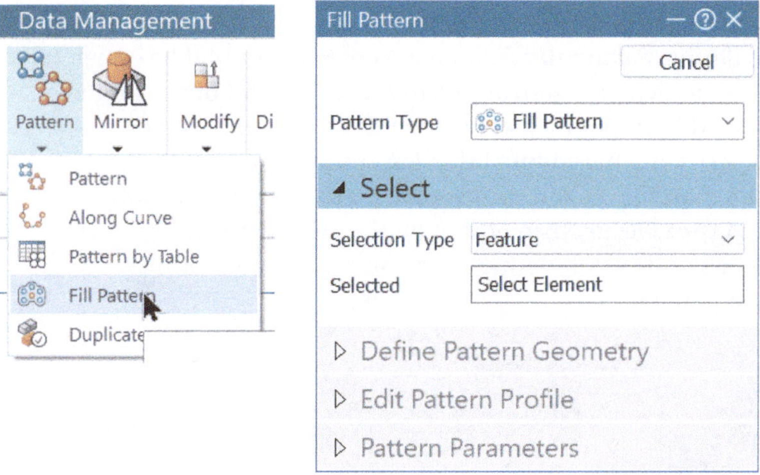

Next, specify the plane where you intend to arrange the pattern; the model is oriented parallel to the selected plane, allowing you to sketch the pattern profile. Create a closed sketch profile using the sketching commands available in the Sketching environment. Next, click **Close Sketch** on the ribbon; the preview of the fill pattern is displayed. Next, specify the settings in the **Pattern Parameters** section. These settings are same as that explained in the **Fill Pattern (Synchronous)** section.

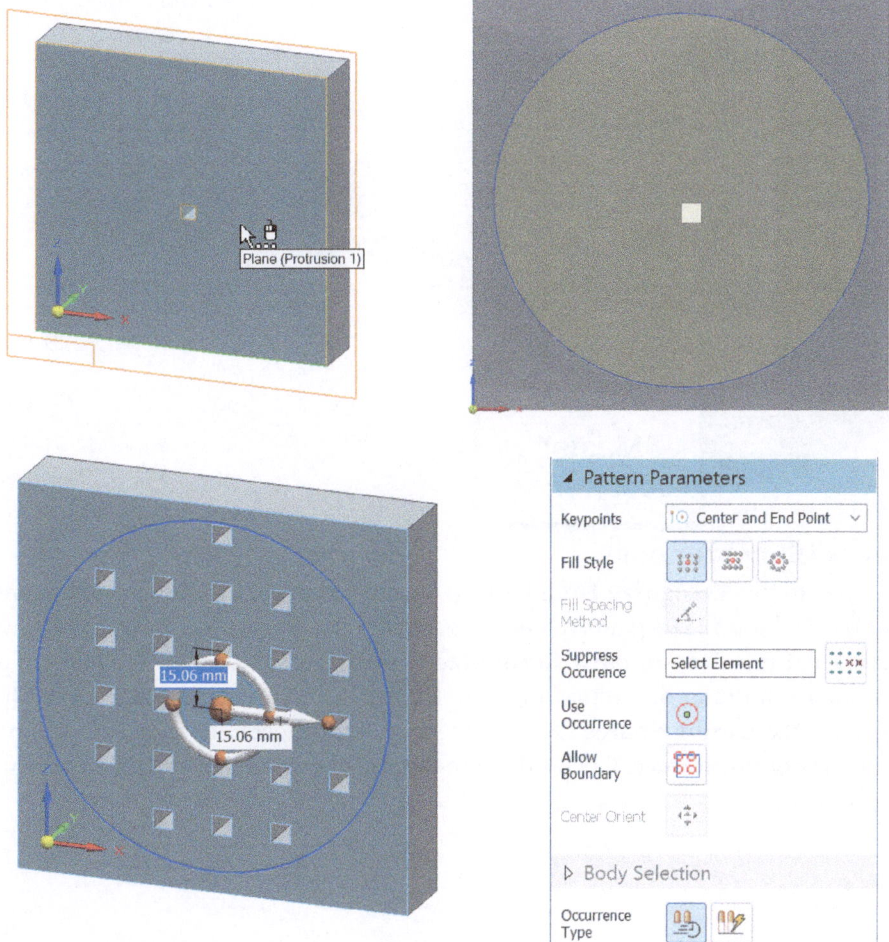

Click **Preview** and **Finish** after specifying the pattern parameters.

Recognize Hole Patterns (Synchronous)

This command converts the holes arranged in a circular or rectangular fashion into patterns. It will be easier for you to modify patterns than individual features. Note that you gain access to this command once you have a minimum of three holes in your model. This command becomes available when these three holes are organized in either a rectangular or circular pattern. Activate this command (click **Home > Pattern > Recognize Hole Patterns** on the ribbon) and select the holes arranged in a circular or rectangular fashion. Right click to accept the selection. Click the **Define Master Occurrence** button on the **Hole Pattern Recognition** dialog. Next, select a hole from the selected hole set to define the master occurrence of the pattern. Click **OK** to convert the group of holes into a pattern.

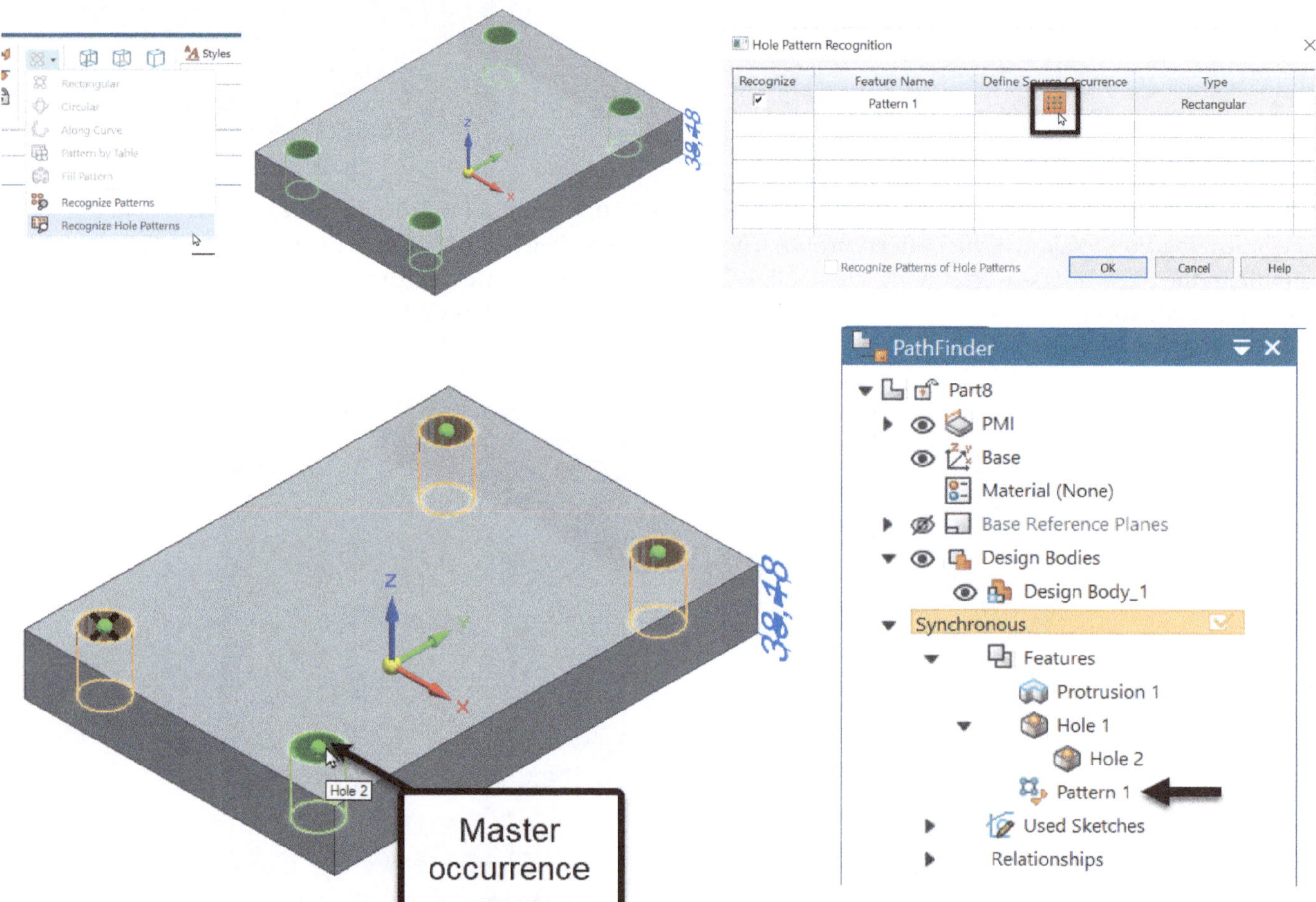

Recognize Patterns (Synchronous)

This command is similar to the **Recognize Hole Pattern** command except that it converts any feature arranged in a rectangular or circular fashion into a pattern feature. Activate the **Recognize Patterns** command (On the ribbon, click **Home > Pattern > Pattern drop-down > Recognize Patterns**) and select all the faces of anyone of the features arranged in the rectangular or circular fashion. Right click to accept the selection. On the **Pattern Recognition** dialog, click the **Define Source Occurrence** icon and select a feature from the pattern. The selected feature will act as the master occurrence. Click **OK** to recognize the arrangement as a pattern feature.

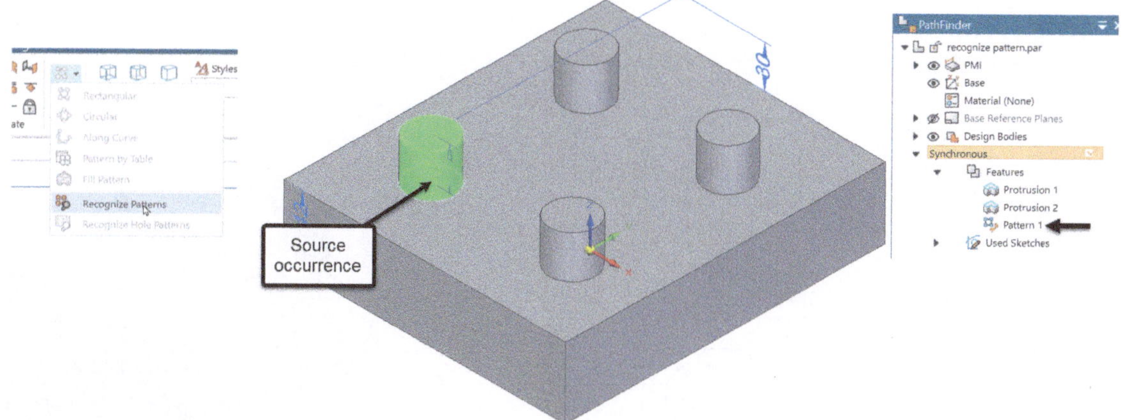

Duplicate (Ordered)

To create duplicates of selected features and define new locations using blocks and coordinate systems, use the **Duplicate** command (on the ribbon, click **Home > Pattern > Pattern** drop-down > **Duplicate**). Begin by selecting the features you want in the pattern. Then, right-click or click the **Accept** button on the command bar. Click a block or coordinate system to set the parent reference, determining how the selected pattern features relate to it.

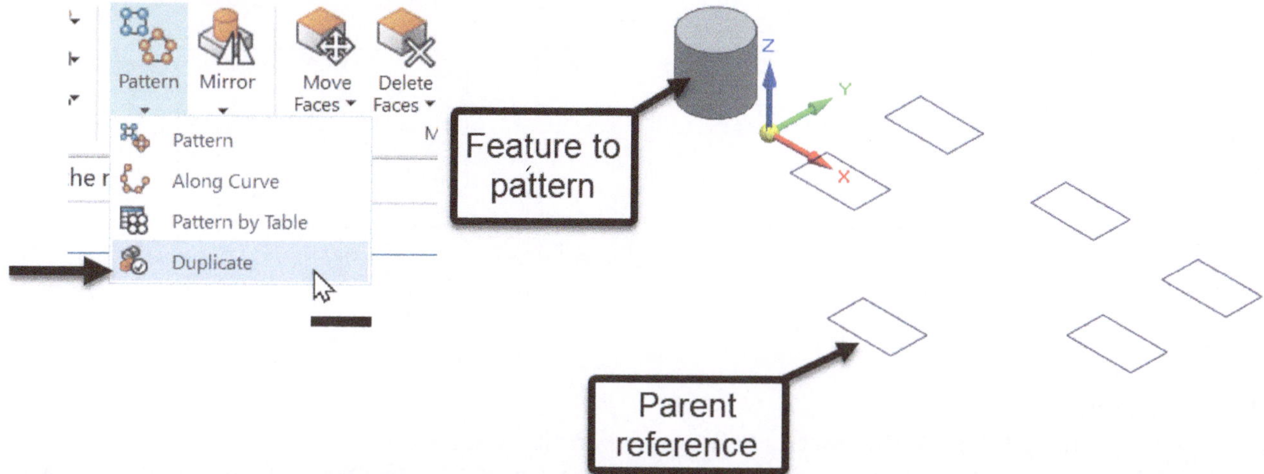

Select a block or coordinate system to establish the duplicate location. You can also click the **All Matching Blocks** button to broaden the selection to all instances of parent and reference blocks. Click **Accept** or right-click to confirm. Click **Finish** to complete the feature to complete the process.

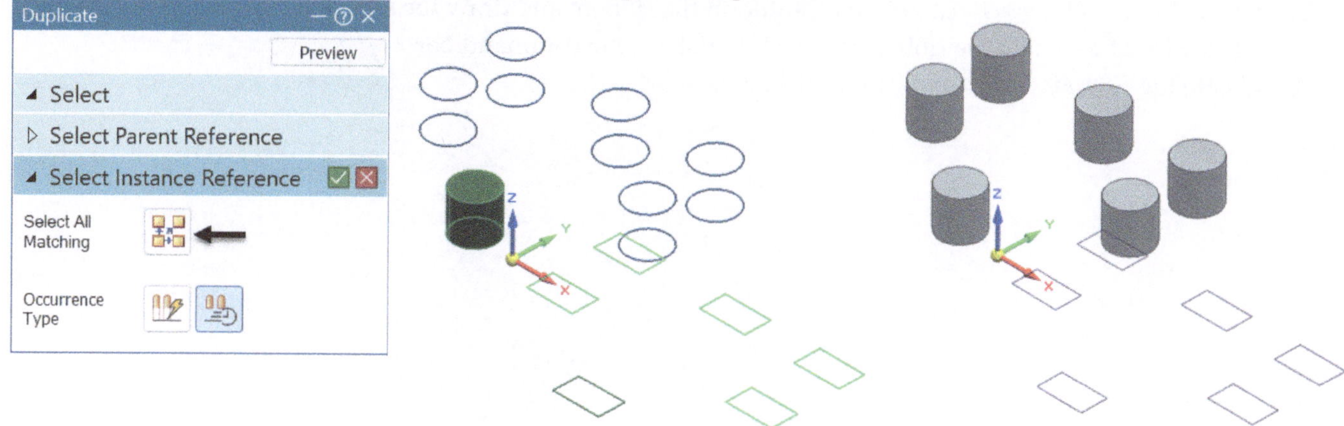

Examples

Example 1 (Millimetres)

In this example, you will create the part shown below.

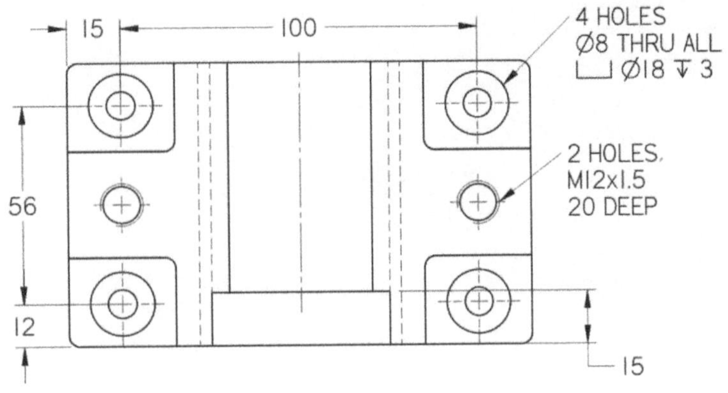

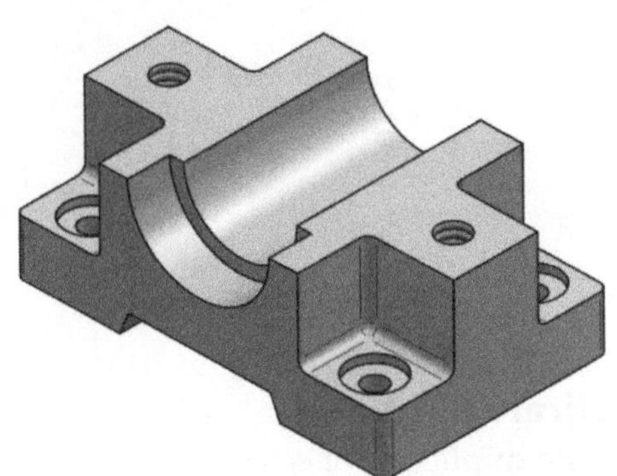

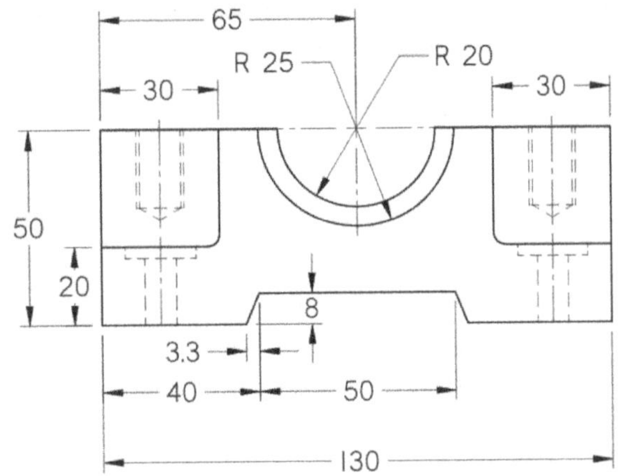

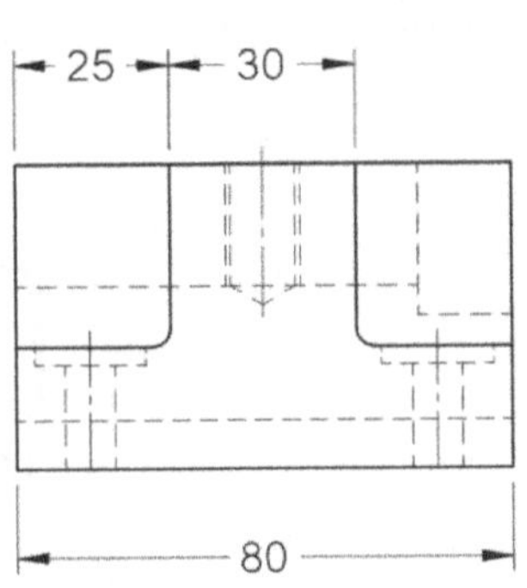

1. Start **Solid Edge 2026.**
2. On the File Menu, click **New > ISO Metric Part**; a new part file is opened.
3. Click **Continue with Ordered** button on the **Ordered as default** dialog; the Ordered environment is set as the default environment.
4. To start a new sketch, **Home > Sketch > Sketch**. Next, select the Front (xz) plane.
5. Click **Home > Draw > Rectangle by Center** on the ribbon, and draw the sketch, as shown below.
6. Click **Close Sketch** on the ribbon and click **Finish** on the command bar.
7. Create the *Extrude* feature of 80 mm thickness.

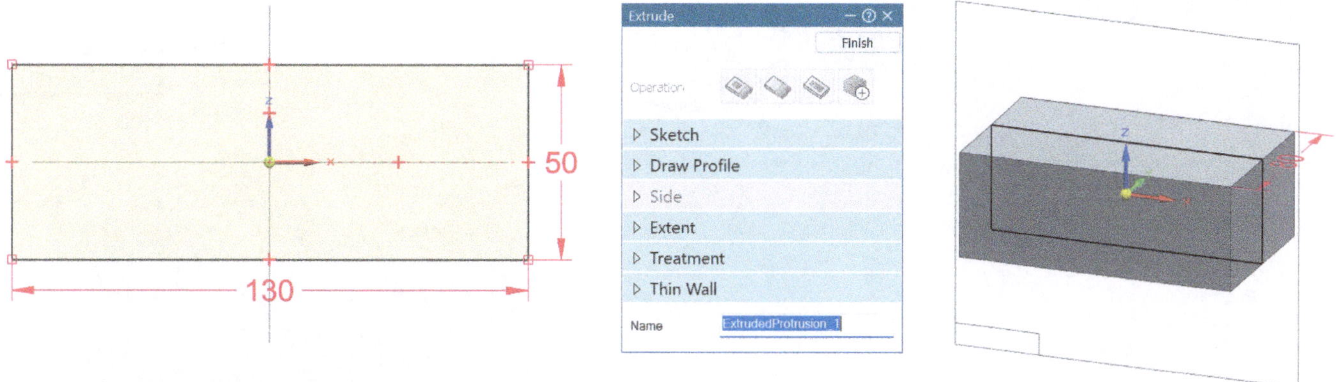

8. On the ribbon, click **Home > Solids > Extrude**. Next, click **Create From Options > Coincident Plane** on the **Extrude** command bar.
9. Click on the top face of the part geometry and draw the sketch.
10. Click **Home > Draw > Rectangle by Center > Rectangle by 2 Points** on the ribbon.
11. Create a rectangle and add dimensions to it. Next, click **Close Sketch** on the ribbon.
12. On the **Extrude** command bar, select **Operation > Cut**.
13. In the **Extent** section, select the **Direction > One-sided Extent** button.
14. Type 30 in the **Distance** box, move the pointer downward and click. Next, click **Finish** and **Cancel**.

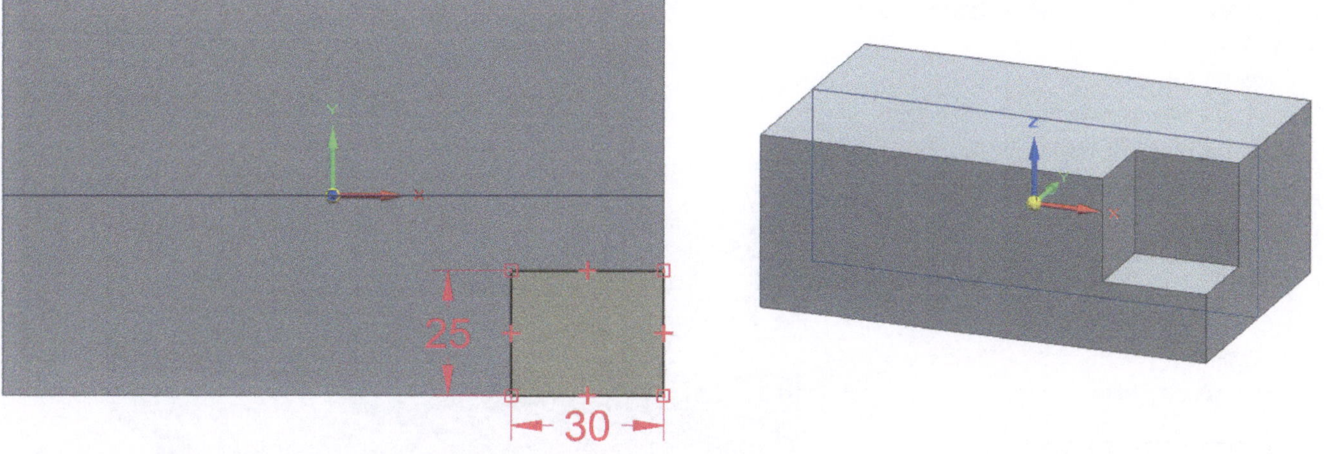

15. Click on the *Cutout* in the Pathfinder.
16. Click **Home > Pattern > Mirror Copy Feature** on the ribbon.
17. Check the **Base Reference Planes** option in the Pathfinder and click on the **Right (yz)** plane.
18. Click **Finish** on the command bar. The selected geometry is mirrored.

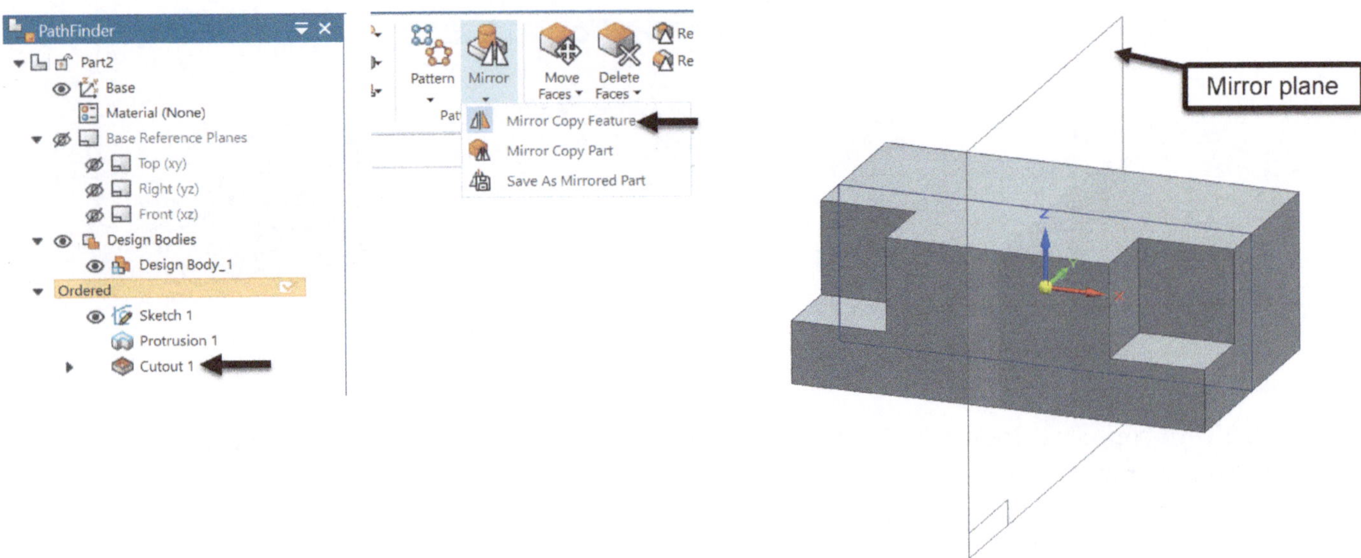

19. Press Shift on the keyboard and click on the *Cutout* and *Mirror* in the Pathfinder.
20. Activate the **Mirror Copy Feature** command.
21. Click on the **Front (xz)** plane to mirror the selected geometry.

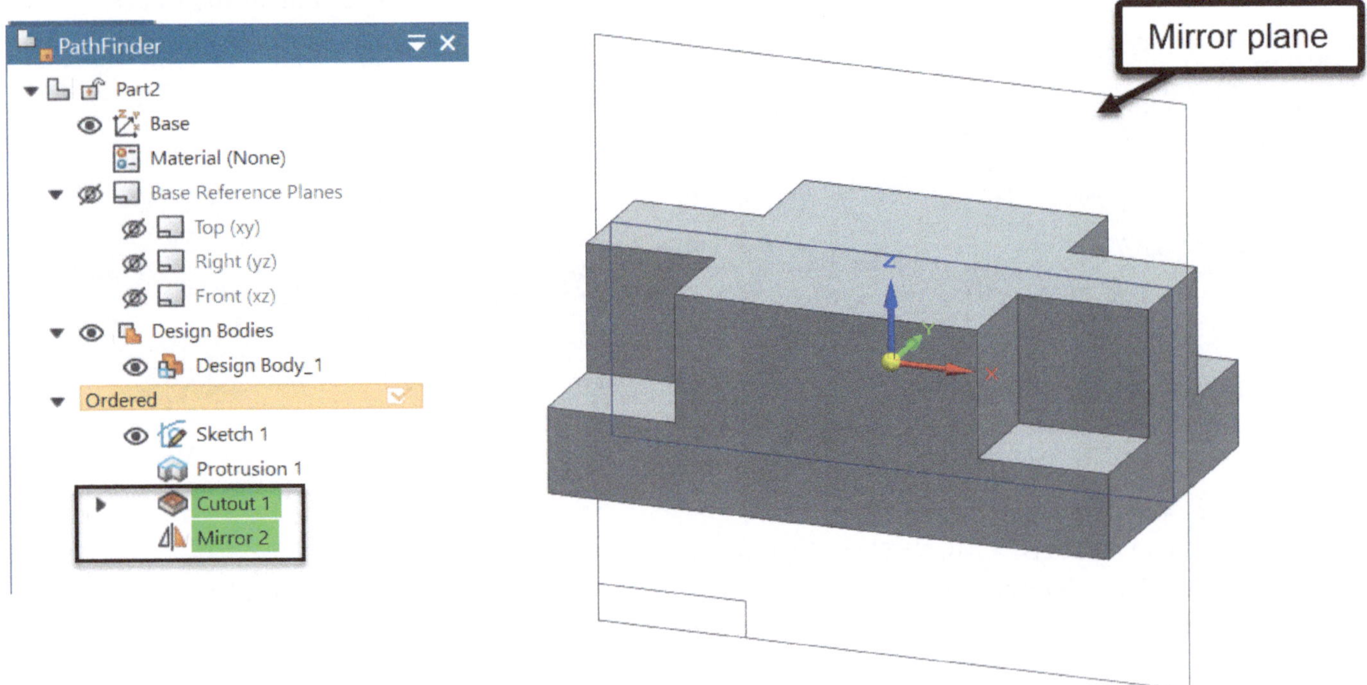

22. Initiate the **Hole** command and select the horizontal face of the *Extruded Cut* feature.
23. Position the hole circle and apply dimensions specifying the distance between its center and the adjacent edges. Next, click **Close Sketch** on the ribbon.

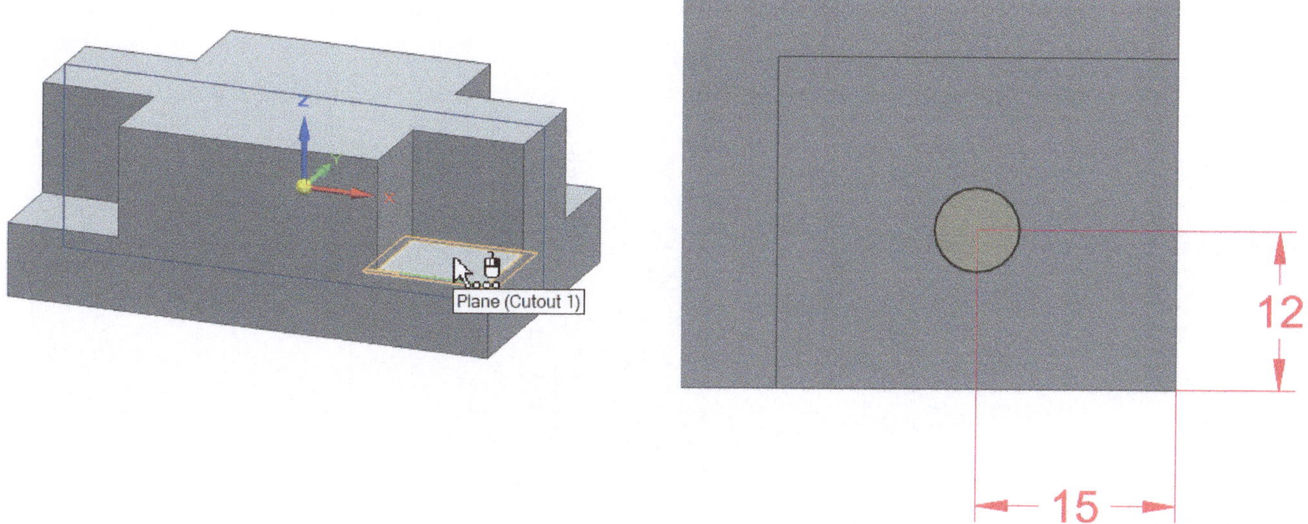

24. Select the **Options** button located on the **Hole** command bar. Subsequently, define the parameters within the **Hole Options** dialog based on the provided illustration, then confirm your selections by clicking **OK**.
25. Conclude the process by selecting both the **Finish** and **Cancel** buttons.

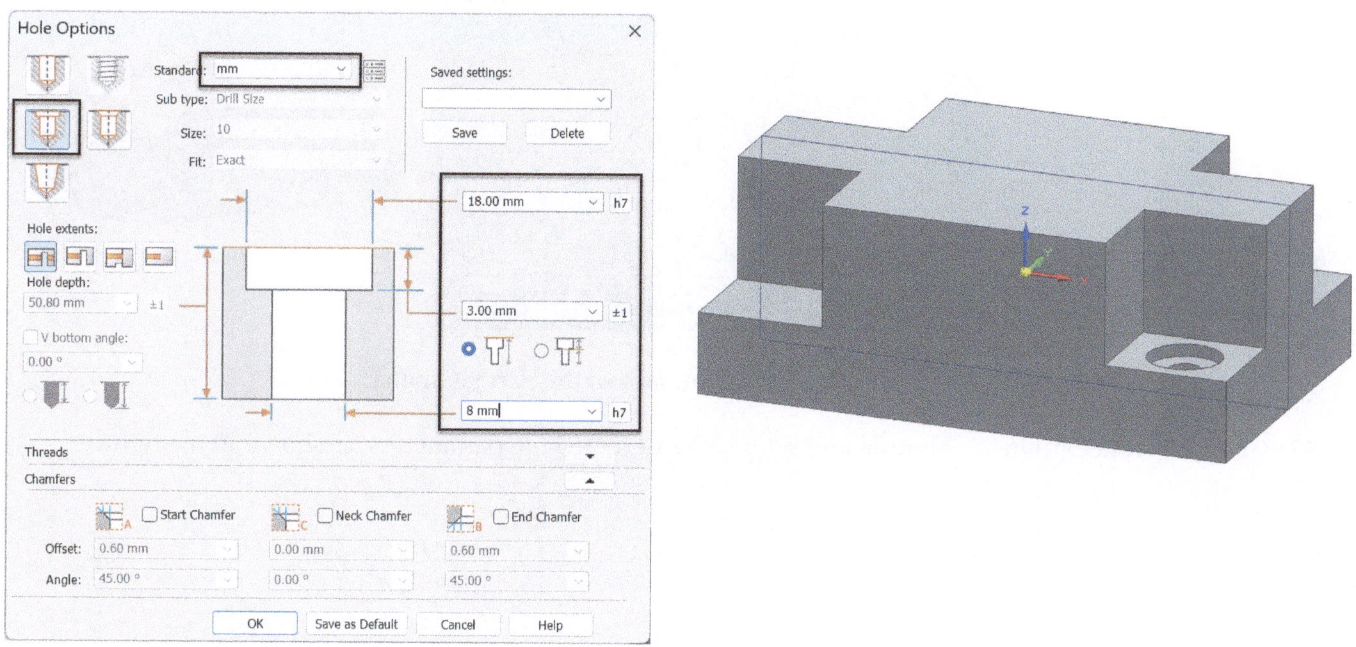

26. In the Pathfinder, click on the *Hole* feature.
27. Click **Home > Pattern > Pattern** on the ribbon. Next, select the ***Hole*** feature.
28. On the **Pattern** dialog, select **Pattern Type > Rectangular Pattern**. Next, select **Placement type > By Sketch.**
29. Select the horizontal face of the extruded cut feature.
30. Select the center point of the counterbore hole.

31. Click on the opposite corner of the part geometry to define the rectangular pattern.

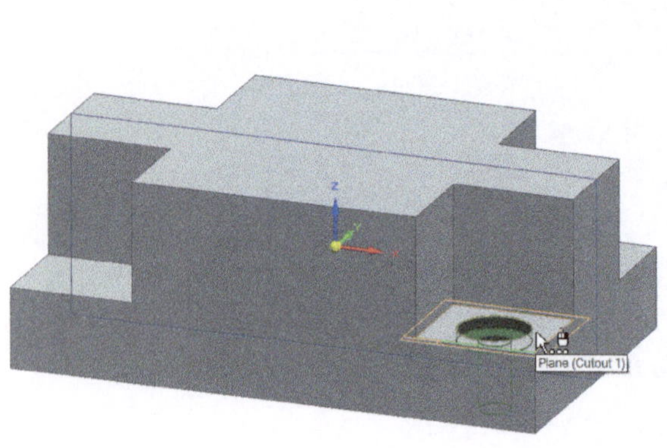

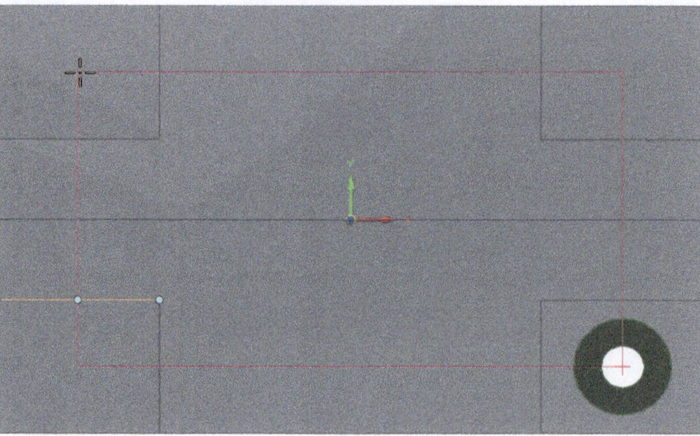

32. On the command bar, set the **Type** option to **Fit**.
33. Type-in **100** in the **Width** box.
34. Type-in **56** in the **Height** box.
35. Type **2** in the X and Y boxes, respectively. Next, click **Close Sketch** on the ribbon.
36. Click the **Finish** on the command bar to create the rectangular pattern.

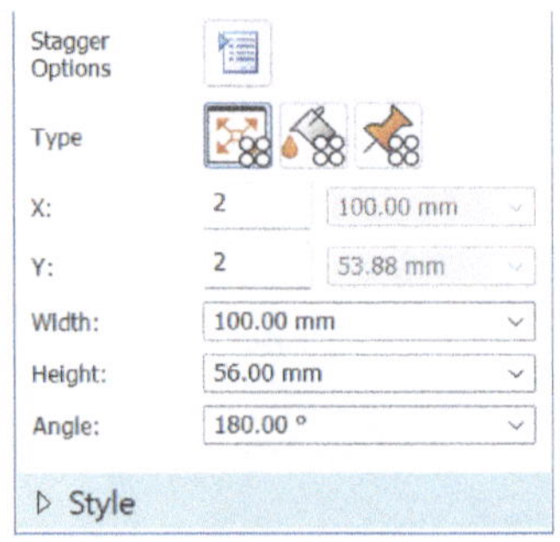

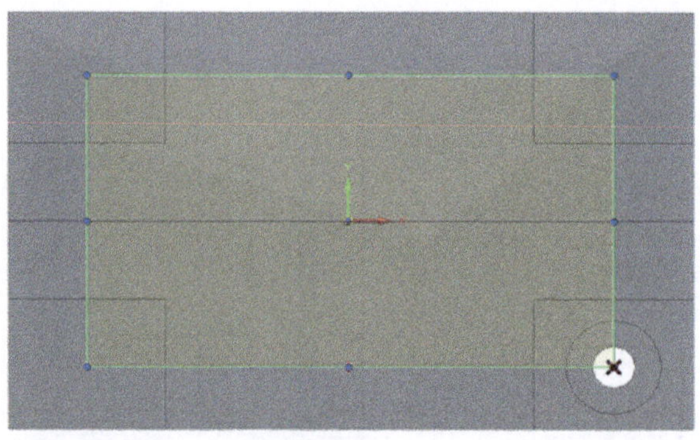

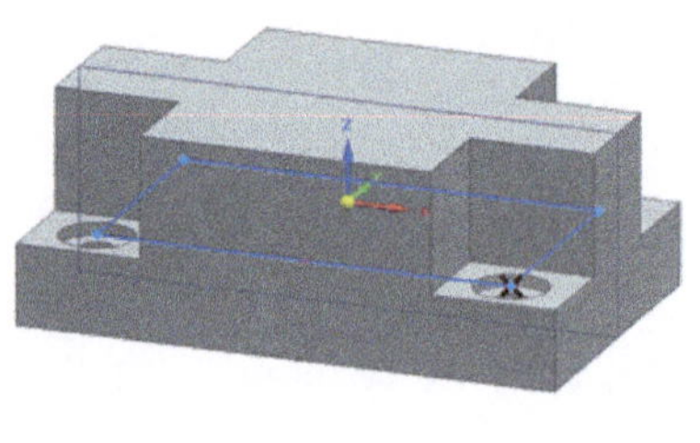

37. Activate the **Hole** command and click on the front face of the part geometry.
38. Click the **Hole Options** button and set the counterbore hole parameters, as shown in the figure.

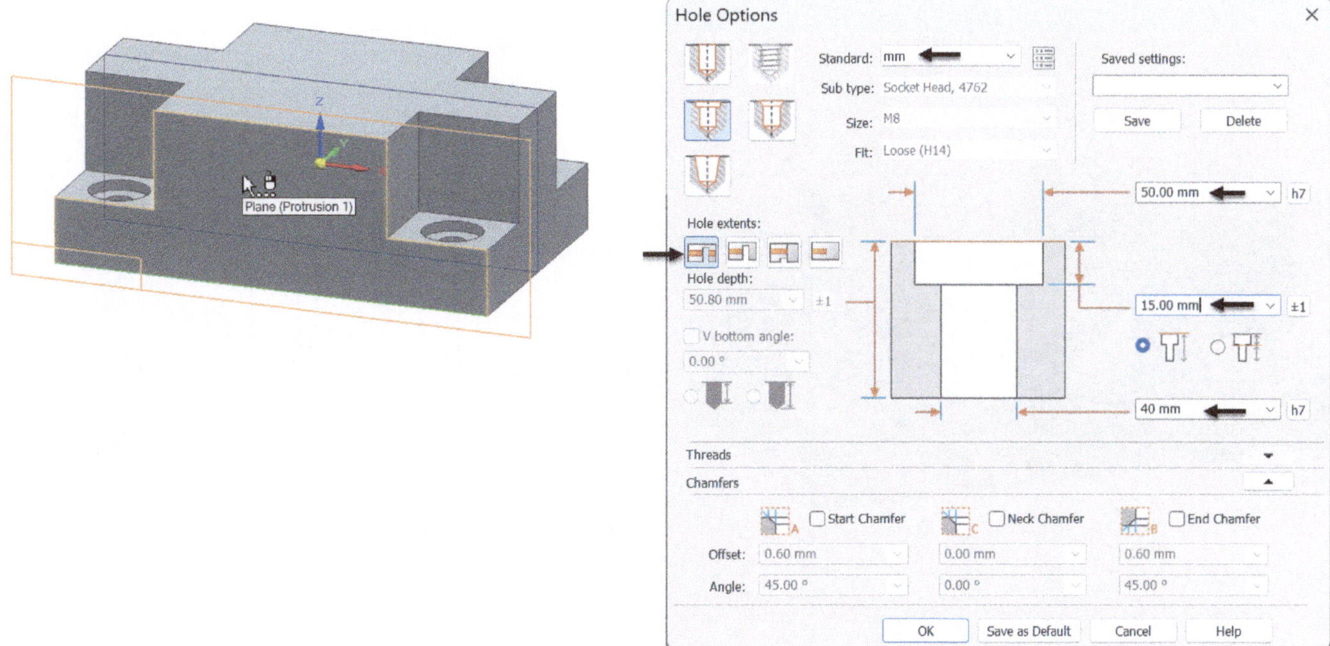

39. Click on the midpoint of the top of the model to place the hole. Next, click **Close Sketch** on the ribbon.
40. Click **Finish** and **Cancel** on the command bar.

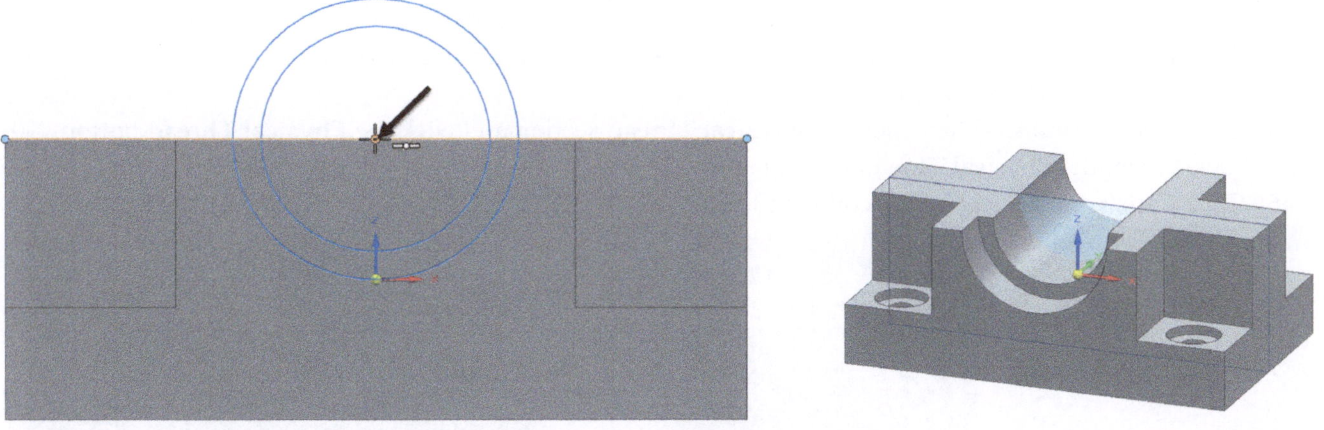

41. Activate the **Hole** command and click on the top face of the part.
42. Click the **Hole Options** button and set the threaded hole parameters, as shown in the figure. Click **OK** to close the dialog.

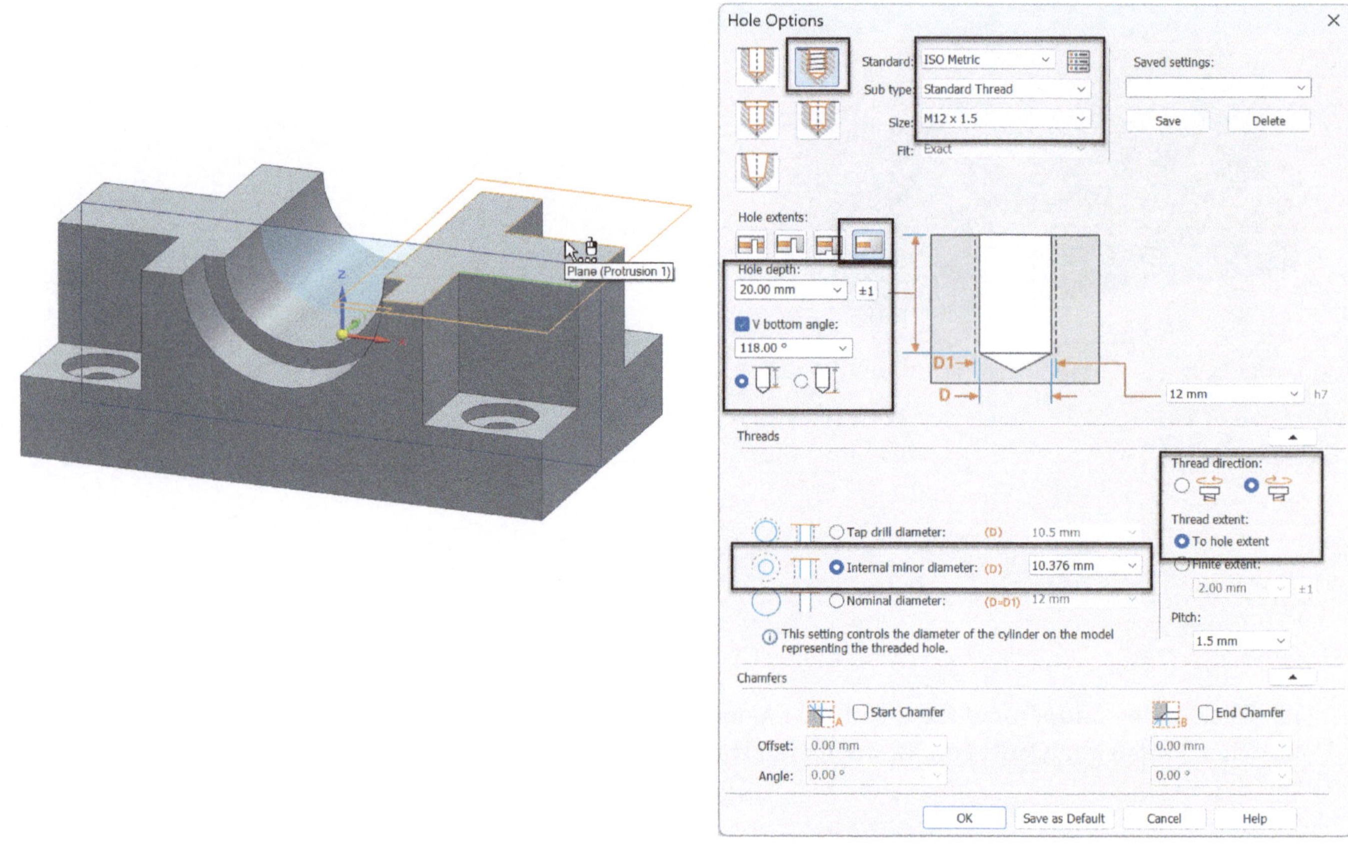

43. Place the hole circle and add dimensions between its center and adjacent edges.
44. Click **Close Sketch** on the ribbon.
45. On the **Hole** command bar, click the **Physical Thread** section and click the **Physical Thread** button. Next, click **Yes** on the **Physical Thread** message box.
46. Click **Finish** and **Cancel** on the command bar.

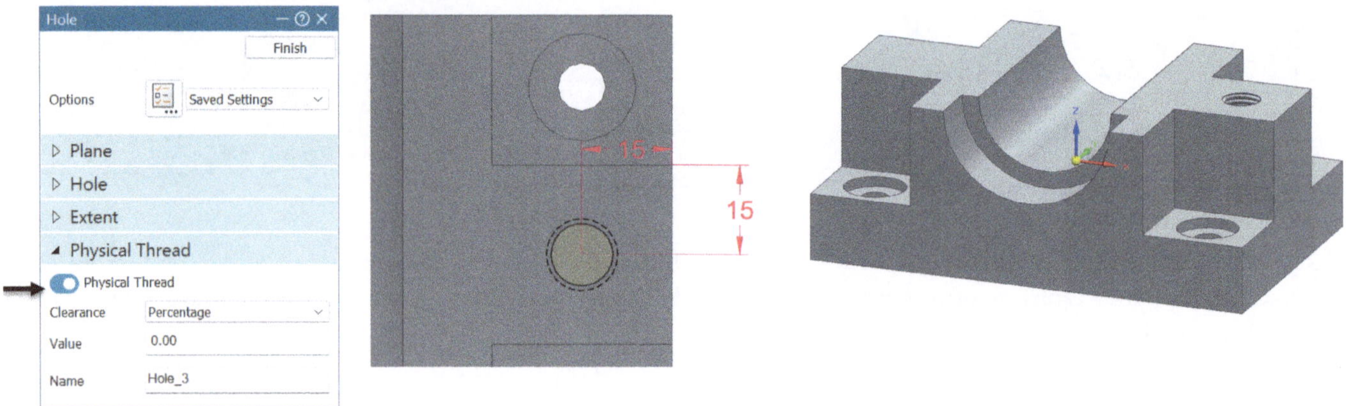

47. Mirror the threaded hole about the YZ plane.

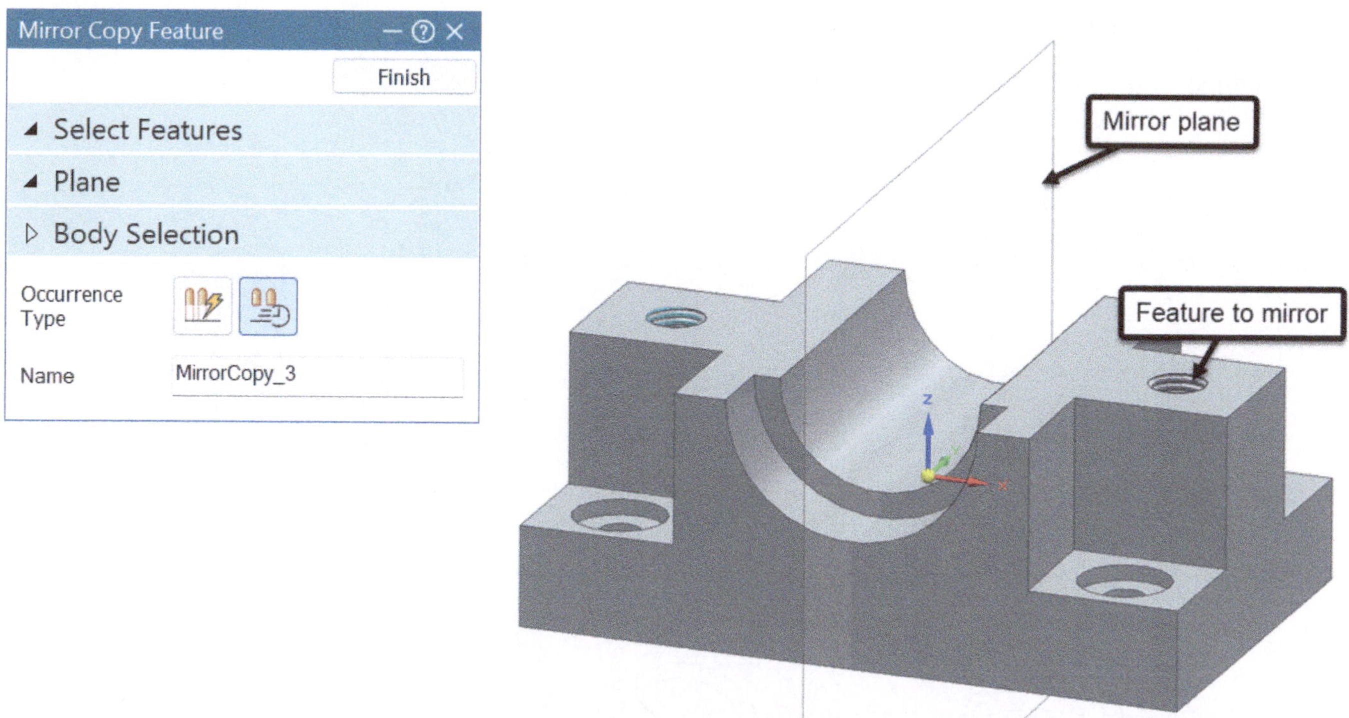

48. Draw a sketch on the front face of the part geometry and create an *Extruded Cut* throughout the model.

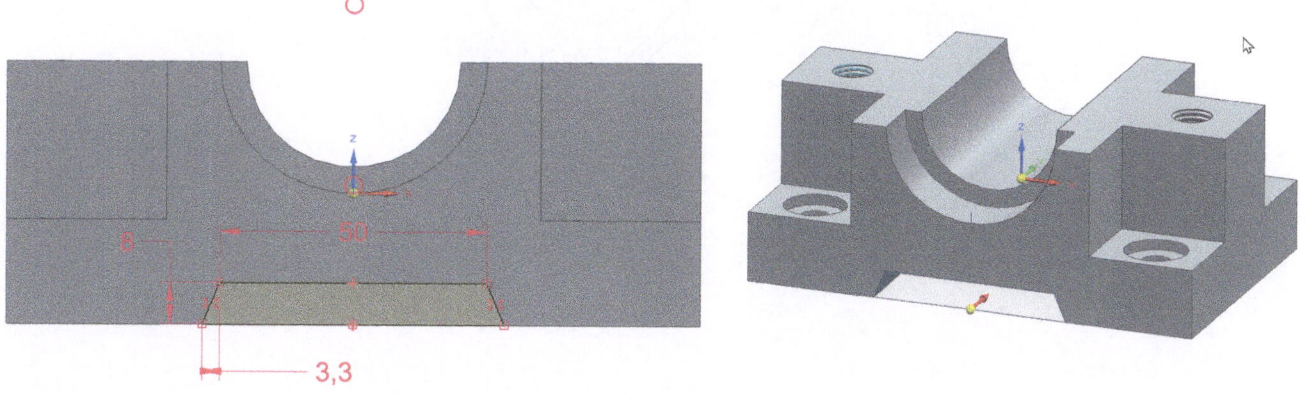

49. Round the sharp edges of the geometry. The round radius is 2 mm.

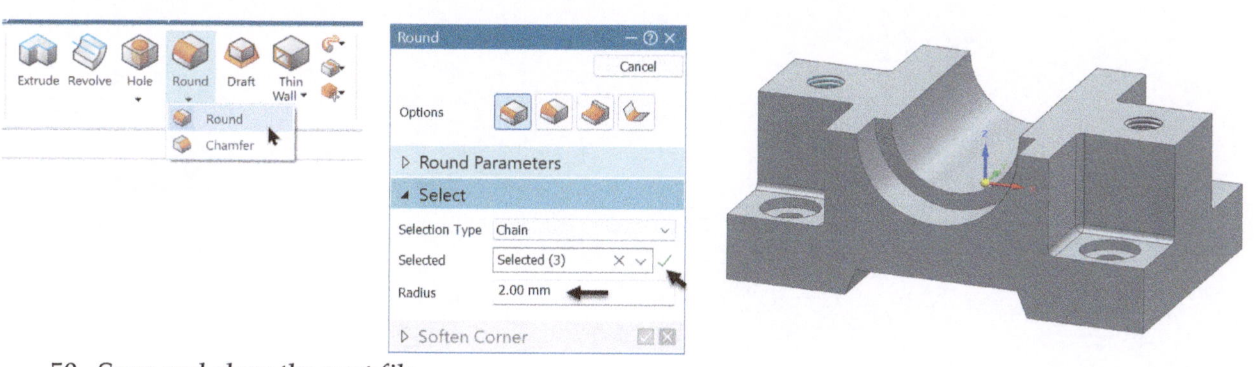

50. Save and close the part file.

Example 2 (Millimeters)

In this example, you will create the part shown below.

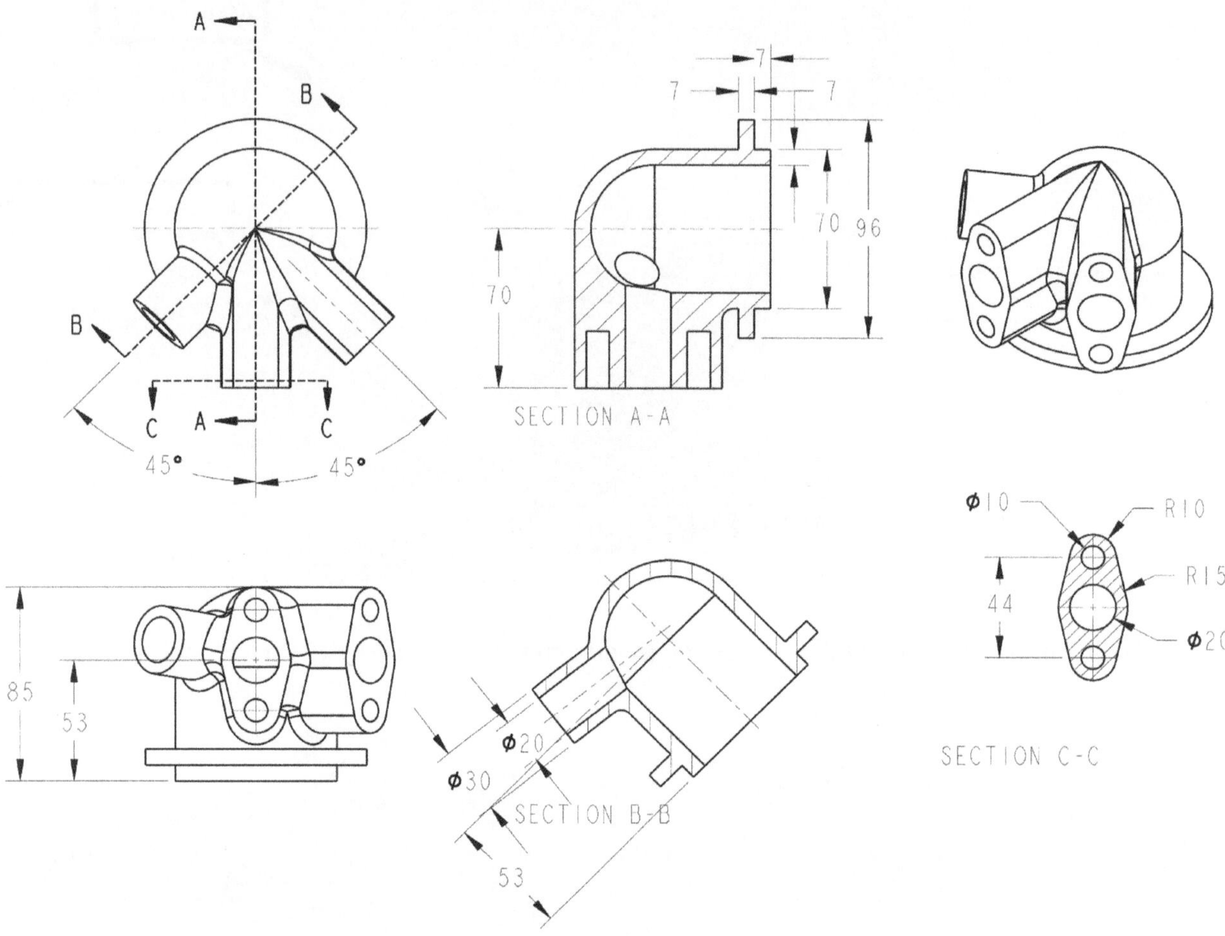

Creating the First Feature

1. Start **Solid Edge 2026**.
2. On the Quick Access Toolbar, click the **New** button.
3. Select **ISO Metric** > **iso metric part.par**. Next, click **OK**; a new part file is opened.
4. Click **Continue with Ordered** button on the **Ordered as default** dialog; the Ordered environment is set as the default environment.
5. On the ribbon, click **Home > Sketch > Sketch** and select the **Front(xz)** plane.
6. Click **Home > Draw > Line** on the ribbon.
7. Specify the start point of the line on the vertical axis.
8. Click on the origin point to define the second point.
9. Move the pointer horizontally toward right and click on the horizontal axis.
10. Move the pointer vertically up to a small distance and click.
11. Move the pointer horizontally toward right up to a small distance and click.
12. Move the pointer vertically up to a small distance and click.
13. Move the pointer horizontally toward left up to a small distance and click.
14. Move the pointer vertically upward and click.

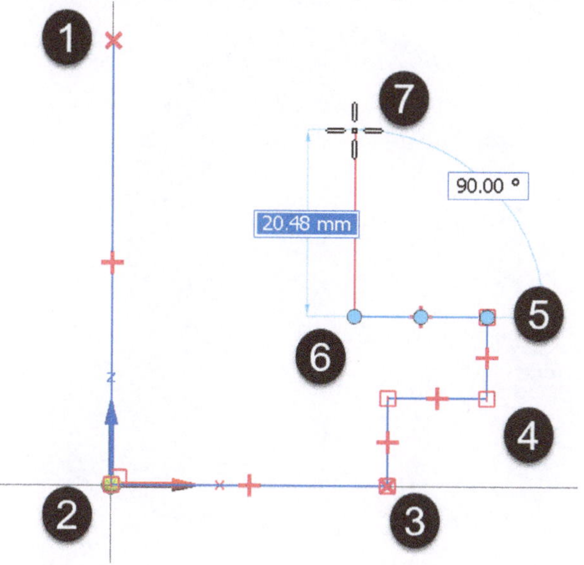

15. On the **Line and Arc** command bar, select **Type > Arc (a)**.
16. Take the mouse pointer to the endpoint of the line.
17. Move it upwards and left. Next, select the endpoint of the right vertical line to create the arc.
18. Press ESC.

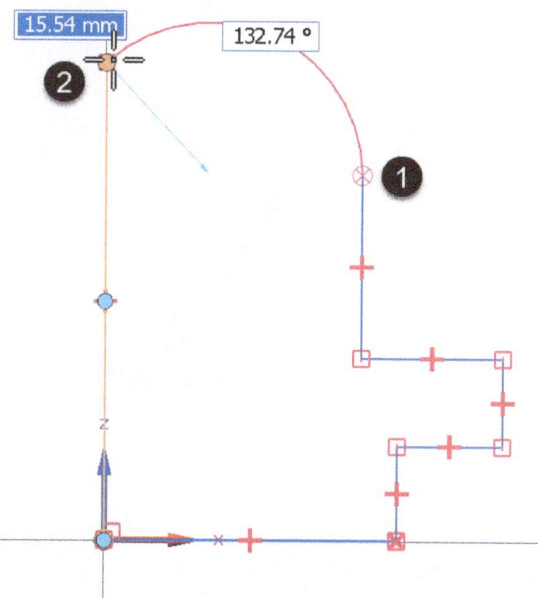

19. Apply the **Connect** relationship between the centerpoint of the arc and the left vertical line.

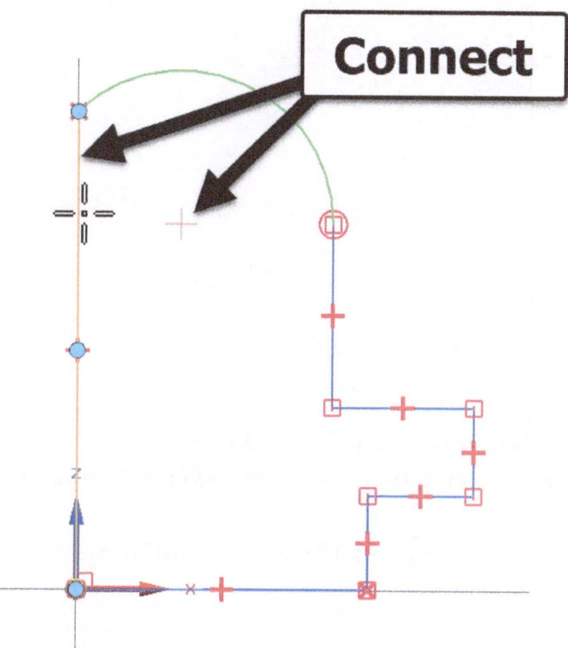

20. Add the Perpendicular relationship between the vertical line and the arc.

21. Add the Equal relationship between the two horizontal lines, as shown.

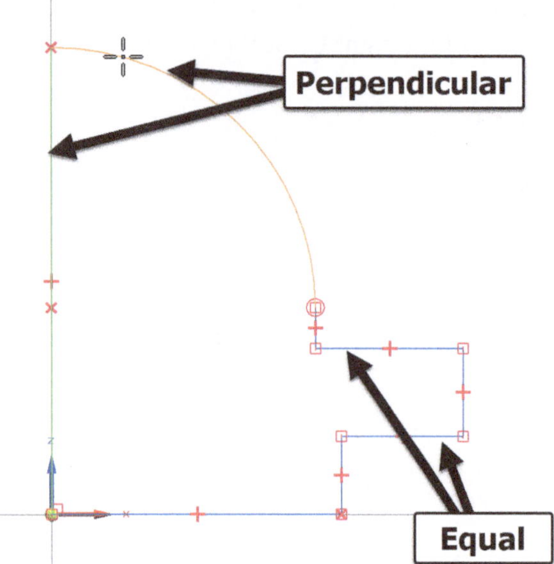

22. Add dimensions to the sketch, as shown.

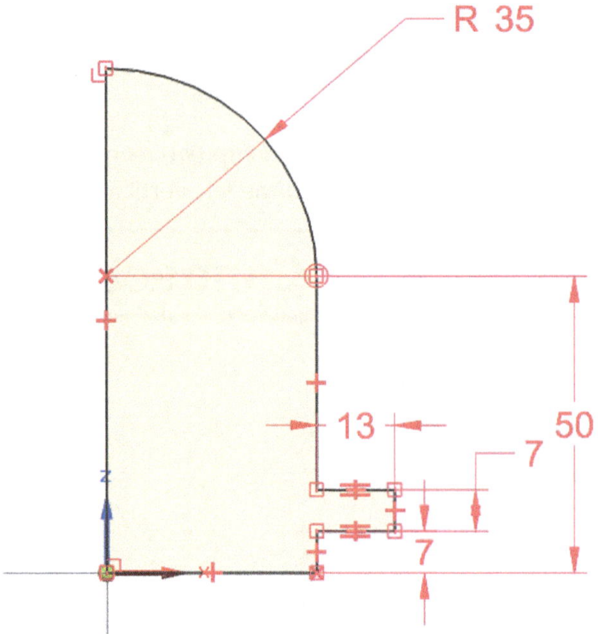

23. On the ribbon, click **Close Sketch**.
24. Click the **Finish** button on the **Sketch** command bar.
25. On the ribbon, click **Home** tab > **Solids** group > **Revolve** .
26. On the **Revolve** command bar, select the **Select from sketch** option from the **Create From** drop-down.
27. Select the sketch and click the green check on the **Revolve** command bar.
28. Select the left vertical line to define the axis of revolution.

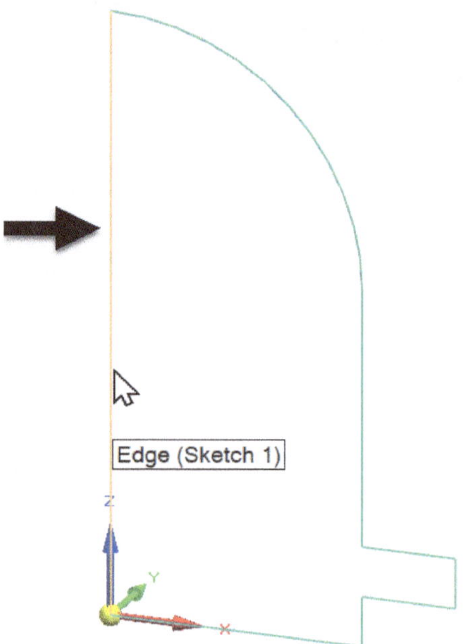

29. On the **Revolve** command bar, click the **Revolve 360** button under the **Extent** section to sketch by 360 degrees.
30. Click the **Finish** button to create the *Revolved* feature.

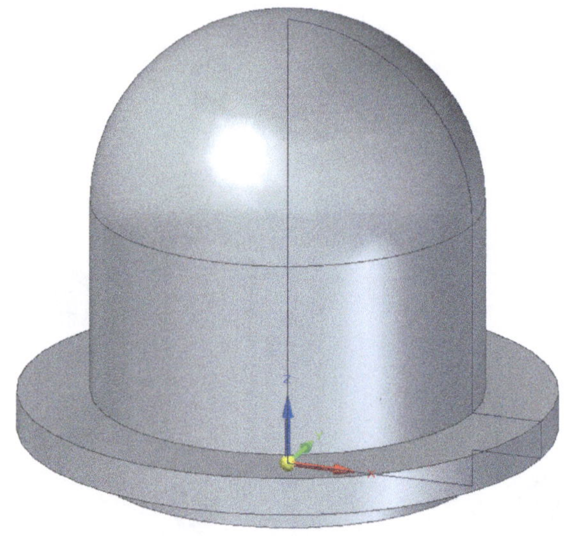

Creating the Second Feature

1. On the ribbon, click **Home** tab > **Sketch** group > **Sketch**.

2. Click the eye icon next to the **Base Reference Planes** node in the Pathfinder.
3. Click on the Front plane.
4. Create three circles, as shown.
5. Apply the **Equal** relationship between the two circles, as shown.

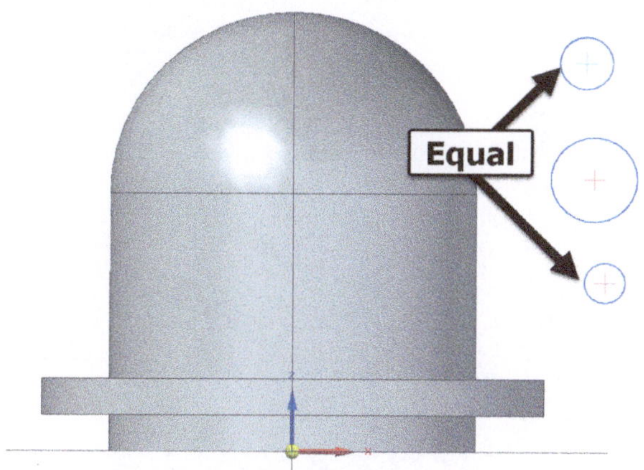

6. Apply the **Vertical** relationship between the center points of the circles.

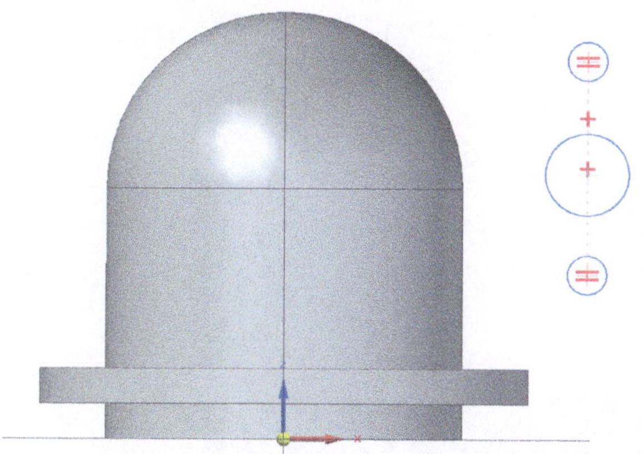

7. On the ribbon, click **Sketch** tab > **Relate** group > **Connect**.
8. Select the centerpoint of anyone of the circles.
9. Select the vertical reference line.

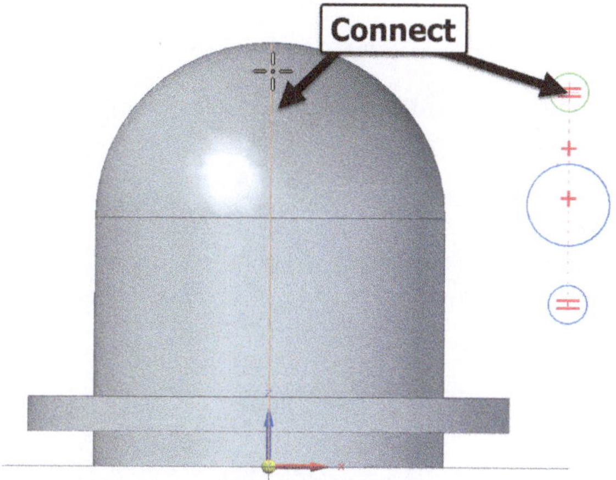

10. On the ribbon, click **Sketch** tab > **Relate** group > **Tangent**.
11. Select the top circle and the curved edge of the model.

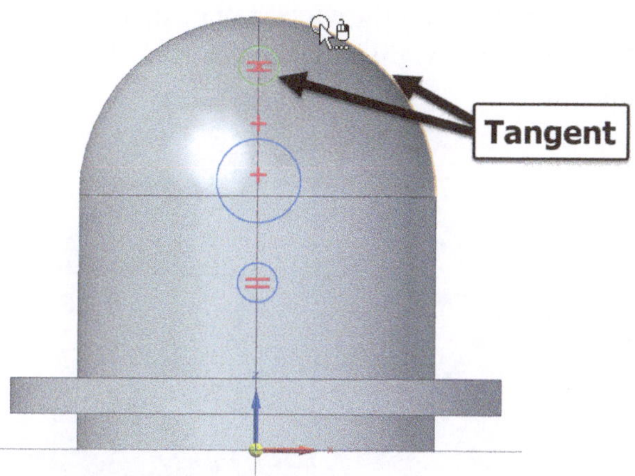

12. On the ribbon, click **Sketch** tab > **Dimension** group > **Smart Dimension**.
13. Create the dimensions, as shown.

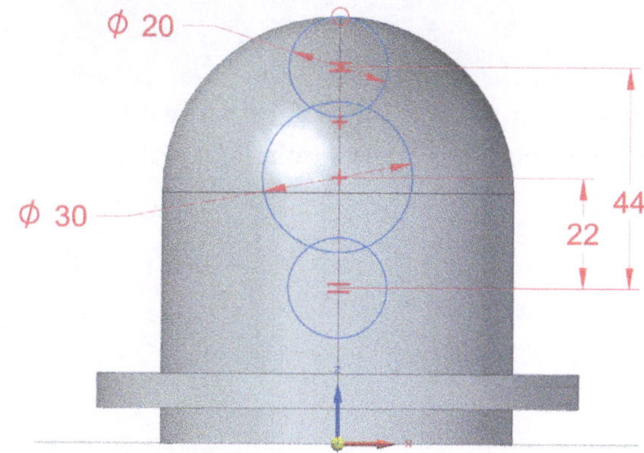

14. Click **Home > Draw > Line** on the ribbon.
15. Select the two circles, as shown.

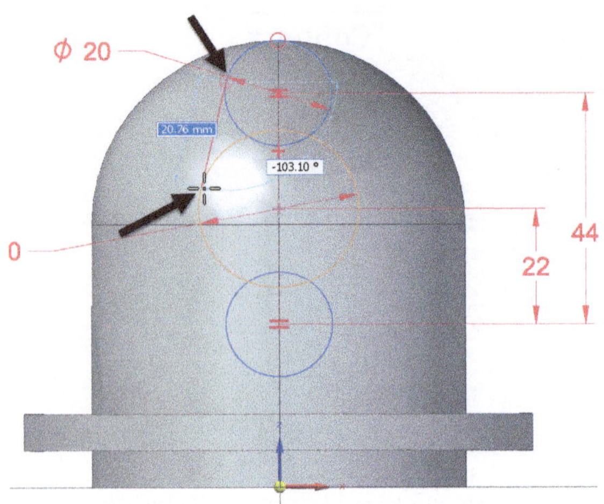

16. Press ESC.
17. On the ribbon, click **Home** tab > **Relate** group > **Tangent**.
18. Select the line and the circle connected to it; the tangent relationship is applied between the line and circle.

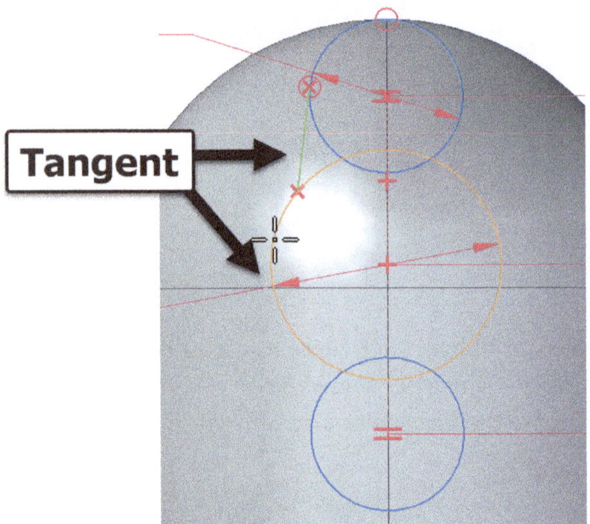

19. Likewise, apply the Tangent relationship between the line and other circle, if not already applied.

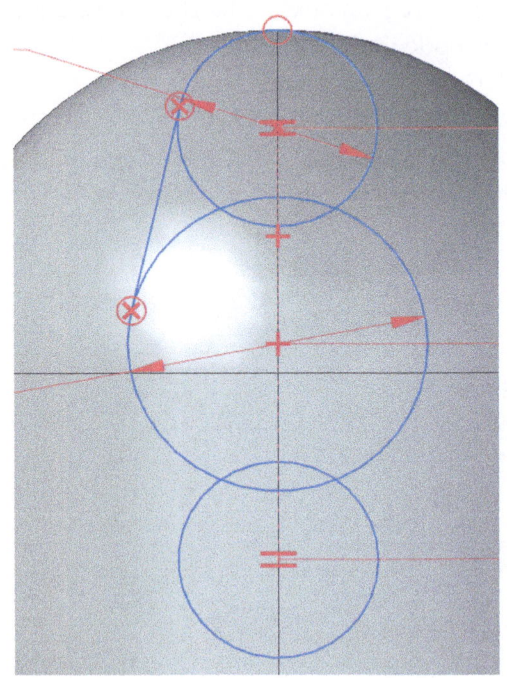

20. Likewise, create three more tangent lines, as shown.

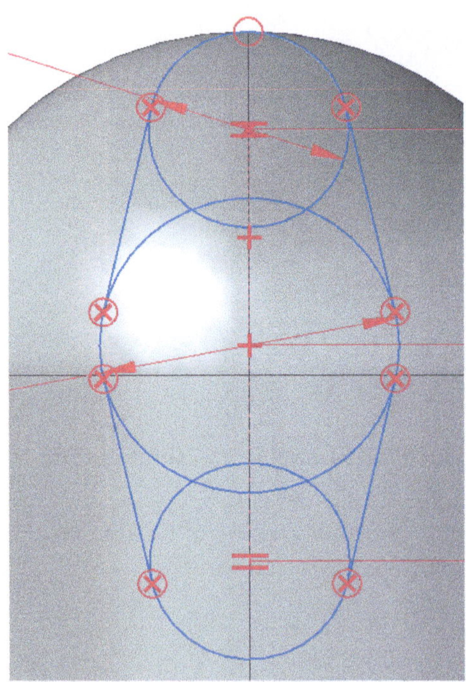

21. On the ribbon, click **Home** tab > **Draw** group > **Trim** drop-down **>** **Trim**.
22. Select the inner segments of the circles, as shown.

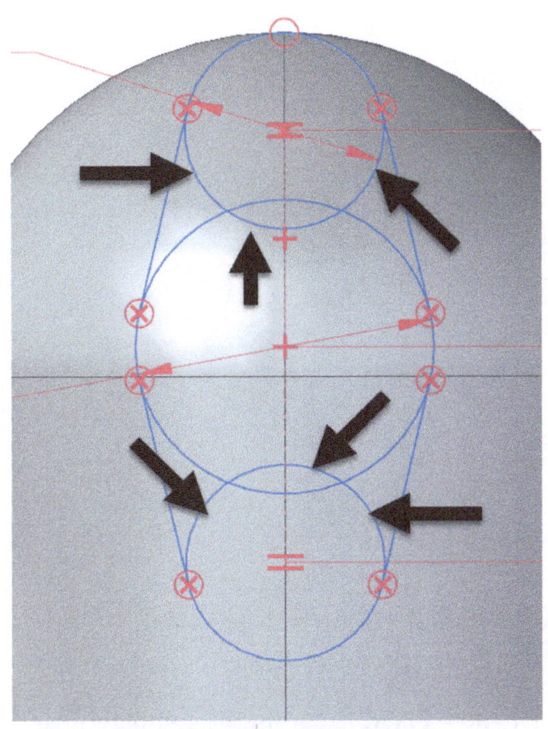

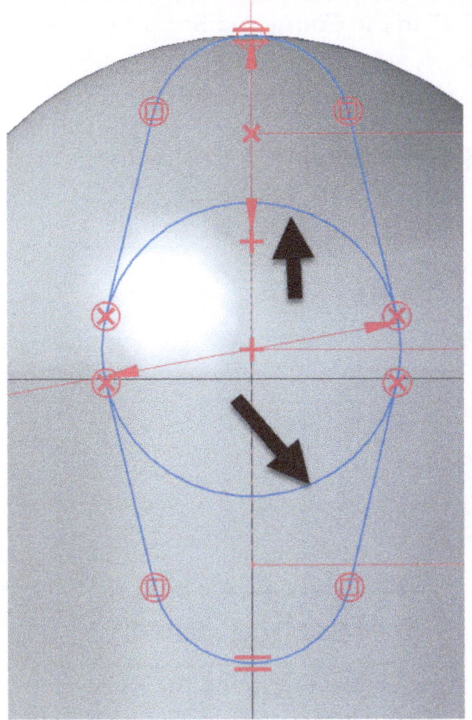

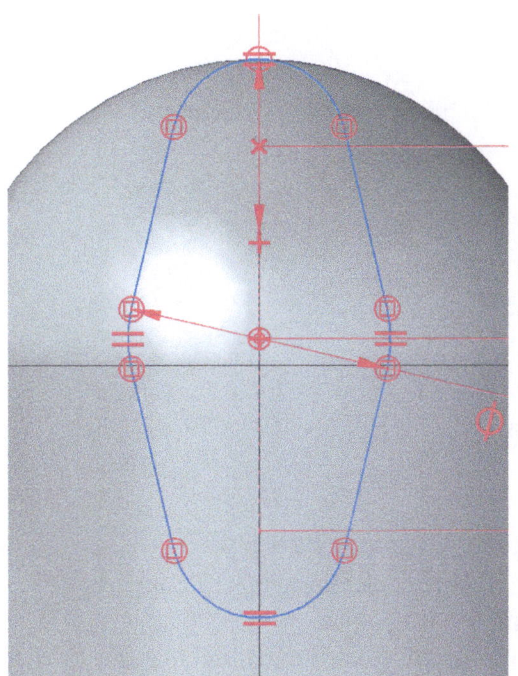

23. Click **Close Sketch** on the **Home** tab of the ribbon.
24. Click **Finish** and **Cancel** on the **Sketch** command bar.
25. On the ribbon, click **Home** tab > **Solids** group > **Extrude**.
26. On the **Extrude** command bar, select **Select from Sketch** option under the **Sketch** section.
27. Select the newly created sketch.
28. Click green check on the command bar.
29. On the **Extrude** command bar, expand **Extent** section and type **70** in the **Distance** box.
30. Move the pointer toward left and click to specify the side of the extrusion.
31. Click **Finish** and **Cancel** on the **Extrude** command bar.

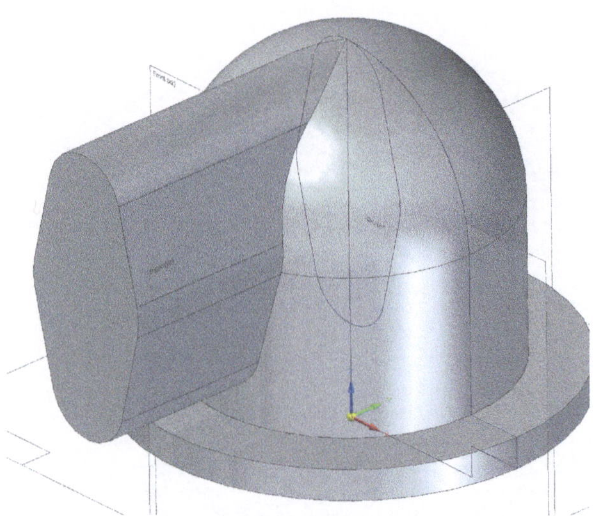

Creating the Circular Pattern

1. On the ribbon, click **Home** tab > **Pattern** > **Pattern**.
2. Select the newly created extruded feature.
3. Click the green check on the command bar.
4. On the **Pattern** dialog, select **Pattern Type > Circular**.
5. Select **Placement Type > By Sketch**.
6. Select the Top plane from the graphics window to sketch the profile of the circular pattern.

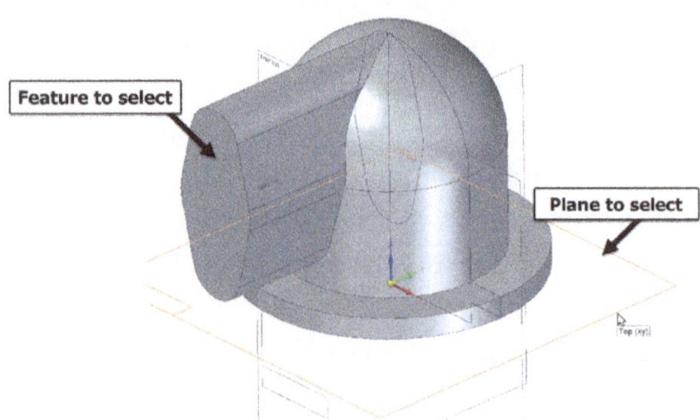

7. Select the sketch origin, move the pointer outward and click.

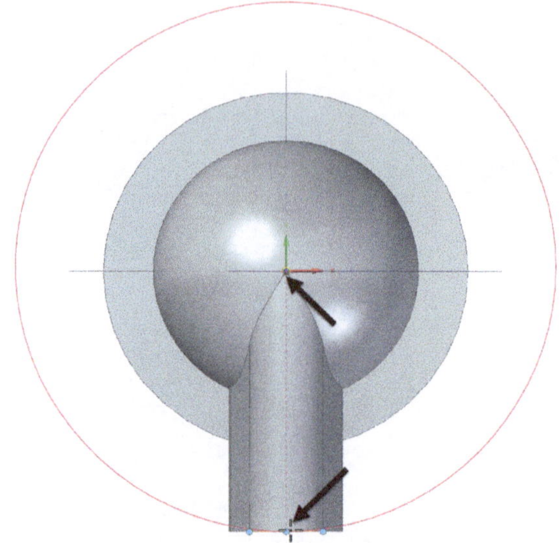

8. Click the **Partial Circle** icon on the **Circular Pattern** command bar.
9. Select **Type** > **Fixed** from the command bar.
10. Type **2** and **45** in the **Count** and **Spacing** boxes, respectively.
11. Move the pointer toward right and click.
12. Click the **Reference point** icon on the command bar.
13. Select the left end point of the arc as the reference point.

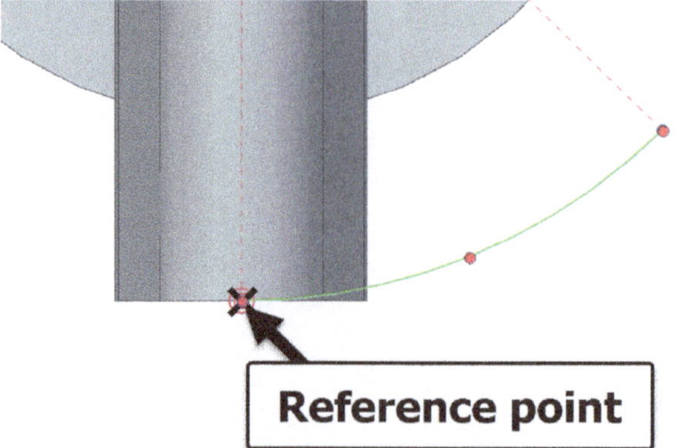

14. Click the **Close Sketch** button on the ribbon.
15. Click **Finish** on the **Pattern** command bar.

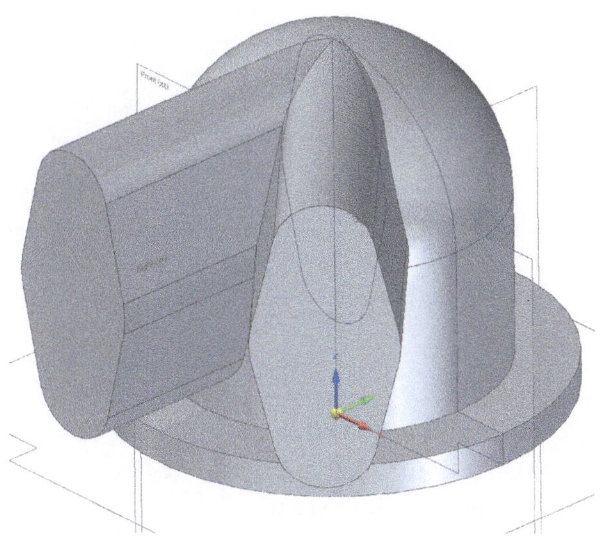

Creating the Inclined Boss

1. On the ribbon, click **Home > Plane > Planes** drop-down **> Angled**.
2. Select the Front and Right planes.
3. Type **45** in the **Angle** box on the command bar.
4. Move the pointer toward left and click to specify the direction on the angled plane.

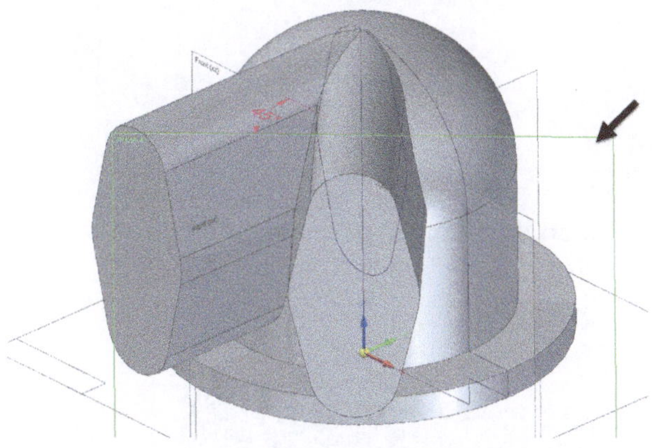

5. On the ribbon, click **Home** tab > **Solids** group > **Revolve**.
6. Select the **Coincident Plane** option from the drop-down available on the command bar.
7. Select the newly created plane.
8. On the ribbon, click **Home > Draw > Rectangle** drop-down > **Rectangle by 3 Points**.
9. Select the two points, as shown.
10. Move the pointer upward and click.

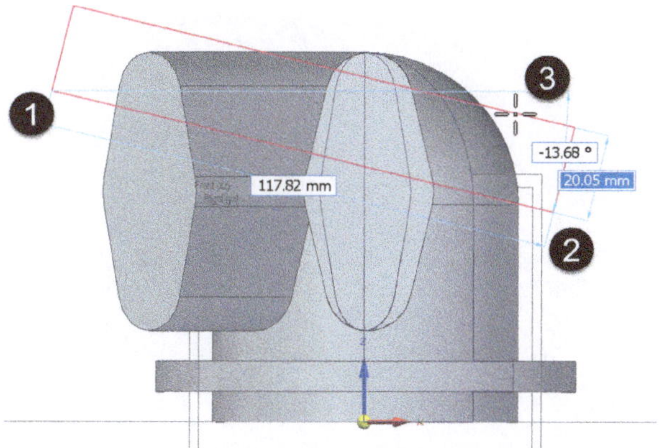

11. Add dimensions to the sketch, as shown.

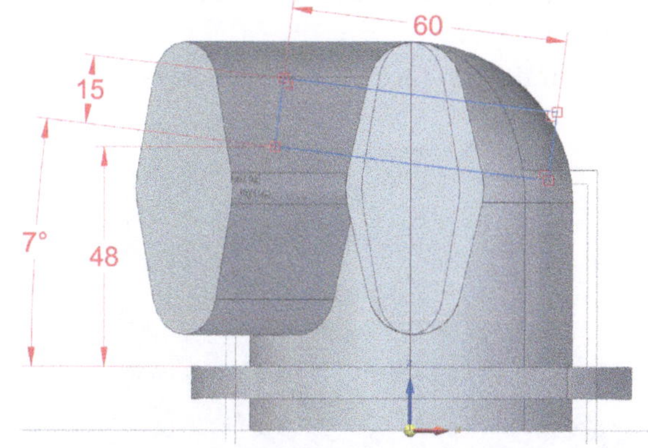

12. On the ribbon, click **Home > Rotate > Connect**.
13. Select the lower right corner of the rectangle.
14. Select the vertical axis of the sketch.

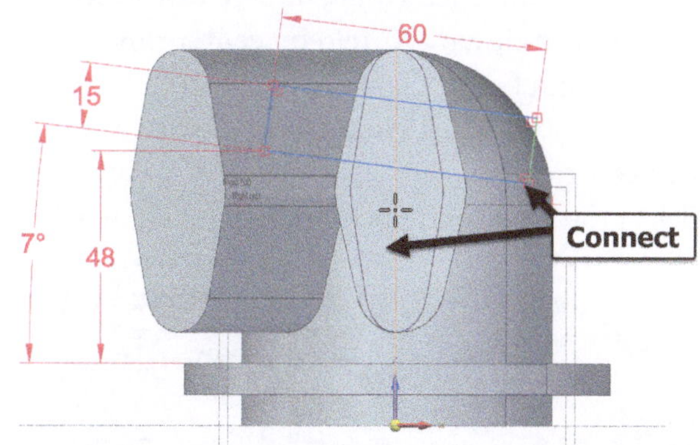

15. On the ribbon, click **Home** tab > **Draw** > **Axis of Revolution**.
16. Select the lower inclined line of the rectangle to define the axis of revolution.
17. Click the **Close Sketch** button on the ribbon.
18. Click the **Finish** button to create the *Revolved* feature.

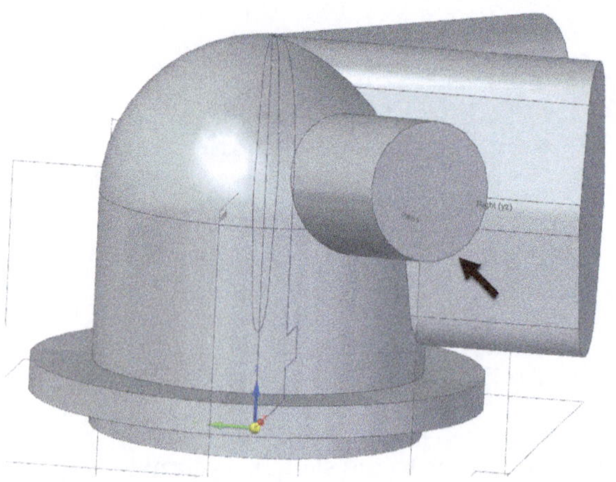

19. On the ribbon, click **Home** tab > **Solids** group > **Extrude**.
20. Click on the flat face of the inclined boss.

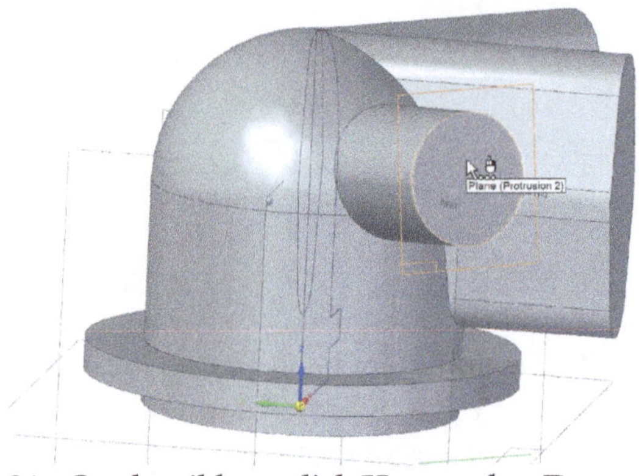

21. On the ribbon, click **Home** tab > **Draw** group > **Circle** drop-down > **Circle by center point**.
22. Create a circle.
23. On the ribbon, click **Home** tab > **Relate** > **Concentric**.
24. Select the circle and circular edge, as shown.

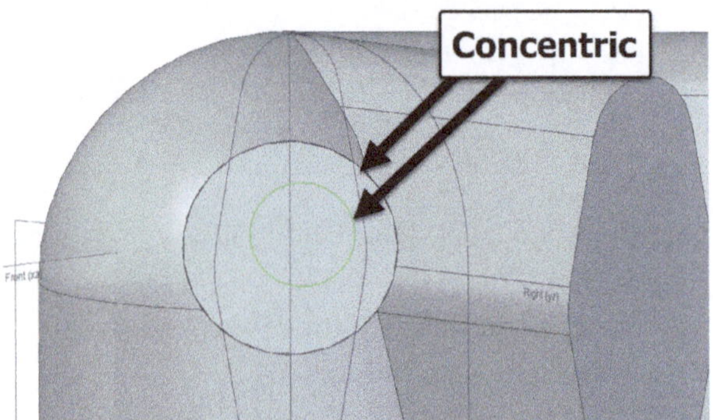

25. Add diameter dimension **20** to the circle.

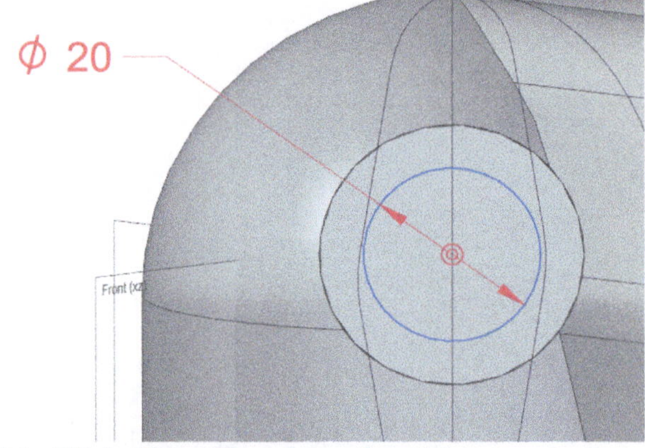

26. Click **Close Sketch** on the ribbon.
27. Click **Direction > One-sided Extent**.
28. Select **Type > Finite Extent**.
29. Type **60** in the **Distance** box and press ENTER.
30. Click in the model to specify the direction of the cut.
31. Click **Finish**.

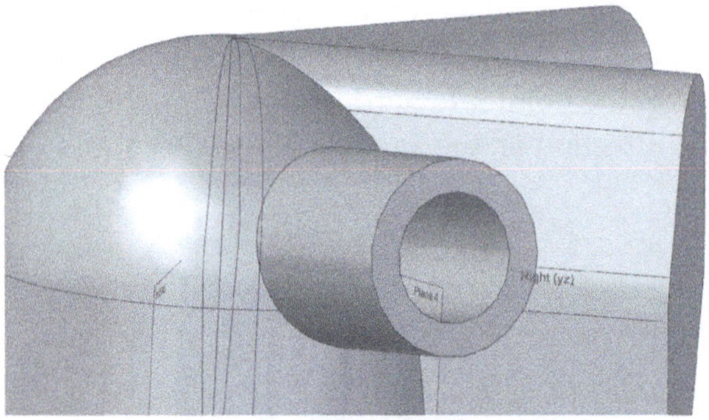

32. Click on the flat face of the second feature.

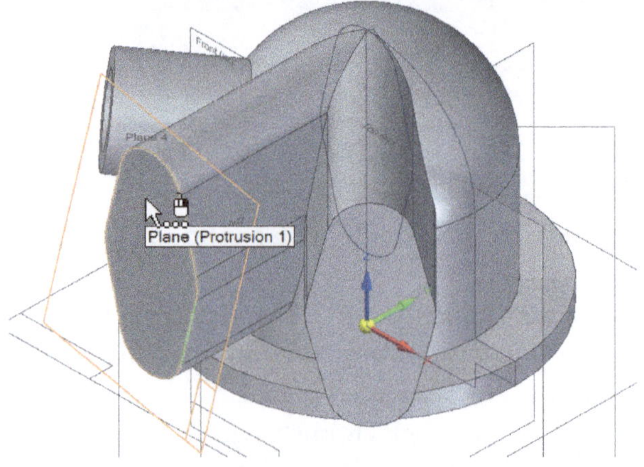

33. Create a circle and apply the **Concentric** relationship between the circle and the curved edge, as shown.

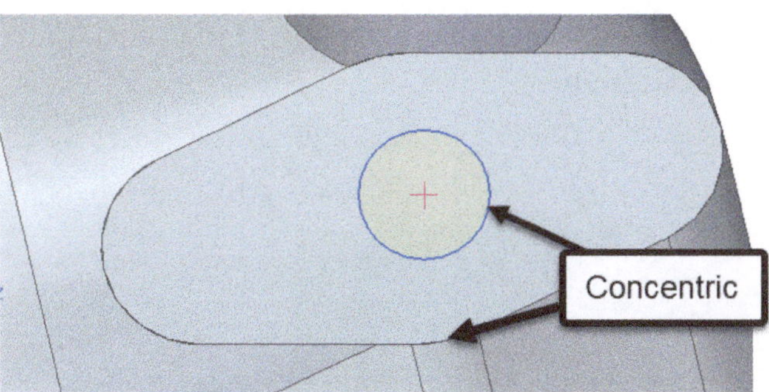

34. Add diameter dimension **20** to the circle.

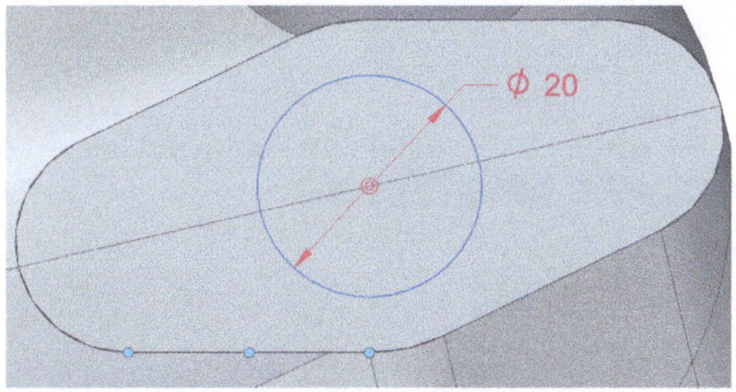

35. Click **Close Sketch** on the ribbon.
36. On the **Extrude** command bar, type **70** in the **Distance** box.
37. Click in the model to specify the direction of the cut.
38. Click **Finish**.

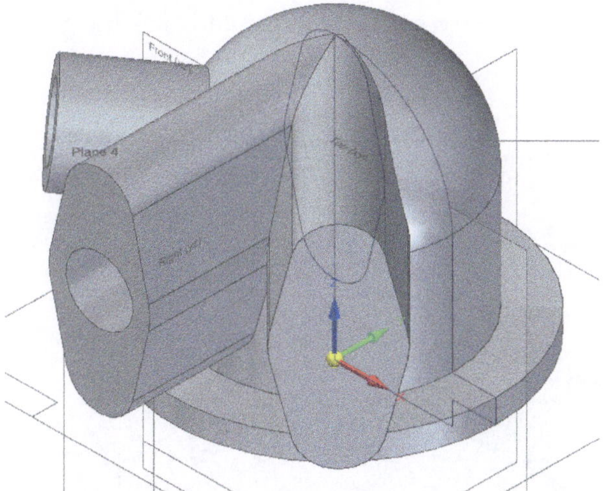

39. Click on the flat face of the second feature.

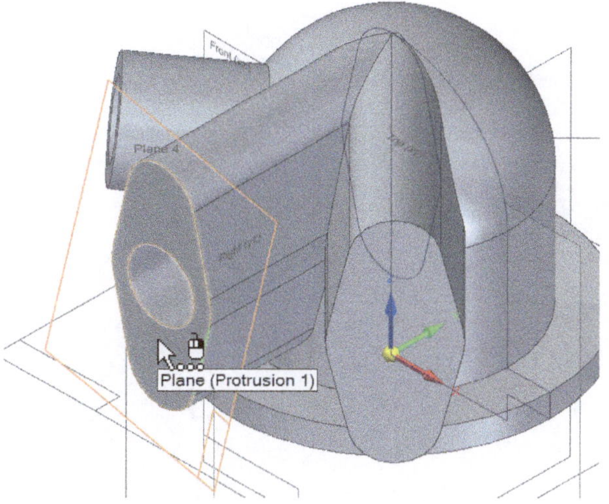

40. Create two circles and apply the **Concentric** relationships between the circles and the curved edges, as shown.
41. Apply the **Equal** relationship between the two circles.
42. Add diameter dimension of **10 mm** to the circles.

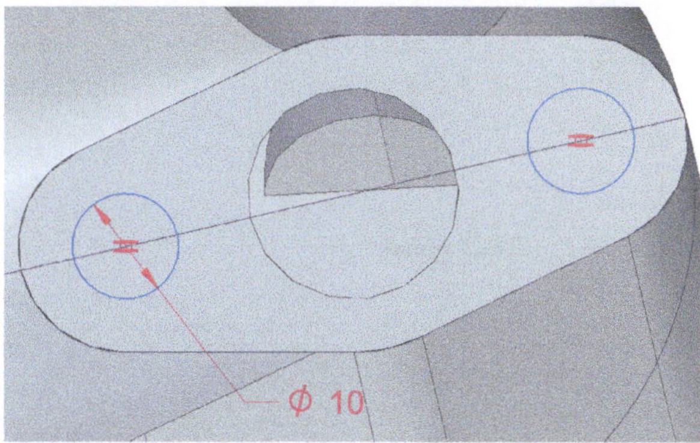

43. Click **Close Sketch** on the ribbon.
44. Type **25** in the **Distance** box and press ENTER.
45. Click in the model to specify the direction of the cut.
46. Click **Finish** and **Cancel**.

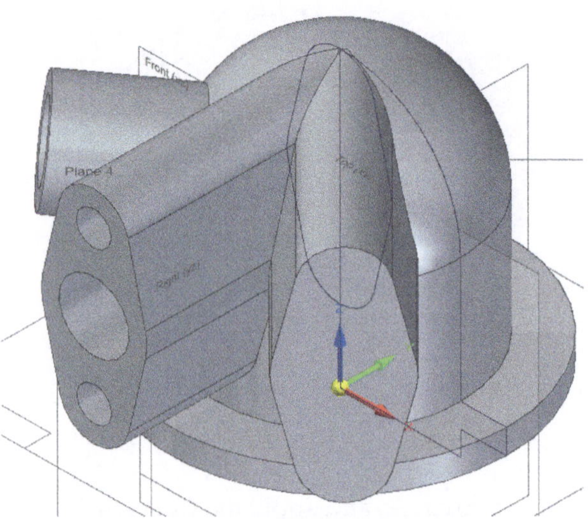

32. Press and hold the left mouse button on the Pattern feature in the Pathfinder.

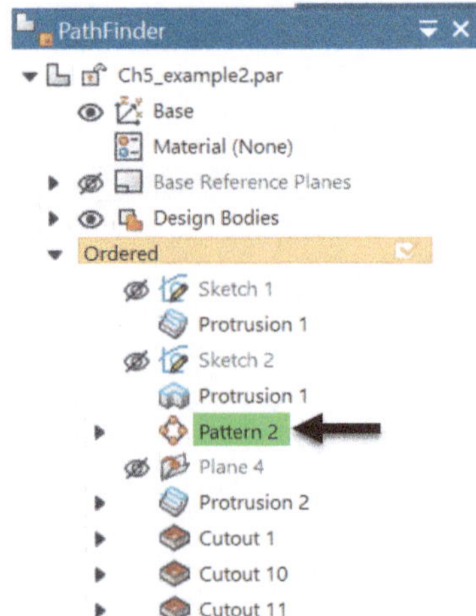

33. Next, drag the pointer down and release it at the bottom of the Pathfinder.

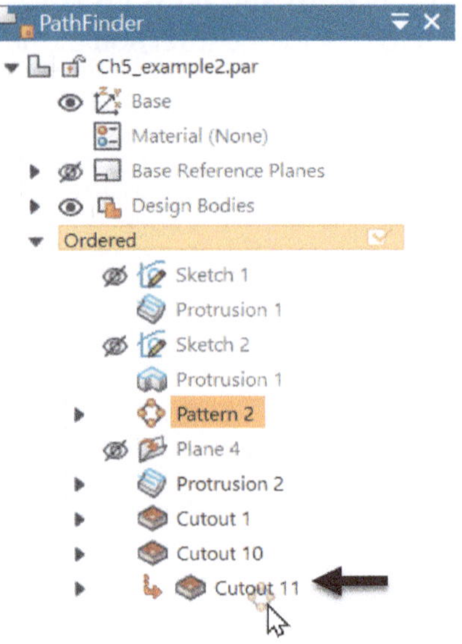

34. Click on the circular pattern, and then click **Edit definition**.

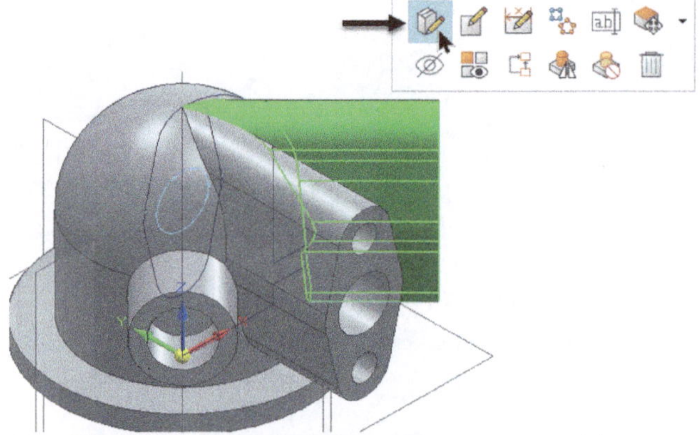

35. Click the **Select** button on the command bar.

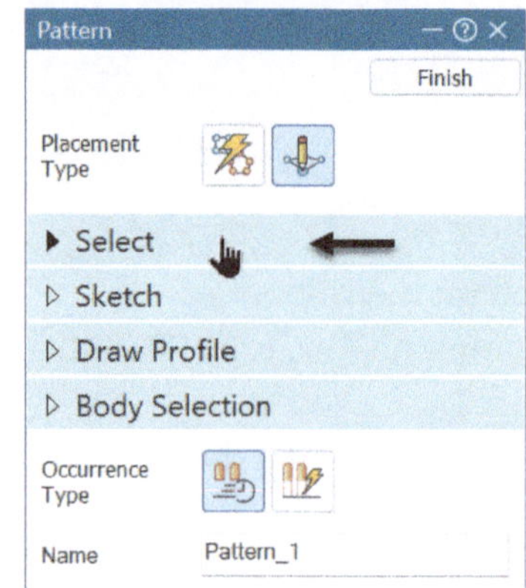

36. Select the two cutout features and click the green check.

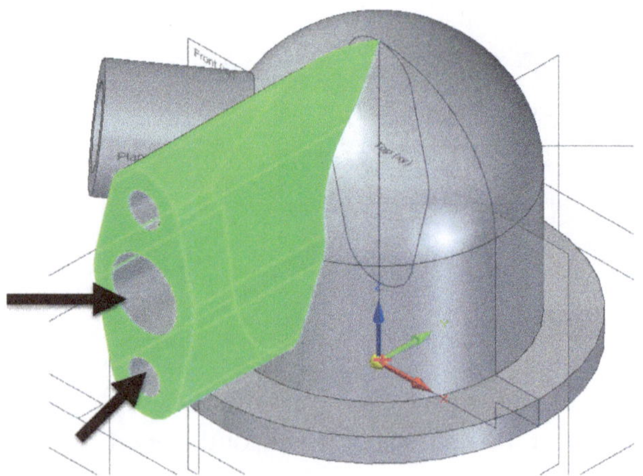

37. Click the **Finish** button.

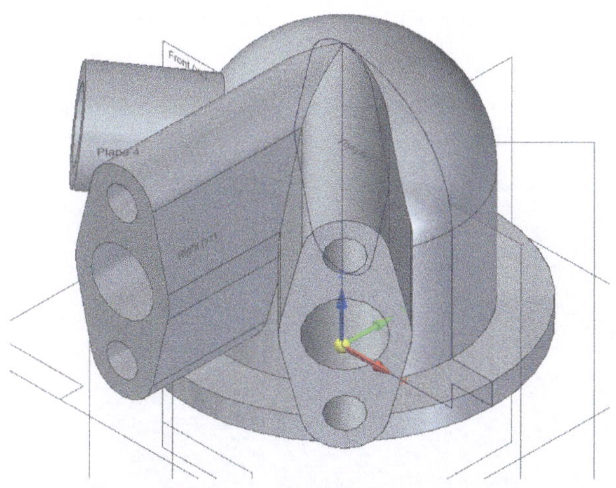

Creating the Revolved Cut Feature

1. On the ribbon, click **Home > Solids > Revolve**.
2. Select the Front plane.
3. Create the sketch, as shown.
4. Apply the **Connect** relationship between the lower right corner of the sketch and the sketch origin.

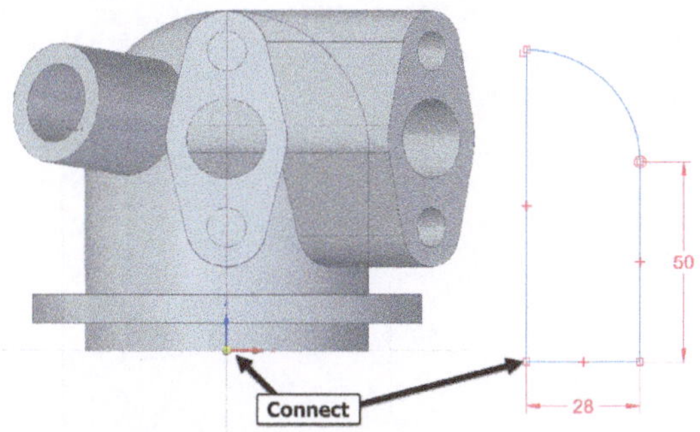

5. On the ribbon, click **Home** tab > **Draw** > **Axis of Revolution**.
6. Select the left vertical line of the sketch to define the axis of revolution.

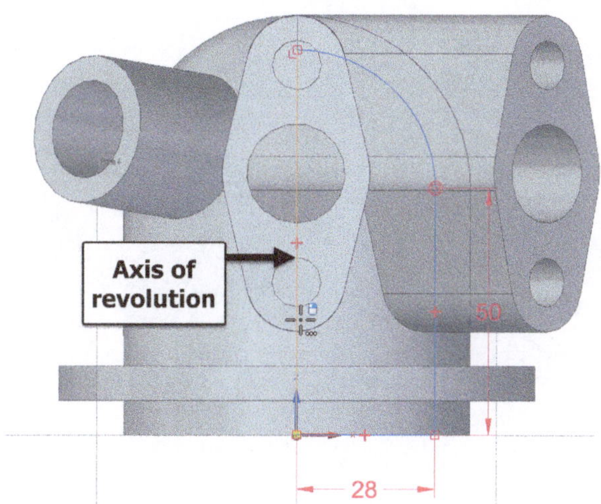

7. Click **Close Sketch** on the ribbon.
8. Click **Finish** and **Cancel**.

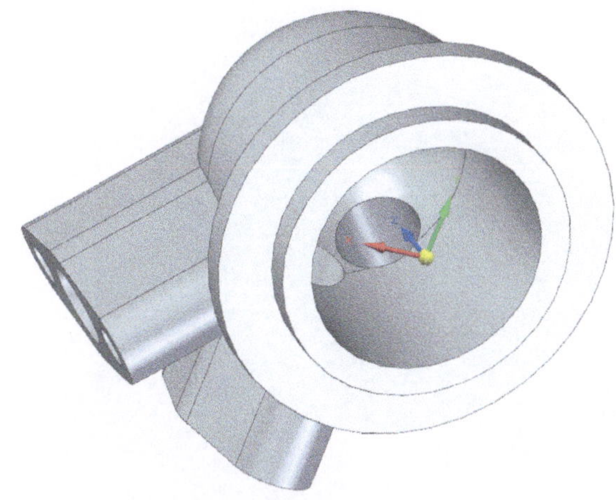

Creating the Rounds

1. On the ribbon, click **Home > Solids > Round**.
2. On the **Round** command bar, type **5** in the **Radius** box.
3. On the command bar, select **Selection Type > Chain**.
4. Select the edges, as shown.

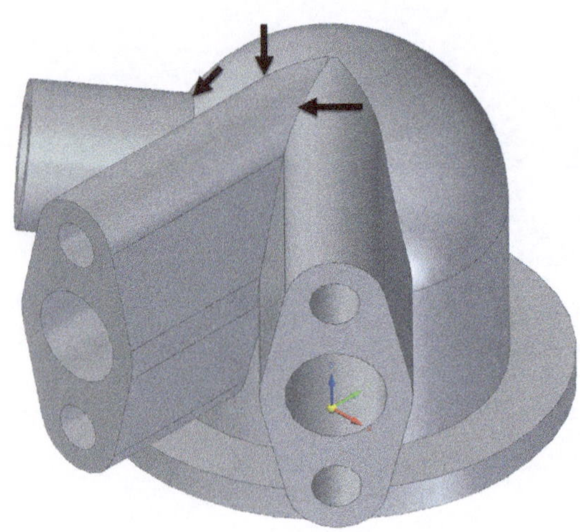

5. Click **Accept**.
6. Click **Preview** and **Finish**.

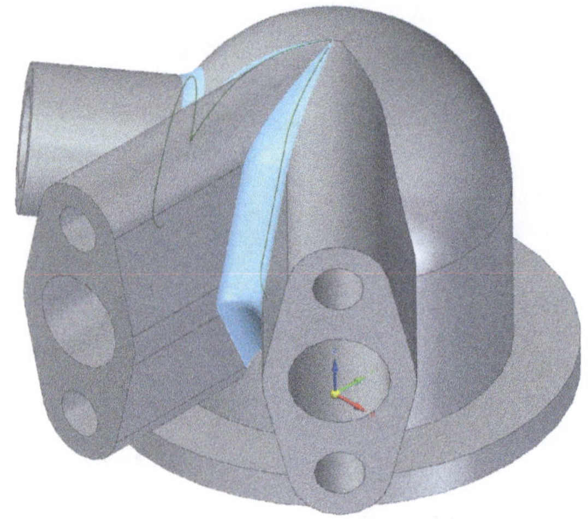

7. Select the edge of the model, as shown.

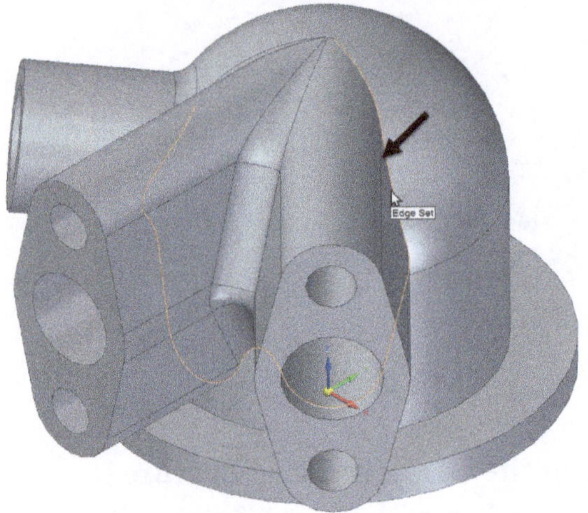

8. Click **Accept**, **Preview**, **Finish**, and **Cancel** on the command bar.
9. Save and close the file.

Questions

1. Describe the procedure to create a mirror feature.
2. List any two commands to create patterns.
3. Why is it important to convert a set of holes into a pattern?
4. How do you add more features to an existing pattern?
5. List the options that define the orientation of the feature in a fill pattern.

Exercises

Exercise 1 (Millimetres)

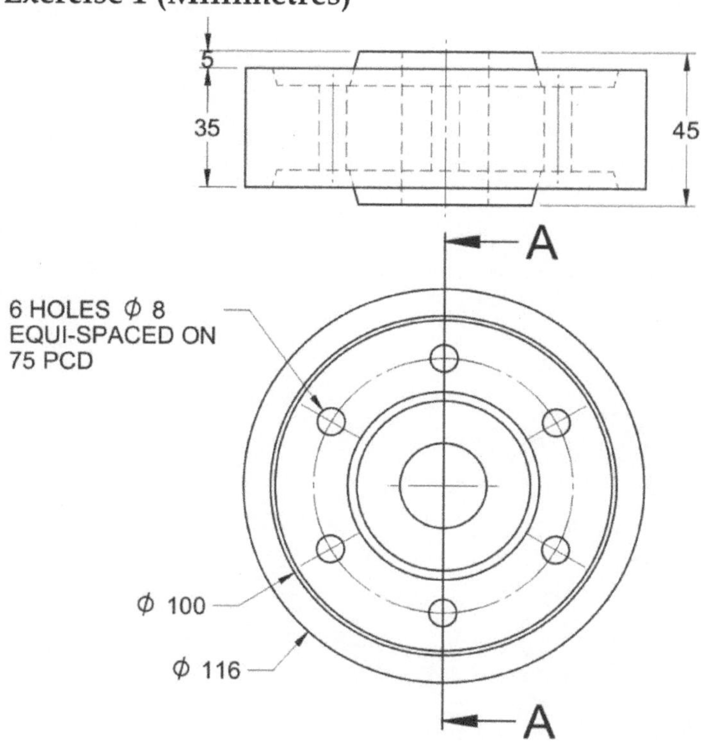

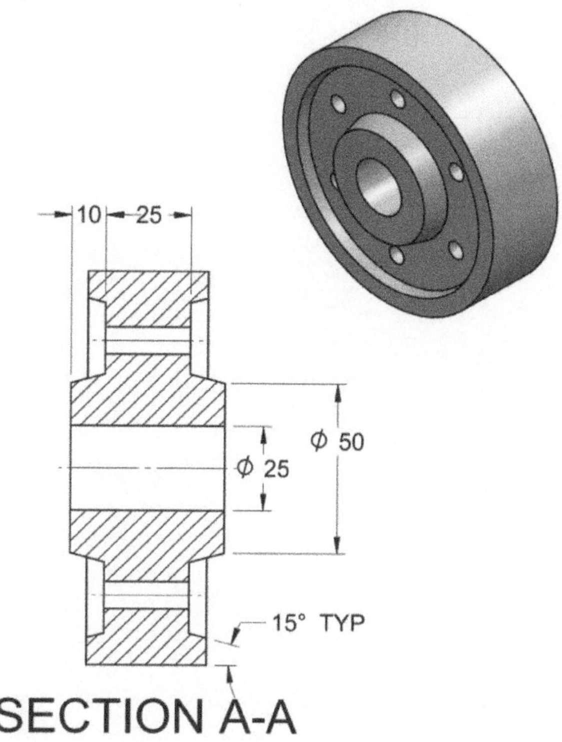

Exercise 2 (Inches)

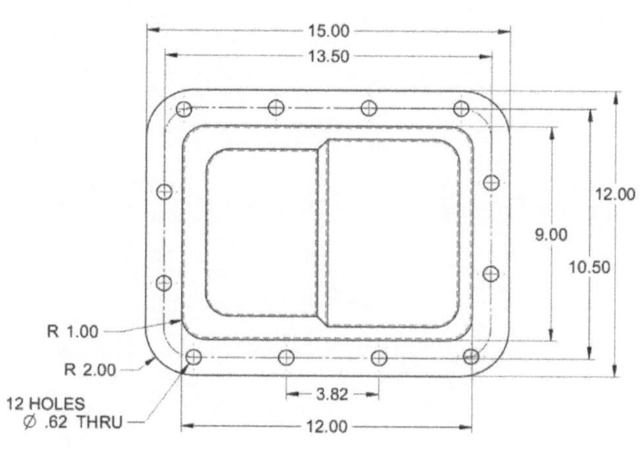

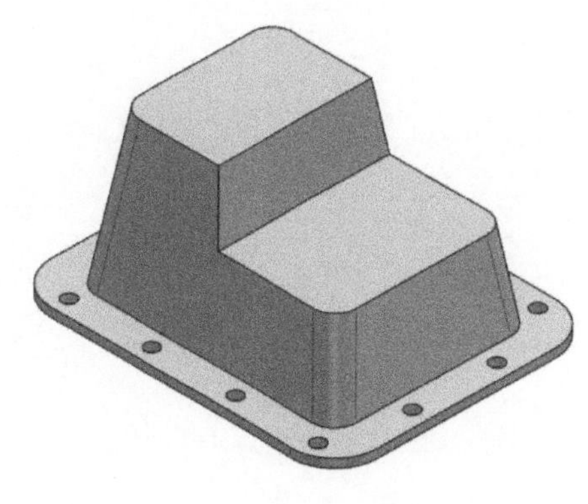

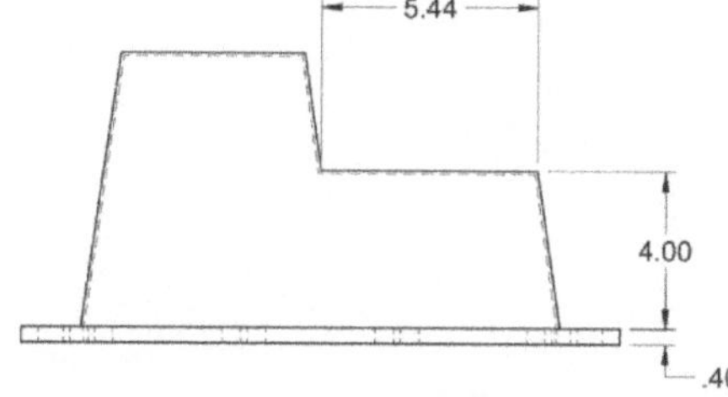

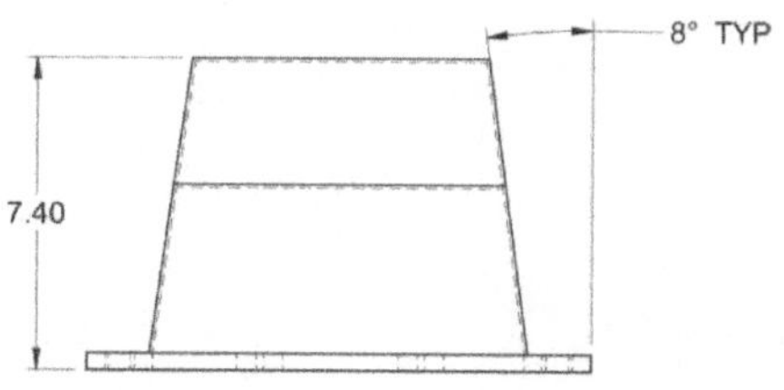

SHEET THICKNESS = 0.079 in

Chapter 6: Sweep Features

The **Sweep** command is one of the basic commands available in Solid Edge that allow you to generate solid geometry. It can be used to create simple geometry as well as complex shapes. A sweep is composed of two items: a cross-section and a path. The cross-section controls the shape of the sweep while the path controls its direction. For example, take a look at the angled cylinder shown in the figure. This is created using a simple sweep with the circle as the profile and an angled line as the path.

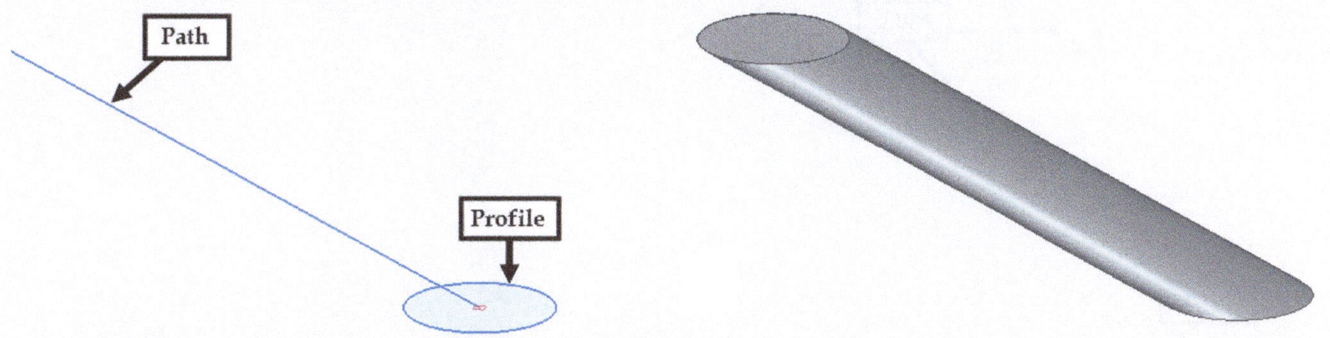

By making the path a bit more complex, you can see that a sweep allows you to create shapes you would not be able to create using commands such as Extrude or Revolve.

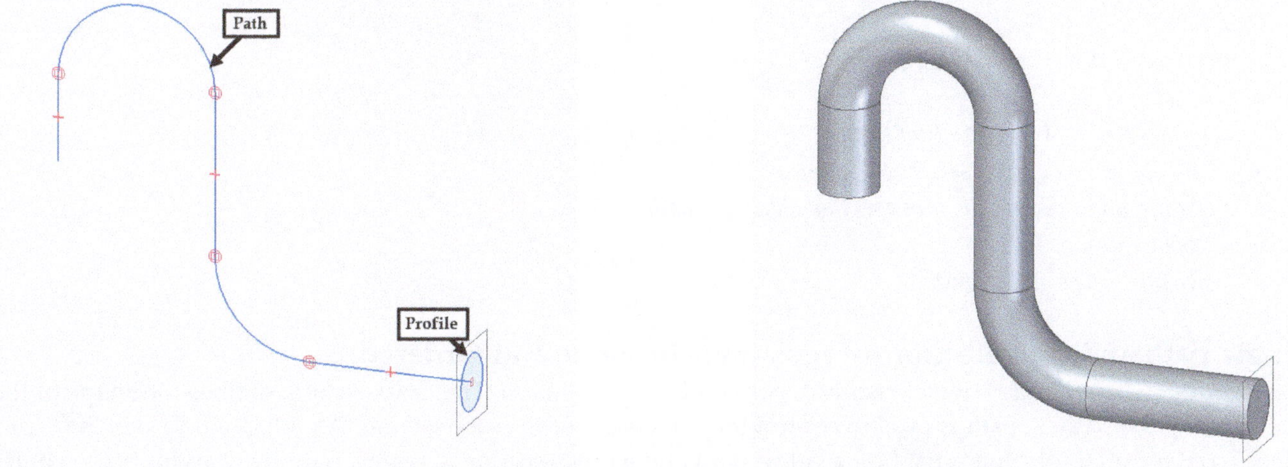

To take the sweep feature to the next level of complexity, you can add multiple paths and cross-sections. By doing so, the shape of the geometry is controlled by multiple cross-sections and paths. For example, the elliptical cross-section in the figure varies in size along the path because an additional path controls it.

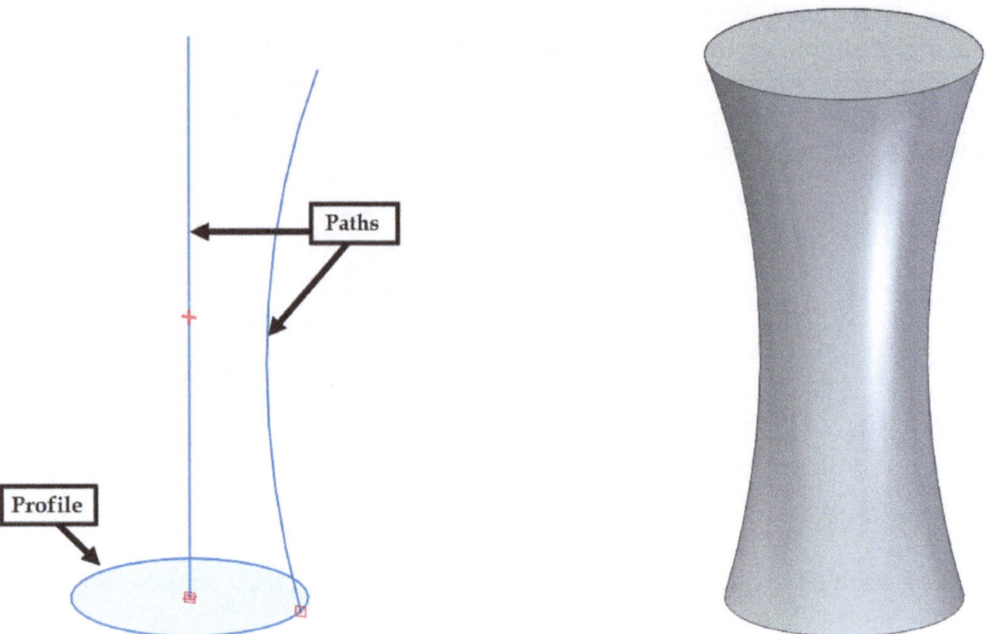

The topics covered in this chapter are:

- *Single Path and cross-section sweeps*
- *Multiple paths and cross-section sweeps*
- *Scaling and twisting the cross-section along the path*
- *Swept Cutouts*
- *Helical sweeps and cutouts*

Single path and cross-section sweeps (Synchronous and Ordered)

This type of sweep requires two elements: a path and a cross-section. The cross-section defines the shape of the sweep along the path. A path is used to control the direction of the cross-section. A path can be a sketch or an edge. To create a sweep, you must first create a path and a cross-section. Create a path by drawing a sketch. It can be an open or closed sketch. Next, click **Home > Planes > More Planes > Normal to Curve** on the ribbon, and then create a plane normal to the path. Sketch the cross-section on the plane normal to the path.

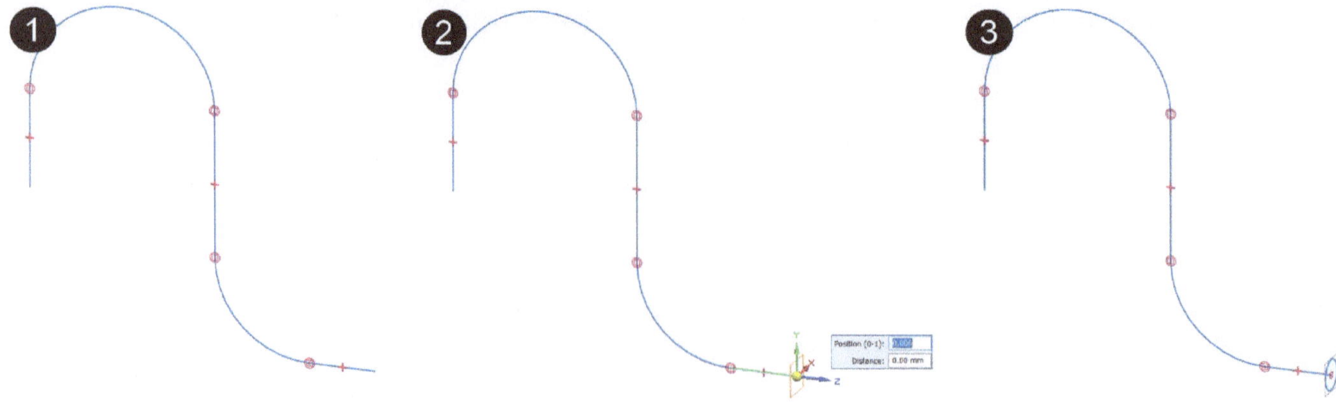

Activate the **Sweep** command (click **Home > Solids > Sweep** on the ribbon). As you activate this command, a dialog appears showing different options to create the sweep. Select the **Single path and cross-section** option on the dialog and click **OK**.

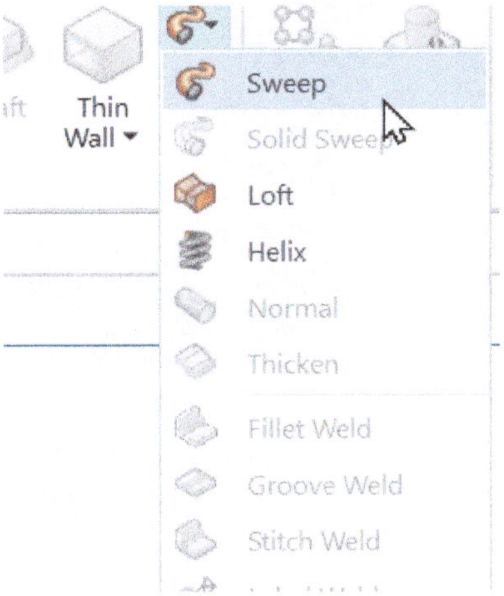

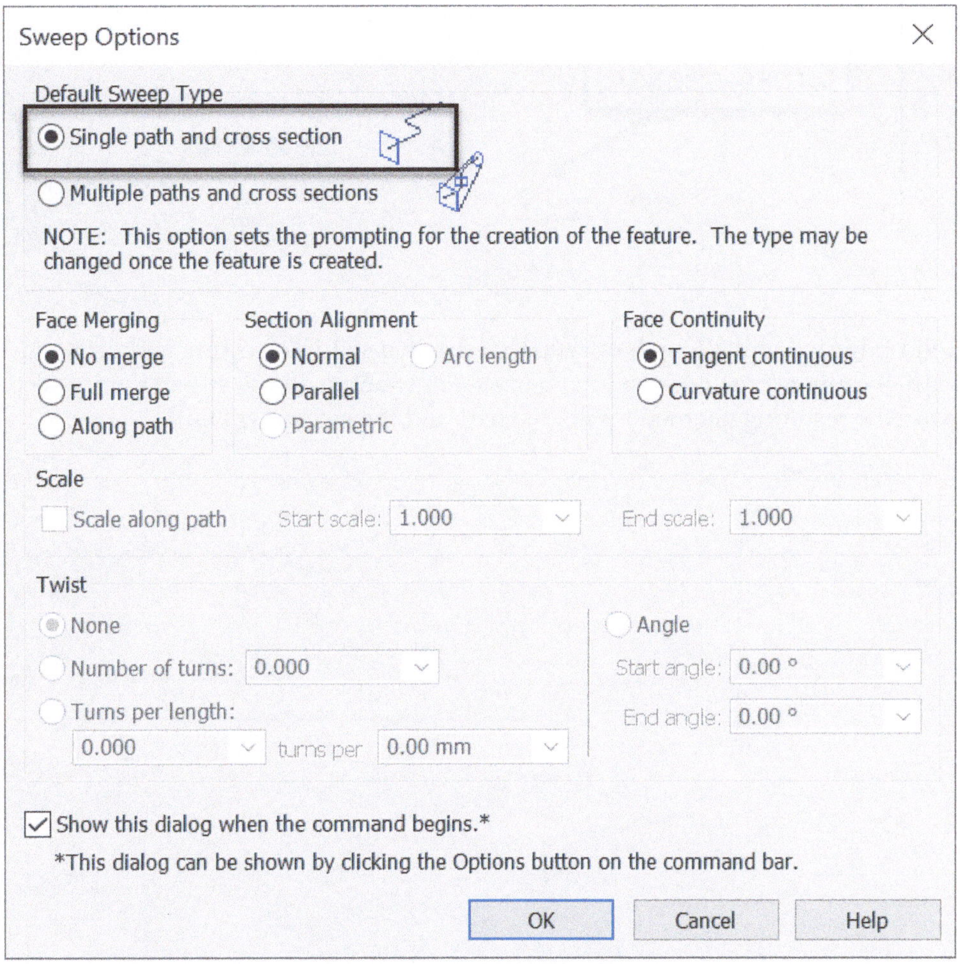

Select the path and click the green check on the command bar.

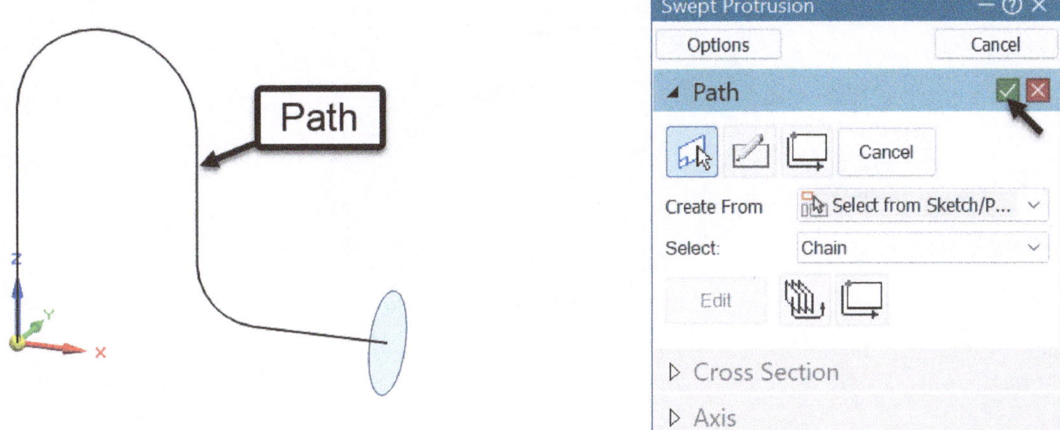

Select the cross-section and click **Finish** on the command bar. Click **Cancel** to deactivate the command.

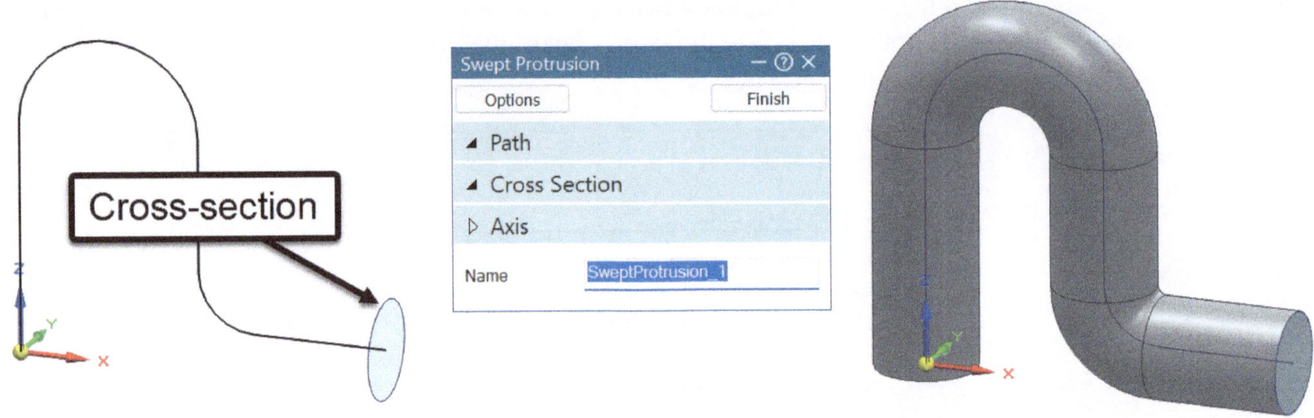

Solid Edge will not allow the sweep to result in a self-intersecting geometry. As the cross-section is swept along a path, it cannot come back and cross itself. For example, if the sweep's cross-section is larger than the curves on the path, the resulting geometry will intersect, and the sweep will fail.

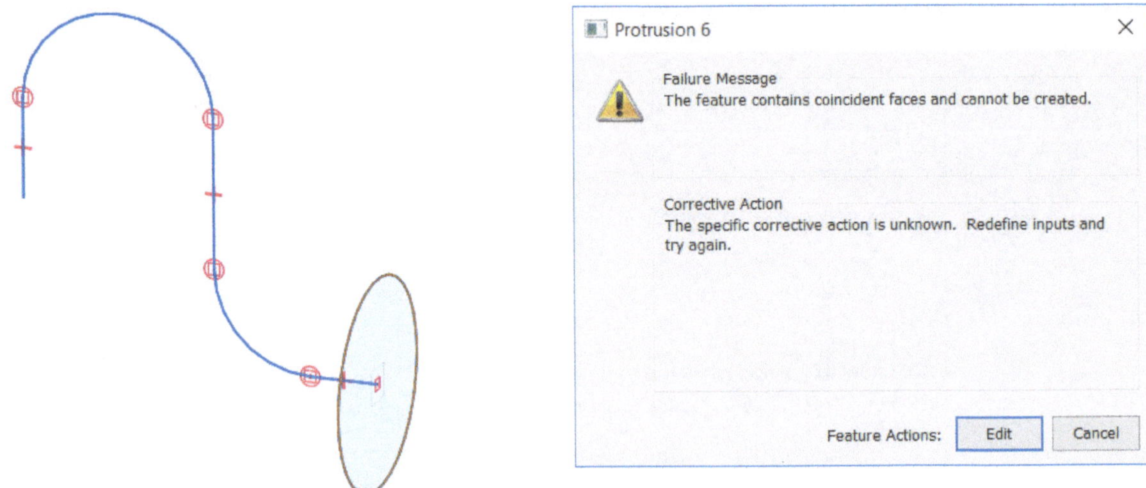

A sweeping profile must be created as a sketch. However, a path can be a sketch, curve, or edge. The following illustrations show various types of paths and resultant sweep features.

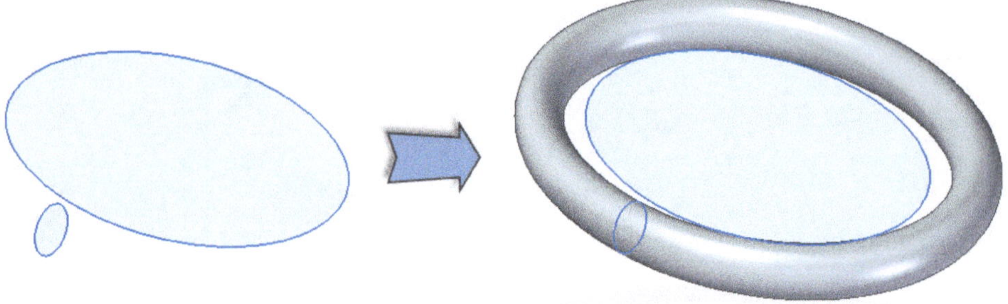

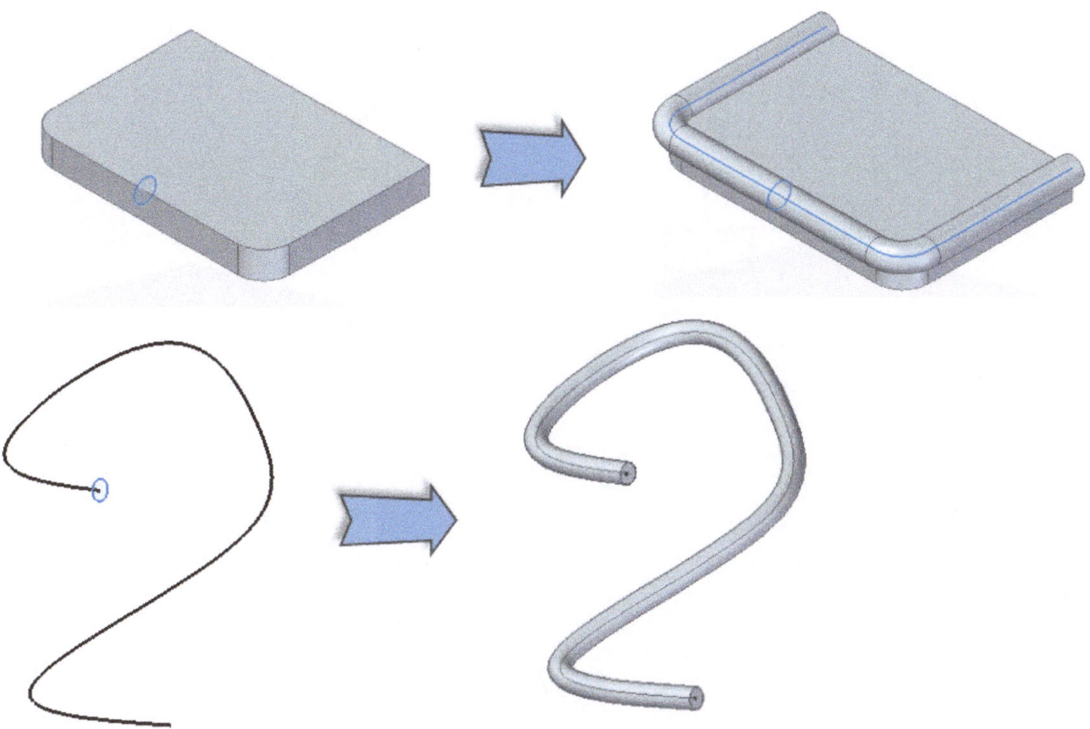

Face Merging

There are three options to merge faces of a sweep feature. These options are available on the **Sweep Options** dialog. The **No Merge** option creates a sweep feature without merging its faces. The **Full Merge** option merges all the faces of a sweep feature. The **Along path** option merges the faces along the direction of the path.

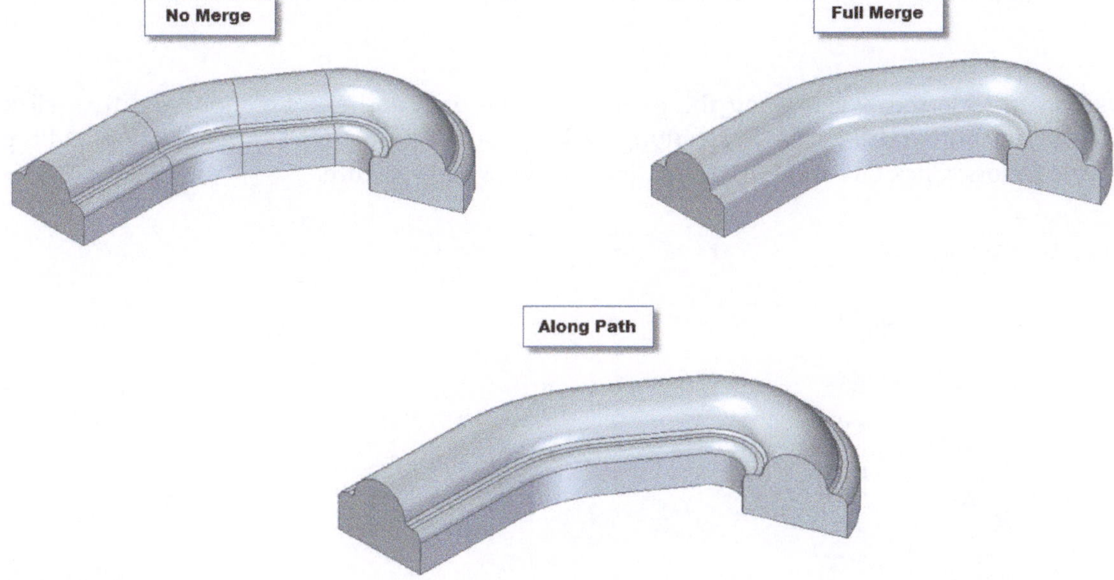

Section Alignment

The section alignment options define the orientation of the resulting geometry. The **Normal** option sweeps the cross-section in the direction normal to the path. The **Parallel** option sweeps the cross-section in the direction parallel to itself.

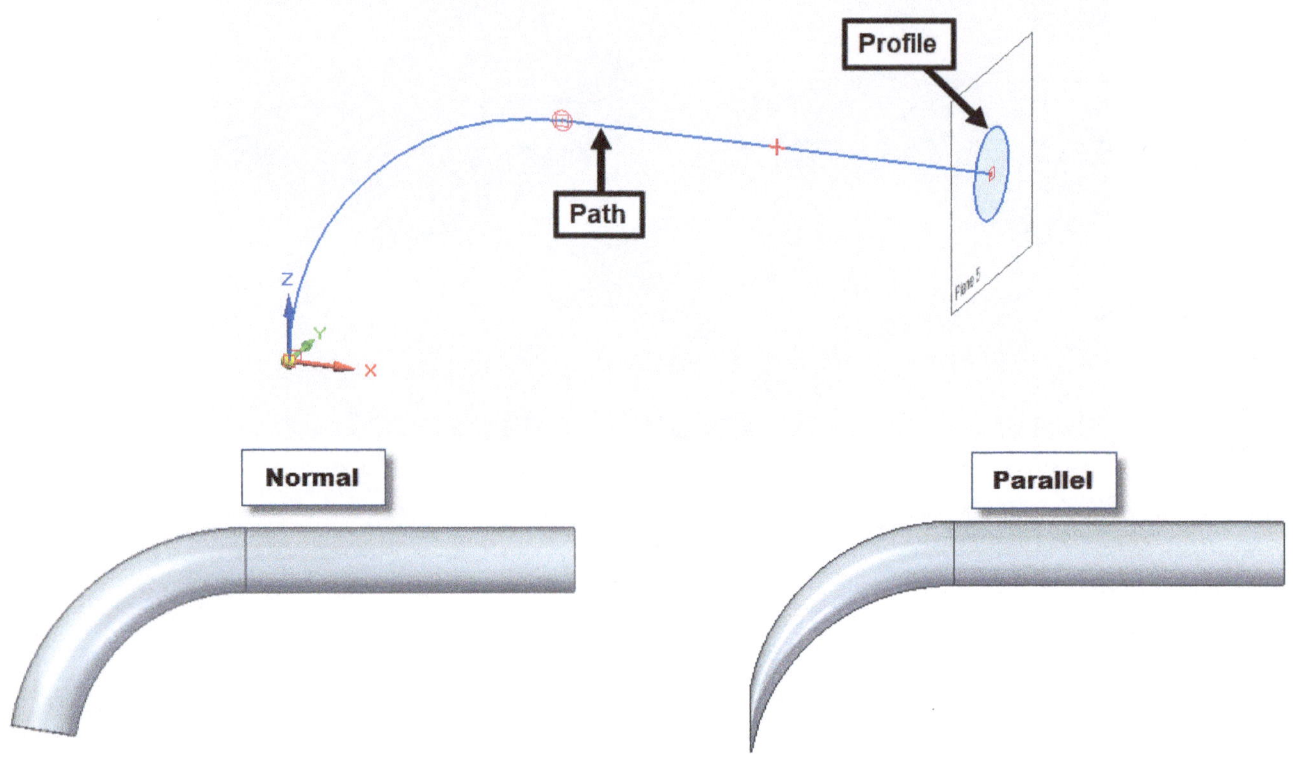

Face Continuity

The **Face Continuity** options define the tangency condition between the faces of a sweep feature. The **Tangent Continuous** option makes two faces tangent and continuous to each other. The **Curvature Continuous** option maintains the tangency and radius of curvature between two faces of a sweep feature.

Scale

Solid Edge allows you to scale the sweep along the path. Select the path and cross-section, and then click the **Options** icon on the command bar. Check the **Scale along path** option on the **Sweep Options** dialog and type-in the start and end scale factors. Click **OK** and **Finish** creating a scaled sweep feature.

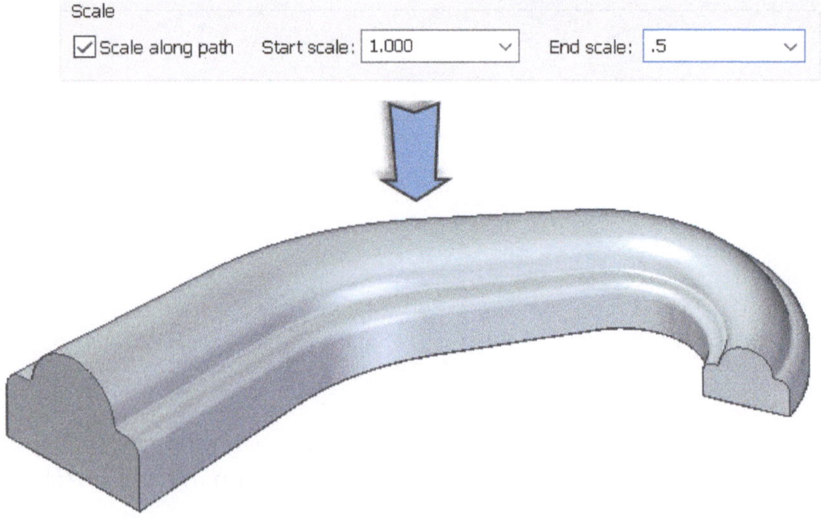

Twist

Solid Edge allows you to twist the cross-section along the path. Define the path and cross-section, and then click the **Options** icon on the command bar. The **Twist** options on the **Sweep Options** dialog help you to apply a twist to the cross-section.

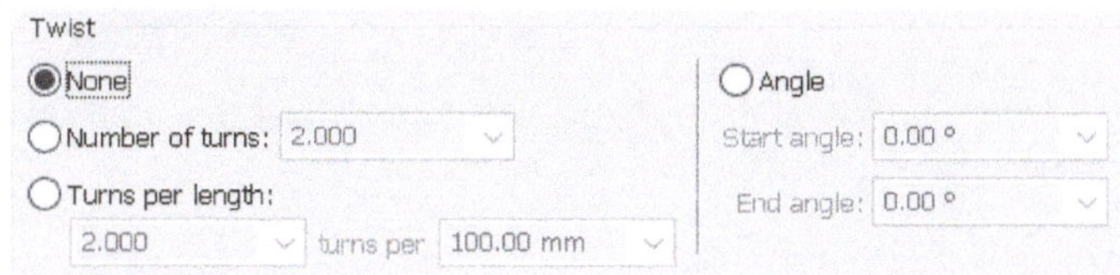

The **Number of Turns** option turns the cross-section by the value you enter in the box.

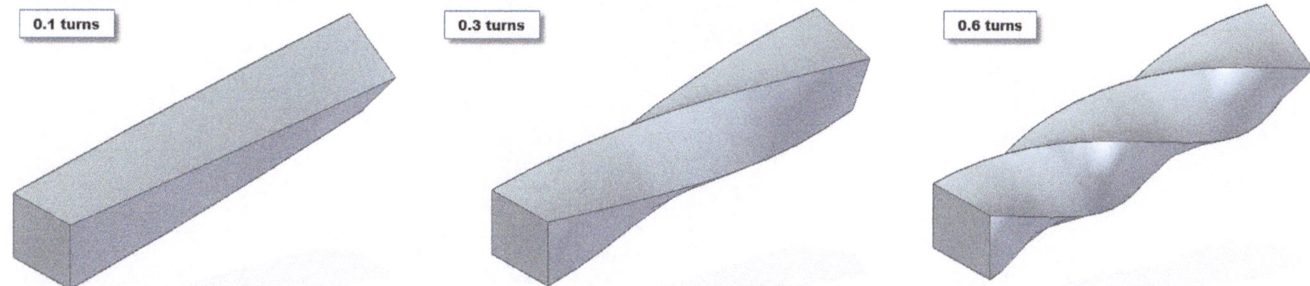

The **Turns per Length** option twists the cross-section by the number of turns and length you enter in the boxes.

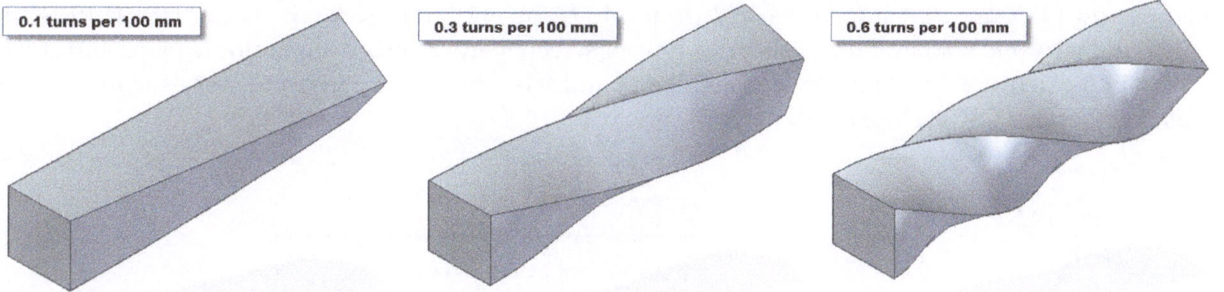

The **Angle** option twists the cross-section by an angle. Select this option and type-in values in the **Start Angle** and **End Angle** boxes.

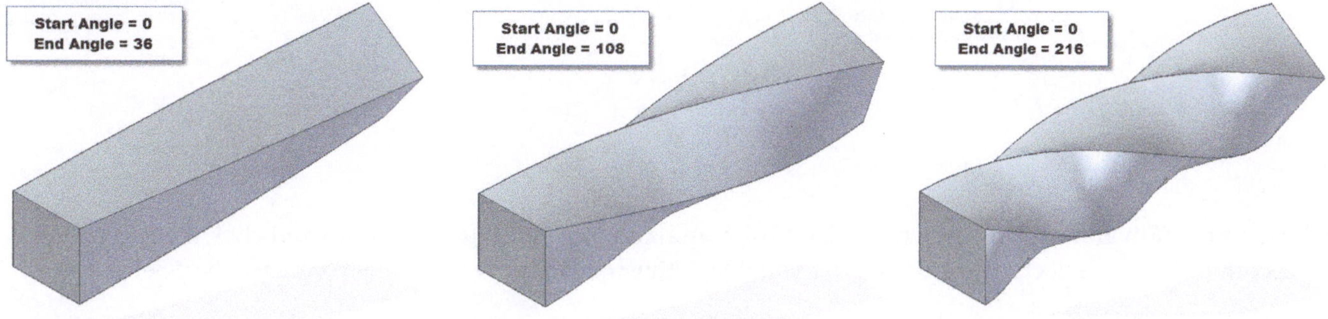

Axis

The **Axis** option on the command bar will be useful while sweeping a cross-section along a non-planar path. For example, define a path and cross-section similar to the one shown in the figure and click the **Axis** option on the command bar. Select a line or axis from the Base coordinate system. The cross-section and the axis will be locked in the same plane. As a result, the cross-section and axis orientation become the same, and the cross-section will be swept while maintaining the axis's orientation.

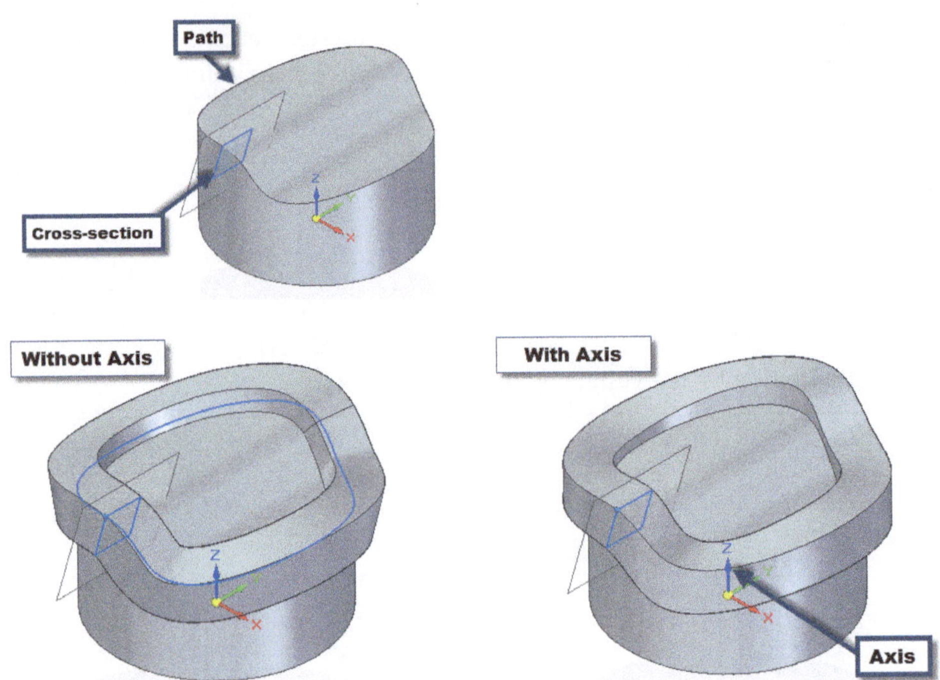

Multiple paths and cross-sections sweeps (Synchronous and Ordered)

Solid Edge allows you to create sweep features with multiple paths and cross-sections. It can be useful while creating complex geometry and shapes. First, create this type of sweep feature and create multiple paths and cross-sections, as shown in the figure. Activate the **Sweep** command and select **Multiple paths and cross-sections** on the **Sweep Options** dialog. Click **OK** to close the dialog.

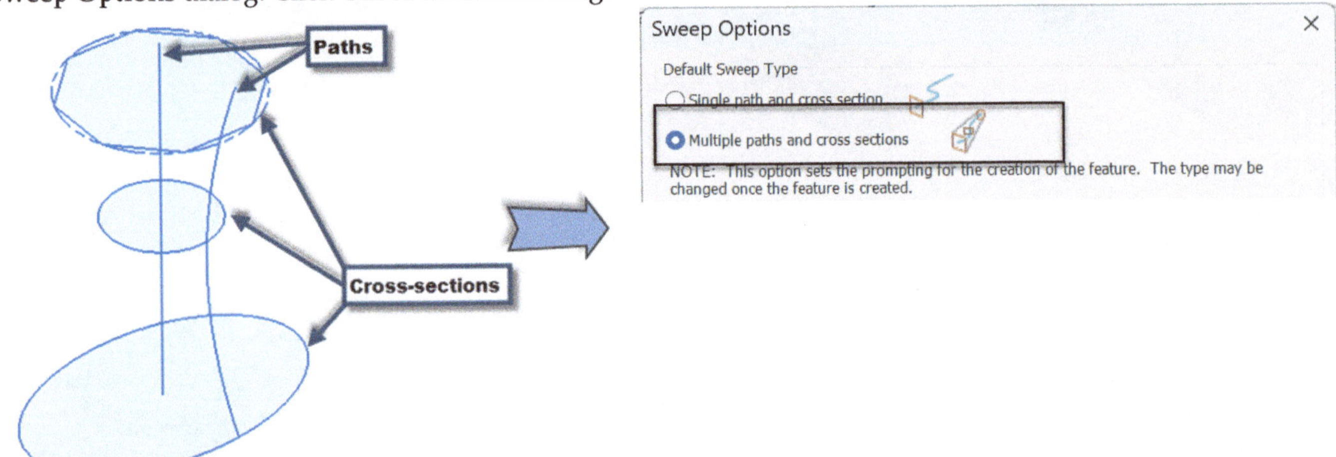

Select the first path and click the green check on the command bar. Select another path and click the green check on the command bar. Select the third path, if available. Otherwise, click **Next** on the command bar. Select the all the cross-sections one-by-one and notice the Clamp Control handles on the selected cross-sections. Click the down-arrow on the Clamp Control handle and notice the two options: **No Clamp** and **Clamp to Section**. The **Clamp to Section** option helps you to maintain the cross-section up to a length specified by the drag handle (magnitude handle). You can click the **Common Clamp Condition** icon on the command bar to apply the same clamp condition to all the sections. Next, click **Preview** on the command bar. A preview of the geometry will appear. Click **Finish** to complete the feature.

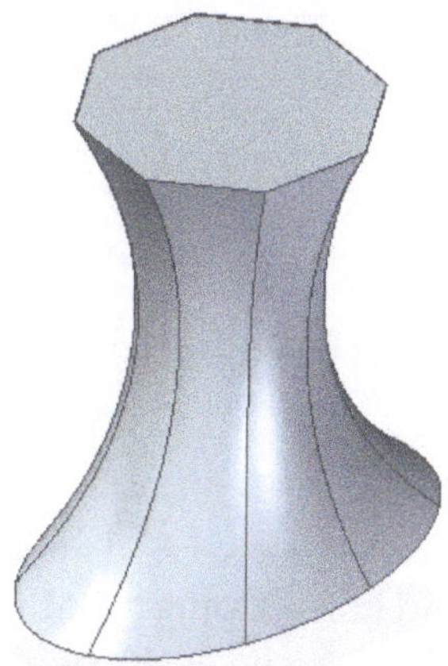

Swept Cutout

In addition to adding swept features, Solid Edge allows you to remove geometry using the **Swept Cutout** command. Activate this command (click **Home > Solids > Cut** drop-down **> Swept Cutout** on the ribbon) and select the sweep type from the **Sweep Options** dialog. Click **OK** and select the path. Click the green check on the command bar to accept the path. Select the cross-section and click **Finish** to create the swept cutout.

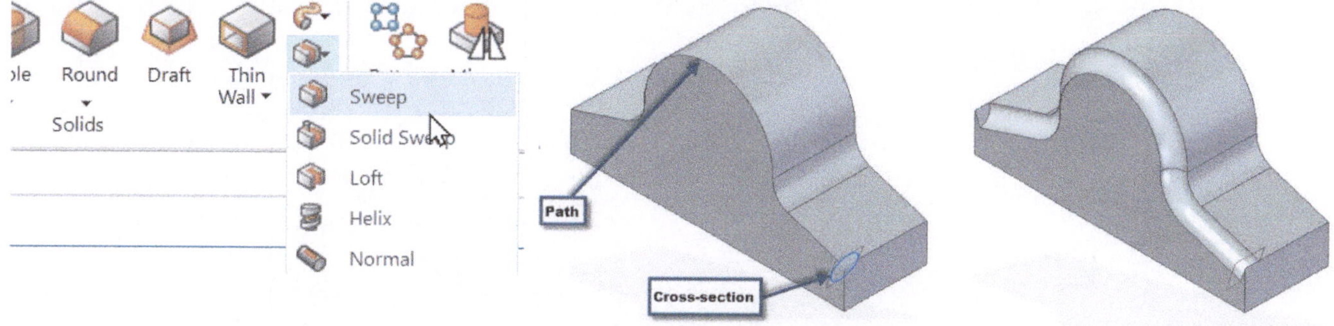

You will notice that the swept cutout is not created throughout the geometry. This is because the cross-section is swept only up to the endpoints of the path. In this case, you must define a new path, which extends beyond the geometry. Delete the swept cutout from the Pathfinder and create two lines, which are continuous and collinear with the path. Activate the **Derived** command (click **Surfacing > Curves > Derived** on the ribbon) and select the edges and lines. Click the green check on the command bar to create a new curve. Now, create a swept cut out by using the curve as the path. The resultant swept cutout will be throughout the geometry.

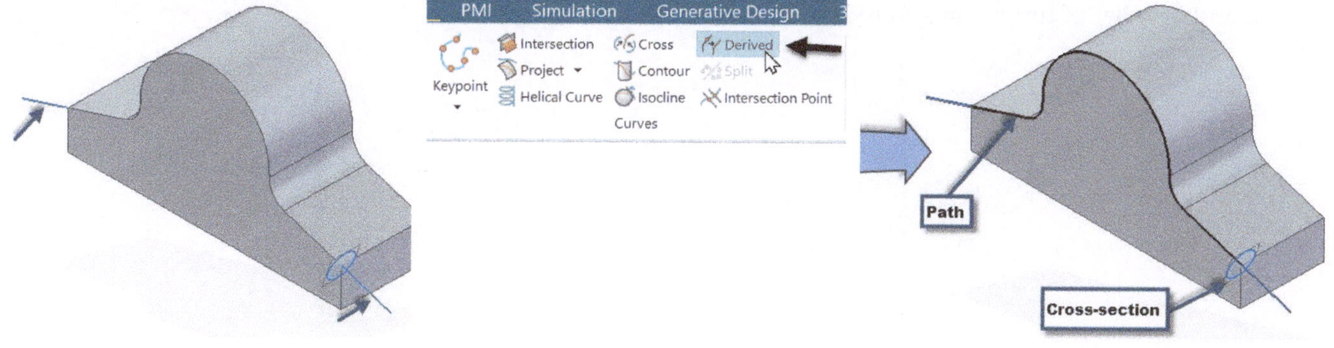

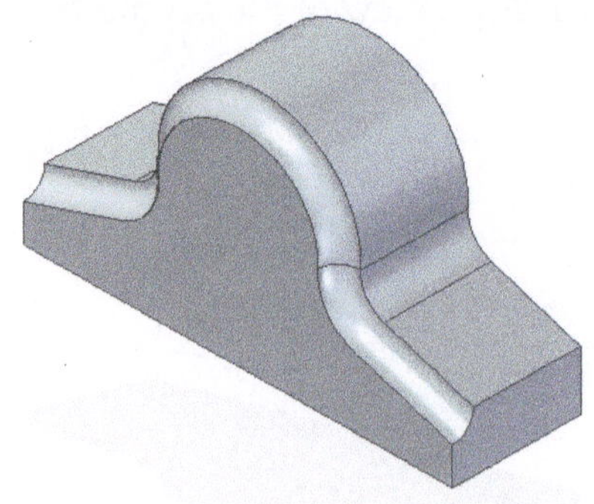

Helix (Synchronous)

This command creates a spring shape feature. To create this type of feature, you must have a cross-section and a line (axis). They can be on the same plane or different planes. Activate the **Helix** command (click **Home > Solids > Add** drop-down **> Helix** on the ribbon), and then select the cross-section and line. Click the green check on the command bar. The preview of the geometry appears on the screen.

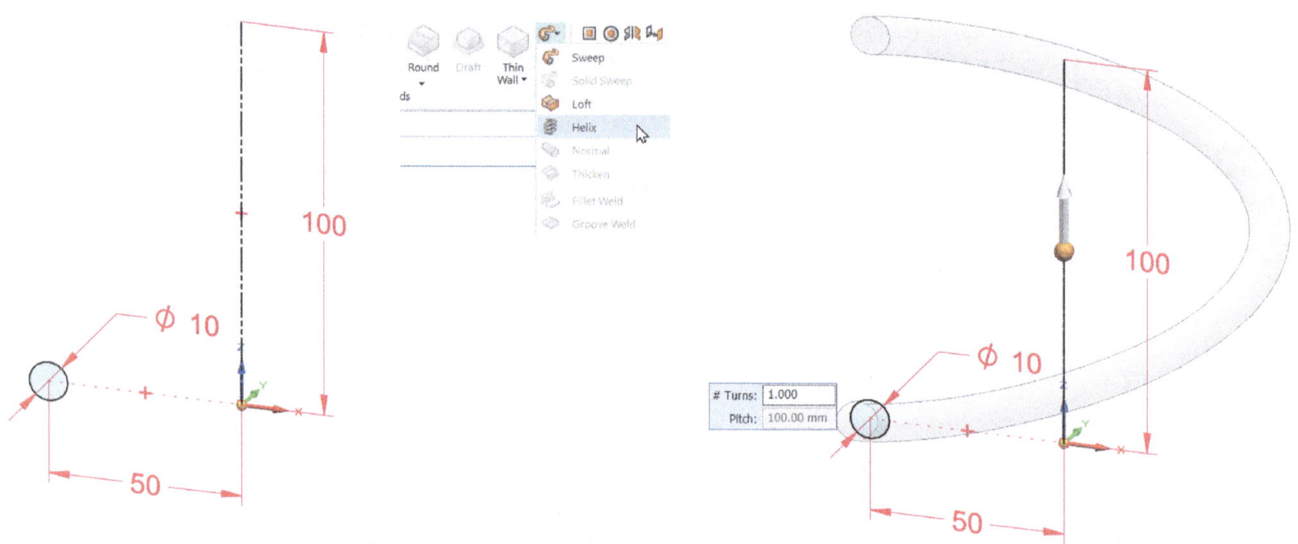

Now, define the **Helix Method** on the command bar. There are three-helix methods: **Axis & Pitch**, **Axis & Turns**, **Pitch & Turns**. The **Axis & Pitch** method creates a helix using the axis's length and distance between the turns. The **Axis & Turns** method creates a helix by using the axis length and number of turns. The **Pitch & Turns** method uses the pitch and number of turns you specify to create the helix.

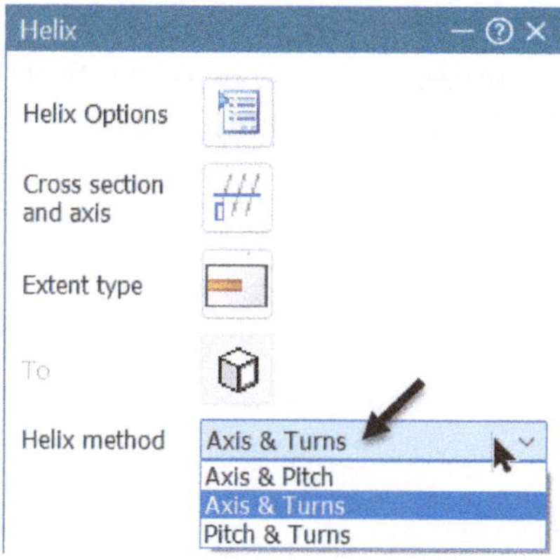

For more helix options, click the **Helix Options** icon on the command bar. The **Helix Options** dialog pops up on the screen. This dialog has many options to define the helix feature's parameters (such as helix direction, taper, and pitch). Define the helix direction by selecting the **Right-handed** or **Left-handed** option.

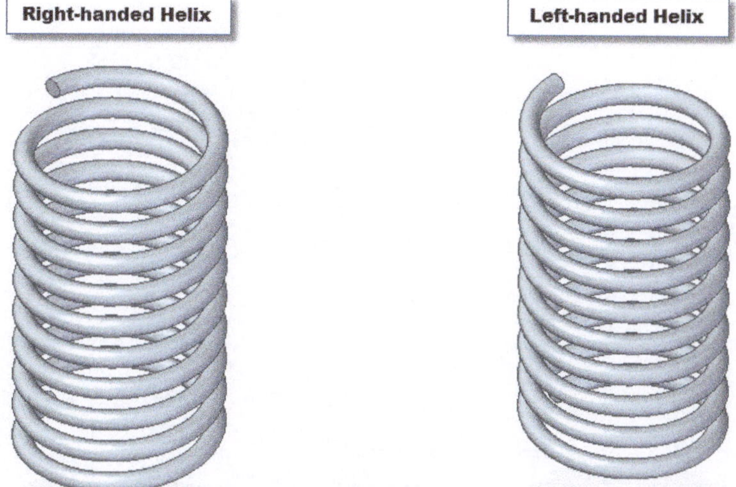

The **Taper** options on the **Helix Options** dialog help you to apply taper to the helix. There are two methods to apply taper to a helix: **By Angle** and **By Radius**. The **By Angle** method applies a taper to the helix using the taper angle you enter in the **Angle** box. The **Inward** or **Outward** options define the taper direction. The **By Radius** method applies a taper to the helix using the start and end radius that you specify.

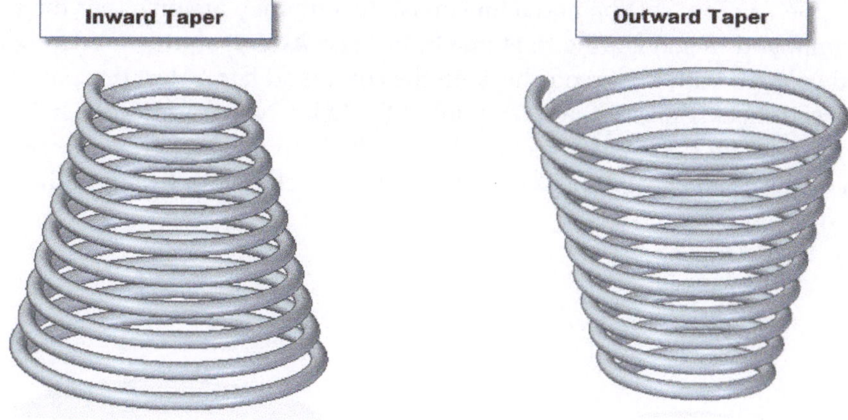

The **Pitch** options on the **Helix Options** dialog help you to create a variable pitch helix. Select the **Variable** option from the drop-down menu and type-in the **Pitch ratio** and **End Pitch** values. For example, if you specify the **Start Pitch =10, Turns = 10**, and **End Pitch = 20**, the helix pitch varies from 10 to 20. The formula calculates the rate of change in the pitch:

$$Rate\ of\ change\ in\ pitch = \frac{End\ Pitch - Start\ Pitch}{No.of\ turns} = \frac{20-10}{10} = 1$$

$$The\ start\ pitch\ = Start\ Pitch + \frac{Rate\ of\ change\ in\ pitch}{2}$$

$$The\ end\ pitch\ = End\ Pitch - \frac{Rate\ of\ change\ in\ pitch}{2}$$

Therefore, the pitch of the first turn = 10+.5 =10.5
Second turn = 10.5+1 = 11.5
Third turn = 11.5+1= 12.5.............................tenth turn=19.5

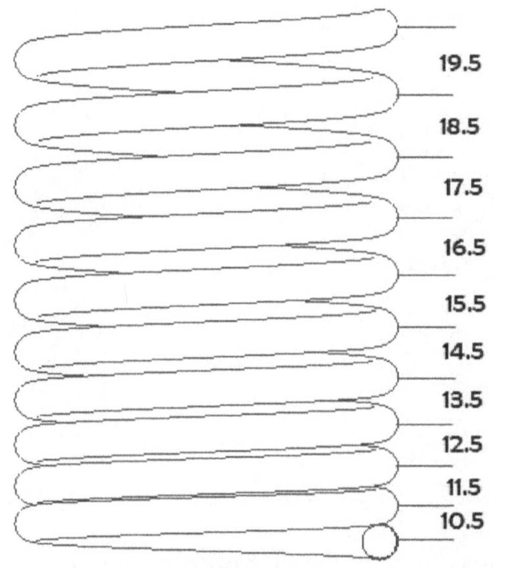

Click **OK** on the **Helix Options** dialog, and then click **Accept** to create the helix.

Helix (Ordered)

To create a spring-shaped feature, you'll need a cross-section and a line (axis). Ensure they are on either the same or different planes. Activate the **Helix** command by navigating to **Home > Solids > Add** drop-down > **Helix** on the ribbon. Choose the cross-section and confirm with the green check on the command bar. Select the axis of revolution and again confirm with the green check. Specify the start point of the helix. Now, specify the helix method using the **Helix method** drop-down in the **Parameters** section. Define the helix parameters in the same step. Click **Next** and then **Preview** to view the geometry on the screen. If satisfied, click **Finish** to accept the helix feature.

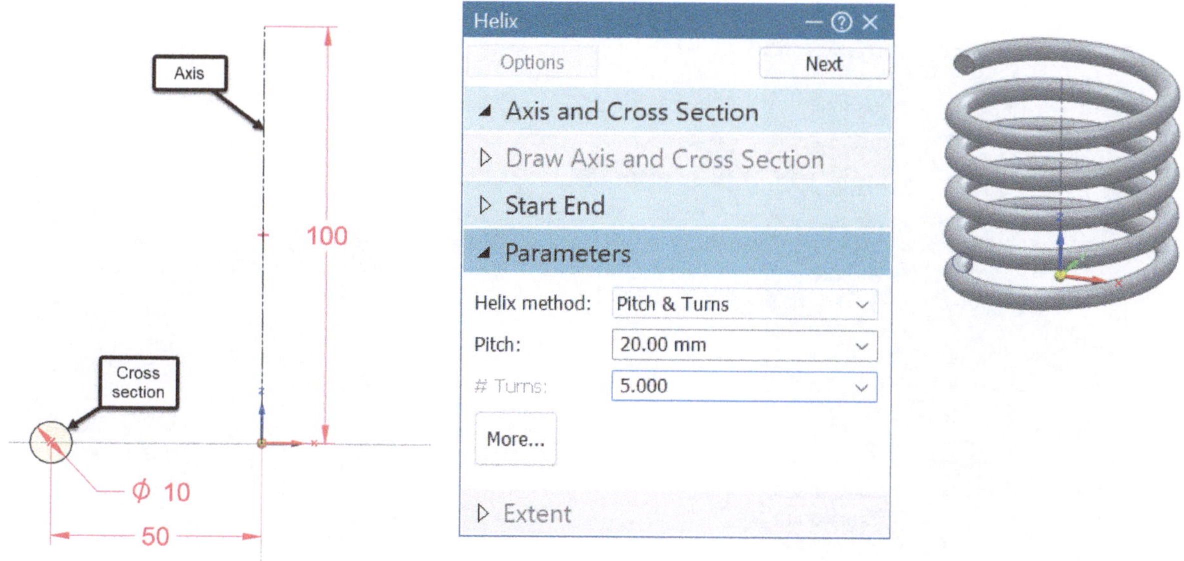

Helical Cutout (Synchronous)

This command removes material from the part geometry by creating a helical feature. First, you must have an existing geometry and the sketches of the cross-section and axis to create this feature. Activate this command (click **Home > Solids > Cut** drop-down **> Helical Cutout** on the ribbon) and select the cross-section and axis. Click the **Accept** button on the command bar to accept the selection. Define the number of turns and pitch using anyone of the **Helix methods** described in the previous topic. Next, right-click to create the helical cutout.

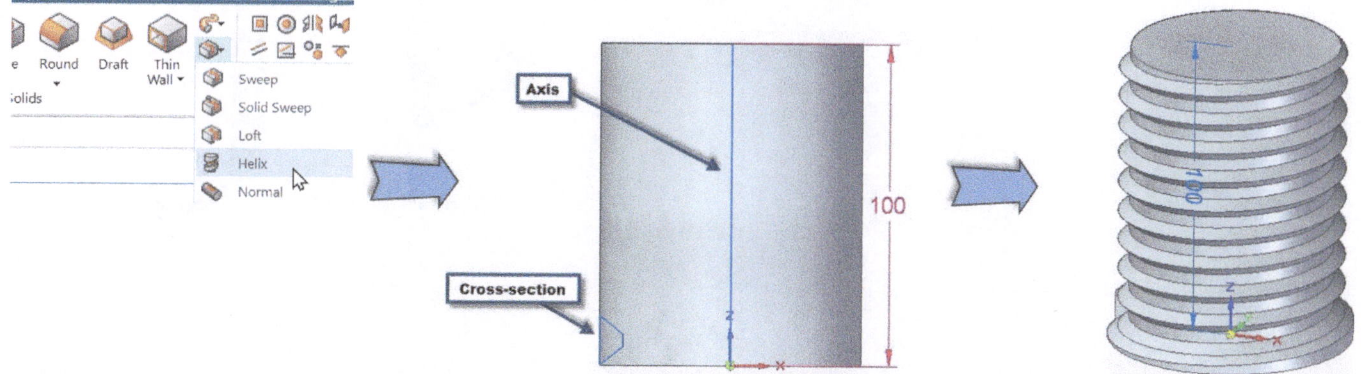

Helical Cutout (Ordered)

To create a helical cutout in the Ordered environment, first make sure that there is an existing geometry. Next, click **Home > Solids > Cut** drop-down > **Helix** on the ribbon. Choose the cross-section and confirm with the green check on the command bar. Select the axis of revolution and again confirm with the green check. Specify the start point of the helix. Now, specify the helix method using the **Helix method** drop-down in the **Parameters** section. Define the helix parameters in the same step. Click **Next** and then **Preview** to view the geometry on the screen. If satisfied, click **Finish** to accept the helix feature.

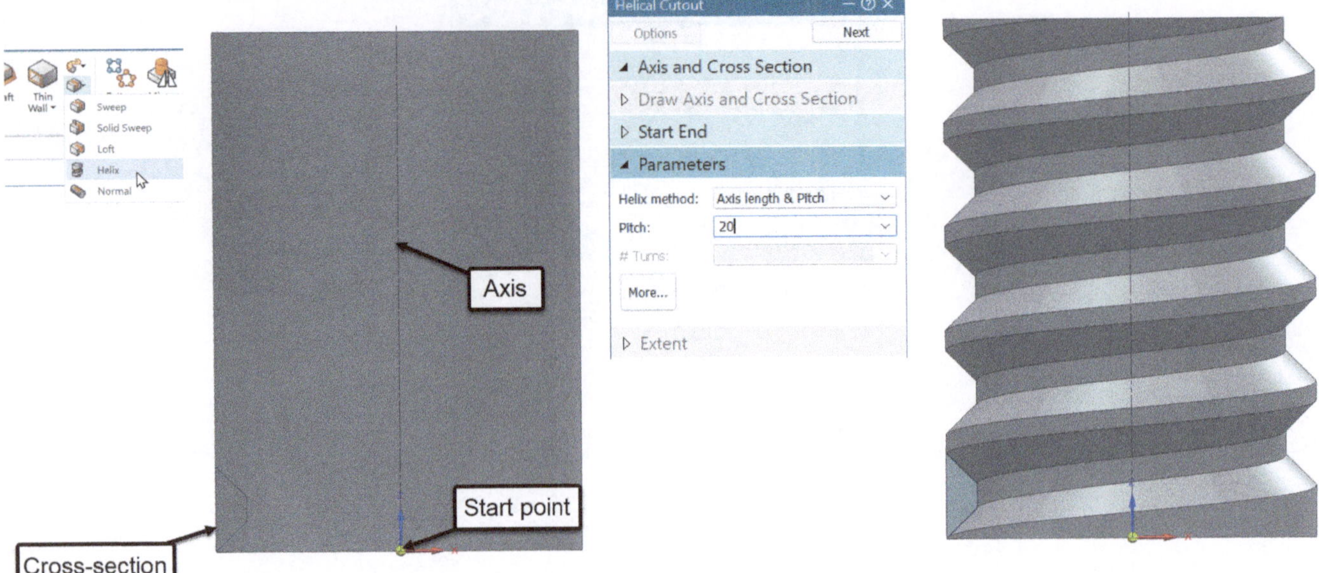

Examples

Example 1 (Inches)

In this example, you will create the part shown below.

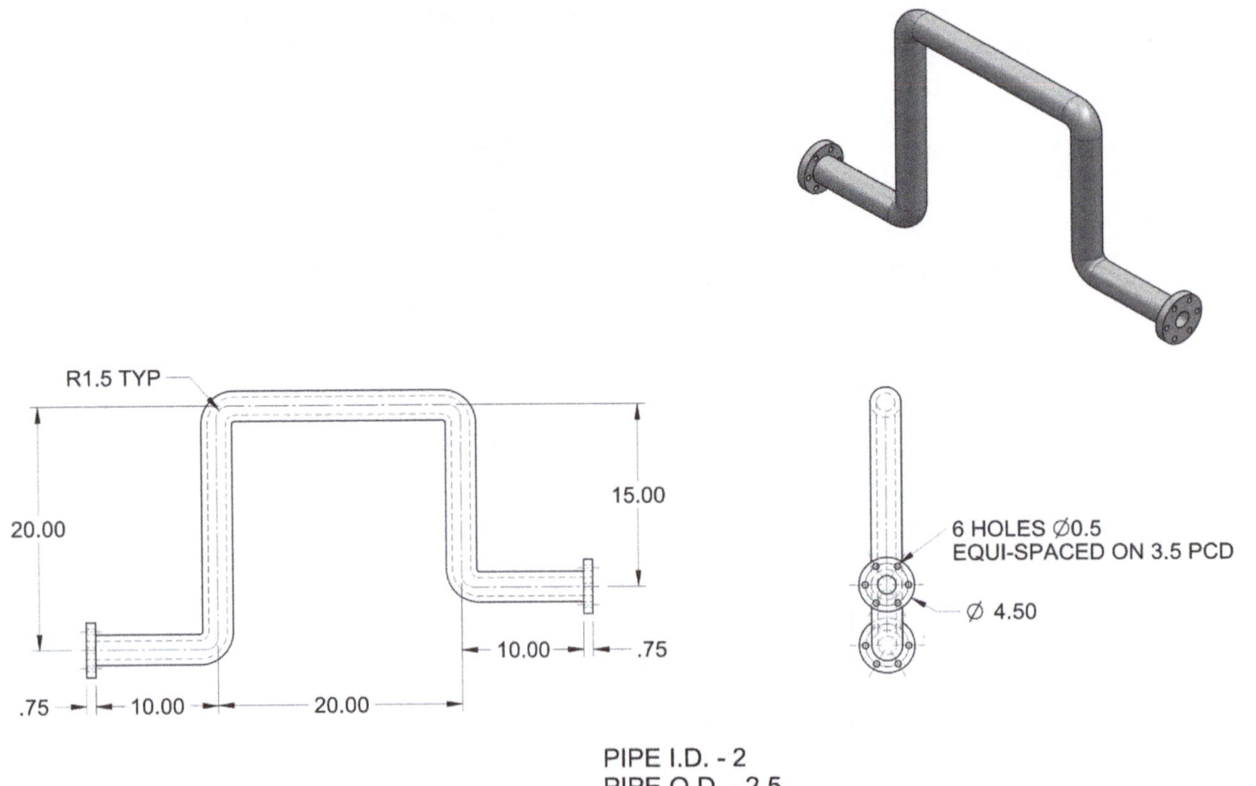

1. Start **Solid Edge 2026.**
2. On the **Quick Access Toolbar**, click **New**; the **New** dialog pops up.
3. On this dialog, click **Standard Templates > ANSI Inch**. Select the **ansi inch part.par** template and click

OK.

4. Right-click in the graphics window and select **Transition to Synchronous**.
5. On the ribbon, click **Home > Draw > Line** and draw the sketch on the XZ plane, as shown below.

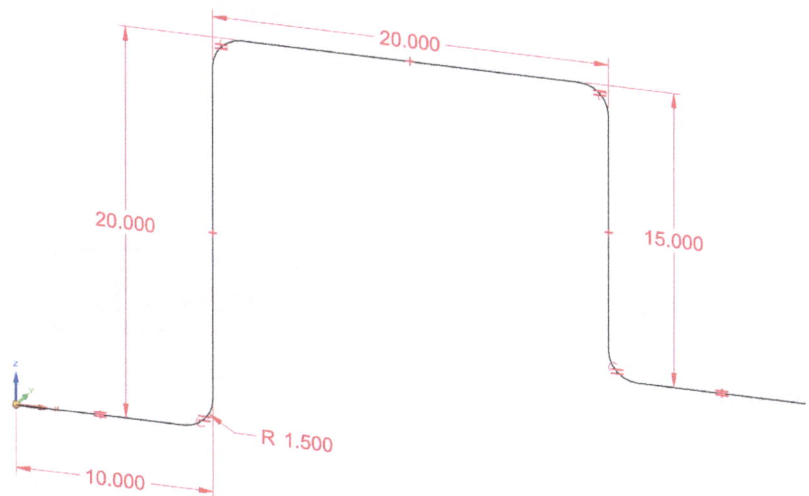

6. Unlock the sketch plane.
7. On the ribbon, click **Home > Planes > More Planes > Normal to Curve** and click on the lower horizontal line.
8. Click on the endpoint of the line to locate the plane.

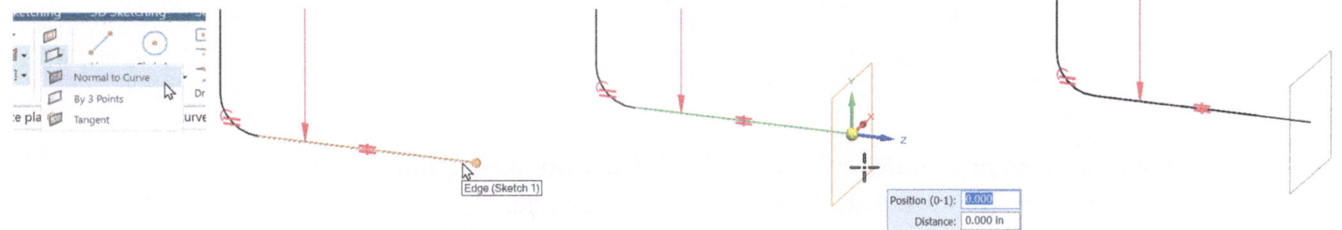

9. On the ribbon, click **Home > Draw > Circle by Center Point** and draw a circle of 2.5-inch diameter on the plane normal to the curve.

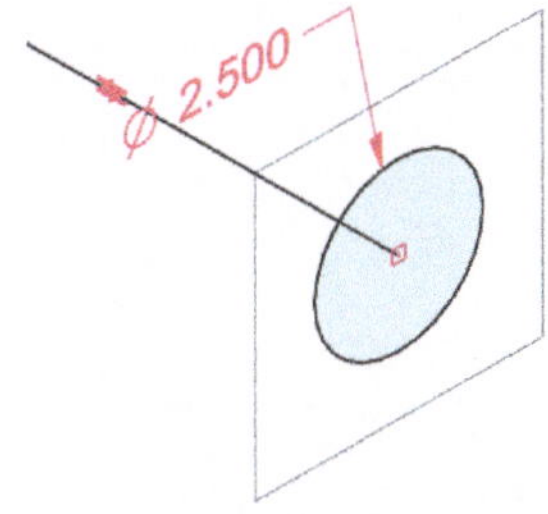

10. On the ribbon, click **Home > Solids > Add** drop-down **> Sweep** ; the **Sweep Options** dialog pops up.
11. On this dialog, set the **Default Sweep Type** to **Single path and cross-section.**
12. Set the **Face Merging** option to **No Merge**.
13. Set the **Section Alignment** option to **Normal**. Click **OK** to close the dialog.
14. Click on the first sketch to define the path of the *Sweep* feature. Click the green check on the command bar.
15. Click on the circle to define the cross-section.

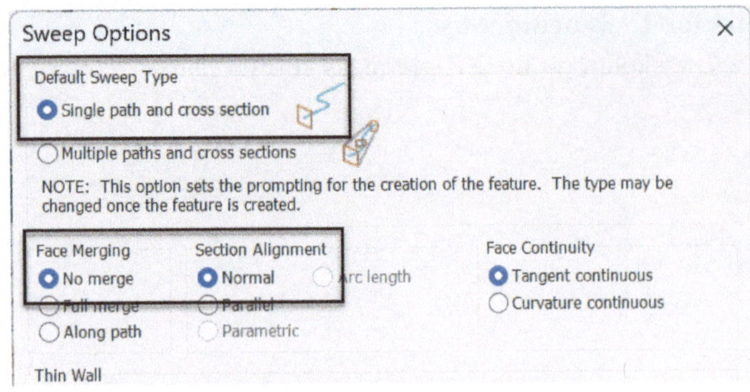

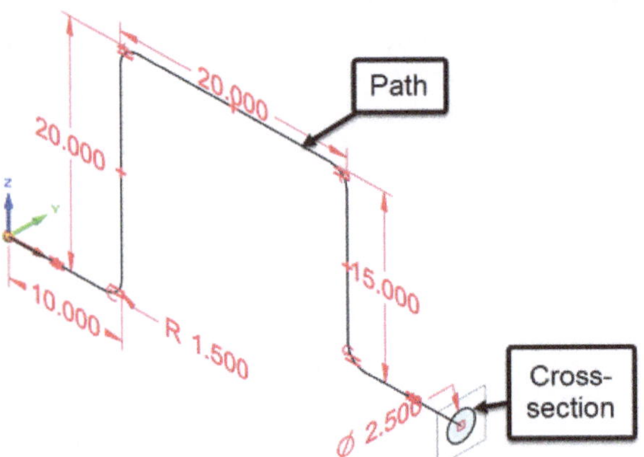

16. Click **Finish** to complete the *Sweep* feature.

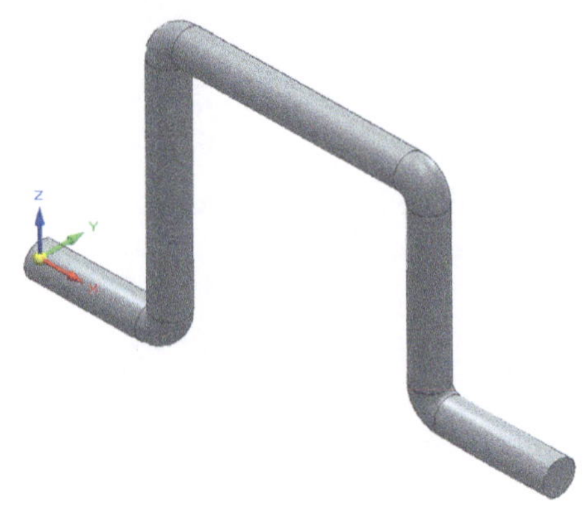

17. On the ribbon, click **Home > Solids > Thin Wall**. Click on the end face of the *Sweep* feature.
18. Rotate the part geometry and click the end face on the other side.
19. Type-in **0.5** in the box that appears on the geometry. Press Enter to shell the *Sweep* feature.

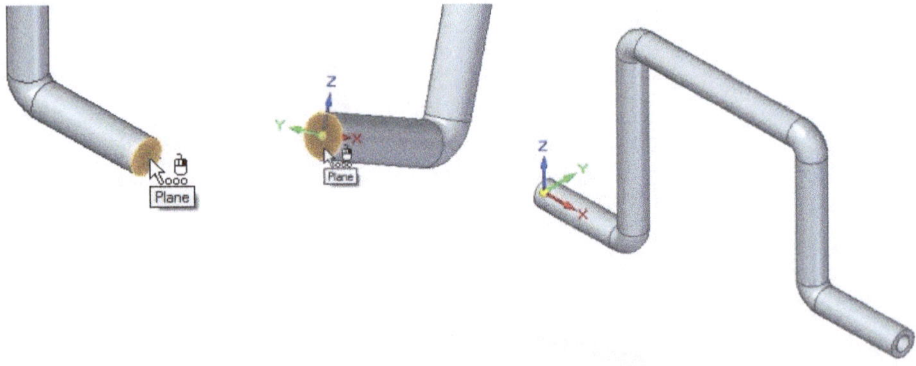

20. On the ribbon, click **Home > Draw > Project to Sketch**. Next, place the cursor on the end face and click on the lock icon.
21. Click on the inner edge of the end face to project it. Next, close the **Project to Sketch** command bar.
22. On the ribbon, click **Home > Draw > Circle by Center Point** and draw a circle of 4.5 in diameter. Unlock the sketch plane.

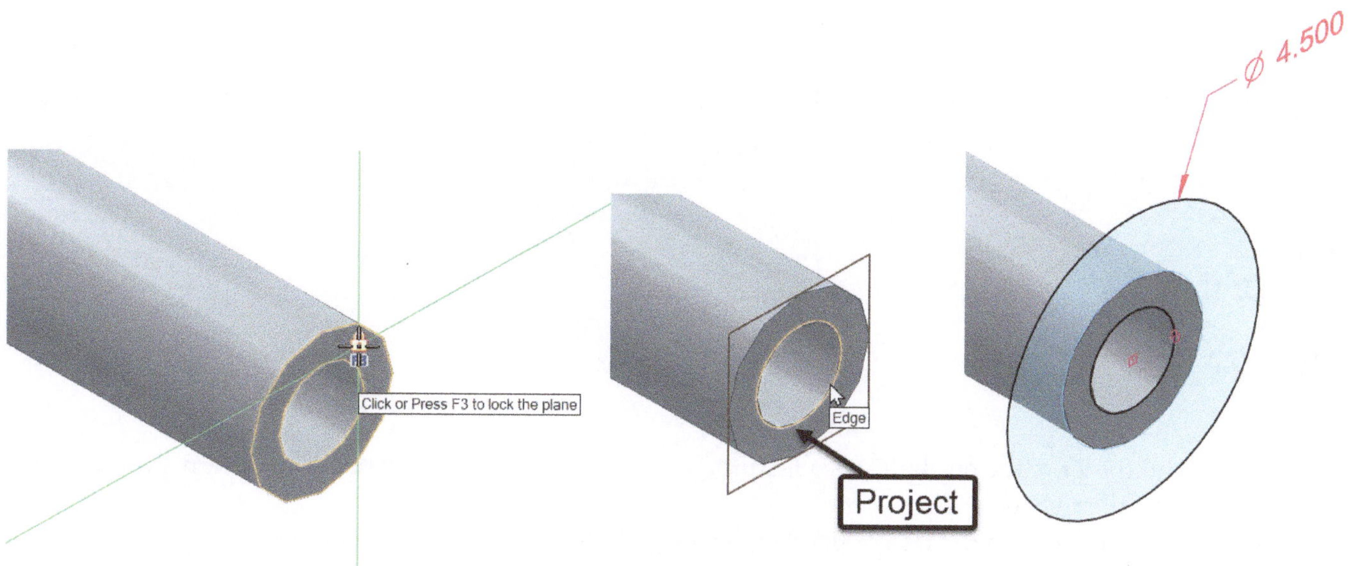

23. Activate the **Extrude** command. Next, click **Selection Type > Face** on the **Extrude** command bar.
24. Click inside the two sketch regions.
25. On the **Extrude** command bar, select the **Include Internal Loops** option.
26. Right-click to accept the selection and move the mouse pointer. Type-in 0.75 in the box that appears on the geometry.
27. Press Enter to create the flange.

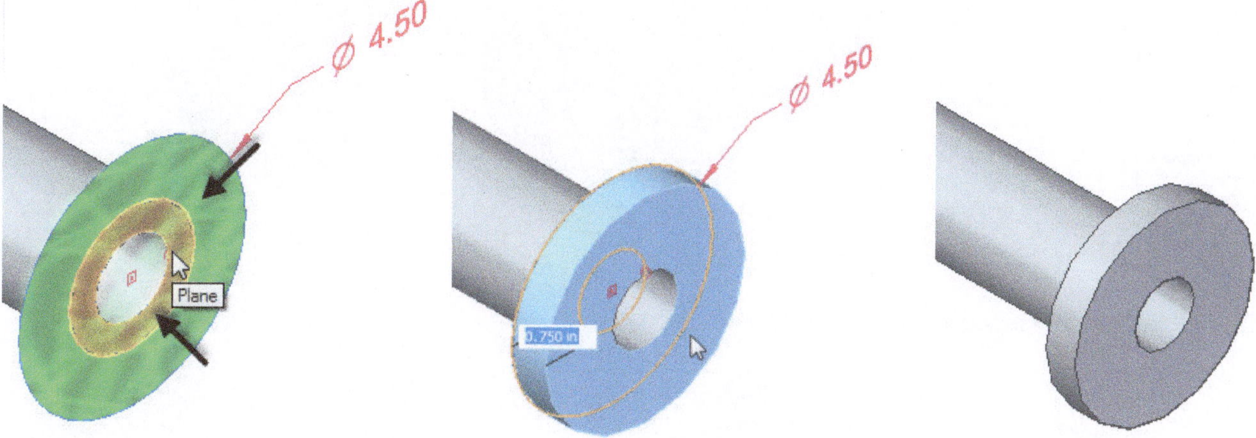

28. Draw a sketch on the flange face and create the *Cutout* feature.

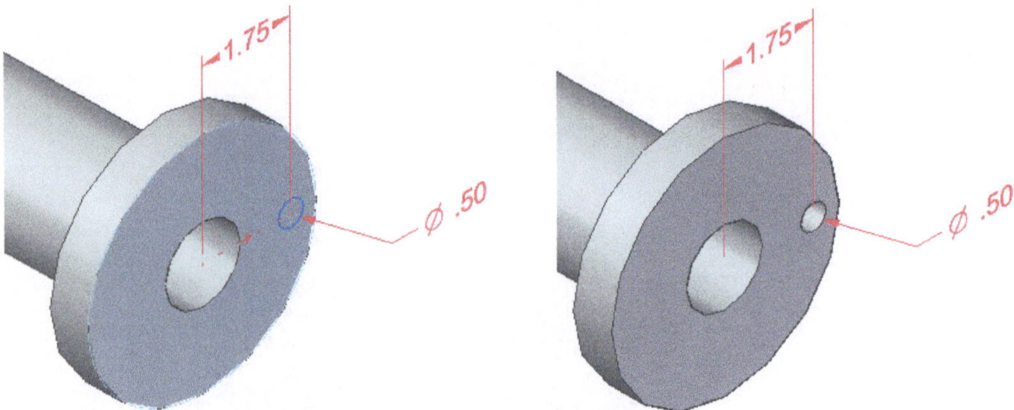

29. In the Pathfinder, click on the *Cutout* feature, and then click **Home > Pattern > Pattern drop-down > Circular** on the ribbon.
30. Place the pointer on the flat face of the flange and click the lock icon. Now, you have to define the axis of the circular pattern.
31. Place the pointer on a circular edge of the flange and click when the circular edge's center point is selected. This defines the pattern axis.
32. Type-in **6** in the **Count** box and click the **Accept** button on the command bar. The cutouts are patterned circularly.

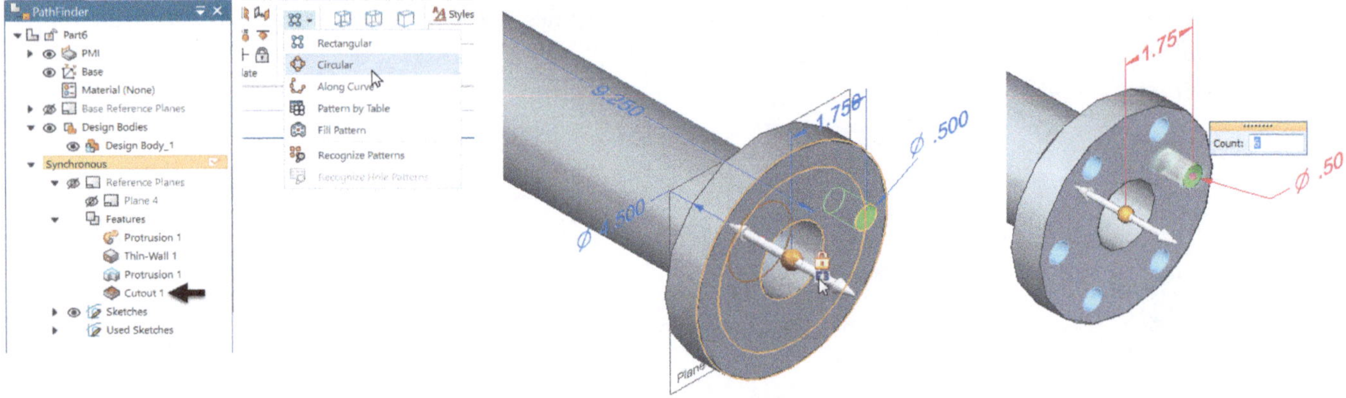

33. Change the model view orientation, as shown.

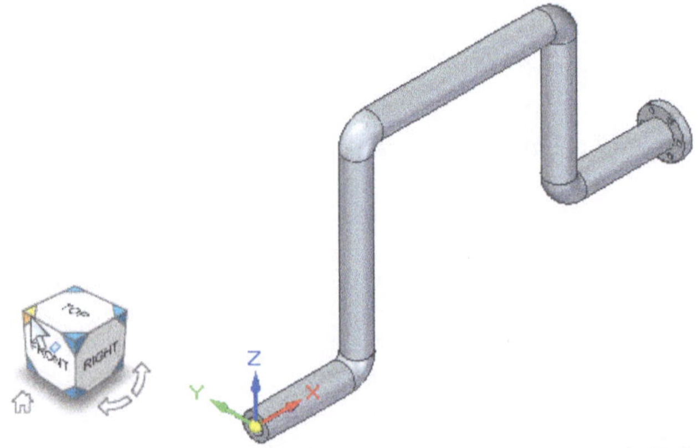

34. Create another flange and circular pattern.

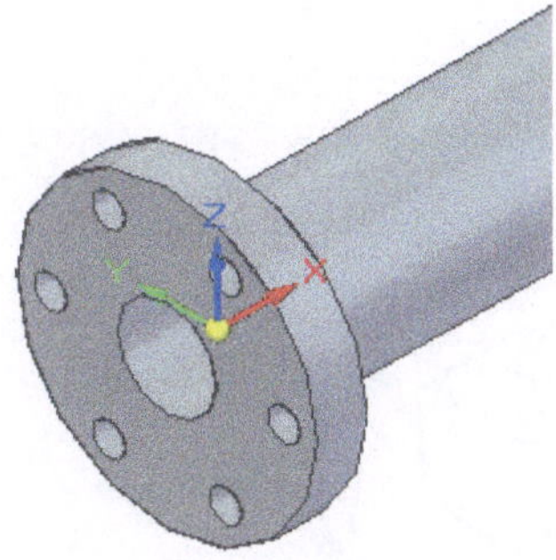

35. Save and close the part file.

Example 2 (Inches & Ordered environment)

In this example, you will create the part shown below.

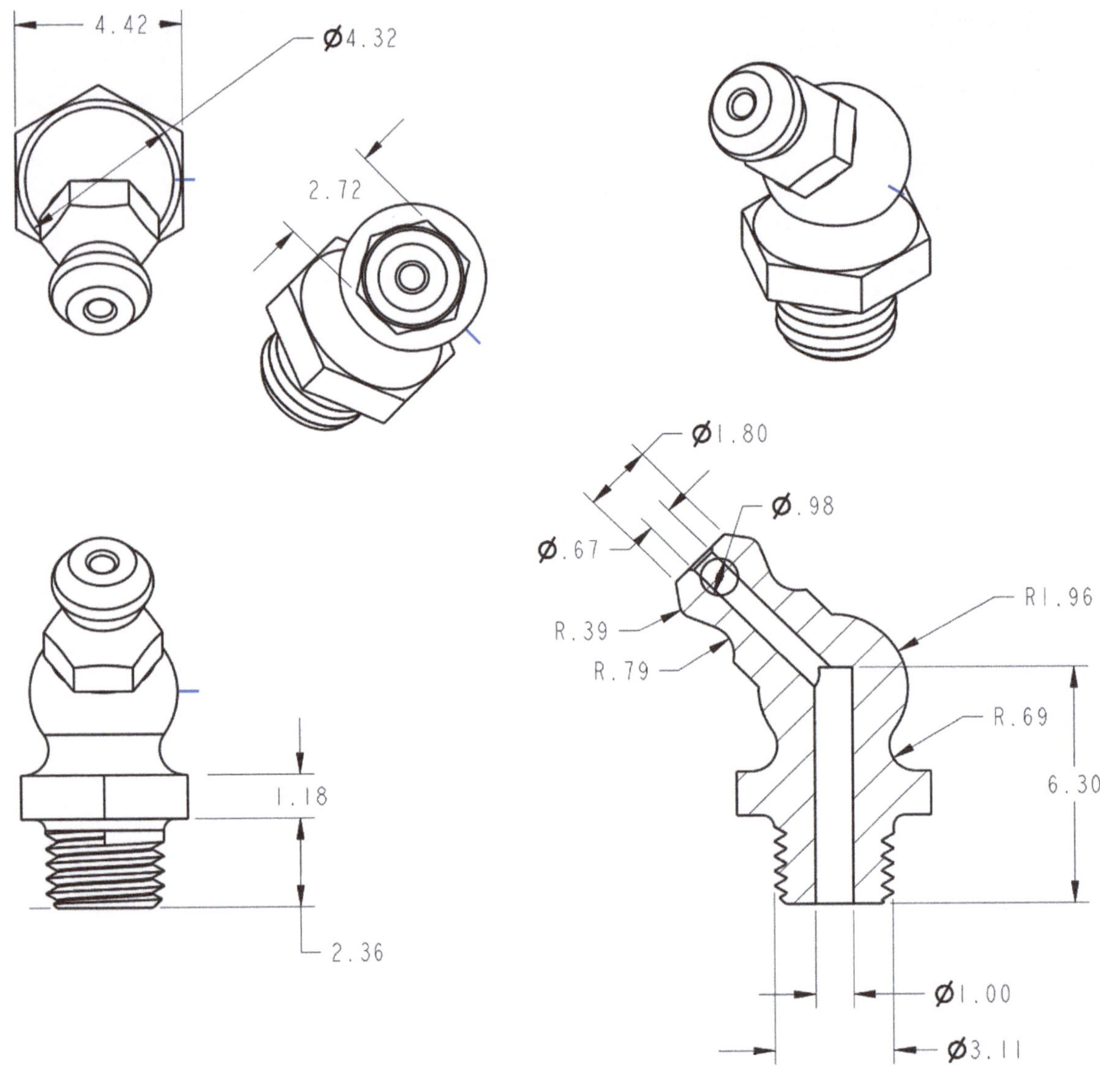

Creating the First Feature

1. Start **Solid Edge 2026.**
2. On the Quick Access Toolbar, click the **New** button.
3. Select **Ansi Inch** > **ansi inch part.par**. Next, click **OK**; a new part file is opened.
4. Click **Continue with Ordered** button on the **Ordered as default** dialog; the Ordered environment is set as the default environment.
5. On the ribbon, click **Home > Solids > Revolve** and select the **Front(xz)** plane.
6. Click **Home > Draw > Line** on the ribbon.
7. Specify the start point of the line on the vertical axis.
8. Click on the origin point to define the second point.
9. Move the pointer horizontally toward right and click on the horizontal reference.

10. Move the pointer vertically up to a small distance and click.
11. Move the pointer horizontally toward right up to a small distance and click.
12. Move the pointer vertically up to a small distance and click.
13. Move the pointer horizontally toward left up to a small distance and click.
14. Move the pointer vertically upward and click.

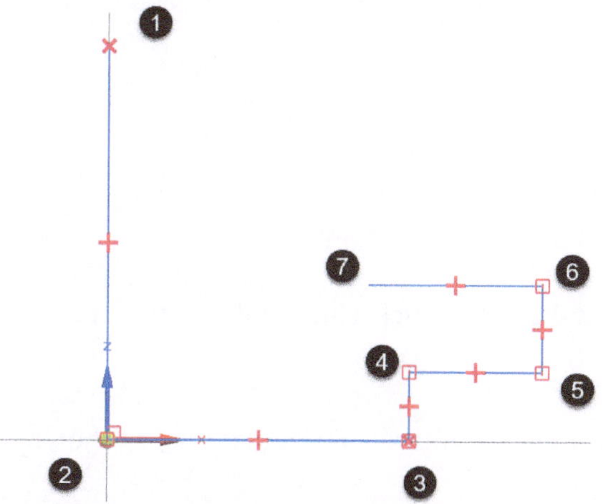

15. Add dimensions to the lines, as shown.

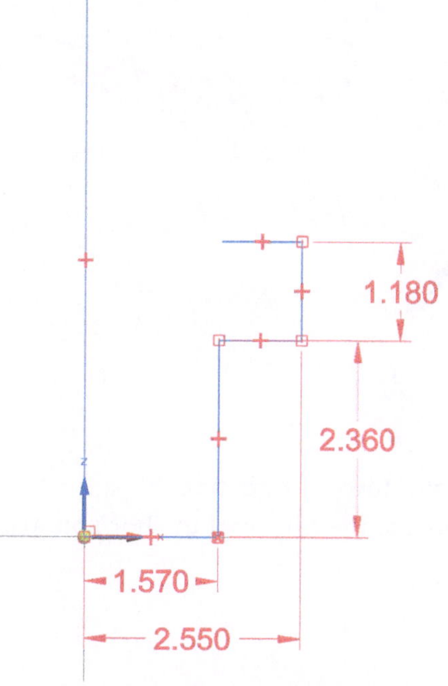

16. On the ribbon, click **Home** tab > **Draw** panel > **Circle** drop-down > **Circle by Center Point**.
17. Select the end point of the left vertical line.
18. Select the endpoint of the horizontal line.

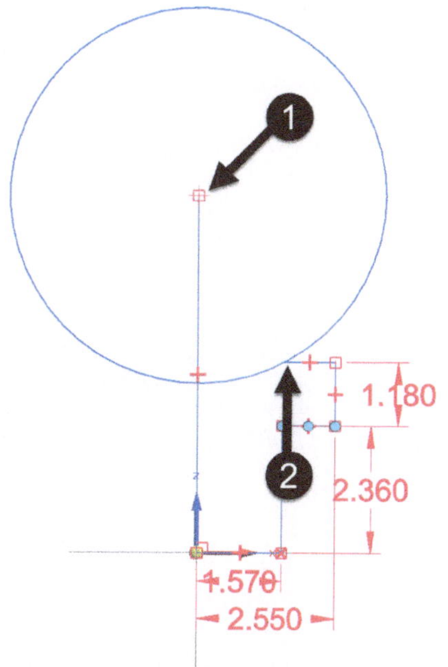

19. On the ribbon, click **Home > Draw > Extend To Next** .
20. Click near the top end of the vertical line; the vertical line is extended up to the circle.

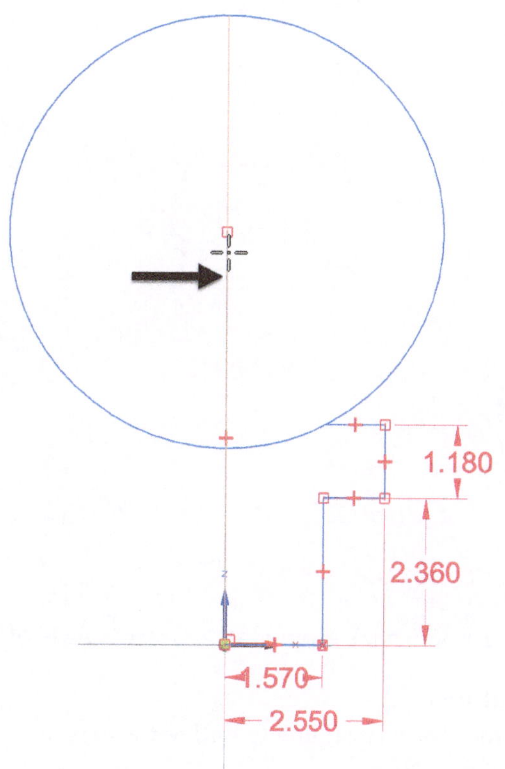

21. On the ribbon, click **Home > Draw > Trim.**
22. Select the edges to trim, as shown.

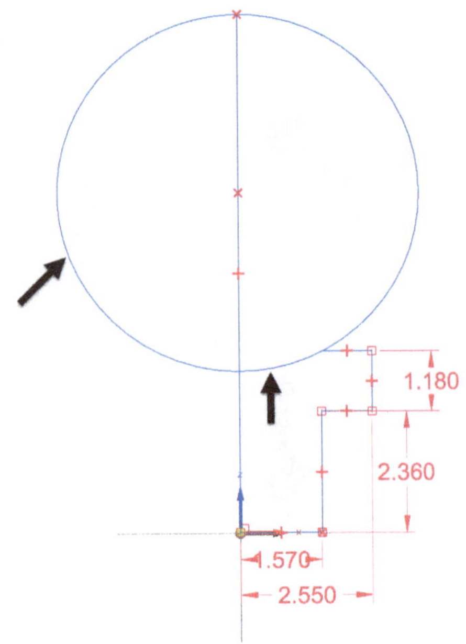

23. Add the radius dimension to the arc.

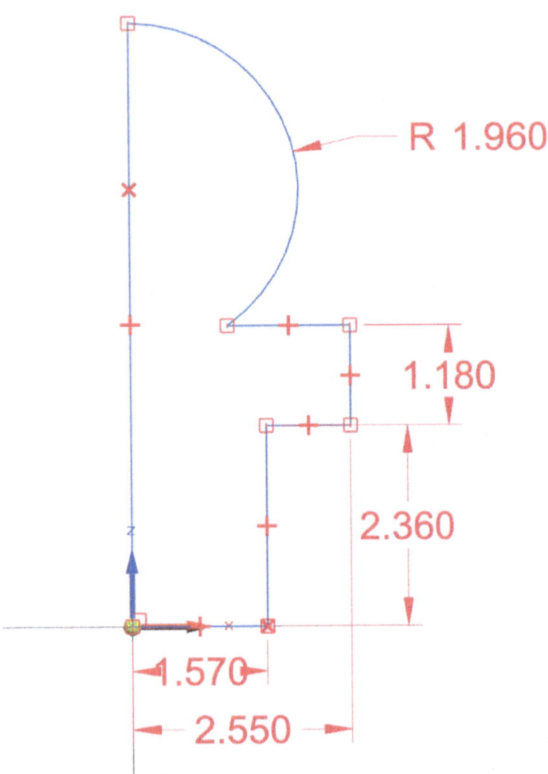

24. On the ribbon, click **Home** tab > **Draw** > **Axis of Revolution** .
25. Select the left vertical line to define the axis of revolution.

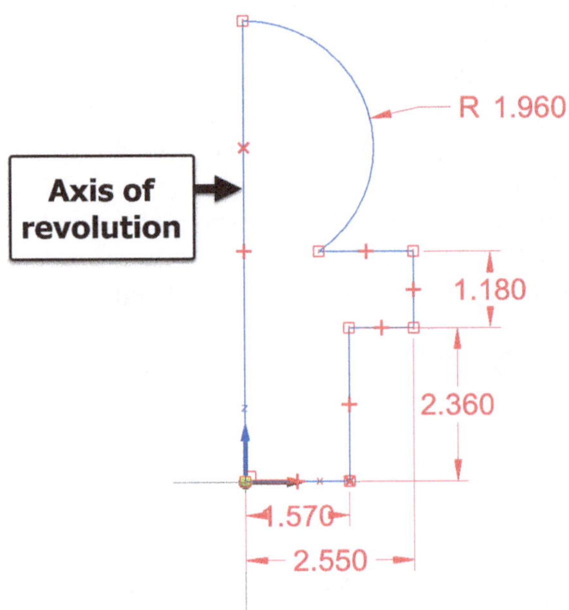

26. On the ribbon, click **Home** tab > **Draw** panel > **Fillet** .
27. Select the arc and the horizontal line, as shown.

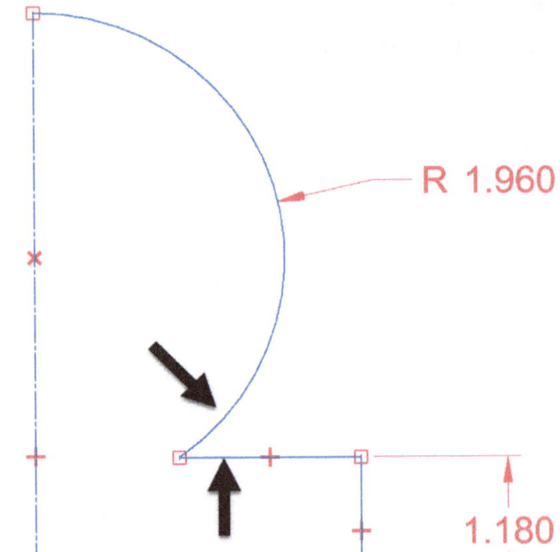

28. Move the pointer toward right and click.
29. Add dimensions to the fillet and the horizontal line, as shown.

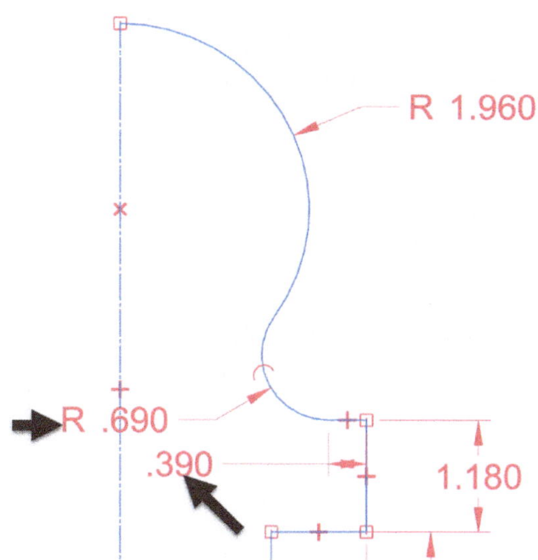

30. Click **Close Sketch** on the ribbon.
31. Click the **Revolve 360** button on the command bar.
32. Click the **Accept** button to create the *Revolved* feature.
33. Click **Finish** and **Cancel**.

Creating the Extruded Cut Features

1. On the ribbon, click **Home** tab > **Solids** panel > **Extrude**.
2. Click on the flat face of the model, as shown.

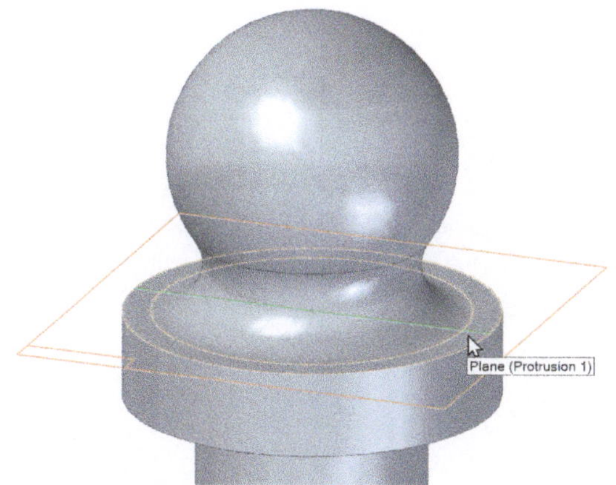

3. On the ribbon, click **Home** tab > **Draw** panel > **Circle** drop-down > **Circle by Center Point**.
4. Select the sketch origin, move the pointer outward and click.

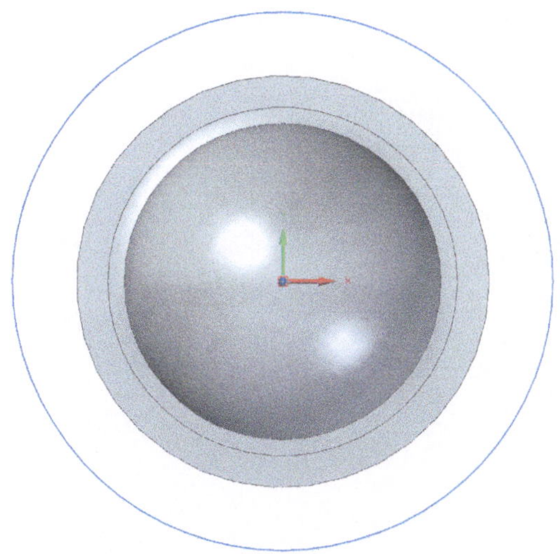

5. On the ribbon, click **Home** tab > **Draw** panel > **Rectangle** drop-down > **Polygon by Center**.

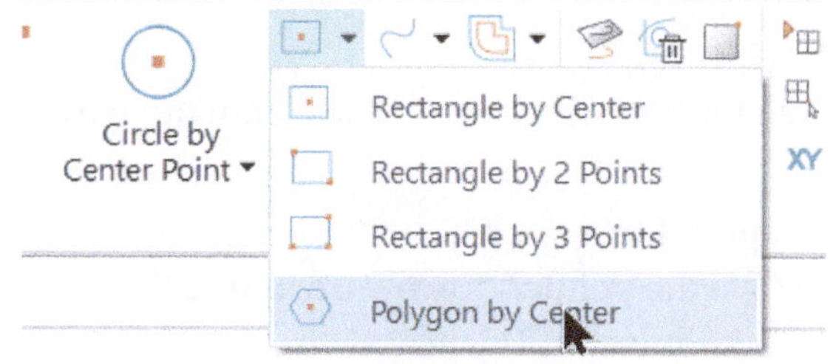

6. Click the **By Vertex** icon on the command bar.
7. Type **6** in the **Sides** box on the command bar.
8. Select the sketch origin, move the pointer outward and click on the circular edge of the model, as shown.

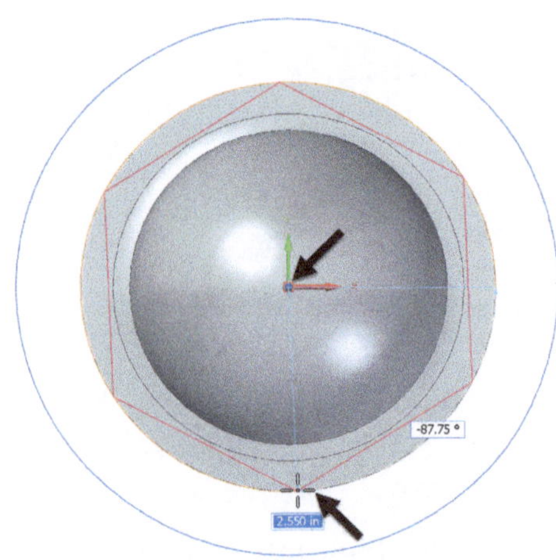

9. On the ribbon, click **Home** tab > **Relate** panel > **Horizontal/Vertical**.
10. Select the right edge of the polygon.

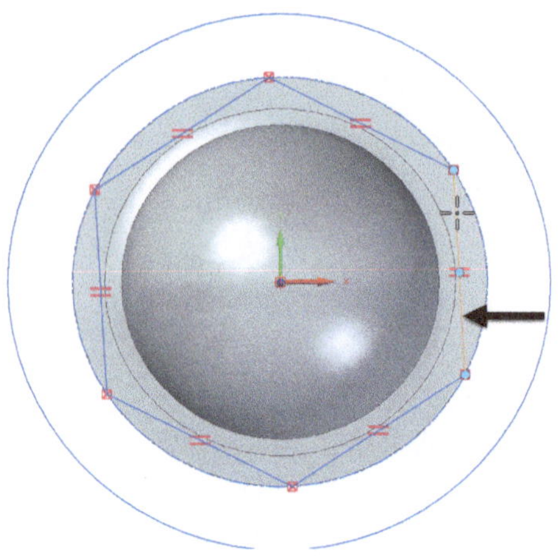

11. Click **Close Sketch** on the ribbon.
12. On the **Extrude** command bar, select **Operation > Cut** .
13. On the **Extent** section of the command bar, select **Type > Through All** icon.
14. Move the pointer downward and click.
15. Click **Finish** and **Cancel**.

16. On the ribbon, click **Home** tab > **Solids** panel > **Extrude**.
17. Click on the bottom face of the model, as shown.

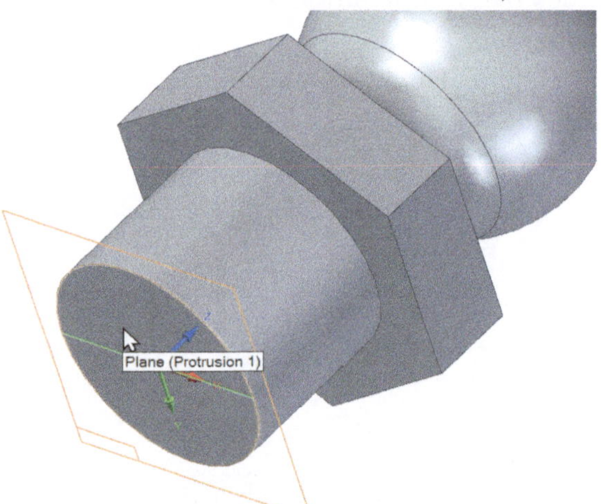

18. Create a circle and add dimension to it, as shown.

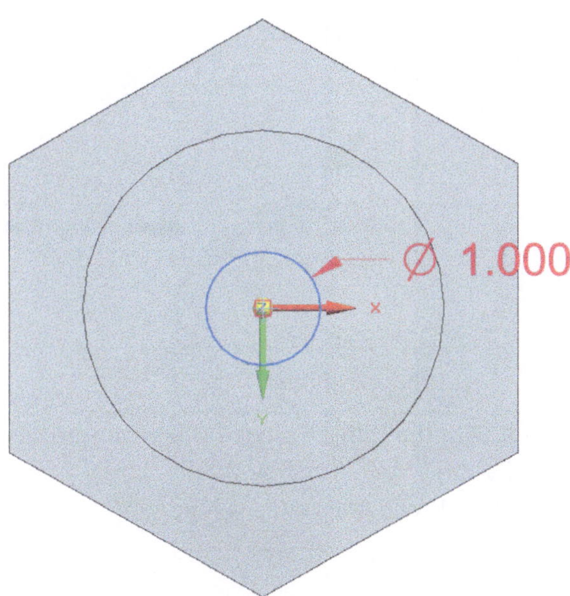

19. Click **Close Sketch** on the ribbon.
20. On the **Extrude** command bar, under the Extent section, select Type > **Finite Extent** 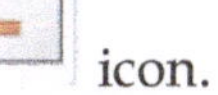 icon.
21. Type **6.3** in the **Distance** box and press ENTER.
22. Move the pointer inside the model and click.
23. Click **Finish** and **Cancel**.

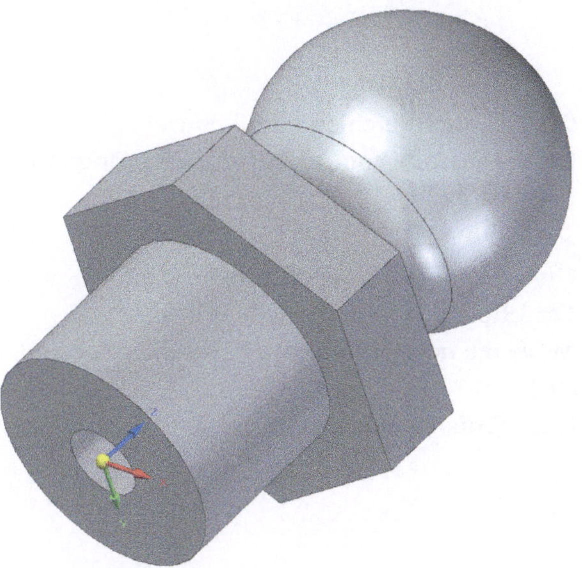

24. On the ribbon, click **Home** tab > **Solids** panel > **Extrude**.
25. Click on the Right plane.
26. Click the **Line** tool on the **Draw** panel of the **Home** ribbon tab.
27. Place the pointer on the silhouette edge of the sphere; the center point of the edge is displayed.
28. Select the centerpoint of the silhouette edge.
29. Move the pointer toward right and click.

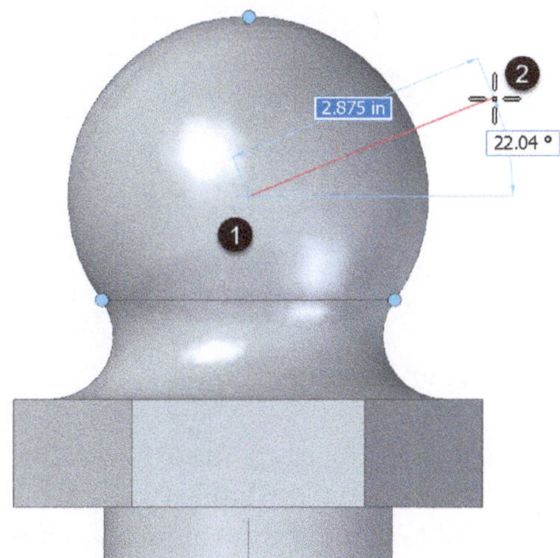

30. Press ESC.
31. Select the line and click the **Construction** button on the toolbar.

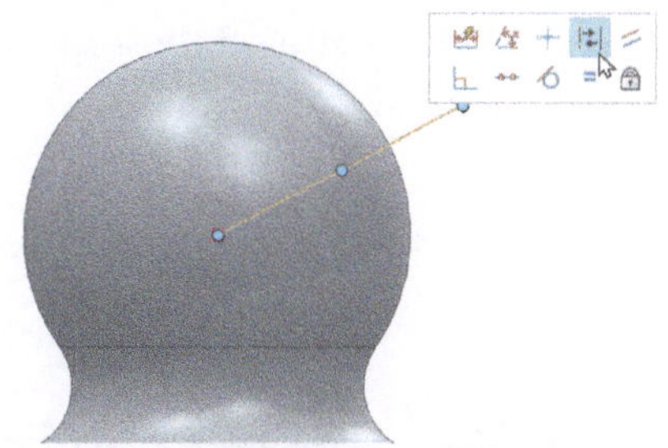

32. Create the angular dimension between the line and horizontal edge of the model, as shown.

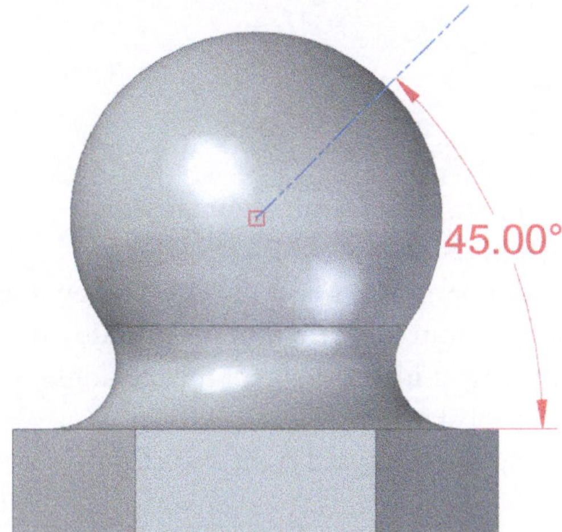

33. On the ribbon, click **Home > Draw > Rectangle** drop-down > **Rectangle by 3 Points**.
34. Select the two points, as shown.

35. Move the pointer upward and click.

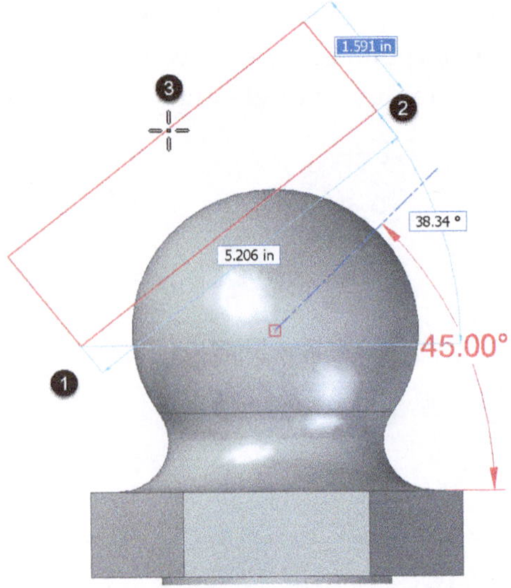

36. Add the Parallel relationship between the construction line and the lower inclined line of the rectangle.
37. On the ribbon, click **Home > Dimension > Dimension Axis** .
38. Select the construction line to set the angle of the dimension to be created.

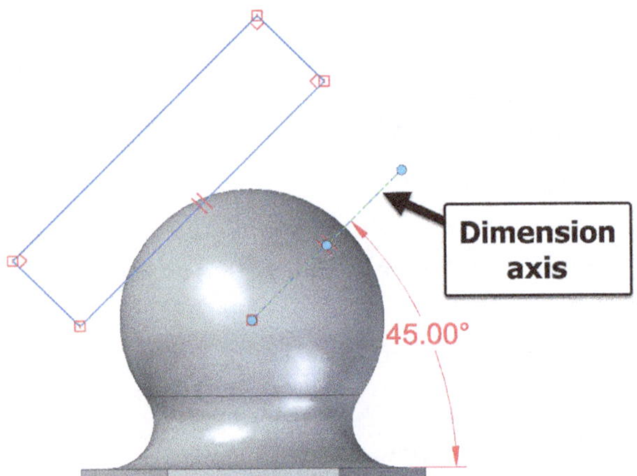

39. On the ribbon, click **Home > Dimension > Smart Dimension**.
40. On the command bar, select the **Use Dimension Axis** option from the **Orientation** drop-down.
41. Select the lower inclined line of the rectangle.
42. Select the construction line.
43. Move the pointer toward right and click.

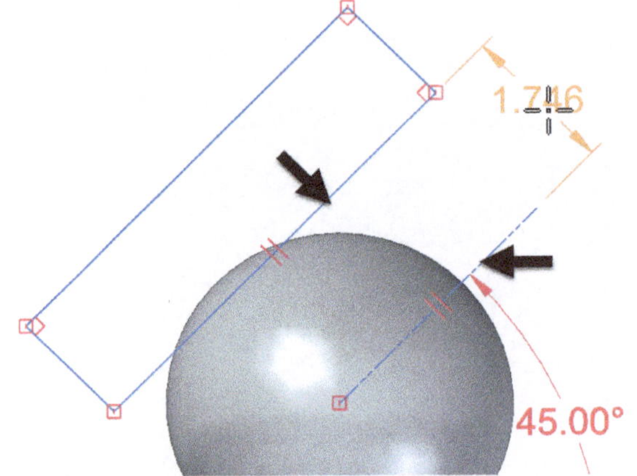

44. Type **1.37** in the **Edit Dimension** box and press ENTER.
45. Add other dimensions to the rectangle.

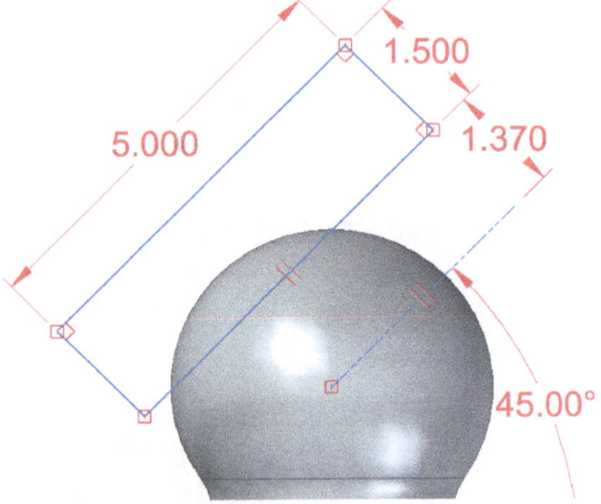

46. Click **Close Sketch** on the ribbon.
47. On the **Extrude** command bar, select **Operation > Cut** .
48. On the **Extent** section of the command bar, select **Direction** > **Symmetric Extent** icon.
49. Move the pointer in the outward direction and click.
50. Click **Finish** and **Cancel**.

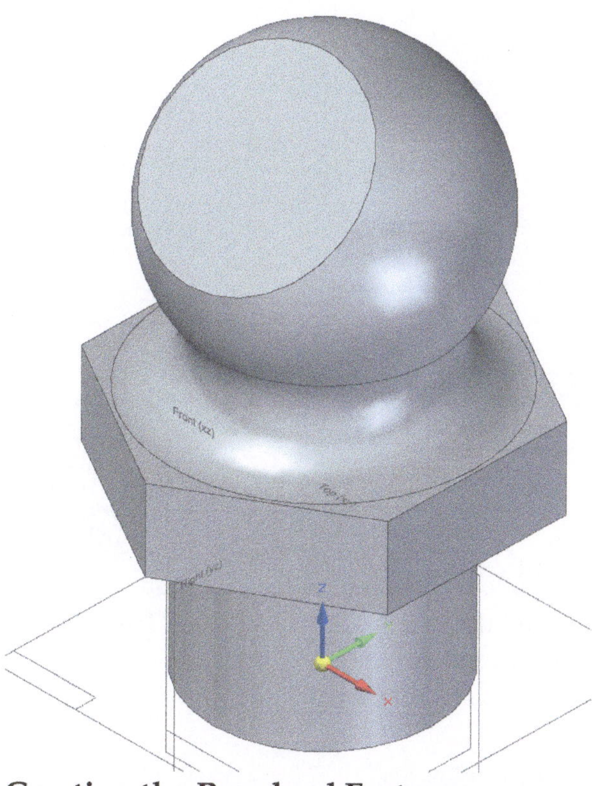

Creating the Revolved Feature

1. On the ribbon, click **Home** tab > **Solids** panel > **Revolve**.
2. Select the right plane.
3. Place the pointer on the inclined edge of the model.
4. Select the midpoint of the inclined edge.
5. Move the pointer toward left and click.
6. On the ribbon, click **Home** tab > **Relate** panel > **Perpendicular**.
7. Select the newly created line and inclined edge.

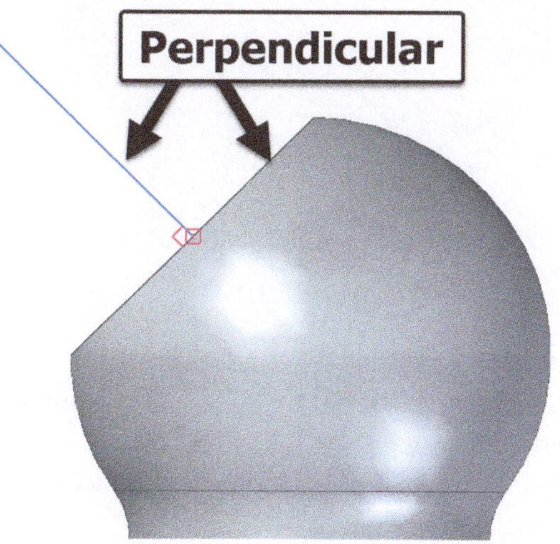

8. Activate the **Line** command and create other lines, as shown.

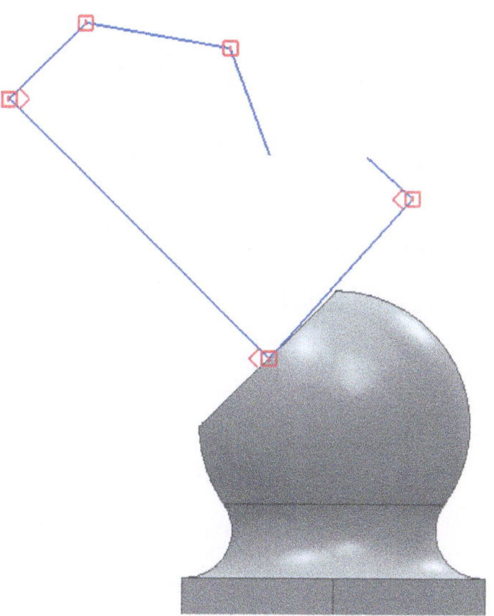

9. On the ribbon, click **Home tab > Draw panel > Arc drop-down > Arc by 3 Points**.
10. Select the endpoint of the two lines, as shown.
11. Move the pointer downward and click.

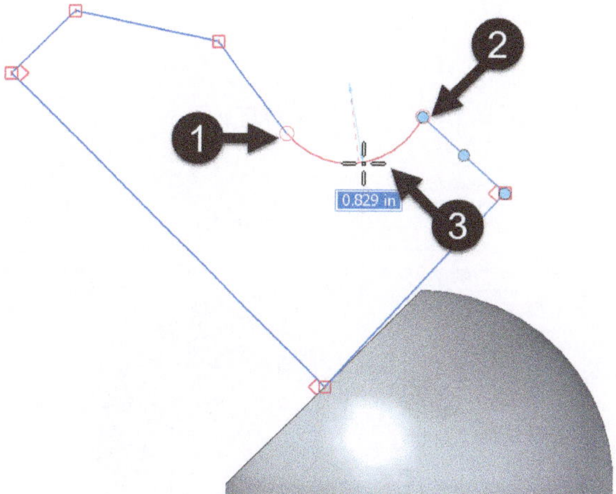

12. Apply the **Tangent** relationship between the arc and the line left to it.
13. Apply the **Collinear** relationship between the horizontal line and the inclined edge.
14. Apply the **Perpendicular** relationship between the two lines, as shown.

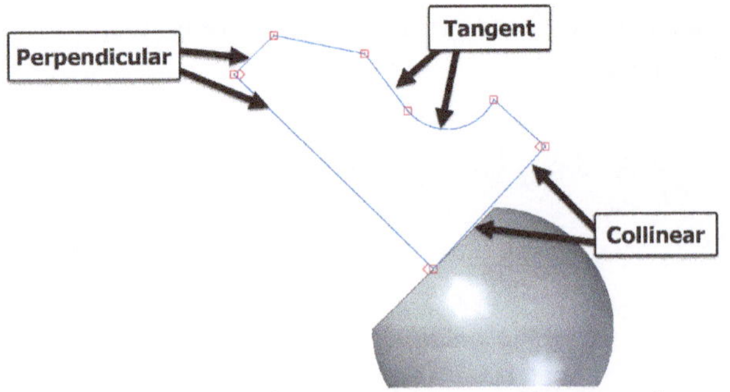

15. Create a fillet between the two lines, as shown.

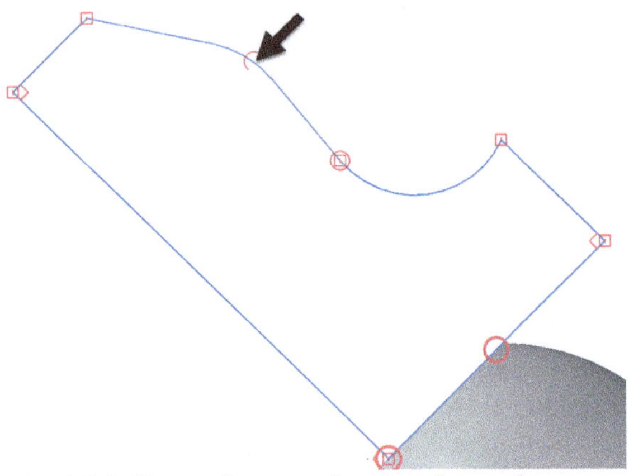

16. Add dimensions to the sketch, as shown.

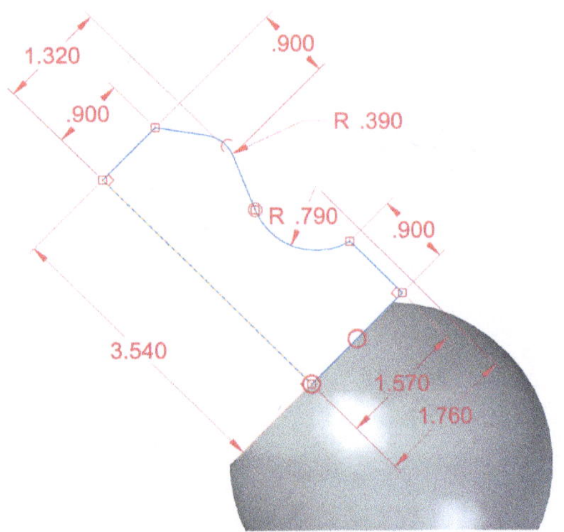

17. On the ribbon, click **Home** tab > **Draw** > **Axis of Revolution**.
18. Select the axis of revolution, as shown.

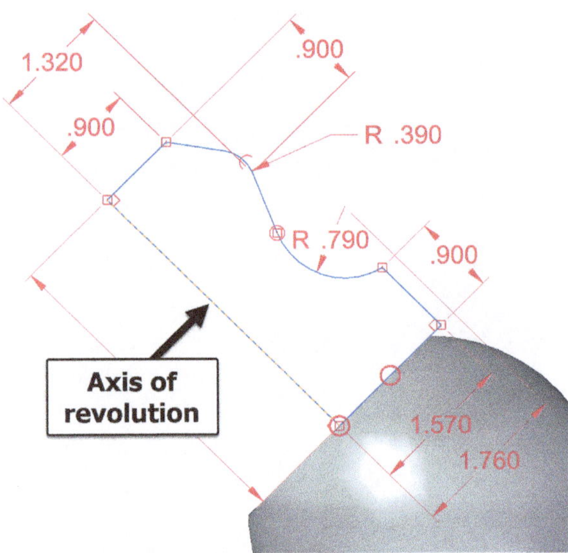

19. Click **Close Sketch** button on the ribbon.
20. Expand the **Extent** section and click **Type > Revolve 360**.
21. Click **Finish** and **Cancel**.

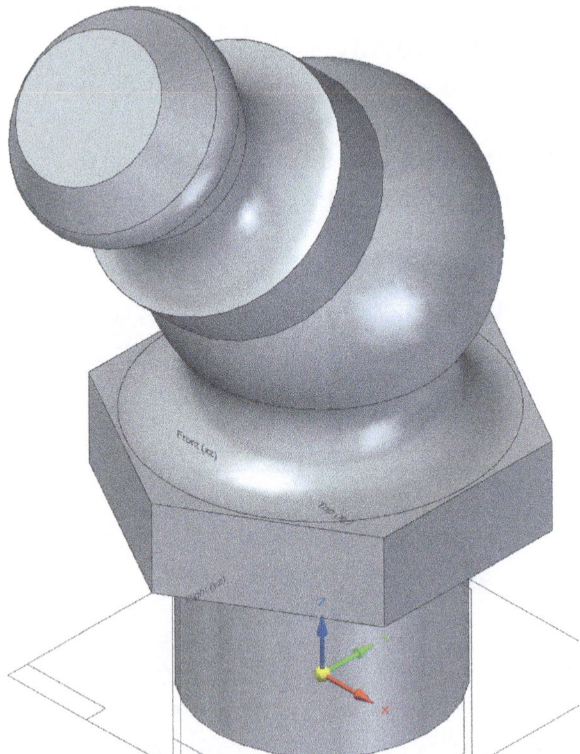

Creating the Extruded Cut Features

1. On the ribbon, click **Home** tab > **Solids** panel > **Extrude**.
2. Rotate the model and click on the flat face of the revolved feature, as shown.

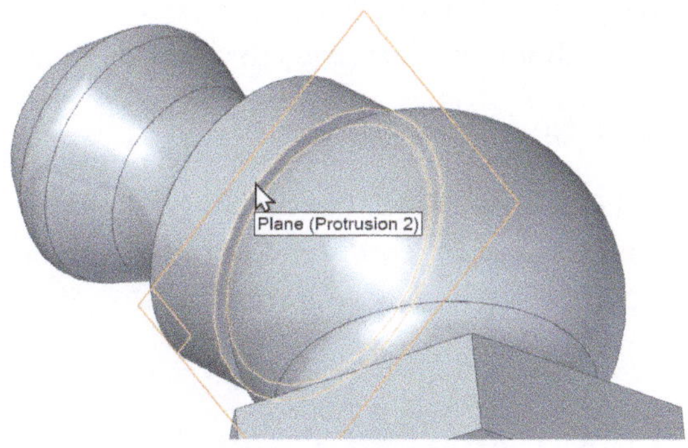

3. Create the sketch, as shown.

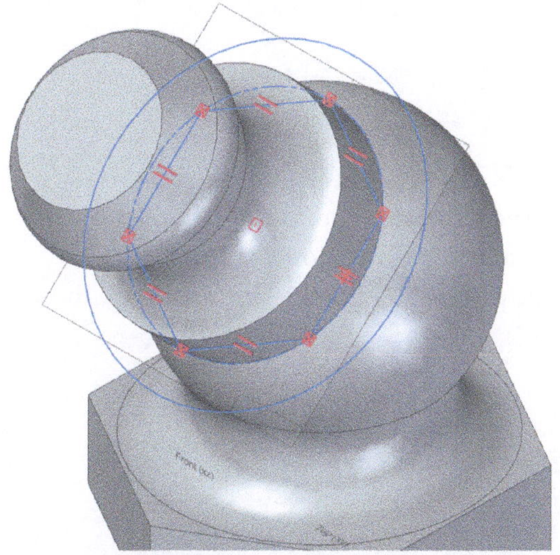

4. Click **Close Sketch** on the ribbon.
5. On the **Extrude** command bar, select **Operation** > **Cut** .
6. On the **Extent** section of the command bar, select **Direction** > **One-sided Extent** icon.
7. Type 1 in the Distance box and press ENTER.
8. Move the pointer upward and click.
9. Click **Finish** and **Cancel**.

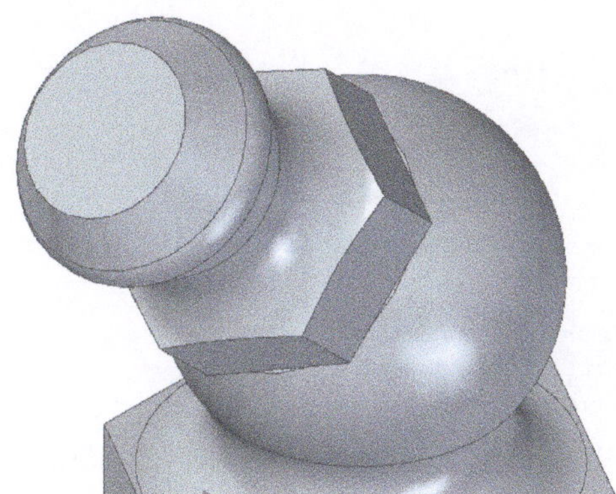

10. On the ribbon, click **Home** tab > **Solids** panel > **Extrude**.
11. Click on the flat face of the revolved feature, as shown.

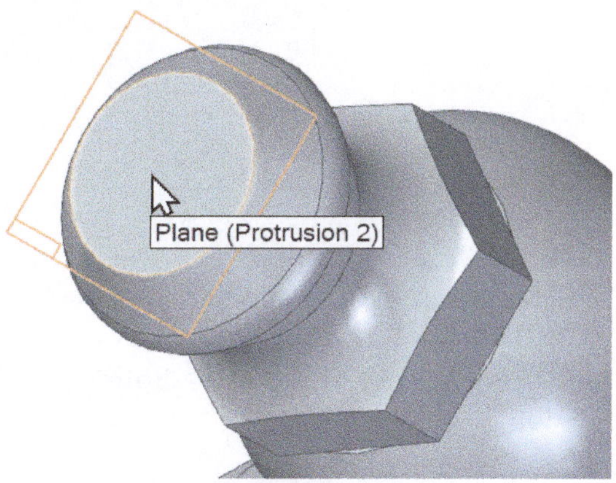

12. Create the sketch, as shown.

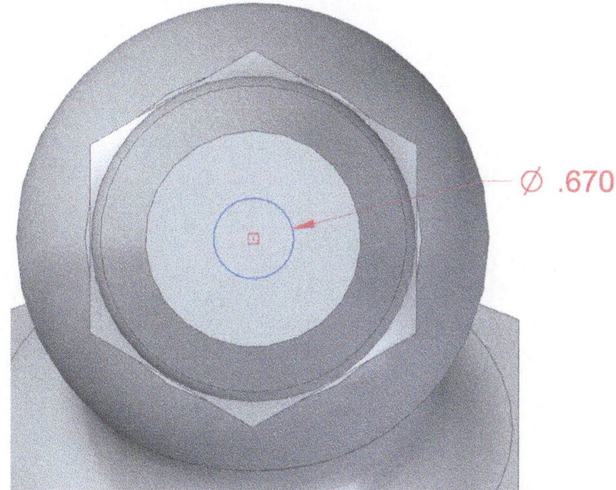

13. Click **Close Sketch** on the ribbon.
14. On the **Extrude** command bar, click the **Finite Extent** icon.
15. Type **5.11** in the **Distance** box and press ENTER.
16. Move the pointer downward and click.
17. Click **Finish** and **Cancel**.

Creating the Ball

1. On the ribbon, click **Home** tab > **Solids** panel > **Revolve**.
2. Select the right plane.
3. Create the sketch, as shown.

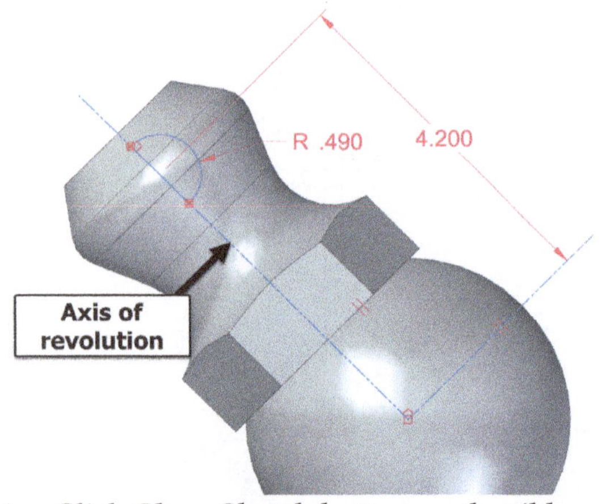

4. Click **Close Sketch** button on the ribbon.
5. Expand the **Extent** section and click **Type > Revolve 360.**
6. Click **Finish** and **Cancel**.

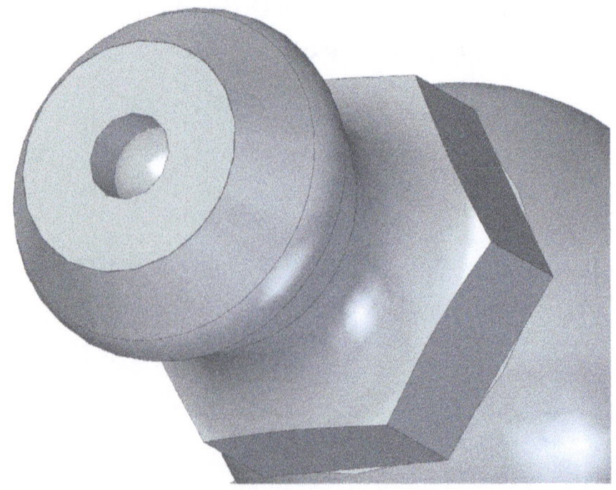

Creating the Chamfers and Rounds

1. On the ribbon, click **Home** tab > **Solids** panel > **Round** drop-down > **Chamfer** .
2. Select **Options** > **Equal Setbacks** option from the **Chamfer** command bar.
3. Select the circular edge, as shown.

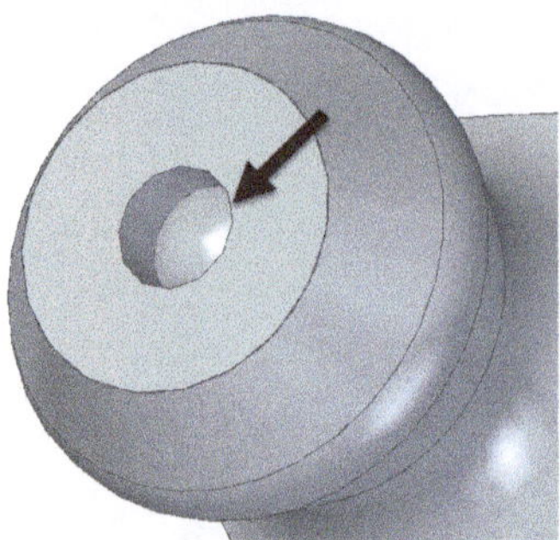

4. On the **Chamfer** command bar, click the **Chamfer Options** icon.
5. Type **0.1** in the **Setback** box and click the green check.

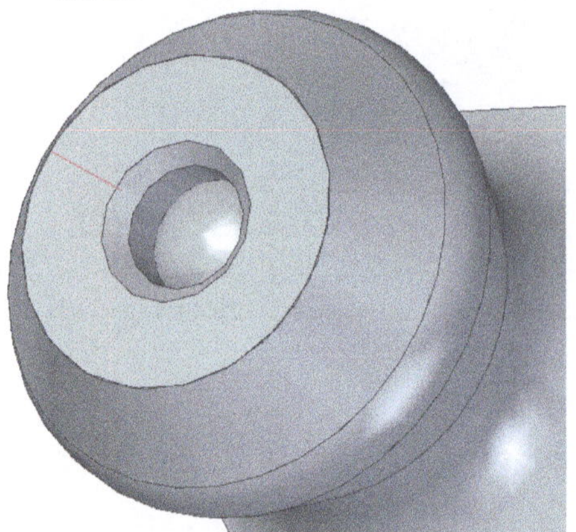

6. Click **Finish**.
7. Likewise, chamfer the circular edge of the bottom face, as shown. The chamfer setback is **0.3.**

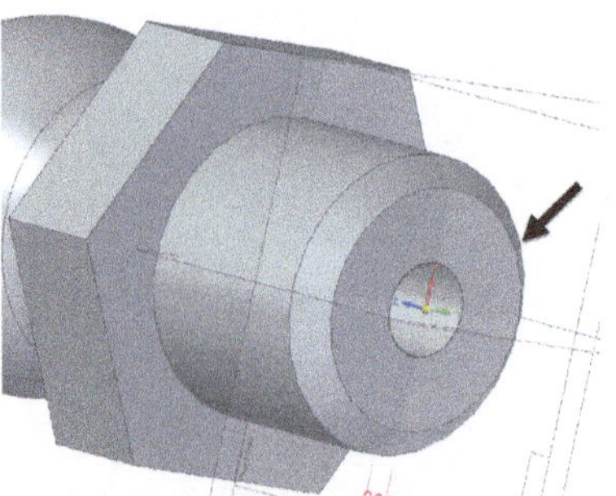

8. On the ribbon, click **Home** tab > **Solids** panel > **Round** drop-down > **Round**.

9. Select the circular edge, as shown.
10. Type **0.3** in the **Radius** box on the **Round** command bar. Next, press ENTER.
11. Click **Preview** and **Finish**.

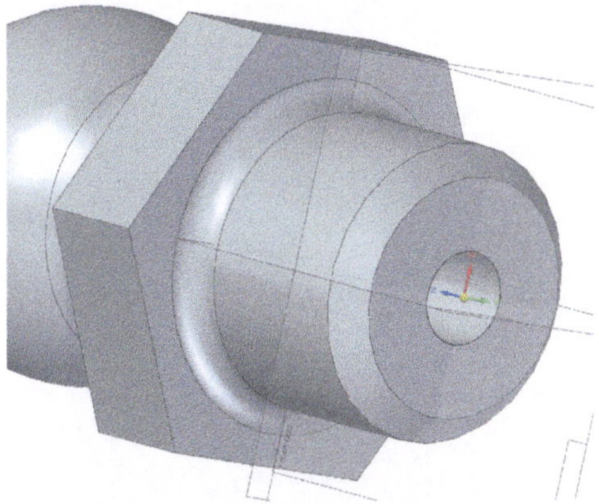

Creating the Helical Swept Cut

1. On the ribbon, click **Home** tab > **Solids** panel > **Cut** drop-down > **Helical Cutout**.
2. Select the Right plane.
3. On the **Sketch** ribbon, click **Sketching > Centerline.**
4. Create a horizontal centerline passing through the sketch origin.

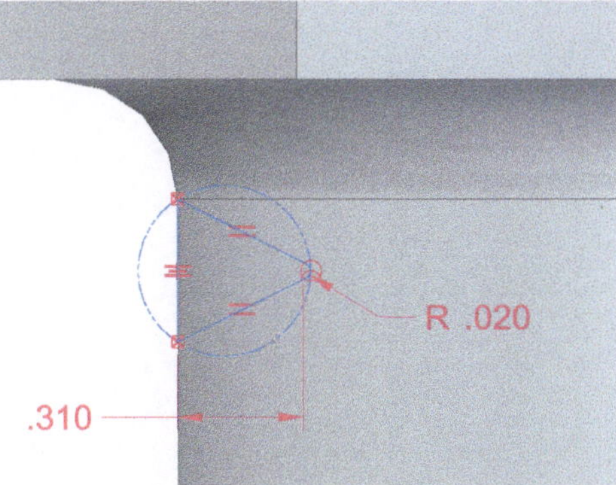

22. Create a vertical line passing through the origin.
23. On the ribbon, click **Home** tab > **Draw** > **Axis of Revolution**.
24. Select the newly created line, as shown.

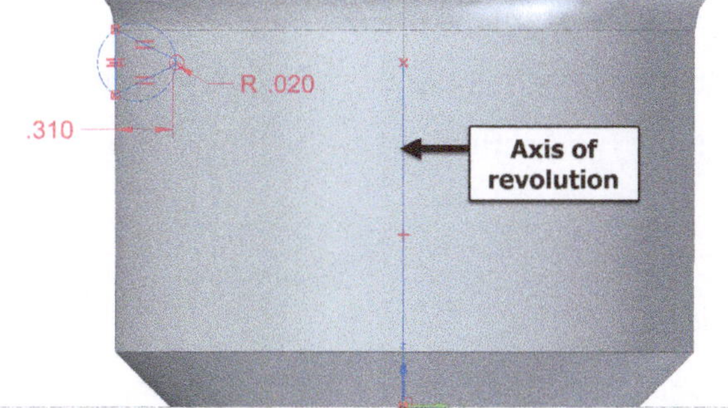

5. Click **Close Sketch** on the ribbon.
6. Click near the top end point of the axis of revolution.

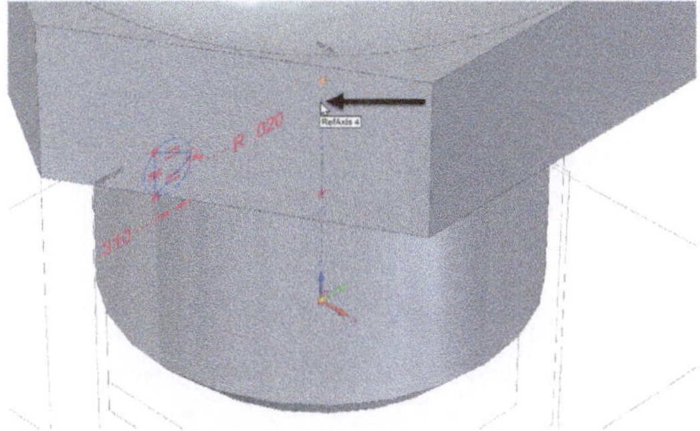

7. Select **Pitch and Turns** from the **Helix Method** drop-down.
8. Type-in **0.394** in the **Pitch** box located on the command bar.
9. Type 5 in the **#Turns** box.
10. Click **Next**.
11. Click **Preview**, **Finish** and **Cancel**.

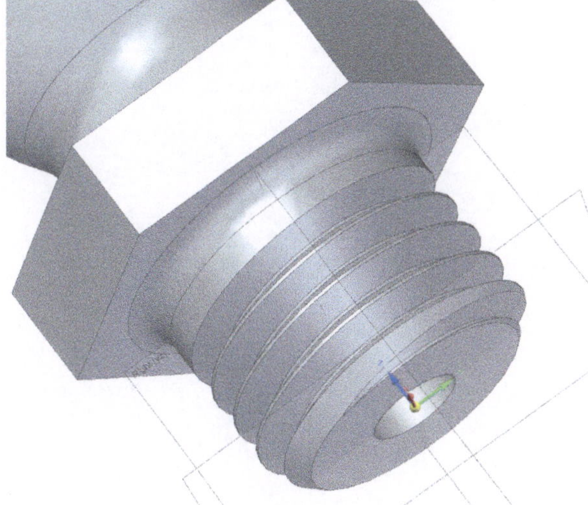

Questions

1. List the methods to create the *Sweep* features.
2. How to apply twist and turns to *Sweep* features?

3. Write the formula to calculate the variable pitch of a helical feature.
4. Why do we define the axis of a *Sweep* feature?
5. List any two methods to create helical features.

Exercises

Exercise1

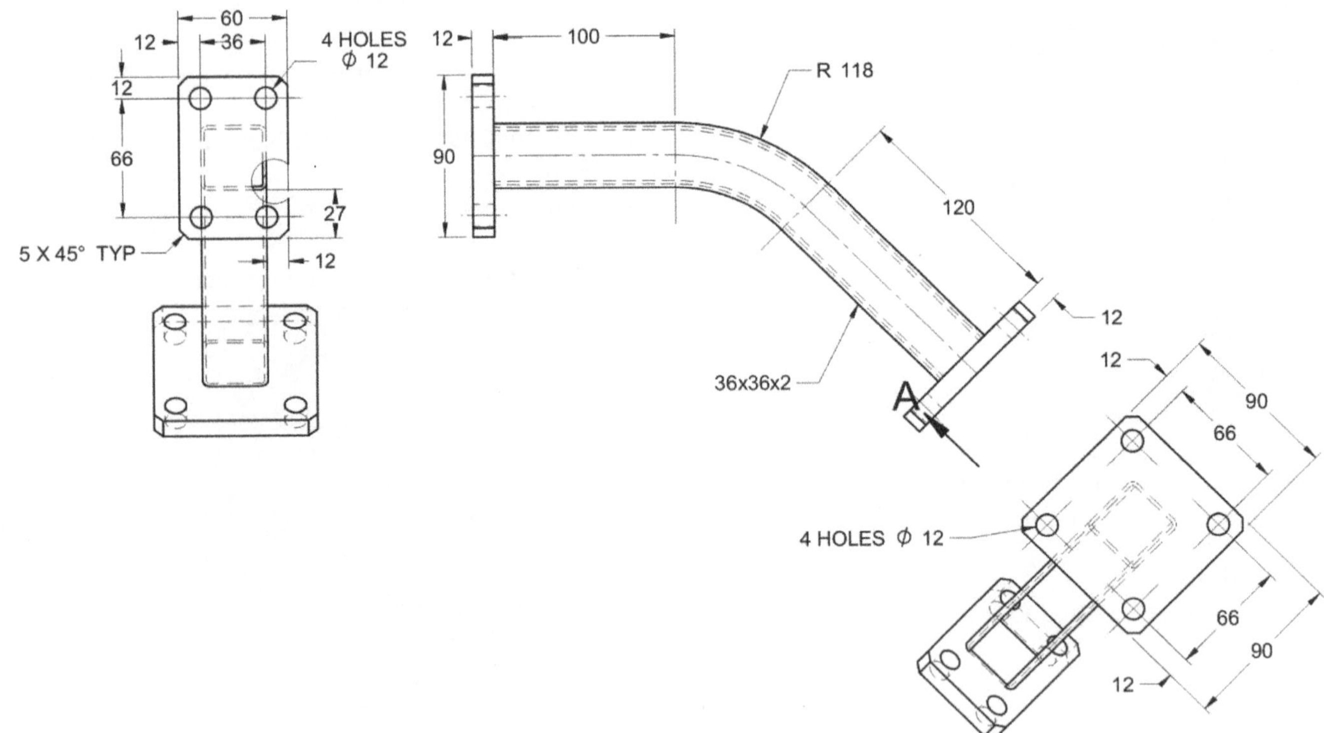

Chapter 7: Loft Features

The **Loft** command is one of the advanced commands available in Solid Edge that allows you to create simple and complex shapes. A basic loft is created by defining two cross-sections and joining them together. For example, if you create a loft feature between a circle and a square, you can easily change the solid's cross-sectional shape. In contrast, the sweep feature allows you to control the cross-section at the start or endpoints.

The topics covered in this chapter are:

- *Basic Lofts*
- *Loft options*
- *Loft Cutouts*

Loft

This command creates a loft feature between different cross-sections. To create a loft, first, create two or more sections on different planes. The planes can be parallel or perpendicular to each other. Activate the **Loft** command (click **Home > Solids > Sweep > Loft** on the ribbon); the **Loft** command bar appears. The **Cross-Section** section is active, and you can select the cross-sections that will define the loft. You need to select two or more cross-sections to define a loft. Select the cross-sections from the graphics window. The loft feature is sensitive to the location at which you will click to select the cross-section. For example, select the first cross-section by clicking near the right corner, and then select the second cross-section by clicking at a corresponding location. Click **Preview** on the command bar; the loft preview immediately appears, as shown below.

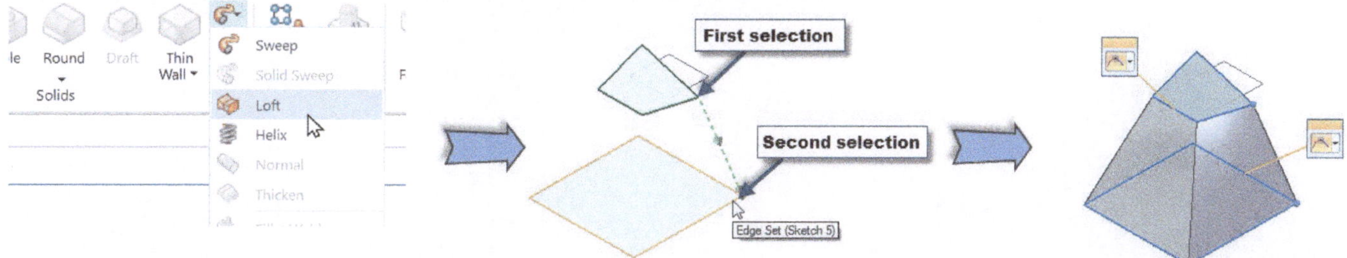

Now, expand the **Cross-Section** section on the command bar, and then click **Define Start Point**. Select the opposite corner on the first cross-section, and then click the **Preview** button; you will notice that a different result appears. For this reason, you have to be careful about where you click to select the cross-sections. However, if you happen to make a mistake, you can use the **Define Start Point** icon to fix any unwanted twisting.

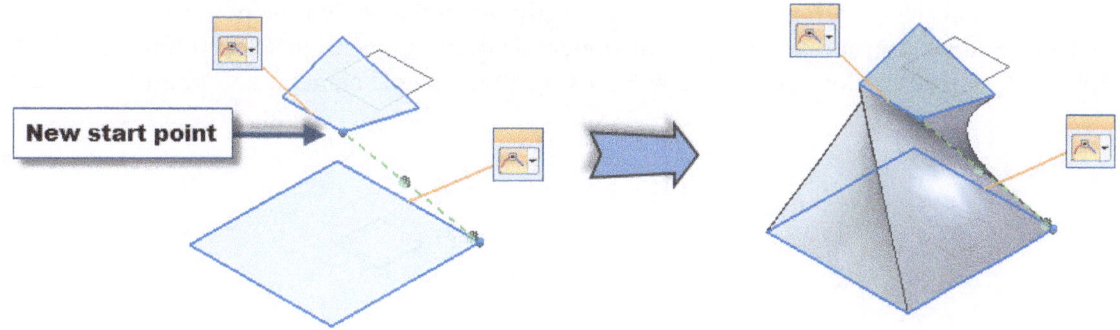

Tangency Controls

The cross-sections and the plane location control the shape of a simple loft. However, the **Tangency Controls** connected to the cross-sections can control the behavior of the side faces. If you would like to change the side faces' appearance, you can use the **Tangency Controls** either at the beginning of the loft, the end of the lofts or both. For instance, click on **Tangency Control** at the beginning of the loft and select **Normal to Section**; the loft updates' preview. You can notice that the beginning of the loft starts in a direction normal to the cross-section. You can control how much influence the **Normal to Section** option will have by adjusting the box's parameter attached to the cross-section. A lower value will have a lesser effect on the feature. As you increase the value, the more noticeable the effect will be, eventually. If you increase the number high enough, the normal effect will lead to some weird results. You can also click and drag the handle attached to the cross-section to control the normal effect. If you want to change the direction of the Normal to Section effect, enter a negative value in the box attached to the section. The same options can also be applied to the end cross-section of the loft.

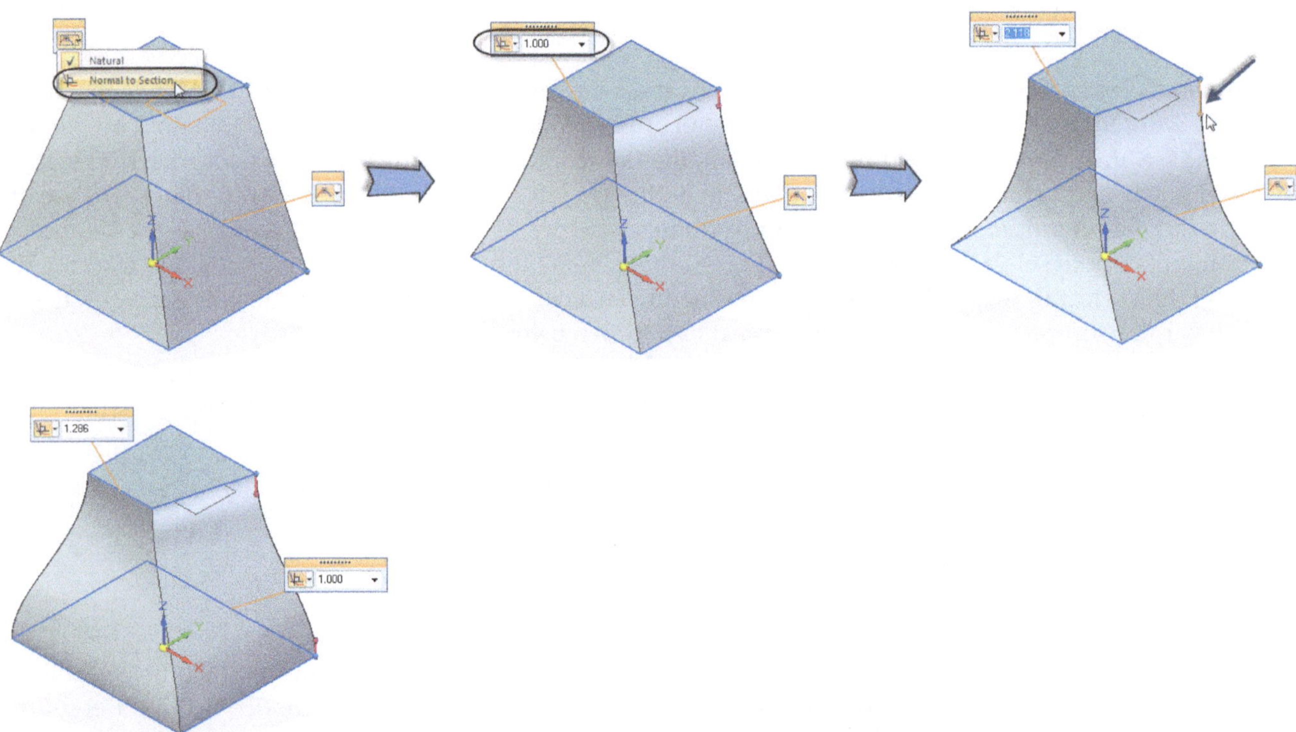

Loft Cross-sections

In addition to 2D sketches, you can also define loft cross-sections by using different element types. For instance, you can use existing model faces, surfaces, curves, and points. The only restriction is that the points can be used at the beginning or end of a loft. Set the appropriate option in the **Select** drop-down menu to select different element types. In the following example, a loft feature is created using a face, single element and point.

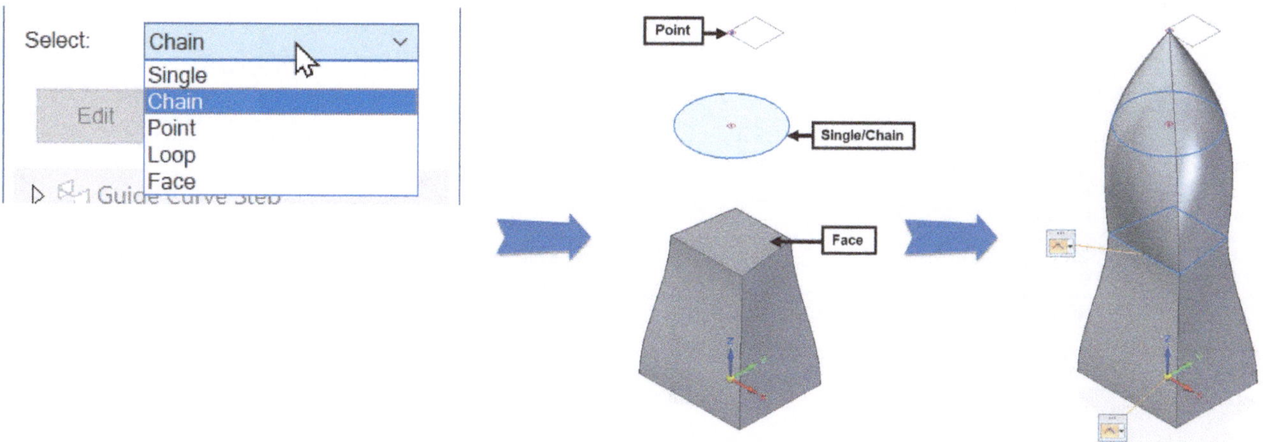

Closed Extent

Solid Edge allows you to create a loft that closes on itself. For example, to create a ring that lofts between each of the shapes, you must select four sketches as shown in the figure, and then click the **Extent** section on the command bar. Next, click the **Closed Extent** icon on the command bar and click **Preview**; this will give you a closed loft.

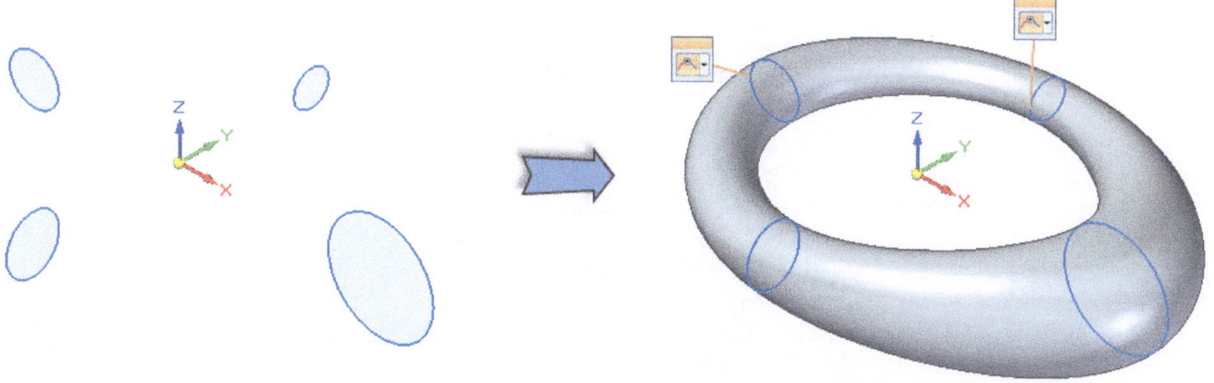

Guide Curves

Similar to **Tangency Controls**, guide curves allow you to control the behavior of a loft between cross-sections. You can create guide curves by using 2D sketches. You can also use the **Keypoint Curve** command to create guided curves. Activate this command (click **Surfacing > Curves > Keypoint Curve** on the ribbon) and select points to create a curve, as illustrated below. Right-click and click **Finish** completing the curve. Likewise, create the other curves.

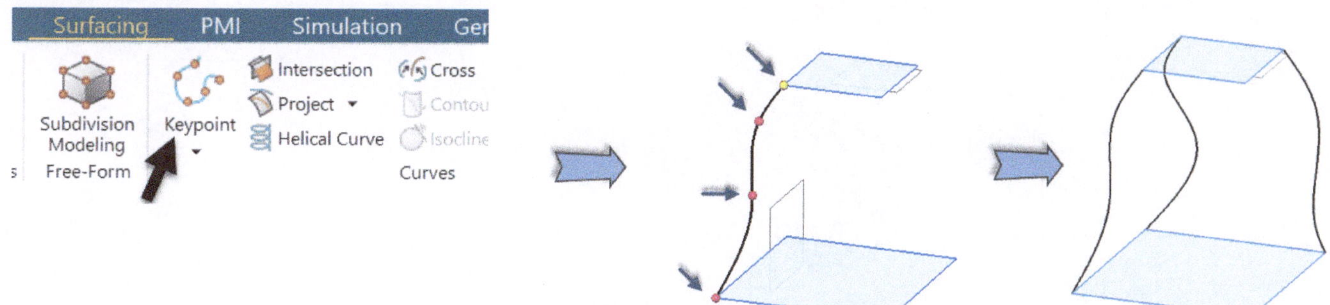

Now, activate the **Loft** command and select the cross-sections. To select guide curves, click the **Guide Curve** section on the command bar, select the first guide curve, and then click the green check on it. Similarly, select the other guide curves and click the **Preview** button; you will see the preview updates. Notice that the edges with guide curves are affected. The one without a guide curve remains as it is.

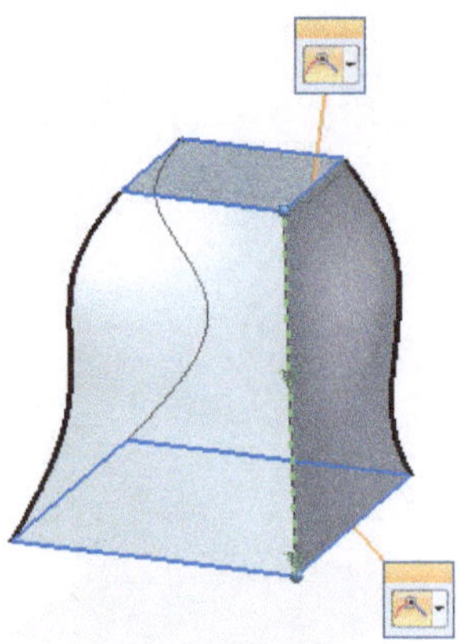

Section Geometry

Sections used for creating lofts should have a matching number of segments. For example, a three-sided section will loft nicely to another three-sided section despite the differences in the individual segments' shape. The **Loft** command does a good job of generating smooth faces to join them.

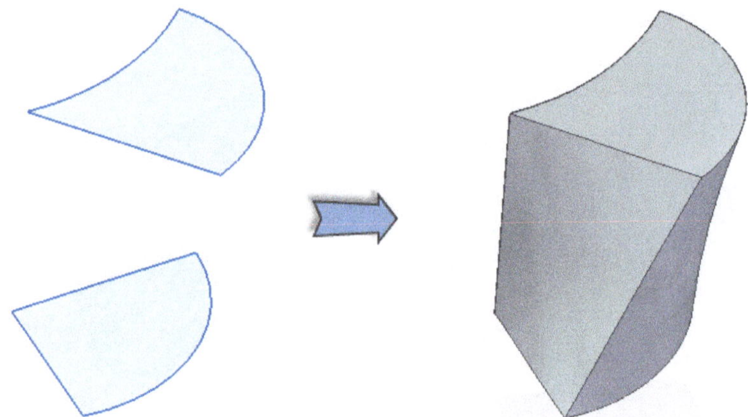

Look at an example for a loft with mismatching segments. Activate the **Loft** command and select the cross-sections. Click the **Extent** section on the command bar, and then click the **Vertex Mapping** icon; the **Vertex Mapping** dialog pops up. You can use this dialog to map vertices of the cross-sections. Click **Set 1** on the dialog and select two vertices. Click **Add** on the dialog and select two vertices; another set of vertices is added to the loft. Similarly, add another set and close the dialog. Click **Finish** to complete the loft.

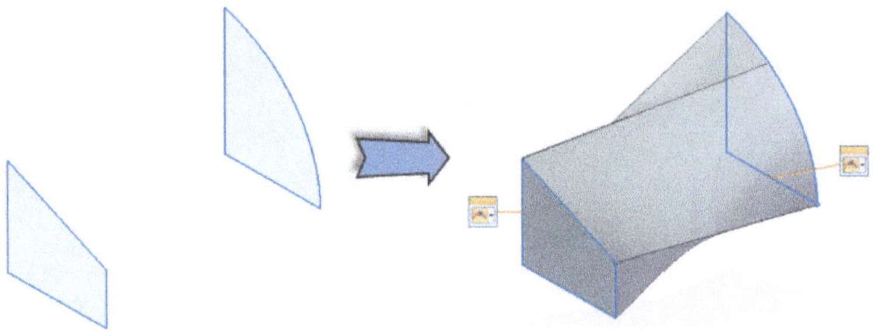

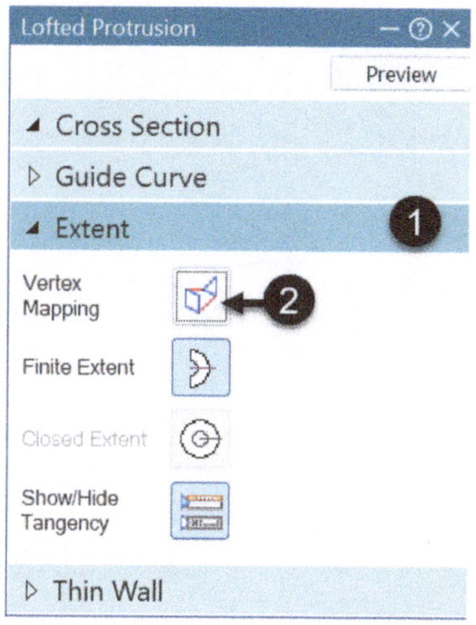

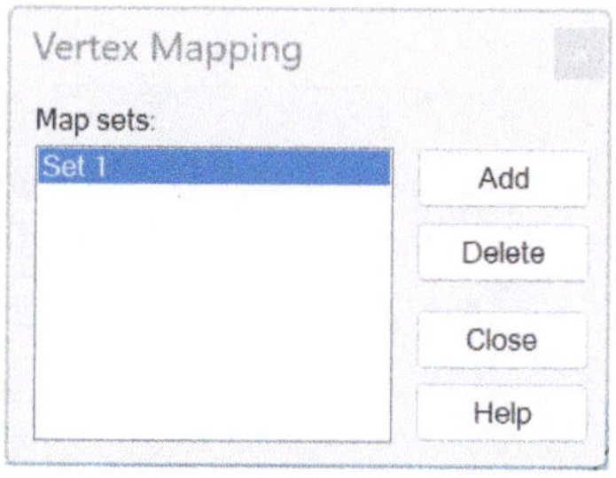

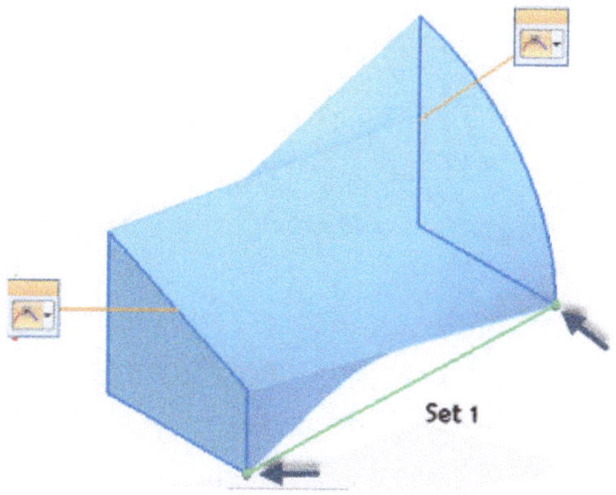

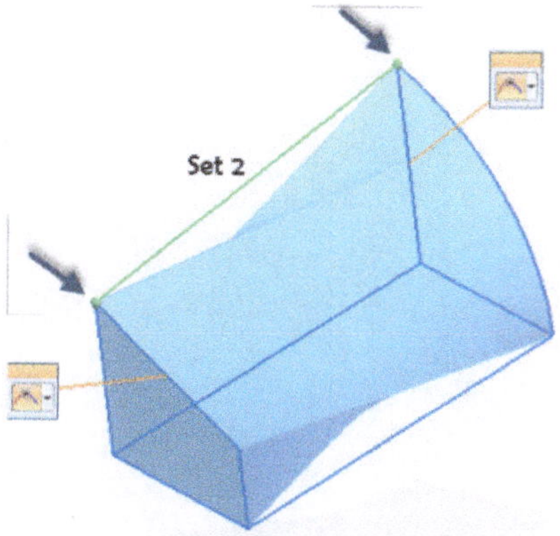

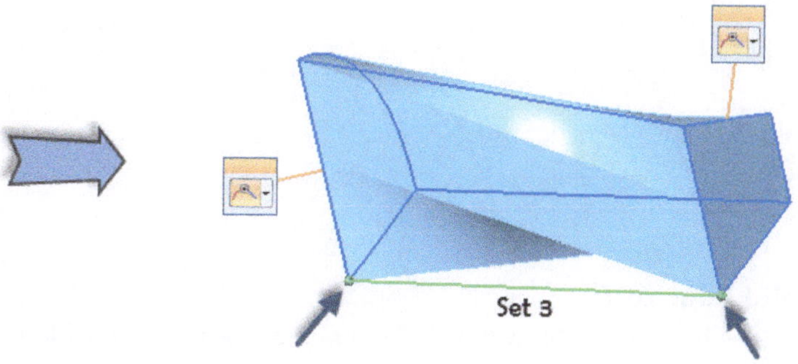

Loft Cutout

Like other standard features such as extrusion, revolve, and sweep, the loft feature can add material or remove material. You can remove material by using the **Loft Cutout** command. Activate this command (click **Home > Solids > Swept Cutout > Loft Cutout** on the ribbon) and select the cross-sections. Click **Preview** and **Finish** to create the loft cutout.

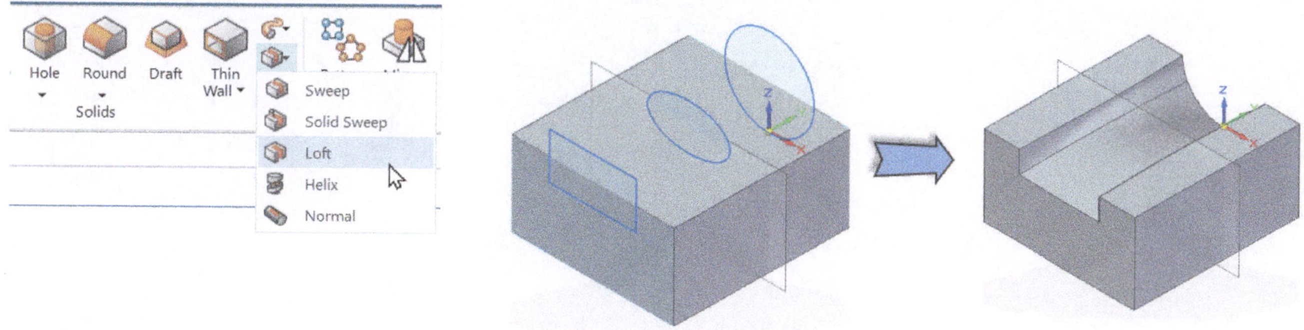

Examples

Example 1 (Millimetres)

In this example, you will create the part shown below.

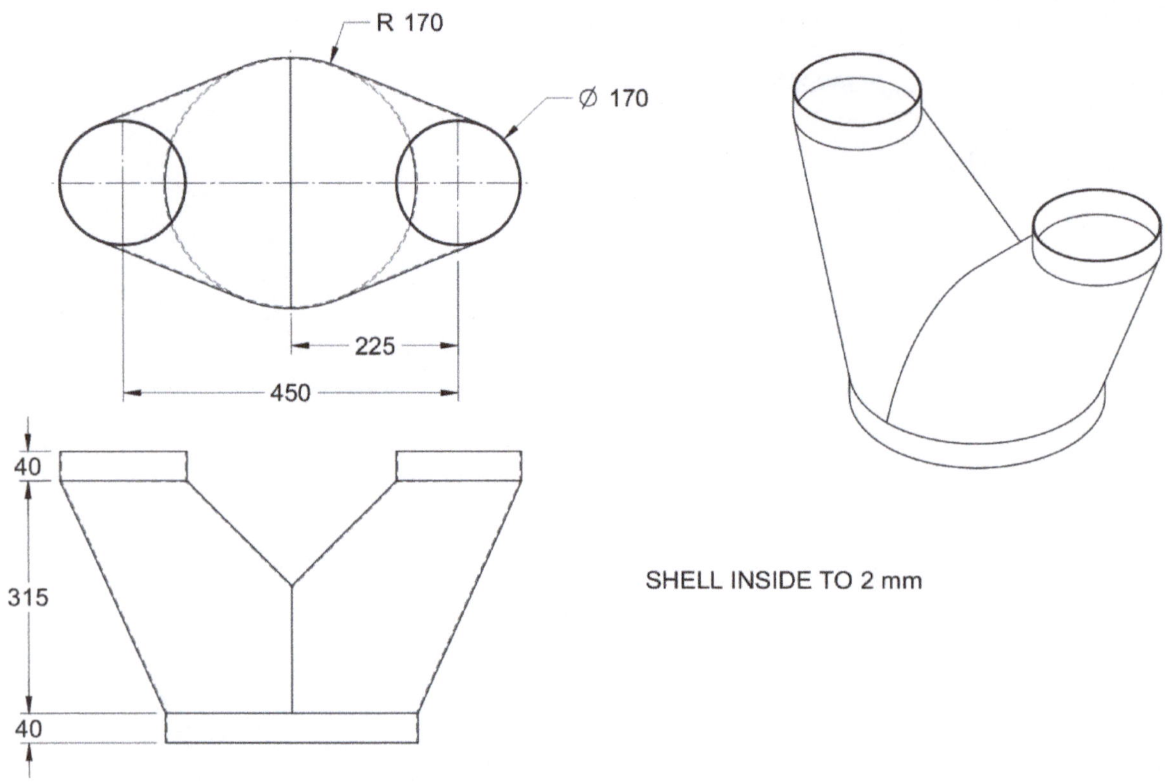

1. Start **Solid Edge 2026**.
2. On the File Menu, click **New > ISO Metric Part**; a new part file is opened.
3. Click **Continue with Synchronous** button on the **Ordered as default** dialog; the Synchronous environment is set as the default environment.
4. To start a new sketch, click **Home > Draw > Circle by Center Point** on the ribbon.
5. Lock the XY plane and draw a circle of 340 mm in diamleter. Unlock the sketch plane.
6. Create the *Extrude* feature with 40 mm thickness.

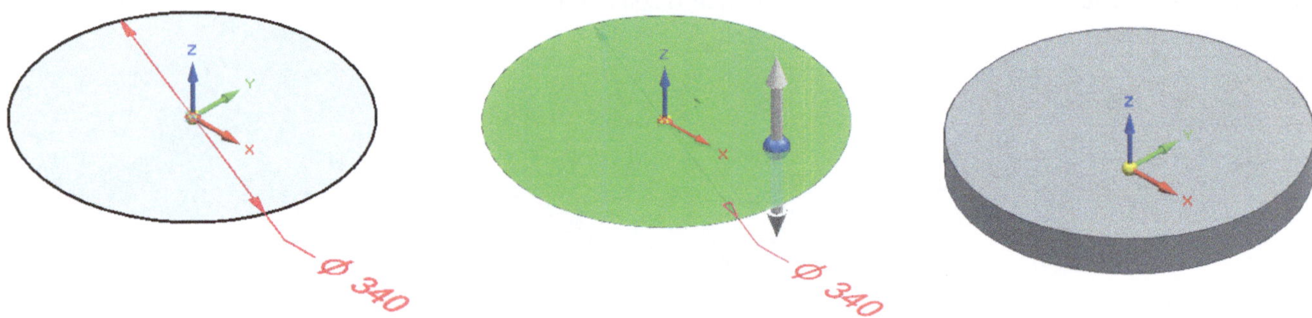

7. On the ribbon, click **Home > Planes > Coincident Plane** .
8. Click on the top face of the geometry to create a coincident plane.
9. Click on the Z-axis of the Steering Wheel tool and move the mouse pointer upward.
10. Type-in 315 mm in the dimension box and press Enter.
11. Activate the **Circle by Center Point** command and draw a circle of 170 mm diameter on the new plane. Also, add dimensions and constraints to the circle, as shown. Unlock the sketch plane.

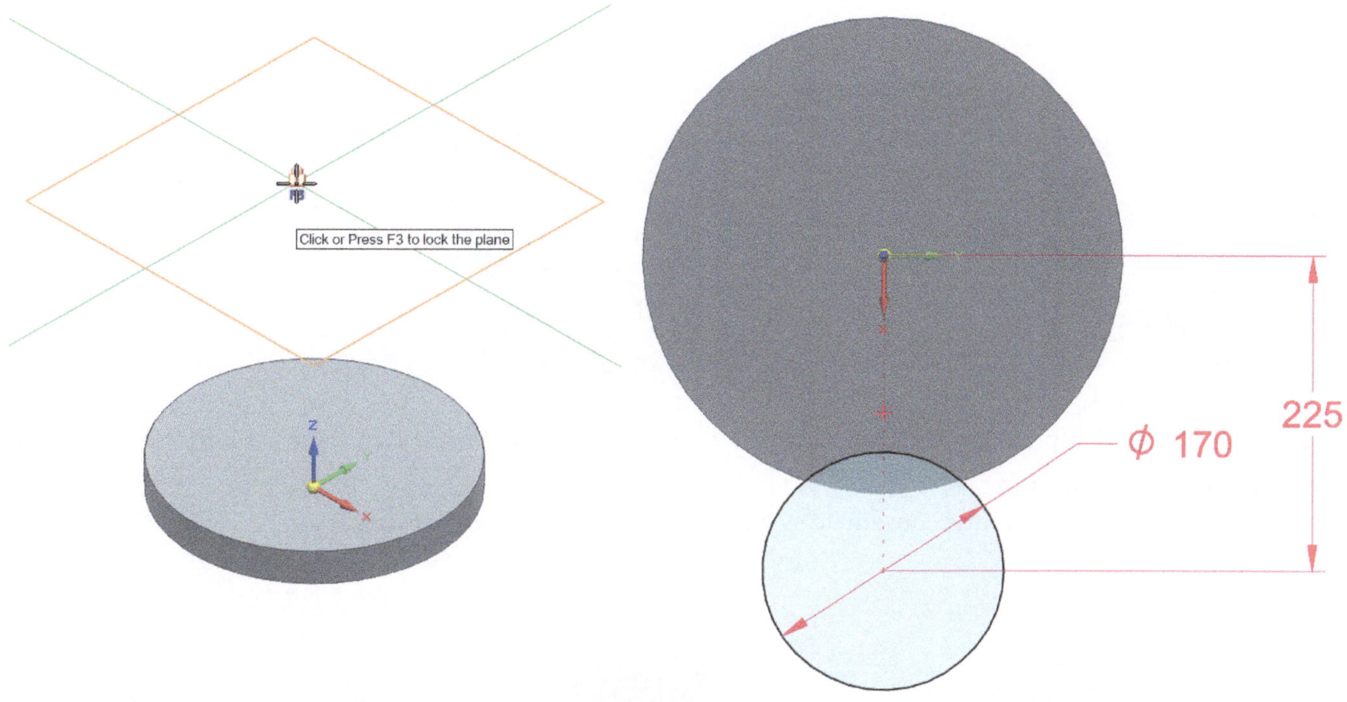

12. Change the model view orientation to ISO View.
13. On the ribbon, click **Home > Solids > Sweep > Loft**.
14. Click on the circle and the top circular edge of the *Extrude* feature.
15. Click **Preview** on the command bar to preview the loft protrusion.
16. Click **Finish** to complete the *Loft* feature.

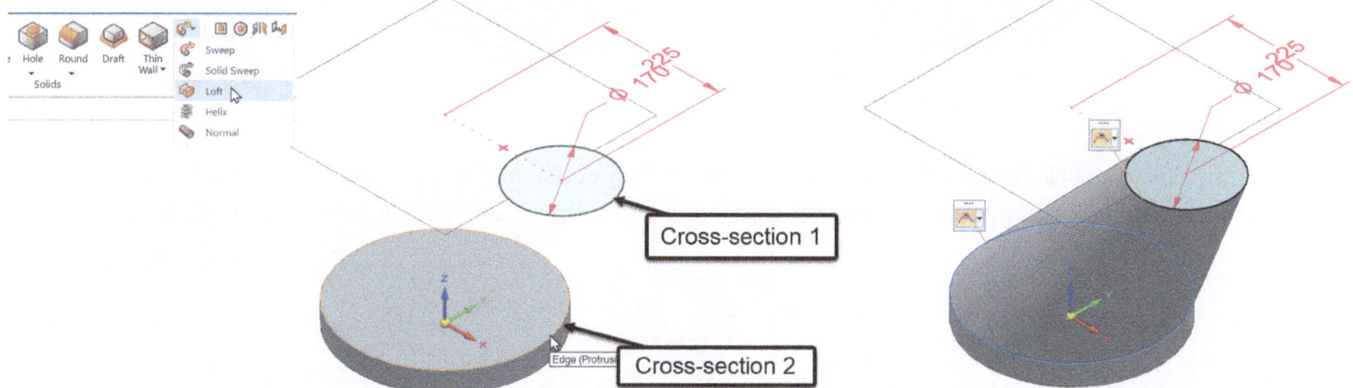

17. Activate the **Extrude** command and click on the top face of the *Loft* feature. Right-click to accept the selection.
18. Move the mouse pointer up and type 40 in the box that appears on the geometry. Press Enter.

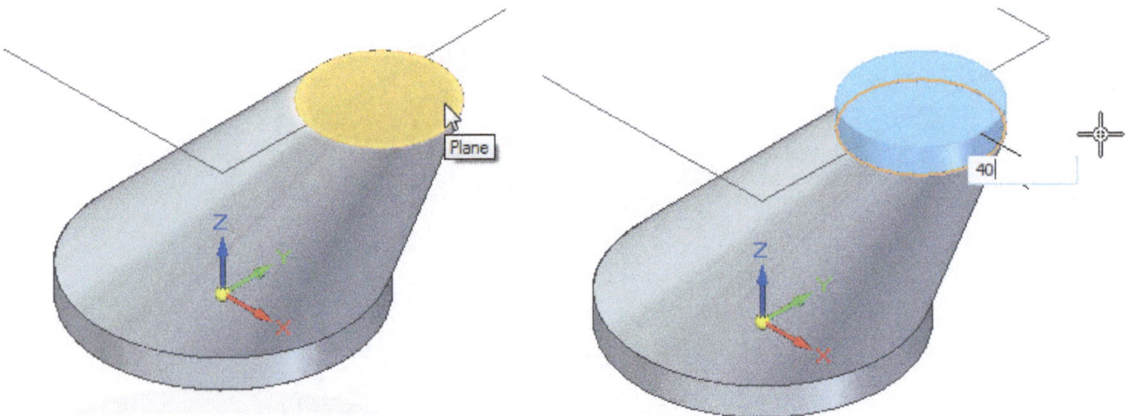

19. In the Pathfinder, press the Shift key and click on the *Loft Protrusion* and two *Extrude Protrusions*. Activate the **Mirror** command.
20. Click on the YZ plane of the coordinate system to mirror the selected features.

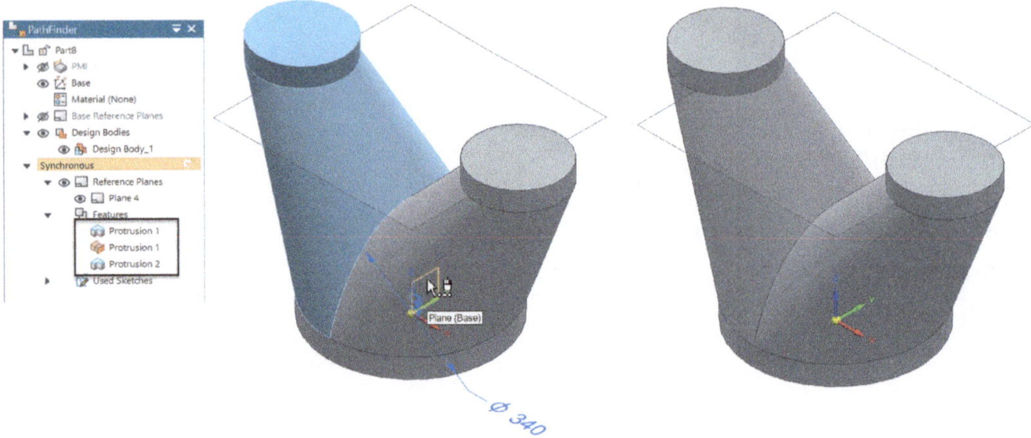

21. On the ribbon, click **Home > Solids > Thin Wall** and click on the part geometry's flat faces.
22. Type **2** in the box that appears on the geometry and press Enter. The part geometry is shelled.

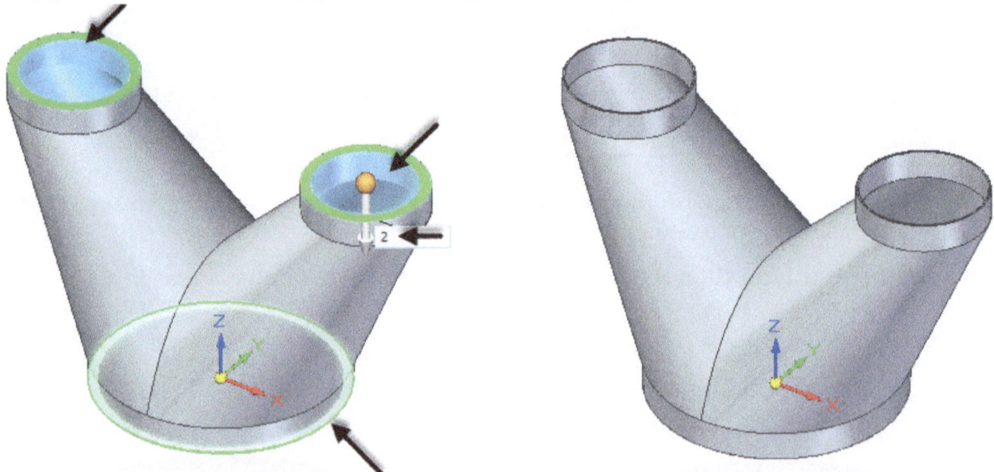

23. Save and close the part file.

Example 2 (Inches)

In this example, you will create the part shown below.

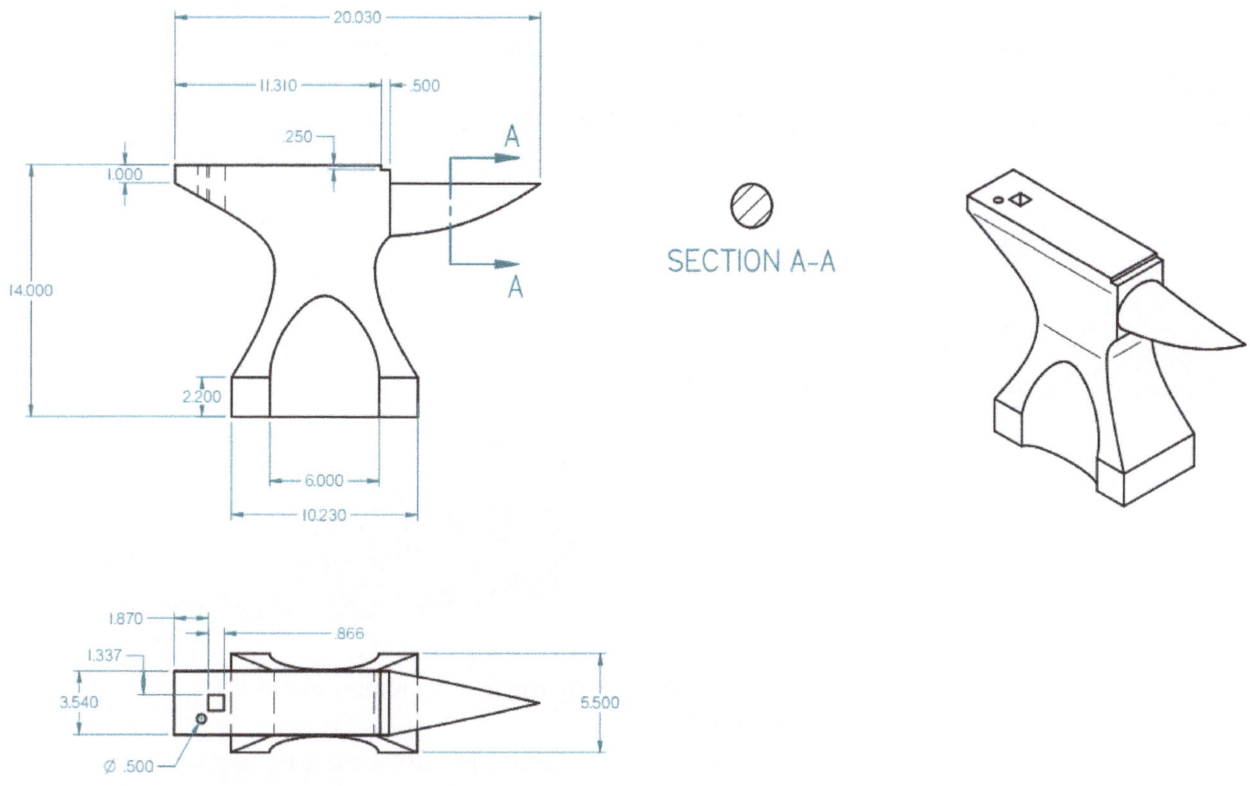

1. Start **Solid Edge 2026**.
2. On the File Menu, click **New > New**; the **New** dialog appears. On this dialog, click **Standard Templates > ANSI Inch**.
3. Select **ansi inch part.par** from the available templates, and then click **OK**.
4. Click **Continue with Ordered** button on the **Ordered as default** dialog; the Ordered environment is set as the default environment.
5. On the ribbon, click **Home > Solids > Extrude** and select the **Top(xy)** plane.
6. To start a new sketch, click **Home > Draw > Rectangle by Center** on the ribbon.
7. Click on the origin point to define the center point of the rectangle. Move the mouse pointer diagonally and click to draw a rectangle.
8. Activate the **Smart Dimension** command and apply dimensions to the sketch, as shown below.

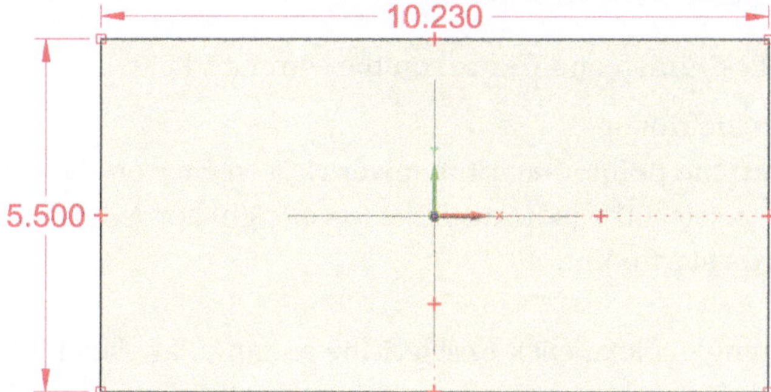

9. Click the **Close Sketch** icon on the ribbon.
10. Click the **Onse-sided Extent** button. Next, type **2.2** in the **Distance** box and press Enter.
11. Move the point upward and click to define the side of the extrusion. Next, click the **Finish** button.
12. Click **Home > Planes > More Planes** drop-down **> Parallel Plane** on the ribbon and click on the top face of the model.
13. Type 6, and then press Enter. Move the pointer upward and click.

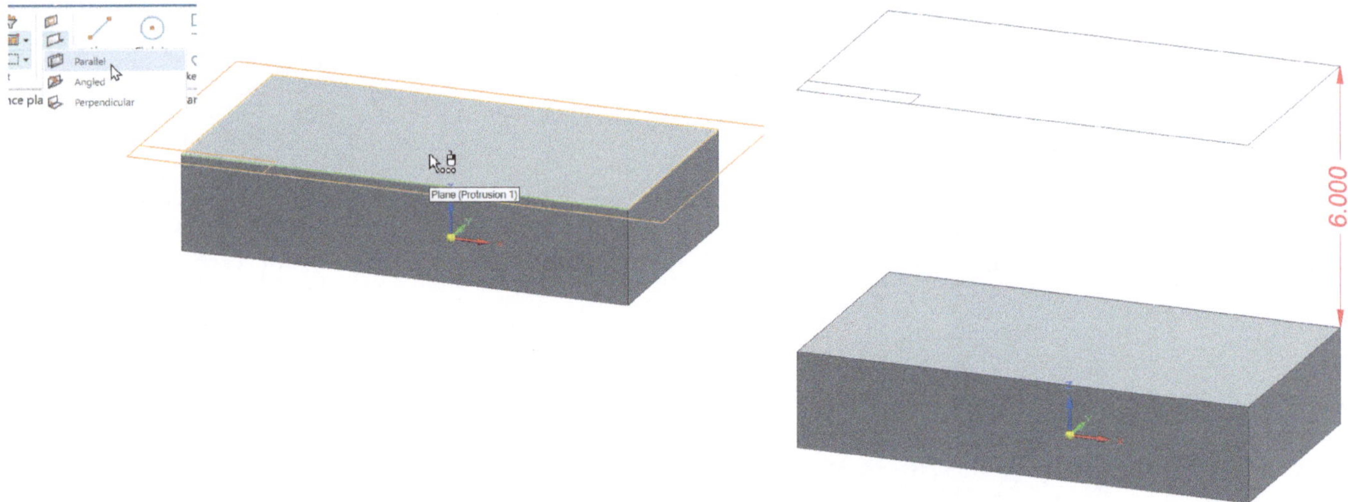

14. Click **Home > Sketch > Sketch** on the ribbon. Next, click on the newly created plane.
15. Click **Home > Draw > Rectangle by Center** on the ribbon.
16. Click on the origin point to define the center point of the rectangle. Move the mouse pointer diagonally and click to draw a rectangle.
17. Activate the **Smart Dimension** command and apply dimensions to the sketch.

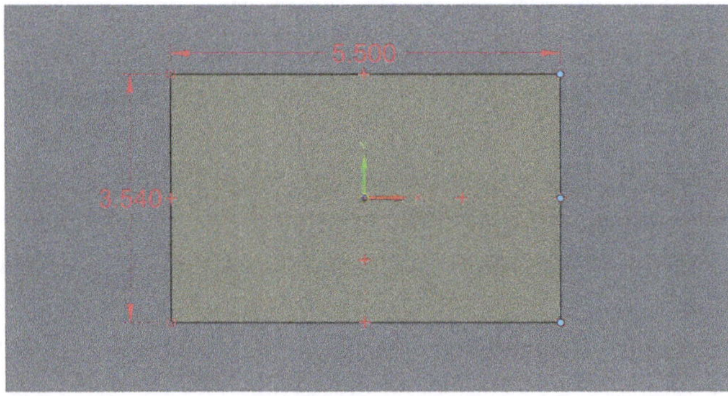

18. Click the **Close Sketch** button on the ribbon. Next, click **Finish** and **Cancel** on the command bar.
19. Click **Home > Solids > Add** drop-down **> Loft** on the ribbon.
20. On the command bar, click **Select > Loop**. Next, place the pointer near the lower right corner on the first feature's top face; the edge loop is highlighted. Click to select the loop; also, the lower right corner point of the first feature's top face is selected as the loft feature's start point.
21. On the command bar, click **Select > Chain**.
22. Place the pointer at the lower right corner of the rectangle. Next, click to select the rectangular sketch; the rectangle's lower right corner point is selected as the loft's endpoint.

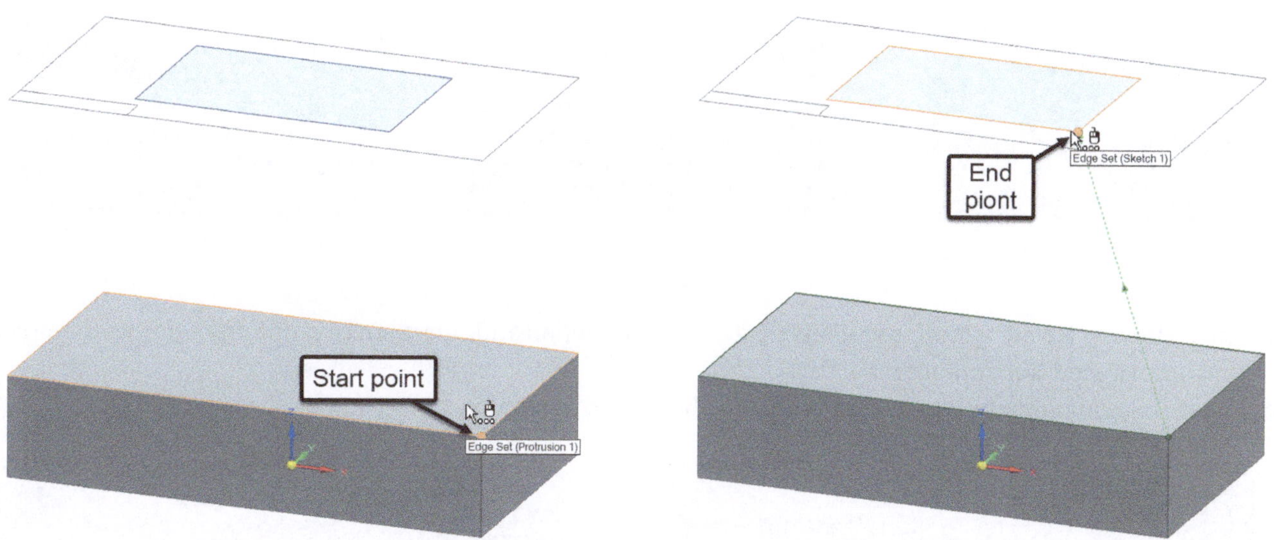

23. Click **Preview** on the command bar. Next, select **Normal to section** from the Tangency control handle attached to the second section. Type 1 in the value box available on the Tangency control handle.
24. Click **Finish** and **Cancel** on the command bar.

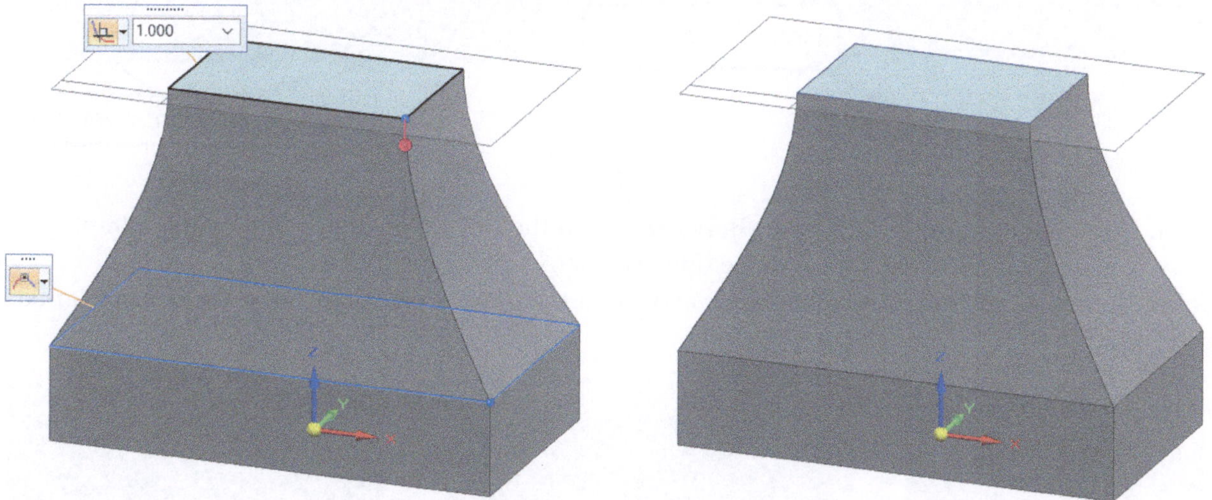

25. Click **Home > Sketch > Sketch** on the ribbon. Next, click on the plane located on the top face of the model.
26. Click **Home > Draw > Circle** drop-down **> Ellipse by Center Point** on the ribbon.
27. Place the pointer on the left vertical edge and select the midpoint. Move the mouse pointer vertically and click to specify the first axis. Next, move the pointer horizontally and click to create the second axis of the ellipse.

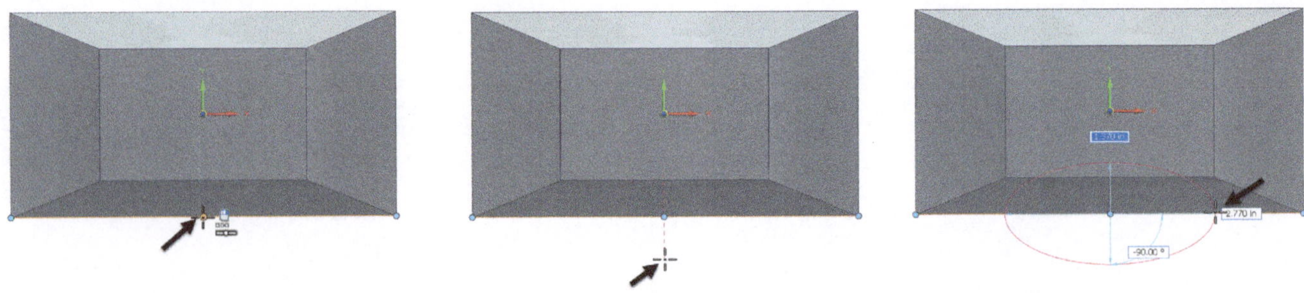

28. Click **Home > Relate > Horizontal/Vertical** on the ribbon and select the two-quadrant points, as shown; they are aligned horizontally.
29. Select the remaining two-quadrant points to align them vertically.

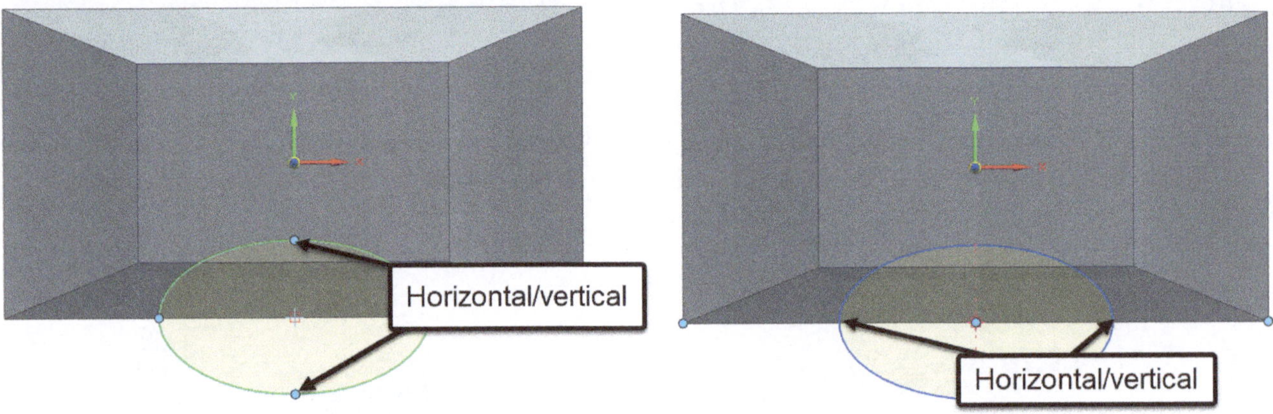

30. Click **Home > Dimension > Distance Between** on the ribbon and select the two-quadrant points, as shown. Place the dimension, type 6 in the dimension box, and press Enter.
31. Select the remaining two-quadrant points and place the dimension. Type 1.8 in the dimension box and press Enter.

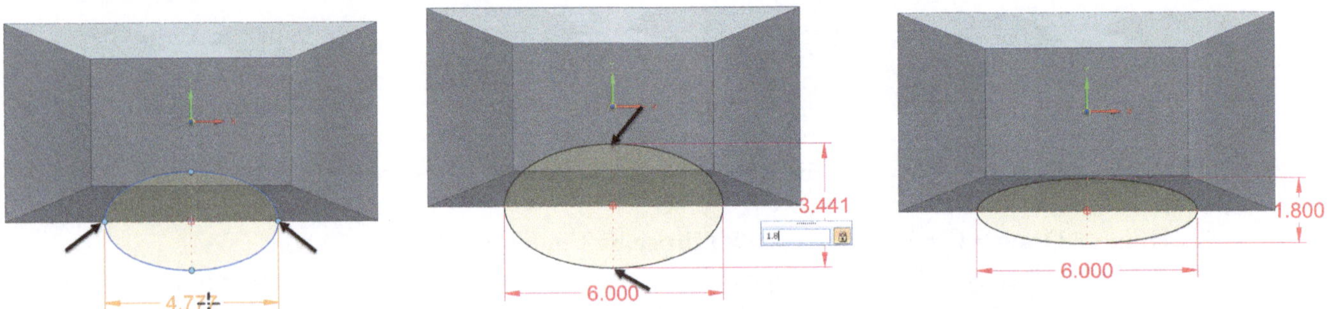

32. Click the **Close Sketch** button on the ribbon. Next, click **Finish** and **Cancel** on the command bar.
33. On the ribbon, click **Home > Solids > Extrude** and select the **Select from sketch** option from the **Create-From Options** drop-down. Next, select the sketch and click the green check.
34. On the command bar, select **Operation** > **Cut**. Next, select the **Extent > Type > Through All.**
35. Move the pointer downward and click in the graphics window to create the extruded cut.
36. Click **Finish** on the command bar.

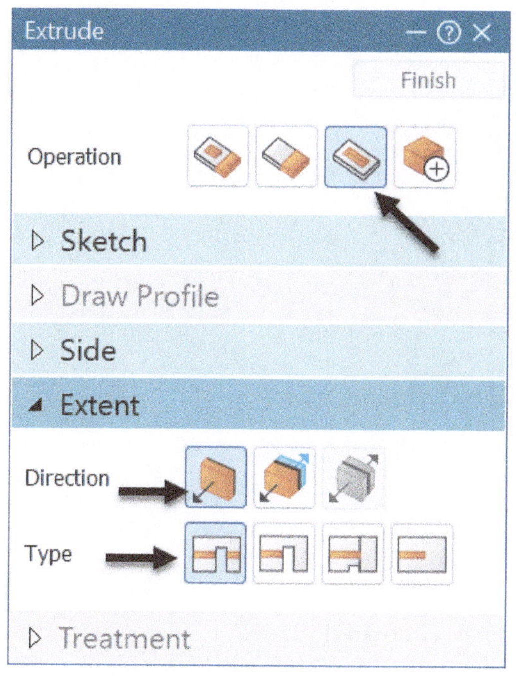

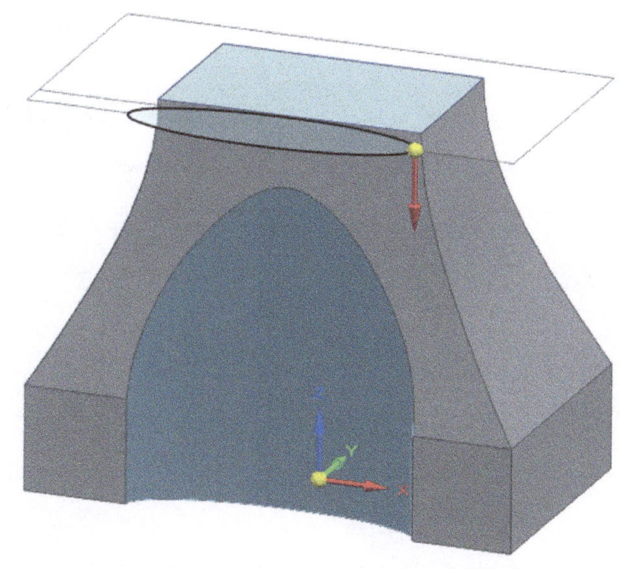

37. Mirror the extruded cut feature about the XZ plane.

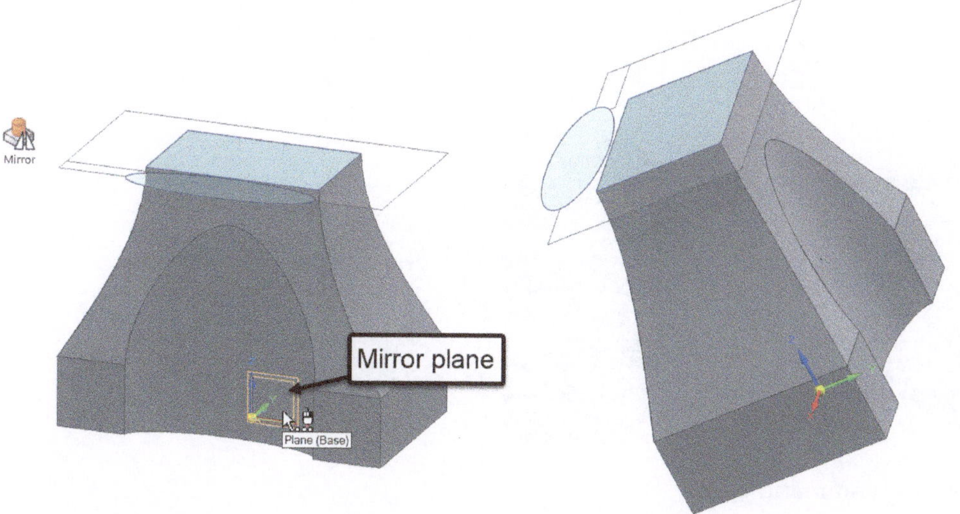

38. Create a plane parallel to the top face of the model. The **Distance** value is 4.8.

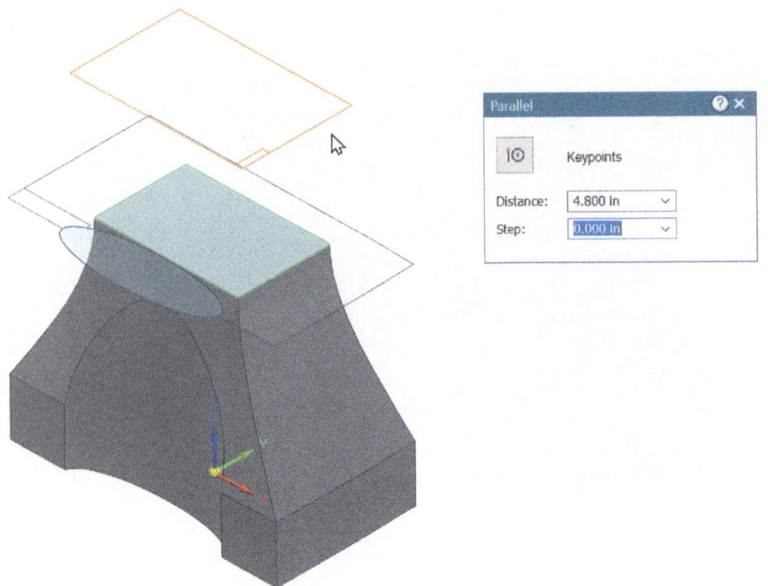

39. Click **Home > Sketch > Sketch** on the ribbon. Next, click on the newly created plane.
40. Click **Home > Draw > Rectangle by Center** on the ribbon.
41. Create a rectangle, as shown. Next, add dimensions to it and click **Close Sketch**.

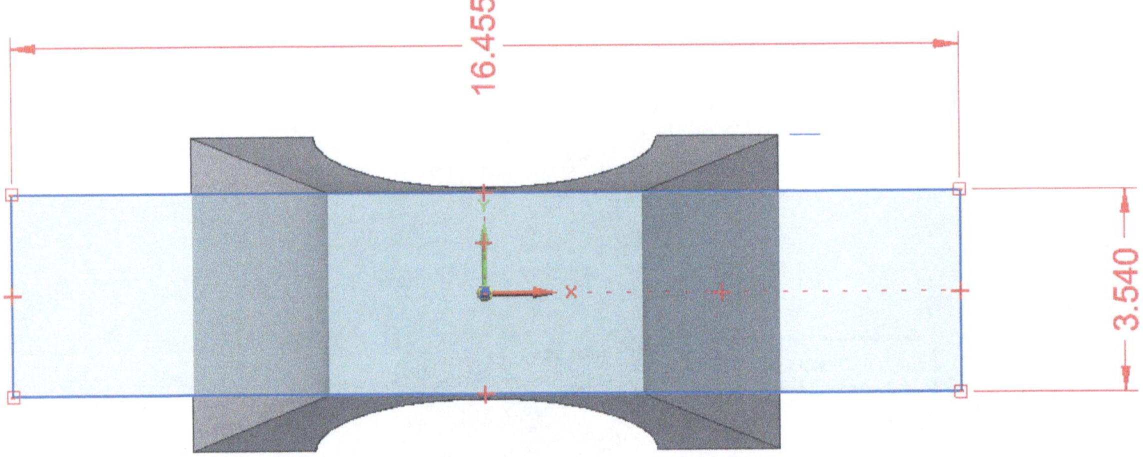

42. Click **Finish** and **Cancel** on the command bar.
43. Click **Home > Solids > Add** drop-down **> Loft** on the ribbon.
44. On the command bar, click **Select > Loop**. Next, place the pointer near the lower right corner on the top face; the edge loop is highlighted. Click to select the loop; the top face's lower right corner point is selected as the start point.
45. On the command bar, select **Select > Chain**.
46. Place the pointer at the lower right corner of the rectangle. Next, click to select the rectangular sketch; the rectangle's lower right corner point is selected as the loft's endpoint.

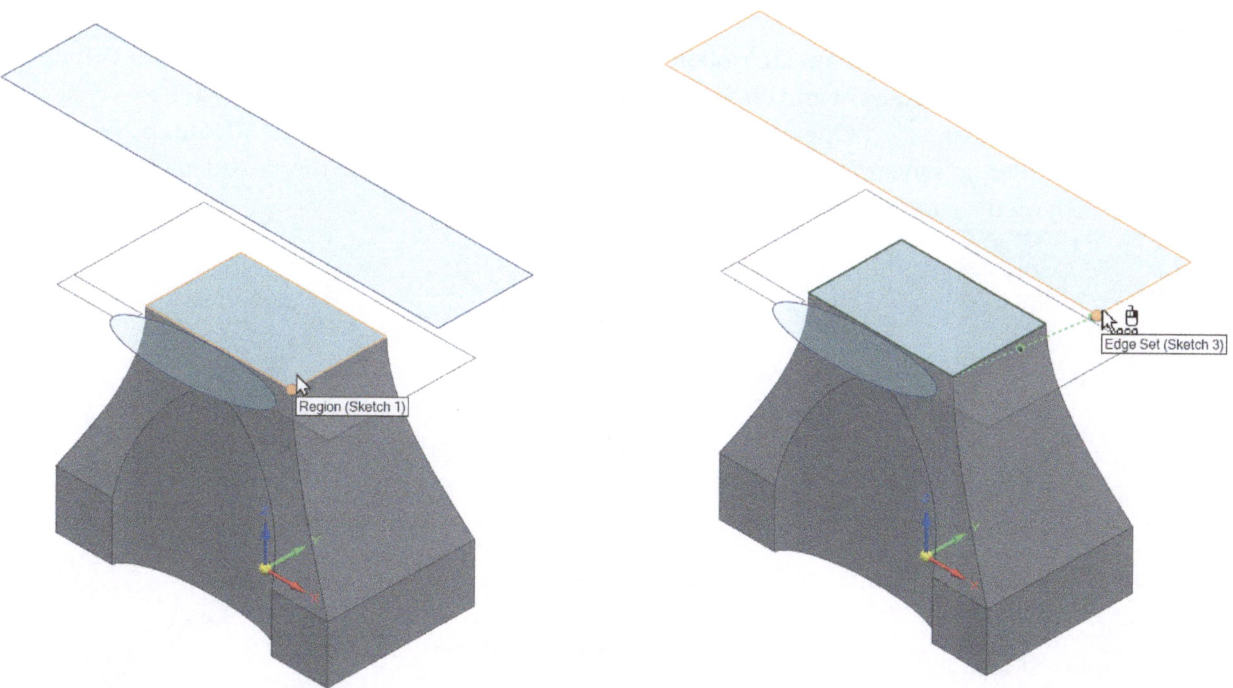

47. Click **Preview** on the command bar. Next, select **Curvature Continuous** from the Tangency control handle attached to the first section. Type 1 in the value box available on the Tangency control handle.
48. Click **Finish** and **Cancel** on the command bar.

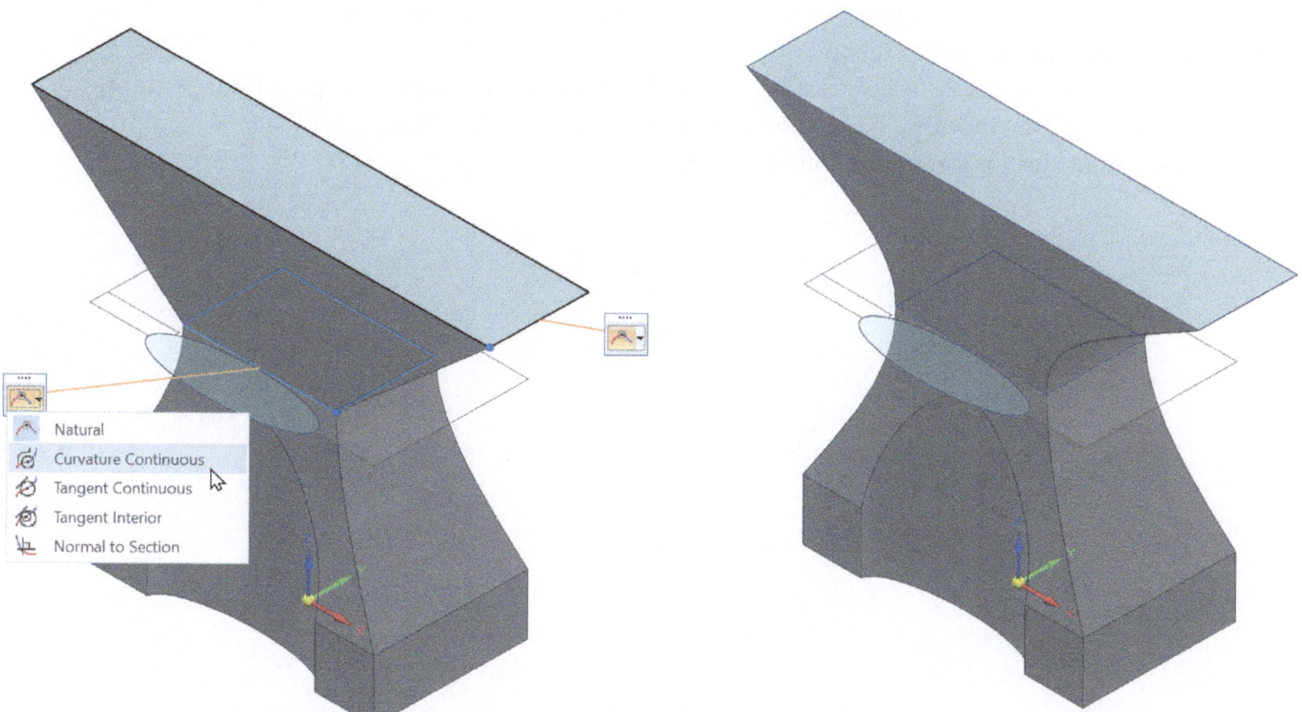

49. On the ribbon, click **Home > Solids > Extrude** and select the **Coincident Plane** option from the **Create-From Options** drop-down. Next, select the top face of the model.

50. Create a rectangle and add a dimension to it, as shown. Press **Esc** to deactivate the **Smart Dimension** command.
51. Click the **Close Sketch** button on the ribbon.
52. Move the pointer toward right and click to define the side of extrusion.
53. On the command bar, select **Operation** > **Cut**. Next, select the **Extent > Type > Through Next**.
54. Move the pointer downward and click in the graphics window to create the extruded cut.
55. Click **Finish** on the command bar.

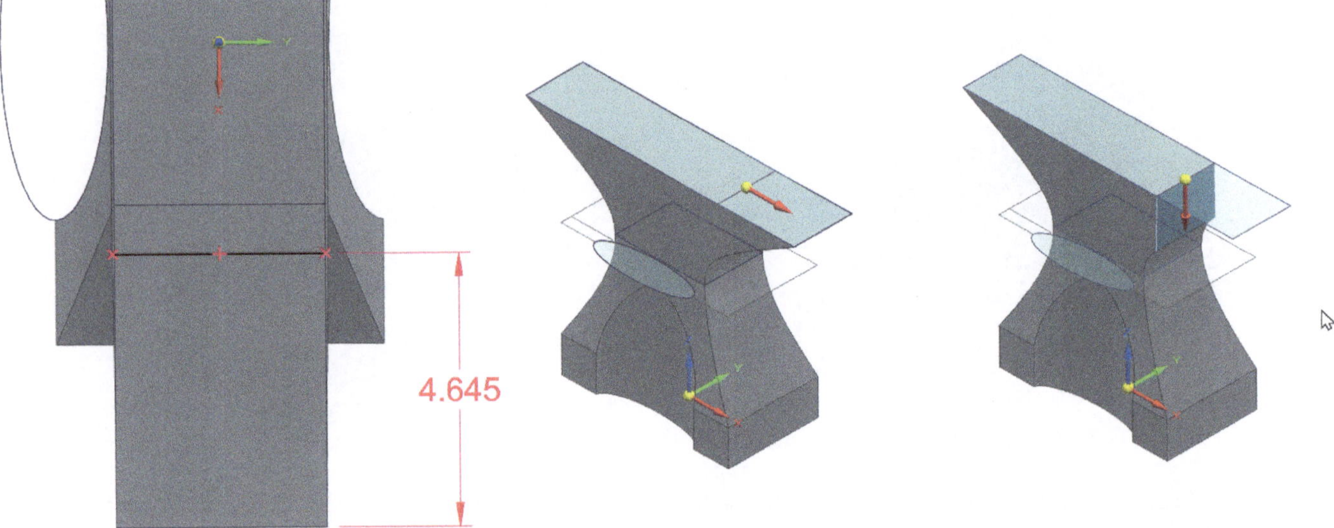

56. Click **Home > Solids > Extrude** on the ribbon, and then click on the top face of the model.
57. Create a rectangle by selecting the corner points of the top face, as shown.
58. Click **Close Sketch** on the ribbon.
59. On the command bar, select **Operation** > **Add**. Next, select the **Extent > Type > Finite Extent**.
60. Type **1** in the **Distance** box. Next, move the pointer upward and click.
61. Click **Finish** and **Cancel** on the command bar.

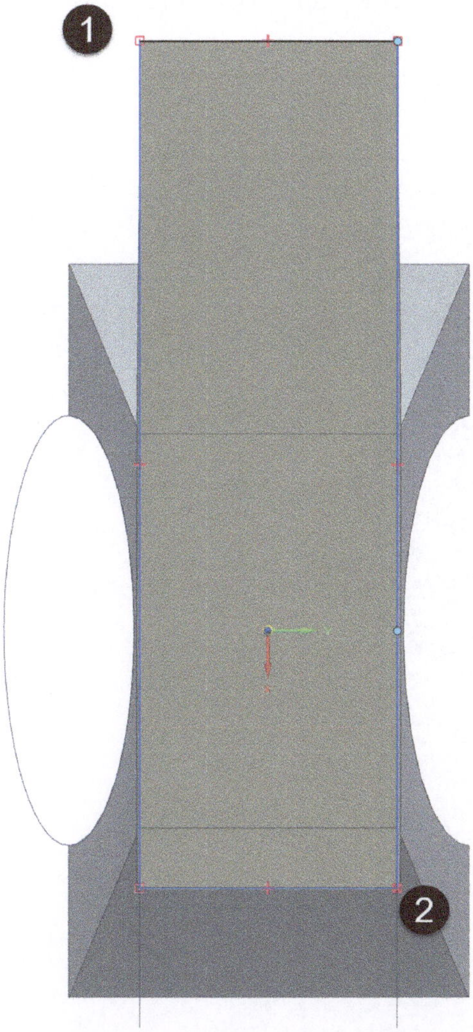

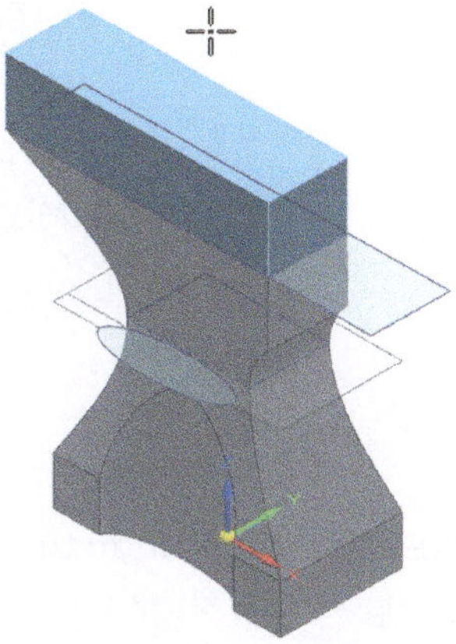

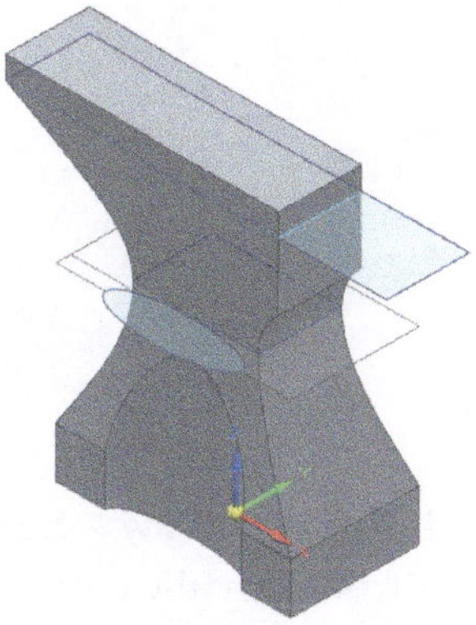

62. Click **Home > Sketch > Sketch** on the ribbon. Next, click on the right face.
63. Click **Home > Draw > Circle drop-down > Ellipse by 3 Points** on the ribbon.
64. Specify the three points of the ellipse, as shown. Next, click **Home > Relate > Connect** on the ribbon.
65. Select the left vertical edge of the sketch plane and the left quadrant of the ellipse.

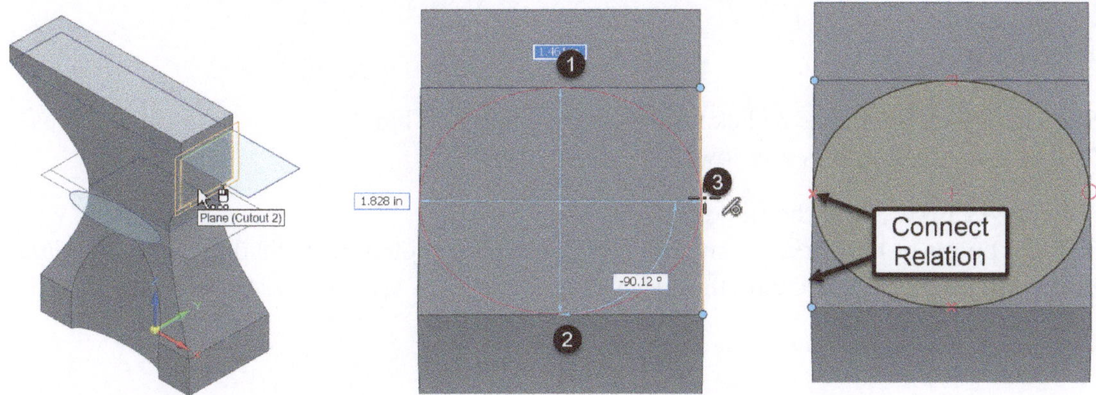

66. Click **Close Sketch** on the ribbon. Next, click **Finish** on the command bar.
67. On the **Sketch** command bar, select **Parallel Plane** from the **Create-From Options** drop-down.

68. Select the right flat face. Type **8.22** in the **Distance** box and press ENTER. Next, move it towards the right and click.

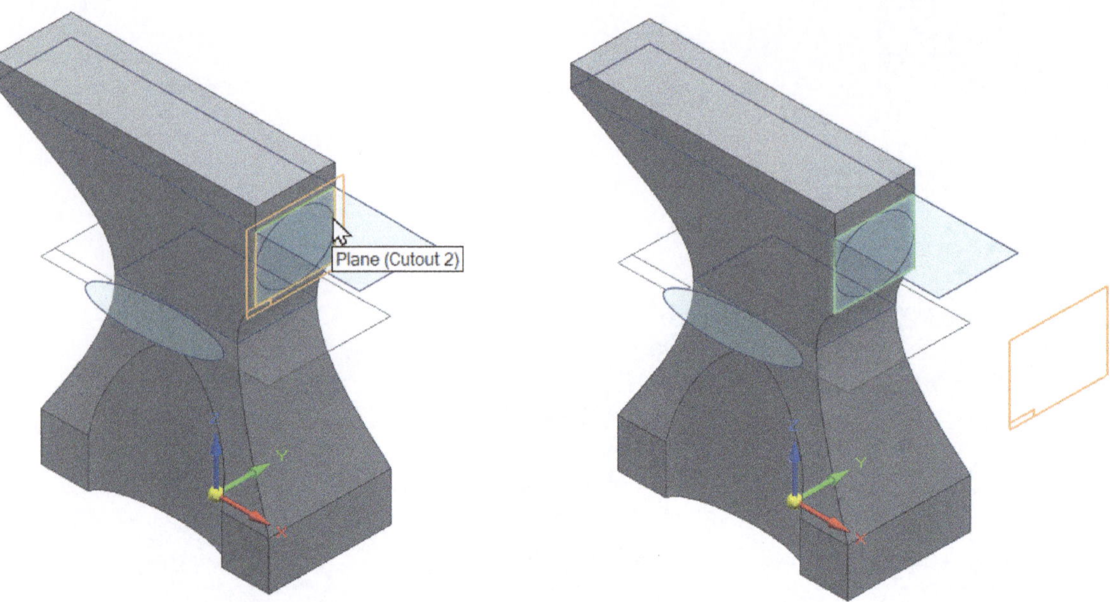

69. Click **Home > Draw > Line** drop-down **> Point** on the ribbon.
70. Click to specify the location of the point, as shown.

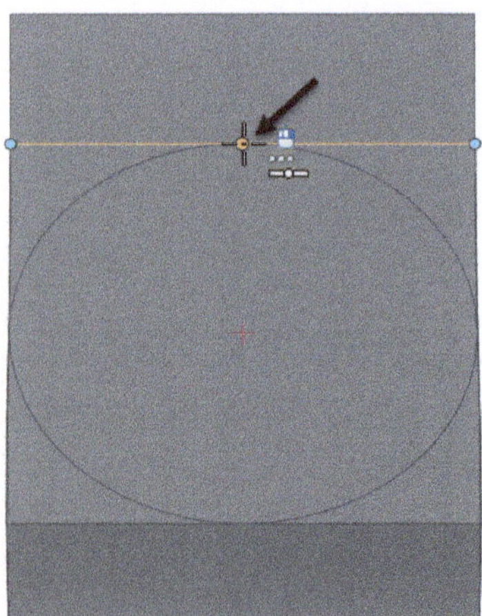

71. Click **Close Sketch** on the ribbon. Next, click **Finish** on the command bar.
72. Select the **XZ** plane from the graphics window.
73. Click **Home > Draw > Curve** on the ribbon.
74. Specify the first two points of the curve, as shown. Next, select the sketch point displayed on the plane to specify the third point. Right click to create the curve.

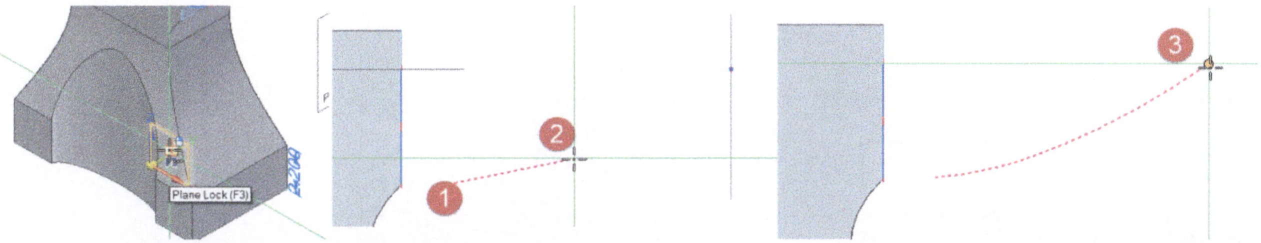

75. Click **Home > Relate > Connect** on the ribbon and select the start point of the curve. Next, select the bottom quadrant point of the ellipse, as shown.

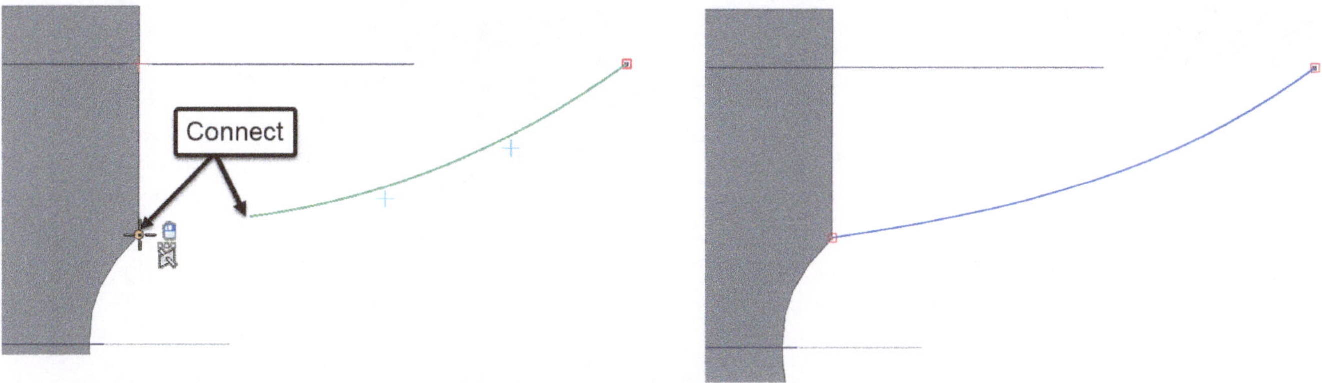

76. Click **Close Sketch** on the ribbon. Next, click **Finish** on the command bar.
77. Select the **XZ** plane from the graphics window.
78. Click **Home > Draw > Line** on the ribbon and create a line connecting the top quadrant point of the ellipse and the sketch point.

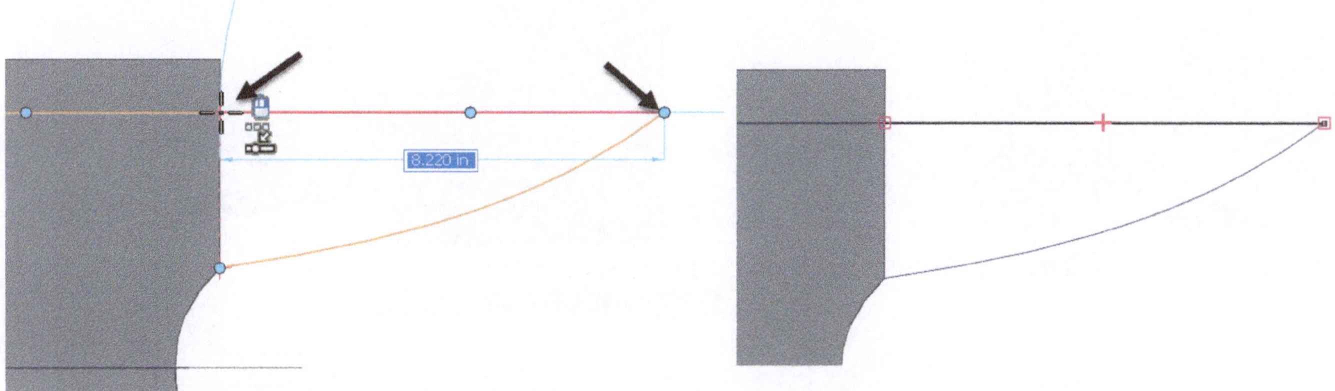

79. Click **Close Sketch** on the ribbon. Next, click **Finish** and **Cancel** on the command bar.
80. Click **Home > Solids > Add** drop-down **> Loft** on the ribbon and select the ellipse.
81. On the command bar, select **Select > Point**, and then select the sketch point.
82. Click the **Guide Curve** section on the command bar and select **Select > Single**.
83. Select the first guide curve, as shown. Next, click the green check button on the command bar.
84. Select the second guide curve, and then click the green button.
85. Click the **Preview** button, and then click **Finish** and **Cancel**.

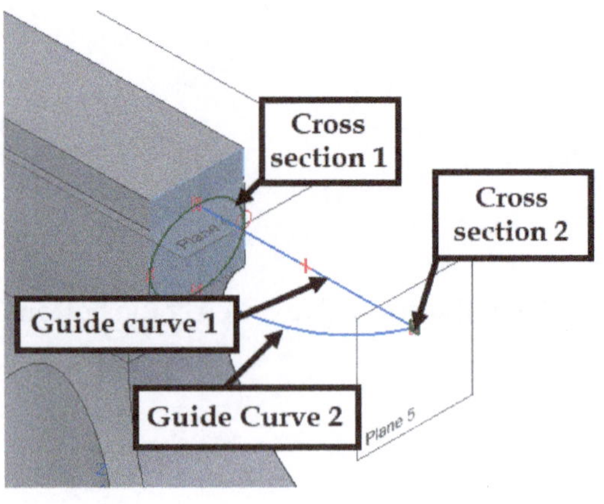

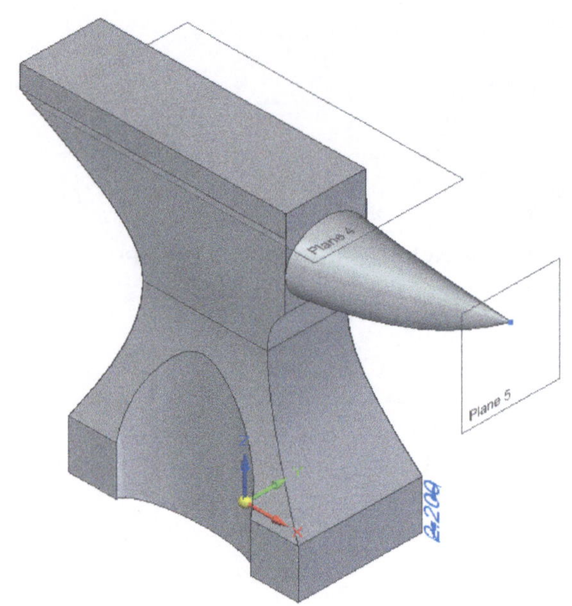

86. Create a cut feature on the side face, as shown.

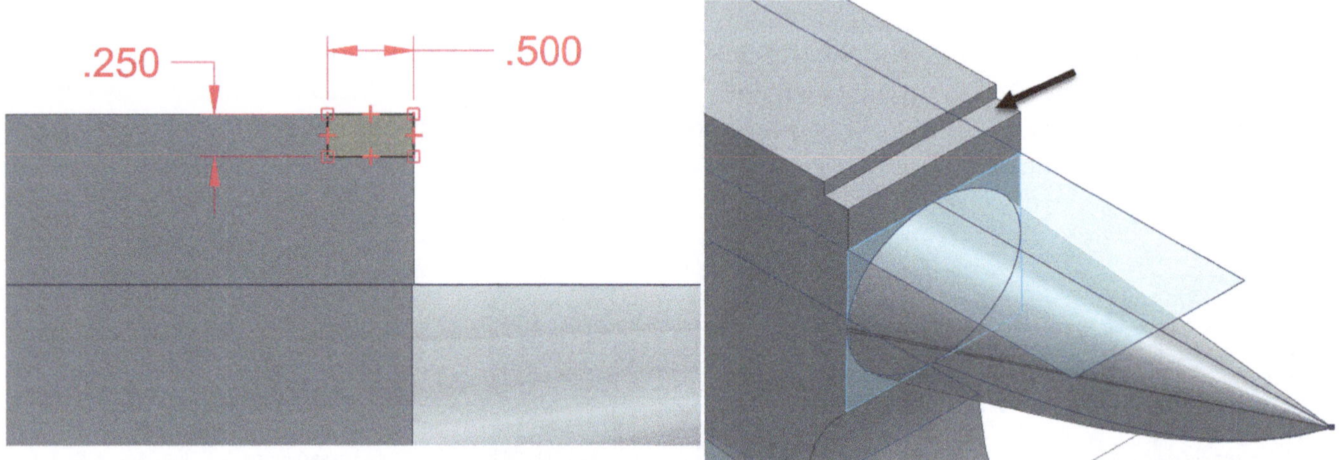

87. Create a hole and the square-cut features on the top face, as shown.

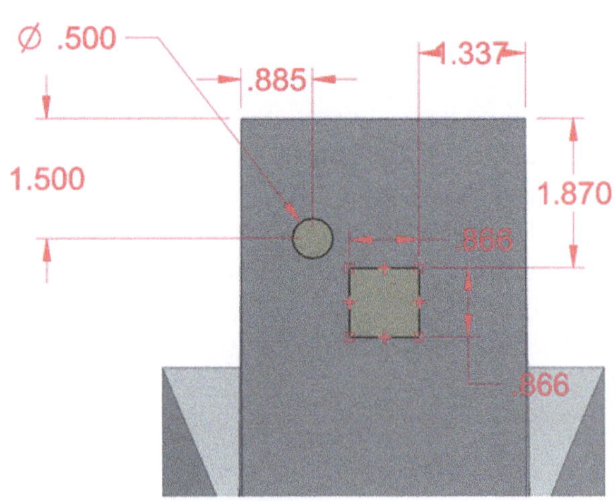

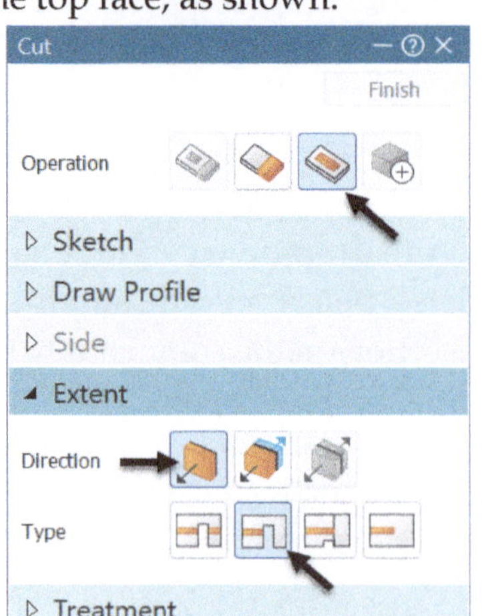

88. Save and close the file.

Questions

1. Describe the procedure to create a *Loft* feature.
2. List any two **Tangency Control** options.
3. List the type of elements that can be selected to create a *Loft* feature.

Exercises

Exercise 1

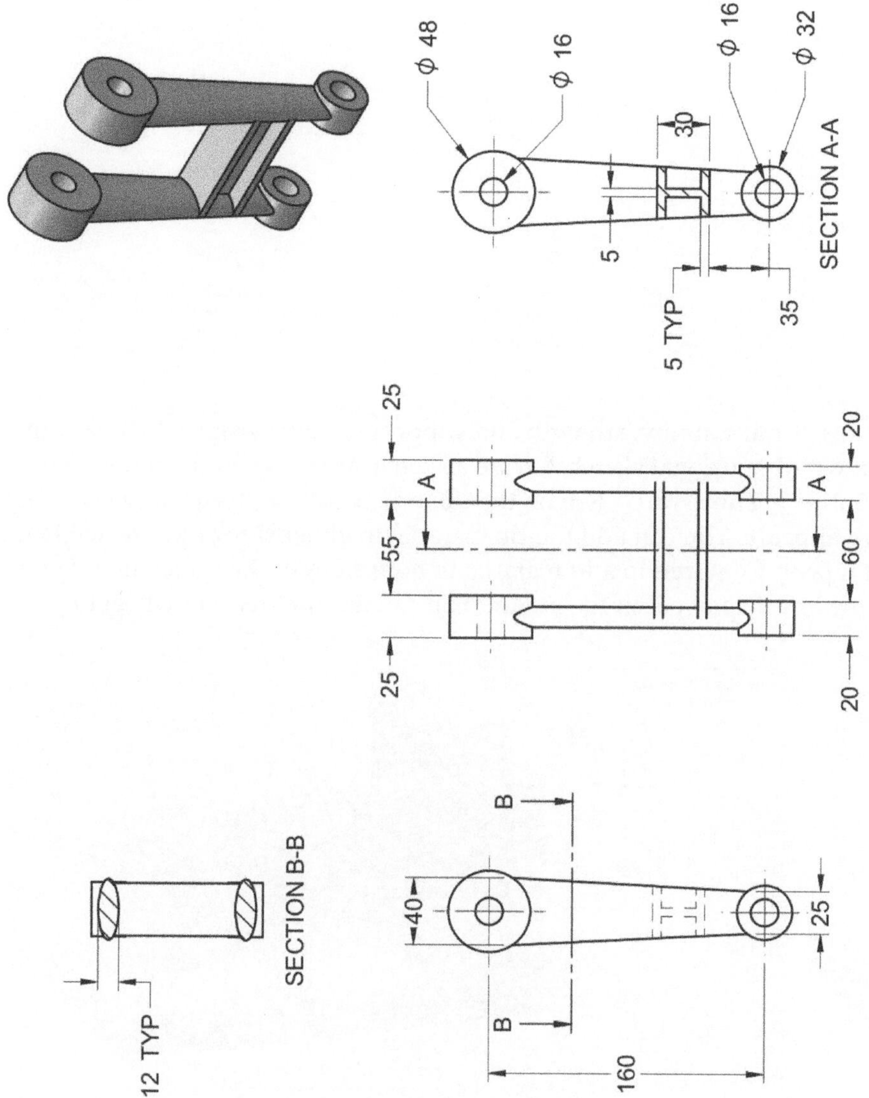

Chapter 8: Additional Features and Multibody Parts

Solid Edge offers you some additional commands and features which will help you to create complex models. These commands are explained in this chapter.

The topics covered in this chapter are:

- *Ribs*
- *Web Network*
- *Mounting bosses*
- *Lips*
- *Vents*
- *Slots*
- *Multi-body parts*
- *Split bodies*
- *Boolean Operations*
- *Emboss features*

Rib (Synchronous)

This command creates a rib feature to add structural stability, strength and support to your designs. Just like any other sketch-based feature, a rib requires a two-dimensional sketch. Create a sketch, as shown in the figure and activate the **Rib** command (click **Home > Solids > Thin Wall > Rib** on the ribbon). Select the sketch and click the **Accept** button; the preview of the geometry appears. You can add the rib material to either side of the sketch line or evenly to both sides. Set the **Alignment** type to **Centered** to add material to both sides of the sketch line. Type-in the thickness value of the rib feature in the box displayed on the model. You can use the steering wheel to change the direction of the rib.

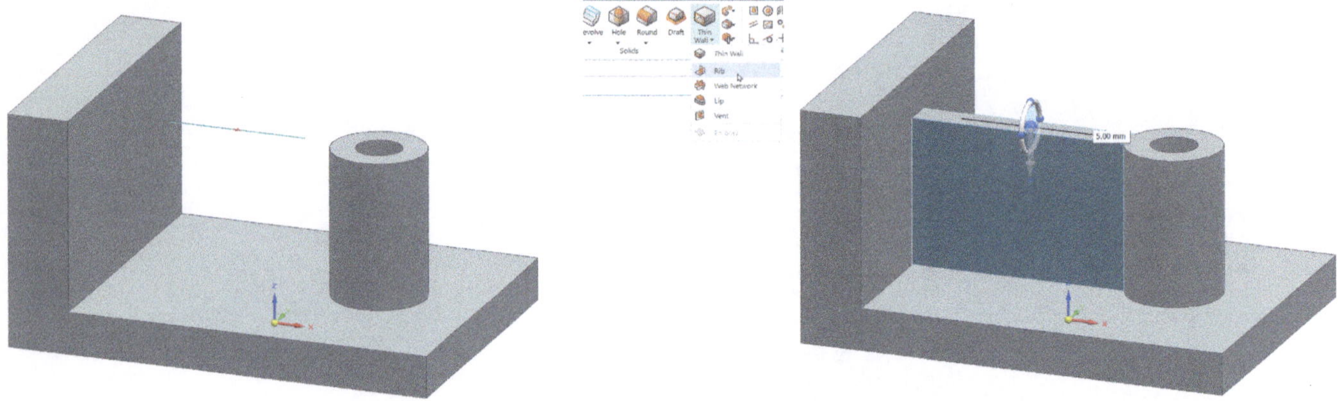

If you activate the **No Extend** option on the command bar, the material will not extend to meet the surrounding features' faces.

Activate the **Finite Depth** option if you want to add material only up to some distance. Click the green check to complete the rib feature.

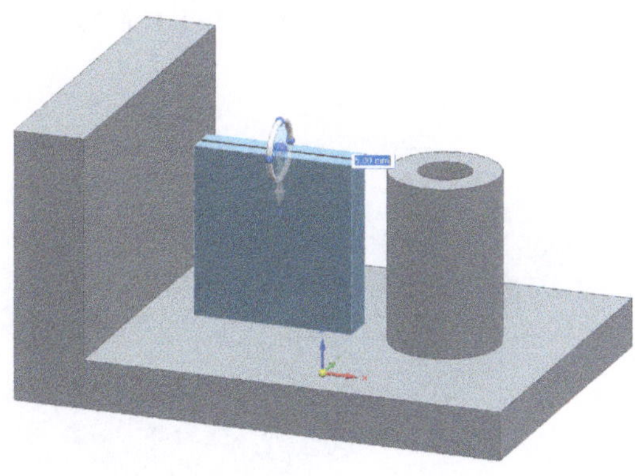

No Extend

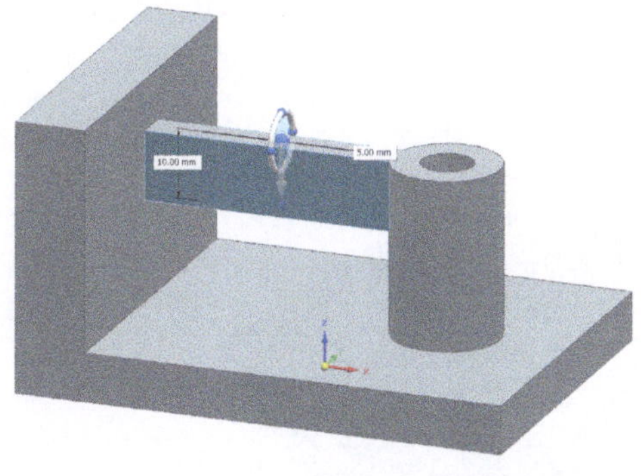

Finite Depth

Rib (Ordered)

Use the **Rib** feature to add structural reinforcement to parts. To create a rib feature, first create a sketch, as shown in the figure and activate the **Rib** command (click **Home > Solids > Thin Wall > Rib** on the ribbon). Choose the sketch and click the green check. Subsequently, input a value in the **Thickness** box. Move the pointer and click to indicate the direction of the rib feature.

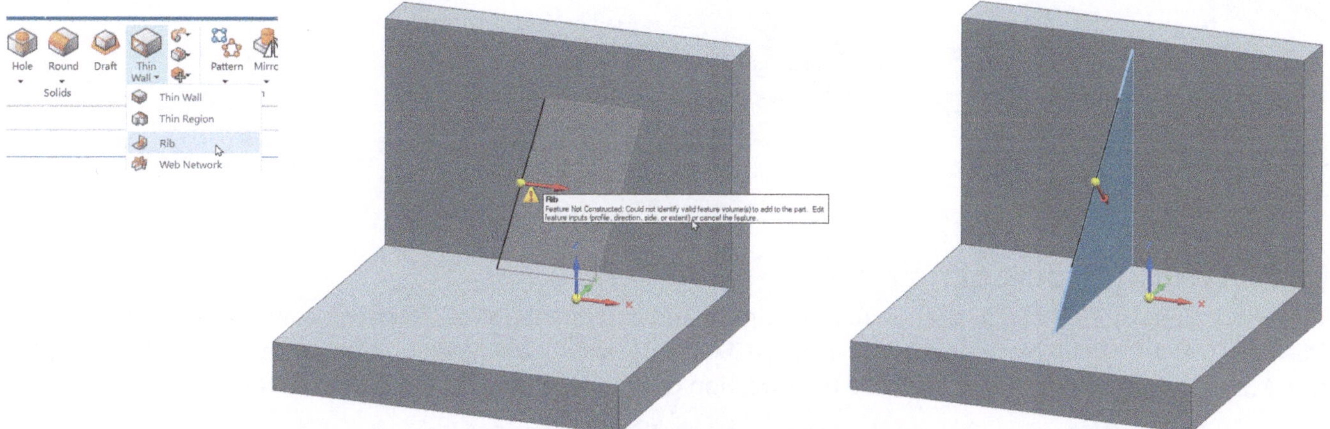

Use the **Side** section to choose which side of the profile will receive the added material. Click on either side of the profile to set the direction, or select the dot on the arrow to create a symmetrical rib. Then click **Finish** or **Cancel** in the command bar.

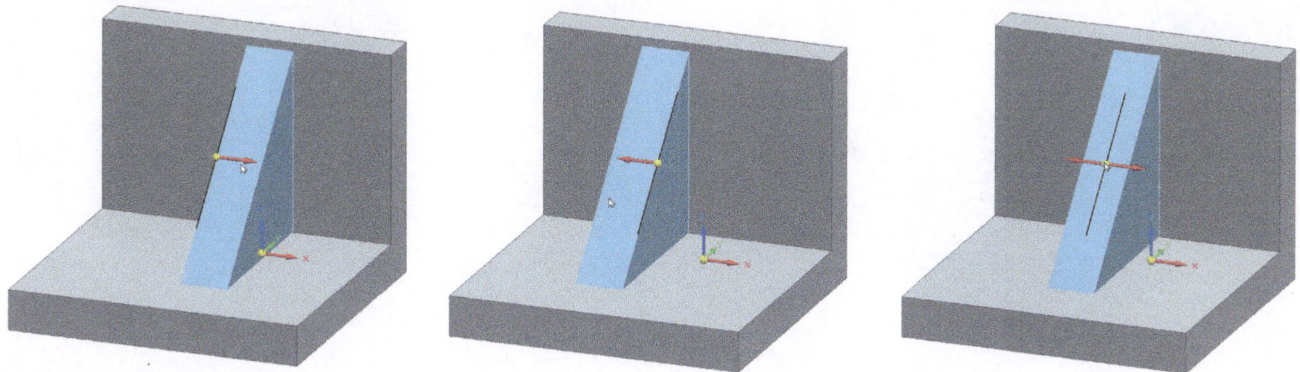

Web Network (Synchronous)

This command is similar to the **Rib** command but creates multiple ribs simultaneously, forming a network. Create a two-dimensional sketch, as shown in the figure and activate the **Web Network** command (Click **Home >**

Solids > Thin Wall > Web Networks on the ribbon). Select the sketch elements one-by-one and click the **Accept** button; the preview of the geometry appears.

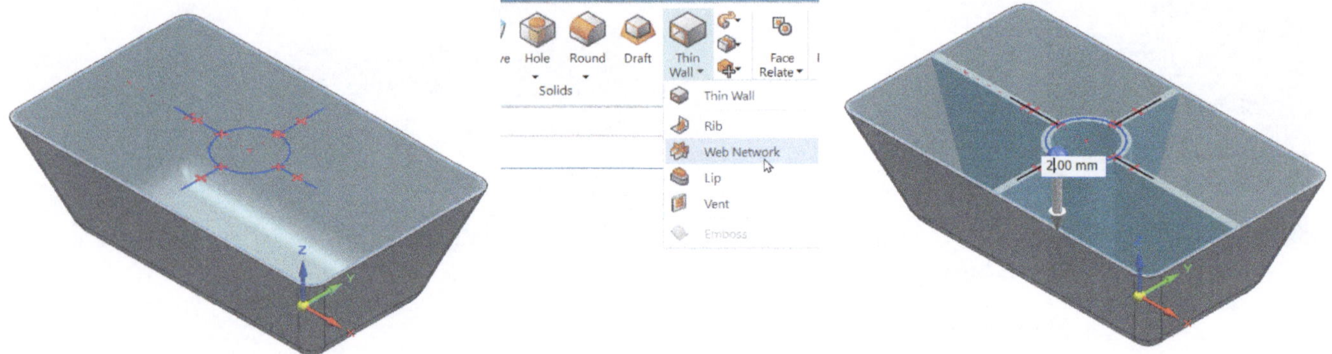

Use the **Draft** option on the command bar to add a draft to the web network feature. Click the **Accept** button to complete the feature.

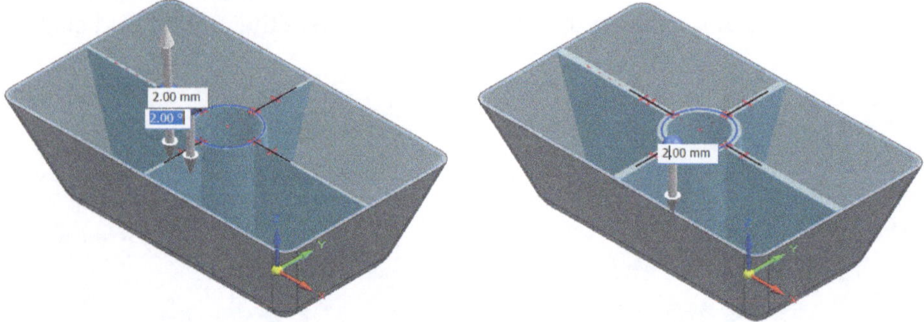

Web Network(Ordered)

Create a two-dimensional sketch, as shown in the figure and activate the **Web Network** command (Click **Home > Solids > Thin Wall > Web Networks** on the ribbon). Select the sketch elements one-by-one and click the **Accept** button. Move the pointer and click to define the direction of the web network. Click the **Finish** button.

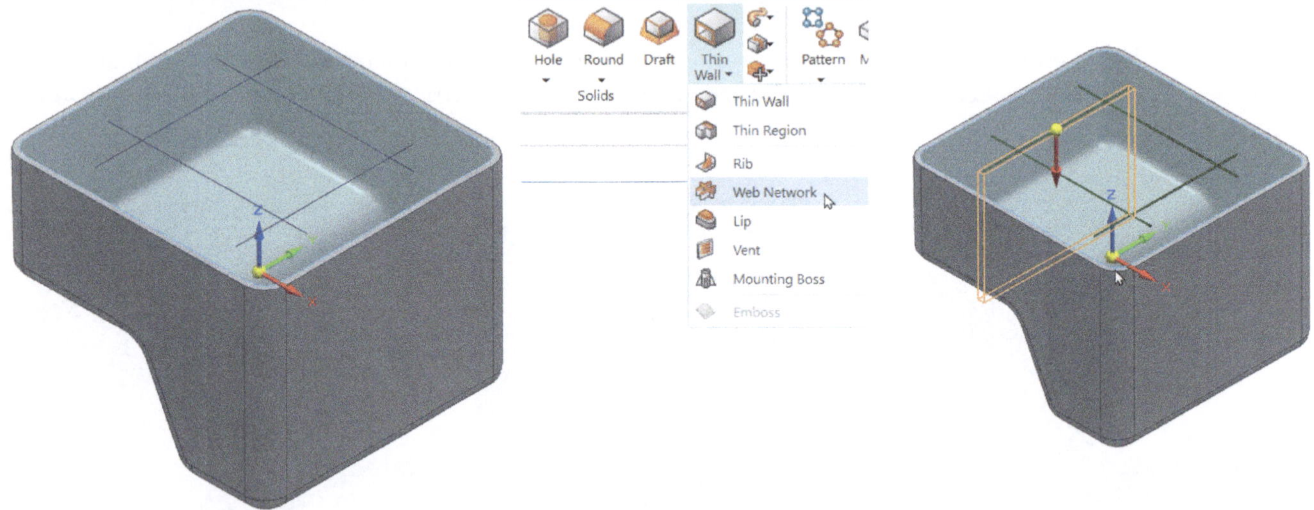

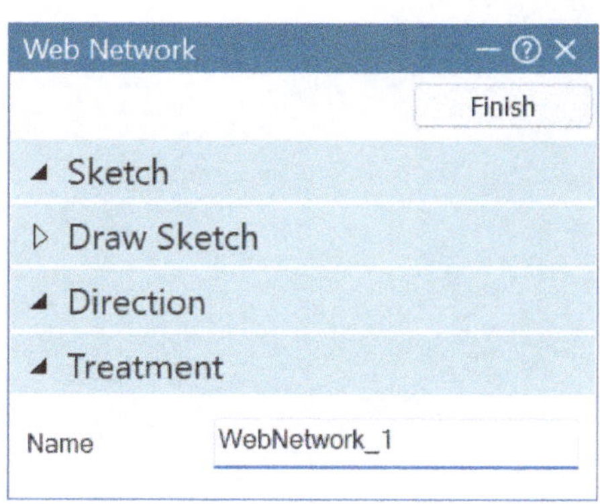

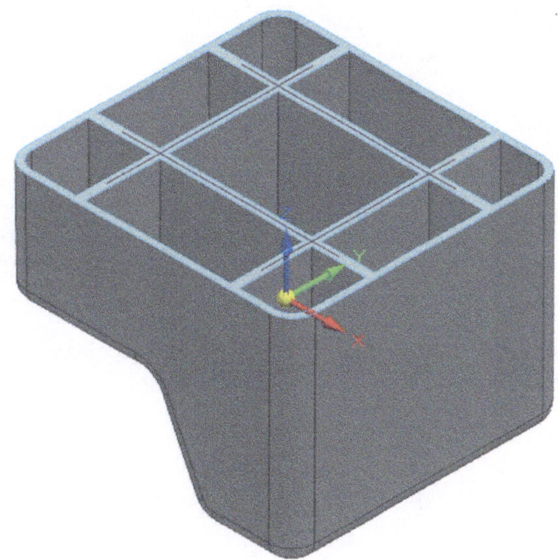

Mounting Boss

The process of creating mounting bosses can be automated using the **Mounting Boss** command. This command is available only in the Ordered mode. Switch to the Ordered mode and activate the **Mounting Boss** command (click **Home > Solids > Thin Wall > Mounting Boss** on the ribbon). On the command bar, select **Coincident Plane** from the **Create from Options** drop-down menu. Select the top face of the model and define the location of the mounting bosses. Click **Close Sketch** on the ribbon and define the side of the bosses.

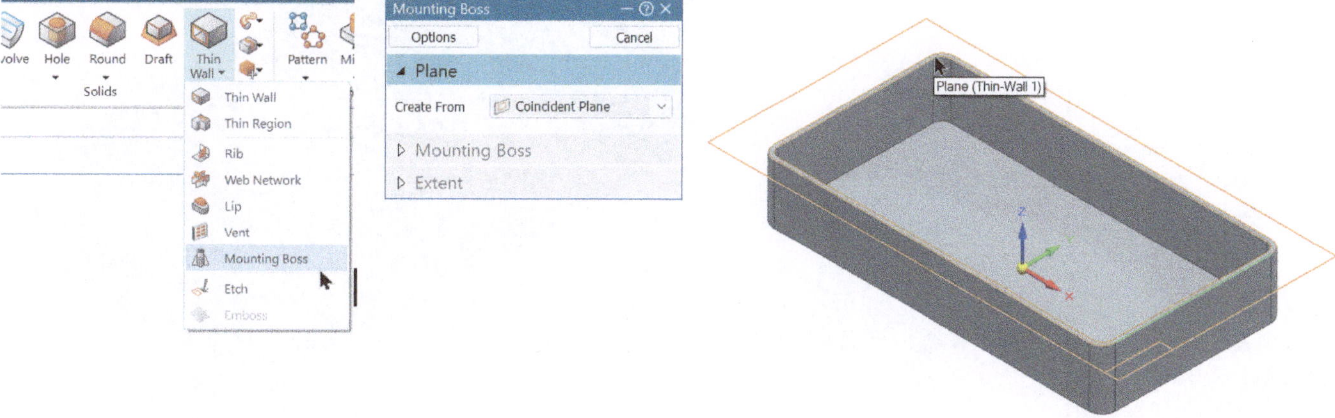

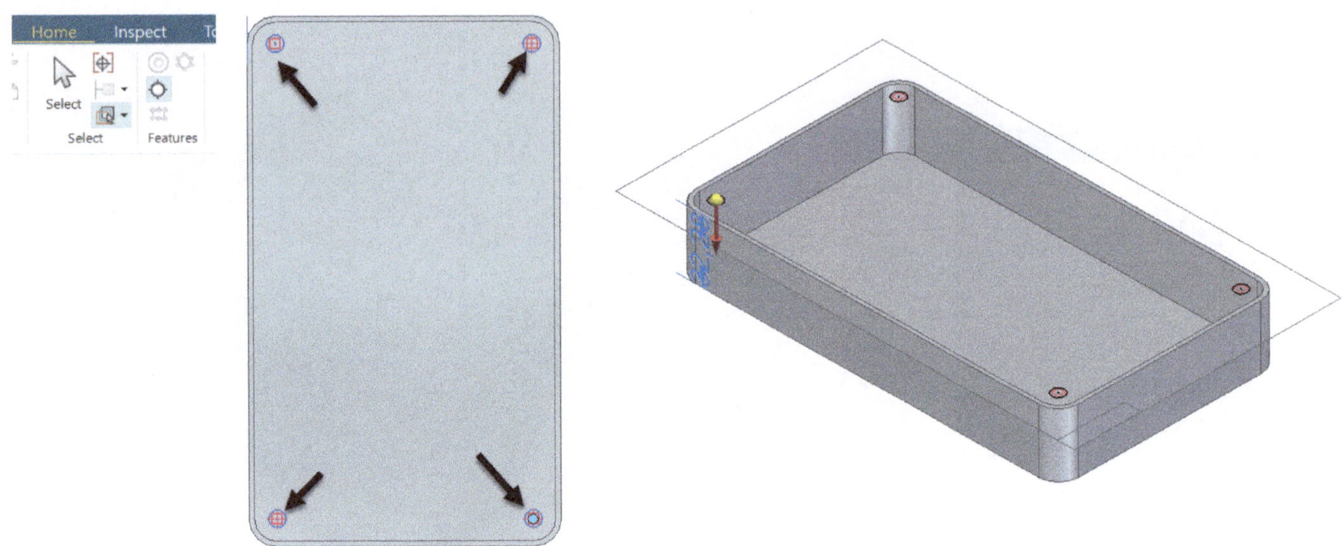

Click the **Options** icon on the command bar; the **Mounting Boss Options** dialog pops up on the screen. Define the parameters of the mounting boss. The parameters are self-explanatory. Click **OK** and then **Finish** completing the feature.

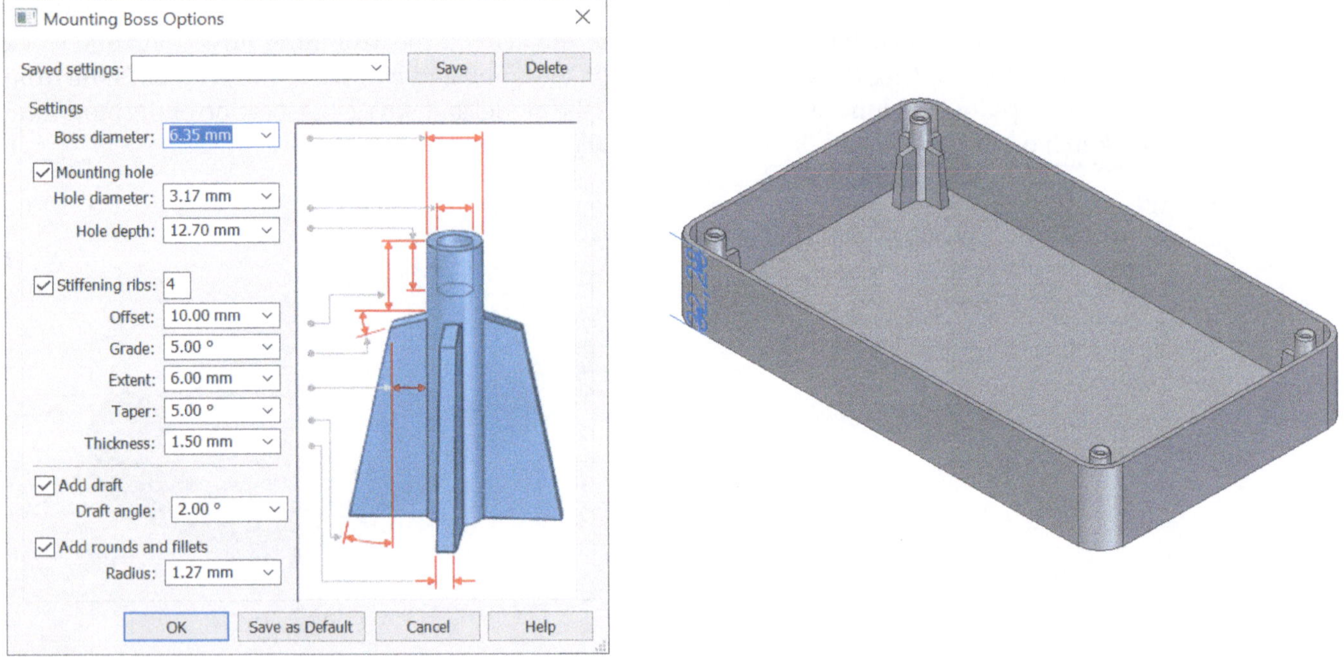

Lip

This command allows you to create lips and grooves on the edges of parts, saving you time by not creating a series of manual cuts. Activate this command (click **Home > Solids > Thin Wall > Lip** on the ribbon) and select a chain of edges. Click the green check on the command bar and define the side of the lip. Click the left mouse button, and then click **Finish** to complete the feature.

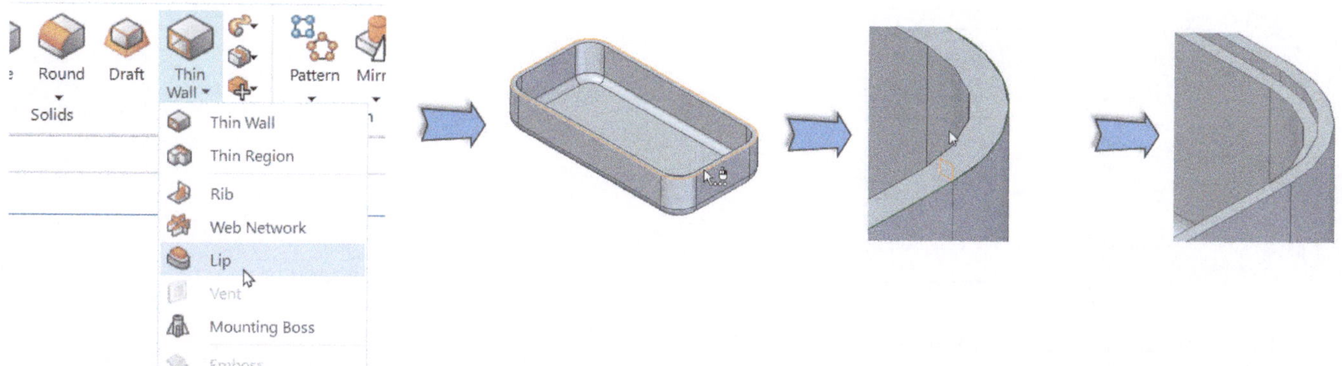

Vent (Synchronous and Ordered)

This command allows you to take a two-dimensional sketch of a vent and convert it into a 3D cutout. To create a vent feature, first, create a 2D sketch and activate the **Vent** command (click **Home > Solids > Thin Wall > Vent** on the ribbon). As you activate this command, the **Vent Options** dialog pops up on the screen.

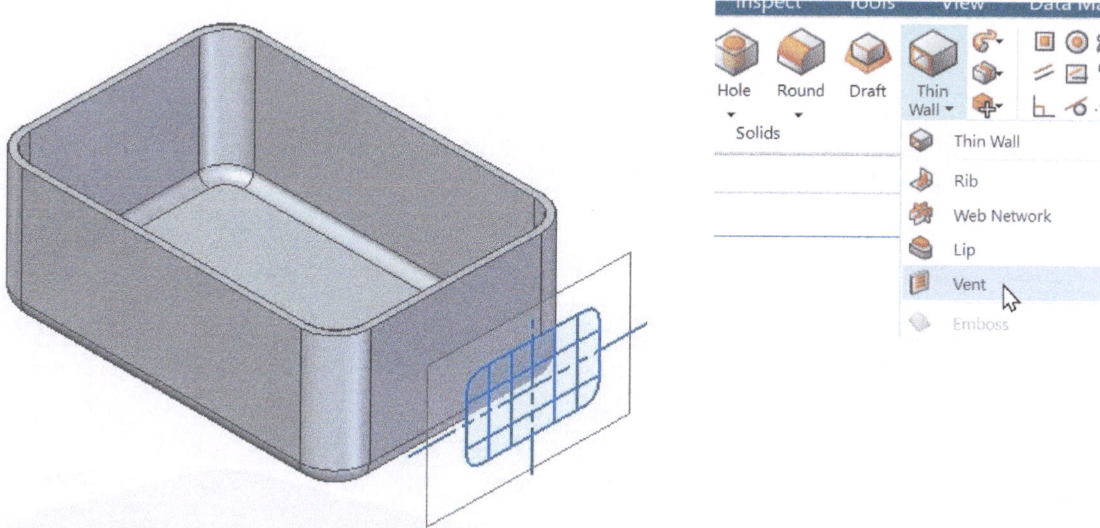

Set the thickness of **Ribs** and **Spars** to 4.

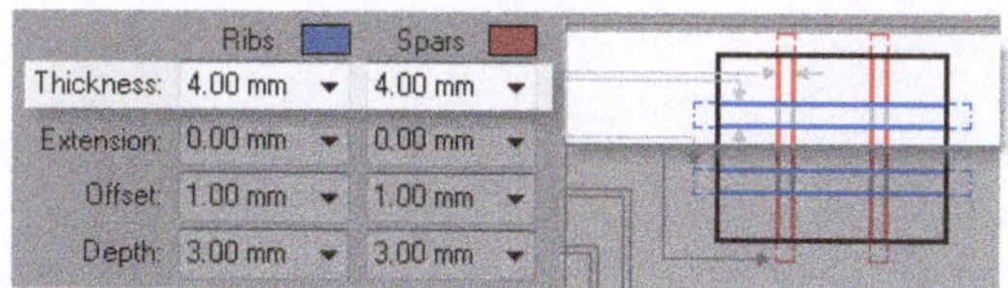

Set the **Offset** values to 1 and **Depth** to 3.

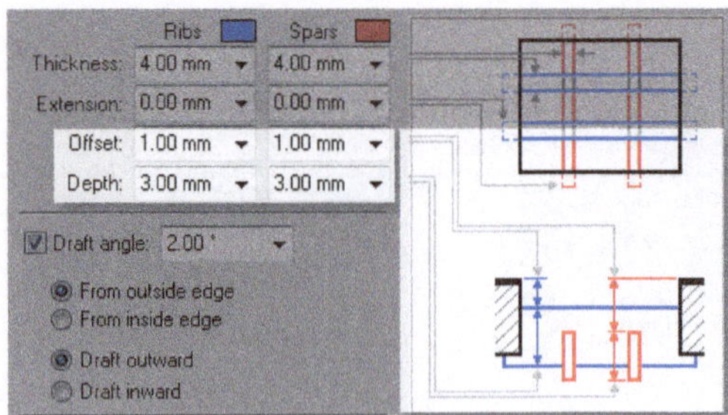

Check the **Draft angle** option and enter 5 in the box.
Check the **Round & fillet radius** option and enter 0.5 in the box. Click **OK** on the dialog.

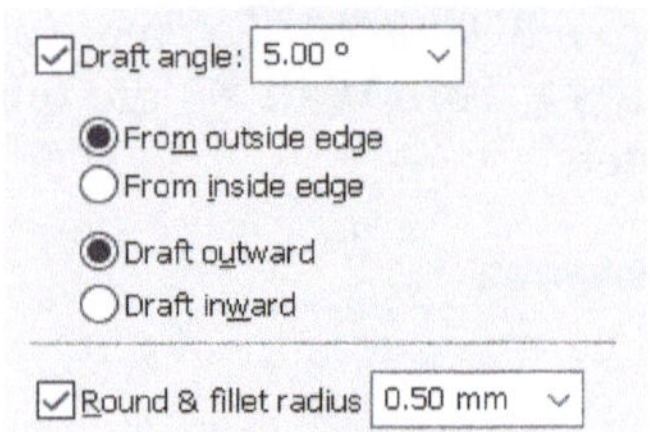

Select the boundary and click the green check on the command bar. Likewise, select the ribs and spars, and then click the **Accept** button. Next, click on the model to define the side of the vent. Click **Finish** to complete the feature.

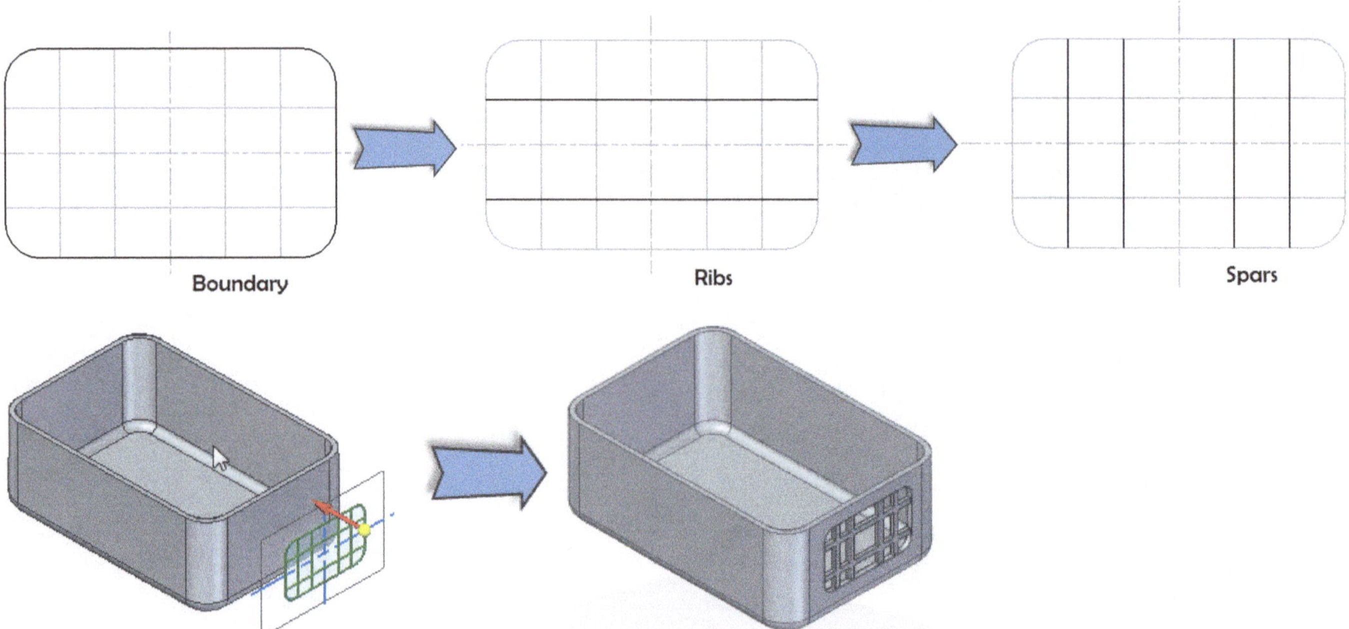

Slot

This command creates a slot by using a 2D sketch. The sketch can have single or multiple elements. If the sketch has multiple elements, they should be tangent and continuous to each other. To create a slot, create a 2D sketch on a face, and then activate the **Slot** command (click **Home > Solids > Hole > Slot** on the command); the command bar pops up on the screen. Click the **Options** icon on the command bar to open the **Slot Options** dialog. Type-in a value in the **Slot width** box and select the end type. Click **OK** and select the sketch. Next, define the extent of the slot feature. Click the right mouse button to complete the slot feature.

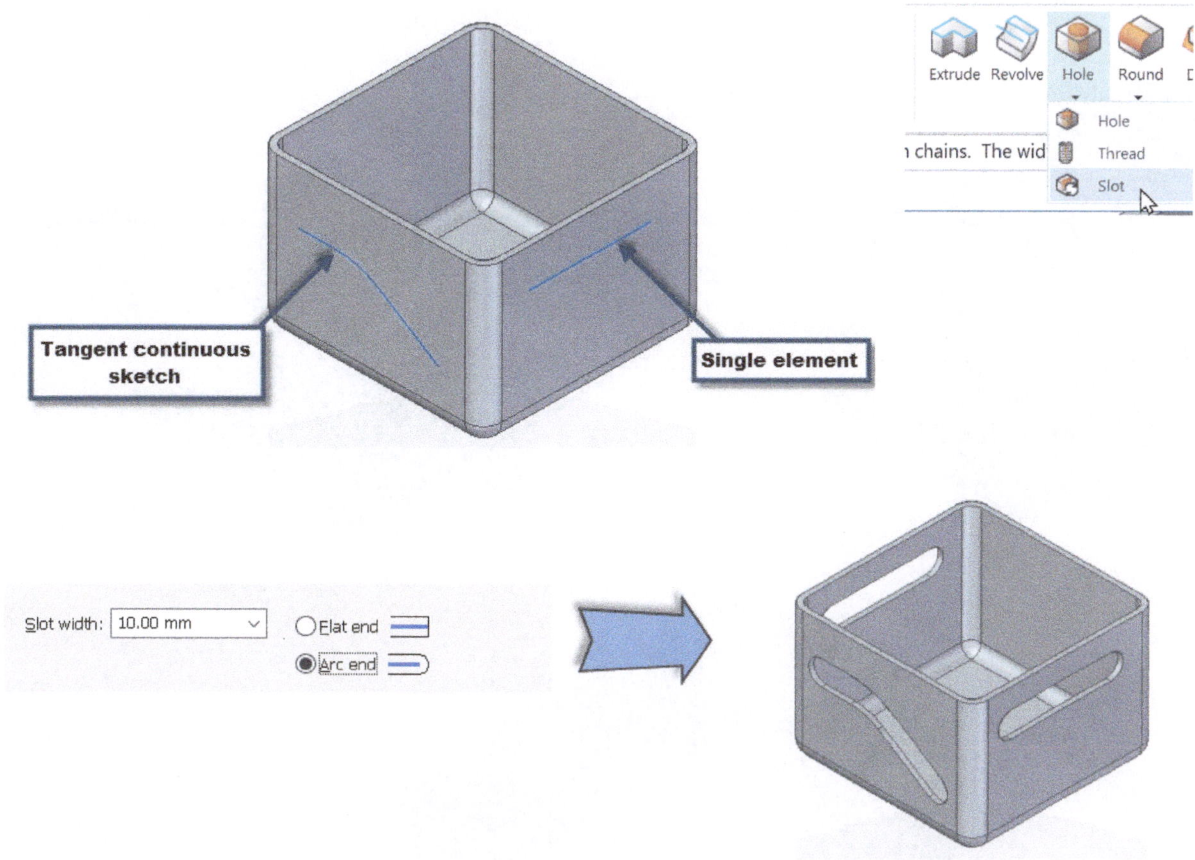

If you want to create a counterbore slot, check the **Counterbore** option on the **Slot Options** dialog and define the **Path Offset** and **Depth Offset** values. You can create two types of counterbore slots: **Recessed** and **Raised**.

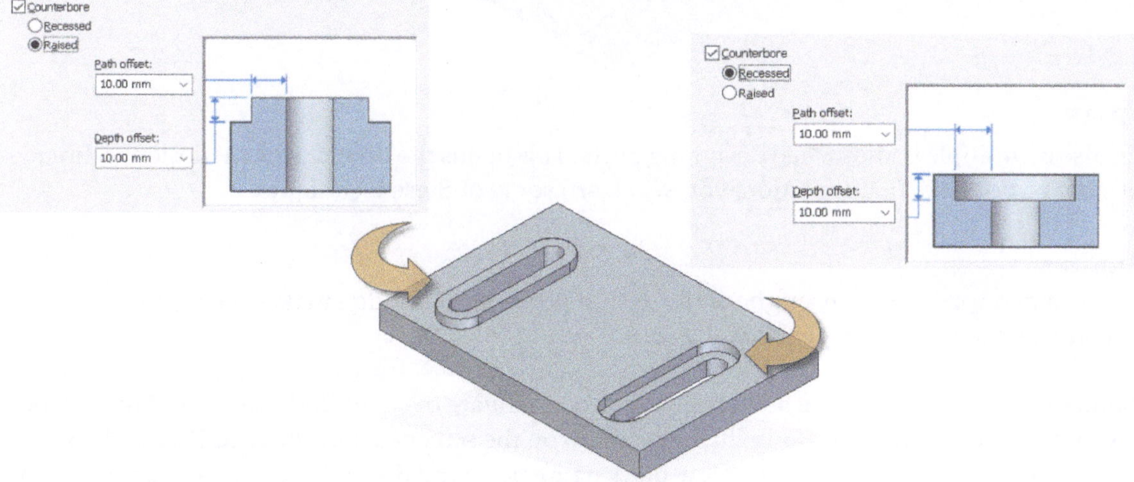

Creating Multiple Slots (Synchronous)

In Solid Edge, you can create multiple slots in a single instance by selecting elements with identical parameters. You can only select the sketch elements lying on the same plane or face. Activate the **Slot** command (on the ribbon, click **Home > Solids > Hole > Slot**), and then select the first sketch element. Next, define the extent of the slot using the options available in the **Extents** drop-down. After defining the extents, select the remaining sketch elements one-by-one or by dragging a selection window across them. You can press hold the Shift or Ctrl key and then click on the selected sketch elements to remove them from the selection. Right-click in the space to complete the feature.

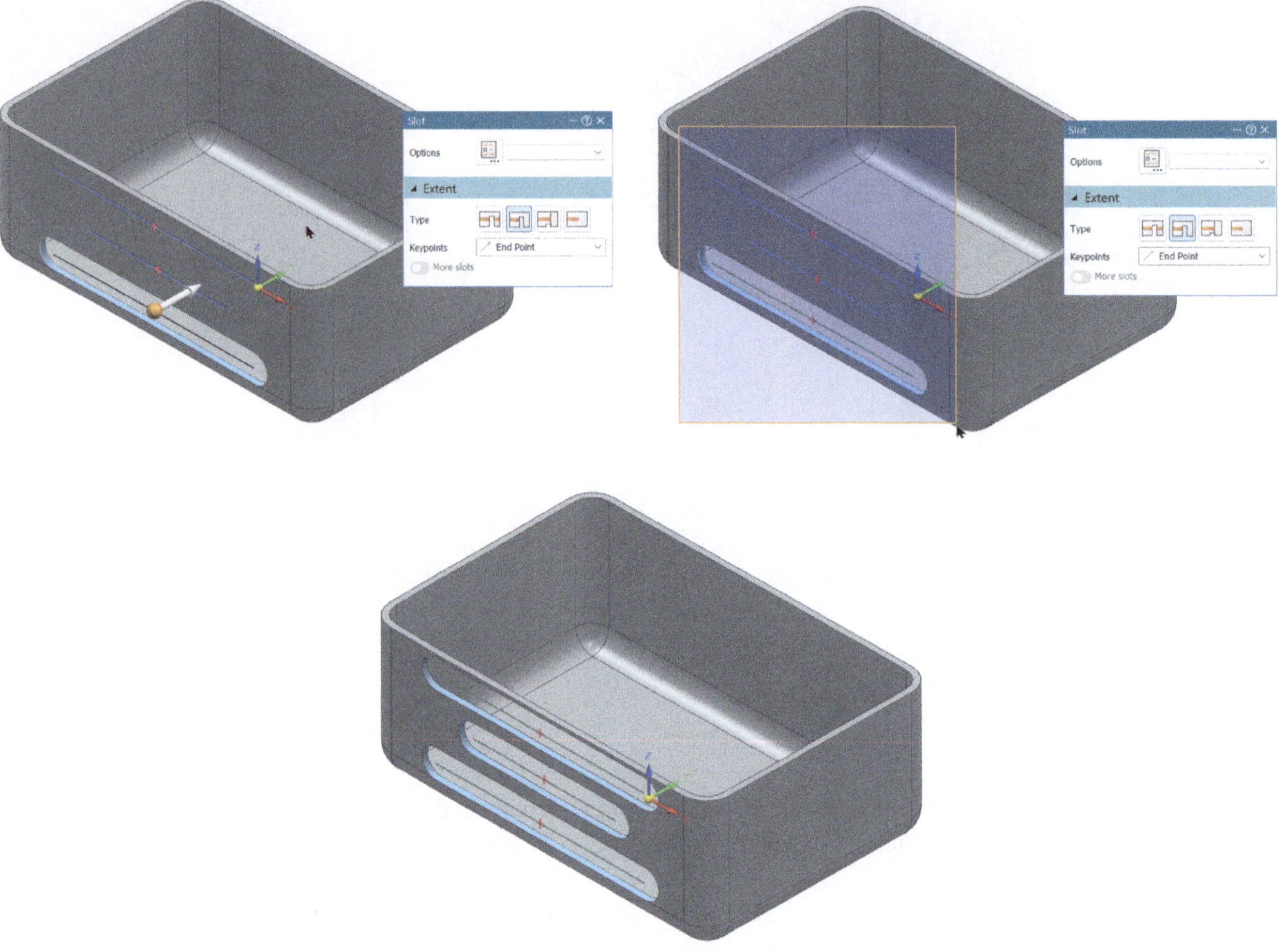

Multi-body Parts

Solid Edge allows the use of multiple bodies when designing parts. This opens the door to several design techniques that would otherwise not be possible. In this section, you will learn some of these techniques.

Creating Multibodies

The number of bodies in a part can change throughout the design process. Solid Edge makes it easy to create multiple bodies and combine them into a single body.

To create multiple bodies in a part, first, create a solid body, and then activate the **Add Body** command (click **Home > Solids > Add Body** on the ribbon); the **Add Body** dialog pops up on the screen. Select the **Add Part body** or **Add Sheet Metal body** option, enter the body name in the **New body name** field, and then click **OK**. Now, create another solid body using any solid modeling tools; the **Design Bodies** entry will be added to the **Pathfinder** tree.

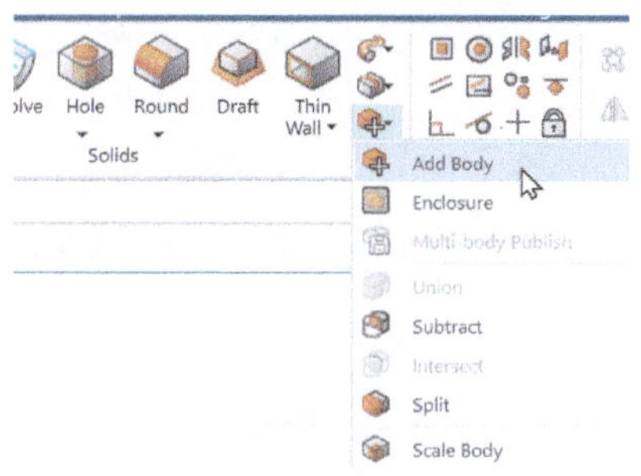

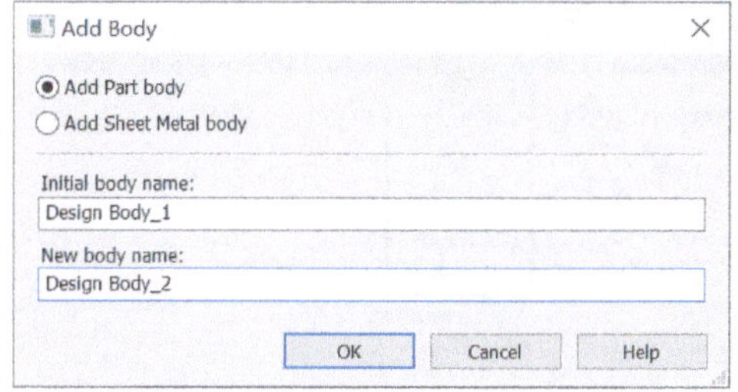

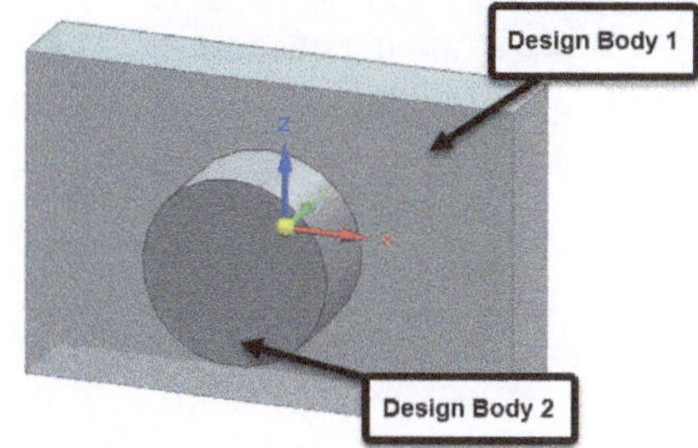

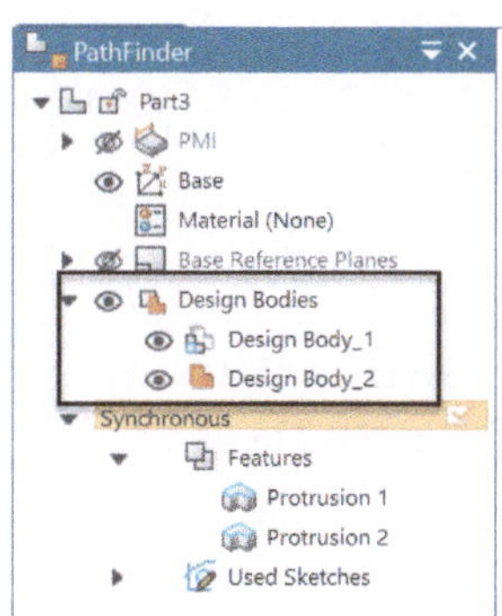

Split

The **Split** command can be used to separate single bodies into multiple bodies. This command can be used to perform local operations. For example, if you apply the shell feature to the front portion of the model shown in the figure, the whole model will be shelled. To solve this problem, you must split the solid body into multiple bodies.

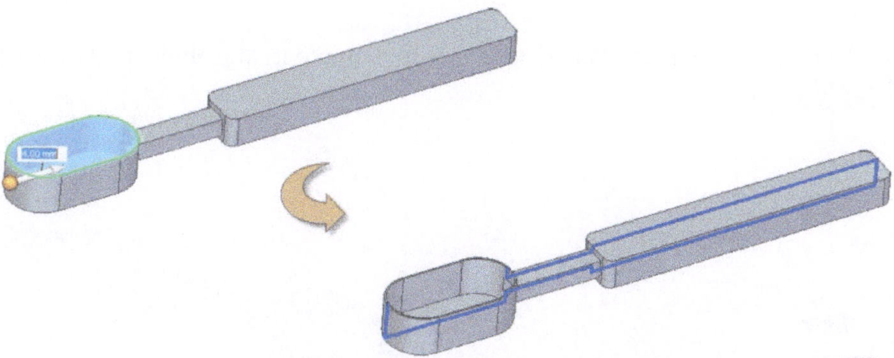

To split a body, you must have a splitting tool such as planes, sketch elements, surfaces, or bodies. In this case, a surface can be used as a splitting tool. To create a surface, activate the **Bounded** command (click **Surfacing > Surfaces > Bounded** on the ribbon) and set the **Selection Type** on the command bar to **Single**. Now, select the edges, as shown in the figure. Click the green check on the command bar and click **Finish** to create the bounded surface.

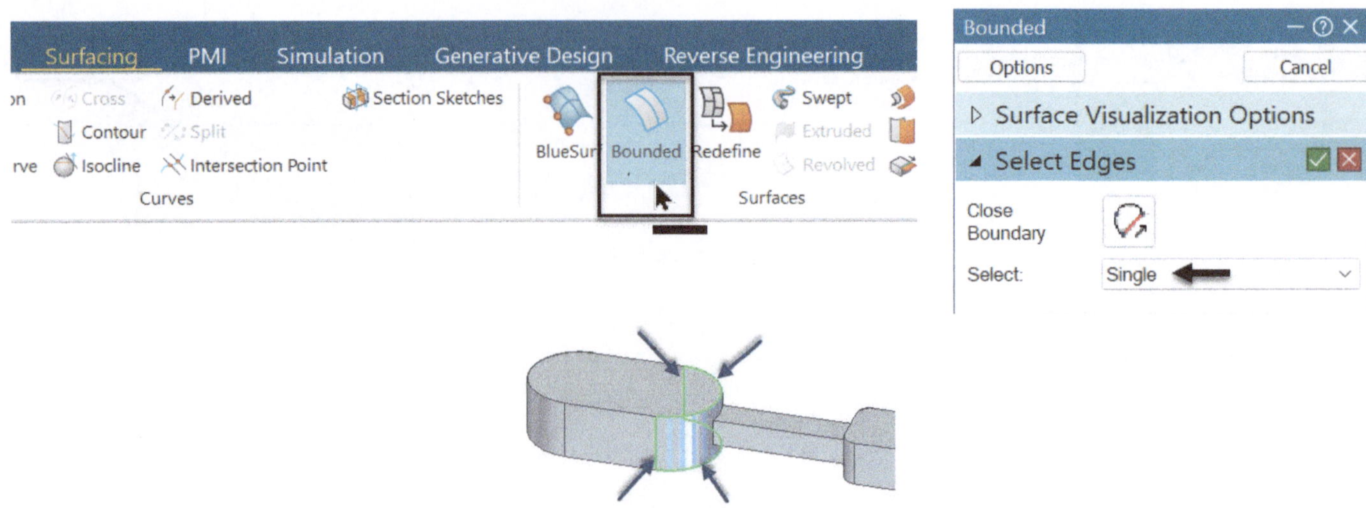

Activate the **Split** command (click **Home > Solids >Add Body** > **Split** on the ribbon) and select the solid body from the graphics window. Next, select the bounded surface as the splitting tool and click the green check on the command bar. This results in two separate bodies. Press Esc to deactivate the **Split** command.

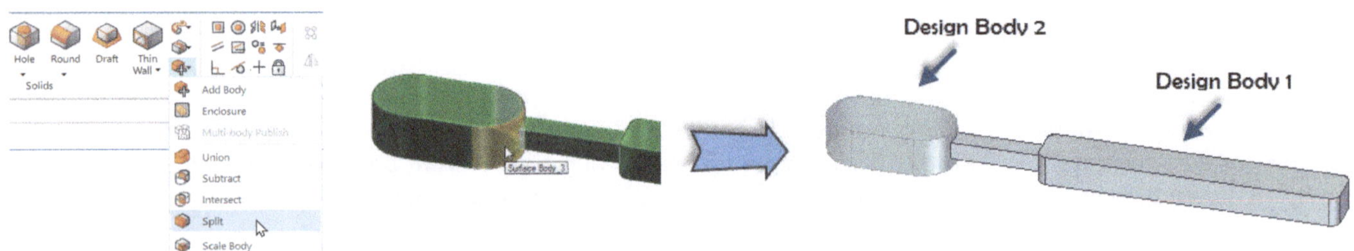

Now, double-click on **Design Body 2** in the **Pathfinder** tree to activate it, and then create the shell feature.

Union

If you apply rounds to edges between two bodies, it will result in a different outcome, as shown in the figure. To solve this problem, you must combine the two bodies using the **Union** command. Activate this command (click **Home > Solids > Add Body > Union** on the ribbon) and select the bodies. Click the green check on the command bar to combine the bodies. Now, apply rounds to the edges.

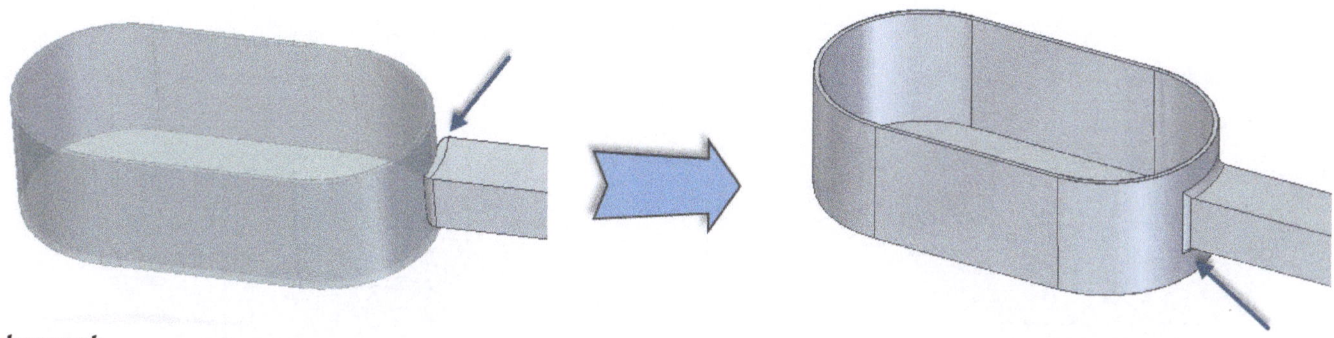

Intersect

By using the **Intersect** command, you can generate bodies defined by the intersecting volume of two bodies. Activate this command (click **Home > Solids > Add Body > Intersect** on the ribbon) and select two bodies. Click the green check to see the resultant single solid body.

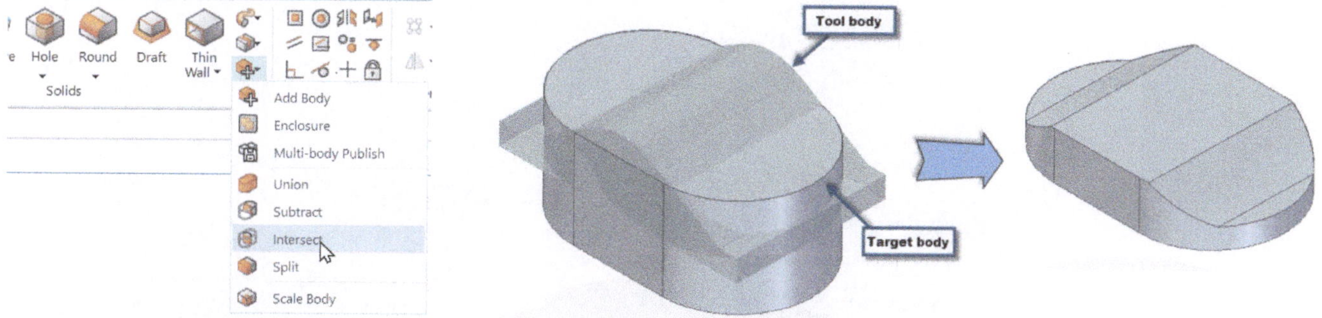

Subtract

This command performs the function of subtracting one solid body from another. Activate this command (click **Home > Solids > Add Body > Subtract** on the ribbon) and select target body. Click the green check, and then select the tool body. Again, click the green check to subtract the tool body from the target. Hide the tool body to see the result.

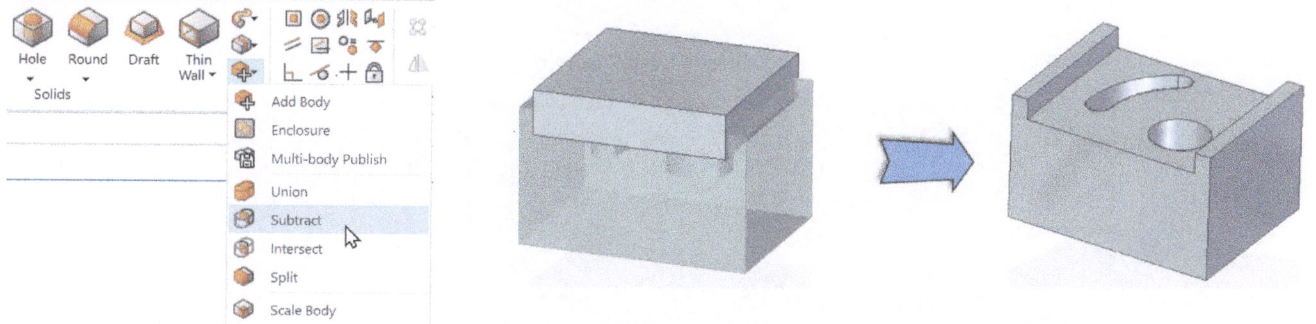

Multi-Body Publish

In addition to creating multiple bodies, Solid Edge also offers an option to generate an assembly from the resulting bodies. For example, create the model shown in the figure and split it into two separate bodies. Next, add the lip/groove feature to the model, and then save the model.

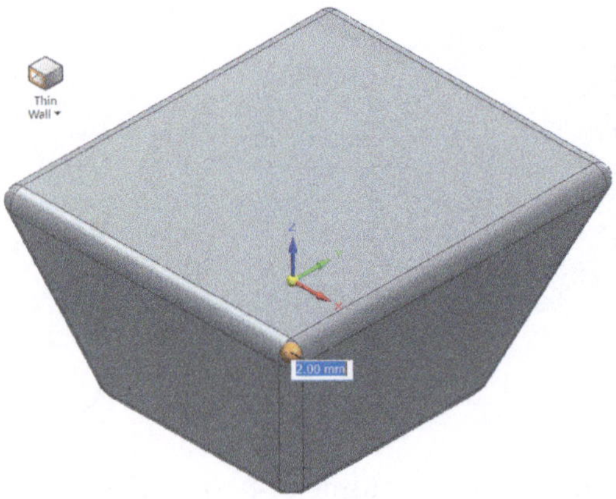

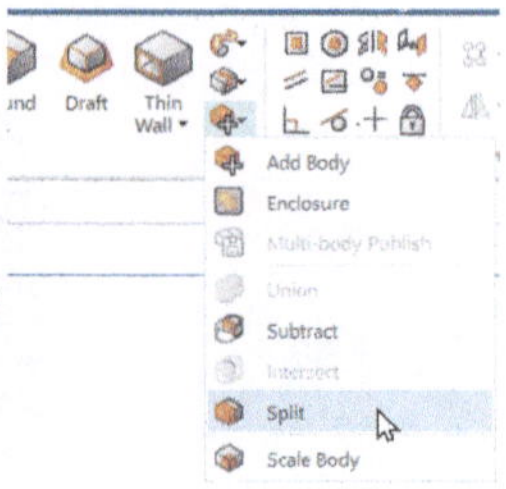

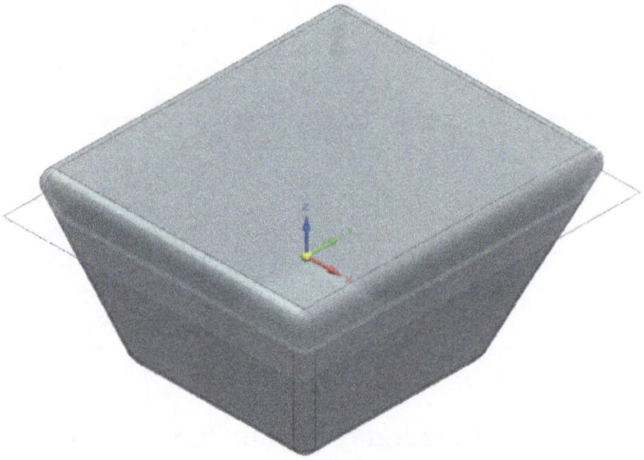

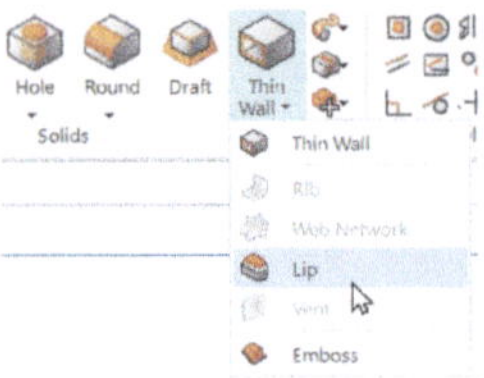

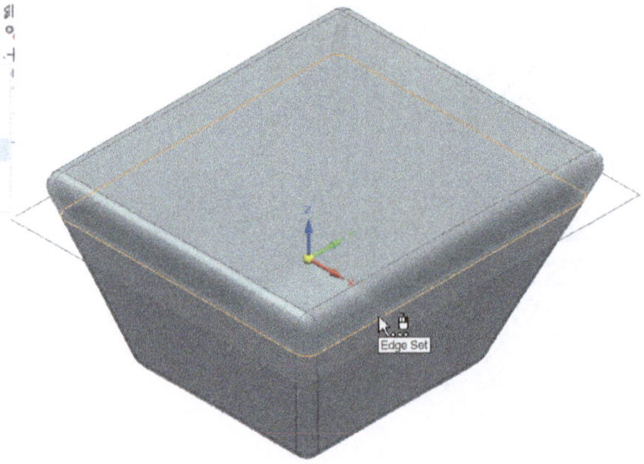

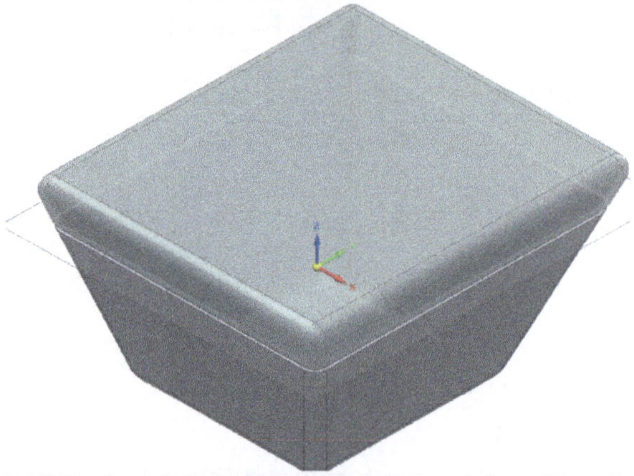

Activate the **Multi Body Publish** command (click **Home > Solids >Add Body > Multi Body Publish** on the ribbon); the **Multi-body Publish** dialog pops up on the screen. Click **Save Files** on the dialog to save the design bodies as individual files and create an assembly. Click the right mouse button on **Create Assembly path** and select **Open**. The newly created assembly is opened. Now, you can apply assembly relationships to the parts.

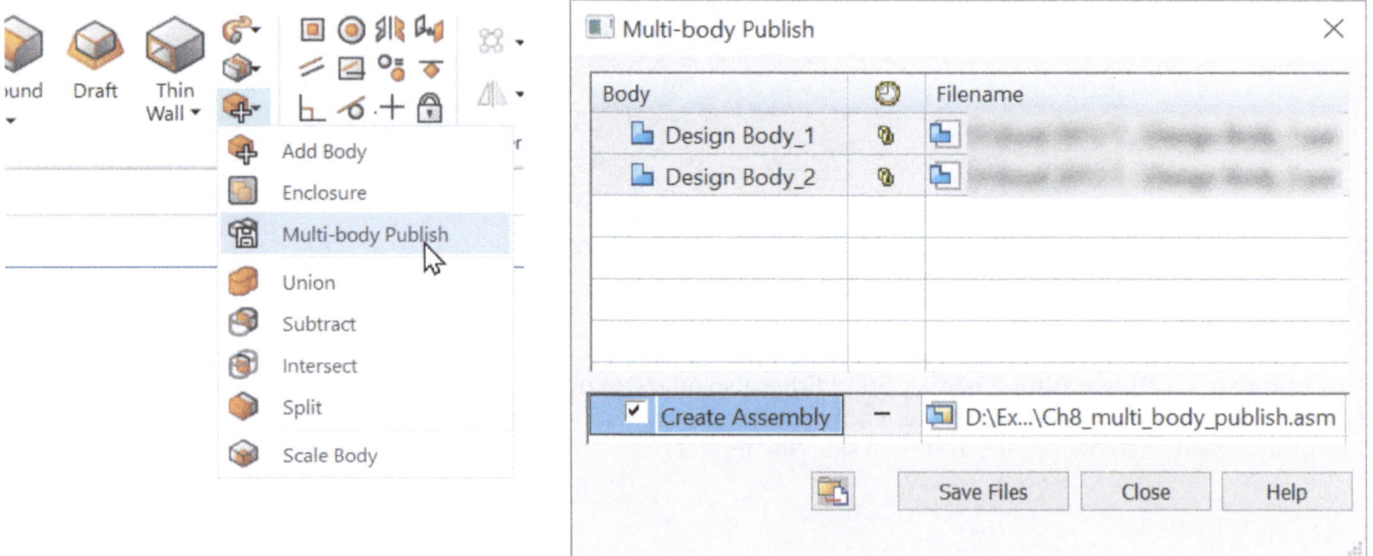

Emboss

This command allows you to change the shape of a solid body by using another solid body. The solid body that is changed is called the target body, and the solid body that causes the changes is called the tool body. To create an emboss feature, you must have two solid bodies in part. Activate the **Emboss** command (click **Home > Solids > Thin Wall > Emboss** on the ribbon) and select the target and tool bodies. Type-in values in the **Clearance** and **Thickness** boxes. Use the **Direction** icon on the command bar to define the side on which the body is embossed. Click the green check on the command bar to complete the emboss feature.

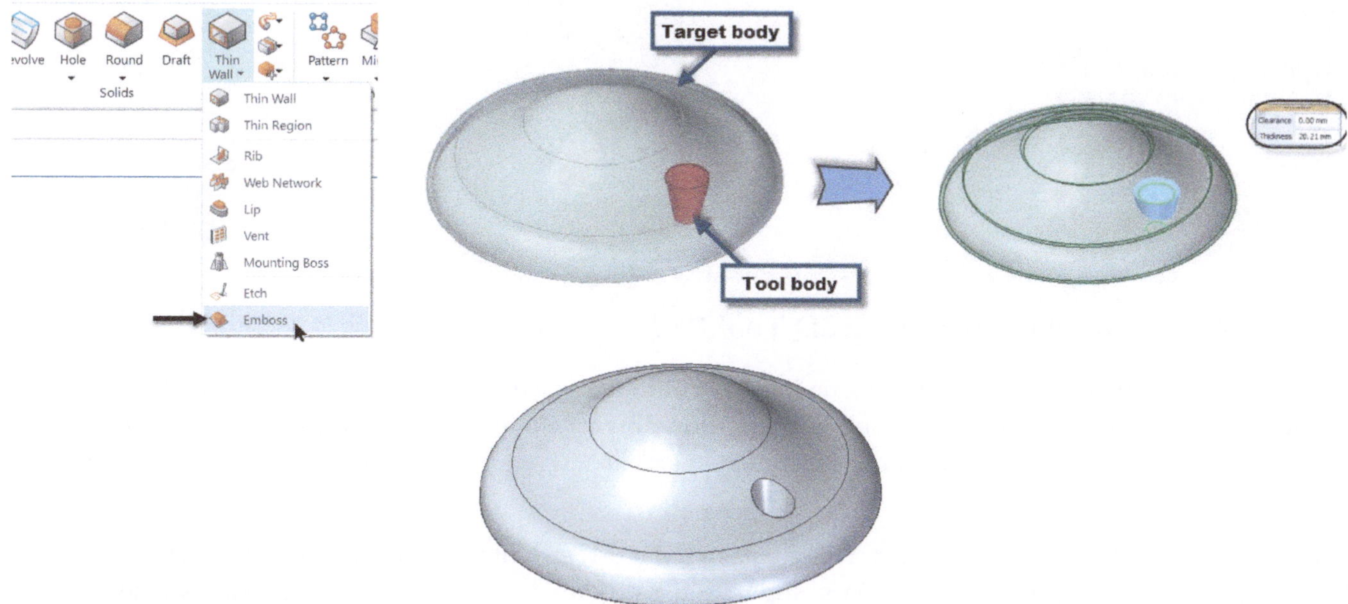

Solid Sweep Cutout

This command removes material by sweeping the volume of another solid body along a planar or non-planar curve. To solid sweep cutout, first, create the target body and the tool path, and then create the tool body. Note that you should create the target and tool bodies as separate bodies (Use the **Add body** command to create the tool body). Also, the tool body should be created in such a way that it intersects the target body. The tool path should be created on the target face. The target face can be planar or non-planar.

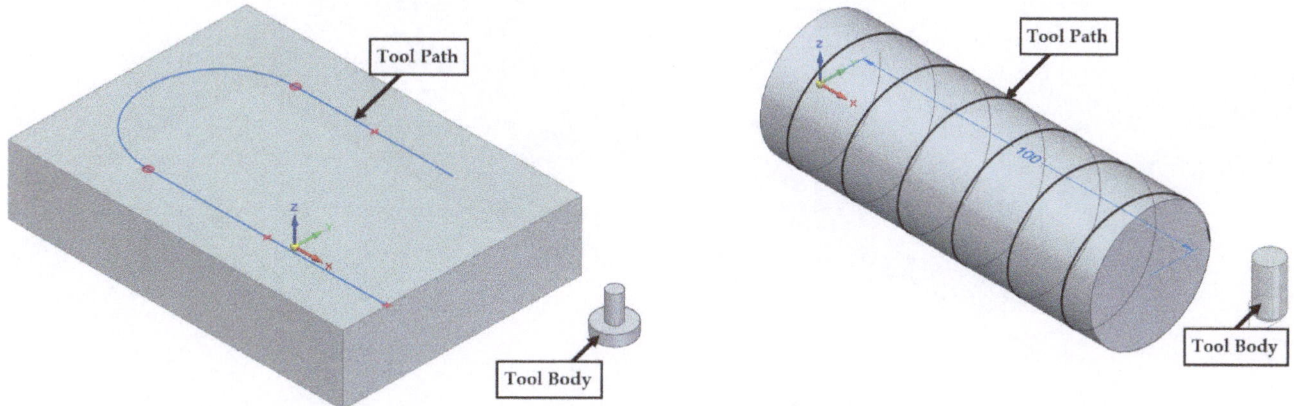

The tool body should be cylindrical or revolved solid. The following figure shows some examples of tool bodies. However, you may need to create the axis manually for the tool similar to the third one.

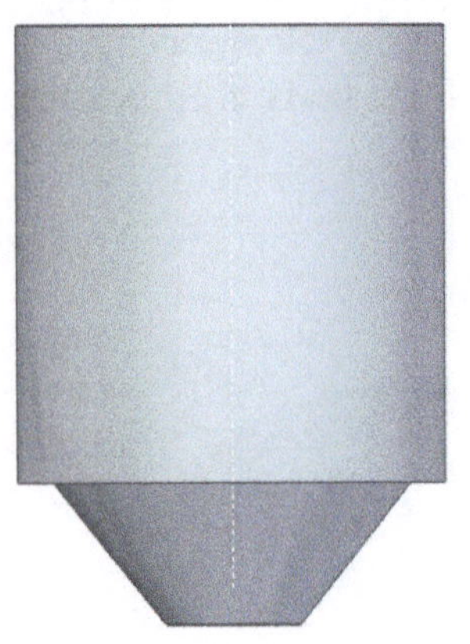
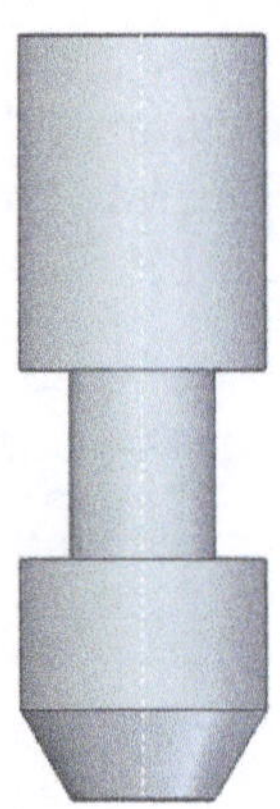

Creating Solid Swept Cutout using 2D Tool Path

Activate the target body by double-clicking on it in the Pathfinder. Activate the **Solid Sweep Cutout** command (on the ribbon, click **Home > Solids > Cut drop-down > Solid Sweep Cutout**). Next, select the tool path and click the **green check** button on the command bar. Next, select the tool body and make sure that the **Place Tool on Path** icon is selected. This creates a Solid Sweep Cutout even when the tool body is not on the tool path. Click the green button; the **Axis step** button is activated, and the axis of the tool body is selected. Select the axis of the tool body if it is not selected. Click green button on the command bar; the tool body's orientation is specified automatically if the tool body is perpendicular to the tool path. However, you need to specify the orientation using the **Lock Direction Step** if the tool body is not perpendicular to the tool path. Click **Finish** and **Cancel** on the command bar to create the Solid Swept cutout.

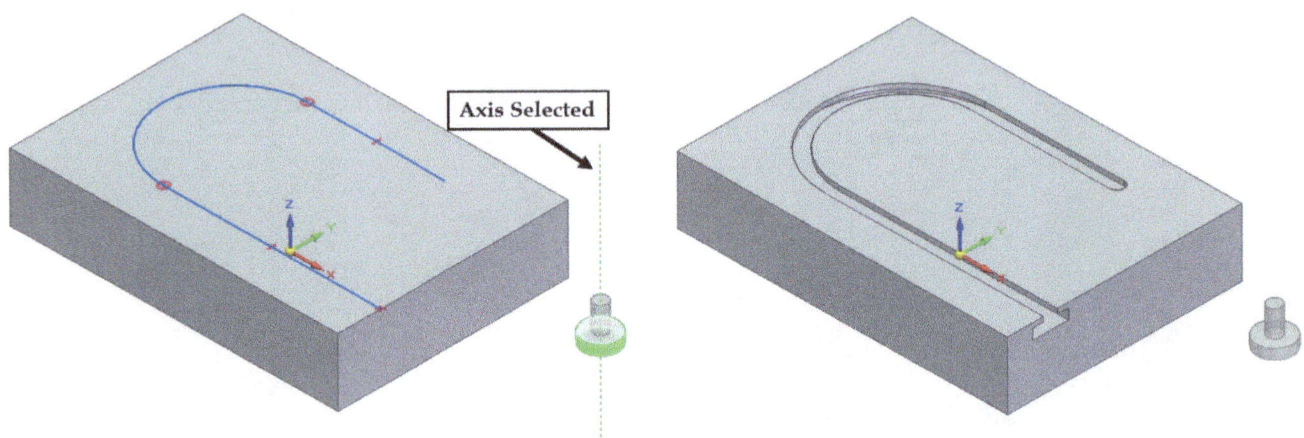

Sweeping Volume using 3D Tool Path

Activate the target body by double-clicking on it in the Pathfinder. Activate the **Solid Sweep Cutout** command (on the ribbon, click **Home > Solids > Cut drop-down > Solid Sweep Cutout**). Next, select the tool path and right-click to accept. Next, select the tool body and right click; the axis is selected automatically. Right click and select the axis perpendicular to the tool body. Click **Finish** and **Cancel** on the command bar to create the Solid Swept cutout.

Note: *Refer to the Helical Curve topic of Chapter 13: Surface Design to learn how to create the following example's helical curve.*

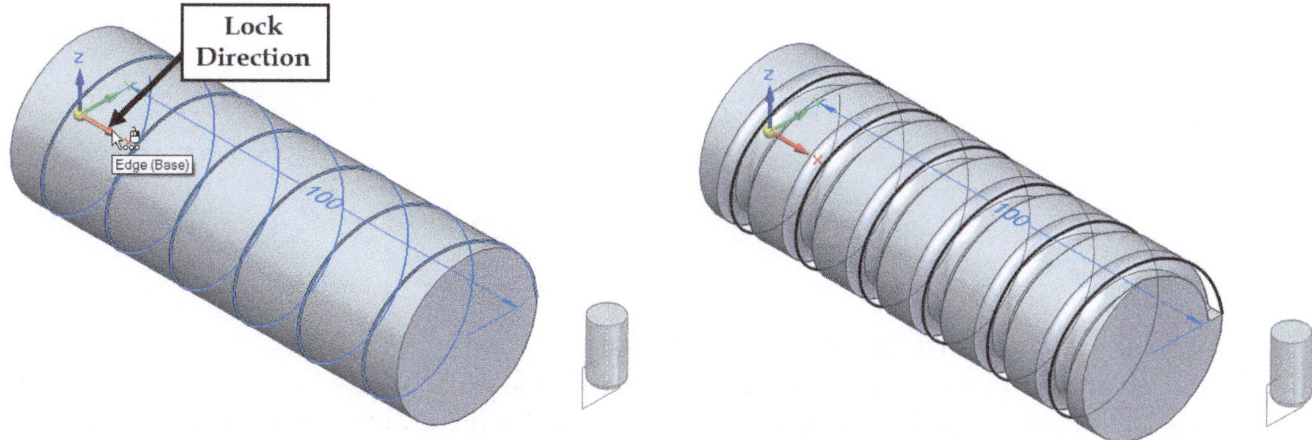

Solid Sweep Protrusion command

This command creates a protrusion by sweeping a solid body along the 2D or 3D path. To create the Solid Sweep Protrusion, first create the solid body and the path, as shown. Activate the **Solid Sweep** command (on the ribbon, click **Home > Solids > Sweep drop-down > Solid Sweep**). Select the path and right click. Next, select the solid body and right click; the solid body axis is selected automatically. Right click to accept the selection. Select an element (planar face, axis, linear edge, or reference plane) to define the solid sweep's orientation. Right click to accept the selection. The following figure shows the solid sweep when the face perpendicular to the solid body axis is selected in the **Lock Direction Step**. Next, click the **Finish** button.

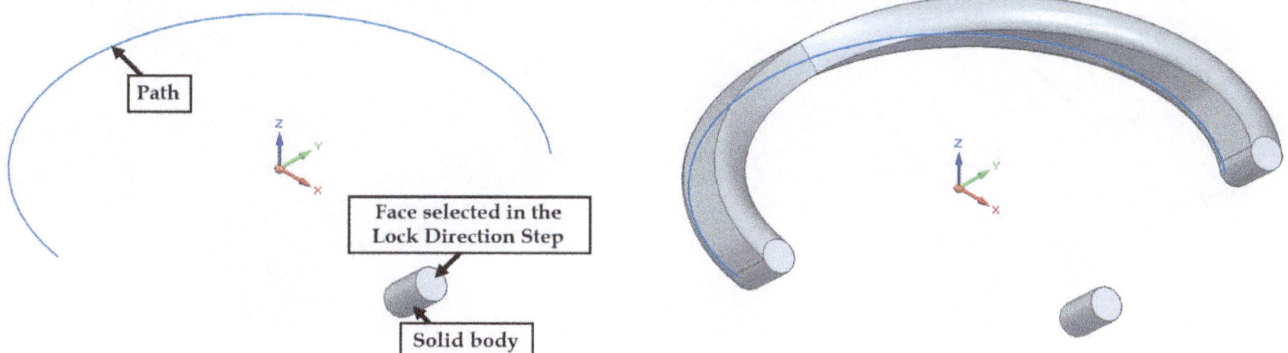

The following figure shows the solid sweep when the Z-axis is selected in the Lock Direction Step.

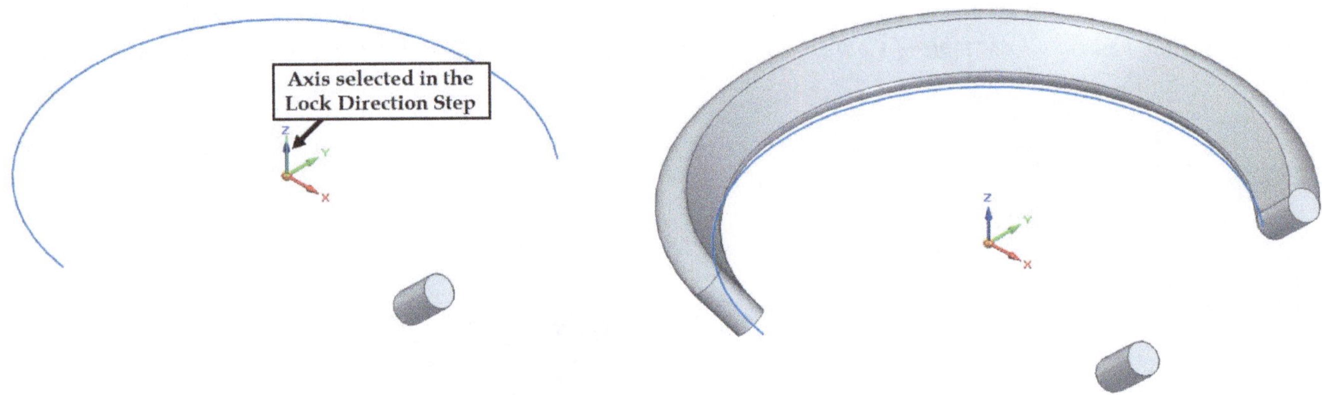

Creating Cut Features in Multi-body Parts

Solid Edge has additional options (**Active Body** and **Selected Bodies**) while creating cuts in Multi-body parts. These options are available on the **Extrude** and **Revolve** command bar in the **Cut Preview** section. However, you can select them only when the **Operation** is set to **Cut**, respectively. These options are explained next.

Active Body

Create three separate bodies in a part file, and then create a sketch on the active body, as shown. Activate the **Extrude** command (on the ribbon, click **Home > Solids > Extrude**). On the **Extrude** command bar, select **Operation > Cut**. Next, select **Active Body** from the **Extent** section. Select sketch region and right click to accept the selection. Move the pointer into the model and click to create the cut feature. Notice the cut is added to the active body only.

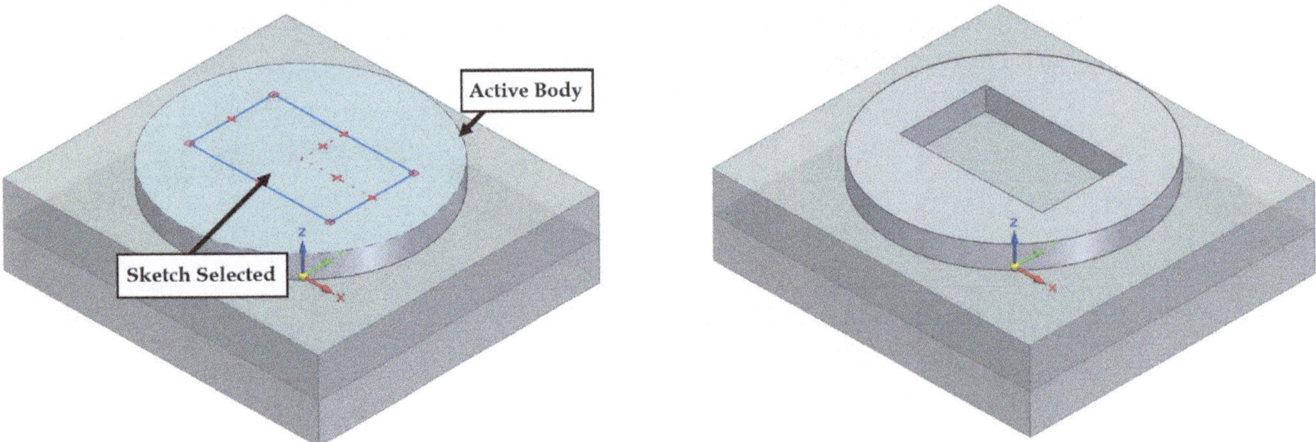

Selected Bodies

Activate the **Extrude** command (on the ribbon, click **Home > Solids > Extrude**). On the **Extrude** command bar, select **Operation > Cut**. Next, select **Selected bodies** from the **Extent** section. Select the sketch region and right click to accept the selection. Move the pointer across all the bodies of the part, and then click. Notice that all the bodies of the part are selected. Click the Body Selection section. Next, press the Shift key and click on the bodies to be removed from the selection. Right click to add the cut to the selected bodies.

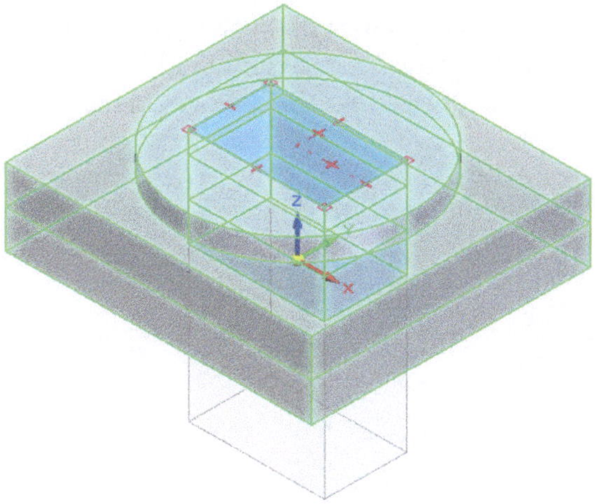

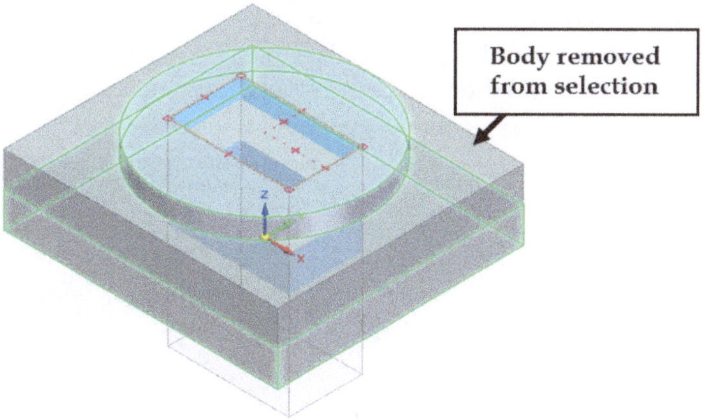

Body removed from selection

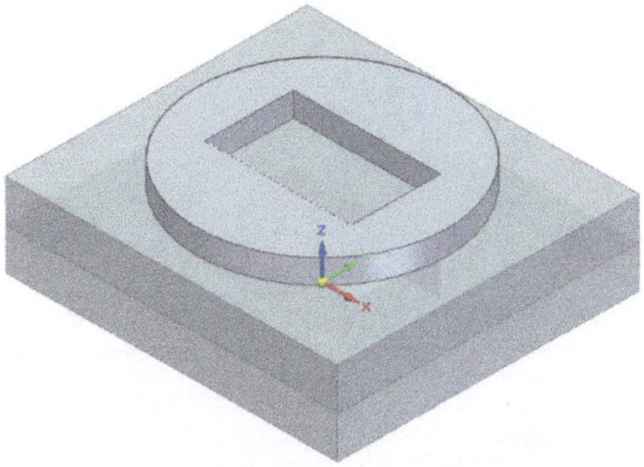

Scale Body

This command scales the part geometry with reference to the Base Coordinate System origin or any other key point you specify. On the **Home** tab of the ribbon, click **Solids** panel > **Add Body** drop-down > **Scale Body**. On the command bar, click the **Options** icon, and then select the **Uniform Scaling** option. Next, click **OK** to close the dialog. Click on the part geometry to scale, and then click green button on the command bar. Next, select a key point on the part geometry to define the scaling reference point (or) leave the Base Coordinate System as the default reference point. Type-in the scaling factor in the **Scale** box.

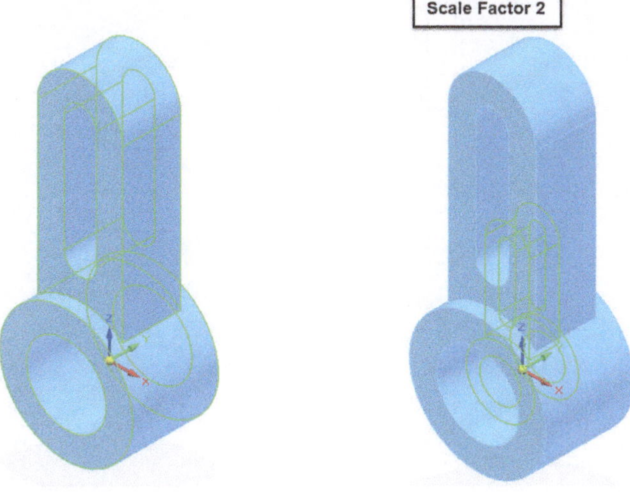

Non-uniform Scaling

This option scales the part geometry along three directions using the coordinate values that you specify. On the **Home** tab of the ribbon, click **Solids** panel > **Add Body** drop-down > **Scale Body**. On the command bar, click the **Options** icon, and then select the **Non-Uniform Scaling** option. Next, click **OK** to close the dialog. On the command bar, type-in values in the X, Y, Z boxes.

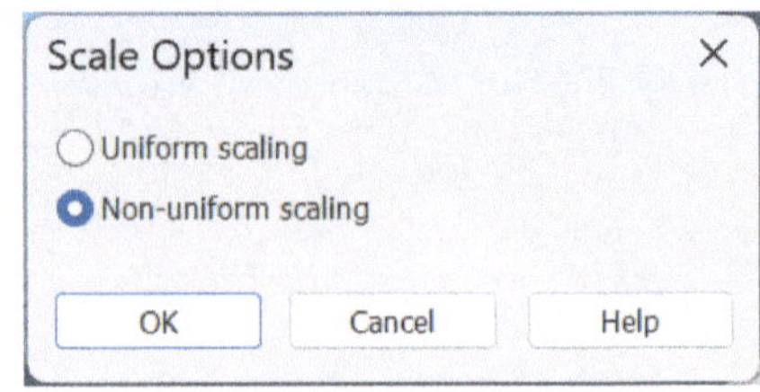

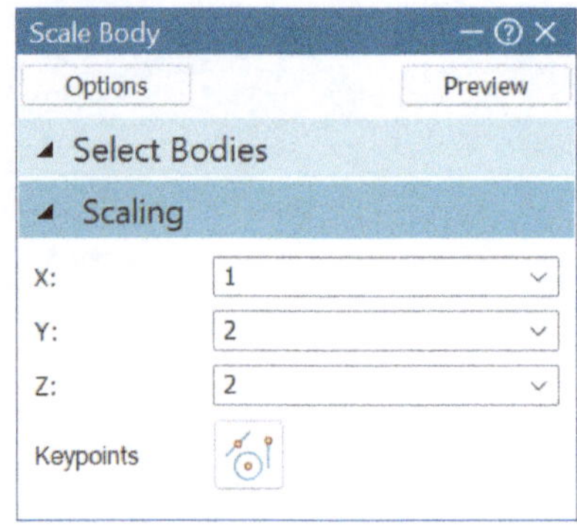

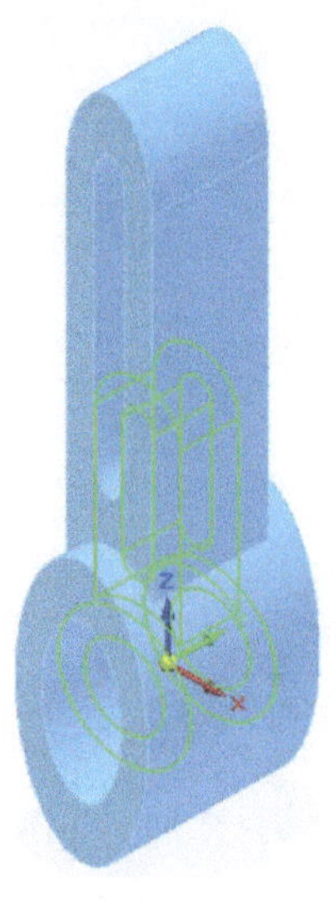

Examples

Example 1 (Millimetres)

In this example, you will create the part shown below.

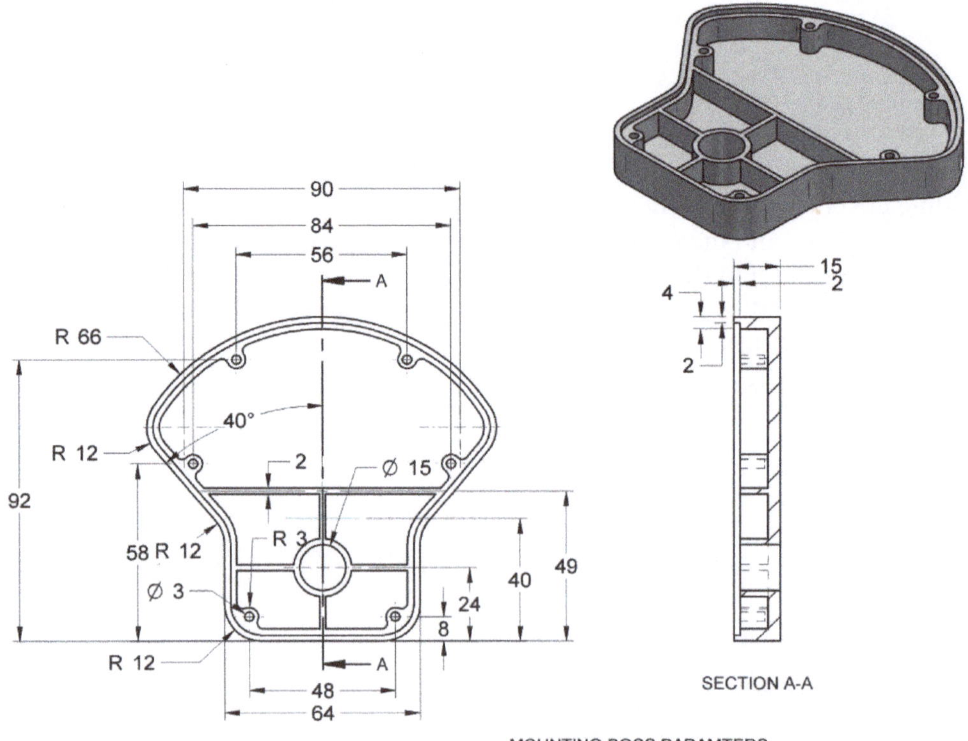

MOUNTING BOSS PARAMTERS:
DIAMETER = 6 mm
HOLE DIAMETER = 3 mm
HOLE DEPTH = 8 mm

FILLET MOUNTING BOSS CORNER 2 mm

1. Start **Solid Edge 2026.**
2. On the File Menu, click **New > ISO Metric Part**; a new part file is opened.
3. Click **Continue with Ordered** button on the **Ordered as default** dialog; the Ordered environment is set as the default environment.
4. On the ribbon, click **Home > Sketch > Sketch** and select the Top (xy) Plane.
5. On the ribbon, click **Home > Draw > Line.**
6. Create the closed sketch, as shown (refer to the examples of **Chapter 2: Sketch Techniques** to learn how to create a closed sketch using the **Line** tool).
7. Add fillets of 12 mm radii to the corners. Also, apply the **Equal** constraint between the fillet.

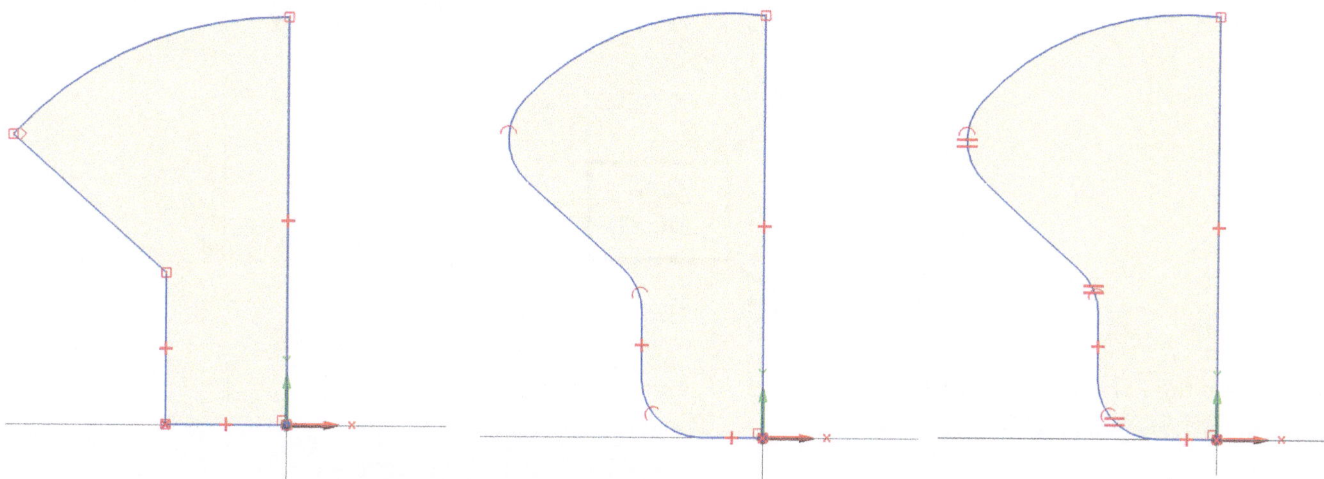

8. Apply dimensions to the sketch.

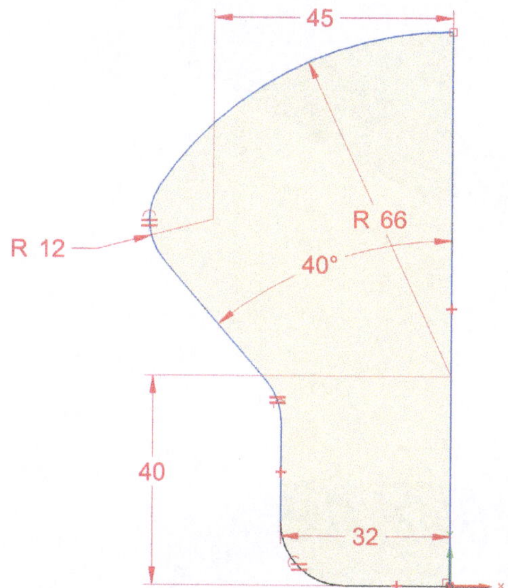

9. On the ribbon, click **Home > Relate > Horizontal/Vertical**. Next, place the pointer on the large arc; its centerpoint is highlighted.
10. Select the centerpoint of the arc and the sketch origin; they are aligned vertically. Next, click **Close Sketch** on the ribbon, and then click **Finish.**

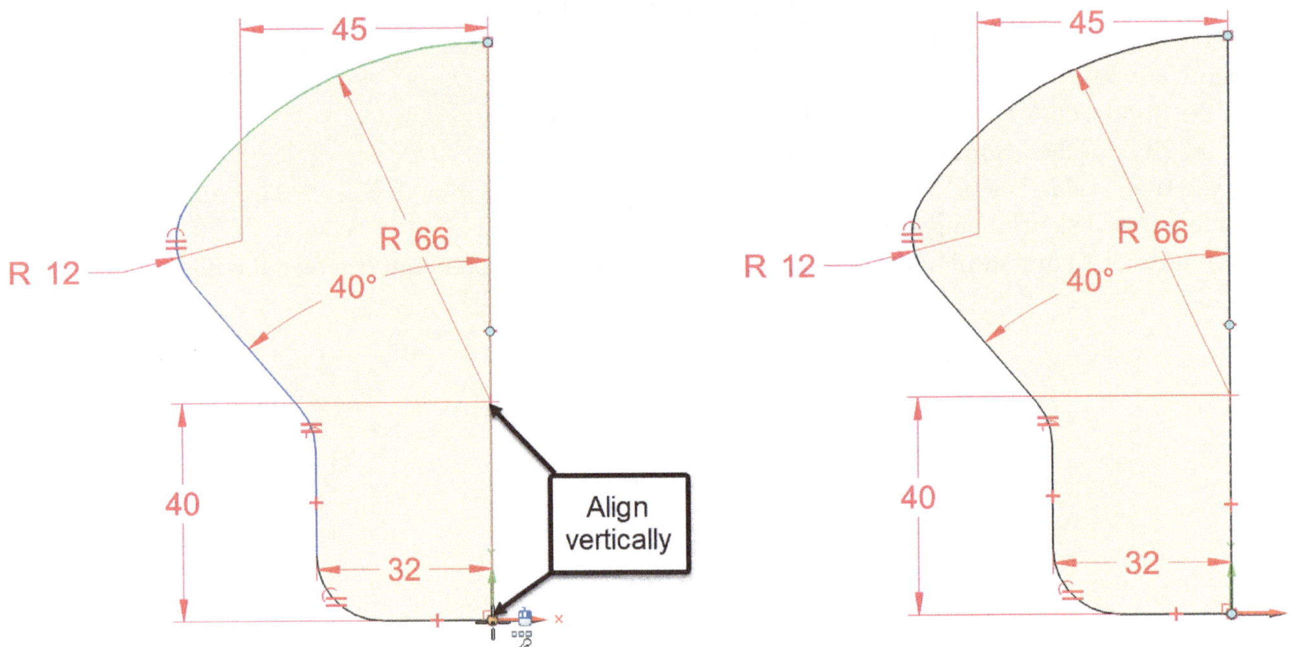

11. Create the *Extrude* feature of 15 mm depth.

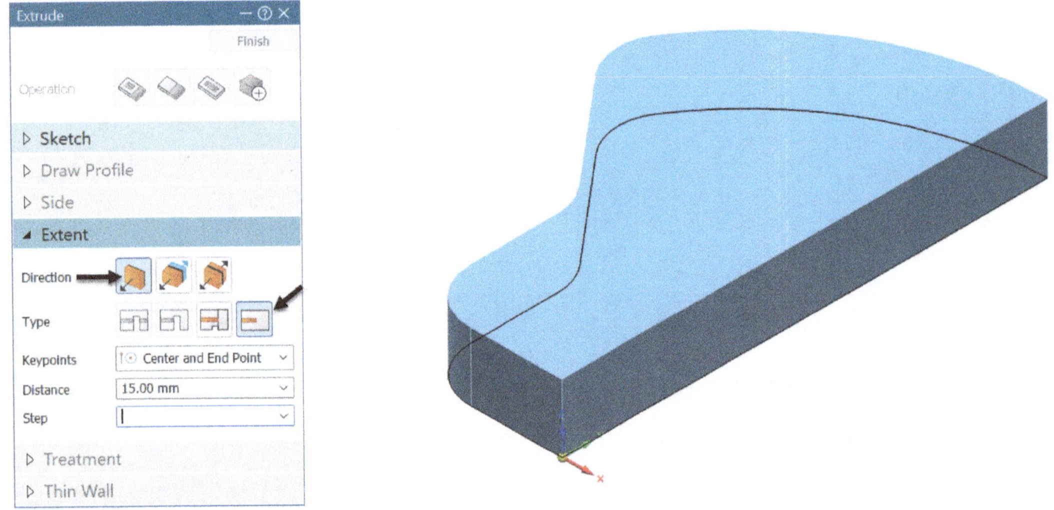

12. Create the *Thin Wall* feature of 4 mm depth.

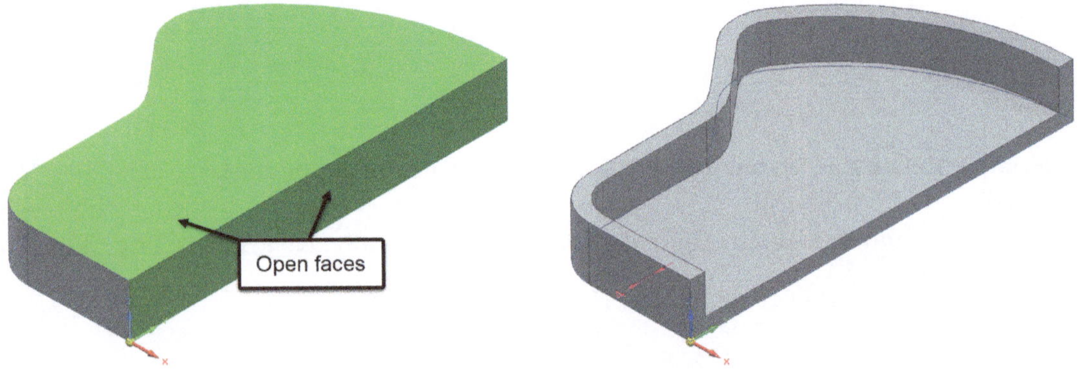

13. On the ribbon, click **Home > Solids > Thin Wall > Lip**.
14. Click on the Thin Wall feature's inner edge and click the green check on the command bar.
15. Type **2** in the **Width** and **Height** boxes, respectively. Click inside the model to define the side of the lip. Click **Finish** and **Cancel** to complete the lip feature.

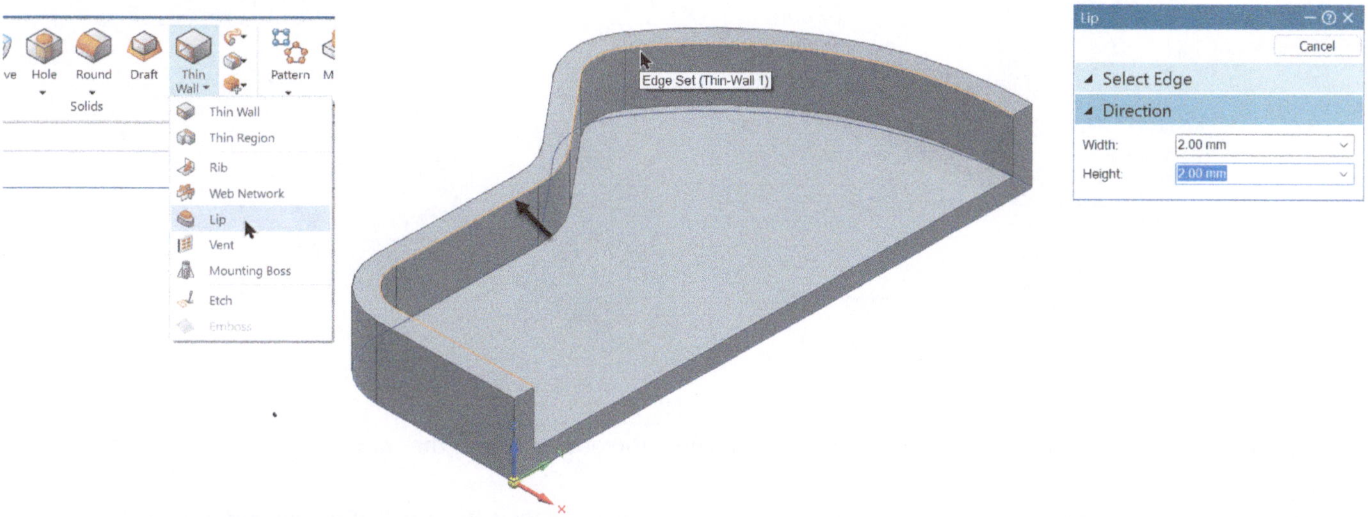

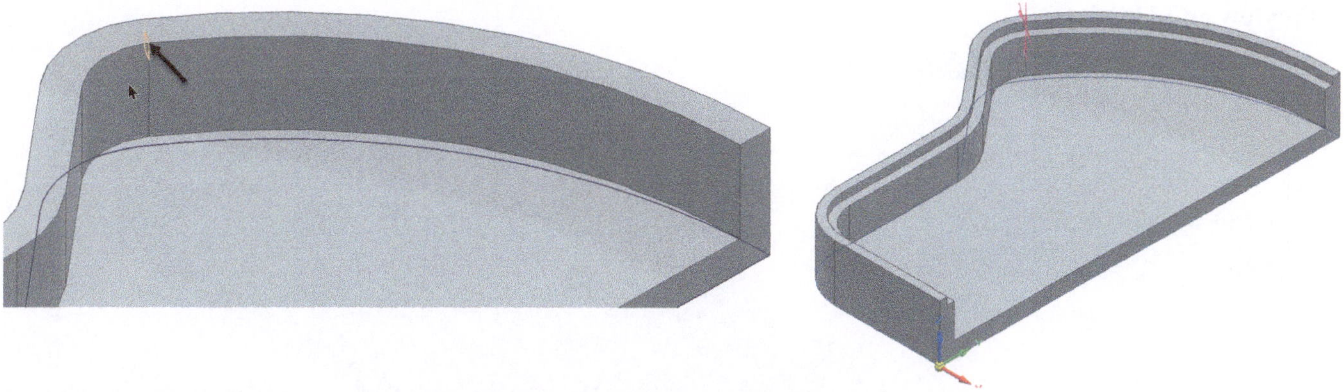

16. Click **Home > Solids > Thin Wall > Mounting Boss** on the ribbon.
17. On the command bar, select **Coincident Plane** from the **Create-From Options** menu.
18. Click on the top face on the lip feature.

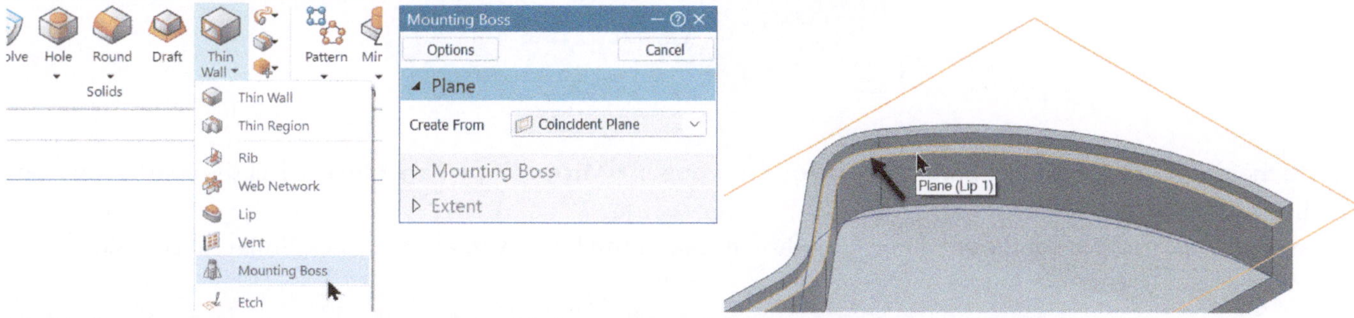

19. Define mounting boss locations and add dimensions. Click **Close Sketch** on the ribbon.
20. On the dialog box, click the **Mounting Boss Options** icon.
21. On the **Mounting Boss Options** dialog, set the **Boss diameter** to 6, check the **Mounting hole** option, and then set the **Hole diameter** to 3 and **Hole depth** to 8. Click **OK** to close the dialog.
22. Move the mouse pointer downward and click to define the side of the mounting boss.

23. Click **Finish** and **Cancel** to complete the mounting boss feature.

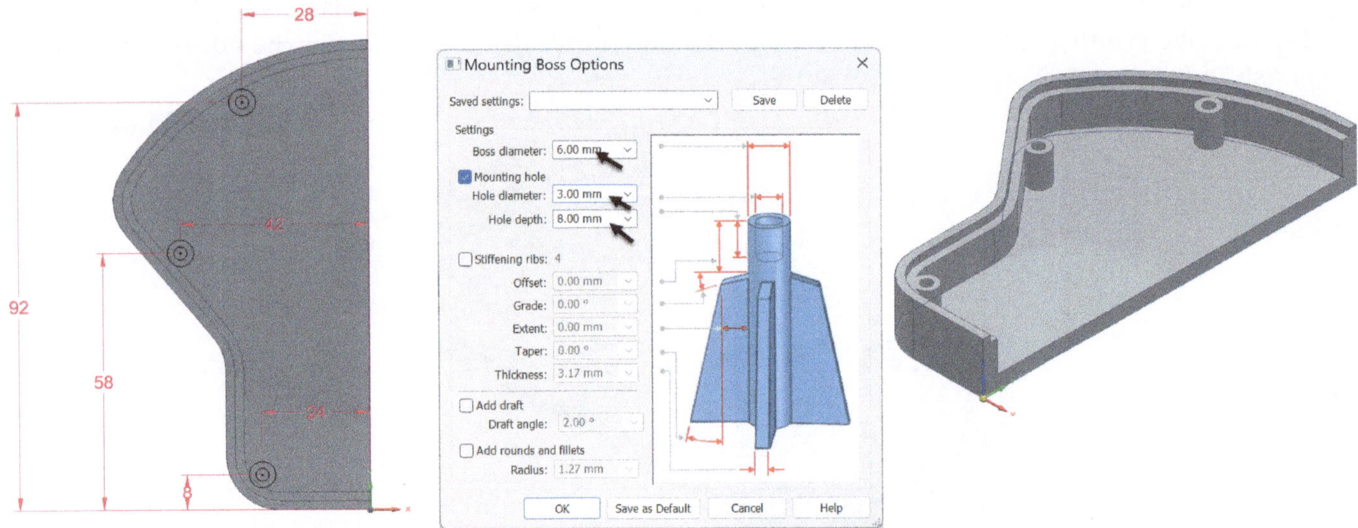

24. On the ribbon, click **Home > Solids > Round** and select the edges where the mounting bosses meet the geometry walls.
25. Type **2** in the box displayed on the geometry. Click the green check to round the selected edges. Next, click **Preview** and **Finish**.

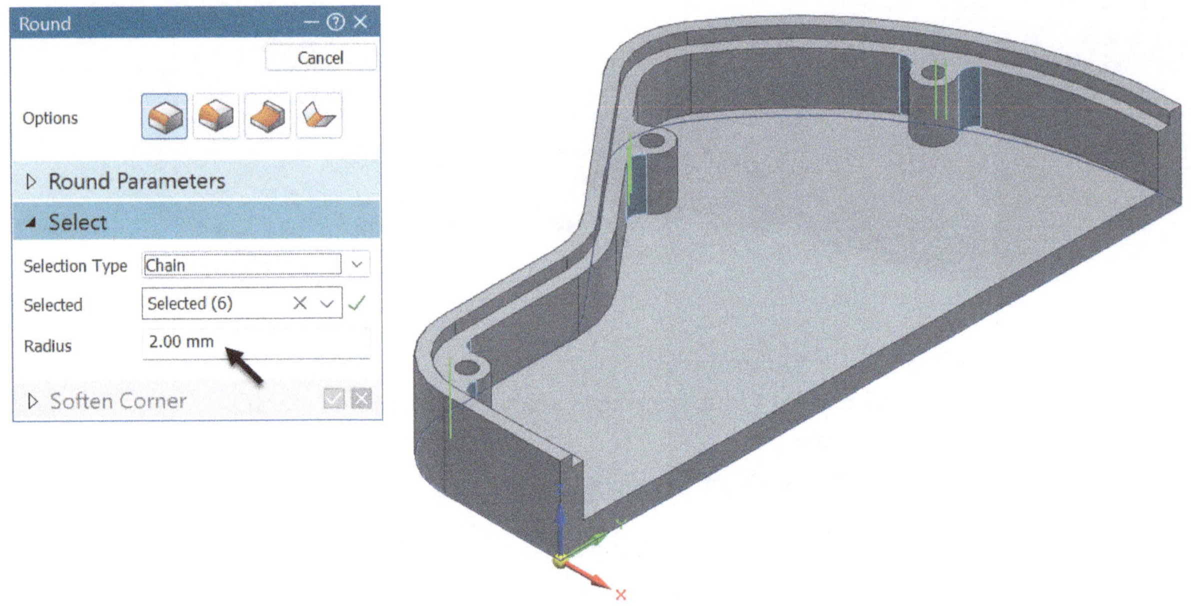

26. On the ribbon, click **Home > Pattern > Mirror** drop-down **> Mirror Copy Part**. Next, select the solid body from the graphics window.
27. Select the flat end face of the solid body, as shown. The entire body is mirrored. Click **Finish** to complete the mirror.

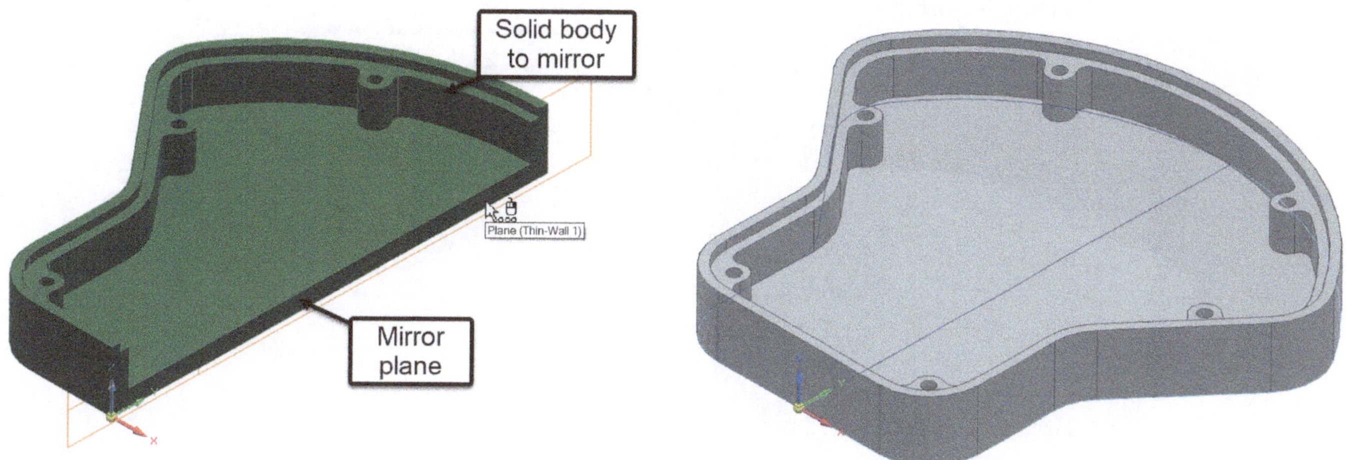

28. Activate the **Hole** command and create a hole on the flat face of the geometry. The hole diameter is 15 mm.

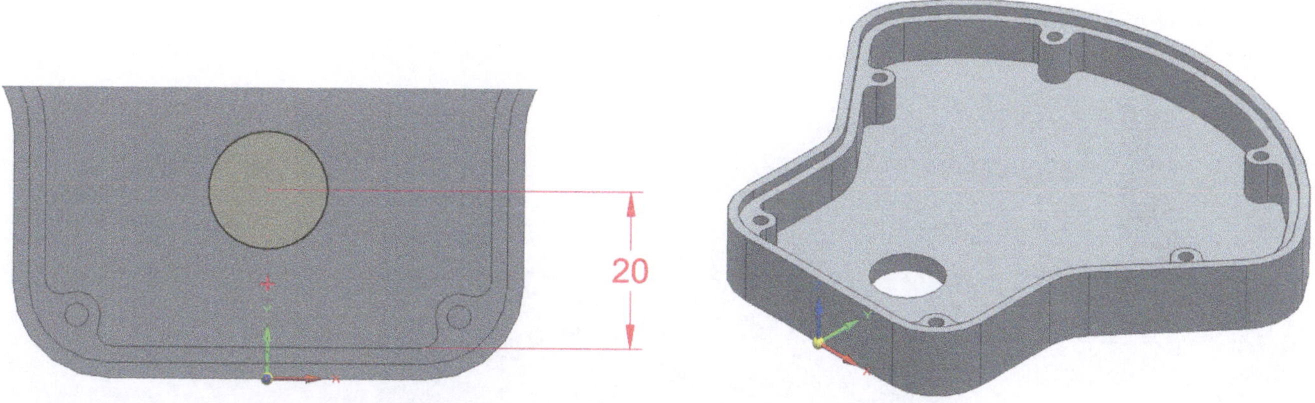

29. On the ribbon, click **Planes > Coincident by Axis**. Click on the top face on the lip feature.
30. Select the horizontal edge of the model, as shown to define the base of the plane.
31. Move the pointer toward left and click to define the origin of the plane.

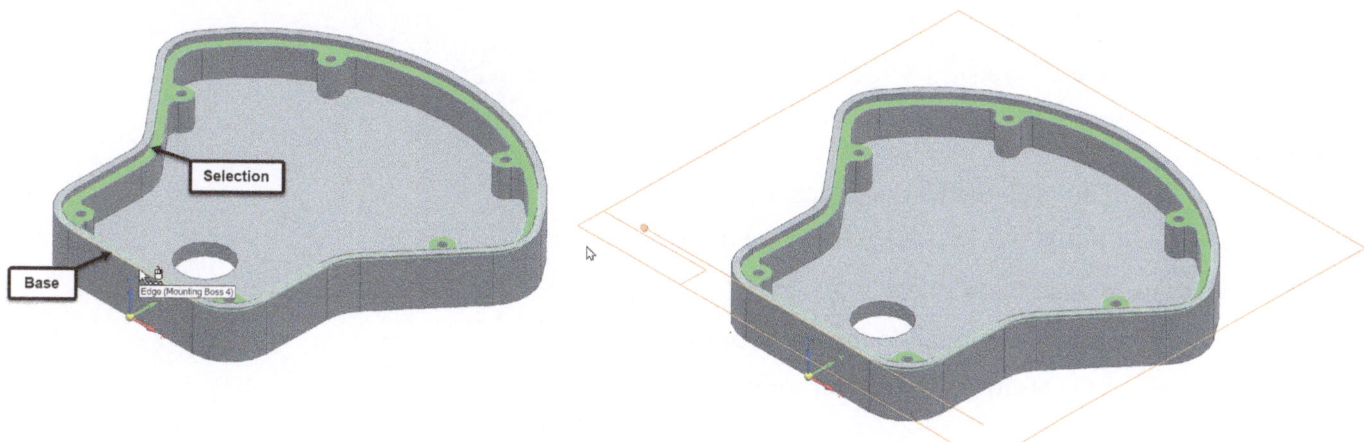

32. Click **Home > Sketch > Sketch** on the ribbon. Next, select the newly created plane.
33. On the ribbon, click **Draw > Circle by Center Point**.
34. Draw the sketch, as shown below. Next, click **Close Sketch** on the ribbon.
35. Click **Finish** and **Cancel** on the command bar.

36. On the ribbon, click **Home > Solids > Thin Wall > Web Network.**

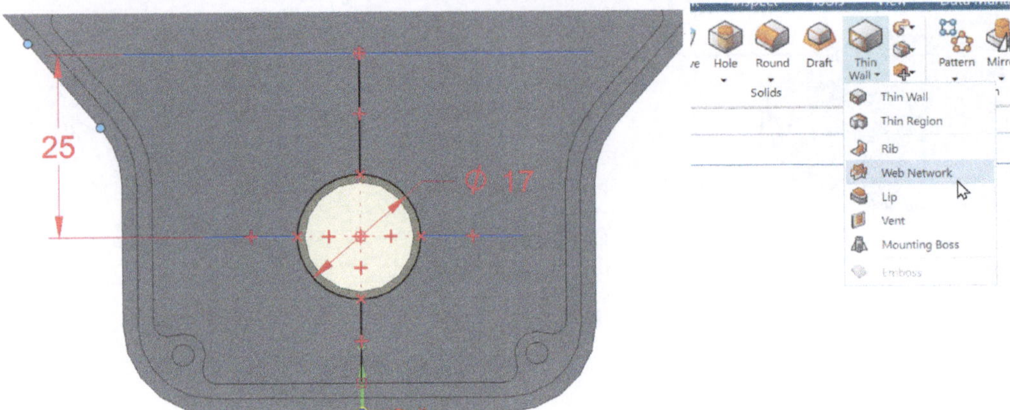

37. Click on the elements of the sketch, and then click the green check on the command bar.
38. Move the pointer downward and click to define the direction of the web network.
39. Type **2** in the **Thickness** box, and then click the green check.
40. Click **Finish** and **Cancel** on the command bar.

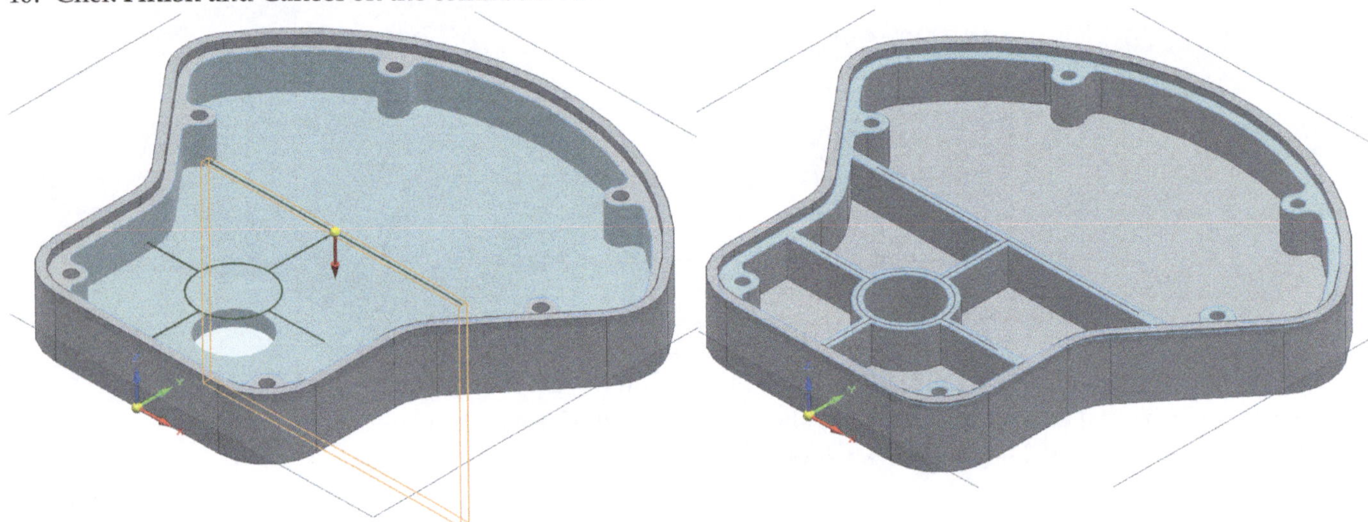

41. Save and close the file.

Questions

1. What is the use of the **Web Network** command?
2. How many types of ribs can be created in Solid Edge?
3. Why do we create multi-body parts?
4. Describe the terms 'Rib' and 'Spar' in the *Vent* feature.
5. What is the use of the **Multi Body Publish** command?

Exercises

Exercise 1

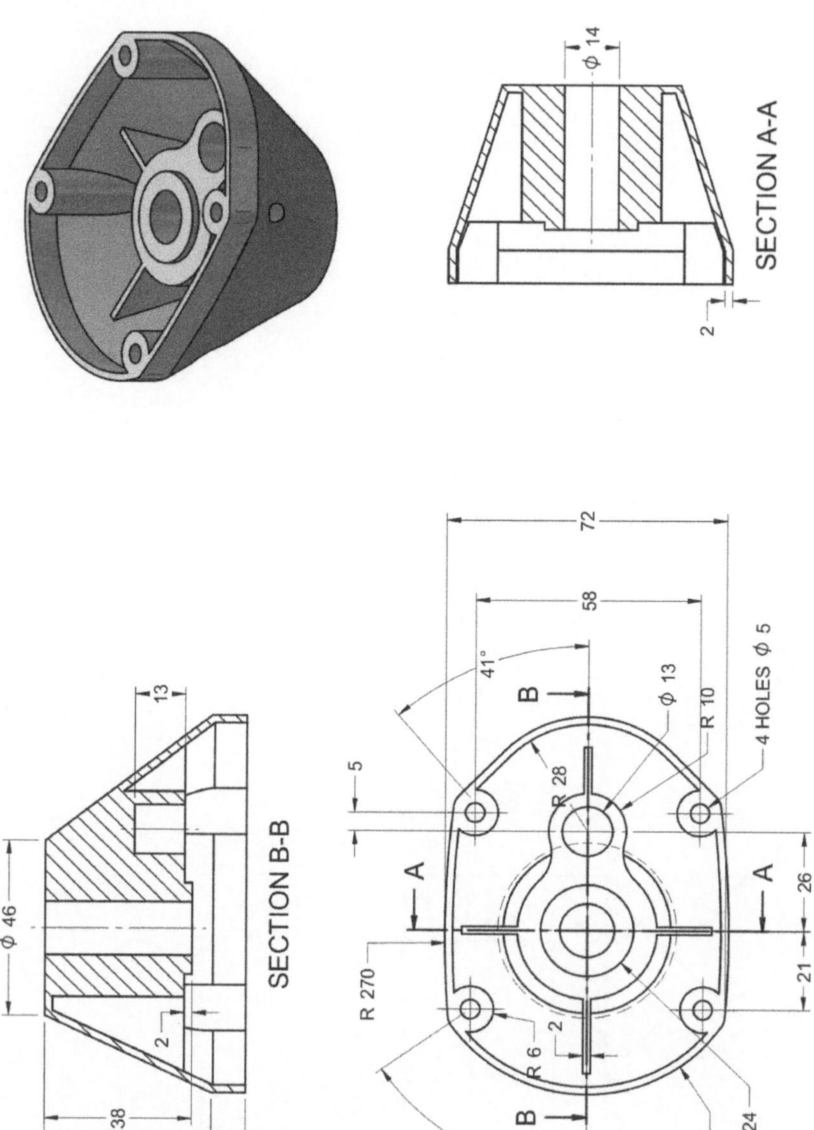

Exercise 2

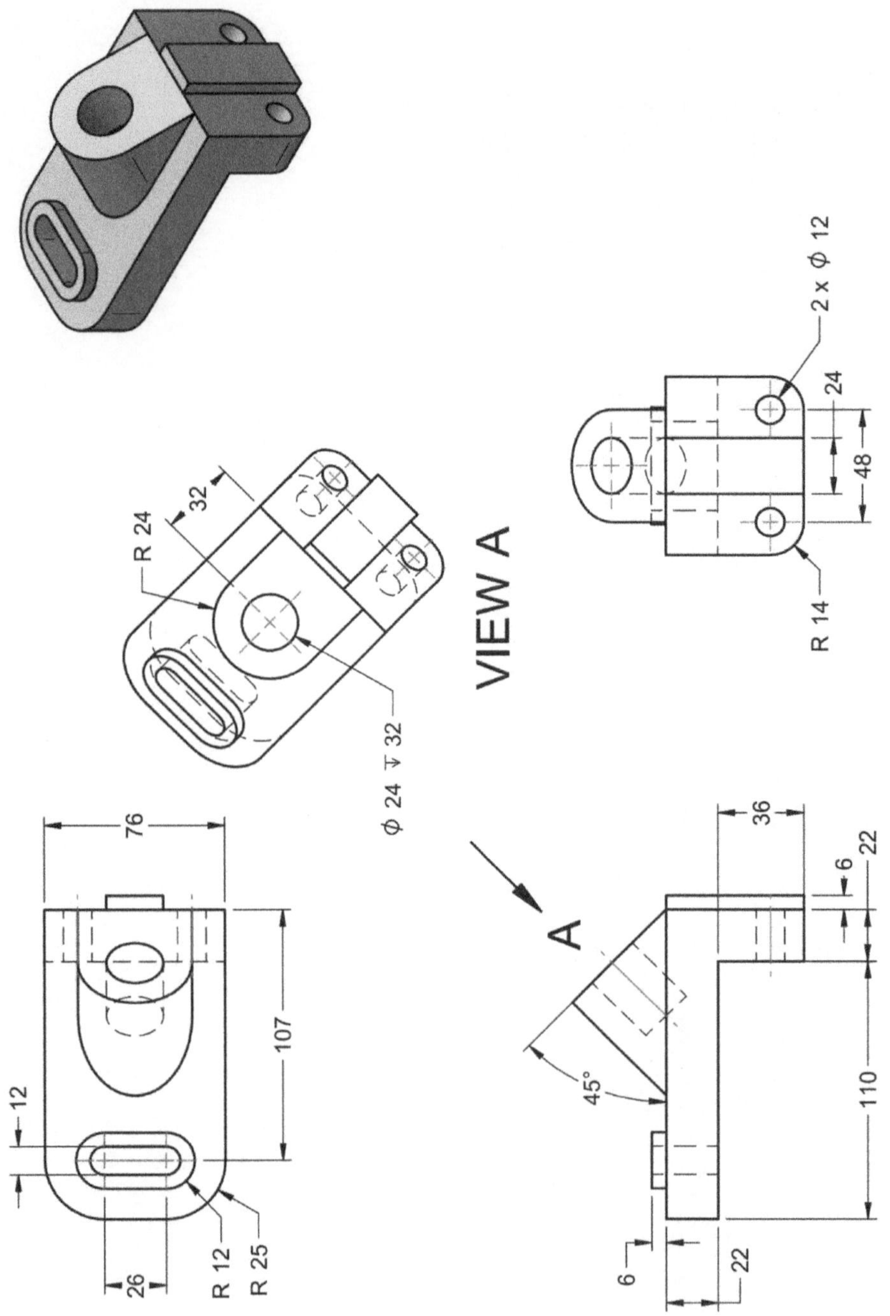
R 24
32
Φ 24 ↧ 32
VIEW A
2 x Φ 12
24
48
R 14
76
107
12
26
R 12
R 25
A
45°
36
6
22
110
6
22

Exercise 3 (Inches)

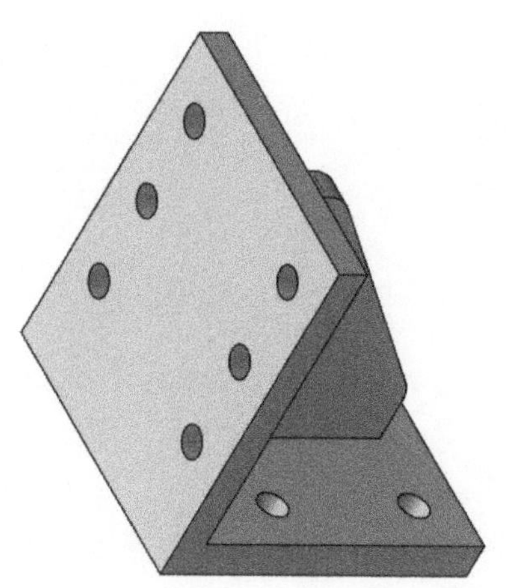

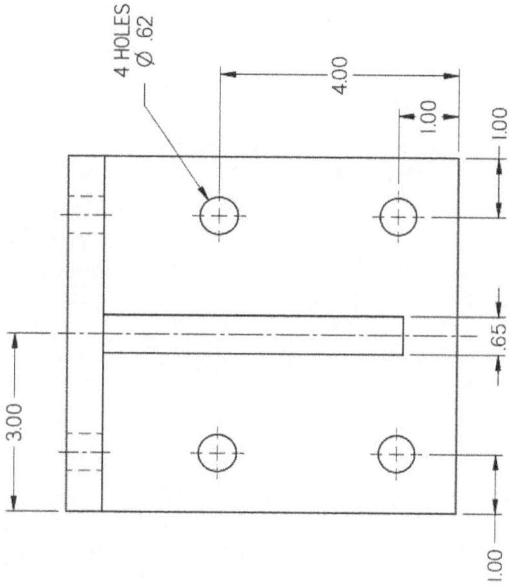

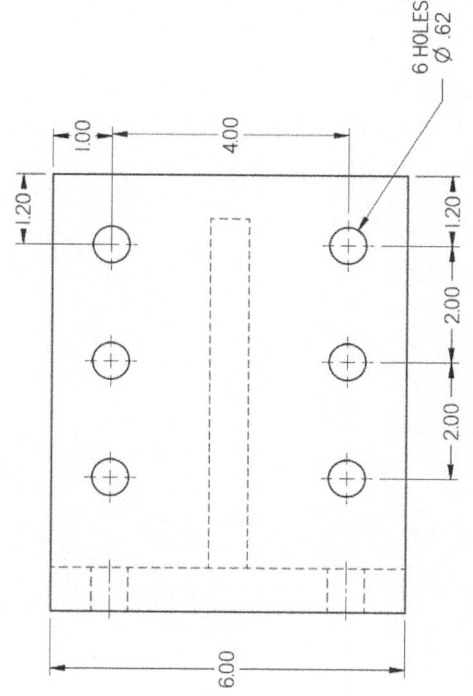

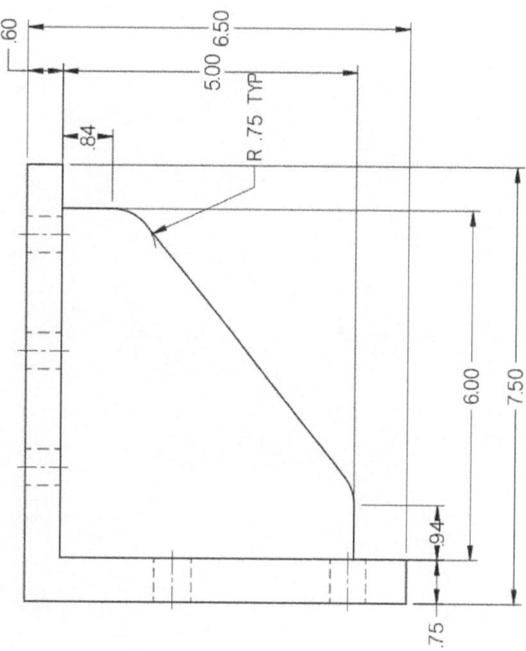

Chapter 9: Modifying Parts

In the design process, it is not required to achieve the final model in the first attempt. There is always a need to modify the existing parts to get the desired part geometry. In this chapter, you will learn various commands and techniques to make changes to a part.

The topics covered in this chapter are:

- *Face Relations*
- *Modify models using the steering wheel*
- *Live Rules*
- *Change model dimensions*
- *Live sections*

Edit Sketches (Ordered)

Sketches form the base of a 3D geometry. They control the size and shape of the geometry. If you want to modify the 3D geometry, most of the time, you are required to edit sketches. To do this, click on the feature to edit and select **Edit Profile**. Now, modify the sketch and click **Close Sketch** on the ribbon. You will notice that the part geometry updates immediately.

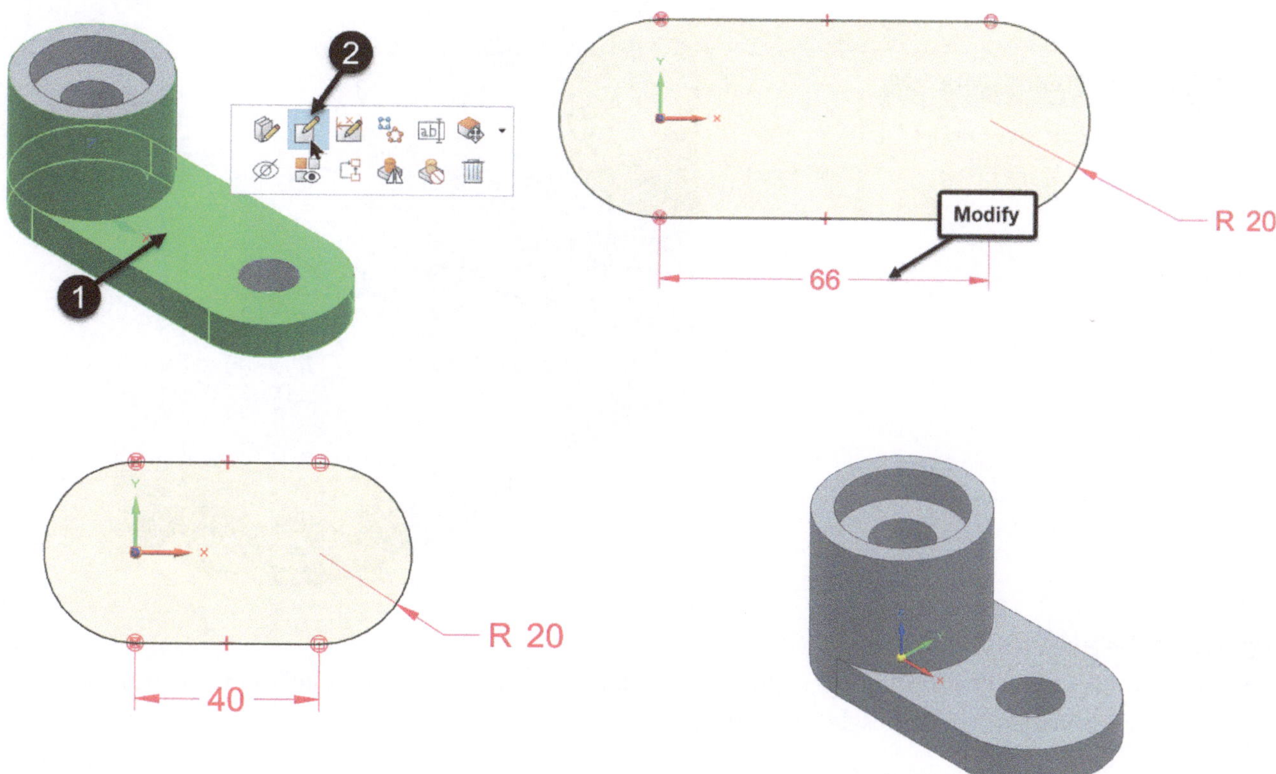

Edit Definition (Ordered)

Features are the building blocks of model geometry. To modify a feature, click on it and select **Edit Definition**. The command bar related to the feature appears. On this dialog, modify the parameters of the feature and click

Finish. The changes take place instantaneously. You can also modify a feature by simply double-clicking on it and changing the parameters.

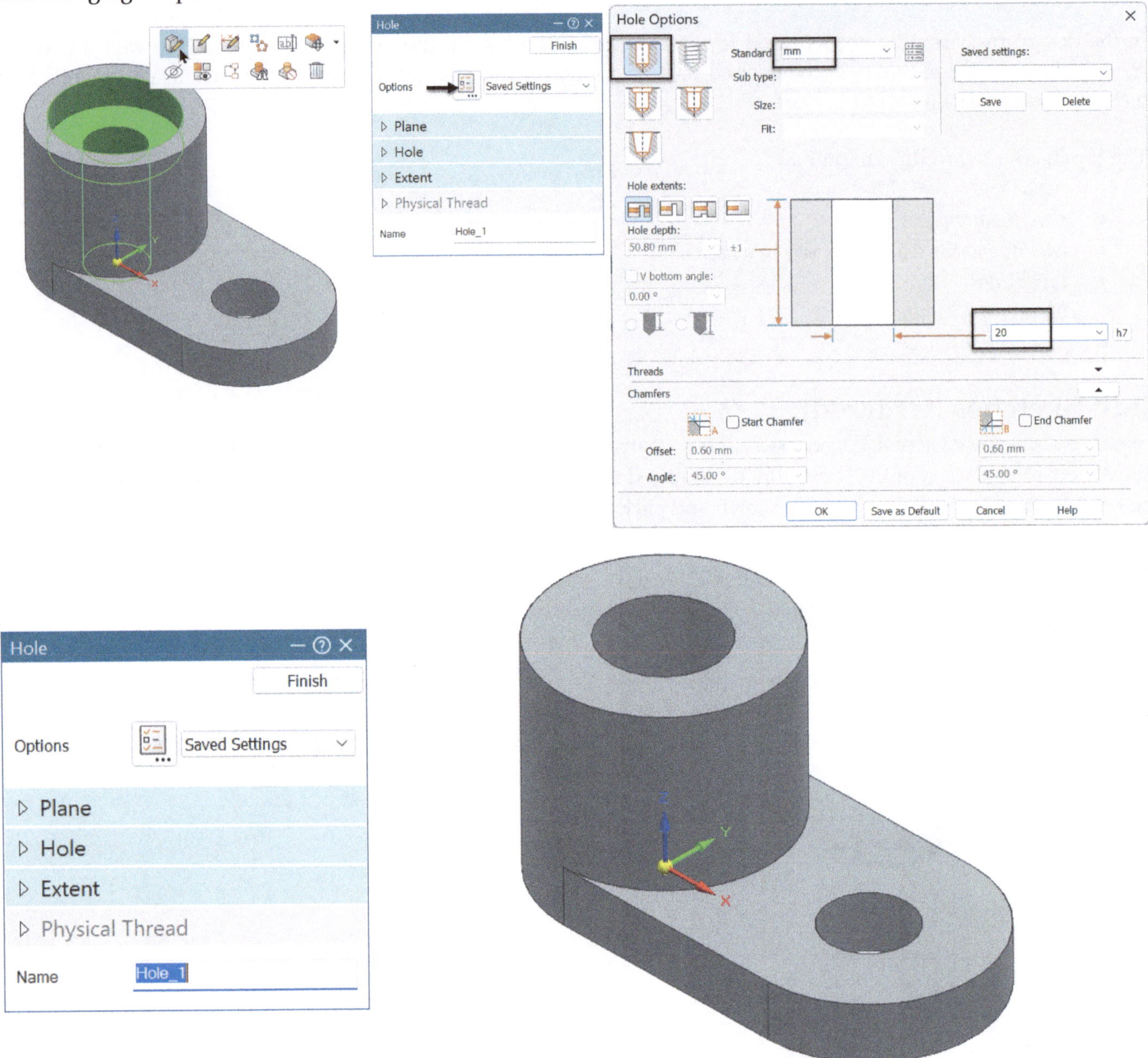

Suppress Features

Sometimes you may need to suppress the features of model geometry. To do this, click on the feature in the **Pathfinder** or graphics window and select **Suppress**.

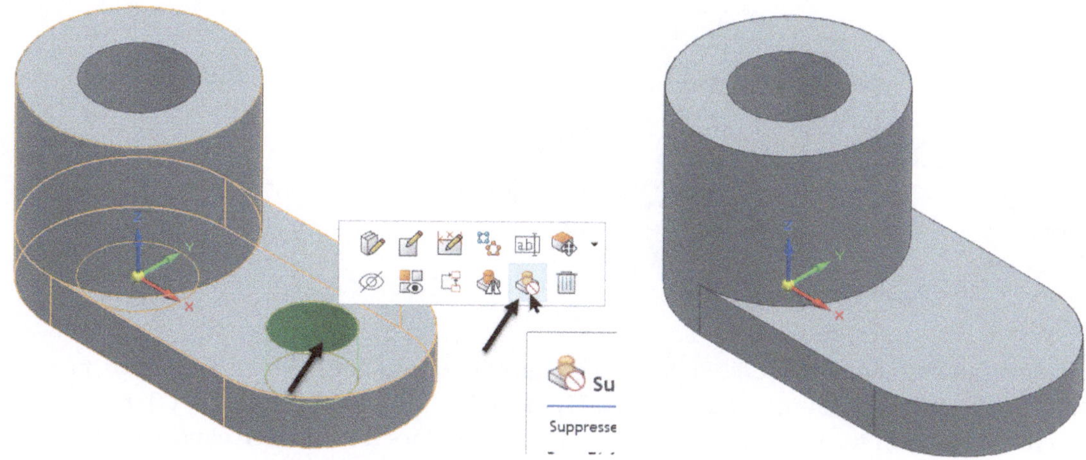

Face Relations (Synchronous)

Solid Edge allows you to define relations between faces. This will help you to control the behavior of the faces when you modify the part geometry. Different relations can be applied between faces. These are explained next.

Coplanar

This command brings the selected faces onto one plane. Activate this command (click **Home > Face Relate > Coplanar** on the ribbon) and select the first face. Right-click and select the second face. Again, right-click to make the two faces coplanar.

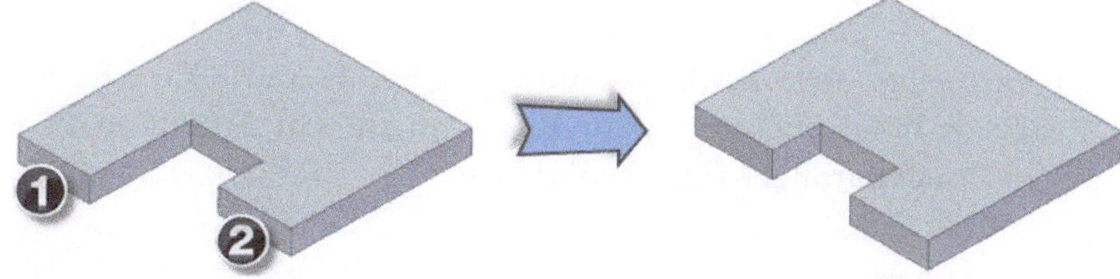

Concentric

This command makes two cylindrical faces share the same centerpoint. Activate this command (click **Home > Face Relate > Concentric** on the ribbon) and select the first cylindrical face. Click the right mouse button and select the second cylindrical face. Click the **Accept** button on the command bar to make the first face concentric to the second one.

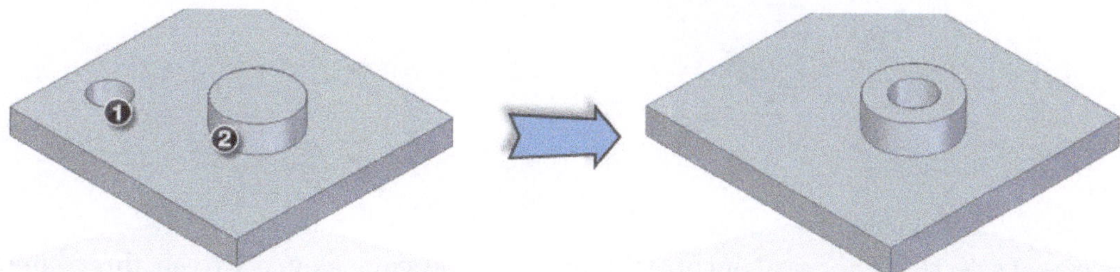

Symmetry

This command makes two faces symmetric about a plane. Activate this command (click **Home > Face Relate > Symmetry** on the ribbon), select the first face and click **Accept** on the command bar. Select the second face and click **Accept** on the command bar. Select the symmetric plane and click **Accept** to make the faces symmetric.

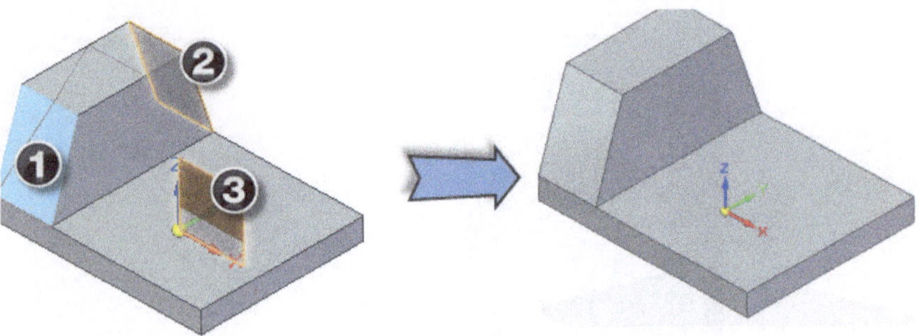

Offset

This command defines an offset distance between two faces. The selected faces should share a common face that is perpendicular to both of them. Activate this command (click **Home > Face Relate > Offset** on the ribbon), select the first face, and then click **Accept** on the command bar. Select the second face and click **Accept**. Type-in an offset value in the box displayed on the model. Click **Accept** on the command bar; the first face will be offset from the second face by the specified value.

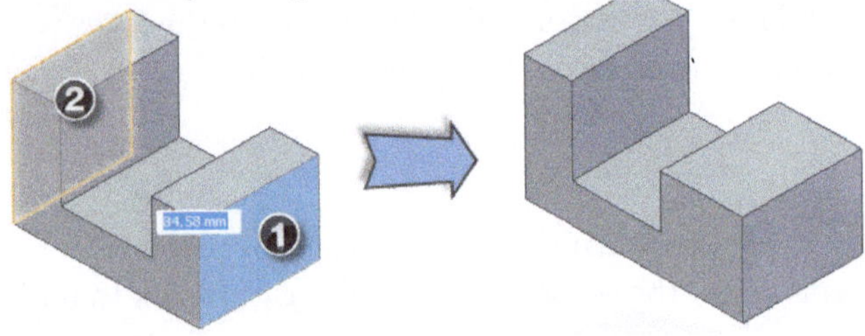

Parallel

This command makes two faces parallel to each other. Activate this command (click **Home > Face Relate > Parallel** on the ribbon), select the first face, and then click **Accept** on the command bar. Select the second face and click **Accept**. The first face will become parallel to the second face.

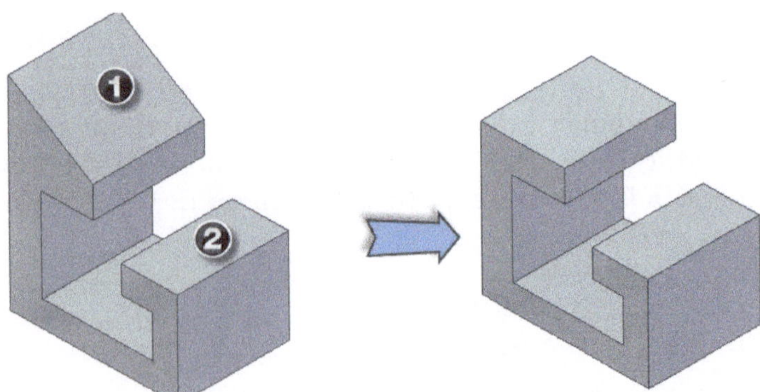

Aligned Holes

This command makes the axes of selected cylindrical or conical faces lie on the same plane. Activate this command and select cylindrical faces from the part geometry. Click **Accept** on the command bar and select a plane or point. Click **Accept** on the command bar; you will notice that selected faces' axes will be moved onto one plane.

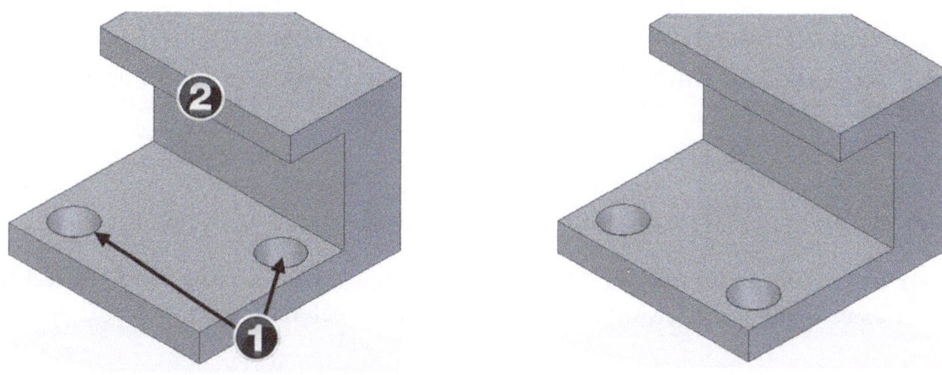

Equal

This command makes the selected cylindrical faces equal in radius. The radius of the first face will be equal to that of the second face.

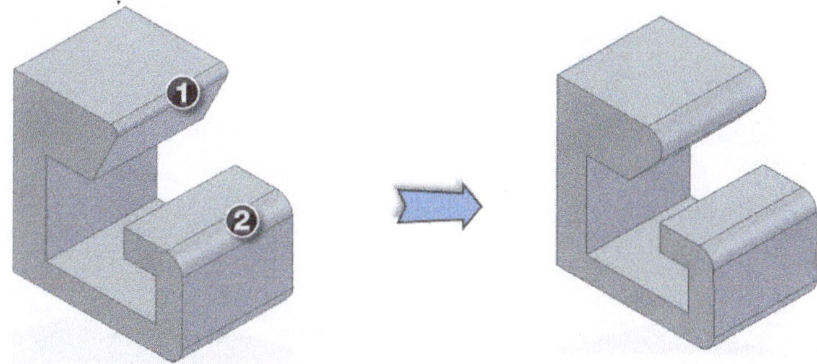

Tangent

This command makes two faces tangent to one another. Select a cylindrical face and right click to accept. Next, select a planar face connected to the selected cylindrical face. Right click to accept the selection; the two faces are made tangent to each other.

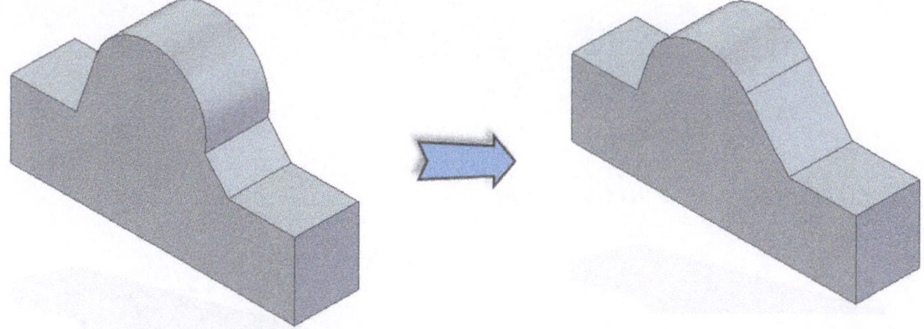

Horizontal/Vertical

This command aligns the selected faces or keypoints vertically/horizontally.

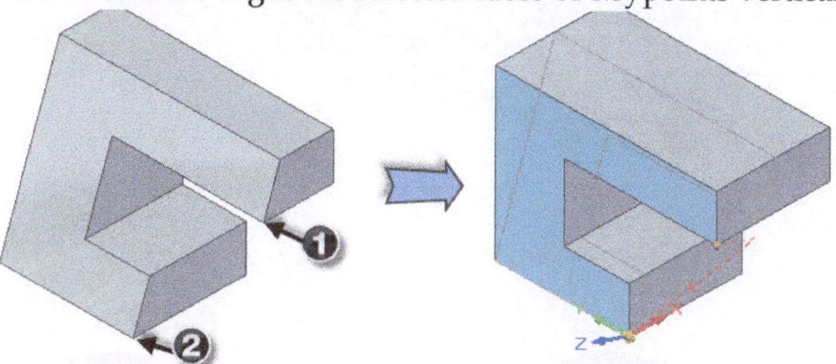

Using the Steering Wheel Tool to Modify Models (Synchronous)

Solid Edge provides you with a special tool called Steering Wheel Tool to modify part geometry faces and planes. You can perform two operations using this tool: **Move** and **Rotate** faces.

Move faces

To move a face, click on it and select the arrow displayed on it. Move the pointer and click to define the distance.

You can also type-in a value in the box displayed on the model. The **Extend/ Trim** option from the **Connected Faces** flyout on the command bar extends or trims the adjacent faces to match the selected face's new location.

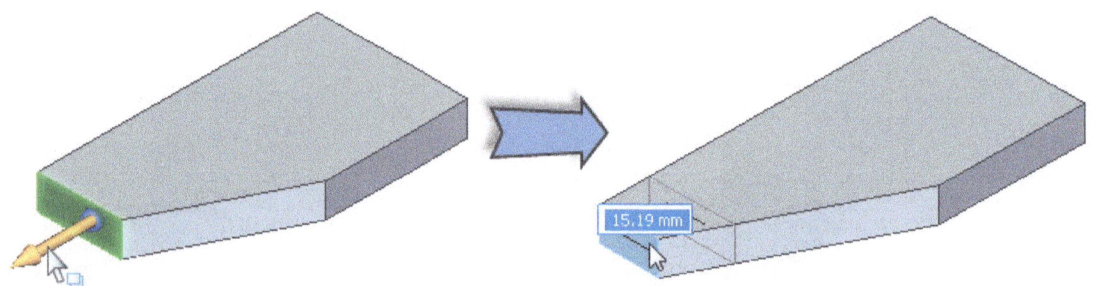

Use the **Tip** option if you want to adjust the faces' orientation connected to the selected face.

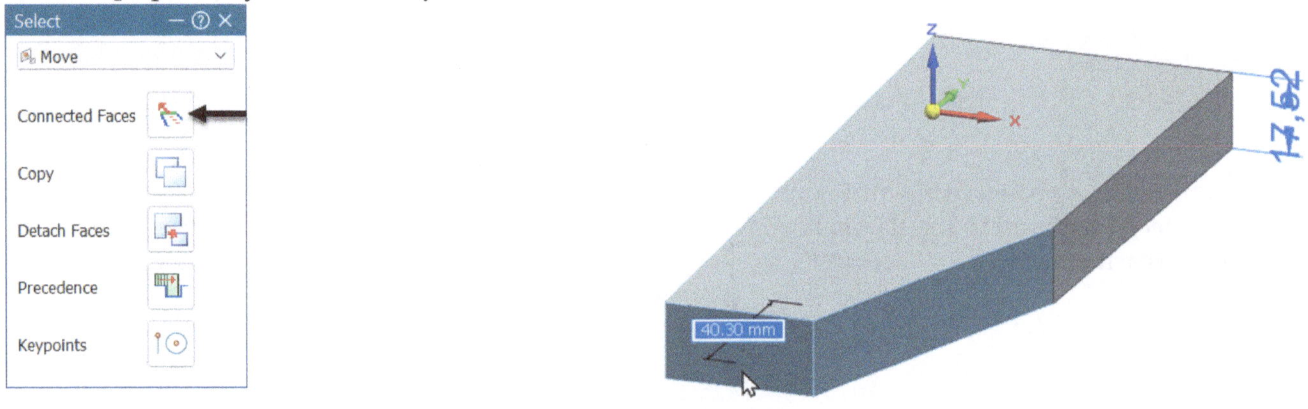

Use the **Lift** option to lift the selected face and add new faces to the model.

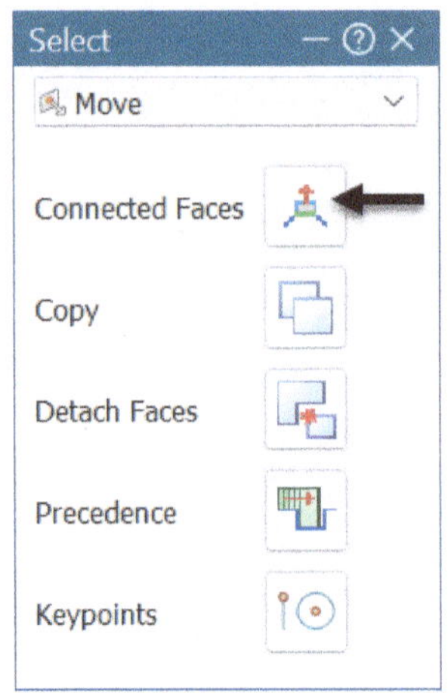

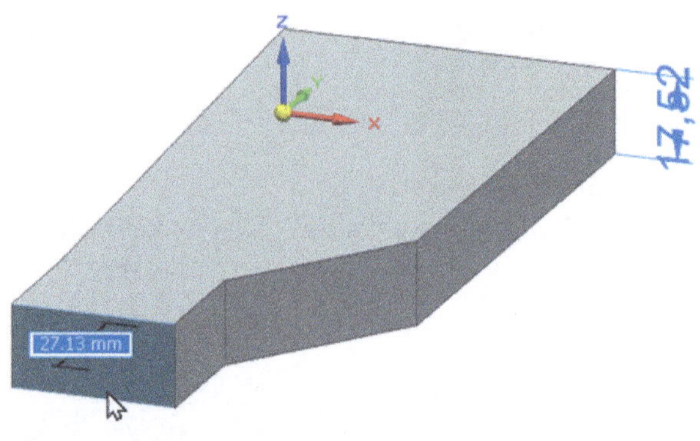

Use the **Detach Faces** option if you want to move and detach the model's selected face.

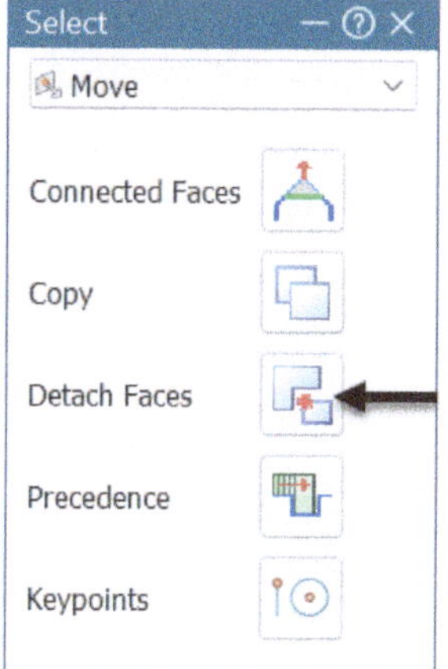

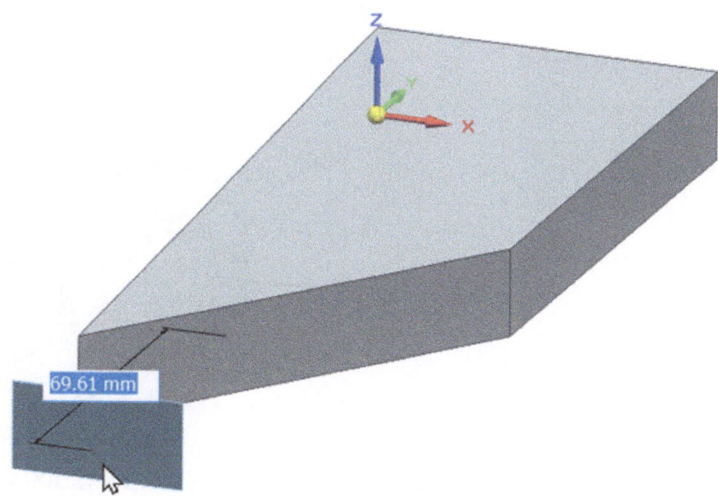

Use the **Copy** option if you want to move and copy the selected face.

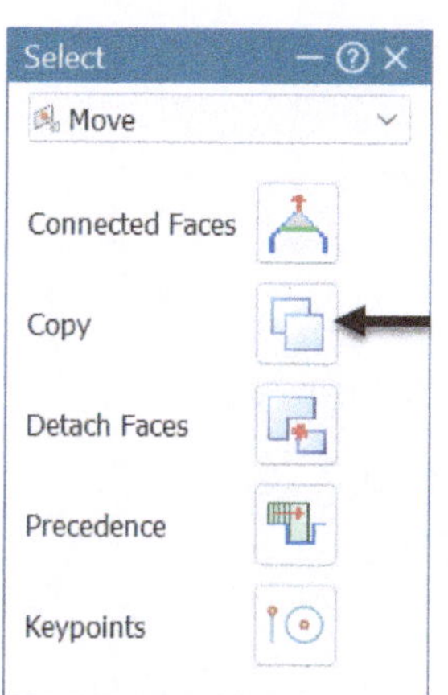

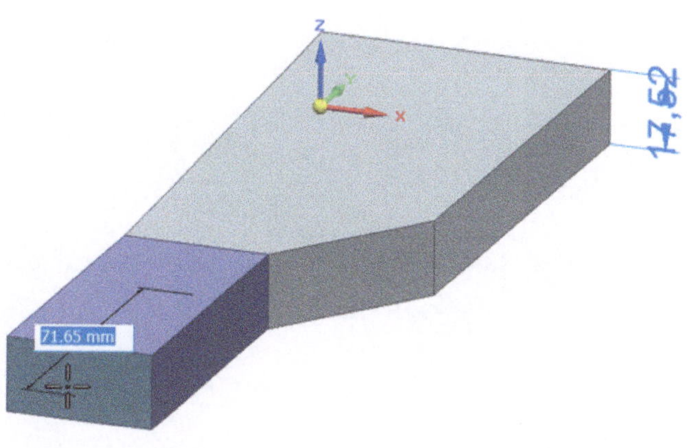

Use the **Model Priority** option to move the selected face only up to the models next face.

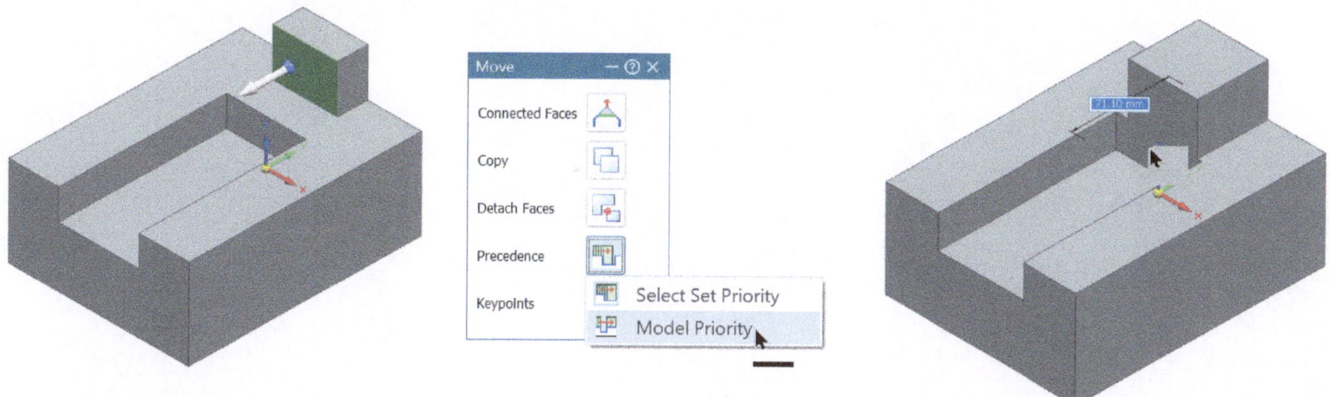

Use the **Select Set Priority** option if you want to move the selected face beyond any faces in the model.

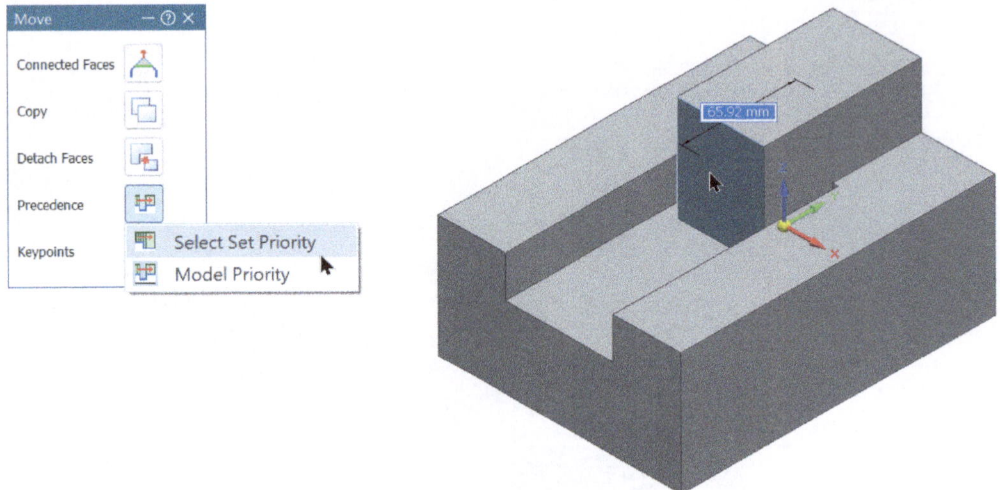

Note that when you move a face adjacent to a chamfer, the chamfer is unaffected.

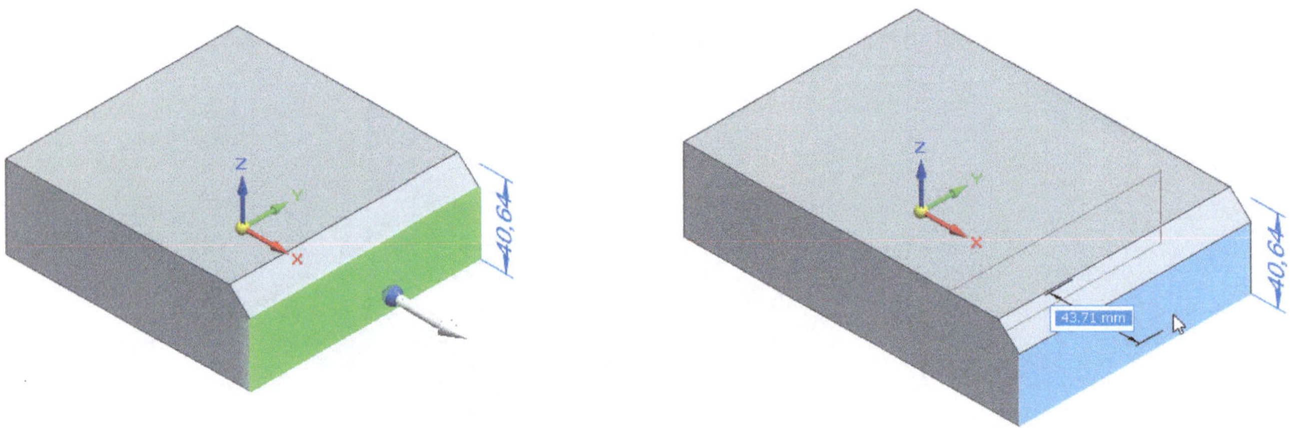

Rotate faces

To rotate a face, you must click on it to display the Steering Wheel arrow. Click and drag the spear attached to the arrow, and then align it to an edge. This defines the axis of rotation. Now, click on the torus of the steering wheel and rotate the face. You can also type-in an angle value in the box displayed on the model.

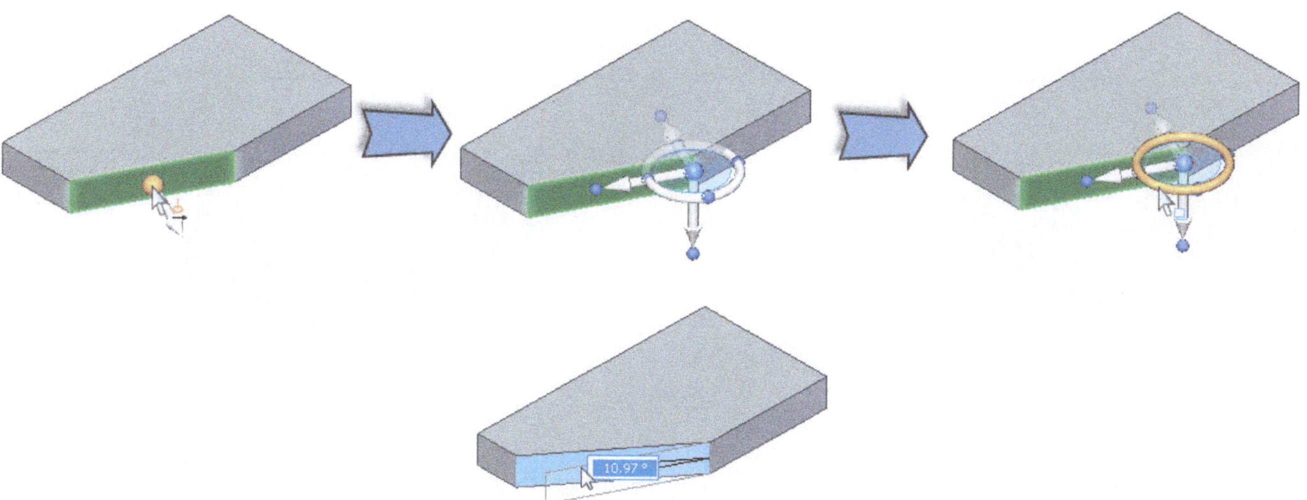

Design Intent Panel

The options on the **Design Intent** panel controls the part geometry when you modify its faces. It appears automatically on selecting any model face. For example, if you move a hole that is concentric to another cylindrical face, the **Relationship** option on the **Design Intent** panel maintains the relationship between the two faces. As a result, both the faces will be moved. If you turn off this option, only the hole will be moved. Similarly, other options maintain the corresponding relationships while modifying the faces.

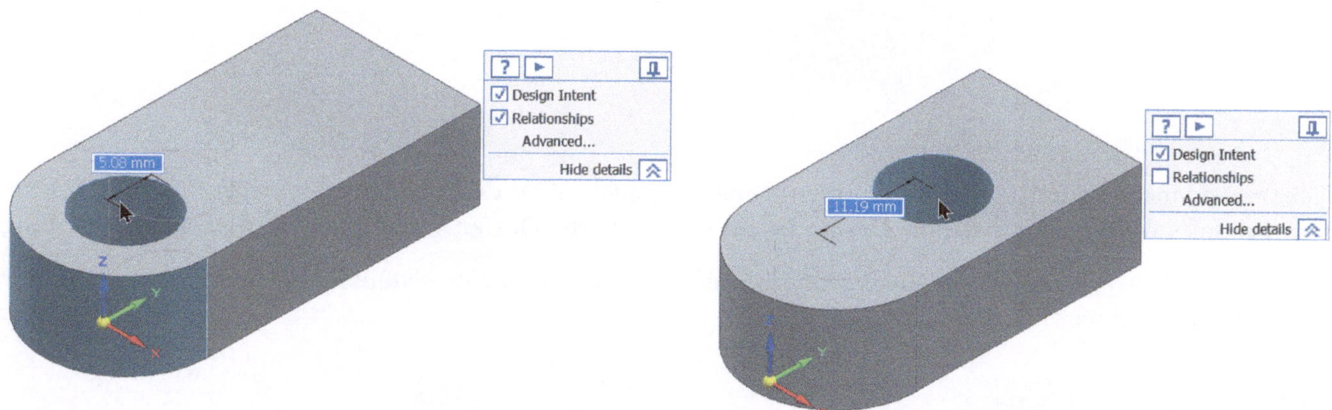

For example, if you move a face symmetric to another face about the YZ plane, the **Symmetric** option maintains the symmetric relationship. As a result, the other face will also be moved in the opposite direction. If you turn off this option, only the selected face will be moved.

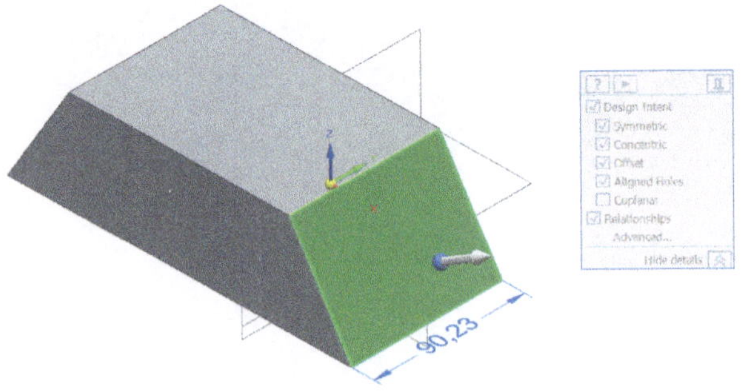

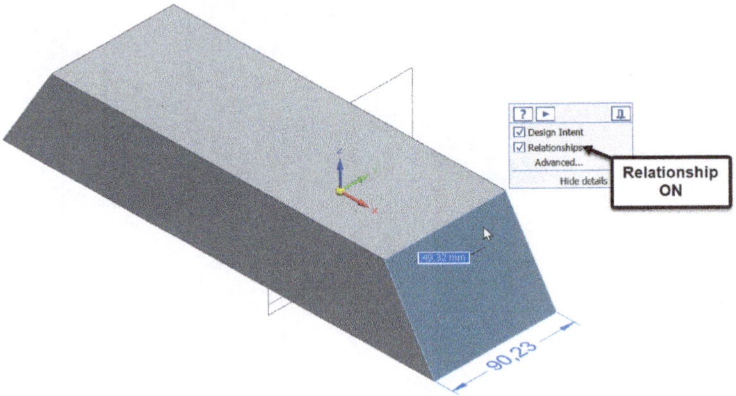

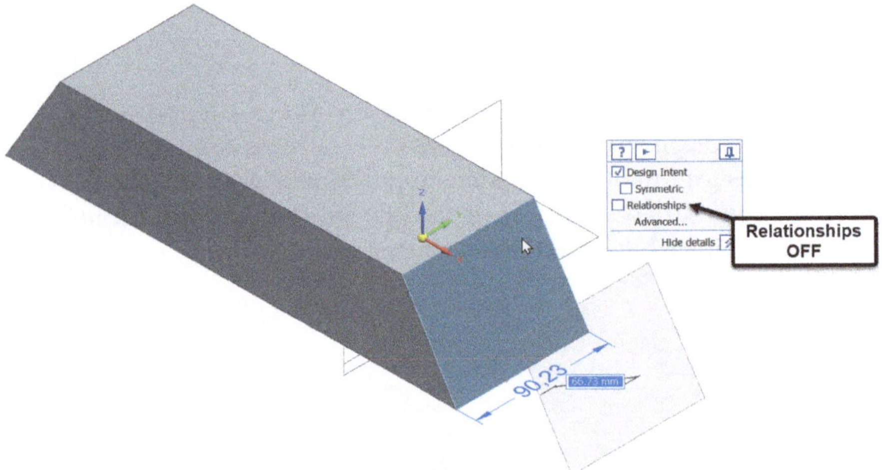

Click the **Advanced** option on the **Design Intent** panel to display all the design intent options on the bottom portion of the graphics window. Uncheck the **Design Intent** option on the **Design Intent** panel to suspend all the design intent options. You can also use the **Relax Dimensions**  and **Relax Persistent Relationships** 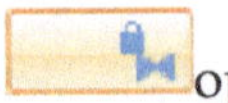 options to relax the dimensions and face relationships.

Use the **Solution Manager** option to solve the errors while moving or rotating faces of the part geometry. Click this option, and you will notice that the model faces are highlighted in different colors. The selected face is highlighted in green color. The error path is highlighted in orange color, and the faces which are being solved are highlighted in blue color. Click on the blue faces if you want to suppress the relationship between the selected face (highlighted in green) and them. Click on the maroon faces if you want to restore the relationship between them and the selected set (green faces). Move or rotate the green face to get the desired result. Click the right mouse button to accept the result.

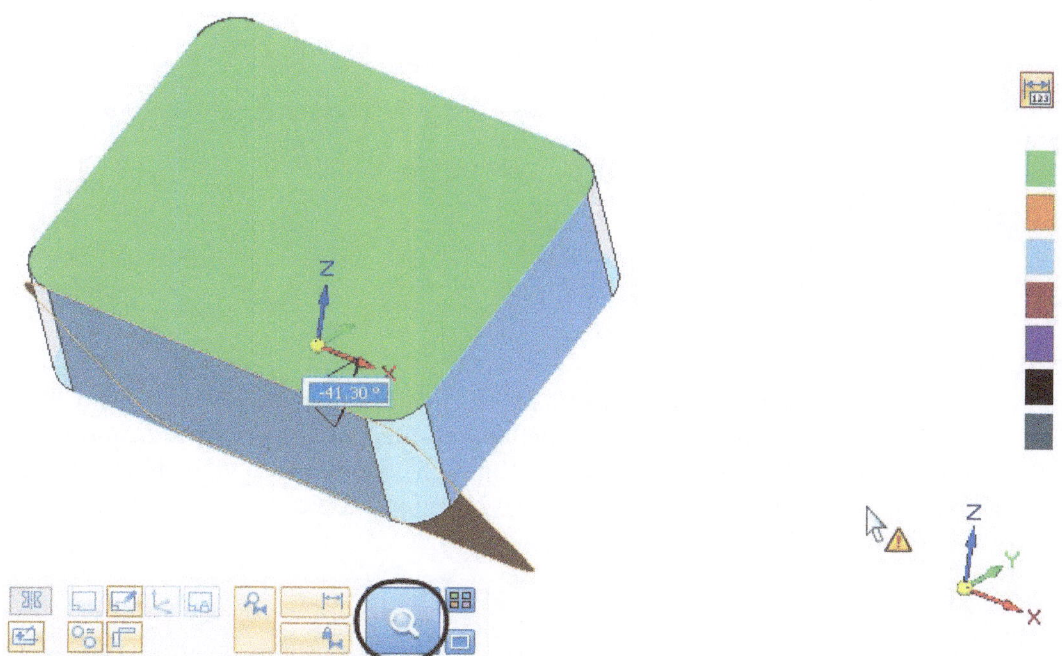

Modify the Part dimensions (Synchronous)

Solid Edge allows you to add and modify dimensions between the faces of the part geometry. This will make the modification process much easy. To add a dimension, activate the **Smart Dimension** command and select an edge connecting two faces. Position the dimension, and you will notice that a box pops up on the screen. Type-in a value in the box and click the arrows displayed on the box to define the face to be affected. Click the double-arrow button if you want to modify both the faces. Click the lock button on the box to lock the dimension. The locked dimension will act as a driving dimension.

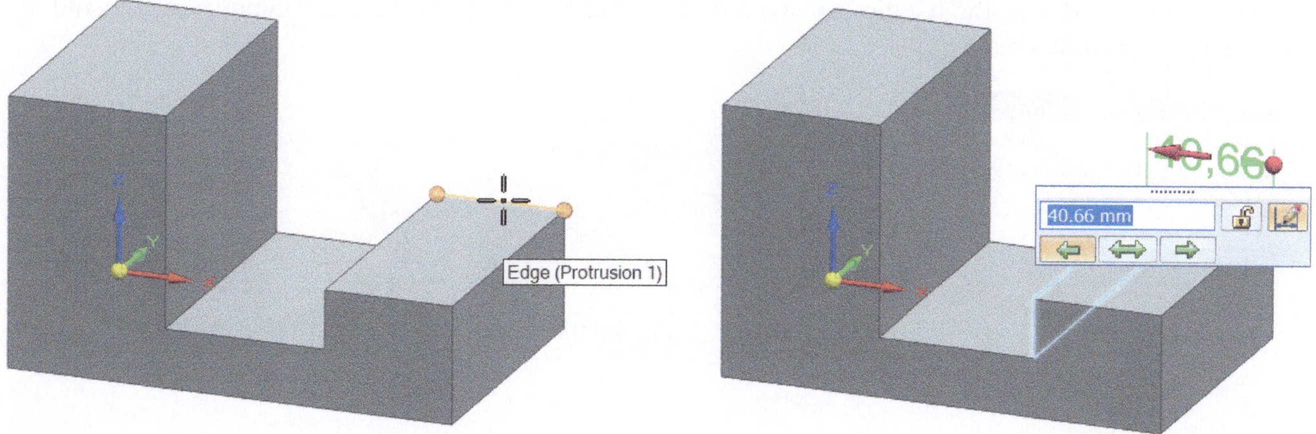

Live Sections

A Live section displays the cross-section at a particular location in part geometry. If you want to create live sections, activate the **Live Section** command (click **Surfacing > Section > Live Section** on the ribbon) and select a plane intersecting with the model. A live section will be created. Use the Steering Wheel Tool to move the live section. You can click and drag the edge of a live section. The part geometry will be modified automatically.

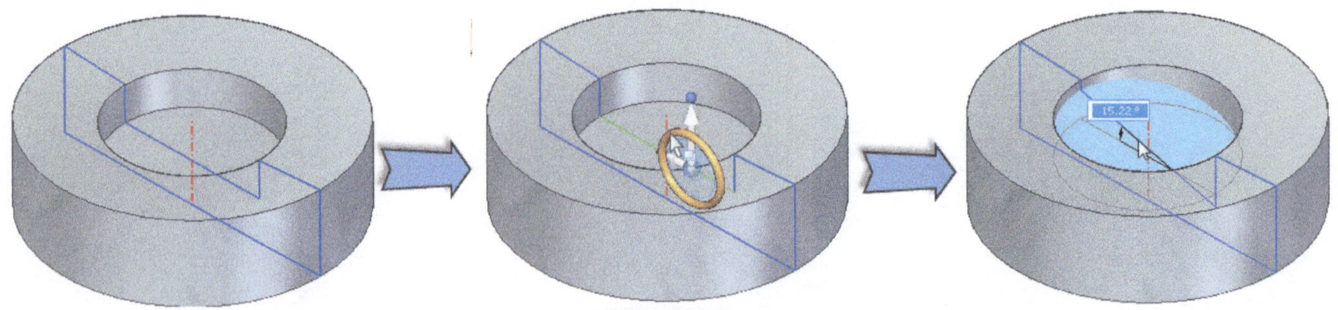

Radiate (Synchronous)

The **Radiate** command helps you to change the diameter of a cylindrical face. In addition to that, you can also move the faces coaxial to the selected cylindrical face. To do this, click **Home** tab > **Solids** panel > **Revolve** drop-down > **Radiate.** Next, select the outer cylindrical face of the model, as shown. Right-click and enter a value in the **Radius** box displayed on the model; the diameter of the selected cylindrical face is changed. However, the faces that coaxial to the selected cylindrical face are not moved.

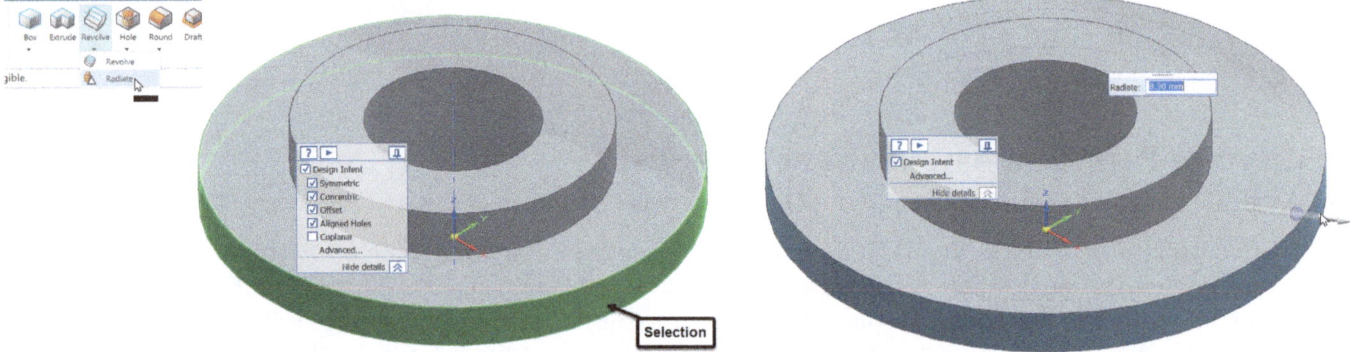

Press ESC and click the **Undo** button on the Quick Access Toolbar. Again, activate the **Radiate** command and select the outer cylindrical face of the model. Next, click the **Include All Coxial Faces** option on the command bar. Click the **Accept** button and drag the handle displayed on the selected cylindrical face; the cylindrical face and all its coaxial faces are resized. Press ESC.

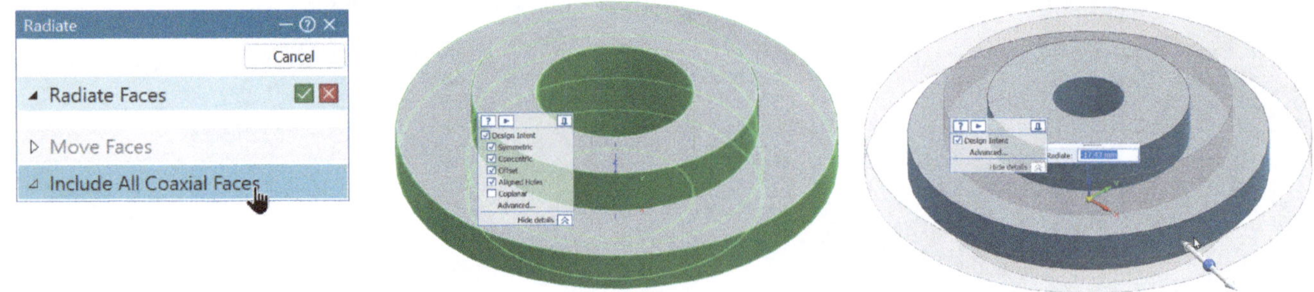

Examples

Example 1 (Millimetres)

In this example, you will create the part shown below and then modify it using the Synchronous editing tools.

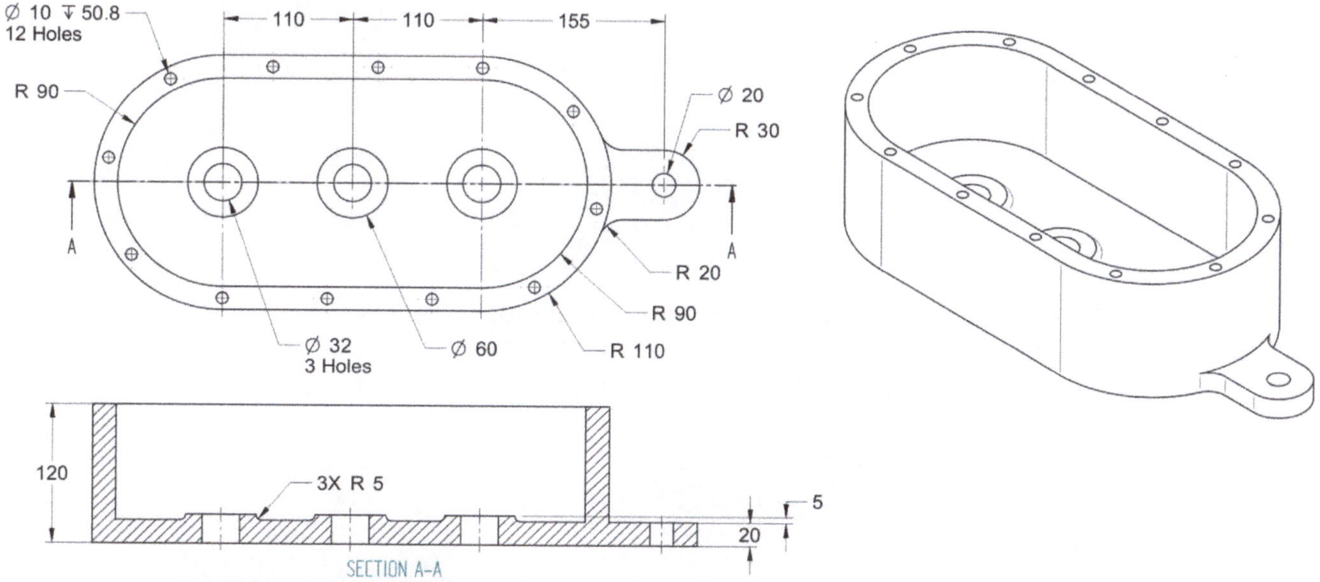

1. Start **Solid Edge 2026.**
2. Click the File Menu located at the top left corner. On the **File Menu**, click **New** > **ISO Metric Part**; a new part file is opened.
3. Create the part in the Synchronous environment using the tools and commands in Solid Edge. You can download the part file from our website if you find it difficult to create it.
4. Click on the 20 mm diameter hole.
5. Click on the dimension value of the hole; the **Hole** command bar pops up on the screen.
6. On the command bar, click the **Hole Options** icon; the **Hole Options** dialog pops up.
7. On the **Hole Options** dialog, set the **Standard** to mm and select the **Counterbore** button.
8. Set the **Counterbore diameter** to 30 and **Counterbore depth** to 10. Click **OK** to close the dialog.
9. Click the right mouse button to accept the changes.

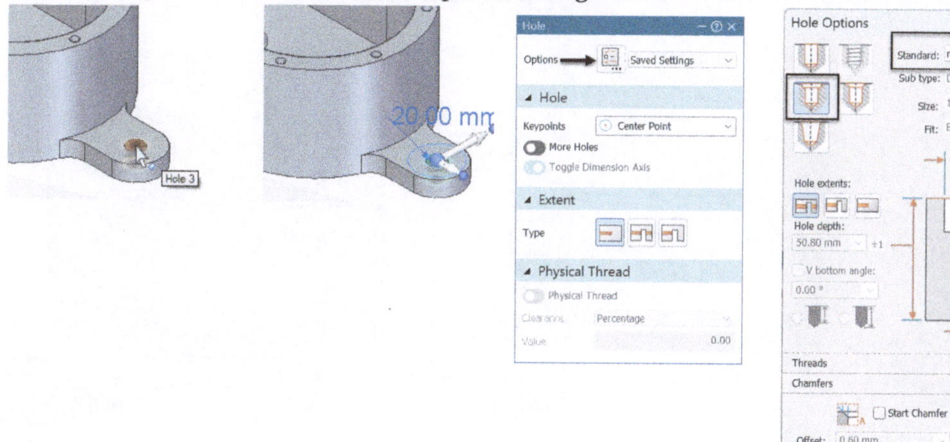

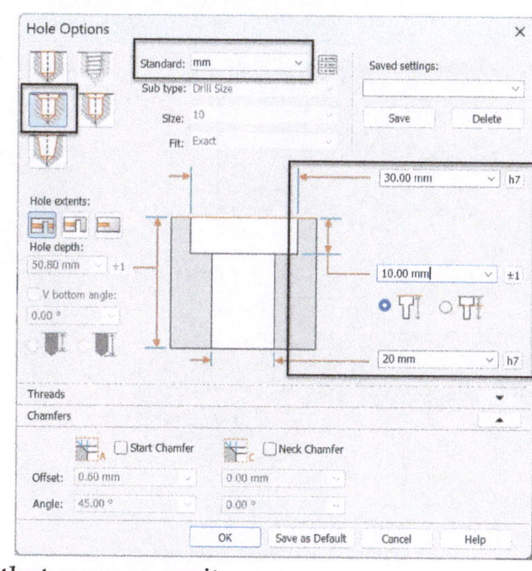

10. Again, click on the counterbore hole and select the small arrow that appears on it.
11. On the **Design Intent** panel, make sure that the **Relationships** option is turned ON.
12. Move the mouse pointer and type 20 in the box that appears on the part geometry. Press Enter to move the hole.

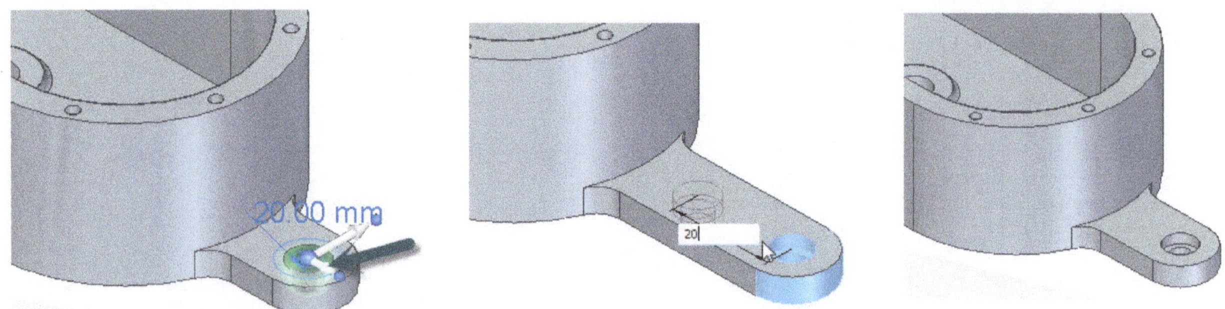

13. Click on the side face of the bottom feature. An arrow handle appears on the face.
14. Click the spear of the handle and drag it; the *Steering Wheel Tool* appears.
15. Align the Z-axis of the *Steering Wheel Tool* to the vertical edge, as shown in the figure.

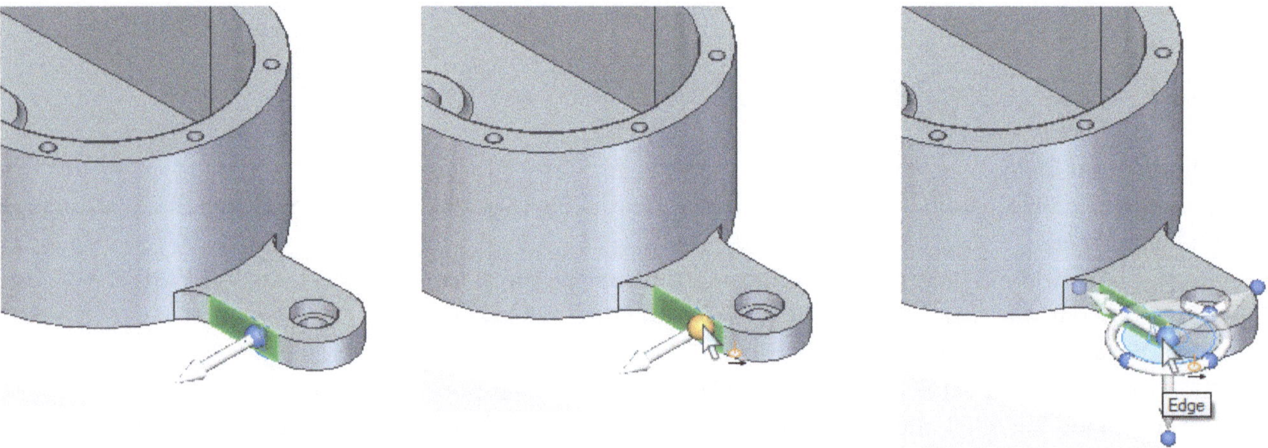

16. Make sure that the **Symmetric** option is turned ON on the **Design Intent** panel.
17. Click on the torus of the *Steering Wheel Tool* and move the mouse pointer outside.
18. Type -20 in the box that appears on the geometry. Press Enter to rotate the faces.

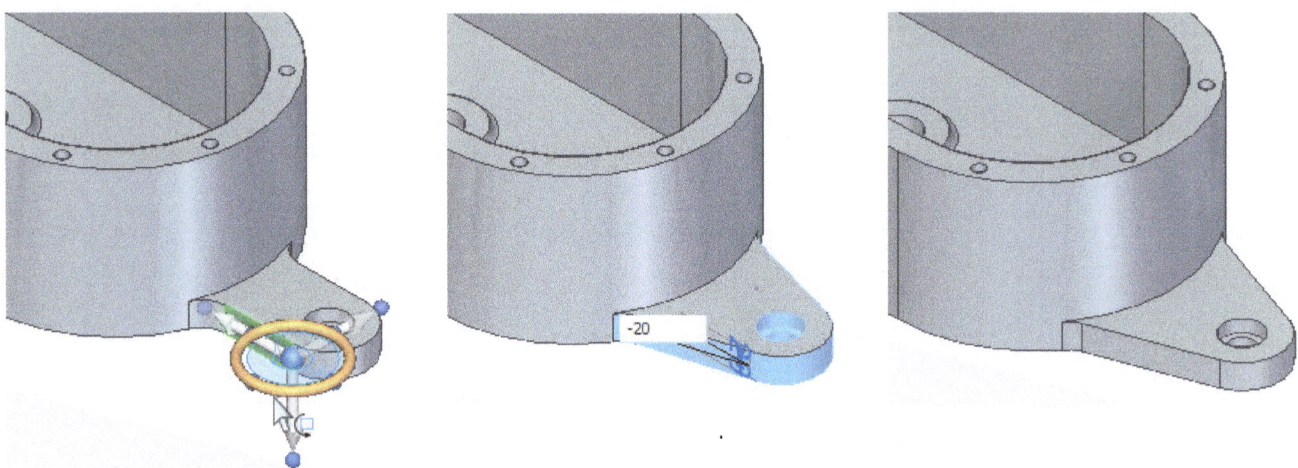

19. Click on any one of the holes of the *Along Curve* pattern; the whole pattern is selected.
20. Click the *Pattern Handle* that appears on the geometry; the **Along Curve** command bar pops up along with the **Count** box.
21. Type 14 in the **Count** box and press Enter to update the pattern.

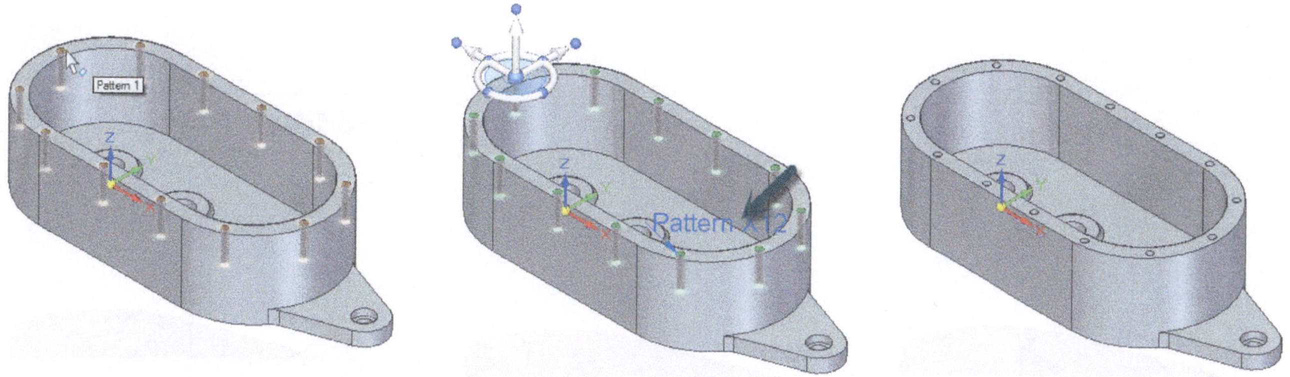

22. Click on the top face of the geometry to display an arrow.
23. Click on the arrow and drag the mouse pointer down. Type 40 in the dimension box and press Enter to update the model.

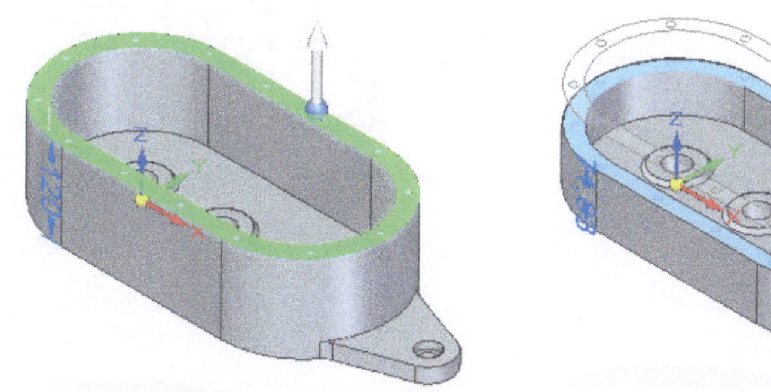
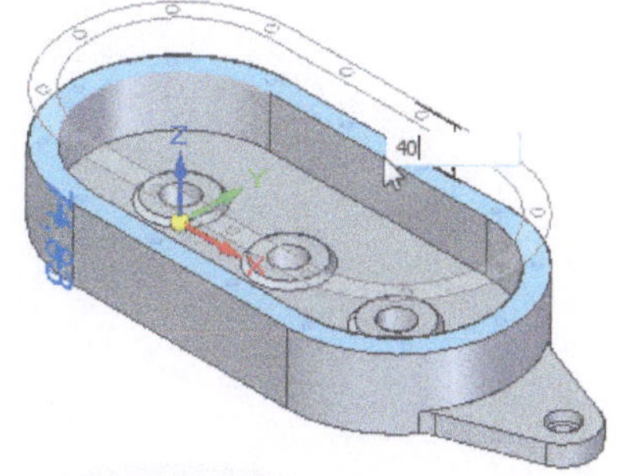

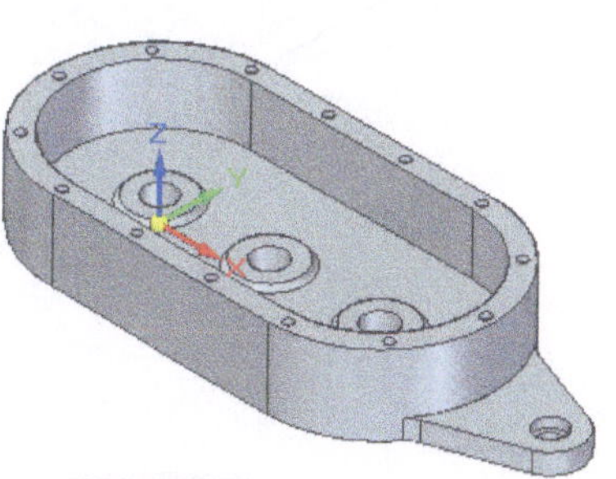

24. Save and close the file.

Questions

1. List any two face relationships.
2. How do you activate the **Move** command?
3. List the three options on the **Move** command bar that help you in moving faces
4. List any two live rules.
5. How do you modify revolved features using Live Sections?
6. What is **Select Set Priority**?

Exercises

Exercise 1

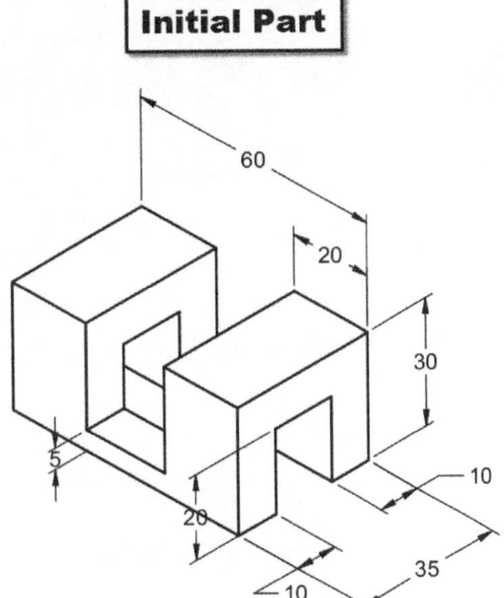

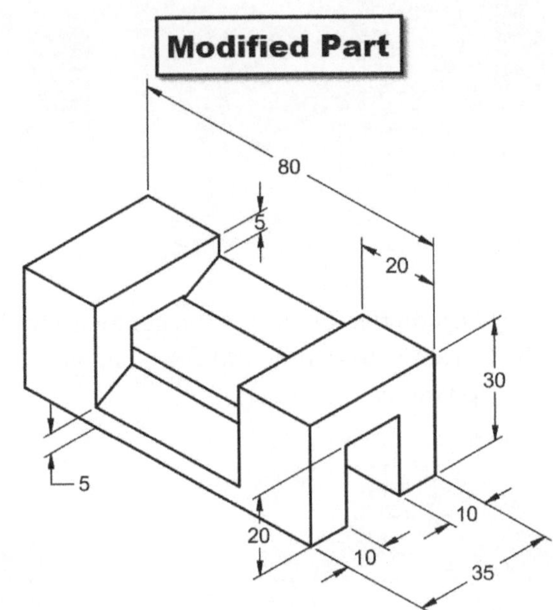

Chapter 10: Assemblies

After creating individual parts, you can bring them together into an assembly. By doing so, it is possible to identify incorrect design problems that may not have been noticeable at the part level. In this chapter, you will learn how to bring parts into the assembly environment and position them.

The topics covered in this chapter are:

- *Starting an assembly*
- *Inserting Parts*
- *Adding Relationships*
- *Dragging and Moving parts*
- *Check Interference*
- *Capture Fit*
- *Editing Assemblies*
- *Replace Parts*
- *Pattern and Mirror Parts*
- *Transfer Parts*
- *Create Subassemblies*
- *Disperse assemblies*
- *Assembly Features*
- *Top-down Assembly Design*
- *Assembly Relationship Assistant*
- *Create Exploded Views*

Starting an Assembly

To begin an assembly file, you can use the **ISO Metric Assembly** option or use the **New** icon and select an assembly template.

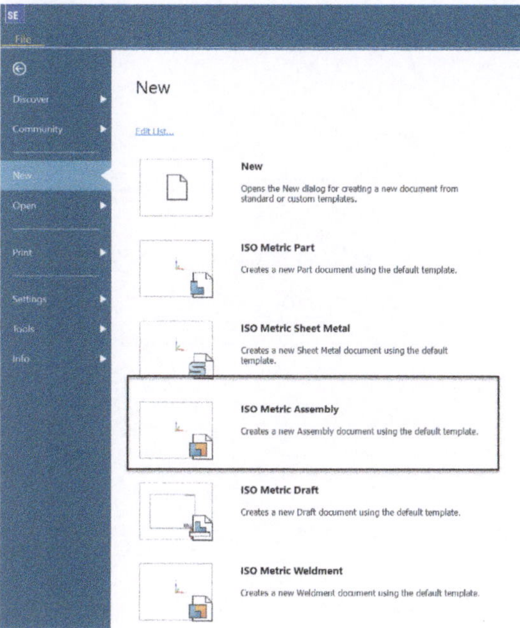

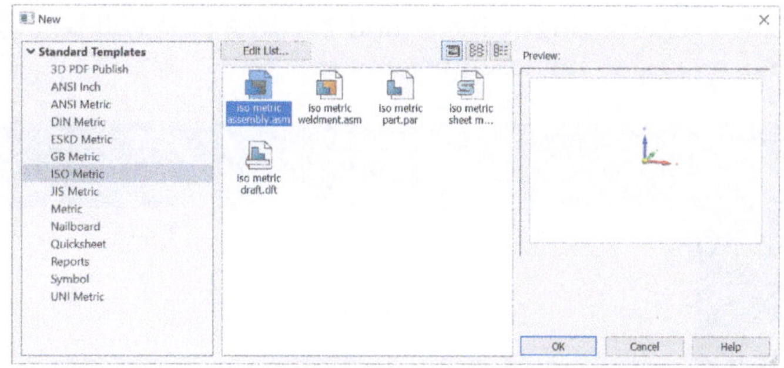

Now, you can insert parts into the assembly by using the **Parts Library** window. On the ribbon, click **Home > Components > Insert Component** to open the **Parts Library**. You can browse to the parts' location by using the drop-down menu on the **Parts Library** window. As you select a component from the list, you can see a preview of the part in the **Preview** box. Now, double-click on the part to drop it into the graphics window.

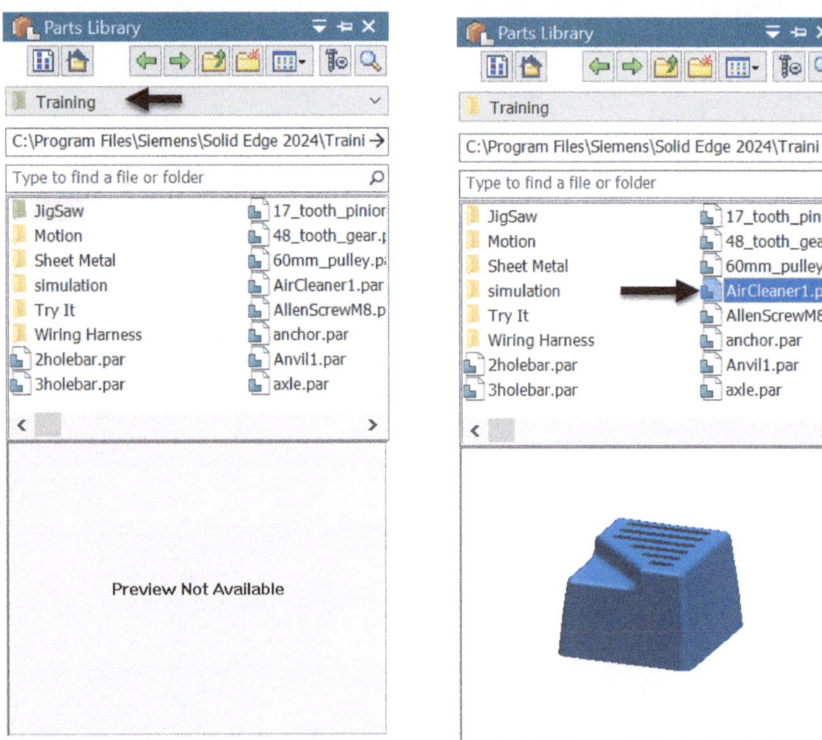

Another way to start an assembly is to create it while a part is open. On the Solid Edge **File Menu**, click **New > Assembly of Active Model**. The **Create Assembly** dialog pops up on the screen. Click the **Browse** button and select an assembly template from the **New** dialog. Click **OK** twice to start the assembly. You will notice that the part will be placed at the origin. By default, the first part will be grounded at the origin. Also, the ribbon displays the commands related to the assembly environment.

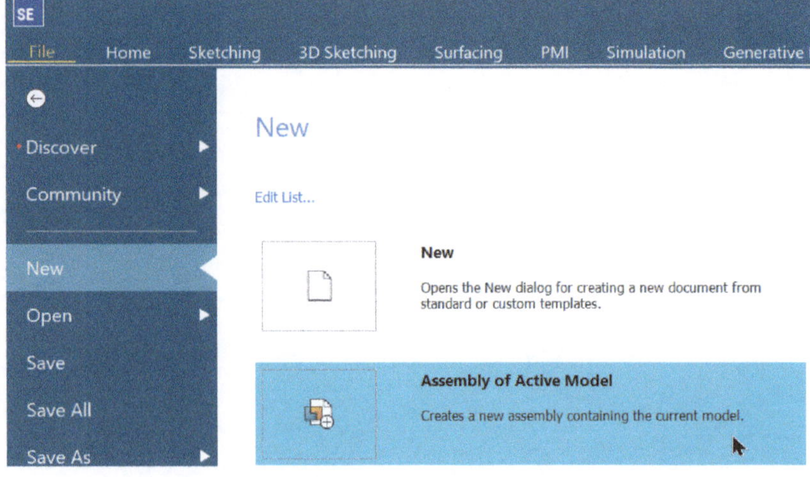

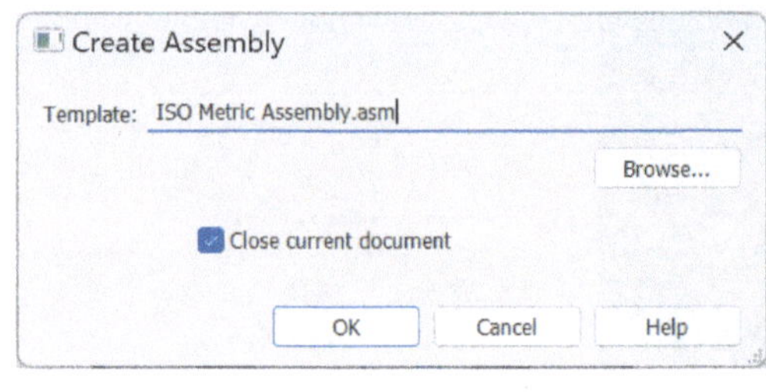

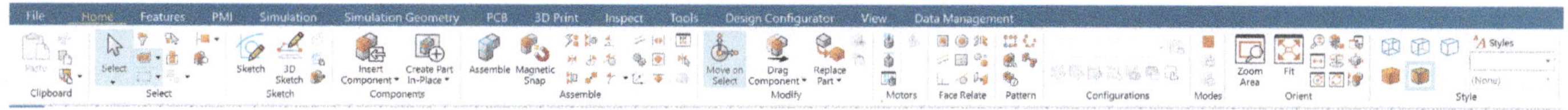

Inserting Parts

There are two different methods to insert an existing part into an assembly. The first one is to drag the part from the **Parts Library** and place it into the graphics window. The second way is to drag it directly from Windows Explorer. In the second method, you are not required to open these parts in Solid Edge. You can simply drag-and-drop the part into the assembly.

Adding Relationships

After inserting parts into an assembly, you have to define relationships between them. By applying relationships, you can make parts to flush with each other or make two cylindrical faces concentric with each other, and so on. As you add relationships between parts, the degrees of freedom will be removed from them. By default, there are six degrees of freedom for a part (three linear and three rotational). Eliminating degrees of freedom will make parts attached and interact with each other as in real life. Now, you will learn to add relationships between parts.

In the **Parts Library**, browse to the folder of the parts to be assembled. Click and drag the first part from the **Parts Library** into the assembly window; it will be fixed at the origin. As a result, all degrees of freedom of the part will be eliminated. Now, drag the second part into the assembly window, the **FlashFit** command bar pops up on the screen. Select a face on the newly inserted part and then click on the fixed part's face. The two selected faces will mate with each other.

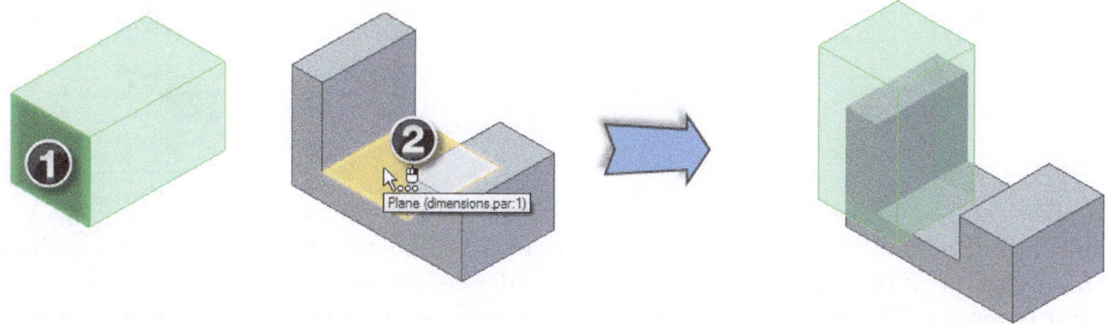

You can use the **Flip** button on the **FlashFit** command bar to flip the part.

Select the second set of faces.

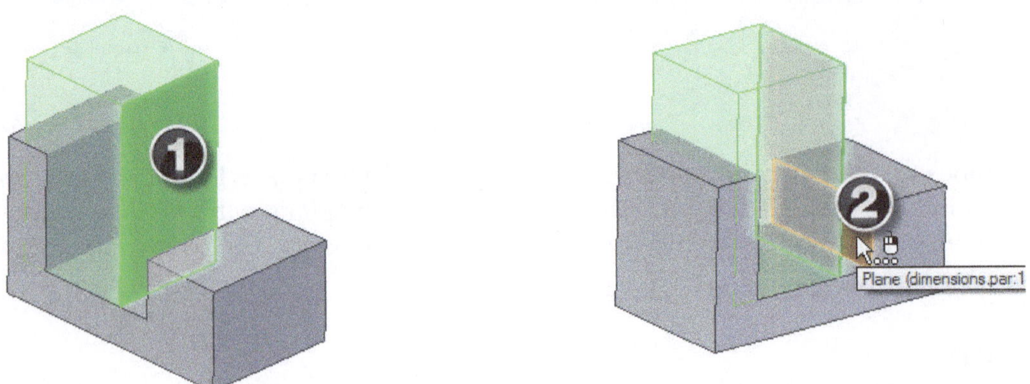

Select the third set of faces; the part will be fully positioned. To confirm this, place the pointer on the corresponding part in the Pathfinder; a message will appear showing that the part is fully positioned.

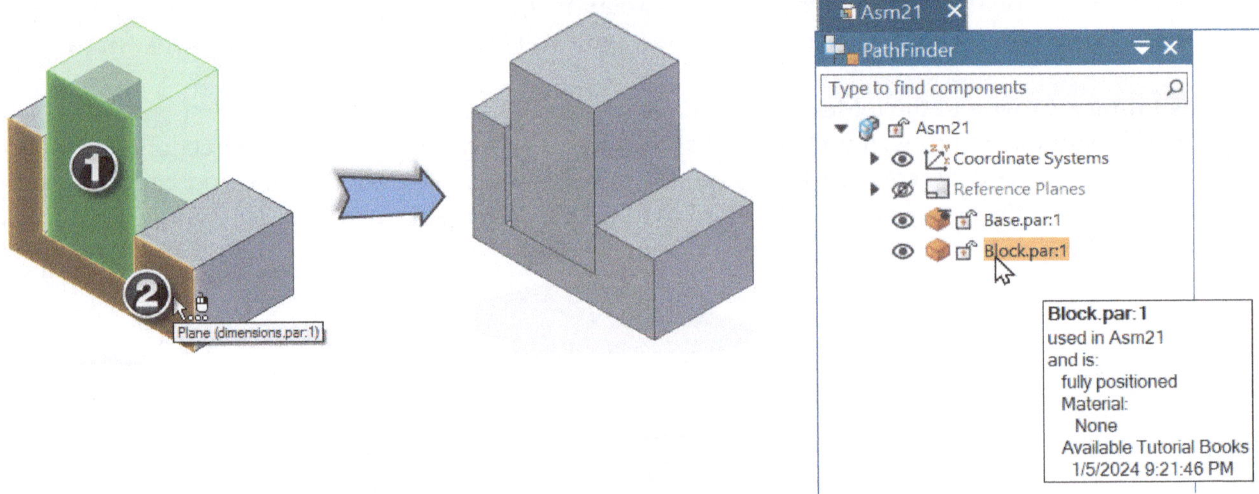

Drag Components

As you insert a part into an assembly, Solid Edge prompts you to define relationships between parts. If you choose not to define any relationships, press the **Esc** key. The part will be under-constrained and free to move and rotate. You can use the **Drag Components** command to move or rotate the under-constrained parts in the assembly window. Activate this command by clicking **Home > Modify > Drag Component** on the ribbon. The **Analysis Options** dialog pops up on the screen. The options on this dialog are self-explanatory. Check the required options on this dialog and click **OK**. Select a part from the assembly window and drag it to a new location.

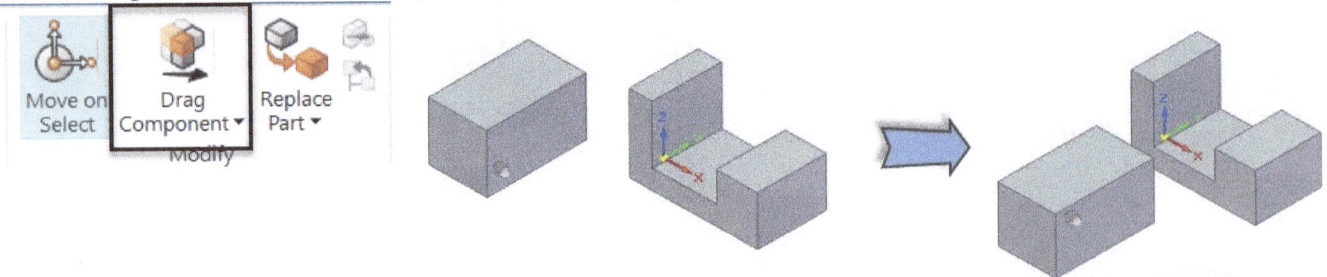

Use the **Move** option on the command bar to move the part in a particular direction. For example, to move the X-direction part, select the X-axis and move it (press and hold the left mouse button and drag the pointer).

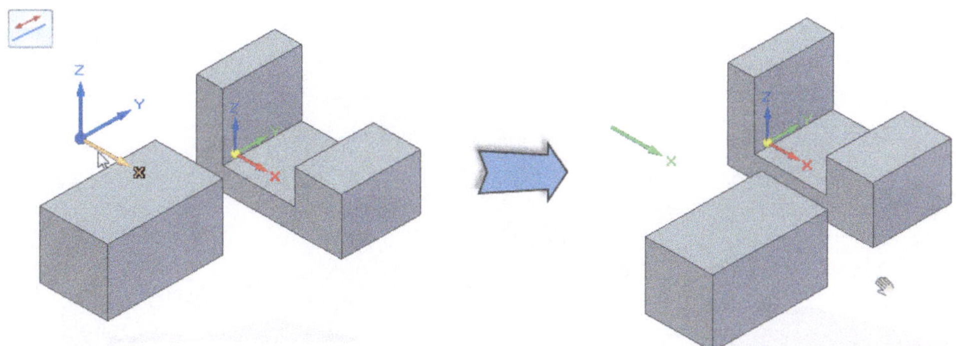

Use the **Rotate** option on the command bar to rotate the part about an axis. For example, to rotate the part about the X-axis, select the X-axis and rotate it (press and hold the left mouse button and drag the pointer).

Likewise, use the **Freeform Move** option on the command bar to move or rotate the component randomly.

Use the **Detect collisions** option on the command bar to detect collisions while moving or rotating the parts.

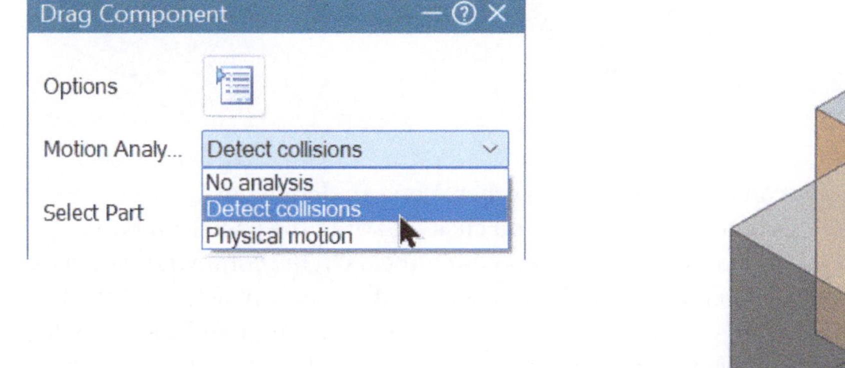

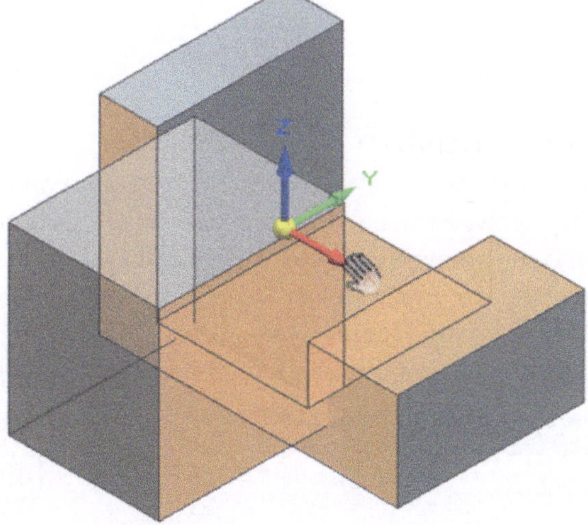

Use the **Physical motion** option on the command bar to stop the part when it collides with another part.

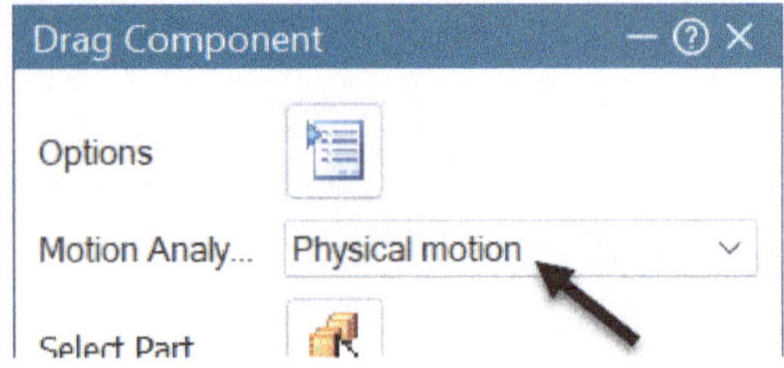

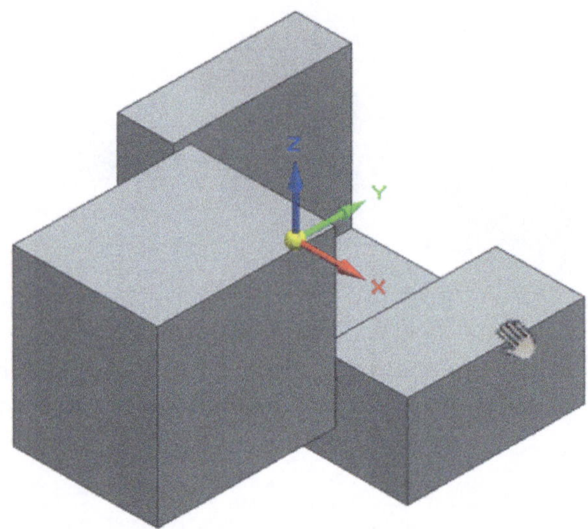

You can also move or rotate grounded parts using the **Drag Component** command. Click the **Options** icon on the command bar and check the **Locate grounded components** option on the **Analysis Options** dialog. Click **OK** on the dialog to close it. Now, select and move (or rotate) the grounded part.

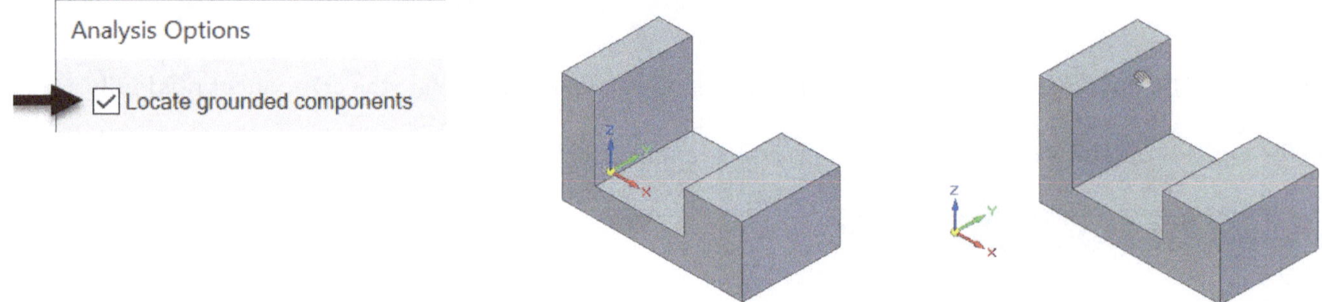

Mate Relationship

The **Mate** relationship makes two faces coincident and opposite to each other. You can define the **Mate** or any relationship between two parts immediately after you insert them. As you click and drag the part from Parts Library into the assembly window, the **FlashFit** command bar pops up on the screen. On the command bar, click the **Types** drop-down and select **Mate**. If the part is already inserted into the assembly, you can activate the Mate command by clicking **Home > Assemble > Mate** on the ribbon. After activating the Mate command select the face of the inserted part and then click on the face of the target part. The two selected faces will mate with each other.

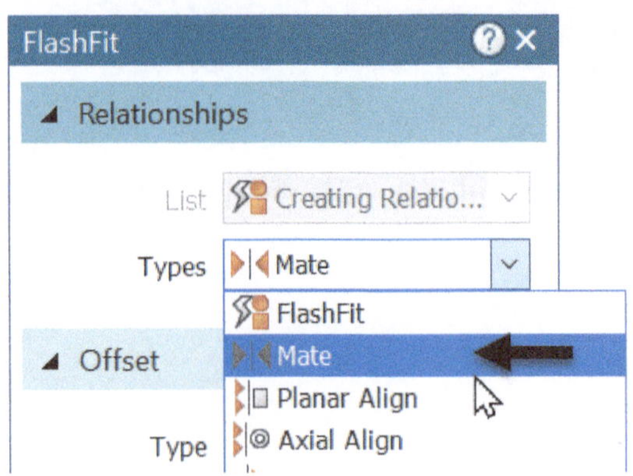

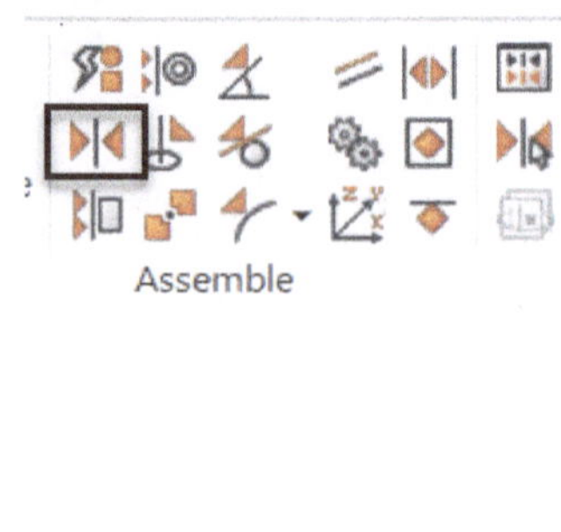

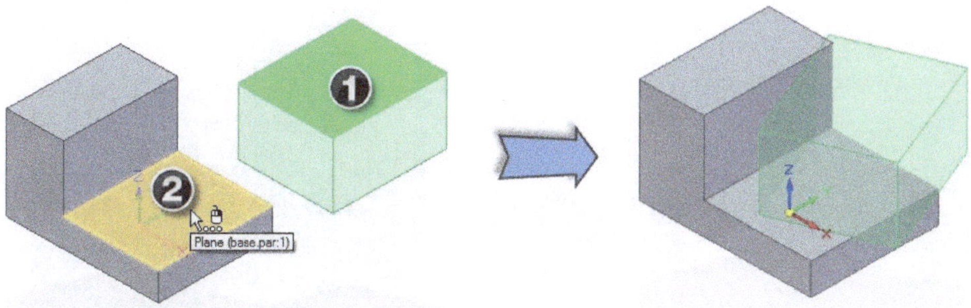

Similarly, select the second set of faces.

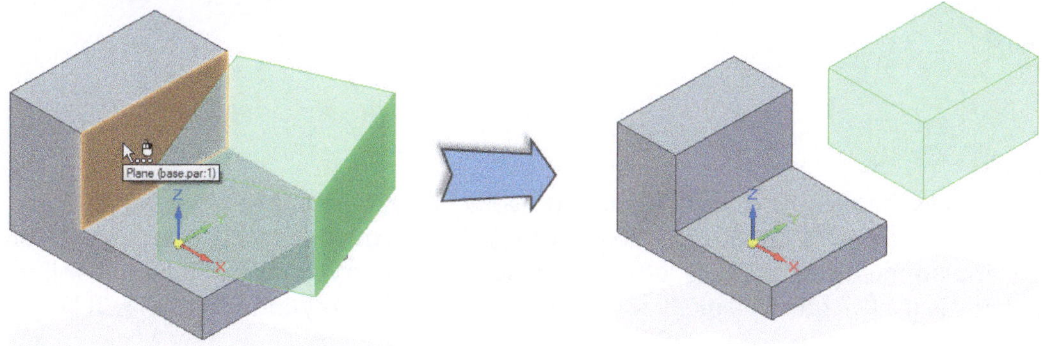

Planar Align Relationship

The **Planar Align** relationship makes two faces flush with each other. To define this relationship, click the **Types** drop-down and select **Planar Align** on the **FlashFit** command bar (or) click **Home > Assemble > Planar Align** on the ribbon. Select a face on the placement part, and then a face on the target part. The two faces will be leveled.

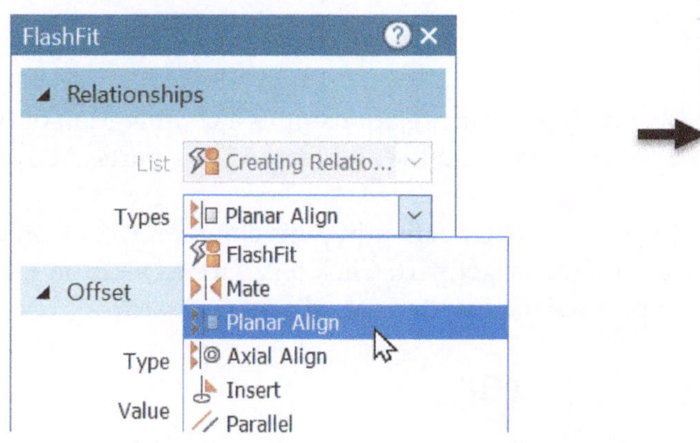

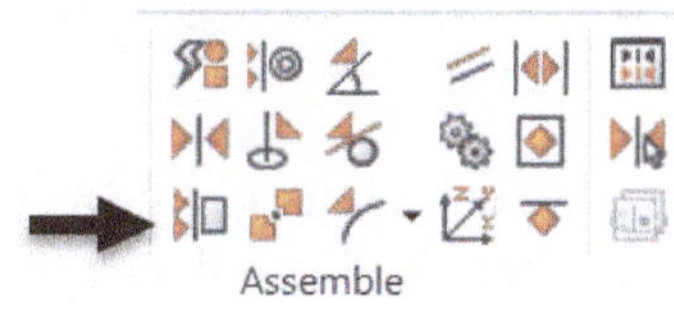

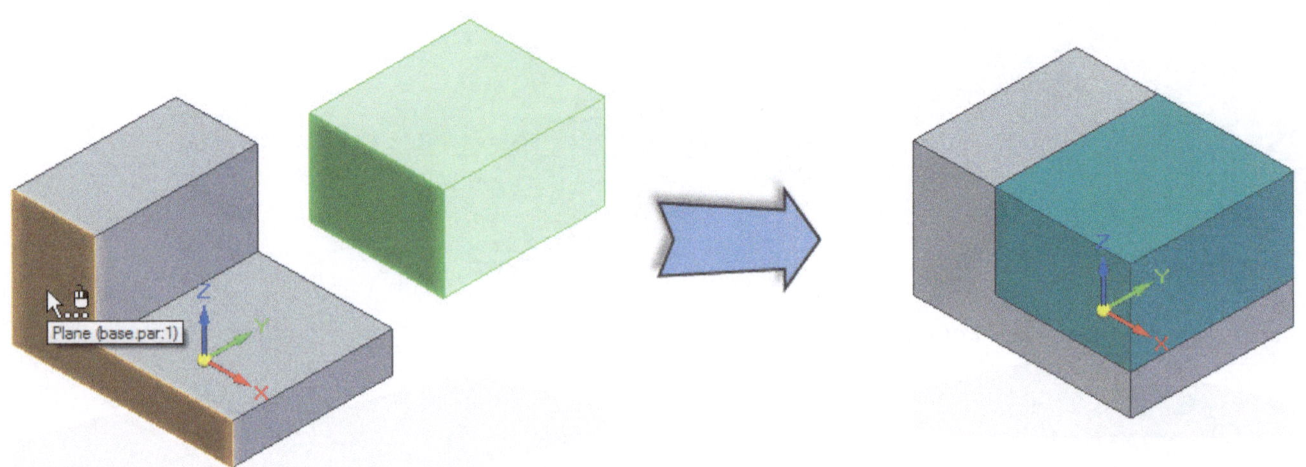

Axial Align Relationship

The **Axial Align** relationship makes the axes of two cylindrical faces coincide with each other. You can activate this command from the ribbon (click **Home > Assemble > Axial Align**). After activating this command, click on a cylindrical face, linear edge, or placement part axis. Click the **Lock axial rotation** icon on the command bar if you want to lock the part's rotation. Next, click on an element on the target part. The two cylindrical axes will be aligned together.

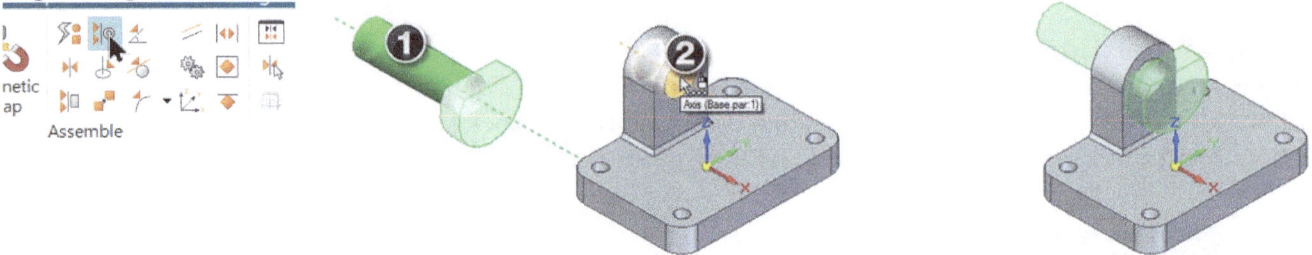

Insert Relationship

The **Insert** relationship helps you to position cylindrical parts into holes. This relationship is a combination of two relationships: **Axial Align** and **Planar Align**. It aligns the cylindrical axes and the end faces of two parts. Activate this command from the ribbon (click **Home > Assemble > Insert**). After activating this command, click on a cylindrical face or axis to align. Next, click on a cylindrical face on the target part. Click on a face to mate on the first part, and then click on a face on the target part. The first part will be inserted into the second part.

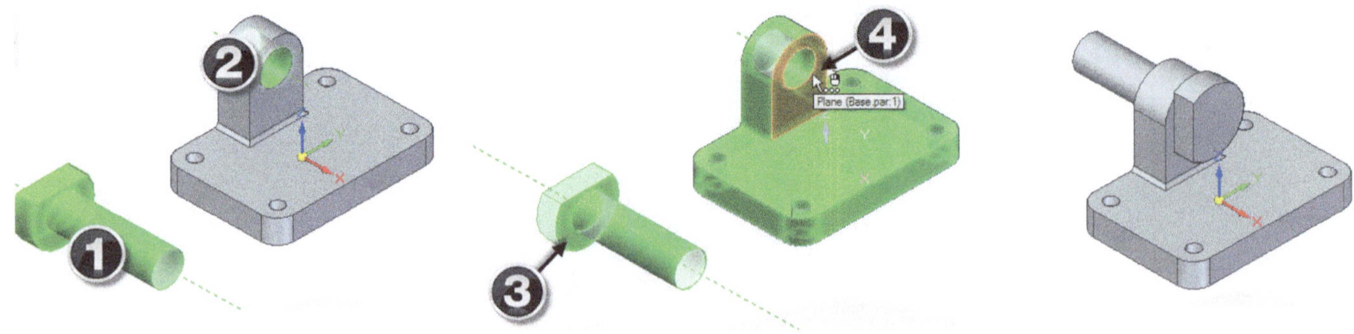

Angle Relationship

The **Angle** relationship is used to position faces at a specified angle. Activate this command from the ribbon (click **Home > Assemble > Angle**). After activating this command, type-in a value in the **Angle Value** box on the command bar and click on a plane or linear element of the first part. Next, click on a plane or linear element of the second part. Click on a plane on which the angle will lie. The first part will be positioned at the specified angle.

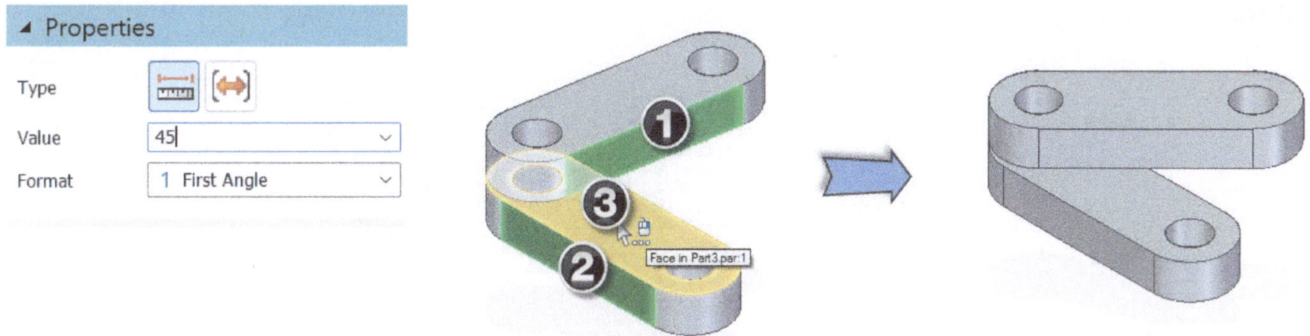

Tangent Relationship

The **Tangent** relationship is often used when working with cylinders and spears. It causes the geometry to maintain contact at a point of tangency. Activate this command from the ribbon (click **Home > Assemble > Tangent**). After activating this command, click on the face to be made tangent. Next, click on the tangent face on the target part. The first part will be made tangent to the target part.

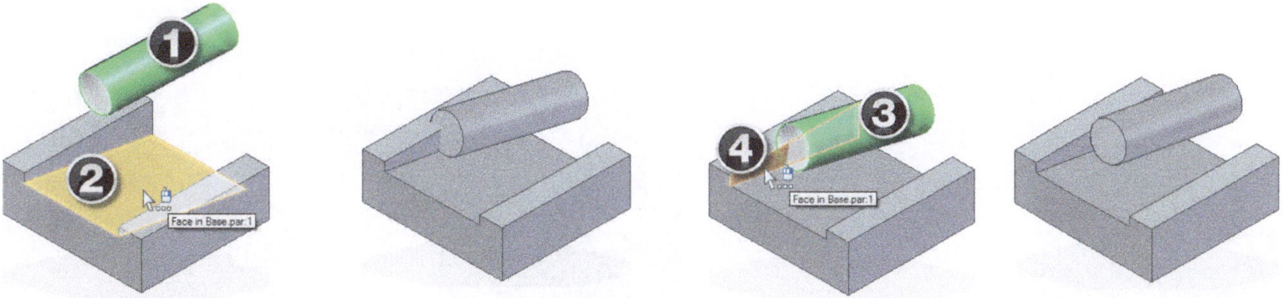

Connect Relationship

The **Connect** relationship connects a key point of one part to that of another part. Activate this command from the ribbon (click **Home > Assemble > Connect**). After activating this command, click on a key point on the first part. Next, click on a keypoint, edge, or face to connect to. The first part will be connected to the second part.

Parallel Relationship

The **Parallel** relationship makes an axis or edge of one part parallel to that of another part. Activate this command from the ribbon (click **Home > Assemble > Parallel**). After activating this command, type-in a value in the **Offset Value** box on the command bar and click on a cylindrical face, linear edge, or axis of the first part. Next, click on an element of the second part. The two selected edges or axes will be parallel to each other.

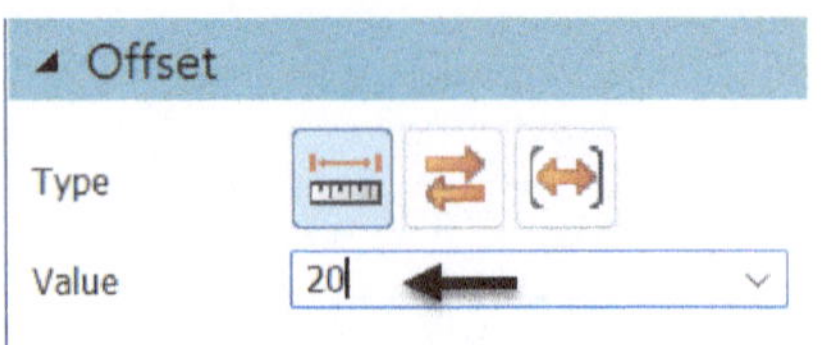

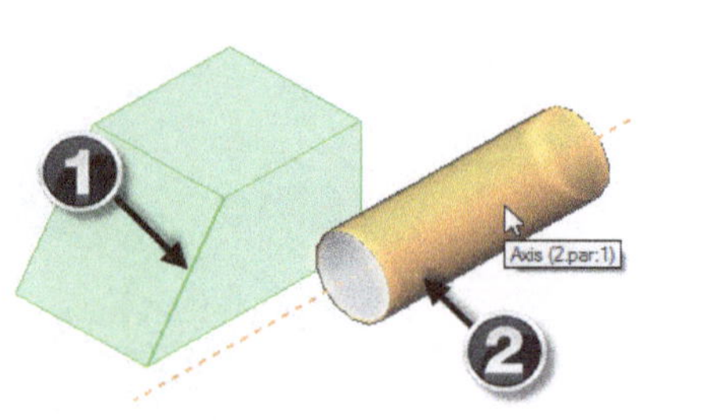

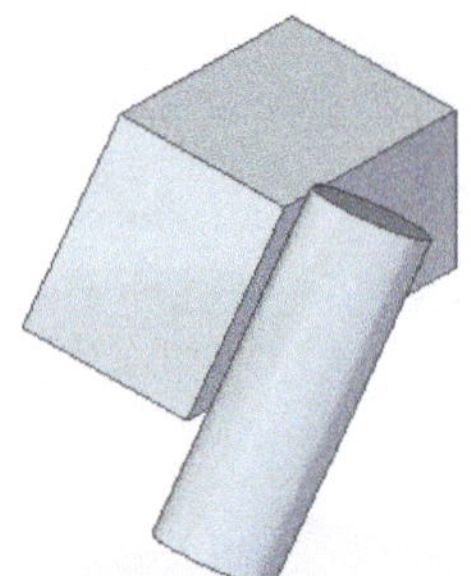

Center-Plane Relationship

The **Center-Plane** relationship allows you to center a part between two faces. Activate this command from ribbon (click **Home > Assemble > Center-Plane**). After activating this command, you must select the object to be positioned at the center of two planes. Click on a planar face, edge, axis, keypoint, or reference plane on the first part. Next, click on two faces or reference planes on the second part. The first part will be centered between the two planes.

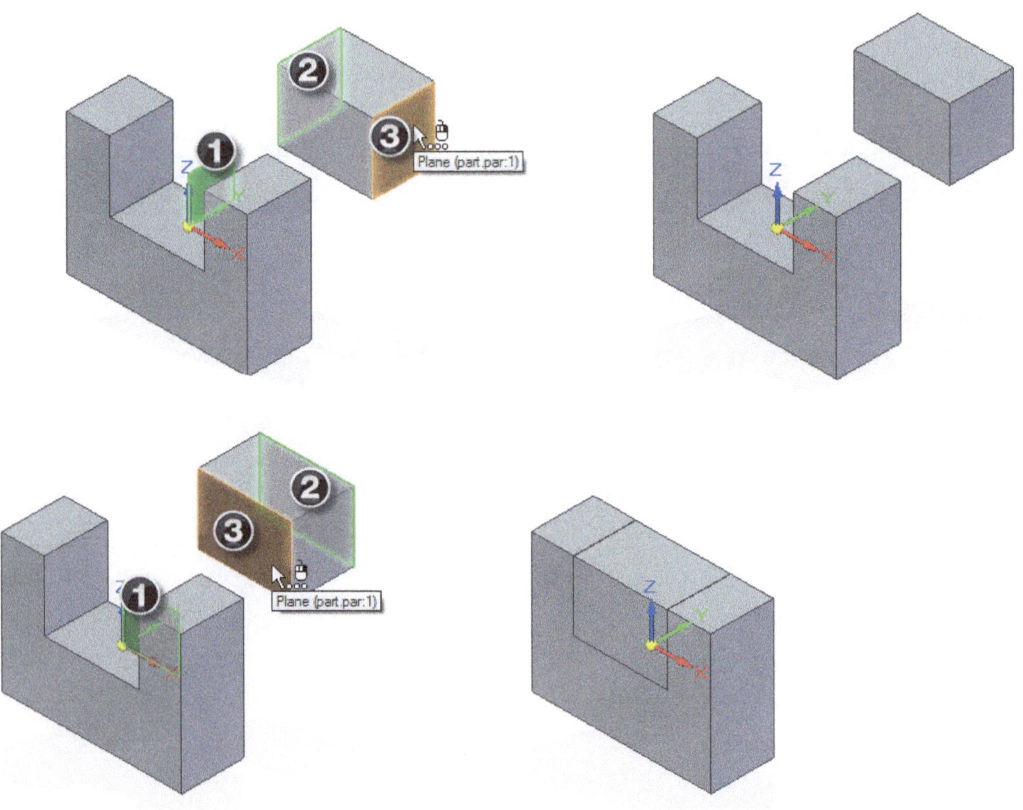

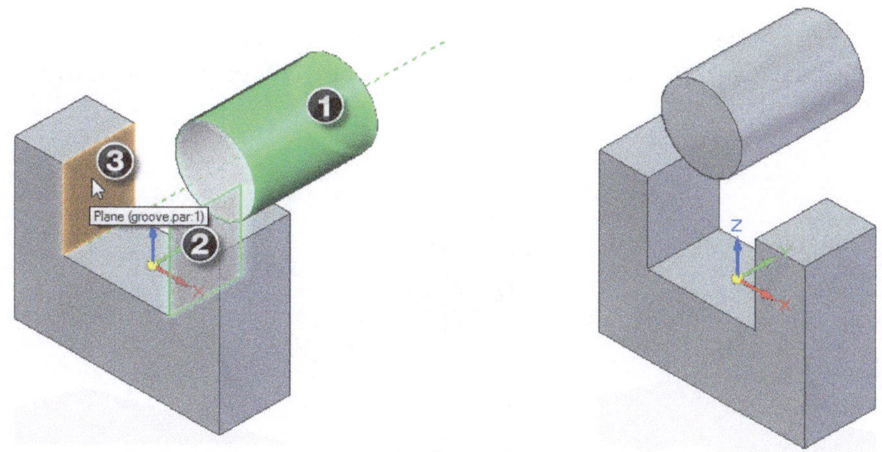

Match Coordinate Systems Relationship

The **Match Coordinate Systems** relationship matches the coordinate systems of two parts. This is the easiest way to constrain parts in an assembly. To apply this relationship, first, you must display the coordinate systems of the parts. You can do so by expanding the **Show** section on the **FlashFit** command bar and selecting the **Coordinate Systems** option (or) by right-clicking on the part, selecting **Show Hide Component**, and then turning on **Coordinate Systems**.

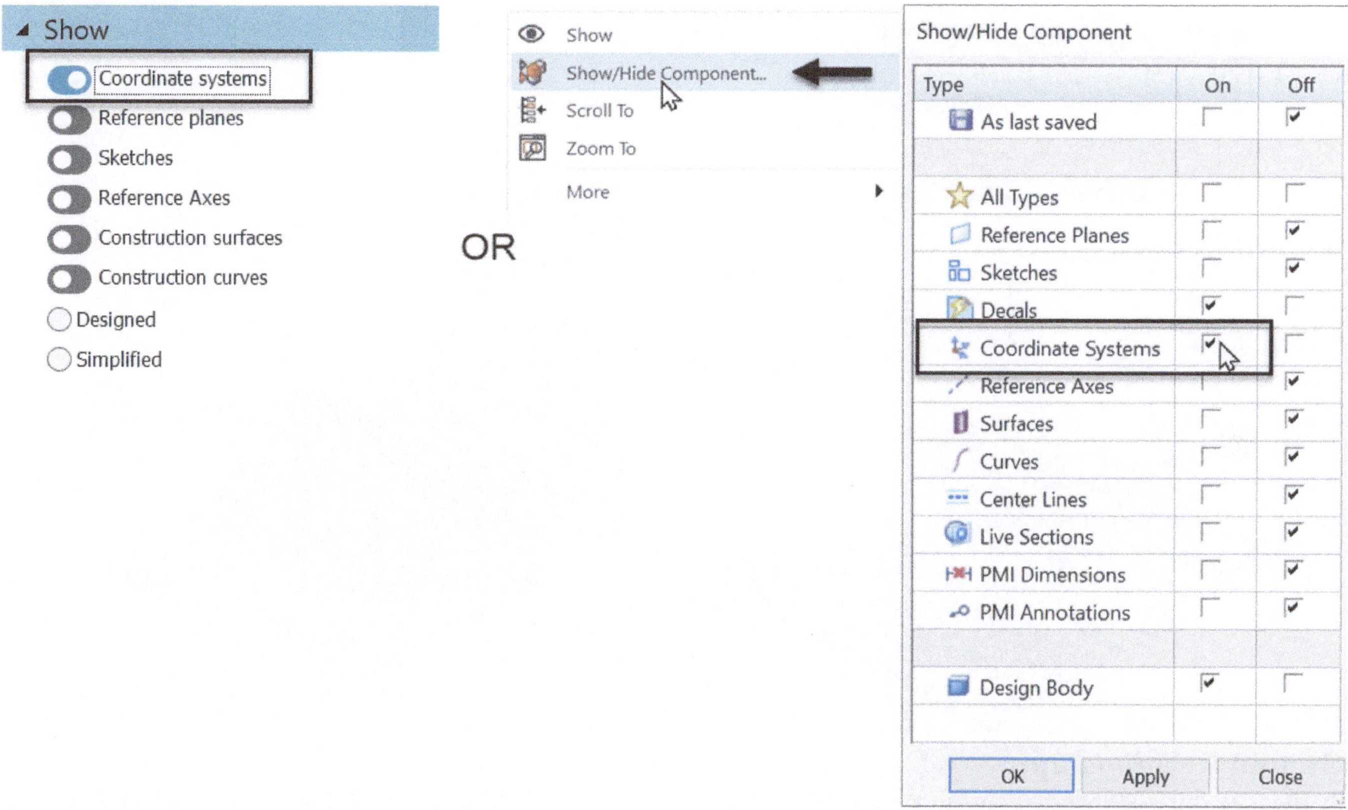

Activate this command from the ribbon (click **Home > Assemble > Match Coordinate Systems**). After activating this command, you have to select the coordinate systems of two parts. They will be positioned together.

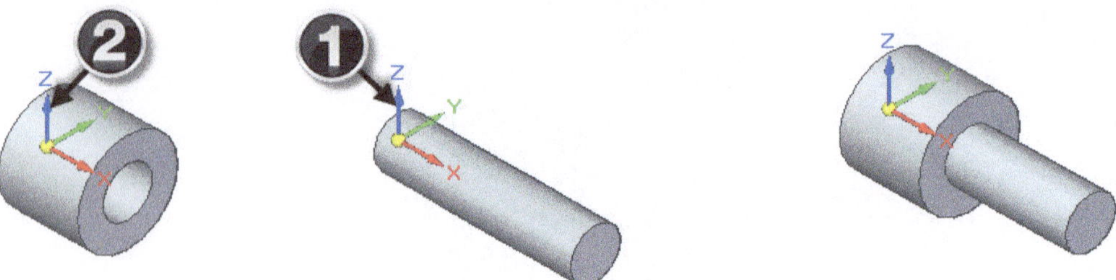

Rigid Set Relationship

The **Rigid Set** relationship makes the selected parts to form a rigid set. As you move a single part of a rigid set, all the other parts will also be moved. Activate this command from the ribbon (click **Home > Assemble > Rigid Set**); a command bar pops up on the screen. On the command bar, select an option from the **Shared Relationships** menu. You can select to **Suppress**, **Delete**, or **Ignore** already existing relationships between the parts. Next, select parts from the assembly window and click the **Accept** button on the command bar. The selected parts will form a rigid set. If you change the position or orientation of one part, all the other parts of the rigid set will also be affected.

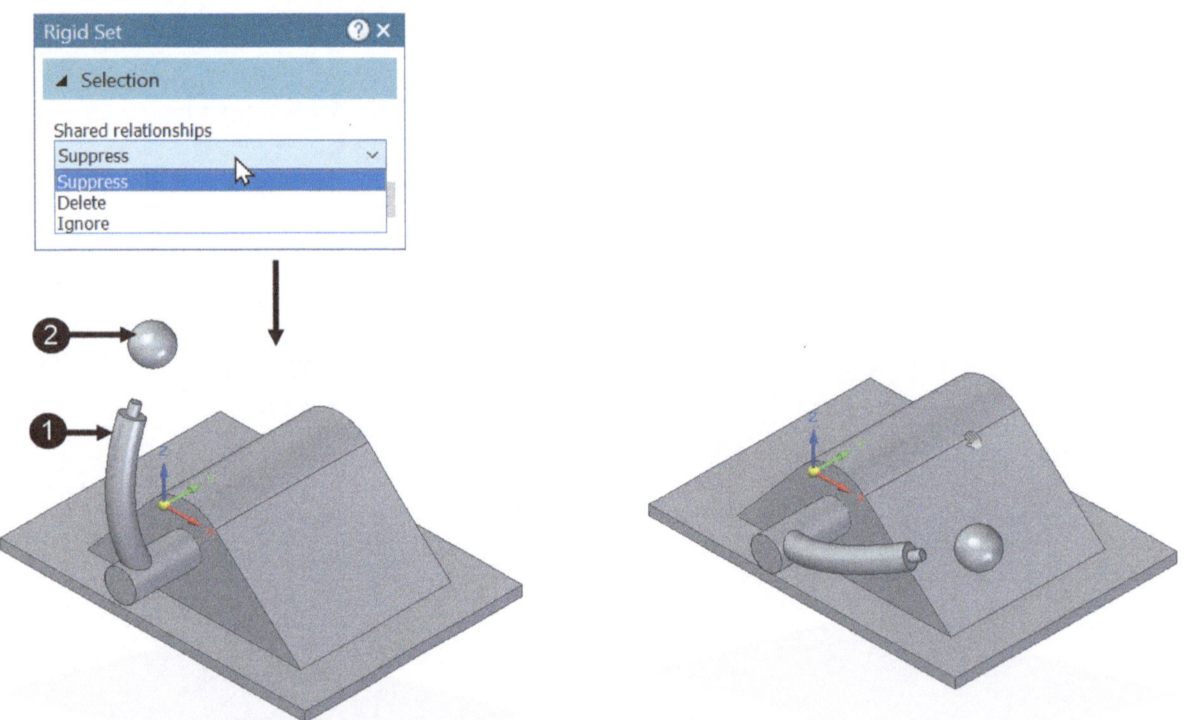

Ground Relationship

By default, the first inserted part in an assembly is grounded or fixed. As a result, all the degrees of freedom of the part are constrained. However, you can make any other part grounded by using the **Ground** command. Activate this command (click **Home > Assemble > Ground** on the ribbon) and select the part to ground. A ground symbol appears on the selected part in the Pathfinder.

Path Relationship

The **Path** relationship is used to constrain a selected point or line along a path. Activate this command from the ribbon (click **Home > Assemble > Path**). After activating this command, click on a point or linear edge to define the follower. Next, click on edge to define the path. Right-click to apply this relationship. Use the **Drag Component** command to drag the follower.

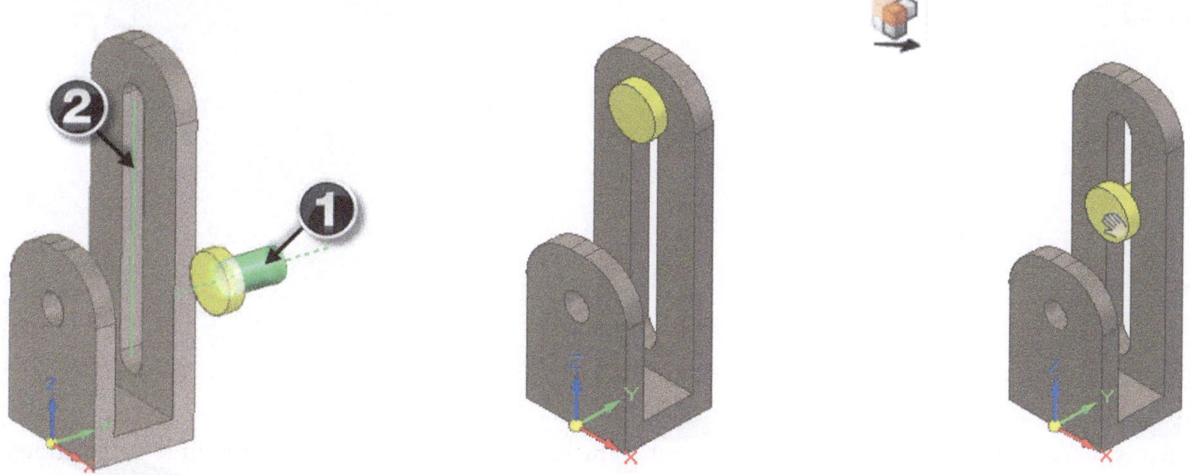

Cam Relationship

The **Cam** relationship is similar to a **Tangent** relationship except that it allows you to mate a cylinder, plane, or point to a series of tangent faces. Activate this command from the ribbon (click **Home > Assemble > Path > Cam**). After activating this command, click on a face or a point to define the follower. Next, click on a face chain to define the cam. Click the green check on the command bar to apply this relationship.

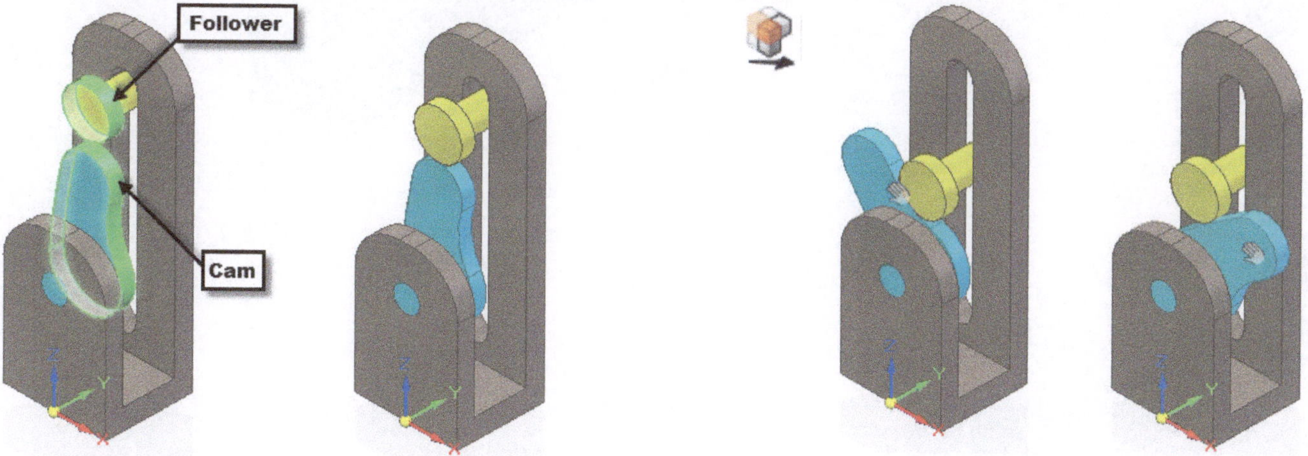

Check Interference

In an assembly, two or more parts can overlap or occupy the same space. However, this would be physically impossible in the real world. When you add relations between parts, Solid Edge develops real-world contacts and movements between them. However, sometimes interferences can occur. To check such errors, Solid Edge provides you with a command called **Check Interference**. Activate this command (click **Inspect > Evaluate > Check Interference** on the ribbon) and select the first set. Click the green check on the command bar and select the second set. Click the green check, and then click the **Process** icon to show the interference. If there is no interference, a message box appears to show no interferences in the assembly.

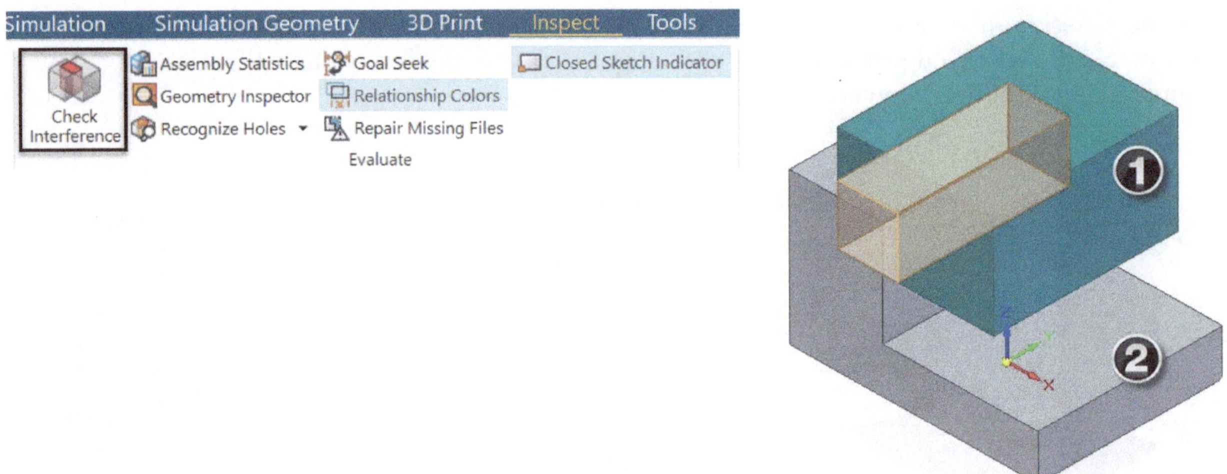

Capture Fit

If you have an assembly where you need to assemble the same part multiple times, it would be a tedious process. In such cases, the **Capture Fit** command will drastically reduce or even eliminate the time used to assemble commonly used parts. To use this command, first, you need to define a relation or set of relations between two parts. For example, define the **Insert** relationship between the screw and the hole.

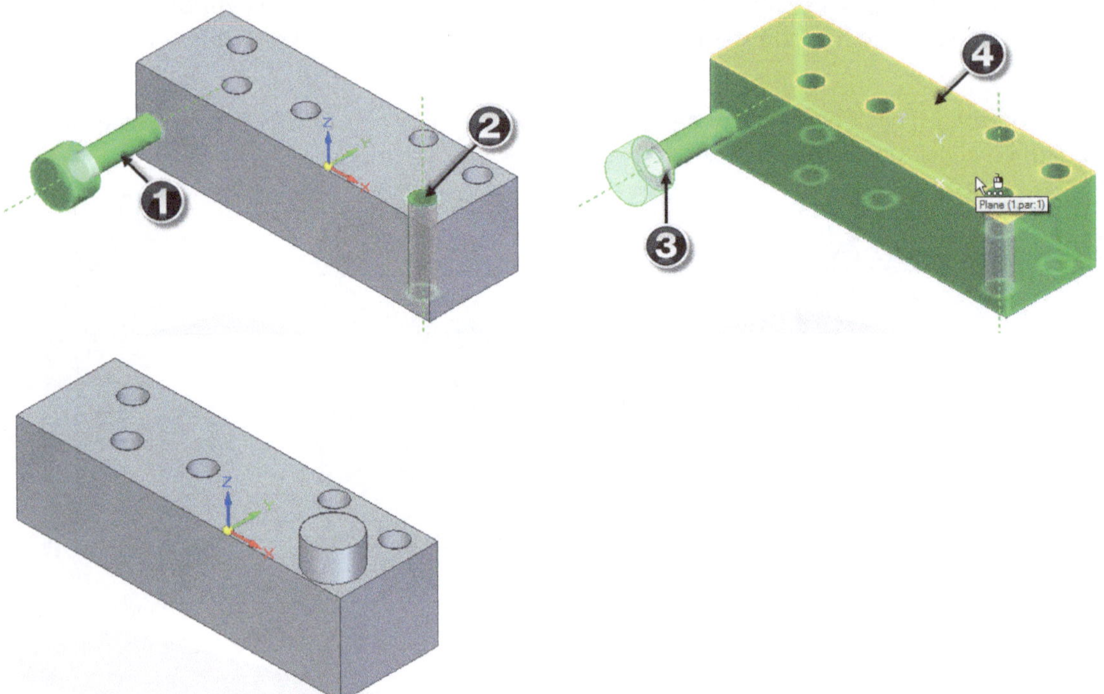

Next, save the assembly and select the screw. Activate the **Capture Fit** command (click **Home > Assemble > Capture Fit** on the ribbon); the **Capture Fit** dialog pops up on the screen. This dialog shows the list of relations that can be captured. If you do not want to capture some relations, select them from the list and click **Remove**. Next, click **OK** on the dialog to capture the relations.

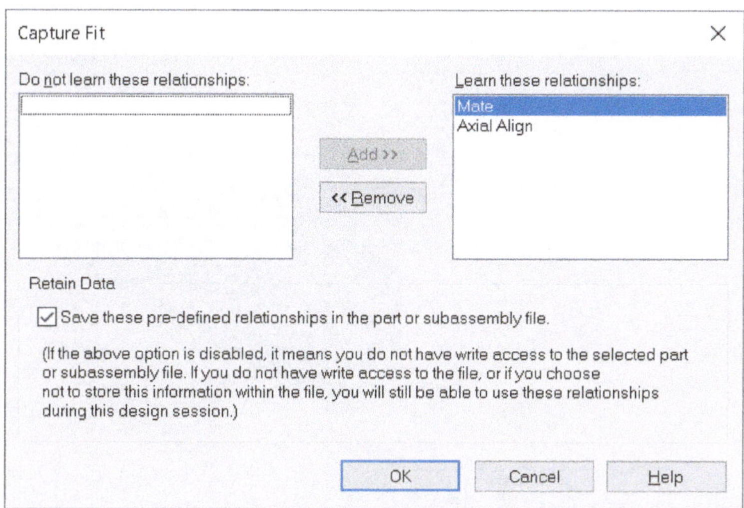

Now, click and drag the screw from the **Parts Library** and place it into the assembly window; you will notice that the flat face on the screw is selected automatically. Select the top face of the block; the axis of the cylinder is selected automatically. Select the holes' axis on the block; the screw is inserted into the hole.

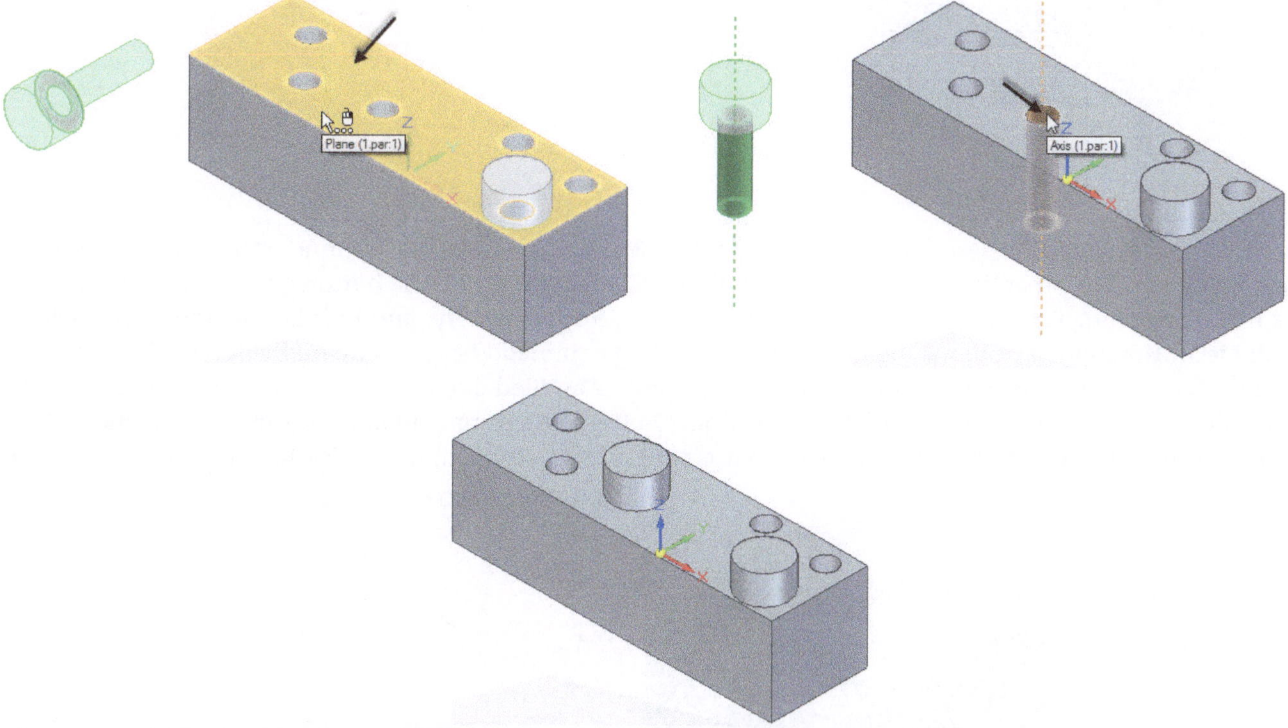

Editing and Updating Assemblies

During the design process, the correct design is not achieved on the first attempt. There is always a need to go back and make modifications. Solid Edge allows you to accomplish this process very easy. To modify a part in an assembly, click on it and select **Open**; the part will be opened in a separate window. Make changes to the part and save it. Next, switch to the assembly window. The part will be updated in the assembly automatically. If it is not updated, click **Tools > Update > Update Active Level** on the ribbon.

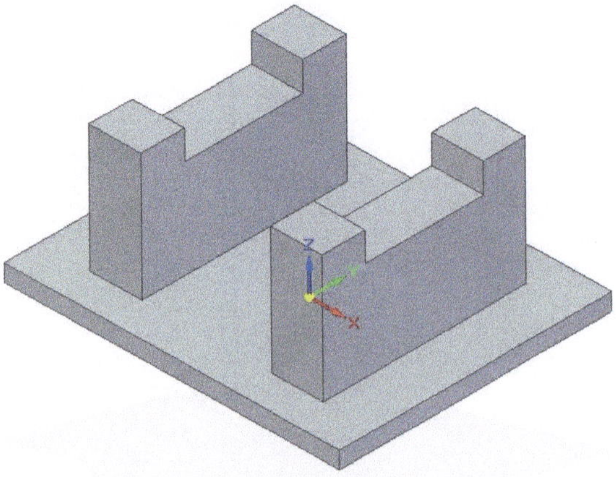

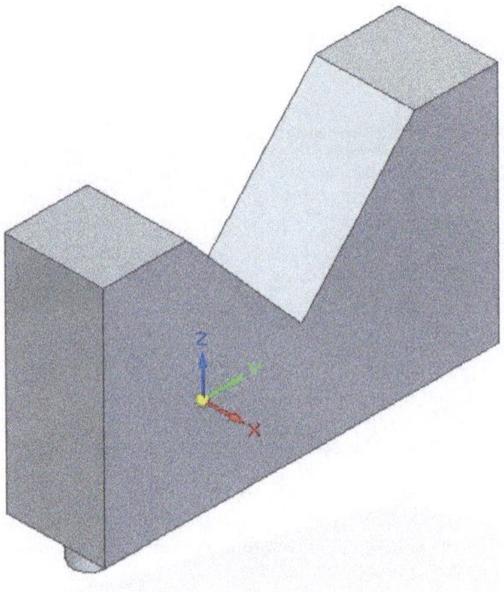

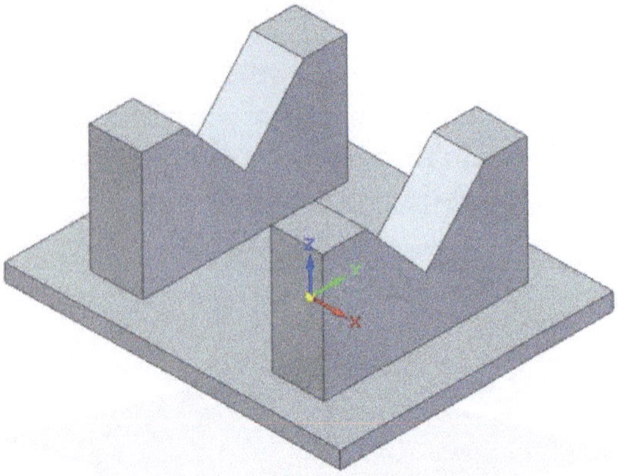

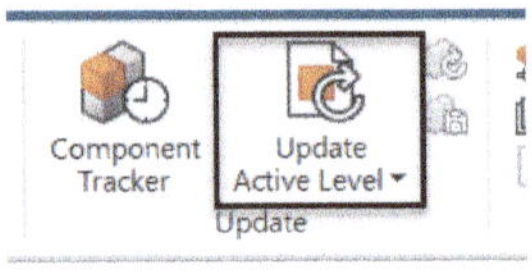

You can also edit relationships in an assembly. To do this, select a part from the Pathfinder; the relationships applied to the part appear at the bottom of the Pathfinder. Click the right mouse button on the relationship to edit; a menu appears with four options: **Delete Relationship**, **Suppress**, **Flip**, and **Edit Definition**. If you select the **Edit Definition** option from the menu, the corresponding command bar pops up on the screen. You can reselect the faces or elements between which the relationship is applied. For example, if you want to edit a **Mate** relationship, right-click on it and select **Edit Definition**. On the **Mate** command bar, click in the **Placement Part – Element** selection box and then click on new the placement part's face. Next, right-click to apply the relationship.

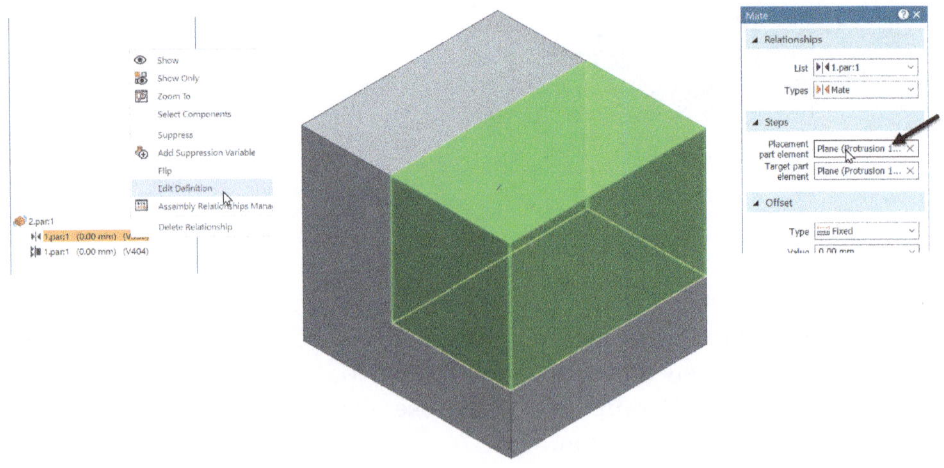

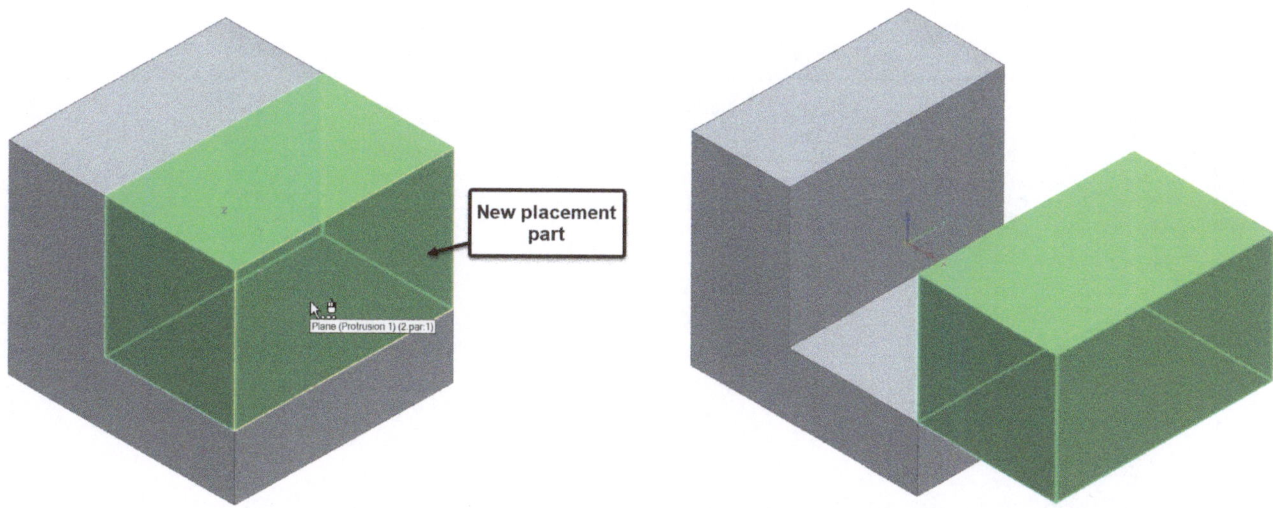

Replace Part

Solid Edge allows you to replace any part in an assembly. Activate the **Replace Part** command (click **Home > Modify > Replace Part** drop-down **> Replace Part** on the ribbon), and then click on parts to replace. Click the **Accept** button on the command bar to accept; the **Replacement Part** dialog pops up on the screen. Browse to the replacement part's location and double-click on it; the **Assembly** message box pops up on the screen. It shows, "The affected Assembly relationships must be either deleted or suppressed to complete the operation." Click **Delete** or **Suppress** on the message box to replace the part. You can suppress or delete relationships based on the differences in the original and replacement part. You can redefine relationships after deleting them.

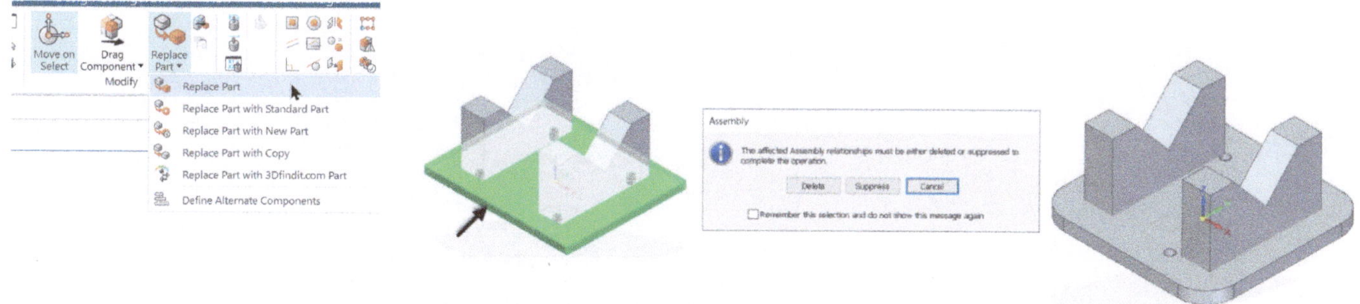

Repair Missing Files

Solid Edge provides a tool to find missing part files of an assembly. Whenever you open an assembly with some missing files, the **Repair Missing Files** dialog appears on the screen. On this dialog, select the missing part and use various options (**Search In**, **Replace Part**, **Replace with Standard Parts**, and **Replace with New Part**) to repair the assembly.

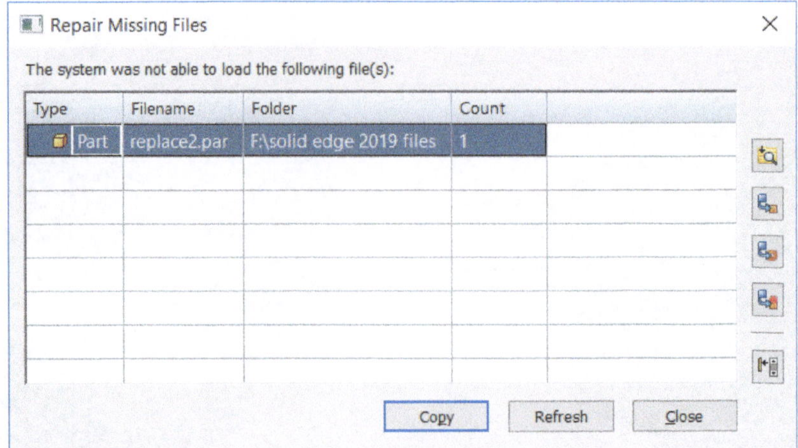

The **Search In** option brings up the **Search In** dialog, which helps you search for various folders on your computer. Click the **Browse** button on the **Search In** dialog, select a folder from the **Browse to Folder** dialog, and click **OK**. On the **Search In** dialog, click the **Add** button to add the selected folder to the **Search in these folders** list. Likewise, add other folders to the list. You can change the order of the folders using the **Move up** and **Move down** buttons. After adding folders to the list, click the **Search and Replace** button to start the search; Solid Edge will search the folder located at the top of the list. If the part file is not found, it will search the next folder.

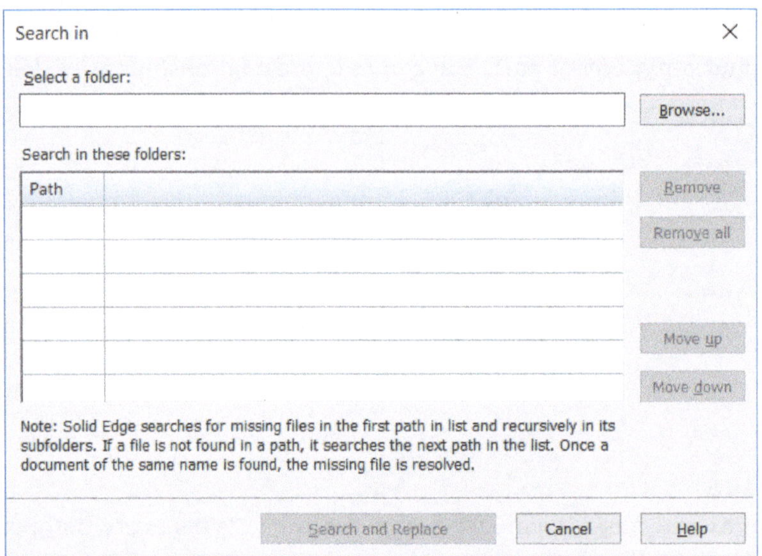

You can also replace the missing parts using the **Replace Part**, **Replace with Standard Parts**, and **Replace with New Part** options.

Pattern

The **Pattern** command allows you to replicate individual parts in an assembly. However, instead of defining layouts of rectangular or circular patterns, you can select an existing pattern as a reference. For example, in the assembly shown in the figure, you can position one screw using relationships and then use the **Pattern** command to place screws in the remaining holes.

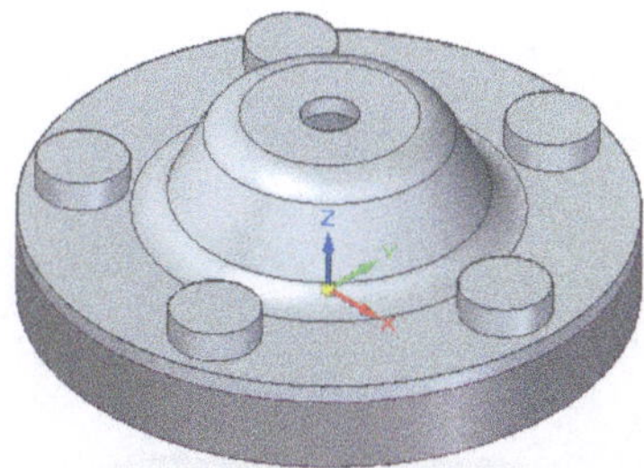

First, position the screw in one hole using the **Insert** relationship. Next, activate the **Pattern** command (click **Home > Pattern > Pattern** on the ribbon) and click on the part to include in the pattern. Click the green check on the command bar to accept the selection. Next, click on the part or sketch which contains the pattern.

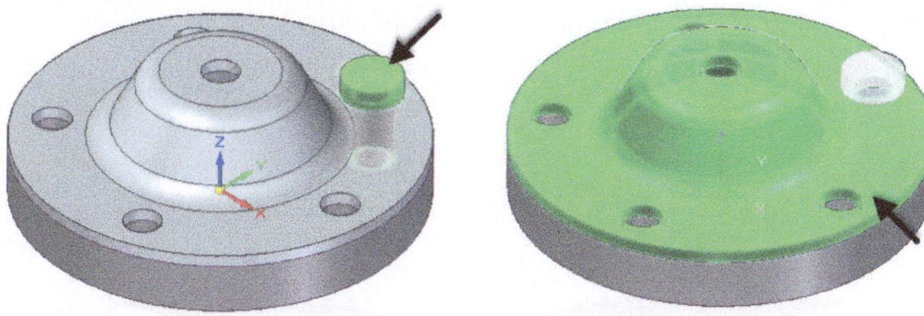

Select the pattern, as shown on the left side in the figure. Next, select the reference feature from the pattern, and then click **Finish** on the command bar to create the pattern.

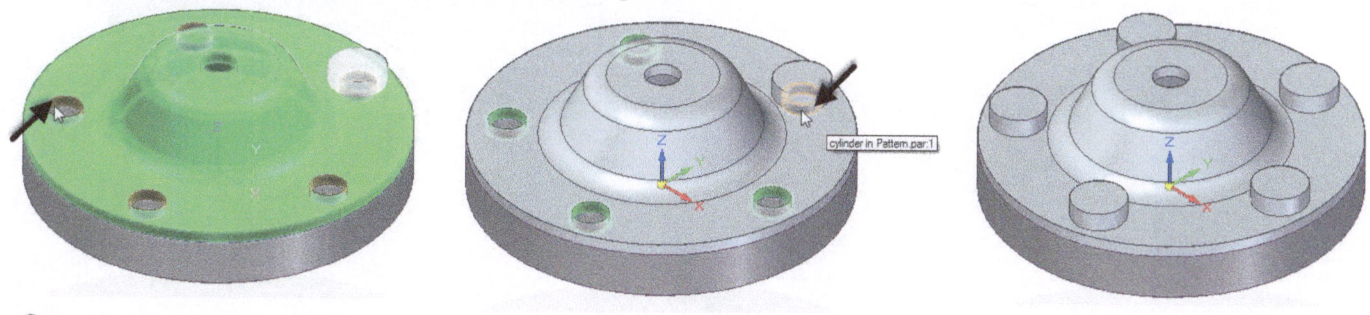

Clone Component

The **Clone Component** command allows you to clone a part or subassembly using the geometry recognition method. Activate this command (on the ribbon, click **Home** tab > **Pattern** panel > **Clone Component**), and then select the part or subassembly to be cloned. Click the **Accept** icon on the command bar. Next, select a reference face to be recognized to place the clones. Right click to accept the selection. Next, select the target component on which the clones are to be placed. Next, select the **Adaptable** or **Exact** button on the command bar. The **Adaptable** option places the clones in similar locations but not the same as the reference face. The **Exact** option places the clones in locations that are the same as the reference face. Click **Accept** on the command bar to accept the selected target component; the occurrence handles (pink dots) appear on the occurrences. Click on an occurrence handle, and then select the **Keep/Remove Occurrence** icon to remove an occurrence. Click the **Flip Orientation** icon if you want to change the orientation of the occurrence. Next, click the **Finish** button to clone the components.

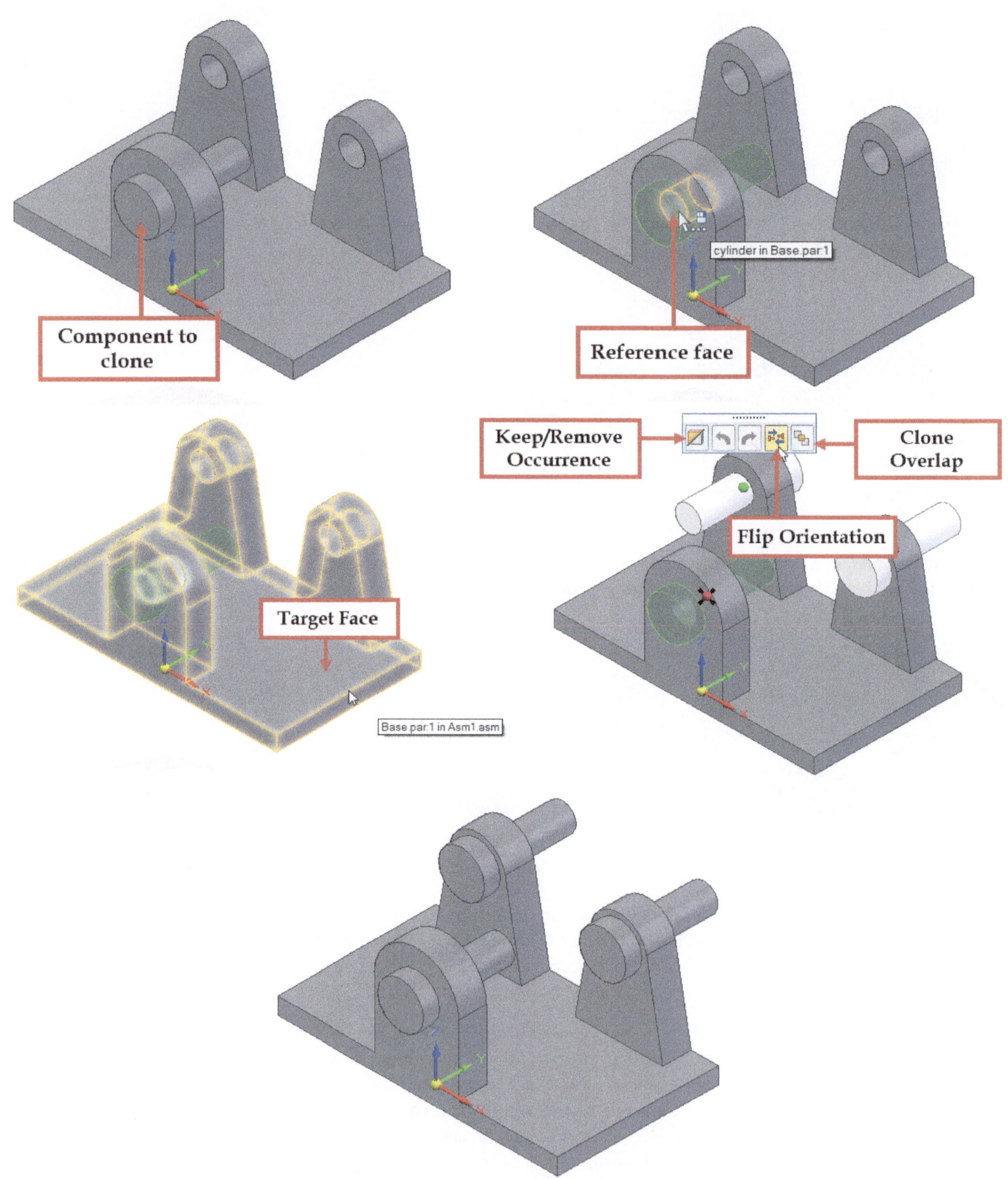

Mirror Components

When designing symmetric assemblies, the **Mirror Components** command will help you save time and capture the design intent. Activate this command (click **Home > Pattern > Mirror Components** on the ribbon) and click on the parts to be mirrored. Click the green check on the command bar, and then click on an assembly reference plane to mirror about; the **Mirror Components** dialog pops up on the screen. On this dialog, select the required action from the **Action** drop-down menu. Type-in the output file name in the **Output File** field and click **OK**. Next, click **Finish** to complete the mirroring.

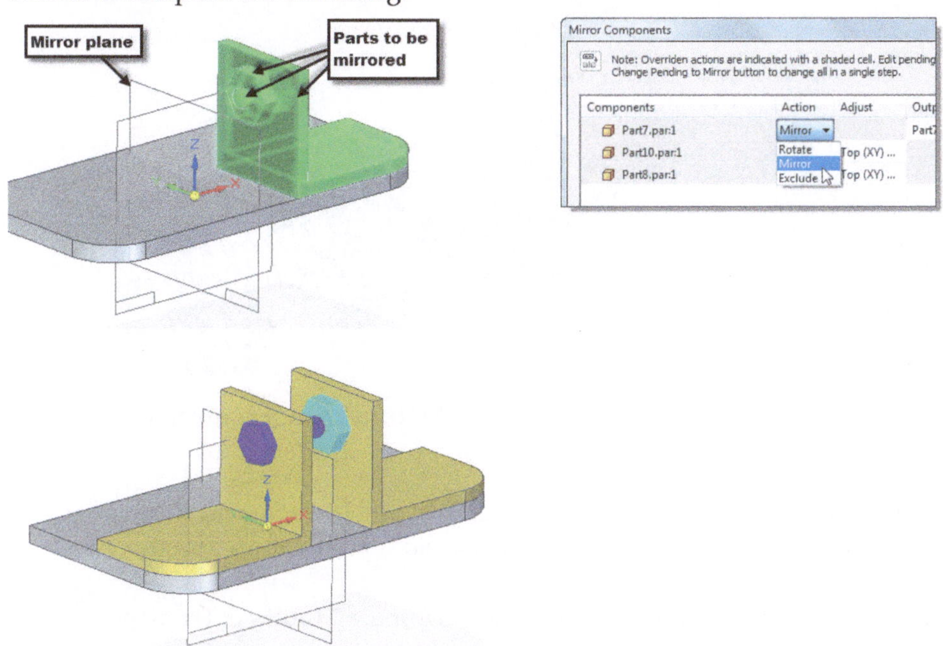

Sub-assemblies

The use of sub-assemblies has many advantages in Solid Edge. Sub-assemblies make large assemblies easier to manage. They make it easy for multiple users to collaborate on a single large assembly design. They can also affect the way you document a large assembly design in 2D drawings. For these reasons, you need to create sub-assemblies in a variety of ways. The easiest way to create a sub-assembly is to insert an existing assembly into another assembly. You need to simply drag and place the assembly from the **Parts Library** window into an existing assembly. Next, apply relationships to constrain the assembly. The process of applying relationships is also simplified. You are required to apply relationships between only one part of a sub-assembly and a part of the main assembly. Also, you can easily hide a group of parts with the help of sub-assemblies. Click the right mouse button on a sub-assembly and select **Hide**.

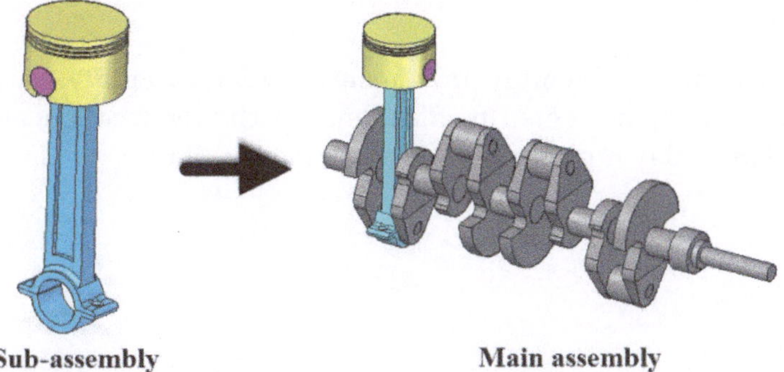

Sub-assembly **Main assembly**

Rigid and Adjustable Sub-Assemblies

By default, Solid Edge makes a sub-assembly as a rigid body. When you move a single part of a sub-assembly, the entire sub-assembly will be moved. If you want the individual parts of a sub-assembly to be moved, you must define the sub-assembly as adjustable. Click the right mouse button on the sub-assembly in the **Pathfinder** and select **Simplified/Adjustable > Adjustable Assembly**. Now, you can move the individual parts of a sub-assembly. If you have multiple occurrences of a sub-assembly, each occurrence can be defined as rigid or adjustable. Solid Edge displays a different icon for each of them in the Pathfinder to help you recognize the difference between the rigid and adjustable assemblies.

Rigid Assembly **Adjustable Assembly**

Transfer

In addition to creating sub-assemblies and inserting them into another assembly, you can also take individual parts in an assembly and make them into a sub-assembly. For example, press and hold the **Shift** key and select the four parts from the assembly. Next, activate the **Transfer** command (click **Home > Modify > Transfer** on the ribbon); the **Transfer to Assembly Level** dialog pops up on the screen.

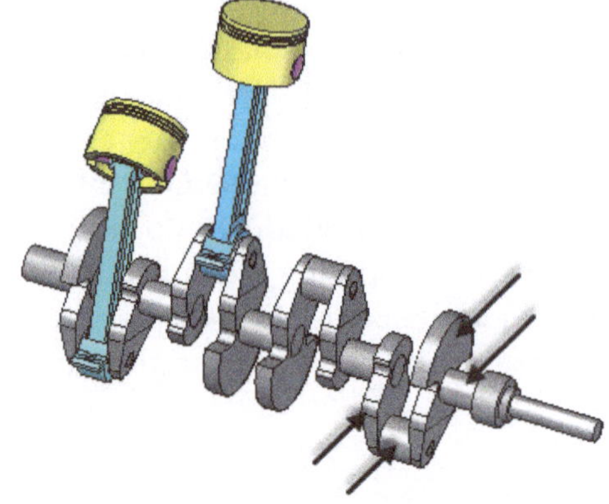

On this dialog, click on the **Assem** option, and then click **New Subassembly**; the **Create New Subassembly** dialog pops up on the screen. On this dialog, select the assembly template, enter the file name, specify the location, and specify the positioning method. Click **OK** twice; the subassembly is created and listed in the Pathfinder.

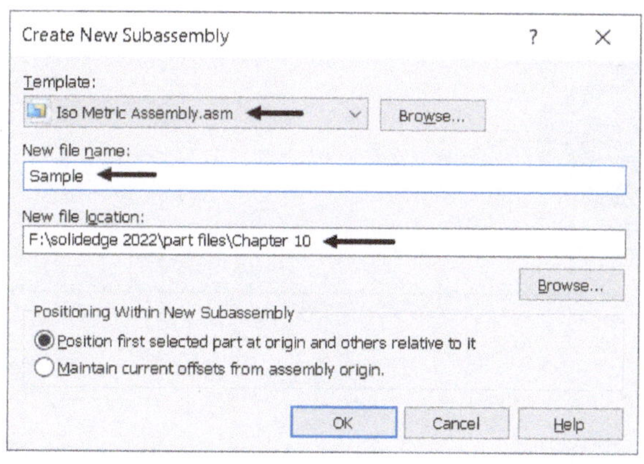

Disperse

After inserting subassemblies, you may require to disperse them into individual parts. Solid Edge provides you with the **Disperse** command to break a subassembly into individual parts. In the Pathfinder, click on the subassembly to disperse, and then activate this command (click **Home > Modify > Disperse** on the ribbon); the **Disperse Assembly** dialog pops up on the screen. On this dialog, click **Disperse Selected Assembly** to disperse the selected assembly (or) click **Disperse All Assemblies** to break down all subassemblies into individual parts. After clicking the required option, a message box pops up showing, "Transfer the parts in the selected assembly to the next higher level, and delete the selected assembly occurrence." Click **Yes** to transfer the parts to the main assembly.

Assembly Features

Assembly features exist only in assemblies, i.e., instead of creating them at the part level, they are created at the assembly level. Most often, the assembly level features are cuts, revolved cuts, holes, and welds. These features are commonly created at the assembly level to represent post assembly machining. For example, add a cut feature to the assembly shown in the figure, activate the **Cut** command (click **Features > Assembly Features > Cut** on the ribbon). On this command bar, select **Feature Type > Assembly Features** from the **Assembly Feature Options** section. Select the top face of the block and sketch the cut feature. Finish the sketch and extrude it using the **Through All** option.

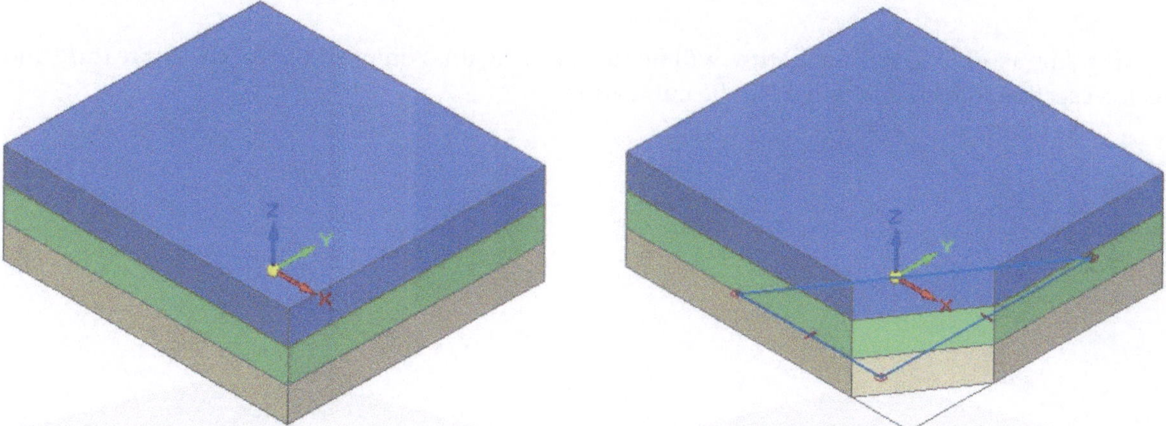

Now, open the individual part in another window. You will notice that the cut feature does not affect the part.

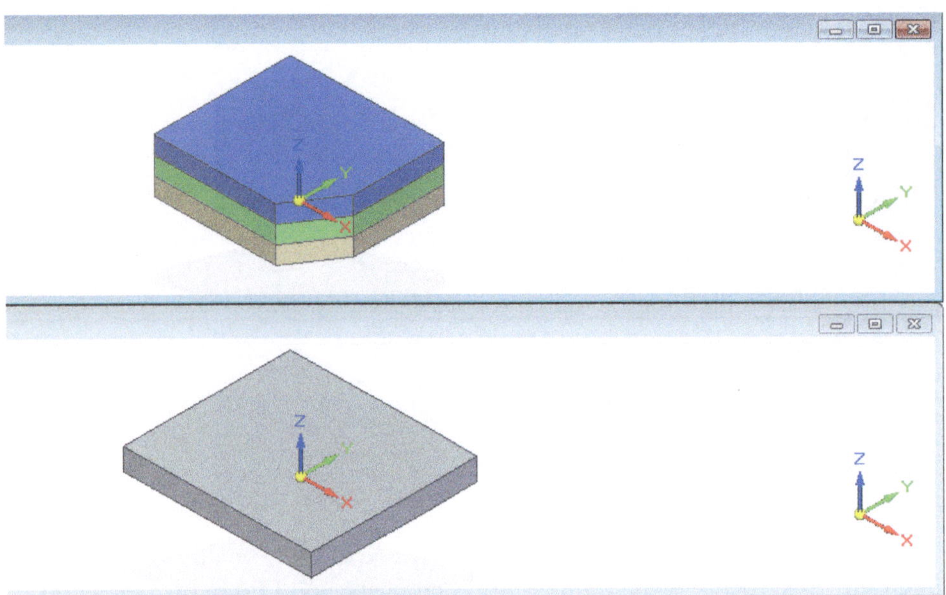

You will also notice that the Cut feature is added to the Pathfinder. You can edit the cut feature by clicking on the **Cut** feature and selecting **Edit Definition**. A command bar pops up on the screen. On the command bar, click the **Body Selection** section, and then press the Shift key and select the parts to be excluded from the cut feature. Click the green check on the command bar, and then click **Finish**; you can see that the cut feature no longer affects the selected components.

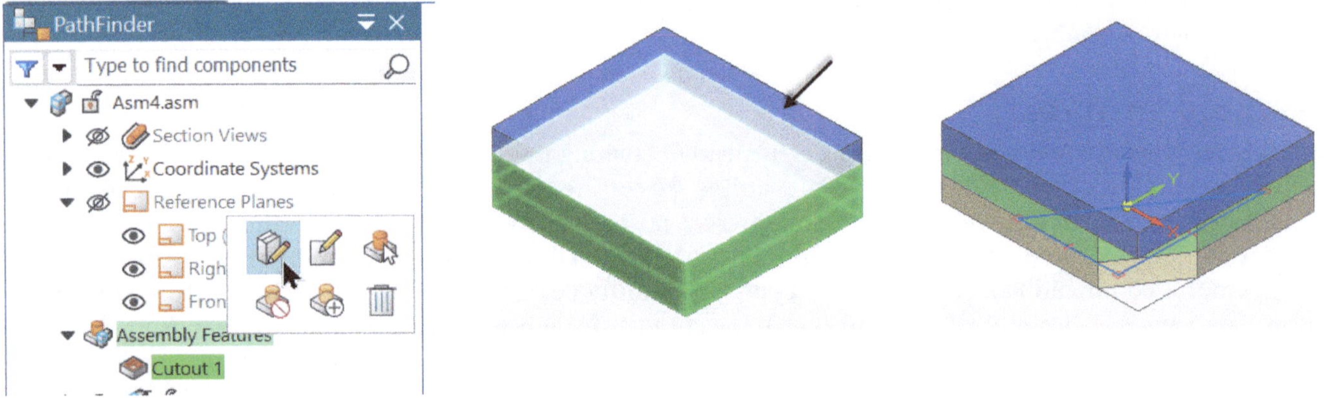

If you add a new part to the assembly, the cut feature will not affect it. Again, you need to edit the cut feature and use the **Body Selection** section to include the part in the cut feature.

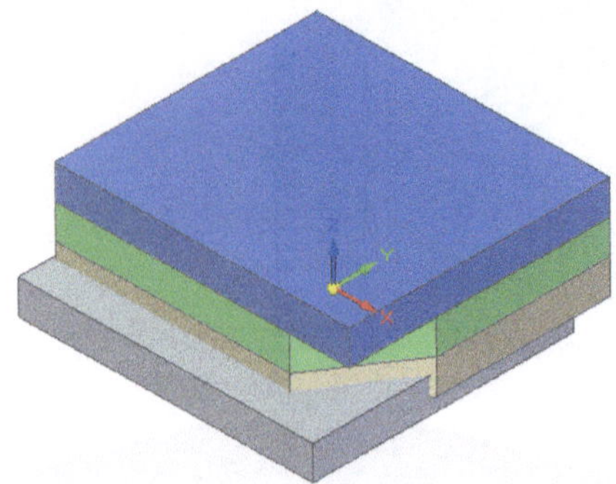

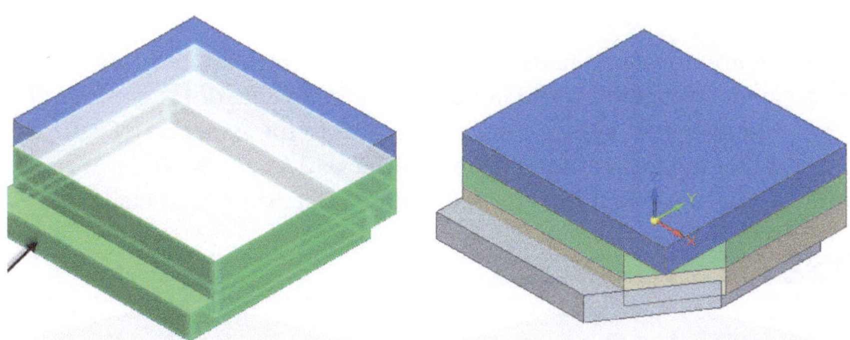

Assembly-Driven Part Features

Assembly-Driven Part features are features created in an assembly and are also reflected in the part documents. To create this type of feature, first, save the assembly file, and then activate any one of the commands available in the **Assembly Features** panel. Next, select **Feature Type > Assembly-Driven Part Features** from the **Assembly Features Options** section. Create the assembly driven feature, and it is listed in the Pathfinder. Now, open the individual part in another window. You will notice that the feature also affects the part. When you update the feature in the assembly file, it will be reflected in the part file.

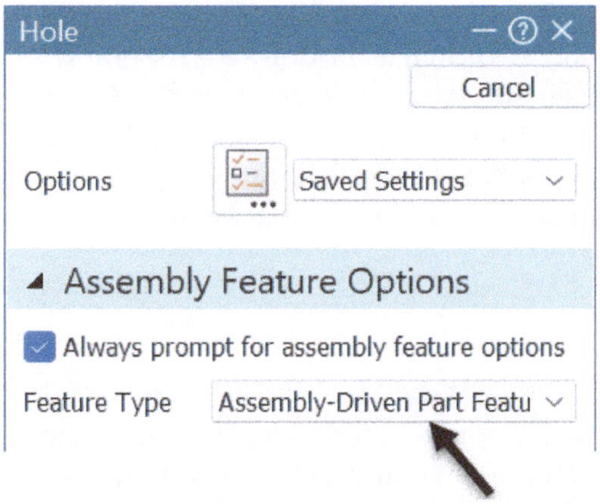

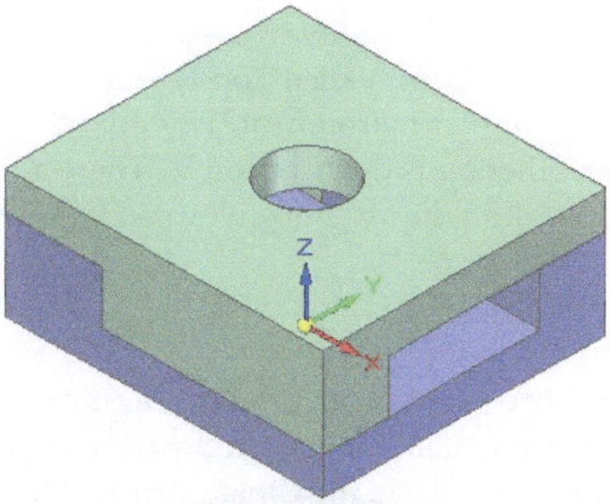

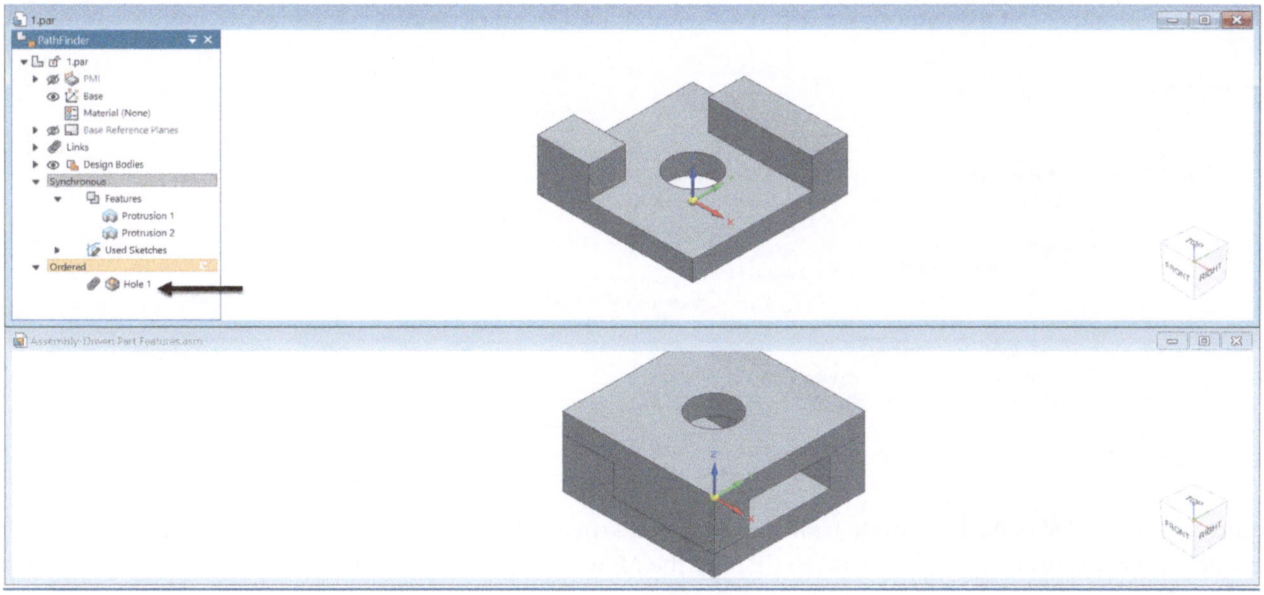

Part Features

Part features are features created in an assembly but are not associated with the assembly. Instead, they are associated with the part file on which they are created. To create a part feature, activate any one of the commands available in the **Assembly Features** panel. Next, select **Feature Type > Part Features** from the **Assembly Features Options** section and create the part feature. Now, open the individual part in another window. You will notice that the feature also affects the part. If you want to edit a part feature, you must open the part file and change it.

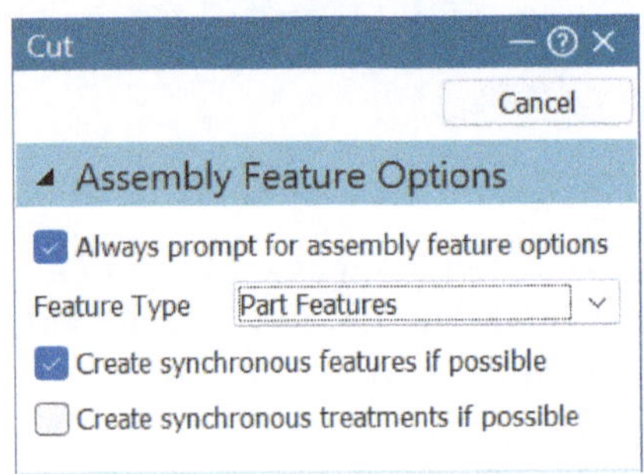

Top-Down Assembly Design

In Solid Edge, there are two methods to create an assembly. The method you are probably familiar with is to create individual parts and then insert them into an assembly. This method is known as Bottom-Up Assembly Design. The second method is called Top-Down Assembly Design. In this method, you will create individual parts within the assembly environment. This allows you to design an individual part while considering how it will interact with other parts in an assembly. There are several advantages to Top-Down Assembly Design. As you design a part within the assembly, you can be sure that it will fit properly. You can also use reference geometry from the other parts.

Create Part In-Place

Top-down assembly design can be used to add new parts to an already existing assembly. You can also use it to create entirely new assemblies. To create a part using the Top-Down Design approach, first, you must save the assembly file and then activate the **Create Part In-Place** command (click **Home > Assemble > Create Part In-Place** on the ribbon); the **Create Part In-Place Options** dialog pops up on the screen. The options available in this dialog are self-explanatory. Set the options on this dialog and click **OK** to close it.

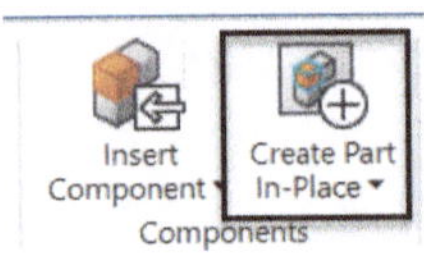

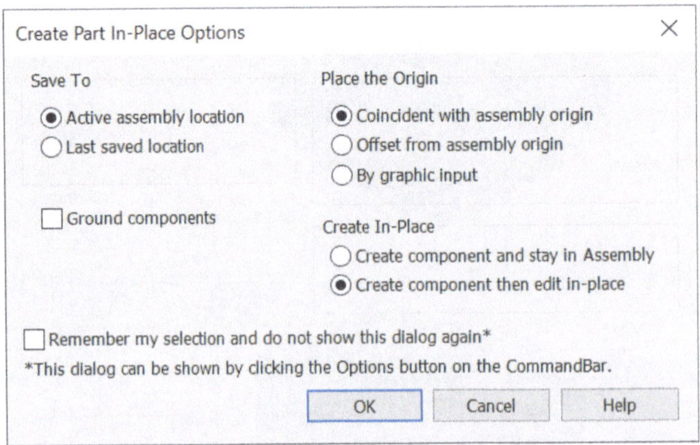

On the command bar, select a part template from the **Template** drop-down menu. If you want to access more templates, click the **Browse for Template** icon to display the **New** dialog. On this dialog, select the template you need and click **OK**.

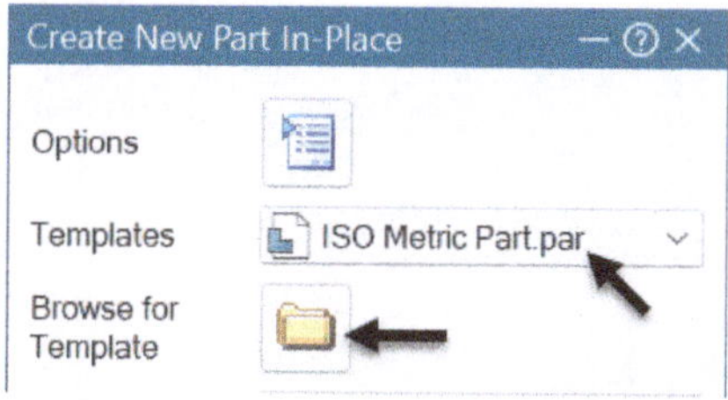

On the command bar, click the **Ground** icon if you want to make the part grounded at the origin.

Use the **Origin** drop-down menu to specify the origin location.

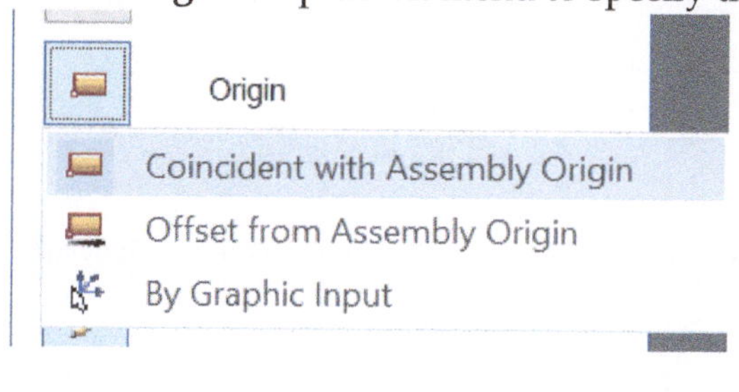

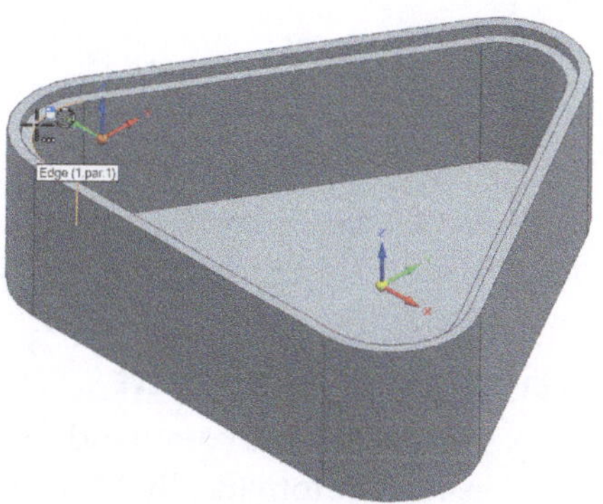

Activate the **Edit In Place** icon to switch to the part environment to create the part directly. Click the **Accept** button on the command bar; the **Save As** dialog pops up on the screen. On this dialog, specify the part name and location on the drive, and then click **Save** to create the part. Now, create the features of the part, and then close and return to the assembly. In the example given in the figure, the **Project to Sketch** command is used to project the edges of the existing part to create a sketch. The projected sketch is then extruded. This makes it easy to create a part using the edges of the existing part.

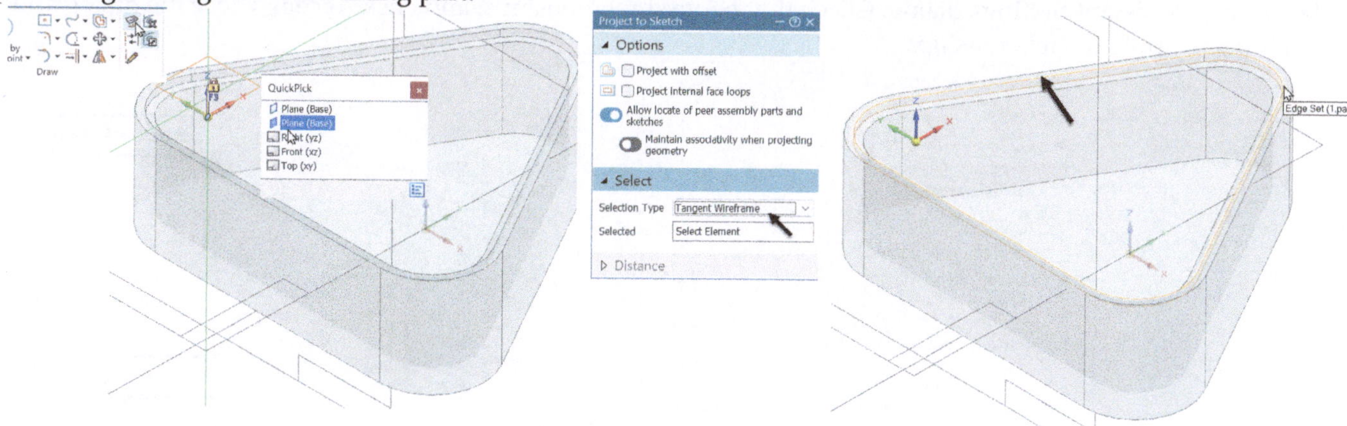

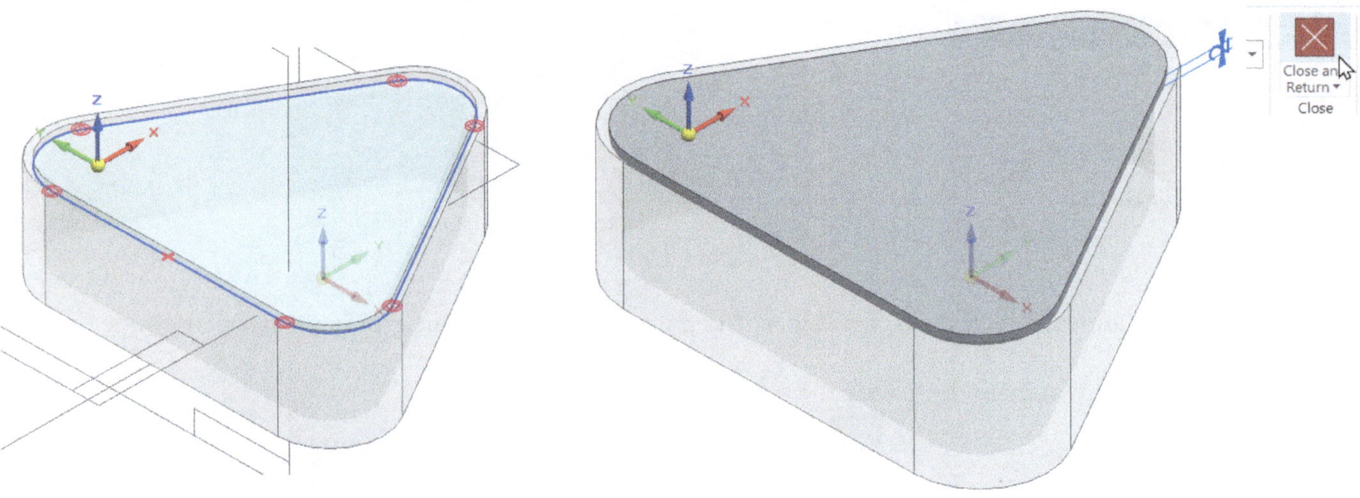

*Tip: You can use the **Thicken** command to create the part features by thickening the adjacent parts' faces. You can learn about the **Thicken** command in Chapter 13: Surface Design.*

Assembly Relationship Assistant

Assembly Relationship Assistant is the command provided by Solid Edge intelligent technology. This command helps you to create relationships automatically based on the position and interaction between the parts. This command is very helpful while creating relationships in a top-down assembly design. Activate this command (click **Home > Assemble > Assembly Relationship Assistant** on the ribbon); the **Relationship Assistant Options** dialog pops up on the screen. Set the options on this dialog and click **OK**. Click on parts to define the first set, and then click the green check on the command bar. Click on parts to define the second set, and then click the green check on the command bar; the **Relationship Assistant Settings** dialog pops up on the screen. On this dialog, check the **Allowable Relationship Types**, and then click **Process**. This will analyze the position and interaction between the parts and then apply relationships between them. The possible relationships are listed on the **Relationship Assistant Settings** dialog. Check the required relationships, and click **Accept**. Close the dialog and click **Finish** to apply the relationships.

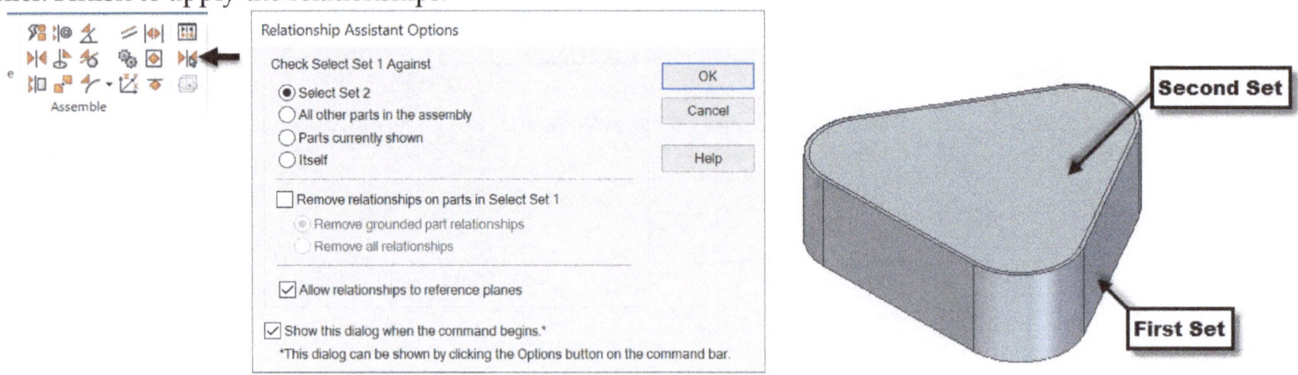

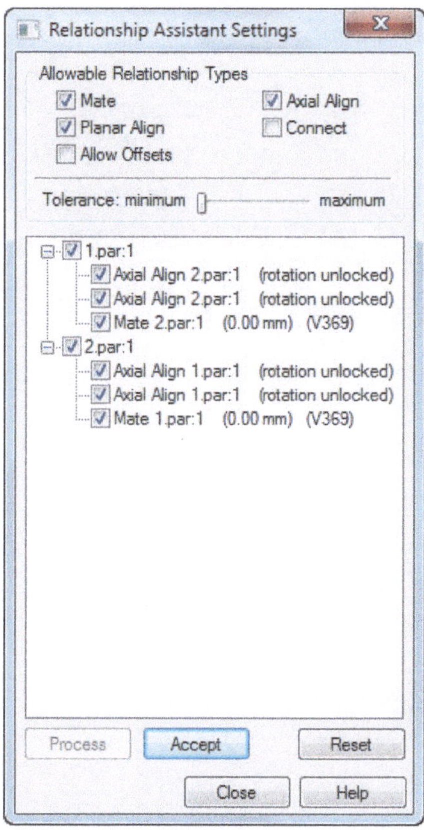

Assembly Relationships Manager

The **Assembly Relationships Manager** command (on the ribbon, click **Home** tab > **Assemble** group > **Assembly Relationships Manager**) displays a table of relationships created in an assembly. You can view and modify the assembly relationships from the table. All assembly relationships are grouped into different categories. For example, all the Axial relationships are grouped into the **Axial** category. Expand the **Axial** category to view all the **Axial** relationships in the assembly. You can further expand each relationship to view its status and the components associated with it. The **Assembly Relationship Manager** dialog provides you with many options when you right click on a relationship or component associated with a relationship. These options help you to solve the relationship error or edit the component. To do this, right click on a relationship and select **Suppress**, **Unsuppress**, **Flip**, **Edit Definition,** or **Delete** from the shortcut menu. Close the dialog after making changes to the relationships.

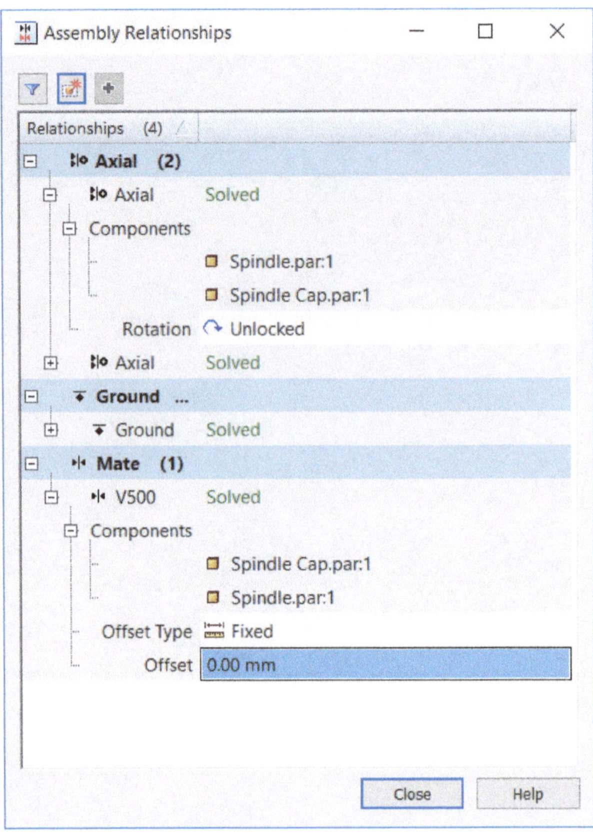

Exploding Assemblies

To document an assembly design properly, it is very common to create an exploded view. In an exploded view, the parts of an assembly are pulled apart to show how they were assembled. To create an exploded view, activate the **ERA** command (click **Tools > Environs > ERA** on the ribbon); the **Explode – Render – Animate** environment is activated.

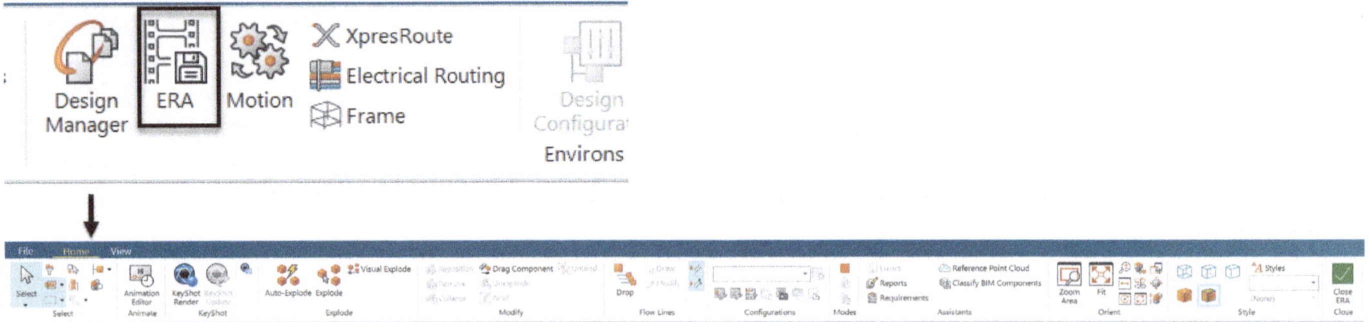

Use the **Auto Explode** command to explode the assembly automatically. On activating this command, the **Auto Explode** command bar pops up on the screen. On the command bar, select **Top-level Assembly** if you want to explode the complete assembly. If you want to explode only selected subassemblies, then select the **Subassembly** option. Next, click the green check on the command bar. Deactivate the **Automatic Spread Distance** icon on the command bar and type-in the spread distance in the **Distance** box. Click **Explode** and **Finish** to explode the assembly.

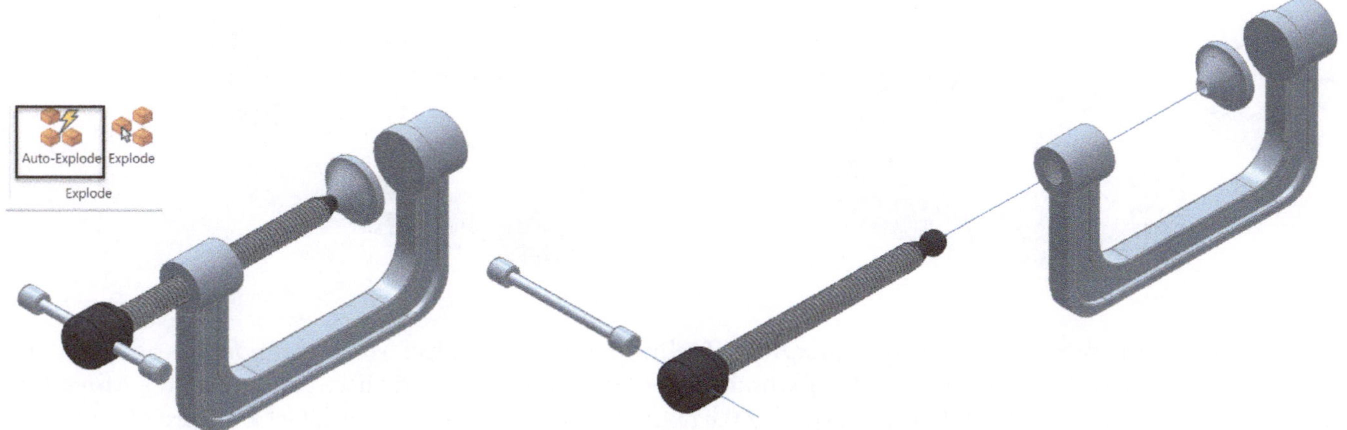

You will notice that the parts are not exploded properly. To get the desired explosion, you need to use the **Explode** command. First, unexplode this assembly using the **Unexplode** command. On clicking this button, the **Solid Edge** message box pops up, showing, "This action will delete the current explosion." Click **Yes** to explode the assembly.

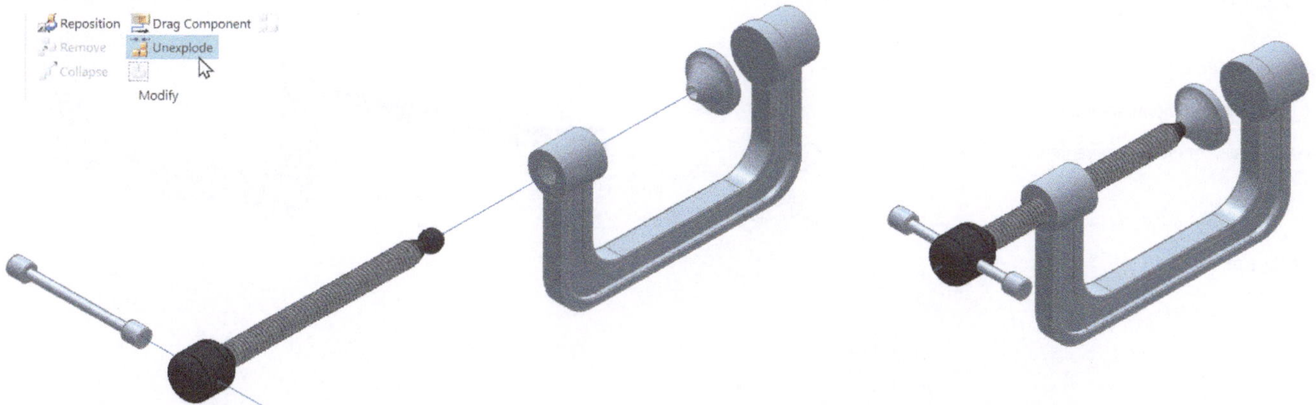

To manually explode an assembly, activate the **Explode** command; the **Explode** command bar pops up. Click on the parts to be exploded, and then click the **Accept** button on the command bar. Click on the part to be remained stationary in the explosion.

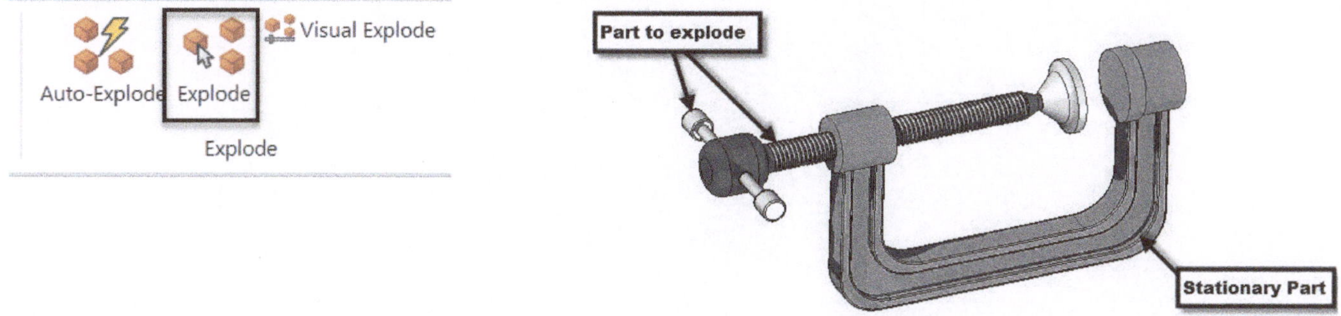

Click on the stationary part face from which you want to explode; an arrow appears on it. Move the pointer and click to define the direction of explosion; the **Explode Options** dialog pops up.

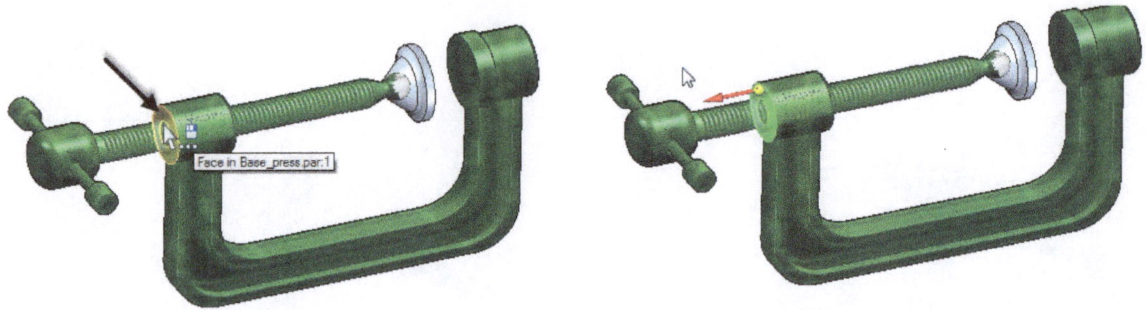

On this dialog, select an option to specify the **Explode Technique**. You can select **Move components as a unit** or **Spread components evenly**. Next, specify the **Explode order** by selecting the parts listed and using the **Move Up** and **Move Down** buttons. Note that you can specify the explode order only when you select the **Spread components evenly** option. Click **OK** to close this dialog.

Type-in a value in the **Distance** box and click **Explode** to explode the parts. Click **Finish** to complete the explosion.

Explode Options

Explode Technique

Move components as a unit

Spread components evenly

Explode order:

Scraw_1.par:1
Crank_1.par:1

Move Up | Move Down

Show this dialog when entering the Explode Step

OK | Cancel | Help

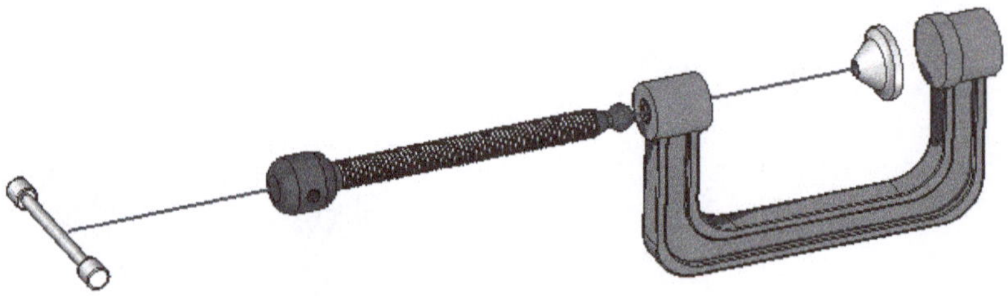

If the distance between the exploded parts is less or more, you can use the **Drag Component** command to adjust the spacing between them. To do this, click the **Drag Component** button on the **Modify** panel of the **Home** tab of ribbon. Next, click the **Move Dependent Parts** icon on the **Drag Component** command bar. Next, select anyone of the exploded components and click the Move icon on the command bar. Click the **Accept** button on the command bar; a triad appears on the selected components. Select anyone of the axes of the triad to define the direction of the movement. Press and hold the left mouse button and drag the cursor to move the selected components.

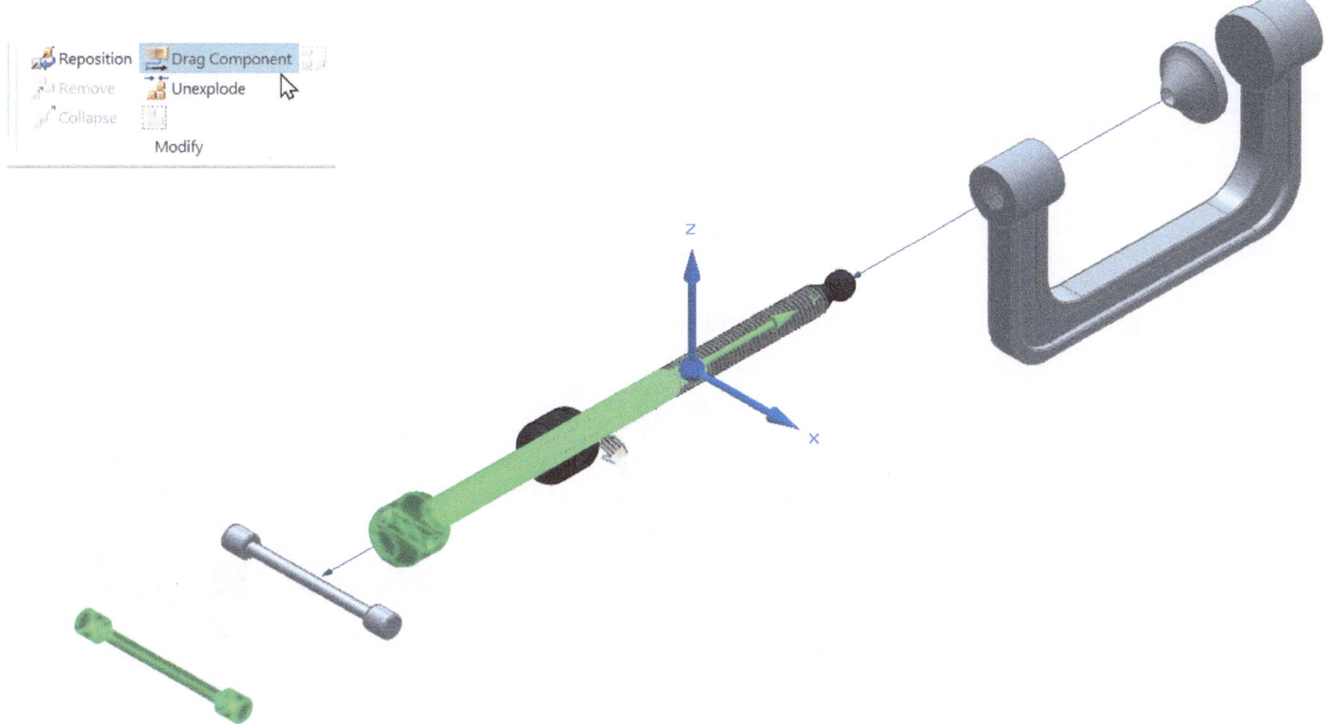

You can also select individual parts and type-in a new explode distance in the **Distance** box.

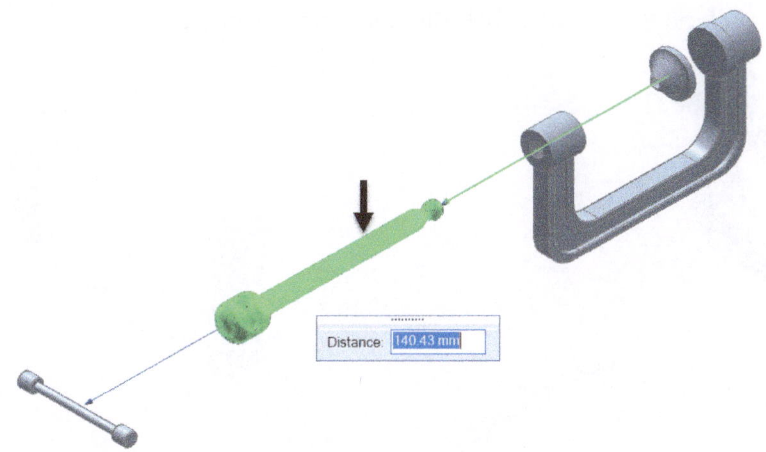

If you want to reorder an exploded component, click **Reposition** on the **Modify** panel and select the component to reorder. Select the component next to it. Click to define the side on which the component will be repositioned.

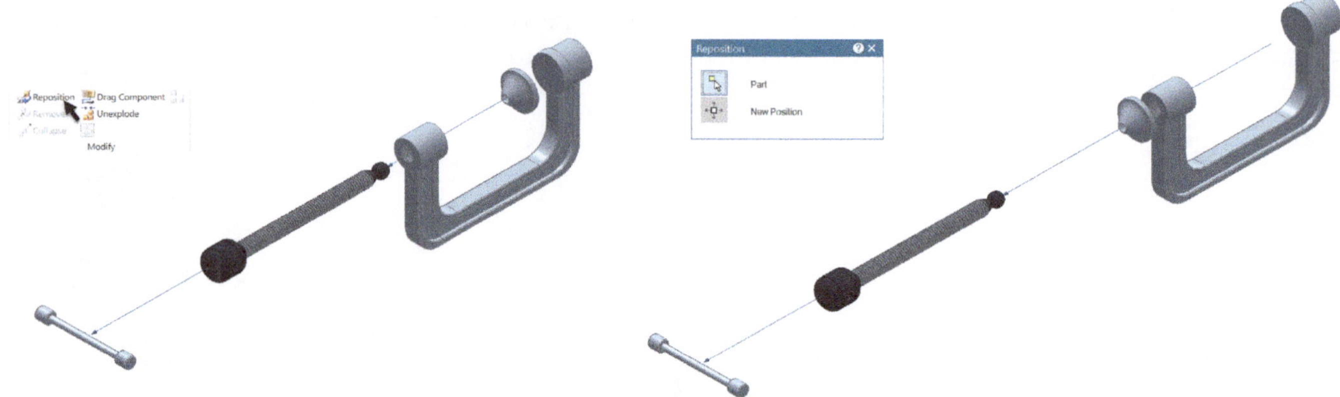

If you want to collapse an exploded part, click on it, and then click **Collapse** on the ribbon.

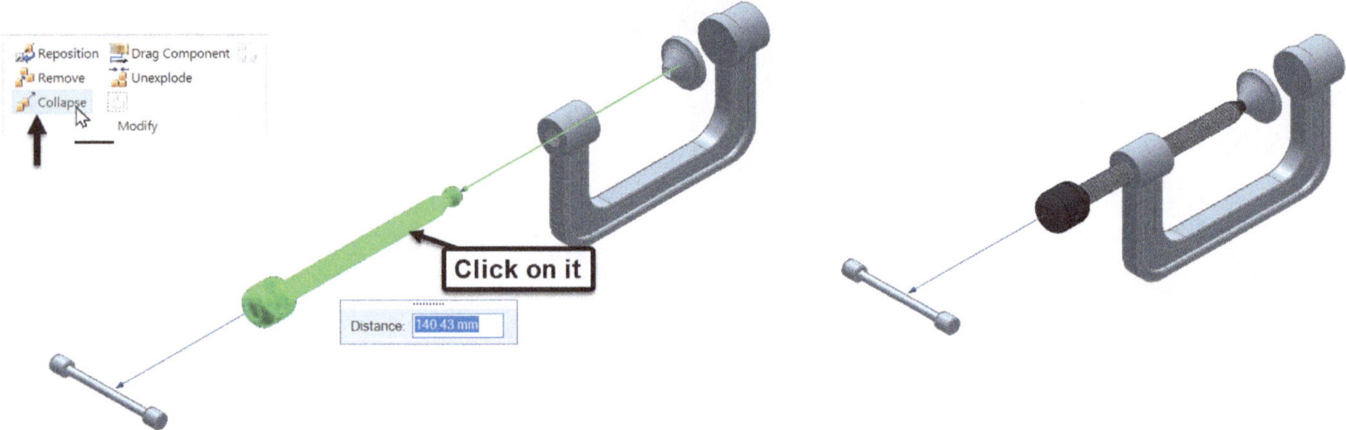

If you want to remove a part from the explosion, click on it, and then click **Remove** on the ribbon.

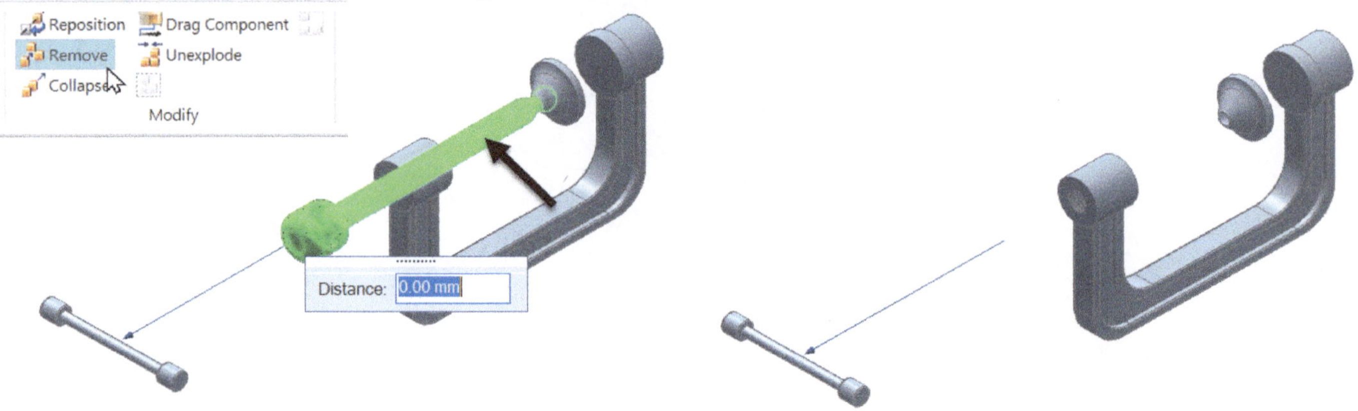

If you want to convert the explosion into a 'move component' operation, click **Drop** on the **Flow Lines** panel. The flow lines are also converted into annotation flow lines.

If you want to modify a flow line, click **Modify** on the **Flow Lines** panel and select the flow line; two handles appear at the flow line's start and endpoints. Click on the start point handle, and then redefine the start point of the flow line. Similarly, redefine the endpoint of the flow line.

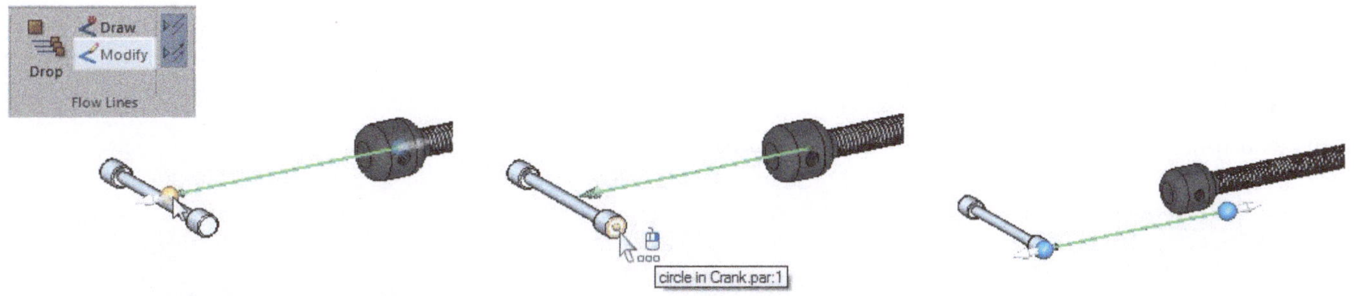

If you want to draw a new flow line, click **Draw** on the **Flow Lines** panel and select the start and end points; a flow line appears between the selected points. On the **Draw** command bar, click the **Next** icon to see different paths of the flow lines. Click **Finish** to complete the flow line creation.

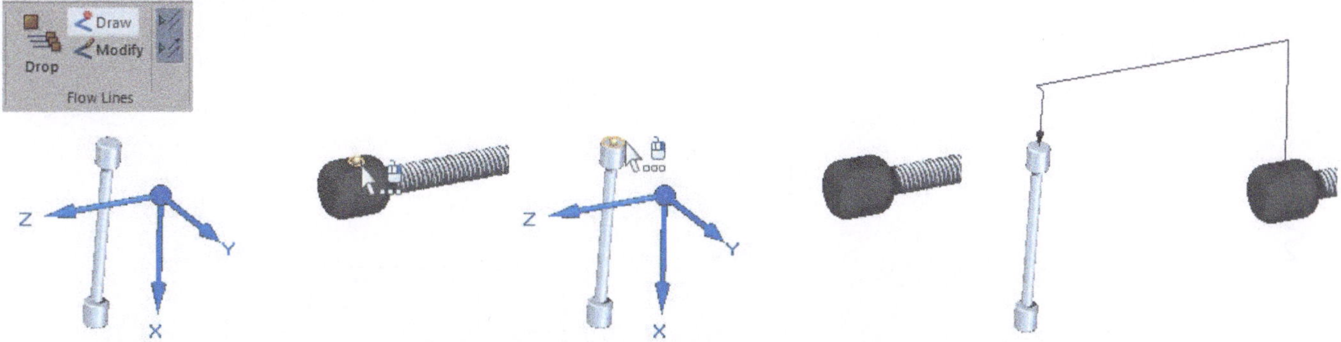

After exploding the assembly, click the **Save** icon on the **Quick Access Toolbar**, specify the assembly file's location, and click **OK**. The **explode, Solid Edge** configuration is created. You can use this configuration to display the exploded view.

Visual Explode

This command allows you to explode the assembly dynamically by dragging the slider. To do this, click **Home > Explode > Visual Explode**. Next, drag the Explode slider on the **Visual Explode** command bar; the assembly is exploded. Adjust the slider to specify the explosion distance. Use the **Explode Stepwise** button to explode the subassemblies inside the main assembly in the step-by-step manner. If you want to save the explosion as a separate configuration, click the **Save Configuration** button; the **New Configuration** dialog appears. Enter the configuration file name in the **Configuration file** box and use the Browse button to specify the location of the configuration file. Next, click **OK** to create the configuration file. Next, close the **Visual Explode** command bar.

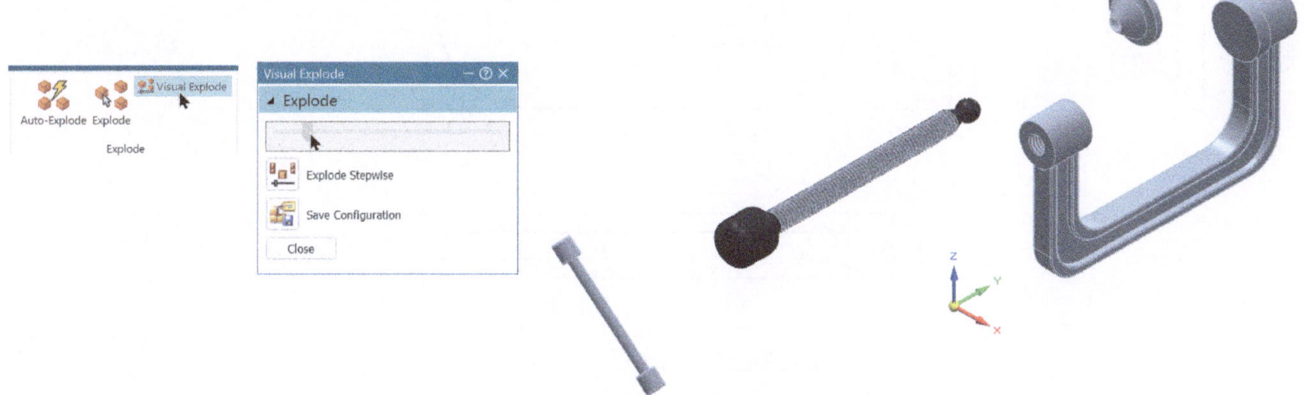

Now, click **Close ERA** on the ribbon; the assembly environment appears.

Examples

Example 1 (Bottom-Up Assembly)

In this example, you will create the assembly shown below.

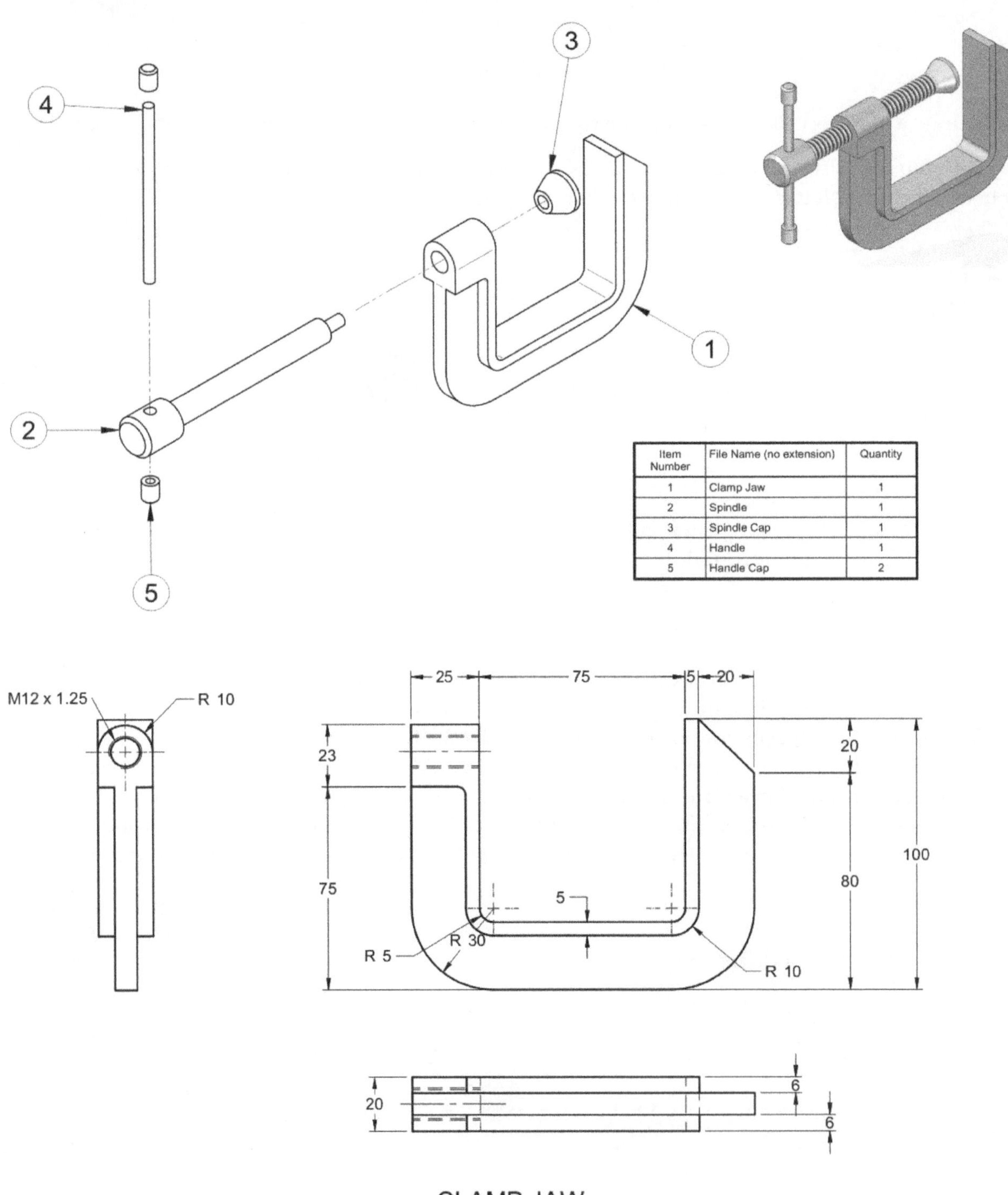

Item Number	File Name (no extension)	Quantity
1	Clamp Jaw	1
2	Spindle	1
3	Spindle Cap	1
4	Handle	1
5	Handle Cap	2

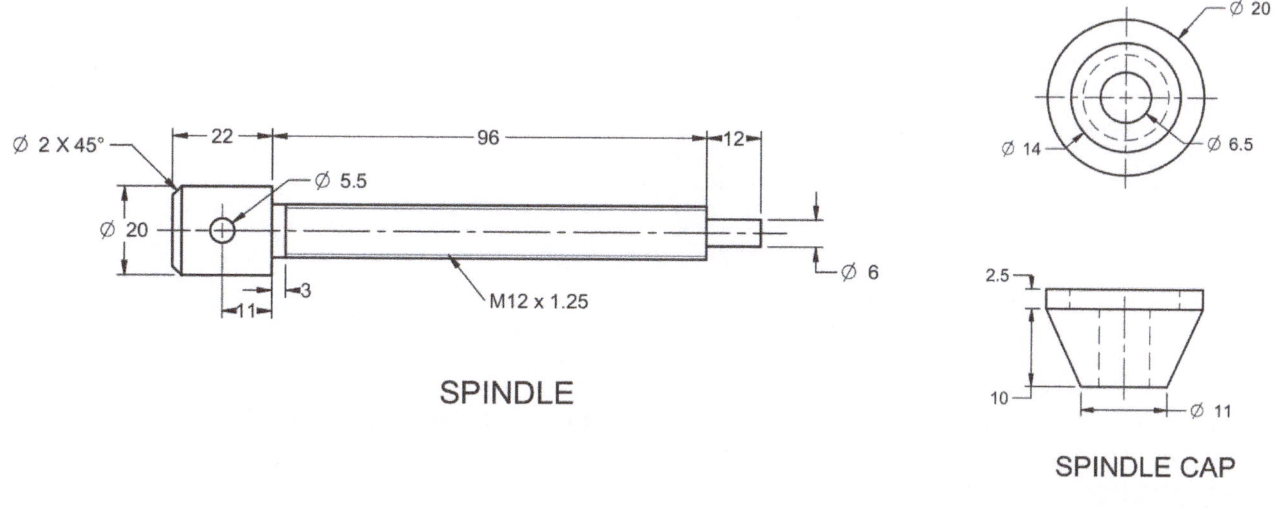

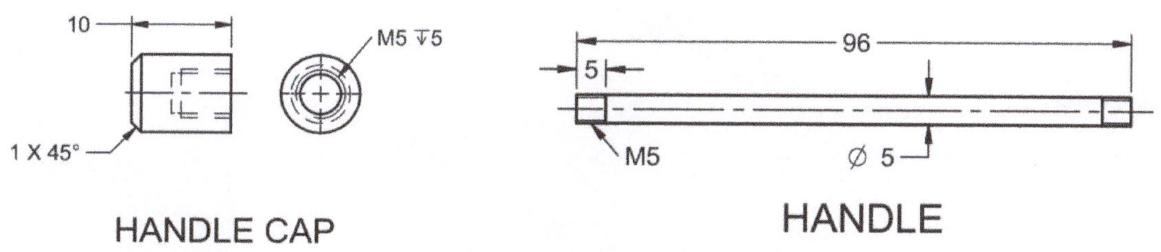

1. Start **Solid Edge 2026.**
2. Create and save all the parts of the assembly in a single folder. Name this folder as *G-Clamp*.
3. On the **File Menu**, click **New > ISO Metric Assembly** to start an assembly file.
4. Click the **Insert Component** button on the ribbon to display the **Parts Library** window.
5. In the **Parts Library** window, use the drop-down menu and go to the *G-Clamp* folder.
6. In the **Parts Library** window, click *Clamp Jaw* and drag it into the assembly window.

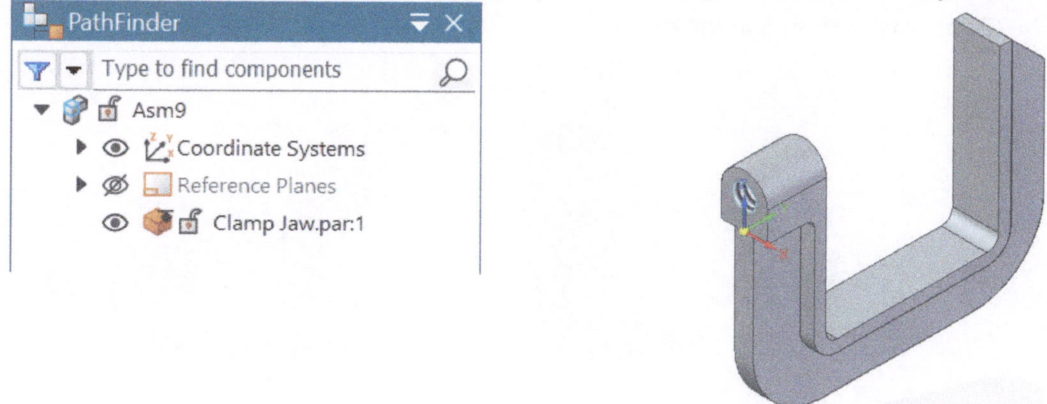

7. In the **Parts Library** window, click *Spindle* and drag it into the assembly window.

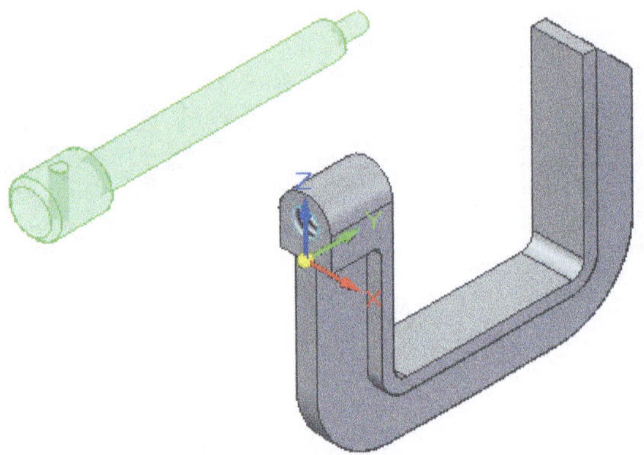

8. On the command bar, click **Relationship Types > Axial Align,** and then select the **Lock axial rotation** option.
9. Click on the cylindrical face of the *Spindle* and hole of the *Clamp Jaw*.

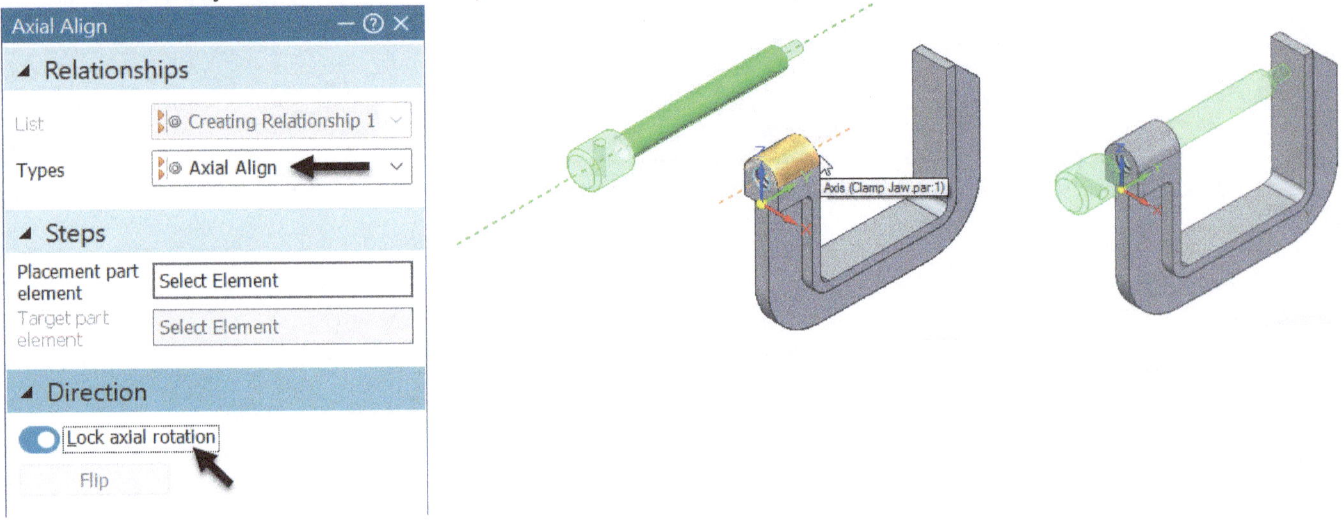

10. On the command bar, click **Types > Planar Align**, and then type **-40** in the **Value** box in the **Offset** section.
11. Click on the back face of the *Spindle* and rotate the view.
12. Click on the flat face of the *Clamp Jaw*, as shown in the figure.

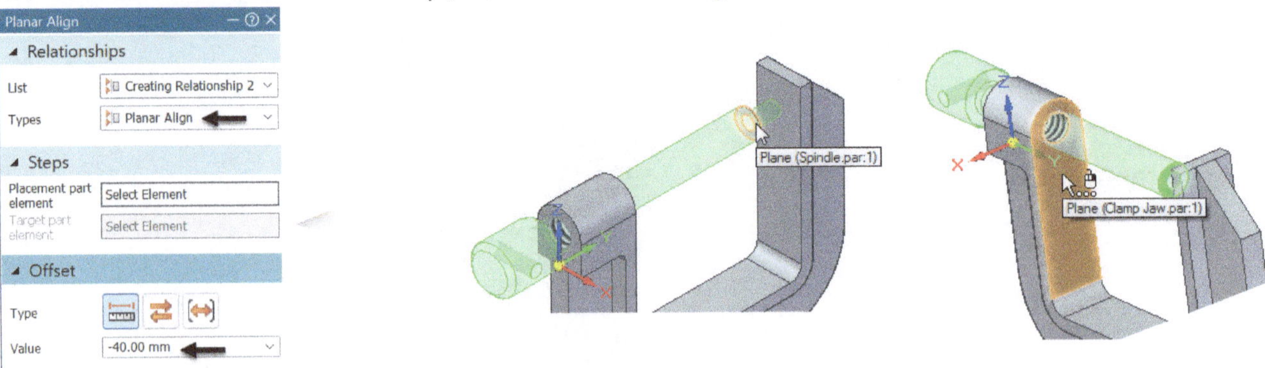

13. In the **Parts Library**, click *Spindle Cap* and drag it into the assembly window.
14. On the command bar, select the **Lock axial rotation** option, and then click on the cylindrical face of the *Spindle Cap* hole.

15. Click on the small cylindrical face of the *Spindle*. The *Spindle* and *Spindle Cap* are axially aligned.

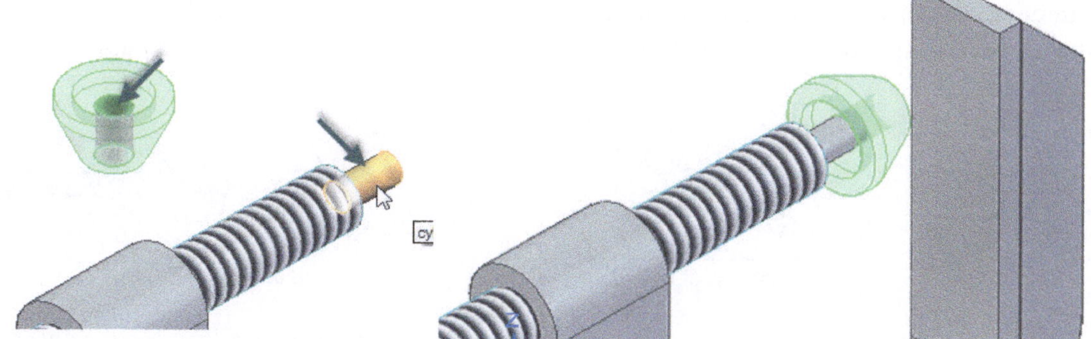

16. Rotate the model view and click on the *Spindle Cap*'s flat face, as shown in the figure.
17. Click on the flat face of the *Spindle*. The *Spindle Cap* is assembled and fully constrained. However, you will notice that the part is oriented in the reverse direction.

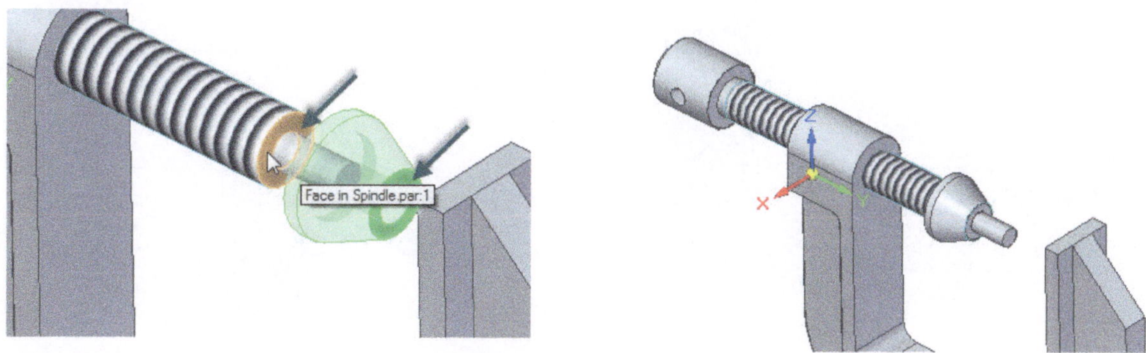

Note: *Skip steps 18 and 19 if the Spindle Cap is oriented properly.*

18. In the **Pathfinder**, click *Spindle Cap*. The relations associated with the part appear at the bottom of the **Pathfinder**.

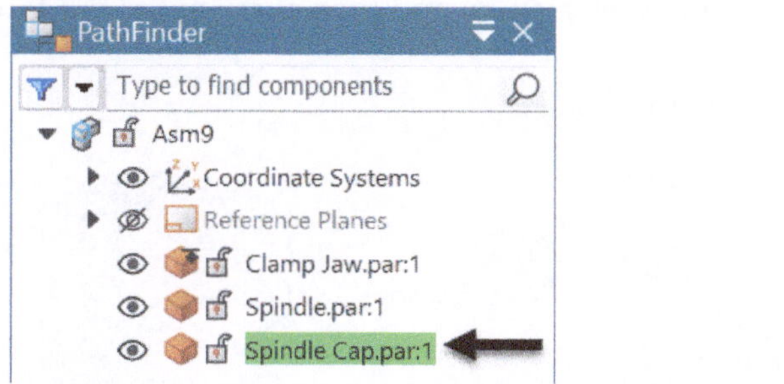

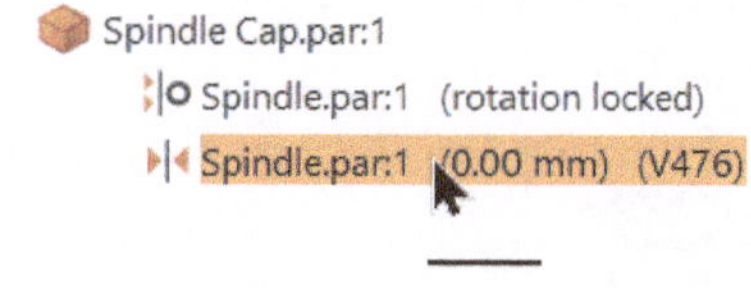

19. Click on the planar align relation, and then click the **Flip** button at the bottom of the screen. The *Spindle Cap* is reversed.

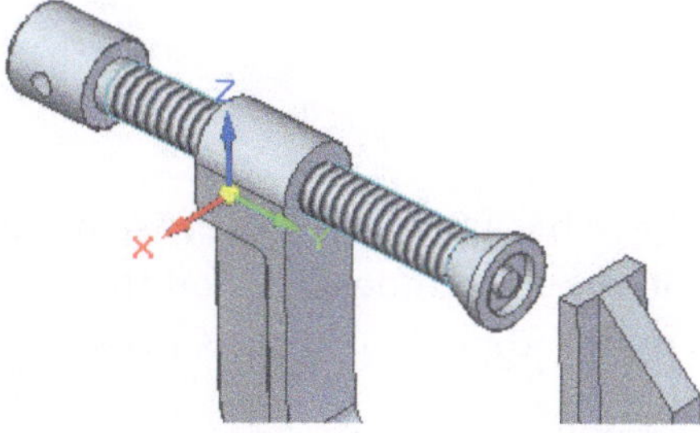

20. In **Parts Library**, click *Handle* and drag it into the assembly window.
21. On the command bar, click **Types > Center-Plane** and select the axis of the *Spindle*.
22. Click on the front face and back face of the *Handle*.

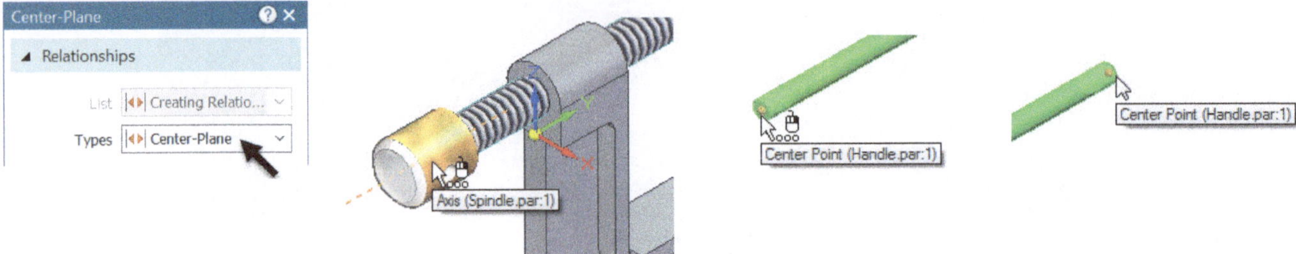

23. On the command bar, click **Types > Axial Align**. Select the **Lock axial rotation** icon, and then click on the cylindrical face of the *Handle*.
24. Click on the hole of the *Spindle*. The *Handle* is axially aligned with the hole.

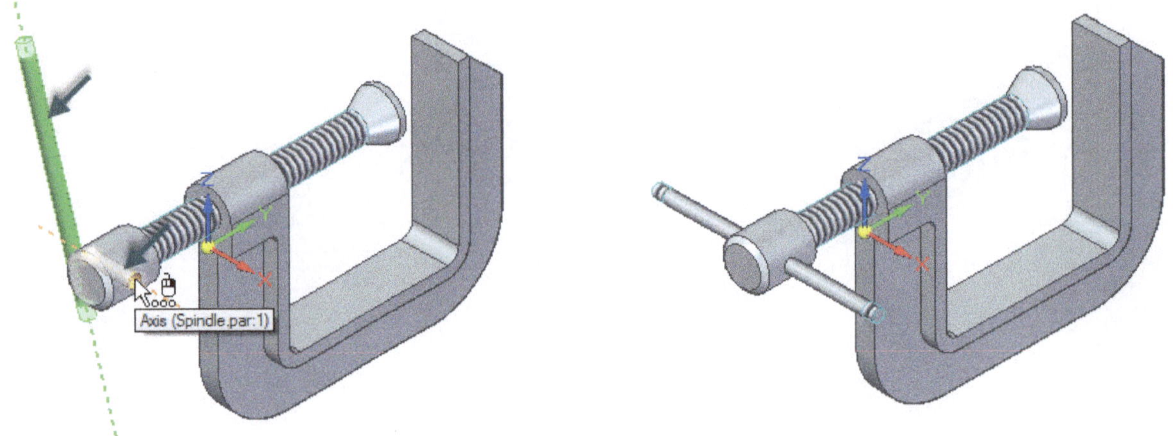

25. In the **Parts Library**, click *Handle Cap* and drag it into the assembly window.
26. On the command bar, click **Types > Insert**, and then click on a cylindrical face of the *Handle Cap*.
27. Click on the cylindrical face of the *Handle*.
28. On the command bar, type 1 in the **Value** box available in the **Offset** section, and then click on the flat face of the hole of the *Handle Cap*.
29. Click the end face of the *Handle*. The *Handle Cap* is inserted into the *Handle*.

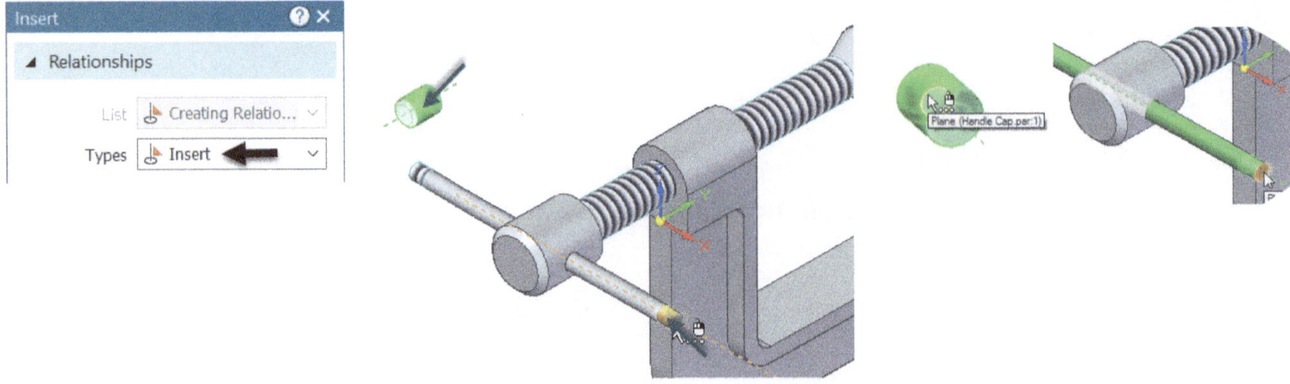

30. Save the assembly with the name **G-Clamp.asm**.
31. In the **Pathfinder**, click on the *Handle Cap*, and then click **Home > Assemble > Capture Fit**. The **Capture Fit** dialog appears. Click **OK** to close the dialog.

32. In the **Parts Library**, click *Handle Cap* and drag it to the assembly window. The **Mate** command is activated, and the flat face of the *Handle Cap* is selected.
33. Type 1 in the **Offset value** box and click on the end face of the *Handle*. The **Axial Align** command is activated, and the axis of the *Handle Cap* is selected.
34. Click on the axis of the *Handle* to complete the assembly.

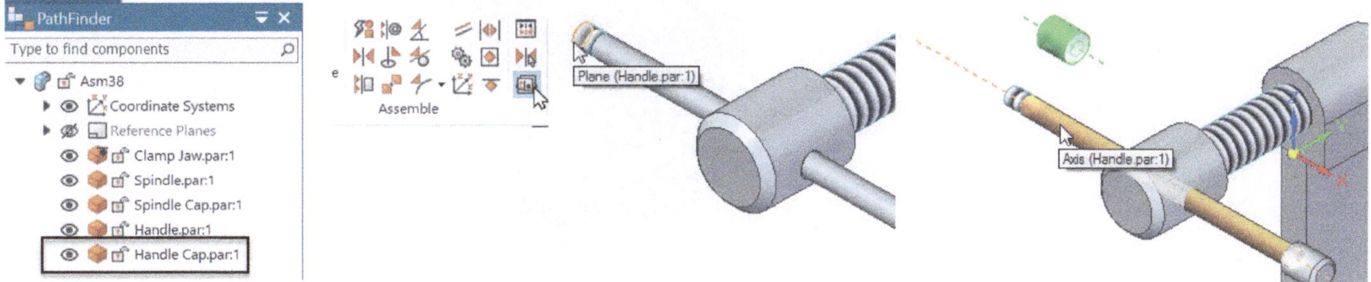

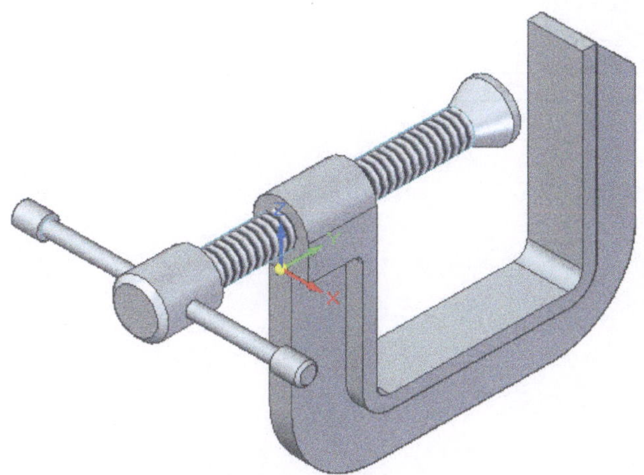

35. Save and close the assembly.

Example 2 (Top-Down Assembly)

In this example, you will create the assembly shown below.

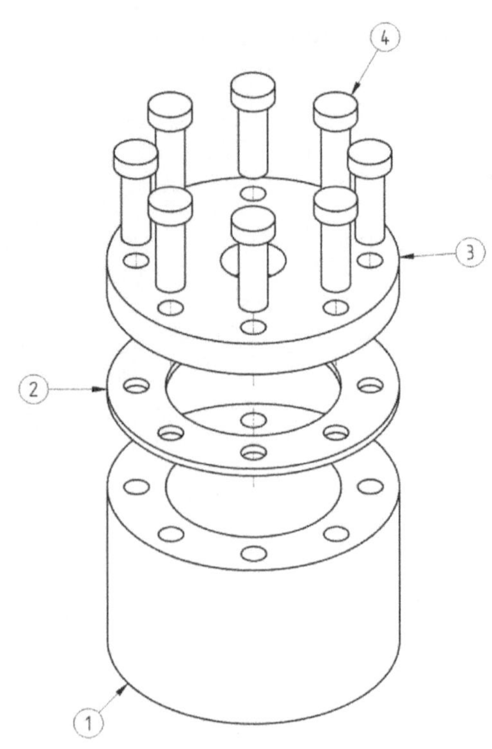

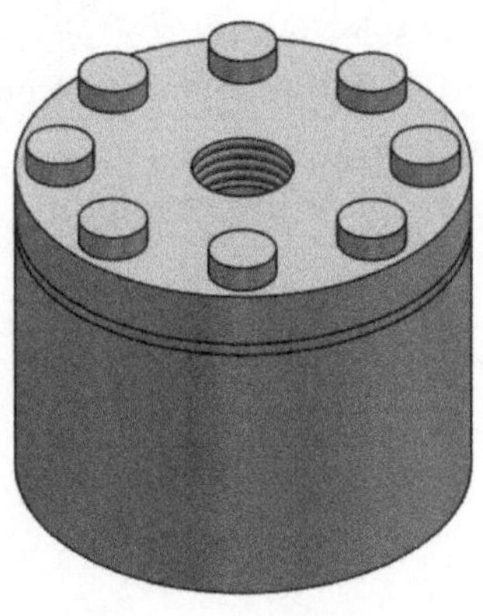

Item Number	File Name (no extension)	Quantity
1	Cylinder base	1
2	Gasket	1
3	Cover plate	1
4	Screw	8

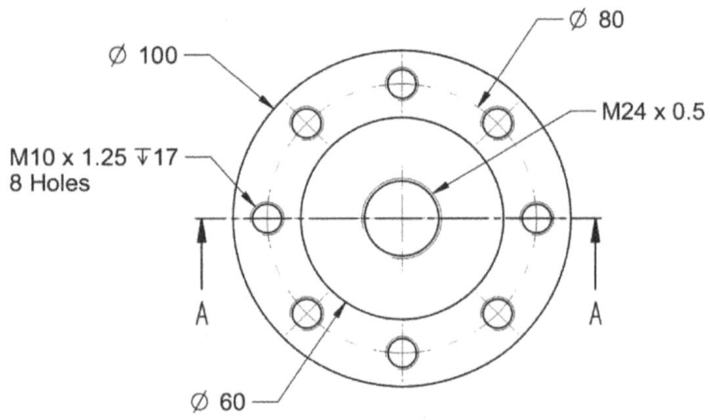

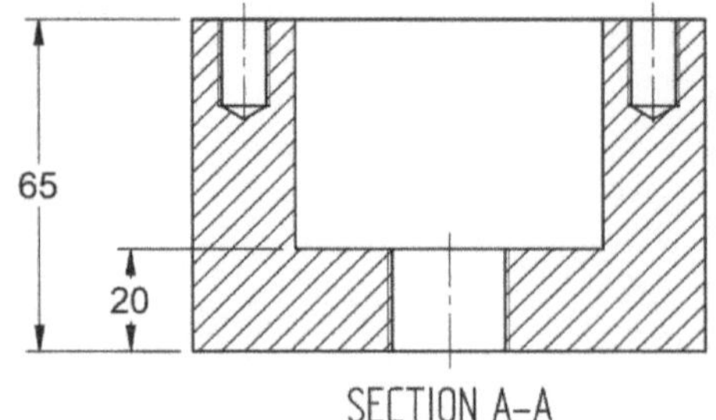

Cylinder Base

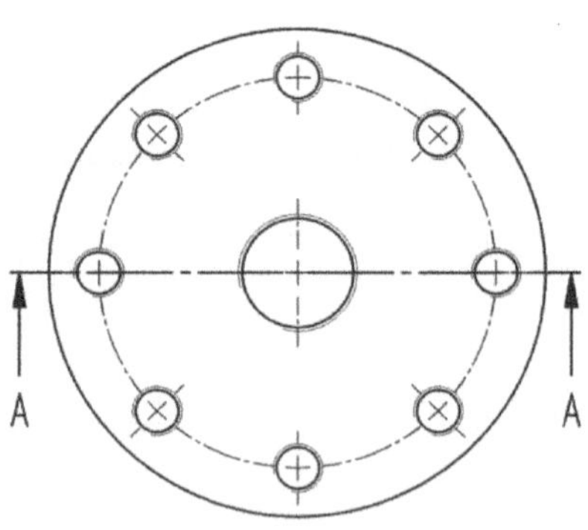

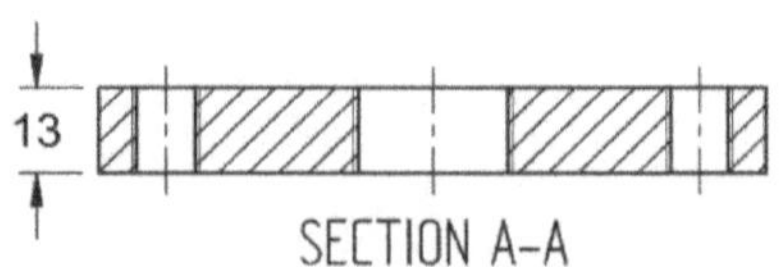

Cover Plate

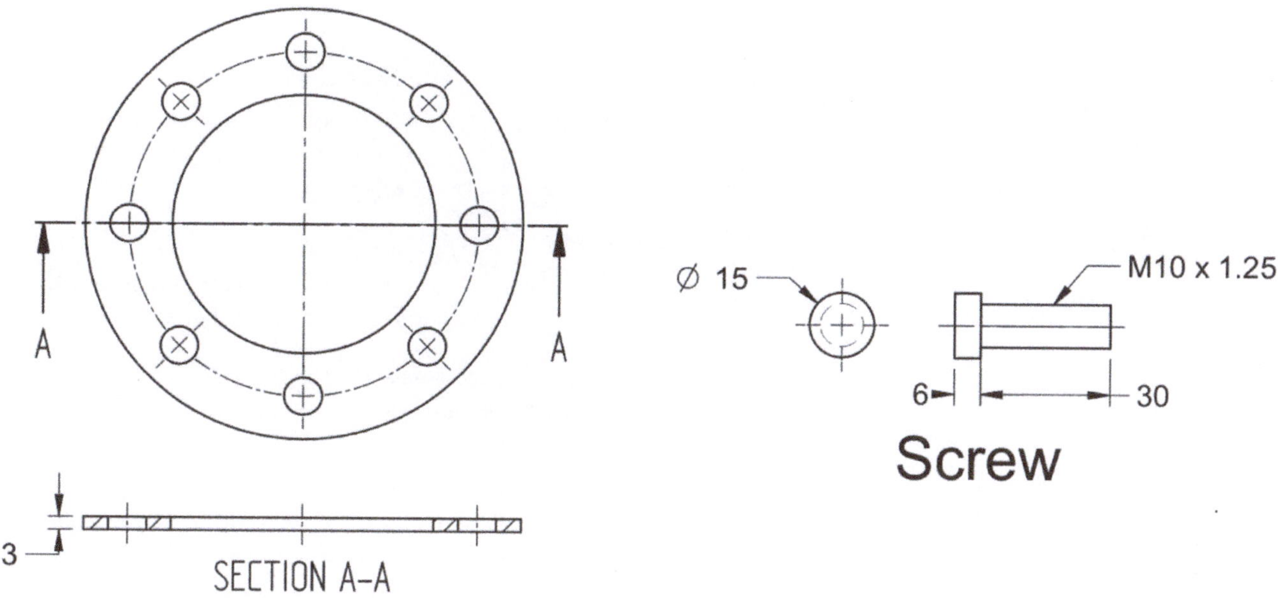

1. Start **Solid Edge 2026**.
2. Start a new part file and create the Cylinder base. Do not create the center hole.

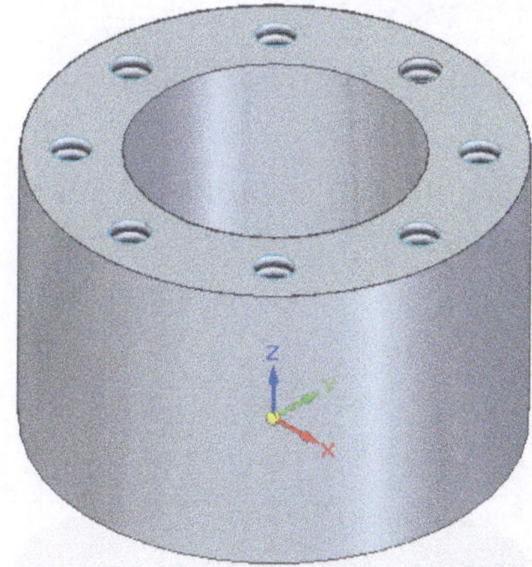

3. Create a new folder with the name *Pressure Cylinder.*
4. Save the file with the name *Cylinder base.*
5. On the **File Menu**, click **New > Assembly of Active Model.** The **Create Assembly** dialog appears.
6. On this dialog, click **OK** to start a new assembly file. The *Cylinder base* is automatically placed at the origin.
7. Save the assembly file in the *Pressure Cylinder* folder.
8. On the ribbon, click **Home > Assemble > Create Part In-Place**. The **Create Part In-Place Options** dialog pops up on the screen.
9. On this dialog, under the **Place the Origin** section, select the **By graphic input** option.
10. Leave the other default options on this dialog and click **OK**. The origin of the new part is attached to the mouse pointer.

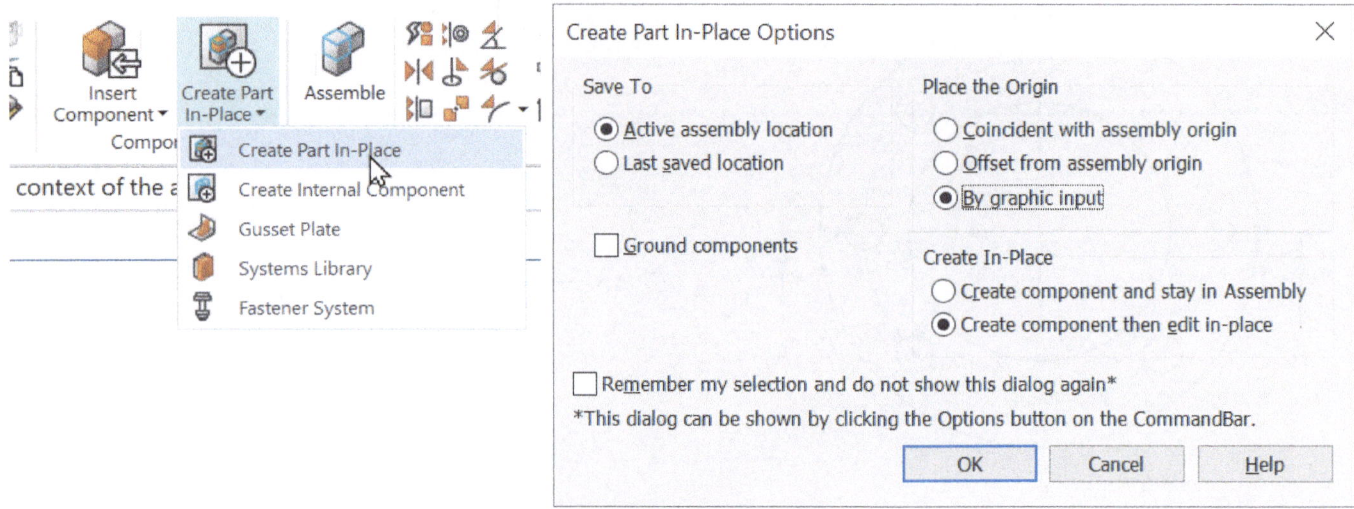

11. Place the mouse pointer on the circular edge of the Cylinder base.
12. Press **N** on your keyboard to change the orientation of the origin.
13. Click when the orientation of the part origin is the same as that of the assembly origin.

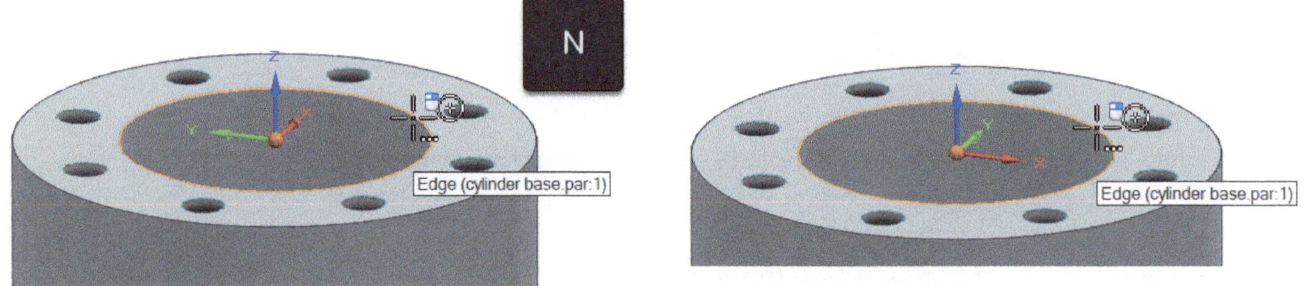

14. On the command bar, click the **Accept** button. The **Save As** dialog pops up.
15. Type *Gasket* in the **File name** field and click **Save**. The part file is created, and the Part environment is activated.
16. On the ribbon, click **Home > Draw > Project to Sketch** and lock the XY plane.

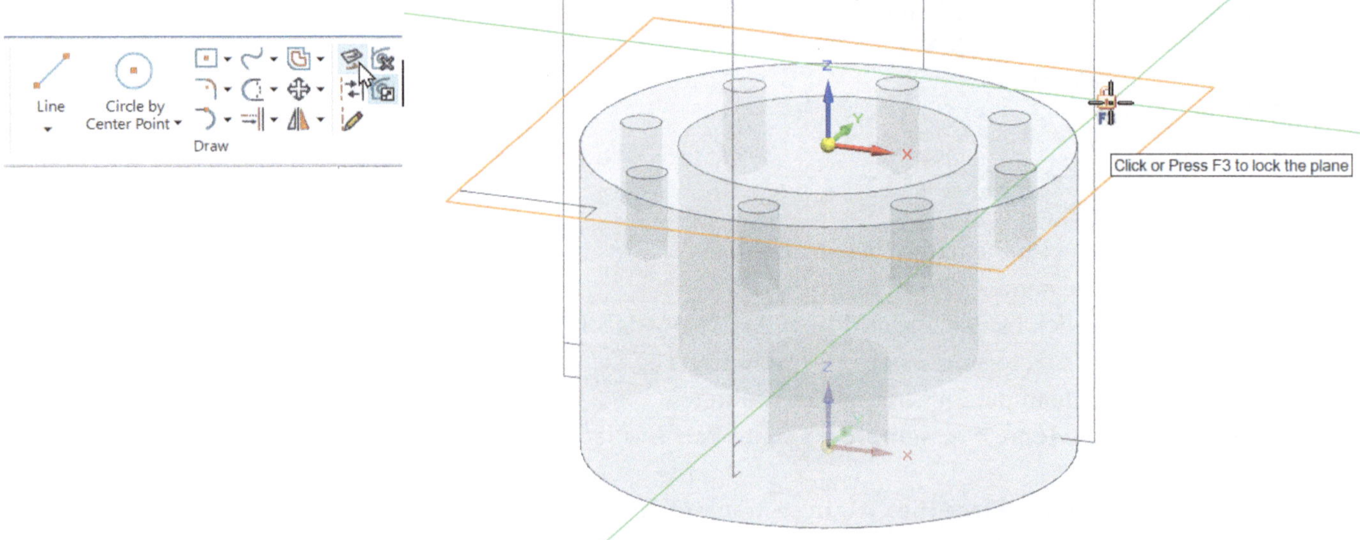

17. Leave the default settings on the **Project to Sketch Options** dialog, and then click **OK**.
18. Click on the circular edges on the top face of the Cylinder base. Click the **Accept** button; the edges are projected to the locked plane.
19. Activate the **Extrude** command and click in the region enclosed by the sketch.

20. Right-click to accept the selection, and then set the **Extent Type** to **Finite**.
21. Move the mouse pointer upward.
22. Type 3 in the dimension box and press Enter to create the *Extrude* feature.

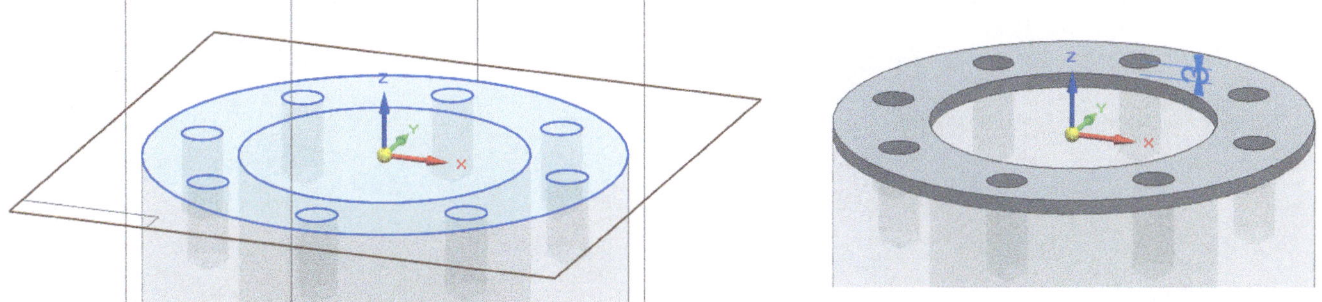

23. On the ribbon, click **Close and Return** to return to the assembly session.
24. On the ribbon, click **Home > Assemble > Create Part In-Place** .
25. On the **Create Part In-Place** dialog, under the **Place the origin** section, select the **Offset from assembly origin** option. Click **OK** to close the dialog. You have to enter X, Y, and Z values (or) select a key point to specify the new part's origin.

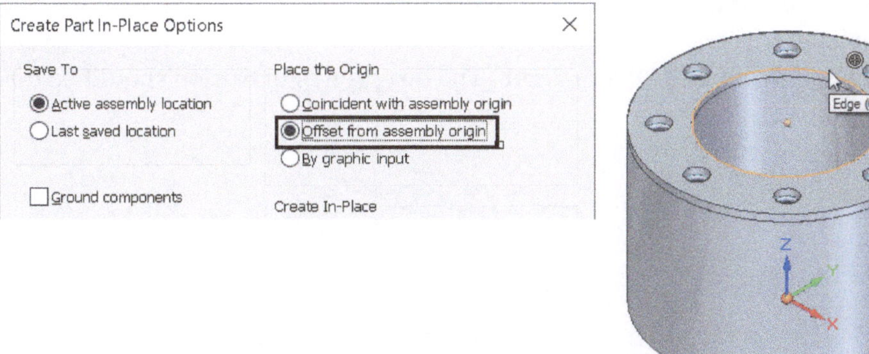

26. Click on the circular edge of the *Gasket* to define the location of the origin.
27. On the command bar, click the **Accept** button.
28. On the **Save As** dialog, type *Cover plate* in the **File name** field and click **Save**.
29. In the **Part** environment, activate the **Project to Sketch** command and lock the XY plane. Next, click **OK** on the **Project Options** dialog.
30. Project the outer and small circular edges.
31. Use the sketch and create an *Extrude* feature. The depth of the extrusion is 13 mm.

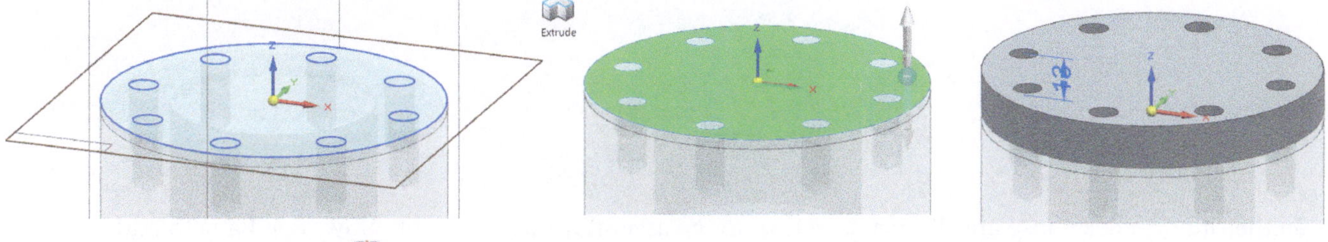

32. Activate the **Thread** command and add M10 x 1.25 to threads to the holes.

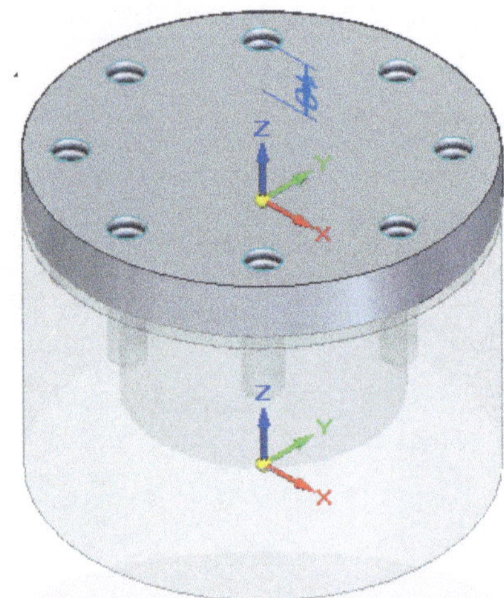

33. On the ribbon, click **Close and Return** to return to the assembly environment.
34. Activate the **Create Part In-Place** command and create the *Screw* on the top face of the *Cover plate*.
35. In the Part environment, activate the **Project to Sketch** command and lock the XY plane.
36. Project the circular edge of the hole.
37. Use the sketch and create an *Extrude* feature of 30 mm depth. The direction of extrusion should be downward.

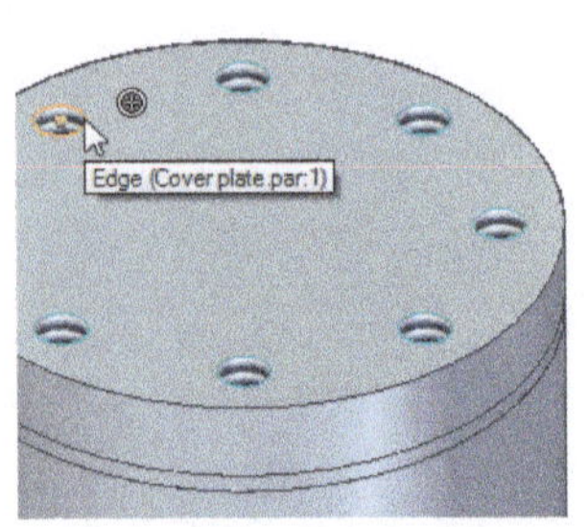

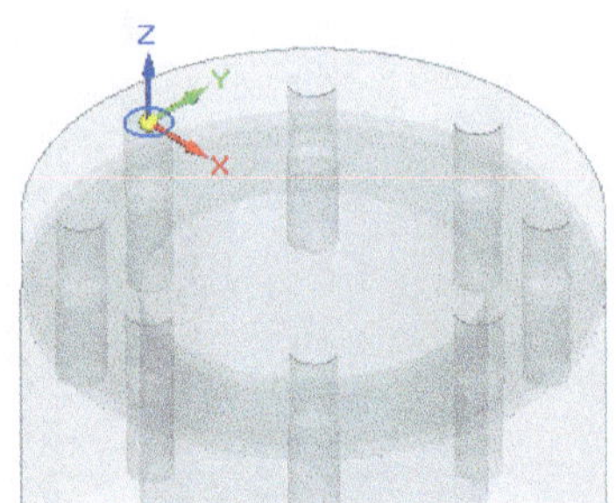

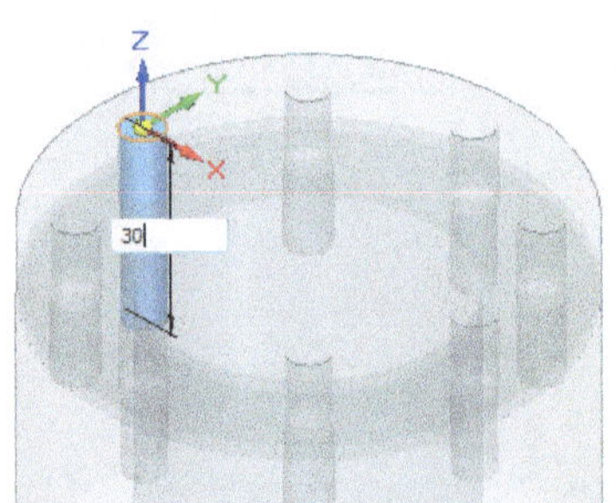

38. Create a circle of 15 mm diameter on the top face and extrude it in the upward direction. The extrude depth is 6 mm.
39. Activate the **Thread** command and add the thread to the lower cylindrical face of the part. The thread size is M10 x 1.25.

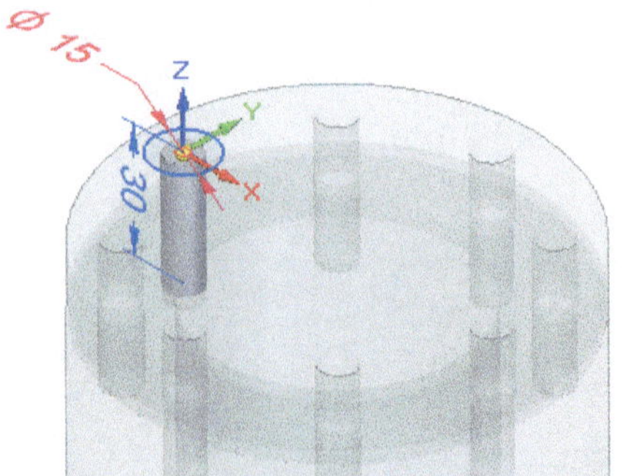

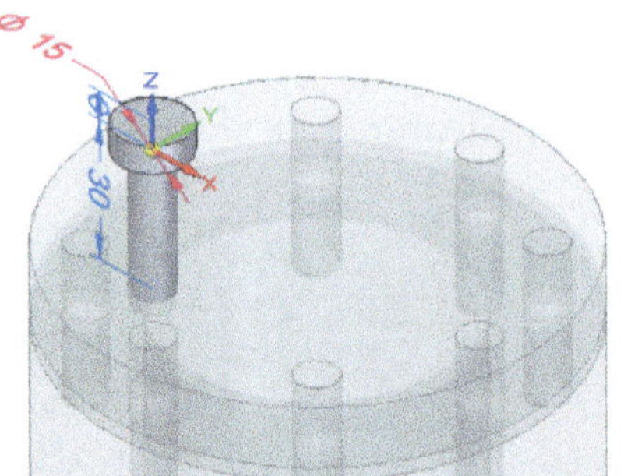

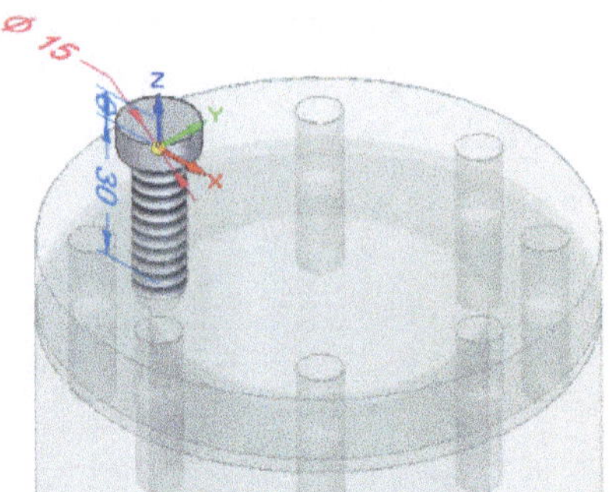

40. On the ribbon, click **Close and Return** to return to the assembly environment. Now, you have to add relationships between parts.
41. On the ribbon, click **Home > Assemble > Assembly Relationship Assistant**. The **Relationship Assistance Options** dialog appears.
42. On this dialog, select the **Select Set 2** option and click **OK**.

43. Click on the *Cylinder base*, and then click the green check on the command bar.
44. Click on the *Gasket*, and then click the green check on the command bar. The **Relationship Assistant Settings** dialog pops up.

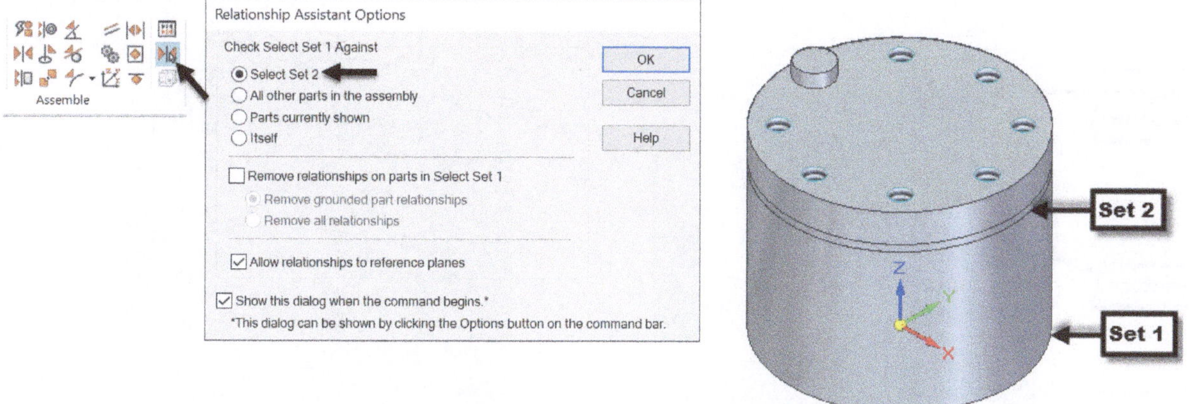

45. In this dialog, make sure that the Mate and Axial Align relationships are turned on. Click the **Process** button to create relationships between the selected parts automatically.

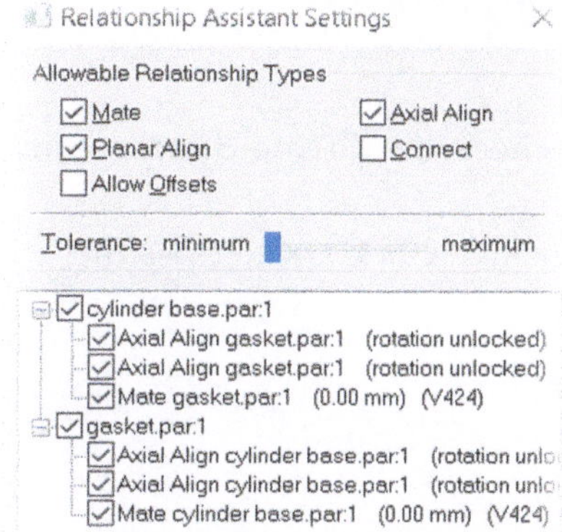

46. Click on the relationships to highlight the faces associated with them.
47. Click **Accept** to create relationships.
48. Close the dialog and click **Finish** to complete creating the relationships. Click **Cancel** to deactivate the command.
49. In the **Pathfinder**, click on the *Gasket*, and then click on the Axial Align relationship at the bottom.
50. At the bottom of the screen, click the **Lock Rotation** icon to arrest the *Gasket* rotation.

51. Use the **Assembly Relationship Assistant** command and create relationships between the other parts of the assembly.

52. On the ribbon, click **Home > Pattern > Pattern**, and then click on the *Screw*. Click the green check on the command bar to accept the selection.

53. Click on the *Cylinder base* and select the circular pattern. Next, select the hole in which the screw in located to define the reference feature of the pattern.
54. On the command bar, click **Finish** to complete the pattern.

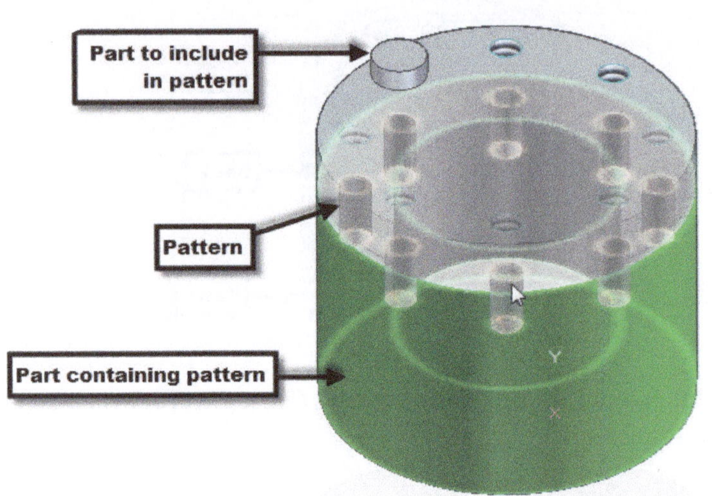

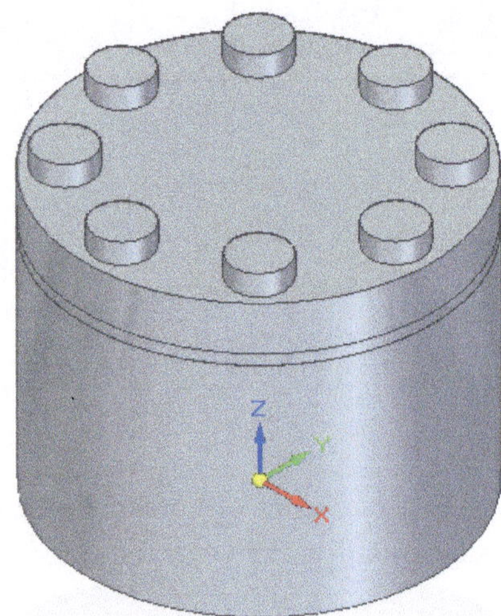

55. On the ribbon, click **Features > Assembly Features > Hole**.
56. On this Hole command bar, select **Feature Type > Part features**, and then check the **Create Synchronous features if possible** option.
57. On the command bar, click the **Options** button and set the options, as shown below. Click **OK** to close the dialog.

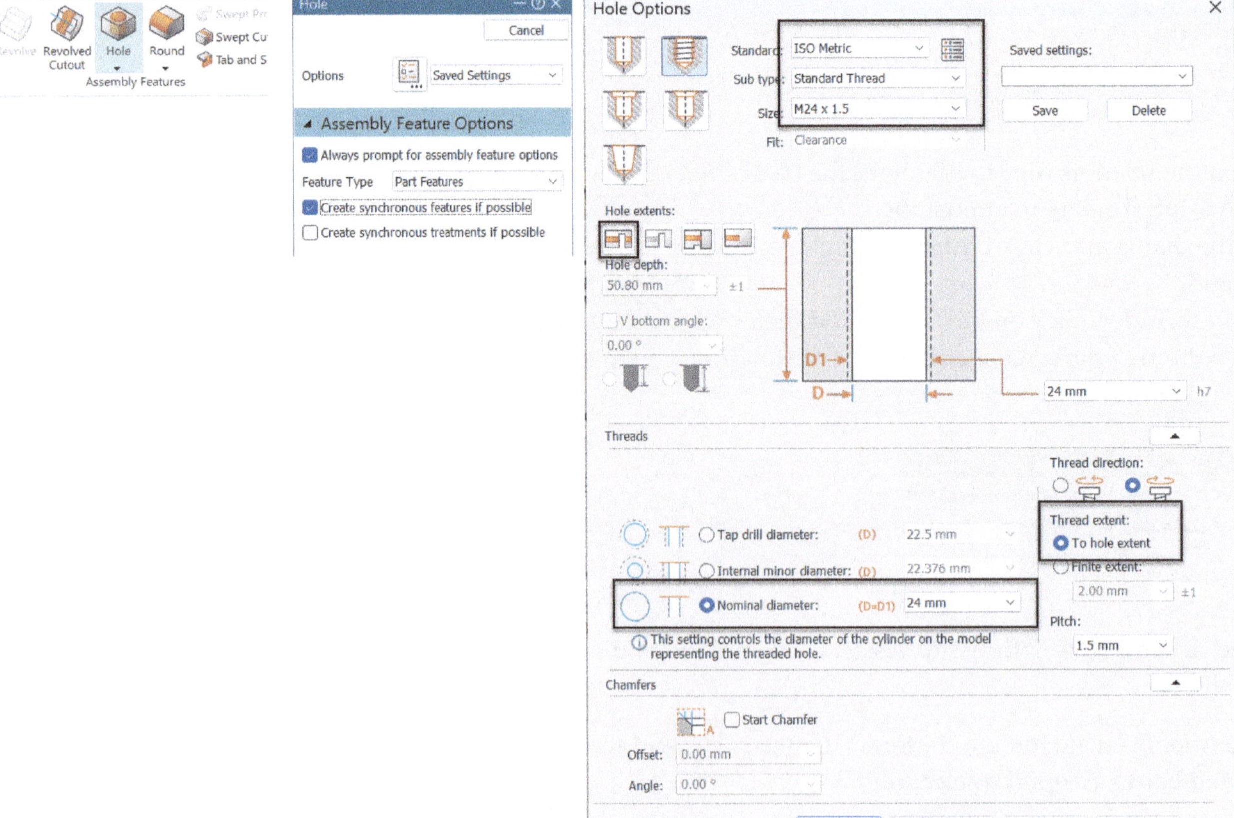

58. Click on the top face of the cover plate and place a hole circle at the center.
59. Click **Close Sketch** to exit the sketch.
60. Move the mouse pointer downwards and click to define the side of the hole.
61. On the command bar, click the green check to create the threaded hole.

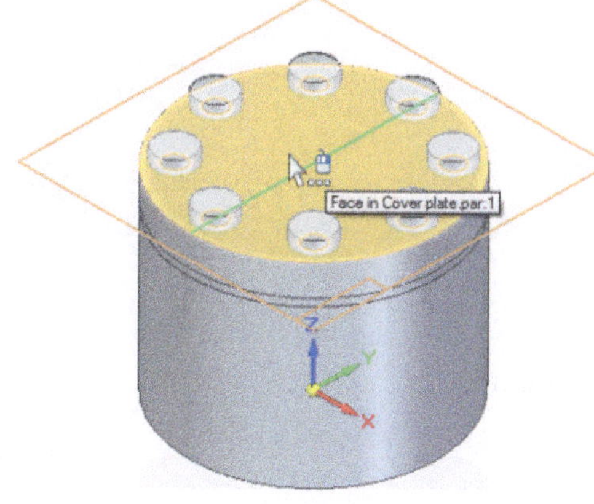

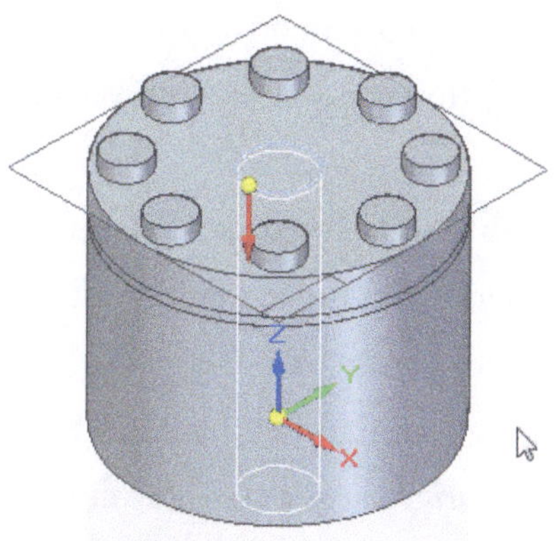

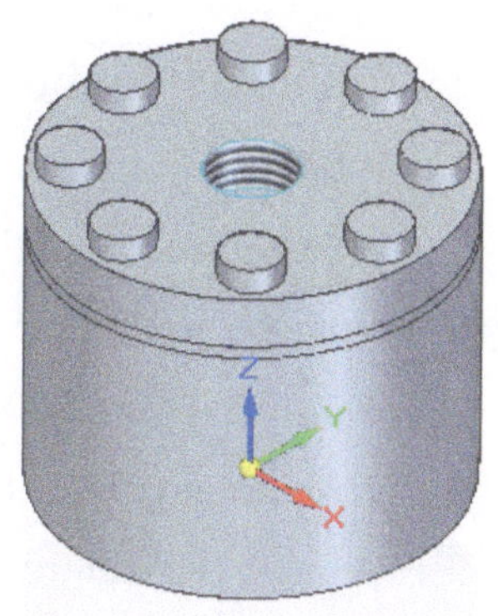

62. On the ribbon, click **PMI > Model Views > Section** .
63. Click on the XZ plane and draw the sketch, as shown in the figure.

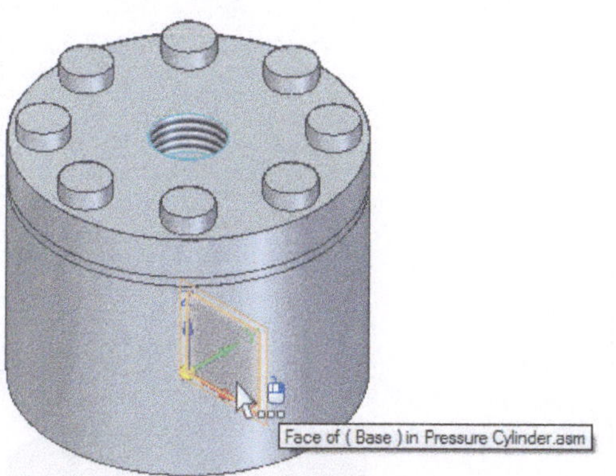

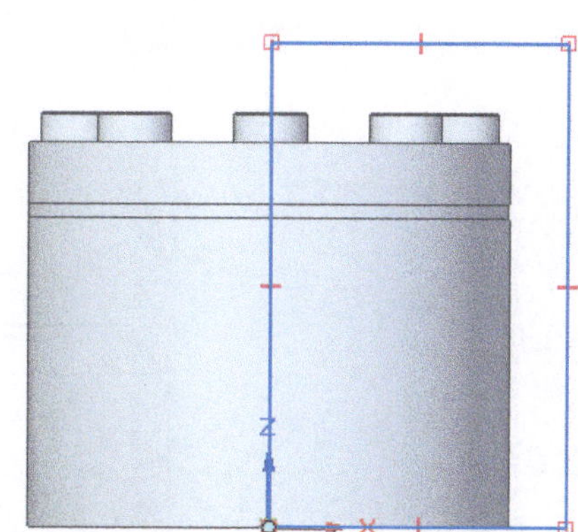

64. On the ribbon, click **Close Sketch** to close the sketch.
65. Move mouse pointer such that the arrow points inside the sketch. Click to define the side of the section cut.
66. Extrude the sketch in the forward direction to create the section cut. Click **Accept** and **Finish** to create the section cut.

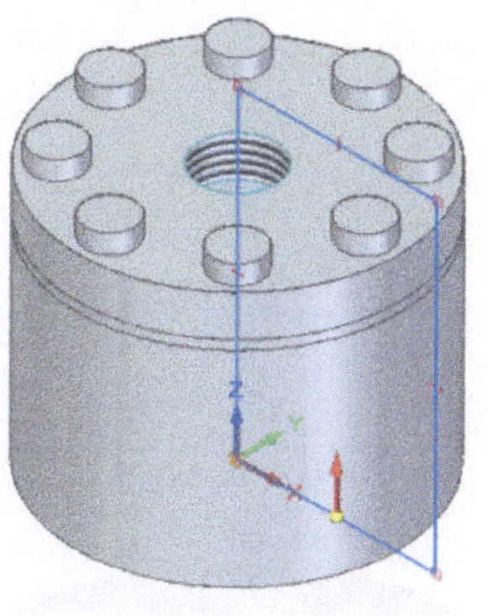

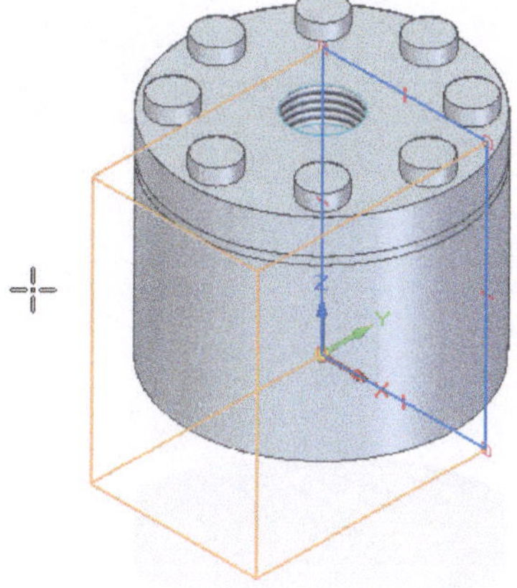

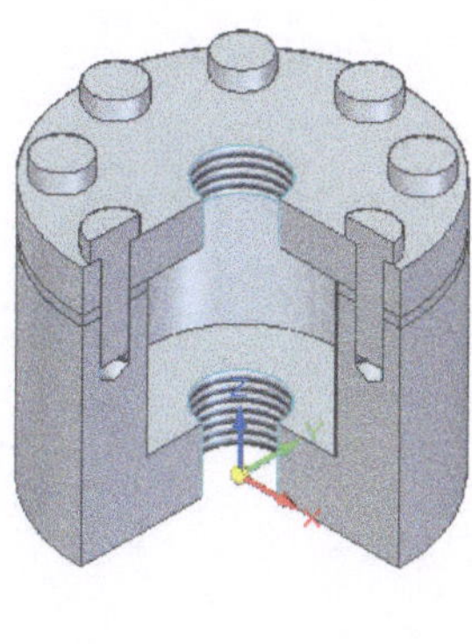

67. Explode, save, and close the assembly file (refer to **Exploding Assemblies** section).

Questions

1. How do you start an assembly from an already opened part?
2. What is the use of the **Capture Fit** command?
3. List the advantages of the Top-down assembly approach.
4. What is a grounded part?
5. What is the use of the **Assembly Relationship Assistant** command?
6. How do you create a sub-assembly in the assembly environment?
7. Briefly explain the **Edit-In Place** command.
8. Why do we prefer the **Explode** command to the **Auto Explode** command?
9. What is the difference between rigid and adjustable subassemblies?
10. How to show or hide reference planes of a part?

Exercise 1

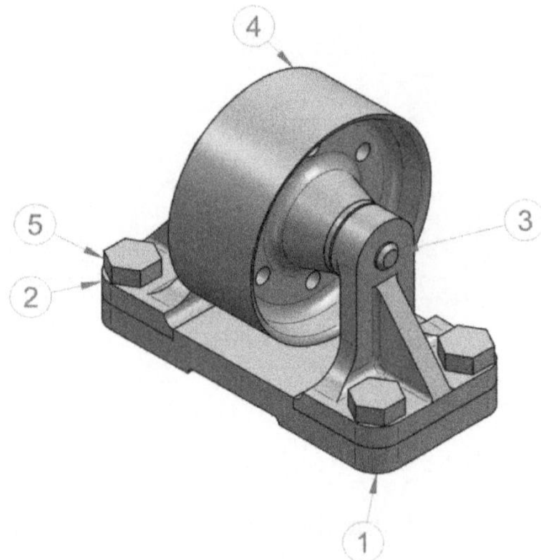

Item Number	File Name (no extension)	Quantity
1	Base	1
2	Bracket	2
3	Spindle	1
4	Roller-Bush assembly	1
5	Bolt	4

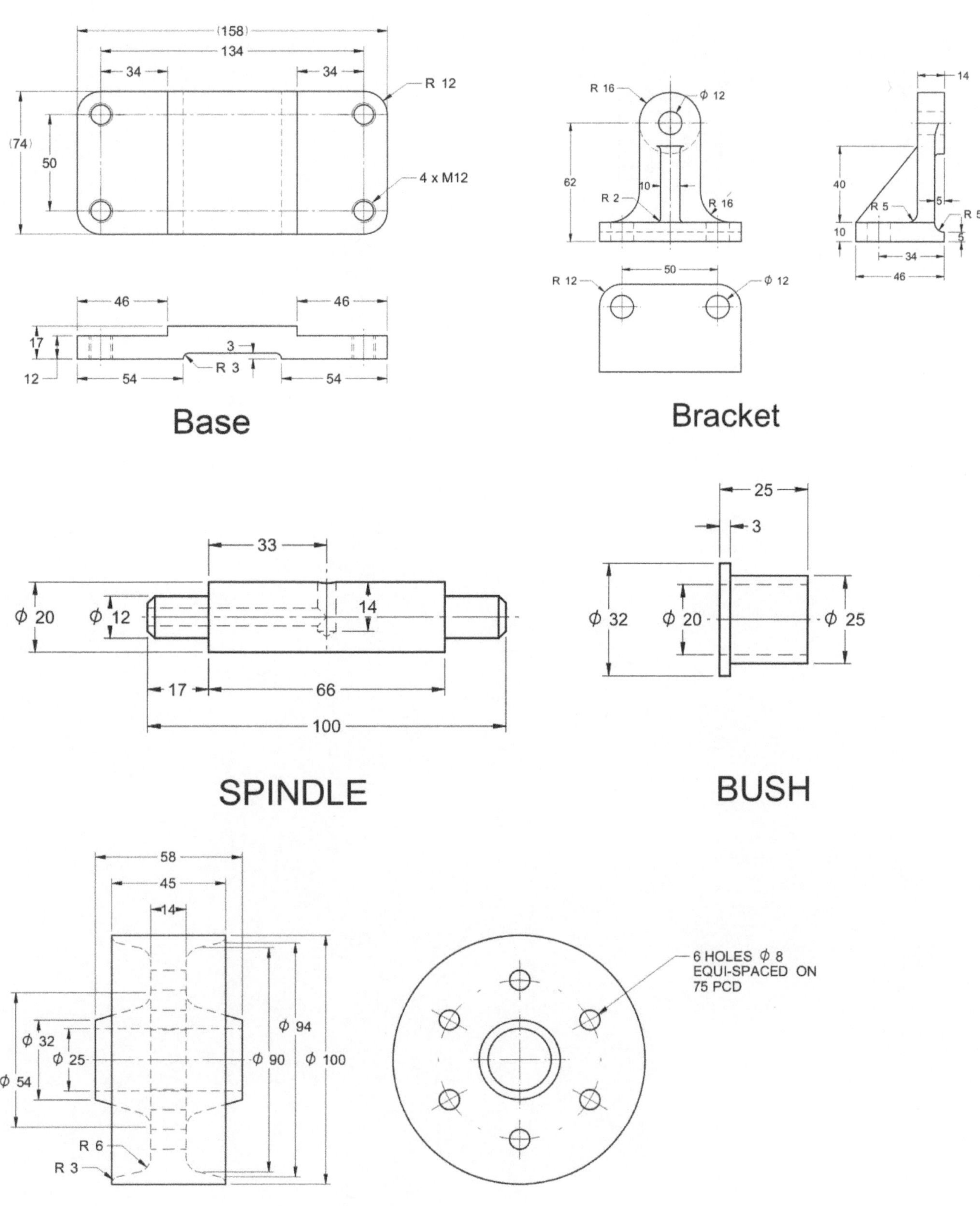

(158)
134
34
34
R 12
(74)
50
4 x M12
46
46
17
3
R 3
12
54
54
Base
R 16
Φ 12
62
10
R 2
R 16
R 12
50
Φ 12
14
40
R 5
5
R 5
10
5
34
46
Bracket
33
Φ 20
Φ 12
14
17
66
100
SPINDLE
25
3
Φ 32
Φ 20
Φ 25
BUSH
58
45
14
Φ 32
Φ 25
Φ 54
Φ 94
Φ 90
Φ 100
R 6
R 3
6 HOLES Φ 8
EQUI-SPACED ON
75 PCD
Roller

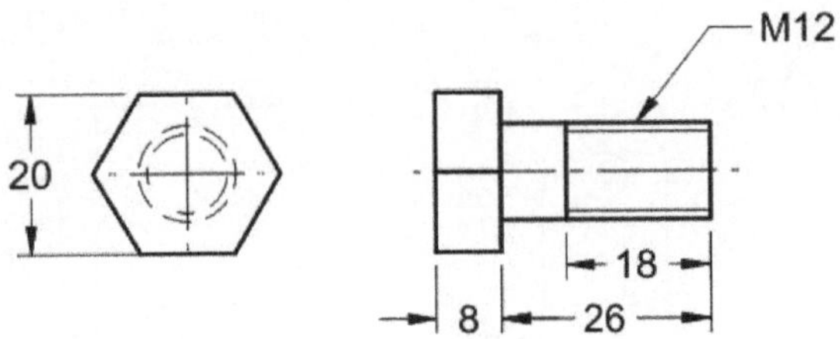

Bolt

Chapter 11: Drawings

Drawings are used to document your 3D models in the traditional 2D format, including dimensions and other instructions useful for manufacturing purposes. In Solid Edge, you first create 3D models and assemblies and then use them to generate drawings. There is a direct association between the 3D model and the drawing. When changes are made to the model, every view in the drawing will be updated. This relationship between the 3D model and the drawing makes the drawing process fast and accurate. Because of the mainstream adoption of 2D drawings in the mechanical industry, drawings are one of the three main file types you can create in Solid Edge.

The topics covered in this chapter are:

- *Create model views*
- *Projected views*
- *Auxiliary views*
- *Section views*
- *Detail views*
- *Broken-Out views*
- *Break Lines*
- *Display Options*
- *View Alignment*
- *Parts List and Balloons*
- *Retrieve Dimensions*
- *Arrange Dimensions*
- *Maintain Alignment*
- *Remove Alignment*
- *Line Up Text*
- *Ordinate Dimensions*
- *Chamfer Dimension*
- *Center Marks*
- *Centerlines*
- *Automatic Centerlines*
- *Bolt Hole Circles*
- *Callouts and Leaders*
- *Notes*

Starting a Drawing

To start a new drawing, click the **File Menu** icon on the initial screen, select **New > ISO Metric Draft** (or) click the **New** icon on the **Quick Access Toolbar**, and then double-click on the **iso metric draft.dft** template on the **New** dialog. If you want to start the drawing in any other standard, select the standard from the **Standard Templates** section and select the required template.

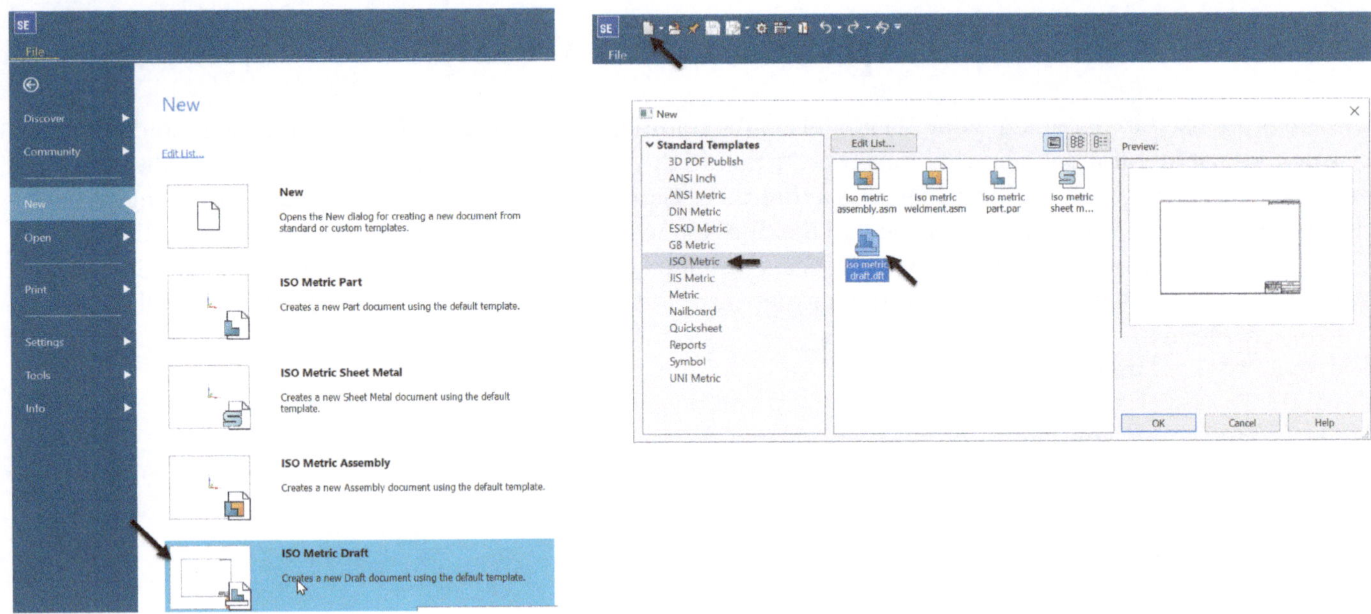

If you already have a part or assembly opened, you can click **File Menu > New > Drawing of Active Model**; the **Create Drawing** dialog appears. On this dialog, click the **Browse** button to access different sheet templates. Select any one of the sheet templates and click **OK**. On the **Create Drawing** dialog, select the **Run Drawing View Creation Wizard** option to start creating drawing views. If you select the **Create standard views** option, the drawing views will be created automatically. Click **OK** on the **Create Drawing** dialog to start a new drawing.

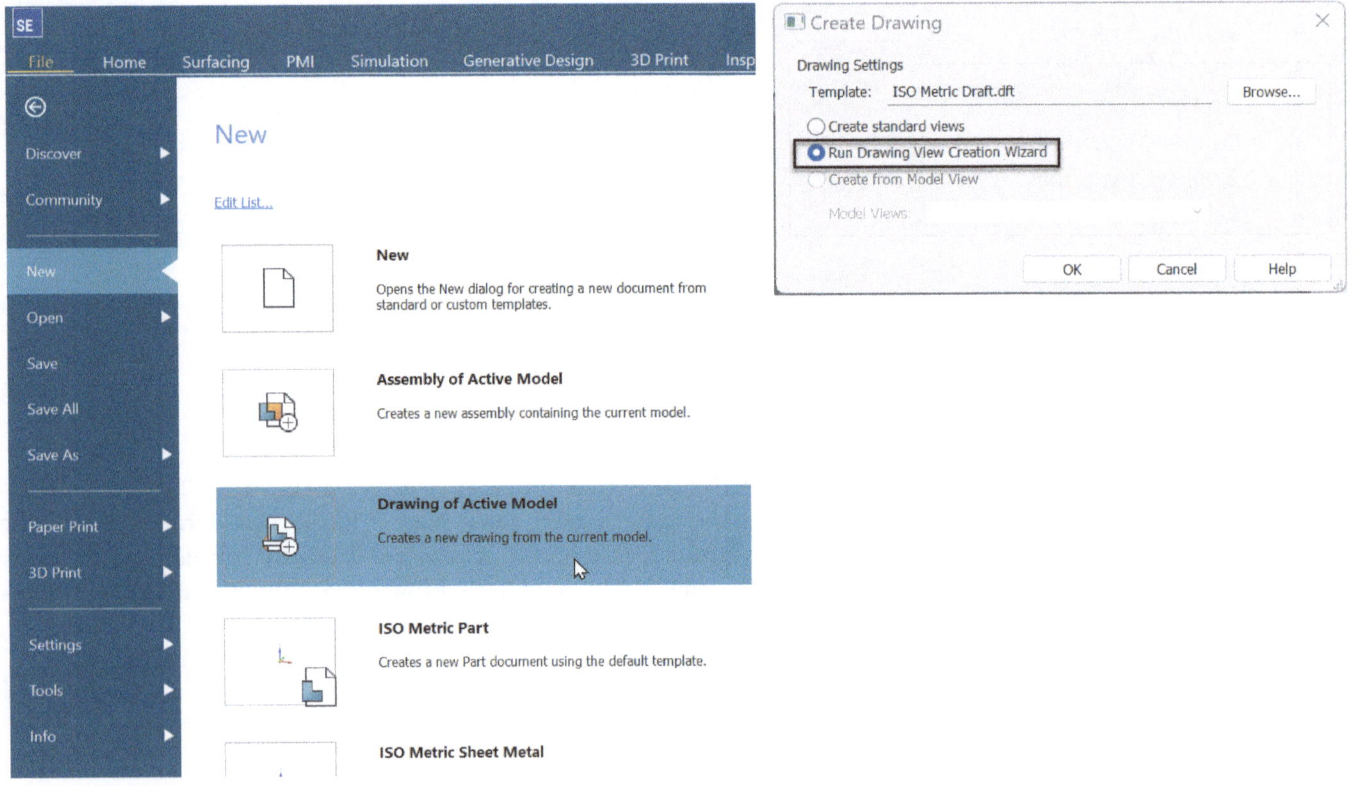

View Creation

There are different standard views available in a 3D part, such as front, right, top, and isometric. In Solid Edge, you can create these views using the **View Wizard** command. This command is activated automatically if you have created a drawing from an already opened part. If it is not activated, click **Home > Drawing Views > View Wizard** on the ribbon. The **Select Model** window appears. Browse to the part or assembly location and double-click on it; a model view will be attached to the pointer. Also, the **View Wizard** command bar pops up on the screen.

Click the **Drawing View Layout** icon on the command bar; the **Drawing View Wizard** dialog pops up on the screen. On this dialog, select the first view from the **Primary View** list. Next, click on the icons that represent the standard views that are to be created. After selecting the standard views, click **OK** on the **Drawing View Wizard** dialog. Click the **Set View Scale** icon to adjust the sizes of the views to sheet size. Click on the sheet to create views. Click and drag the views to position them.

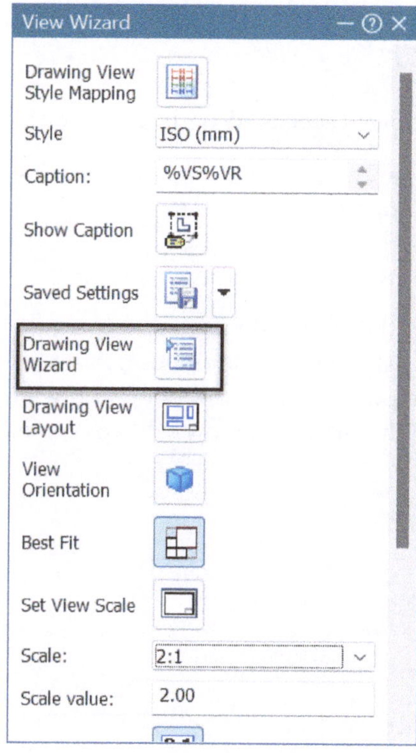

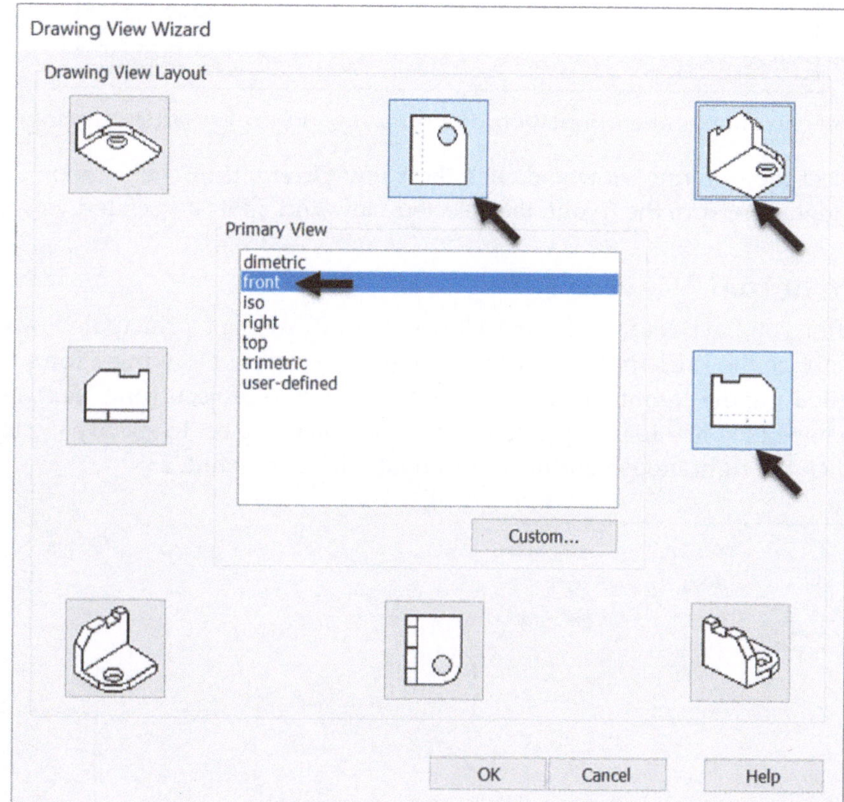

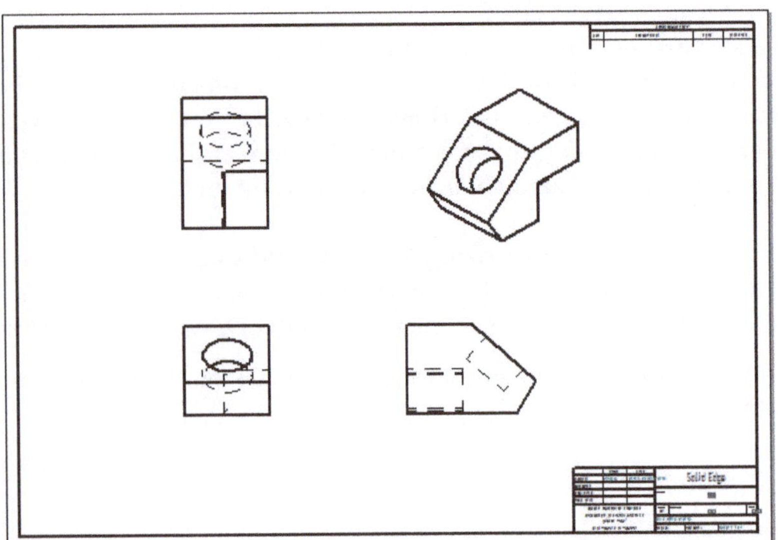

You can change the orientation of a drawing view, even after creating all the views associated with it. To do this, select the drawing view and click the **View Orientation** icon on the command bar. Next, select the required orientation from the flyout; the selected view and all its associated views are changed.

Principal View

After you have created the first view in your drawing, a principal view is one of the simplest views to create. Activate the **Principal View** command (click **Home > Drawing Views > Principal View** on the ribbon). After activating the command, select a view you wish to project from. Next, move the pointer in the direction you wish to have the view to be projected. Next, click on the sheet to specify the location; the projected view will be created. Click the right mouse button to deactivate this command.

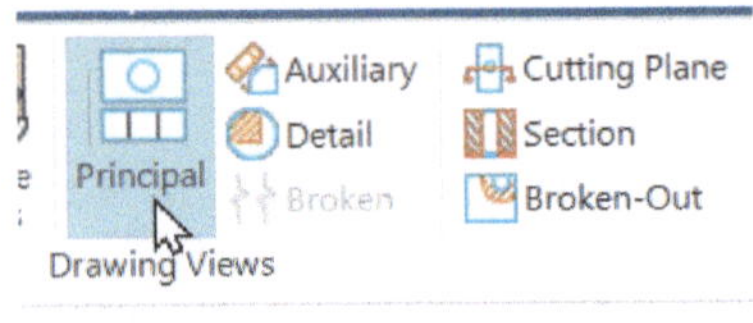

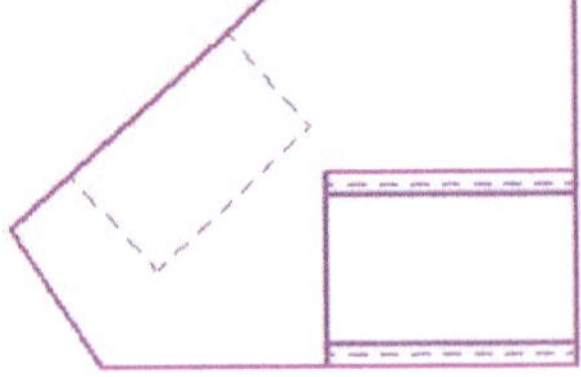

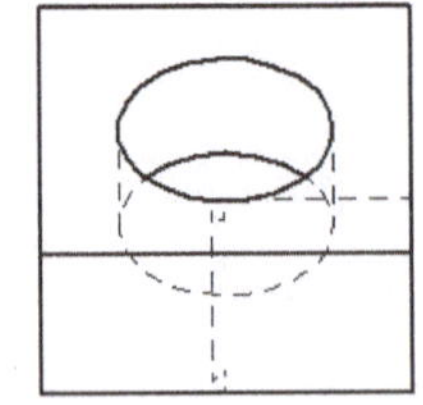

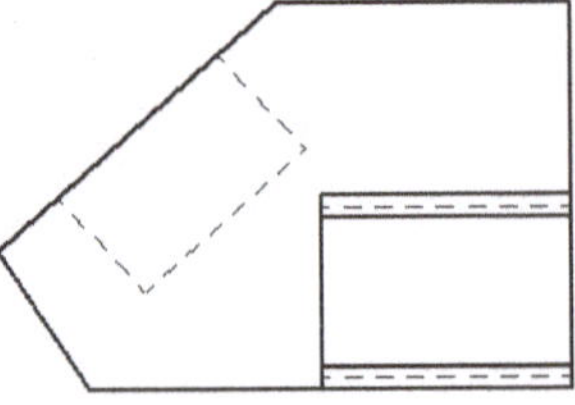

Auxiliary View

Most of the parts are represented using orthographic views (front, top and/or side views). However, many parts have features located on inclined faces. You cannot get the true shape and size for these features by using the orthographic views. To see an accurate size and shape of the inclined features, you need to create an auxiliary view. An auxiliary view is created by projecting the part onto a plane other than horizontal, front or side planes. To create an auxiliary view, activate the **Auxiliary** command (click **Home > Drawing Views > Auxiliary** on the ribbon). Click the angled edge of the model to establish the direction of the auxiliary view. Next, move the pointer to the desired location and click to locate the view.

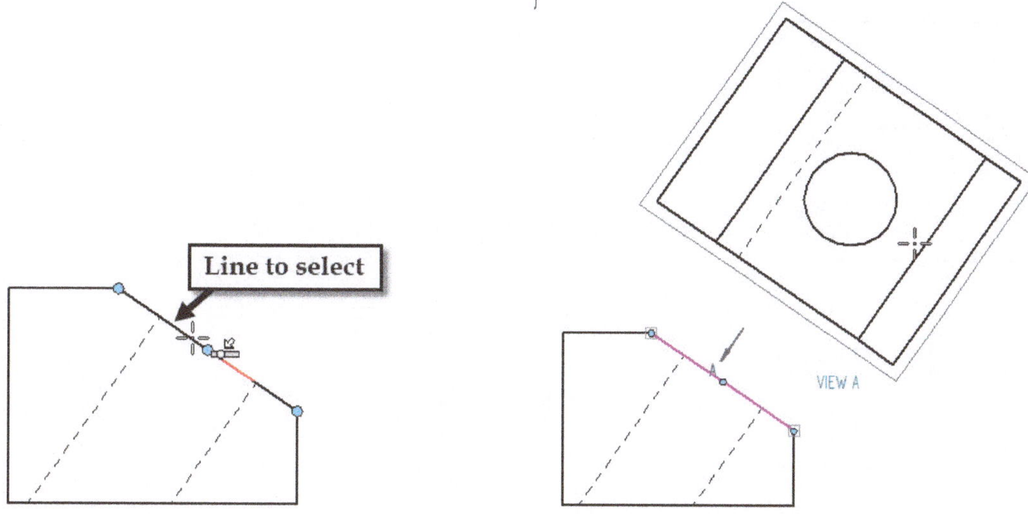

Section View

One of the more common views used in 2D drawings is the section view. Creating a section view in Solid Edge is very simple. Once a view is placed on the drawing sheet, you need to draw a line to section the drawing view.

Activate the **Cutting Plane** command (click **Home > Drawing Views > Cutting Plane** on the ribbon) and click on a drawing view. Now, you have to draw a line to define the cutting plane. You can use the geometry of the drawing view to draw the line. After drawing a line, click **Close Cutting Plane** on the ribbon. Next, click on either side of the cutting plane to indicate the view direction.

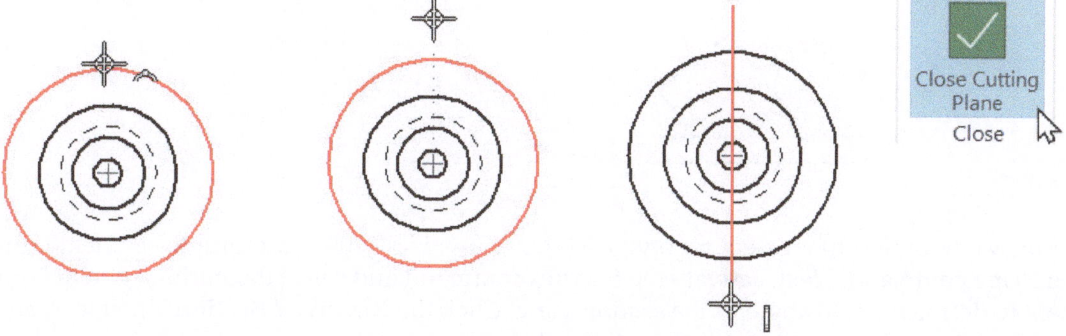

Activate the **Section** command (click **Home > Drawing Views > Section** on the ribbon) and click on a cutting plane. Move the pointer and click to position the section view.

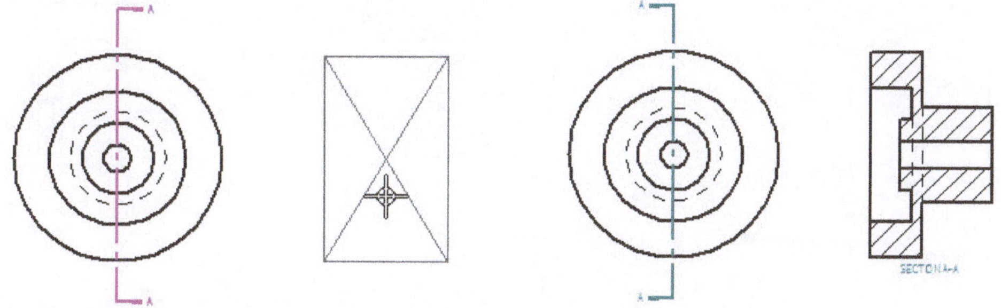

You can also use a multi-segment cutting line to create a section view.

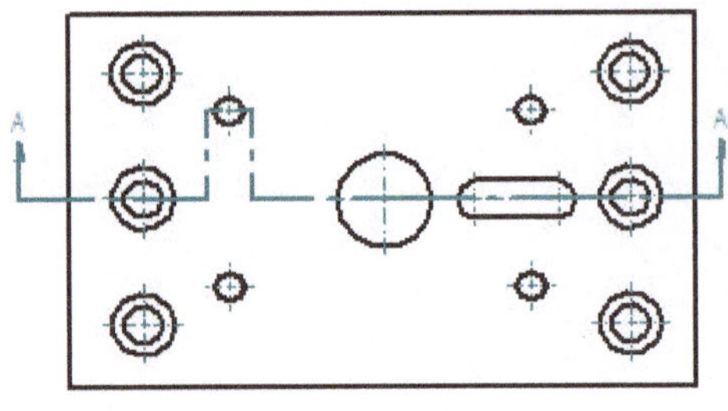

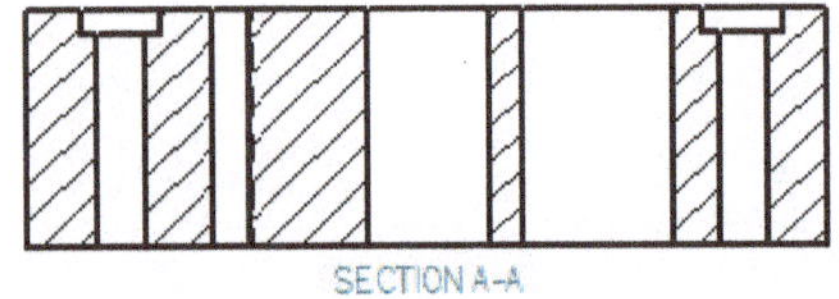

Use the **Section Only** option to display only the geometry on the cutting plane.

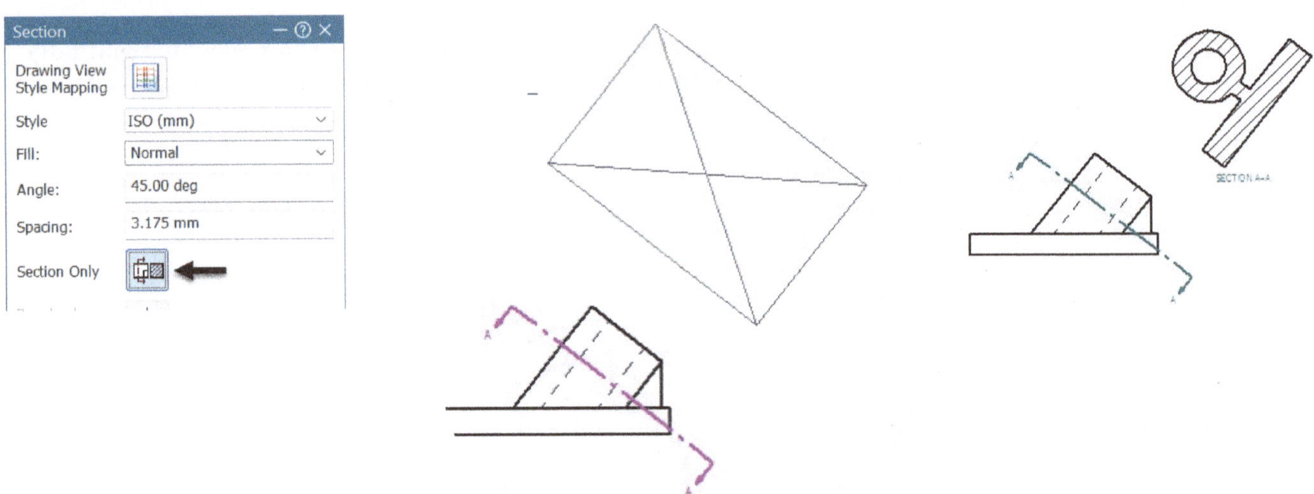

Use the **Revolved Section View** option to create a revolved section view. First, draw a multiple segment cutting plane using the **Cutting Plane** command. Next, activate the **Section** command and select the multi-segment cutting plane. Click on a segment to define the fold angle of the section view. Click the **Revolved Section View** icon on the command bar. Move the pointer and click to position the revolved section view.

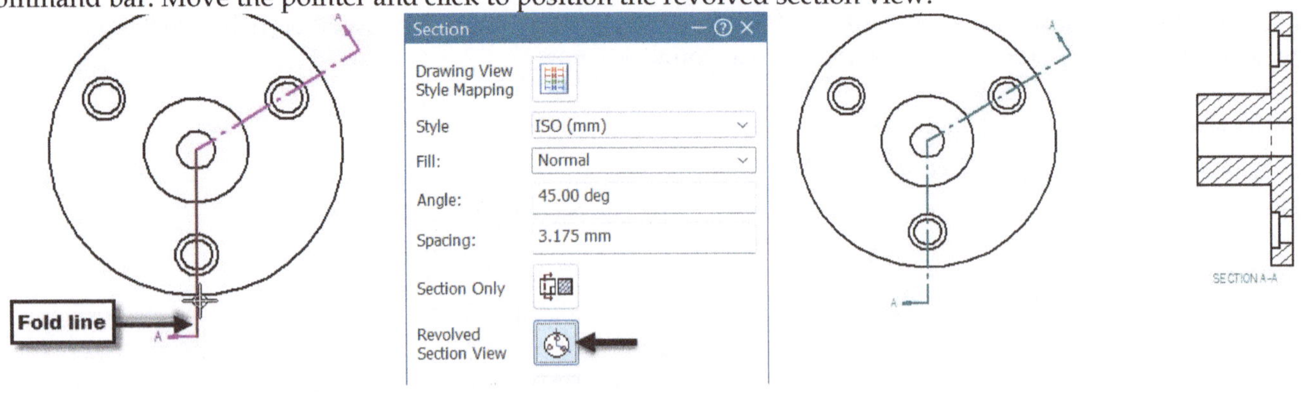

When creating a section view of an assembly, you can choose to exclude one or more components from the section cut. For example, to exclude the pneumatic cylinder's piston, click the **Model Display Settings** icon on the command bar; the **Drawing View Properties** dialog pops up on the screen. On this dialog, select **piston** from the

Parts list and uncheck the **Section** option. Click **OK** and locate the section view. You will notice that the piston is not cut.

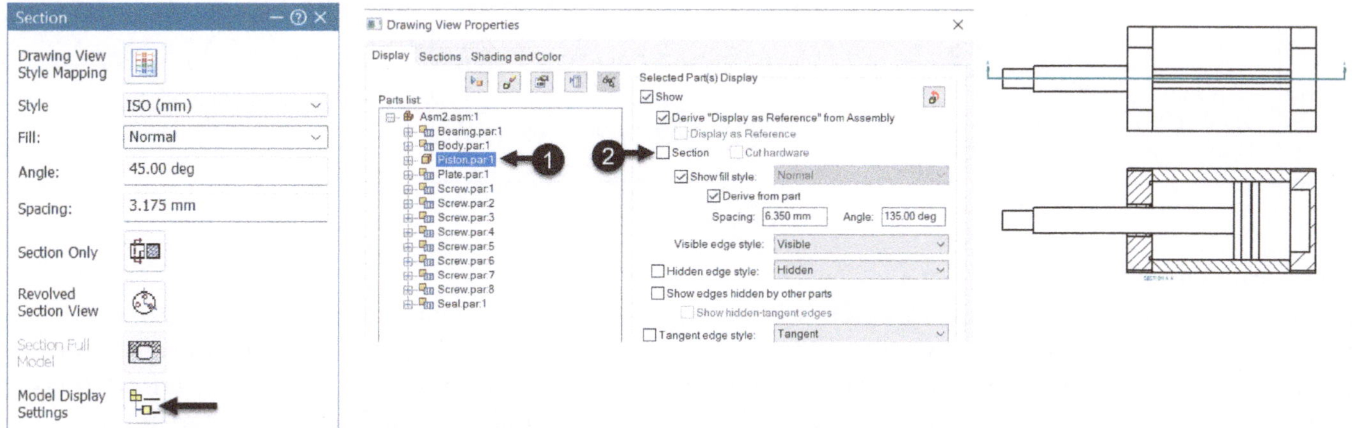

Solid Edge allows you to change the section view type even after creating it.

Detail View

If a drawing view contains small features that are difficult to see, a detailed view can be used to zoom in and clarify. To create a detailed view, activate the **Detail** command (click **Home > Drawing Views > Detail** on the ribbon); this automatically activates the circle tool. Draw a circle to identify the area that you wish to zoom into. Once the circle is drawn, type in a value in the **Multiplier** box available on the command bar; the detail view is scaled by the number you enter in the **Multiplier** box. Next, move the pointer and click to locate it; the detail view will appear with a label.

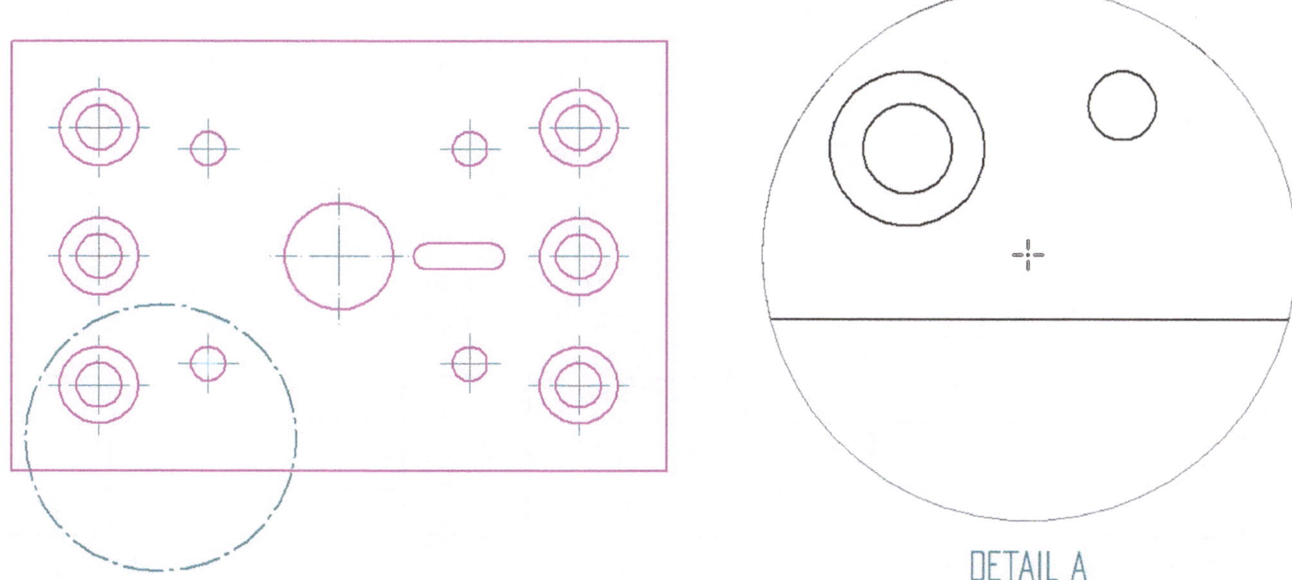

Solid Edge allows you to create a custom profile of the detail view. To do this, click the **Define Profile** icon on the command bar, and then select the drawing view; the **Detail Profile** environment is activated. Draw the profile for the detail view using the commands available in the **Draw** panel of the ribbon. Next, click the **Close Detail Envelope** icon on the ribbon. Move the pointer and click to position the detail view.

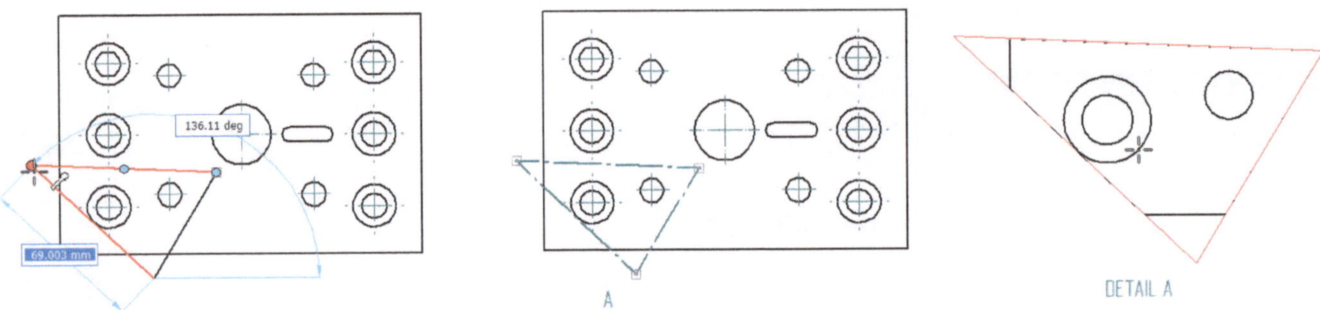

Broken View

Break lines are added to a drawing view, which is too large to fit on the drawing sheet. They break the view so that only important details are shown. To add break lines, select the view and click **Home > Drawing Views > Broken View** on the ribbon; the **Broken** command bar pops up. On this command bar, click the **Vertical Break** or **Horizontal Break** icon and define the **Break Line Type**. Type in the desired value in the **Break gap** box and move your pointer to the area of the view where you would like to start the break. Click once to locate the beginning of the break. Move the pointer and click again to locate the end of the break. You can select the key point of view to create associative break lines. The resultant break lines update when the model is updated. Click **Finish** on the command bar; the view is automatically broken.

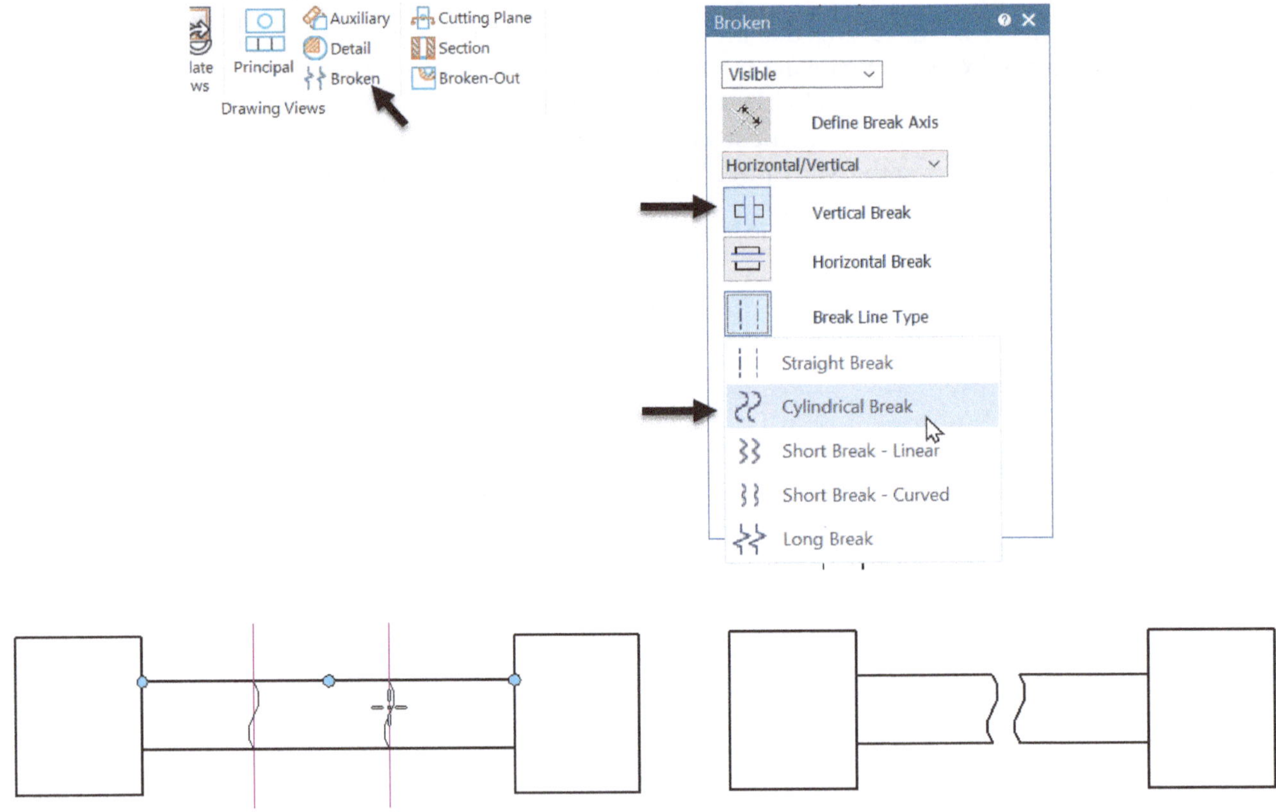

Tip: If you want to add a break line to another view in the drawing, then select the view, right click and select ***Inherit Break Lines*** *from the shortcut menu. Next, select the view with break lines.*

Broken Out

The **Broken-Out** command alters an existing view to show the hidden portion of a part or assembly. This command is very useful to show the parts which are hidden inside an assembly view. You need to have a closed profile to break-out a view. For example, if you want to show the piston inside a pneumatic cylinder, activate the **Broken-Out** command (click **Home > Drawing Views > Broken-Out** on the ribbon) select a drawing view to draw the profile. Draw a closed profile on the selected drawing view and click **Close Broken Out Section** on the ribbon.

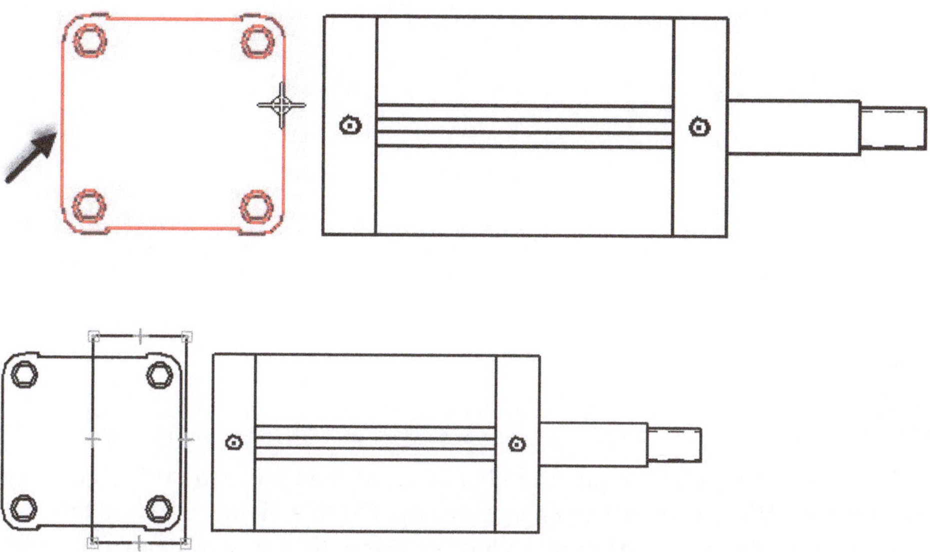

Now, move the pointer and click to specify the depth of the cutout. Select the drawing view to applying the cutout.

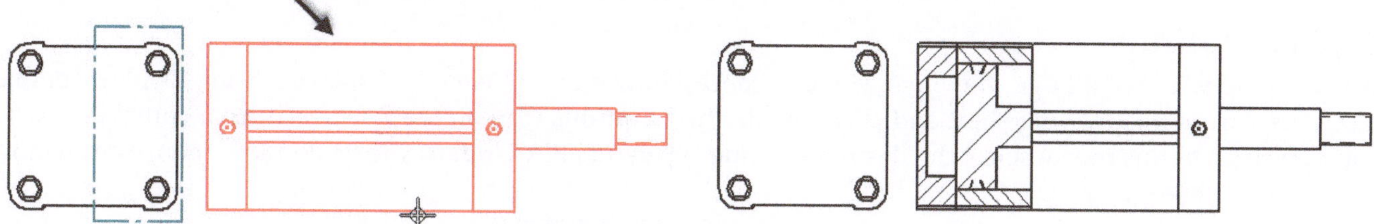

Exploded View

You can display an assembly in an exploded state as long as the assembly already has an exploded view defined. If you want to add an isometric exploded view, activate the **View Wizard** command and select the assembly from the **Select Model** dialog. On the command bar, click the **Drawing View Wizard Options** icon; the **Drawing View Creation Wizard** dialog pops up. On this dialog, select **explode, Solid Edge** from the **.cfg, PMI model view, or Zone** drop-down menu and click **OK**. Click on the drawing sheet to locate the exploded view.

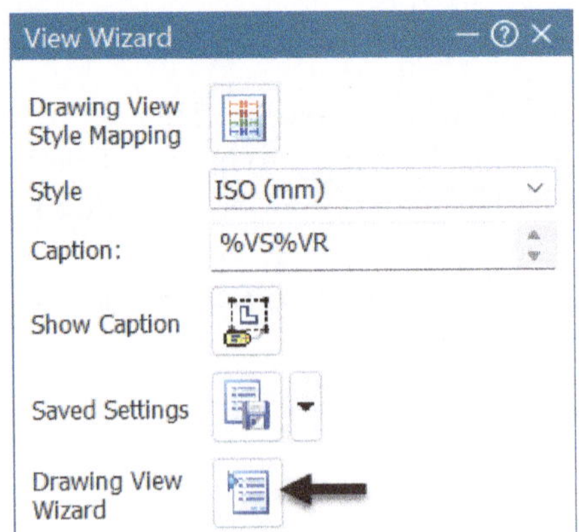

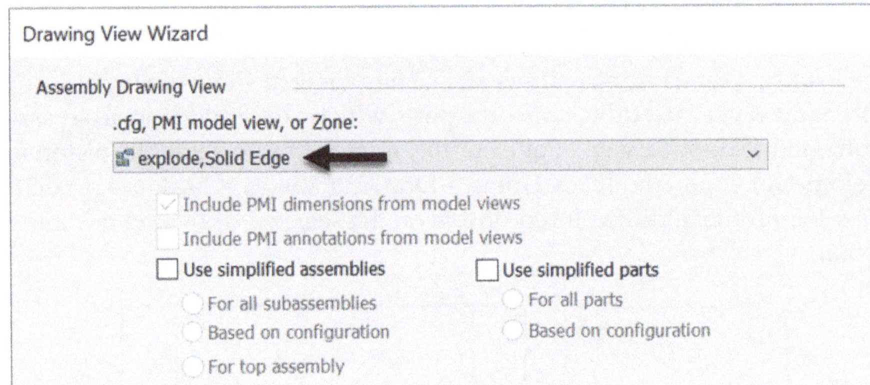

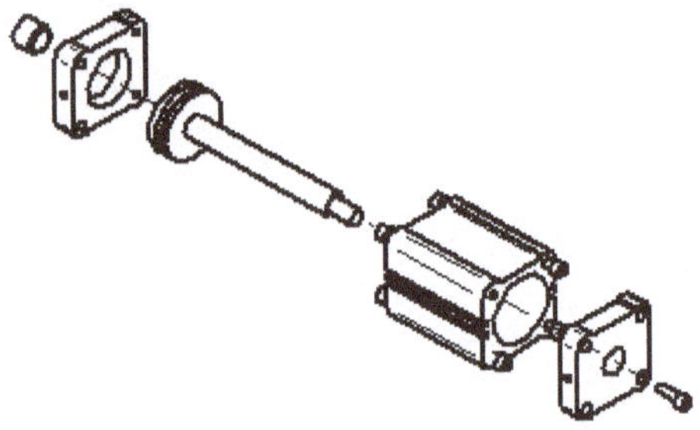

If you want to show an already existing isometric view in an exploded state, all you have to do is right-click the view and select **Properties**; the **High Quality View Properties** dialog pops up. On this dialog, click the **Display** tab and select the explode configuration file from the **.cfg, PMI model view, or Zone** drop-down menu and click **OK**. Next, click **Update Views** on the ribbon; the view will be updated.

Display Options

When working with Solid Edge drawings, you can control how a model view is displayed using display options. Select a view from the drawing sheet and click the **Shading Options** icon on the **Edit Definition** command bar; a menu appears. On this menu, select the desired shading type and click **Update Views** on the ribbon. The shading type of view will be changed.

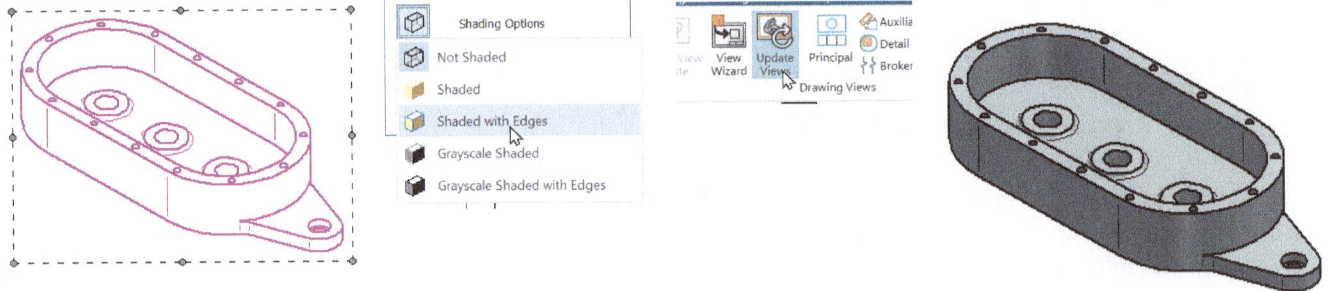

If you want to hide the hidden lines of multiple views, select them and click **Properties** on the command bar; the **High Quality View Properties** dialog pops up. On this dialog, uncheck the **Hidden edge style** option on the **Display** tab and click **OK**. The hidden lines will disappear from the model view.

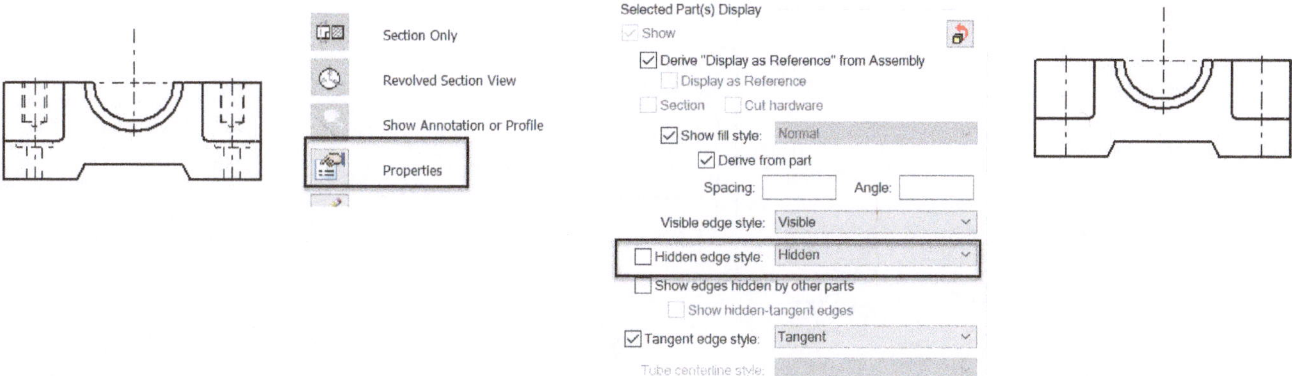

View Alignment

Several types of views are automatically aligned to a parent view. These include section views, auxiliary views, and projective views. If you move down a view, the parent view associated with it will also move.

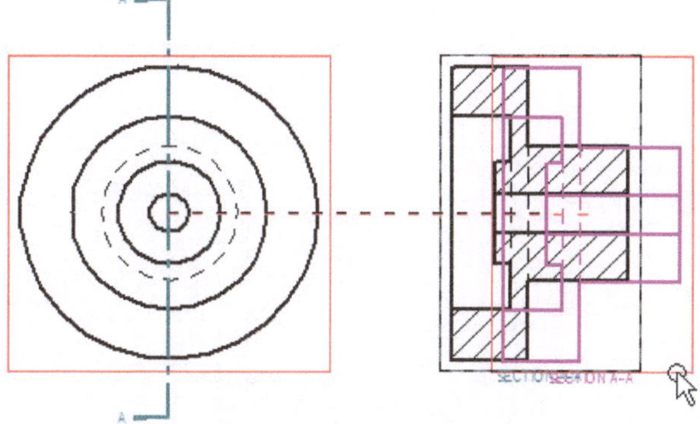

You need to break the alignment between them to move the view separately. Click the right mouse button on the view and select **Delete Alignment**. Now, click on the alignment line that appears between the two views.

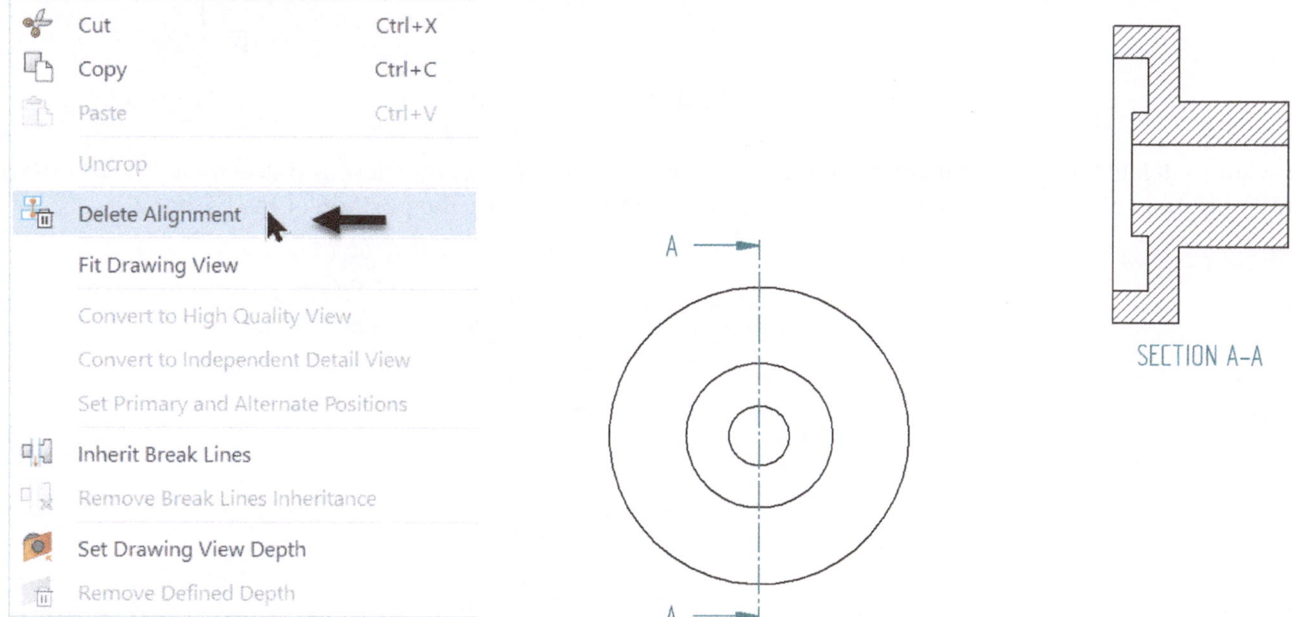

If you want to create alignment between the views, click on the parent view and select **Create Alignment**. On the command bar, select the required alignment option and click on the view to be aligned.

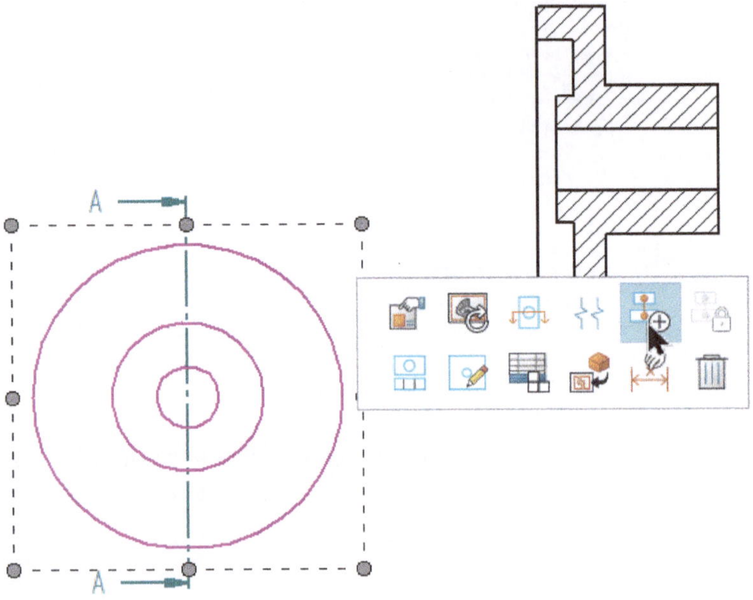

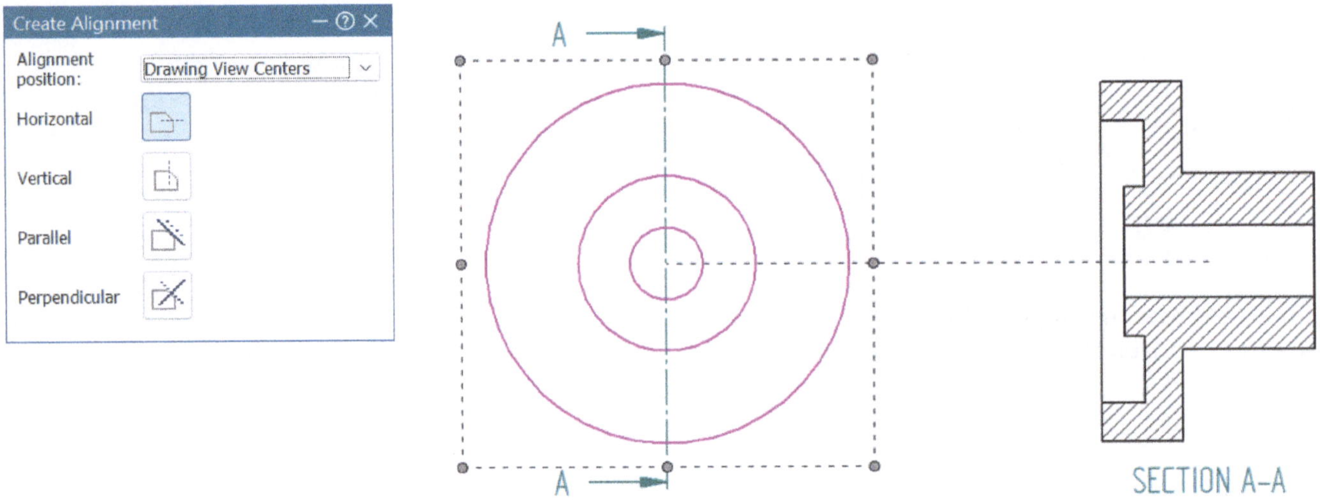

If you want to delete the alignment between the views temporarily, click on the view and deactivate the **Maintain Alignment** option. Now, drag the view to a new location without affecting the position of the parent view.

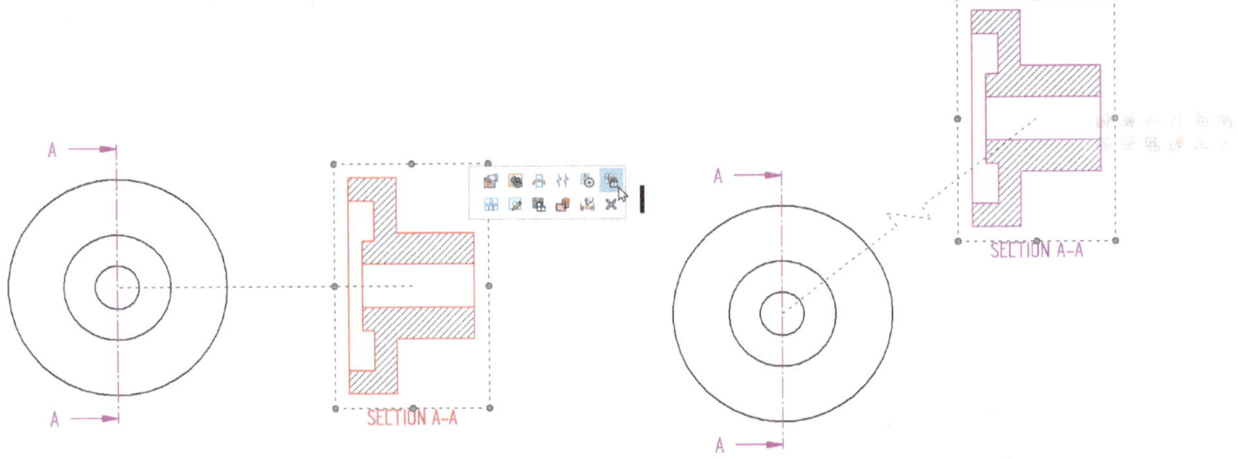

Parts List and Balloons

Creating an assembly drawing is very similar to creating a part drawing. However, there are few things unique in an assembly drawing. One of them is creating a parts list. A parts list identifies the different components in an assembly. Generating a parts list is very easy in Solid Edge. First, you need to have a view of the assembly. Next, click **Home > Tables > Parts List** on the ribbon, and then click on the drawing view. On the command bar, click the **Properties** icon to open the **Parts List Properties** dialog. On this dialog, click the **List Control** tab and select an option from the **Global** section. You can select the **Top-level list**, **Atomic list**, or **Exploded list** option. Next, select the required configuration and click the **Columns** tab.

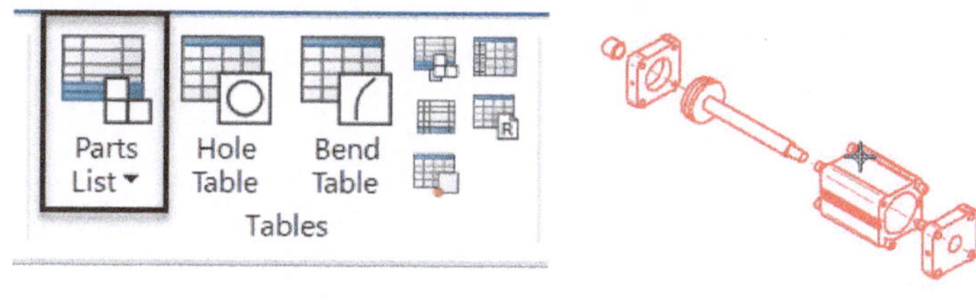

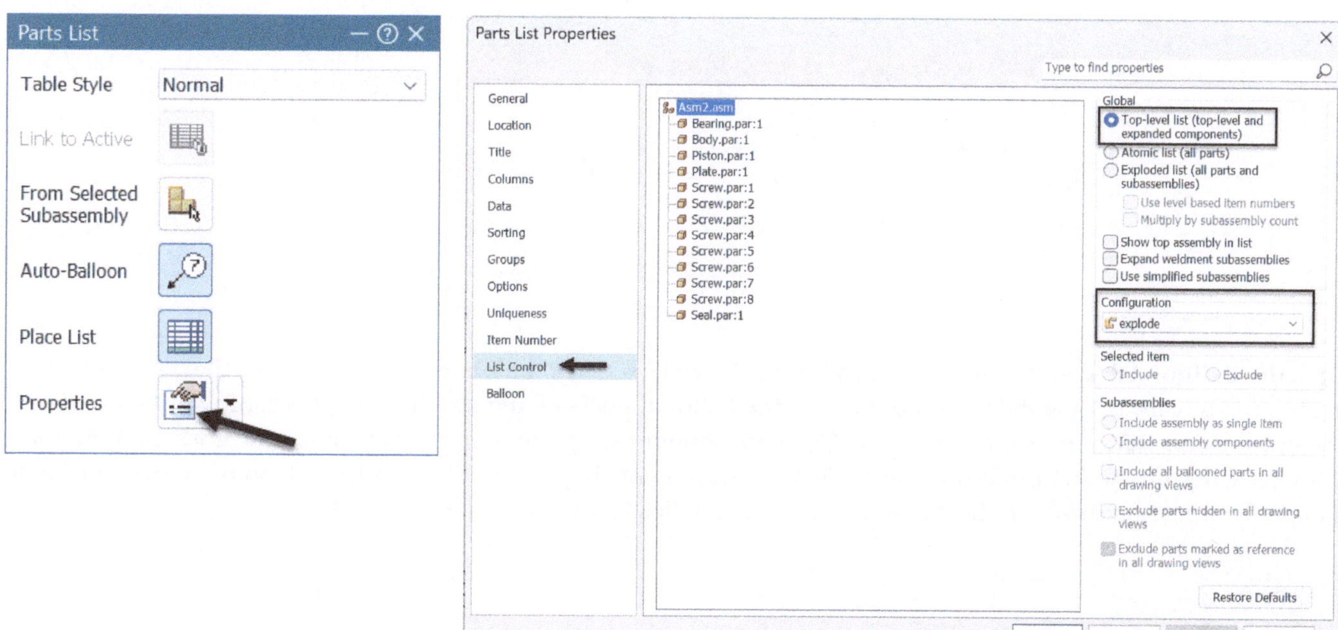

In this tab, select the column names from the **Columns** section and arrange them using the **Move Up** and **Move Down** buttons. To add a new column, select the column name from the **Properties** section and click **Add Column**. To remove a column, select the column name from the **Columns** section and click **Delete Column**. Type-in a value in the **Column width** box.

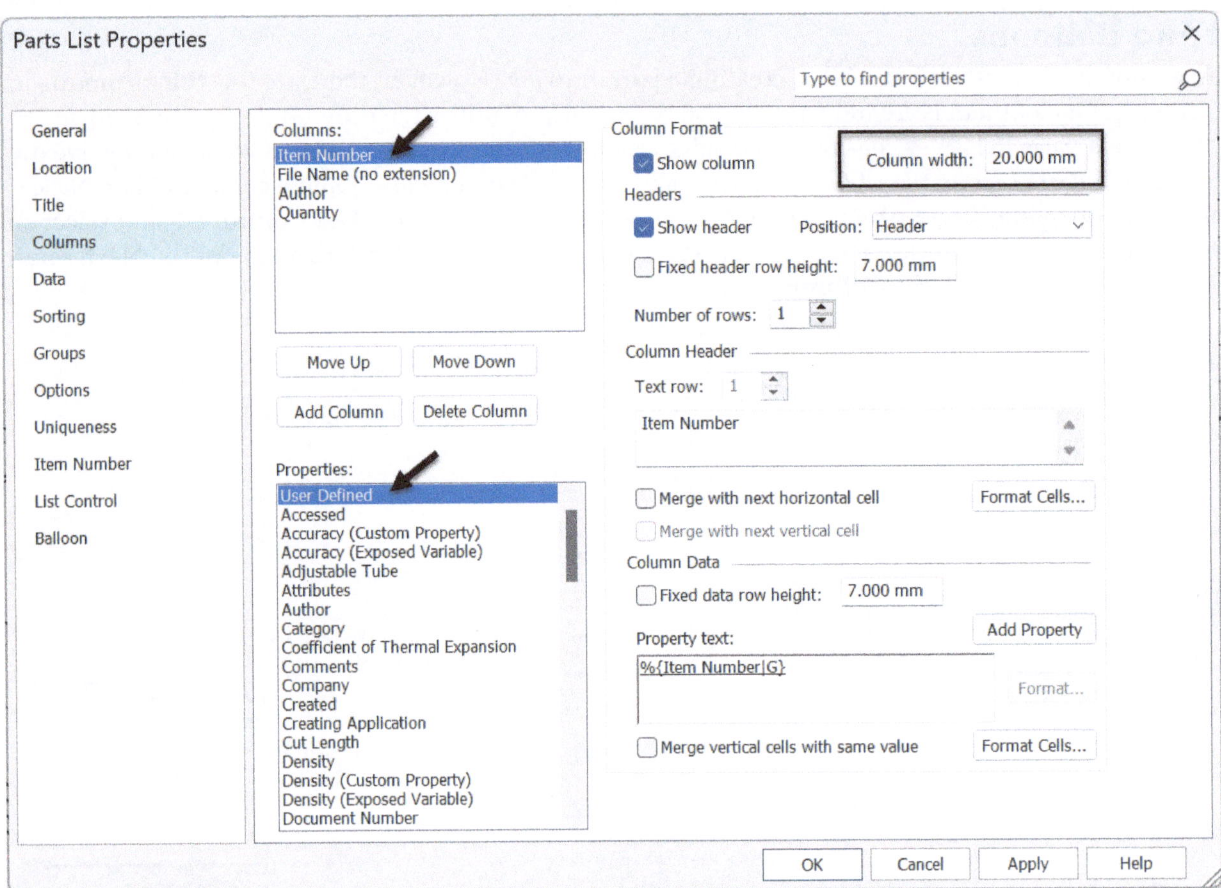

Click the **Balloon** tab and type-in a value in the **Text size** box. Click the **Shape** icon and select the desired balloon shape. If you want to hide the item count inside the balloon, uncheck the **Use Item Count for lower text** option. Under the **Auto-Balloon** section, check the **Create alignment shape** option to create magnetic lines aligning the balloons. Click on the **Pattern** button and select the alignment shape from the menu. Click on the **Order** button to change the direction in which the balloons are created. Click **OK** on the dialog to close it.

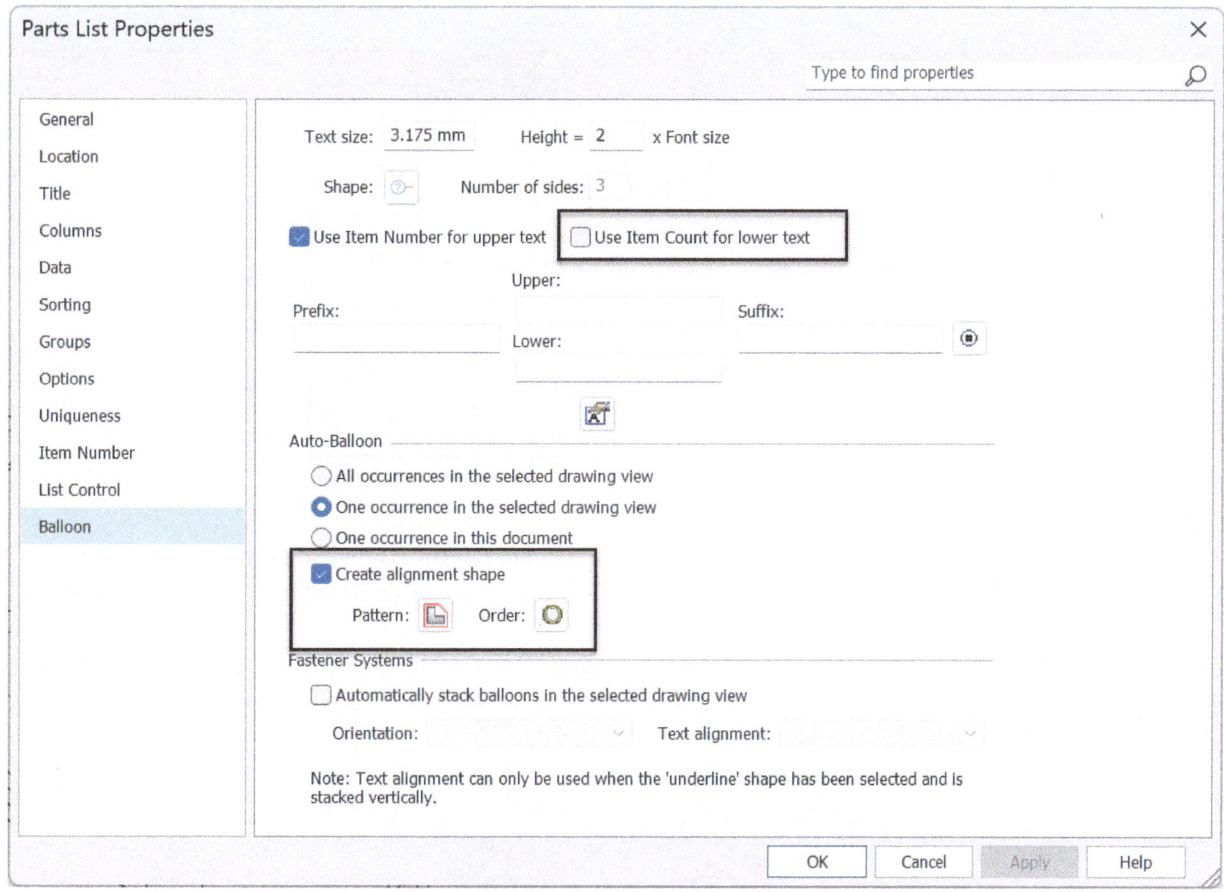

Click on the drawing sheet to place the parts list. The balloons are created automatically.

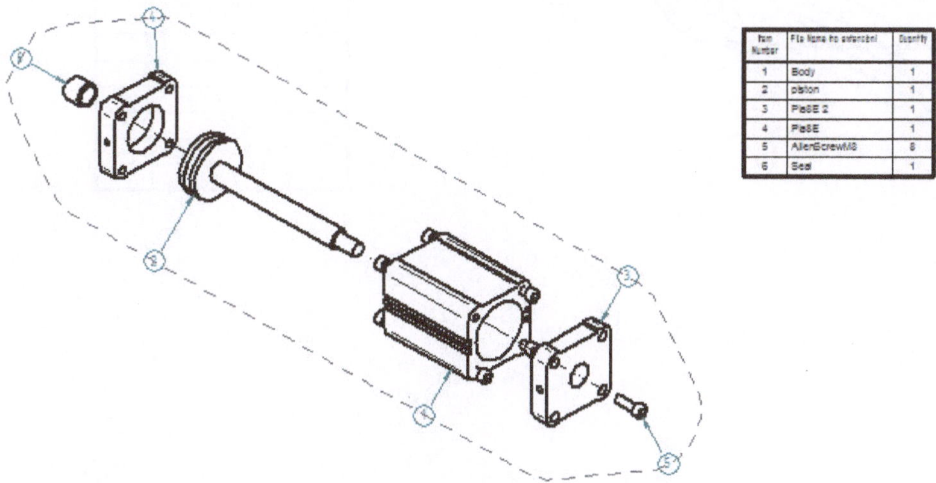

Item Number	File Name (no extension)	Quantity
1	Body	1
2	piston	1
3	Plate 2	1
4	Plate	1
5	AllenScrewM8	8
6	Seal	1

After creating the table, you can change the font type, size, orientation, and alignment using the direct edit. To do this, double click on the table and select the icon that appears at the top left corner. Next, change the options on the direct edit and click anywhere in the drawing sheet.

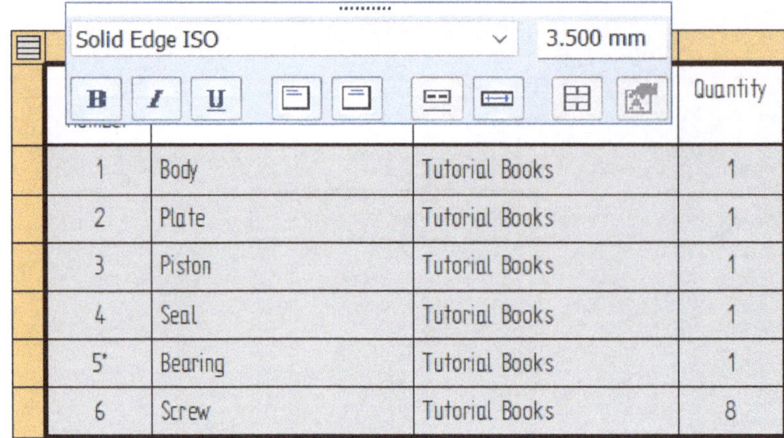

			Quantity
1	Body	Tutorial Books	1
2	Plate	Tutorial Books	1
3	Piston	Tutorial Books	1
4	Seal	Tutorial Books	1
5*	Bearing	Tutorial Books	1
6	Screw	Tutorial Books	8

Creating a Subassembly Parts List and Balloons

Solid Edge allows you to create a parts list of a subassembly, which is part of the main assembly. Activate the **Parts List** command (**Home > Tables > Part List** on the ribbon). Select the assembly view from the drawing sheet and click the **From Selected Subassembly** icon on the command bar. On the **Select Assembly** dialog, select the subassembly from the Assemblies list and click **OK**. Click on the drawing sheet to position the part list table; the balloons are attached to the selected subassembly parts.

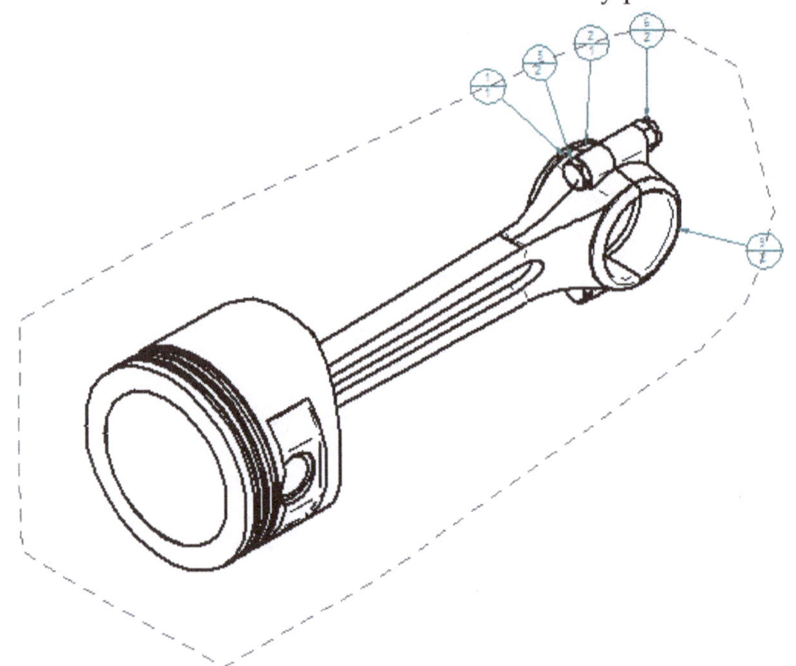

Item Number	File Name (no extension)	Quantity
1	Rod	1
2	Cap	1
3	Bearing_Brass	2
4*	Bearing_Bush	1
5	Bolt	2
6	Nut	2

Dimensions

Solid Edge provides you with different ways to add dimensions to the drawing. One of the methods is to retrieve the dimensions that are already contained in the 3D part file. Click **Home > Dimension > Retrieve Dimensions** on the ribbon. On the command bar, select the dimension types that you want to retrieve. You can click the **Multiple Views** icon on the command bar to retrieve the linear dimensions into multiple views of the drawing view. Click on the drawing view where you want to display the dimensions.

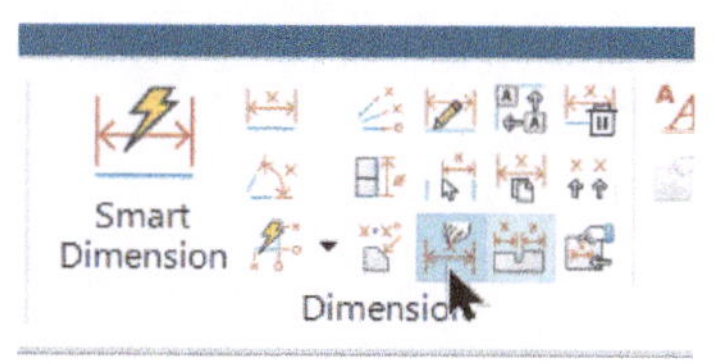

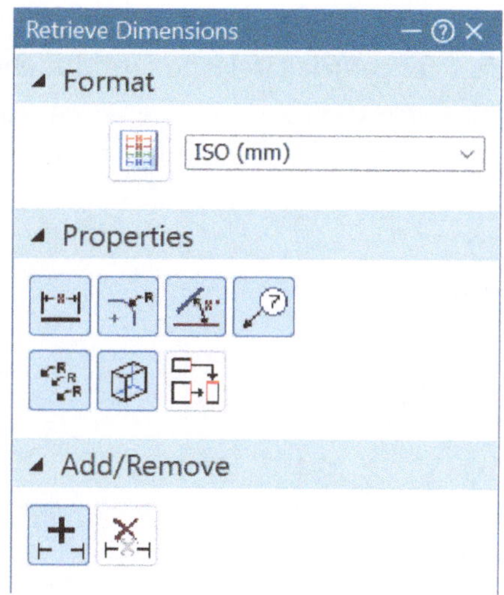

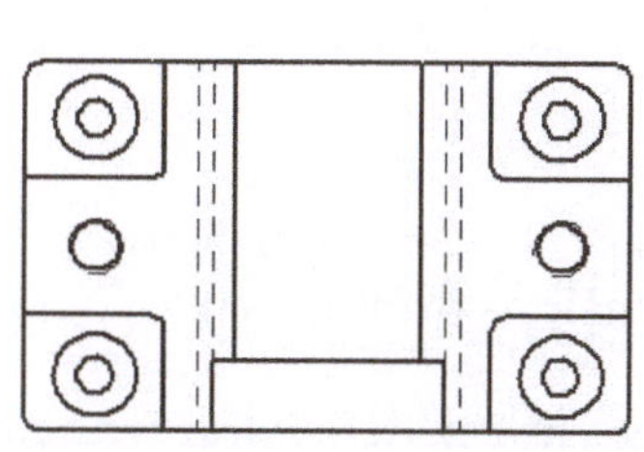

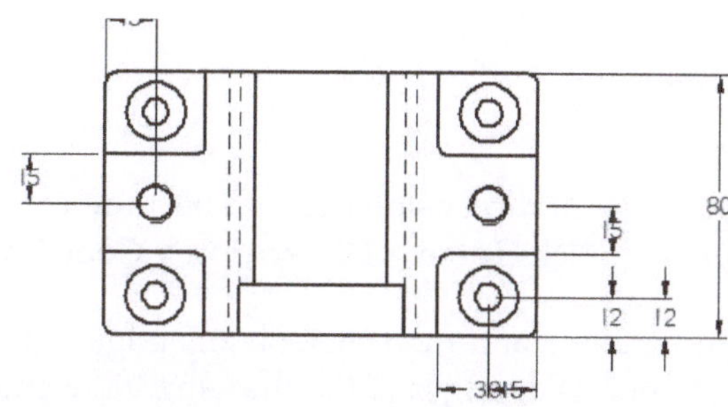

You may notice that there are some unwanted dimensions. Simply select them and press Delete to remove them. Also, the dimensions may not be positioned properly. To arrange them properly, activate the **Arrange Dimensions** command (click **Home > Dimension > Arrange Dimension** on the ribbon). Click on the dimensions, and then click the green check on the command bar. The dimensions will be arranged properly.

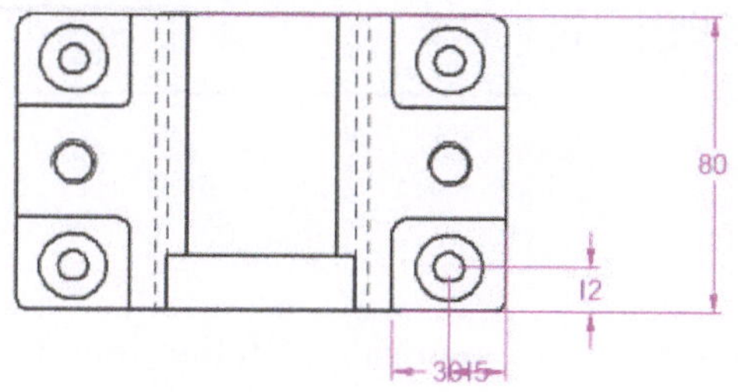

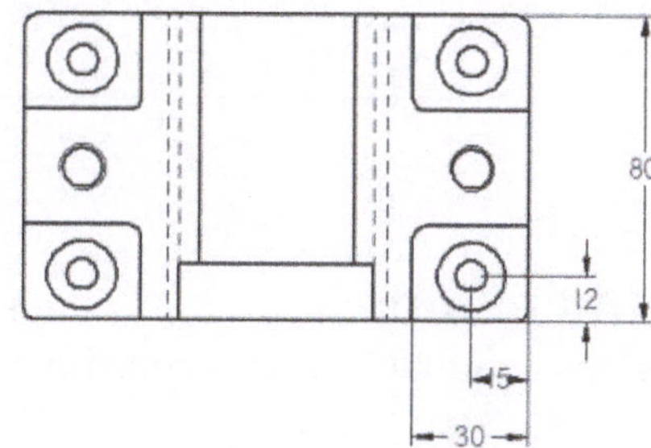

If you want to add some more dimensions necessary to manufacture a part, activate the **Smart Dimension** command and add them to the view. You can also use the **Distance Between** command to add linear dimensions.

Note: *You can use the dimension handles to modify the position of the dimension and size of the dimension and extension lines. The dimension handles are displayed on selecting a dimension.*

Concentric diameter Dimensions

Solid Edge has a new option to create concentric diameter dimensions. Activate the **Smart Dimensions** command (on the ribbon, click **Home > Dimension > Smart Dimension**), and then select the drawing view's circular edge.

On the **Smart Dimension** command bar, click **Show More Options** and select the **Concentric Dimension** icon. Place the diameter dimension, and then select a concentric circle; the second dimension is placed automatically. Likewise, select other concentric circles to add dimensions to them.

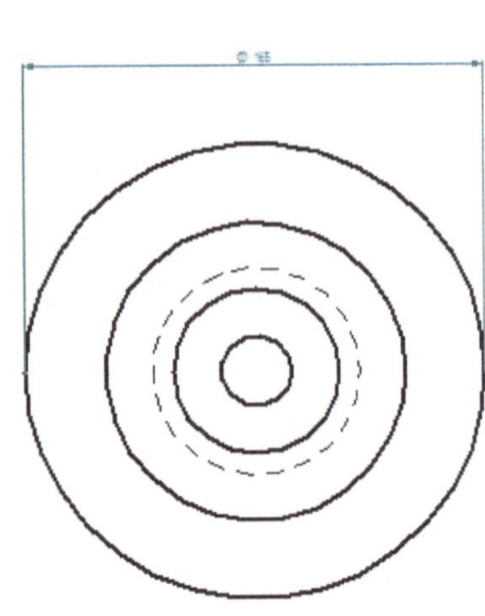

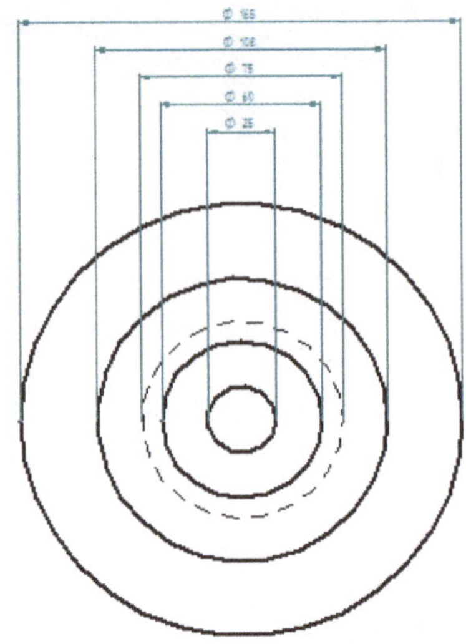

Coordinate Dimensions

Coordinate dimensions are another type of dimension that can be added to a drawing. To create them, activate the **Coordinate Dimension** command (click **Home > Dimension > Coordinate Dimensions** drop-down > **Coordinate Dimension** on the ribbon), and then click on any edge of the drawing view to define the ordinate or zero reference. Now, click on the points or edges of the drawing view and place the coordinate dimensions.

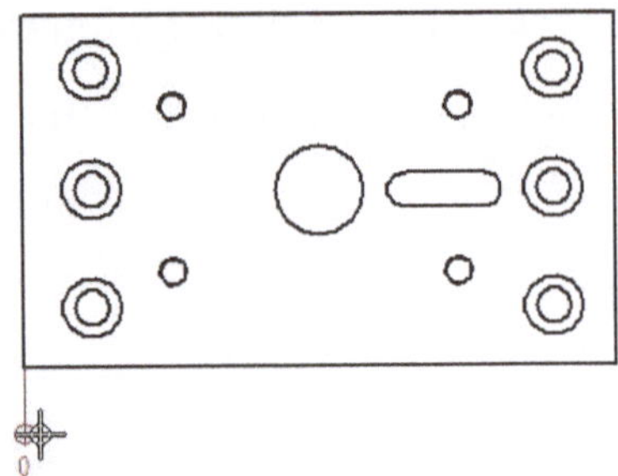

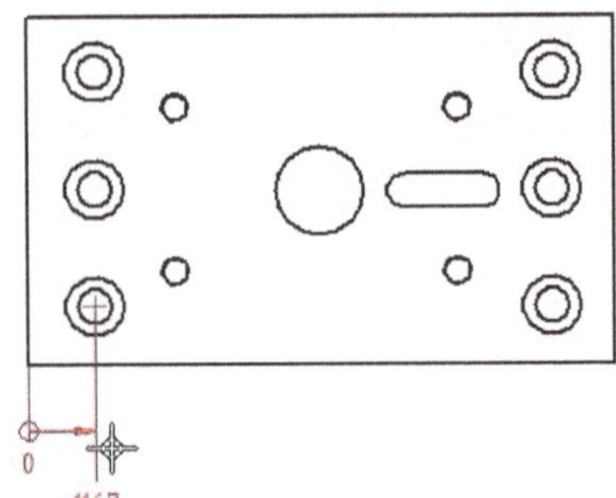

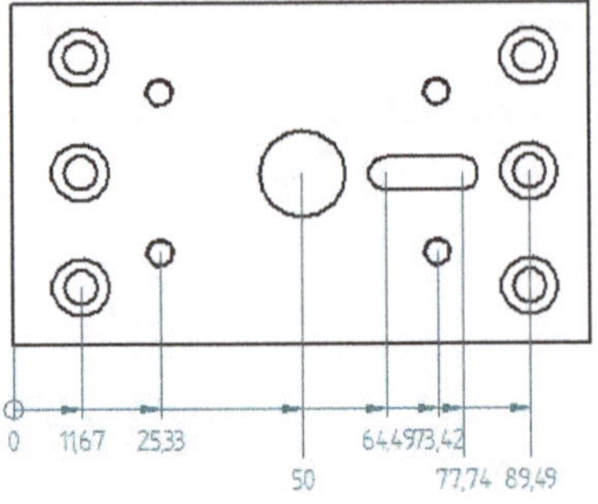

Automatic Coordinate Dimensions

The **Automatic Coordinate Dimensions** command creates coordinate dimensions automatically. On the ribbon, click **Home > Dimension > Coordinate Dimensions** drop-down > **Automatic Coordinate Dimensions** , and click the **Keypoint Options** button on the command bar. On the **Keypoint Options** dialog, select the type of the points selected to create the coordinate dimensions. Click **OK** and select the drawing view. Click **Accept** and select a point on the drawing view to define the origin. Move the pointer vertically or horizontally and click to position the coordinate dimensions.

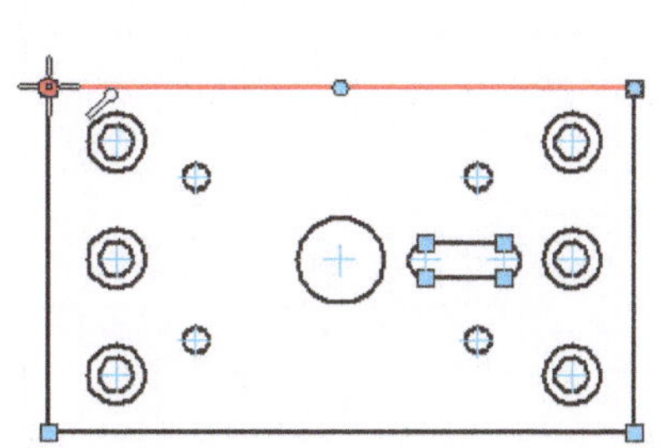

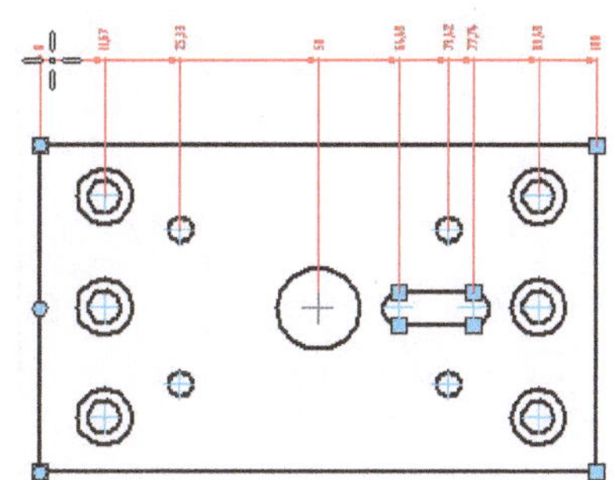

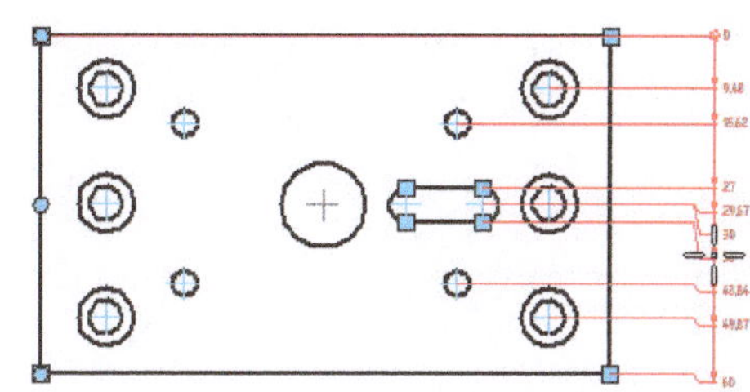

Change Coordinate Origin

The **Change Coordinate Origin** command is used to change the origin of the coordinate dimensions. Activate is command (On the ribbon, click **Home > Dimension > Coordinate Dimensions** drop-down **> Change Coordinate Origin**), and click on a coordinate dimension to change it as the origin.

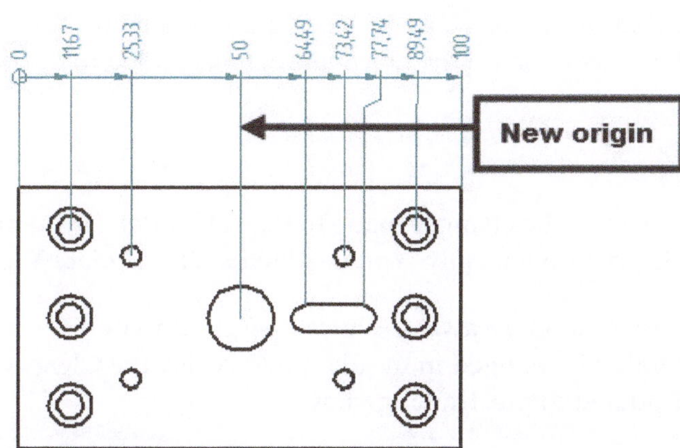

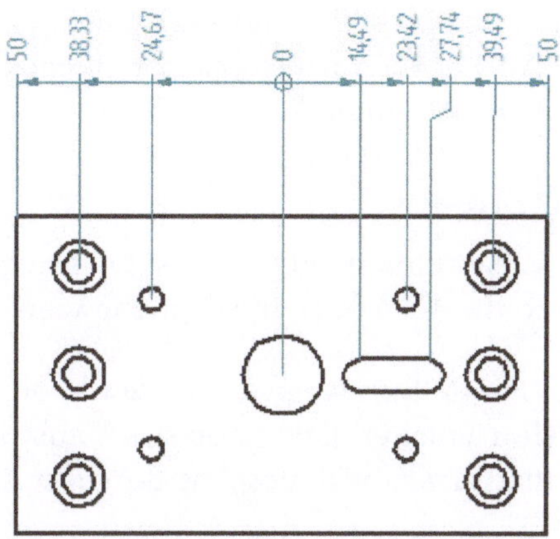

Hole Table

The **Hole Table** command creates a table showing the X, Y, and Z coordinates of the hole, sizes, and other properties. Activate the **Hole Table** command (on the ribbon, click **Home** tab > **Tables** panel > **Hole Table**), and then click on the point of the drawing view to define the origin of the coordinate system. Next, move the pointer vertically and click to place the X1 axis. Again, click on the origin point, move the pointer horizontally, and then click to place the Y1 axis. On the command bar, click the **Properties** icon to open the **Hole Table Properties** dialog. In this dialog, specify the options for table columns, callout, and data. Next, click **OK** on the dialog. On the command bar, click **Selection Method** > **By User Selection**, and then select the hole features one-by-one. The numbering of the holes will be generated based on the order in which you select the holes. You can also drag a selection box across all the hole features if the numbering order does not matter.

If you set the **Selection Method** to **By Drawing View**, you need to define the origin and X1 and Y1 axes. Next, click on the drawing view; all the hole features in the selected drawing view are selected automatically.

Click the **Accept** icon on the command bar after selecting the holes. Click on the drawing sheet to place the hole table.

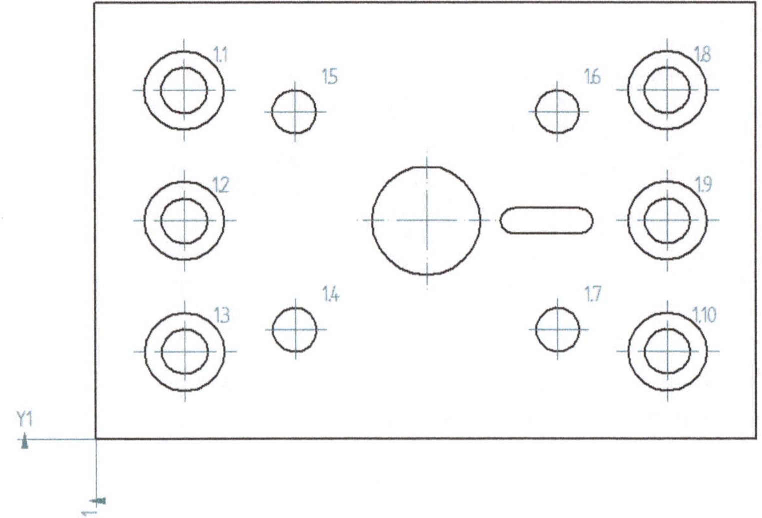

Hole	X	Y	Size
1.1	20 mm	80 mm	10.5 mm
1.2	20 mm	50 mm	10.5 mm
1.3	20 mm	20 mm	10.5 mm
1.4	45 mm	25 mm	10 mm
1.5	45 mm	75 mm	10 mm
1.6	105 mm	75 mm	10 mm
1.7	105 mm	25 mm	10 mm
1.8	130 mm	80 mm	10.5 mm
1.9	130 mm	50 mm	10.5 mm
1.10	130 mm	20 mm	10.5 mm

You can add more holes to the hole table using the **Add or Remove Holes** icon. To do this, select the hole table and click the **Add or Remove Holes** icon on the command bar. Next, select the hole feature to be added to the table, and then click the **Accept** icon.

Update Views

The **Update Views** command updates the drawing view to reflect the changes made to the 3D model. If you make any changes to the 3D model, the drawing view is not updated automatically. You need to use the **Update Views** command to update the changes. On the ribbon, click the **Home** tab > **Drawing Views** panel > **Update Views** ; the **Dimension Tracker** dialog appears if any dimension value is changed in the 3D model. Click the **Clear All** button, and then close the dialog; the dimension value is updated in the drawing view.

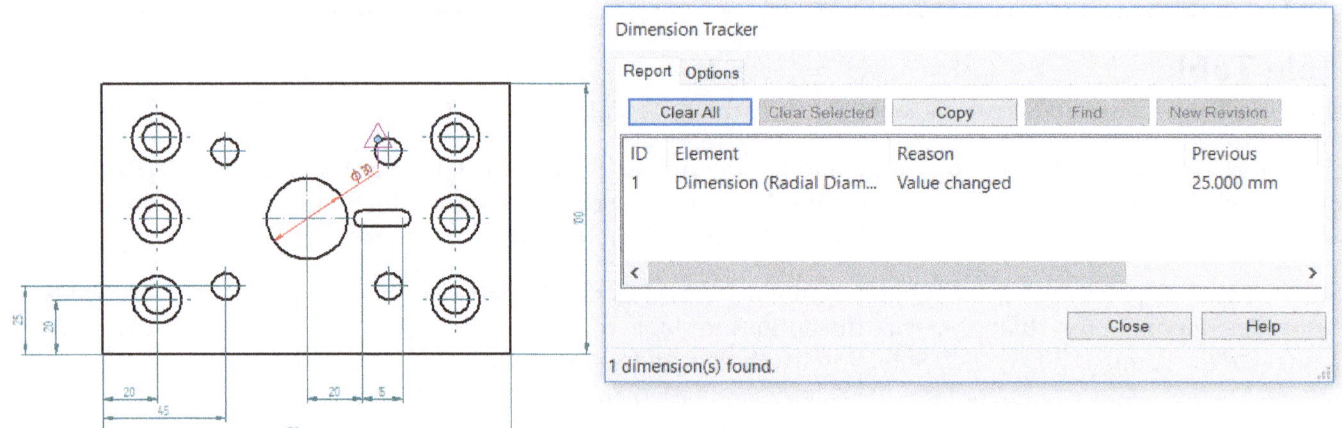

Center Marks and Centerlines

Centerlines and Centermarks are used in engineering drawings to denote hole centers and lines. To add center marks to the drawing, activate the **Center Mark** command (click **Home > Annotation > Center Mark** on the ribbon) and click on the hole circles. On the Command bar, click the **Projection Lines** icon if you want to add projected centermarks to the circle.

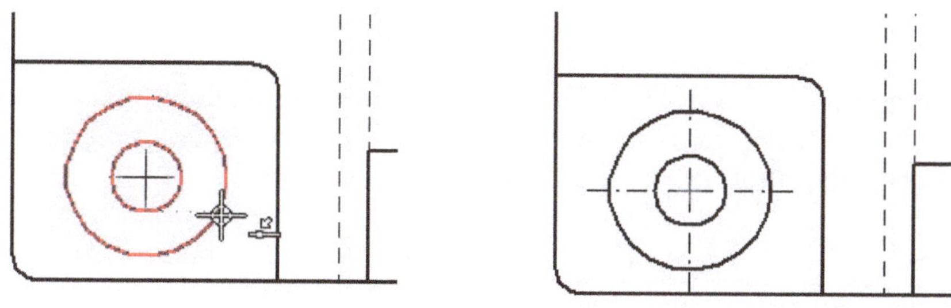

To add centerlines, activate the **Centerline** command (click **Home > Annotation > Centerline** on the ribbon). On the command bar, select **Placement Options > By 2 Lines**, and then click on two parallel edges of the drawing view. A centerline will be created between the two lines.

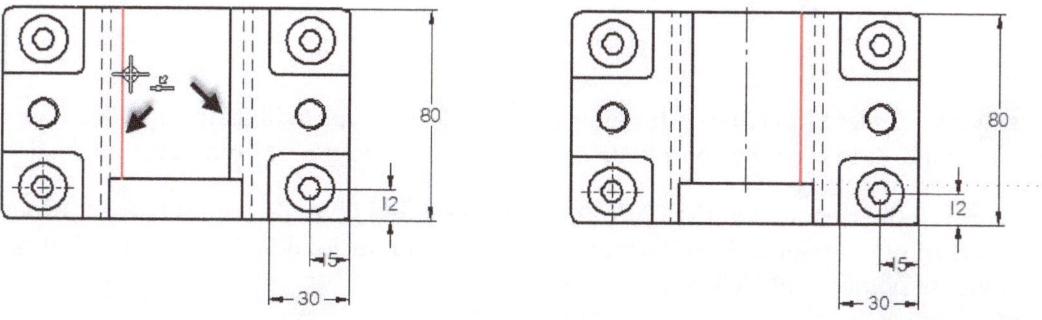

If you want to add centrelines automatically, activate the **Automatic Centerlines** command (click **Home > Annotation > Automatic Centerlines** on the ribbon). The **Automatic Centerlines** command bar pops up. On the command bar, click the **Options** icon to open the **Center Line and Center Mark Options** dialog. On the dialog, select the element to which the centerlines and center marks are to be added. Click **OK** to close the dialog. Click the drawing view to add centerlines and center marks.

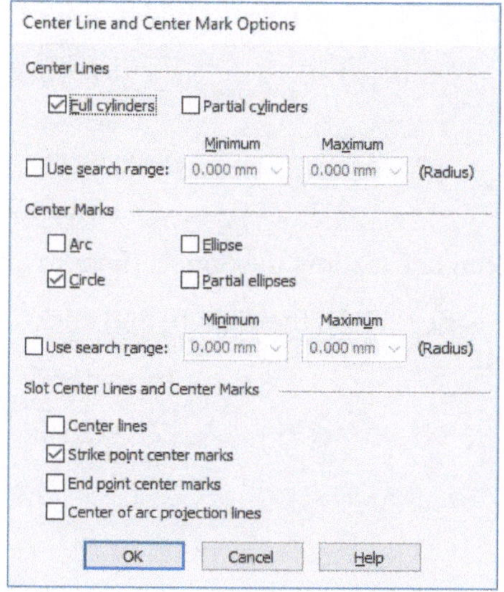

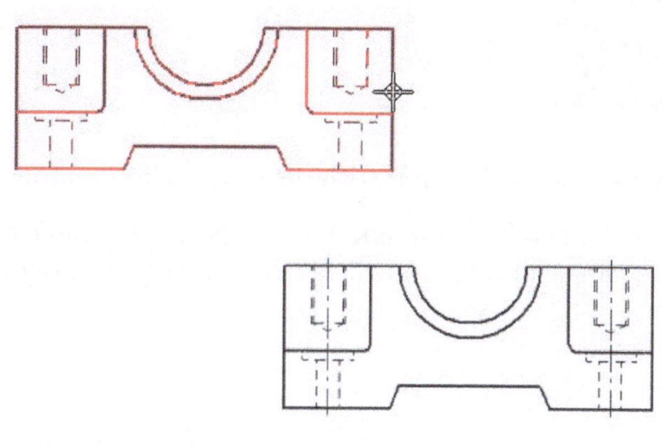

Bolt Hole Circle

The **Bolt Hole Circle** command (click **Home > Annotation > Bolt Hole Circle** on the ribbon) allows you to add center marks to the holes arranged circularly. Activate this command and click for the center of the bolt hole circle. Drag the pointer and click for the radius point of the bolt hole circle. A bolt circle will be created.

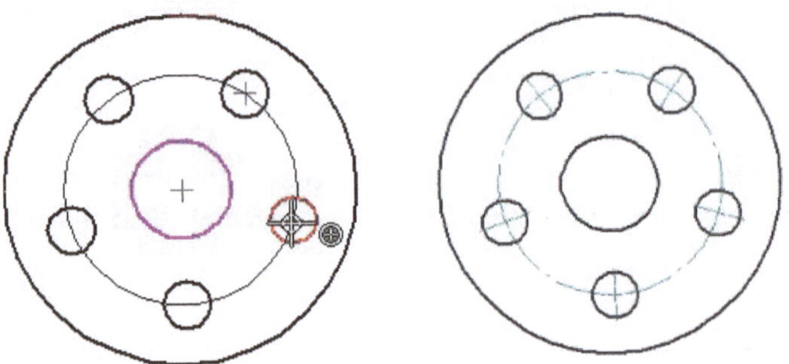

Callouts and Leaders

Callouts and leaders are an essential element in creating drawings. In this section, you will learn to add callouts and leaders to a drawing. For example, add a counterbore hole callout and activate the **Callout** command (click **Home > Annotation > Callout** on the ribbon). On the **Callout Properties** dialog, type-in values in the **Callout text** and **Callout text 2** boxes. You can use the **Special Character** icons available on the dialog. Click the **OK** button and click on the hole. Drag the mouse pointer and click to place the callout.

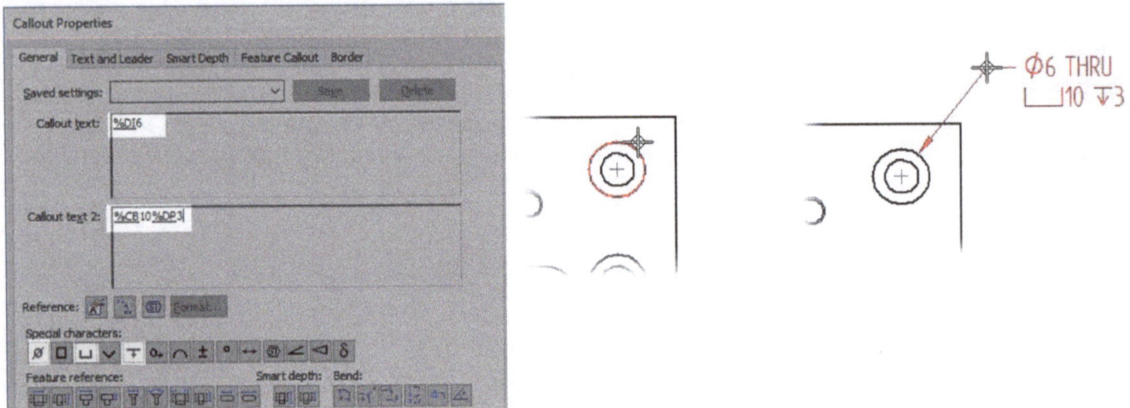

If you have multiple elements in a drawing with the same callout value, you can use leaders to connect them to an existing callout. Activate the **Leader** command (click **Home > Annotation > Leader** on the ribbon) and click on an element. Drag the mouse pointer and click on an already existing callout.

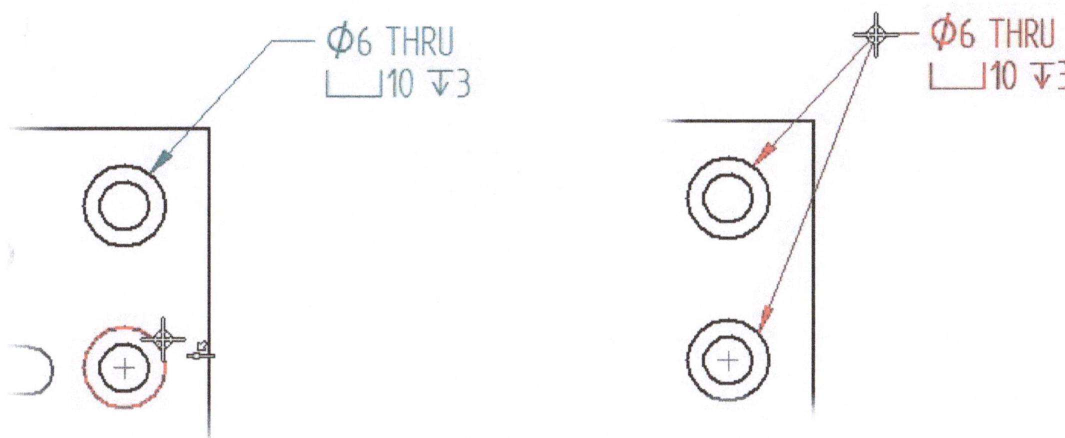

Notes

Notes are an important part of a drawing. You add notes to provide additional details, which cannot be done using dimensions and annotations. To add a note or text, activate the **Text** command (click **Home > Annotation > Text** on the ribbon). On the command bar, select the font and font size. Create a box and type text inside it.

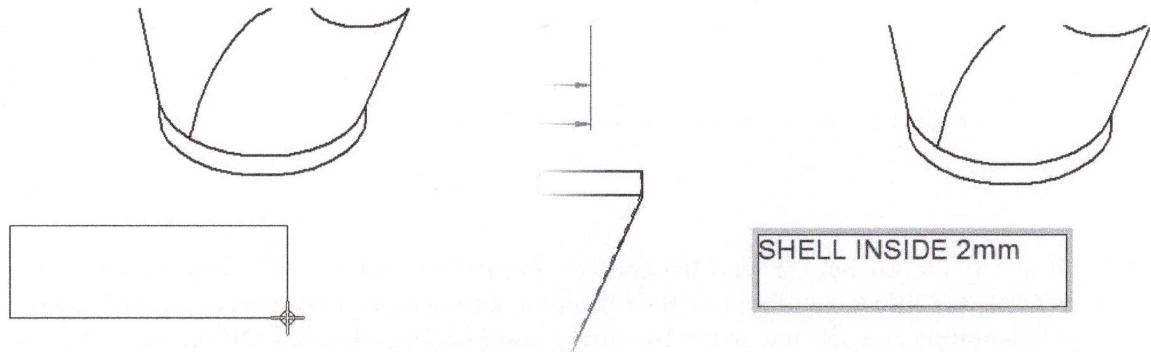

You can use the **Text** command to insert associative text (reference and property texts). To insert an associative text in the drawing, activate the **Text** command and click to define the text position. On the **Text** command bar, click the Insert **Symbols, Characters or Property Text** icon. Select **Insert Property Text** from the flyout. On the **Insert Property Text** dialog, click the **Property Text** icon to open the **Select Property Text** dialog. On this dialog, select a property from the **Properties** list and click **Select.** Click **OK** on the **Select Property Text and Insert Property Text** dialogs; the property text will be inserted on the drawing sheet.

Adding Technical Requirements

Solid Edge has an option to add technical requirements to the drawing. On the ribbon, click **Home > Annotation > Text** drop-down **> Technical Requirements**. On the **Technical Requirements Properties** dialog, click the **General** tab and type-in the technical requirement in the box available at the top. Click **Insert** to add the technical requirement. Likewise, type-in another technical requirement and insert it into the table available at the bottom. Select the bullet style and format from the **Style** and **Format** drop-downs.

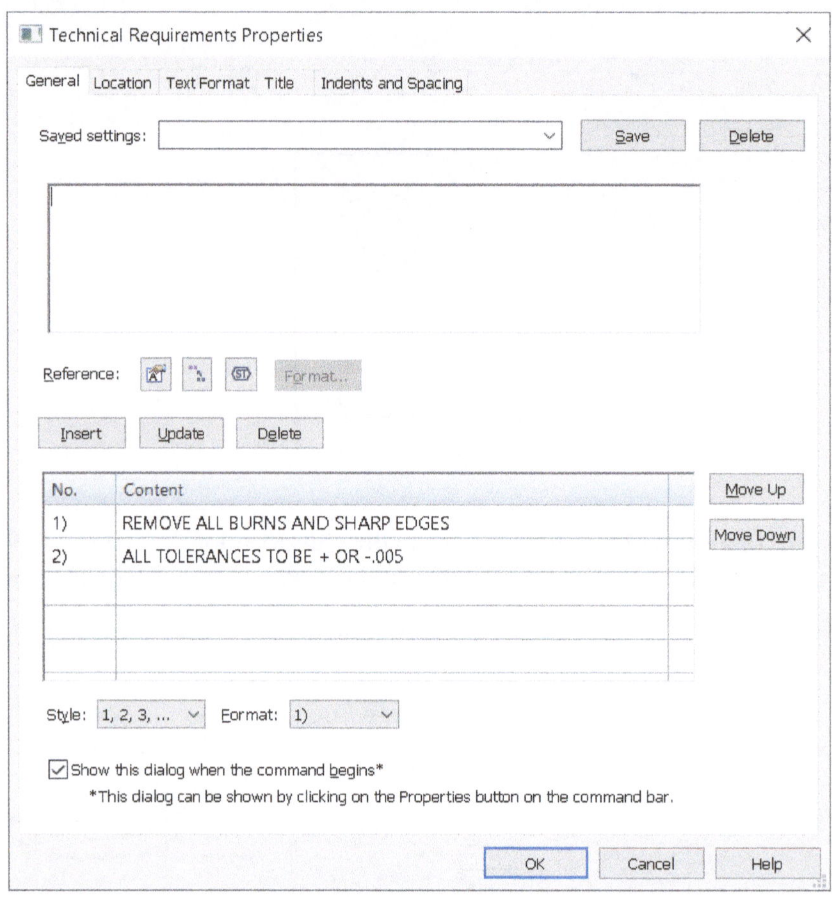

Click the **Location** tab and specify the **Anchor corner**. Click the **Text Format** tab and set the Font type, size, color, aspect ratio, and fit width. Click the **Title tab** and type-in the title of the technical requirements in the **Title text** box. Likewise, specify the Indentation and spacing on the **Indenting and Spacing** tab. Click **OK** on the Technical **Requirement Properties** dialog, and then position the drawing sheet's technical requirements.

GENERAL NOTES: UNLESS OTHERWISE SPECIFIED
1) REMOVE ALL BURRS AND SHARP EDGES
2) ALL TOLERANCES TO BE + OR - .005

Compare Drawings

Solid Edge allows you to compare two different versions of a drawing file. It is very useful when a drawing file is shared between different members of a team. To compare the two drawings, click **File Menu > Tools > Compare Drawings** . Under the Configure New Comparison section, click the Browse button next to the File 1 drop-down on the **Compare Drawings** dialog. On the **Open File** dialog, select the first version of a drawing file, and then click **Open**. Likewise, click the **Browse** button next to the **File 1** drop-down and select the second version of the drawing. Select the sheets to be compared from the **Sheet** drop-downs, and then click **Compare**. The differences between the two versions of the drawing are displayed in the **Differences** section. You can use the **Zoom Area**, **Fit**, **Pan**, and **Zoom** buttons under the **Display** section to view various drawing portions. You can also save the comparison file for future use with the help of the **Save** button. You can load an existing comparison file using the **Browse** button in the **Open Existing Comparison** section.

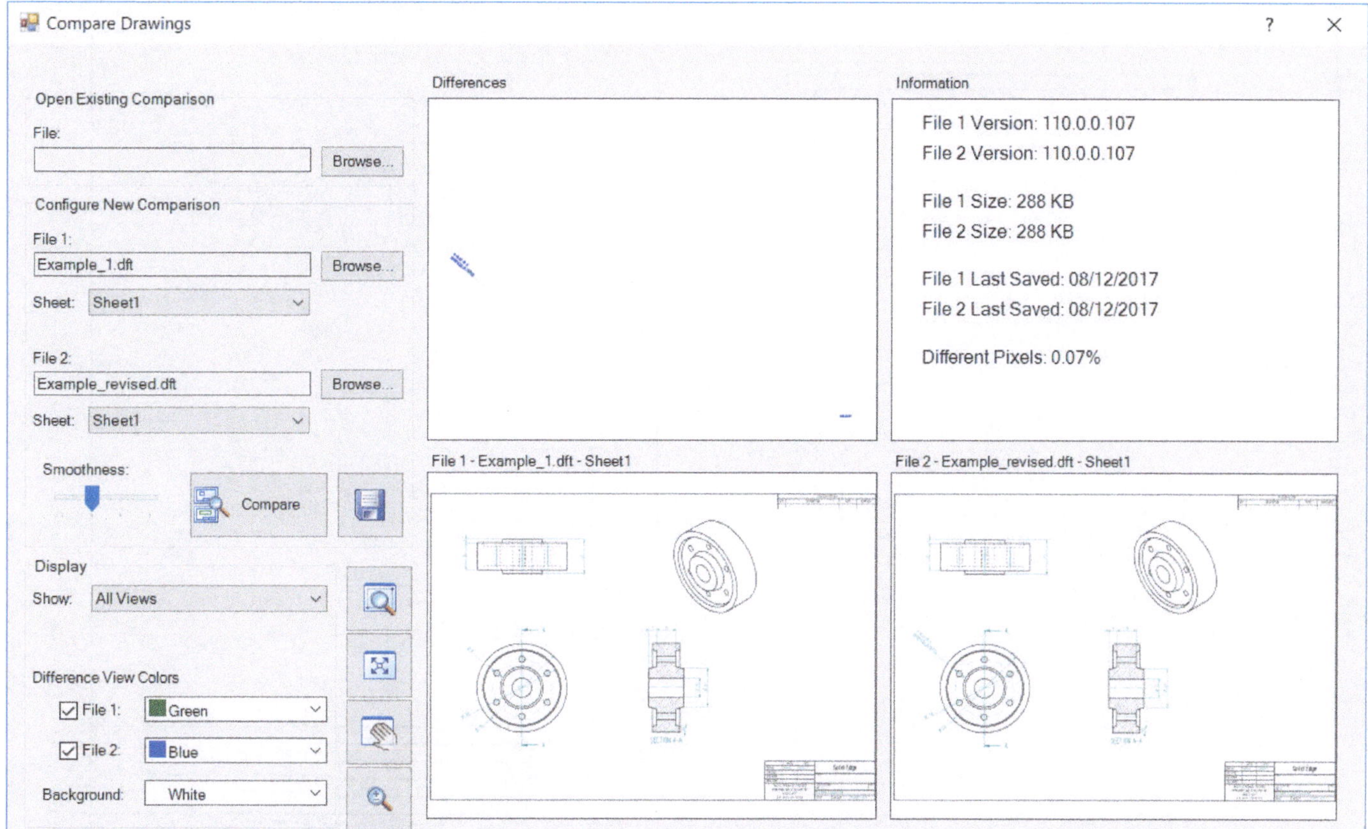

Examples

Example 1

In this example, you will create the 2D drawing of the part shown below.

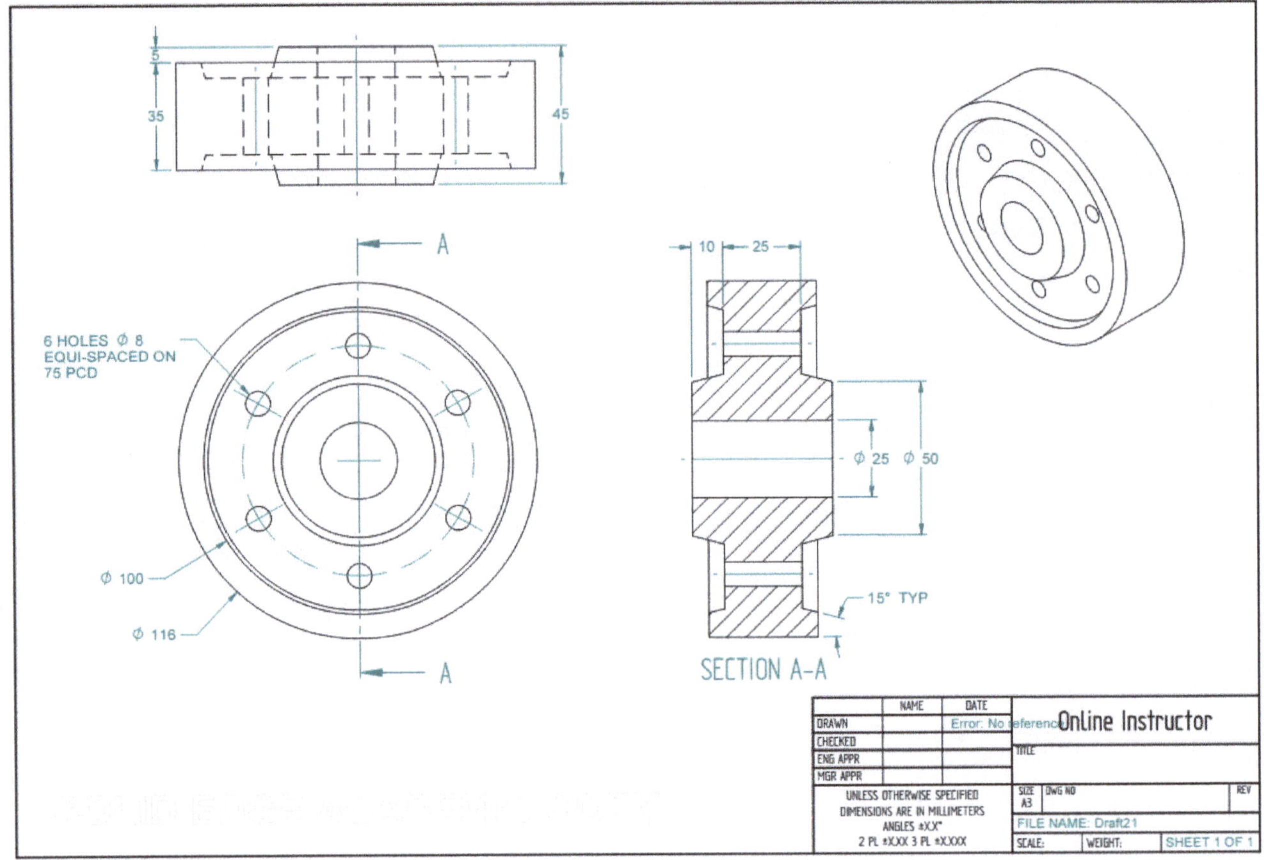

1. Start **Solid Edge 2026.**
2. On the **File Menu**, click **New > ISO Metric Draft** to start a new drawing.
3. At the bottom of the window, right-click on the **Sheet 1** tab and select **Sheet Setup**.
4. On the **Sheet Setup** dialog, click the **Size** tab and select the **Standard** option. Set the sheet size to **A3 Wide (420mm x 297mm).**
5. Click the **Background** tab and set the **Background sheet** to **A3-Sheet**. Click **OK** to close the dialog.

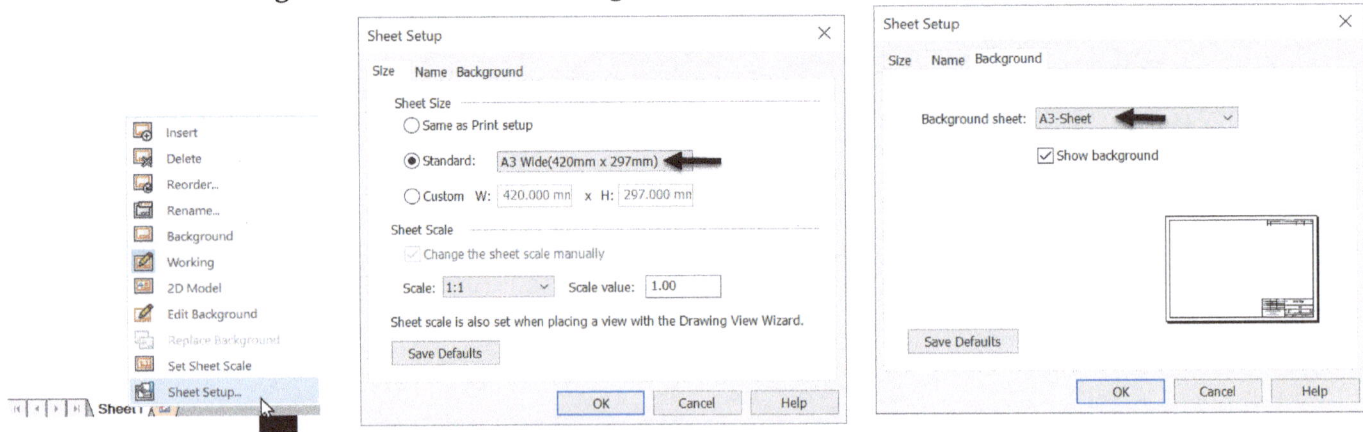

6. On the ribbon, click **View > Sheet Views > Background** to activate the background. Deactivate the **Working** icon located below the **Background** icon.

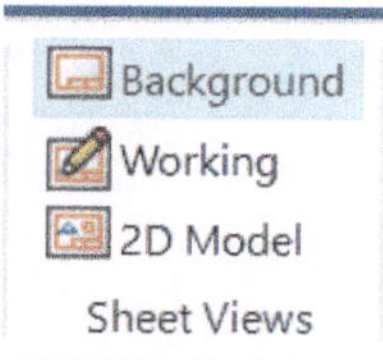

7. At the bottom of the sheet, click **A3-Sheet.**
8. Select the revision table and press Delete on your keyboard.

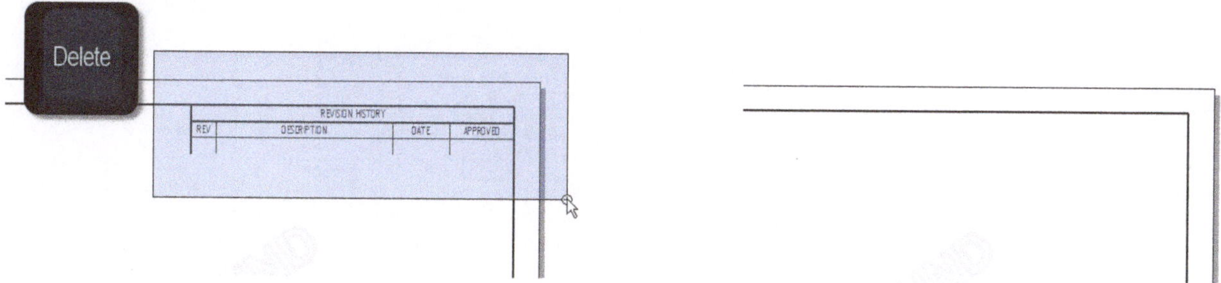

9. In the Title Block, change the company name to Online Instructor.

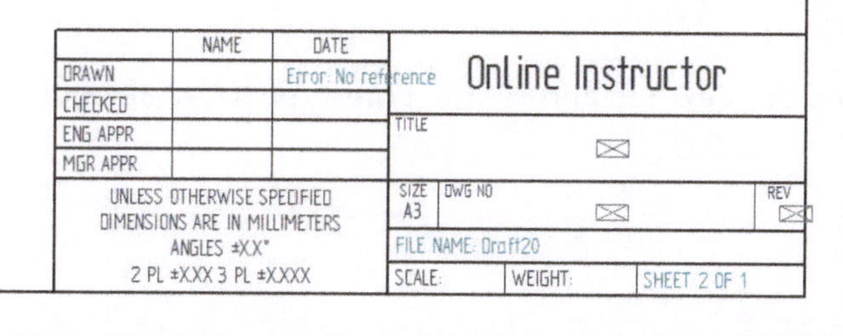

10. Activate the **Working** icon on the **Sheet views** panel, and then deactivate the **Background** icon.
11. On the **File Menu**, click the **Settings > Options** button. On the **Solid Edge Options** dialog, click the **Drawing Standards** tab. Set the **Projection Angle** to **Third** and click the **OK** button.

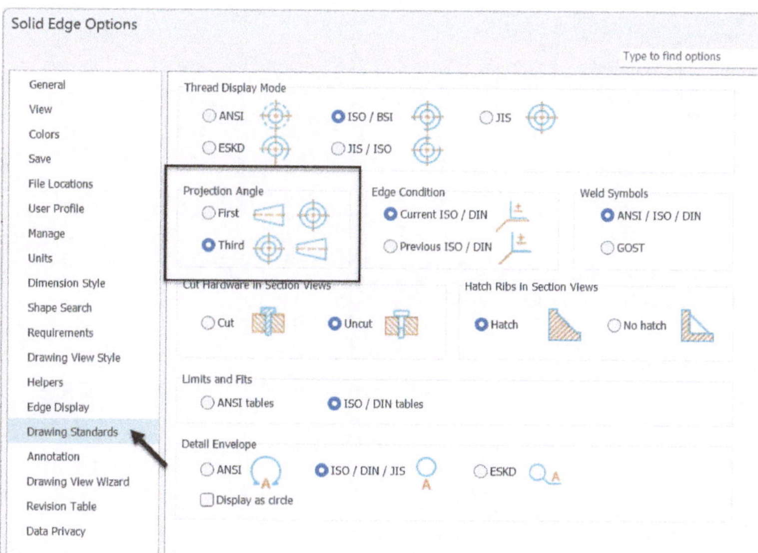

12. Activate the **Styles** command (click **Home > Dimension > Styles** on the ribbon). On the **Style** dialog, set the **Style type** to **Dimension**. Select **ISO (mm)** from the **Styles** box and click the **Modify** button.

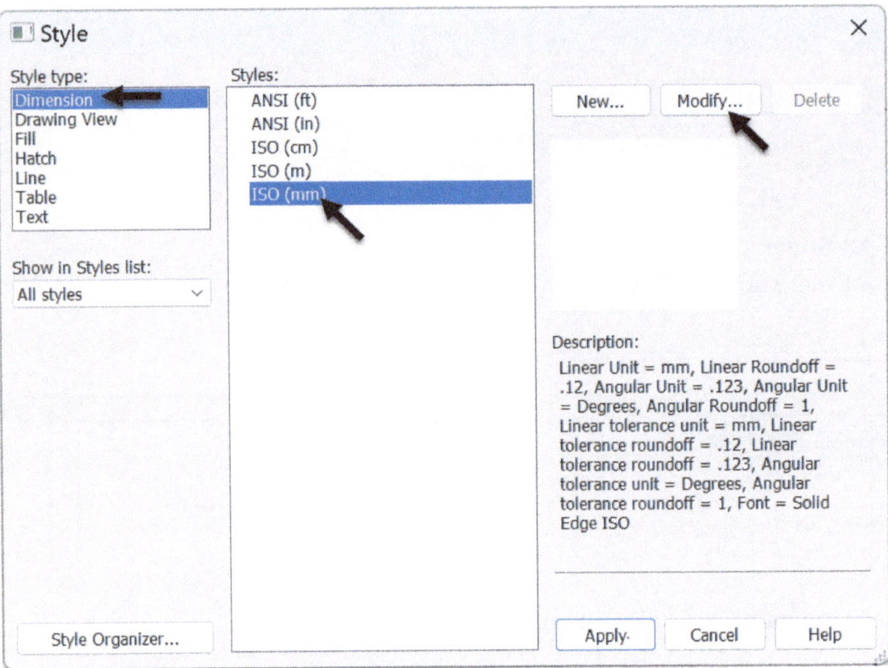

13. On the **Modify Dimension Style** dialog, click the **Text** tab and set the **Font** type to **Arial**. Set the **Orientation** to **Horizontal** and **Position** to **Embedded**.

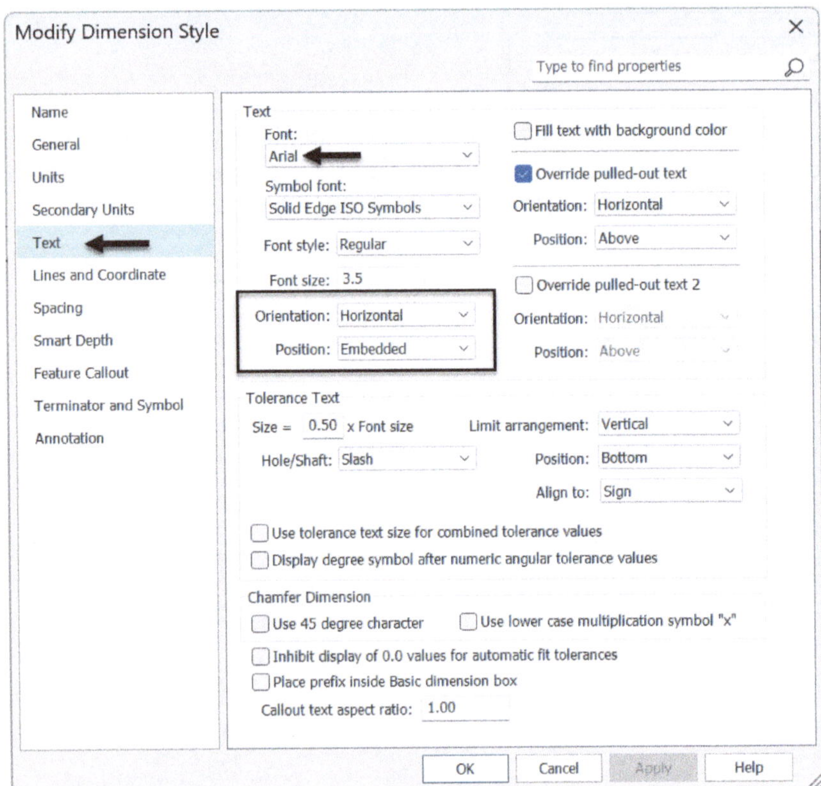

14. Click the **Units** tab and set the **Round-off** value to **1**.

15. Click the **Lines and Coordinate** tab and set the **Element gap** to 0.5 x Font Size. Under **Dimension Lines**, uncheck the **Connect** option. Click **OK** and then **Apply** to make changes to the dimension style.

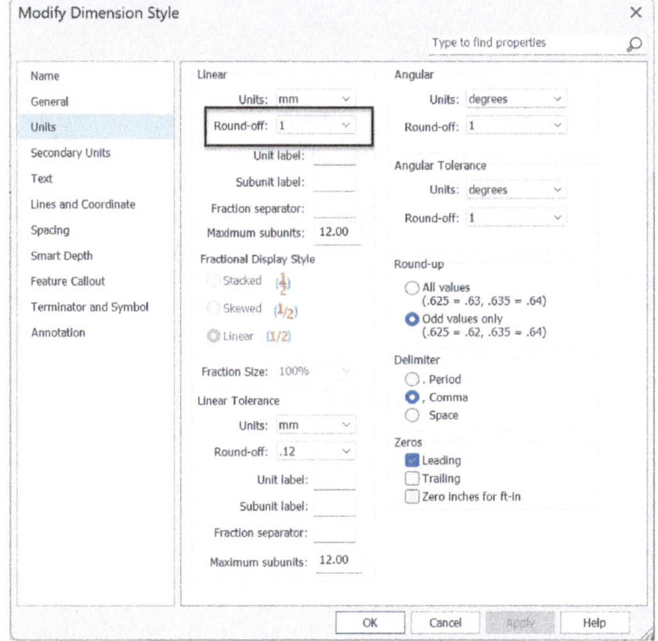

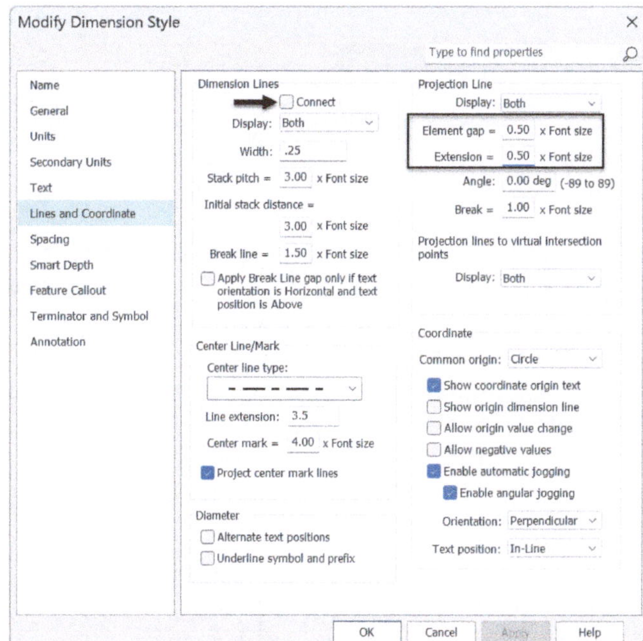

16. On the **Quick Access Toolbar**, click the **Save** icon and browse to the location C:\Program files\Solid Edge 2026\Template\ISO Metric. Type **Online Instructor** in the **File name** box and click **Save**. Close the file.
17. On the **File Menu**, click the **New** icon to open the **New** dialog. On this dialog, click **Standard Templates > ISO Metric** and select **Online Instructor.dft**. Click **OK** to start a new drawing file.

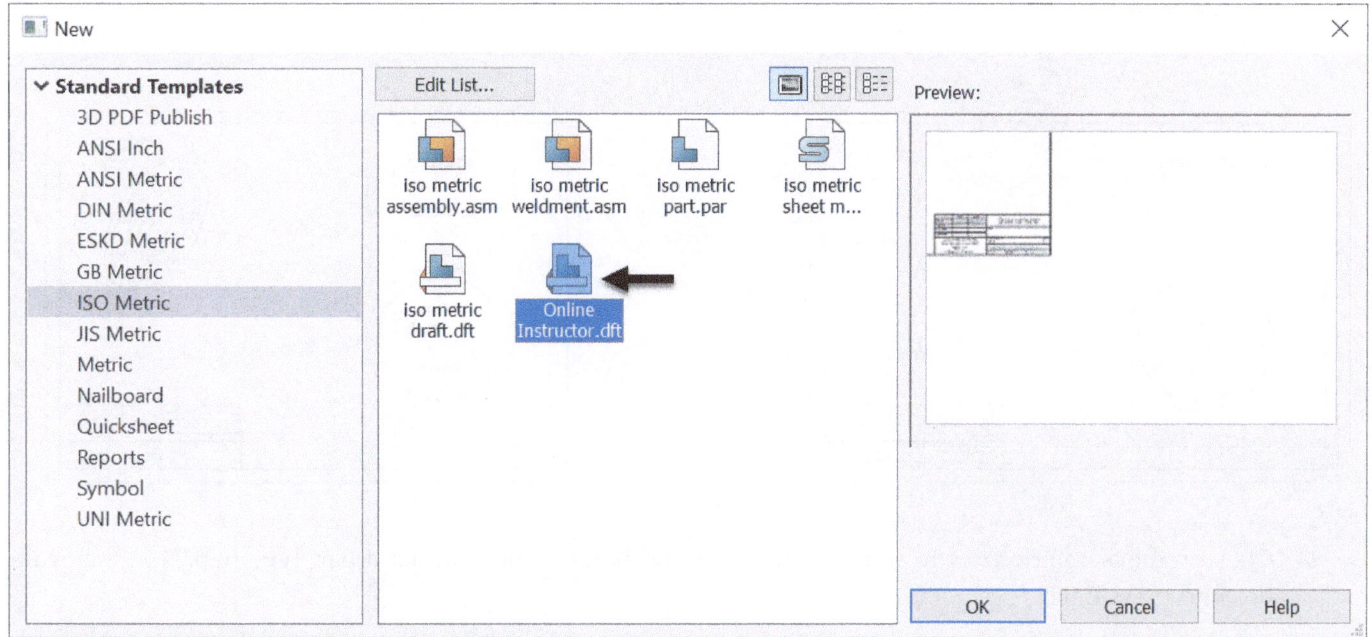

18. Activate the **View Wizard** command (click **Home > Drawing Views > View Wizard** on the ribbon).
19. Browse to the location of Exercise 1 of Chapter 5 and click on the part file. Click the **Open** button.

20. On the command bar, click the **Drawing View Layout** icon.
21. On the **Drawing View Wizard** dialog, set the **Primary View** to **front**. Click on the top view and isometric view icons. Click the **OK** button to close the dialog.

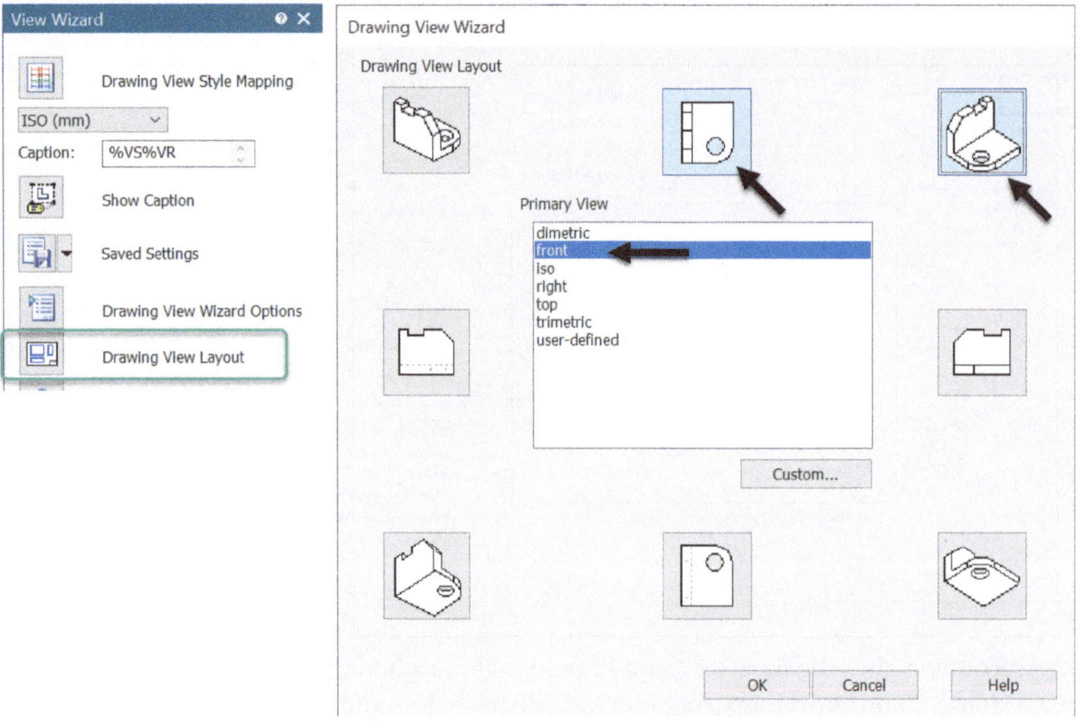

22. On the command bar, set the **Scale** to **1:1**
23. Click on the left portion of the sheet to place the drawing views. Drag the isometric view and position it at the top right corner.

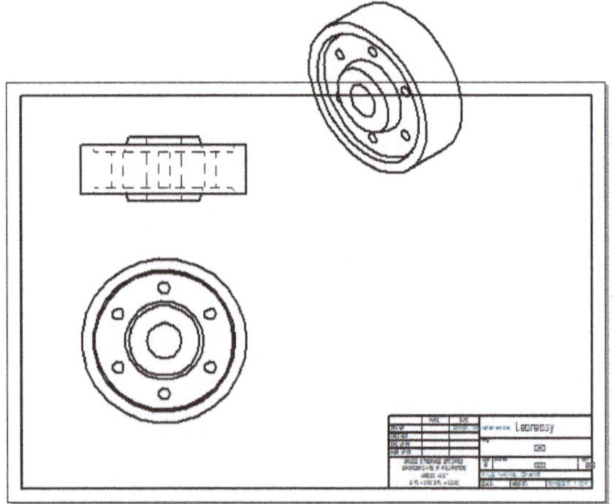

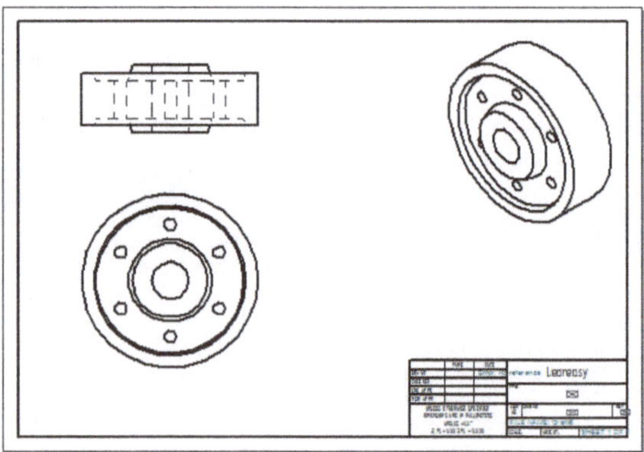

24. Click on the isometric view to activate the command bar. On the command bar, type-in **0.75** in the **Scale** box and press Enter.

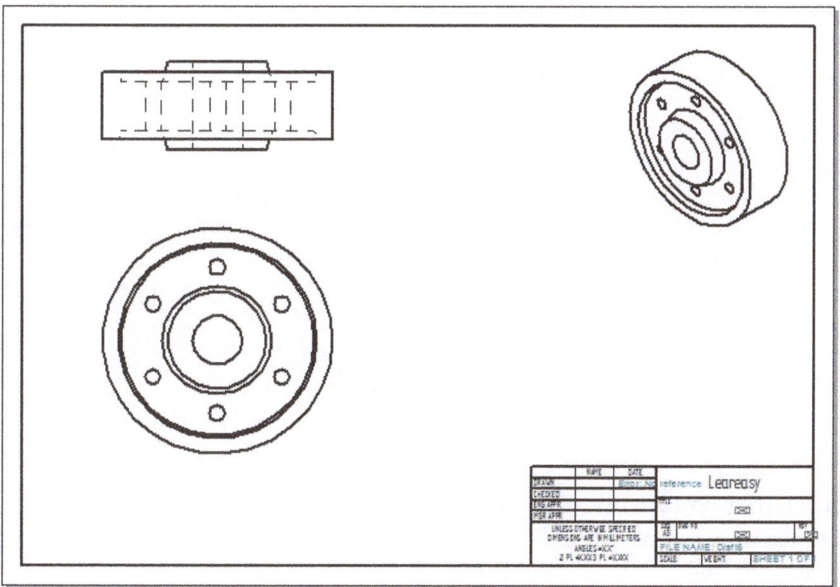

25. Activate the **Cutting Plane** command (click **Home > Drawing Views > Cutting Plane** on the ribbon) and select the front view. Create a cutting plane passing through the center of the front view.

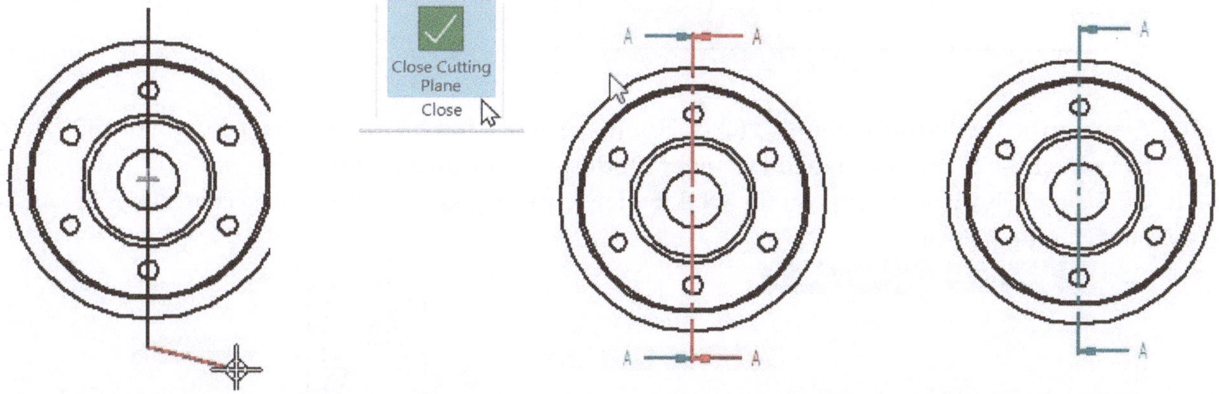

26. Activate the **Section** command (click **Home > Drawing views > Section** on the ribbon) and click on the cutting plane.
27. On the command bar, click the **Model Display Settings** icon. On the **Drawing View Properties** dialog, uncheck the **Hidden edge style** option and click **OK** twice.

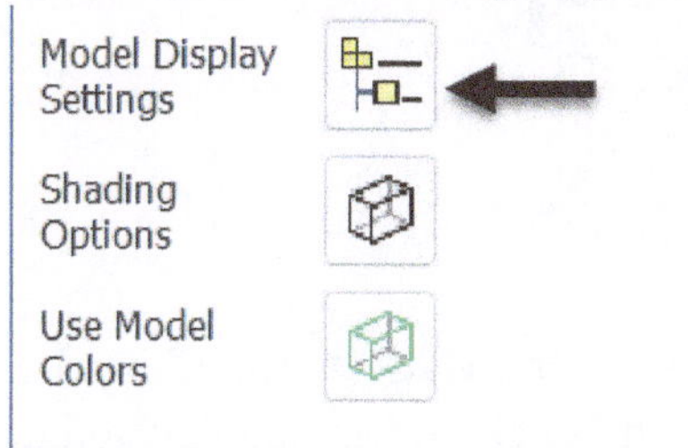

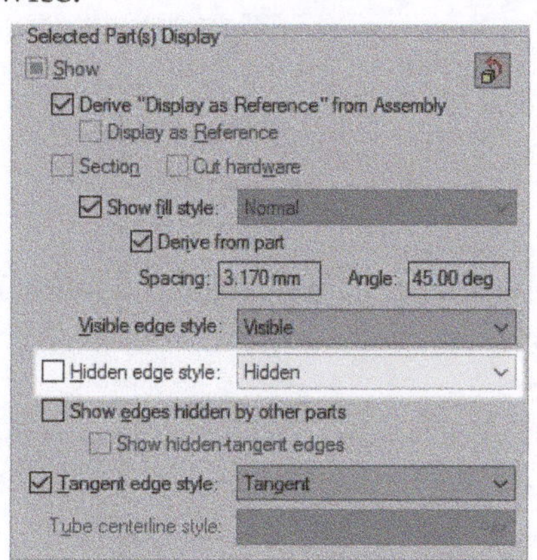

28. Drag the mouse pointer toward the right and click to position the view.

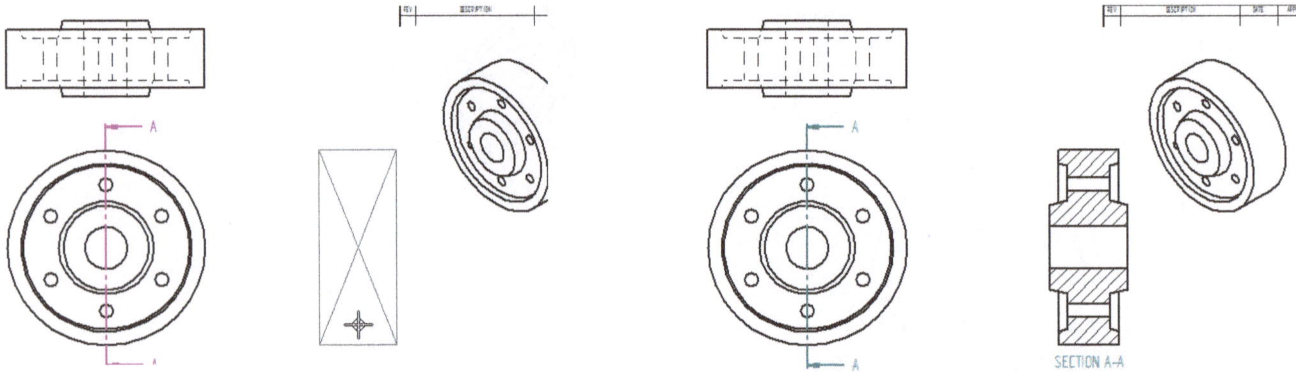

29. Activate the **Automatic Centerlines** command (click **Home > Annotation > Automatic Centerlines** on the ribbon). Click on the top view to apply centerlines.

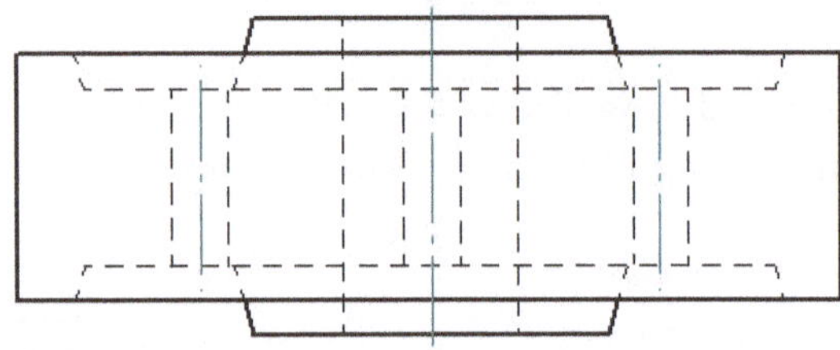

30. Activate the **Centerline** command (click **Home > Annotation > Centerline** on the ribbon). On the command bar, select **By 2 Lines** from the **Placement Options** drop-down menu.
31. Click on the horizontal lines on the section view corresponding to holes. The centerlines are created between the hole lines.

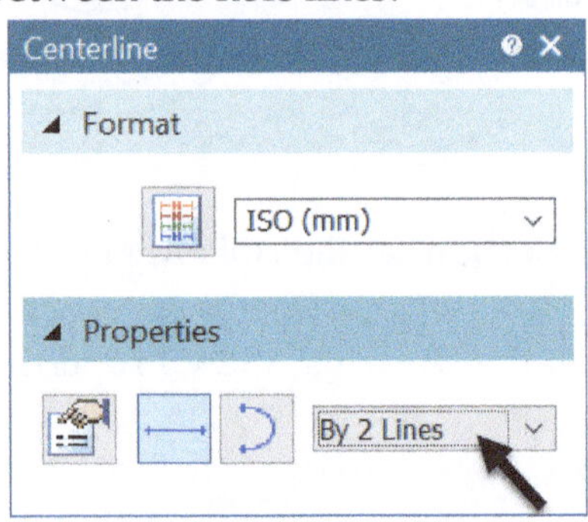

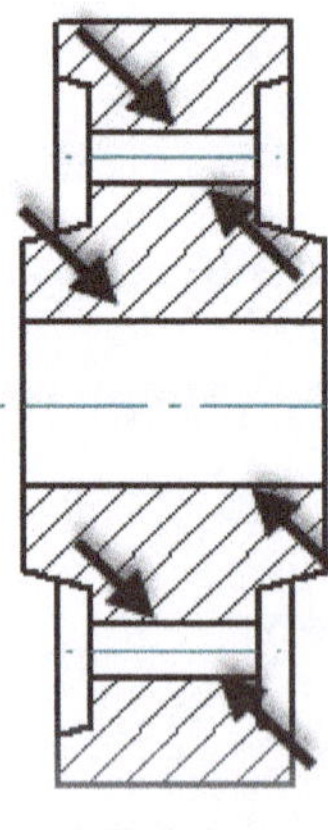

32. Activate the **Center Mark** command (click **Home > Annotation > Center Mark** on the ribbon)
33. On the command bar, set the **Orientation** to **Horizontal/Vertical** and click on the hole located at the front view center.
34. Activate the **Bolt Hole Circle** command (click **Home > Annotation > Bolt Hole Circle** on the ribbon) and click on the hole located at the center of the front view. Drag the mouse pointer and click on any one of the small holes. A bolt hole circle is created.

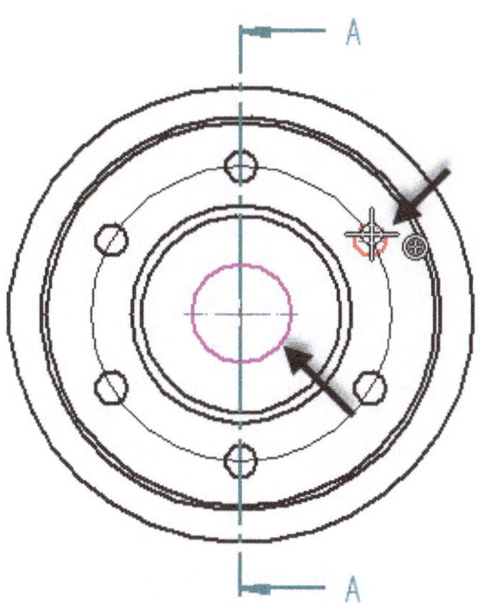

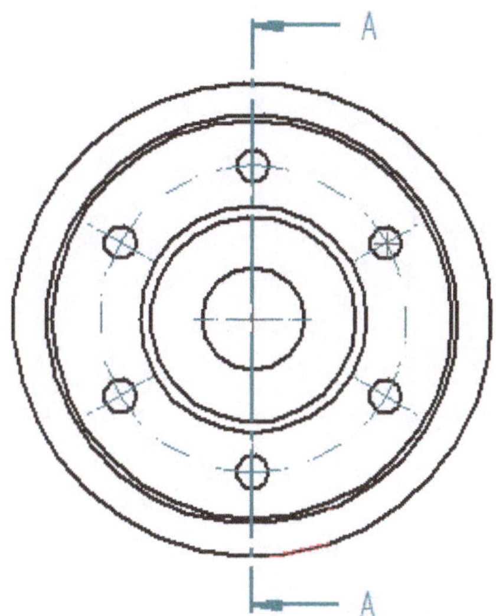

35. Activate the **Smart Dimension** command and apply dimensions to the top view.

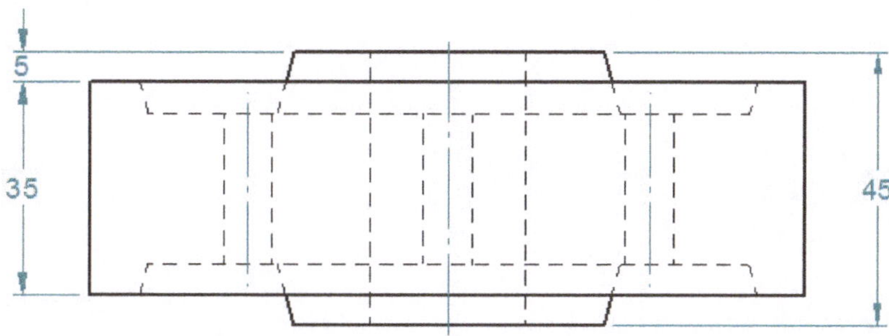

36. Activate the **Symmetric Diameter** command (click **Home > Dimension > Symmetric Diameter** on the ribbon). On the command bar, check the **Diameter- Full** option.
37. Click the centerline of the section view and horizontal line of the large hole. Drag the mouse pointer toward the right, and position the diameter dimension.

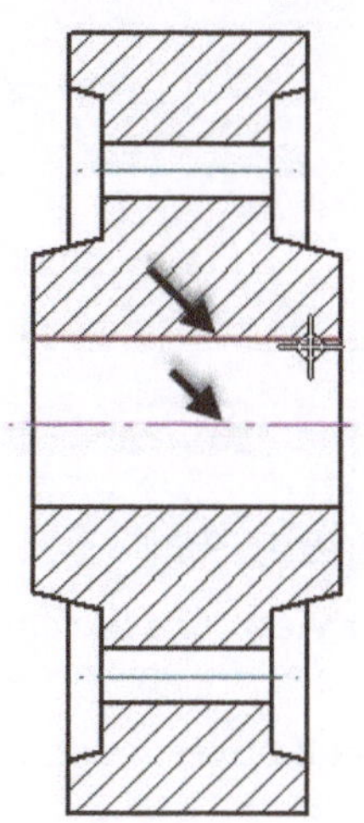

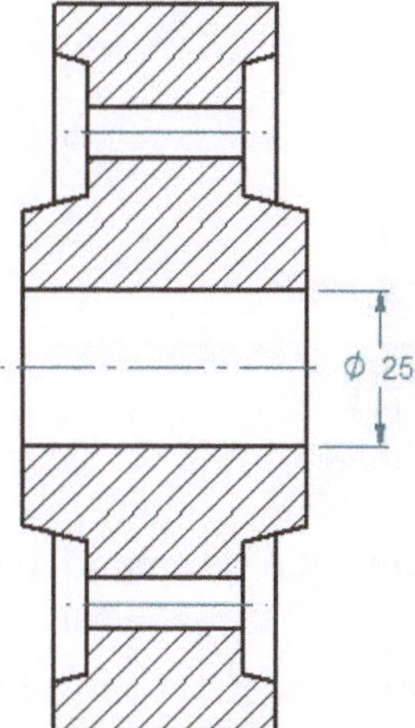

38. Click on the angled edge of the section view and create another diameter dimension.

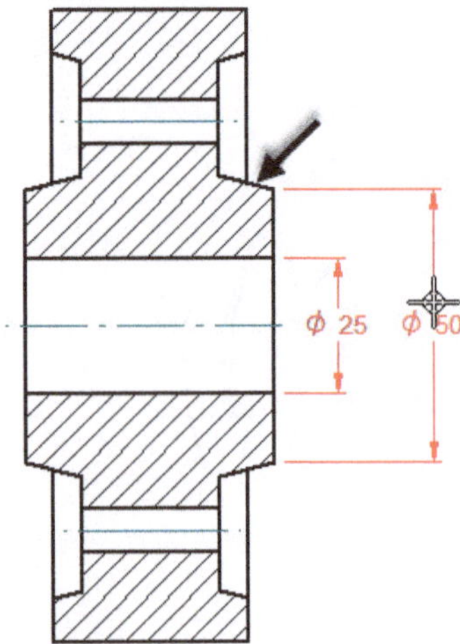

39. Activate the **Smart Dimension** command and click on the lower horizontal edge of the section view. On the command bar, activate the **Angle** icon and click on the inclined edge. Drag the pointer and click to position the angle dimension. Press Esc to deactivate the **Smart Dimension** command.

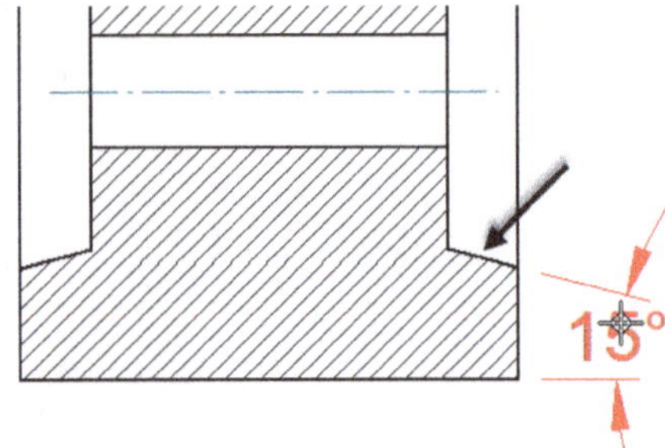

40. Click on the angle dimension and drag upward. On the command bar, click the **Prefix** button to open the **Dimension Prefix** dialog.
41. On the **Dimension Prefix** dialog, type-in **TYP** in the **Suffix** box and click **OK**.

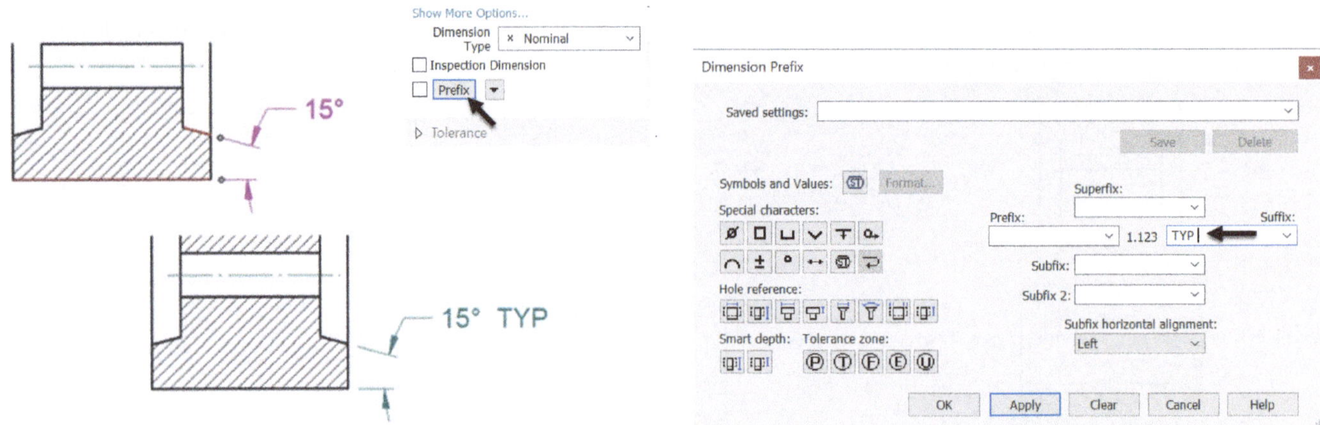

42. Activate the **Smart Dimension** command and click on the small hole in the front view. On the command bar, click the **Prefix** icon.
43. On the **Dimension Prefix** dialog, type-in values in the **Prefix**, **Subfix**, and **Subfix 2** boxes, as shown. Click **OK** and position the hole dimension.

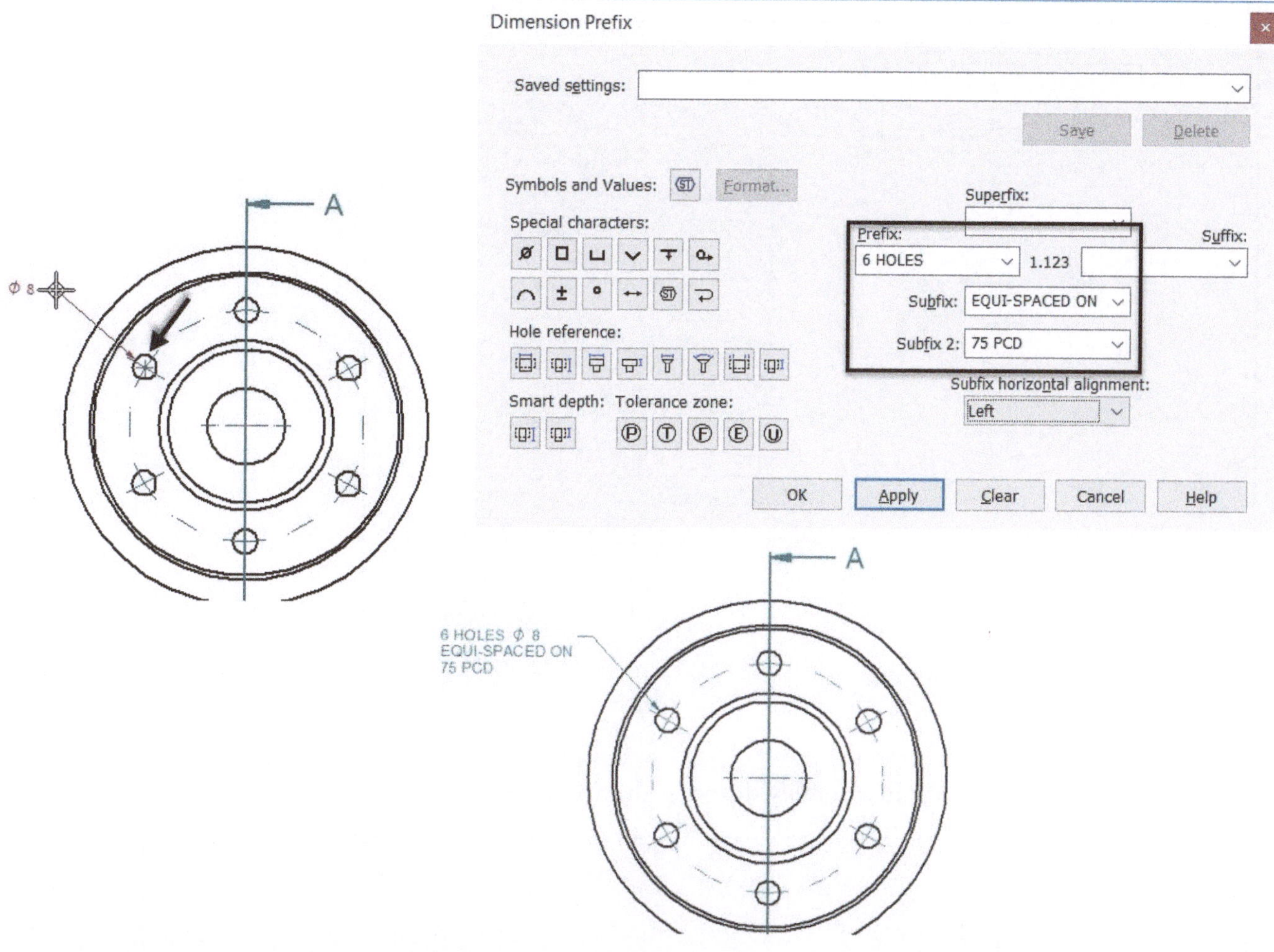

44. Activate the **Smart Dimension** command and open the **Dimension Prefix** dialog. On this dialog, empty the **Prefix**, **Subfix**, and **Subfix 2** boxes and click **OK**.
45. Create other dimensions in the drawing.

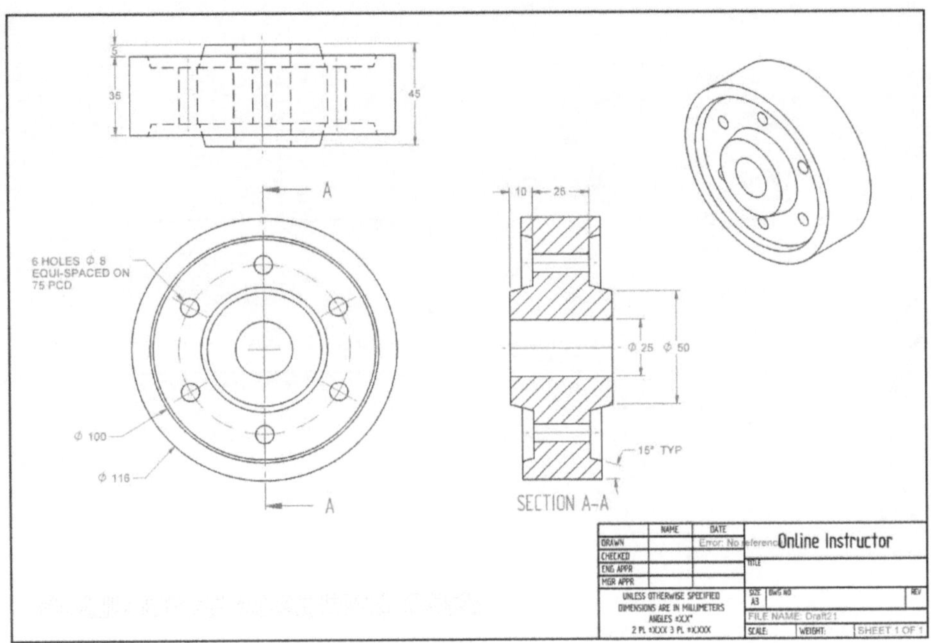

46. Save and close the drawing.

Example 2

In this example, you will create an assembly drawing shown below.

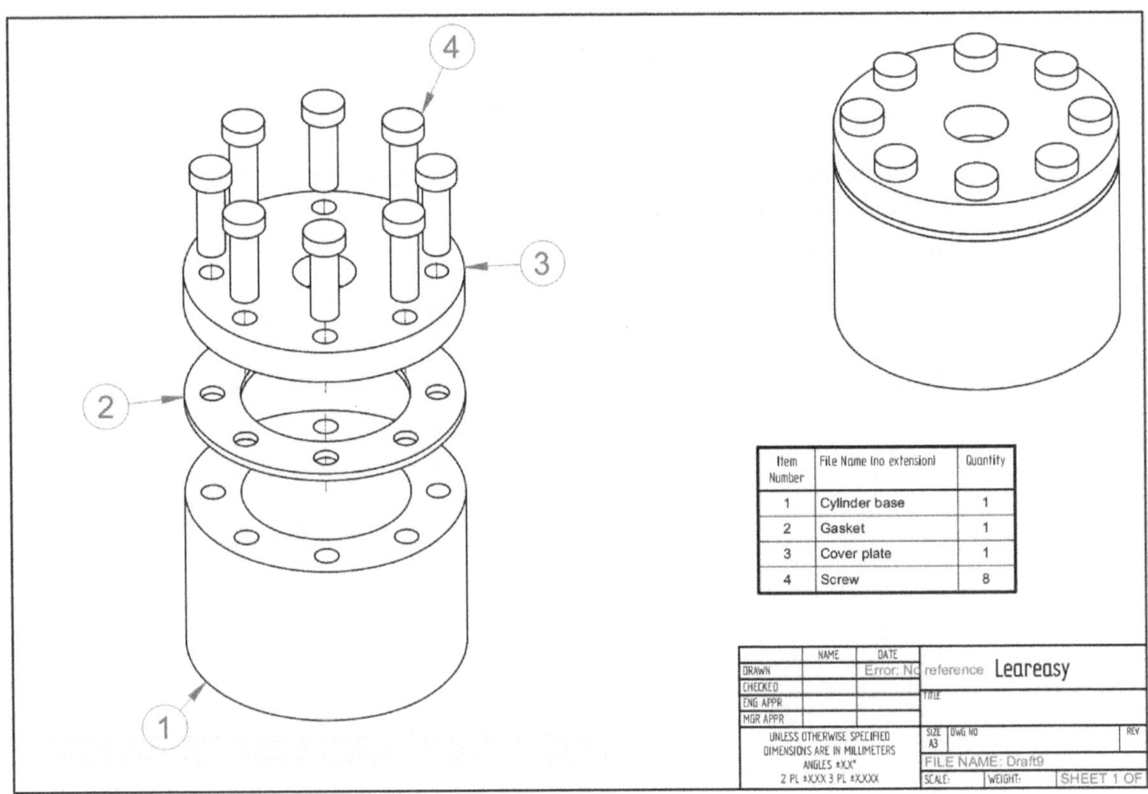

Item Number	File Name (no extension)	Quantity
1	Cylinder base	1
2	Gasket	1
3	Cover plate	1
4	Screw	8

1. Start **Solid Edge 2026.**

2. On the **Quick Access Toolbar**, click the **New** icon. On the **New** dialog, click on the **Online Instructor.dft**, and then click **OK**.
3. Activate the **View Wizard** command (click **Home > Drawing Views > View Wizard** on the ribbon).
4. Browse to the location of Example 2 of Chapter 10 and click on the assembly file. Click the **Open** button.
5. Click on the top right corner to place the isometric view of the assembly. Press Esc to stop view projection.
6. Again, activate the **View Wizard** command. On the **Select Attachment** dialog, check the **Create drawing view independent of assembly** option and set the **Configuration** to **explode, Solid Edge**. Click **OK**.
7. On the command bar, set the **Scale** to 1:1. Click on the drawing sheet to position the exploded view.

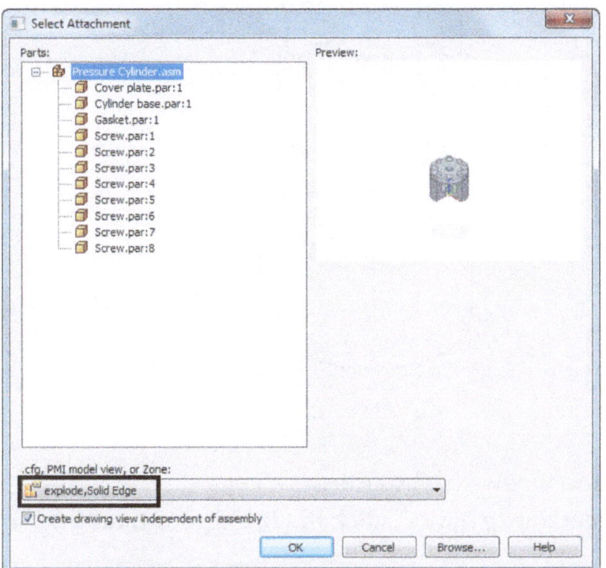

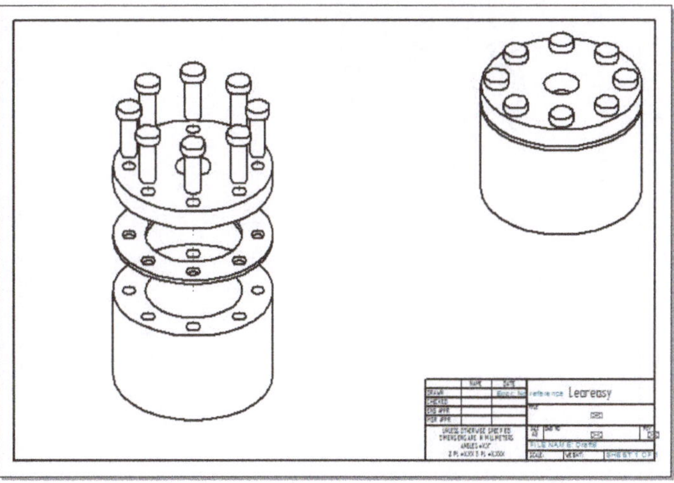

8. Activate the **Parts List** command (click **Home > Tables > Parts List** on the ribbon) and click on the exploded view.
9. On the command bar, click the **Properties** icon to open the **Parts List Properties** dialog.
10. On this dialog, click the **Columns** tab. In the **Columns** box, click on the **Author** option, and then click the **Delete Column** button.
11. On the **Data** tab, press the Shift key and select all the cells of the table. Change the **Font** type to **Arial**.

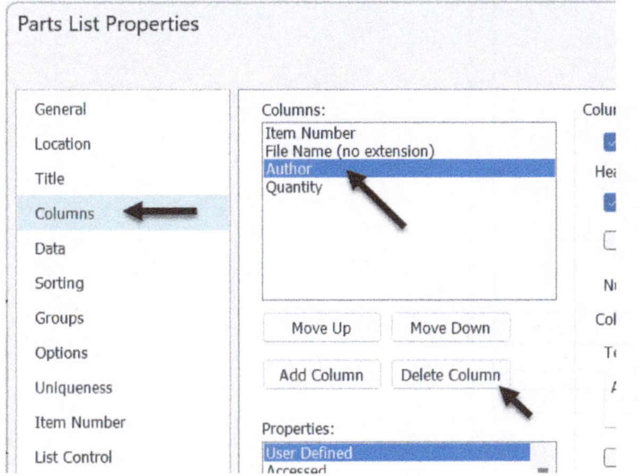

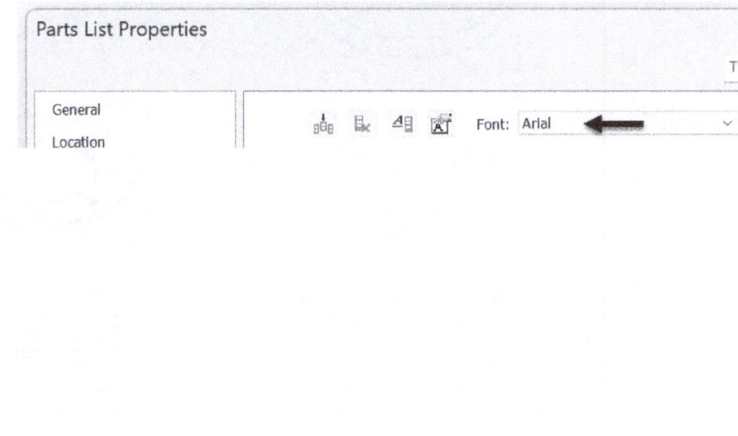

12. On the **Balloon** tab, set the **Text Size** to **8** and uncheck the **Use Item Count for lower text** option. Click **OK.**
13. Position the parts list below the isometric view. You will notice that some balloons are placed outside the sheet.
14. Click on the alignment line connecting the balloons. Square and circle grips appear on it.
15. Click on a square grip and reduce the size of the alignment shape.

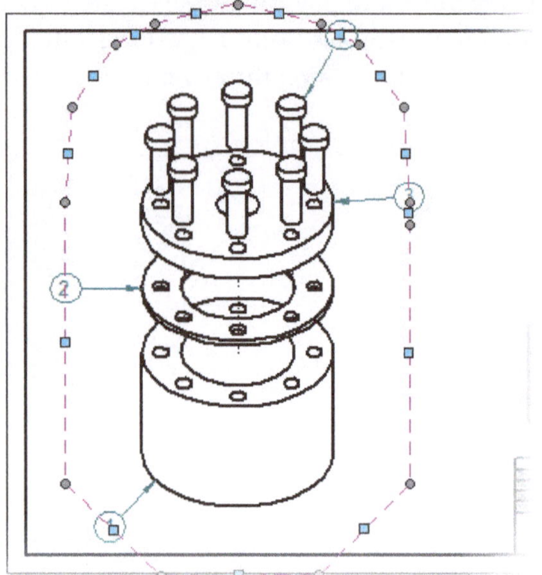

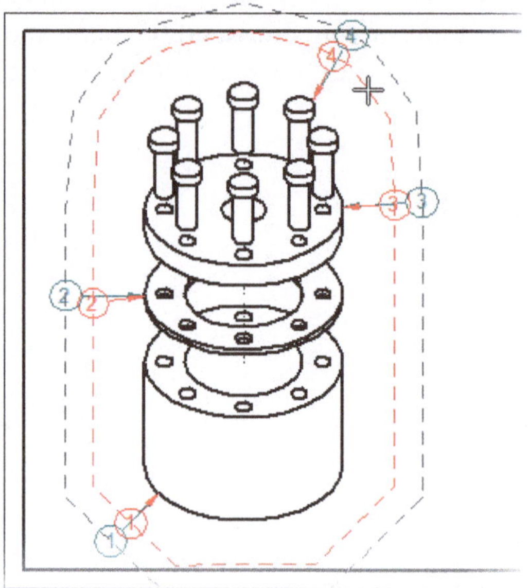

16. At the bottom of the sheet, click the **New Sheet** icon to add a new sheet to the drawing.
17. Right-click on **Sheet2** and select **Sheet Setup**. On the **Sheet Setup** dialog, click the **Background** tab and set the **Background sheet** to **A3-Sheet**. Click **OK**.
18. Activate the **View Wizard** command and uncheck the **Create drawing view independent of assembly** option.
19. From the Parts list, click the Cylinder Base.par file. Click **OK** and place the drawing view on the sheet.
20. Likewise, use the **View Wizard** command and place other part views, as shown below.

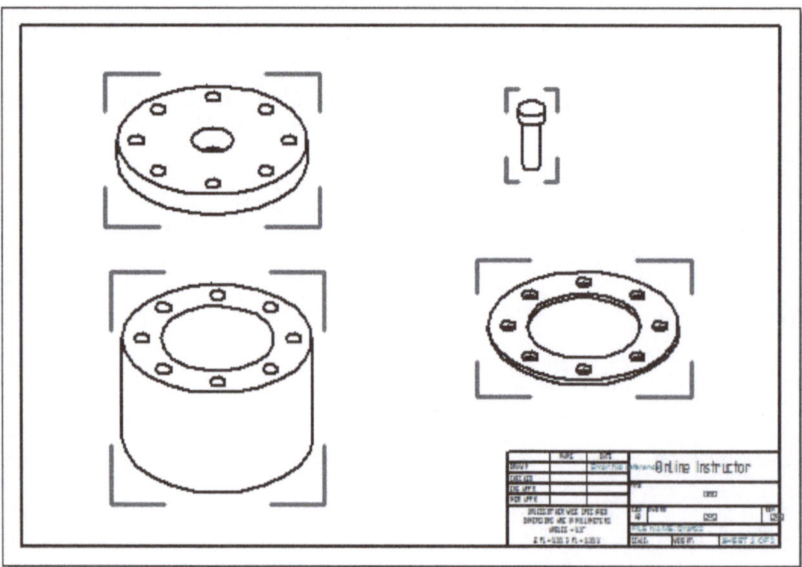

21. On the ribbon, click **Home > Annotation > Balloon** .

22. On the command bar, type-in 2 in the **Text Scale** and **Height** boxes.

23. On the command bar, check the **Link to Parts list** option and click the **Link to Parts List** icon. Next, check the **Display item number in parts list** option.

24. Select a point on the cover plate to attach a balloon to it. Move the pointer and click to define the location of the balloon.

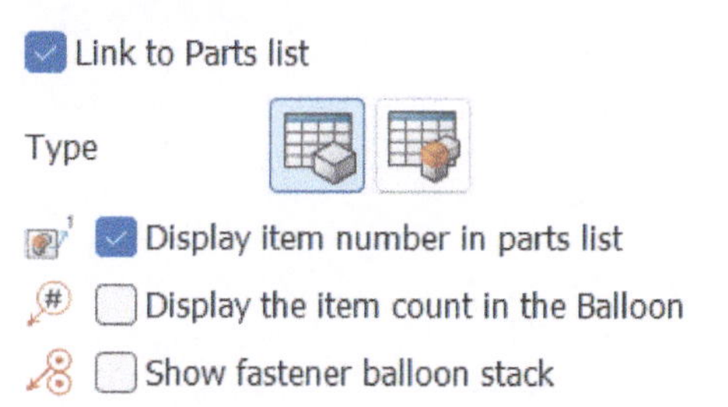

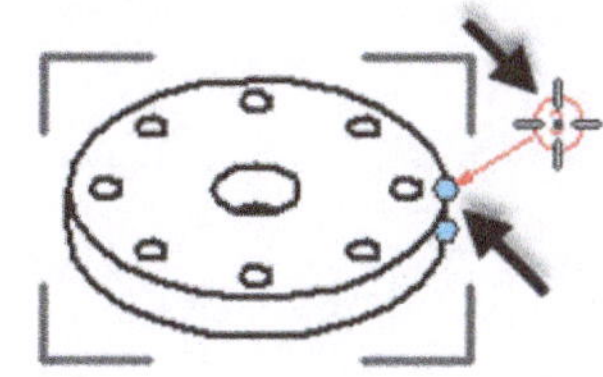

25. Likewise, add balloons to other views.

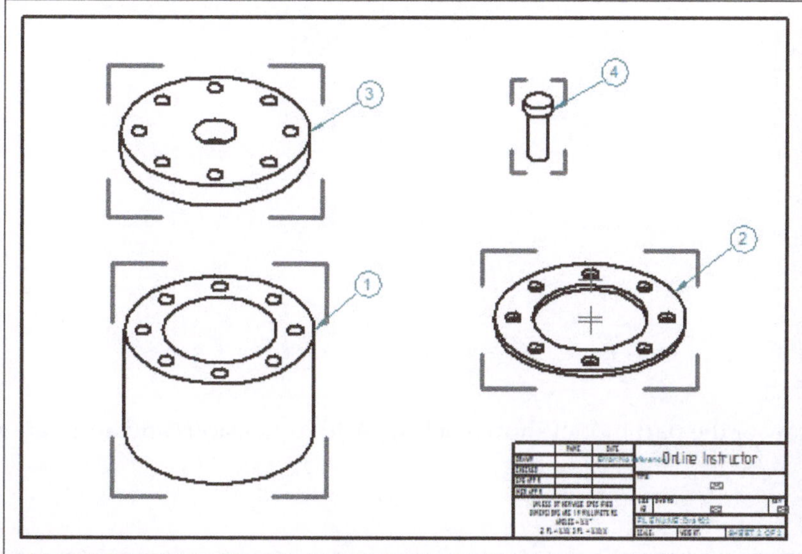

26. Save and close the drawing.

Questions

1. How to create drawing views using the **View Wizard** command?
2. How do you hide the hidden edges of a drawing view?
3. How do you change the display style of a drawing view?
4. How do you update drawing views when the part is edited?
5. How do you control the properties of dimensions and annotations?
6. List the commands used to create centerlines and center marks.
7. How do you add symbols and texts to a dimension?
8. How do you add break lines to a drawing view?
9. How do you create revolved section views?

10. How do you create an exploded view of an assembly?

Exercises

Exercise 1

Create orthographic views of the part model shown below. Add dimensions and annotations to the drawing.

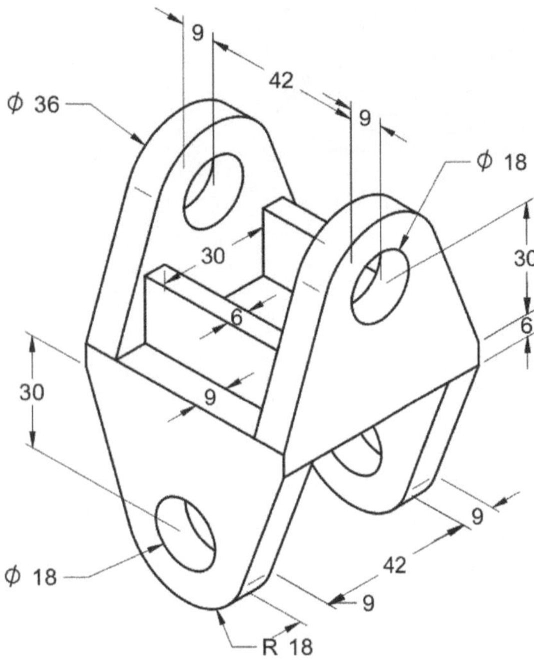

Exercise 2

Create orthographic views and an auxiliary view of the part model shown below. Add dimensions and annotations to the drawing.

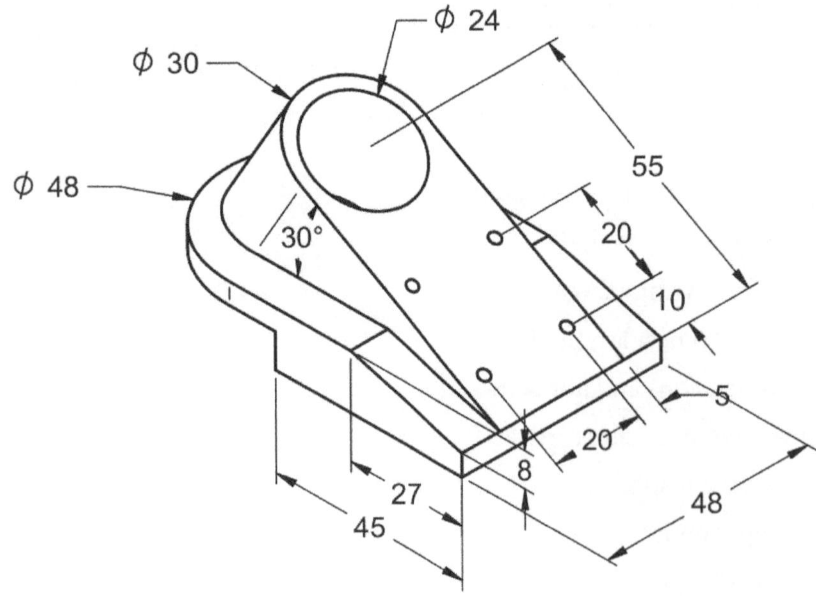

Chapter 12: Sheet Metal Design

Sheet metal parts are made by bending and forming flat sheets of metal. In Solid Edge, sheet-metal parts can be folded and unfolded, enabling you to show them in the flat pattern as well as their bent-up state. There are two ways to design sheet metal parts in Solid Edge. You either start the sheet-metal part from scratch using sheet-metal features throughout the design process or design it as a regular solid part and convert it to a sheet-metal part. Most commonly, sheet-metal parts are designed in a Sheet Metal environment from the beginning. In this chapter, you will learn both approaches.

The topics covered in this chapter are:

- *Tabs*
- *Flanges*
- *Bend Allowance*
- *Bend Tables*
- *Counter Flanges*
- *Hems*
- *Close 2-Bend Corners*
- *Bends*
- *Jogs*
- *Dimples*
- *Louvers*
- *Drawn Cutouts*
- *Beads*
- *Gussets*
- *Etches*
- *Embosses*
- *Cuts*
- *Convert to Sheet Metal*
- *Rip Corners*
- *Flat Pattern*
- *Export to DXF or DWG*

Starting a Sheet Metal part

To start a new sheet metal part, click the **File** tab on the top left corner. On the **File Menu**, click **New** tab > **ISO Metric Sheet Metal** option (or) click the **New** icon on the **Quick Access Toolbar**, and then double-click on the **iso sheet metal.psm** template on the **New** dialog. If you want to start the sheet metal part using any other template, select a standard from the **Standard Templates** section, and then select the sheet metal template corresponding to the selected standard.

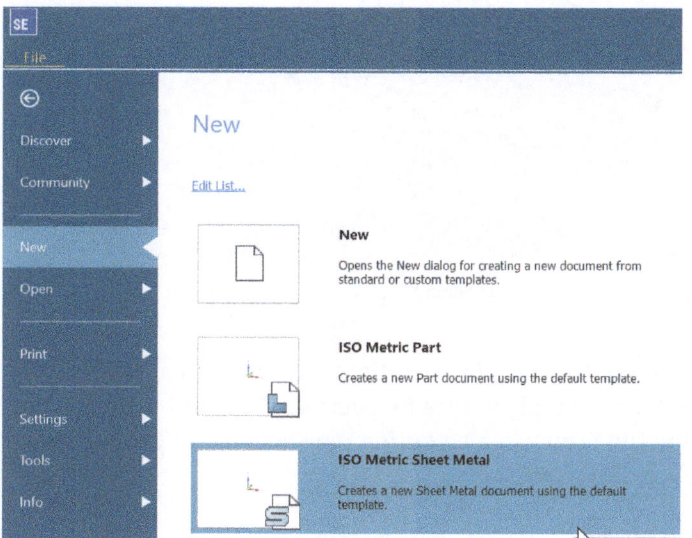

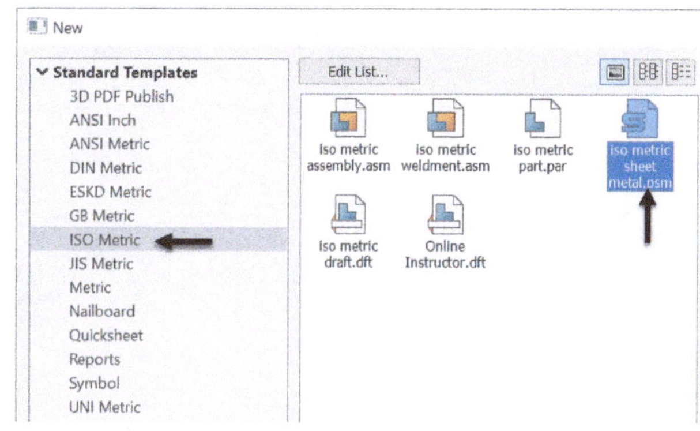

Tab (Synchronous)

The tab is a basic type of sheet metal feature. To create a tab, create a closed sketch on a plane and click inside it.

An arrow handle appears along with the command bar. On the command bar, click the **Material Table** icon to open the **Material Table** dialog. On this dialog, select a material from the Materials tree; its properties are displayed in the **Material Properties** tab. You can change the properties of the material in the **Properties** table.

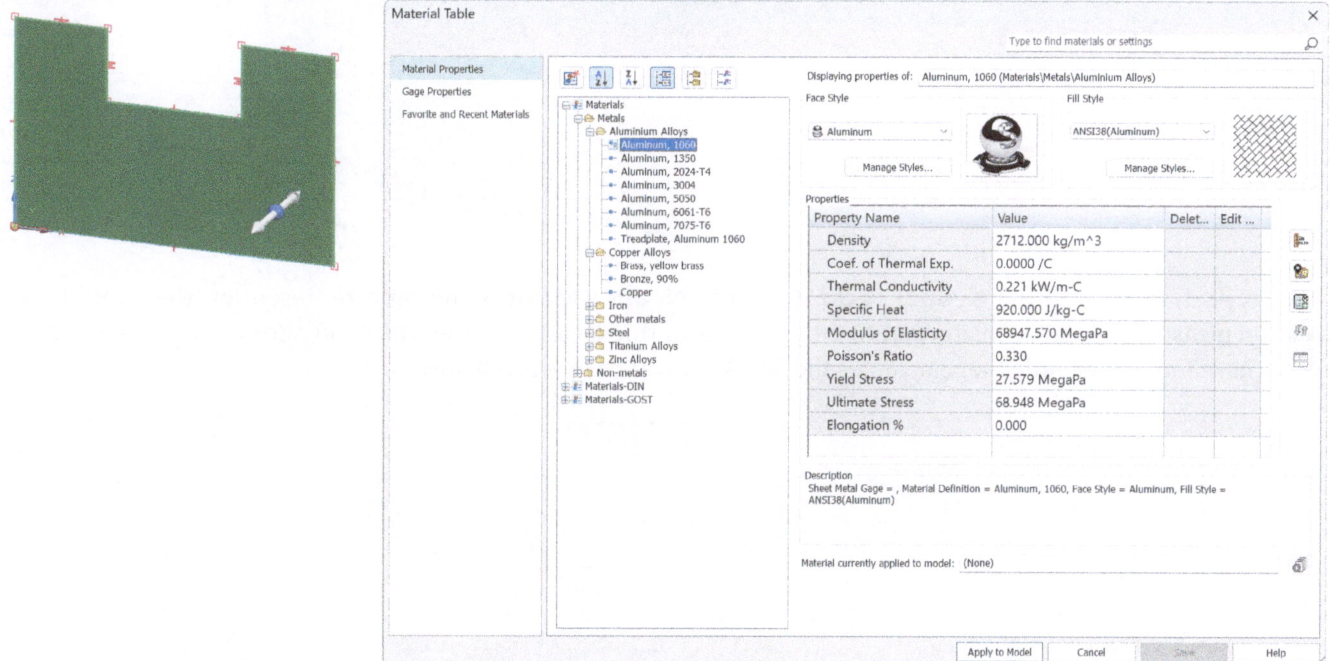

Open the **Gage Properties** tab and define the gage properties of the sheet metal part. Type-in values in the **Material thickness**, **Bend radius**, **Relief depth**, and **Relief width** boxes.

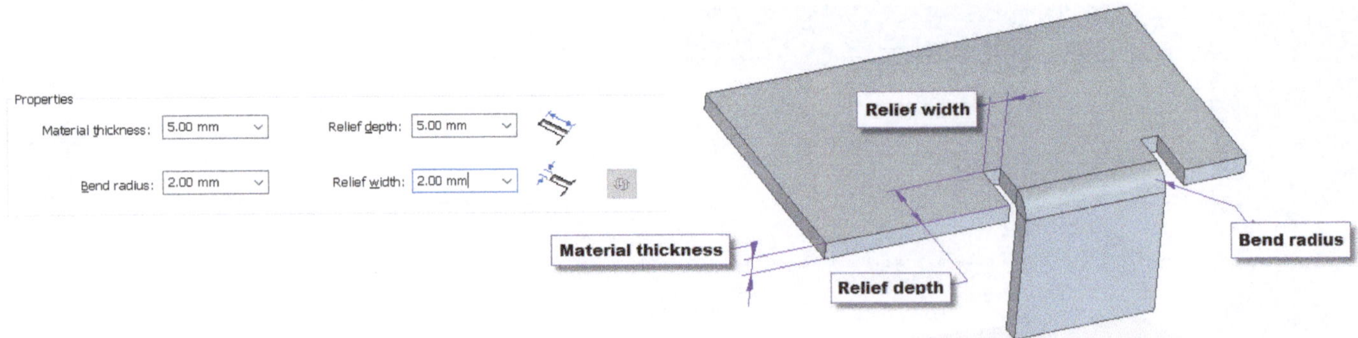

You can also use a spreadsheet to define these values. Check the **Use Excel file** option and select a gage table from the **Use Gage Table** drop-down menu. You can edit the gage table values by clicking the **Edit** button. In the spreadsheet, modify the values, and then save and close the file. You can also define the sheet metal properties by selecting any sheet metal gages in the **Sheet metal gage** drop-down menu.

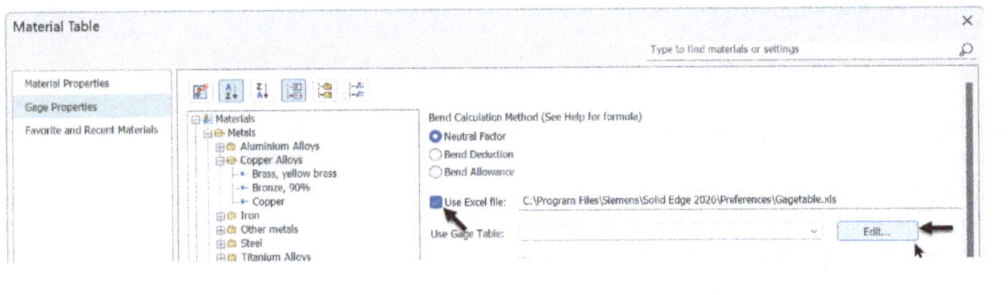

	A	B	C	D	E
1	Process Type				
2	Units	mm			
3	-100				
4	Gage Name	10 Gage Al			
5	Material Thickness	2.59			
6	Bend Radius	20			
7	Relief Depth	5			
8	Relief Width	2.75			
9	-200	Radius			
10	Angle	10	20	25	30
11	5	0.1	0.1	0.15	0.2
12	15	0.17	0.1	0.15	0.25
13	30	0.19	0.15	0.2	0.3
14	45	0.2	0.2	0.25	0.35
15	60	0.21	0.2	0.25	0.4
16	75	0.22	0.3	0.35	0.45
17	90	0.23	0.3	0.35	0.5
18	120	0.24	0.4	0.4	0.65
19	135	0.25	0.4	0.5	0.68
20	180	0.3	0.5	0.6	0.7

Next, type-in a value in the **Neutral Factor** box. The **Neutral Factor** is the ratio representing the neutral sheet's location measured from the inside face to the sheet-metal thickness. It defines the bend allowance of the sheet metal part. The standard formula that calculates the bend allowance is given below.

$$BA = \frac{\pi(R + KT)A}{180}$$

BA = Bend Allowance

R = Bend Radius

K = Neutral Factor = t/T

T = Material Thickness

t = Distance from inside face to the neutral sheet

A = Bend Angle

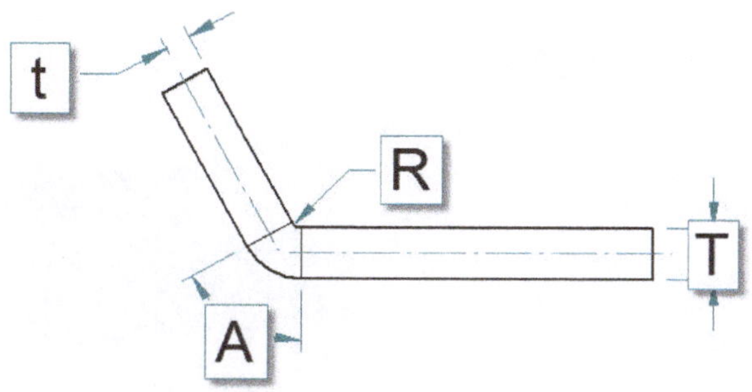

You can also define the bend allowance by using your formula. Select the **Custom formula** option and type-in a value in the **ProgramID.ClassName** box. Click the **Apply to Model** button to apply the material and gage properties to the model. Now, click on the arrow handle to define the side of the tab feature. Click the right mouse button to create the tab feature.

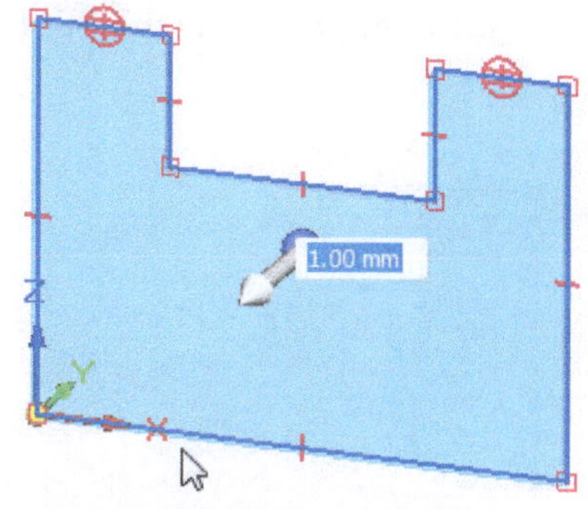

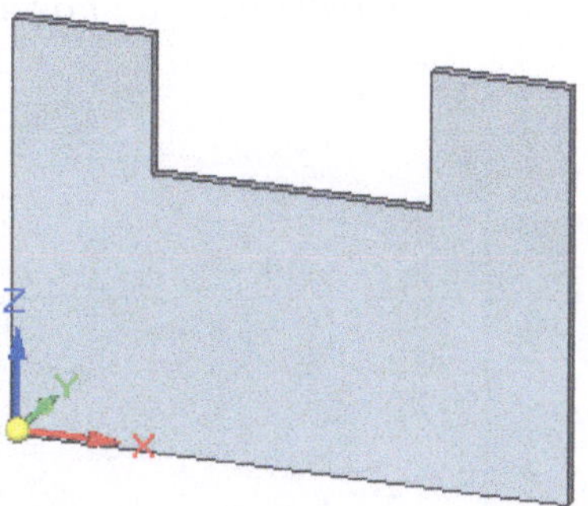

Tab (Ordered)

Before creating the **Tab** feature in the Ordered environment, it is necessary to specify the material properties. To achieve this, right-click on the **Material** node in the Pathfinder and select the **Material Table** option. The resulting Material Table dialog provides configuration options, as detailed in the preceding section.

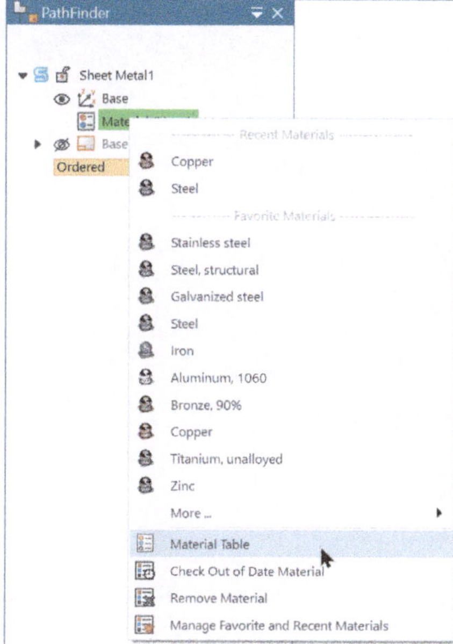

After applying the material properties, click **Home > Sheet Metal > Tab** on the ribbon and select an existing close sketch (or) create a sketch. Next, type-in a value in the **Thickness** box available in the **Thickness** section. Move the pointer and click to define the side of the tab feature. Click **Finish** on the command bar.

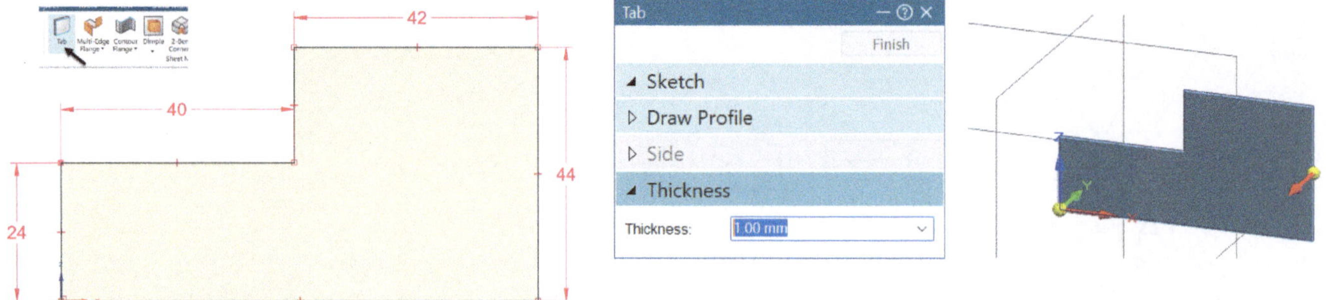

Flange (Synchrnous)

The second feature after creating a tab is a flange. This feature can be created along an edge or multiple edges of a sheet metal part. To create a flange, all you need is to click an end face of the tab feature. The flange handle appears on the selected face. Click the small arrow and drag the pointer. A flange feature appears attached to the mouse pointer.

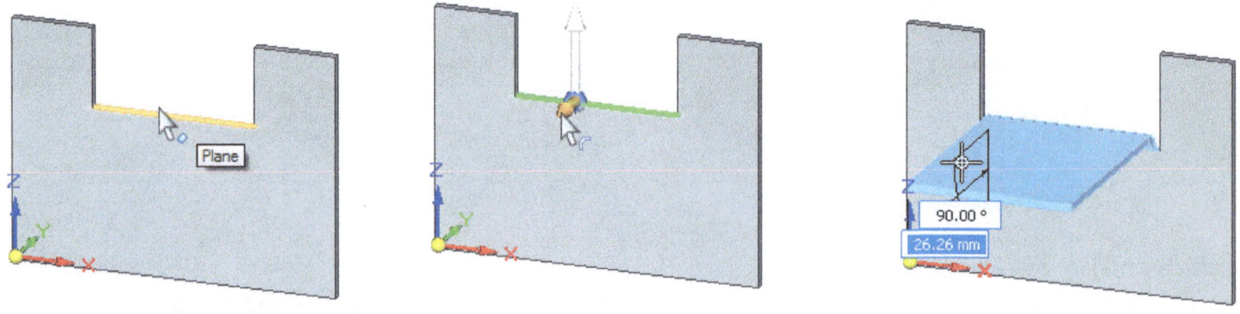

On the command bar, click the **Flange Options** icon to open the **Flange Options** dialog. You can override the gage properties by checking the **Override global value** options available next to each of the gage properties on this dialog.

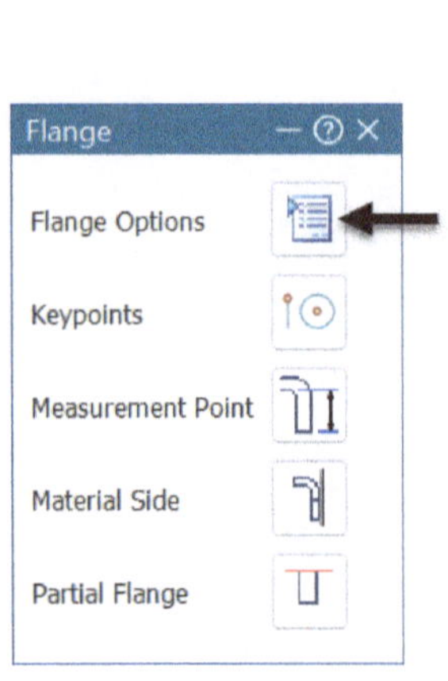

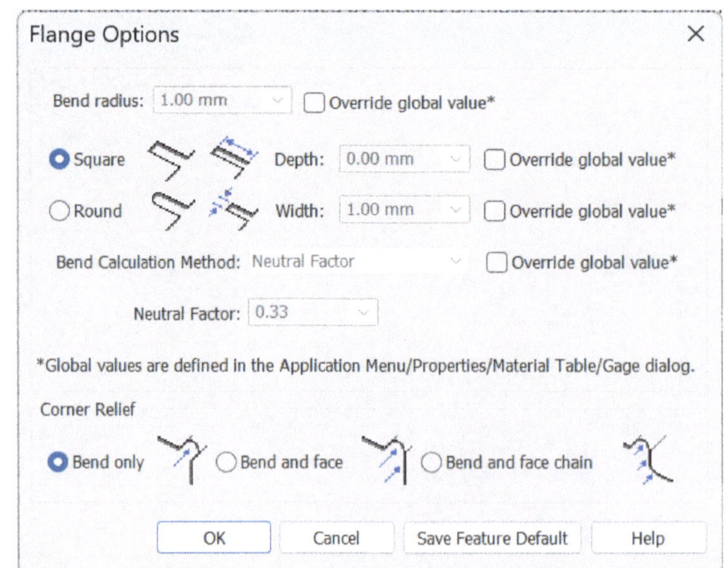

Under the **Corner Relief** section, select an option to define the type of corner relief. The three types of corner reliefs are shown below. Click **OK** to close the dialog.

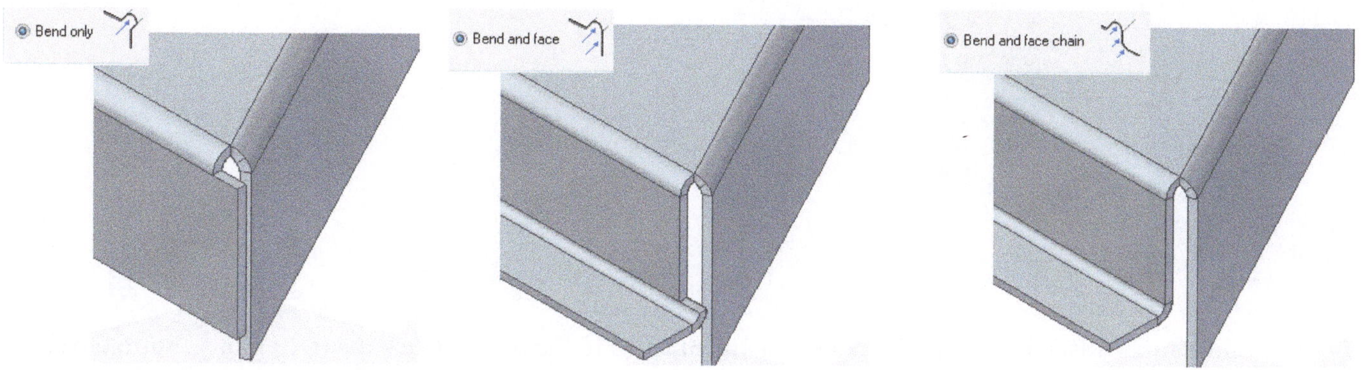

On the command bar, select an option from the **Measurement Point** drop-down menu. Both the measurement points are explained in the illustration below.

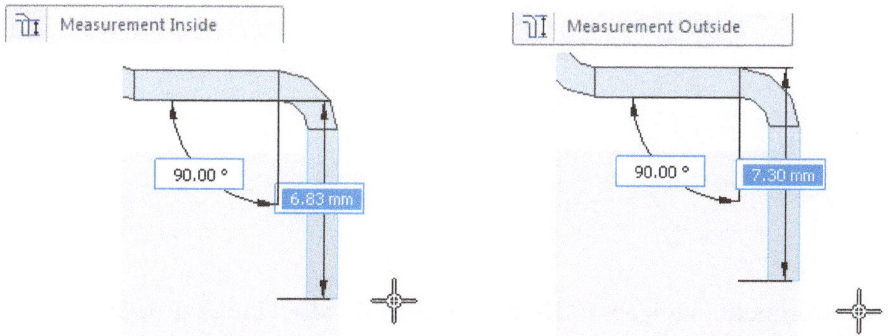

Define the material side using the **Material Side** drop-down menu. The three types of material sides are shown below.

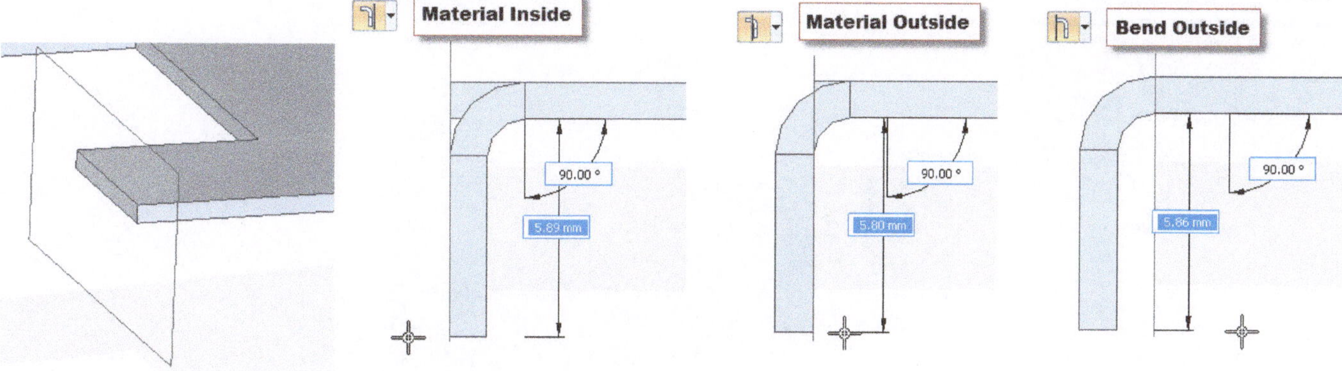

Click the **Partial Flange** icon to create the flange at the middle of the selected edge.

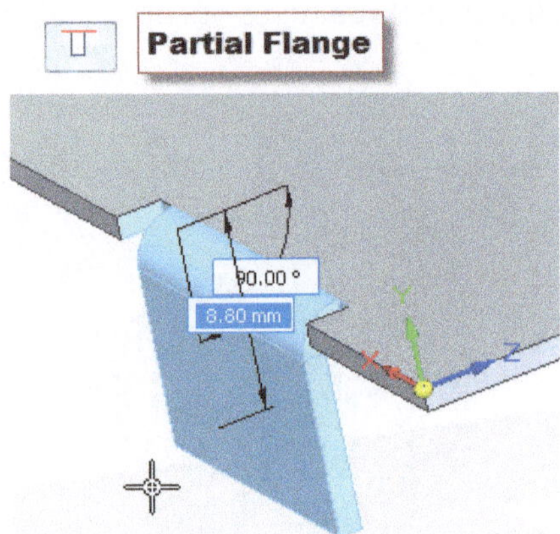

Type-in values in the distance and angle boxes that are attached to the flange. Click the right mouse button to create the flange.

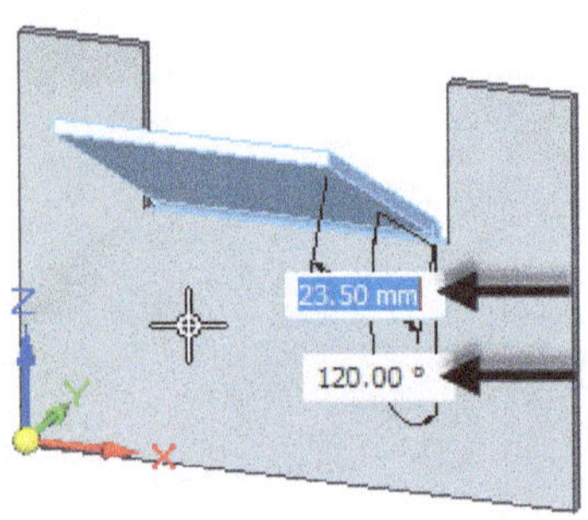

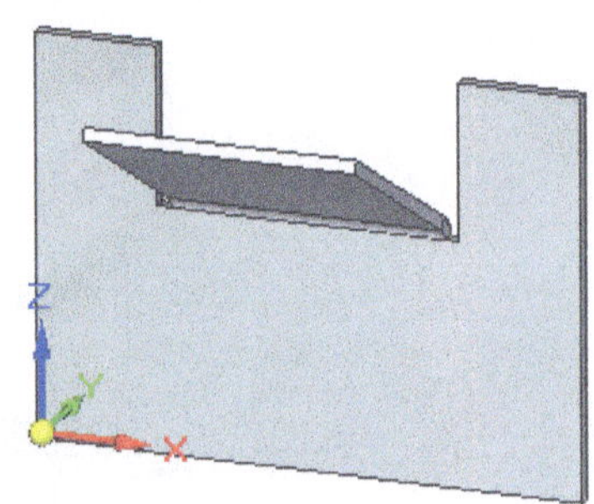

Flange (Ordered)

To generate a flange within the Ordered environment, navigate to **Home > Sheet Metal > Flange** drop-down > **Flange**. Subsequently, designate the edge where the flange is to be added. Then, define the material side of the flange by selecting the **Material Outside**, **Material Inside**, or **Bend Outside** icons, as discussed previously in the Synchronous part. Next, select an option from the **Flange Placement** drop-down: the **Full Width**, **Centered**, **At End**, **From Both Ends**, or **From End** option.

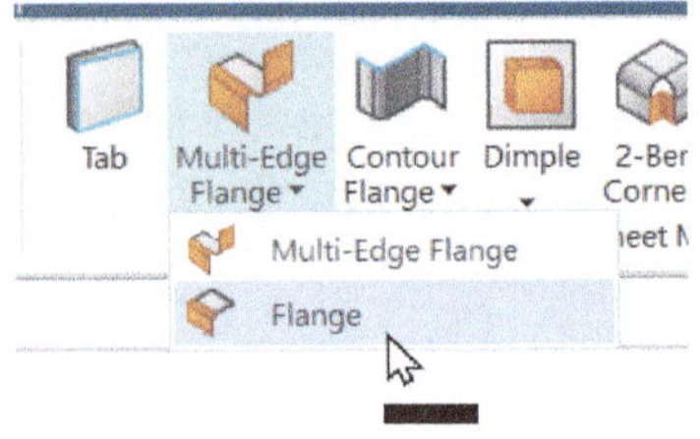

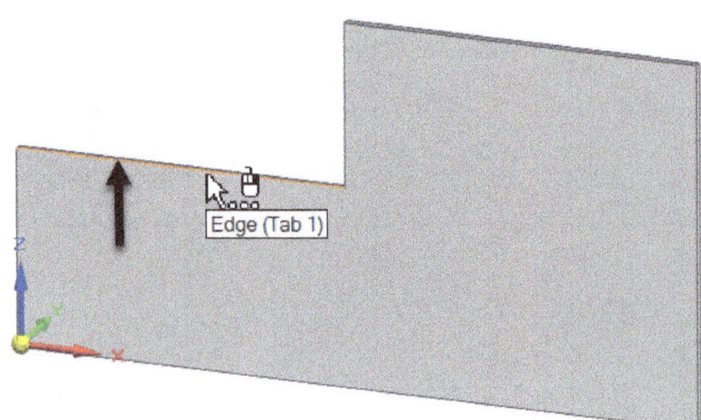

The **Full Width** option produces a flange along the entire length of the chosen edge.

The **Centered** option generates a flange at the center of the selected edge.

The **At End** option forms a flange at one end of the selected edge.

The **From Both Ends** option constructs a flange measured from both ends of the selected edge.

The **From End** option constructs a flange measured from the chosen end of the selected edge.

Choose either the **Inside Dimension** or **Outside Dimension** icon from the **Dimension Placement** section. Hover the cursor on either side of the sheet metal face to designate the extrusion's side. Enter a value in the **Distance** box and press ENTER to establish the flange length.

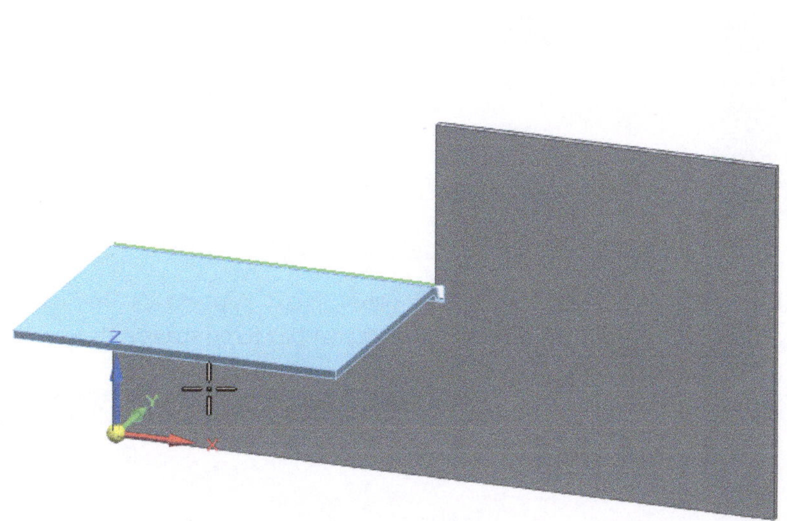

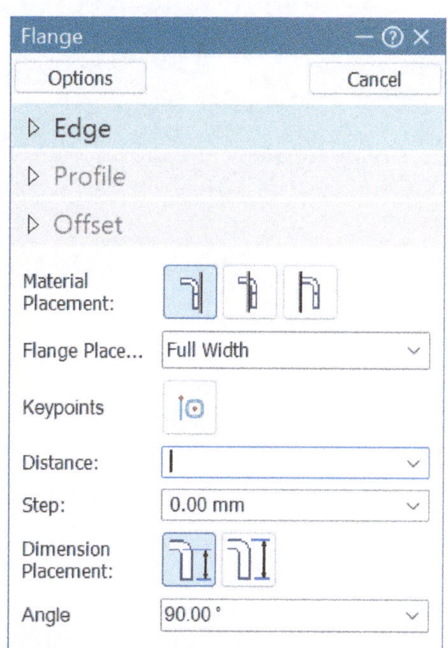

Click the **Offset** section if desiring to displace the flange from the chosen edge. This section comprises three icons: **Offset Flange**, **Match Face**, and **No Offset**. The **Offset Flange** option permits the specification of the offset distance from the chosen edge. The **Match Face** option enables the selection of a face or plane against which the flange is to be offset. As implied by its name, the **No Offset** option facilitates the creation of a flange without an offset.

Click the **Finish** button on the command bar to create the flange.

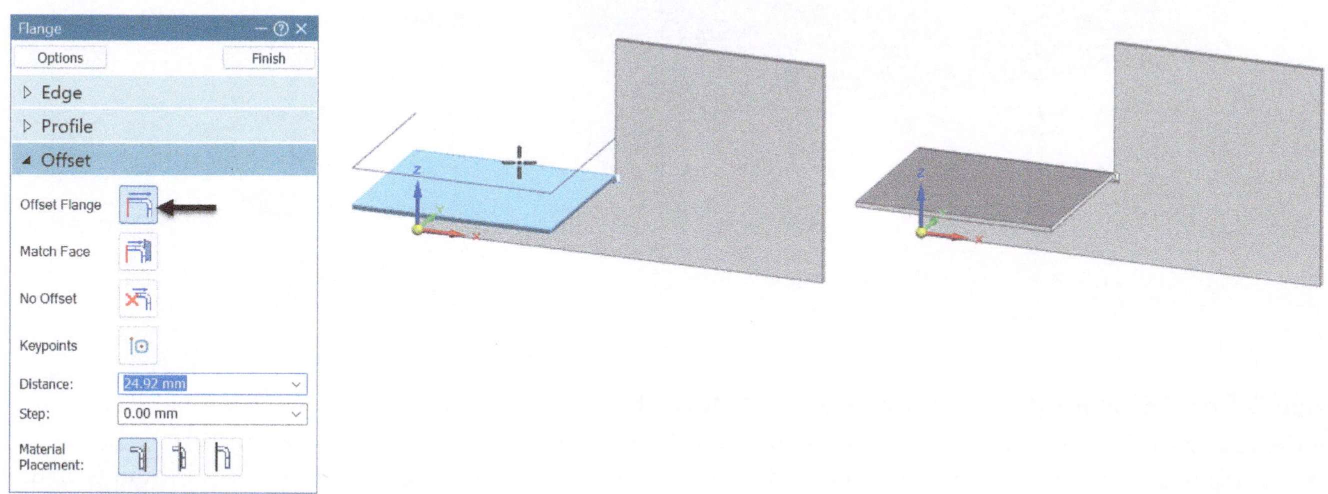

Multi-Edge Flange (Ordered)

Use the **Multi-Edge Flange** command to create flanges by selecting multiple edges at a time. On the ribbon, click

Home > **Sheet Metal** > **Flange** drop-down > **Multi-Edge Flange** . Select the two or more edges from the sheet metal geometry. Click the green check on the command bar to accept the selection. Move the pointer on either side of the sheet metal face to define the side of the extrusion.

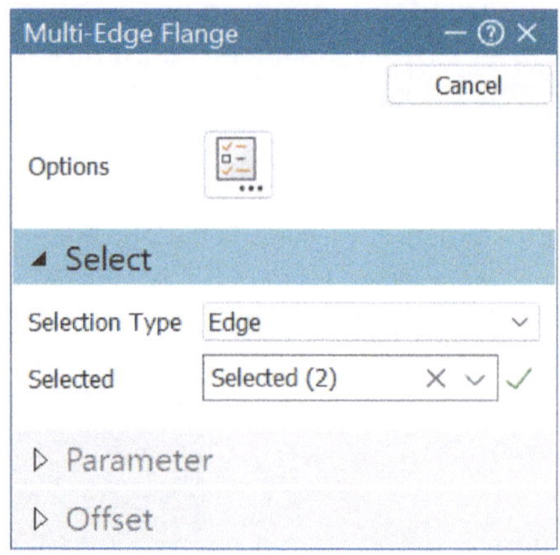

Select the **Trim** option on the command bar if the flanges intersect with each other. Next, type-in a value in the **Distance** box and press ENTER to define the flange length. Click **Finish** on the command bar to complete the multi-edge flange.

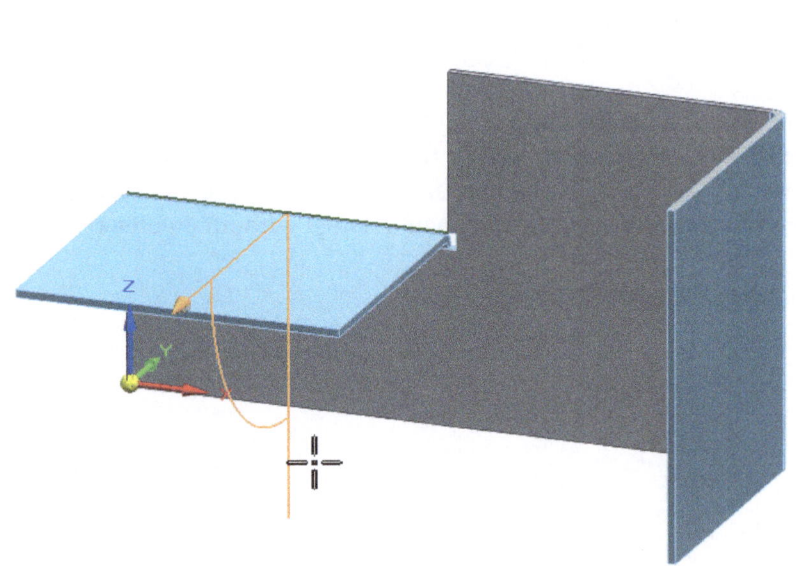

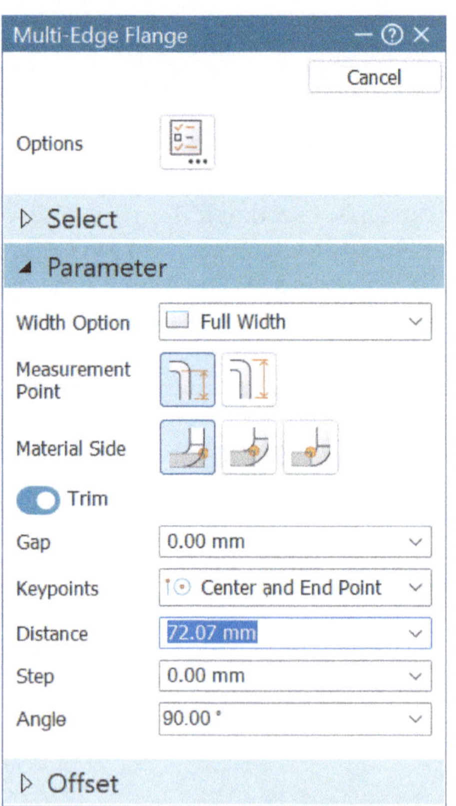

Close 2-Bend Corner (Synchronous and Ordered)

The **Close 2-Bend Corner** command allows you to control the appearance of sheet metal seams. For example, when two flanges meet at a corner, this command allows you to close the gap between them. In addition to that, it applies a corner treatment. Activate this command (click **Home > Sheet Metal > Close 2-Bend Corner** on the ribbon) and click on two bends that meet at a corner. On the command bar, select the required corner treatment.

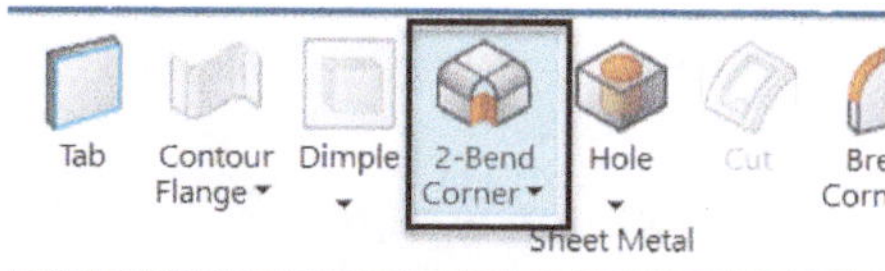

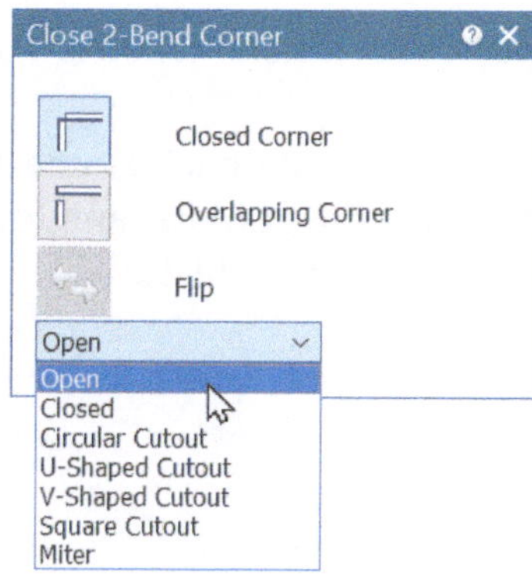

There are seven types of corner treatments available in the **Corner Treatment** drop-down menu, as shown below.

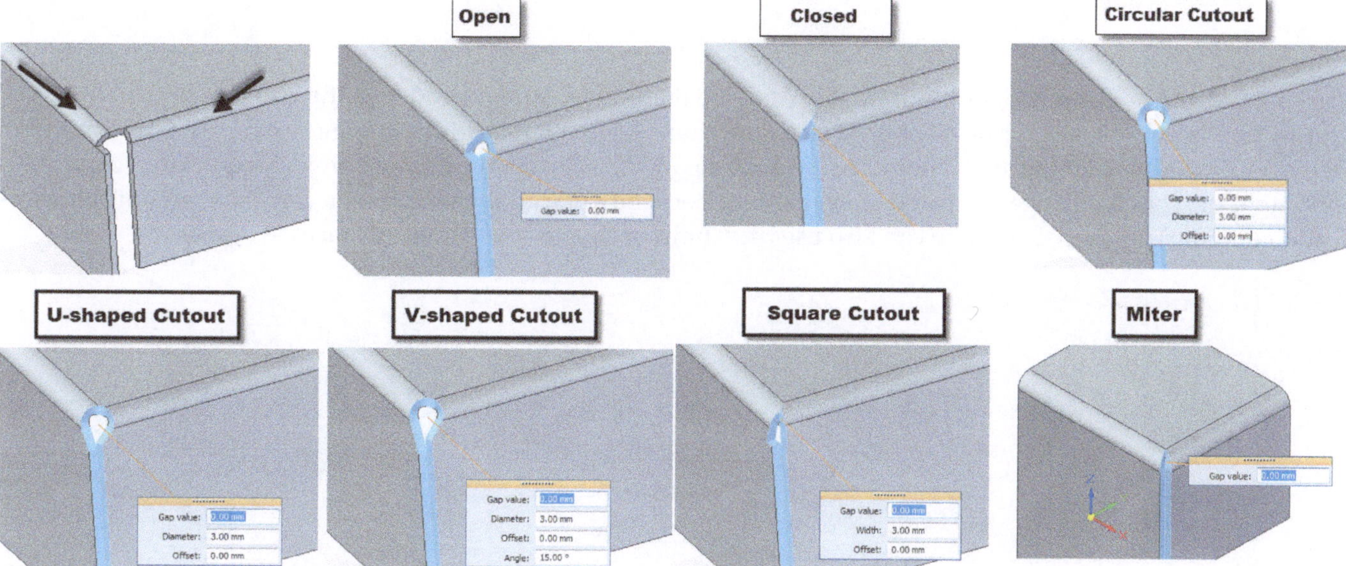

Note: The **Miter** corner treatment can be created only when the flanges are similar and perpendicular to each other.

On the command bar, click the **Overlap** icon to overlap one flange on the other. Next, type-in a value in the **Overlap ratio** box. Click the **Flip** icon to change the overlapping side.

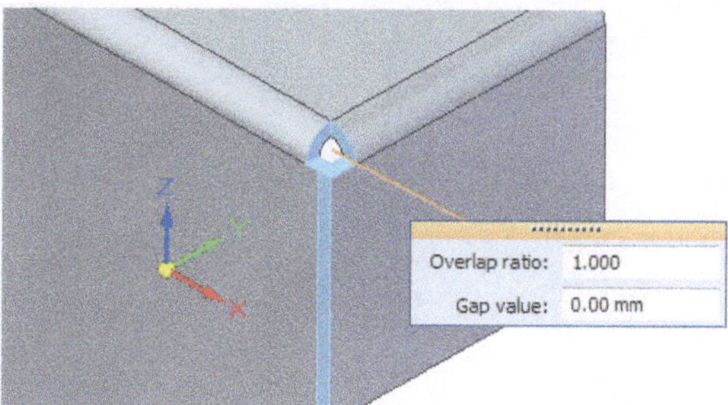

Contour Flange (Synchronous)

The contour flange is another basic type of sheet metal feature. To create a contour flange, you need to have an open sketch. Activate the **Contour Flange** command (click **Home > Sheet Metal > Contour Flange** on the ribbon) and click on the open sketch. Drag the mouse pointer and type-in a value in the distance box that is attached to the preview. Press Enter to create the contour flange feature.

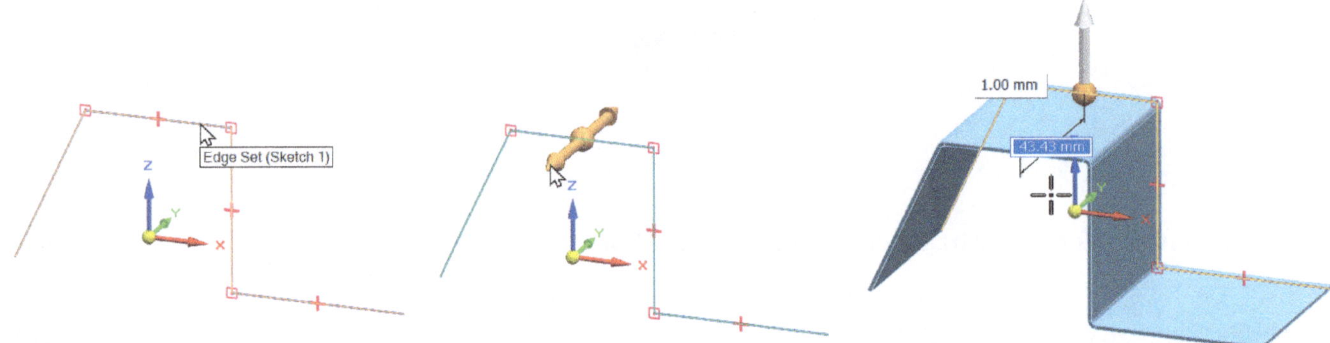

You can also add contour flanges to a base tab. Activate the **Line** command and lock the end face of the tab feature. On the locked face, draw an open sketch, and then activate the **Contour Flange** command. Click on the sketch, and then click on the arrow pointing towards the model. The contour flange preview appears. You will notice that the contour flange is created along the face perpendicular to the sketch. You can click on multiple faces to add contour flanges to them. You can also use the **Chain** option to select multiple faces at a time.

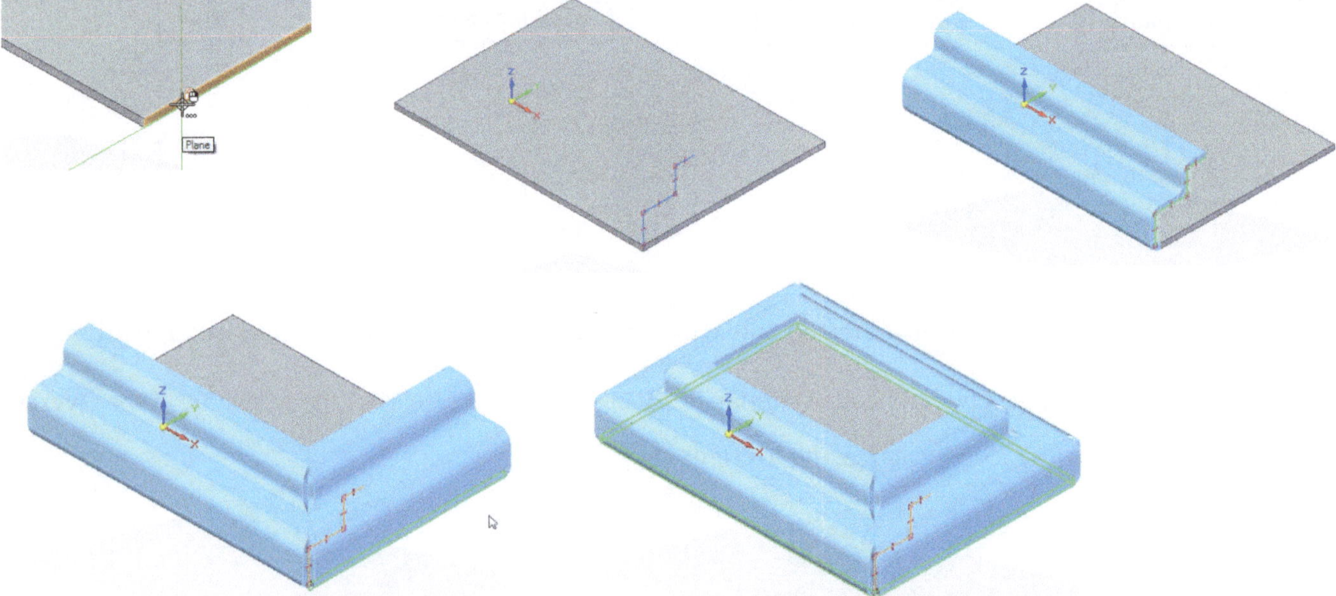

If you want to create a contour flange only up to a certain distance, click the **Partial Flange** icon on the command bar and type-in the distance value.

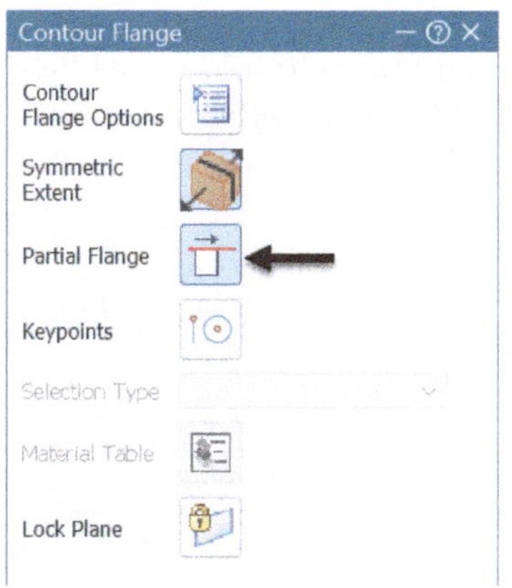

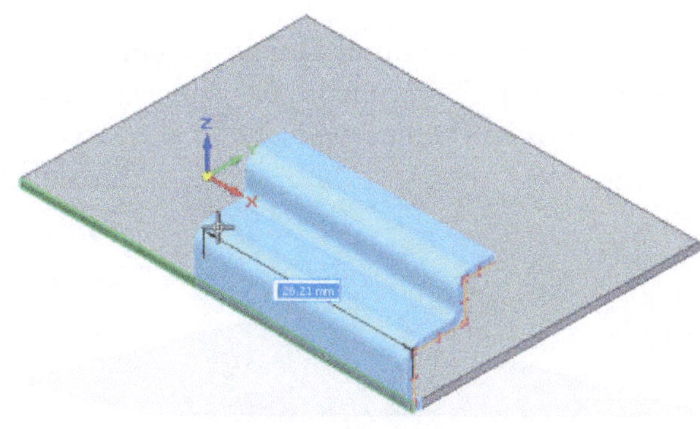

On the command bar, click the **Contour Flange Options** icon to open the **Contour Flange Options** dialog. On this dialog, click the **Miters and Corners** tab and check the **Miter** option to apply miter to the contour flange's ends. Under the **Interior Corners** section, check the **Close Corner** option to apply treatment to the corners.

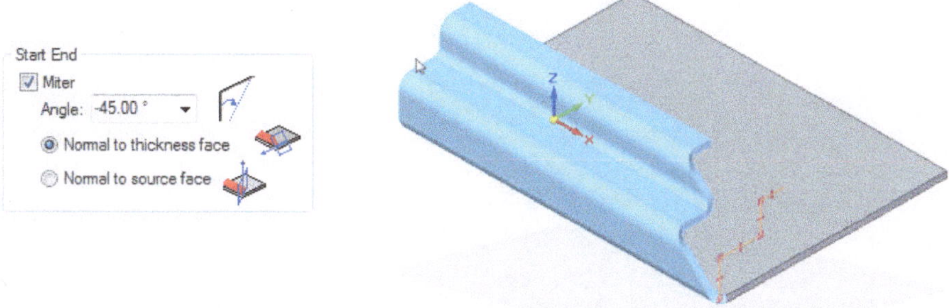

Click **OK** on the dialog to close it. Right click to create the counter flange.

Contour Flange (Ordered)

To generate a contour flange in the ordered environment, navigate to **Home > Sheet Metal > Flange** drop-down **> Contour Flange** on the ribbon. Subsequently, choose the sketch from the graphics window, and click the **Accept** button. Enter a value in the **Thickness** box. Position the pointer on either side of the sketch to delineate the thickness side of the contour flange. Move the pointer and click to establish the extrusion distance of the contour flange. Conclude the process by selecting **Finish** on the command bar.

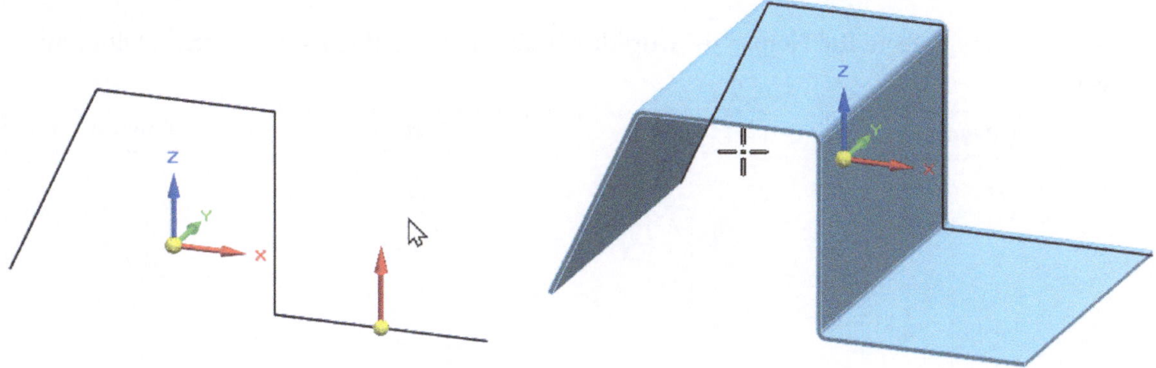

Hem (Synchronous and Ordered)

The **Hem** command is used to fold an edge of a sheet metal part. To add a hem, activate the **Hem** command (click

Home > Sheet Metal > Contour Flange > Hem on the ribbon) and select the edge you need to fold over (click the **Accept** button on the command bar after selection the Ordered environment). The **Material Setback** drop-down menu controls whether the material is added inside or outside the existing edge on the command bar.

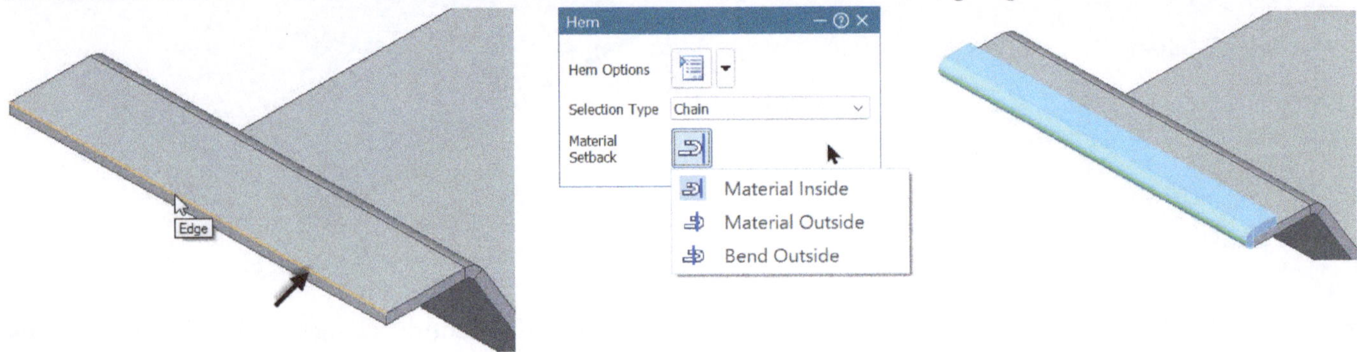

On the command bar, click the **Hem Options** icon to open the **Hem Option** dialog.

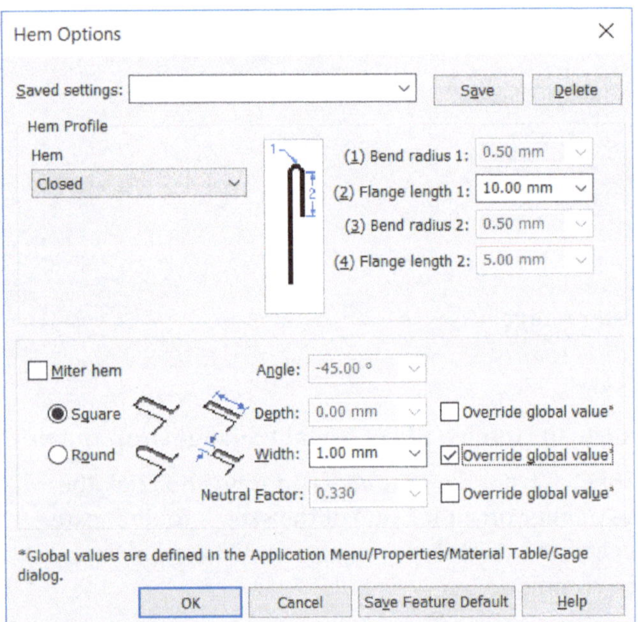

On this dialog, select a hem type from the **Hem type** drop-down menu and define its parameters. Different hem types are shown below.

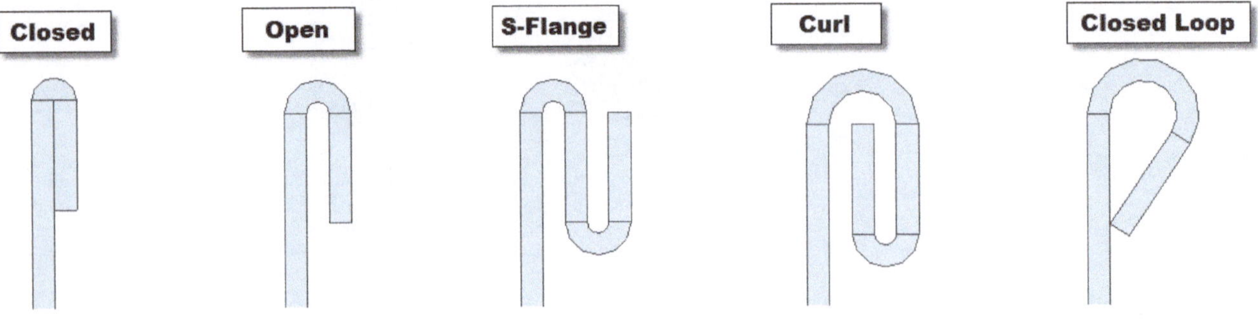

If you want to bevel the hem's end faces, check the **Miter hem** option and type-in a value in the **Angle** box. Click the **OK** button to close the dialog, and then right-click to complete the hem feature.

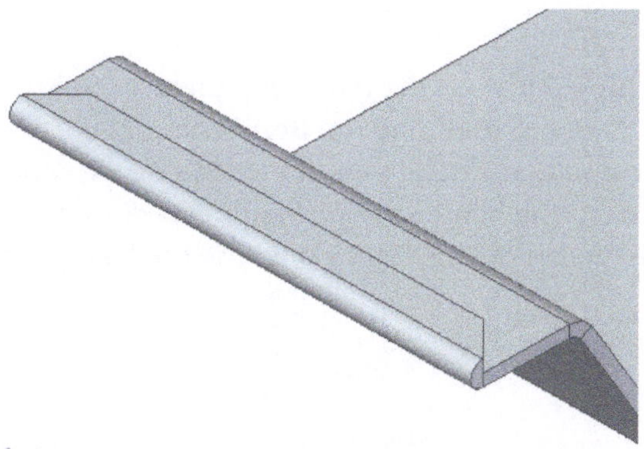

Bend (Synchronous)

In addition to adding flanges and contour flanges, you can also bend a flat sheet using the **Bend** command. First, draw a sketch line on the flat sheet. Activate the **Bend** command (click **Home > Sheet Metal > Bend** on the ribbon) and click on the sketched line. A two-sided arrow appears on the line. Click on either side of the arrow to define the side to be folded. Type-in a value in the angle box to change the folding angle. Click on the arrow attached to the folded face to reverse the folding direction.

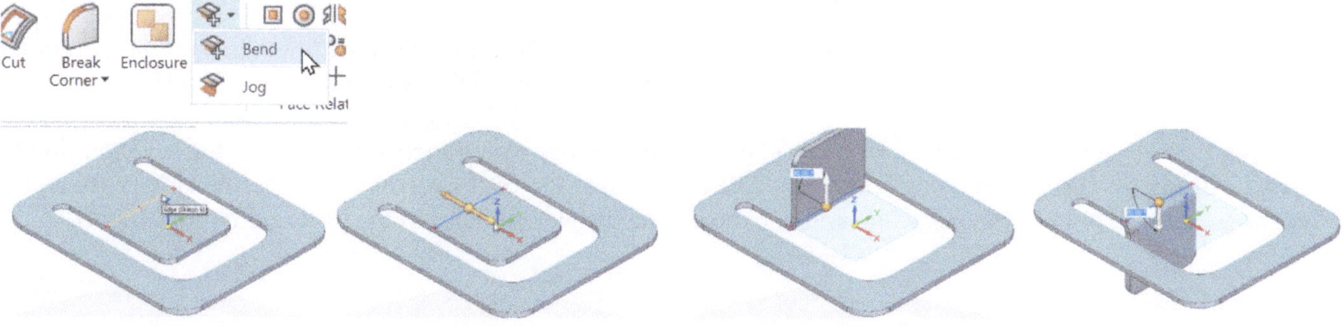

On the Command bar, click **Material Side > Center of Mold Lines** option to position the bend's center on the sketched line. Click **Material Side > Mold Lines** option to position the sketch line on the left or right edge of the bend.

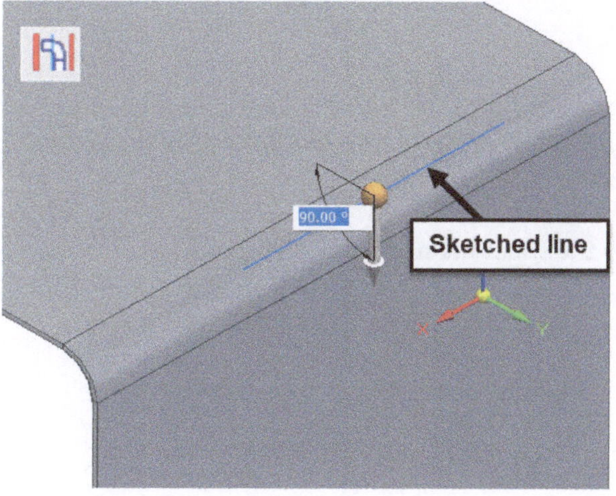

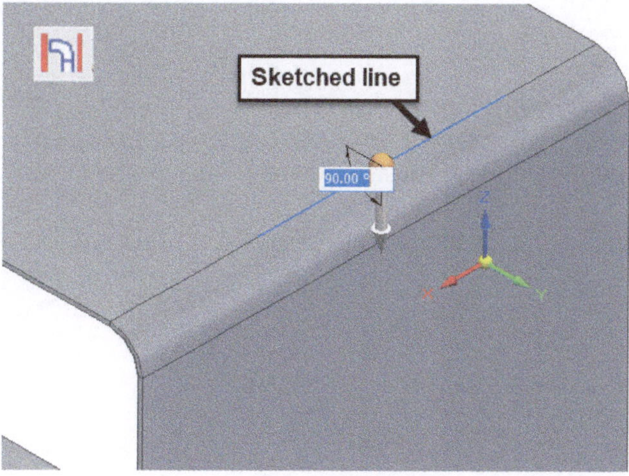

Click anywhere in the graphics window to complete the bend creation.

Bend (Ordered)

To initiate a bend feature in the Ordered environment, begin by sketching a line on the flat sheet. Ensure the line comprises a singular linear element to indicate the approximate bend location. Activate the **Bend** command (navigate to **Home > Sheet Metal > Bend** drop-down > **Bend** on the ribbon) and select the sketched line. Accept the selection by clicking the **Accept** button on the command bar. Establish the bend location with respect to the profile, specify the side of the part undergoing movement, and define the bend direction. Conclude the feature by clicking **Finish**.

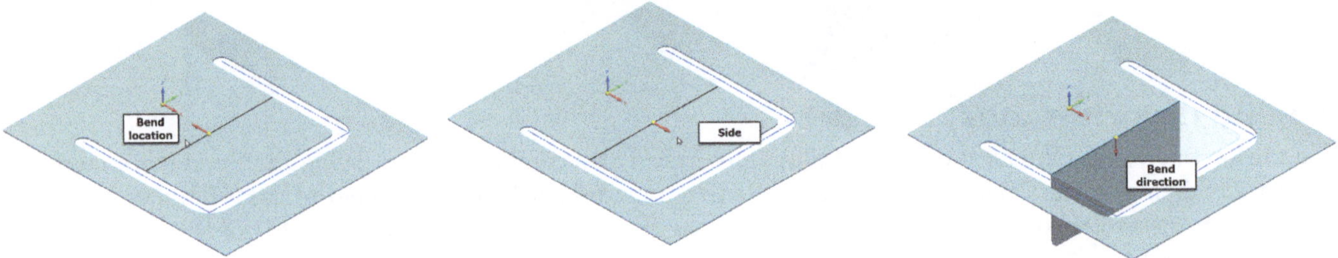

Jog (Synchronous and Ordered)

The **Jog** command is used to add a jog or offset to a flat sheet. To add a jog to the sheet metal part, first, you must define its location. You can do this by drawing a sketch line. Next, activate the **Jog** command (click **Home > Sheet metal > Jog** on the ribbon) and click on the sketched line. A two-sided arrow appears on the selected line (a red arrow appears in the Ordered environment). Click on either side of the arrow to define the side of the bend (Move the pointer on either side of the line and click to define the side of bend in the Ordered environment).

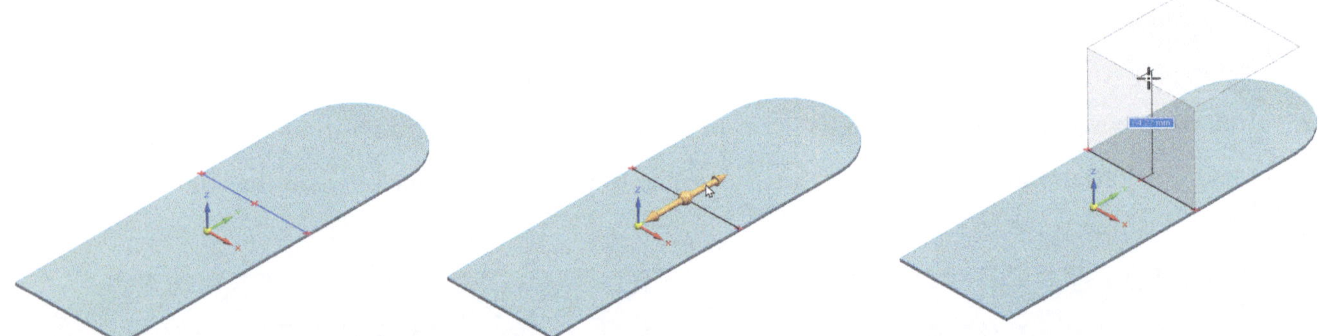

To define measurement points, select an option from the **Measurement Point** drop-down menu on the command bar within the Synchronous environment, or utilize the **Offset Dimension** or **Full Dimension** icons in the Ordered environment. Both measurement point types are illustrated below.

Type-in a value in the distance box and press Enter to add a jog to the sheet metal part.

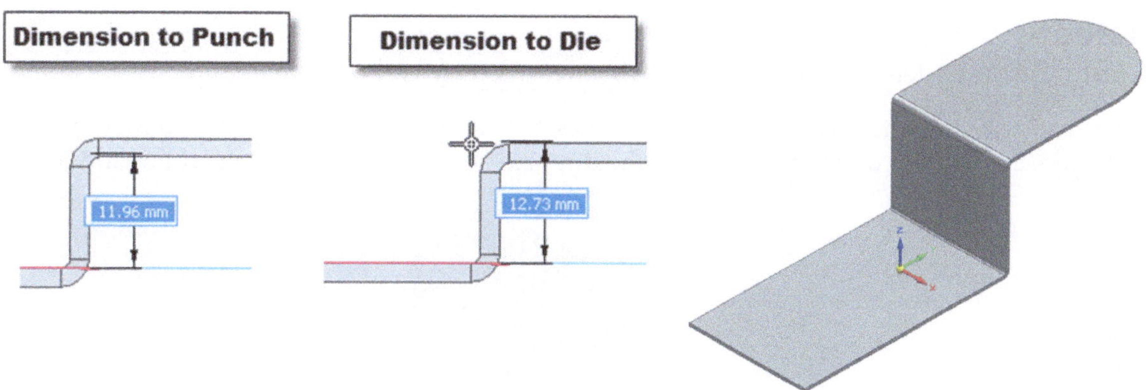

Dimple (Synchronous)

The **Dimple** command is used to add a dimple to a flat sheet by deforming it. To add a dimple to a sheet metal part, first, you must define its shape, size, and location. You can do this by drawing a closed sketch. After creating a closed sketch, activate the **Dimple** command (click **Home > Sheet Metal > Dimple** on the ribbon) and click in the sketch region. The sketch will be converted into a dimple shape. Type-in a value in the value box displayed in on the preview of the dimple to define its depth. Click the arrow that appears on the dimple to change its direction.

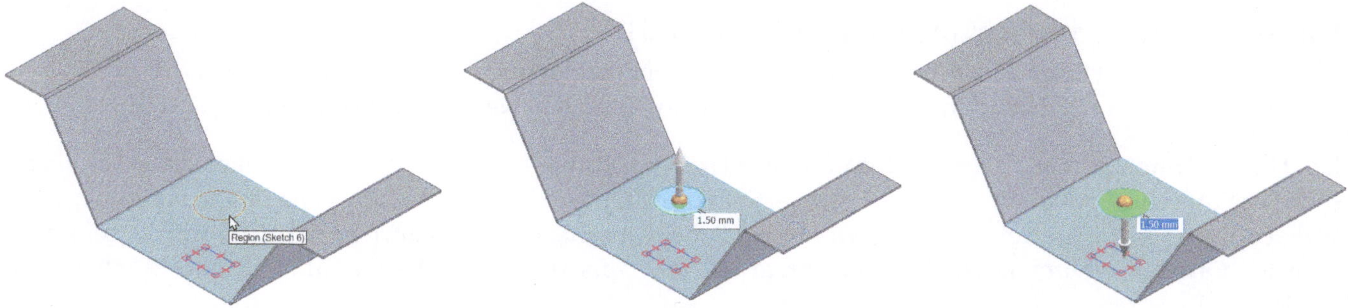

On the command bar, click the **Dimple Options** icon to open the **Dimple Options** dialog. On this dialog, type-in the values of taper angle, punch radius, die radius, and corner radius. Click **OK** to close the dialog. On the command bar, define the representation of the profile. You can select **Profile Represents Die** or **Profile Represents Punch**. Type-in a value in the distance box attached to the feature, and then press Enter to create the dimple.

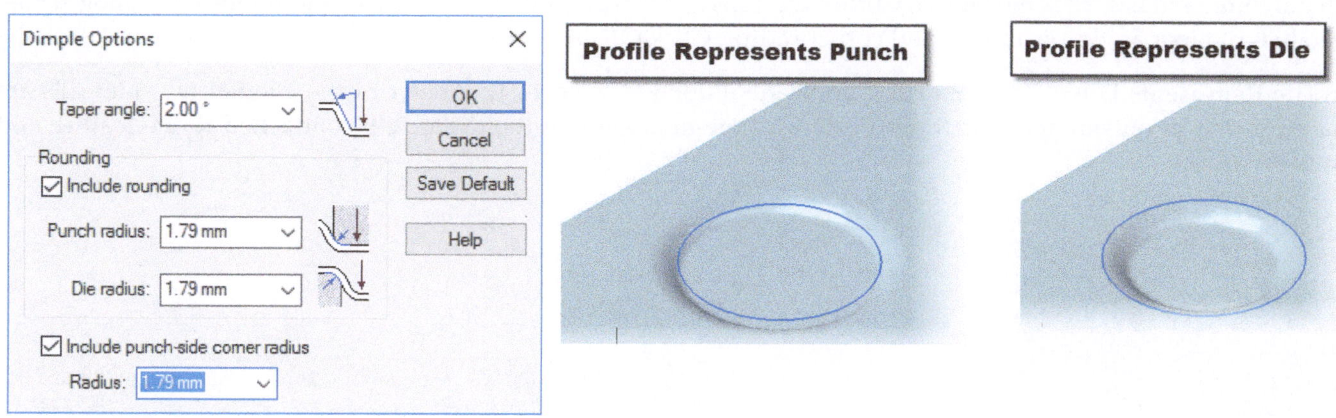

Dimple (Ordered)

To create a dimple feature in the Ordered environment, click **Home > Sheet Metal > Dimple** drop-down > **Dimple** . Next, select a sketch located on the sheet metal face and click the **Accept** button. Move the pointer on either side of the sheet metal face and click to define the extent of the dimple. Next, click **Finish** on the command bar.

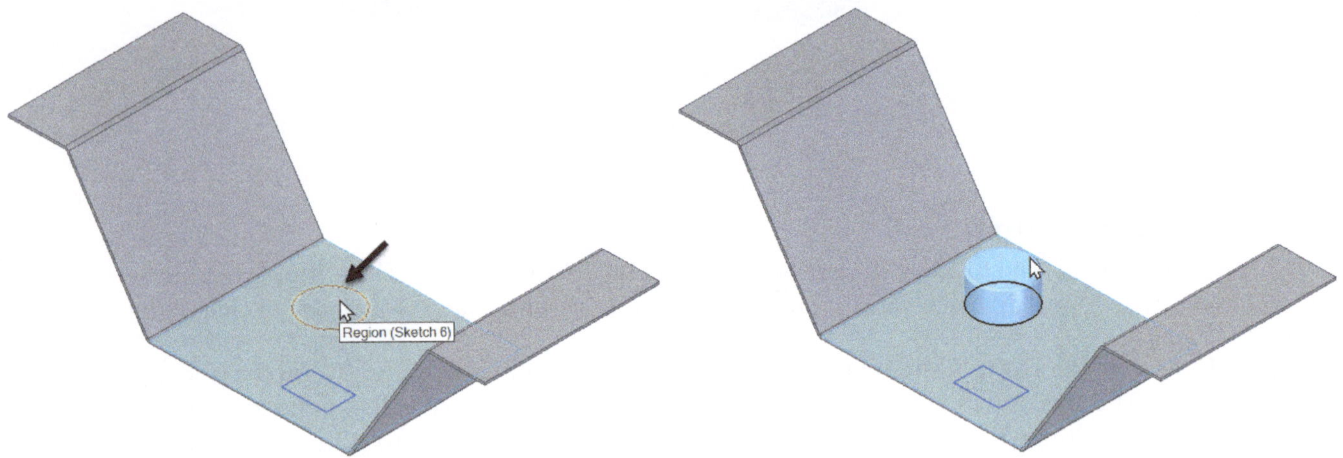

Drawn Cutout (Synchronous and Ordered)

The drawn cutout and dimple feature are almost alike, except that an opening is created in case of a drawn cutout. In order to create a drawn cutout, first, you must have a closed sketch. Next, activate the **Drawn Cutout** command (click **Home > Sheet Metal > Dimple drop-down > Drawn Cutout** on the ribbon) and click inside the sketch region (click the Accept button to accept the selection in the Ordered environment). Type-in a value in the value box that appears on the preview of the drawn cutout (Type-in a value in the Distance box available on the command bar in the Ordered environment). Click on the arrow that appears on the drawn cutout feature to change its direction.

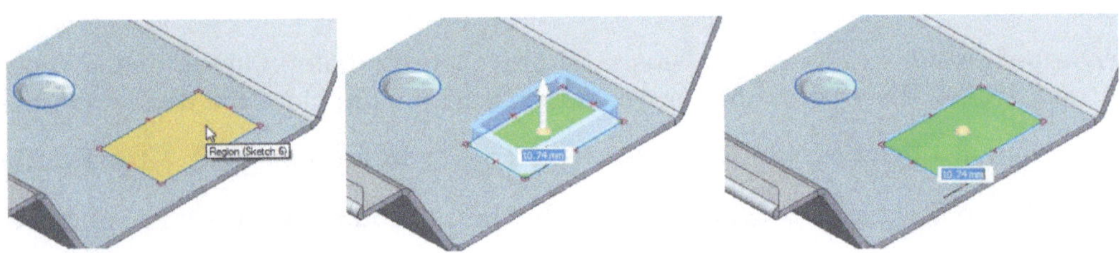

On the command bar, click the **Drawn Cutout Options** icon to open the **Drawn Cutout Options** dialog. Type-in values of taper angle, die radius, and corner radius. Click **OK** to close the dialog. On the command bar, click the **Profile Represents Die** or **Profile Represents Punch** icon. This determines whether the sidewalls are placed inside or outside the sketch profile. Next, type-in a value in the distance box attached to the feature and press Enter.

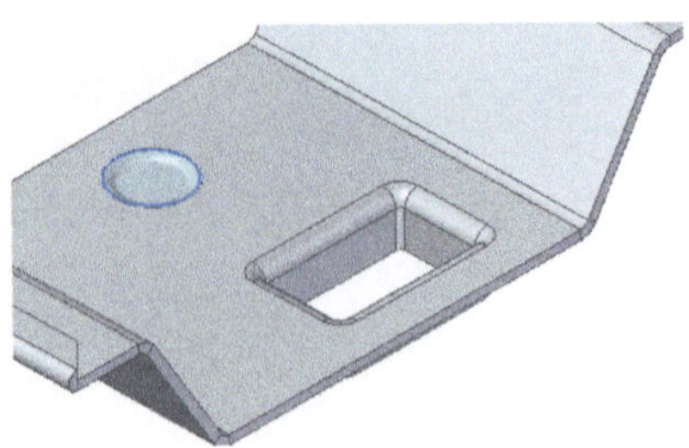

Bead (Synchronous and Ordered)

The **Bead** command creates a bead feature, which stiffens the sheet metal part. First, you must have a sketch, which defines its size and shape to create a bead feature. If the sketch has curved edges, then ensure that they are tangent continuous. Next, activate the **Bead** command (click **Home > Sheet Metal > Dimple drop-down > Bead** on the ribbon) and click on the sketch (click the Accept button to confirm the selection in the Ordered environment). Click on the arrow that appears on the bead feature to change its direction.

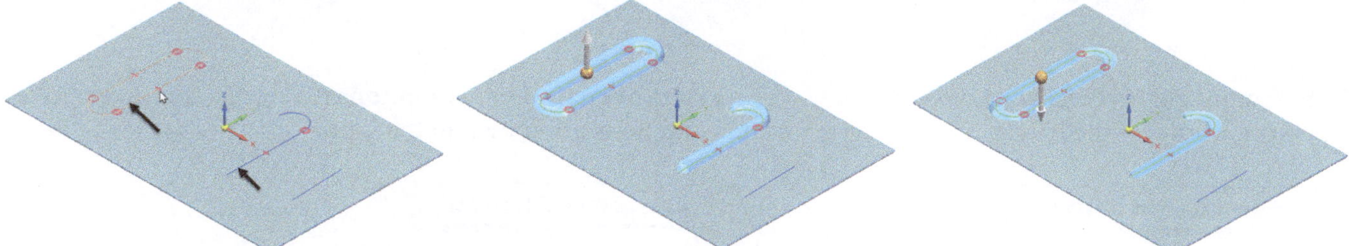

On the command bar, click the **Options** button to open the **Bead Options** dialog. On this dialog, under **Cross Section**, select the cross-section type and define the size parameters. Check the **Include Rounding** option to apply rounds to the edges of the bead feature. Under the **End Conditions** section, select the desired option and click **OK** to close the dialog. Click the right mouse button to complete the bead feature.

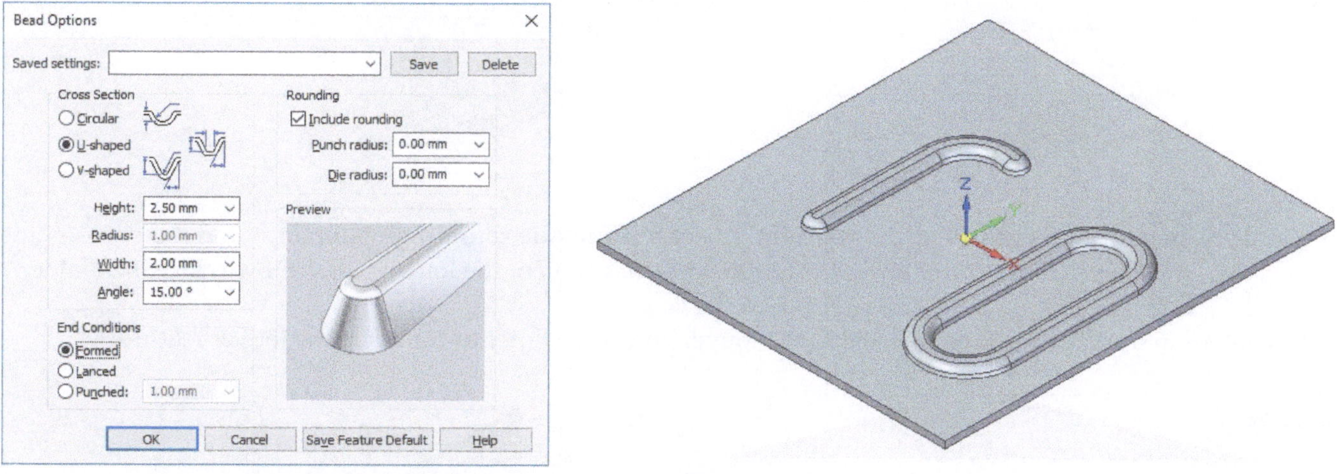

Louver (Synchronous)

Solid Edge provides you with the **Louver** command, which makes it easy to create louvers. Activate this command (click **Home > Sheet Metal > Dimple > Louver** on the ribbon) and place the mouse pointer on a face. You will notice that a louver appears parallel to an edge. Press N or B on your keyboard to change the orientation of the louver. Press F3 on your keyboard to lock the face, and then place the mouse pointer on an edge and press E to add location dimension.

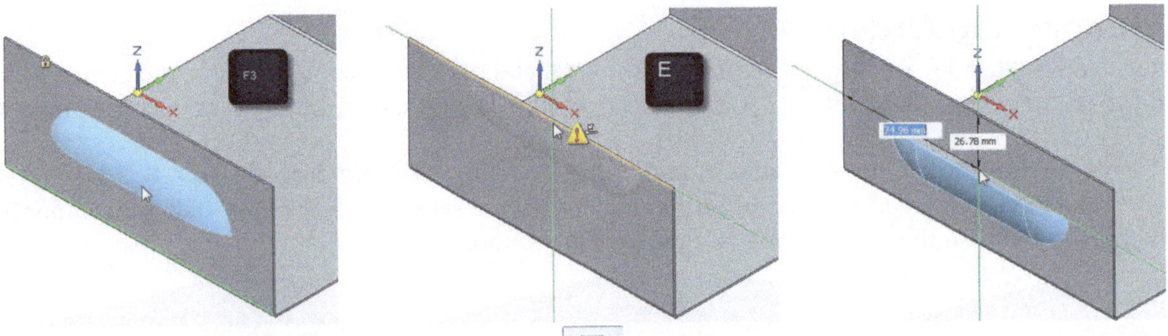

On the command bar, click the **Louver Options** icon to open the **Louver Options** dialog. On this dialog, select the end condition of the louver. The two types of end conditions are shown in the figure.

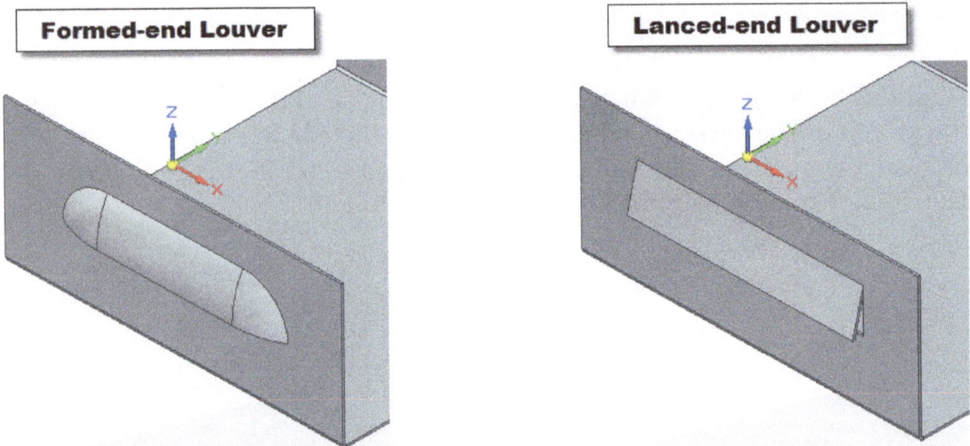

Type-in the values of the length, depth, and height. Check the **Include rounding** option to round the edges of the louver. Type-in values in the **X** and **Y** boxes to shift the default origin of the louver. Click **OK** to close the dialog.

Type-in values in dimension boxes attached to the louver and press Enter to complete the louver feature.

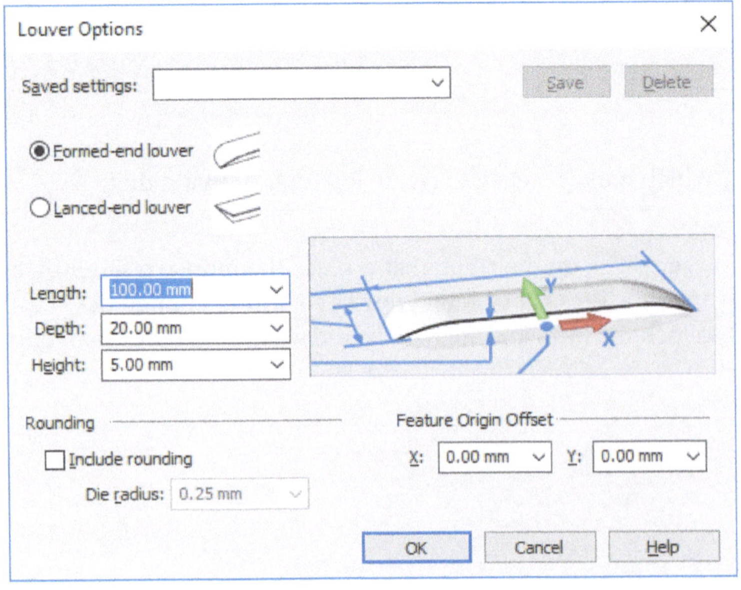

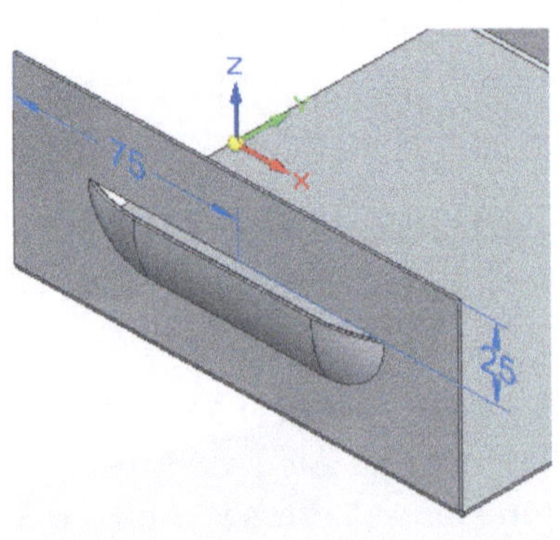

Louver (Ordered)

Solid Edge provides you with the **Louver** command, which makes it easy to create louvers. Activate this command (click **Home > Sheet Metal > Dimple > Louver** on the ribbon) and click on a face. Draw a line on the selected face and click **Close Sketch** on the ribbon. On the **Louver** command bar, type-in a value in the **Distance** box. Next, specify the depth side. Type-in a value in the **Height** box to define the height of the louver. Next, define the side of the height. You should ensure that the louver height should be less than or equal to width minus the material thickness. Click **Finish** on the command bar.

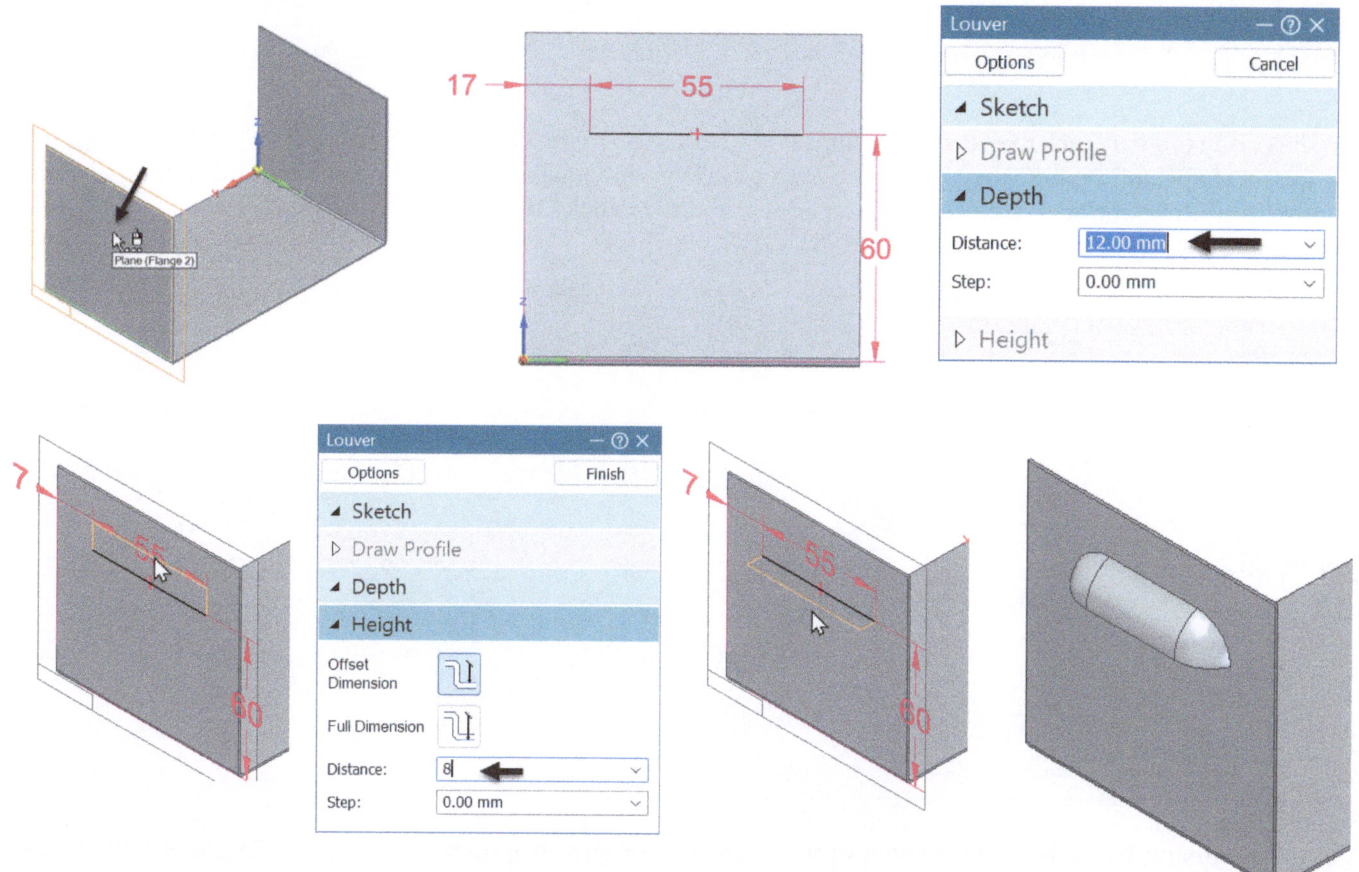

Gusset (Synchronous and Ordered)

Gussets are stiffening features created across a bend to reinforce the sheet metal part. To create a gusset, activate the **Gusset** command (click **Home > Sheet Metal > Dimple > Gusset** on the ribbon) and click on a bend face. A gusset feature appears along with a dimension box attached to it.

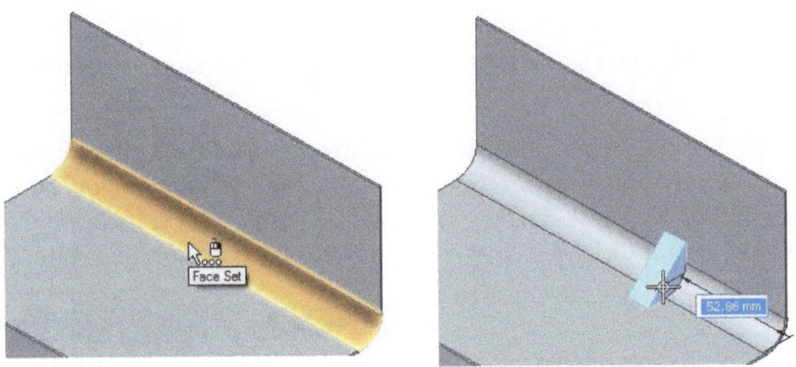

On the command bar, click the **Gusset Options** icon to open the **Gusset Options** dialog. On this dialog, select the gusset shape and type-in a value in the **Depth** box. Type-in values of taper angle, width, and radius. Check the **Include rounding** option to round the gusset edges, and then click **OK** to close the dialog.

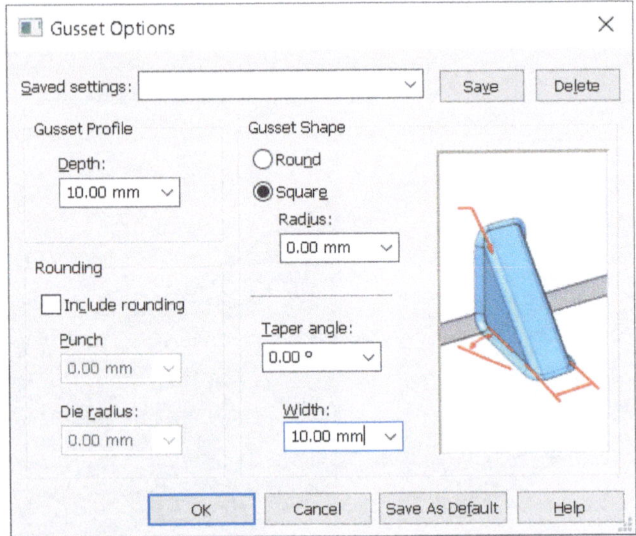

On the command bar, select a patterning option from the **Pattern** drop-down menu. The **Single** option creates a single gusset. The **Fit** option creates a pattern along the bend's total length using the count value you specify. The **Fill** option creates a pattern along the bend's total length using the spacing value you specify. The **Fixed** option creates a pattern by using the spacing and the count values that you specify.

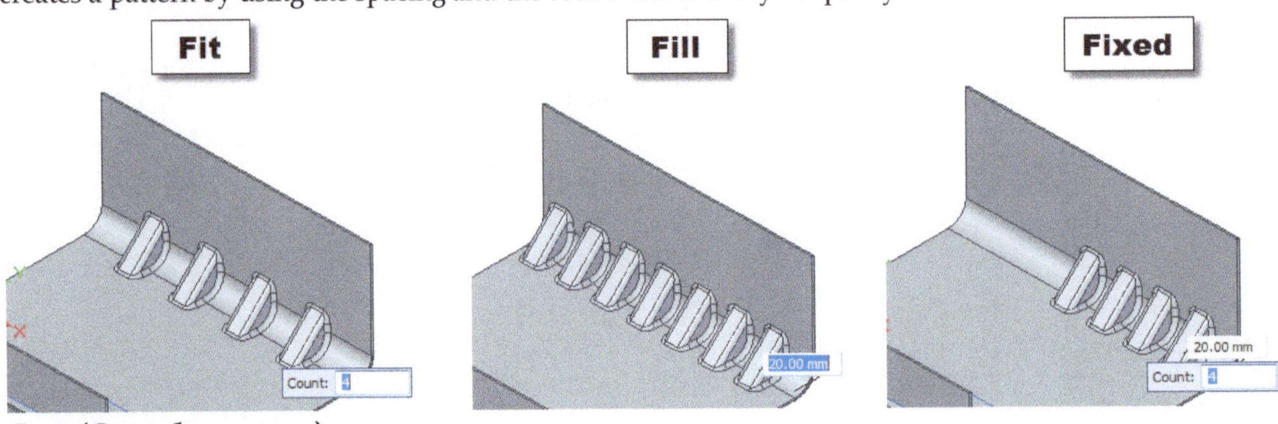

Cut (Synchronous)

When it is necessary to remove material from a sheet metal part, you must use the **Cut** command. First, draw a sketch and click inside it; a two-sided arrow appears. Click on this arrow and drag the mouse pointer into the geometry. On the command bar, select the extent type from the **Extents** drop-down menu. Click the right mouse button to create the cut.

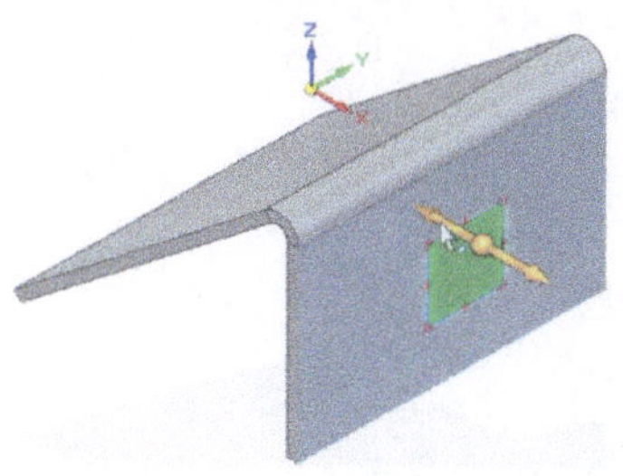

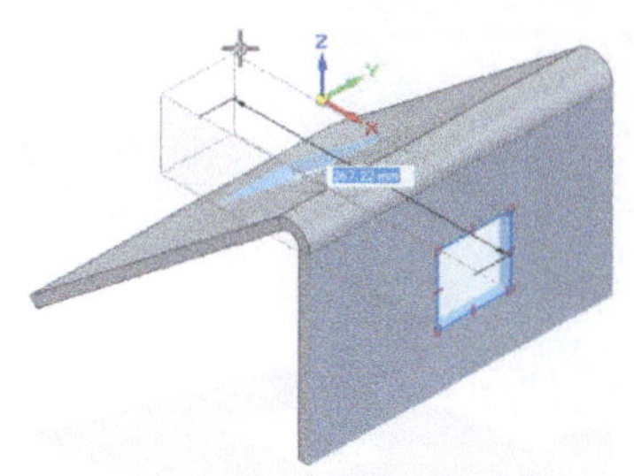

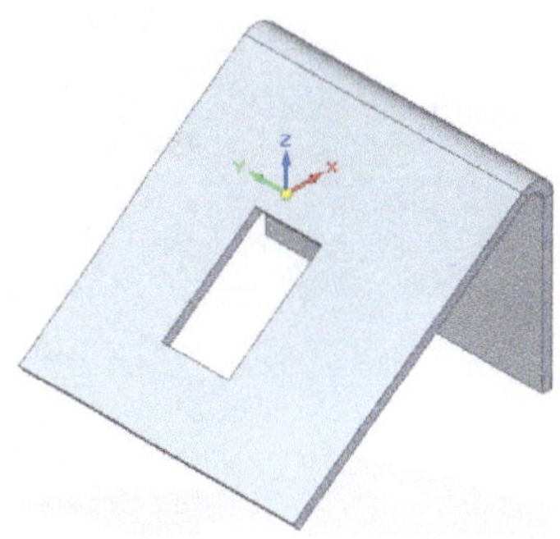

Creating Cut across Bends

If you need to create a cut across a bend, you must use the **Wrapped Cut** 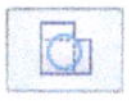 option. First, you must create a closed sketch across a bend. Press the Shift key and select all portions of the sketch region. On the command bar, activate the **Wrapped Cut** icon, and then click on the arrow handle pointing toward the model. You will notice that the sheet metal part is flattened, and a cut is created across the bend. Click the right mouse button to complete the cut.

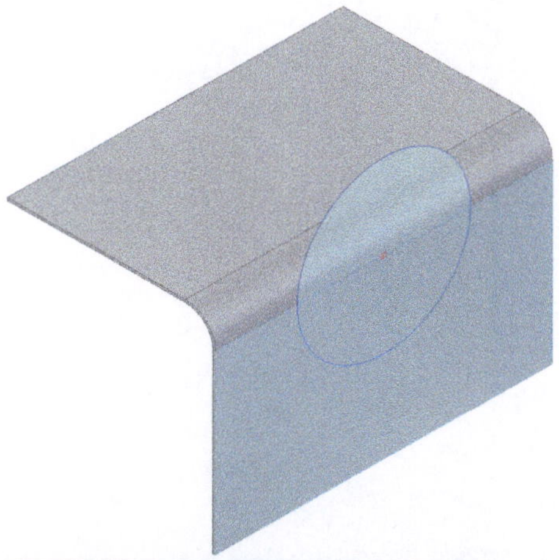

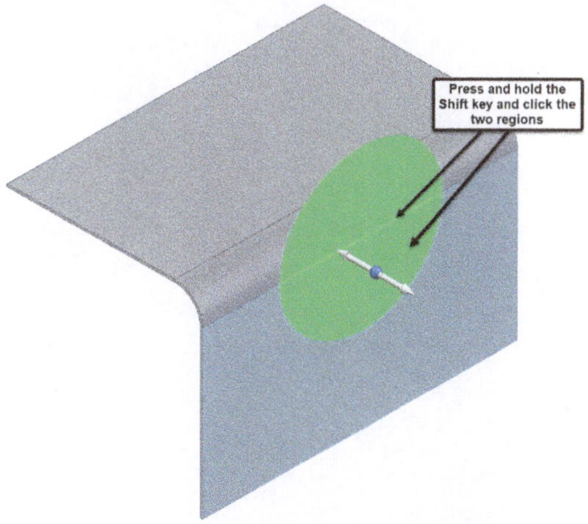

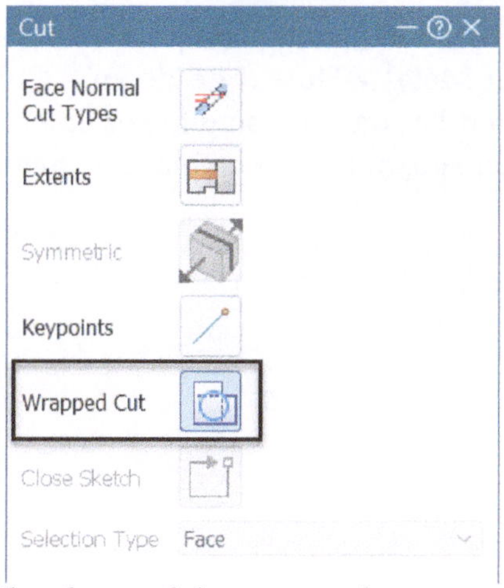

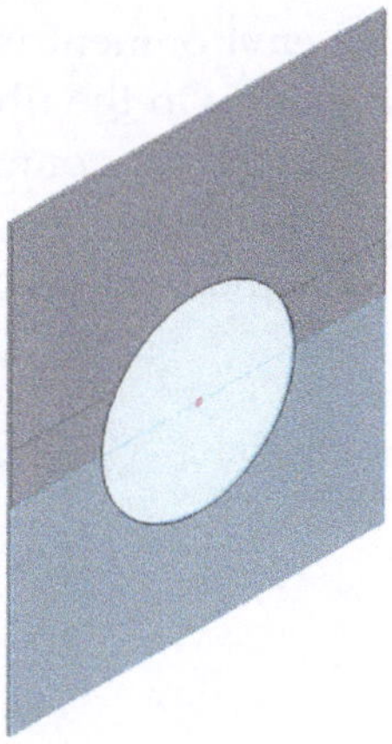

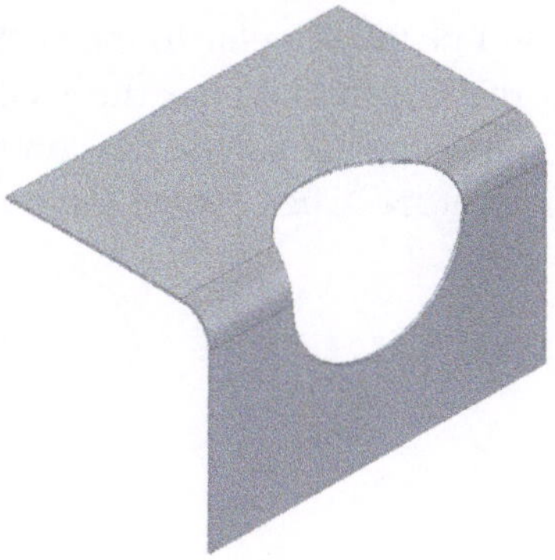

The shape of the wrapped cut-out remains constant even if you move the sheet metal face connected to the bend.

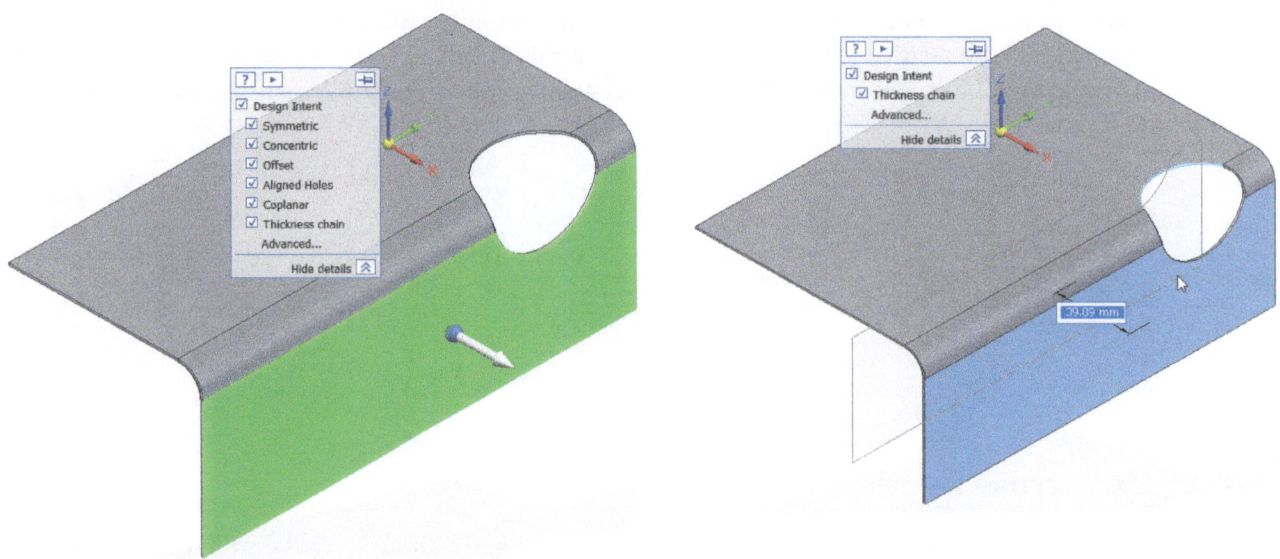

Also, the cut-out maintains its shape when you move its face. However, it displays an error message when you try to move the face over the bend.

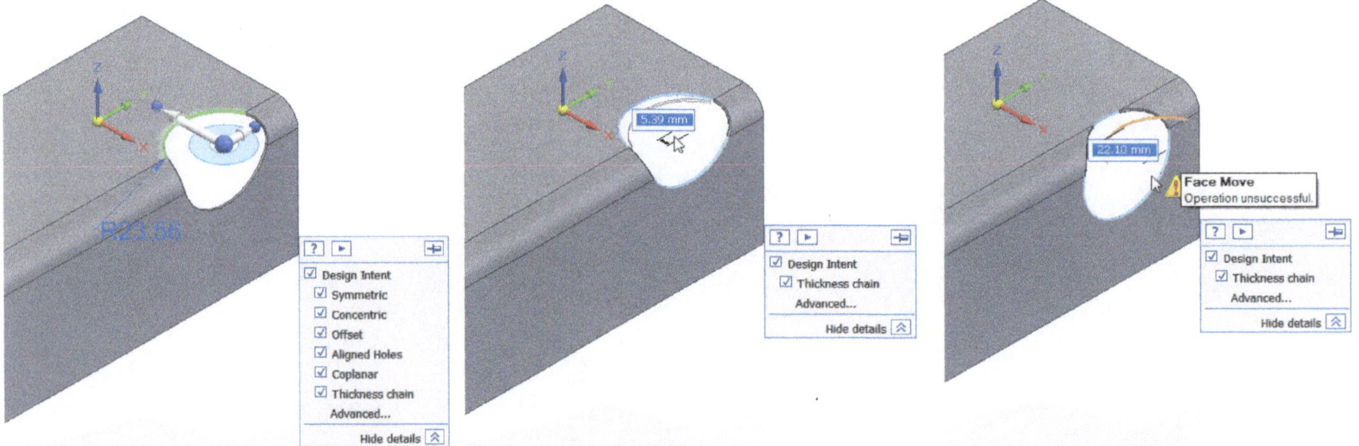

Cut (Ordered)

The **Cut** command in the Ordered environment is used to remove material by extruding the profile in the direction perpendicular to the sketch plane. On the ribbon, click **Home > Sheet Metal > Hole** drop-down > **Cut**. Select the sketch and click the green check on the command bar. Specify the extend of the cut using the options in the Extent Step section on the command bar. Move the pointer and click on either side of the sketch plane to create the cut feature. Click **Finish** on the command bar.

Break Corner (Synchronous and Ordered)

The **Break Corner** command is used to round or chamfer the sharp corner of a sheet metal part. Activate this command (click **Home > Sheet Metal > Break Corner** drop-down **> Break Corner** on the ribbon) and click on the corner edges of the sheet metal part. If you want to break all the sheet metal part corners, drag a window across the geometry. All the corners of the sheet metal part will be selected (click the **Accept** button on the command bar after selection in the Ordered environment).

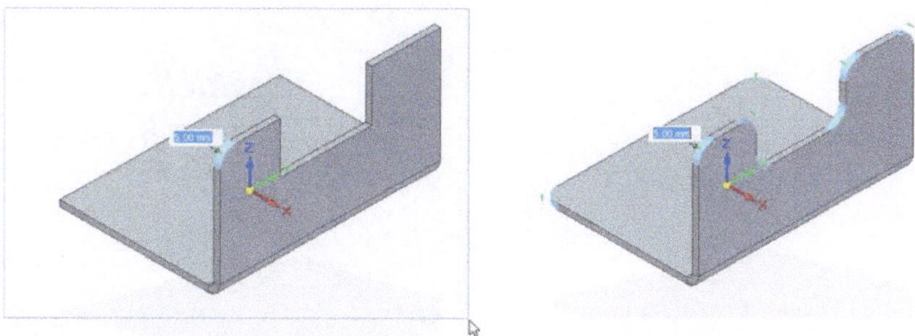

On the command bar, click the **Chamfer Corner** icon to apply chamfers to the corner edges. Type-in a value in the box that is attached to the round or chamfer. Press Enter to complete the break corner feature.

Flat Pattern

The **Flat Pattern** command flattens the part so that the manufacturing information can be displayed easily. To create a flat pattern, activate the **Flat Pattern** command (click **Tools > Model > Flatten** on the ribbon) and click on a base sheet. Next, click on an edge to define the x-axis of the flat pattern. Click the right mouse button to create the flat pattern.

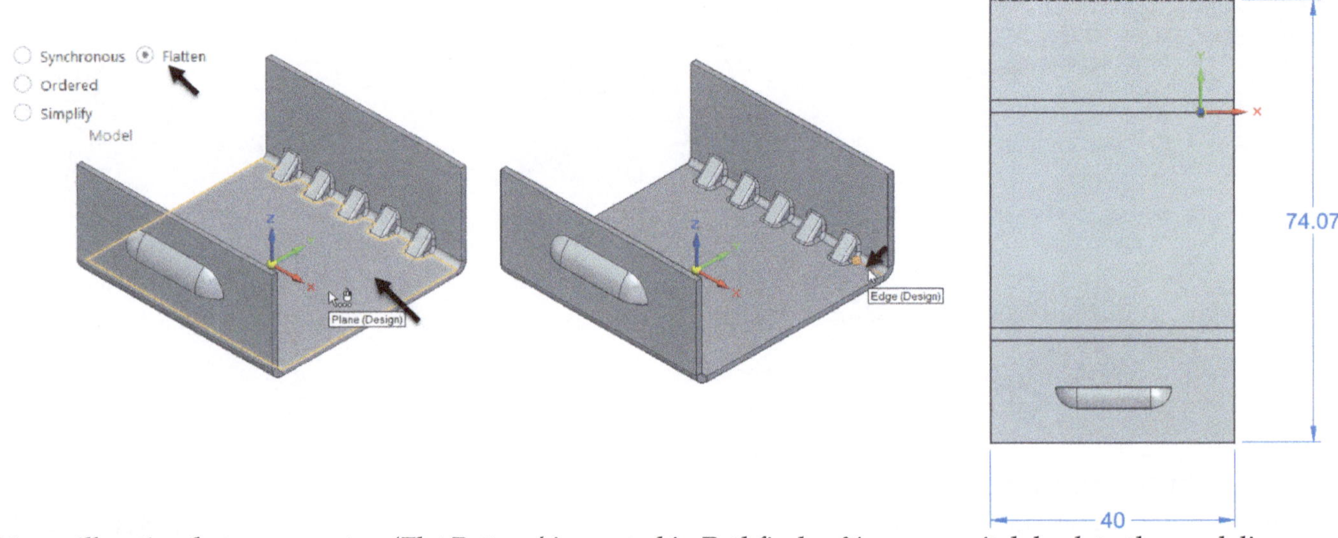

You will notice that a new entry, 'Flat Pattern' is created in Pathfinder. You can switch back to the modeling mode by clicking **Tools > Model > Synchronous** on the ribbon.

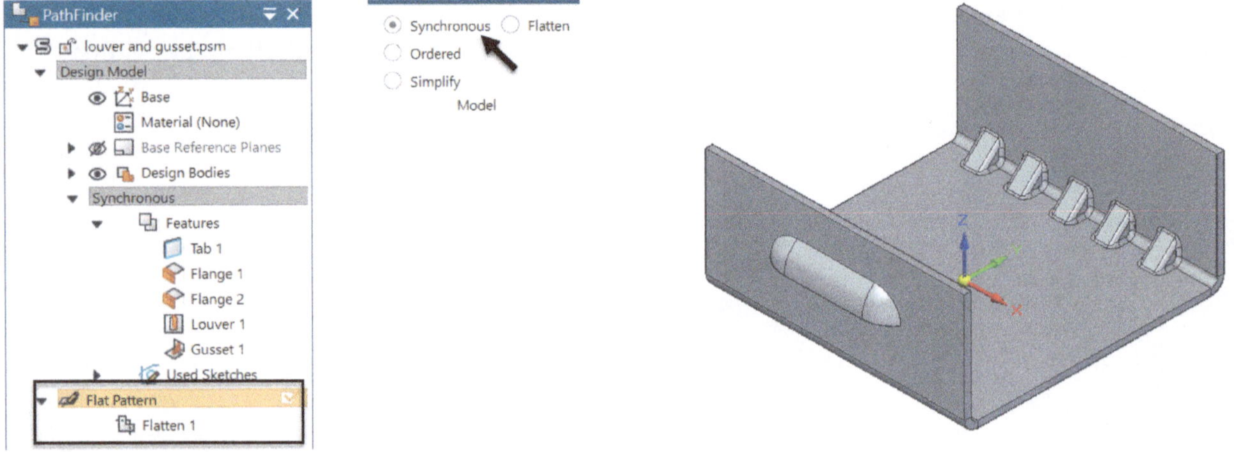

Lofted Flange

The **Lofted Flange** command allows you to create a lofted flange that can be unfolded into a flat pattern. In Solid Edge, the **Lofted Flange** command is available only in the **Ordered** environment. Transit to the **Ordered** environment and create two sketches on planes parallel to each other. Ensure that the sketches are not closed. Also, the openings should be in the same direction.

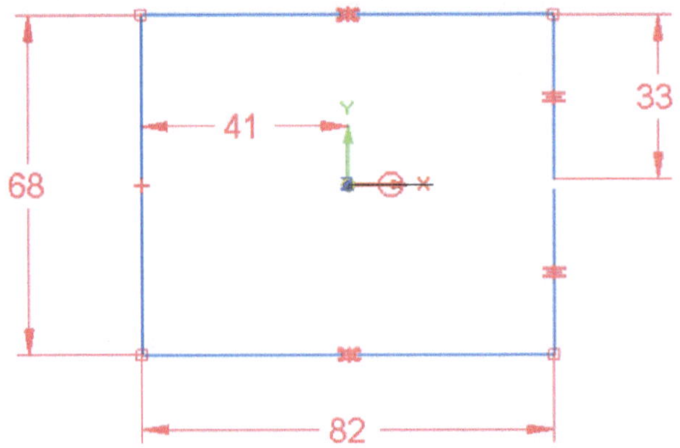

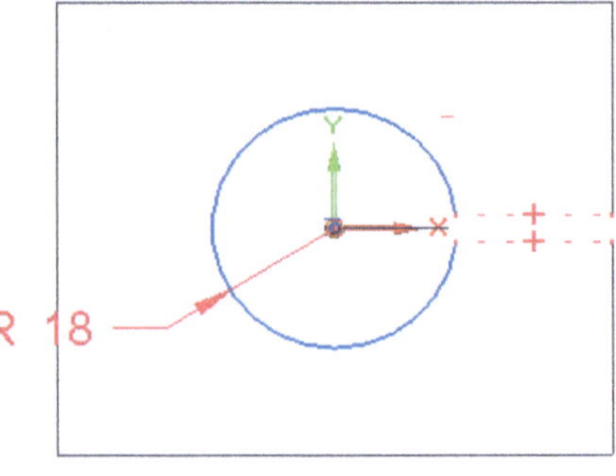

Activate the **Lofted Flange** command (click **Home > Sheet Metal > Contour Flange > Lofted Flange** on the ribbon) click on the first cross-section. Click the green check on the command bar to accept the selection. Click on the second cross-section and click the green check.

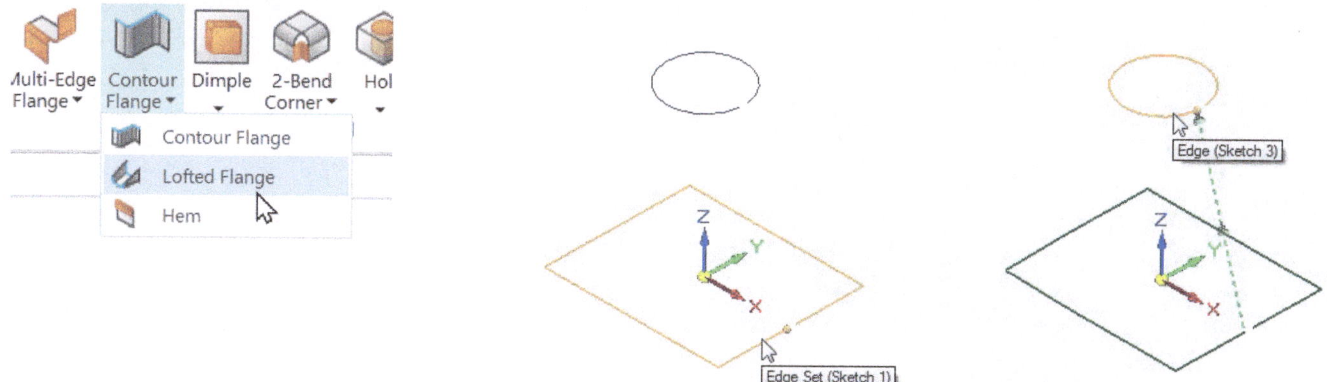

On the command bar, type-in a value in the **Thickness** box. Click inside or outside the sketch to define the side of sheet metal. Click **Finish** to complete the lofted flange feature.

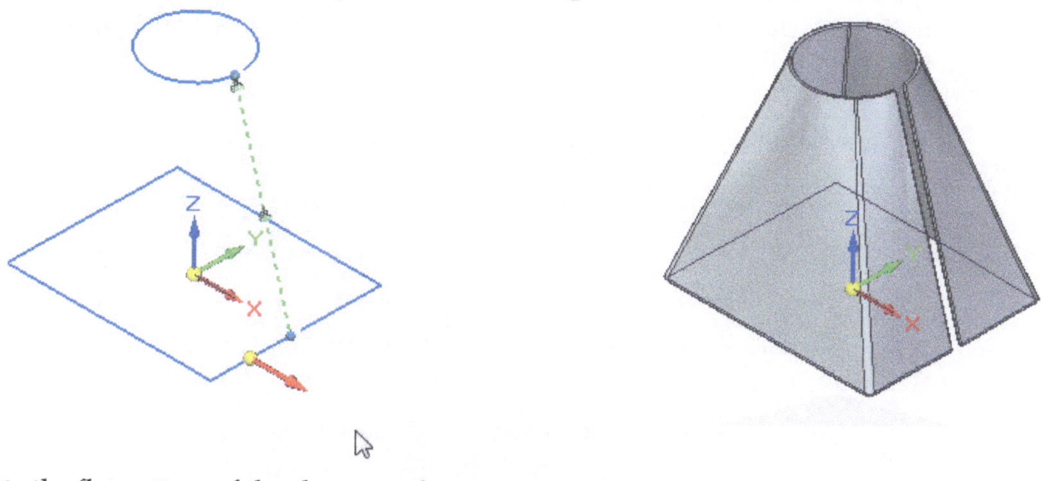

Create the flat pattern of the sheet metal part.

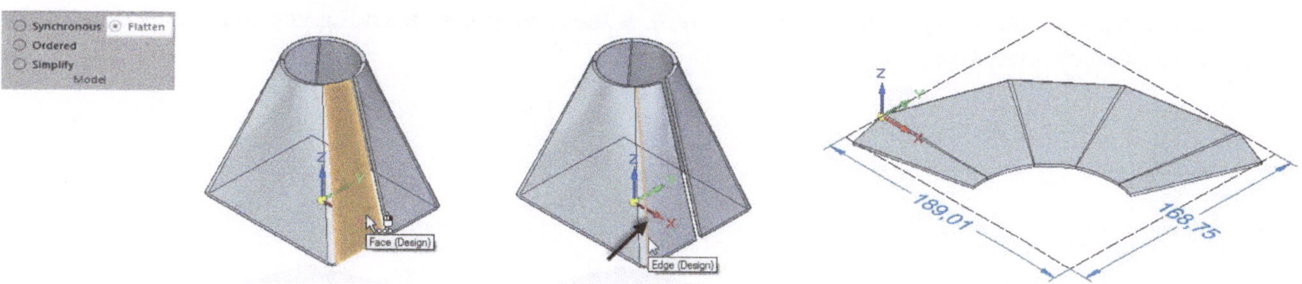

Thin Part to Synchronous Sheet Metal

Solid Edge has a special command, which converts an already existing part into a sheet metal part. This command is called **Thin Part to Synchronous Sheet Metal**. First, create a part in the Synchronous environment, and then shell it using the **Thin Wall** command. Next, click **Tools > Transform > Thin Part to Synchronous Sheet Metal** on the ribbon.

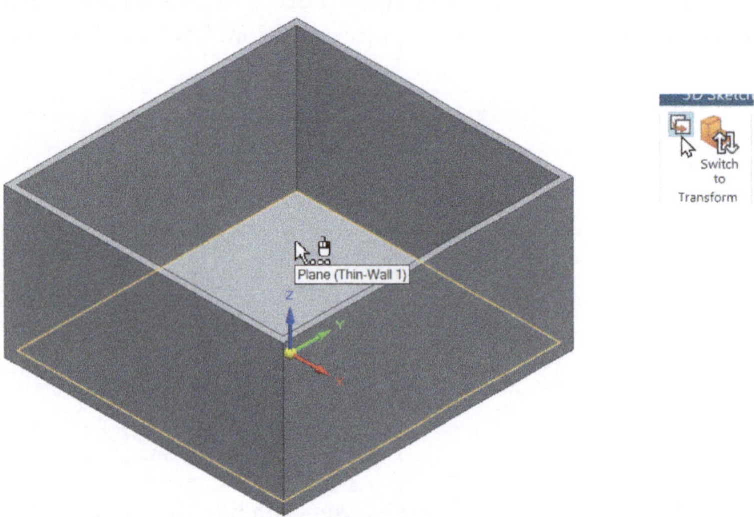

On the command bar, click the **Options** icon to open the **Transform to Sheet Metal Options** dialog. On this dialog, set the relief type: **Square** or **Round**. Next, check the **Override global value** option and specify the **Depth**, **Width**, **Bend radius**, and **Neutral Factor** values. Click **OK** to close the dialog.

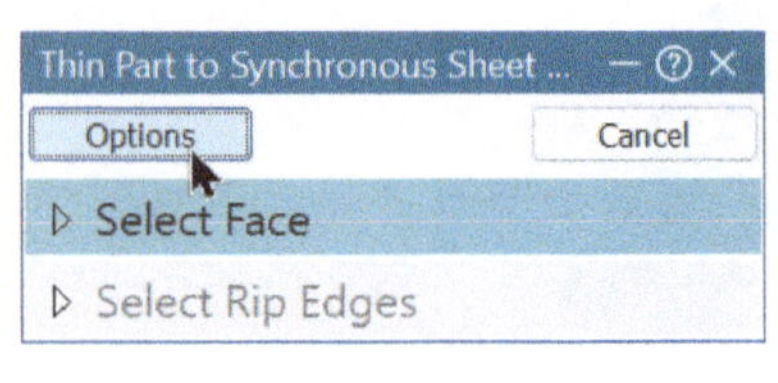

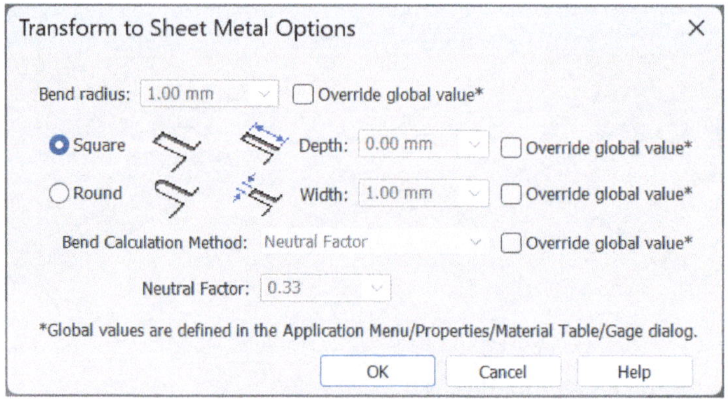

Click on the face of the part geometry to define the base face. A message pops up asking you to rip the edges of the part. Click **OK** to close the message.

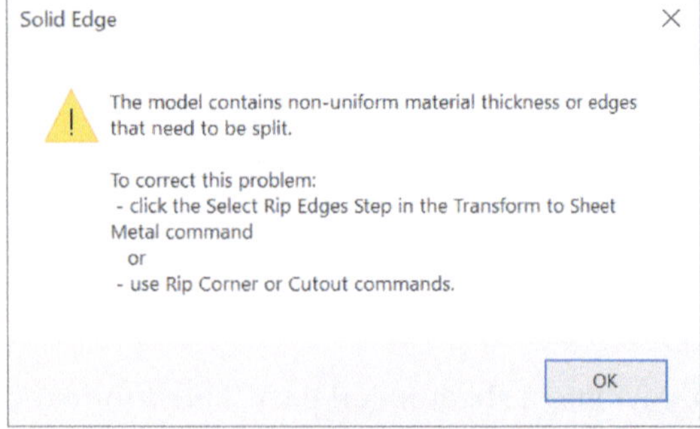

On the command bar, click the **Select Rip Edges** section and click on the part's side edges. Click the green check to complete the conversion process. Now, you can save and close the file.

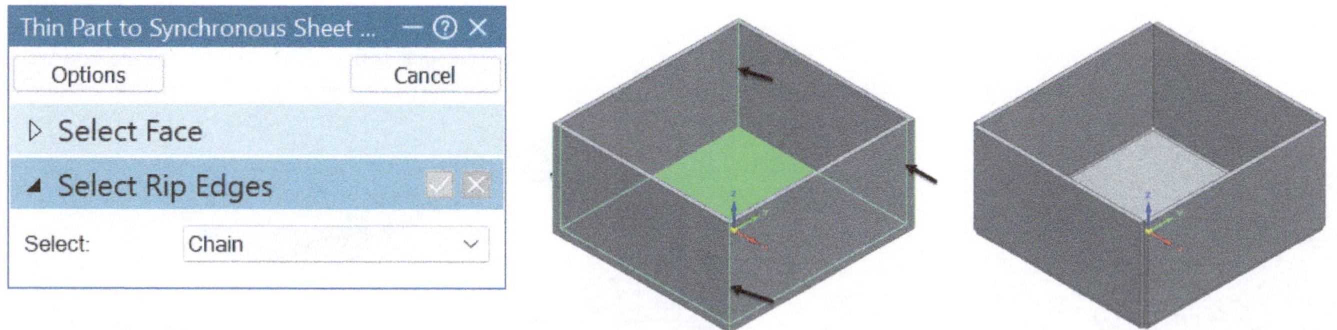

Part to Sheet Metal

The **Part to Sheet Metal** command creates a sheet metal part from a set of planar faces of a solid body. This command is available in the **Ordered** environment only. First, create a solid body using the solid modeling commands, and then activate the **Part to Sheet Metal** command (On the ribbon, click **Tools > Transform > Part to Sheet Metal**). On the **Part to Sheet Metal Options** dialog, specify the sheet metal properties (refer to the **Tab** section) and click **OK**. Click on linear edges of the solid body. The faces connected to the selected edge are highlighted.

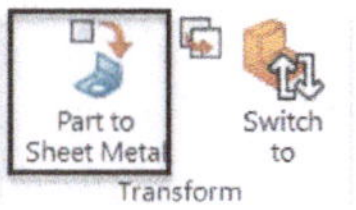

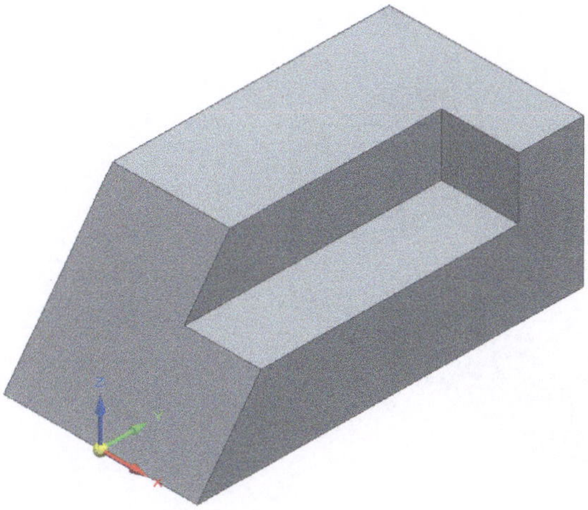

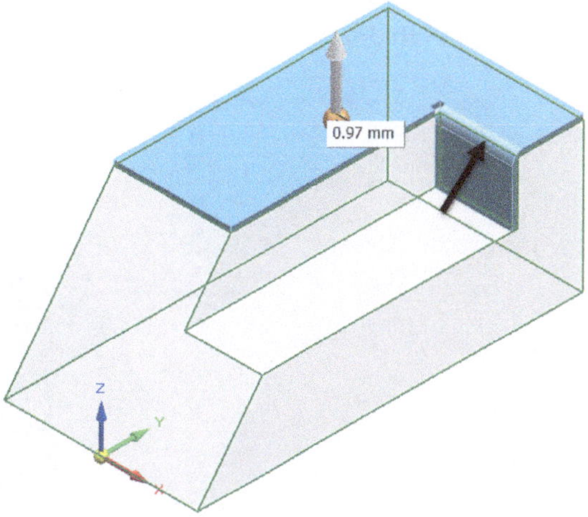

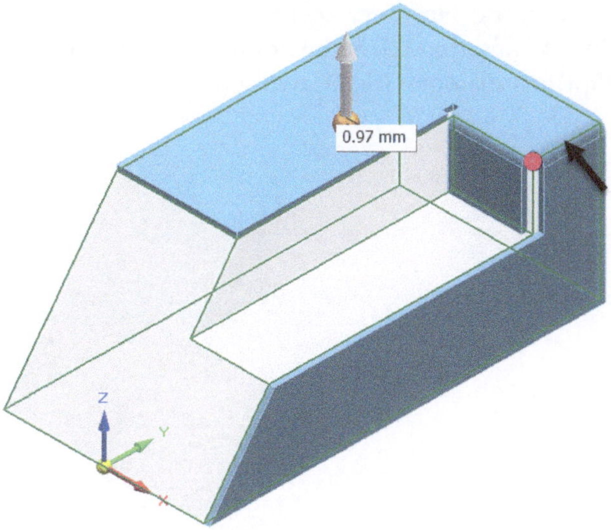

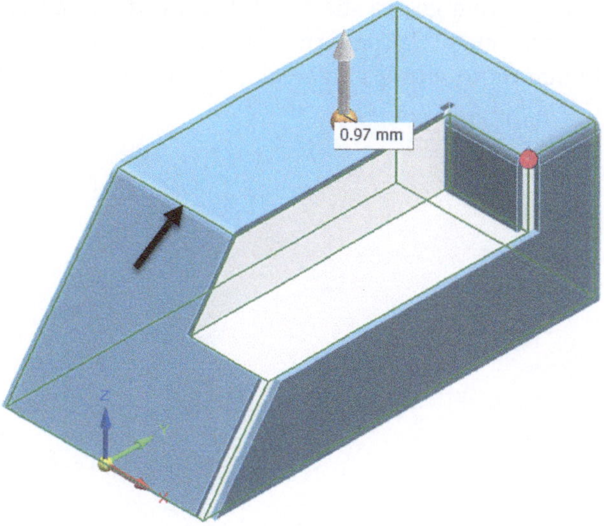

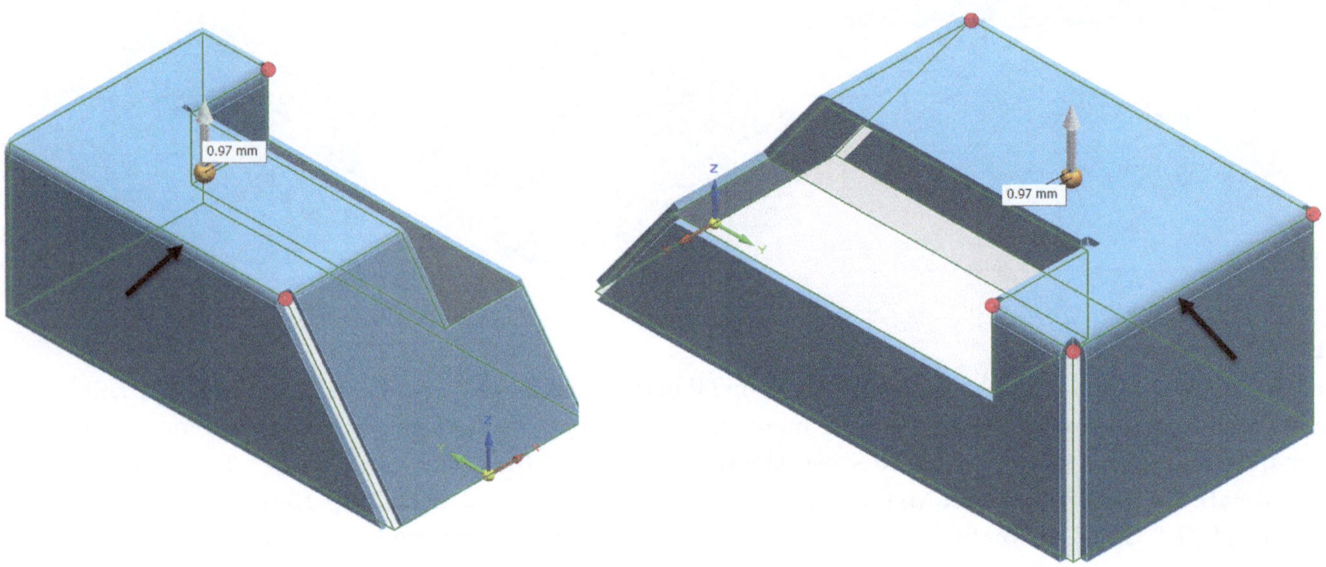

Click the arrow to change the side of the sheet metal. Type-in the sheet metal thickness and right-click to convert the solid to sheet metal.

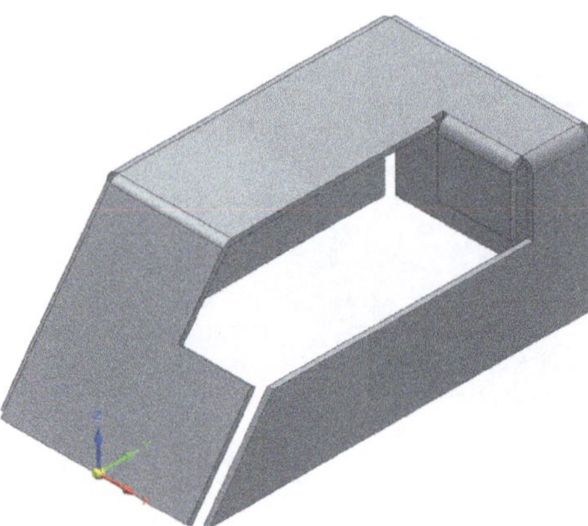

Sheet Metal Drawings

Creating drawings of a sheet metal part is the same as any other drawing. However, there are some settings specific to the sheet metal flat pattern. You can access these settings in the **Annotation** tab of the **Solid Edge Options** dialog. Note that these settings are available only in the **Solid Edge Options** dialog of the **Drawing** file.

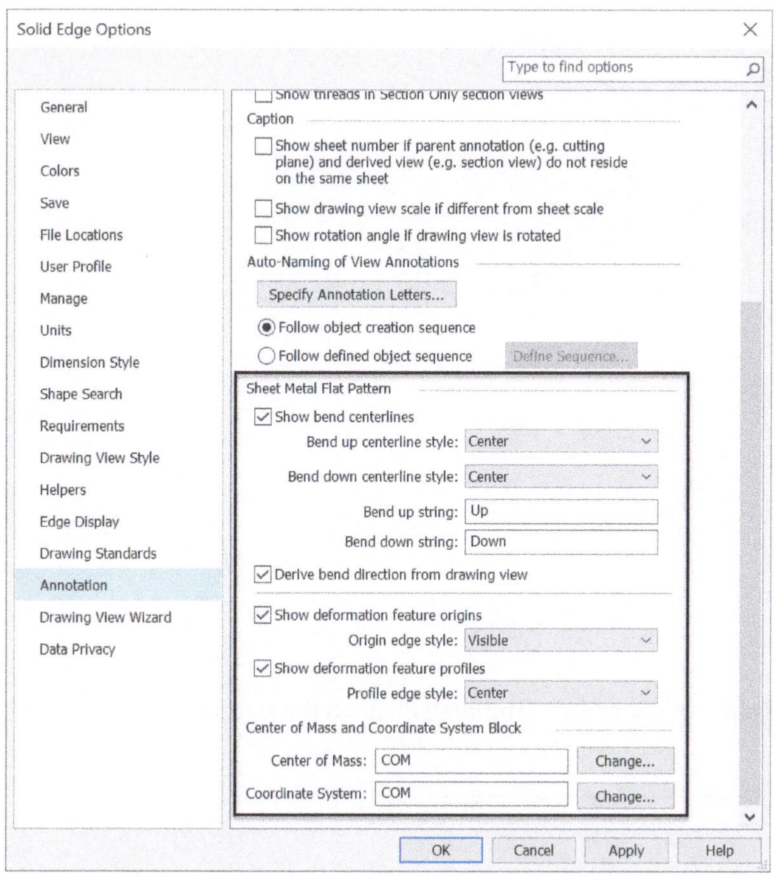

To create a flat pattern view, activate the **View Wizard** command and select the sheet metal part. On the command bar, click the **Drawing View Wizard Options** icon to open the **Drawing View Creation Wizard** dialog. On this dialog, select the **Flat pattern** option and click **OK**.

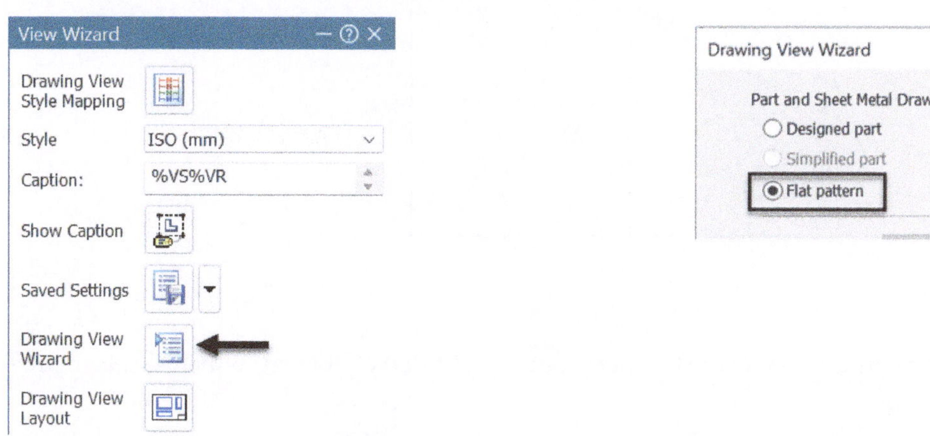

On the command bar, set the **Scale** value and click to place the view. You will notice that centrelines represent the bends.

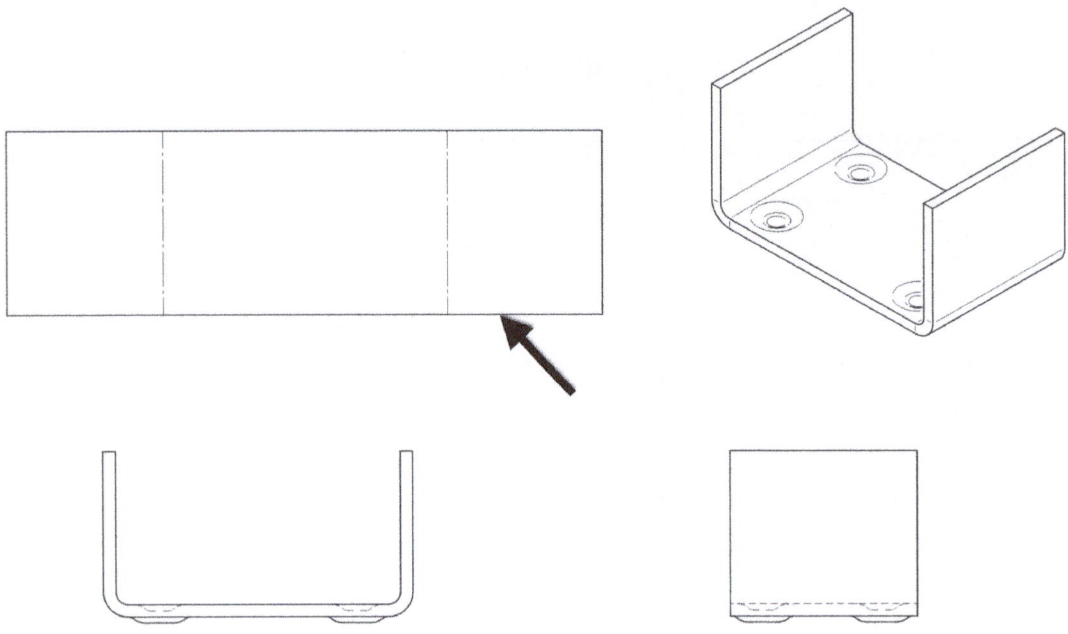

To add a bend table, click **Home > Tables > Bend Table** on the ribbon, and then click on the flat pattern view. Click on the sheet to position the bend table.

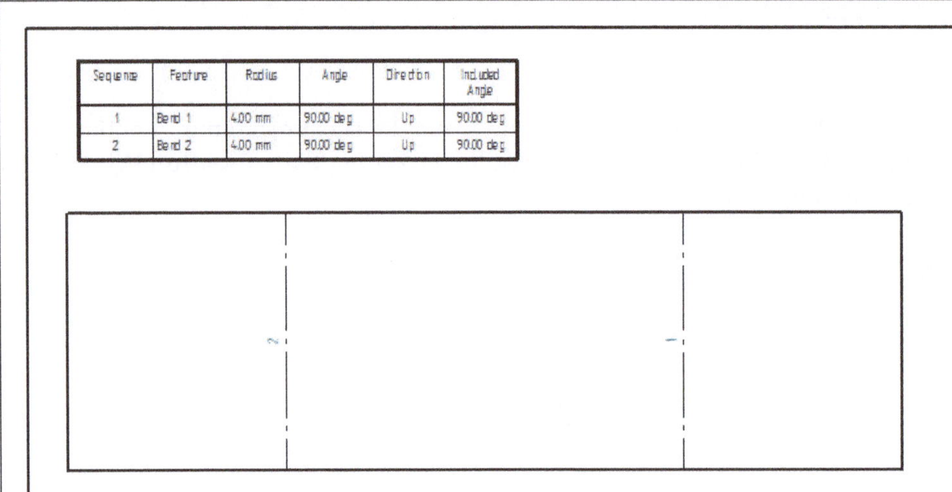

Sequence	Feature	Radius	Angle	Direction	Included Angle
1	Bend 1	4.00 mm	90.00 deg	Up	90.00 deg
2	Bend 2	4.00 mm	90.00 deg	Up	90.00 deg

Export to DWF

In addition to creating drawings, you can directly export a sheet metal part to DWF format, which can be opened in AutoCAD. All you have to do is click **File Menu > Save As > Save As Flat** . Select the sheet metal face that will be orientated upwards. Click on the edge of the selected face to define the x-axis of the DWF file. On the **Save As Flat** dialog, click the **Options** button to open the **Save As Flat DXF Options** dialog. On this dialog, set the layer properties and bend data, and then click **OK**. Type-in a name in the **File name** box and click **Save**. Now, you can open the DWF file in AutoCAD.

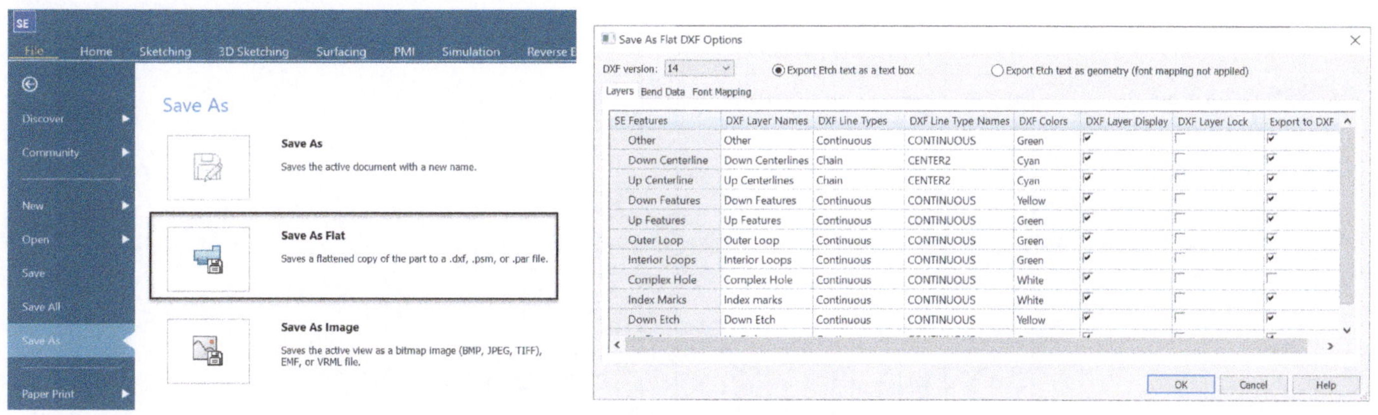

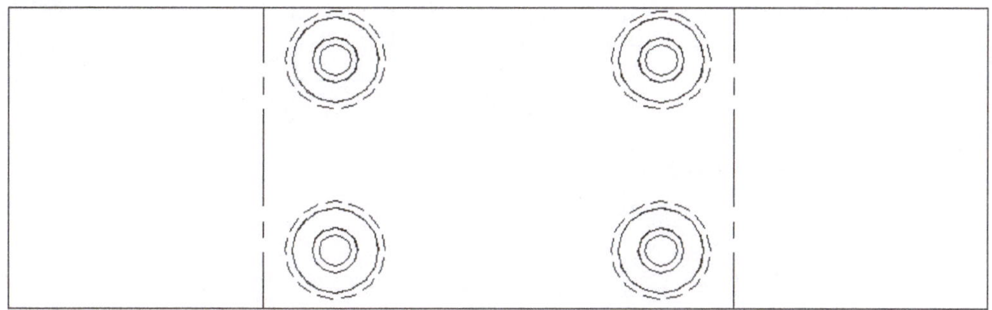

Examples

Example 1

In this example, you will design the sheet metal part shown below.

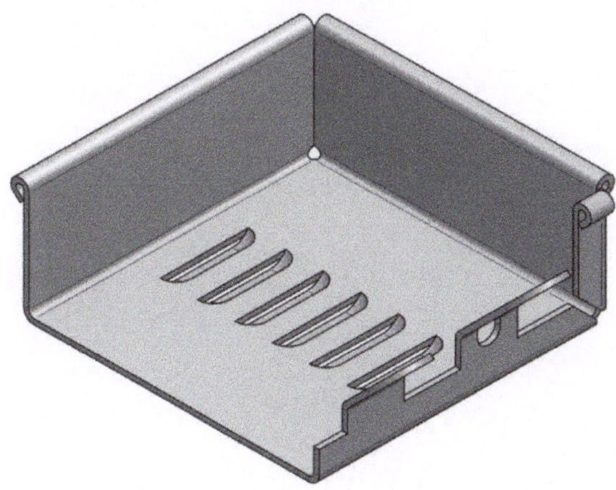

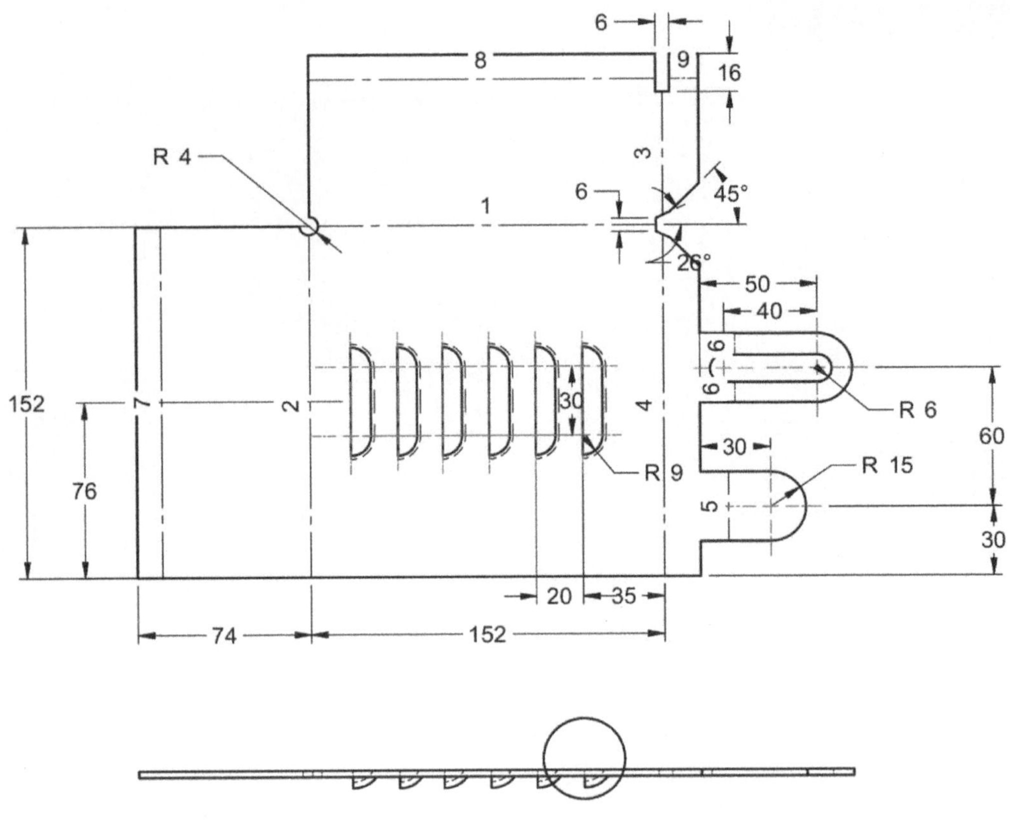

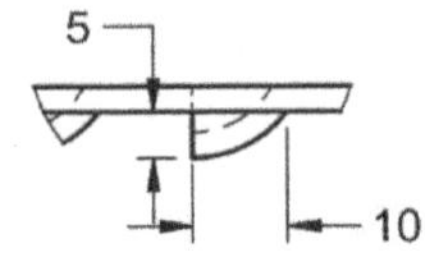

DETAIL A

Sequence	Feature	Radius	Angle	Direction	Included Angle
1	Bend 1	2.77 mm	90.00 deg	Up	90.00 deg
2	Bend 2	2.77 mm	90.00 deg	Up	90.00 deg
3	Bend 4	2.77 mm	90.00 deg	Up	90.00 deg
4	Bend 3	2.77 mm	90.00 deg	Up	90.00 deg
5	Bend 5	2.77 mm	45.00 deg	Down	135.00 deg
6	Bend 9	2.77 mm	45.00 deg	Down	135.00 deg
7	Bend 12	2.00 mm	136.44 deg	Down	43.56 deg
8	Bend 11	2.00 mm	136.44 deg	Down	43.56 deg
9	Bend 10	2.00 mm	136.44 deg	Down	43.56 deg

1. Start **Solid Edge 2026.**
2. On the **File Menu**, click **New > ISO Metric Sheet Metal** to start a new sheet metal file.
3. Right-click in the graphics window and select **Transition to Synchronous**.
4. Create a sketch on the top (XY) plane. Change the orientation of the model to the ISO View.

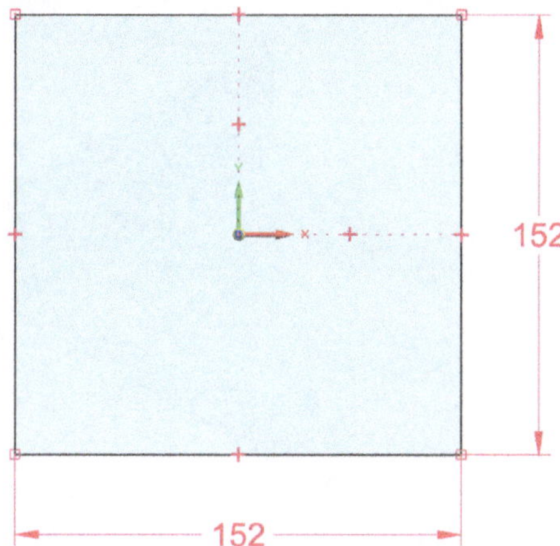

5. Click inside the region enclosed by the sketch. On the command bar, click the **Material Table** icon to open the **Material Table** dialog. On this dialog, open the **Gage Properties** tab and set the **Sheet metal gage** to **12 gage**. Set the **Neutral Factor** to 0.5. Click **Apply to Model** and then click **No** on the **Save Changes** message box. Next, close the dialog.
6. Click on the arrow handle to make it point upwards. Click the right mouse button to complete the tab feature.

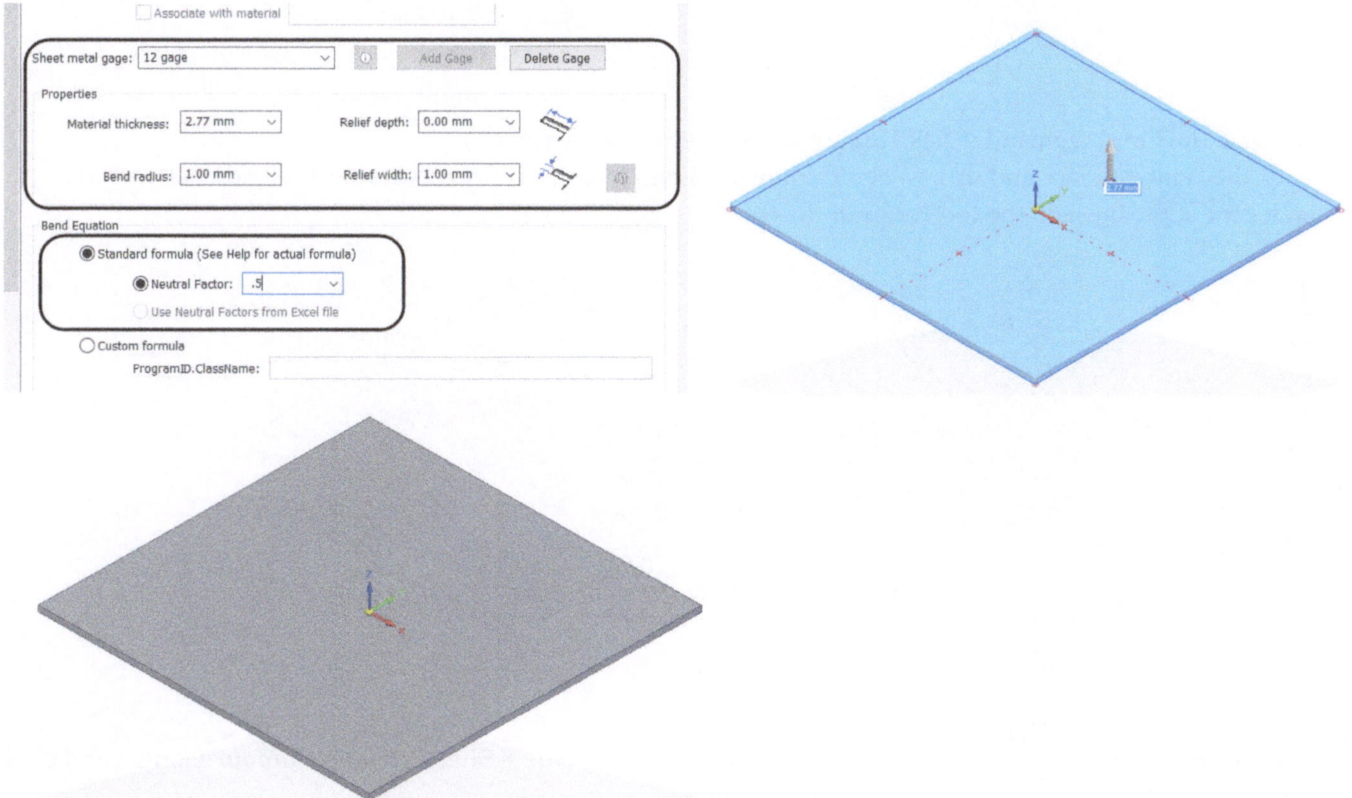

7. Click on the back-end face to display the flange handle on it. On the flange handle, click the arrow pointing upwards, and then drag the mouse pointer.
8. On the command bar, set the **Measurement Point** to **Measurement Outside**. Set the **Material Side** to **Material Outside**.
9. Move the mouse pointer up and type-in **65** in the distance box. Press Enter to create the flange.

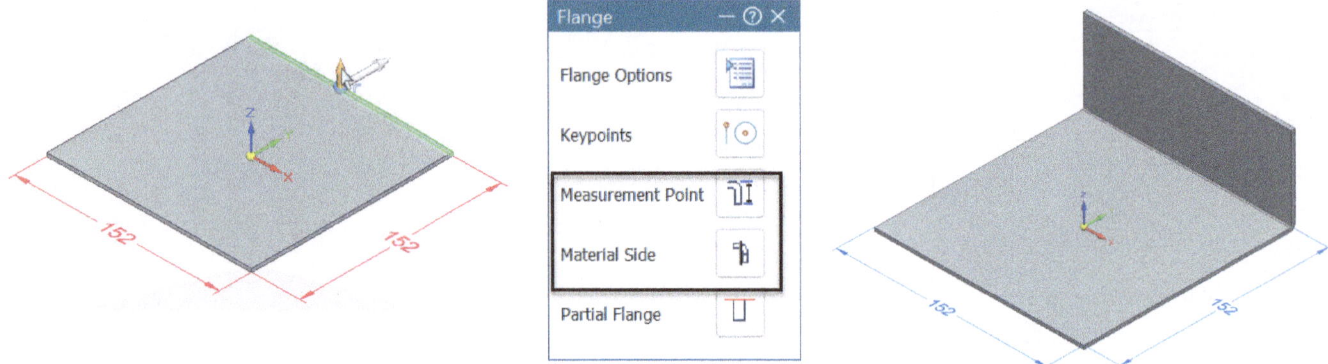

10. Create another flange on the left side. The flange length is 65 mm.

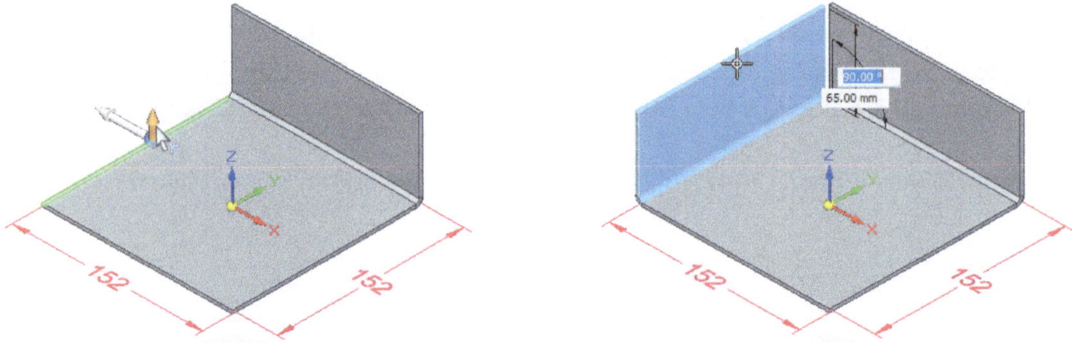

11. Activate the **Line** command (Click **Home > Draw > Line** on the ribbon).
12. Lock the front-end face and draw a vertical line of **15** mm length. Apply the Connect relation between the endpoint of the line and the top vertex of the corner.

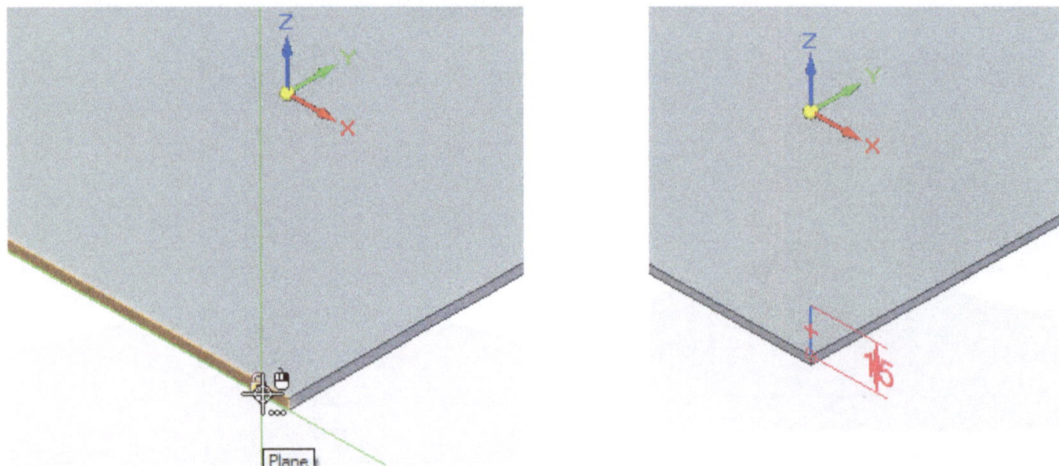

13. Activate the **Contour Flange** command (on the ribbon, click **Home > Sheet Metal > Contour Flange**) and click on the line. Click the arrow pointing toward the right.

14. Select the end face of the flange perpendicular to the tab feature. Click the **Contour Flange Options** icon on the Command Bar. On the **Contour Flange Options** dialog, click the **Miters and Corners** tab, and then type in 2.77 in the **Gap** box of the **Interior Corners** section. Click **OK** to close the dialog. Click the right mouse button to create the contour flange.

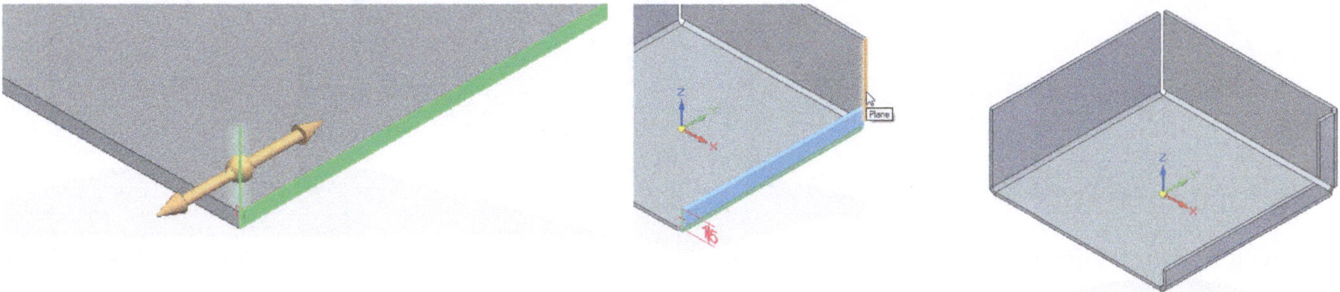

15. Activate the **Line** command (Click **Home > Draw > Line** on the ribbon).
16. Lock the outer face of the contour flange and draw the sketch shown below. Create a tab feature using the sketch.

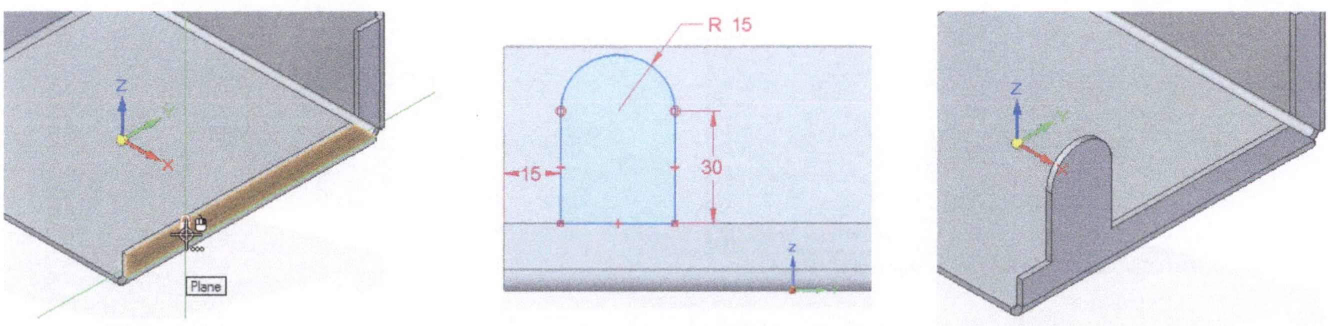

17. Draw a horizontal line on the outer face of the tab. Activate the **Bend** command (click **Home > Sheet Metal > Bend** on the ribbon) and click on the line.
18. Click on the arrow pointing upwards. Type-in **135** in the angle box and press Enter to bend the tab feature.

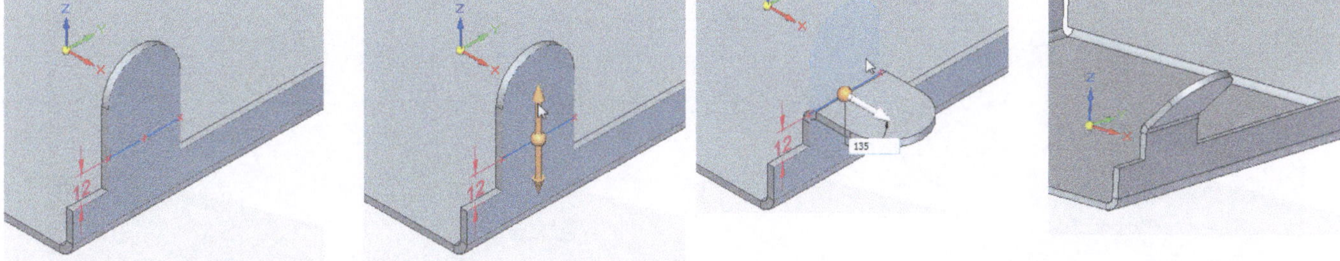

19. Draw another sketch on the outer face of the contour flange.
20. Activate the **Tab** command and create a tab feature using the sketch.

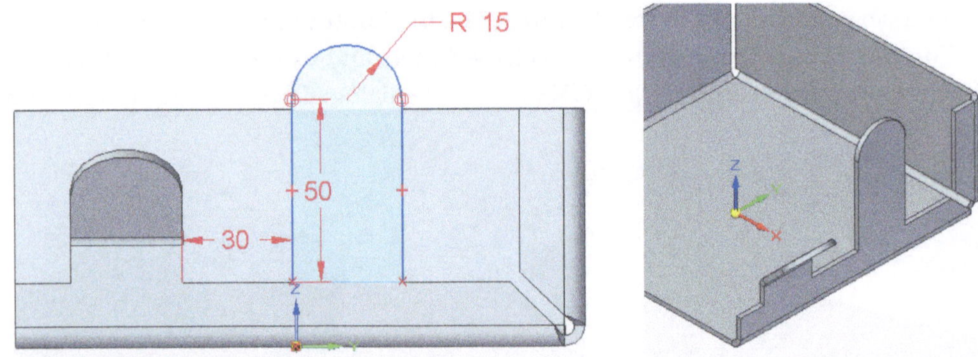

21. Draw a horizontal line on the outer face of the tab feature. Activate the **Bend** command (click **Home > Sheet Metal > Bend** on the ribbon) and click on the sketched line.

22. Click on the arrow pointing upwards. Type-in **135** in the angle box and press Enter to bend the tab feature.

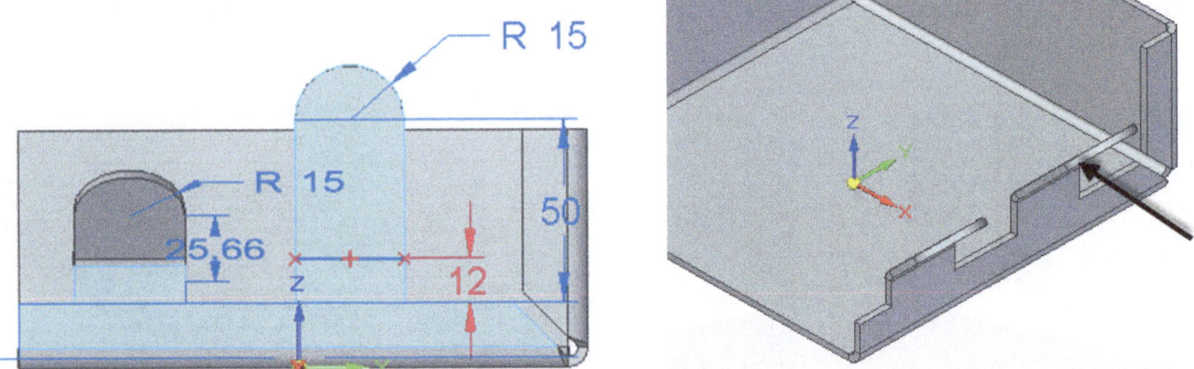

23. Create the sketch on the bend feature's vertical face (use the **Symmetric Offset** command), as shown in the figure.

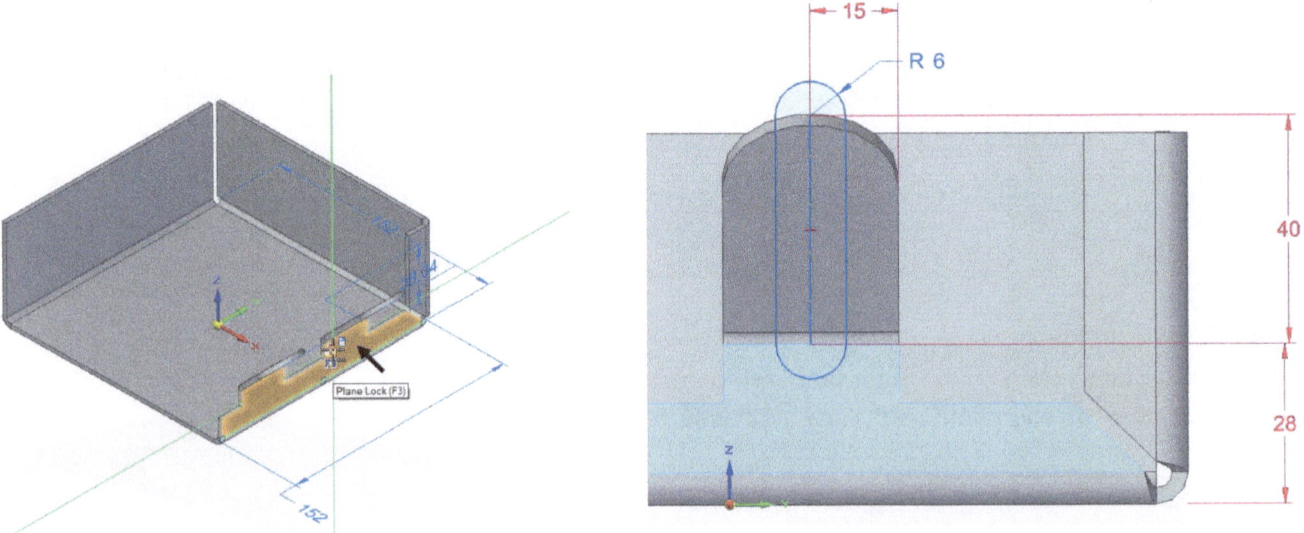

24. On ribbon, click **Home > Sheet Metal > Hole > Cut**.
25. Press the Ctrl key and click inside the regions enclosed by the sketch. Click the right mouse button to accept the selection.

26. On the command bar, click the **Wrapped Cut** icon.
27. Click the right mouse button to complete the cut feature.

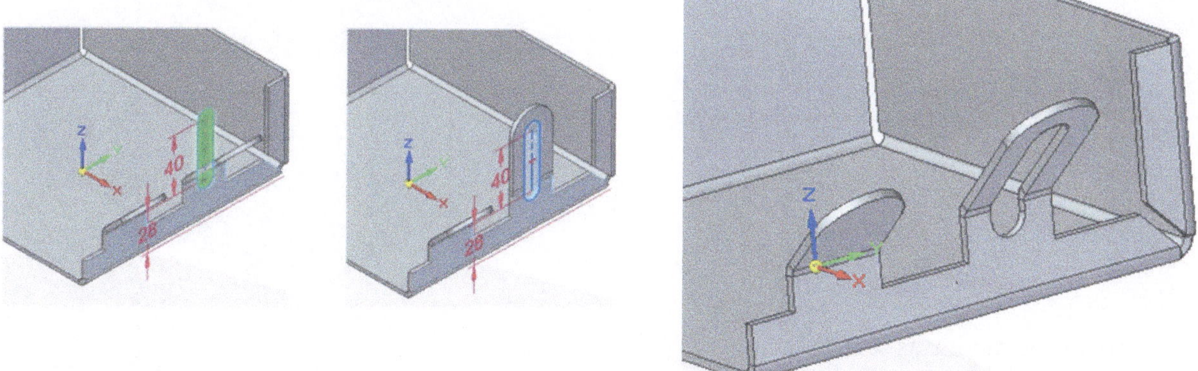

28. Activate the **Close 2-Bend Corner** command (click **Home > Sheet Metal > Close 2 Bend Corner** on the ribbon) and click on the flange features' bends.
29. On the command bar, set the **Corner Treatment** to **Circular Cutout**. Click the **Closed Corner** icon on the command bar. Set the **Diameter** value to 8 mm. Click the right mouse button to close the bends.

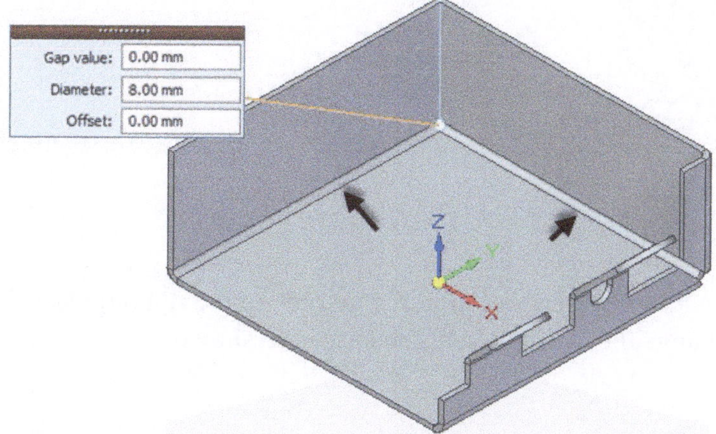

30. Activate the **Hem** command (click **Home > Sheet Metal > Contour Flange > Hem** on the ribbon).
31. On the command bar, click the **Hem Options** icon to open the **Hem Options** dialog. On this dialog, set the **Hem type** to **Closed Loop**. Set the **Bend radius1** to 2 and **Flange length1** to 8. Click **OK** to close the dialog. On the command bar, select **Material Setback > Material Outside** .

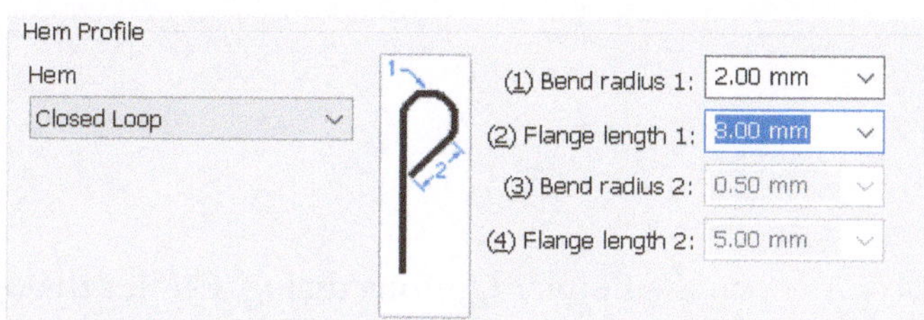

32. Click on the outer edges of the flange features. Click the right mouse button to create the hem features.

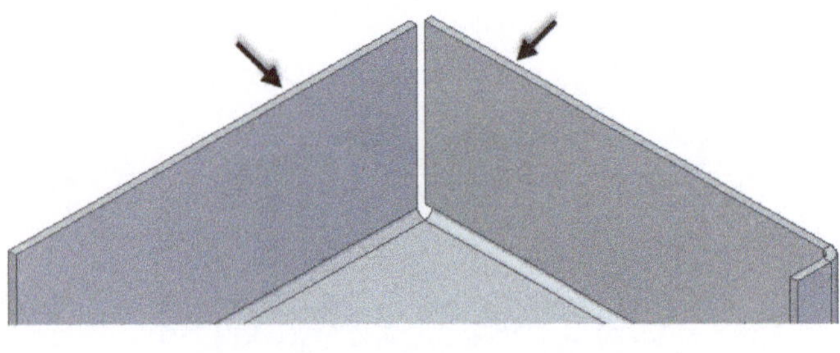

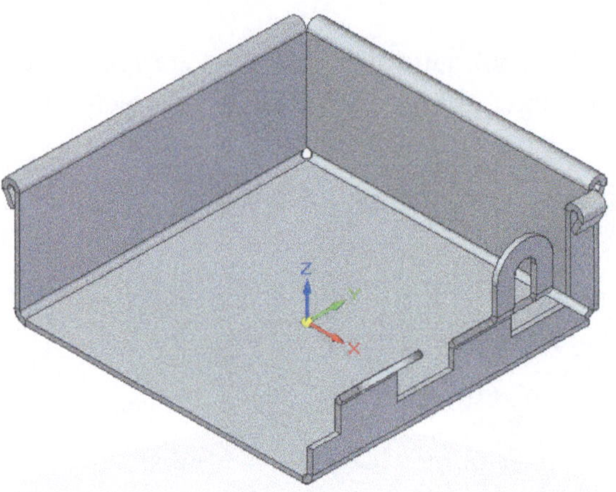

33. Rotate and orient the model, as shown below.

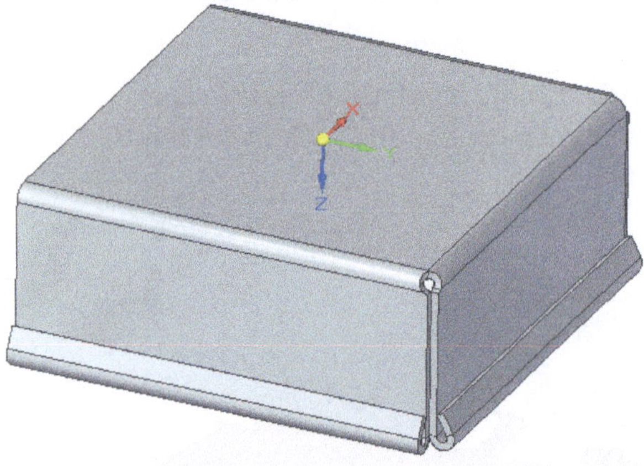

34. Activate the **Louver** command (click **Home > Sheet Metal > Dimple > Louver** on the ribbon) place the mouse pointer on the top face. Use the **N** key to change the orientation of the louver, as shown.

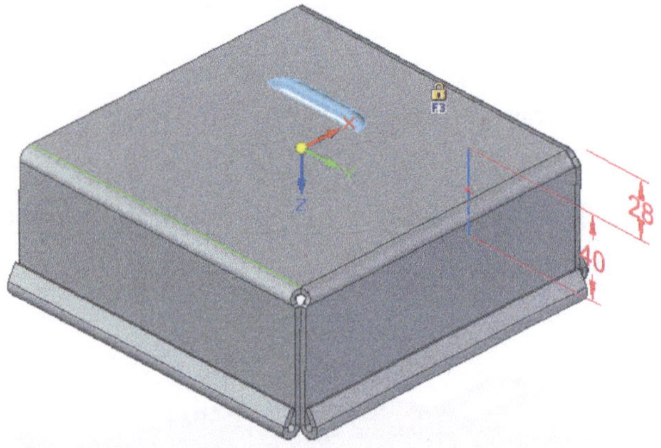

35. Press F3 on your keyboard to lock the plane.

36. On the command bar, click the **Louver Options** icon to open the **Louver Options** dialog. On this dialog, set the **Length**, **Depth** and **Height** values to 50, 10, and 5, respectively. Check the **Formed-end louver** option. Next, check the **Include rounding** option and set the **Die radius** to 1. Click **OK** to close the dialog.

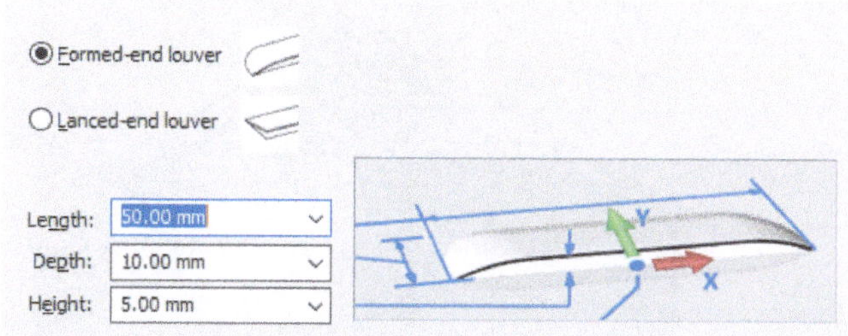

37. Place the mouse pointer on the left edge and press E twice. The location dimensions appear.
38. Type-in 76 and 120 in the dimension boxes. Press Enter to create the louver feature.

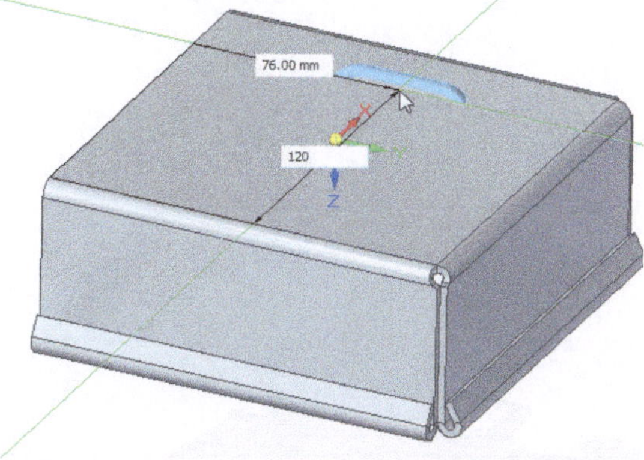

39. Select the louver feature and create a rectangular pattern.

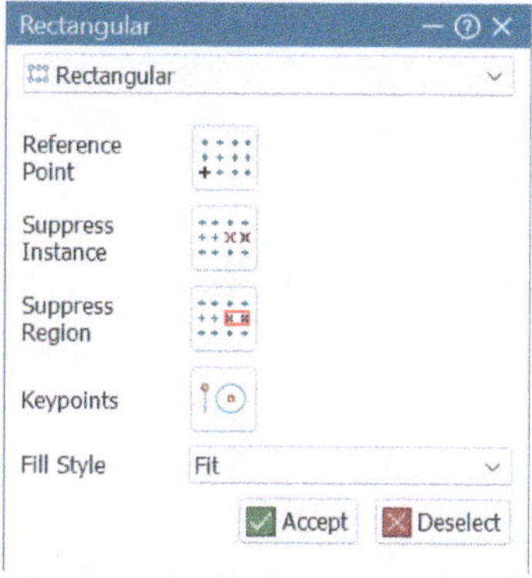

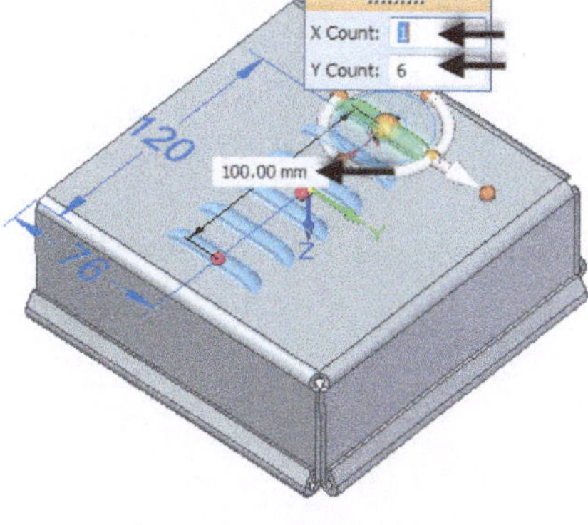

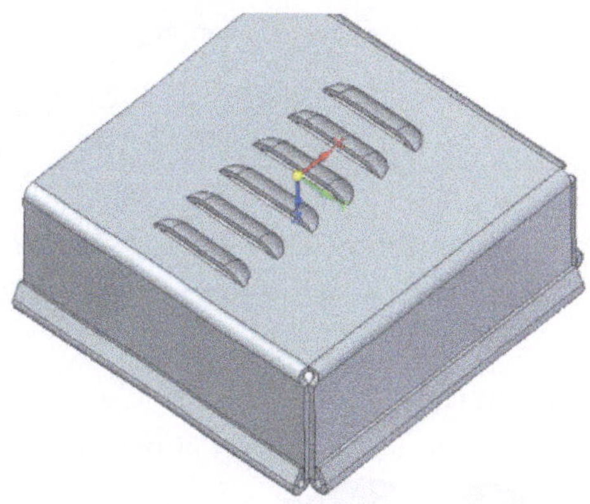

40. Change the view orientation of the sheet metal to Isometric.
41. On the ribbon, click **Tools > Model > Flatten** on the ribbon. The **Flat Pattern** command is activated.
42. Click on the top face of the tab feature.
43. Click on the front edge of the tab feature to define the x-axis of the flat pattern. The flat pattern is created.

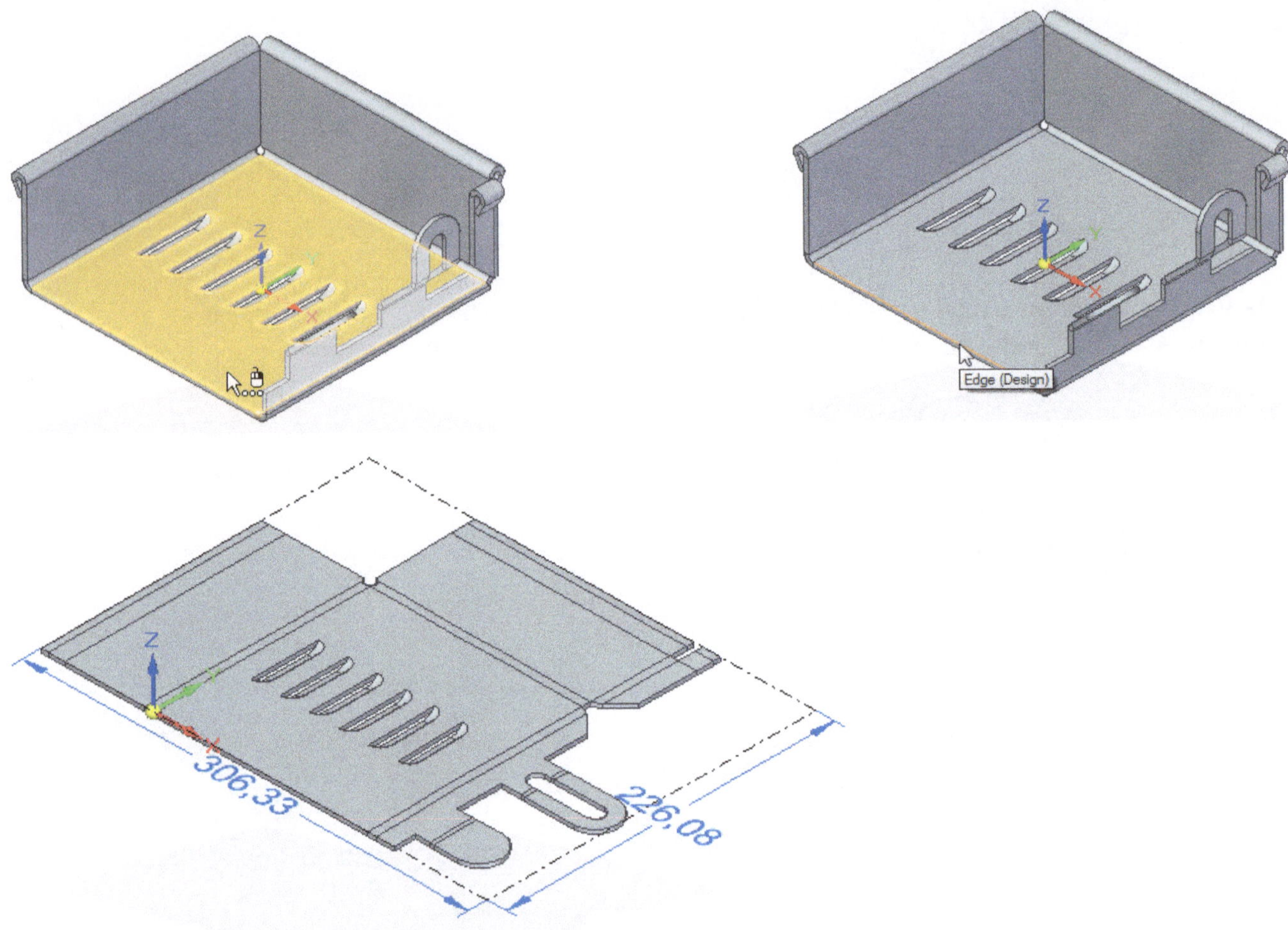

44. On the ribbon, click **Tools > Model > Synchronous** to switch back to the Synchronous environment.
45. Save and close the sheet metal part.

Questions

1. How do you insert a flat pattern into a drawing?
2. Describe parameters that can be specified on the **Material Table** dialog.
3. Define the term 'Neutral Factor.'
4. List any two parameter settings of a gage table that can be overridden when creating a feature.
5. What is the use of the **Cut** command?
6. Which command is used to apply rounds and chamfers to the corners of a sheet metal part?
7. List the types of hems that can be created in Solid Edge.
8. What is the use of the **Close 2-Corner** command?
9. What are the corner treatment options when closing a corner?
10. What is the difference between a dimple and a drawn cutout?

Exercises

Exercise 1

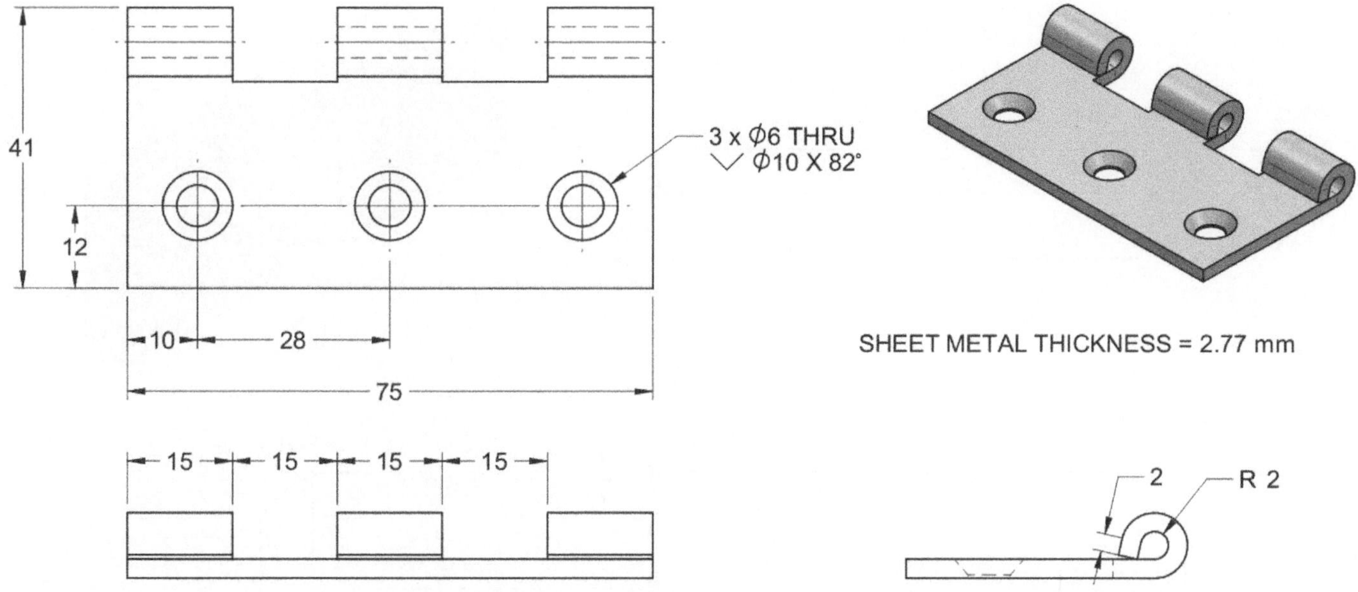

Exercise 2

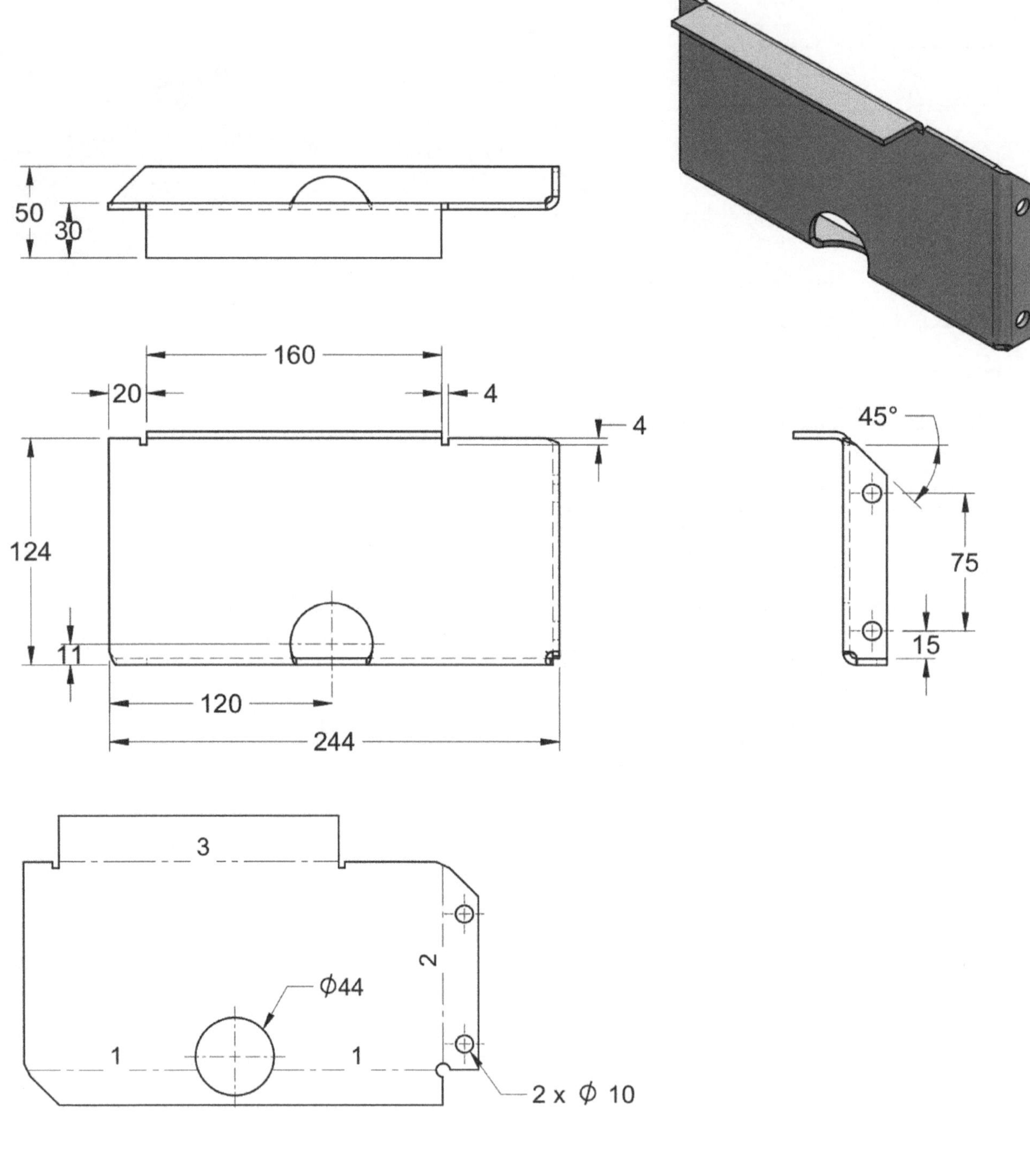

Sequence	Feature	Radius	Angle	Direction	Included Angle
1	Bend 1	3.58 mm	90.00 deg	Down	90.00 deg
2	Bend 2	3.58 mm	90.00 deg	Down	90.00 deg
3	Bend 3	3.58 mm	90.00 deg	Up	90.00 deg

Chapter 13: Surface Design

The topics covered in this chapter are:

- *Basic surfaces*
- *Curves*
- *Swept command*
- *BlueSurf*
- *Ruled*
- *Bounded*
- *Offset*
- *Copy*
- *Redefine*
- *Intersect*
- *Extend*
- *Replace Face*
- *Trim*
- *Extend*
- *Split*
- *Stitched*

Solid Edge Surfacing commands can create complex geometries that are very difficult to create using standard extruded bosses and revolve bosses. They can also be used to edit and fix the broken imported parts. In this chapter, you learn the basics of surfacing commands that are mostly used. The surfacing commands are available in the **Surfacing** tab.

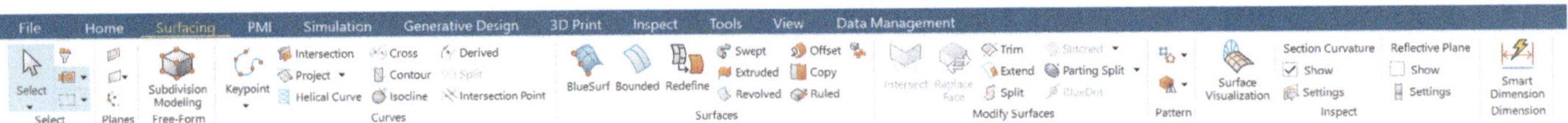

Solid Edge offers a rich set of surface design commands. A surface is an infinitely thin piece of geometry. For example, consider a cube shown in the figure. It has six faces. Each of these faces is a surface, an infinitely thin piece of geometry that acts as a boundary in 3D space. Surfaces can be simple or complex shapes.

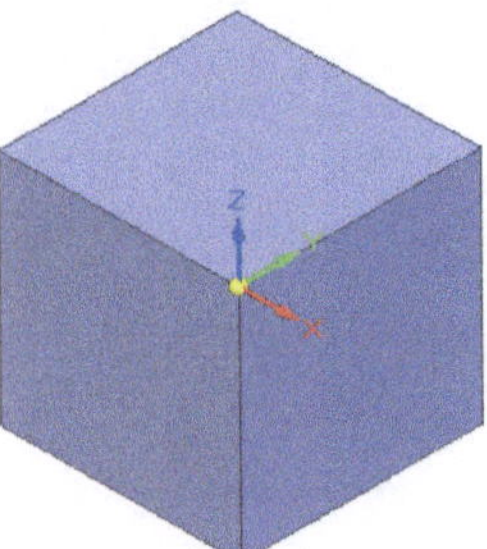

In solid modeling, when you have created solid features such as an Extruded feature or a Revolved feature, Solid Edge creates a set of features (surfaces) that enclose a volume. The airtight enclosure is considered as a solid body. The advantage of using the surfacing commands is that you can design a model with more flexibility. You can create surfaces in Synchronous and Ordered environments. However, the Ordered environment offers history-based modeling, which makes it easy to edit surfaces. This chapter explains the surface modeling commands by using them in the Ordered environment.

Extruded Surface

To create an extruded surface, first, create an open or closed sketch and activate the **Extruded** command (on the ribbon, click **Surfacing > Surfaces > Extruded** ). Select the sketch and right-click. Next, type-in a value in the **Distance** box available on the command bar and press Enter. On the command bar, click the **Close Ends** button in the **End Conditions** section to create an extruded surface with closed ends. You can also use the **Treatment** section to apply the draft or crown to the extruded surface. Click **Finish** to create the extruded surface.

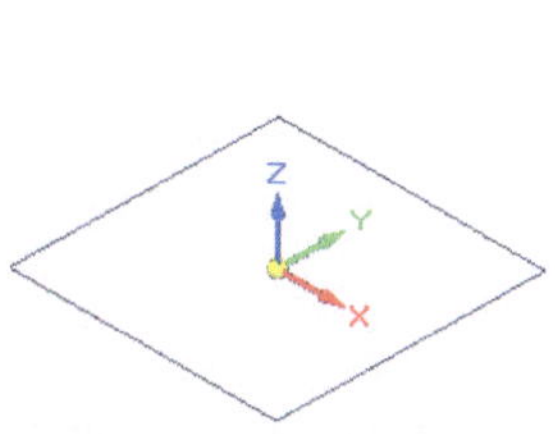

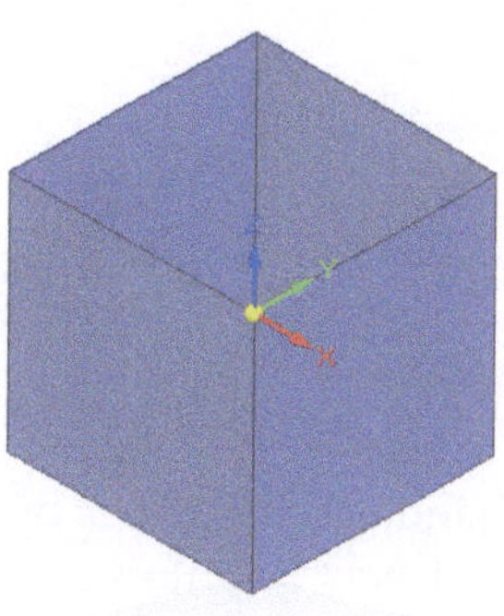

Revolved Surface

To create a revolved surface, first, create an open or closed profile and the axis of revolution. Activate the **Revolved** command (on the ribbon, click **Surfacing > Surfaces > Revolved**). Select the sketch and right-click. Specify the axis of revolution. Next, click the Extent section and type-in the angle of revolution in the **Angle** box or click **Type > Revolve 360** button. Click to define the side of the revolution, in case you have specified the angle value. Click **Finish** to complete the feature.

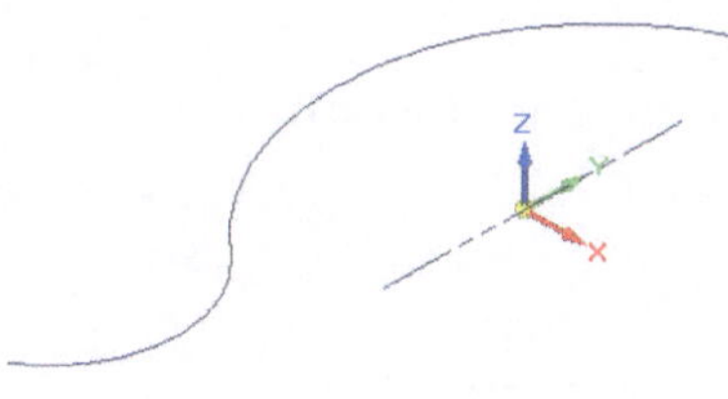

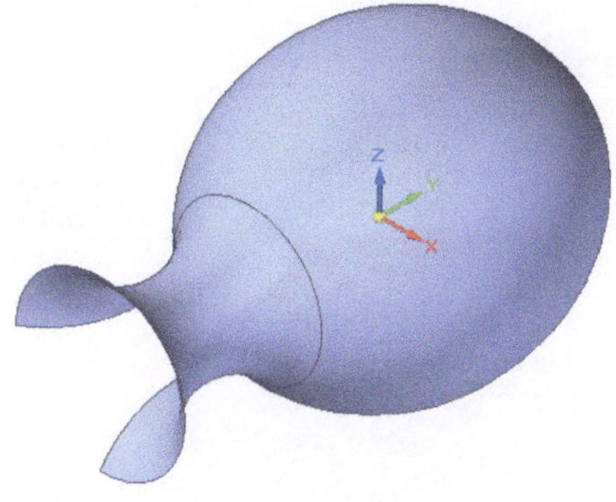

Even if you create an enclosed surface, Solid Edge will not recognize it as a solid body. You can examine this by activating the **Physical Properties** command (on the ribbon, click **Inspect > Physical Properties > Physical Properties**). On the **Physical Properties** dialog, click the **Change** button under the **Density** section. The **Material Table** dialog appears. On this dialog, select a material from the **Material** tree, and click **Apply to Model**. Next, click **Update** on the **Physical Properties** dialog. You will notice that all the physical properties are displayed as zero. This means that there exists no solid body. You will learn to convert a surface body into a solid later in this chapter.

Keypoint Curve

The **Keypoint Curve** command creates curves through selected keypoints. You can click in the graphics window to specify points or select existing points. Activate this command (on the ribbon, click **Surfacing > Curves > Keypoint Curve**) and select key points from the graphics window. Click **Accept** and **Finish** on the command bar.

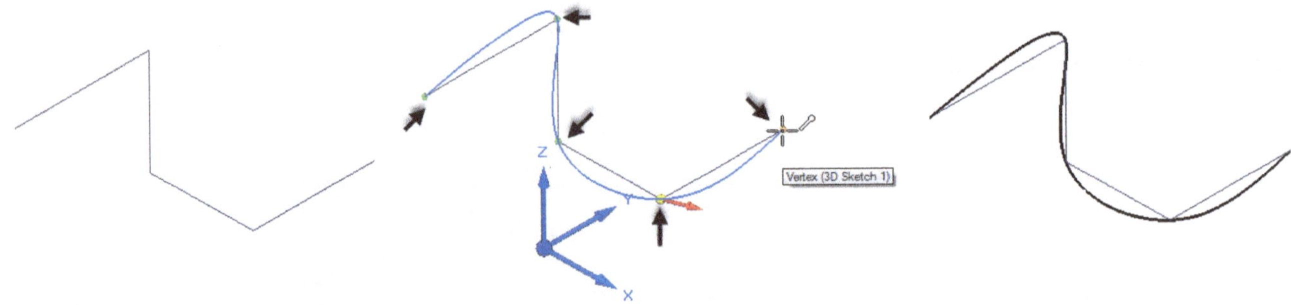

Curve by Table

The **Curve by Table** command creates curves by using the X, Y, Z points. These points can be defined using a spreadsheet. Create a spreadsheet by entering values in the A, B, and C columns and save it. The values in the A, B, C columns of the spreadsheet represent the X, Y, Z values. Activate the **Curve by Table** command (on the ribbon, click **Surfacing > Curves > Keypoint** drop-down **> Curve by Table**). On the **Insert Object** dialog, select the **Create from file** option and click the **Browse** button. Go to the location of the spreadsheet and double-click on it. Click **OK** to close the dialog. You will notice that a curve appears.

On the command bar, click the **Parameters** section. On the **Curve by Table Parameters** dialog, set the **Curve fit** type. You can select **Linear segments**, **Smoothing off**, and **Smoothing on**. The **Linear segments** option creates a linear curve. The **Smoothing off** option creates a curve directly passing through the points. The **Smoothing on** option creates a curve whose path is controlled by the **Tolerance** value.

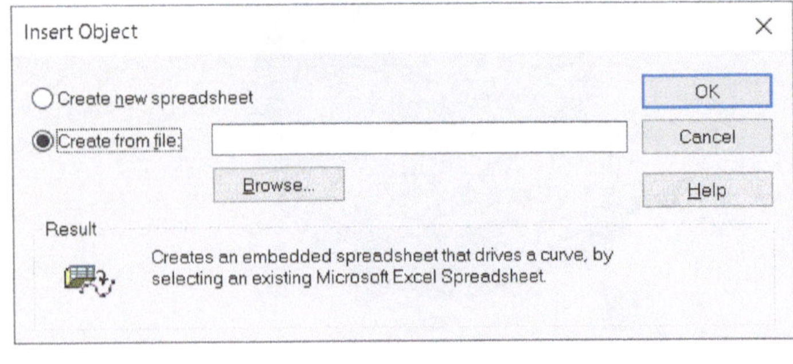

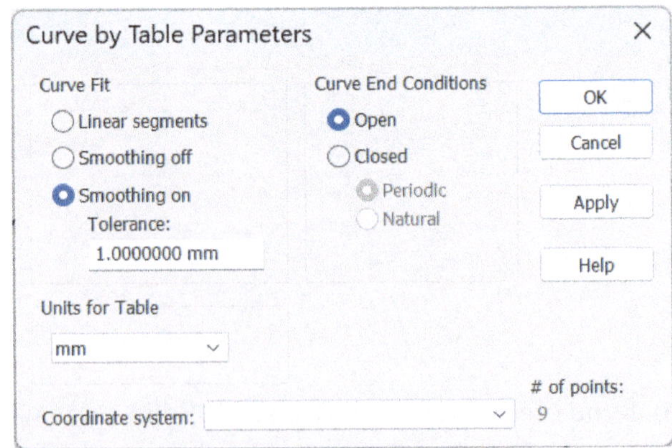

Next, set the **Curve End Conditions** options. You can define open or close curves. Specify the **Units for Table** and **Coordinate system**, and then click **OK**. Click **Finish** to complete the curve.

Helical Curve

This command allows you to create a helical curve.

Constant Pitch Helical Curve

A constant pitch helical curve has an equal distance between the turns. Activate this command (on the ribbon, click **Surfacing > Curves > Helical Curve**); the **Axis** section is activated, and you need to define the axis of the helical curve. Select a key point, arbitrary point in the graphics window, line, circle, cylindrical face, cone face, or type-in values in the X, Y, and Z boxes on the command bar.

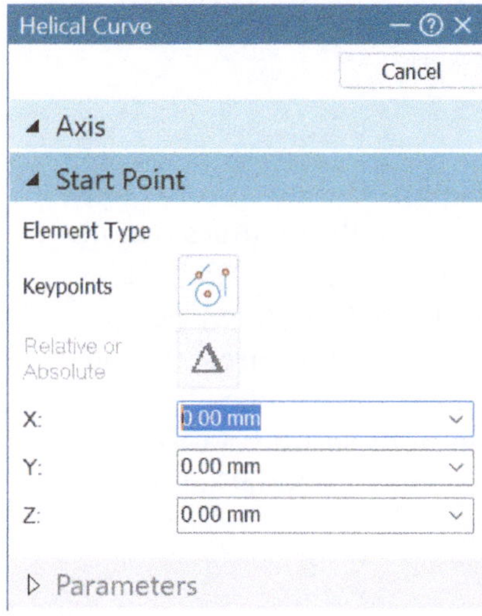

If you select a key point or an arbitrary point in the graphics window, move the pointer in the graphics window. Click to specify the second point of the axis. After specifying the axis, the **Start Point** section is activated, and you need to specify the start point of the helical curve. Move the pointer in the direction perpendicular to the axis and click to specify the helical curve's start point; the **Helical Curve Parameters** dialog pops up on the screen. On the dialog, select **Type > Constant Pitch**. Next, specify the helix creation method by selecting an option from the **Method** drop-down. The options in this drop-down are **Length and Turns**, **Length and Pitch**, and **Pitch and Turns**.

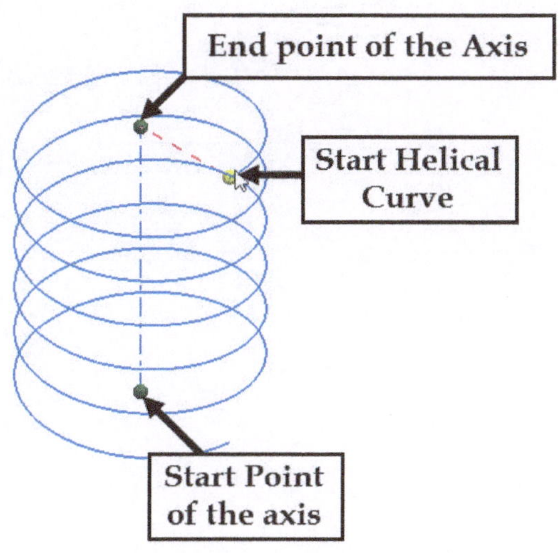

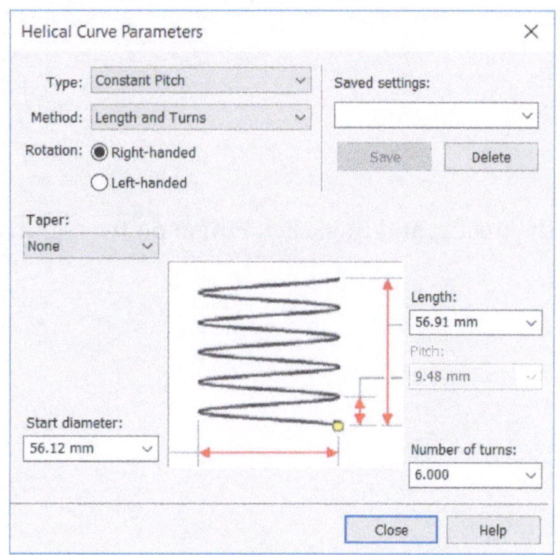

Length and Turns: In this method, you need to specify the total length of the helix and its number of turns in the **Length** and **Number of turns** boxes, respectively.

Length and Pitch: In this method, you need to specify the helix's total length and the distance between the turns.

Pitch and Turns: In this method, you need to specify the distance between the turns and the number of turns.

Next, specify the rotation direction of the helix. You can select the **Right-handed** or **Left-handed** direction of the rotation. Next, type-in a value in the **Start diameter** box. Use the arrow handle that appears on the helical curve to change its side. You can also apply taper to helix using the **Taper** drop-down. Next, click **Close** on the **Helical Curve Parameters** dialog. Next, click **Finish** on the command bar to create the helical curve.

Variable Pitch Helical Curve

Activate the **Helical Curve** command (on the ribbon, click **Surfacing > Curves > Helical Curve**); the **Axis** section is activated, and you need to define the axis of the helical curve. Select a line from the graphics window to define the axis. Move the pointer and click to define the start point of the helical curve. On the **Helical Curve Parameters** dialog, select **Type > Variable Pitch**. Next, select an option from the **Method** drop-down. For example, select the **Pitch and Turns** option. Next, specify the **End pitch**, **Pitch**, and **Number of turns**; the pitch value increases or decreases from the start point to the helical curve's endpoint. For example, if Pitch = 10, End pitch = 3, and Number of turns = 15, the pitch value varies from 10 to 3 (refer to the **Helix** section of *Chapter 6: Sweep Features* for the rate of change in pitch value). Next, specify the **Start diameter** and the **Rotation** direction.

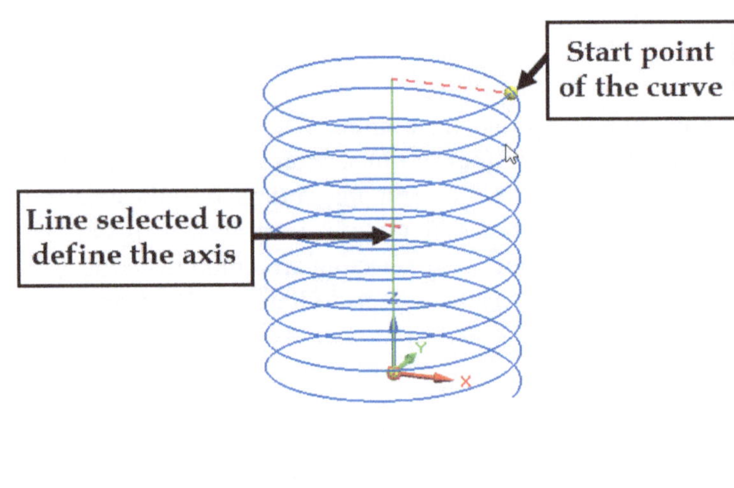

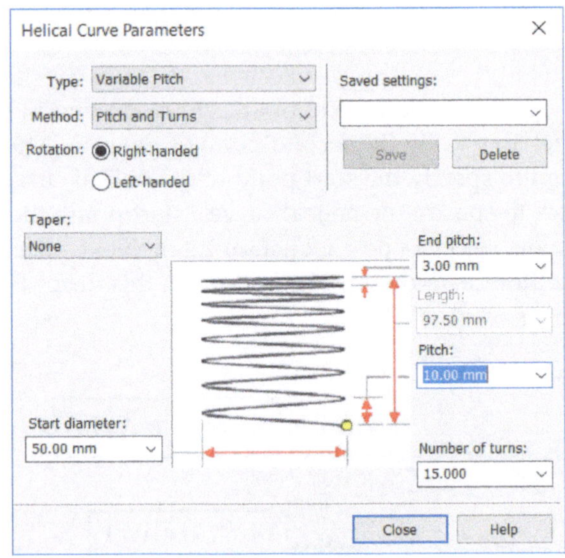

Click **Close** on the dialog, and then click **Finish** on the command bar.

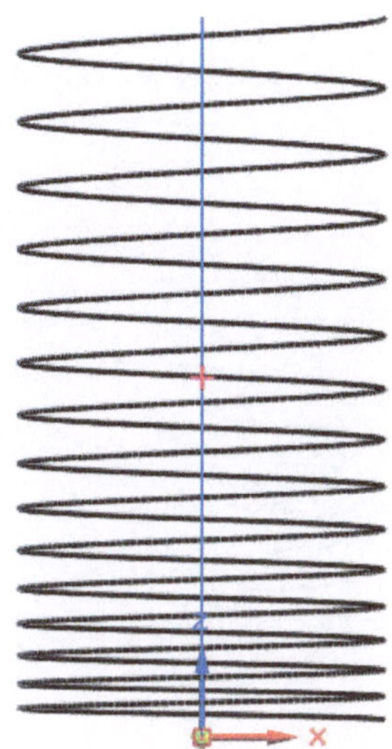

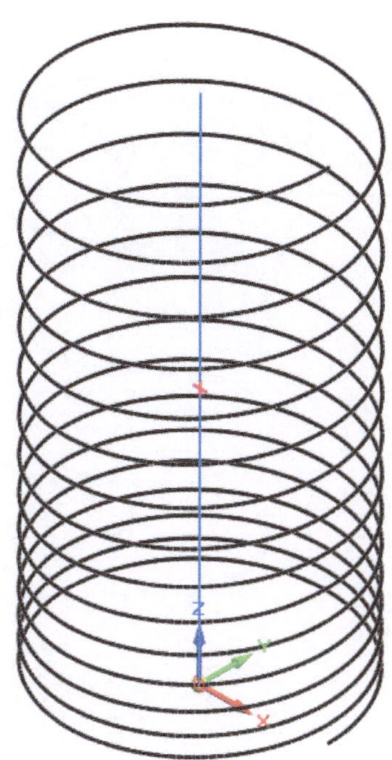

Compound Helical Curve

Activate the **Helical Curve** command (on the ribbon, click **Surfacing > Curves > Helical Curve**); the **Axis** section is activated, and you need to define the axis of the helical curve. Select a circle from the graphics window; the center point of the circle acts as the axis point, and a quadrant point on the circle is used to define the start point of the helical curve. On the **Helical Curve Parameters** dialog, select **Type > Compound**; a table appears at the bottom of the dialog. The parameters in the table are annotated in the figure displayed on the dialog. The table has four parameters and three-point sets. You need to specify the parameters for the three-point sets. However, you can add more point sets using the **Insert** button located at the bottom. Next, select an option from the **Method** drop-down. For example, select the **Pitch and Turns** option and notice that the **Length** fields of all the point sets are greyed out. Also, the **Turns** and **Diameter** fields of the first point are greyed out. You need to specify the **Pitch** values of the point sets. Also, specify the **Turns** and **Diameter** values for all the point sets except for the first point set. The following figure shows the values of the parameters in the table and the output achieved.

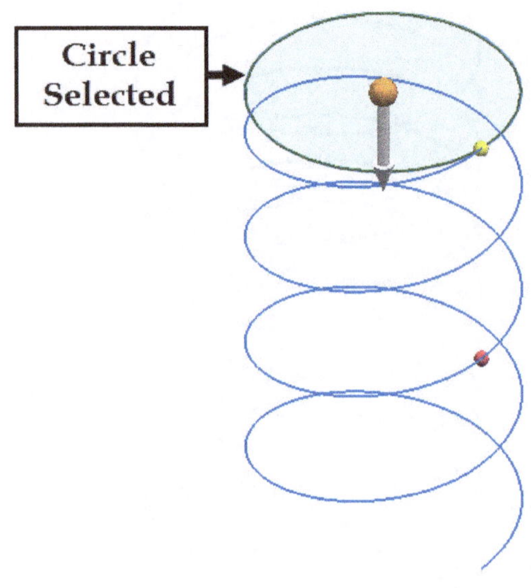

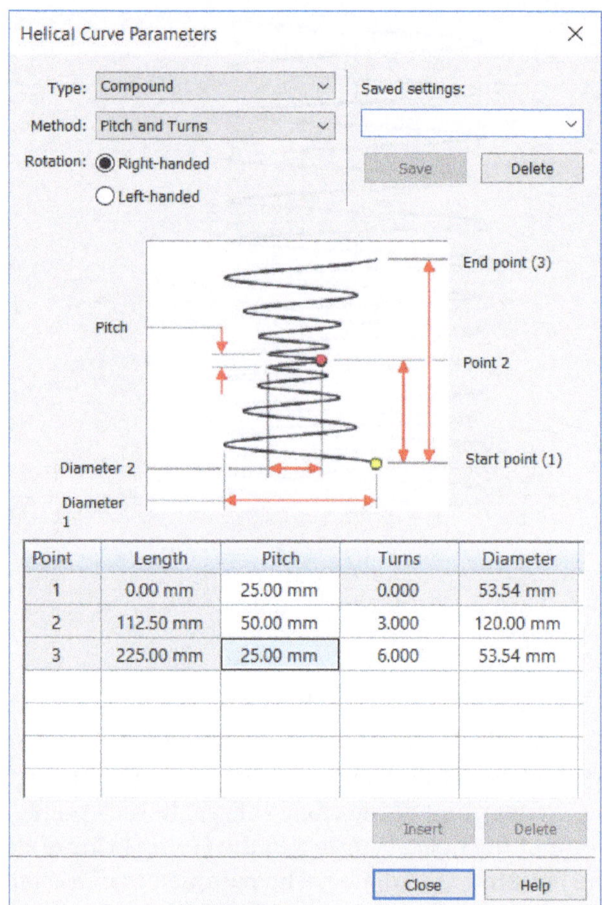

Point	Length	Pitch	Turns	Diameter
1	0.00 mm	25.00 mm	0.000	53.54 mm
2	112.50 mm	50.00 mm	3.000	120.00 mm
3	225.00 mm	25.00 mm	6.000	53.54 mm

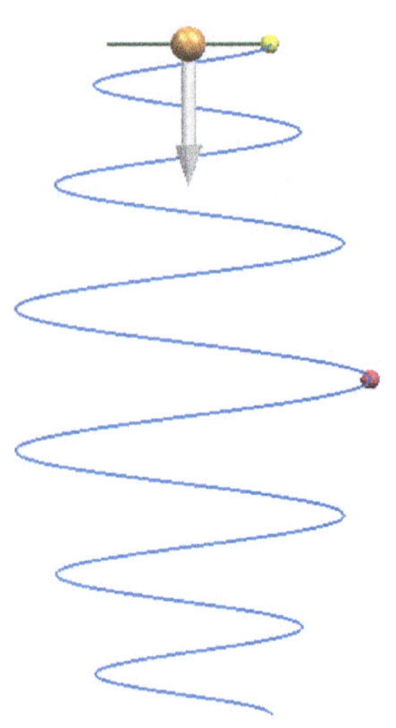

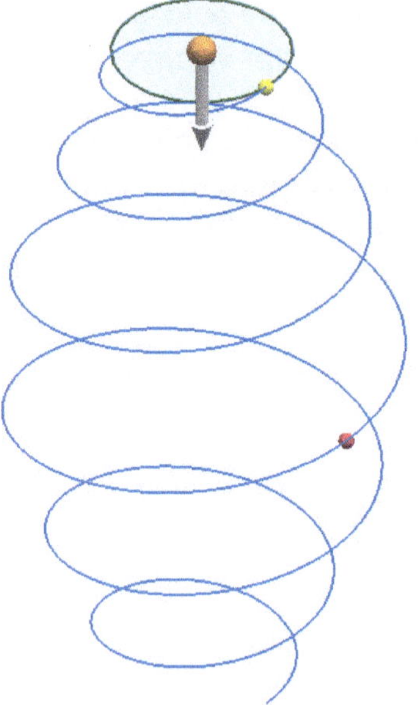

Click **Close** on the dialog, and then **Finish** on the command bar.

Spiral Curve

Activate the **Helical Curve** command (on the ribbon, click **Surfacing > Curves > Helical Curve**); the **Axis** section is activated, and you need to define the axis of the spiral curve. Select a circle from the graphics window; the center point of the circle acts as the axis point, and a quadrant point on the circle is used to define the start point of the spiral curve. On the **Helical Curve Parameters** dialog, select **Type > Spiral**. Next, specify the spiral curve creation method by selecting an option from the **Method** drop-down. The options in this drop-down are **End diameter and Turns, End diameter and Radial pitch**, and **Radial pitch and Turns.**

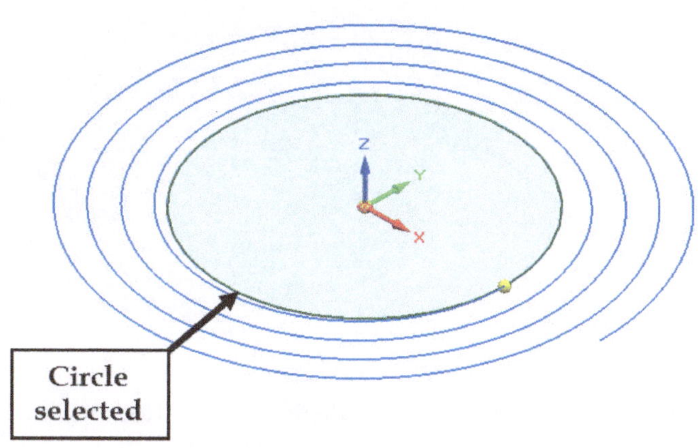

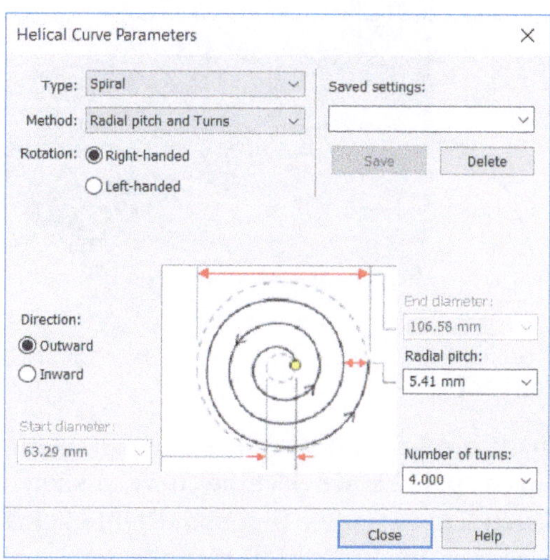

End diameter and Turns: In this method, you need to specify the outer or inner diameter of the spiral curve for the Outward or Inward spiral curve, respectively. Next, you need to specify the **Number of turns** value.

End diameter and Radial pitch: In this method, you need to specify the end diameter and the radial distance between the turns.

Radial pitch and Turns: In this method, you need to specify the radial distance between the turns and the number of turns. Also, you need to specify the **Direction** of the spiral curve. It can be **Outward** or **Inward**.

Next, select the **Rotation** direction and specify the parameters (**End diameter**, **Radial pitch**, and **Number of turns**) depending on the option selected from the **Method** drop-down. Click **Close** on the dialog, and then click **Finish**.

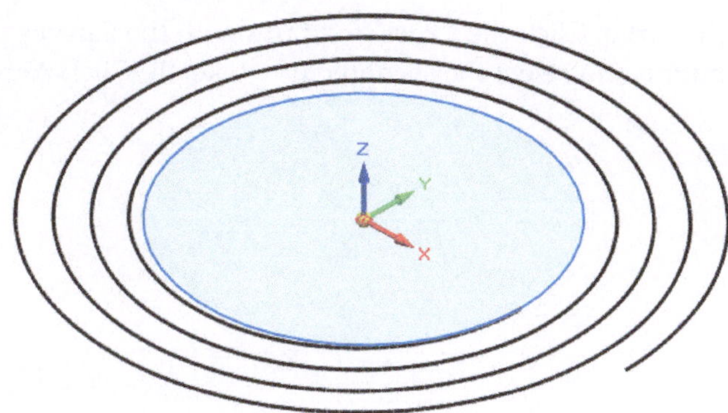

Intersection

The **Intersection** command creates a curve at the intersection of the surface and plane, or two surfaces, or solid and surface, or solid and plane. Activate the **Intersection** command (on the ribbon, click **Surfacing > Curves > Intersection**) and select the two intersecting surfaces. Click **Finish** to create the intersection curve.

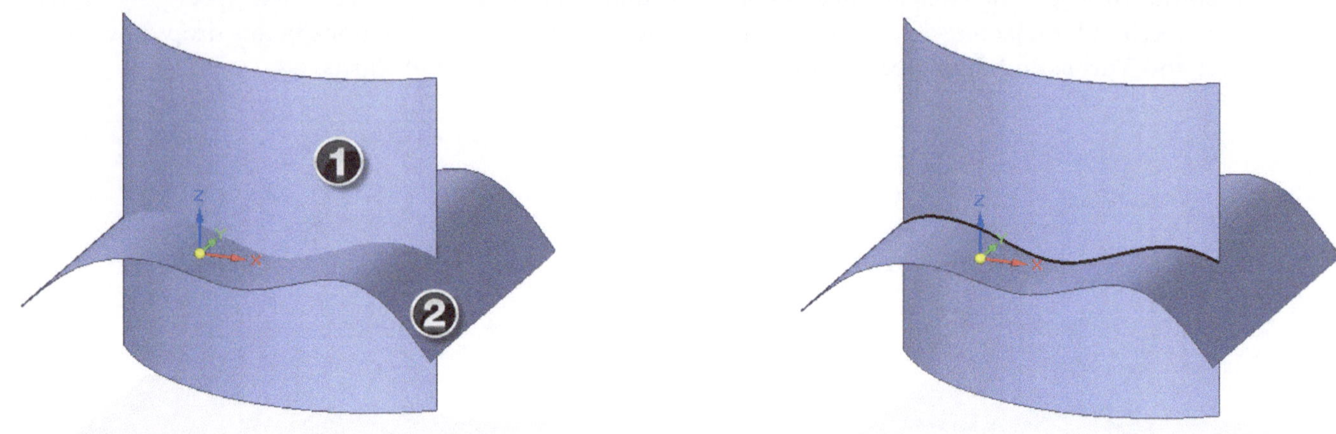

Project

The **Project** command takes a sketch or curve and maps it onto a surface. Click the **Project** button on the **Curves** panel and select the curve or sketch to project. Right-click and select the surface onto which the sketch/curve will be mapped. Right-click, and then define the side of the projection. If you have selected a curve to project, the **Projection Plane** section is activated, and you need to select a plane to define the projection direction. The curve will be projected in the direction normal to the selected plane. Click **Finish** to complete the projection.

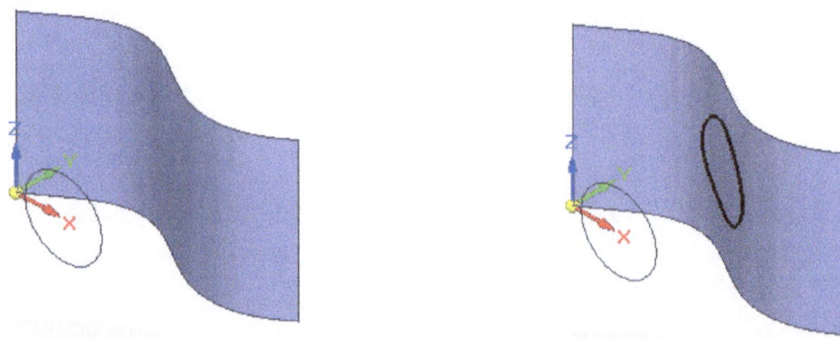

Cross

The **Cross** command is similar to the **Project** command except that it creates a curve by projecting one sketch/curve onto another sketch/curve. Click the **Cross** button on the **Curves** panel and select the first sketch/curve. Click the **Accept** button and select the second curve/sketch. Click **Accept** and **Finish** to create the cross curve.

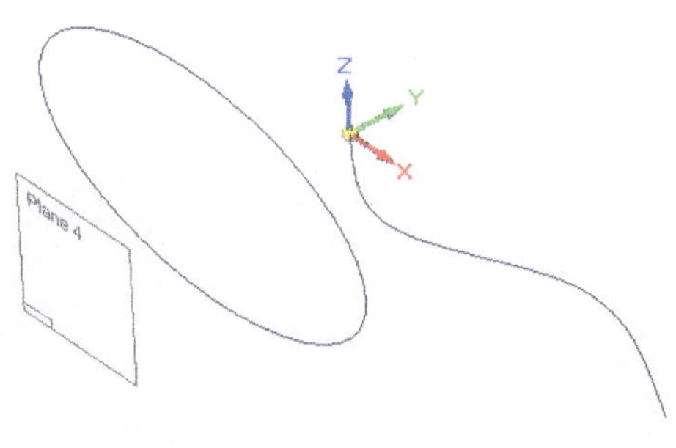

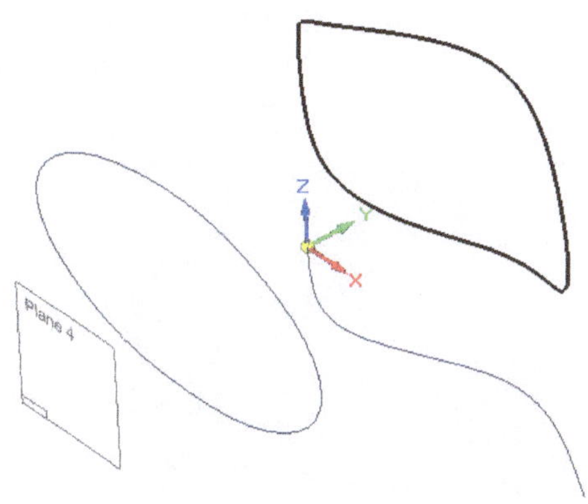

Wrap Sketch

The **Wrap Sketch** command wraps a sketch around the solid or surface body. First, create a sketch on the plane tangent to the surface onto which the sketch is wrapped. Next, click **Project > Wrap Sketch** on the **Curves** panel. Select the surface on which you want to wrap the sketch, and then right-click. Select the sketch and right-click. Click **Finish** to wrap the sketch.

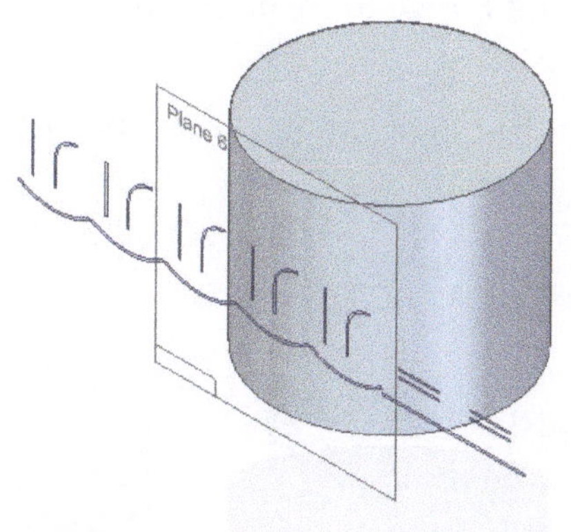

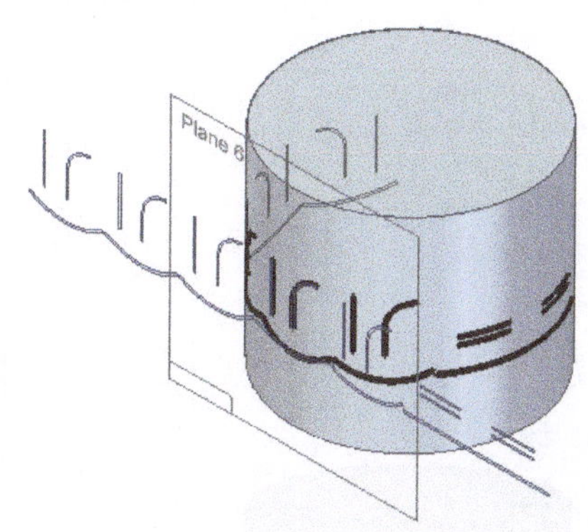

Contour

The **Contour** command creates curves on a surface. Activate this command (on the ribbon, **Surfacing > Curves > Contour**) select the surface. You can select a single or chain of surfaces. Click **Accept** after selecting the surface. Start selecting points on the surface. On the command bar, click the **Close** button if you want to close the curve. Click **Accept** and **Finish** to create the contour curve.

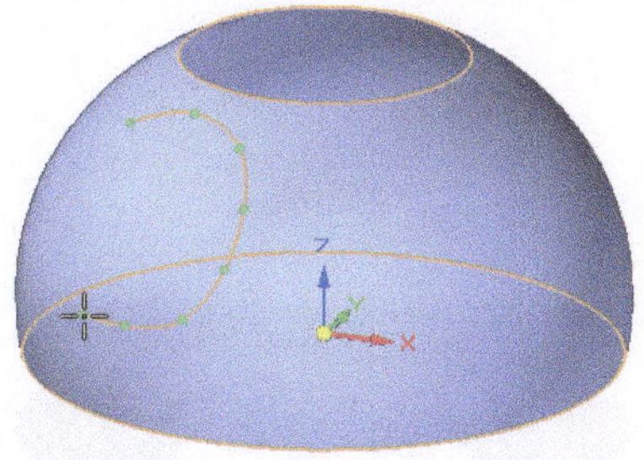

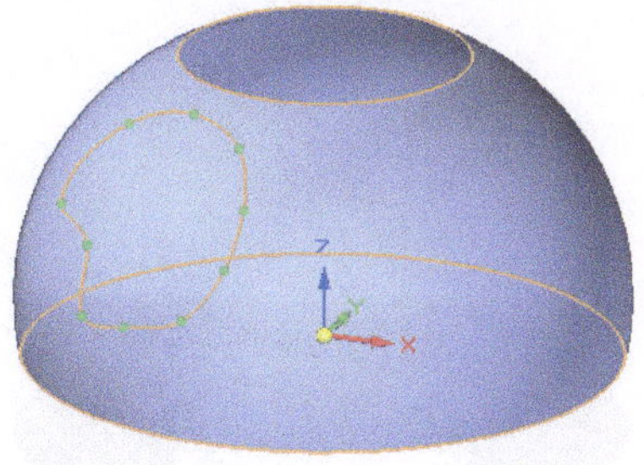

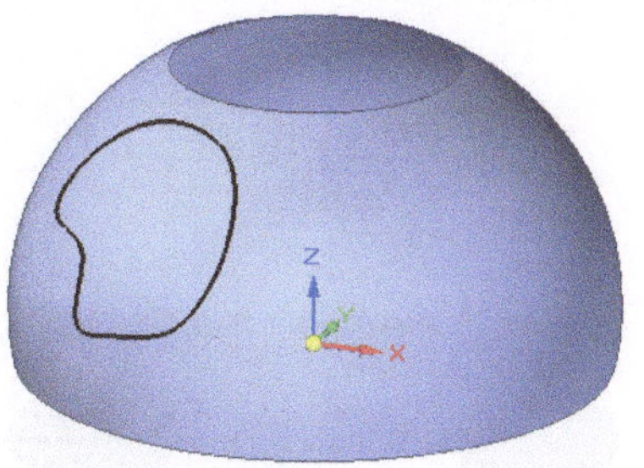

Isocline

The **Isocline** command creates a curve on a surface by using a plane. You need to select a plane and then specify an angle; a curve will be created at the point where the selected plane touches the surface when inclined at the specified angle. For example, click the **Isocline** button on the **Curves** panel and select the Front(XZ) plane.

Select the solid or surface body. Type-in the inclination angle and click the arrow to define the side of the isoclines curve. Click **Accept** and **Finish** to create the curve.

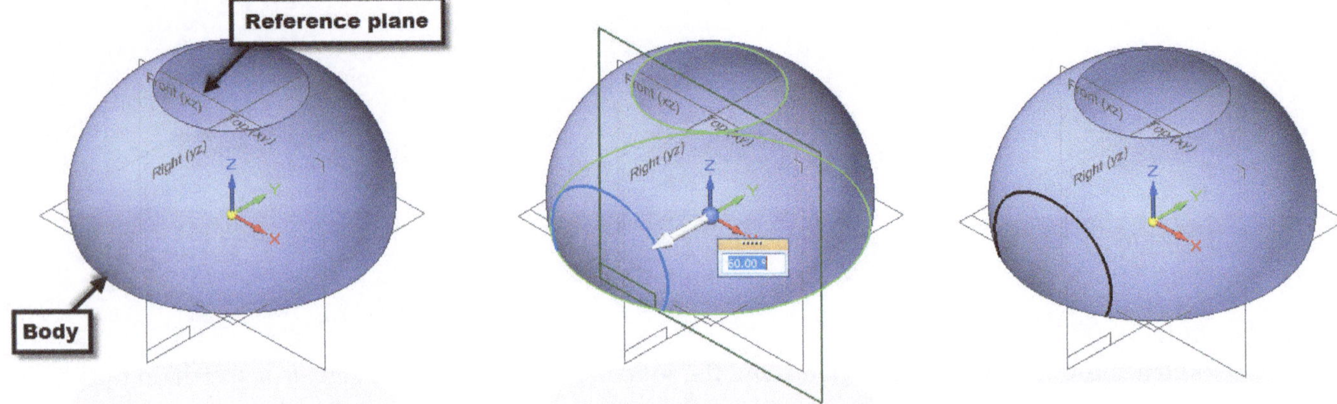

Derived

The **Derived** command creates a curve from the selected edges of solid/surface geometry. Click the **Derived** button on the **Curves** panel and select the edges of the geometry. Click **Accept** and **Finish** to create the derived curve.

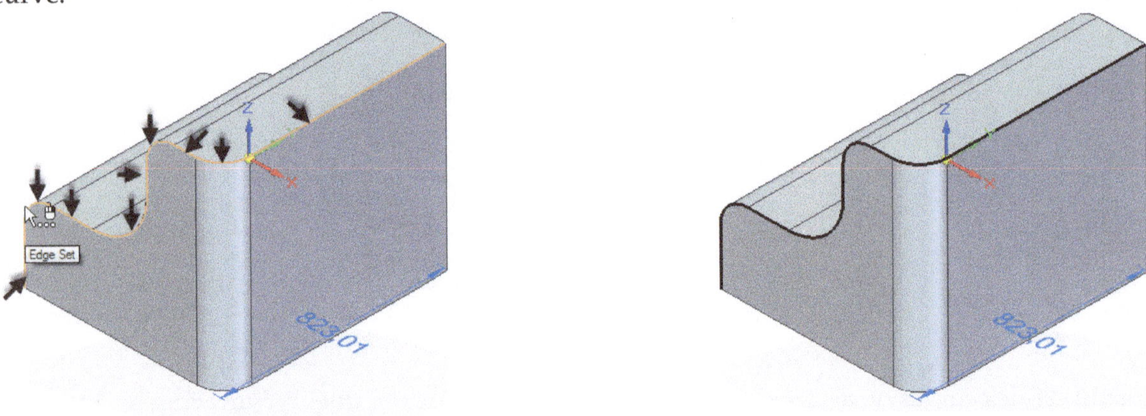

Split

The **Split** command splits a curve using an intersecting plane, curve, body, or point. Click the **Split** command on the **Curves** panel and select the curve. Right-click and select the intersecting elements. Click **Accept** and **Finish**.

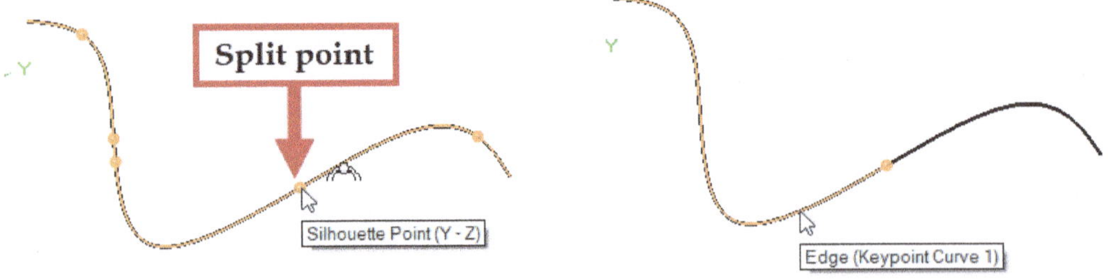

Intersection Point

The **Intersection Point** command creates points at the intersection of a curve/edge and another element. Click the **Intersection Point** button on the **Curves** panel. Select a curve/edge and right-click. Select a plane, axis or body. Click **Accept** and **Finish**.

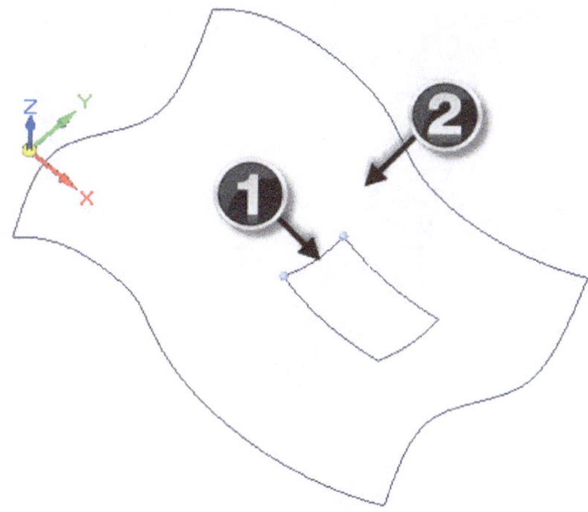

Swept Surfaces

The **Swept** command creates a surface by sweeping one or more cross-sections along guide curves. It also provides various options to control the shape along the guides. To create a swept surface, first, create a sweep profile and a path. On the ribbon, click **Surfacing > Surfaces > Swept** . On the **Sweep Options** dialog, select the **Single path and cross section** option and click **OK**. Select the path and right-click. Select the cross-section and right-click. Click **Finish** on the command bar.

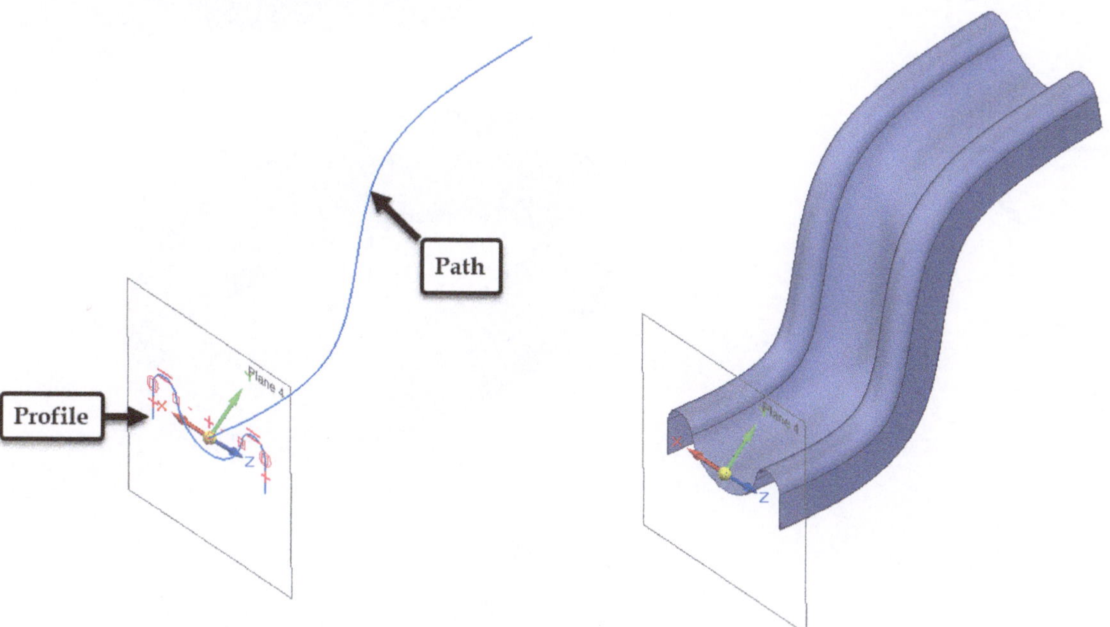

Various ways of creating swept surfaces are given next.

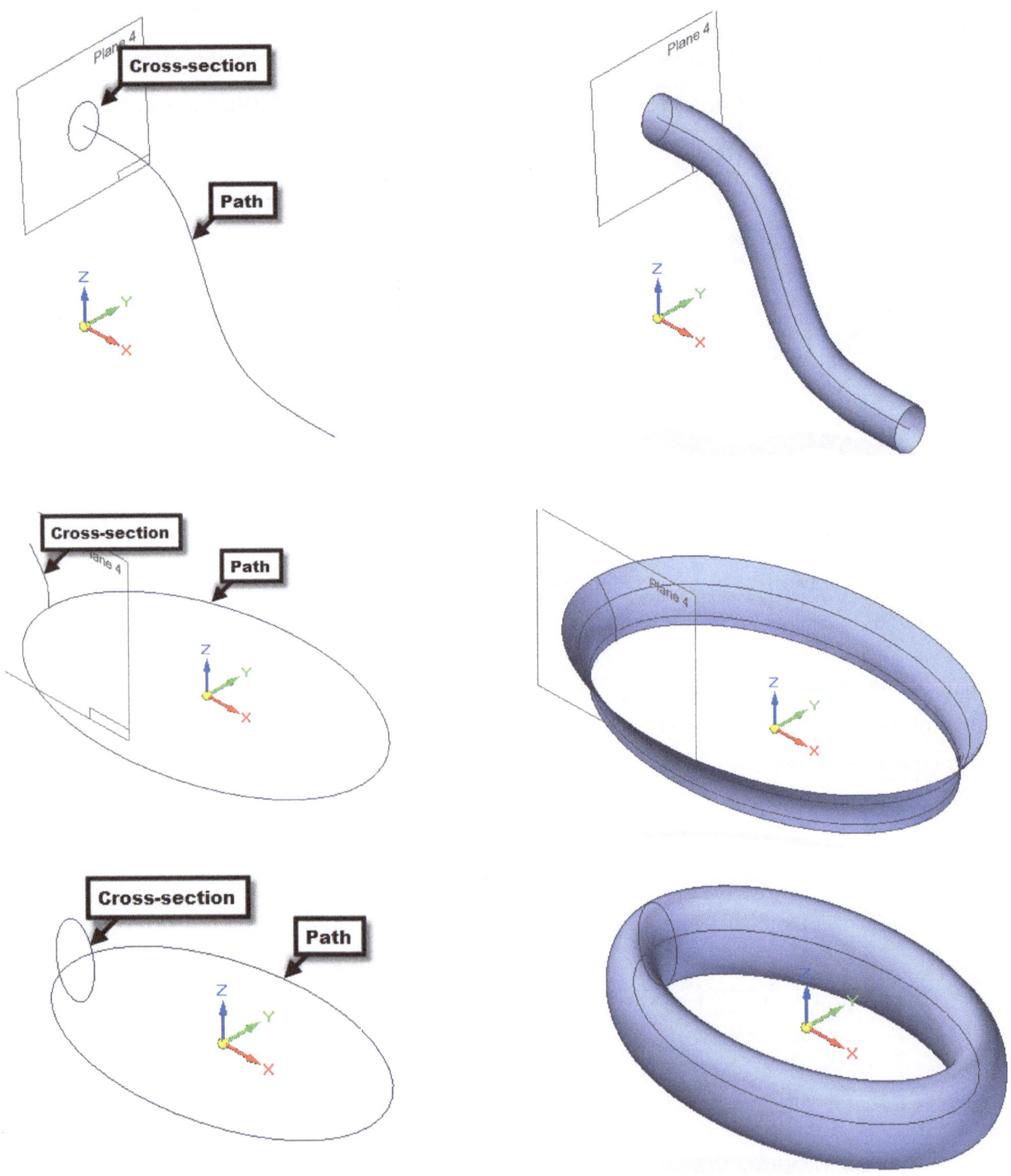
Plane 4
Cross-section
Path
Z
Y
X
Plane 4
Z
Y
X
Cross-section
Plane 4
Path
Z
Y
X
Plane 4
Z
Y
X
Cross-section
Path
Z
Y
X
Y
X

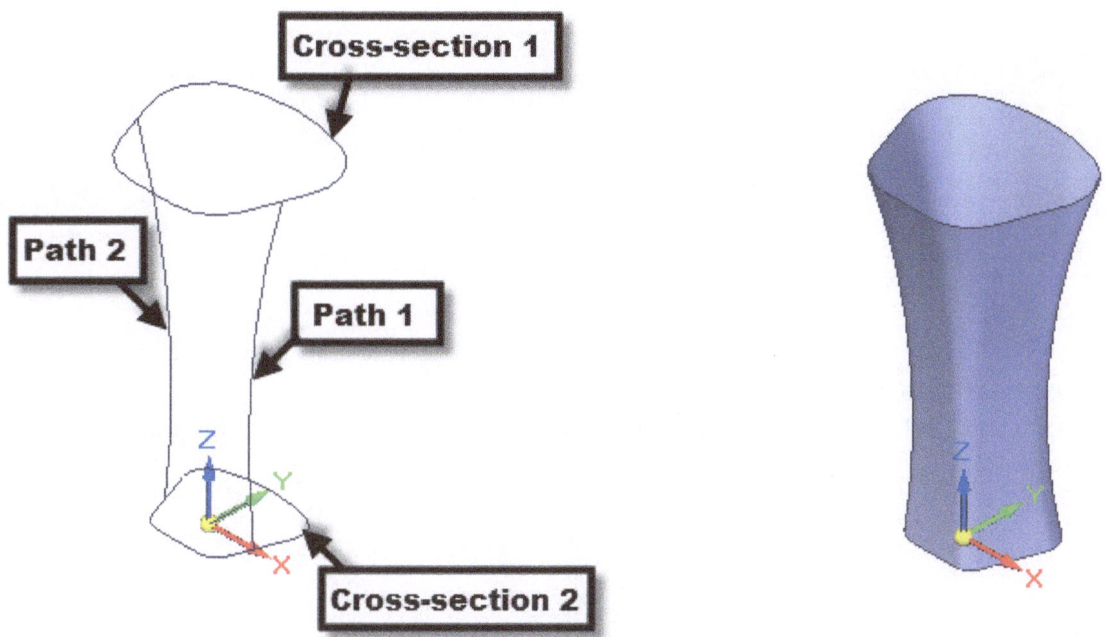

BlueSurf

This command creates a surface between two or more cross-sections. You can also add guide curves to specify the shape between two sections. Make sure that the guide curve is continuous without any sharp edges and touches the cross-sections as well.

BlueSurf between cross-sections

Activate the **BlueSurf** command (on the ribbon, click **Surfacing > Surfaces > BlueSurf**). Select the first cross-section and right-click. Likewise, select the second and third cross-sections.

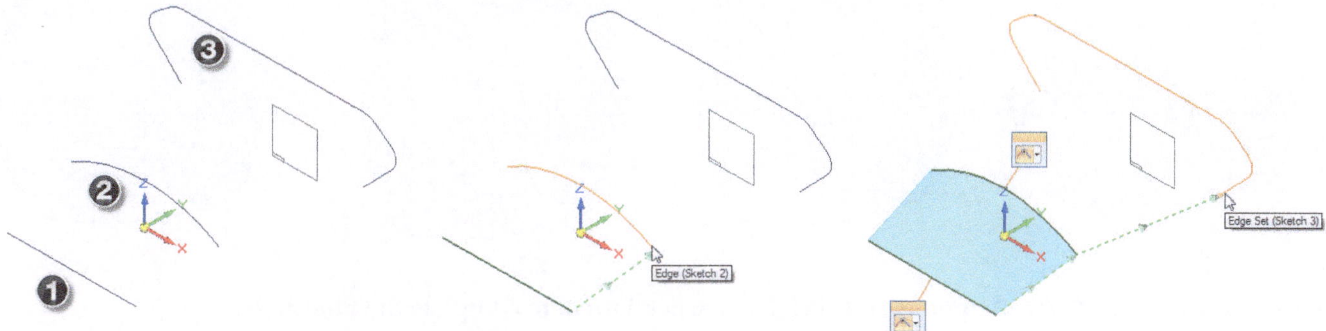

You can use the **Deselect All** icon to deselect all the selected cross-sections.

Select an option from the **Tangency Control** handles attached to the cross-sections. Click **Next** and **Finish** on the command bar.

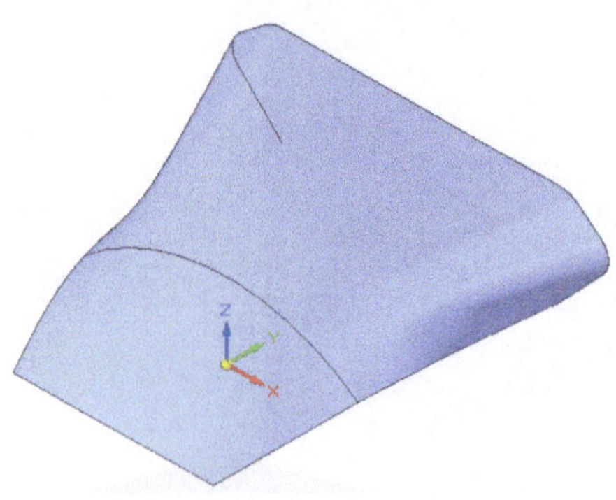

BlueSurf using Cross-sections and Guide Curves

Activate the **BlueSurf** command and select the cross-sections. Click **Accept** (green check) on the command bar after selecting each cross-section.

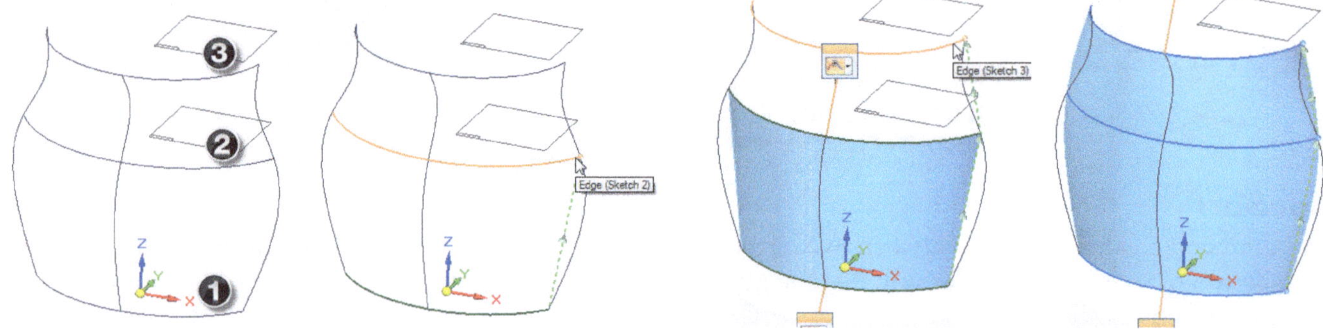

Click **Guide Curve** section after selecting all the cross-sections. Now, select the guide curves one-by-one. Click **Accept** after each selection.

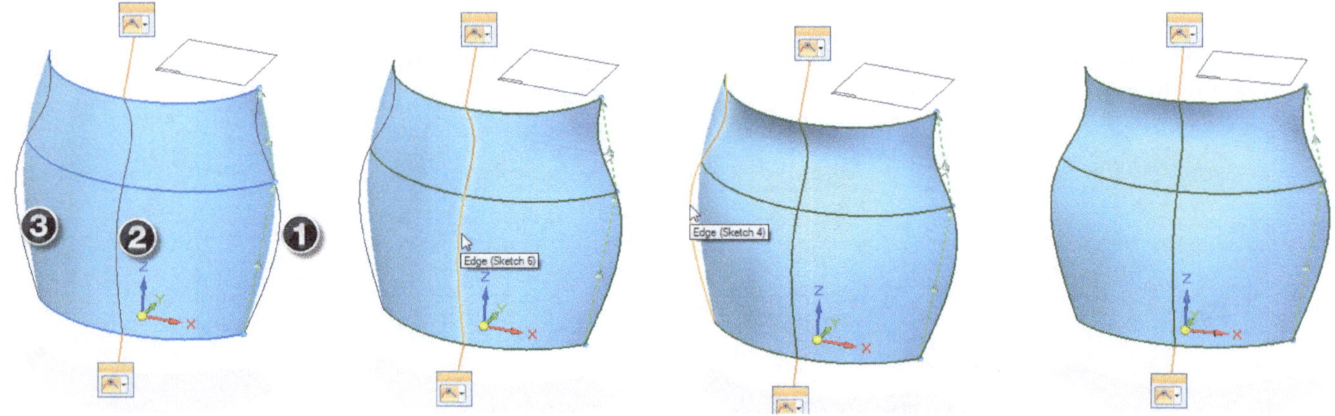

Select the **Tangency Control** options and click **Next**. Click **Finish** to complete the Bluesurf.

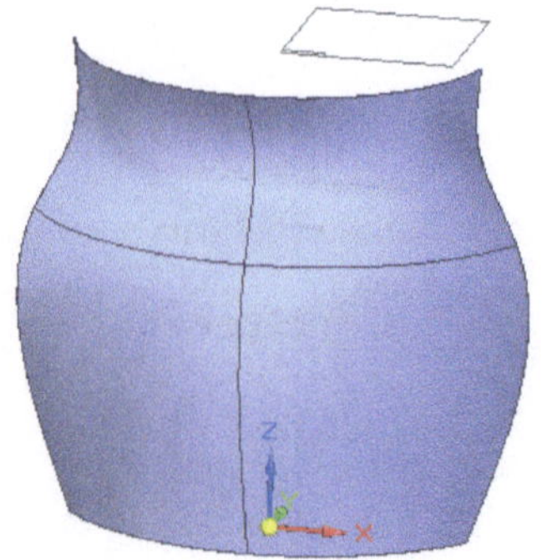

If you want to modify the shape of the Bluesurf by adding a new section, click on the surface and select **Edit Definition** . Note that this option is available only when the surface is created in the **Ordered** mode. On the command bar, click the **Insert Sketch** section and define the location of the new cross-section plane. Click **Next** and **Finish** to complete the bluesurf. You will notice that a new sketch appears in the Pathfinder. Modify the shape of this sketch to modify the bluesurf.

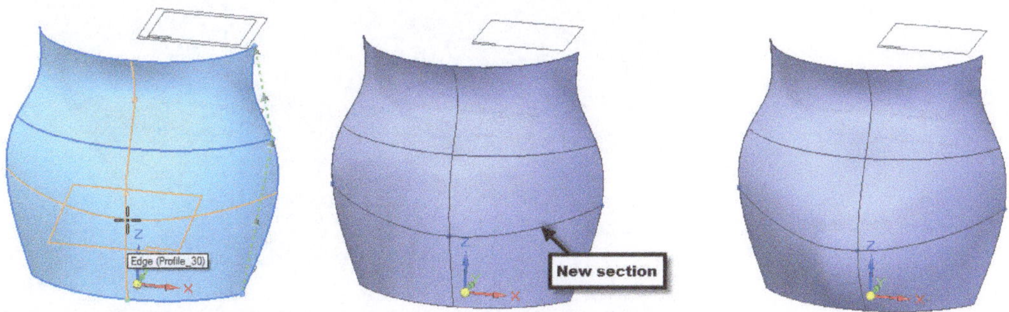

Section Sketches

This command creates multiple 2D cross-section sketches. Activate this command (on the ribbon, click **Surfacing** tab > **Curves** group > **Section Sketches**) and select the surface. Next, click the **Accept** button or press ENTER. Next, select the reference plane from the graphics window. On the command bar, type-in values in the **Number of offset** and **Offset** boxes, respectively. Next, click the **Section Sketches Options** section on the command bar to display the **Section Sketches Options** dialog. In this dialog, select the elements to be recognized from the cross-section sketch. Next, click **OK** on the **Section Sketches Options** dialog. Make sure that the arrow is pointing inside the model. Click on the arrow to change its direction. Click **Accept** on the command bar.

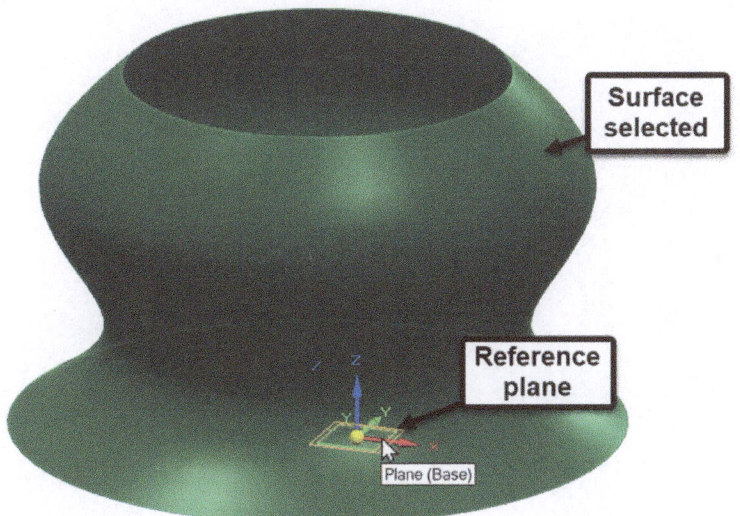

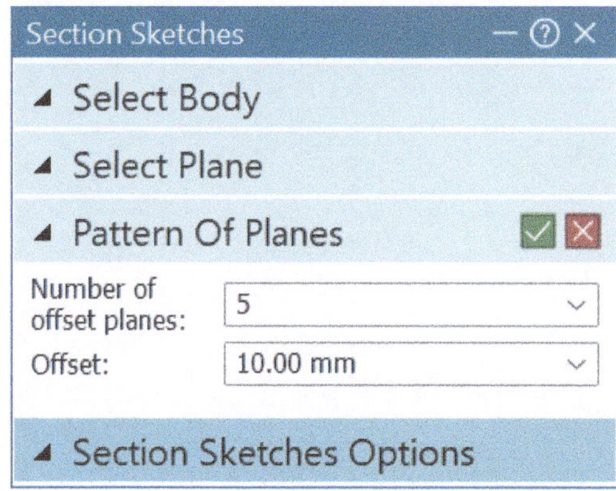

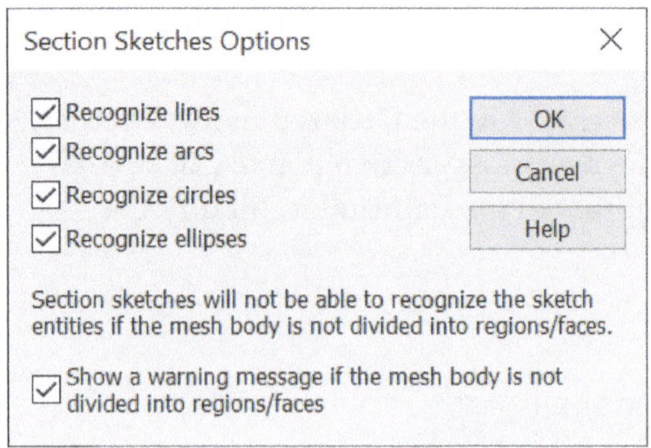

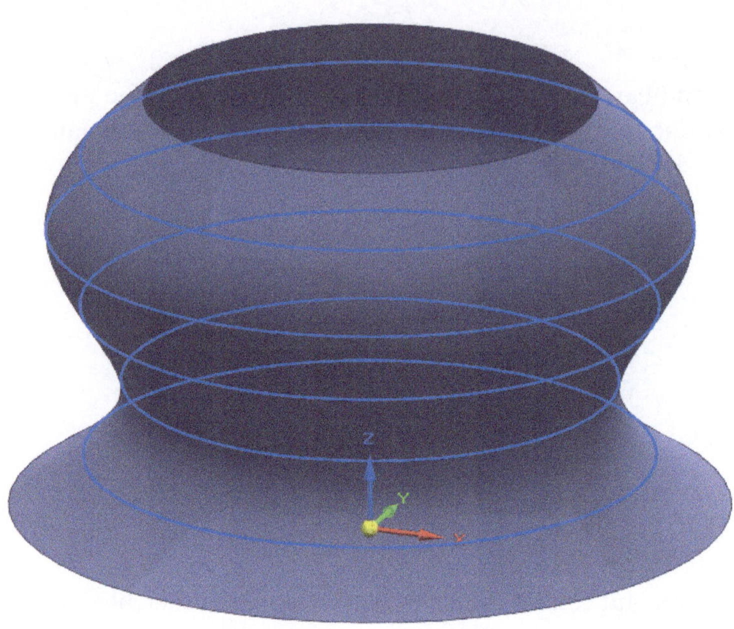

Bounded

The **Bounded** command can be used either to patch holes in models or to create complex surfaces. As a patching tool, the **Bounded** command is more robust than deleting holes. It provides more discrete control over the definition of the resultant patch. For example, consider the model shown in the figure. You can see that the face is missing. In a case like this, the **Bounded** command can be used to fill the gap.

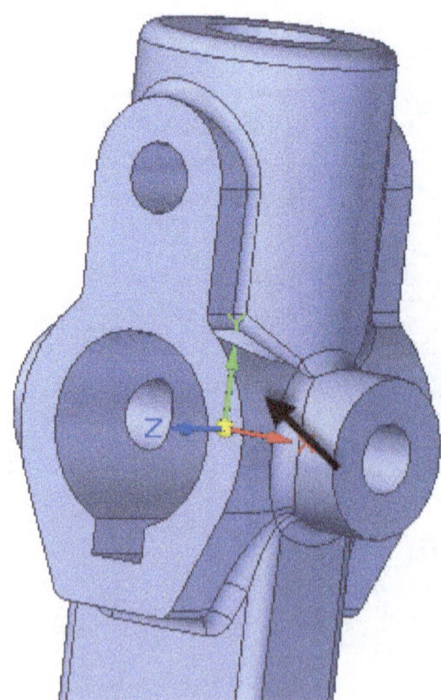

To create a bounded surface, click **Surfacing > Surfaces > Bounded**. Next, you need to select the patch boundaries. To select the patch boundaries, set the **Selection Type** to **Chain** and click on any one of the open edges. Now, you need to set the tangent condition. You can use the **Tangency Control** handle attached to the selected boundary. The options in this handle are **Natural**, **Tangency Continuous**, and **Curvature Continuous**. Most of the gap edges should be tangent to the surrounding faces. For this example, the bounded surface should be natural, as shown in Figure. Use the **Common Tangent Condition** 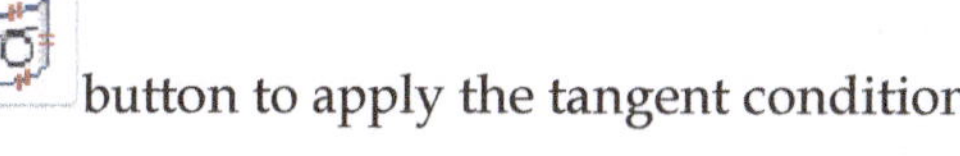 button to apply the tangent condition to all edges.

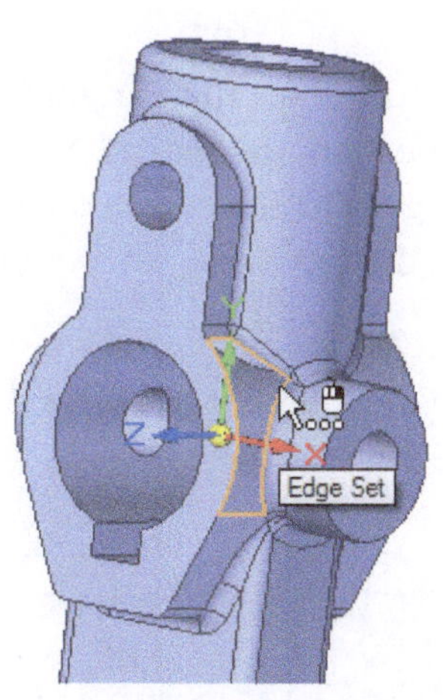

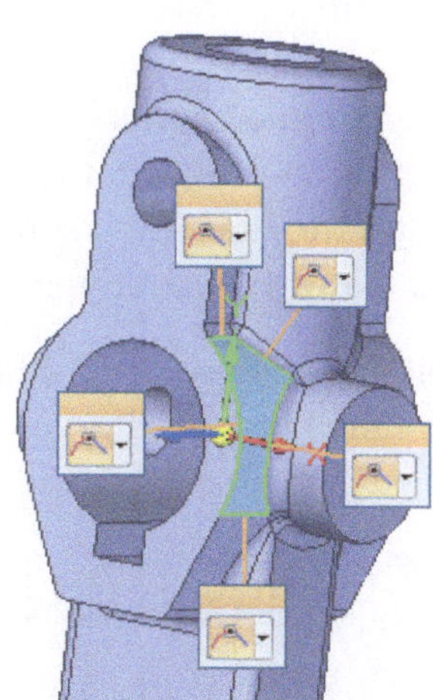

After specifying the required settings, click **Accept** and **Finish** to create the bounded surface, as shown below.

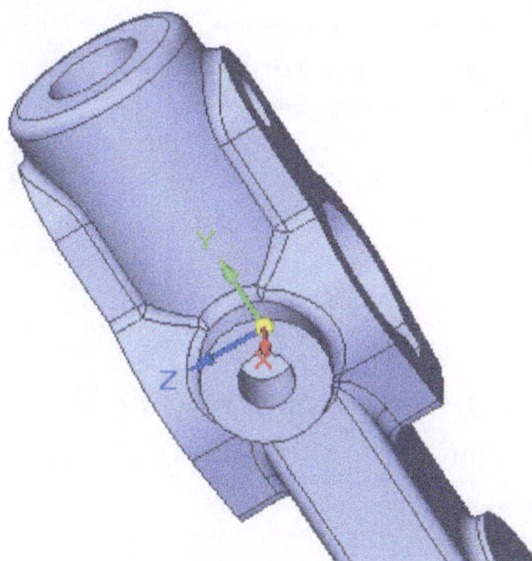

You can also use the **Bounded** command for creating a new surface. Activate this command and select the boundary. Right-click to accept the selection. Click the **Guide Curve** section and then select the guide curves. The preview of the bounded surface appears. After defining the required settings, click **Accept** and **Finish** to create the bounded surface

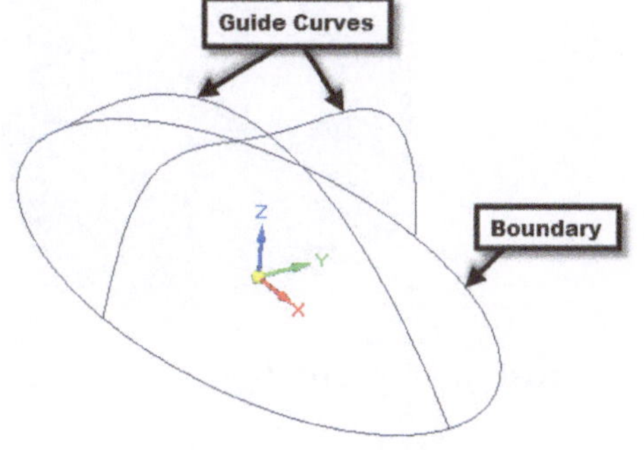

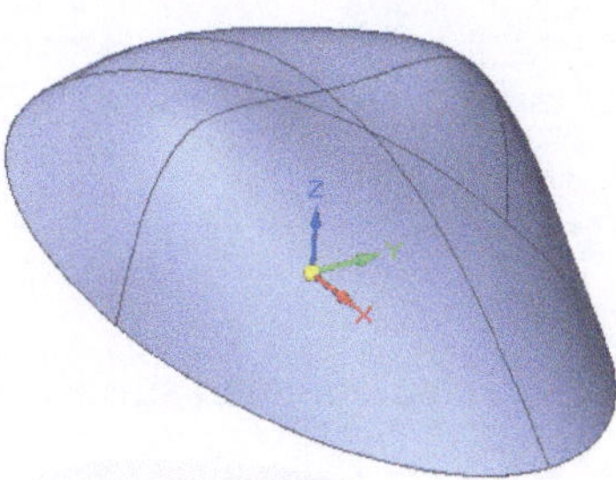

Ruled Surfaces

The **Ruled** command creates surfaces attached to the edges of existing surfaces. You can find the **Ruled Surface** command on the **Surfaces** panel. You can create five types of ruled surfaces using the options in the command bar. These five types of ruled surfaces are discussed next.

The first type is the tangent ruled surface. To create a tangent ruled surface, select the **Tangent Continuous** option from the **Ruled Options** drop-down on the command bar. Select an edge from the model. You will notice that the preview of the ruled surface appears. The resultant surface will be tangent to the selected edge. In this case, the selected edge is associated with two reference surfaces (the vertical and the top surfaces). As a result, there will be two solutions available from the selected edge. Click the **Alternate Face/Side** button on the command bar to view the alternate solution. Enter a distance value in the **Distance** box. Click **Accept** to create the ruled surface.

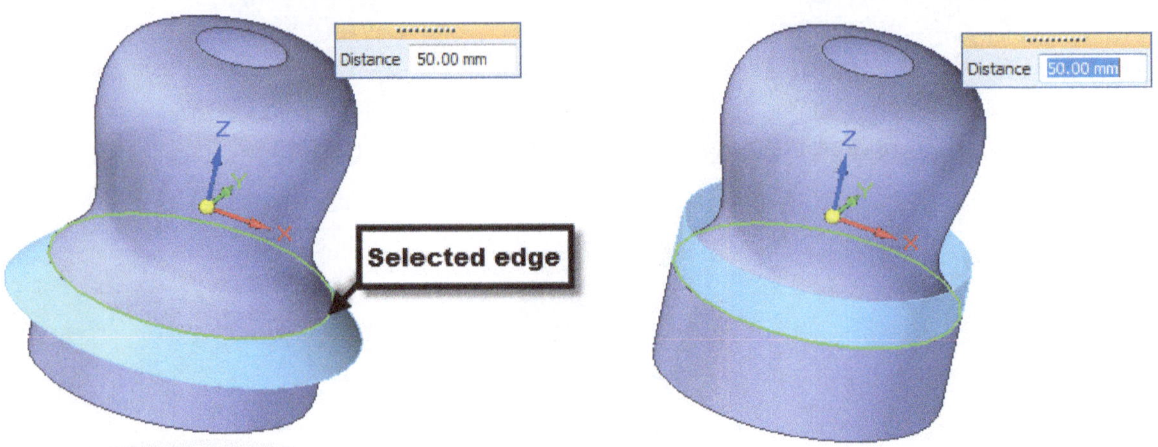

Select the **Normal to face** option from the **Ruled Options** drop-down to create a ruled surface normal to the supporting surface. Use the arrow to change the direction of the surface.

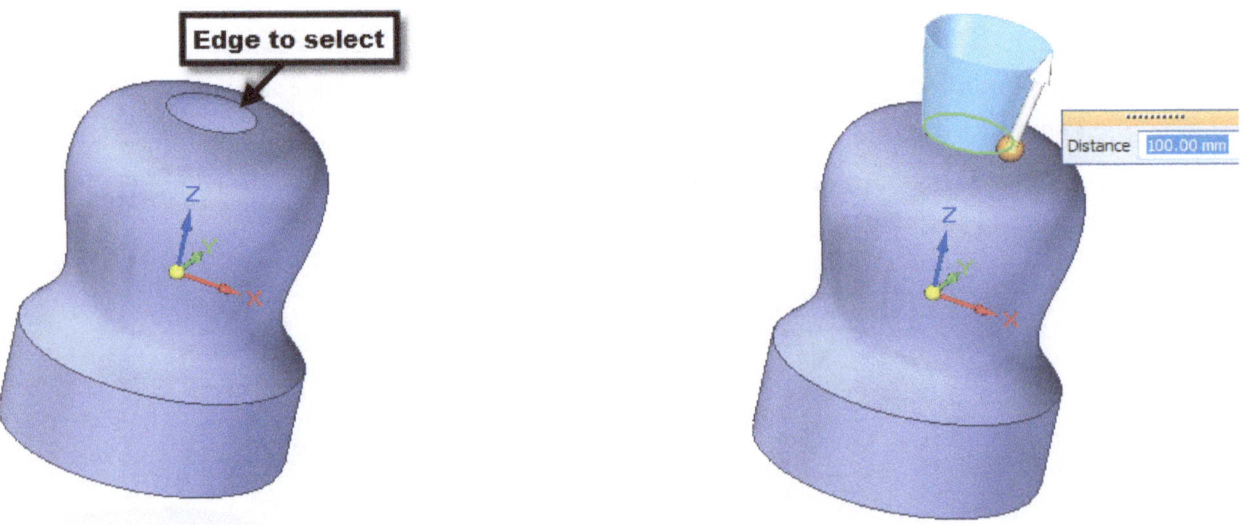

Use the **Natural** option to create a ruled surface without any constraining condition.

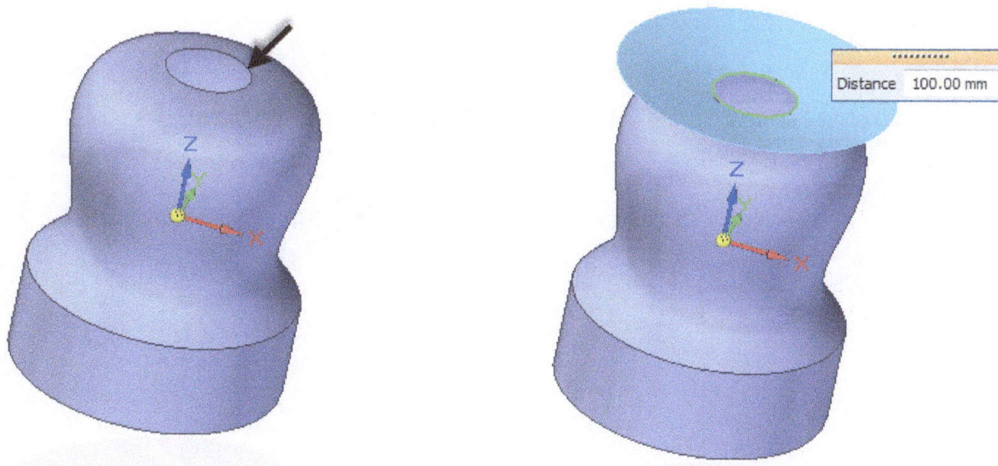

Use the **Along an axis** option to create a ruled surface by sweeping the selected edge along an axis. Select a sketch, edge, or curve to define the reference axis. Select the edge, and then define the **Distance** and **Angle** values.

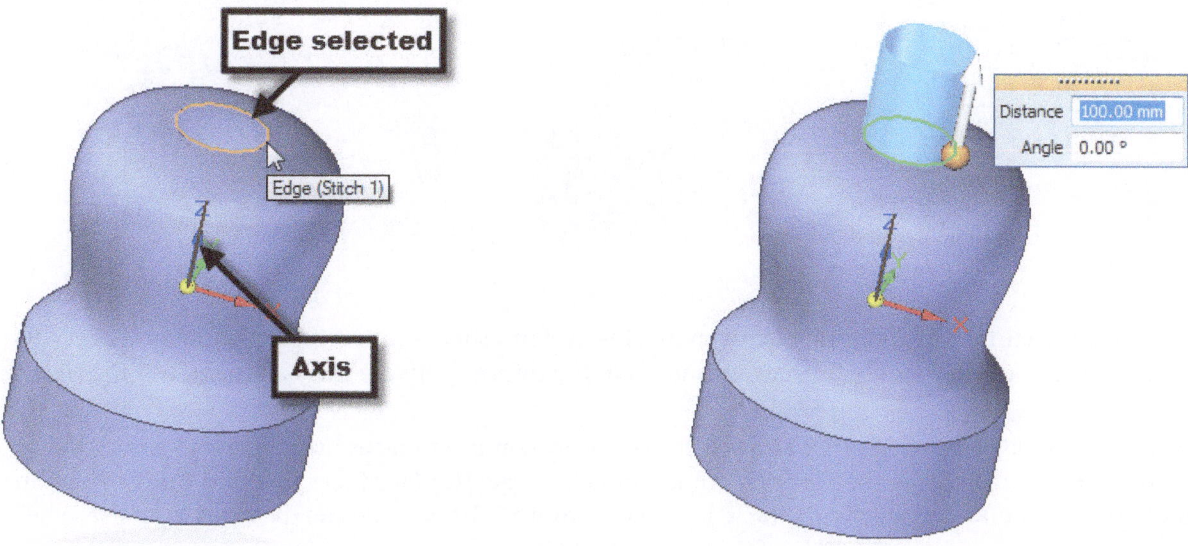

Select the **Tapered to plane** option from the **Ruled Options** drop-down to create a ruled surface at an angle to a plane. Select a planar face or plane to define the reference. Select an edge from the model.

Specify the distance and taper angle of the ruled surface in the **Distance** and **Angle** boxes. Click the arrow to change the direction of the ruled surface. Click **Accept** to create the ruled surface.

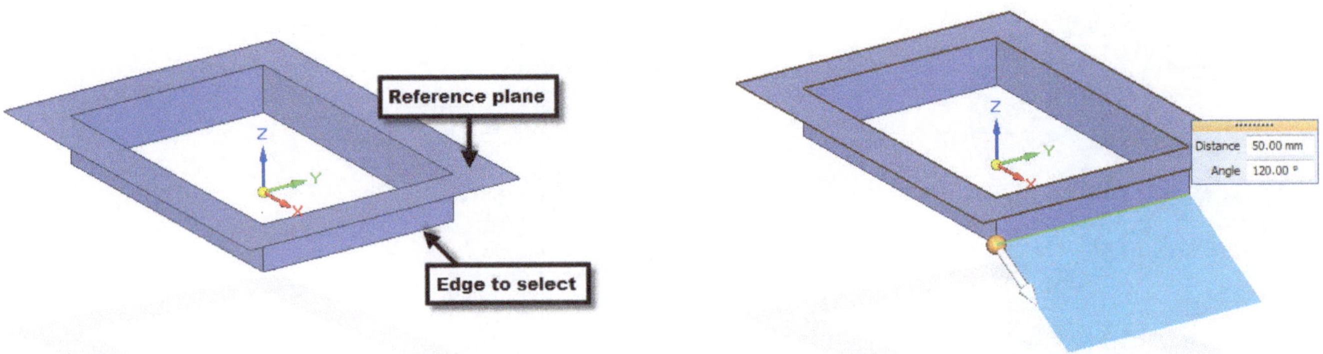

Offset

To create an offset surface, activate the **Offset** command (click **Surfacing > Surfaces > Offset** on the ribbon) and select the faces to offset. Right-click to accept the selection. Next, type-in a value in the **Distance** box and click to define the offset surface's side. Click **Finish** to complete the offset surface.

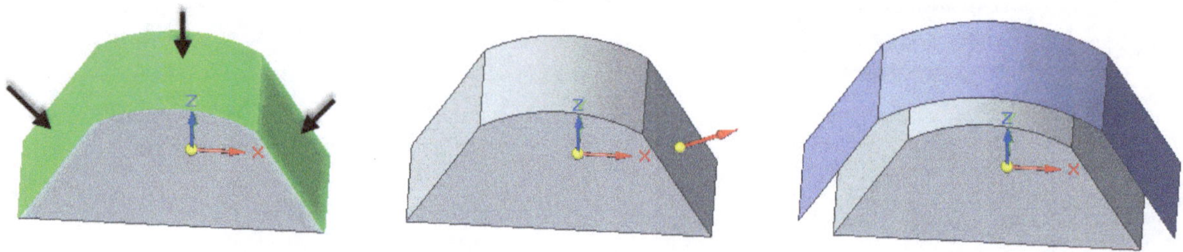

Redefine

This command creates a surface by merging two or more closely connected surfaces. This command is very useful when a solid or surface body contains split faces, as shown in the figure. Activate this command (on the ribbon, click **Surfacing > Surfaces > Redefine**) and select the closely connected faces. Right-click to accept the selection. On the command bar, click the **Options** button and check the **Replace faces on solid body** option in case of a solid body. Click **OK** to close the dialog. Click **Accept** and **Finish** to redefine the faces.

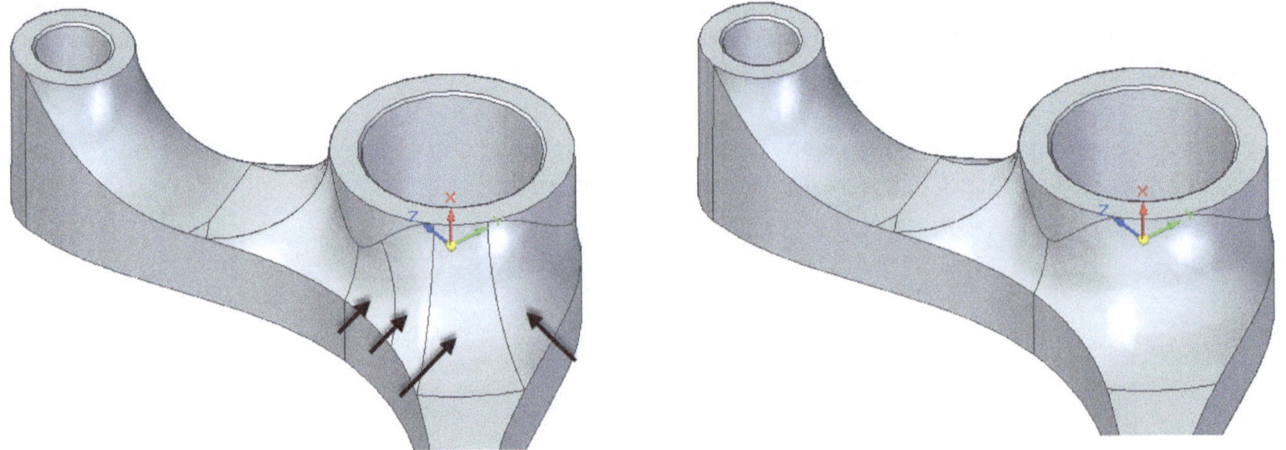

Copy

This command creates a copy of the existing surfaces. Activate this command (on the ribbon, click **Surfacing > Surfaces > Copy**) and select the surfaces to copy. Right-click to accept the selection, and then click **Finish**. Hide the original body to view the copied surface.

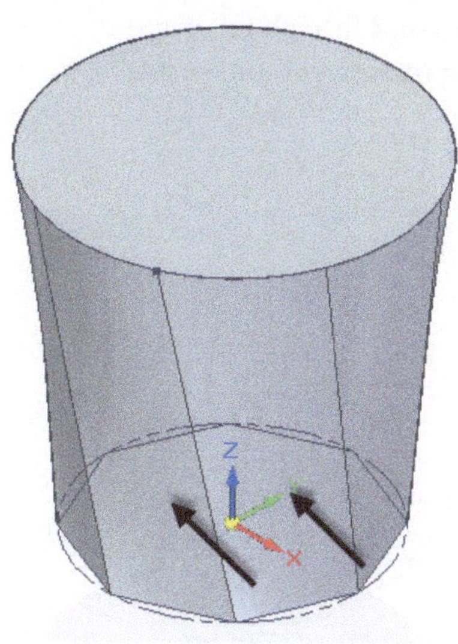
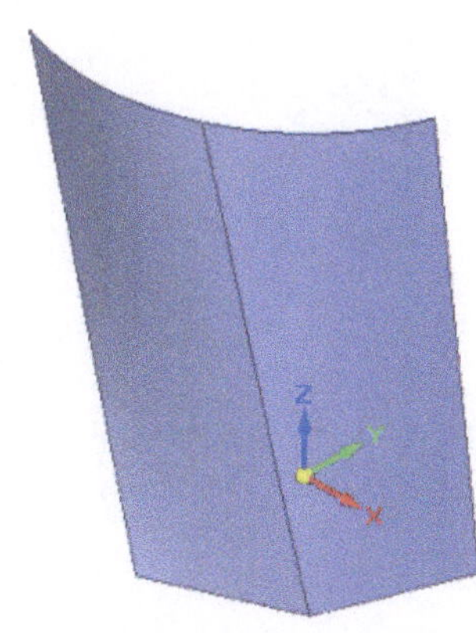

The **Remove Internal Boundaries** button will copy the surface by removing the internal boundaries.

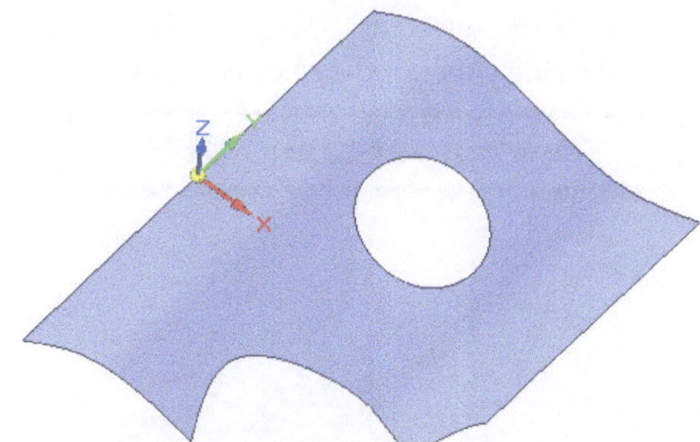
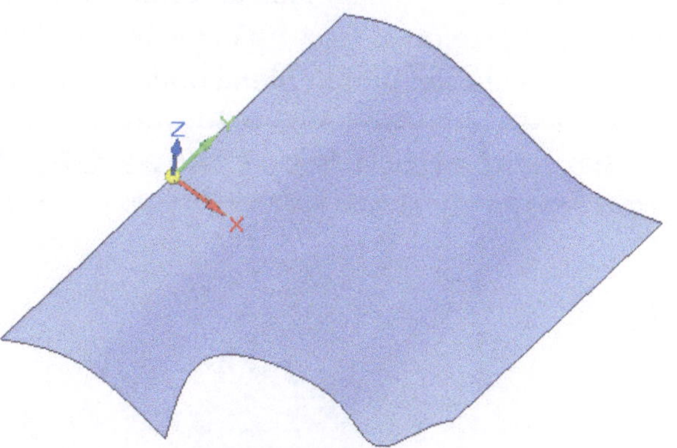

The **Remove External Boundaries** button will copy the surface by removing the external boundaries.

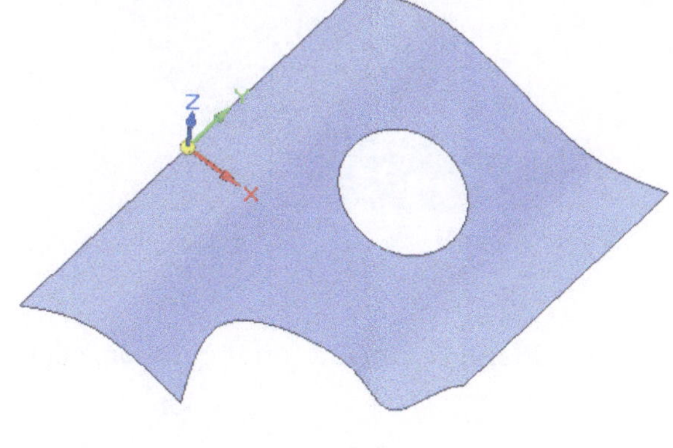
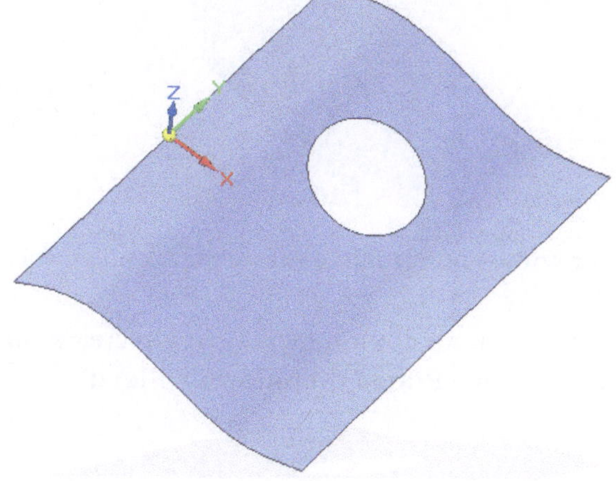

Creating Surface Blends

Surface blends have several uses. They can span across gaps between faces or can be useful in blending complex surfaces. For example, you can create a surface blend, which spans across a gap between two faces. To do this in the Ordered environment, activate the **Round** command (on the ribbon, click **Home > Solids > Round**) and select the **Surface blend** option from the command bar. Select the first face and second face chain. Type-in a value in the **Radius** box and click **Accept**. Note that the radius value depends on the gap between the surfaces. Now, click to define the side of the blend. Make sure that the arrows point inwards.

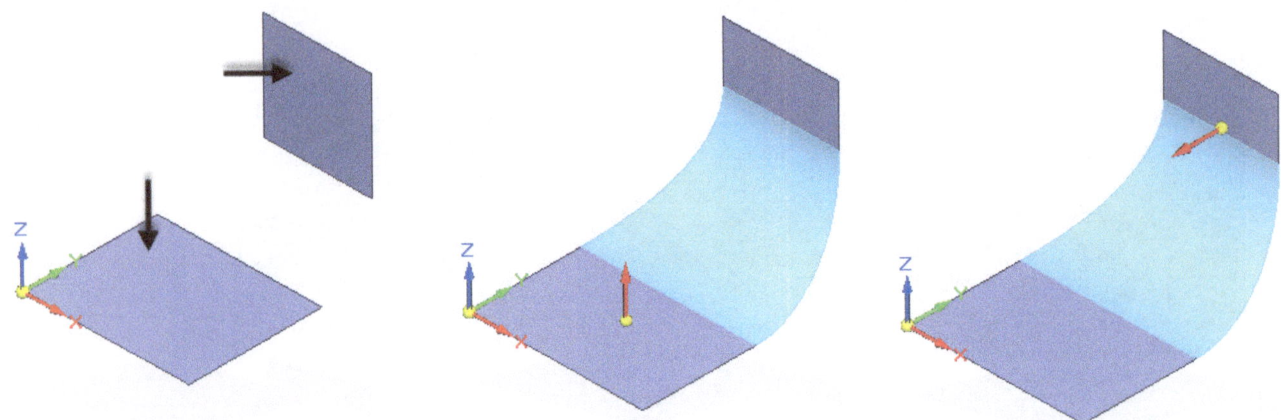

Click the **Surface Blend Parameters** section on the command bar. The **Trim and stitch input faces** option in this section trims the selected faces up to the blend edges and stitches them. If you select this option, the faces will not be trimmed. The **Trim output blend** option trims the blend to match the side edges of the selected faces.

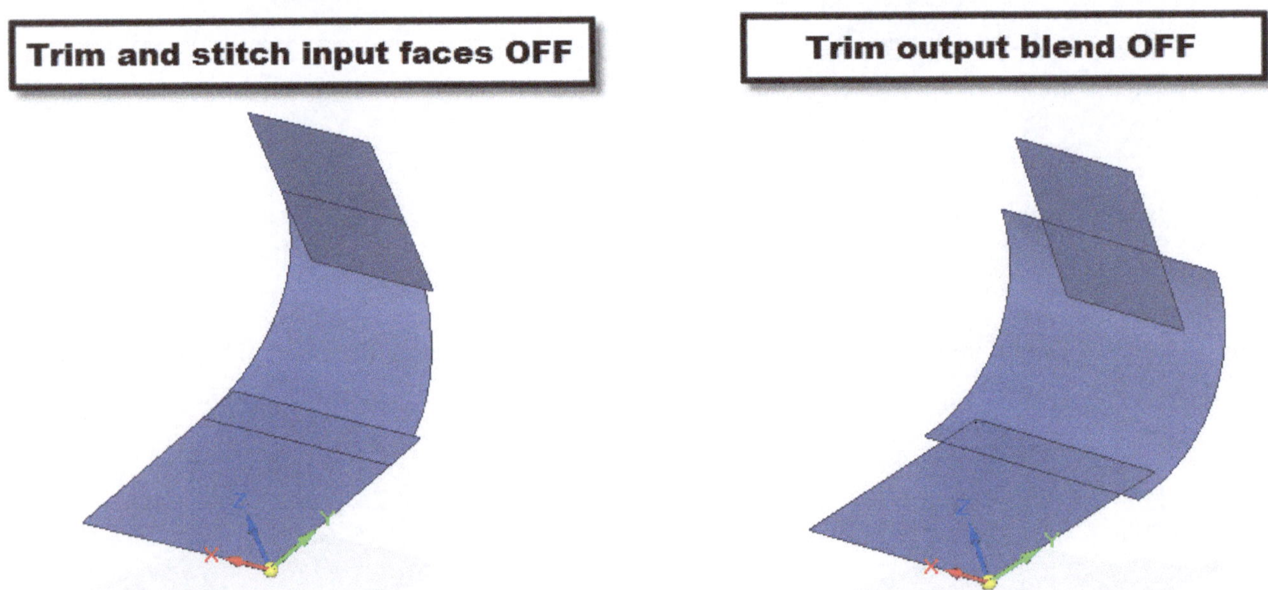

Click **Preview** and **Finish** to create the blend surface.

In the Synchronous environment, you can create surface blends using the **Blend** command (on the ribbon, click **Home > Solids > Round** drop-down **> Blend**).

Trim

This command trims a portion of a surface using a trimming tool. The trimming tool can be a surface, plane or a sketched entity. Activate this command (click **Surfacing > Modify Surfaces > Trim** on the ribbon) and select the target body. Right-click to accept the selection. On the command bar, set the **Selection type**, and then click on the trimming tool. Click **Accept** on the command bar. Next, select the region to remove. You can use the **Invert** button to select the opposite side of the selected portion. Next, click the **Accept** button to accept the selection. Click **Finish** to trim the surface.

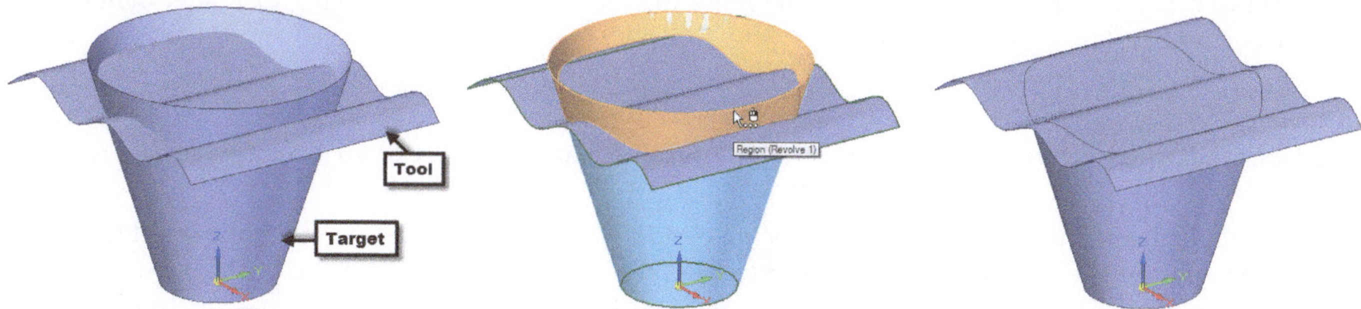

You can also trim a surface using a sketch. Activate the **Trim** command and select the target body. On the command bar, click **Accept**, and then click on the sketch. Right-click and select the region to remove. Click **Accept** and **Finish** to complete the trim operation.

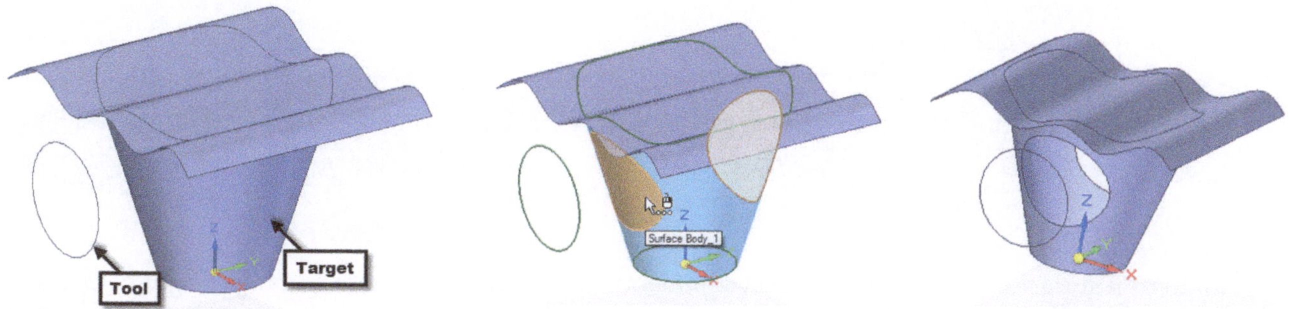

Extend

During the design process, you may sometimes need to extend a surface. You can extend a surface using the **Extend** command. Activate this command (On the ribbon, click **Surfacing > Modify Surfaces > Extend**) and click the surface to extend. Right-click to accept.

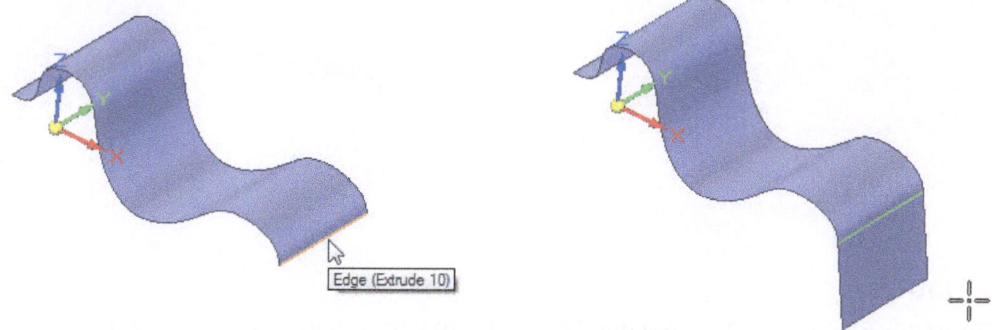

After selecting an edge, you can define the extension surface's distance using the **Finite Extent** and **Extend To**

options. If you select the **Finite Extend** option, you can define the distance by entering a value in the **Distance** box. If you select the **Extend To** option, you can define the distance by selecting a boundary surface.

When the surface you have selected is not a planar one, you can decide the extension using the **Extend Type** options. Use the **Curvature Continuous** option to extend the surface by maintaining the curvature of the original surface. If you select the **Linear** option, the extended surface will be created tangent to the original surface. The **Reflective** option extends the surface by reflecting the original surface. Click **Finish** after defining the distance of the extension.

Intersect

This command trims or extends a set of surfaces by the distance that you specify or up to another surface.

Activate this command (on the ribbon, click **Surfacing > Modify Surfaces > Intersect**) and select two surfaces. If you want to extend a surface, you need to select the surface to be extended and the boundary surface. Right-click and click on edge to extend. Click **Accept** and **Finish** to extend the surface.

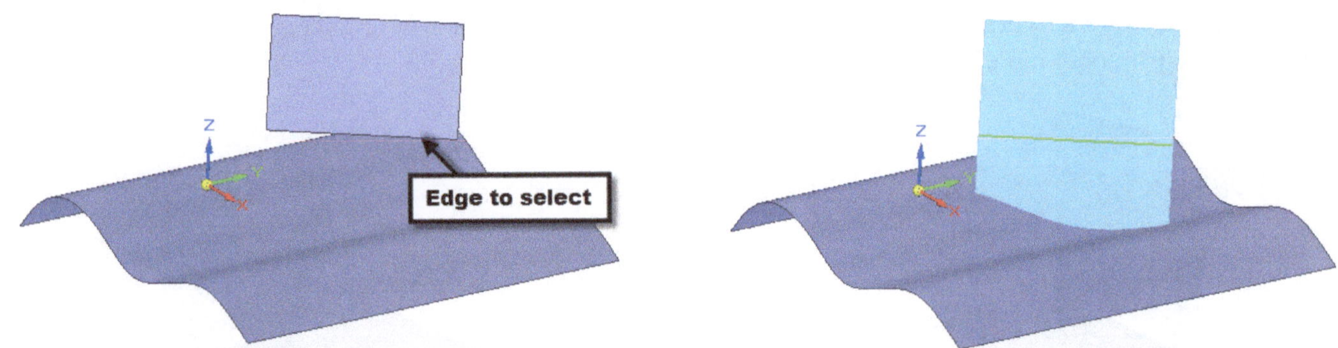

If you want to trim surfaces, activate the **Intersect** command and select two or more surfaces. Right-click and select the region to remove. On the command bar, click the **Stitch** button to stitch surfaces. Click **Accept** and **Finish** to trim the surface.

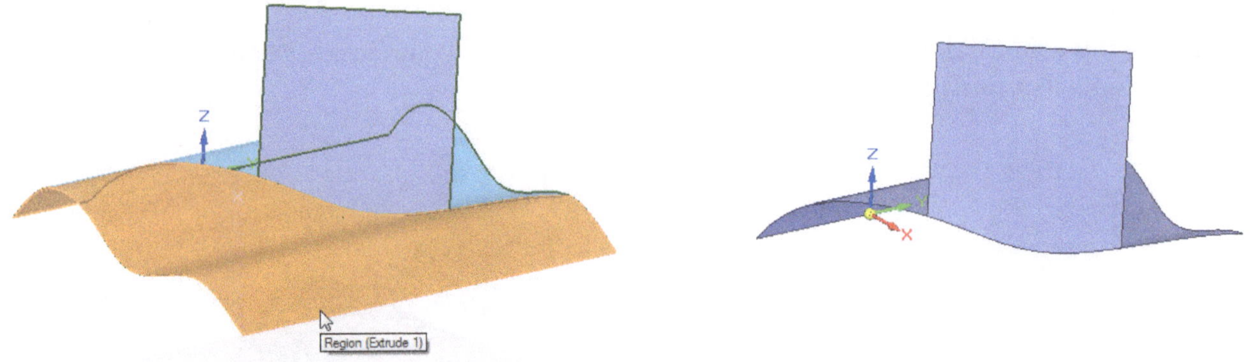

Create design Bodies

The **Intersect** command can create a design using two or more surfaces intersecting and forming a closed volume. To do this, click activate the **Intersect** command and select **Options > Create design Bodies** . Select the intersecting surfaces and click the **Accept** button on the command bar; the **Volume Regions** dialog displays the intersecting surfaces' regions. You can uncheck the regions that you do not want. Click the **Close** button on the **Volume Regions** dialog. Click the **Accept** button to create the design body. Next, hide the surface bodies to view the design body.

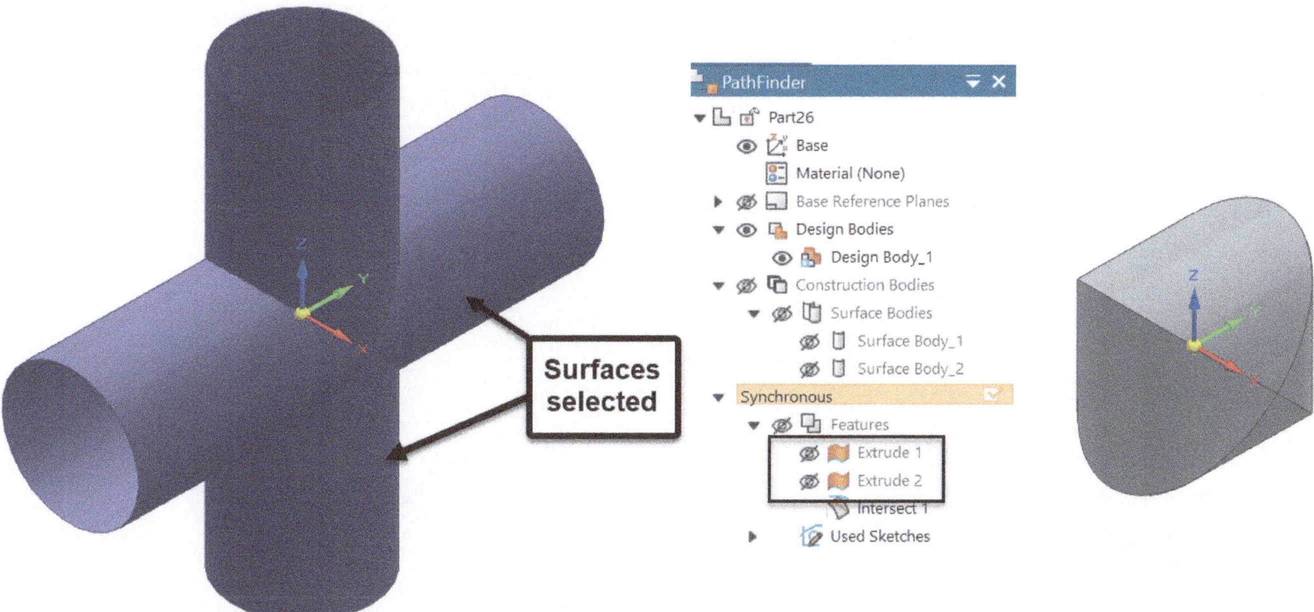

Solid Edge allows you to select solid bodies if it is intersecting with a surface or solid body. If a void is created from the intersection, you can select it to create a new body. For example, create a solid body, as shown. Next, create a flat surface body intersecting it.

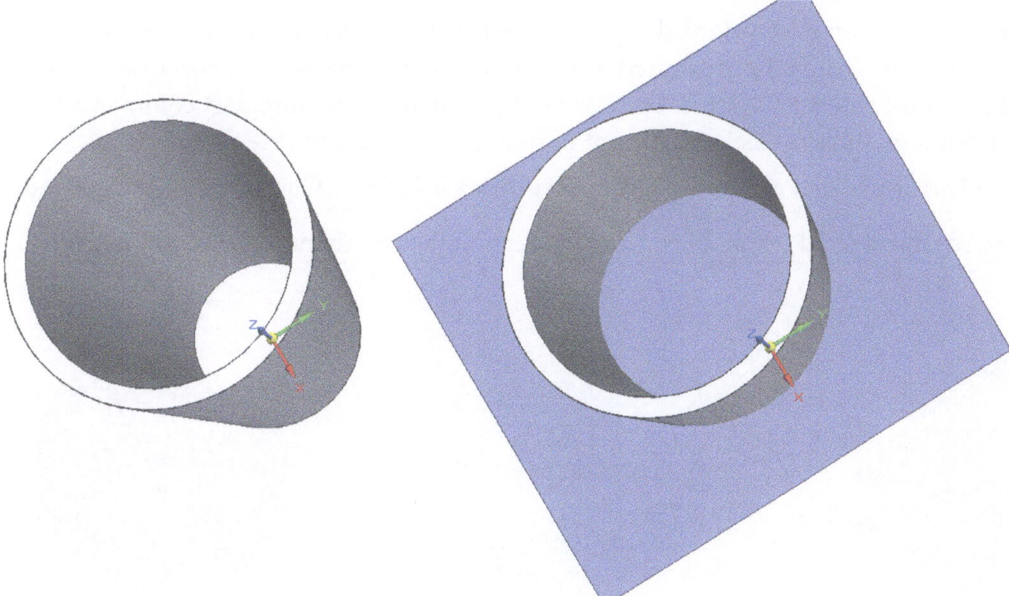

Activate the **Intersect** command and select **Intersect Options > Create design bodies**. Select the intersecting solid and surface and click the **Accept** button on the command bar; the **Volume Regions** dialog displays the intersecting bodies' regions. It also displays the regions detected from the voids. Keep the **Void Regions** option checked. Next, uncheck the **Solid Regions** option. Click the **Close** button on the **Volume Regions** dialog. Click the **Accept** button to create the design body. Next, hide the surface and solid bodies to view the design body.

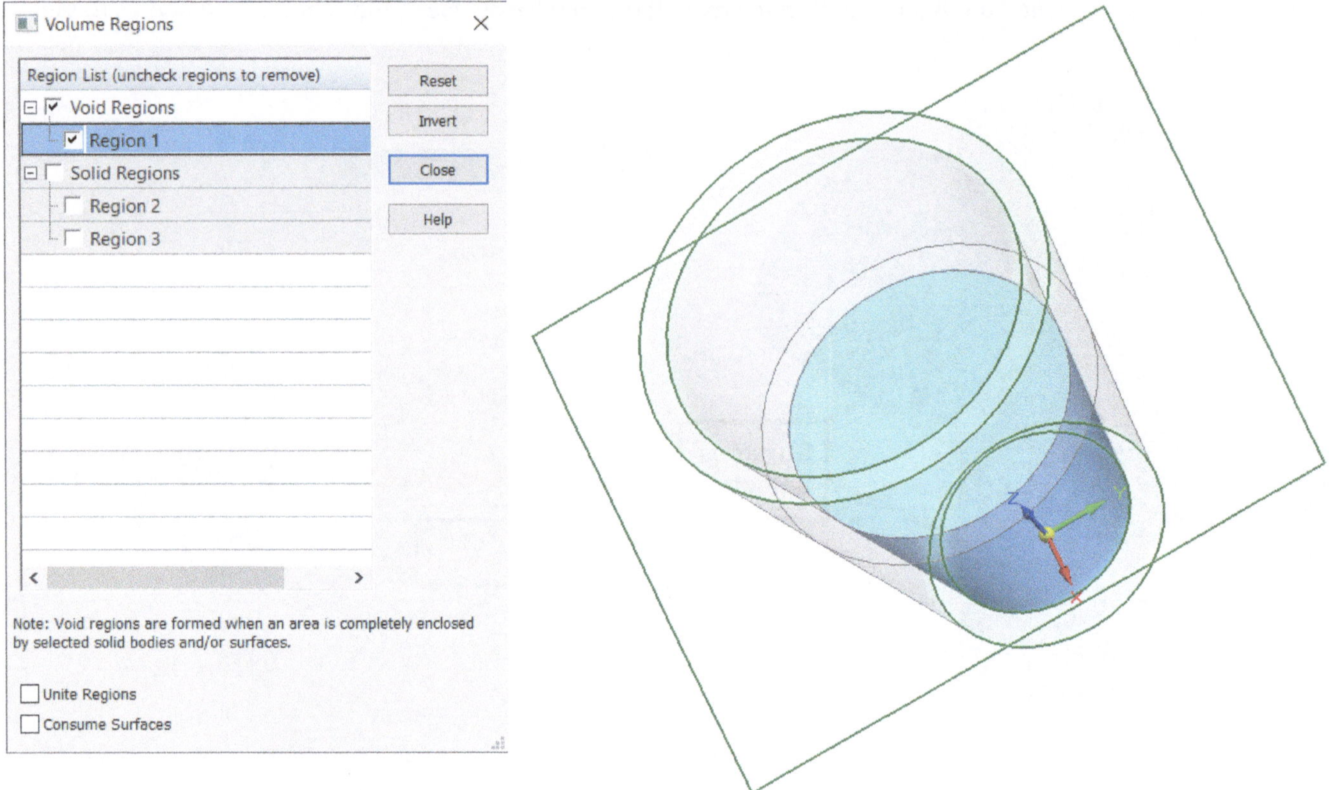

Auto-trim intersecting surfaces

The **Auto-trim** option available in the **Intersect Options** drop-down makes it easy to trim the intersecting surfaces' unwanted portions. This option trims the unwanted portions such that a closed volume, closed-loop, or continuous surface is formed out of the intersecting surfaces. For example, activate the **Intersect** command and select the three intersecting surfaces, as shown. Click the **Accept** button, and then select **Intersect Options > Auto-trim** on the command bar; notice that a closed volume of surfaces is created. Click the **Invert Selected Regions** icon if you do not see the desired result. Next, click **Accept** on the command bar to complete the feature.

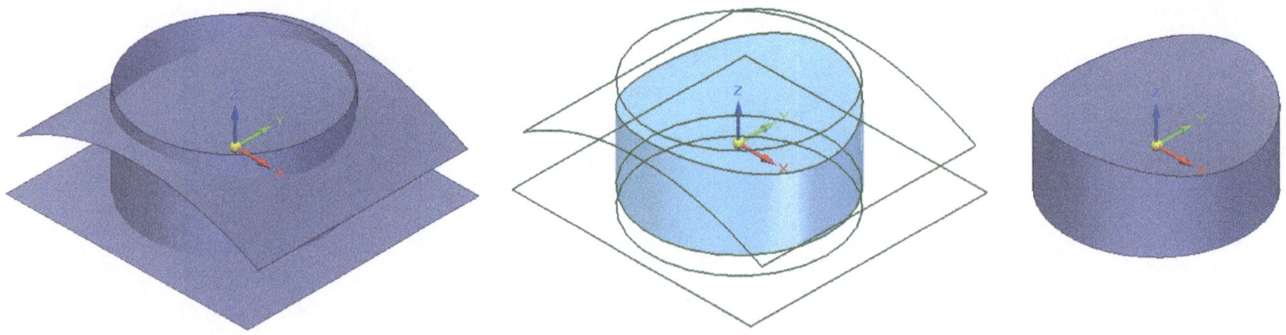

Stitched Surfaces

The surfaces created act as individual surfaces unless they are stitched together. The **Stitched** command lets you combine two or more surfaces to form a single surface. To stitch surfaces, activate this command (click **Surfacing > Modify Surfaces > Stitched** on the ribbon). On the **Stitched Surface Options** dialog, type-in a value in the **Stitched tolerance** box. The value you type in this box defines the tolerance gap. All the surfaces within the tolerance gap will be stitched. The **Heal stitched surfaces** option closes the gap between the stitched surfaces. Click **OK** and select the surfaces to stitch.

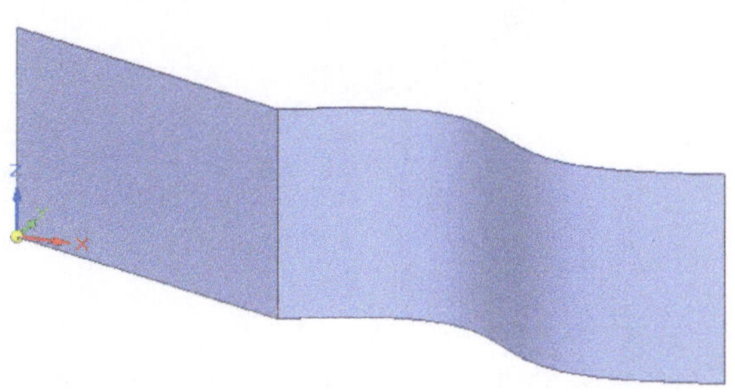

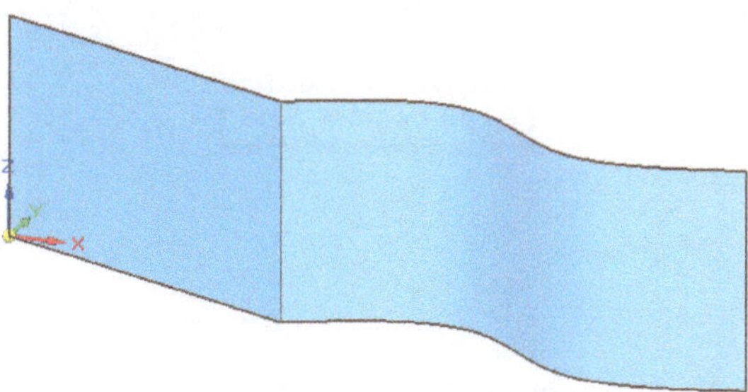

Click the **Accept** and **Finish** buttons to stitch the surfaces.

Thicken

Creating a solid from a surface can be accomplished by simply thickening a surface. To add thickness to a surface, activate the **Thicken** command (on the ribbon, click **Home > Solids > Add** drop-down **> Thicken**) and click on a face of the surface geometry. Enter the thickness value in the **Distance** box. Move the pointer inwards or outwards to define the side of material addition. Place the pointer on the surface body and click to add material on both sides of the surface. Click **Finish** to thicken the surface.

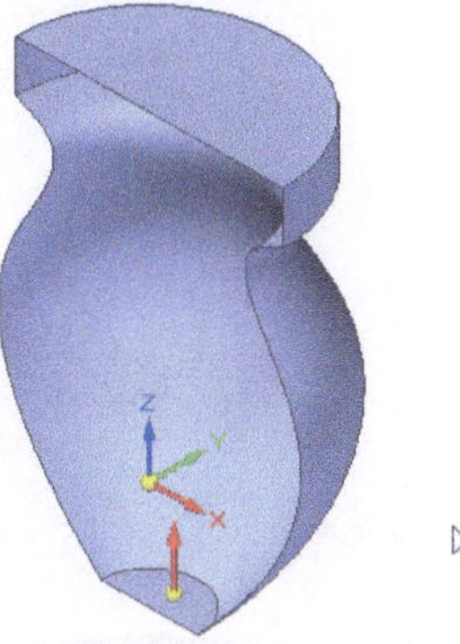

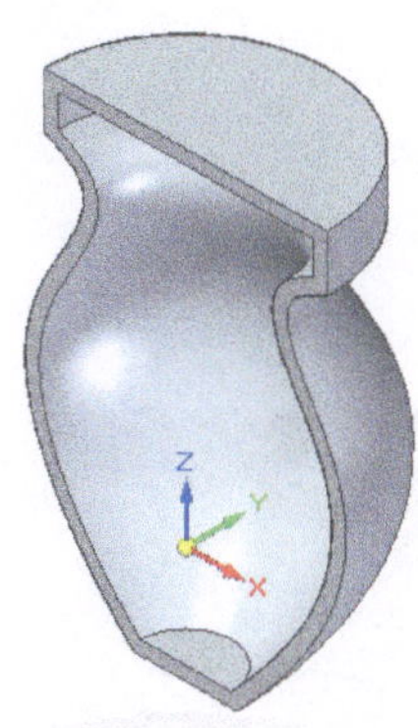

Replace Face

The **Replace Face** command replaces a face or group of faces with another face or group of faces. To replace a face, activate this command (on the ribbon, click **Surfacing > Modify Surfaces > Replace Face**). Select the faces to replace and click **Accept**. Select the replacement surface and click **Finish**.

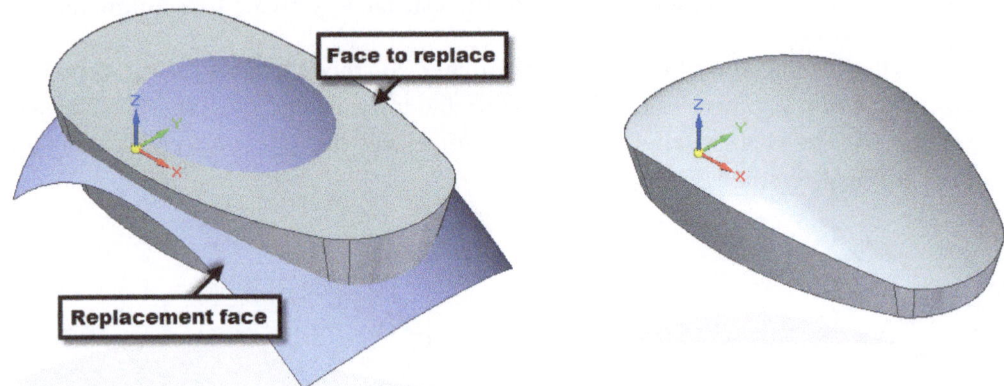

Split

The **Split** command splits a face or a body using a plane, body, curve or sketch. Click the **Split** button on the **Modify Surfaces** panel and select a face or body. Right-click and select a splitting element. Click **Accept** and **Finish.**

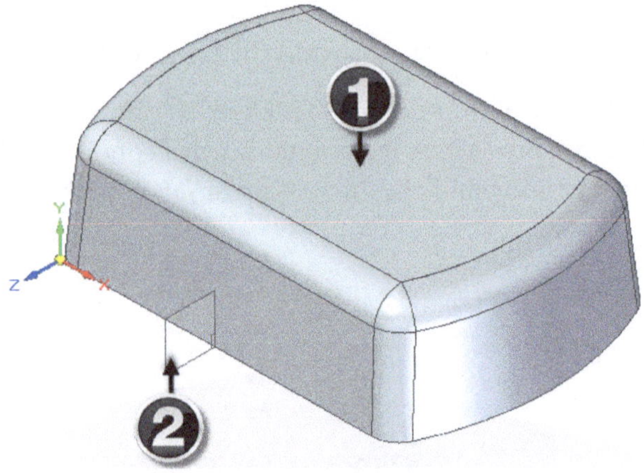

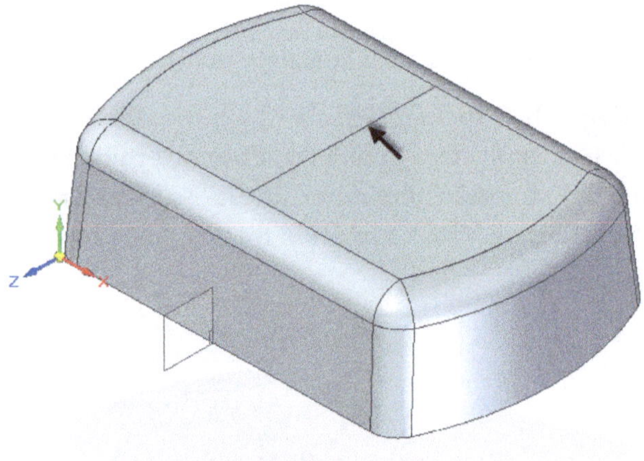

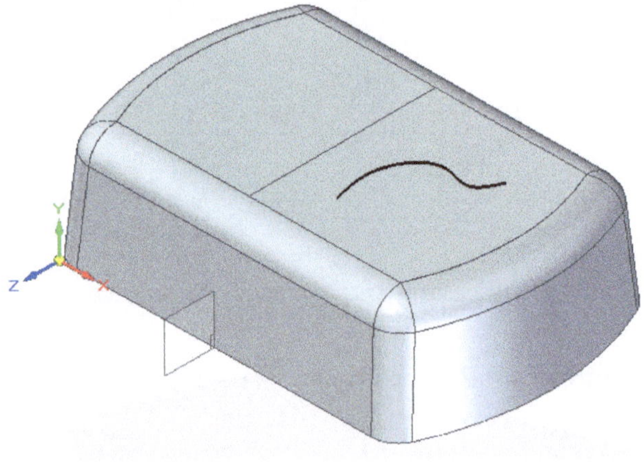

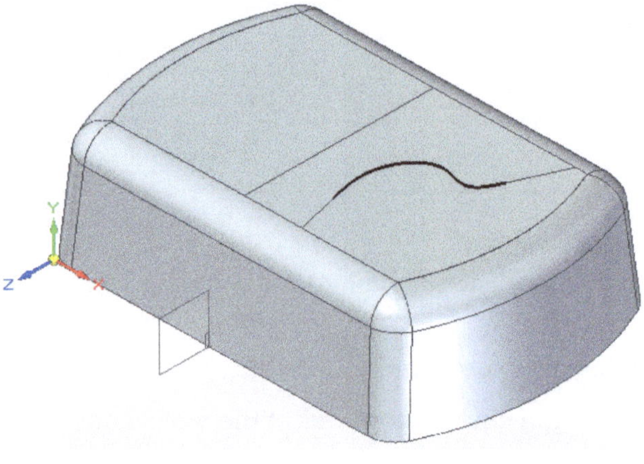

Example

In this example, you will construct the model shown below.

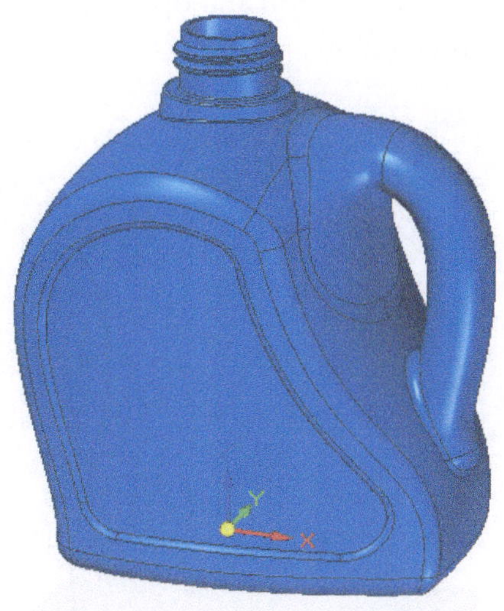

Drawing the Layout Curves

1. Start **Solid Edge 2026**.
2. Start a new part file using the **ISO Metric Part** template.
3. Click the **Continue with Ordered** to continue with the ordered environment. In this tutorial, you will create the surface model in the **Ordered** environment as you can edit the surfaces easily. You can also create this model in the **Synchronous** environment.
4. Create a spreadsheet with the following values and save it as Curve1. You can also download this file from our website.
5. On the ribbon, click **Surfacing > Curves > Keypoint** drop-down **> Curve by table**.
6. On the **Insert Object** dialog, select the **Create from file** option and click the **Browse** button. Go to the location of the **Curve1** spreadsheet, select it, and click **Open**. Click **OK** on the dialog.
7. On the Command bar, click the **Parameters** section and set the **Curve Fit** to **Smoothening on**. Set the **Curve End Conditions** to **Open**. Set the **Coordinate System** to **Base** and click **OK**.
8. Click **Finish** to create the curve, as shown below.

	A	B	C	D	E
1	-75	0	-20		
2	-65	0	18		
3	-67	0	32		
4	-80	0	125		
5	-66	0	160		
6	-45	0	182		
7	0	0	200		
8	60	0	182		
9	80	0	160		
10					

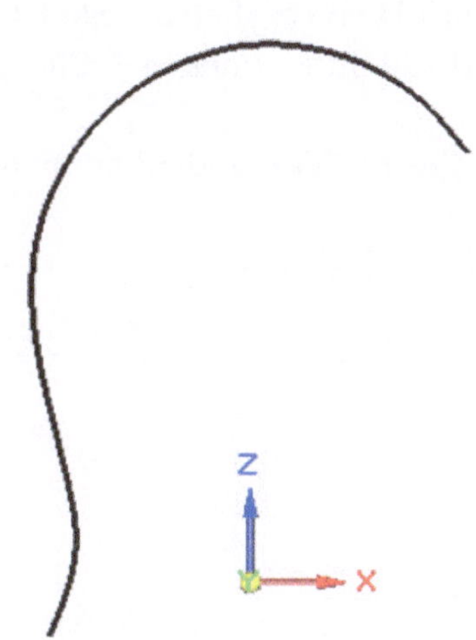

9. Create another spreadsheet with the following values and save it as Curve2.
10. On the ribbon, click **Surfacing > Curves > Keypoint** drop-down **> Curve by table**.

11. On the **Insert Object** dialog, click the **Browse** button and open the **Curve2** spreadsheet. Click **OK** on the dialog.
12. Click **Finish** to create the curve, as shown below.

	A	B	C	D
1	110	0	-5	
2	113	0	20	
3	110	0	45	
4	86	0	90	
5	60	0	155	
6	55	0	210	
7				
8				
9				
10				

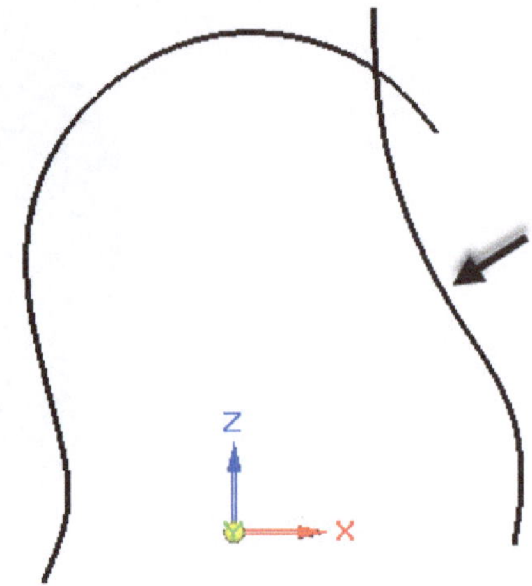

13. Create another spreadsheet with the following values and save it as Curve3.
14. Activate the **Curve by table** command and select the Curve3 spreadsheet. Click **Finish** to create the third curve.

	A	B	C	D
1	120	0	45	
2	110	0	65	
3	112	0	85	
4	117	0	120	
5	114	0	155	
6	95	0	185	
7	60	0	195	
8	35	0	175	
9				

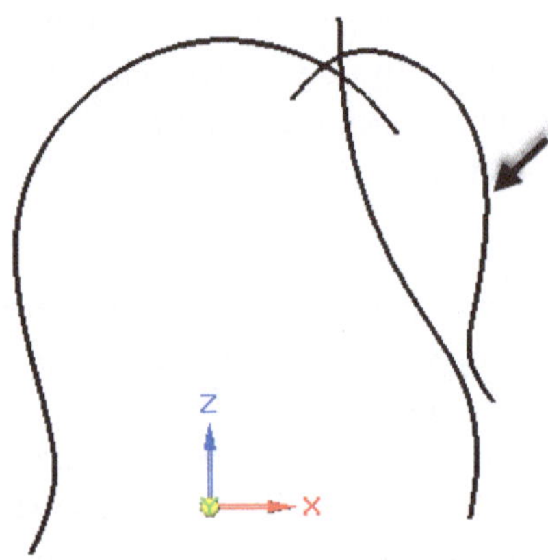

Creating the Front Surface

1. On the ribbon, click **Home > Sketch > Sketch** and select the XY plane
2. Create an arc and add dimensions to it. Click the **Close Sketch** button on the ribbon. Click **Finish** on the command bar.
3. Create an arc on the YZ Plane and add dimensions to it. Finish the sketch.

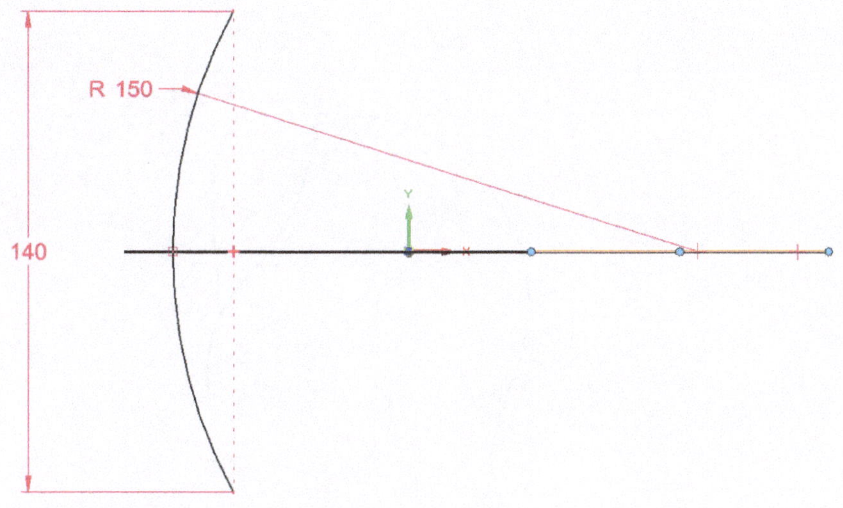

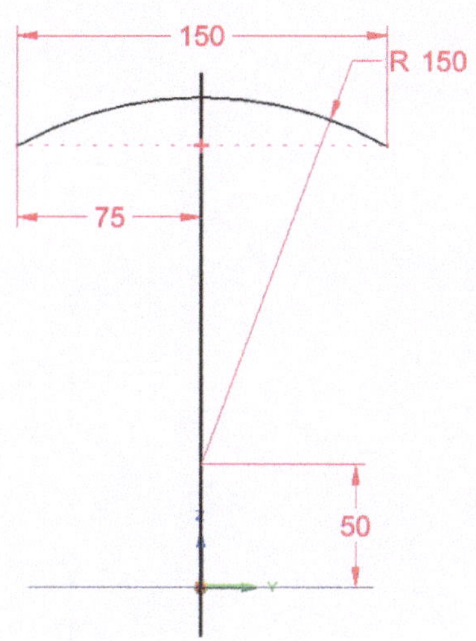

4. Create a plane normal to the first curve.

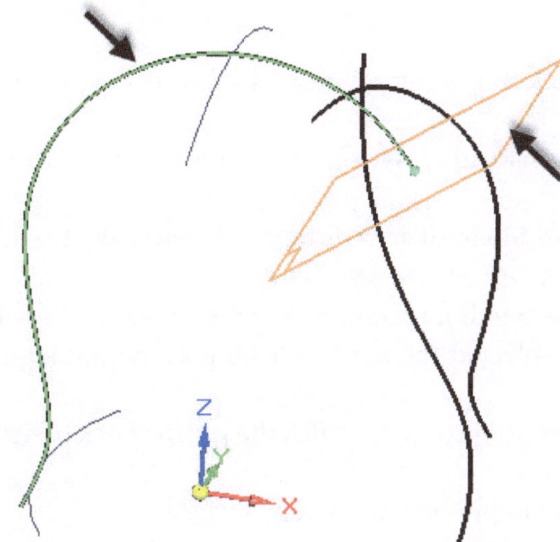

5. Create an arc on the plane normal to the curve. Finish the sketch.

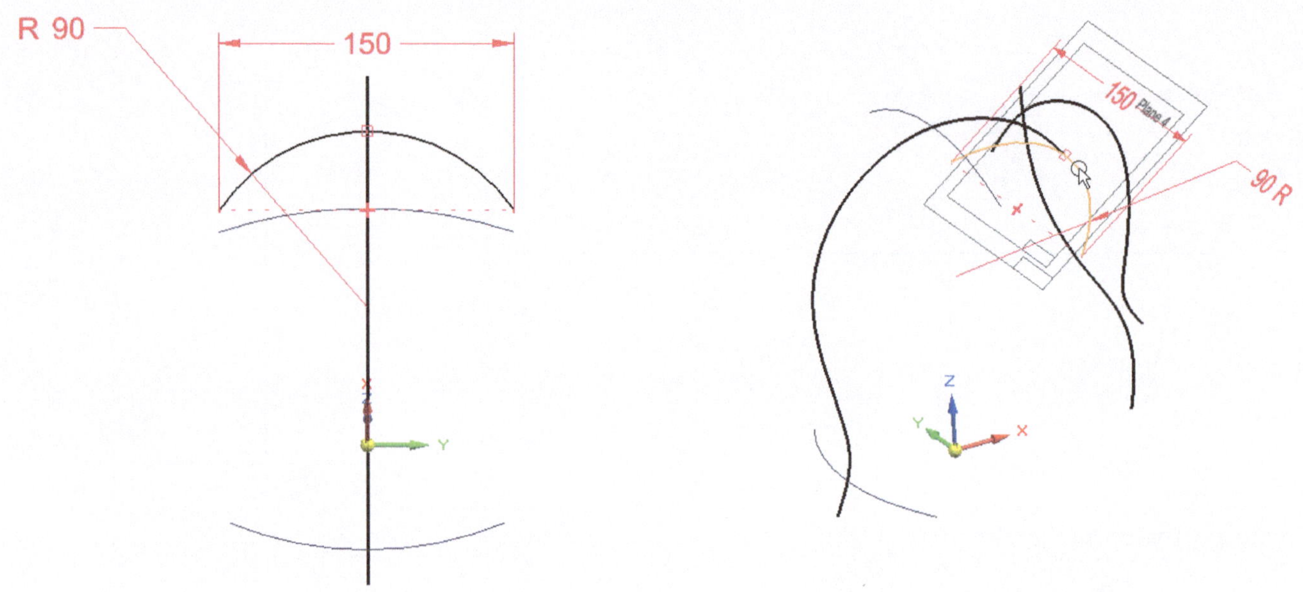

6. Activate the **Swept** command (on the ribbon, click **Surfacing > Surfaces > Swept**). Next, click the **Options** button
7. On the **Sweep Options** dialog, select the **Multiple paths and cross section** option. Select the **Along path** option from the **Face Merging** section and click **OK.**
8. In the **Path** section, select **Create From > Select from Sketch/Part Edges**. Next, select the first curve to define the path. Click the green check on the command bar to accept the selection.
9. On the command bar, click **Next** to activate the **Cross Section** section. Select the arc located on the XY plane to define the first cross section. Ensure that you have selected the arc by clicking at the point, as shown in the figure. Click the green check on the command bar.
10. Select the second arc by clicking at the point, as shown in the figure. Click the green check to define the second cross section.
11. Likewise, select the third cross section. Click **Preview** to preview the swept surface.
12. Click **Finish** to complete the swept surface. Click **Cancel** to deactivate the command.

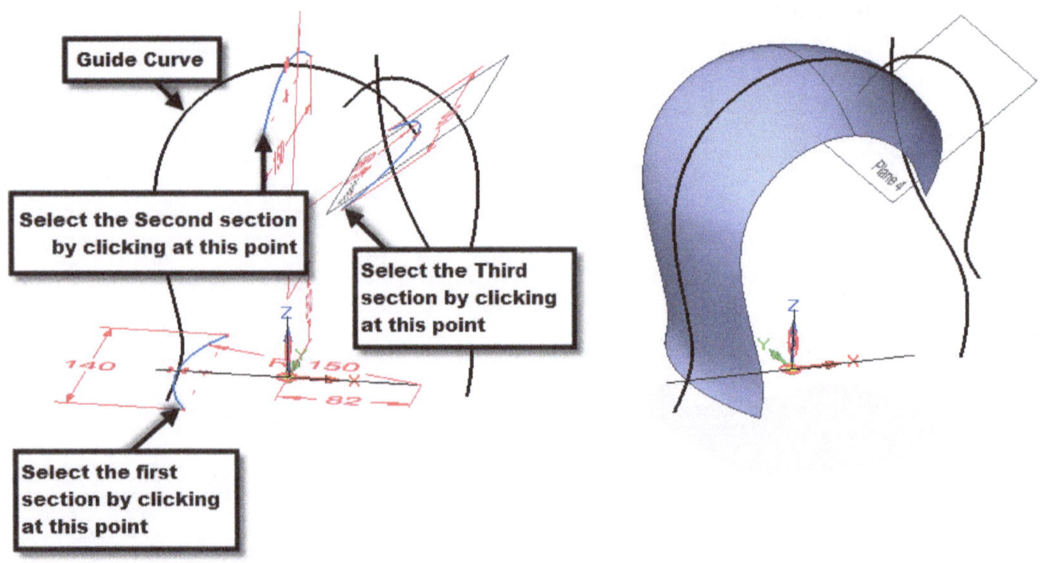

13. Save the file. As you are creating a complex geometry, you should save the model after each operation.

Creating the Label surface

1. Create an arc on the XY plane. Finish the sketch.

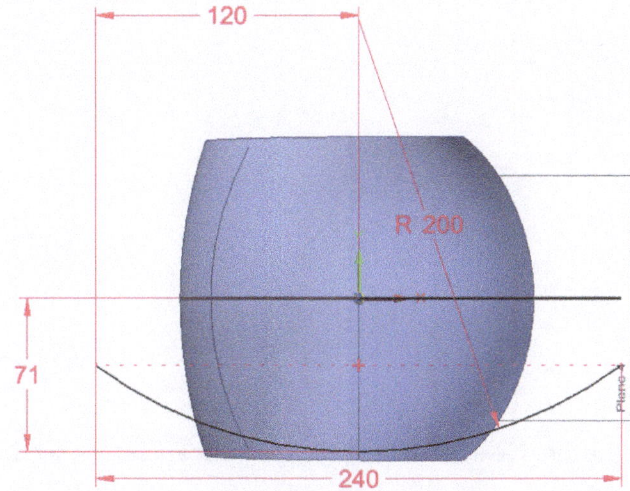

2. Activate the **Extruded** command (on the ribbon, click **Surfacing > Surfaces > Extruded**). On the command bar, click **Create-From Options** drop-down **> Select from Sketch**.
3. Select the sketch and click the green check on the command bar220. Type-in 220 in the **Distance** box on the command bar. Move the pointer upward and click to define the side of the extrusion. Click **Finish** to complete the extruded surface.
4. On the ribbon, click **Surfacing > Pattern > Mirror Copy Part**. Select the extruded surface and right-click.
5. Select the XZ plane and click **Finish** to mirror the extruded surface.

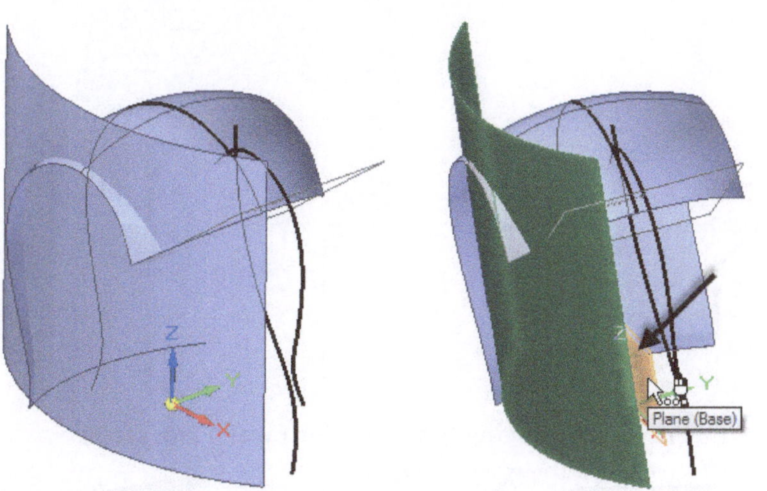

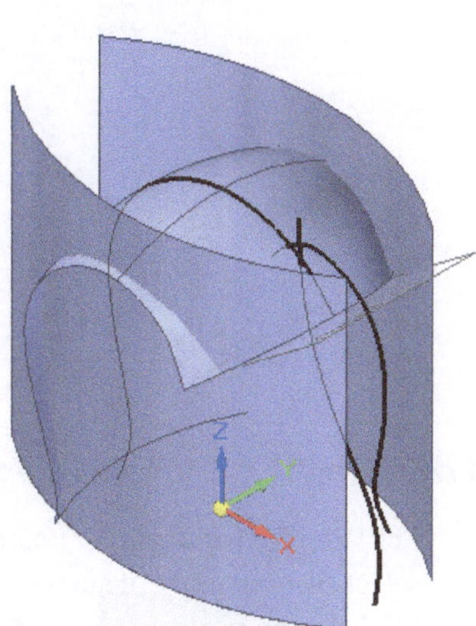

Creating the Back surface

1. Create an arc on the XY plane. Finish the sketch.

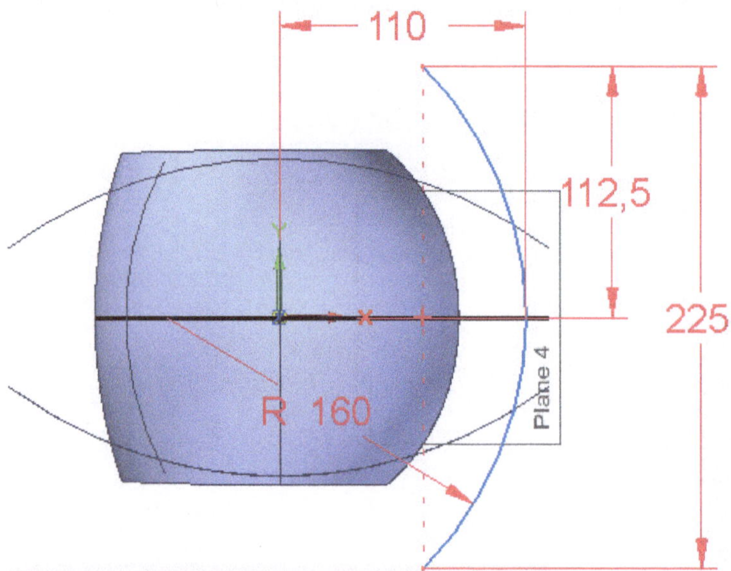

2. Activate the **Swept** command and click the **Options** button. Next, select the **Single path and cross section** option on the **Sweep Options** dialog. Click **OK**.
3. Select the second curve to define the path of the swept surface. Click the green check to accept the selection.
4. Select the arc and click the green check to define the cross section. Click **Finish** and **Cancel** to complete the swept surface.

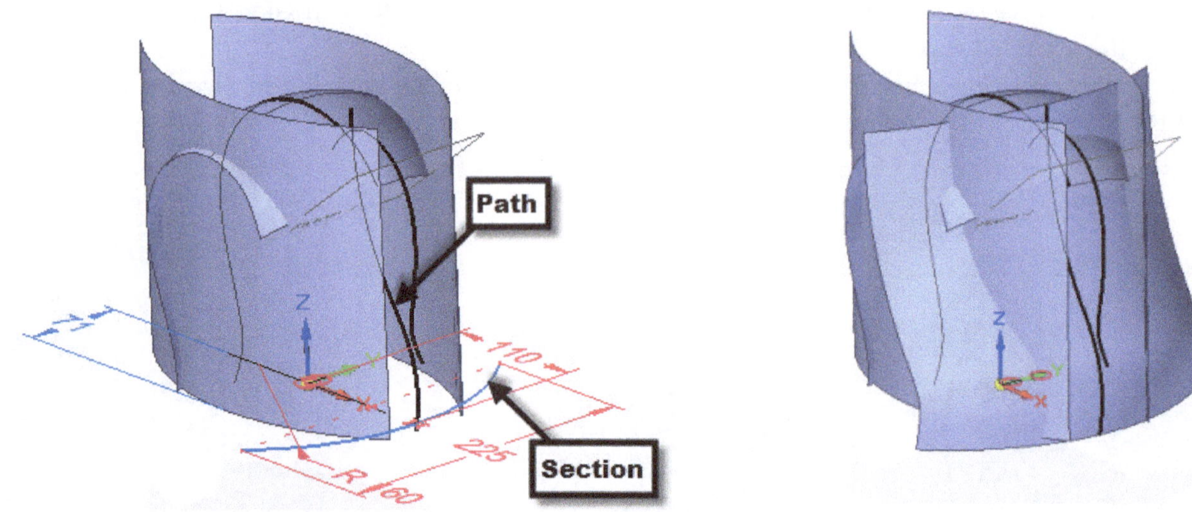

Trimming the Unwanted Portions

1. Activate the **Intersect** command (on the ribbon, click **Surfacing > Modify Surfaces > Intersect**).
2. Select the front swept surface and extruded surfaces. Click the green check.
3. Click on the portions to trim, as shown in the figure.

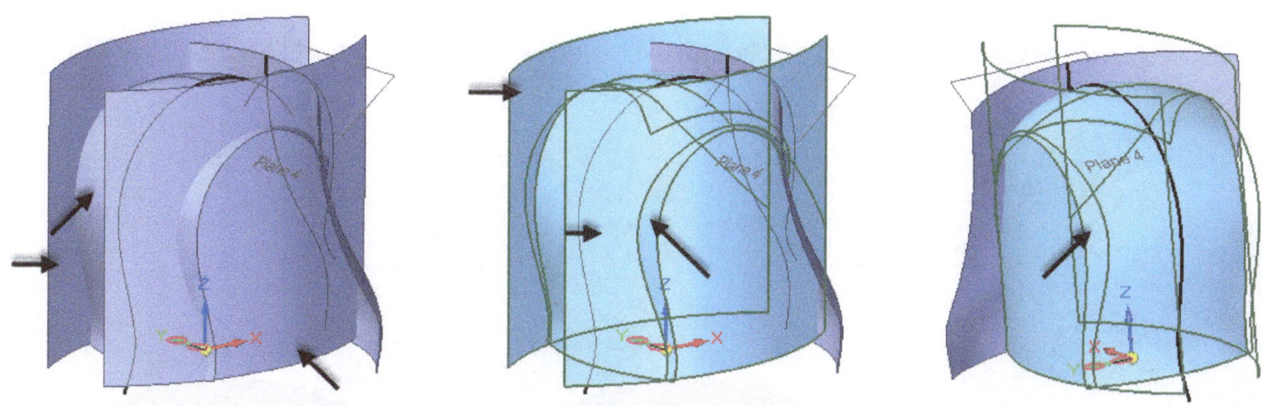

4. Click the **Stitch** button on the command bar. Click the green check to trim the selected portions. Click **Finish**.
5. With the **Intersect** command still active, select the back swept surface and the stitched surface. Click the green check.
6. Select the portions of the back swept surface and stitched surface, as shown below. Click the green check.

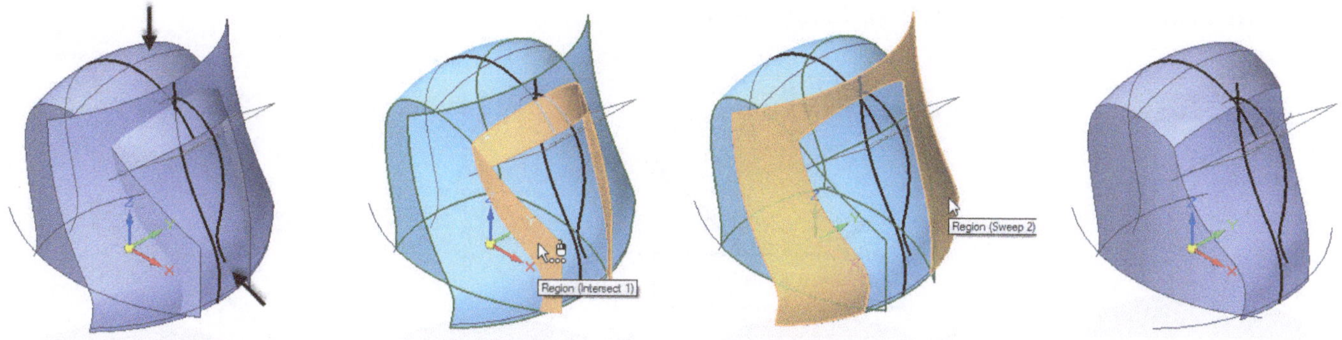

7. Click **Finish** and **Cancel**.

8. Activate the **Trim** command (on the ribbon, click **Surfacing > Modify Surfaces > Trim**) and click on the surface body. Click the green check.
9. Select the XY Plane, and then click the green check.
10. Select the portion of the target surface, as shown. Click the **Accept** button on the command bar.
11. Click **Finish** and **Cancel**.

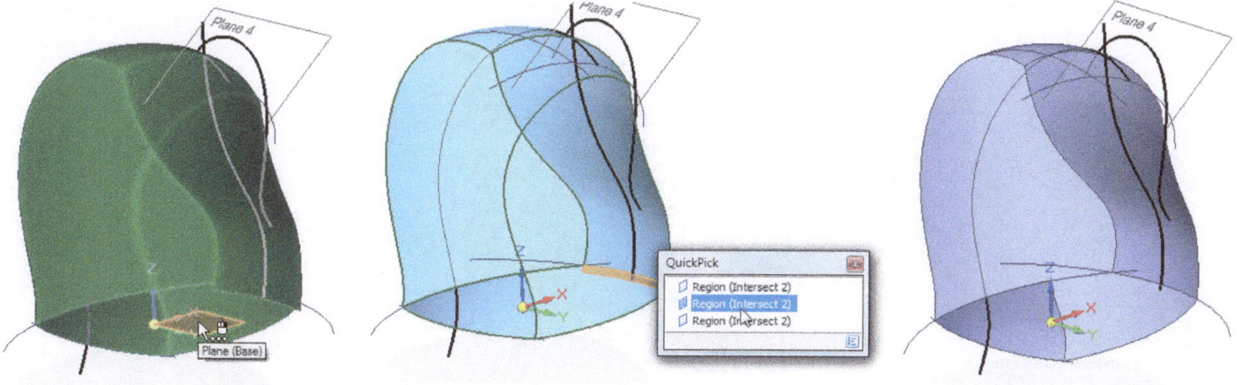

Creating the Handle Surface

1. Activate the **Normal to Curve** command and click on the lower end-point of the third curve. Left-click to create the plane normal to the curve.

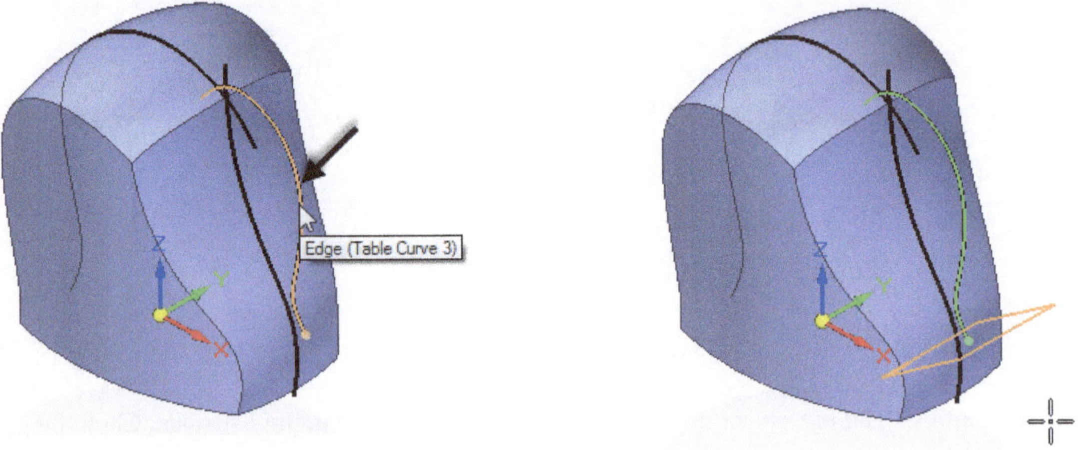

2. Start a sketch on the plane normal to the curve.
3. Create an ellipse on the sketch plane. Apply the **Horizontal** relation between the two-quadrant points, as shown. Add dimensions and relations to the sketch.

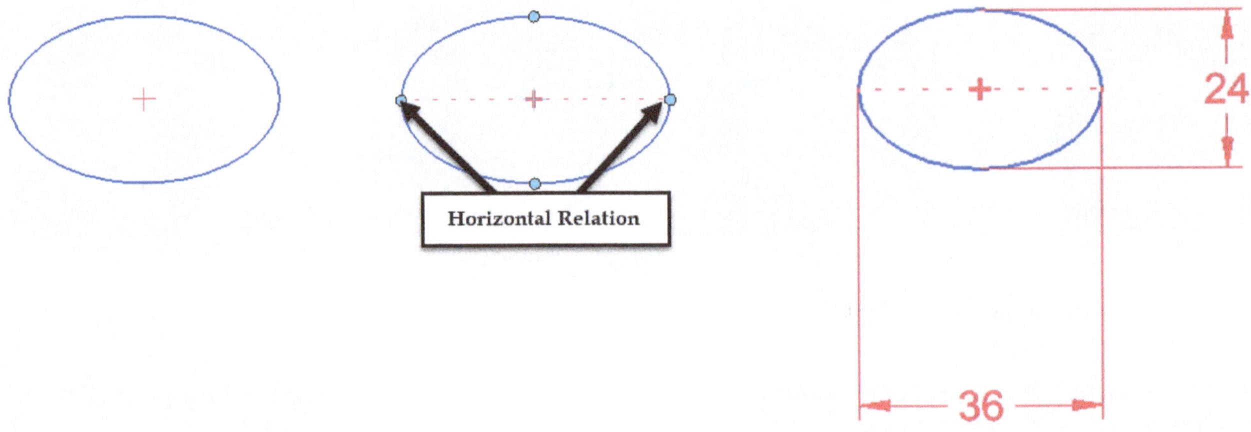

4. Make the upper quadrant point of the ellipse coincident with the end-point of the curve. Finish the sketch.

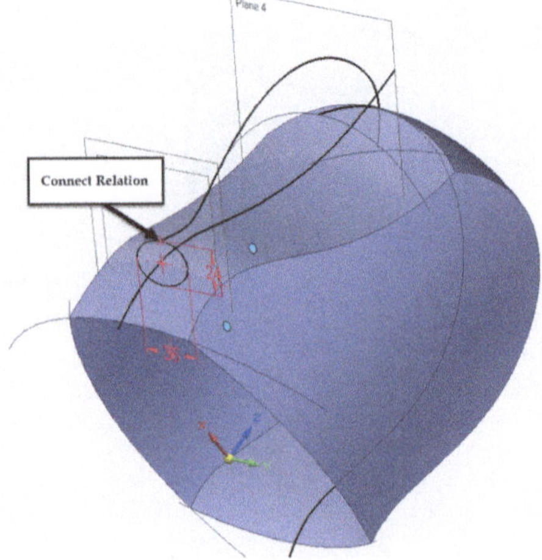

5. Activate the **Swept** command and create the handle surface (refer to the **Swept Surfaces** section).

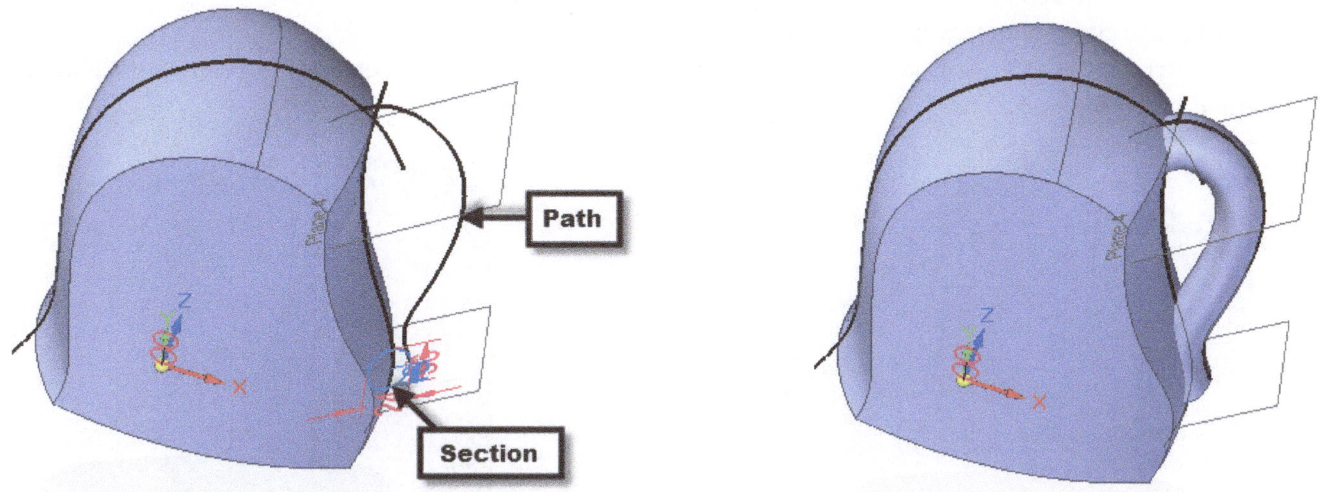

6. Activate the **Round** command (click **Home > Solids > Round**) and select the edge between the front and back surfaces. Type **25** in the **Radius** box and click the green check on the command bar. Click **Preview**, **Finish**, and **Cancel** and on the command bar.

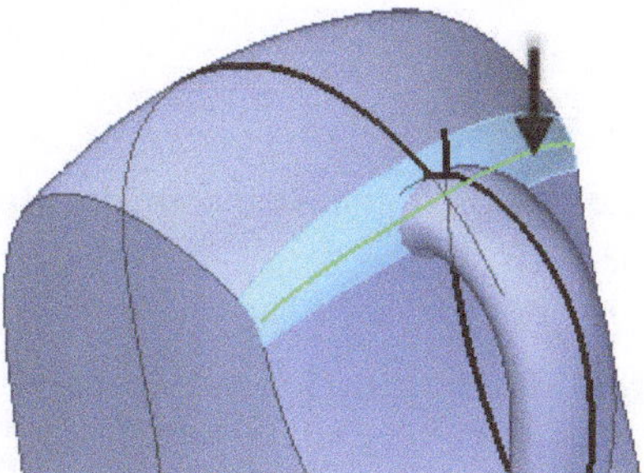

Trimming the Handle

1. On the ribbon, click **Surfacing > Planes > More Planes** drop-down **> Parallel.**
2. Select the YZ plane from the Base Coordinate System. Type-in 75 in the **Distance** box and press Enter. Move the pointer toward the right and click.
3. Activate the **Trim** command and click on the Handle surface. Right-click to accept the selection.
4. Select the parallel plane and right-click to accept.
5. Select the region of the handle, as shown below. Click the green check on the command bar, and then click **Finish**.

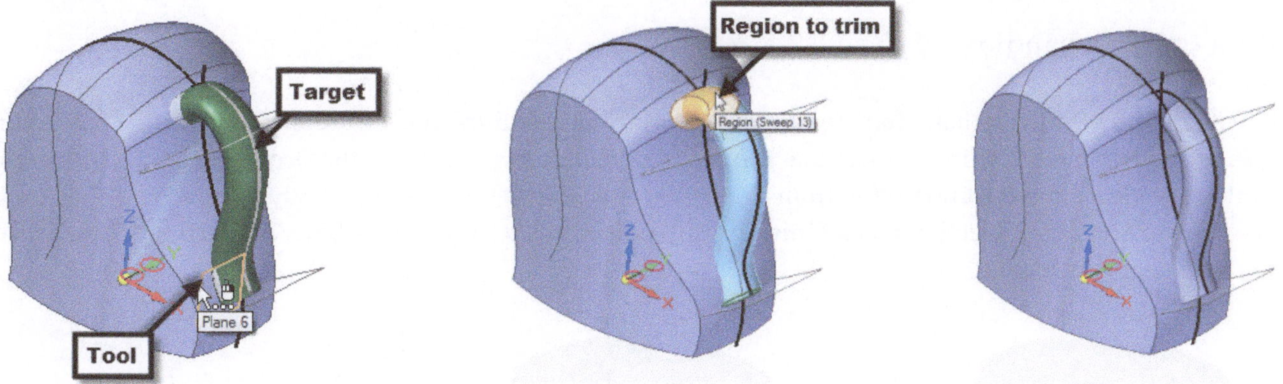

6. On the ribbon, **Surfacing > Planes > More planes > Normal to Curve** .
7. Select the path curve of the swept surface and then its top endpoint.
8. Start a sketch on the plane normal to the curve and draw an ellipse. Add dimensions to position the ellipse, and then finish the sketch.

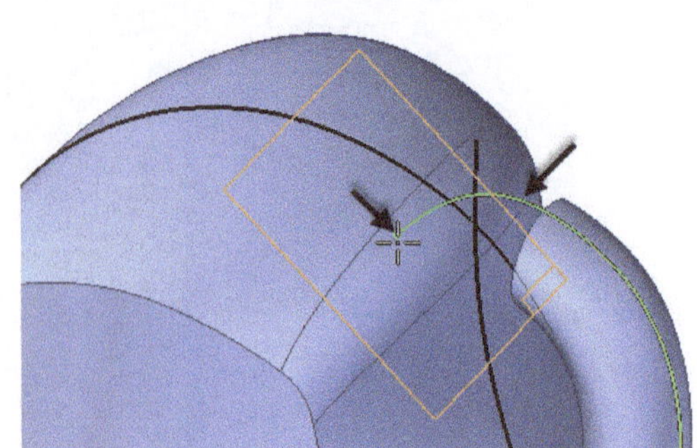

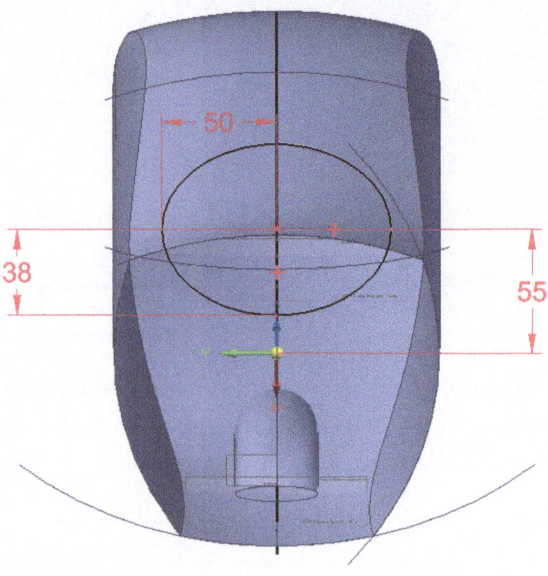

9. Activate the **Trim** command (on the ribbon, click **Surfacing > Modify Surfaces > Trim**) and click on the main body. Right-click to accept the selection.
10. Select the ellipse and right-click.
11. Select the surface region enclosed by the sketch. Right-click to accept the selection. Next, click **Finish** and **Cancel** on the command bar.

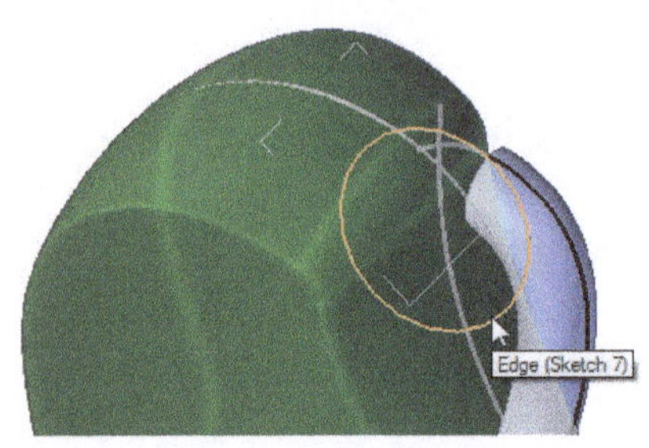

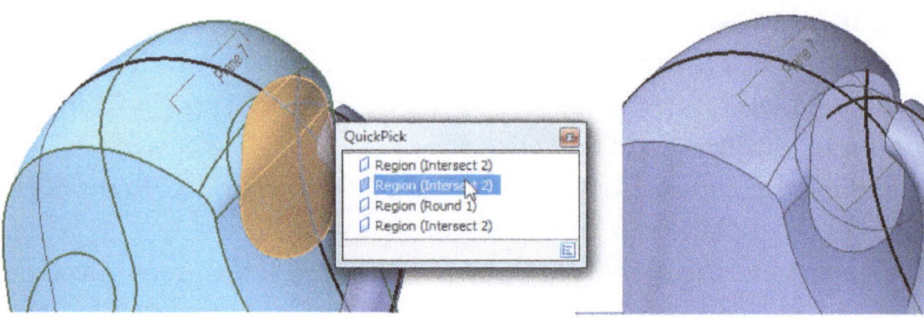

Blending the Top handle

1. Activate the **BlueSurf** command (on the ribbon, click **Surfacing > Surfaces > BlueSurf**) and click on the edges of the trimmed openings. Select the **Tangent Continuous** option from the drop-down attached to the handle edge. Select the **Natural** option from the drop-down attached to the main body edge.
2. Click **Next** to accept the selection. Click **Finish** on the command bar to create the BlueSurf surface. Click **Cancel** to deactivate the command.

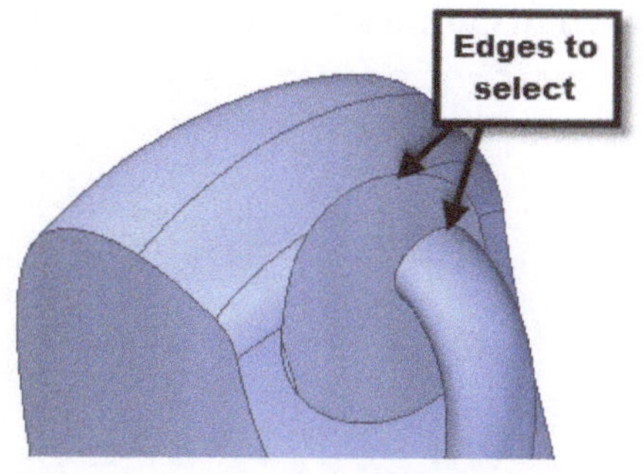

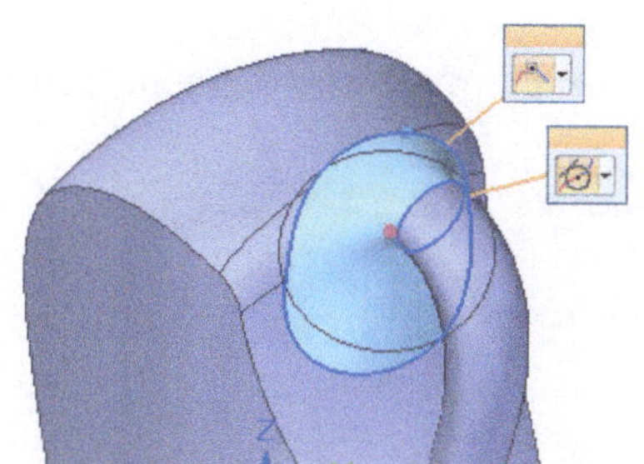

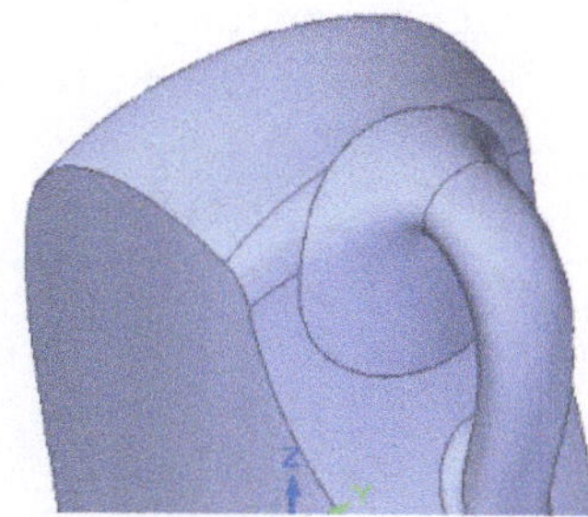

Blending the Bottom handle

1. On the ribbon, click **Surfacing > Planes > More Planes** drop-down **> Tangent** and select the handle surface.
2. On the Command bar, click **Keypoints** drop-down **> Silhouette**. Select the top silhouette point of the handle's lower edge. A plane tangent to the handle surface is created.

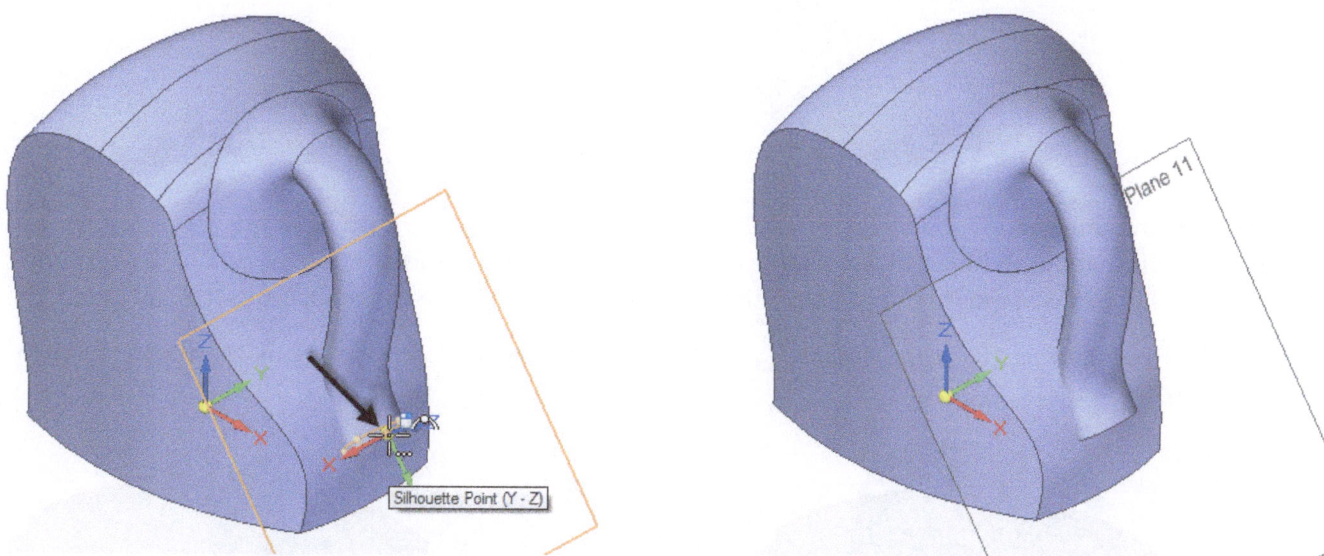

3. Create an ellipse on the new plane and trim it by half. Finish the sketch. Ensure that the sketch lies inside the handle surface.

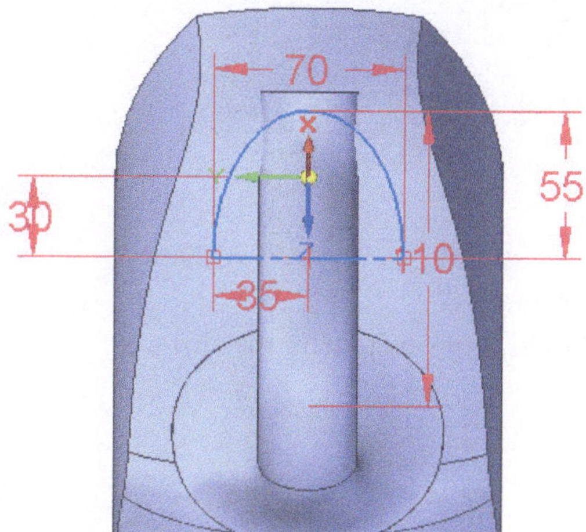

4. On the ribbon, click **Surfacing > Surfaces > Extruded**. Next, select **Create from Options > Select from Sketch** on the command bar.
5. Select the sketch and extrude it up to an arbitrary distance in both directions.

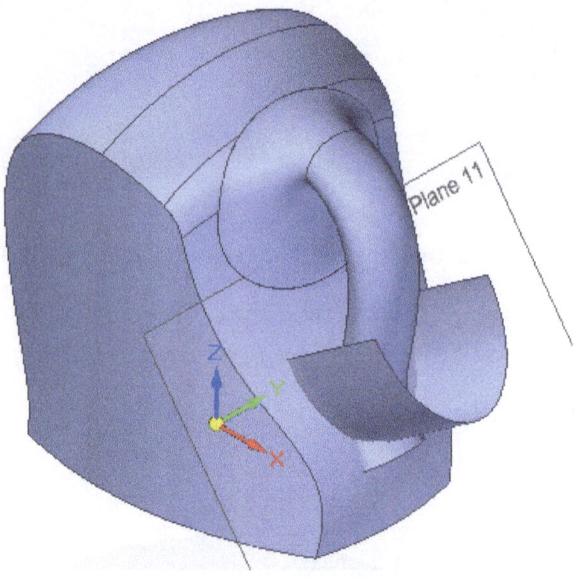

6. Activate the **Intersect** command.
7. Click on the handle and the extruded surfaces, and then right-click to accept.
8. Select the portions of the handle and extruded surfaces in the sequence shown below.
9. On the command bar, click the **Stitch** button, and then right-click. Click **Finish** to trim and stitch the surfaces.

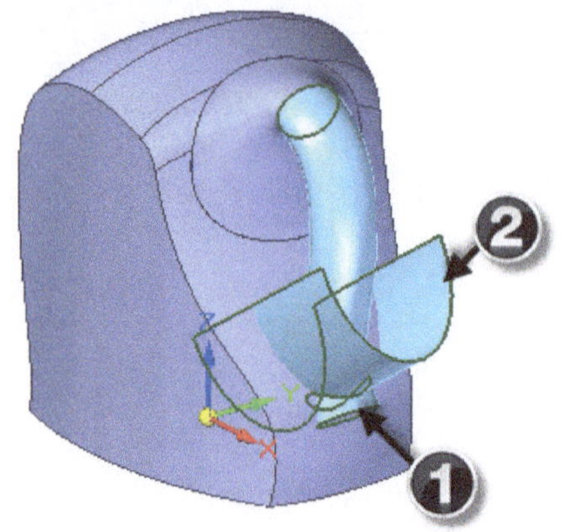

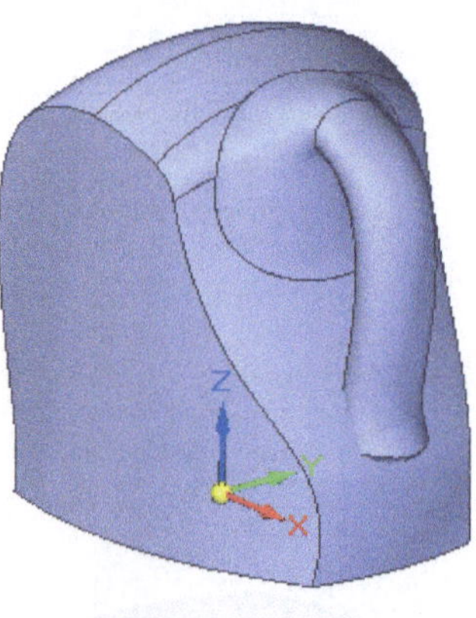

10. Select the handle and main body, and then right-click to accept the selection.
11. Rotate the model, select the intersecting portion, and stitched portion.
12. Make sure that the **Stitch** button is active. Click the **Accept** and **Finish** buttons to trim the surface.

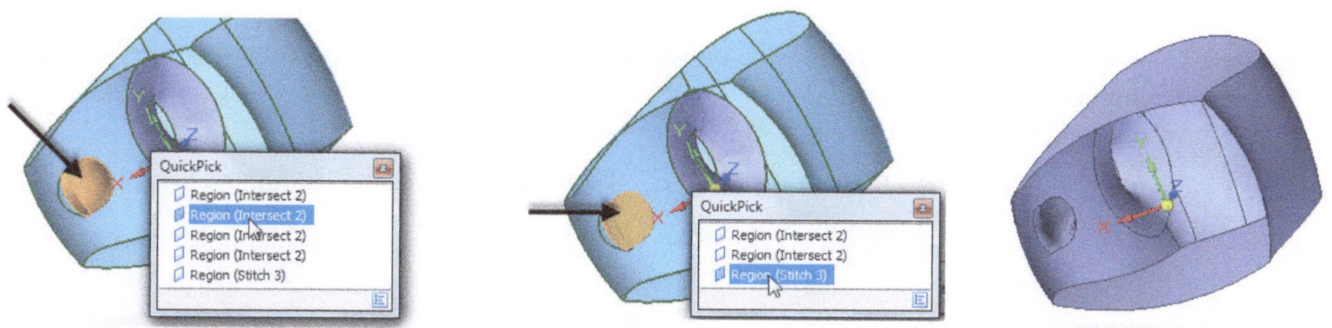

13. Activate the **Round** command (On the ribbon, click **Home > Solids > Round**) and round the edge of the handle. The round radius is 6 mm.
14. Round the intersection between the main surface and handle. The round radius is 5 mm.

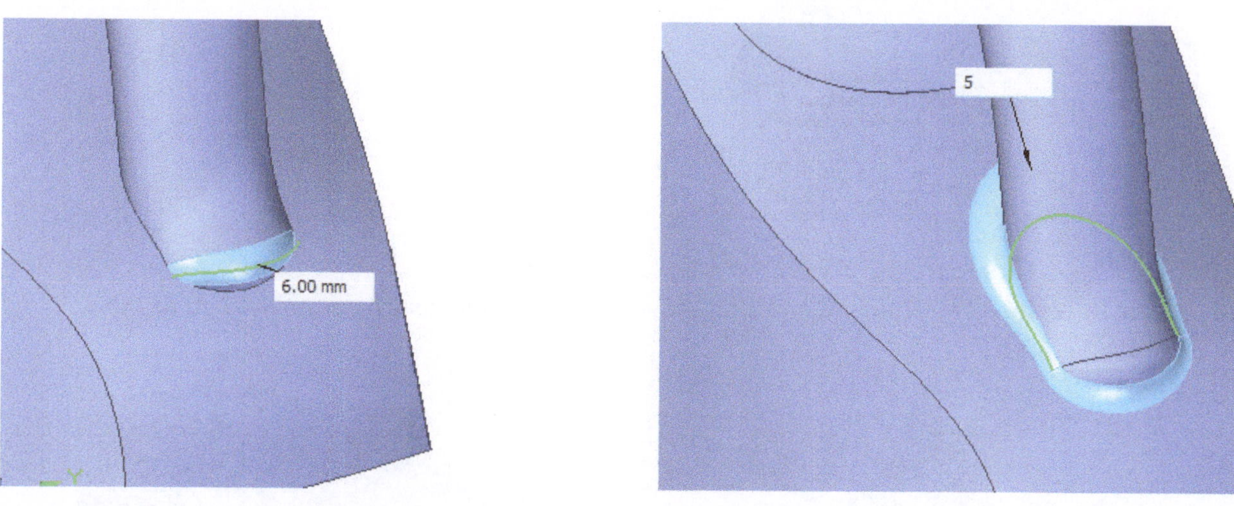

Creating the Neck and Spout

1. Draw a sketch on the XZ Plane for the revolved surface. Finish the sketch.

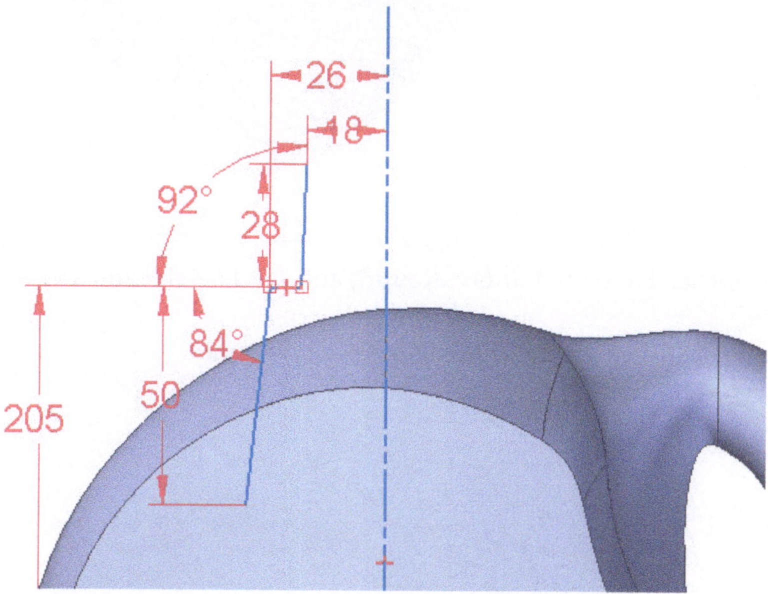

2. On the ribbon, click **Surfacing > Surfaces > Revolved**. On the command bar, set the **Create-From Options** type to **Select from Sketch**.
3. Select the sketch and right-click to accept.
4. Select the centerline and click the Extent section. Next, click the **Revolve 360** button on the command bar. Click **Finish** and **Cancel**.

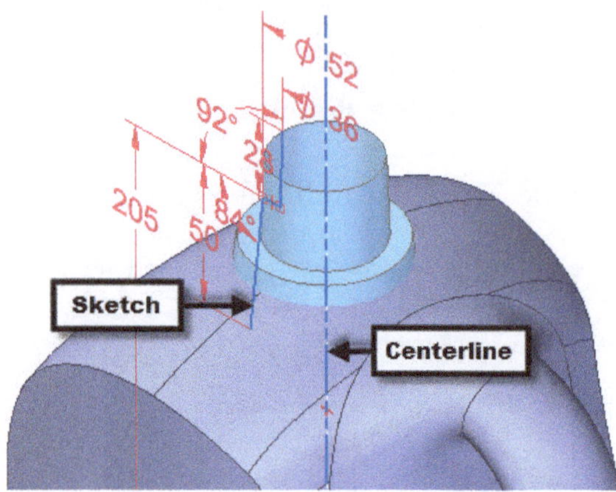

5. Activate the **Intersect** command and trim the revolved and main surface. Stitch them together.

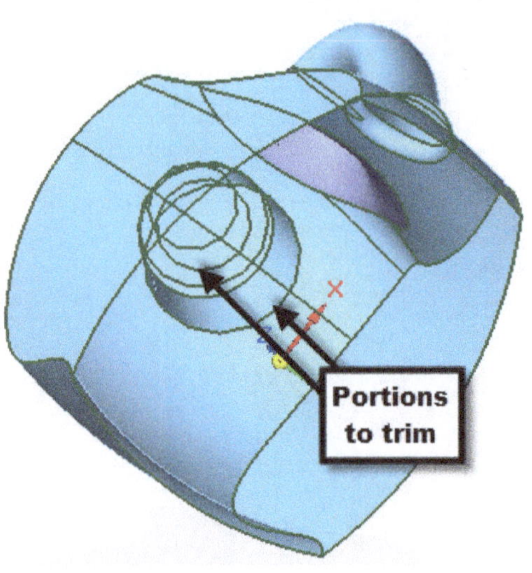

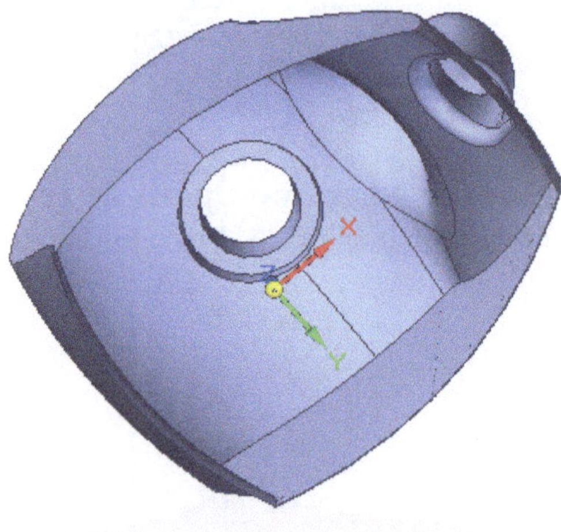

Rounding the Label Faces

1. Activate the **Round** command (on the ribbon, click **Home > Solids > Round**) and set the **Selection Type** to **Face**. Click on the front and back label faces.
2. Type-in **10** in the **Radius** box and right-click. Click **Preview** and **Finish** to create the round.

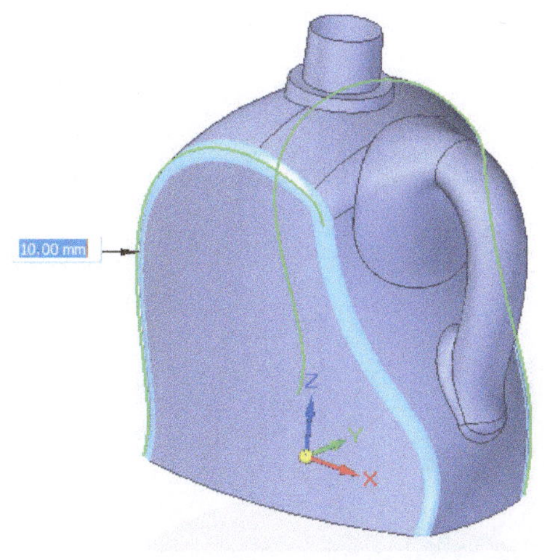

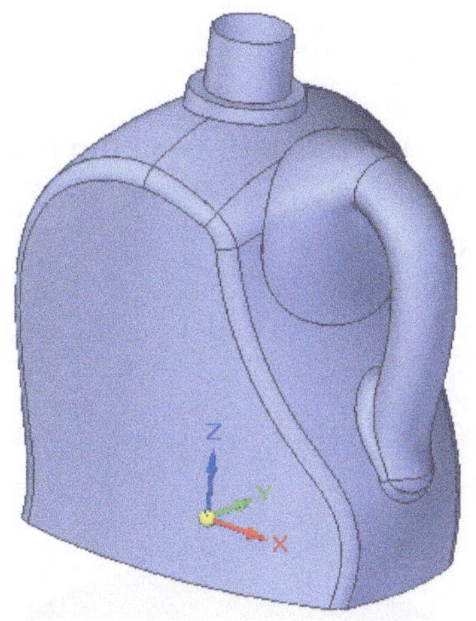

Creating the Bottom Face

1. Start a sketch on the XZ plane and draw a curve, as shown below. Click **Close Sketch** on the ribbon.

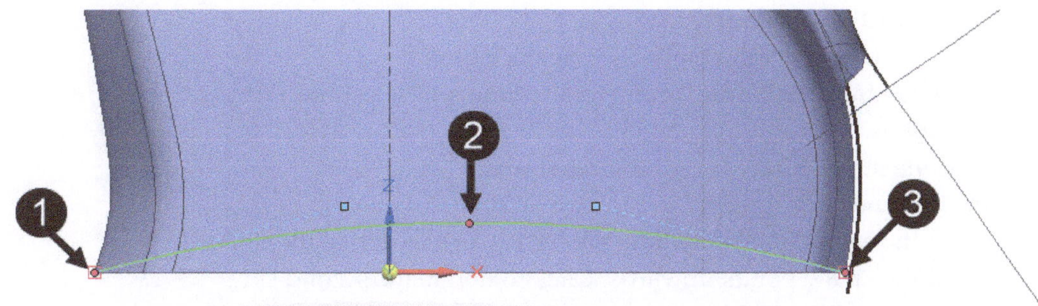

2. Activate the **Bounded** command (on the ribbon, click **Surfacing > Surfaces > Bounded**) and click on the edge-set at the bottom of the surface model. Right-click to accept the selection.
3. On the command bar, click the **Guide Curve** section and select the spline.
4. On the command bar, make sure that the **Common Tangent Condition** button is activated. Click the green check to accept the guide curve selection.
5. Click **Finish** and **Cancel**.

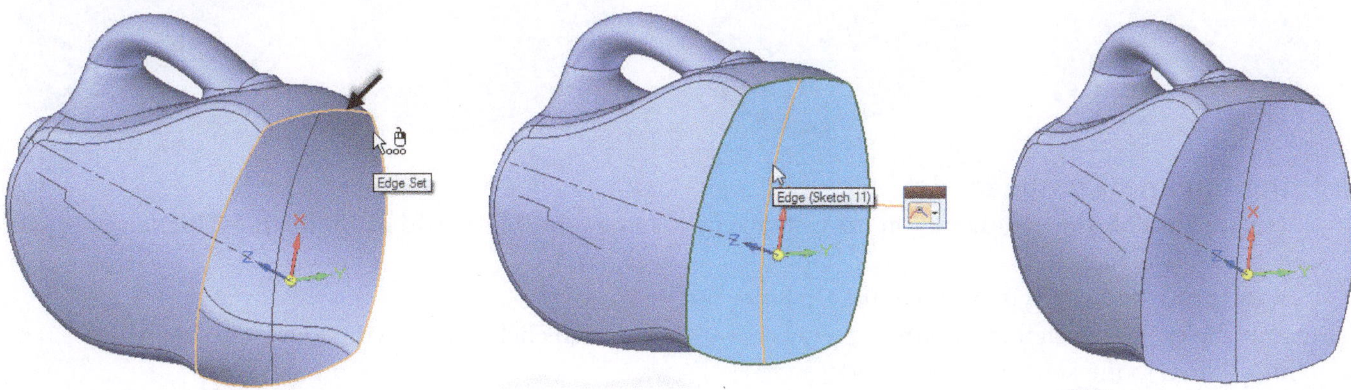

Rounding the Bottom Face

1. On the ribbon, click **Surfacing > Modify Surfaces > Stitched** . Click **OK** on the **Stitched Surface Options**

dialog.
2. Select all the surfaces. Click the green check on the command bar.
3. Click **Finish** and **Cancel**.
4. Activate the **Round** command and select the **Selection Type** to **Loop**.
5. Select the edge set at the bottom and type-in 10 in the **Radius** box. Right-click and click **Preview**.
6. Click **Finish** and **Cancel**.

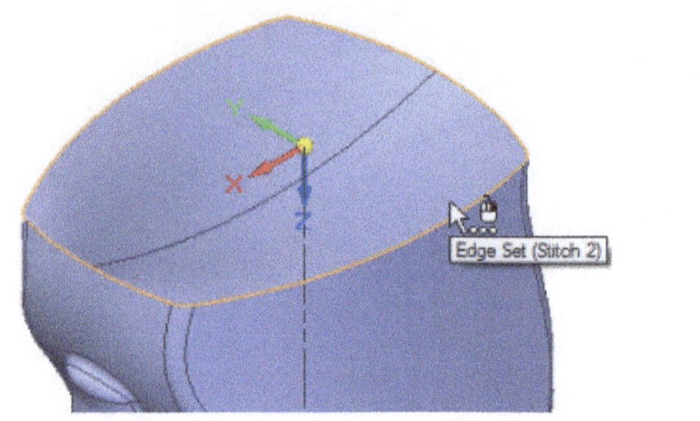

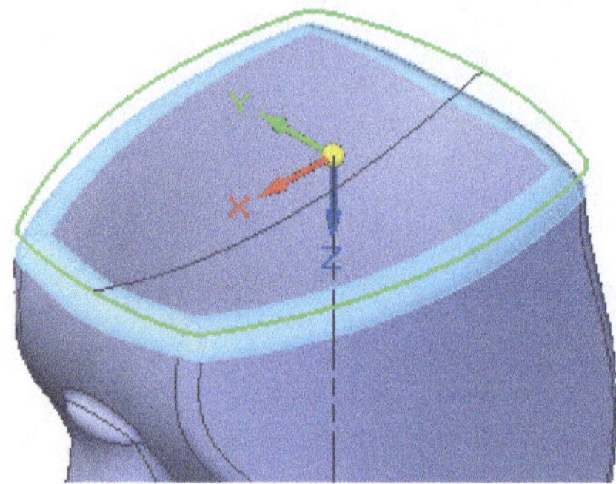

Blending the Bluesurface and Main body

1. Activate the **Round** command and select the **Options** > **Surface blend**.
2. On the command bar, click the **Surface Blend Parameters** section and select the **Trim and stitch input faces** and **Trim output blend** options.
3. Select the bluesurface and the main surface body connected to it.
4. Type-in 30 in the **Radius** box and click **Accept**.
5. Move the pointer such that the arrow points towards the back. Click to define the first side.
6. Move the pointer such that the arrow points upwards. Click to define the second side.
7. Click **Preview** and **Finish** to complete the blend surface.

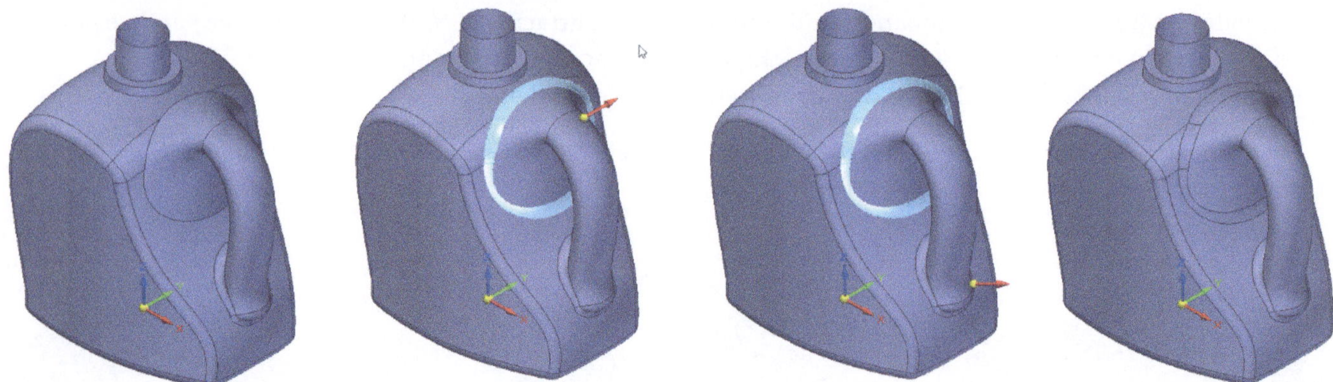

Adding thickness to the model

1. Activate the **Thicken** command (on the ribbon, click **Home > Solids > Add drop-down > Thicken**) and click on the surface body.
2. On the command bar, type-in 1.5 in the **Distance** box.
3. Move the pointer such that the arrow points outward, and then click to define the thickness side.
4. Click **Finish** to thicken the surface model.

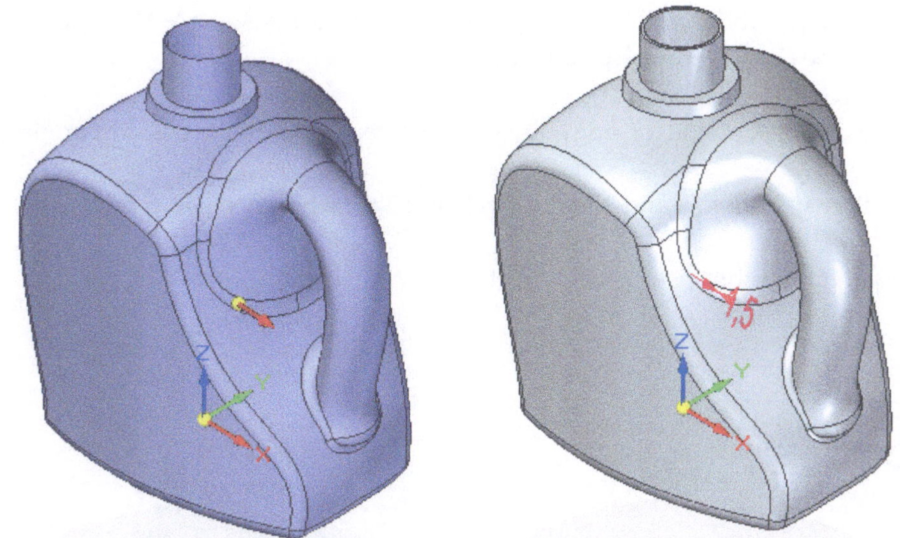

5. Activate the **Round** command, and then blend the sharp edges of the neck and spout. The blend radius is 1 mm.

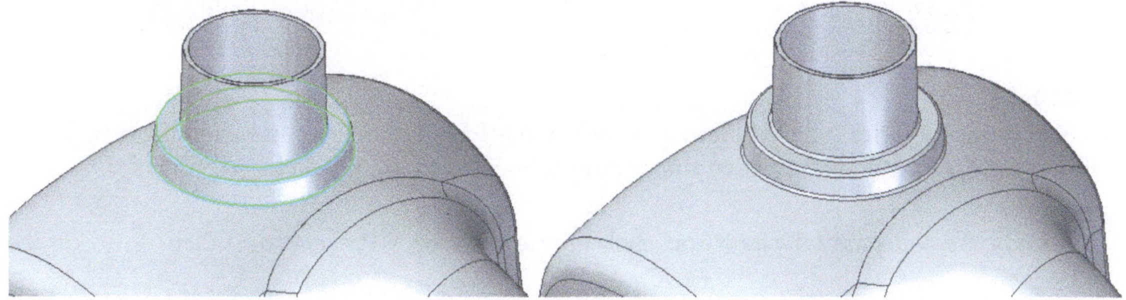

Creating threads

1. Create the cross-section and axis of the thread on the XZ Plane, as shown below. Click **Close Sketch**.

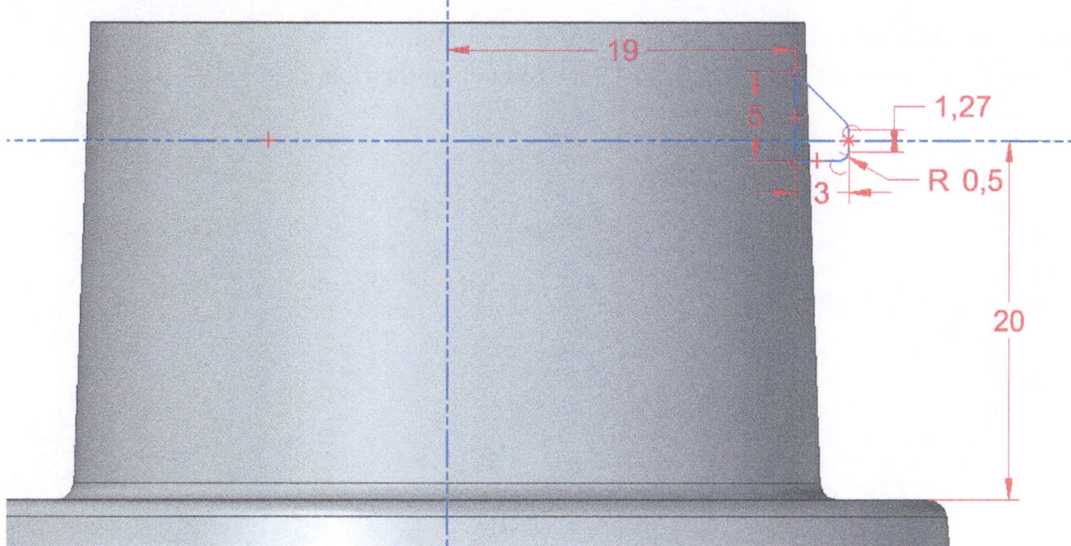

2. Activate the **Helix** command (on the ribbon, click **Home > Solids > Add** drop-down **> Helix**) and select the **Select from sketch** option from the **Create-From Options** drop-down.
3. Select the cross-section and right-click.
4. Select the centerline to define the axis. Click on the top endpoint of the centerline to define the start point of the helical protrusion.
5. Set the **Helix method** to **Pitch & Turns**. Type-in 6 and 2 in the **Pitch** and **Turns** boxes, respectively. Click **Next** and **Preview** to view the helix.
6. Click **Finish** to complete the helical protrusion.

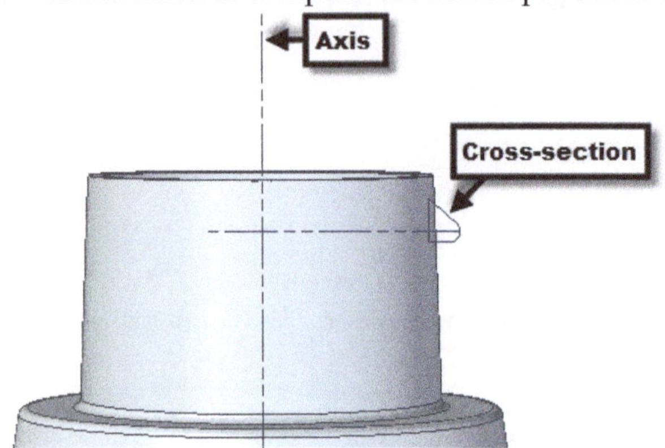

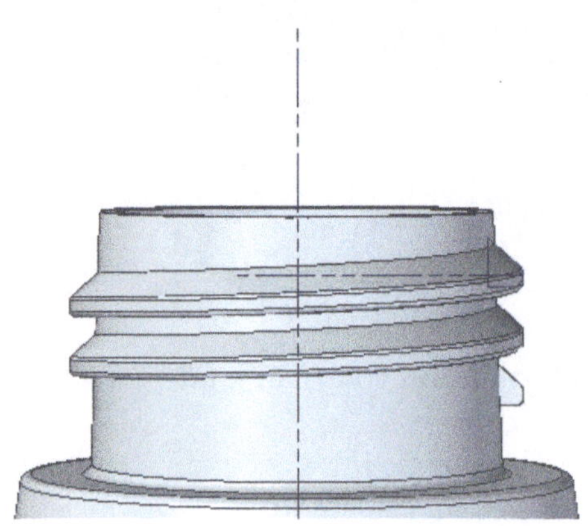

Embossing the label faces

1. On the ribbon, click **Surfacing > Planes > More Planes** drop-down **> Parallel.** Select the XZ plane, type 100 in the **Distance** box, and then press Enter. Next, move the pointer toward the left and click.
2. Start a sketch on the newly created parallel plane and click **Home > Draw > Project to Sketch**  on the ribbon.
3. On the command bar, check the **Project with offset** option. Click **OK**.
4. Set the **Selection Type** to **Loop** and click on the round's inner edge, as shown below. Click the green check.
5. Type-in **15** in the **Distance** box and click inside the loop. The edge loop will be projected. Next, press Esc to deactivate the **Project to Sketch** command.
6. Click on the offset constraints displayed on the sketch and press **Delete**.
7. Add 12 radius fillets to the corners of the sketch. Click **Close Sketch** on the ribbon.
8. Click **Finish** and **Cancel**.

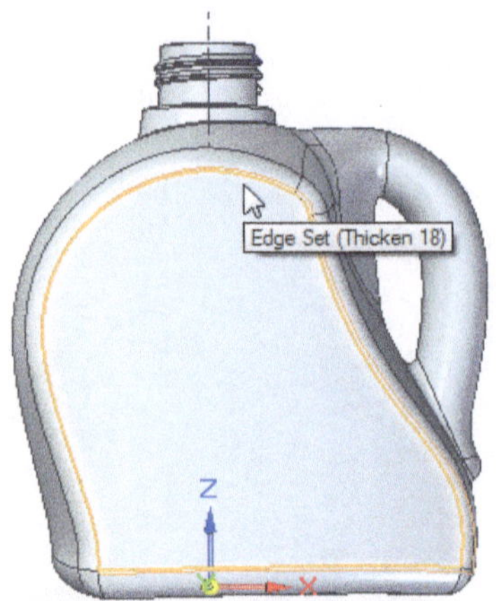

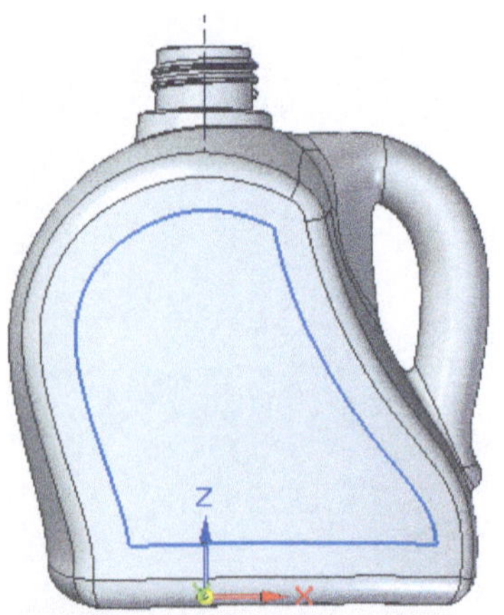

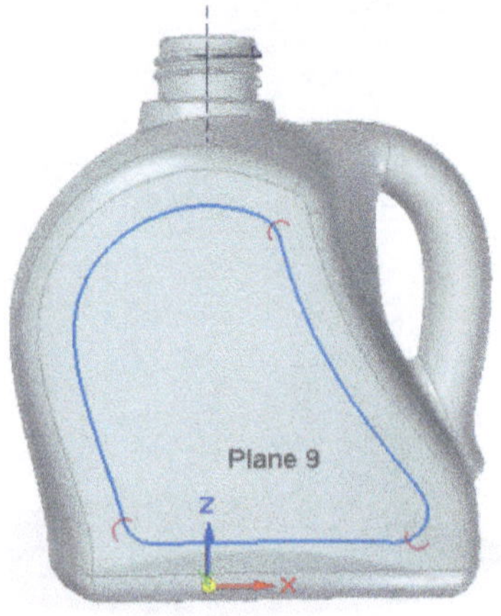

9. On the ribbon, click **Home > Solids > Add Body** and click **OK** on the **Add body** dialog. A new body is created within the part file.
10. On the ribbon, click **Home > Solids > Extrude**. Select **Create-From Options** drop-down > **Select from Sketch** on the command bar. Select the sketch. Click the green check.
11. On the command bar, click the **From/To Extent** button and select the sketch plane to define the 'From' surface.
12. Rotate the model and select the inner face of the label face to define the 'To' surface.

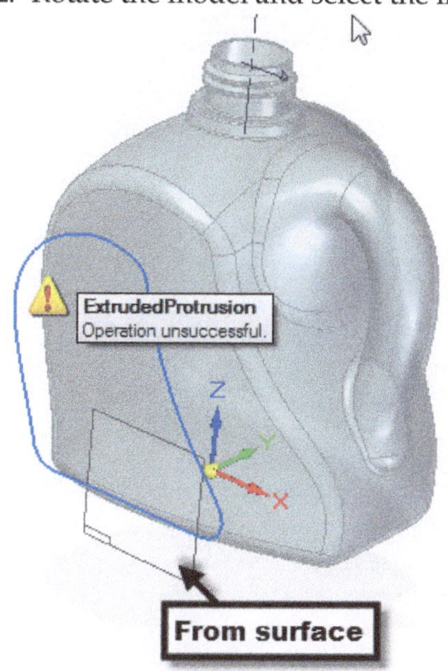

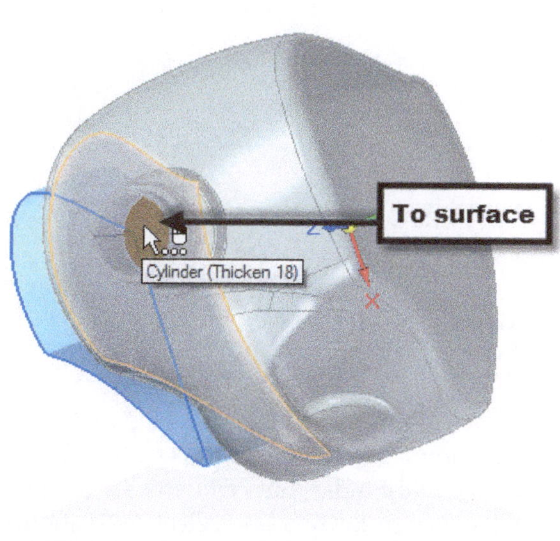

13. On the command bar, click **Treatment** section and select the **Draft** button.
14. Type-in **5** in the **Angle(a)** box. Use the **Flip Side** button to make sure that arrow 2 points outwards.
15. Click **Preview** and **Finish** to create the *Extrude* feature.

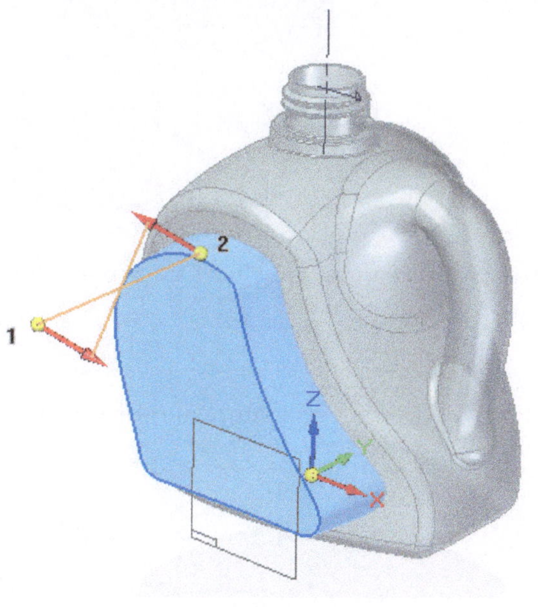

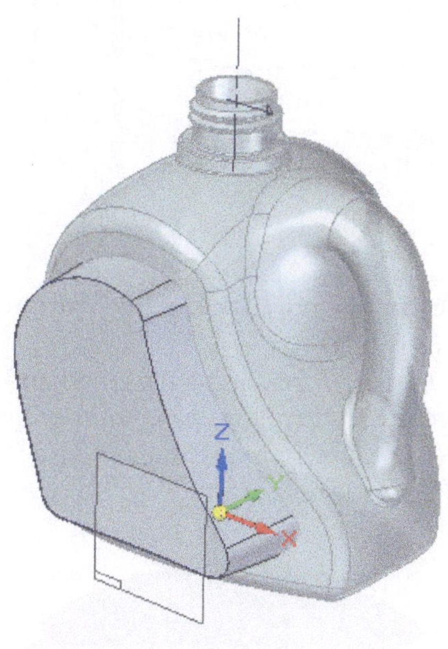

16. On the ribbon, click **Home > Solids > Thin Wall** drop-down > **Emboss** .

17. Select the target and tool bodies, as shown in the figure. Click the **Direction** button on the command bar to reverse the direction of the emboss feature.
18. Type-in 0.5 and 1 in the **Clearance** and **Thickness** boxes, respectively.

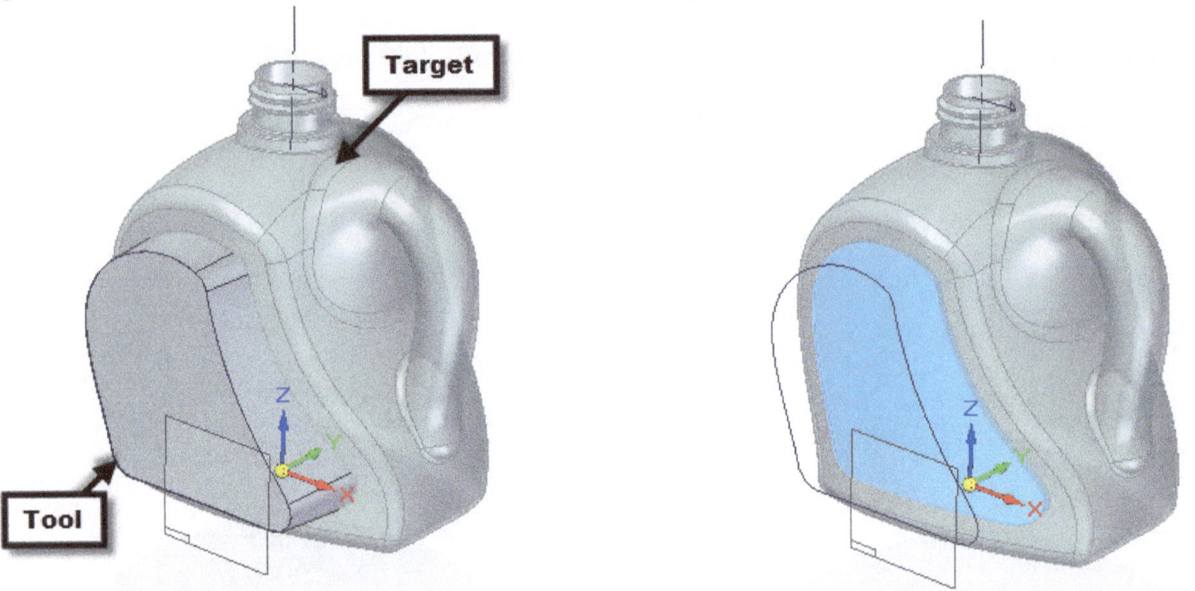

19. Click **Accept** to create the emboss feature. Press Esc to deactivate the **Emboss** command.
20. Under the PathFinder, turn OFF the eye icon next to the **Design Body_2** to hide it.
21. Click on **Design Body_1** and select **Activate Body**. This activates the main body.

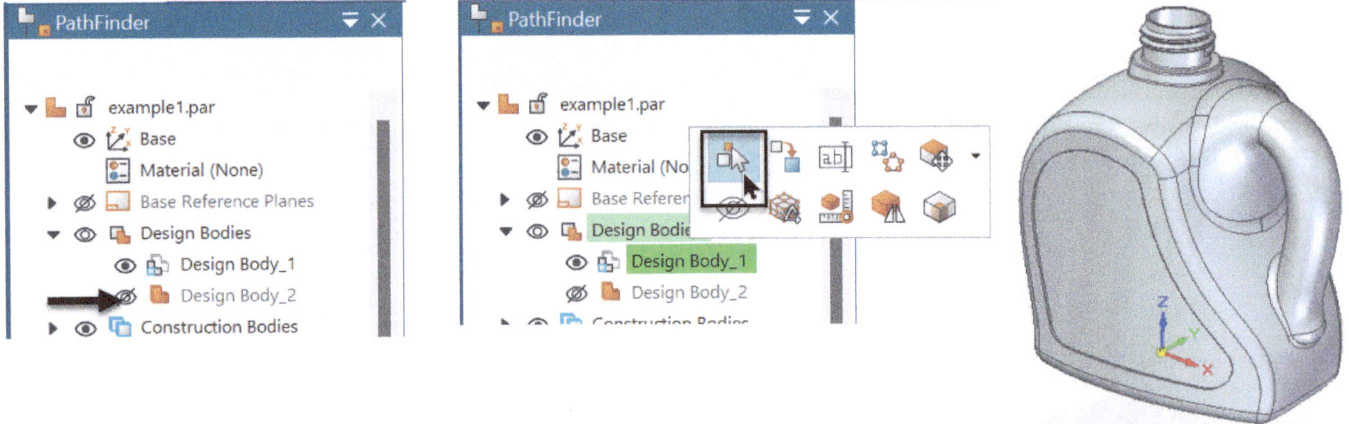

22. On the ribbon, click **Home > Pattern > Mirror drop-down > Mirror Copy Feature** and click **Occurrence Type > Fast** button on the command bar.
23. Select the emboss feature and right-click.
24. Select the XZ plane from the Base Coordinate system and click **Finish**. The emboss feature is mirrored about the XZ plane.

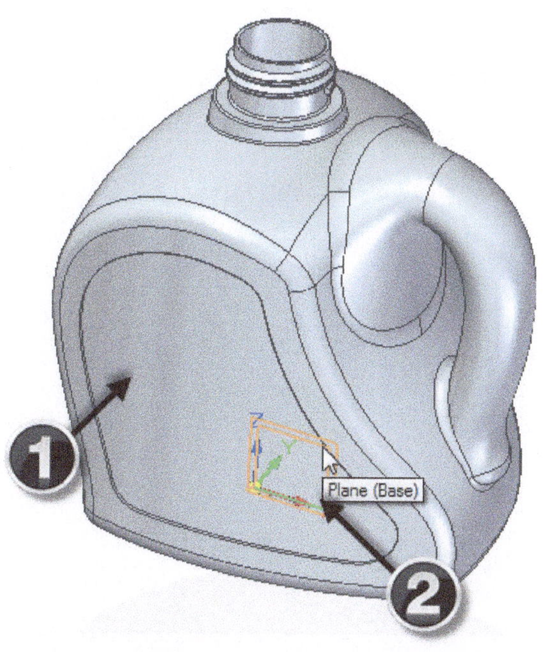

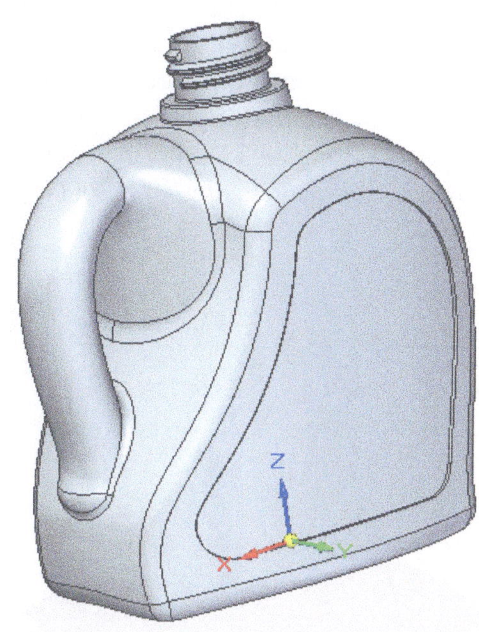

25. Activate the **Round** command and set the **Selection Type** to **Chain**.
26. Select the outer edges of the emboss features and type-in 3 in the **Radius** box. Click **Accept**.
27. Click **Preview** and **Finish** to complete the round feature.

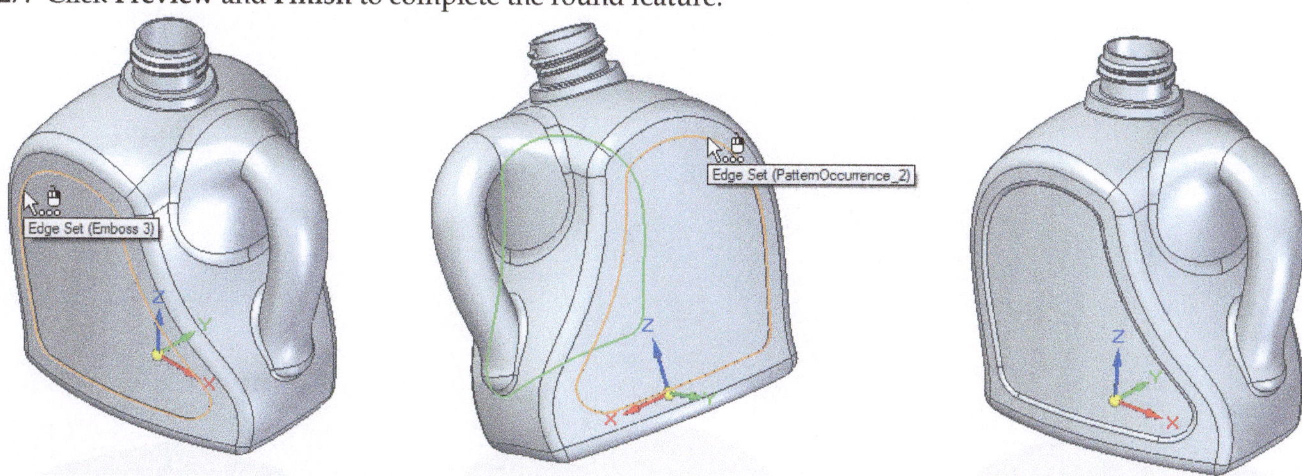

Measuring the Volume of the bottle

1. Activate the **Physical Properties** command (on the ribbon, click **Inspect > Physical Properties > Physical Properties**).
2. On the **Physical Properties** dialog, click the **Change** button under the **Density** section.
3. On the **Solid Edge Material Table** dialog, click **Material > Non-metals > Plastics > Polyethylene, low density**. Click **Apply to Model**. Click **Update** to display the physical properties of the bottle on the dialog.
4. View the **Volume** box on the **Physical Properties** dialog. Next, click **Close**.
5. Save and close the file.

Questions

1. What is the use of the **Stitched** command?
2. How many types of rounds can be created in Solid Edge?

3. Why do we use the **Boundary** command?
4. Which command can be used to bridge the gap between two surfaces?
5. Name the command that can be used to perform a variety of operations.
6. How do you add thicknesses to a surface body?
7. Which command is used to extend surfaces from an edge?
8. Which command is used to offset faces?

Chapter 14: Subdivision Modeling

Subdivision Modeling in Solid Edge allows you to create organic smooth solid or surface models by manipulating and subdividing the primitive shapes such as spheres, boxes, and cylinders. To activate this environment, click the **Surfacing** tab > **Free-Form** group > **Subdivision Modeling** on the ribbon.

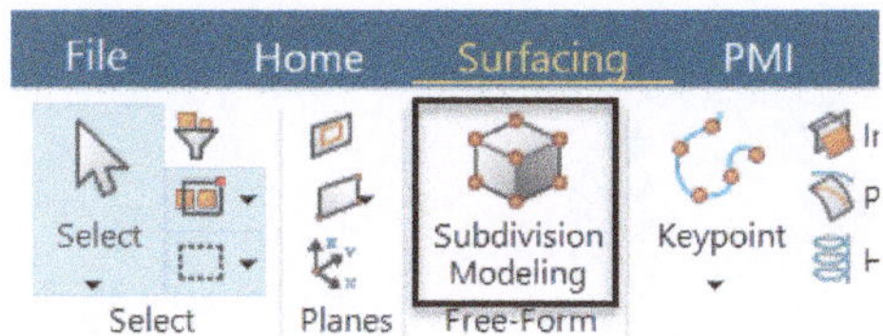

The topics covered in this chapter are:

- *Primitive Shapes*
- *Transform Cage faces*
- *Extrude Cage Faces*
- *Scale Cage faces*
- *Fill*
- *Blend*
- *Start Symmetric Modeling*
- *Split Face*
- *Delete*

Creating Primitive Shapes

In the **Subdivision Modeling** environment, first, you create primitive shapes and then refine them into finished models. The primitive shapes are simple geometric models such as a sphere, cylinder, box, and torus. They are completely airtight closed surfaces. The commands on the **Shapes** group help you to create different primitive shapes. The procedures to create different primitive shapes are explained next.

Creating a Sphere

To create a sphere, activate the **Sphere** command (on the ribbon, click **Home > Shapes > Sphere**). On the command bar, the **At Origin** option is selected from the **Selection Type** drop-down. As a result, the sphere appears at the origin of the Coordinate System. Next, specify the sphere size by entering a value in the size box.

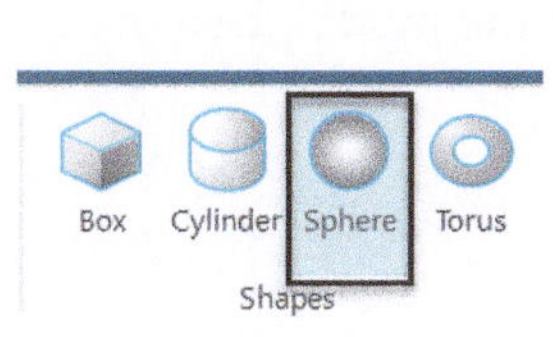

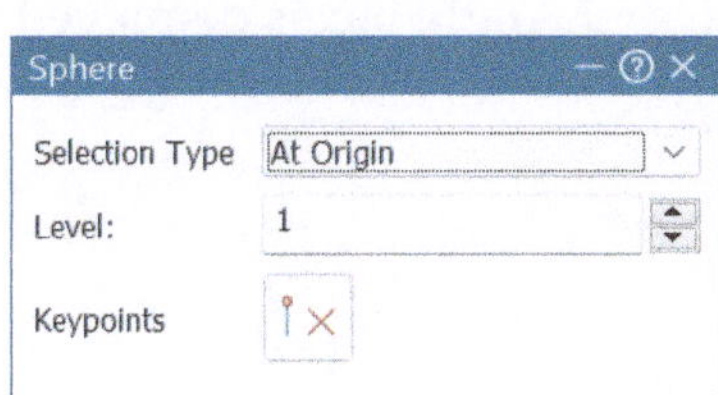

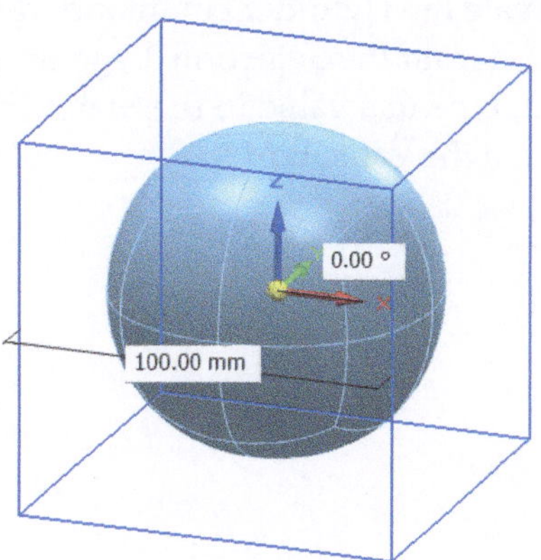

You can also select the **2 Points** option from the **Selection Type** drop-down and then select two points in the graphics window to define the sphere's location and size.

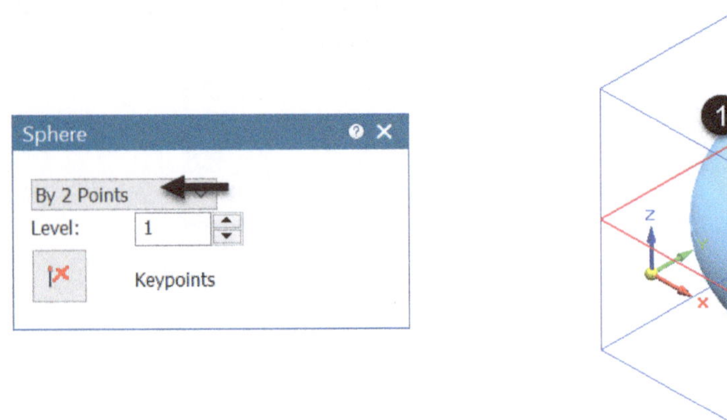

Next, you need to define the number of segments by selecting an option from the **Level** drop-down (**1**, **2** and **3**). The **1** option creates a sphere with six segments. The **2** option creates a ninety-six segmented sphere. The **3** option creates a sphere with more segments. Right-click to create the sphere.

Level 1 **Level 2** **Level 3**

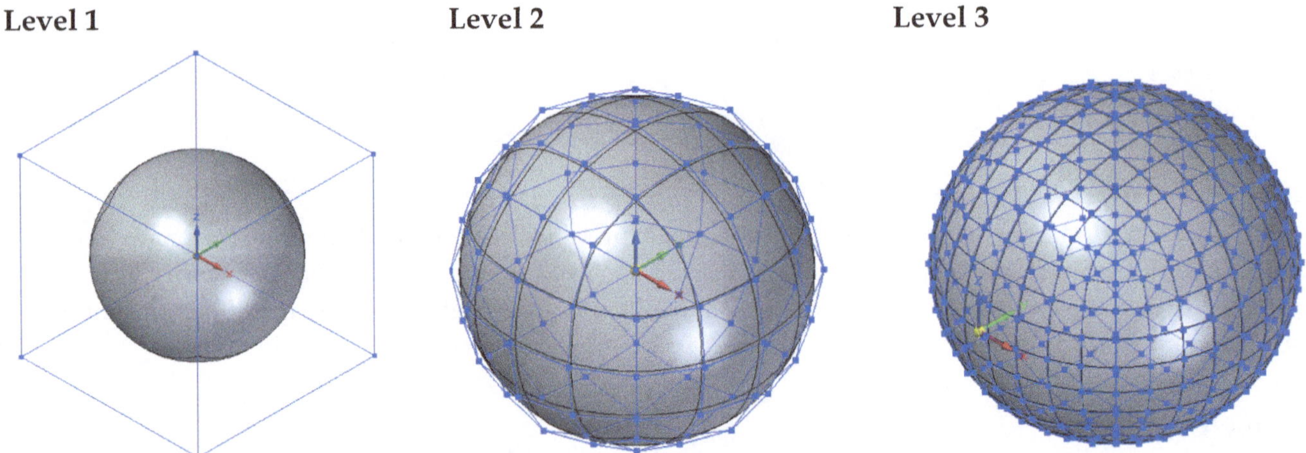

Creating a Cylinder

To create a cylinder, activate the **Cylinder** command (on the ribbon, click **Home > Shapes > Cylinder**). Next, select the **At Origin** option from the **Selection Type** drop-down. The cylinder is placed at the origin of the Coordinate System. Next, type in a value in the **Size**, **Height**, and **Angle** boxes displayed on the model. Use the TAB key to switch between the value boxes.

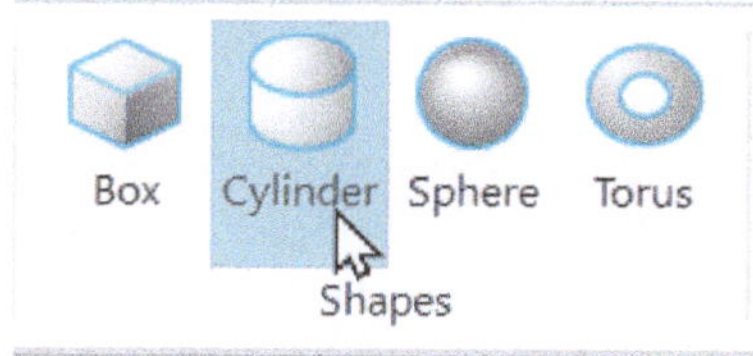

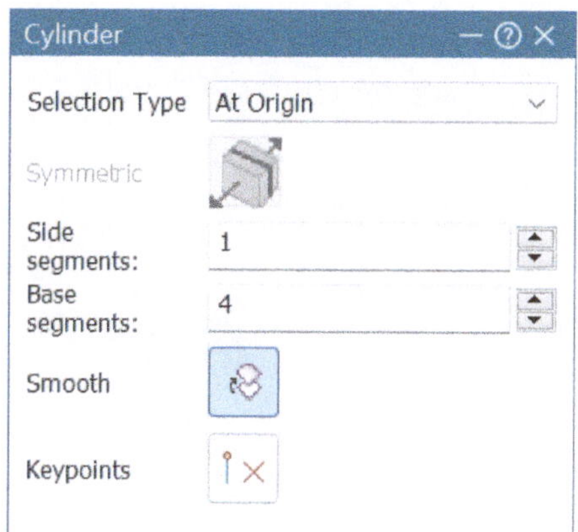

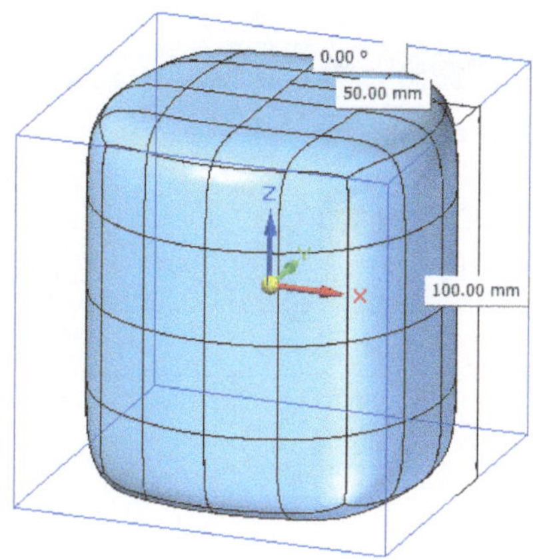

Next, specify the number of segments in the linear and circular direction by entering values in the **Side Segments** and **Base Segments** boxes available on the command bar. Note that the number of segments in the circular direction should be between 3 and 25. Simultaneously, the number of segments in the linear direction should be between 1 and 25. The **Smooth** icon is activated by default on the command bar. As a result, the cylinder is smoothened. Deactivate this icon if you want to remove the smoothness of the cylinder. Right-click to complete the cylindrical shape.

Side Segments: 3
Base Segments: 4

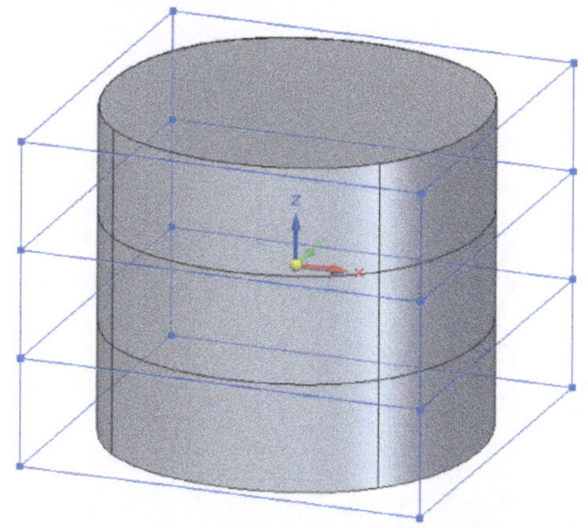

Side Segments: 4
Base Segments: 6

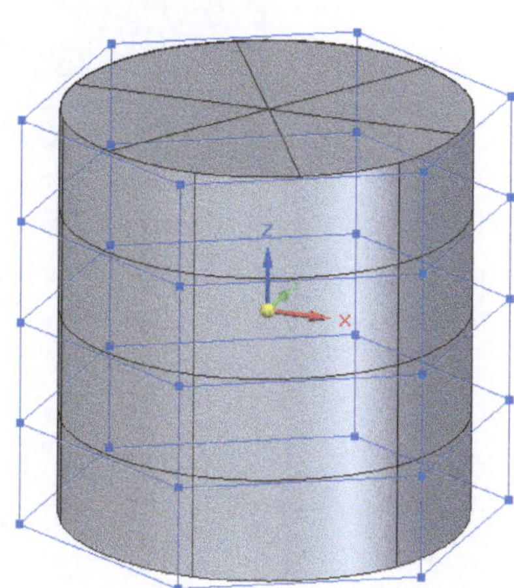

Creating a Cylinder using the By 2 Points option

On the ribbon, click **Home > Shapes > Cylinder**. Next, select the **By 2 Points** option from the **Selection Type** drop-down available on the command bar. Select a plane from the graphics window. Click in the graphics window to define the center point of the cylinder. Next, move the pointer outward and enter the diameter value of the cylinder. Press the TAB key and specify the orientation of the cylinder cage. Next, move the pointer upward and click to define the height of the cylinder.

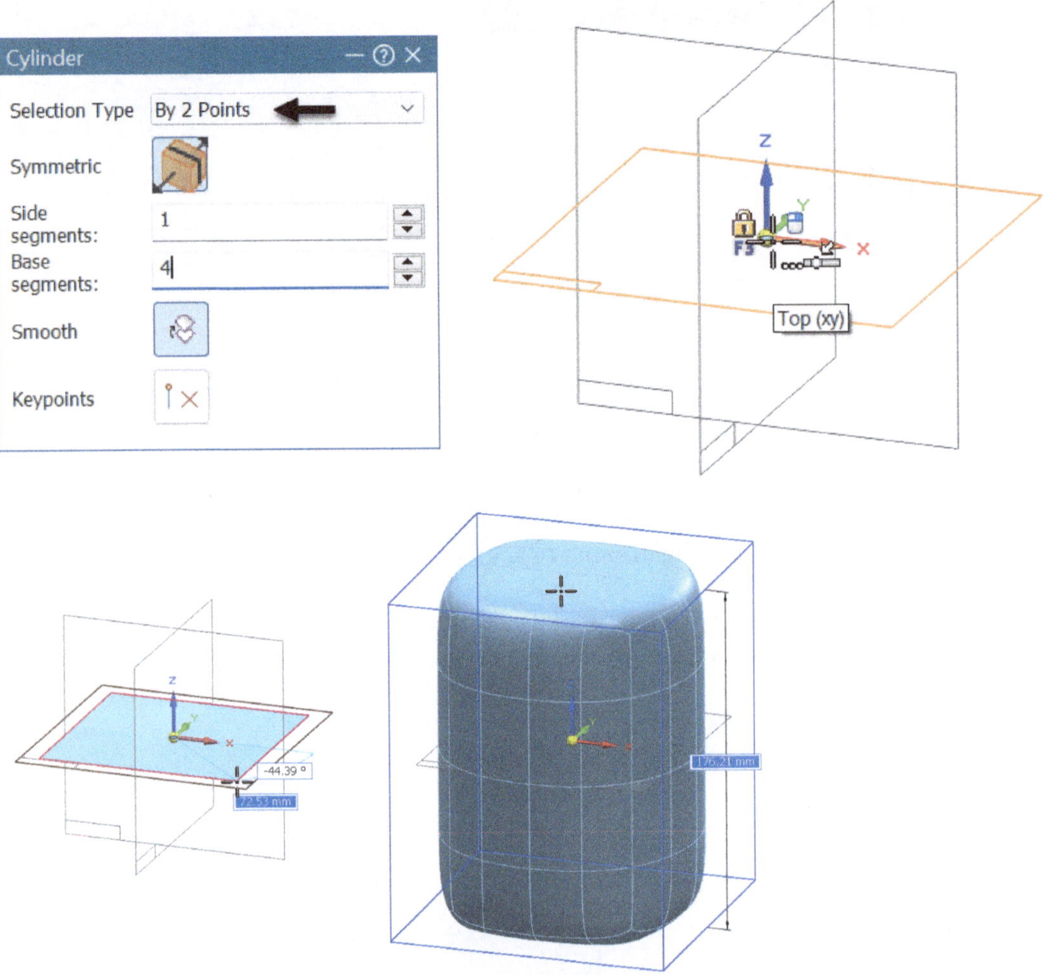

The **Symmetric** icon is activated on the command bar. As a result, the cylinder is created symmetrical on both sides of the sketch plane. Deactivate the **Symmetric** icon if you want to create the cylinder only on one side of the sketch plane. Right-click to complete the cylinder.

Symmetric-ON

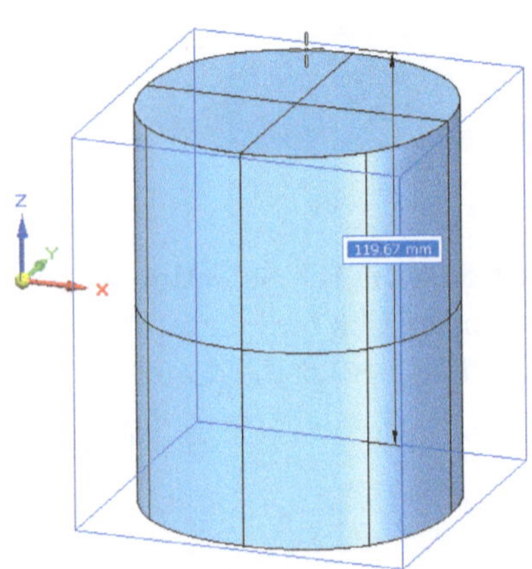

Symmetric-OFF

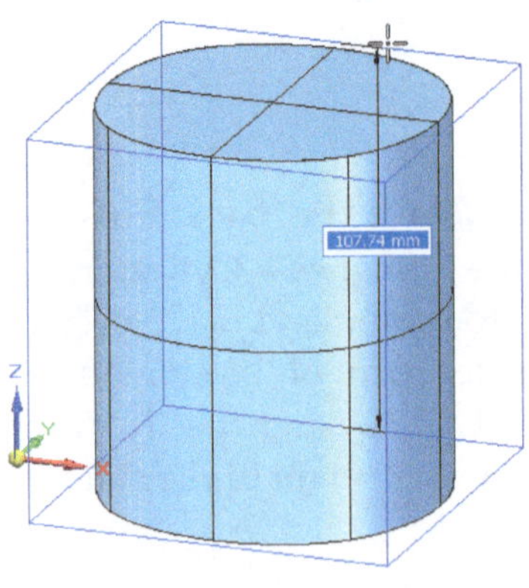

Creating Box

To create a box, activate the **Box** command (on the ribbon, click **Home > Shapes > Box**. Next, specify the box's location and size using any one of the options available in the **Selection Type** drop-down.

At Origin

Select this option from the **Selection Type** drop-down; the box is placed at the Coordinate system's origin. Next, specify the length, width, height, orientation angle of the box in the value boxes displayed on the box.

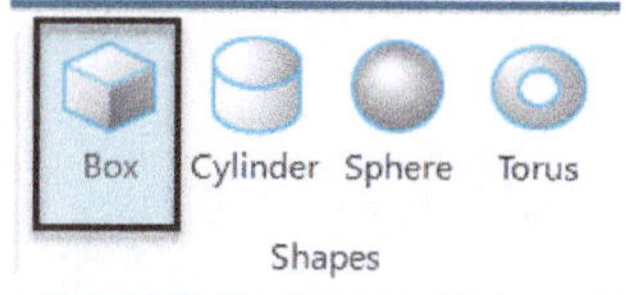

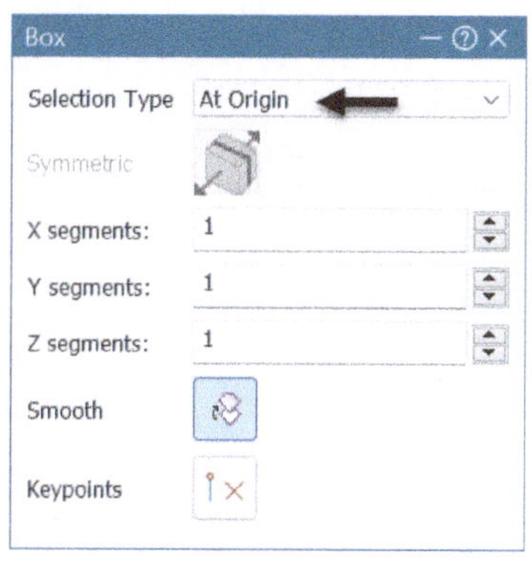

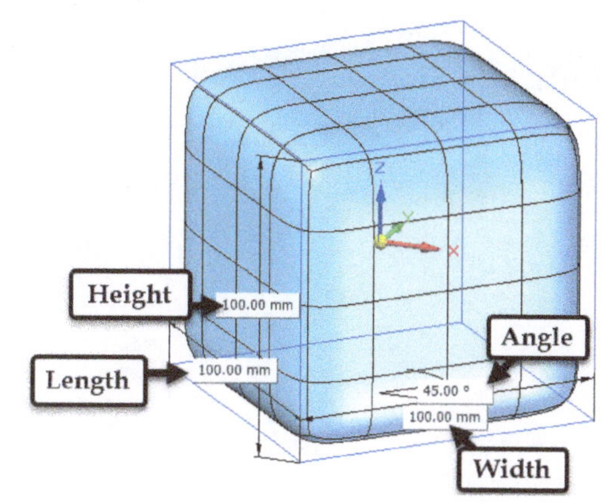

By Center

Select this option from the **Selection Type** drop-down. Next, click on the XZ Plane to specify the center of the rectangle. Move the pointer outward and click (or) enter the length, width, and angle values in the value boxes displayed in the graphics window. Move the pointer in the direction perpendicular to the sketch, and then click to create the box.

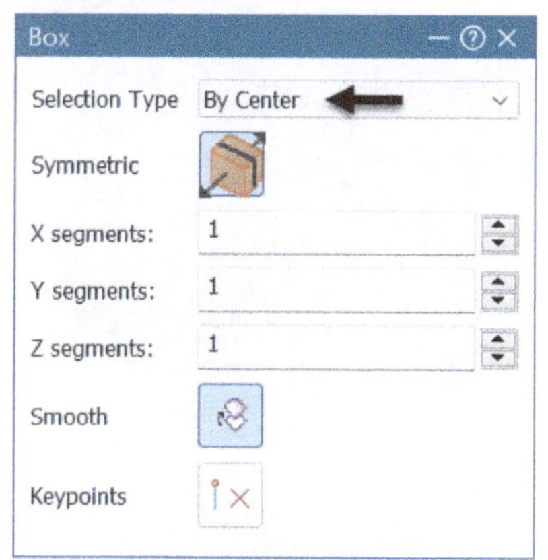

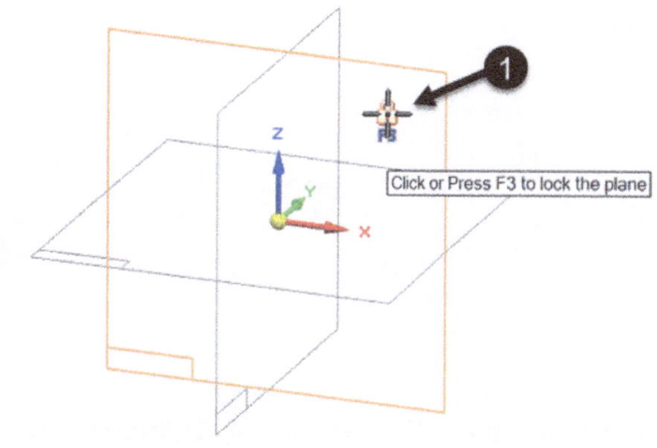

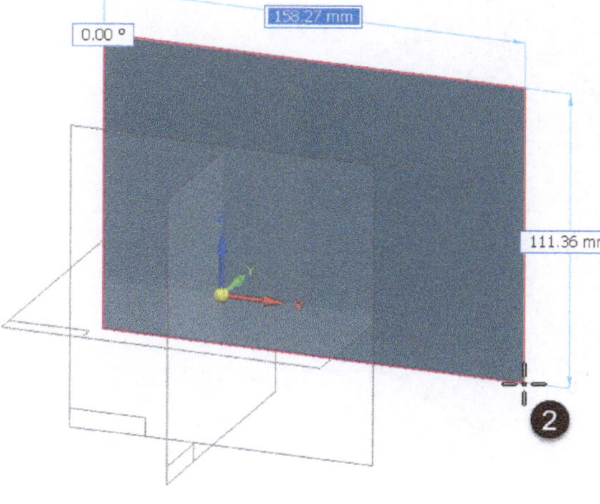

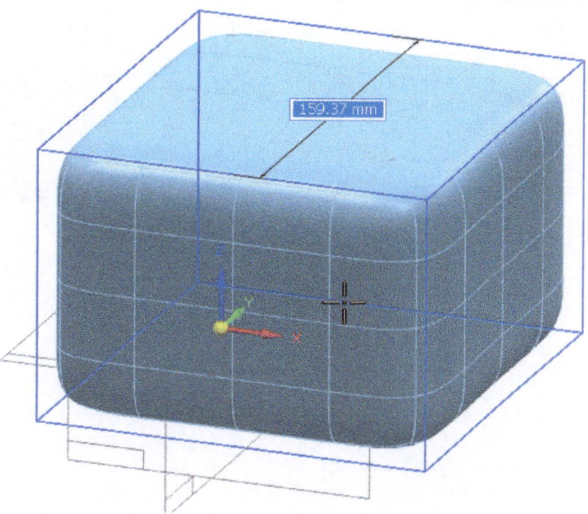

By 2 Points

Select this option from the **Selection Type** drop-down. Next, click on the XZ plane to specify the first corner rectangle. Move the pointer diagonally and click to specify the second corner of the rectangle. Next, move the pointer in the direction perpendicular to the sketch and click to create the box.

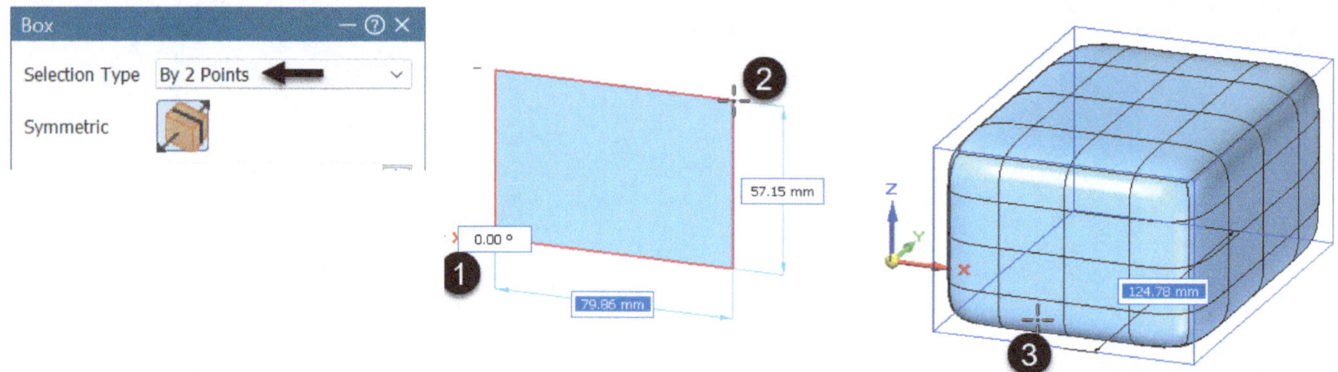

By 3 Points

Select this option from the **Selection Type** drop-down. Next, select a plane. Specify the first, second, and third corners of the rectangle. Move the pointer in the direction perpendicular to the rectangle and click. Next, change the dimensions of the box. Use the TAB key to switch between the value boxes.

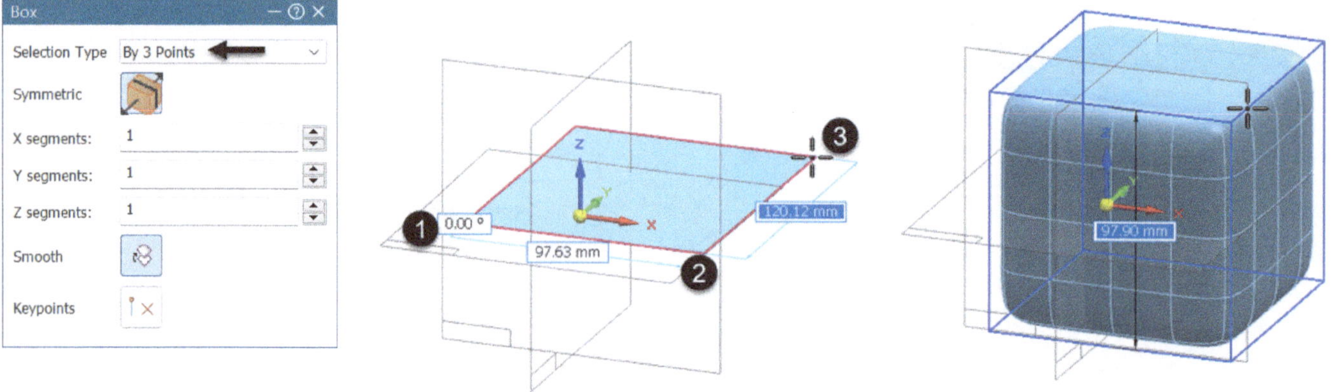

Next, type-in values in the **X segments**, **Y segments**, and **Z segments** boxes to add segments along the X, Y, and Z directions, respectively. Right-click to complete the block.

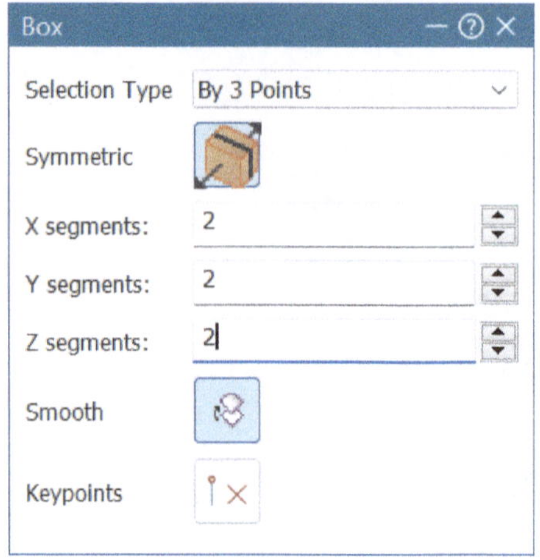

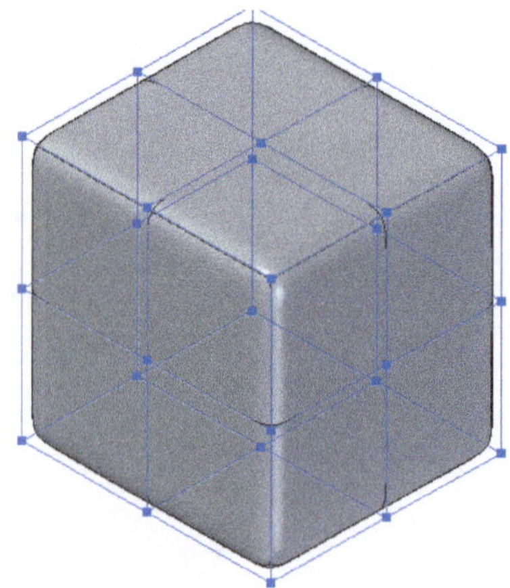

Creating a Torus

To create a torus, activate the **Torus** command (on the ribbon, click **Home > Shapes > Torus**). Specify the location of the torus using the **At Origin** or the **By Axis and 2 Points** option.

At Origin

The **By Origin** option define the location of the torus at the origin of the Coordinate System. After defining the torus' location, specify its Outer radius of the and minor radius.

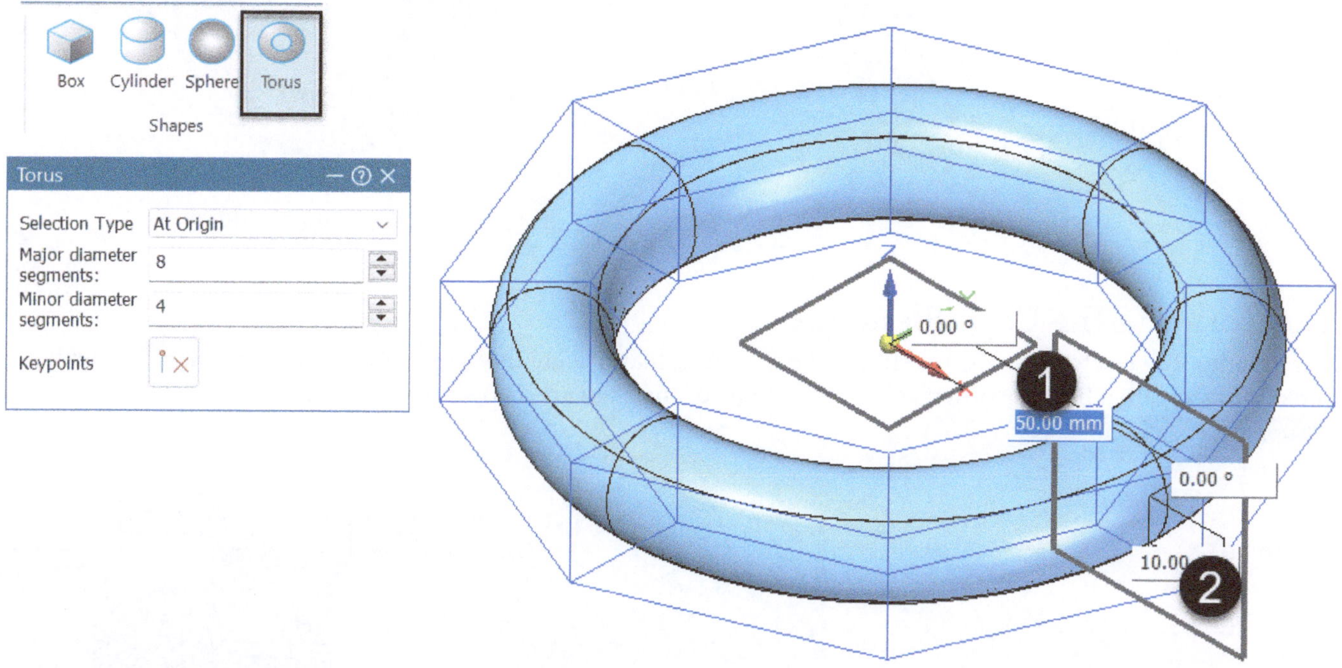

By Axis and 2 Points

Select this option from the **Selection Type** drop-down and specify the location of the torus axis. Next, select a line or Coordinate System axis to define the orientation of the torus axis. Move the pointer outward and click to specify the outer radius of the torus. Next, move the pointer inward or outward to change the minor radius of the torus. Click to create the torus. Change the outer and minor radius of the torus, if required.

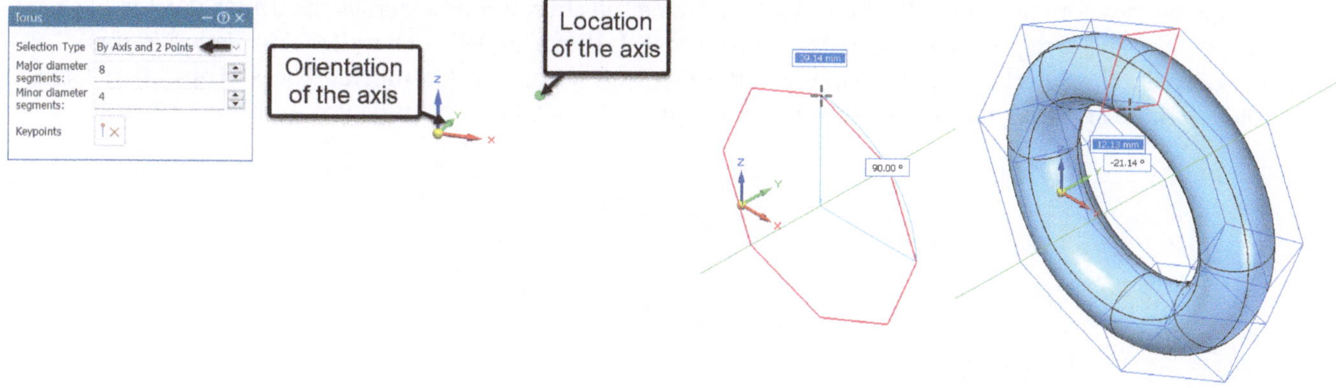

Next, specify the number of segments in the radial and circular direction by entering values in the **Major diameter segments** and **Minor diameter segment** boxes. Right-click to create the torus.

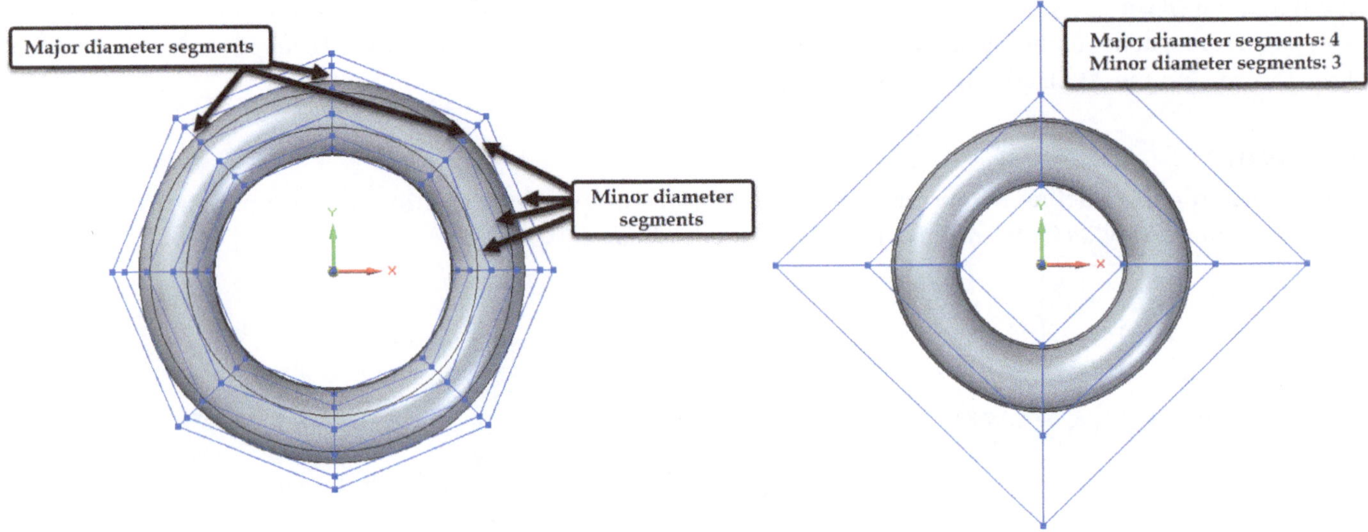

Transforming the Cage Elements

After creating the freeform primitive shapes, you need to manipulate them by transforming the cage elements. For example, create a box, as shown below. Elements of the cage are also shown in the figure.

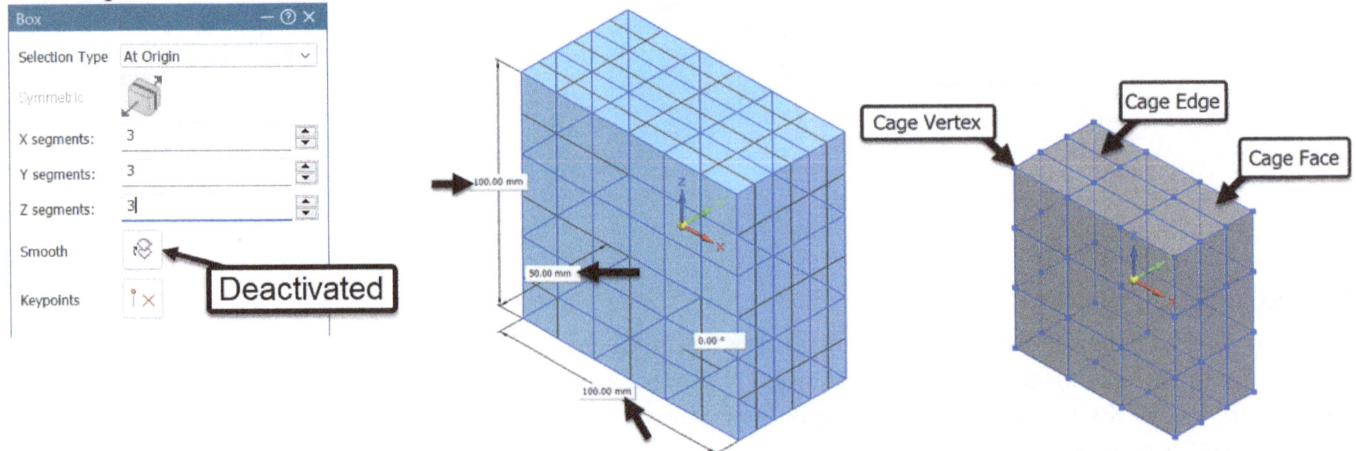

Next, change the view orientation to **Right**. Click and drag a selection window across the upper portion of the box, as shown; the entire region is selected. Also, notice that the Steering Wheel handle is displayed in the selected region. On the **Select** command bar, select the **Tip** option from the **Connected Faces** drop-down. Click on the rotate handle and drag the pointer to rotate the region. Type **15** in the Angle box and press ENTER.

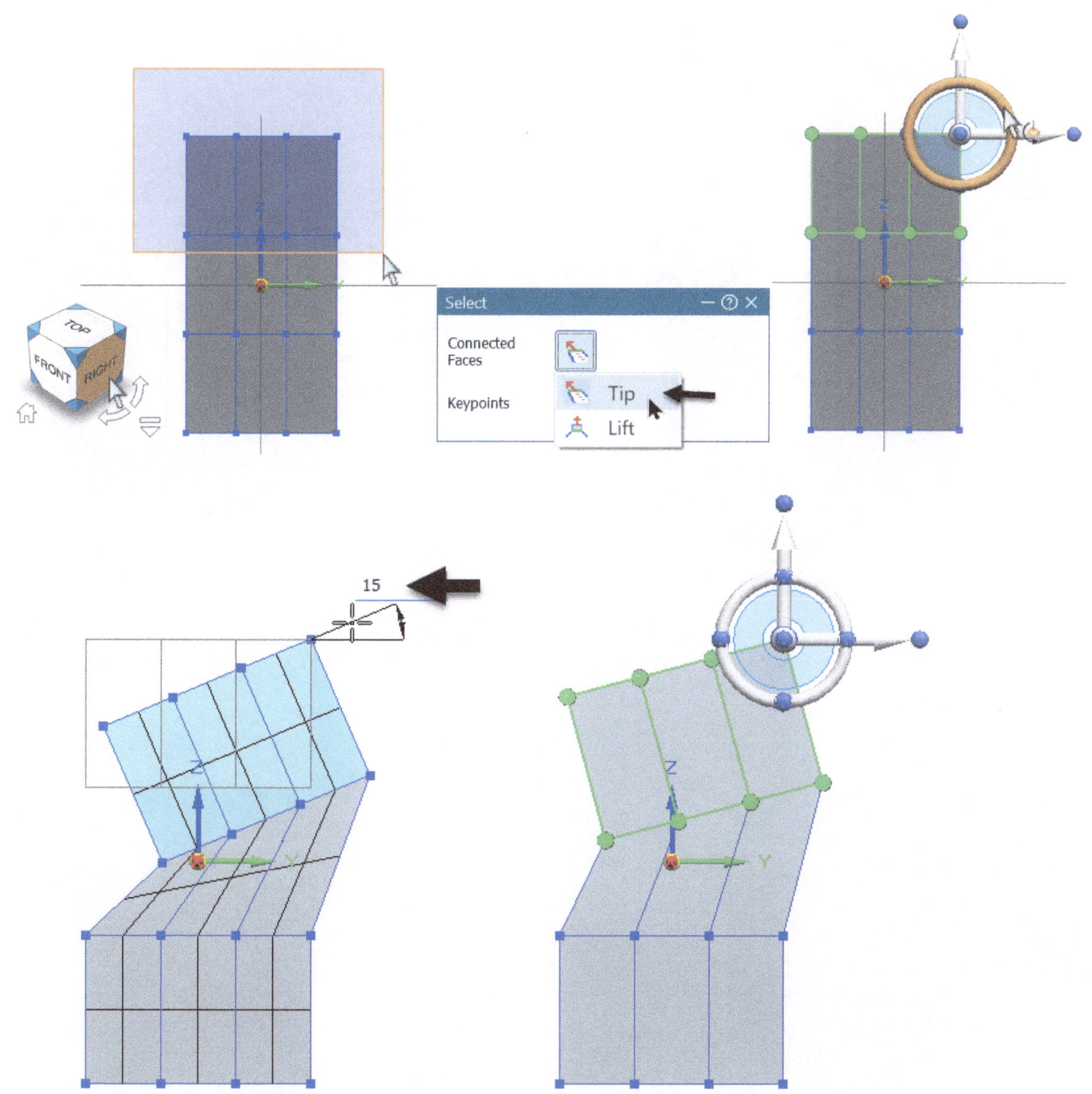

Scaling the Cage Elements

The **Scale** command allows you to scale the cage elements. Press ESC to deselect the selected cage elements. Change the view orientation to **Isometric**. Press and hold the CTRL key and select the top faces of the cage, as shown. On the ribbon, click the **Home** tab > **Modify** panel > **Scale**. Next, click the **Planar Scaling** on the command bar; the selected face will be scaled along with the X and Y directions. Make sure that the **Uniform** icon is selected. Click and drag the scale handle, as shown; the selected faces are scaled uniformly in the X and Y directions.

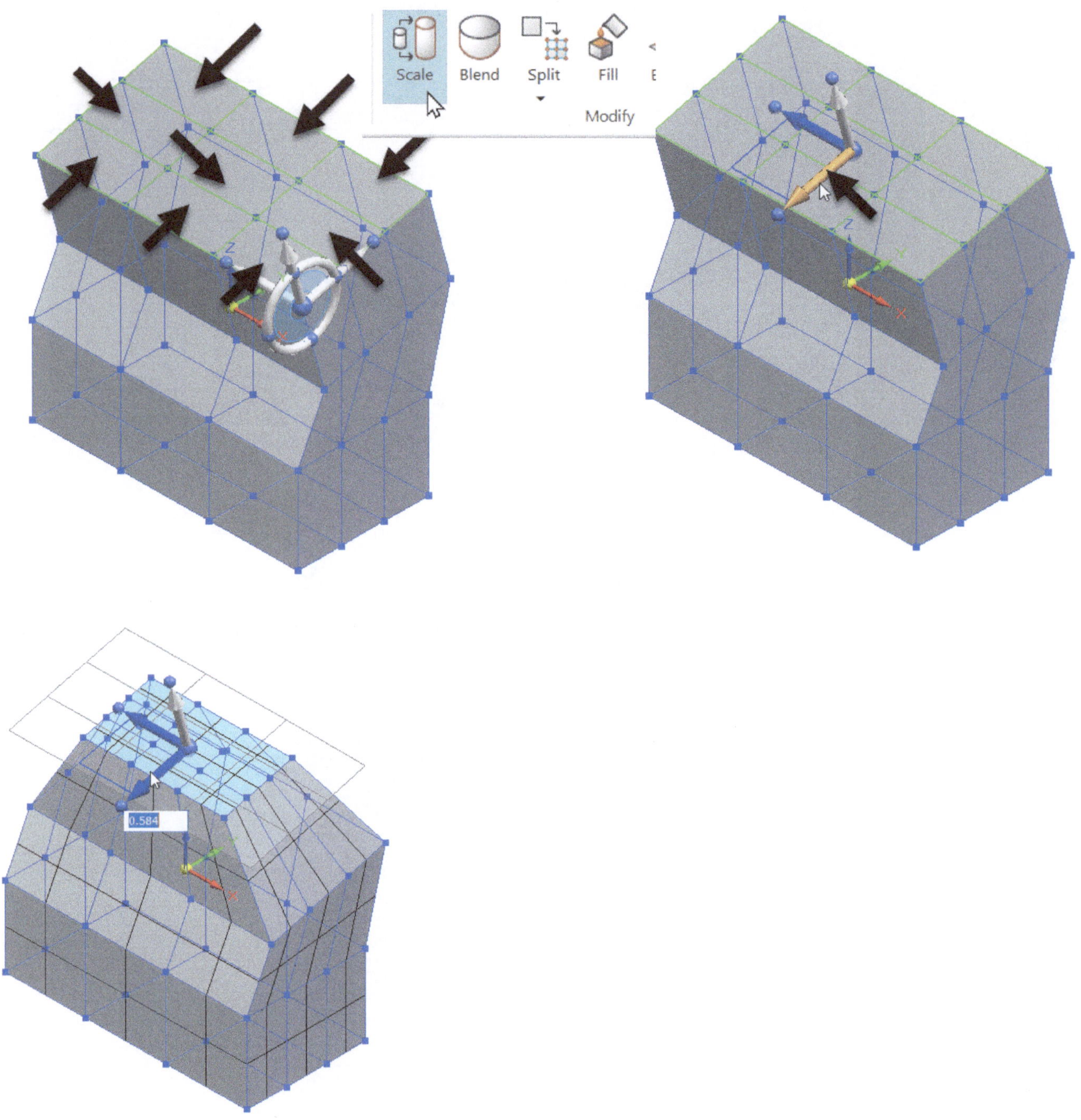

Deactivate the **Uniform** icon on the command bar. Next, type 0.5 in the scale box along the X-direction and press the TAB key. Type 0.75 in the scale box along the Y direction. Right-click to scale the face.

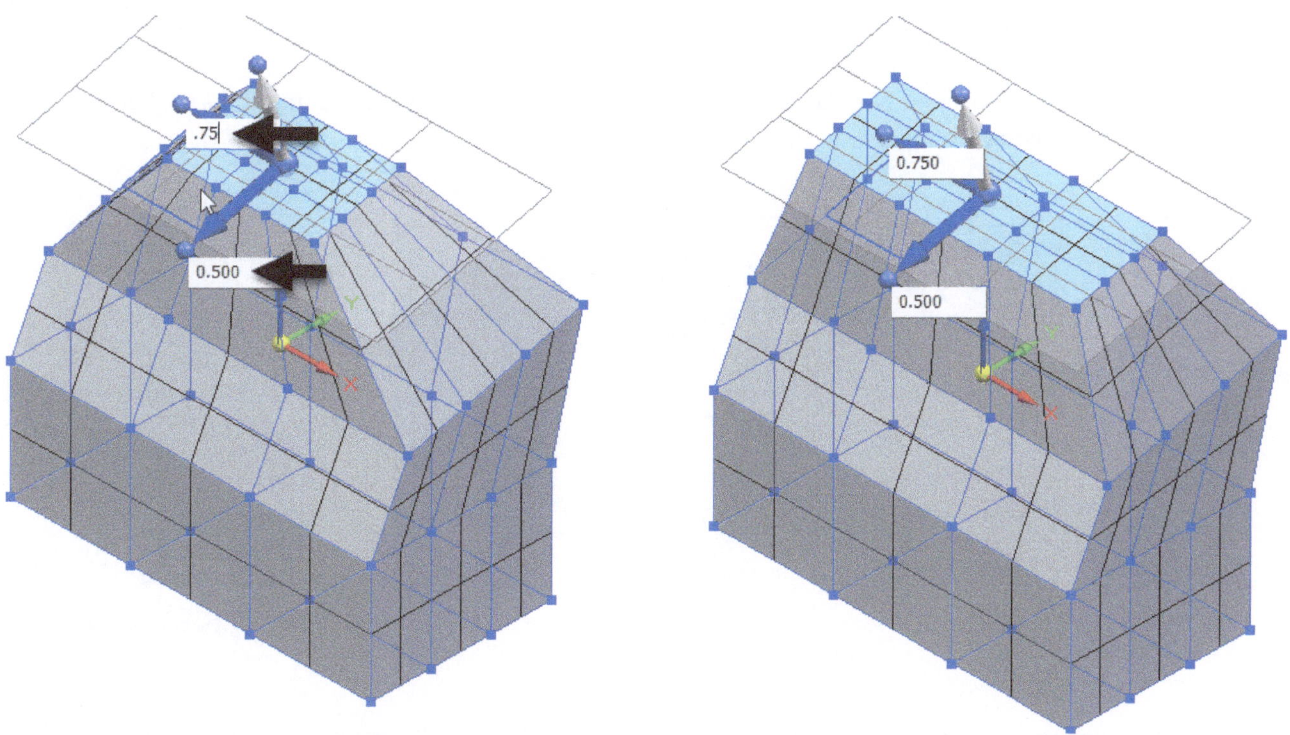

On the ribbon, click the **Home** tab > **Modify** panel > **Scale**. On the command bar, click the **Linear Scaling** icon. Click on the front edges of the inclined top face, as shown. Click and drag the blue arrow handle that appears on the selected edges. Type 0.5 and press ENTER. Right-click to scale the edges.

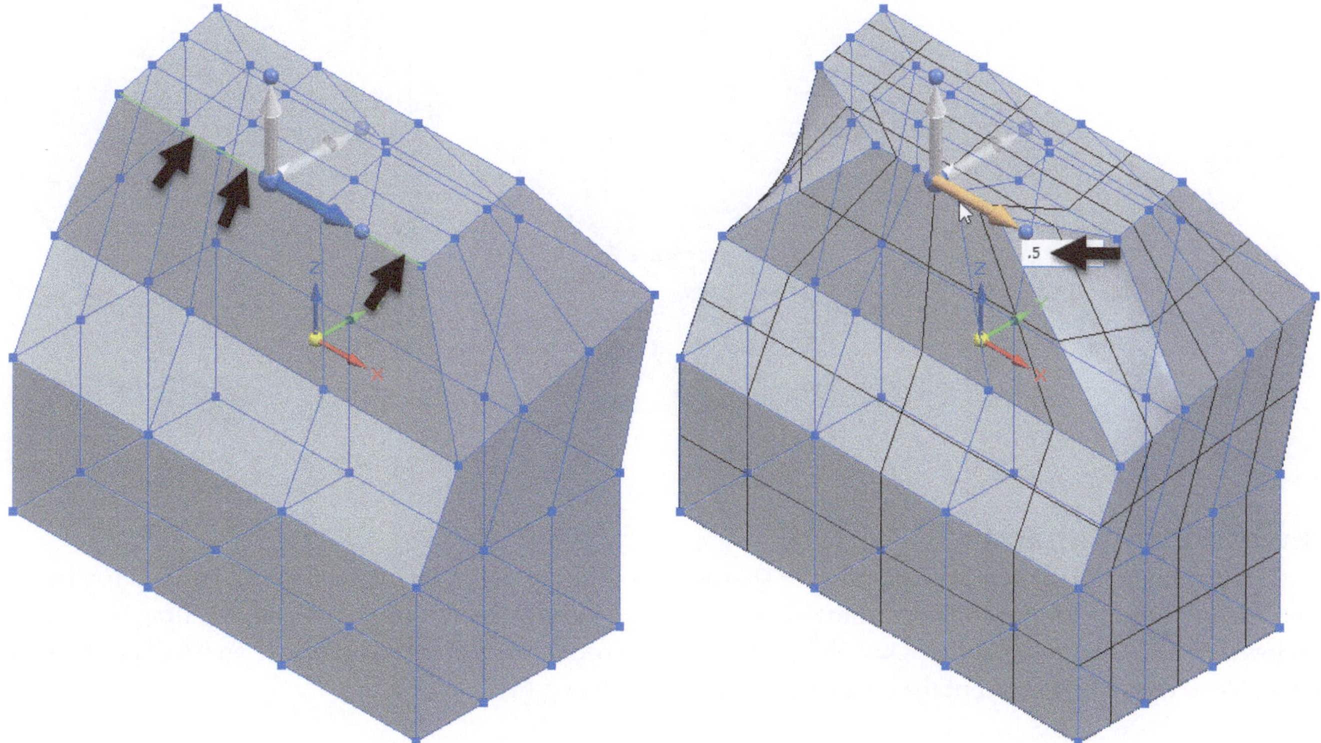

Change the View Orientation to right. Next, click **Home** tab > **Modify** panel > **Scale**, and then click the **3 Axes Scaling** icon on the command bar. Activate the **Uniform** icon on the command bar. Click and drag the origin of the steering wheel to the lower-left corner.

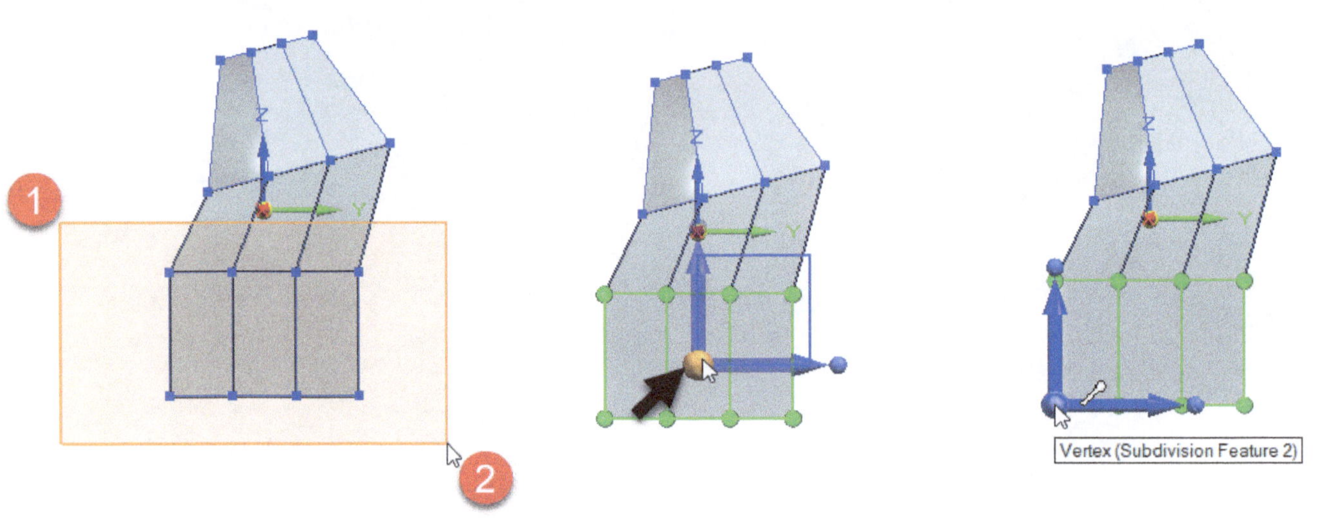

Click the **Recenter** icon on the command bar; the steering wheel is placed at the selection set's geometric center. Change the view orientation to Isometric. Click on any one of the arrows of the steering wheel and drag it. Type 0.75 and press ENTER. Right-click to scale the selection set.

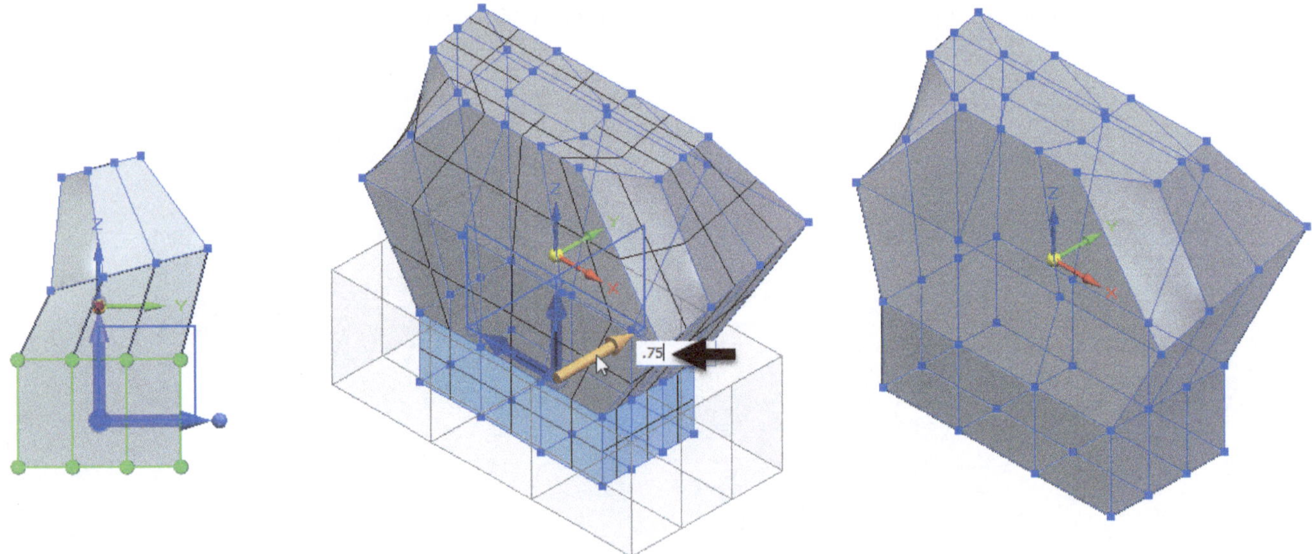

The Blend command

The **Blend** command helps you to smoothen or sharpen the edges of the cage. Activate this command (on the ribbon, click **Home > Modify > Blend**) and select a cage edge to set the continuity. You can also drag the selection window across the entire model to select all its edges. Next, specify the smoothness scale from 0 to 3 on the **Blend** dialog. Next, right-click to accept the result. Close the **Blend** dialog.

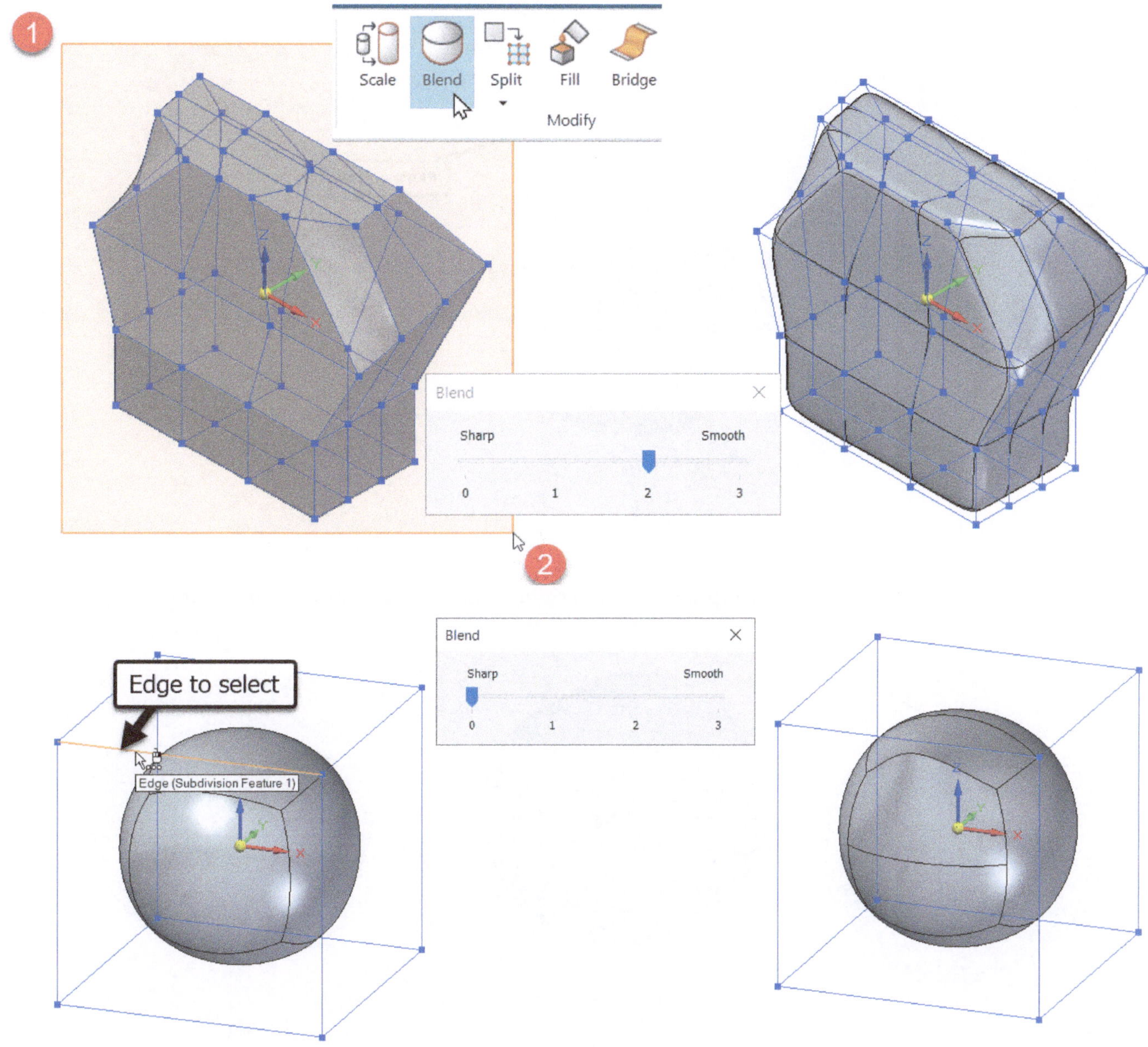

Start Symmetry

The **Start Symmetry** command helps you to create subdivision models that are symmetrical about a plane. Activate this command (on the ribbon, click **Home > Symmetry > Start Symmetry**) and select a plane from the graphics window to define the symmetric plane.

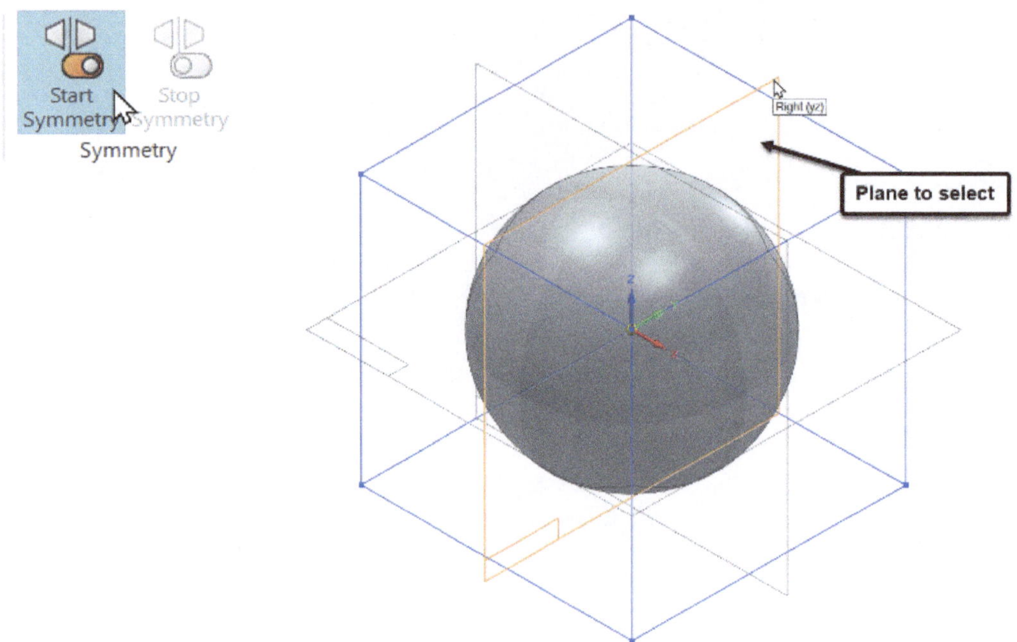

Click the arrow to change the side to be manipulated. Next, right-click to start symmetric modeling.

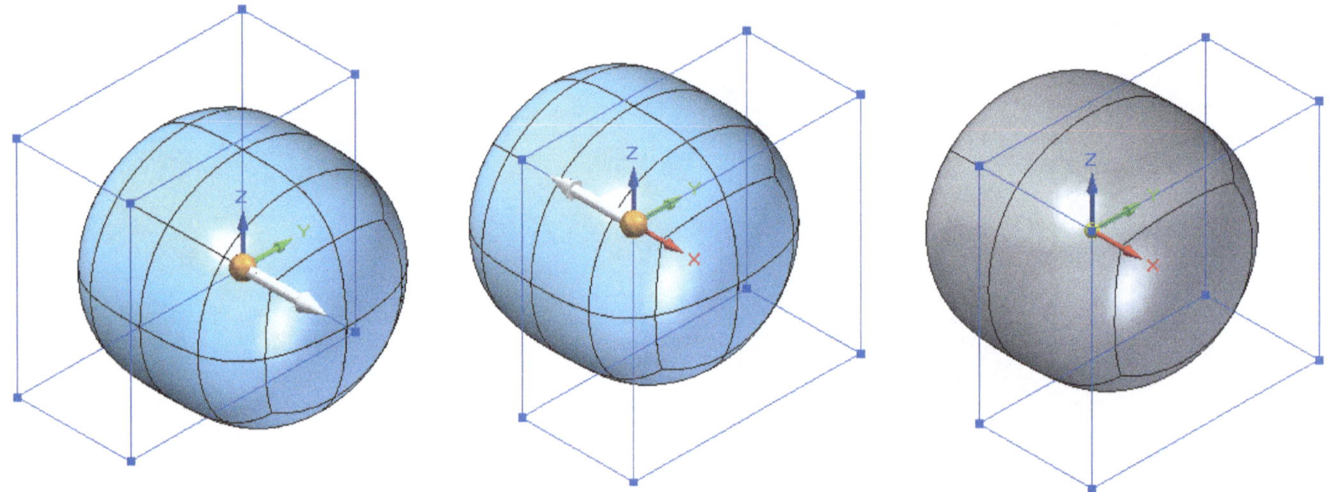

Now, click on the side face of the cage and notice an arrow. Click and drag the arrow toward the right; the cage is modified symmetrically. Press ESC.

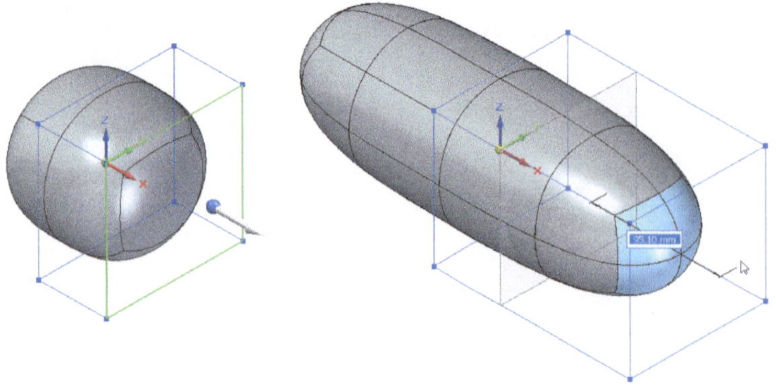

Select the right vertical edge of the cage and drag it in the forward direction.

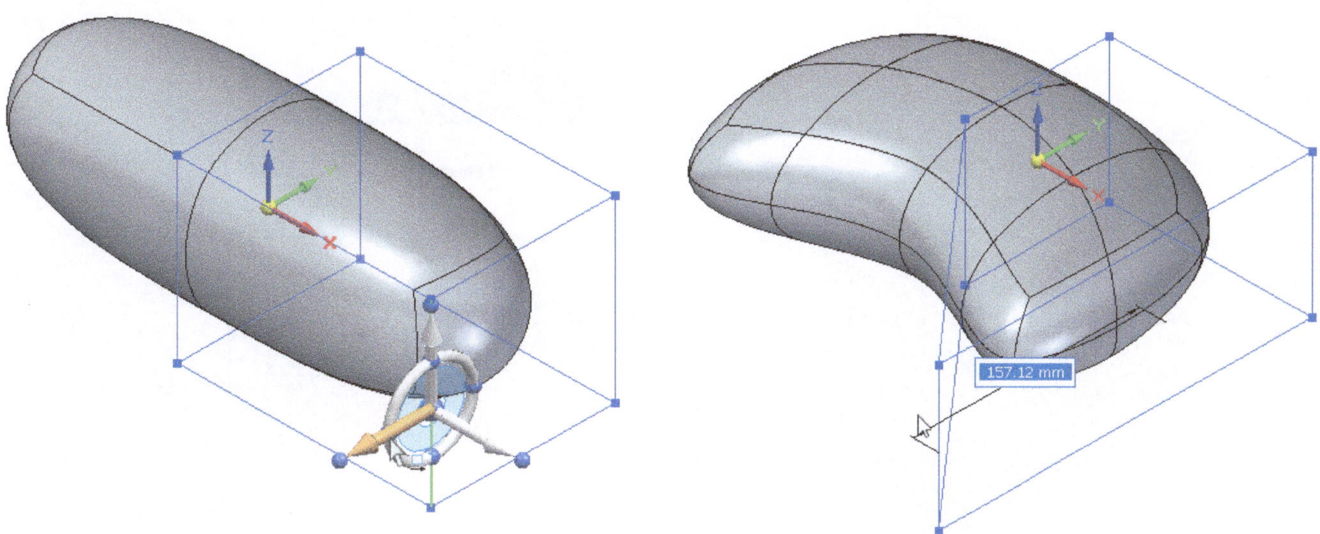

You can use the **Stop Symmetry** command to stop manipulating the model symmetrically. Activate this command (on the ribbon, click **Home > Symmetry > Stop Symmetry**) and notice that the cage is displayed on both sides of the model. You can manipulate the model independently on both sides.

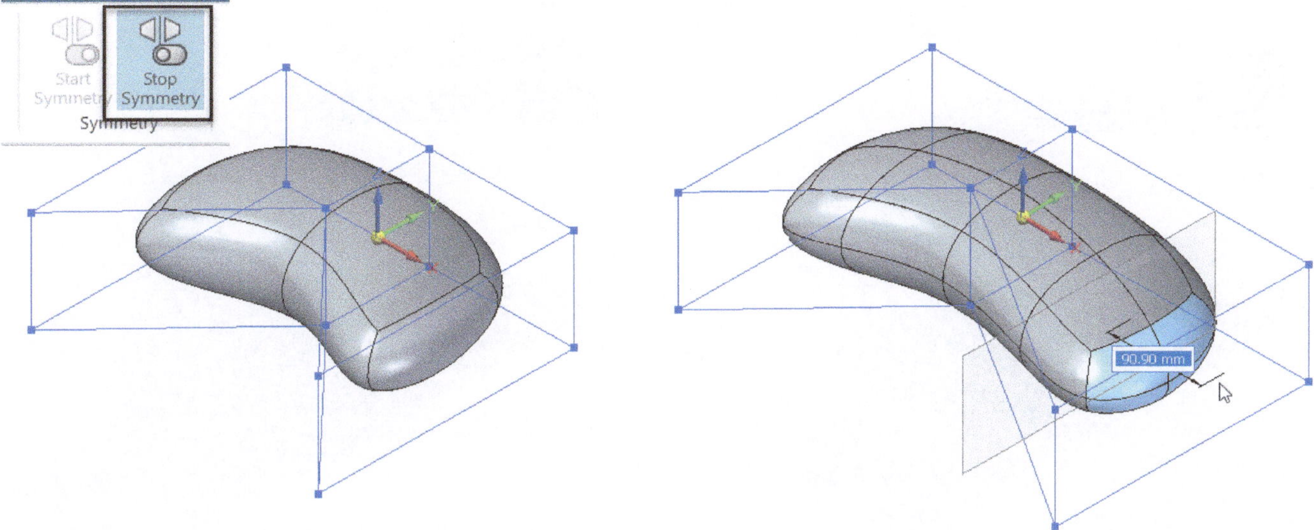

Rotating and Moving the Cage Faces

Create a selection window across the side face of the box, as shown. Click and drag the steering wheel's origin and place it at the model's lower horizontal edge, as shown. Click on the rotate handle of the steering wheel and move the pointer. Type 10 in the angle box and press ENTER; the selected face set is rotated.

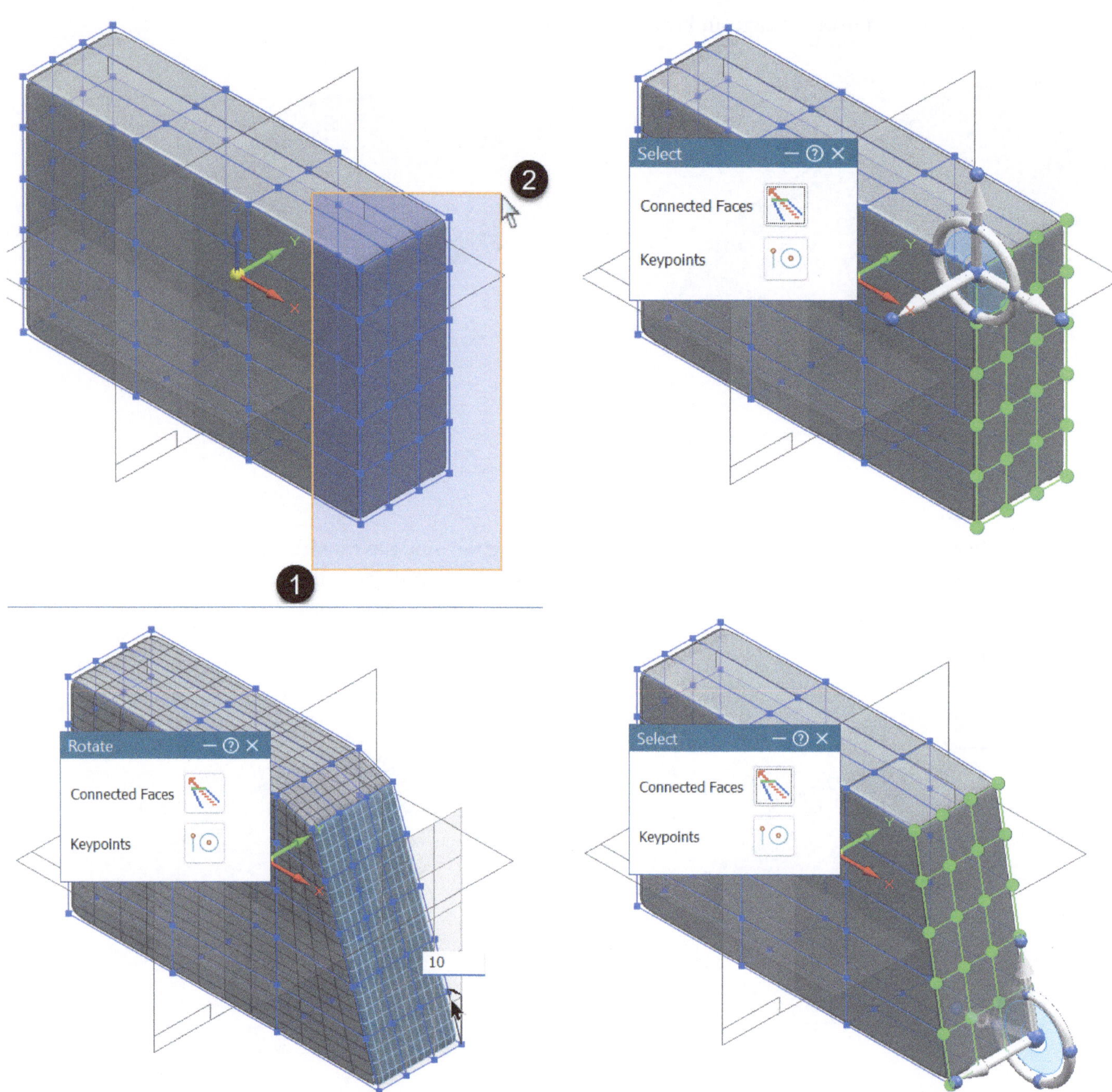

Click and drag the steering wheel's origin and place it on the cage vertex, as shown. Click on the Arrow of the steering wheel pointing towards the right. Drag it toward the right and click to move the selected face set.

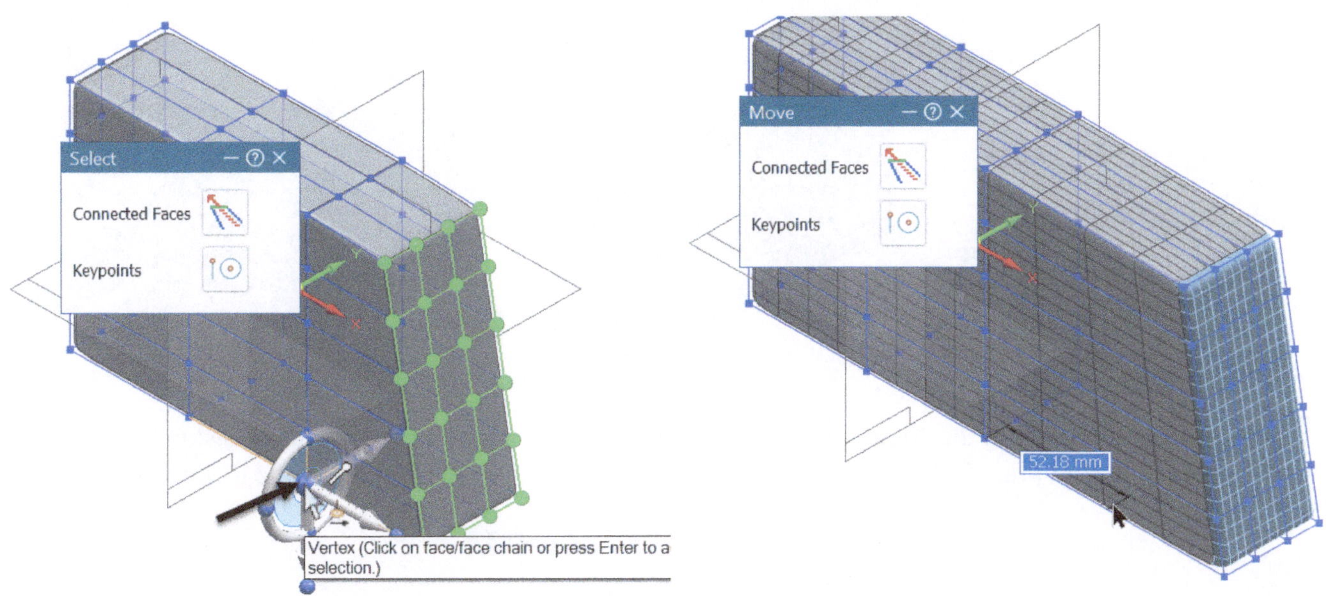

Extruding the Cage Faces

You can use the steering wheel to extrude the cage faces. Click on the top-center segment of the inclined face, as shown (You can also activate the **Offset** command and select the face to extrude). Next, select the **Lift** option from the drop-down located on the **Move** command bar. Drag the arrow handle displayed on the selected face. Notice that the cage face is extruded in the direction perpendicular to the inclined face. Press ESC to stop the extrusion.

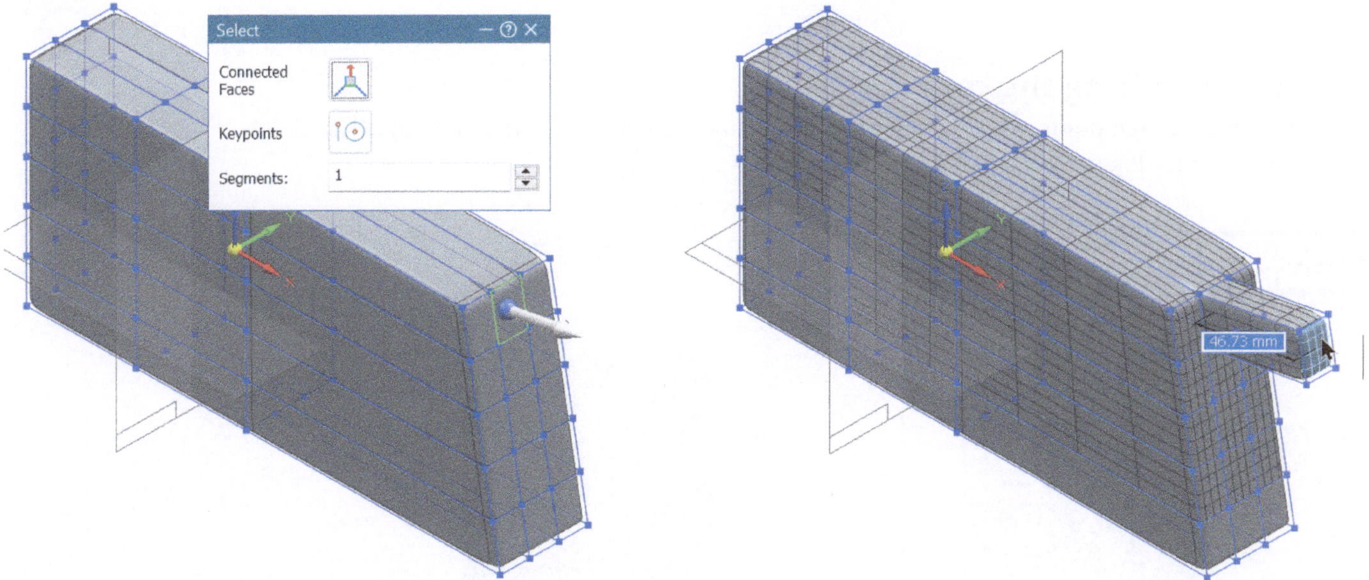

Click and drag the steering wheel's origin and place it on the cage's horizontal edge, as shown. The steering wheel is aligned to the horizontal edge. Click on the arrow align to the horizontal edge and drag the pointer toward the right.

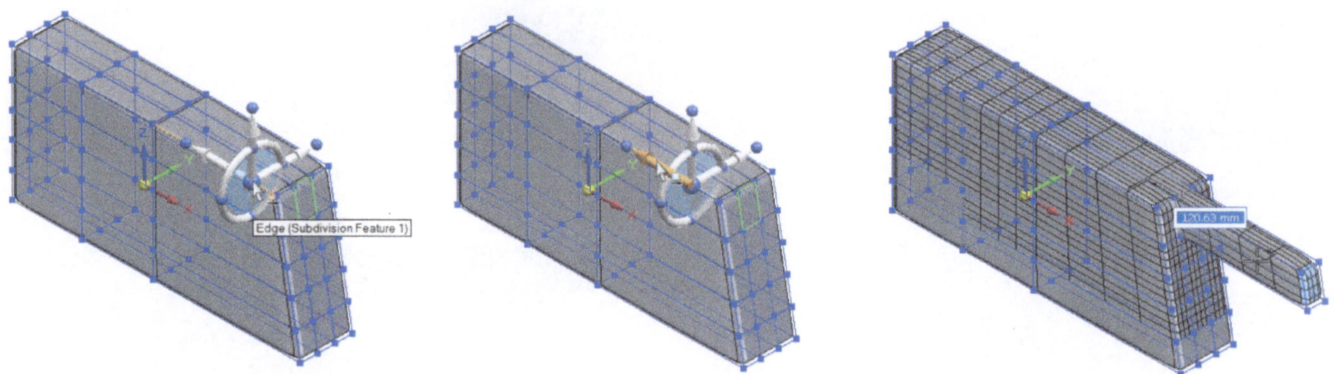

On the command bar, type 3 in the **Segments** box; three segments are added on the extrusion's side faces. Type **75** in the dimension box and press ENTER. Likewise, extrude the bottom-center segment of the inclined face, as shown.

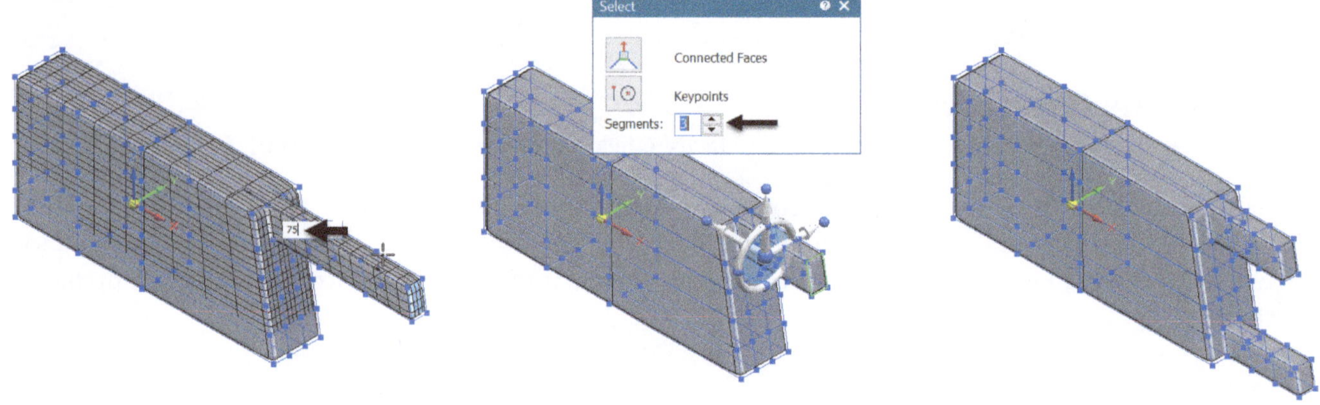

Delete and filling the cage faces

You can delete a cage point, edge, face, or the entire cage. To do this, select the objects to delete. Press DELETE on your keyboard to delete the face.

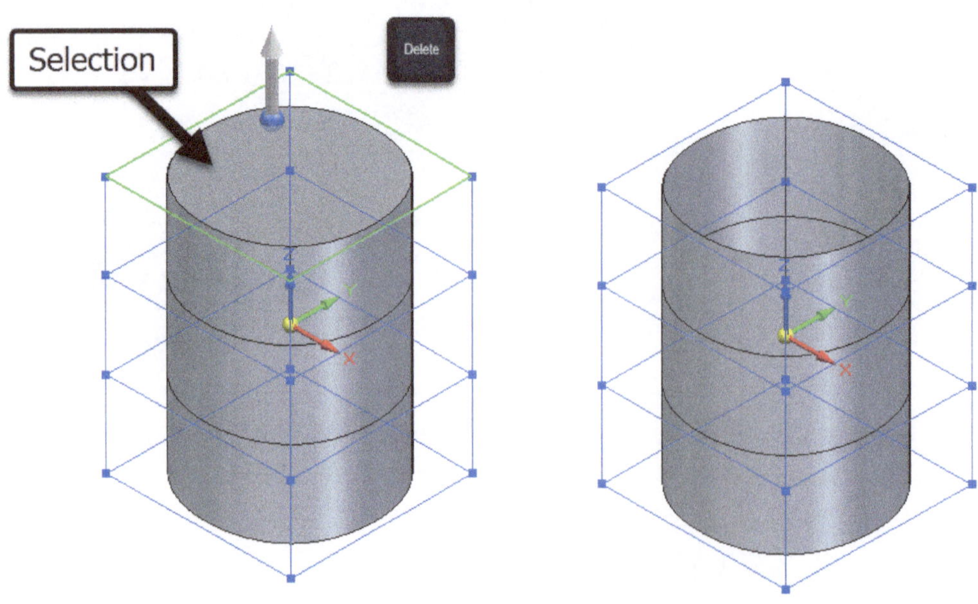

The **Fill** command adds a new face to the cage using two or more cage edges. Activate this command (on the ribbon, click **Home > Modify > Fill**) and click on the open edges of a cage. Click the green check on the command bar.

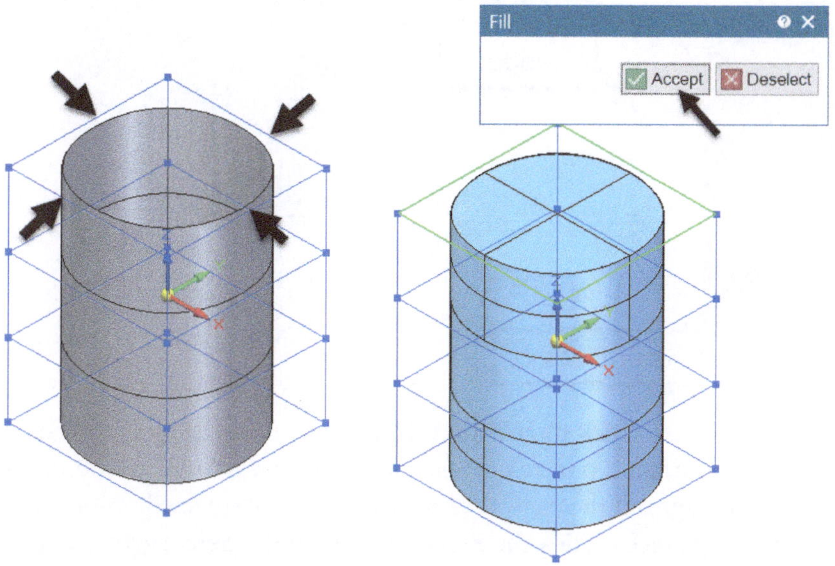

Split

The **Split** command splits a cage face into multiple faces uniformly or through selected points. The following example illustrates the use of this command. First, create a cylinder with the specifications, as shown.

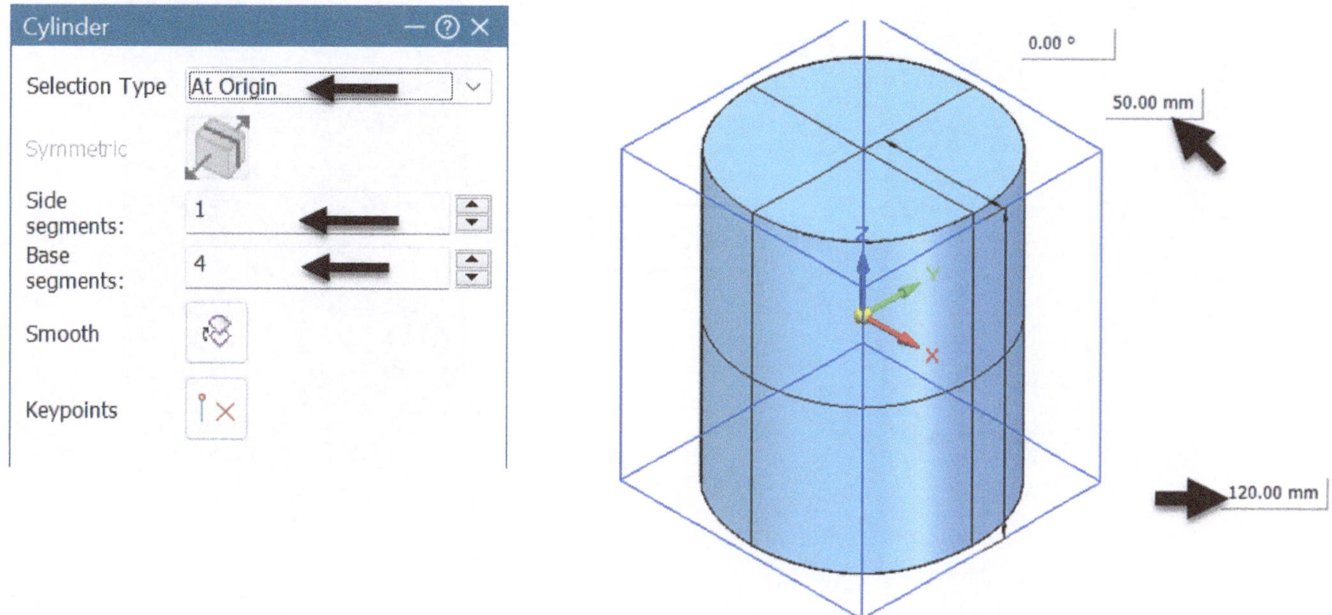

Activate the **Split** command (on the ribbon, click **Home > Modify > Split**), and then select **Selection Type > Single** on the command bar. Click on the face to split, and then select an edge of the selected cage face. Next, specify the number of splitting edges in the **Number** box. Click the **Accept** button to split the face.

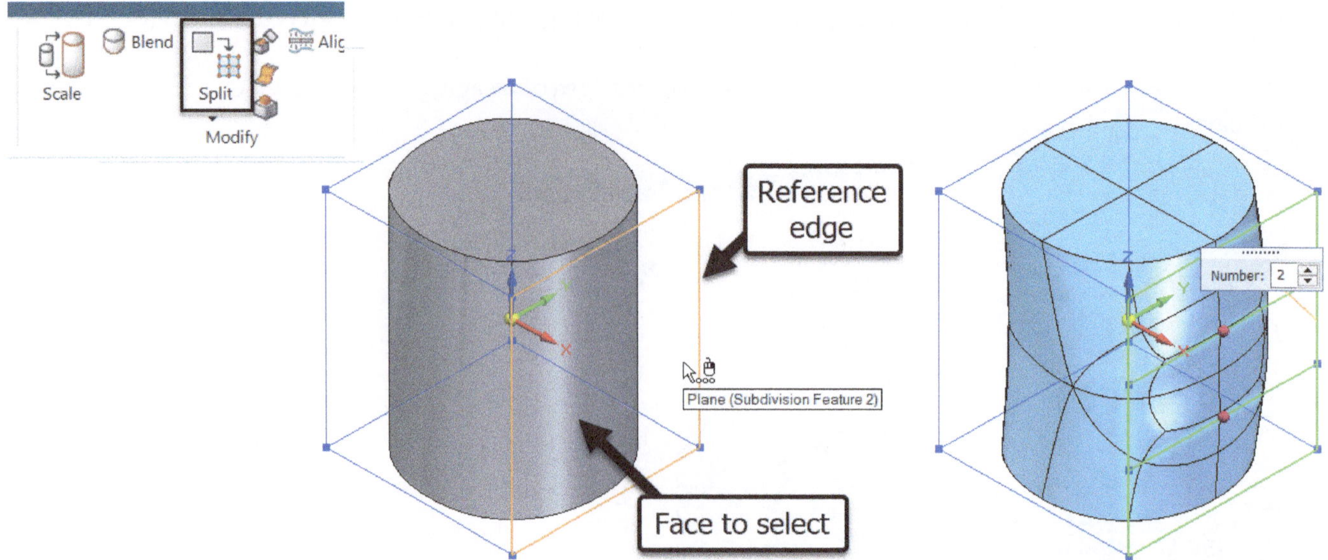

Notice that the adjacent faces of the split face are affected. Click the **Undo (CTRL+Z)** icon on the Quick Access Toolbar. Next, activate the **Split** command. On the command bar, select Selection **Type > Chain**. Click on the side face of the previously selected face near the vertical edge; all the cage's cylindrical faces are selected. Type **2** in the **Number** box and click **Accept** to split the selected cage faces. Click the **Select** button on the **Select** group of the **Home** ribbon tab.

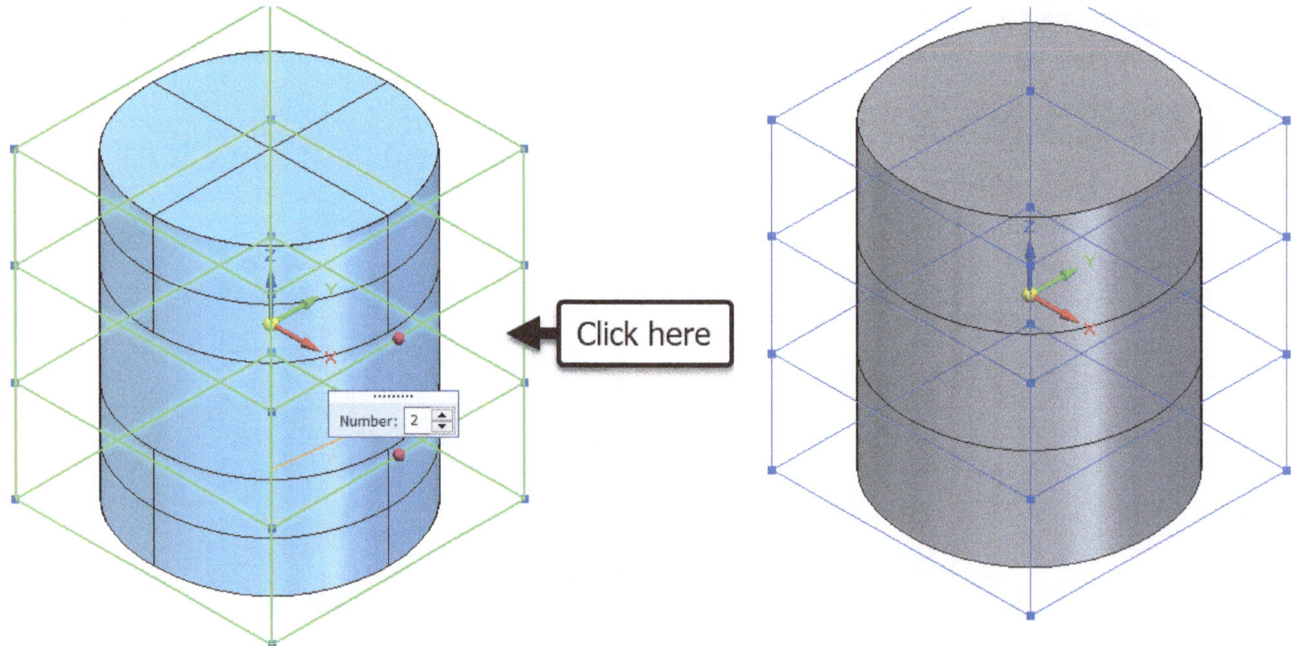

Bridge

The **Bridge** command creates a closed tunnel-like surface between two faces. The following example illustrates the use of this command. First, create a torus with the specifications, as shown. Next, create a sphere of 200 mm size at the center of the torus.

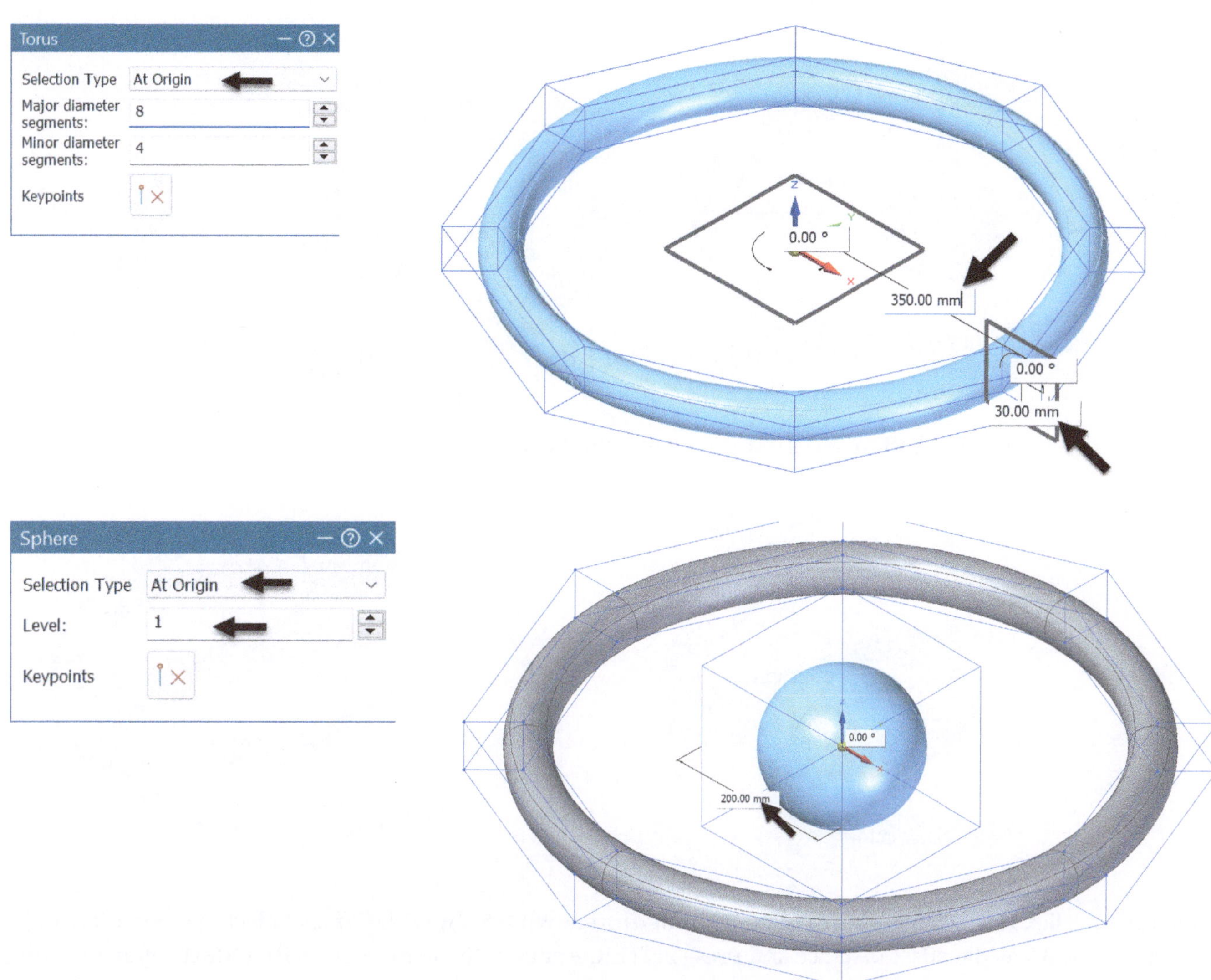

Activate the **Bridge** command (on the ribbon, click **Home > Modify > Bridge**) and click on the right face of the sphere, as shown. Click the **Accept** button on the command bar. Rotate the model and click on the inner face of the torus, as shown. Make sure that the origin points of the two selected faces are on the same side. On the command bar, change the **Segments** value to **2**. Click the **Accept** button. Next, you can select a curve to define the shape of the bridge. However, you can right-click without selecting a shape curve to create bridge face between the selected face.

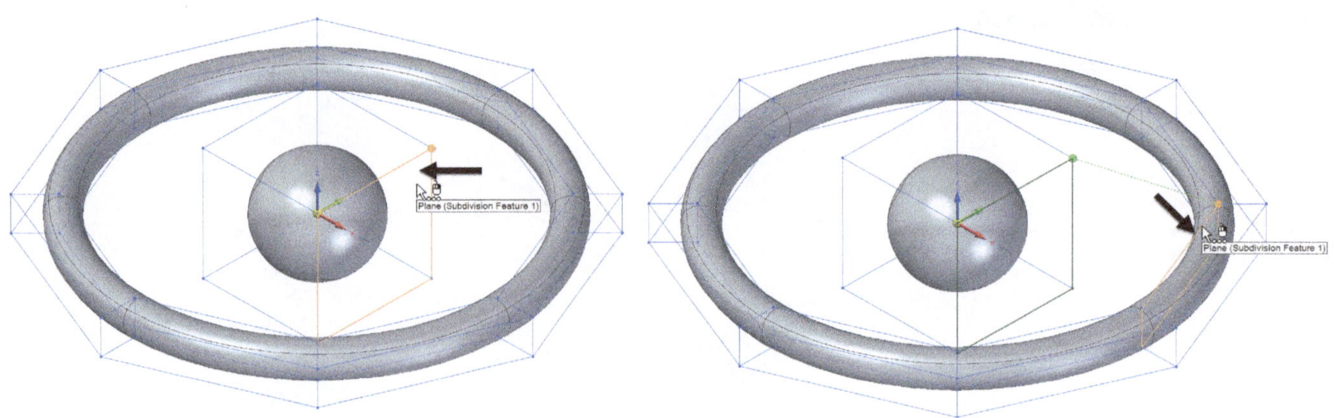

Likewise, bridge the left and bottom faces of the sphere with the torus.

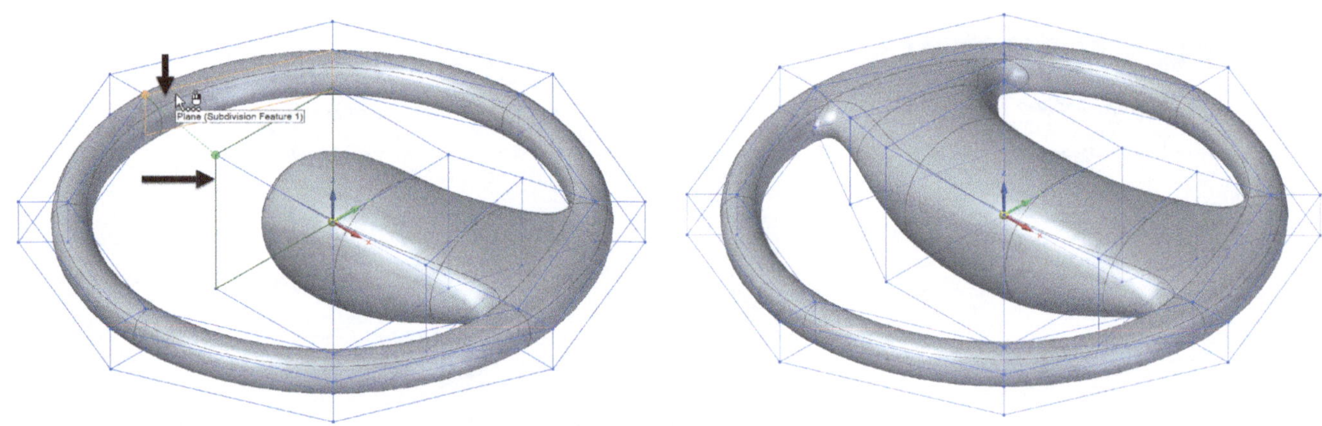

On the ribbon, click **Home** tab > **Modify** panel > **Split** drop-down > **Split with Offset**. Select the center face of the model. Type **0.3** as the offset distance and press ENTER. Again, activate the **Split with Offset** command and rotate the model. Select the center face of the model, type 0.3, and press ENTER.

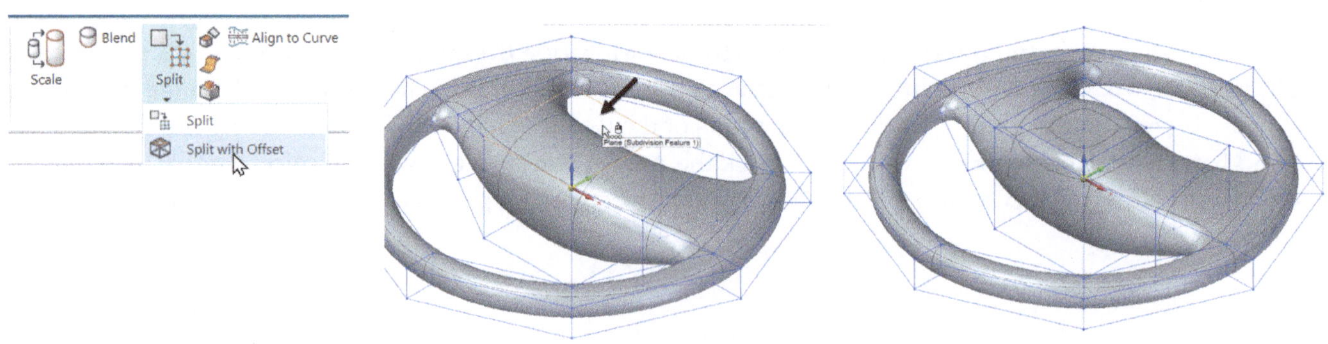

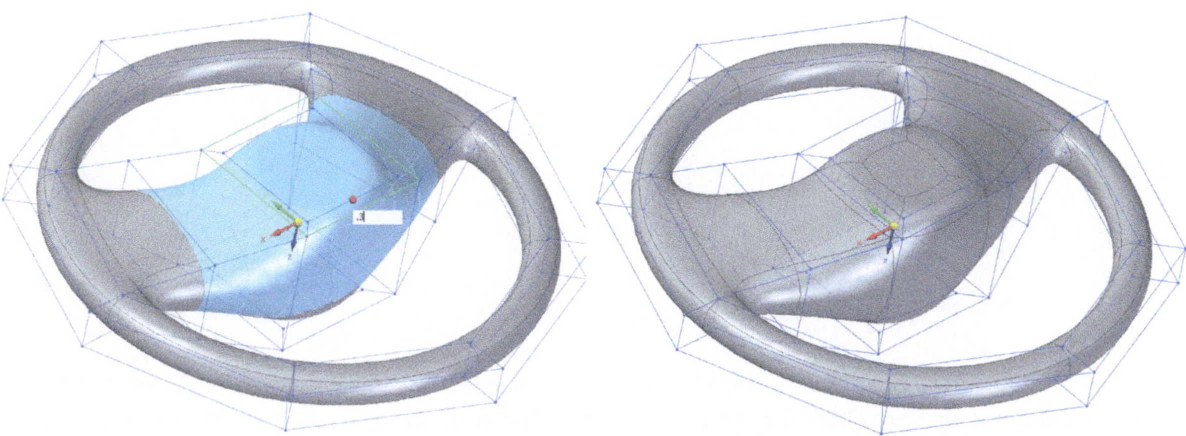

Activate the **Bridge** command and select the split center face on the front side. Next, click **Accept**. Rotate the model and select the split center face on the back side. Change the **Number of Segments** value to 1. Click **Accept** and right-click to create a tunnel between the two selected faces.

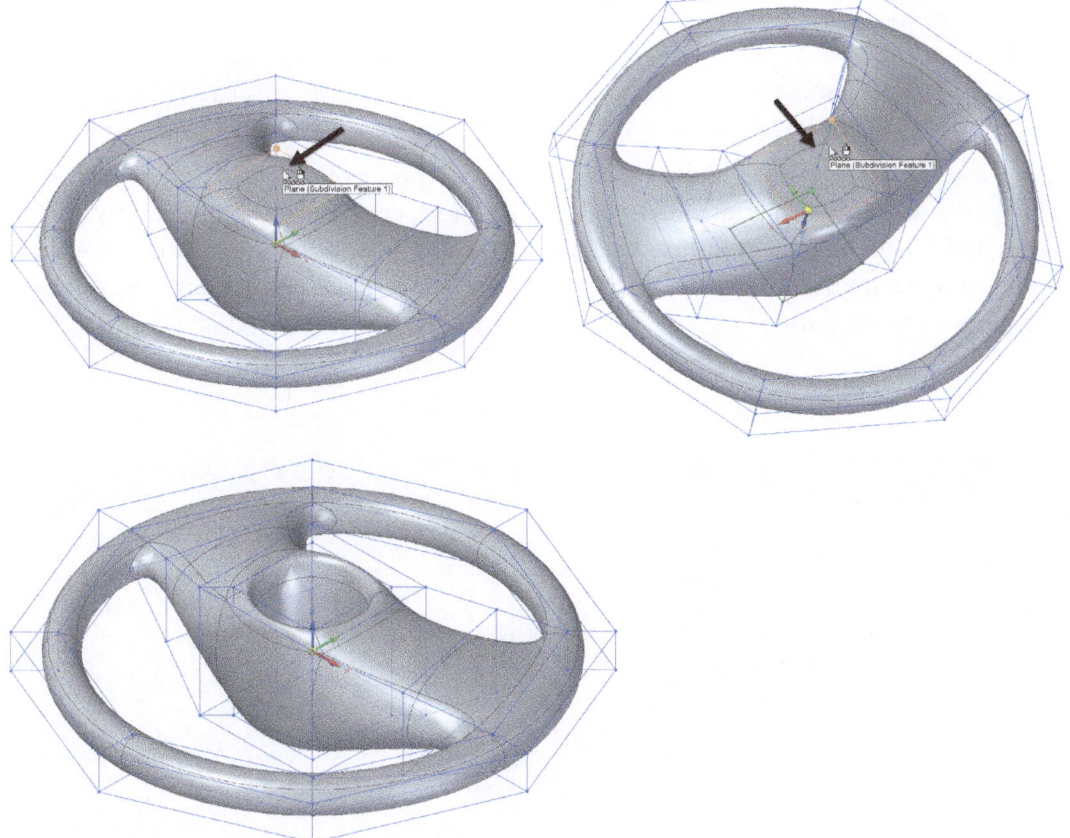

Align to Curve

The **Align to Curve** command aligns the vertices up to a selected curve. For example, create a box and the curve, as shown. Next, change the view orientation to Front using the ViewCube. Activate this command (on the ribbon, click **Home > Modify > Align to Curve**). Next, create a selection window from left to right on the top portion of the box. Change the view orientation to ISO View. Notice that the vertices on the top face of the box are selected. Click the **Accept** button on the command bar.

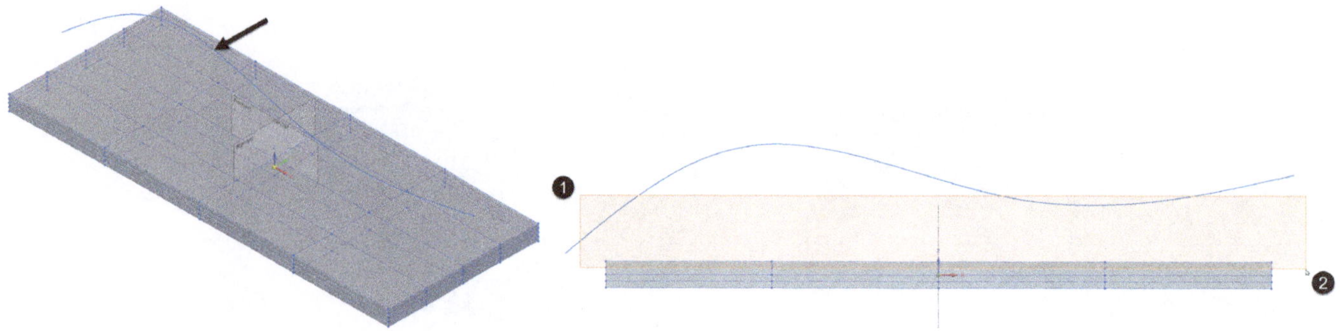

Again, change the view orientation to **Front** using the ViewCube. Next, select the Z-axis from the Base Coordinate System to define the alignment direction. Click the **Accept** button on the command bar. Select the curve to graphics window, and then click the **Accept** button. Right-click and press ESC.

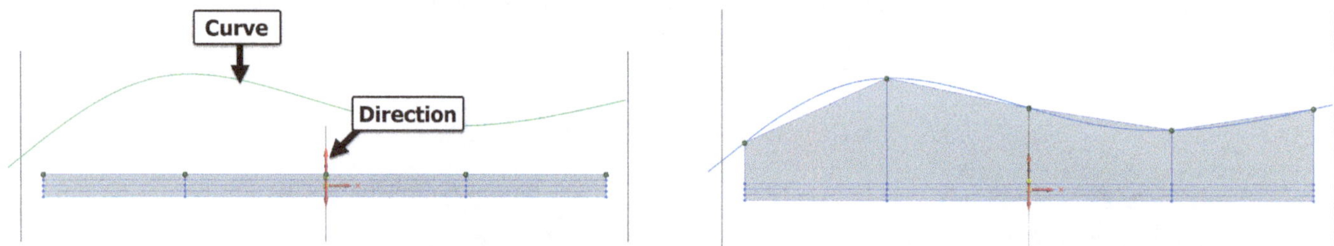

You can also align the selected vertices of the cage by drawing a curve. To do this, activate the **Align to Curve** command and change the view orientation to Front (any other side view). Next, create a selection window enclosing the vertices to be aligned. Click the **Accept** button and specify the alignment direction. Next, press and hold the left-mouse button and drag the pointer to create a curve, as shown. Release the pointer, and then right-click; the selected vertices are aligned to the curve.

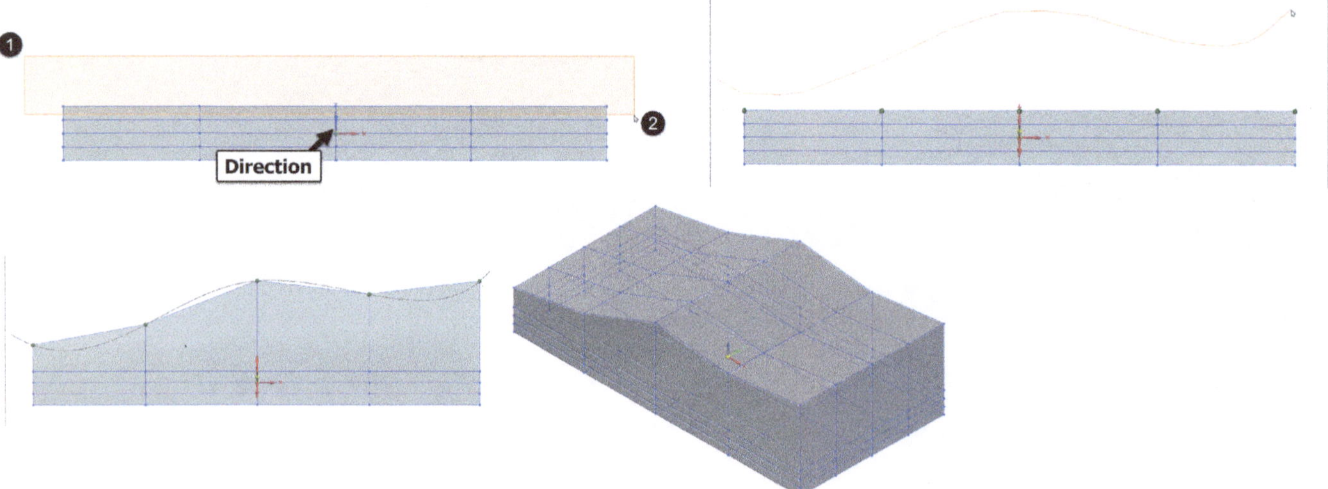

Example 1

In this example, you will construct the model shown below.

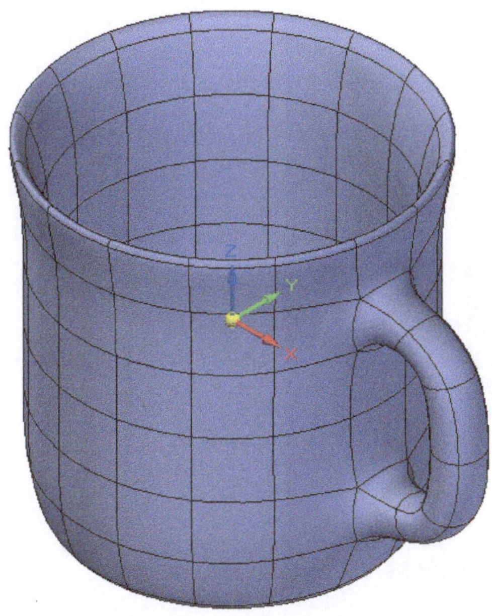

Activating the Subdivision Modeling Environment

1. Start **Solid Edge 2026**.
2. Start a new part file using the **ANSI Metric Part** template.
3. On the ribbon, click **Surfacing > Free-Form > Subdivision Modeling**.

Creating a Cylinder Shape

1. On the ribbon, click **Home > Shapes > Cylinder**. Next, select the **At Origin** option from the drop-down located on the command bar.
2. In the graphics window, type **40** and **90** in the **Radius** and **Height** boxes, respectively. Next, type 6 and 16 in the **Side segments** and **Base segments** boxes of the command bar. Right-click to create the cylinder.

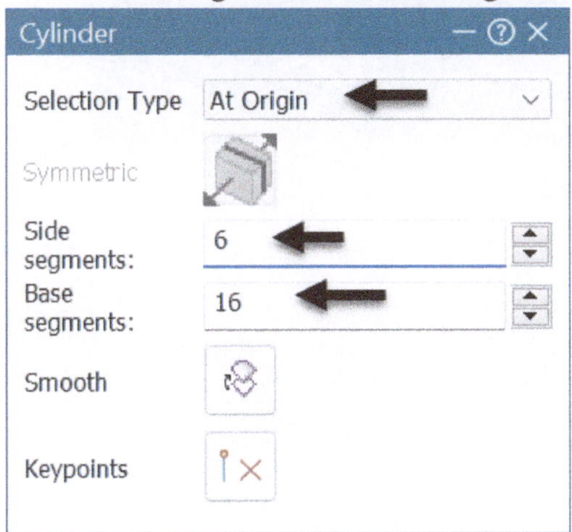

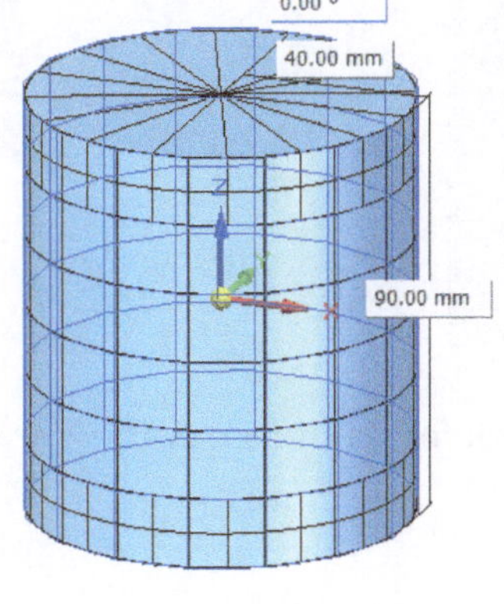

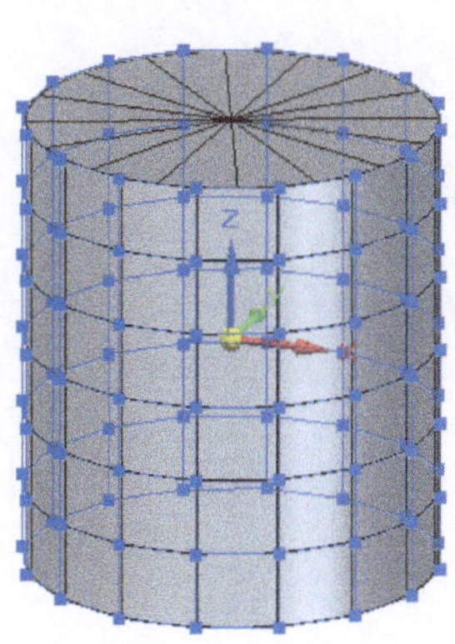

Adding Symmetry to the model

1. On the ribbon, click **Home > Symmetry > Start Symmetry**.
2. Click on the **Top (xy)** plane from the Pathfinder. Next, click the arrow such that the arrow points in the downward direction. Right-click to start symmetry.

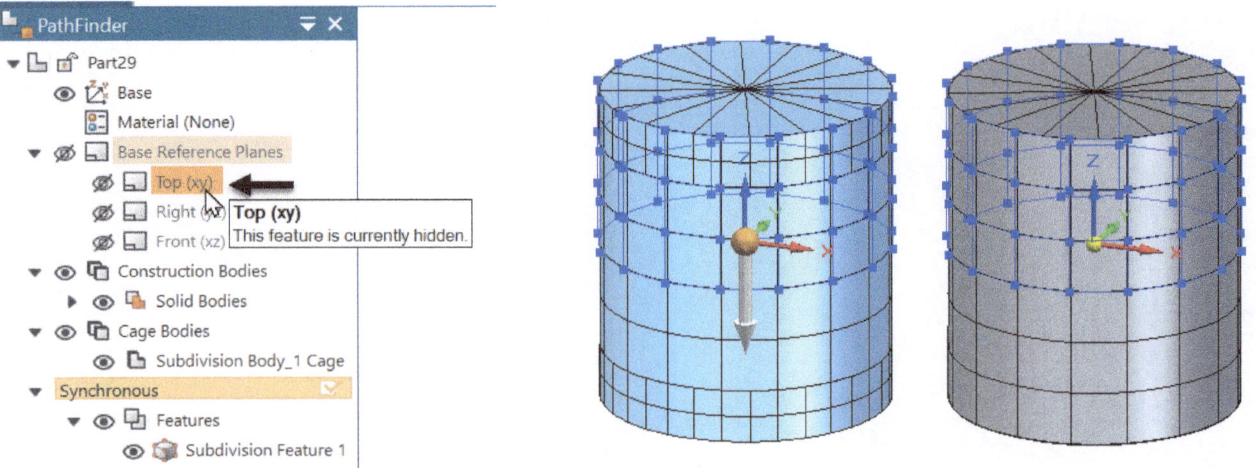

Creating the Handle

1. Click the Right face of the ViewCube; the view orientation is changed to right. Next, activate the **Scale** command (on the ribbon, click **Home > Modify > Scale**).
2. Click on the cage face, as shown. Next, click the **3 Axes Scaling** and **Uniform** icons on the **Scale** dialog.
3. Click on the arrow, pointing downwards. Next, type **0.6** in the **Percentage** box.
4. Right-click to scale the face. Next, press ESC to deactivate the command.

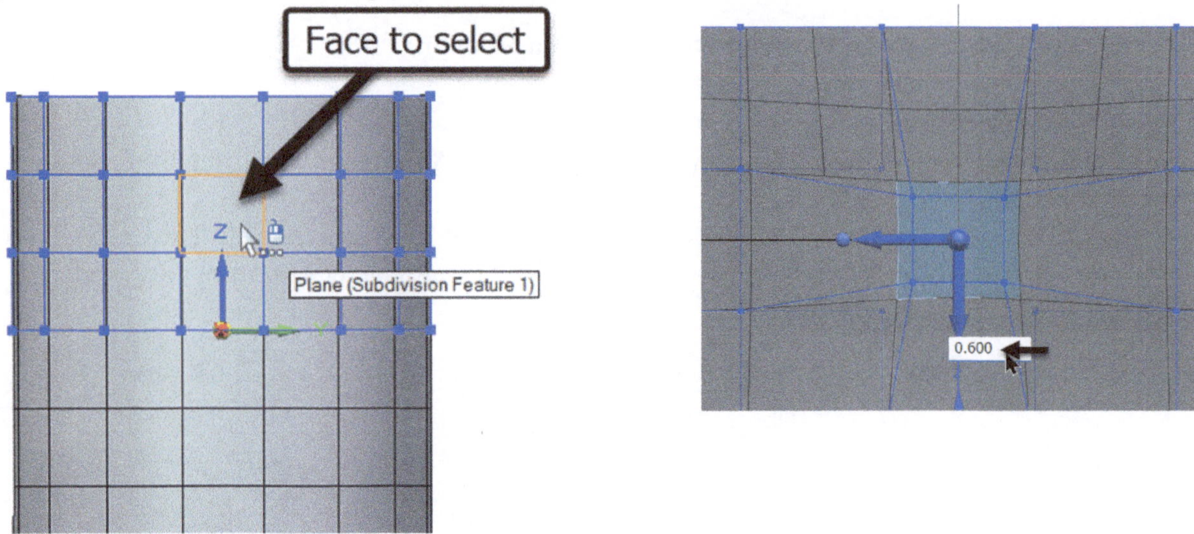

5. Click on the scaled face, and then click the front face of the ViewCube.

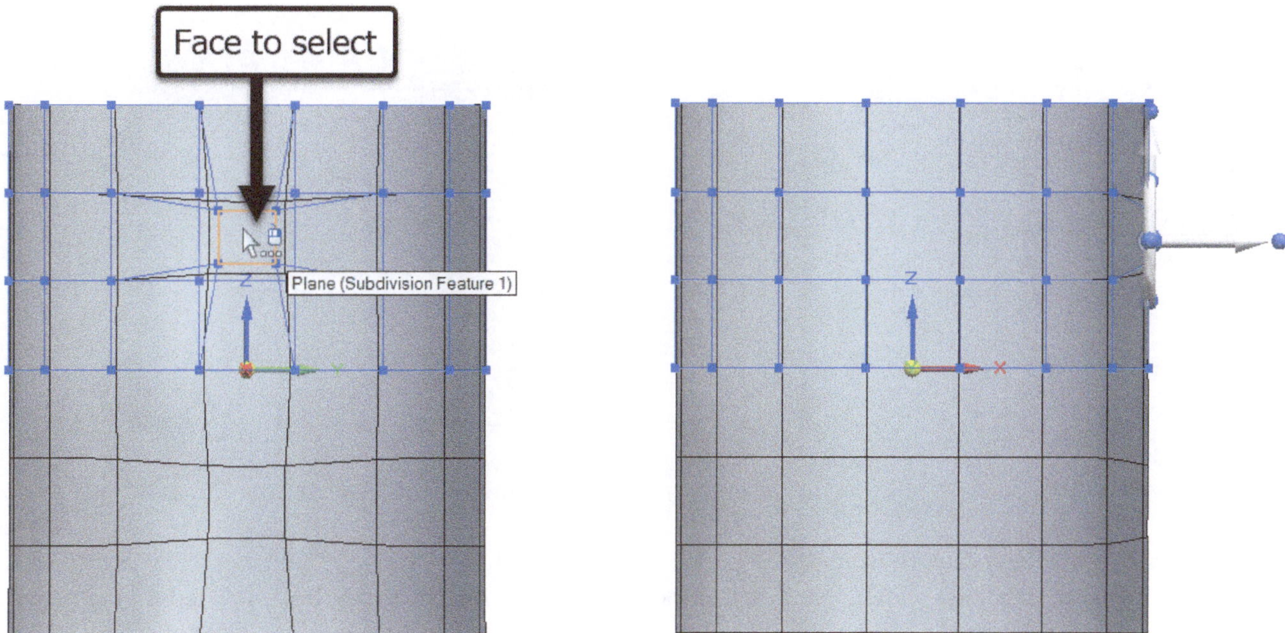

6. On the Move command bar, select the **Lift** option from the drop-down. Type 1 in the **Segments** box.
7. Click and drag the arrow, pointing toward right up to a small distance. Type 10 and press ENTER.

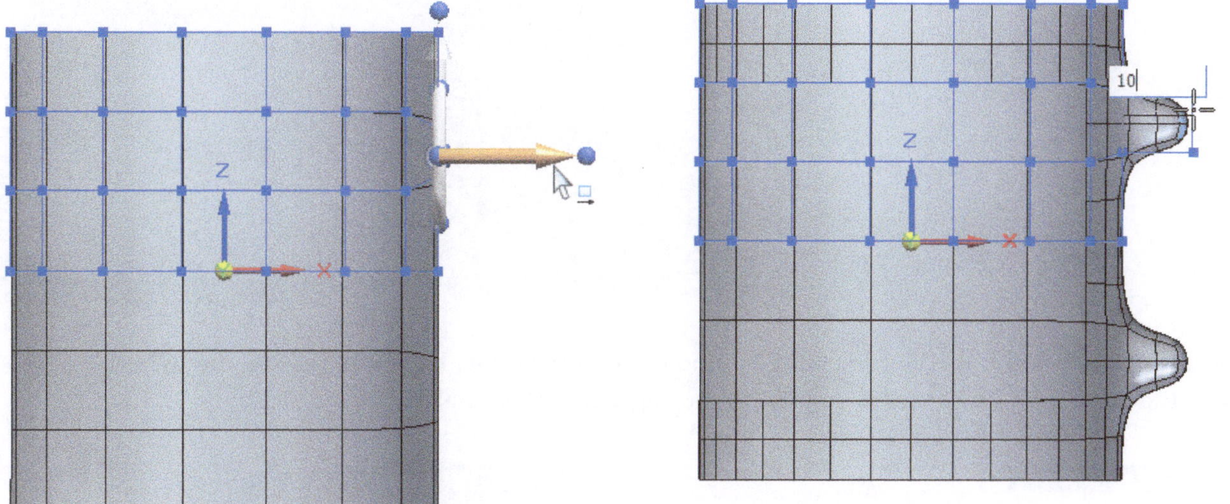

8. Click on the rotation handle of the steering wheel. Next, select the **Tip** option from the drop-down located on the command bar.
9. Move the pointer downward and type -23 in the angle box, and press ENTER. Press ESC to deselect the face.

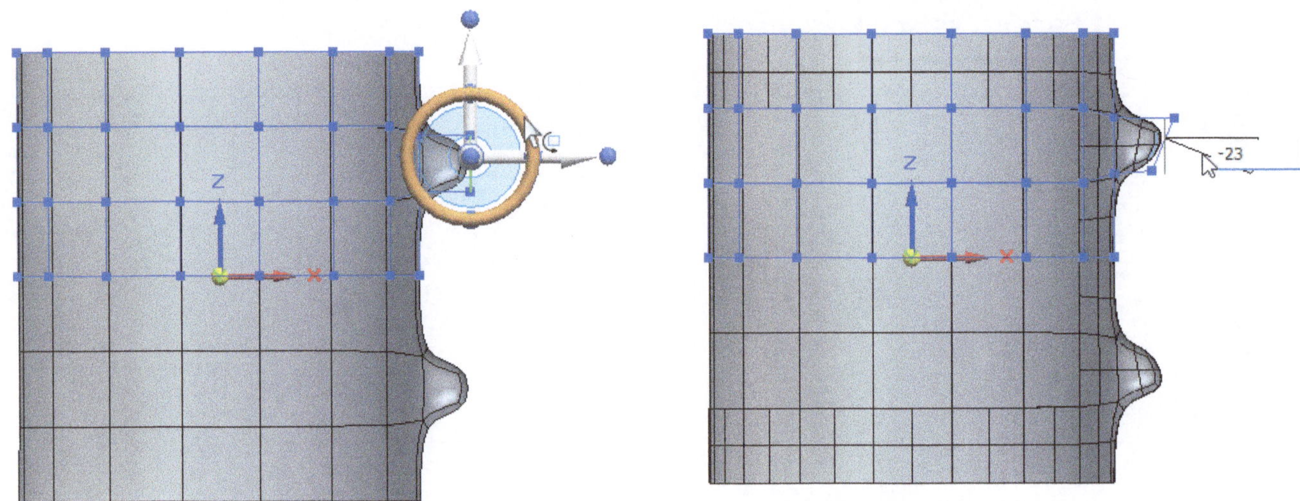

10. Change the view orientation to Isometric.
11. Click on the rotated face, as shown. Next, select the **Lift** option from the drop-down located on the command bar.
12. Click and drag the arrow handle, as shown. Type 10 in the distance box and press ENTER.

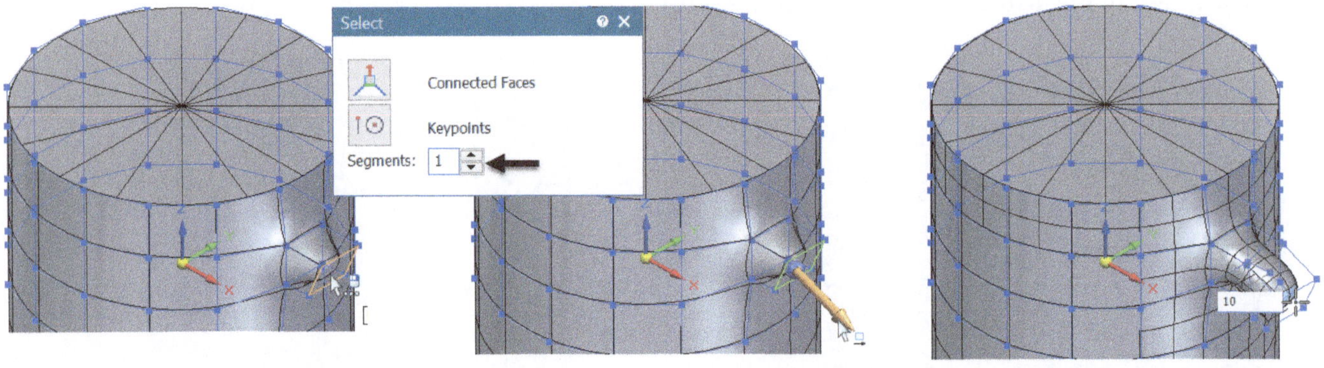

13. Select the **Tip** option from the command bar and click on the rotate handle of the steering wheel.
14. Move the pointer downward and type -60 in the angle box. Press ENTER.
15. Press ESC to deselect the rotated face.

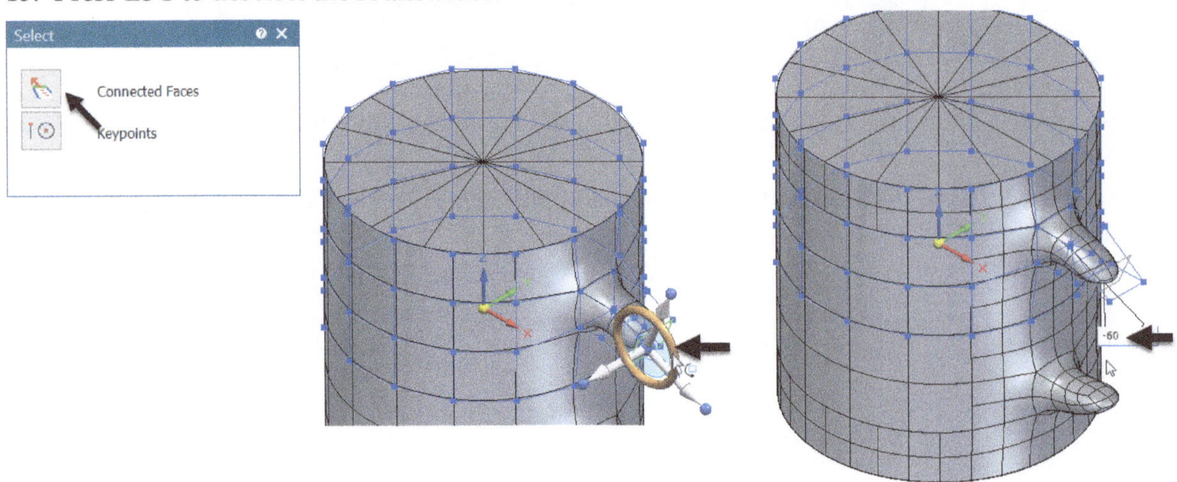

16. Select the rotated face and select the **Lift** option from the drop-down.
17. Click on the arrow displayed on the selected face and drag it downward. Notice that the end faces are bridged, as shown.

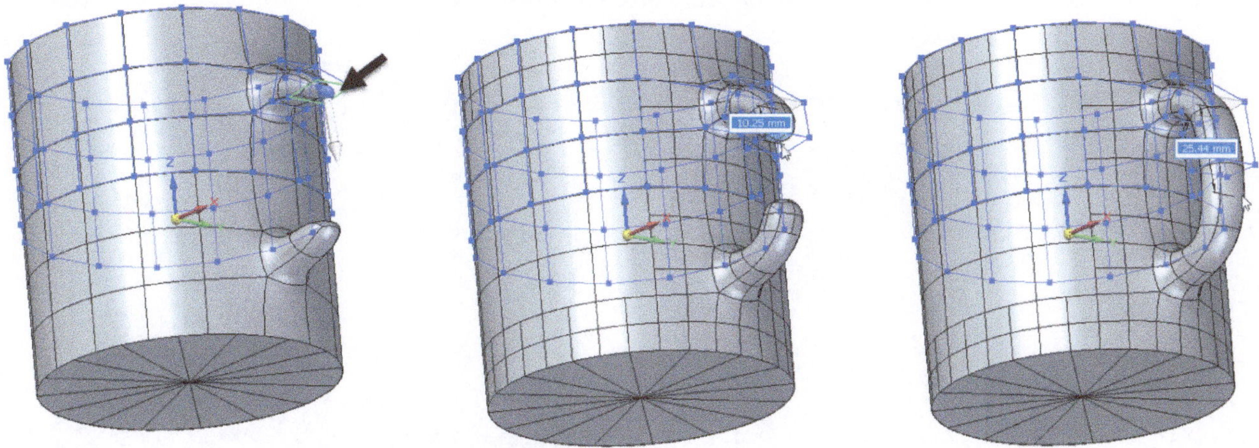

18. On the ribbon, click **Home > Symmetry > Stop Symmetry**.

Scaling the Top and bottom Faces

1. On the ribbon, click **Home > Modify > Scale.** Click on the top face of the model.
2. Click on the arrow of the steering wheel, as shown. Type **1.1** in the **Percentage** box and right-click to scale the face. Press ESC to deselect the scaled face.

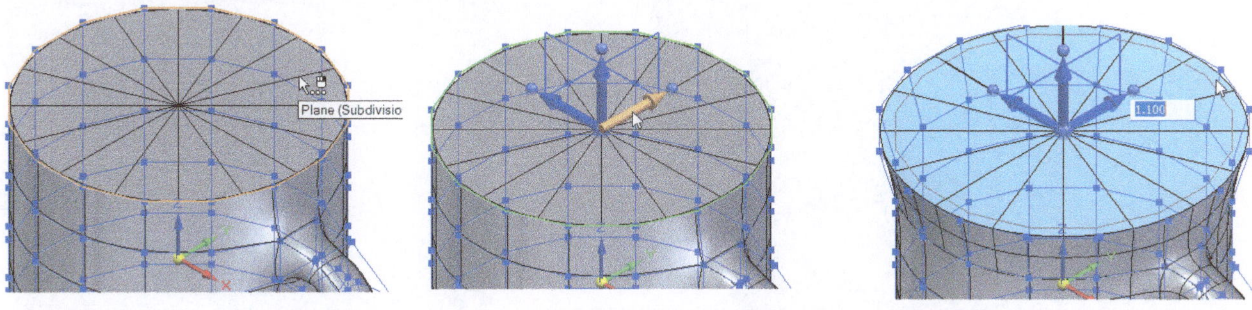

3. Click the top face of the model. Next, select the **Lift** option from the command bar.
4. Click on the arrow displayed on the selected face. Drag the pointer downward and type 2 in the distance box. Press ENTER and right-click to lift the selected face.

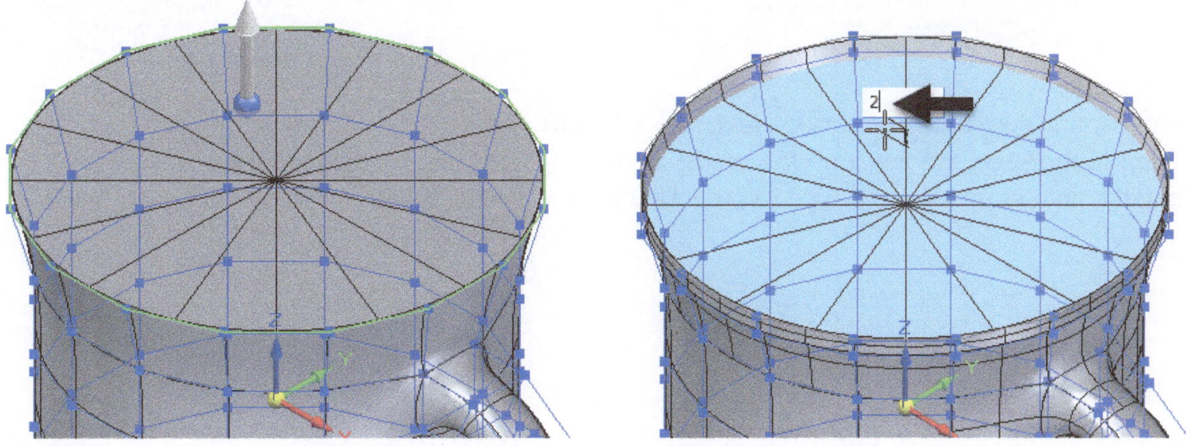

5. On the ribbon, click **Home > Modify > Scale** . Click on the facelifted in the previous step.
6. Click on the arrow, as shown. Type 0.9 in the scale box and press ENTER. Next, right-click to scale the face.

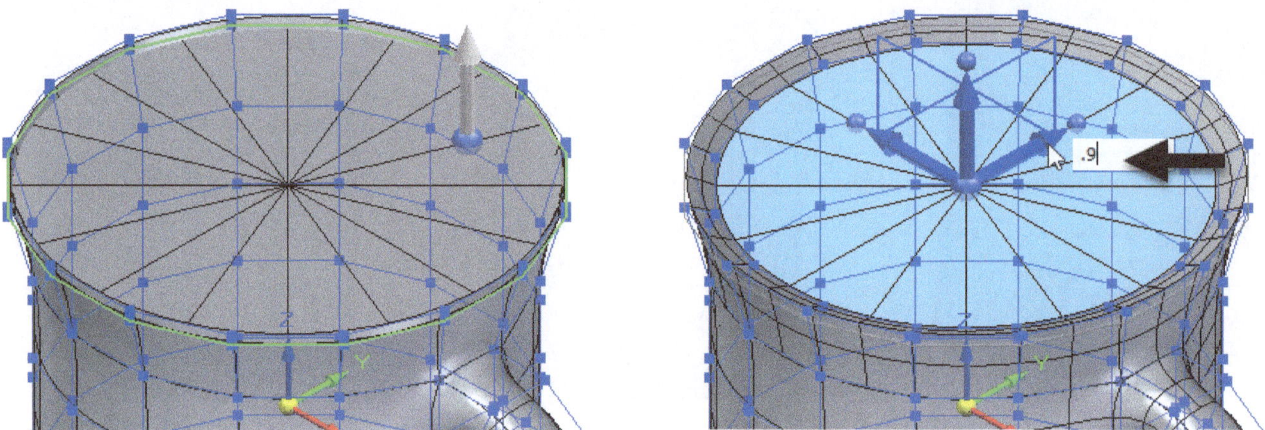

7. Press ESC and rotate the model such that the bottom face of the model is displayed.
8. On the ribbon, click **Home > Modify > Scale** . Click on the bottom face of the model.
9. Click on the arrow of the steering wheel, as shown. Type **0.9** in the **Percentage** box and right-click to scale the face. Press ESC to deselect the scaled face.

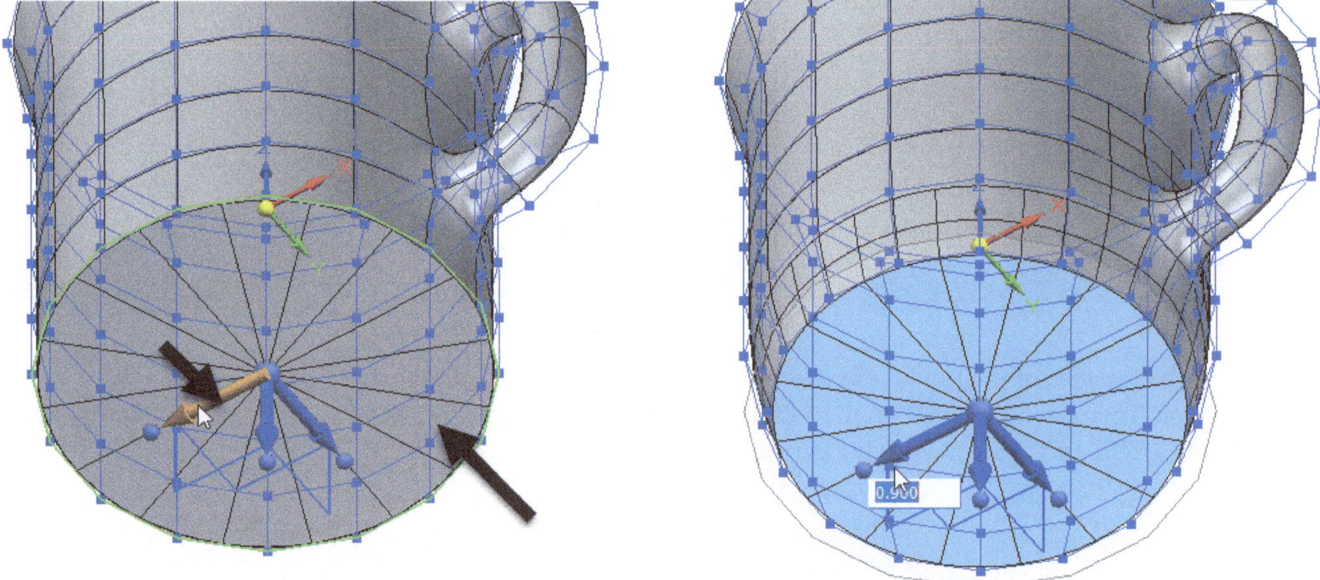

10. Press Esc and select the scaled face. Next, select the **Lift** option from the command bar.
11. Type 1 in the **Segments** box and click on the arrow displayed on the selected face.
12. Drag the pointer upward and type 2 in the distance box. Press ENTER and right-click to lift the selected face.

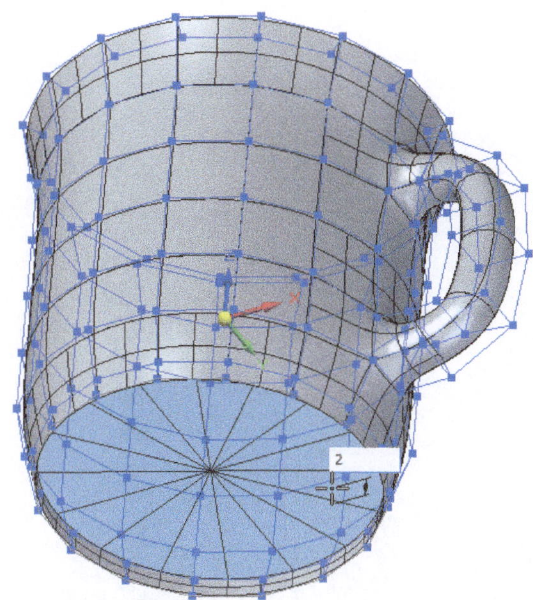

13. On the ribbon, click **Home > Modify > Scale**. Click on the facelifted in the previous step.
14. Click on the arrow of the steering wheel, as shown. Type **0.9** in the **Percentage** box and right-click to scale the face. Press ESC to deselect the scaled face.

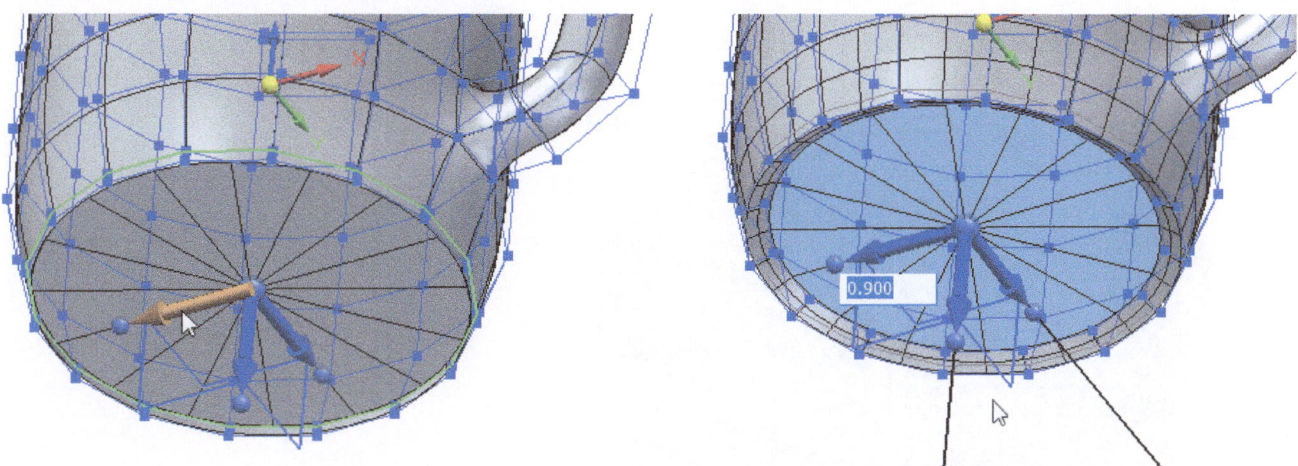

Shelling the Mug

1. Click on the center face on the top surface. Next, select the **Lift** option from the drop-down available on the command bar.
2. Click on the arrow pointing upwards. Drag the pointer downward, type 15 in the distance box, and press ENTER.

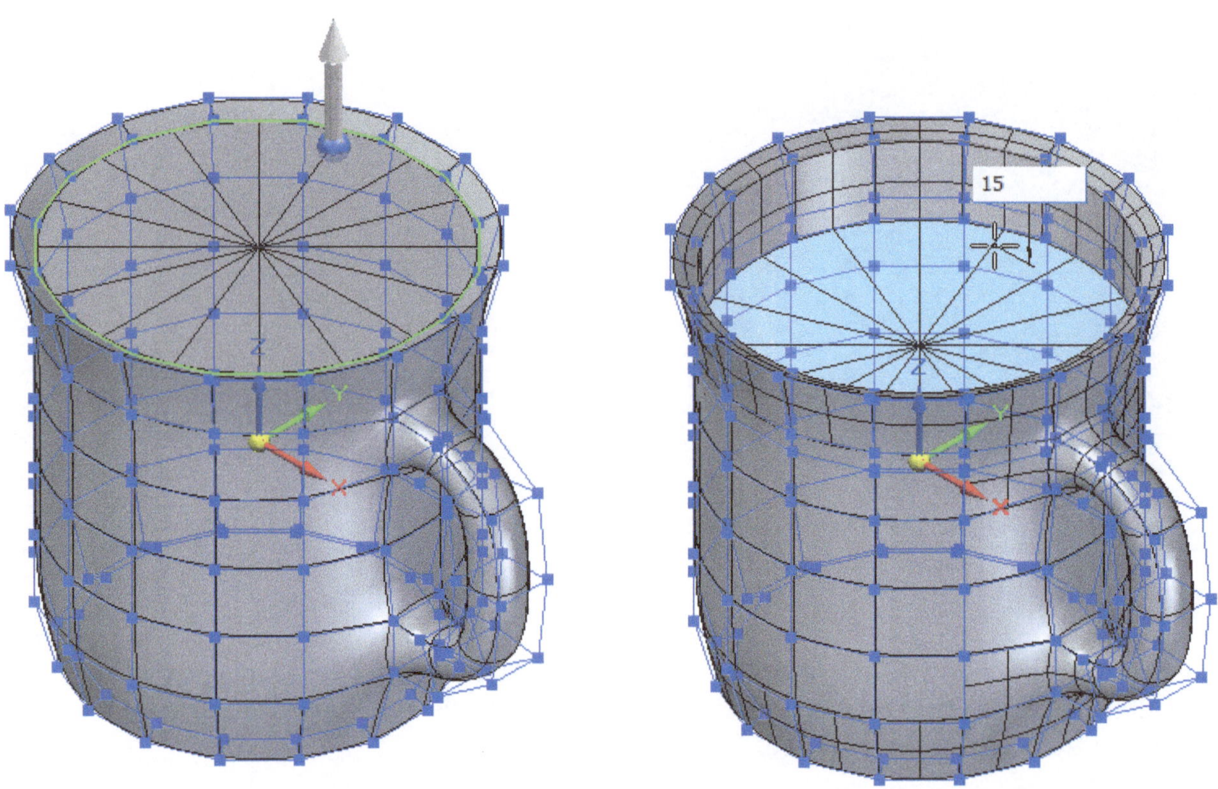

3. On the ribbon, click **Home > Modify > Scale.** Click on the facelifted in the previous step.
4. Click on the arrow of the steering wheel, as shown. Type 0.9 and press ENTER. Next, right-click to scale.

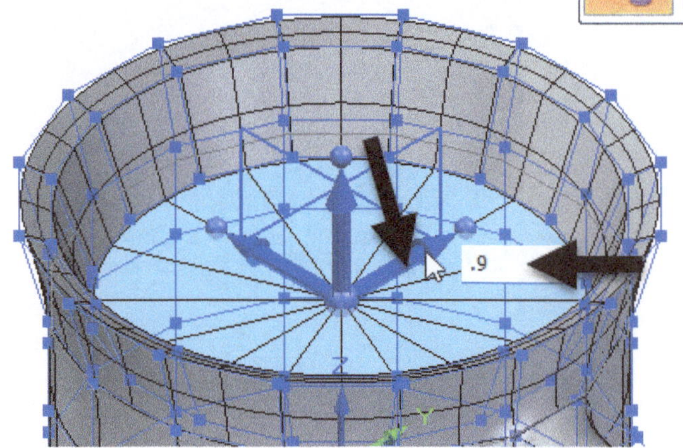

5. Press ESC and select the face scaled in the previous step. Next, type **4** in the **Segments** box.
6. Click on the arrow pointing upwards. Drag the pointer downward, type **60** in the distance box, and press ENTER.

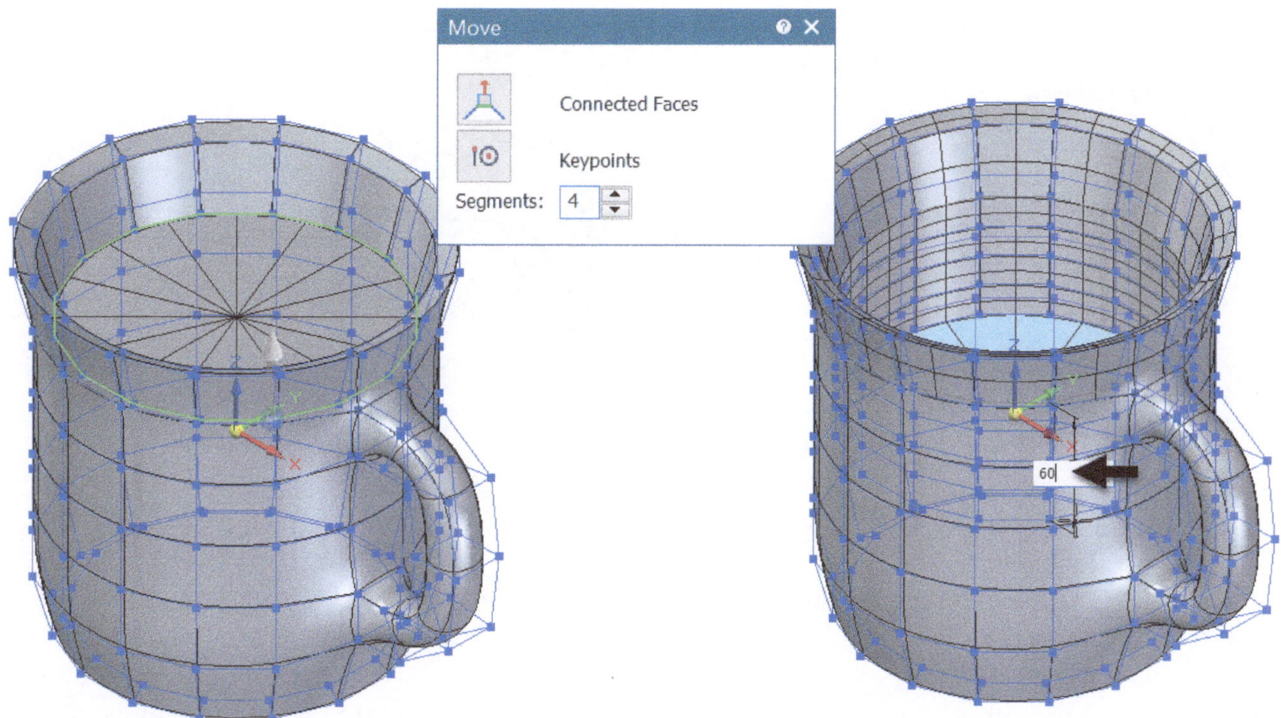

7. On the ribbon, click **Home > Modify > Scale.** Click on the facelifted in the previous step.
8. Click on the arrow of the steering wheel, as shown. Type 0.9 and press ENTER. Next, right-click to scale.
9. Press ESC and select the face scaled in the previous step. Next, type **1** in the **Segments** box.
10. Click on the arrow pointing upwards. Drag the pointer downward, type **6** in the distance box, and press ENTER. Next, press ESC.

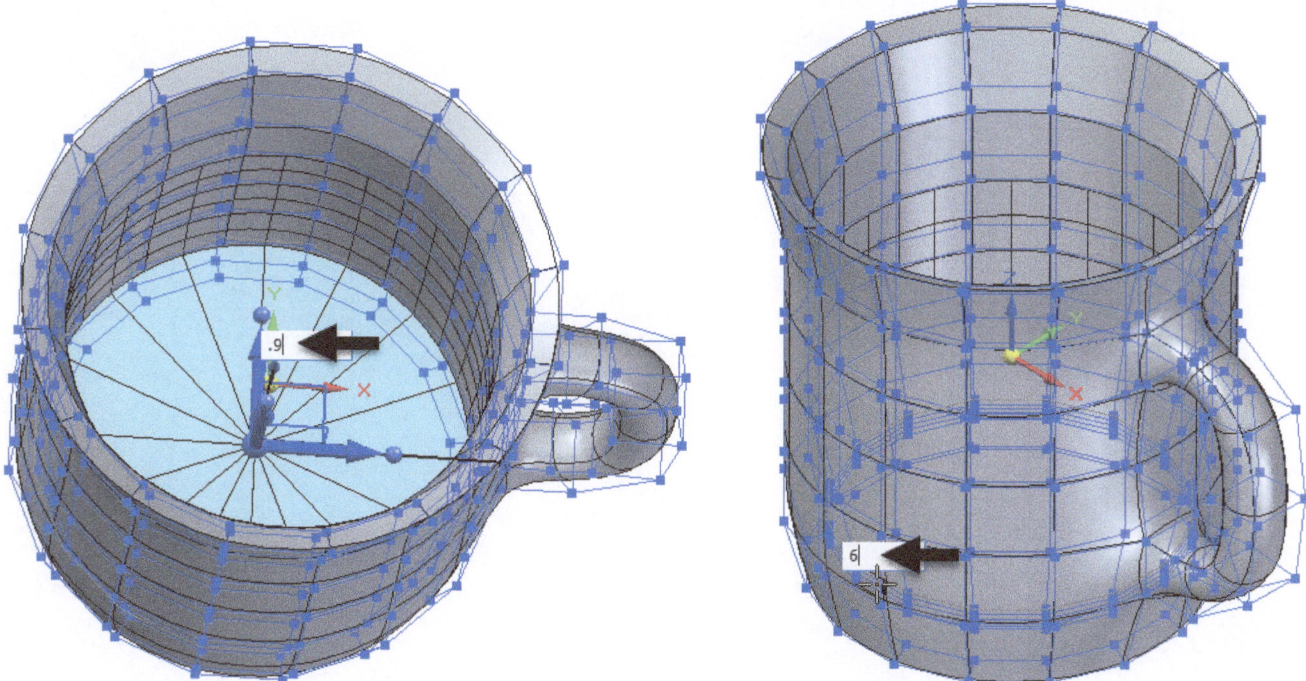

11. On the ribbon, click **Home > Modify > Blend**. Create a selection window across the entire model.

12. On the **Blend** dialog, drag the slider to **Smooth**. Next, right-click to smooth the model.

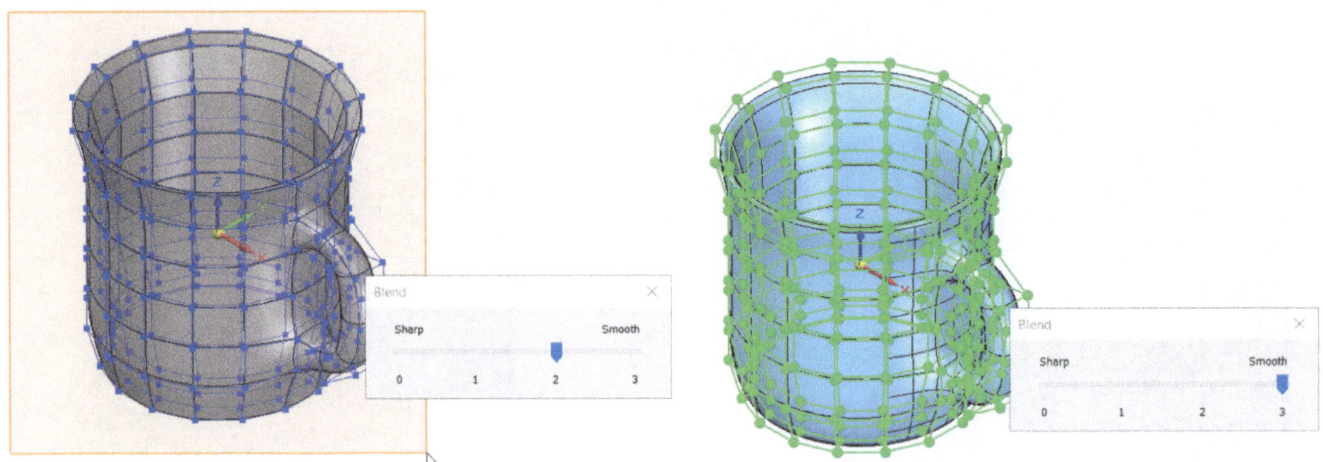

13. On the ribbon, click **Home > Close > Close Subdivision Modeling** .
14. Save and close the part file.

Questions

1. What are primitive shapes that you can create in Subdivision Modeling?
2. How can you change the size of a face using the **Scale** command?
3. What is the difference between the **Scale** and the **Split** command?

Index

9 788199 428928

Printed at Repro India Ltd.